1994 Income Tax Fundamentals

The Editorial Review Board for
Everett, Raabe, and Fortin, *1994 Income Tax Fundamentals*

The Dryden Press is proud to announce the Editorial Review Board chosen to review this 1994 edition upon publication for ongoing improvement and quality control. They are

Ronald E. Celotto
Rancho Santiago College

David B. Davidson
Califonria State University, Long Beach

Barbara Gerrity
Berkeley College

Harry Gray
Indiana Vocational Technical College

Jean Hunting
Heald Business College

Joe McCauley
Monroe Community College

Lee Kantin
Madison Area Technical College

Tim Rupert
Northeastern University

Vicki Vorell
Cuyahoga Community College

Joe Webster
Albuquerque T-VI Community College

Terry Witt
University of Texas at Arlington

1994 Income Tax Fundamentals

John O. Everett

Virginia Commonwealth University

William A. Raabe

University of Wisconsin—Milwaukee

Karen A. Fortin

Georgia Southern University

The Dryden Press
Harcourt Brace College Publishers
Fort Worth Philadelphia San Diego
New York Orlando Austin San Antonio
Toronto Montreal London Sydney Tokyo

Publisher	Liz Widdicombe
Acquisitions Editor	Tim Vertovec
Managing Editor	Cheryl Hauser
Production Manager	Ann Coburn
Production Services	Seaside Publishing Services

Copyright © 1994, 1993, 1992 by Harcourt Brace & Company.

All rights reserved. No part of this publication may be reproduced or transmitted in any form or by any means, electronic or mechanical, including photocopy, recording, or any information storage and retrieval system, without permission in writing from the publisher.

Although for mechanical reason all pages of this publication are perforated, only those pages imprinted with a Harcourt Brace & Company copyright notice are intended for removal.

Requests for permission to make copies of any part of the work should be mailed to: Permissions Department, Harcourt Brace College Publishers, Orlando, FL 32887.

Address for Editorial Correspondence
The Dryden Press, 301 Commerce Street, Suite 3700, Fort Worth, TX 76102

Address for Orders
The Dryden Press, 6277 Sea Harbor Drive, Orlando, FL 32887
1-800-782-4479, or 1-800-433-0001 (in Florida)

ISBN: 0-03-098184-0
Printed in the United States of America
Library of Congress Catalog Number: 93-74378
    3 4 5 6 7 8 9 0 1   085   9 8 7 6 5 4 3 2 1
The Dryden Press

The Dryden Press Series in Accounting

Introductory

Bischoff
Introduction to College Accounting
Second Edition

Principles

Hanson, Hamre, and Walgenbach
Principles of Accounting
Sixth Edition

Hillman, Kochanek, and Norgaard
Principles of Accounting
Sixth Edition

Computerized

Bischoff and Wanlass
The Computer Connection
Second Edition

Brigham and Knechel
Financial Accounting Using Lotus 1-2-3

Wanlass
Computer Resource Guide: Principles of Accounting
Fourth Edition

Yasuda and Wanlass
The Real Time Advantage

Financial

Backer, Elgers, and Asebrook
Financial Accounting: Concepts and Practices

Beirne and Dauderis
Financial Accounting: An Introduction to Decision Making

Hanson, Hamre, and Walgenbach
Financial Accounting
Seventh Edition

Kochanek, Hillman, and Norgaard
Financial Accounting
Second Edition

Stickney and Weil
Financial Accounting: An Introduction to Concepts, Methods, and Uses
Seventh Edition

Managerial

Ketz, Campbell, and Baxendale
Management Accounting

Maher, Stickney, and Weil
Managerial Accounting: An Introduction to Concepts, Methods, and Uses
Fifth Edition

Intermediate

Williams, Stanga, and Holder
Intermediate Accounting
Fourth Edition

Advanced

Huefner and Largay
Advanced Financial Accounting
Third Edition

Pahler and Mori
Advanced Accounting
Fifth Edition

Financial Statement Analysis

Stickney
Financial Statement Analysis: A Strategic Perspective
Second Edition

Auditing

Guy, Alderman, and Winters
Auditing
Third Edition

Rittenberg and Schwieger
Auditing: Concepts for a Changing Environment

Theory

Belkaoui
Accounting Theory
Third Edition

Bloom and Elgers
Accounting Theory & Policy: A Reader
Second Edition

Taxation

Everett, Raabe, and Fortin
Income Tax Fundamentals

Sommerfeld, Madeo, Anderson, and Jackson
Concepts of Taxation

Duncan
Essentials of U.S. Taxation

Reference

Miller and Bailey
HBJ Miller GAAS Guide
College Edition

Williams and Miller
HBJ Miller GAAP Guide
College Edition

The Harcourt Brace College Outline Series

Campbell, Grierson, and Taylor
Principles of Accounting I
Revised Edition

Emery
Principles of Accounting II

Emery
Intermediate Accounting I
Second Edition

Emery
Intermediate Accounting II

Frigo
Cost Accounting

Preface

This textbook was prepared for students taking an introductory course in federal taxation. Our objective is to provide a self-contained and practical course on the basic fundamentals of taxation without overwhelming the reader with technical details. Through the use of a self-study format, we have attempted to provide coverage of those provisions of the tax law that students will most frequently encounter in their personal and professional lives. The coverage does not assume that the student has had an introductory course in accounting.

In attempting to meet our objective, we have included several features in the textbook that are designed to help students in dealing with the complexities of federal tax law:

(1) Each chapter is divided into several units, with at least four self-study, multiple-choice questions following each unit. Answers are provided on following pages to allow students to check their comprehension of the material immediately.

(2) A list of the relevant sections of the Internal Revenue Code is included at the beginning of each chapter unit. These citations provide a reference point for students who want to do additional reading or research on a particular issue.

(3) Actual tax law is quoted briefly throughout the textbook in boxed inserts. These excerpts introduce students to the actual language used by Congress in addressing a tax issue. Then, the specific legal concept is explained in uncomplicated terminology in the following text discussion.

(4) Numerous examples are included in each chapter to explain the application of the law and its exceptions. These examples bring the tax law into true life situations and make it more interesting.

(5) Numerous tax tips are included as boxed inserts in each chapter. These tips offer practical advice on reducing tax liability and planning for future tax return considerations.

(6) Each chapter includes a number of filled-in tax forms that illustrate practical tax reporting procedures on the latest forms released by the Internal Revenue Service.

(7) Several of the chapters include appendixes to explore certain tax issues in greater depth. These optional appendixes provide the flexibility of additional coverage without unduly lengthening each chapter.

(8) Every chapter includes a variety of problem materials. These end-of-chapter exercises include:

   (a) *Problems*—These are keyed to specific units in each chapter and provide practical applications of the material discussed in the chapter.

   (b) *Tax Return Problems*—Each chapter includes at least two tax form problems based on the forms illustrated in the chapter. Blank forms are provided for each problem at the end of each chapter.

   (c) *How Would You Rule?*—Each chapter includes two problems on a controversial tax issue that has been subject to litigation. These questions allow students to act as "judges" and can be used to generate lively class discussions. Optionally, the questions can be used as tax research problems by those instructors who choose to introduce basic tax research procedures in their courses.

(9) A comprehensive tax return problem follows Chapters 2, 4, 6, 8, and 9. These five tax problems reinforce the topics covered in the preceding group of chapters, and blank tax forms are provided for each problem.

(10) Appendix A of the text includes a comprehensive "portfolio" problem that involves the preparation of several tax returns for the Neilson family. This is an ongoing set of tax returns that students work on throughout the textbook. A specific set of instructions is provided for each chapter so that students can apply the knowledge gained in studying the chapter to a practical "real world" tax return. The portfolio problem provides unity to information covered throughout the text. In addition, two optional extensions are provided for those instructors who wish to cover the advanced topics of the alternative minimum tax and employment tax returns.

(11) Also accompanying the textbook is Tax Prep software by Ten Key Publishing, Inc. This quality tax software is provided free to adopters in the form of a master diskette and brief documentation. The software is available on high-density 5¼ inch and 3½ inch diskettes for DOS-based personal computers with a hard disk drive. With the program installation disk comes a program to allow the software to print on most laser printers. Enhancements to the latest edition of Tax Prep include

    (a) An improved interface to allow users to step through tax return preparation more logically and easily.

    (b) Context-sensitive help to provide instant access to Tax Prep's expanded Help system.

    (c) New forms added to support almost every form appearing in the Comprehensive Tax Return Problem and Portfolio Tax Problem. The newly available forms include Form 4797—Sales of Business Property, Form 4684—Casualties and Thefts, Form 6252—Installment Sales Income, and Form W-4—Employee's Withholding Allowance Certificate.

(12) Several icons are used throughout the text to help students focus on the purpose of the particular section being read. Icons are provided for the following features:

 The Law (extracts from the Internal Revenue Code)

 Tax Planning Tips

 Unit Reviews

 How Would You Rule? Problems

 Tax Problems Solvable with Tax Prep Software

In addition to these standard text features, an accompanying Instructor's Manual contains a variety of pedagogical aids. These include (1) solutions to all text problems, comprehensive tax returns, and portfolio tax returns; (2) a comprehensive test bank of over 300 questions and solutions, furnished in both the instructor's manual and in ExaMaster software for easy test preparation; (3) comprehensive lecture notes for each chapter, including "instructor comments," demonstration problems, and selected transparency masters; (4) objective achievement tests with answers for classroom use; and (5) suggested course syllabi and assignment schedules for various combinations of chapters and coverage. Our goal is to offer the most complete and useful resource guide on the market today for instructors.

Many people have made important contributions to the development of *Income Tax Fundamentals*. We would especially like to thank James S. Gale, Northern Virginia Community College, J.U. Gray, Jr., Northern Virginia Community College, Professor G.L. Kantin, Madison Area Technical College, Professor Mike Milliren, Milwaukee Area Technical College, and Professor James D. Sherrifs, Paradise Valley Community College. For their useful comments on the current edition we wish to thank Catherine Berg, Nassau Community College; Gregory A. Carnes, Louisiana State University; C. Dorsey Dyer, Jr., Davidson County Community College; Dann G. Fisher, Kansas State University; Nancy J. Foran, Wichita State University; Joyce Griffin, Kansas City Kansas Community College; Norma Jean Hunting, Heald Business College—Hayward; G.L. Kantin, Madison Area Technical College; Al McKinnie, Northeast State Technical Community College; Deanne R. Pannell, Pellissippi State Technical Community College; Timothy J. Rupert, Northeastern University; Roy Sanchez, Jr., San Jacinto College—South; Vicki S. Vorell, Cuyahoga Community College; Joe Webster, Albuquerque T-VI Community College; John F. Wells, Triton Community College; Jane G. Wiese, Valencia Community College; Lee C. Wilson, Mesa College; and Terry J. Witt, University of Texas at Arlington. In addition, we owe a special debt of gratitude to Tim Vertovec and Bill Teague of Dryden Press and Lynne Bush of Seaside Publishing Services for directing the current edition.

John O. Everett
William A. Raabe
Karen A. Fortin

Contents

1 Filing the Individual Return
    I. Introduction to the Tax Process   1-1
        Review   1-6
    II. Overview of the Individual Tax Computation   1-8
        Review II   1-16
    III. The Standard Deduction, Filing Status, and Requirements to file   1-17
        Review III   1-25
    IV. Personal Exemption Deductions and Inflation Adjustments   1-27
        Review IV   1-38
    V. Filing the Individual Return   1-39
        Review V   1-48

    Chapter Appendix: Responsibilities of Taxpayers and Tax Preparers   1-52
    Chapter Problems   1-54

2 Gross Income of Individuals: Inclusions
    I. Gross Income: General concepts and Methods of Reporting   2-1
        Review I   2-9
    II. Special Inclusions: Interest, Dividends, and Annuities   2-10
        Review II   2-23
    III. Miscellaneous Inclusions: Rents and Alimony   2-24
        Review III   2-30
    IV. Assignment of Income and the Allocable Parental ("Kiddie") Tax   2-31
        Review IV   2-39

    Chapter Appendix: Annuity Calculations Based on Life Expectancies   2-41
    Chapter Problems   2-44
    Comprehensive Tax Return Problem 1   2-53

3 Gross Income of Individuals: Exclusions
    I. Donative Transfers and Life Insurance   3-1
        Review I   3-7
    II. Accident, Health, and Other Compensation Payments   3-8
        Review II   3-12
    III. Employee Benefits   3-12
        Review III   3-21
    IV. Miscellaneous Exclusions   3-28
        Review IV   3-18

Chapter Appendix: Measuring the Value of an Exclusion   3-28
Chapter Problems   3-30

4 Deductions for Personal Expenses of Individuals

    I. The Medical Expense Deduction   4-3
       Review I   4-7
    II. Interest Deductions   4-7
       Review II   4-14
    III. Deductions for Taxes and Charitable Contributions   4-14
       Review III   4-25
    IV. Personal Casualty and Theft Losses and the Moving Expense Deduction   4-25
       Review IV   4-35
    V. Employee Business Expenses and Other Miscellaneous Deductions   4-36
       Review V   4-53
    VI. Miscellaneous Deductions for Adjusted Gross Income   4-56
       Review VI   4-61

    Chapter Problems   4-62
    Comprehensive Tax Return Problem 2   4-71

5 Individual Tax Credits and Prepayments

    I. Credits Available to Lower-Income Taxpayers   5-2
       Review I   5-15
    II. Child and Dependent Care Credit   5-16
       Review II   5-20
    III. Miscellaneous Credits   5-21
       Review III   5-23
    IV. Estimated Tax Payments for Individuals   5-26
       Review IV   5-30

    Chapter Appendix: The Tax Return Audit and Appeals Process   5-32
    Chapter Problems   5-34

6 Gain and Loss Recognition: An Introduction

    I. Concepts of Gain, Loss, and Amount Realized   6-1
       Review I   6-5
    II. Determining the Adjusted Basis of Property   6-6
       Review II   6-12
    III. Capital Assets and the Netting Process   6-13
       Review III   6-26
    IV. Installment Sales   6-27
       Review IV   6-34
    V. Sale of a Personal Residence   6-35
       Review V   6-45

    Chapter Appendix: Capital Asset Status—Special Classifications   6-45
    Chapter Problems   6-49
    Comprehensive Tax Return Problem 3   6-61

7 Special Tax Computations for Individuals

 I. The Alternative Minimum Tax 7-2
   Review I 7-14
 II. Lump Sum Distributions from Retirement Plans 7-15
   Review II 7-21
 III. Passive Loss Limitations 7-23
   Review III 7-26
 IV. Extensions and Amended Returns 7-28
   Review IV 7-31

Chapter Appendix: Interest Charges and Penalties 7-32
Chapter Problems 7-34

8 Deductions: Income Producing Activities and Trades or Business

 I. Requirements of a Deduction 8-1
   Review I 8-10]
 II. Business Expenses: Inventories and Cost of Goods sold 8-10
   Review II 8-17
 III. Depreciation, MACRS, and ACRS Deductions 8-18
   Review III 8-33
 IV. Retirement Plans for Self-Employed Individuals 8-36
   Review IV 8-42
 V. Miscellaneous Business Expenses 8-42
   Review V 8-55

Chapter Appendix: Employment Taxes—An Introduction 8-57
Chapter Problems 8-70
Comprehensive Tax Return Problem 4 8-87

9 Special Computations and Credits for Business Taxpayers

 I. Like-Kind Exchanges 9-2
   Review I 9-9
 II. Involuntary Conversions 9-10
   Review II 9-15
 III. Section 1231 Treatment 9-16
   Review III 9-24
 IV. Depreciation Recapture 9-27
   Review IV 9-32
 V. General Business Tax Credits 9-33
   Review V 9-49

Chapter Appendix: Net Operating Loss Deductions 9-50
Review Appendix 9-59
Chapter Problems 9-60
Comprehensive Tax Return Problem 5 9-75

10 Formation and Taxation of Business Entities

    I.   Introduction to Partnership Taxation   10-2
          Review I   10-8
   II.   Partnership Income—Partnership Taxation   10-9
          Review II   10-20
  III.   Introduction to C Corporation Taxation   10-21
          Review III   10-28
  IV.   Taxation of Corporate Income   10-29
          Review IV   10-45
   V.   S Corporations   10-46
          Review V   10-58

Chapter Appendix: Comparison of Tax Consequences of Business Forms   10-60
Chapter Problems   10-60

Appendix A: Portfolio Problem   A-1
                  Portfolio Problem Checklist   A-15

Appendix B.   Tax Rate Schedules   B-1

Appendix C: 1992 Tax Tables   C-1

Appendix D: Earned Income Credit Tables   D-1

Appendix E: MACRS Rates for Property Other Than Residential Rental and Nonresidential Real Property   E-1

Appendix F: MACRS Straight-Line Rates for Residential Rental and Nonresidential Real Property   F-1

Appendix G: ACRS Rates for Personalty   G-1

Appendix H: ACRS Rates for Realty   H-1

Appendix I: ADS Rates for the Alternative Minimum Tax—Personalty   I-1

Appendix J: Tax Law Changes Effective in 1994   J-1

Appendix K: Instructions for Commonly Used Tax Forms   K-1

Index by the Internal Revenue Code Section   S-1
Top Index   T-1

Chapter 1

Filing the Individual Tax Return

The U.S. income tax system reflects an attempt by Congress to achieve a variety of objectives. It is a system designed primarily to raise revenue, but it has also been used over the years in bringing about economic, social, and political change.

Unfortunately, this multipurpose function of the tax law complicates any attempt to simplify and explain the current provisions. The purpose of this chapter is to provide an overview of the tax legislative process and to introduce the various components of the tax calculation for an individual.

Part I of the chapter describes the legislative process by which a tax bill becomes law. Part II introduces the format for the individual tax computation, and Parts III and IV examine in detail two important components of this calculation: the standard deduction and the personal exemption deduction. Finally, Part V of the chapter introduces the basic tax forms that individuals use in reporting their tax liabilities: Form 1040EZ, Form 1040A, and Form 1040.

Before we get into the "nitty-gritty" of the tax law, a word of caution (and, we hope, reassurance!): This entire textbook will be devoted to a detailed examination of the components of the individual tax computation. By the end of Chapter 1, however—other than the standard deduction and the personal exemption deduction—you will not be expected to know the fine points of the components of the income tax calculation. In this chapter, we will merely observe the forest; the "trees" will come later!

I INTRODUCTION TO THE TAX PROCESS
(Code Section 7805)

Our federal income tax laws are contained in Title 26 of the U.S. Code and are more commonly referred to as simply "The Internal Revenue Code." It is important to understand how a tax bill eventually becomes part of the "Code," because the process produces several by-products that are sometimes used to interpret congressional intent. Before turning to an examination of this legislative process, we will first trace the history of the federal income tax.

HISTORY OF THE U.S. INCOME TAX

The first federal income tax was passed during the Civil War to assist the Union's war effort. Prior to this time, the nation had relied primarily on excise and custom charges to raise revenues. This first income tax was very modest (3% on the income exceeding an $800 exemption), and the tax was allowed to expire in 1873.

The federal income tax was revived in 1894, but the next year the Supreme Court found it to be unconstitutional. The Court reasoned that the tax was a "direct tax," which was required by the Constitution to be divided among the states based on the results of a census. Congress solved this problem in 1909 by enacting the Sixteenth Amendment to the Constitution, which stated that "Congress shall have the power to lay and collect taxes on income from whatever source derived, without apportionment among the several states, and without regard to any census or enumeration." This amendment was ratified by the states in 1913, and Congress once again reinstated the income tax with the Revenue Act of 1913.

During the next 25 years Congress passed many other tax bills, often without paying any attention to prior laws that would be affected by the new provisions. In 1939 Congress combined all prior tax bills into one comprehensive set of tax laws know as the Internal Revenue Code of 1939 (the term *code* is short for "codification"). Subsequent changes in the law led to another major codification in 1954. Finally, in 1986 Congress decided that the changes enacted that year were so major that the Code was retitled as "The Internal Revenue Code of 1986."

HOW A TAX BILL BECOMES LAW

The Internal Revenue Code is amended through essentially the same process as other bills introduced in Congress. This process is summarized chronologically in Figure 1-1. Each step is described briefly in the following sections.

House of Representatives. In general, all revenue bills must originate in the House of Representatives, although occasionally a revenue proposal is "tacked on" as a rider to a Senate bill. The bill is introduced by a House member, but it may represent the collective wisdom of several members of Congress, the Treasury Department, and/or technical staff committees, such as the Joint Committee on Taxation.

The first stop for a bill in the House is the Ways and Means Committee. This committee is composed of a varying number of members (dominated by the majority party) and is currently chaired by Representative Dan Rostenkowski (D) of Illinois. The Committee holds public hearings, discusses the relative merits of the bill (sometimes in executive session), and eventually votes on the bill. If the bill passes by a simple majority, it is then introduced to the full House of Representatives. After another round of hearings and debate (with possible amendments), the House votes on the merits of the bill. If a simple majority vote in favor of the bill, it moves on to the Senate; if the bill fails, it receives no further consideration.

Senate. In the Senate the first stop for proposed tax legislation is the Senate Finance Committee. This committee is composed of a varying number of members

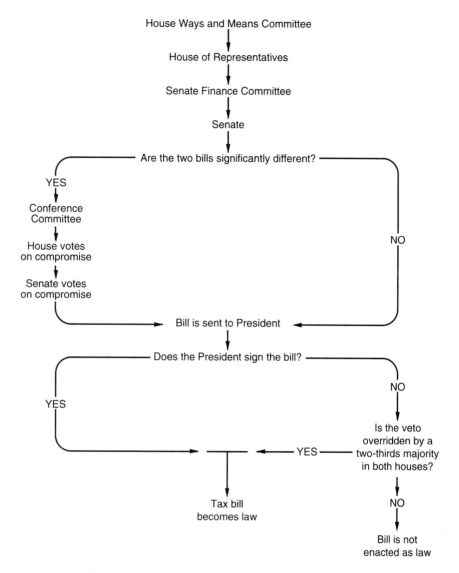

Figure 1-1   Legislative History of A Tax Bill

and is currently chaired by Senator Patrick Moynihan (D) of New York. This committee follows the same general procedure as the House Ways and Means Committee, although the Senate committee is free to amend (or scrap) the House version of the bill. If the Senate Finance Committee passes the bill, then the provision is sent to the full Senate for hearings, debate (including possible amendments), and a final vote.

Conference Committee. If the Senate passes essentially the same version of the legislation as the House of Representatives, then the bill is sent to the President for his or her signature. However, if the two versions of the bill are significantly different, a Conference Committee is formed to draft a compromise bill before the President considers the legislation. The Conference Committee is usually composed of the ranking members of the House Ways and Means Committee and the Senate Finance Committee. The compromise legislation must be approved by both houses before it can be sent on to the President.

Presidential Signature. If the President signs the final bill, the legislation becomes part of Title 26 of the United States Code. If the President does not sign the bill, the legislation can become law only by once again passing both houses of Congress, this time by a two-thirds majority. This requirement for overriding a Presidential veto ensures the active participation of the executive branch in the legislative process.

When talking about the tax law in this text, we will refer to "sections" of the Code. For convenience, the Code is broken down into various parts, subparts, chapters, subchapters, and sections. A reference to Code Section 61 will be abbreviated as "Sec. 61." Throughout the text, we will quote (in "boxes") various sections of the Code (and Regulations) in order to illustrate the actual wording used in the tax law. (However, have no fear; we will translate the law into plain English where necessary!)

SOURCES OF TAX AUTHORITY

Legislative Authority. Obviously, the Internal Revenue Code and the Constitution are the ultimate sources of *legislative* authority. However, the wording of the various Code sections can never cover every conceivable set of facts. Therefore, we must sometimes attempt to determine congressional intent when analyzing a particular tax provision.

As part of the legislative process, the House Ways and Means Committee and the Senate Finance Committee are required to publish final reports that summarize the old law, explain the reasons for changing the law, explain the new provisions, and estimate the total revenue effect of the proposed changes. These reports are valuable sources for determining congressional intent. In addition, any Conference Committee must issue a report, and finally, the Joint Committee on Taxation will issue perhaps the most comprehensive explanation of the legislation.

There is also one other source of legislative authority. The President, with the approval of a majority of the Senate, may enter into tax treaties with foreign countries.

TAX TIP

The House Ways and Means and the Senate Finance reports both summarize the tax bills in the form they were voted on in the two tax-writing committees. If a committee bill is amended on the floor of either the House or the Senate, the committee bill will not contain an explanation of the amendment. In such a case, the Congressional Record must be consulted for additional information on possible congressional intent regarding the amendment.

Two other sources of tax authority are the Treasury Department (through the Internal Revenue Service) and the courts. These two sources are referred to as administrative and judicial authorities, respectively.

THE LAW

Sec. 7805(a). Except where such authority is expressly given by this title to any other person other than an officer or employee of the Treasury Department, the Secretary shall prescribe all needful rules and regulations for the enforcement of this title, including all rules and regulations as may be necessary by reason of any alteration of law in relation to internal revenue.

Administrative Authority. The primary source of administrative authority is the *Income Tax Regulations*, issued by the Treasury Department. These are official interpretations of the tax law by the Treasury and are considered to have the force and effect of law. In addition, the Internal Revenue Service (IRS) publishes various other announcements, technical advice memoranda, and revenue procedures. The most common of these are the published *revenue rulings*, which represent the IRS's interpretation of how the law applies to a particular set of facts. Often, these revenue rulings result from *letter ruling requests*, which are written requests for rulings from taxpayers.

Judicial Authority. The federal courts have played a prominent role in the development of tax authority. Although the purpose of the courts is to interpret—not to enact—the laws of the country, many of the questions encountered in everyday tax practice are answered by court decisions.

A taxpayer who decides to take an issue to court has three initial choices: the U.S. Tax Court, the U.S. District Court, or the U.S. Claims Court. The *U.S. Tax Court* is a federal court composed of 19 judges who hear only tax matters. (This court also has a small-claims division that hears cases involving deficiencies of less than $10,000; although legal representation is not required, there is no appeal of this court's decision.) The *U.S. District Court* is a federal court that hears all types of cases, and this court offers the taxpayer the only opportunity of having his or her case heard by a jury (though questions of law must be answered by a judge). Finally, the *U.S. Claims Court* is a federal court composed of 16 judges who hear claims against the U.S. government (including nontax issues).

If the taxpayer loses in the lower courts, appeals of the decision are made to the *Circuit Courts of Appeal*. Tax Court and District Court decisions are appealed to one of 12 geographically located circuit courts of appeal; appeals from the Claims Court are made to a special Court of Appeals for the Federal Circuit. Decisions of the circuit courts of appeal have more precedent value than do lower court decisions; a lower court must generally follow any circuit court of appeal decision in its circuit. The only avenue of appeal from this level is the *U.S. Supreme Court*, which traditionally agrees to hear very few tax cases.

TAX TIP

A taxpayer must consider several factors when selecting a court to hear his or her tax case. One consideration is financial; if the taxpayer would prefer to wait for a final court decision to pay a deficiency, then the Tax Court offers the only opportunity to postpone payment; in both the District Court and the Claims Court, the proposed deficiency first must be paid and then the taxpayer may file a claim for refund. Also, the Tax Court guarantees that a taxpayer's case will be heard by a tax specialist. However, the District Court offers the only opportunity of having one's case heard by a jury (if the case involves a question of fact). Perhaps the most important consideration is the "track record" of the court; since courts must follow their previous decisions, a taxpayer may choose a court that has ruled favorably on similar issues in the past.

Figure 1-2 (page 1-7) summarizes the sources of legislative, executive, and judicial authority. Throughout this textbook, portions of the appropriate legislative authority (Code sections) will be quoted in a boxed format to highlight the actual wording of important tax provisions. (All relevant Code sections are also listed at the beginning of each chapter unit.) In addition, an occasional reference will be made to various administrative and court decisions of importance. We hope this review of tax authority will help you to understand the origins of these laws and their various interpretations.

REVIEW I

1. The federal income tax was declared unconstitutional in 1895 by the U.S. Supreme Court because
    (a) the tax violated the principle of taxation without representation.
    (b) the tax was not apportioned according to a census.
    (c) the tax had not been approved by both houses of Congress.
    (d) the bill originated in the Senate.
2. Which of the following statements concerning the legislative process of a tax bill is incorrect?
    (a) Most tax bills originate in the House of Representatives.
    (b) A conference committee is required for all tax bills.
    (c) The Senate is free to amend or scrap a House bill.
    (d) Two-thirds of both houses of Congress must approve a tax bill in order to override a Presidential veto.
3. The only court that allows a taxpayer to have his or her case heard by a jury is the
    (a) U.S. Tax Court.
    (b) U.S. District Court.
    (c) U.S. Claims Court.
    (d) any of the courts listed above

I. Introduction to the Tax Process   1-7

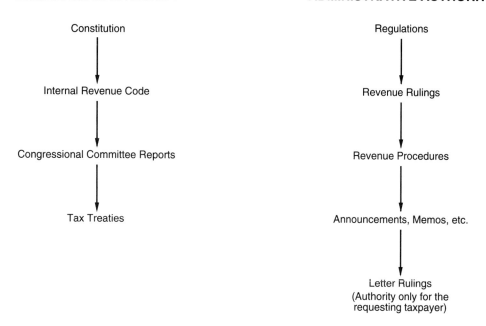

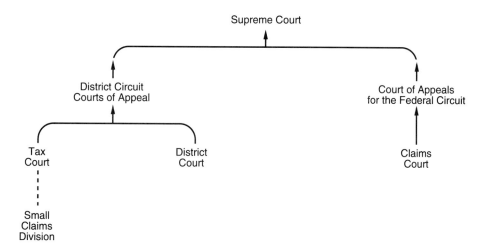

Figure 1-2   Sources of Tax Authority

4. Which of the following is an example of administrative authority?
   (a)   a U.S. Tax Court decision
   (b)   the Internal Revenue Code
   (c)   an Income Tax Regulation
   (d)   All of these are examples of administrative authority.

Answers are on page 1-8.

II. OVERVIEW OF THE INDIVIDUAL TAX COMPUTATION
(Code Sections 1, 2, 3, 21, and 441)

The purpose of this section is to provide an overview of the components of the income tax calculation for individuals. Obviously, the determination of income must depend on some unit of time measurement. An individual must file a tax return on an annual basis, with each tax return due within 3 ½ months of the end of his or her taxable year.

A taxpayer may choose as his or her "taxable year" a calendar year, a fiscal year, or a 52–53-week year. A *calendar year* is simply a tax year ending on December 31. A *fiscal year* is a tax year ending at the end of a month other than December. Finally, a "*52–53-week*" year is a tax year ending on the same day of the week at the end of a particular month (or simply the same day nearest the end of the month; an example would be a year ending on the Friday closest to December 31).

The best way to introduce the individual income tax calculation is to walk through a hypothetical example. Table 1-1 illustrates the computational format for a hypothetical taxpayer named Anne Wilson. Each of the major components of the calculation is discussed briefly in the following sections.

GROSS RECEIPTS

Gross receipts is the broadest definition of income found in the Internal Revenue Code. The term refers to total income flows (other than loan proceeds) received during the year, regardless of whether the inflow is from a taxable or a nontaxable source. No expense deductions (reductions in income) are allowed at this point. (However, gross sales would always be reduced by the cost of the item sold to determine gross receipts.) In Table 1-1, Wilson's gross receipts consist of a salary, dividends, two types of interest income, lottery winnings, and a gain on the sale of corporate stock.

Since the "gain" on the sale of the stock is a net figure, the $6,000 actually represents the difference between the selling price of the stock and its cost basis for tax purposes. For example, the stock may have cost $14,000 in 1982 and then sold for $20,000 in 1993. Since the stock was held longer than a year, the gain is classified as a "long-term capital gain." This treatment of capital gains and losses is discussed in Chapter 6.

ANSWERS TO REVIEW I

1. (b) The lack of apportionment according to a census violated the requirements of a "direct tax."
2. (b) A conference committee is not required if both tax bills substantially agree on all major points.
3. (b) Only the U.S. District Court offers the option of a jury trial for questions of fact (but not questions of law).
4. (c) Income Tax Regulations are sources of administrative authority drafted by the Treasury Department.

Table 1-1 Example of Individual Tax Computation—1993

FACTS: Anne Wilson, age 34, is divorced and supports her minor son. She elects to itemize her deductions for the year.

Gross receipts:		
Salary	$ 58,300	
Gross dividend income (IBM stock)	4,100	
Interest (certificates of deposit)	2,400	
Interest (state of Virginia bonds)	3,000	
Lottery winnings (District of Columbia)	5,000	
Gain on sale of stock (acquired in 1982)	6,000	$78,800
Less exclusions *from* income:		
Municipal bond interest exclusion		(3,000)
Gross income		$ 75,800
Less deductions *for* adjusted gross income:		
Alimony paid to former spouse		(6,000)
Adjusted gross income (AGI)		$ 69,800
Less deductions *from* adjusted gross income:		
Personal exemptions (2 @ $2,350)		(4,700)
Larger of:		
(a) Standard deduction (head of household)	$ 5,450	
(b) Itemized deductions:		
Medical	$ 0	
Interest (home mortgage)	5,700	
Taxes (state income and property)	3,000	
Contributions	2,794	
Casualty	0	
Miscellaneous itemized	0	
Total itemized deductions	11,494	
Larger of standard deduction or itemized		(11,494)
Taxable income		$ 53,606
Gross tax liability (HH - Tax on $53,606 @ 1993 rates)		$ 11,167
Less credits and prepayments:		
Dependent care credit ($2,400 maximum × .20)		(480)
Federal income tax withholdings (from salary)		(12,020)
Net refund due		$(1,333)

EXCLUSIONS

Exclusions are those items of income specifically exempted from taxation by Congress. Generally, the tax law assumes that all sources of income are taxable unless specifically excluded by Congress through a provision in the Code. Table 1-1 assumes that Wilson qualifies for only one exclusion, the exclusion for interest on state, local, or municipal bonds (in this case, the interest on state of Virginia bonds). This exclusion is specifically listed in the Internal Revenue Code (Sec. 103). Other common exclusions to be discussed in Chapter 3 include certain death benefits (Sec. 101), gifts and inheritances (Sec. 102), amounts received under accident and health plans (Sec. 105), employer payments of accident and health-plan insurance premiums for employees (Sec. 106), and scholarships (Sec. 117).

GROSS INCOME

Gross income is the term used in the tax law to represent total income less all allowable exclusions. Note that this number is derived *before* any deductions are subtracted. Gross income is used as a key figure for other purposes in the Code. For example, the requirements to file a tax return are based on gross income, and one of the five tests for dependency exemptions discussed later in this chapter is a gross income test. In Table 1-1, Wilson's gross income is $75,800 (the $78,800 gross receipts less $3,000 of allowable exclusions).

DEDUCTIONS FOR ADJUSTED GROSS INCOME

Deductions are items specifically provided by Congress in the Internal Revenue Code as reductions in the income that is subject to taxation. Deductions for an individual are grouped into two broad categories: deductions "for" adjusted gross income (AGI), and deductions "from" AGI. Alternately, some publications refer to the deductions as "above the line" (deductions for AGI) and "below the line" (deductions from AGI).

Deductions "for" AGI are composed mainly of business-related expenditures, although over the years Congress has added some personal expenditures, such as alimony and payments to individual retirement accounts, to the "for AGI" category. The example assumes that Wilson qualifies for only one deduction for AGI: alimony paid to a former spouse.

Section 62 specifies a variety of deductions for AGI for individual taxpayers. Among the other most commonly used deductions in this category are (1) trade or business deductions of self-employed individuals, (2) losses from the sale or exchange of property (e.g., capital losses), (3) deductions attributable to rents and royalties, (4) contributions to self-employed retirement plans, (5) contributions to individual retirement accounts, and (6) forfeiture penalties for premature withdrawals of funds from savings accounts and deposits. All of these items will be discussed in detail later in the text.

☑ **Example 1.** Billy Allen has $10,000 on deposit at a savings and loan. The normal interest rate is 10% per year; however, if the depositor withdraws any of the principal during the year, the rate drops to 6%. During the current year, Billy withdrew some of the principal and as a result received only $600 of interest; however, his Form 1099-INT (statement of interest income) shows the gross interest of $1,000 reported to the government. To show the correct amount of $600 on his tax return, Billy must report a deduction for AGI of $400, the amount of the forfeiture penalty.

☑ **Example 2.** During 1993 Sara Vann incurred $600 of repair expenses related to a rental house that she owns. During 1993 Sara received $4,800 of gross rents from the tenants. On her 1993 tax return, Sara will include the $4,800 gross rents in gross income and deduct the $600 repair expense in determining adjusted gross income.

ADJUSTED GROSS INCOME

Adjusted gross income (AGI) is defined as gross income less all allowable deductions for AGI. AGI is another key income figure used for different purposes in the Code. For example, certain itemized deductions are allowed only to the extent that they exceed a certain percentage of AGI, and one deduction, the charitable deduction, is limited to a percentage of AGI. In Table 1-1, Wilson's AGI is $69,800.

DEDUCTIONS <u>FROM</u> ADJUSTED GROSS INCOME

The Internal Revenue Code permits taxpayers to use two broad categories of deductions *from* adjusted gross income in arriving at taxable income. These are the deductions for personal exemptions and the larger of the standard deduction or itemized deductions. The personal exemption deduction and the standard deduction are discussed in detail in the next two sections of this chapter, and itemized deductions are discussed in detail in Chapter 4. Following is a brief description of how these two categories of deductions enter into the tax computation.

Personal Exemption Deductions

As part of the very first U.S. income tax law, Congress granted every individual a taxfree subsistence level of income for himself or herself and all family members. This amount has been increased over the years and is currently established at $2,350 in 1993, with automatic annual increases for inflation. Obviously, the $2,350 is an unrealistically low amount for subsistence in today's economy, but the revenue cost to the government of increasing the amount to a true subsistence level would be prohibitive. In Table 1-1, it is assumed that Wilson qualifies for two exemptions, one for herself and one for her son.

Itemized Deductions and the Standard Deduction

Over the years, Congress has granted a variety of personal deductions to individual taxpayers as deductions from AGI. These deductions are allowed for a variety of reasons; for example, casualty losses and medical losses are deductible when the amounts are considered to be extraordinary in nature. Similarly, a deduction is allowed for personal state and local income taxes paid to alleviate double taxation on the same amount of income. These qualifying personal expenditures became known as "itemized deductions" because the taxpayer had to list the items individually on his or her tax return.

To simplify the tax calculation and reduce the administrative burden on the IRS, Congress instituted the concept of a "standard deduction" during World War II. The standard deduction was a fixed percentage of AGI, subject to certain dollar minimums and maximums. A taxpayer was given the choice of either itemizing his or her deductible personal expenditures or simply subtracting the standard deduction, if this amount was larger than itemized deductions. One advantage of using the standard deduction was that it relieved the taxpayer of the responsibility of keeping records of his or her personal expenditures, thereby lessening the possibility of an IRS audit.

The standard deduction is currently fixed at one of four amounts (based on filing status), each of which is adjusted annually for an inflation factor. The 1993 amounts are $3,700 for a single taxpayer, $6,200 for married-filing jointly taxpayers, $3,100 for married-filing separately taxpayers, and $5,450 for qualifying heads of household. As explained later in the chapter, the standard deduction amount is increased for taxpayers (and spouses) who are age 65 or older and/or are legally blind. Additionally, certain taxpayers may be limited to a standard deduction smaller than the base amounts given above.

As an alternative to using the standard deduction, a taxpayer may elect to itemize his or her personal deductions. Table 1-1 illustrates the major categories of itemized deductions. Note that taxpayer Wilson elected to itemize, since the total ($11,494) exceeded her standard deduction (based on "head of household" filing status) of $5,450 in the tax year 1993.

Obviously, there are many details concerning itemized deductions that are not covered in this brief introduction. Many restrictions apply to each of the major categories, and some categories are deductible only to the extent that the total exceeds a specified percentage of adjusted gross income. The specific requirements and limitations related to each deduction are discussed (in somewhat excruciating detail!) in Chapter 4.

TAX TIP

Occasionally a taxpayer may have the opportunity to "bunch" itemized deductions into one particular year and use the standard deduction in another year. For example, assume that a single taxpayer has accumulated approximately $2,000 of itemized deductions near the end of the tax year, and that the taxpayer owes $1,500 of deductible real estate taxes at the end of the year. In this case, the taxpayer would be better off to postpone the property tax payment until the beginning of the next year. That way, the taxpayer can use the $3,700 standard deduction this year and use the $1,500 next year, if the taxpayer itemizes.

TAXABLE INCOME

Taxable income is the final income figure after all allowable deductions. This figure is used to compute the gross tax liability. If taxable income is less than $100,000, the taxpayer must use the tax tables reproduced in Appendix C to determine the tax liability. If the taxable income is $100,000 or greater, the taxpayer must use the tax rate schedules (reproduced in Appendix B) to compute tax liability. The first step in computing tax liability is to determine the taxpayer's filing status. There are five possible filing statuses: single, married-filing jointly, married-filing separately, head of household, and surviving spouse. The requirements for each filing status are discussed in Part IV of this chapter. In Table 1-1, Wilson would qualify for "head of household" status, since she is unmarried and provides over half the support of her minor child.

COMPUTATION OF TAX LIABILITY

The Tax Tables

Taxpayers with less than $100,000 of taxable income must generally use printed tax tables to determine tax liability. These tables, shown in Appendix C for 1993, disclose the computed tax liability for each filing status for taxable income amounts under $100,000, in $50 increments ($25 increments for the first $3,000 of taxable income). Each tax liability is computed from the tax rate schedules using the midpoint of the bracket. As discussed later, the tax tables for Forms 1040EZ and 1040A are limited to $50,000 of taxable income.

☑ **Example 3.** In the example of Table 1-1, Anne Wilson had taxable income of $53,606 in 1993. She qualifies as a "head of household." Her tax liability must be computed from the tax tables, and this amount is $11,167 (the "head of household tax" for the $53,600–$53,650 bracket). This is the same tax that would be computed from the tax rate schedules using $53,625 of taxable income (i.e., the midpoint of the bracket).

The Tax Rate Schedules

The tax rate schedules for the various filing statuses are disclosed in Figure 1-3 (reproduced in Appendix B) for 1993. These rate schedules illustrate the progressive nature of the federal income tax; the larger the income, the larger the tax rate applicable to that income. Note that the third column for each rate schedule discloses the cumulative tax due on all lower brackets; for 1993, for example, the $17,544 in Schedule Z (Head of Household) is the cumulative tax on the first $76,400 of taxable income of the taxpayer.

The 36% and 39.6% brackets in each tax rate schedule were actually added by the Revenue Reconciliation Act of 1993; prior to this time, only the 15%, 28%, and 31% tax brackets were applicable for each possible filing status. Although this tax legislation was not signed into law by President Clinton until August 10, 1993, the rate increases were made *retroactive* to January 1, 1993.

In order to soften the impact of these rate increases, Congress enacted a special installment payment provision whereby any 1993 tax liability caused by the addition of the 36% and 39.6% brackets can be paid in three equal annual installments, beginning

1993 Tax Rate Schedules

Schedule X—Use if your filing status is **Single**

If the amount on Form 1040, line 37, is: Over—	But not over—	Enter on Form 1040, line 38	of the amount over—
$0	$22,100	.... 15%	$0
22,100	53,500	$3,315.00 + 28%	22,100
53,500	115,000	12,107.00 + 31%	53,500
115,000	250,000	31,172.00 + 36%	115,000
250,000	....	79,772.00 + 39.6%	250,000

Schedule Y-1—Use if your filing status is **Married filing jointly** or **Qualifying widow(er)**

If the amount on Form 1040, line 37, is: Over—	But not over—	Enter on Form 1040, line 38	of the amount over—
$0	$36,900	.... 15%	$0
36,900	89,150	$5,535.00 + 28%	36,900
89,150	140,000	20,165.00 + 31%	89,150
140,000	250,000	35,928.50 + 36%	140,000
250,000	....	75,528.50 + 39.6%	250,000

Schedule Z—Use if your filing status is **Head of household**

If the amount on Form 1040, line 37, is: Over—	But not over—	Enter on Form 1040, line 38	of the amount over—
$0	$29,600	.... 15%	$0
29,600	76,400	$4,440.00 + 28%	29,600
76,400	127,500	17,544.00 + 31%	76,400
127,500	250,000	33,385.00 + 36%	127,500
250,000	....	77,485.00 + 39.6%	250,000

Schedule Y-2—Use if your filing status is **Married filing separately**

If the amount on Form 1040, line 37, is: Over—	But not over—	Enter on Form 1040, line 38	of the amount over—
$0	$18,450	.... 15%	$0
18,450	44,575	$2,767.50 + 28%	18,450
44,575	70,000	10,082.50 + 31%	44,575
70,000	125,000	17,964.25 + 36%	70,000
125,000	....	37,764.25 + 39.6%	125,000

Figure 1-3 1993 Tax Rate Schedule

with the 1993 tax return. In order to determine this tax increase, the computed 1993 gross tax liability must be compared with a hypothetical 1993 liability computed at a 31% maximum rate. These computations are best illustrated with an example.

Example 4. Marlon and Stella Corleone have $300,000 of taxable income in 1993, and they file a joint return. Their 1993 gross tax liability, computed from Rate Schedule Y-1 in Figure 1-3, is $95,328.50 ($75,528.50 plus 39.6% of the $50,000 taxable income exceeding $250,000). However, if the maximum tax rate for 1993 was only 31%, their tax liability would be $85,528.50 ($20,165 plus 31% of the $210,850 taxable income exceeding $89,150). The additional tax due in 1993 because of the 36% and 39.6% brackets is $9,800 ($95,328.50 − $85,528.50). The Corleones may elect to pay 1/3 of this amount, or $3,267, in 1993. The Corleones will pay $88,795.50 of tax in 1993 ($85,528.50 plus $3,267), and then increase their 1994 and 1995 tax payments by $3,267 each.

CREDITS AGAINST THE TAX LIABILITY

Credits are dollar-for-dollar reductions in tax liability that are specified in the Code. In recent years, Congress has used credits to provide different forms of tax relief, since a credit is worth more dollar for dollar to a taxpayer than a deduction, which reduces only the income subject to tax. Table 1-1 assumes that taxpayer Wilson qualifies for one tax credit—the special credit for child and dependent care expenses.

As discussed later in this text, this credit is generally limited to a "specified percentage" of child or dependent care expenses, not to exceed a maximum of $2,400 qualifying expenses (one child or dependent) or $4,800 (two or more children or dependents). The "specified percentage" is 30% for taxpayers with adjusted gross incomes of $10,000 or less, and this percentage is reduced one point (but never below 20%) for each $2,000 of adjusted gross income exceeding $10,000. Thus, the "specified percentage" for taxpayers with adjusted gross incomes exceeding $28,000 will always be 20%.

In Table 1-1, it is assumed that Wilson qualifies for the maximum credit for one dependent, or $480 ($2,400 maximum qualifying expenses times 20%, the "specified percentage" for taxpayers with adjusted gross incomes exceeding $28,000). Other details concerning the child and dependent care credit are covered in Chapter 5. Table 1-2 provides some additional examples of this credit computation.

PREPAYMENTS OF TAX LIABILITY

The federal income tax system operates on a pay-as-you-go principle. Employees prepay some (or all) of their federal tax liabilities during the tax year through employer withholdings from their salaries. Taxpayers not covered by tax withholding, such as self-employed individuals, must prepay their tax liabilities in quarterly estimates. In Table 1-1, it is assumed that Wilson had $12,020 of federal income tax withheld from her salary. Since this amount represents a prepayment of tax, the withholdings are used as a direct reduction in tax liability.

NET TAX PAYABLE OR REFUND DUE

All individual taxpayers are required to file a return and pay any balance due within 3 ½ months of the end of their tax year. Since most individual taxpayers file their returns on a calendar-year basis, this means that April 15 is the "witching hour" for tax returns. If April 15 falls on a weekend, the deadline is extended to the following Monday. Failure to pay any balance due on time may subject a taxpayer to interest penalties.

In the case of a refund due to an overpayment of tax, a taxpayer can elect to receive the refund by check (usually in four to eight weeks) or elect to apply the refund to the next year's tax liability. In Table 1-1, Wilson is due a refund of $1,333.

Table 1-2 Examples—Child and Dependent Care Credit Computation

AGI of Taxpayer	Qualifying Dependents	Dependent Care Expenses	Credit Computation	Credit
$ 8,000	1	$2,000	($2,000 × .30)	$600
12,020	1	2,000	($2,000 × .28)	560
19,000	1	2,800	($2,400 × .25)	600
29,000	1	3,200	($2,400 × .20)	480
40,000	2	4,500	($4,500 × .20)	900
40,000	2	5,100	($4,800 × .20)	960
63,000	3	7,100	($4,800 × .20)	960

TAX TIP

In the case of a refund, a taxpayer usually should elect to receive the refund, rather than applying it to the next year's tax liability. The reason is simple: The government does not pay any interest on amounts deposited for the next year's tax liability. As a general rule, taxpayers want to adjust their withholdings and/or estimated tax payments so that the total prepayments are close to the expected final tax liability. More planning possibilities are discussed in Chapter 5.

This concludes an overview of the individual tax computation. Again, our purpose at this point is obtain an overview of the tax computation, to look at the forest rather than the individual trees. In the next two sections of this chapter, three of the "trees" are examined in more detail: the standard deduction, filing status, and the personal exemption deduction.

REVIEW II

1. Yvonne Hartfield had $60,000 of salary, $4,000 of dividend income, $2,000 of interest on state of Mississippi bonds, and $500 of Louisiana lottery winnings. Her only deductions are $2,000 of qualifying alimony, $5,000 of home mortgage interest, $2,000 of property taxes, and three personal exemptions for herself and her two daughters. Yvonne's 1993 *gross income* is
   (a) $60,000.
   (b) $64,000.
   (c) $64,500.
   (d) $66,000.
2. Refer to Problem 1. Yvonne's deductions *for* adjusted gross income for 1993 are
   (a) $0.
   (b) $2,000.
   (c) $7,000.
   (d) $9,000.
3. Refer to Problem 1. Yvonne's deductions *from* adjusted gross income for 1993 are
   (a) $2,000.
   (b) $7,000.
   (c) $12,050.
   (d) $14,050.
4. During 1993 Roy Hayes, a qualifying head of household, is entitled to two exemptions (one for himself and one for his 10-year-old daughter Joanne). During the year, Roy incurred $4,300 of legitimate itemized deductions. The standard deduction for a head of household in 1993 is $5,450. Roy's total 1993 deductions from adjusted gross income (AGI) are

(a) $4,700.
(b) $5,450.
(c) $9,000.
(d) $10,150.

Answers are on page 1-18.

III. THE STANDARD DEDUCTION, FILING STATUS, AND REQUIREMENTS TO FILE
(Code Sections 1, 2, and 63)

THE STANDARD DEDUCTION

As mentioned in Part II of this chapter, the standard deduction is fixed at one of four amounts, depending on the taxpayer's filing status. The 1993 amounts are

Filing Status	1993 Standard Deduction
Single	$3,700
Married-filing jointly (and qualified widow(er))	6,200
Married-filing separately	3,100
Head of household	5,450

THE LAW

Sec. 63(b). *Individuals who do not itemize their deductions.*

In the case of an individual who does not elect to itemize his deductions for the taxable year, for purposes of this subtitle, the term "taxable income" means adjusted gross income, minus—

(1) the standard deduction, and
(2) the deduction for personal exemptions provided in section 151.

Most taxpayers have a choice of either taking the standard deduction or itemizing deductions. One of the purposes of the standard deduction is to reduce the need for most taxpayers to itemize deductions and retain the relevant documentation. In turn, this eases the audit burden on the IRS.

TAX TIP

Taxpayers who have itemized deductions that exceed the relevant standard deduction by only a few dollars should not elect the standard deduction merely because this "alleviates the need to keep records." It is unlikely that such a return will be selected for audit, since the IRS must always allow at a minimum the standard deduction. For example, if a married couple filing jointly has itemized deductions of $6,400 in 1993, the IRS is unlikely to audit these deductions because the largest adjustment that the agent could make would be $200 (since the taxpayers will receive a $6,200 standard deduction).

Additional Standard Deduction Amounts

Taxpayers (and spouses) who are age 65 or older before the end of the tax year, or are legally blind, qualify for higher standard deductions. For each instance of a taxpayer or his or her spouse being 65 or older or legally blind, the basic standard deduction is increased by an "additional standard deduction." This "additional" amount is $900 for single taxpayers and $700 for married taxpayers and qualifying widow(er)s in 1993. These additions apply only to the taxpayer and his or her spouse; they do not apply to dependents, such as children. Both amounts are indexed for inflation.

Example 5. Mary Allen, a divorced taxpayer of age 66, provides all of the support of her blind dependent grandson. Mary Allen's standard deduction for 1993 would be $6,350, the $5,450 "basic" standard deduction for a head of household and the $900 "additional" amount for a single person, age 65 or older.

Example 6. Wayne and Wanda Sharp, both age 71, file a joint return in 1993. Wanda is legally blind. Their 1993 standard deduction is $8,300 ($6,200 "basic" standard deduction and $2,100 "additional" standard deduction for three instances of being age 65 or older or legally blind).

ANSWERS TO REVIEW II

1. (c) All amounts are taxable except the $2,000 municipal interest, which is specifically excludable under the Code.
2. (b) Only the alimony is specifically allowed as a deduction for adjusted gross income in the Code. If an item is not specifically listed in the Code as a deduction for adjusted gross income, it can be deducted only from adjusted gross income (if at all).
3. (d) All expenses other than the alimony are deductible from adjusted gross income, and none are subject to any "floor" reductions. In addition, Yvonne may deduct $2,350 for each of the three personal exemptions, or a total of $7,050.
4. (d) Ray will deduct $5,450 as a standard deduction (since it exceeds the $4,300 of itemized deductions) and will deduct $4,700 for two personal exemptions.

☑ **Example 7.** Martin and Maria Steinberg, both age 42, provide all of the support of their 15-year-old daughter, who is legally blind, and all of the support of Martin's 68-year-old father. Their standard deduction for 1993 is the basic amount of $6,200; additional amounts are available only for the taxpayer and spouse.

For purposes of the "additional amount," a taxpayer or spouse is presumed to reach age 65 on the day *before* his or her 65th birthday. Therefore, a taxpayer whose birthday is on January 1 may claim the additional amount for the tax year before he or she reaches age 65. A taxpayer is legally blind if his or her vision is no better than 20/200 in the better eye corrected, or if his or her field of vision is not more than 20 degrees. In these cases, a certified statement from an eye physician or registered optometrist must be submitted with the tax return.

Limits on the Standard Deduction

All taxpayers do not have the choice of taking the standard deduction or itemizing deductions. For example, a standard deduction is not available for taxpayers filing a tax return for a "short" tax year (i.e., a year of less than 12 months). Two other special limitations on the use of the standard deduction are imposed on (1) married taxpayers filing separate returns and (2) dependents with unearned income.

Married Taxpayers Filing Separate Returns. When married taxpayers file separately, they must both consent either to itemizing or to using the standard deduction. Stated differently, if one spouse elects to itemize deductions, the other spouse is barred from using the standard deduction. This consistency requirement makes sense; if one spouse uses all of the itemized deductions and the other spouse uses the standard deduction, they would in effect be "doubling up" deductions (since the standard deduction is *in lieu of* itemized deductions).

☑ **Example 8.** Juan and Nan Perez elect to file married-filing separately in 1993. Juan's itemized deductions total $4,700, and Nan's total $1,200. If Juan itemizes, then Nan *must* also itemize, reporting $1,200 of deductions. Optionally, both could elect the standard deduction, and each would claim a $3,100 deduction (the basic standard deduction for the married-filing separately option).

Dependents with Unearned Income. If a taxpayer can be claimed as a dependent on another person's tax return, his or her standard deduction amount may be limited. The limitation comes into play when the taxpayer has *unearned income,* defined as passive income sources such as interest, dividends, rents, and royalty income. This is in contrast to *earned income,* which represents payments for work actually performed, such as salaries, wages, tips, and professional fees. Scholarship or fellowship income is earned income only if it must be included in gross income under the rules described in Chapter 2.

THE LAW

Sec. 63(c)(5). Limitation on basic standard deduction in the case of certain dependents. In the case of an individual with respect to whom a deduction under section 151 is allowable to another taxpayer for a taxable year beginning in the calendar year in which the individual's taxable year begins, the basic standard deduction applicable to such individual for such individual's taxable year shall not exceed the greater of—
  (A) $500 [$600 in 1993], or
  (B) such individual's earned income.

If a taxpayer is eligible to be claimed as a dependent on another person's return, the general rule is that the standard deduction is limited to $600 in 1993. This amount is increased for inflation each year. One reason this rule was enacted was to prevent wealthy taxpayers from shifting income to related taxpayers with lower tax brackets. For example, a parent in the 39.6% bracket may gift income-producing properties, such as stocks or bonds, to his or her child, whose marginal tax rate is 15%. With the current rule, such "unearned" income (dividends or interest) can only be offset with a standard deduction of $600. However, if the dependent also has *earned income*, the standard deduction can be increased to offset this amount (not to exceed the normal standard deduction for a single taxpayer of $3,700 in 1993).

Example 9. Harriet Schloss, age 13, earned $400 from a paper route and received $1,200 interest income in 1993. She is eligible to be claimed as a dependent on her parents' tax return. Her standard deduction for 1993 is $600, since this minimum amount exceeds her $400 of earned income.

Example 10. Assume the same facts as Example 9, except that Harriet's paper route earnings were $830. In this case, her standard deduction would equal the $830 of earned income, since this exceeds the minimum amount of $600.

In summary, the standard deduction of a person who can be claimed as a dependent on another person's return is limited to the *larger* of $600 or the taxpayer's earned income. However, in either case, the standard deduction cannot exceed the basic amount of $3,700. Any taxpayer subject to these limitations still has the option of itemizing deductions. Table 1-3 displays several examples of these rules.

Three other points need to be made regarding the standard deduction for such taxpayers. First, the special limitations apply in any case where the taxpayer is *eligible* to be claimed as a dependent; whether the taxpayer was actually claimed as a dependent on the other person's return is irrelevant. Thus, a parent cannot elect to forgo claiming the exemption in order to ensure that the child's standard deduction will not be limited. Second, the source of the unearned income is irrelevant for purposes of these rules. Thus, a child who invests his or her own earned income and earns interest or dividends will also be subject to the limitations. Third and finally, a dependent who is blind or age 65 or older may increase the limited standard deduction by the $700 or $900 additions discussed earlier.

Table 1-3 Examples—Standard Deduction of Dependent Taxpayers—1993

	A	B	C	D	E
Facts:					
Earned income (wages)	$ 0	$ 400	$1,000	$2,300	$3,750
Unearned income (interest)	700	1,100	2,900	1,400	1,900
Total itemized deductions	300	650	1,200	1,600	2,100
Deduction:					
Maximum standard deduction (larger of $600 or earned income, limited to $3,700)	600	600	1,000	2,300	3,700
Larger of itemized deductions or standard deduction	600	650	1,200	2,300	3,700

FILING STATUS

A taxpayer's filing status is used for several important tax computations in the Code. Most important, the filing status determines the rate(s) at which income is taxed. And, as discussed in the preceding section, filing status is used to determine a taxpayer's standard deduction. Finally, a taxpayer's filing status may qualify him or her for special deductions and credits. There are five possible filing statuses: (1) single, (2) married-filing jointly, (3) married-filing separately, (4) head of household, and (5) qualifying widow or widower. Each status is discussed below.

Single

A taxpayer's filing status is single if he or she is unmarried or is separated under either a divorce decree or a separate maintenance decree. A person's marital status is determined on the last day of the taxable year. The single tax rates are higher than the married-filing jointly and head of household rates. In certain cases, single taxpayers may qualify to file as a head of household, as described below.

Married-Filing Jointly

Taxpayers may elect to file a joint return if they are legally married at the end of the tax year and both agree to file jointly (as evidenced by both signatures on a single return). In such a case, all income, expense, and credit items of both spouses are combined on one tax return.

Generally, the tax due from this rate schedule on the combined income will be less than the tax due on married-filing separately returns. However, this would not necessarily be true if both spouses were allowed to use the *single* rate schedules on separate returns. This option is not available to married individuals; their only two choices are married-filing jointly and married-filing separately. This has led to the much-discussed "marriage penalty," where a married couple will pay more tax on a joint return than they would if they were unmarried taxpayers with the same incomes using single filing status.

Example 11. Hank and Rose Goodlove are two single taxpayers who are considering marriage. Hank and Rose each earned salaries of $25,000 in 1993, and each has approximately $2,000 of itemized deductions. Tax liabilities under three possible filing statuses are computed as follows:

	Hank (Single)	Rose (Single)	Hank (M-Sep.)	Rose (M-Sep.)	Both (M-Jt.)
Salary	$25,000	$25,000	$25,000	$25,000	$50,000
Std. deduction	(3,700)	(3,700)	(3,100)	(3,100)	(6,200)
Exemption(s)	(2,350)	(2,350)	(2,350)	(2,350)	(4,700)
Taxable inc.	$18,950	$18,950	$19,550	$19,550	$39,100
Gross tax	$ 2,846	$ 2,846	$ 3,083	$ 3,083	$ 6,158
Combined tax		$ 5,692		$ 6,166	$ 6,158

If Hank and Rose marry, their total tax liability will be at least $6,158, regardless of whether they file jointly or separately. If they remain single, their combined tax will be $5,692. Therefore, their marriage "penalty" is $466 ($6,158 less $5,692).

Married-Filing Separately

The married-filing separately status is available only to taxpayers who are legally married at the end of the tax year. As Example 11 above indicates, this status will normally not result in a smaller combined tax liability for the couple. (The $8 difference was due to rounding in the tables.) An inspection of the tax rate schedules in Appendix B discloses that these rates are approximately one-half of the married-filing jointly rate schedules. One possible advantage of filing separate returns is that it limits a taxpayer's liability for tax; if a joint return is filed, each spouse is jointly and severally liable for the *total* tax liability shown on the return.

TAX TIP

In some cases, the married-filing separately option may reduce the total tax liability. For example, one spouse may have large medical expense deductions and little adjusted gross income (AGI). As will be discussed in Chapter 4, medical expenses are deductible only to the extent that they exceed 7.5% of the taxpayer's adjusted gross income. By filing a separate return, this spouse would avoid the problem of combining income with his or her spouse and therefore increasing the 7.5% of AGI floor applicable to such expenses. The same logic may apply for casualty and theft losses and miscellaneous itemized deductions, both of which are also subject to an AGI floor.

Head of Household

The head of household filing status was established to provide tax relief to unmarried individuals who incur expenses related to providing a home for dependent individuals. Congress felt that such family responsibilities justified a tax rate schedule with rates approximately half way between the single and married-filing jointly rates. (Recall that a head of household also qualifies for a different standard deduction.) Because of the special tax breaks available for a head of household, Congress has established specific requirements to be met for this filing status. To qualify as a head of household, a taxpayer must (1) be a qualified individual who (2) provides a household for (3) a qualified relative.

"Qualified Individual." A qualified individual must either be unmarried at the end of the tax year or qualify as an "abandoned spouse." An abandoned spouse is a married taxpayer who (1) files a separate return, (2) pays more than half of the cost of keeping up his or her home during the year, (3) has a dependent child, stepchild, or adopted child living in the home for more than half of the year, and (4) has a spouse who did not live in the home during the last six months of the tax year. (The requirement that the child be a dependent of the abandoned spouse is waived if all other tests are met and the abandoned spouse has waived the exemption deduction in favor of the noncustodial parent.) Thus, a qualifying abandoned spouse is not forced to file a married-filing separately return just because it is not possible to file a joint return with his or her spouse.

✓ Example 12. Gretchin Davis provides all of the support of her 11-year-old daughter, who lived with her for the entire year. Gretchin's husband Marty left home last year and has not been seen or heard from since that time. Were it not for the special rule for "abandoned spouses," Gretchin would have to file married-filing separately and pay the highest tax rates, since Marty is not around to sign a joint return. Because Gretchin meets all of the requirements, she may file as a head of household.

"Provides a Household." The qualified individual must provide over one-half of the cost of upkeep of a household. These household costs include expenditures for such items as rent, taxes, mortgage interest, repairs, utilities, domestic help, and food. Estimates for values of food consumed and/or rent may be used, but these must withstand scrutiny by the Internal Revenue Service.

"Qualified Relative." In general, a head of household must provide over half of the household costs for a home in which a *dependent* relative resides (i.e., a person claimed as a dependency exemption on the head of household's tax return). A relative includes all blood relationships defined under the "relationship test" for dependency deductions described in the next part of this chapter. In general, this includes all blood relatives other than cousins.

There are two general exceptions to the qualified-relative requirement. First, an unmarried child of the taxpayer does not have to qualify as a dependent for tax purposes (married children must qualify as dependents). As long as the taxpayer provides over half of the living costs of the unmarried child, the head of household filing status is still available.

☑ **Example 13.** Ken Bright provides over half of the living costs of a household in which his unmarried 22-year-old son resides. His son does not qualify as a dependent because he violates the gross income test for dependency exemptions (described below). Nonetheless, Ken may use head of household filing status.

☑ **Example 14.** Assume the same facts as Example 13, except that Ken's son is married and he and his wife live with Ken. Since neither the son nor the daughter-in-law qualifies as a dependent, Ken must file as a single person.

Second, a dependent parent (or parents) does not have to live with the taxpayer, as long the taxpayer provides over half of the living costs of the home of the parent(s). This provision permits a taxpayer to claim head of household status when his or her parent(s) resides in a convalescent home. For all other dependent relatives, the dependent must reside with the taxpayer.

Qualifying Widow or Widower

A special filing status is available for certain qualifying widows or widowers. This special status allows the widow(er) to use the married-filing jointly rate schedules, standard deduction amounts, and other deductions or credits based on marital status. This special status is available only for the two years *following* the year of death of the spouse; in the year of death of the spouse, a joint return (with all accompanying elections) is available under the general rules. For example, a dependency exemption may be claimed for the deceased spouse in the year of death.

To qualify for this special filing status, the widow(er) must be unmarried and provide over half the household costs of his or her residence that was the home of a dependent child for the entire year. (Temporary absences of the child due to school, vacation, or military service do not violate the "entire year" requirement.) Without this special filing status, qualifying widow(er)s would at best qualify as a head of household and pay higher taxes.

☑ **Example 15.** Andrea North's husband Robert died in 1992. Andrea provided over half of the household costs of a residence in which her 20-year-old dependent daughter Sue lived in 1992, 1993, and 1994. Andrea may file a joint income tax return in 1992, the year of death of Robert, and claim three personal exemption deductions (for herself, Robert, and Sue). In 1993 and 1994, Andrea is a "qualifying widow" and may use the joint return rate schedule and standard deduction; however, she may claim only two exemption deductions (for herself and Sue).

☑ **Example 16.** Assume the same facts as Example 15, except that Sue does not qualify as a dependent in 1994. In this case, Andrea may be able to qualify as a head of household, assuming that Sue is unmarried at year-end.

REQUIREMENTS TO FILE A RETURN

In order to minimize the possibility that taxpayers will unnecessarily file a return when no tax is due, the tax return instructions specify certain minimum requirements for filing a return. These minimum requirements are specified in terms of "gross income," defined earlier in this chapter as gross receipts less all allowable exclusions. The tax return instructions include a table listing these amounts of gross income for various situations. This table (for 1993) is reproduced as Figure 1-4.

A close inspection of Figure 1-4 reveals that a general rule may be used to determine the minimum requirements to file a return. As a rule, the minimum filing requirement is the sum of (1) the personal exemption deductions for a taxpayer and his or her spouse (but *not* dependents) plus (2) the standard deduction for the taxpayer(s). The only exceptions to this rule would be for taxpayers who are not guaranteed a personal exemption deduction or a full standard deduction.

☑ **Example 17.** Aaron Jastrow is a single taxpayer of age 67. In 1993 his gross income must exceed $6,950 before he is required to file a return. The $6,950 is the sum of his personal exemption deduction of $2,350 and a standard deduction of $4,600 ($3,700 basic standard deduction plus $900 additional standard deduction for age 65 or older).

☑ **Example 18.** Ada Henry, age 12, is claimed as a dependent on her parents' tax return. Her minimum required gross income to file a return in 1993 is only $600, because (1) her standard deduction will be limited to this amount if her earned income does not exceed $600 and (2) as explained below, she may not claim a personal exemption for herself.

REVIEW III

1. Ralph Issen elects to file married-filing separately in 1993. His spouse Inga has already filed a separate return on which she itemized her deductions. Ralph's itemized deductions total $1,900. In addition to his personal exemption deduction of $2,350, Ralph will deduct the following amount from adjusted gross income:
   (a) $0.
   (b) $1,900.
   (c) $2,850.
   (d) $3,400.
2. Ellen Waitz, age 11, is claimed as a dependent on her parents' tax return. During 1993 she earned $350 selling magazines and received $1,300 interest on a savings account. Her standard deduction for 1993 will be

Chart A—For Most People

To use this chart, first find your marital status at the end of 1993. Then, read across to find your filing status and age at the end of 1993. You must file a return if your gross income was at least the amount shown in the last column. Gross income means all income you received in the form of money, goods, property, and services that is not exempt from tax, including any gain on the sale of your main home.

Marital status	Filing Status	Age	Gross Income
Single (including divorced and separated	Single	under 65	$ 6,050
		65 or older	$ 6,950
	Head of household	under 65	$ 7,800
		65 or older	$ 8,700
Married with a child and living apart from your spouse during the last 6 months of 1993	Head of household (see page 10)	under 65	$ 7,800
		65 or older	$ 8,700
Married and living with your spouse at end of 1993 (or on the date your spouse died)	Married, joint return	under 65 (both spouses)	$10,900
		65 or older (one spouse)	$11,600
		65 or older (both spouses)	$12,300
	Married, separate return	any age	$ 2,350
Married, not living with your spouse at end of 1993 (or on the date your spouse died)	Married, joint or separate return	any age	$ 2,350
Widowed before 1993 and not remarried in 1993	Single	under 65	$ 6,050
		65 or older	$ 6,950
	Head of household	under 65	$ 7,800
		65 or older	$ 8,700
	Qualifying widow(er) with dependent child	under 65	$ 8,550
		65 or older	$ 9,250

Chart B—For Children

If your parent (or someone else) can claim you as a dependent, and any of the conditions listed below applies to you, you must file a return.

In this chart, unearned income includes taxable interest and dividends. Earned income includes wages, tips, and taxable scholarships and fellowships.

Single dependents under 65
You must file a return if—

Your unearned income was	and	the total of that income plus your earned income was
$1 or more		more than $600
$0		more than $3,700

Figure 1-4 Requirements to File a Return

(a) $350.
(b) $600.
(c) $950.
(d) $3,600.

3. Brenda Irby's husband Charles died in 1992. In 1993 Brenda provided over half of the household costs of her home in which her 19-year-old daughter Ann and Ann's husband William reside. Neither qualifies as Brenda's dependent for tax purposes. Brenda's filing status for 1993 is
   (a) single.
   (b) head of household.
   (c) qualifying widow.
   (d) married-filing separately.

4. Thomas Ivy is a 68-year-old single person who qualifies as a head of household because he provides over half of the support of his 15-year old grandson. Thomas must file a tax return in 1993 if his gross income exceeds
   (a) $5,450.
   (b) $7,800.
   (c) $8,500.
   (d) $8,700.

Answers are on page 1-28.

IV PERSONAL EXEMPTION DEDUCTIONS AND INFLATION ADJUSTMENTS
(Code Sections 1, 63, 151, 152, and 153)

PERSONAL EXEMPTION DEDUCTIONS

As mentioned earlier in this chapter, the personal exemption deduction was originally enacted by Congress to exempt a subsistence level of income from taxation. This subsistence level was loosely based on the number of individuals in a taxpayer's household. Although the amount of the exemption deduction today is hardly adequate to cover a subsistence level of existence, taxpayers obviously will claim all exemptions allowed under the Code.

Each personal exemption deduction is worth $2,350 in 1993. However, as discussed later in this section, taxpayers with incomes above certain levels may lose a portion or all of their exemption deductions under a special "phaseout" rule applicable to 1991 and later years.

A taxpayer can deduct an exemption for himself or herself and an exemption for his or her spouse. However, taxpayers who are eligible to be claimed as dependents by another person are *not* entitled to an exemption deduction. The rationale for this rule is the same as for the rule limiting the standard deduction of such a taxpayer when unearned income is present; Congress wanted to remove the incentive to shift income to family members with lower marginal tax rates.

☑ **Example 19.** Terry Moore, age 10, is claimed as a dependent on his parents' tax return. During 1993 Terry's parents transferred 1,000 shares of stock to Terry by depositing the shares in a trusteed account. This account earned $6,000 interest during the year. If this is Terry's only income for the year, his taxable income will be $5,400 ($6,000 less a $600 standard deduction). Terry may not claim a personal exemption for himself, since he is eligible to be claimed as a dependent by his parents. (And, to add insult to injury, some of the $5,400 will be taxed at Terry's parents' marginal tax rate! See the discussion of the "allocable parental tax" in Chapter 2.)

A taxpayer may also deduct additional personal exemption amounts for anyone who qualifies as a "dependent." The Code specifies five tests that must be met before an individual can be claimed as a dependent. All five tests must be met by a dependent, unless one of several exceptions applies. The five tests are (1) citizenship, (2) gross income, (3) relationship, (4) support, and (5) filing status.

Citizenship Test

An eligible dependent must be a U.S. citizen or resident, or a resident of Canada or Mexico for a portion of the taxpayer's tax year. Special rules are provided for adopted children of U.S. citizens living abroad; normally, these children meet the citizenship test if they live with the taxpayer for the entire year.

Gross Income Test

As a general rule, the gross income of a dependent may not exceed the amount of a personal exemption ($2,350 in 1993). Recall that gross income is total income (i.e., gross receipts) less allowable exclusions; no expenses are deducted in determining gross income.

ANSWERS TO REVIEW III

1. (b) Since the taxpayer's spouse itemized, the taxpayer must also itemize on a separate return, even though these deductions are less than the normal standard deduction for a married-filing separately return if both spouses had elected to use the standard deduction.
2. (b) For a person claimed as a dependent on another's return, the deduction is limited to the larger of $600 (in 1993) or the earned income of the taxpayer (here $350).
3. (a) Brenda is not a "qualified widow" because her daughter does not qualify as her dependent. And since her daughter is married, Brenda will not qualify as a head of household. The only option left is that of a single taxpayer.
4. (d) The minimum requirement to file a return is the sum of the personal exemption of the taxpayer ($2,350) plus the standard deduction for a head of household ($5,450 basic deduction plus $900 for being age 65 or older). Note that the possible exemption deduction for the grandson is not included for these purposes; only a spouse's exemption would be added to the taxpayer's.

☑ **Example 20.** During 1993 John Vale had $1,300 of interest from state of Illinois bonds, $2,600 of gross rental receipts, and $600 of rental expenses. John may not be claimed as a dependent by another person, since his gross income is $2,600. The interest income is not included in gross income because it is excludable by law. However, the $2,600 of gross rents are included, and he *cannot* reduce this amount by expenses when determining "gross income."

The gross income test is waived for a child of the taxpayer who is either under age 19 or a full-time student under age 24. A full-time student must attend a recognized educational organization for at least parts of five calendar months during the tax year and must be enrolled as a "full-time" student, as defined by the educational organization. This special rule applies only to a child of the taxpayer; it does not apply to other relatives. Furthermore, this exception is a waiver of only one of the five dependency tests; the other four tests (most notably the support test) must still be met.

☑ **Example 21.** Dora Herring provides over half of the support of her 22-year-old son Dave, who is a full-time student at a local community college. During the summer of 1993, Dave worked full-time and earned $4,200. Dora may claim Dave as a dependent on her 1993 return.

☑ **Example 22.** Assume the same facts as Example 21, except that Dave used the $4,200 to provide over half of his own support. In this case, Dora may not claim Dave as an exemption. Even though the gross income test is waived, the support test (described below) is not met.

☑ **Example 23.** Assume the same facts as Example 21, except that Dave is 27 years old. In this case Dora may not claim an exemption for Dave; the exception for a full-time student applies only if the child is under 24 years of age.

Relationship Test

To qualify as a dependent, an individual must be either a blood relative of the taxpayer (as defined in Code Sec. 152) or a member of the taxpayer's household for the entire year. For purposes of the household test, temporary absences (e.g., sickness, school, military) will not disqualify the individual as a dependent.

The qualifying relationships are shown in Figure 1-5. Cousins do not meet the test of being blood relatives; they have to qualify as a member of the taxpayer's household for the entire year. Note that step and in-law relationships also qualify, although foster children must live with the taxpayer for the entire year.

☑ **Example 24.** Darlene Bringle's cousin Martha lived with her during 1993, except for eight months that she lived in a college dormitory as a full-time student. Martha meets the relationship test as a member of Darlene's household for the entire year; the temporary absence due to school has no effect on her status.

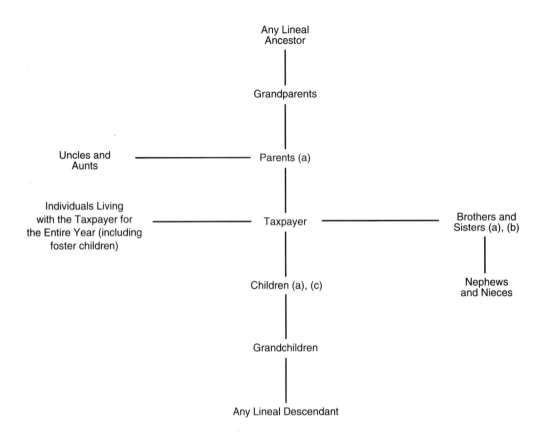

(a) Includes step and in-law relationships.
(b) Half-brothers and half-sisters are also included.
(c) Adopted children are treated as children by blood.

Figure 1-5 Qualifying Dependency Relationships

Support Test

General Requirements. Perhaps the most important of the five tests for a dependency exemption is the support test. As a general rule, a taxpayer must provide over half of the total support of a dependent during the calendar year; however, two notable exceptions are discussed later in this section.

Support includes amounts *actually spent* for basic living necessities such as food, clothing, shelter, medical expenses, education, and transportation. Support may also include some amounts for recreation. It is permissible to use an estimate of the fair rental value of food and lodging, rather than attempting to allocate such expenditures. In calculating total support, the taxpayers should include all expenditures other than those made from educational scholarships, regardless of whether the amount comes from a taxable source or a nontaxable one. The exception for scholarship expenditures reflects a desire of Congress not to penalize parents (by denying personal exemption deductions) for scholarship awards earned by their children during the tax year.

Form **2120** (Rev. August 1989)	Department of the Treasury—Internal Revenue Service **Multiple Support Declaration**	OMB No. 1545-0071 Expires 6-30-91 Attachment Sequence No. **50**

During the calendar year 19 _93_, I paid more than 10% of the support of

Rebecca Todd
(Name of person)

I could have claimed this person as a dependent except that I did not pay more than 50% of his or her support. I understand that this person is being claimed as a dependent on the income tax return of

Laurie A. Cridlin
(Name)

2205 Chancellor St., New Orleans, LA 70148
(Address)

I agree not to claim an exemption for this person on my Federal income tax return for any tax year that began in this calendar year.

Alice G. Todd   418 : 77 : 4031
(Your signature)   (Your social security number)

_3-2-94_   _1265 Sunset Ave., Phoenix, AZ 85281_
(Date)   (Address)

Figure 1-6 Multiple Support Agreement Waiver (Form 2120)

☑ **Example 25.** During 1993 Rebus McIntyre incurred $5,300 of personal support expenditures from the following sources: $800 from part-time employment, $2,100 from nontaxable social security, and $2,400 received from his daughter Elizabeth. Elizabeth may not claim her father as a personal exemption because he provided over half of his own support ($2,900 of the $5,300). Expenditures made from the social security are counted as support payments, even though this source of income is excludable in this case.

☑ **Example 26.** During 1993 a total of $5,600 was spent on Debra White's support. Debra's parents provided all of the support except for $3,000 received from a college scholarship. The $3,000 expenditure is ignored for purposes of the support test, and Debra's parents are treated as providing 100% of her support.

Exception for Multiple Support Agreements. A special exception to the support test applies in cases where several individuals (but no one person *individually*) contribute over half of the support of an individual. In this situation, only one person can claim the dependency exemption, and to do so he or she must (1) contribute at least 10% of the total support and otherwise qualify for the exemption and (2) obtain written waivers (Form 2120) from other 10%-or-more contributors, stating that they will not claim the dependency exemption on their tax returns. Form 2120 is illustrated in Figure 1-6, which incorporates the facts of the following example.

☑ **Example 27.** During 1993 Rebecca Todd received $8,200 of total support from the following sources: $1,800 from her own social security, $3,000 from her daughter Alice, $2,800 from her sister Laurie Cridlin, and $600 from her brother Charles Todd. In this case, only Alice or Laurie may claim Rebecca as an exemption, since each provided at least 10% of the total support. Assuming that Laurie claims the exemption, she must attach a signed waiver Form 2120 from Alice to her tax return (see Figure 1-6). Since Charles provided less than 10% of the total support, he cannot claim the exemption, and he is not required to sign a waiver.

☑ **Example 28.** Assume the same facts as Example 27, except that Rebecca received $7,000 of social security and spent it on her own support. In this case, Rebecca will claim an exemption for herself, and no one else can claim the exemption, because she provided over half of her own total support of $13,400 ($7,000 + $3,000 + $2,800 + $600).

TAX TIP

In multiple support situations, the individuals who provided more than 10% of the total support may be unable to agree as to who should claim the exemption. In such a case, it would make sense for the person with the highest marginal tax rate to claim the exemption and then divide the tax savings among the various contributors. For example, a $2,350 deduction for a 15% bracket taxpayer generates $352 of tax savings, while the same deduction for a 39.6% bracket taxpayer generates $931 of tax savings. The parties should reach some kind of agreement, because the exemption cannot be claimed without the signed waivers.

Exception for Children of Divorced Parents. Another exception to the support test applies to children of divorced parents. In 1984 Congress attempted to simplify the dependency deduction question for such children by enacting a relatively straightforward rule: The parent who maintains custody for the majority of the year is presumed to be entitled to the exemption deduction. However, the custody parent may waive this right in writing by signing a Form 8332, which will be attached to the noncustody parent's tax return (see Figure 1-7).

☑ **Example 29.** Hal and Jena Haikey were divorced in 1993. Jena was awarded custody of their six-year-old daughter Jan. Jena is entitled to claim an exemption deduction for Jan in 1993. Hal can claim the exemption only if Jena signs a Form 8332 waiving her right to claim the exemption. If this occurs, Hal must attach the Form 8332 to his return.

This general rule applies for divorce decrees entered into after 1984. Unfortunately, a more complicated set of rules applies for divorce decrees granted prior to 1985. Under pre-1985 law, a similar assumption is made—that the custody parent normally qualifies for the dependency deduction. However, there is one circumstance where the noncustody parent may claim the exemption.

If the divorce decree states that the noncustody parent is entitled to the exemption, and the noncustody parent contributes at least $600 of support during the year for each child, then the noncustody parent is entitled to the exemption. This rule still applies to divorces granted prior to 1985, since the post-1984 rules were not made retroactive.

IV. Personal Exemption Deductions and Inflation Adjustments   1-33

Form 8332
(Rev. September 1990)
Department of the Treasury
Internal Revenue Service

Release of Claim to Exemption for Child of Divorced or Separated Parents
▶ Attach to Tax Return of Parent Claiming Exemption.

OMB No. 1545-0915
Expires 6-30-93

Attachment Sequence No. **51**

Name(s) of parent claiming exemption: Martha M. Washington

Social security number: 106 : 32 : 4041

Part I Release of Claim to Exemption for Current Year

I agree not to claim an exemption for _Thomas J. Washington_
                                      Name(s) of child (or children)

for the tax year 19 _93_.

George Washington   463-20-1239   4/6/94
Signature of parent releasing claim to exemption   Social security number   Date

If you choose not to claim an exemption for this child (or children) for future tax years, complete Part II, as explained in the instructions below.

Part II Release of Claim to Exemption for Future Years

I agree not to claim an exemption for _____
                                       Name(s) of child (or children)

for tax year(s) _____
                 (Specify. See instructions.)

_____   _____   _____
Signature of parent releasing claim to exemption   Social security number   Date

Paperwork Reduction Act Notice.— We ask for the information on this form to carry out the Internal Revenue laws of the United States. You are required to give us this information. We need it to ensure that you are complying with these laws and to allow us to figure and collect the right amount of tax.

The time needed to complete and file this form will vary depending on individual circumstances. The estimated average time is:

Recordkeeping . . . . . . 7 min.
Learning about the law
or the form . . . . 5 min.
Preparing the form . . . . 7 min.
Copying, assembling,
and sending the form
to IRS . . . . 14 min.

If you have comments concerning the accuracy of these time estimates or suggestions for making this form more simple, we would be happy to hear from you. You can write to both the IRS and the Office of Management and Budget at the addresses listed in the instructions for the return with which this form is filed.

Purpose of Form.—This form may be used by a **custodial parent** to release his or her claim to a child's exemption. This form is completed by the custodial parent and is given to the **noncustodial parent** who will claim the exemption. The noncustodial parent who will claim the child's exemption must attach this form or a similar statement to his or her tax return.

The **custodial parent** is the parent who had custody of the child for most of the year. The **noncustodial parent** is the parent who had custody for the shorter period or who did not have custody at all.

Instead of using this form, a similar statement may be used. The similar statement must contain the same information that is required by this form.

Children of Divorced or Separated Parents.—Special rules apply to determine if the support test is met for children of parents who are divorced or legally separated under a decree of divorce or separate maintenance or separated under a written separation agreement. The rules also apply to children of parents who did not live together at any time during the last 6 months of the year, even if they do not have a separation agreement.

The general rule is that the custodial parent is treated as having provided over half of the child's support if **both 1 and 2** below apply. This means that the custodial parent can claim the child's exemption if the other four dependency tests in the Instructions for Form 1040 or Form 1040A are also met.

1. The child receives over half of his or her total support from both of the parents; **AND**
2. The child was in the custody of one or both of his or her parents for more than half of the year.

Note: *Public assistance payments, such as Aid to Families with Dependent Children, are not support provided by the parents.*

Exception.—The general rule does not apply if any of the following applies:

• The custodial parent agrees not to claim the child's exemption by signing this form or similar statement, and the noncustodial parent attaches the form or similar statement to his or her tax return for the tax year. (See **Instructions for Custodial Parent,** later.)

• The child is treated as having received over half of his or her total support from a person under a multiple support agreement (**Form 2120,** Multiple Support Declaration).

• A qualified divorce decree or written agreement went into effect before 1985 and it states that the noncustodial parent can claim the child as a dependent. But the noncustodial parent must have given at least $600 for the child's support during the year. (The noncustodial parent must also check the box on line 6d of Form 1040 or Form 1040A.) This rule does not apply if the decree or agreement was changed after 1984 to say that the noncustodial parent cannot claim the child as a dependent.

Additional Information.—For more information, get **Pub. 504,** Tax Information for Divorced or Separated Individuals.

Instructions for Custodial Parent.—You may agree to release your claim to the child's exemption for the current tax year or for future years, or both.

Part I should be completed if you agree to release your claim to the child's exemption for the current tax year.

Part II should be completed if you agree to release your claim to the child's exemption for a specified number of future years, or for all future years. If you are releasing claim for all future years, write "all future years" in the space provided in Part II.

Instructions for Noncustodial Parent.— Attach Form 8332 or a similar statement to your tax return for the tax year in which you claim the child's exemption. If the custodial parent completed Part II, you must attach a copy of this form to your tax return for each succeeding year in which you claim the exemption.

You may claim the exemption **only** if the other four dependency tests in the Form 1040 or 1040A Instructions are met.

Form **8332** (Rev. 9-90)

Figure 1-7   Form 8332

☑ **Example 30.** James and Kathleen Hethcox were divorced in 1983. The divorce decree granted custody of their 10-year-old son Allen to Kathleen, and specifically stated that Kathleen was entitled to the personal exemption deduction for Allen. During 1993 James contributed $1,000 and Kathleen contributed $800 toward Allen's support. Since the divorce decree did not specify that James could claim the exemption, Kathleen will claim the exemption for Allen.

☑ **Example 31.** Assume the same facts as Example 30, except that the divorce decree specifies that James can take the exemption. In this case, James may claim the exemption deduction, since his contribution was at least $600.

Filing Status Test

The filing status test (sometimes referred to as the "joint return test") denies an exemption deduction for a dependent who otherwise qualifies if he or she files a joint tax return. The purpose of this rule is to deny the double benefit of using joint return filing status to reduce tax liability and at the same time allowing someone else to claim a spouse's exemption deduction. However, a special exception to the joint return test may apply. Specifically, if a joint return is filed solely for purposes of receiving a refund of tax withheld (i.e., no tax liability exists for either spouse on separate returns), then the filing status test will not apply.

☑ **Example 32.** Ron Howard provided over half of the support of his 22-year-old son Donald and Donald's wife Sue. Donald and Sue had $11,400 of gross income in 1993 and filed a joint return showing a gross tax liability of $75. Because the joint tax return created a gross tax liability, Ron may not claim personal exemption deductions for either Donald or Sue. (This would be true even if Donald and Sue received a refund of tax for the year because of excess tax withholdings.)

☑ **Example 33.** Assume the same facts as Example 32, except that Donald and Sue had only $2,000 of adjusted gross income and no gross tax liability; however, they filed a joint return for 1993 solely for the purpose of receiving a refund of $220 of taxes withheld from Sue's salary. In this case, the filing status test would not be violated, because the joint return was filed solely for the purpose of receiving a refund when no gross tax is due on separate returns. Therefore, Ron may claim exemption deductions for both Donald and Sue, assuming that the other dependency tests are met.

To summarize, any person claimed as a dependent on another individual's return may not claim an exemption for himself or herself on his or her own return. A dependency exemption may be claimed for another person only if five tests are met: (1) citizenship, (2) gross income, (3) relationship, (4) support, and (5) filing status. Each dependency test is subject to one or more exceptions, as summarized in Table 1-4.

Phaseout of the Personal Exemption Deductions

In 1993, the personal exemption deduction is phased out (reduced) by an *applicable percentage*, defined as 2% for each $2,500 (or fraction thereof) of adjusted gross income

Table 1-4 Five Tests for Dependency Exemptions and Related Exceptions

Dependency Test	Exception(s)
1. CITIZENSHIP TEST (the taxpayer must be a U.S. citizen or resident, or a resident of Canada or Mexico for part of the year)	Adopted children of U.S. citizens living abroad qualify if they live with the taxpayer for the entire tax year
2. GROSS INCOME TEST (the gross income of a dependent may not exceed the amount of a personal exemption—i.e. $2,350 in 1993)	A child of the taxpayer who is either under 19 years of age or is a full-time student under 24 years of age
3. RELATIONSHIP TEST (a dependent must be a blood relative of the taxpayer—i.e., most relationships other than cousins)	A person who is a member of the taxpayer's household for the entire year
4. SUPPORT TEST (the taxpayer must provide over half of the total support—e.g., food, clothing—of the dependent during the year)	Expenditures from scholarship income are excluded from the test, and special rules are provided for multiple support agreements and children of divorced parents
5. FILING STATUS TEST (a dependent may not file a joint tax return with another person)	A joint return filed solely for a refund of tax (when no gross tax liability is due) is permitted

exceeding (a) $162,700 on joint returns (or those of surviving spouses), (b) $135,600 for heads of household, and (c) $108,450 for single taxpayers. For married-filing separately taxpayers, the reduction is 2% for each *$1,250* (or fraction thereof) of adjusted gross income exceeding $81,350.

In effect, the exemption deduction is completely phased out (for taxpayers other than those filing married-filing separately) when the taxpayer(s) adjusted gross income(s) is *more than* $122,500 greater than the beginning of the phaseout (i.e., 49 "bundles" of 2% phaseouts at $2,500 per bundle equals $122,500). For a married-filing separately taxpayer, the deduction is completely phased out when the taxpayer(s)' adjusted gross income is more than $61,250 greater than the $81,350 beginning of the phaseout. Thus, the exemption phaseout may be summarized as follows:

Filing Status	Beginning of Phaseout (AGI)	End of Phaseout (AGI)
Married-filing jointly	$162,700	$285,200
Head of household	135,600	258,100
Single	108,450	230,950
Married-filing separately	81,350	142,600

Example 34. Kay Quevas, a single individual, qualifies for one initial exemption deduction of $2,350 in 1993 and has $119,650 of adjusted gross income (AGI). Her AGI in excess of the $108,450 phaseout beginning for a single person is $11,200, which represents five "bundles" of $2,500 amounts (*rounded up*). Thus, her reduction in the $2,350 exemption deduction for 1993 will be 10% (2% × 5), or $235. Kay's exemption

deduction is reduced to $2,115. The following worksheet is provided in the 1040 instructions for computing the correct deduction (using the facts of this example):

Deduction for Exemptions Worksheet—Line 36 (keep for your records)

Use this worksheet **only** if the amount on Form 1040, line 32, is more than the dollar amount shown on line 3 below for your filing status. If the amount on Form 1040, line 32, is equal to or less than the dollar amount shown on line 3, multiply $2,350 by the total number of exemptions claimed on Form 1040, line 6e, and enter the result on line 36.

1. Multiply $2,350 by the total number of exemptions claimed on Form 1040, line 6e . . . . 1. __2,350__
2. Enter the amount from Form 1040, line 32 . . 2. __119,650__
3. Enter on line 3 the amount shown below for your filing status:
   - Married filing separately, enter $81,350
   - Single, enter $108,450
   - Head of household, enter $135,600
   - Married filing jointly or Qualifying widow(er), enter $162,700

   3. __108,450__
4. Subtract line 3 from line 2. If zero or less, **stop here;** enter the amount from line 1 above on Form 1040, line 36 . . . . 4. __11,200__

   Note: If line 4 is more than $122,500 (more than $61,250 if married filing separately), **stop here;** you **cannot** take a deduction for exemptions. Enter -0- on Form 1040, line 36.
5. Divide line 4 by $2,500 ($1,250 if married filing separately). If the result is not a whole number, round it up to the next higher whole number (for example, round 0.0004 to 1) . . . . 5. __5__
6. Multiply line 5 by 2% (.02) and enter the result as a decimal amount . . . . 6. __.10__
7. Multiply line 1 by line 6 . . . . 7. __235__
8. **Deduction for exemptions.** Subtract line 7 from line 1. Enter the result here and on Form 1040, line 36 . . . . 8. __2115__

✓ **Example 35.** Assume the same facts as Example 34, except that Kay files as a married-filing separately taxpayer. In this case, her AGI in excess of the $81,350 beginning of the phaseout for married-filing separately is $38,300, which represents 31 "bundles" of $1,250 amounts (rounded up). In this case, her reduction will be 62% of $2,350, or $1,457, and her net exemption deduction will be $893.

✓ **Example 36.** Al and Nan Bacon, married, qualify for two exemption deductions in 1993, or an initial deduction of $4,700 ($2,350 × 2). The net exemption deduction for various levels of adjusted gross income (AGI) after the phaseout is reflected as follows:

AGI	AGI in Excess Beginning of Phaseout	Number of 2% Reductions (rounded up)	Reduction Amount	Net Exemption Deduction
$162,700	$ 0	0 (0%)	$ 0	$ 4,700
167,700	5,000	2 (4%)	188	4,512
167,701	5,001	3 (6%)	282	4,418
263,700	101,000	41 (82%)	3,854	846
285,200	122,500	49 (98%)	4,606	94
285,201	122,501	50 (100%)	4,700	0
312,700	150,000	50 (100%)	4,700	0

TAX TIP

In Example 36, when the taxpayers' AGI increased $1 from $167,700 to $167,701, the personal exemption deduction was decreased 2%, or $92. Since these taxpayers would likely be in the 36% tax bracket, $1 more of AGI creates $34 more of tax liability! Obviously, it would pay the taxpayers to find or create $1 more of deductions for AGI before the end of the year, assuming that it is too late to postpone recognition of any gross income.

ANNUAL INFLATION ADJUSTMENTS

As part of the Economic Recovery Tax Act of 1981, Congress instituted a special annual adjustment to compensate taxpayers for the effects of inflation. This inflation adjustment is made to three items: (1) the taxable income brackets used in the tax rate schedules, (2) the standard deduction (including the $600 minimum standard deduction), and (3) the personal exemption deduction (including the phaseout thresholds beginning in 1993). Each amount is adjusted to prevent the problem of "bracket creep," which can cause a taxpayer to pay more taxes solely because of inflation.

The IRS determines the inflation adjustment each August, first by computing the increase in the consumer price index from the previous August. The computed increase is then used to adjust the numbers for the following tax year. After some rounding, each tax bracket (for each filing status) is "widened" by the inflation adjustment. (However, the new 36% and 39.6% brackets will not be adjusted for inflation until 1995.) Each standard deduction amount and each personal exemption amount are also increased by the same inflation percentage. As a result, these amounts usually change each year. While this complicates any attempt to simplify the tax law, it does produce savings for taxpayers.

TAX TIP

As we went to press, the IRS released the 1994 inflation-adjusted numbers for the tax rate schedules, standard deduction, and personal exemption. In order to avoid confusion in this text, we will strictly work with the 1993 numbers, since all tax returns used are for the year 1993. However, two tables in Appendix B of this text include the rate schedules and a table of all other inflation-adjusted numbers for 1994. These numbers would be relevant for tax planning for 1994 and beyond.

✓ **Example 37.** The 1994 inflation adjustment was determined in August 1993 to be approximately 3.0%. In this case, the 1994 standard deduction for a single individual was increased to $3,800, each personal exemption deduction was increased to

$2,450, and each tax bracket was increased approximately 3.0% (for example, the 15% bracket for a single individual was increased from $22,100 to $22,750). Finally, the exemption phaseout threshold of $108,450 for a single taxpayer was increased to $111,800. All amounts were subject to Code rounding rules.

REVIEW IV

1. Linda Folkes provides more than half of the support of her sister Ellen and her aunt Mary. Ellen earned $300 of interest income from a savings account during 1993 and received $3,600 from her typing business (her expenses related to the typing totaled $2,000). Mary received $2,200 of social security income and $1,700 of dividends in 1993. On her 1993 return, Linda may claim exemption deductions for
   (a) Ellen only.
   (b) Mary only.
   (c) neither Ellen nor Mary.
   (d) both Ellen and Mary.

2. Hank and Jean Aaron (both age 45) provide all of the support of their blind 14-year-old daughter Dawn. They also contributed $4,000 toward the support of their 21-year old son Jim, who spent $4,300 on his own support from a university scholarship (he is a full-time student). Assuming that the Aarons file a joint return, they may claim
   (a) two exemption deductions.
   (b) three exemption deductions.
   (c) four exemption deductions.
   (d) five exemption deductions.

3. Teena Seigo, age 74, received her total support of $9,000 in 1993 from the following individuals: $700 from her sister Jeena, $4,000 from her brother Alfred, and $4,300 from her daughter Wilma. Assuming that the proper waiver forms are signed, the following individuals could potentially claim Teena as an exemption deduction:
   (a) none; only Teena can claim her own exemption.
   (b) only Alfred.
   (c) Alfred or Wilma.
   (d) Jeena, Alfred, or Wilma.

4. Ray and Norma Holden file a joint return in 1993 and claim a total of four personal exemption deductions. Their 1993 AGI is $210,600. What net amount may they deduct for personal exemptions on their 1993 return?
   (a) $9,400
   (b) $5,828
   (c) $5,640
   (d) $3,880

Answers are on page 1-41.

V FILING THE INDIVIDUAL RETURN
(Code Sections 1, 2, 3, and 63)

The basic tax return required for individual taxpayers is Form 1040. However, in some cases, an individual may be able to file one of two simplified returns, Form 1040EZ or Form 1040A. Each of these forms is discussed in the following text, and each is illustrated with simple examples.

Form 1040EZ

Form 1040EZ is the simplest tax return individuals can file. To file this form, taxpayers (1) must file as a single individual or married-filing jointly; (2) must not be 65 or older or blind; (3) must not claim any dependents; (4) must have taxable income of less than $50,000 (the limit on the Form 1040EZ tax table), consisting only of wages, salaries, tips, taxable scholarships, and/or interest (of $400 or less); and (5) must not itemize deductions or claim any adjustments to income or credits.

Figure 1-8 illustrates a completed Form 1040EZ for a taxpayer named Gwendolyn Nance. Note that the taxpayer has the option of contributing $1 to the presidential election campaign fund (without affecting the tax or refund due on the return). All figures are to be entered in the boxes, because this form is designed to be machine readable. The tax (line 7) is computed from the Form 1040EZ tax tables for single individuals.

In Figure 1-8, Gwendolyn is entitled to a $425 refund due to excess federal tax withholdings. The withholdings total, as well as the total wages figure, is obtained from her Form W-2, which is illustrated in Figure 1-9. Employers are required to furnish this wage statement to taxpayers no later than January 31 following the close of the tax year. This form is discussed in more detail in the appendix to Chapter 8.

Form 1040A

Taxpayers who are unable to use Form 1040EZ may be able to file Form 1040A, another simplified tax return. This form allows the reporting of a few more types of income (e.g., unlimited interest income, dividends, and unemployment compensation) and allows one deduction (contributions to individual retirement accounts) and three credits (child and dependent care credit, earned income credit, and the tax credit for the elderly or disabled) that are not reportable on the Form 1040EZ. The Form 1040A also permits all possible filing statuses and deductions for personal exemptions of a spouse and dependents. Just as on the Form 1040EZ, a taxpayer using the 1040A may not itemize deductions, claim other deductions or credits, or have taxable income of $50,000 or more (the limit on the Form 1040A tax tables).

Figure 1-10 illustrates a completed Form 1040A for William T. and Muriel P. Schwartz, married taxpayers who file a joint return and claim an exemption for their daughter Alexis. Note that the Form 1040A includes three optional schedules that may be applicable to certain taxpayers. For example, Schedule 1 (Interest and Dividend Income) must be filed by any taxpayer who has either interest or dividend income exceeding $400 (which is the case for William and Muriel Schwartz).

Schedule 2 (Child and Dependent Care Expenses) is used to compute and report the tax credit for child and dependent care (as well as a special exclusion discussed in Chapter 3). In the case of the Schwartzes, who incurred $2,600 of such expenses, the

Filing the Individual Tax Return

Form 1040EZ — Department of the Treasury—Internal Revenue Service
Income Tax Return for Single and Joint Filers With No Dependents 1993

OMB No. 1545-0675

Use the IRS label (See page 10.) Otherwise, please print.

Print your name (first, initial, last): Gwendolyn Nance
If a joint return, print spouse's name (first, initial, last):
Home address (number and street). If you have a P.O. box, see page 11. Apt. no.: 463 Chere Drive
City, town or post office, state and ZIP code. If you have a foreign address, see page 11.: Toledo, Ohio 43606

Your social security number: 414 20 6060
Spouse's social security number:

See instructions on back and in Form 1040EZ booklet.

Presidential Election Campaign (See page 11.)
Note: Checking "Yes" will not change your tax or reduce your refund.
Do you want $3 to go to this fund? ▶ Yes [X] No [ ]
If a joint return, does your spouse want $3 to go to this fund? ▶ Yes [ ] No [ ]

Filing status
1. [ ] Single   [ ] Married filing joint return (even if only one had income)

Report your income

Attach Copy B of Form(s) W-2 here. Attach any tax payment on top of Form(s) W-2.

Note: *You must check Yes or No.*

	Dollars	Cents
2. Total wages, salaries, and tips. This should be shown in box 1 of your W-2 form(s). Attach your W-2 form(s).	18,640	00
3. Taxable interest income of $400 or less. If the total is over $400, you cannot use Form 1040EZ.	200	00
4. Add lines 2 and 3. This is your **adjusted gross income**.	18,840	00
5. Can your parents (or someone else) claim you on their return? [ ] Yes. Do worksheet on back; enter amount from line G here. [X] No. If **single**, enter 6,050.00. If **married**, enter 10,900.00. For an explanation of these amounts, see back of form.	6,050	00
6. Subtract line 5 from line 4. If line 5 is larger than line 4, enter 0. This is your **taxable income**.	12,790	00

Figure your tax

7. Enter your Federal income tax withheld from box 2 of your W-2 form(s).	2,341	00
8. **Tax.** Look at line 6 above. Use the amount on **line 6** to find your tax in the tax table on pages 24–28 of the booklet. Then, enter the tax from the table on this line.	1,916	00

Refund or amount you owe

9. If line 7 is larger than line 8, subtract line 8 from line 7. This is your **refund**.	425	00
10. If line 8 is larger than line 7, subtract line 7 from line 8. This is the **amount you owe**. For details on how to pay, including what to write on your payment, see page 16.		

Sign your return

Keep a copy of this form for your records.

I have read this return. Under penalties of perjury, I declare that to the best of my knowledge and belief, the return is true, correct, and accurately lists all amounts and sources of income I received during the tax year.

Your signature: Gwendolyn Nance
Date: 4/15/94
Your occupation: Secretary
Spouse's signature if joint return:
Date:
Spouse's occupation:

For IRS Use Only — Please do not write in boxes below.

Figure 1-8 Form 1040EZ

Form W-2

1 Control number		OMB No. 1545 0008							
2 Employer's name, address, and ZIP code Gunn's Glass Works 1211 Maumee Drive Toledo, OH 43609			6 Statutory employee ☐	Deceased ☐	Pension plan ☐	Legal rep. ☐	942 emp. ☐	Subtotal ☐	Deferred compensation ☐ Void ☐
			7 Allocated tips				8 Advance EIC payment		
			9 Federal income tax withheld 2,341				10 Wages, tips, other compensation 18,640		
3 Employer's identification number 87-1123410	4 Employer's state I.D. number 87-1123410		11 Social security tax withheld 1,425.96				12 Social security wages 18,640		
5 Employee's social security number 414-20-6061			13 Social security tips				14 Nonqualified plans		
19 Employee's name, address and ZIP code Gwendolyn Nance 463 Chere Drive Toledo, OH 43606			15 Dependent care benefits				16 Fringe benefits incl. in Box 10		
			17				18 Other		
20	21		22				23		
24 State income tax 372.80	25 State wages, tips, etc. 18,640	26 Name of state OHIO	27 Local income tax			28 Local wages, tips, etc.		29 Name of locality	

Copy B To be filed with employee's FEDERAL tax return   Dept. of the Treasury—Internal Revenue Service

Figure 1-9   Form W-2

allowable credit is $528 ($2,400 maximum qualifying expenses times a .22 "applicable percentage"). Finally, Schedule 3 (Credit for the Elderly or Disabled) is used to report a special credit that is discussed in Chapter 5.

ANSWERS TO REVIEW IV

1. (b) For purposes of the gross income test, no deductions are allowed in computing gross income; therefore, Ellen's gross income exceeds $2,350, and she may not be claimed as an exemption.
2. (c) For purposes of the support test, any support payments made from scholarship funds are ignored; therefore, both children qualify as dependents.
3. (c) Individuals eligible to claim the exemption must contribute at least 10% of the total support; therefore, Jeena is not able to claim the exemption deduction.
4. (c) The Holdens' AGI is $47,900 above the $162,700 phaseout threshold for married-filing jointly status. This represents 20 "bundles" of $2,500 amounts ($47,900/$2,500, rounded up). Thus, the reduction percentage is 40% (20 × 2%), and the net reduction is $3,760 ($9,400 × .40). The final exemption deduction would then be $5,640, or $9,400 less $3,760.

1-42 *Filing the Individual Tax Return*

Form **1040A**	Department of the Treasury—Internal Revenue Service **U.S. Individual Income Tax Return**	**1993**	IRS Use Only—Do not write or staple in this space.

OMB No. 1545-0085

Label
(See page 15.)

Use the IRS label. Otherwise, please print or type.

L A B E L H E R E

Your first name and initial: **William T.** Last name: **Schwartz**

If a joint return, spouse's first name and initial: **Muriel P.** Last name: **Schwartz**

Home address (number and street). If you have a P.O. box, see page 16. **1623 Pacific Drive** Apt. no.

City, town or post office, state, and ZIP code. If you have a foreign address, see page 16. **Stockton, CA 95211**

Your social security number: **633:01:2234**

Spouse's social security number: **584:67:3032**

For Privacy Act and Paperwork Reduction Act Notice, see page 4.

Presidential Election Campaign Fund (See page 16.)
Do you want $3 to go to this fund? .... Yes [ ] No [X]
If a joint return, does your spouse want $3 to go to this fund? Yes [ ] No [X]

Note: Checking "Yes" will not change your tax or reduce your refund.

Check the box for your filing status
(See page 16.)
Check only one box.

1 [ ] Single
2 [X] Married filing joint return (even if only one had income)
3 [ ] Married filing separate return. Enter spouse's social security number above and full name here. ▶ _____
4 [ ] Head of household (with qualifying person). (See page 17.) If the qualifying person is a child but not your dependent, enter this child's name here. ▶ _____
5 [ ] Qualifying widow(er) with dependent child (year spouse died ▶ 19___). (See page 18.)

Figure your exemptions
(See page 19.)

If more than seven dependents, see page 22

6a [X] **Yourself.** If your parent (or someone else) can claim you as a dependent on his or her tax return, **do not** check box 6a. But be sure to check the box on line 18b on page 2.

b [X] **Spouse**

c Dependents:

(1) Name (first, initial, and last name)	(2) Check if under age 1	(3) If age 1 or older, dependent's social security number	(4) Dependent's relationship to you	(5) No. of months lived in your home in 1993
Alexis B. Schwartz		410:22:6612	Daughter	12

No. of boxes checked on 6a and 6b: **2**

No. of your children on 6c who:
• lived with you: **1**
• didn't live with you due to divorce or separation (see page 22): ___

Dependents on 6c not entered above: ___

d If your child didn't live with you but is claimed as your dependent under a pre-1985 agreement, check here ...... ▶ [ ]
e Total number of exemptions claimed.

Add numbers entered on lines above: **3**

Figure your total income

Attach Copy B of your Forms W-2 and 1099-R here.

If you didn't get a W-2, see page 24

If you are attaching a check or money order, put it on top of any Forms W-2 or 1099-R

7 Wages, salaries, tips, etc. This should be shown in box 1 of your W-2 form(s). Attach Form(s) W-2. — 7 — **24,060**
8a **Taxable** interest income (see page 25). If over $400, also complete and attach Schedule 1, Part I. — 8a — **510**
b **Tax-exempt** interest. DO NOT include on line 8a. 8b _____
9 Dividends. If over $400, also complete and attach Schedule 1, Part II. — 9 — **430**
10a Total IRA distributions. 10a _____ 10b Taxable amount (see page 26). 10b _____
11a Total pensions and annuities. 11a _____ 11b Taxable amount (see page 26). 11b _____
12 Unemployment compensation (see page 30). 12 _____
13a Social security benefits. 13a _____ 13b Taxable amount (see page 30). 13b _____
14 Add lines 7 through 13b (far right column). This is your **total income.** ▶ 14 **25,000**

Figure your adjusted gross income

15a Your IRA deduction (see page 32). 15a _____
b Spouse's IRA deduction (see page 32). 15b _____
c Add lines 15a and 15b. These are your **total adjustments.** 15c _____
16 Subtract line 15c from line 14. This is your **adjusted gross income.** If less than $23,050 and a child lived with you, see page 63 to find out if you can claim the "Earned income credit" on line 28c. ▶ 16 **25,000**

Cat. No. 11327A   1993 Form 1040A page 1

Figure 1-10   Form 1040A

1993 Form 1040A page 2

Name(s) shown on page 1 | Your social security number

Figure your standard deduction, exemption amount, and taxable income

17 Enter the amount from line 16. — 17 | 25,000

18a Check if: ☐ You were 65 or older ☐ Blind / ☐ Spouse was 65 or older ☐ Blind — Enter number of boxes checked ▶ 18a | 0

b If your parent (or someone else) can claim you as a dependent, check here . . . . ▶ 18b ☐

c If you are married filing separately and your spouse files Form 1040 and itemizes deductions, see page 36 and check here ▶ 18c ☐

19 Enter the **standard deduction** shown below for your filing status. **But if you checked any box on line 18a or b,** go to page 36 to find your standard deduction. **If you checked box 18c, enter -0-.**
- Single—$3,700
- Head of household—$5,450
- Married filing jointly or Qualifying widow(er)—$6,200
- Married filing separately—$3,100

19 | 6,200

20 Subtract line 19 from line 17. If line 19 is more than line 17, enter -0-. 20 | 18,800

21 Multiply $2,350 by the total number of exemptions claimed on line 6e. 21 | 7,050

22 Subtract line 21 from line 20. If line 21 is more than line 20, enter -0-. This is your **taxable income.** ▶ 22 | 11,750

Figure your tax, credits, and payments

If you want the IRS to figure your tax, see the instructions for line 22 on page 37.

23 Find the tax on the amount on line 22. Check if from: ☐ Tax Table (pages 50–55) or ☐ Form 8615 (see page 38). 23 | 1,766

24a Credit for child and dependent care expenses. Complete and attach Schedule 2. 24a | 528

b Credit for the elderly or the disabled. Complete and attach Schedule 3. 24b |

c Add lines 24a and 24b. These are your **total credits.** 24c | 528

25 Subtract line 24c from line 23. If line 24c is more than line 23, enter -0-. 25 | 1,238

26 Advance earned income credit payments from Form W-2. 26 |

27 Add lines 25 and 26. This is your **total tax.** ▶ 27 | 1,238

28a Total Federal income tax withheld. If any tax is from Form(s) 1099, check here. ▶ ☐ 28a | 1,620

b 1993 estimated tax payments and amount applied from 1992 return. 28b |

c **Earned income credit.** Complete and attach Schedule EIC. 28c |

d Add lines 28a, 28b, and 28c. These are your **total payments.** ▶ 28d | 1,620

Figure your refund or amount you owe

29 If line 28d is more than line 27, subtract line 27 from line 28d. This is the amount you **overpaid.** 29 | 382

30 Amount of line 29 you want **refunded to you.** 30 | 382

31 Amount of line 29 you want **applied to your 1994 estimated tax.** 31 | 0

32 If line 27 is more than line 28d, subtract line 28d from line 27. This is the **amount you owe.** For details on how to pay, including what to write on your payment, see page 42.

33 Estimated tax penalty (see page 43). Also, include on line 32. 33 |

Sign your return

Keep a copy of this return for your records.

Under penalties of perjury, I declare that I have examined this return and accompanying schedules and statements, and to the best of my knowledge and belief, they are true, correct, and accurately list all amounts and sources of income I received during the tax year. Declaration of preparer (other than the taxpayer) is based on all information of which the preparer has any knowledge.

Your signature: William T. Schwartz | Date: 4-15-94 | Your occupation: Brick mason

Spouse's signature. If joint return, BOTH must sign.: Muriel P. Schwartz | Date: 4-15-94 | Spouse's occupation: Lab assistant

Paid preparer's use only

Preparer's signature | Date | Check if self-employed ☐ | Preparer's social security no.

Firm's name (or yours if self-employed) and address | E.I. No. | ZIP code

Figure 1-10 (continued) Form 1040A

**Schedule 1
(Form 1040A)**

Department of the Treasury—Internal Revenue Service

Interest and Dividend Income for Form 1040A Filers

1993

OMB No 1545-0085

Name(s) shown on Form 1040A: William T. & Muriel P. Schwartz

Your social security number: 584 67 3032 | 633 : 01 : 2234

Part I

Interest income

(See pages 25 and 56.)

Note: *If you received a Form 1099–INT, Form 1099–OID, or substitute statement from a brokerage firm, enter the firm's name and the total interest shown on that form.*

1. List name of payer. If any interest is from a seller-financed mortgage and the buyer used the property as a personal residence, see page 56 and list this interest first. Also, show that buyer's social security number and address.

Payer	Amount
First National Bank	510

2. Add the amounts on line 1. — **510**
3. Excludable interest on series EE U.S. savings bonds issued after 1989 from Form 8815, line 14. You MUST attach Form 8815 to Form 1040A.
4. Subtract line 3 from line 2. Enter the result here and on Form 1040A, line 8a. — **510**

Part II

Dividend income

(See pages 25 and 57.)

Note: *If you received a Form 1099–DIV or substitute statement from a brokerage firm, enter the firm's name and the total dividends shown on that form.*

5. List name of payer

Payer	Amount
XYZ Common Stock	430

6. Add the amounts on line 5. Enter the total here and on Form 1040A, line 9. — **430**

For Paperwork Reduction Act Notice, see Form 1040A instructions.   Cat. No. 12075R   1993 Schedule 1 (Form 1040A) page 1

Figure 1-10 (continued) Form 1040A

**Schedule 2
(Form 1040A)**

Department of the Treasury—Internal Revenue Service

Child and Dependent Care Expenses for Form 1040A Filers

1993

OMB No. 1545-0085

Name(s) shown on Form 1040A		Your social security number
William T. & Muriel P. Schwartz	584-67-3032	633 : 01 : 2234

You need to understand the following terms to complete this schedule: **Dependent care benefits, Earned income, Qualified expenses,** and **Qualifying person(s).** See **Important terms** on page 58. Also, if you had a child born in 1993 and line 17 of Form 1040A is less than $23,050, see **A change to note** on page 59.

Part I

Persons or organizations who provided the care

You MUST complete this part.

	(a) Care provider's name	(b) Address (number, street, apt. no., city, state, and ZIP code)	(c) Identifying number (SSN or EIN)	(d) Amount paid (see page 61)
1	Toddler Nursery	112 Westwood Stockton, CA 95211	66-44108	2,600

(If you need more space, use the bottom of page 2.)

2 Add the amounts in column (d) of line 1. .... 2 2,600

3 Enter the number of **qualifying persons** cared for in 1993 ... ▶ ☐

Did you receive **dependent care benefits?** — NO ⟶ Complete only Part II below.
— YES ⟶ Complete Part III on the back now.

Part II

Credit for child and dependent care expenses

4 Enter the amount of **qualified expenses** you incurred and paid in 1993. DO NOT enter more than $2,400 for one qualifying person or $4,800 for two or more persons. If you completed Part III, enter the amount from line 25. .... 4 2,400

5 Enter YOUR **earned income.** 5 14,060

6 If married filing a joint return, enter YOUR SPOUSE'S earned income (if student or disabled, see page 61); **all others,** enter the amount from line 5. .... 6 10,000

7 Enter the **smallest** of line 4, 5, or 6. .... 7 2,400

8 Enter the amount from Form 1040A, line 17. .... 8 25,000

9 Enter on line 9 the decimal amount shown below that applies to the amount on line 8.

If line 8 is—		Decimal amount is	If line 8 is—		Decimal amount is
Over	But not over		Over	But not over	
$0	10,000	.30	$20,000	22,000	.24
10,000	12,000	.29	22,000	24,000	.23
12,000	14,000	.28	24,000	26,000	.22
14,000	16,000	.27	26,000	28,000	.21
16,000	18,000	.26	28,000	No limit	.20
18,000	20,000	.25			

9 × .22

10 Multiply **line 7** by the decimal amount on line 9. Enter the result. Then, see page 61 for the amount of credit to enter on Form 1040A, line 24a. .... 10 = 528

Caution: *If you paid $50 or more in a calendar quarter to a person who worked in your home, you must file an employment tax return. Get Form 942 for details.*

For Paperwork Reduction Act Notice, see Form 1040A instructions.   Cat. No. 107491   1993 Schedule 2 (Form 1040A) page 1

Figure 1-10 (continued)   Form 1040A

1993 Schedule 2 (Form 1040A) page 2

Name(s) shown on page 1 | Your social security number

Part III

Dependent care benefits

Complete this part **only** if you received these benefits.

11	Enter the total amount of **dependent care benefits** you received for 1993. This amount should be shown in box 10 of your W-2 form(s). DO NOT include amounts that were reported to you as wages in box 1 of Form(s) W-2.	11	
12	Enter the amount forfeited, if any. See page 62.	12	
13	Subtract line 12 from line 11.	13	
14	Enter the total amount of **qualified expenses** incurred in 1993 for the care of the qualifying person(s).	14	
15	Enter the **smaller** of line 13 or 14.	15	
16	Enter YOUR **earned income.**	16	
17	If married filing a joint return, enter YOUR SPOUSE'S earned income (if student or disabled, see the line 6 instructions); if married filing a separate return, see the instructions for the amount to enter; **all others,** enter the amount from line 16.	17	
18	Enter the **smallest** of line 15, 16, or 17.	18	
19	**Excluded benefits.** Enter here the **smaller** of the following: • The amount from line 18, or • $5,000 ($2,500 if married filing a separate return **and** you were required to enter your spouse's earned income on line 17).	19	
20	**Taxable benefits.** Subtract line 19 from line 13. Also, include this amount on Form 1040A, line 7. In the space to the left of line 7, write "DCB."	20	

To claim the child and dependent care credit, complete lines 21–25 below, and lines 4–10 on the front of this schedule.

21	Enter the amount of qualified expenses you incurred and paid in 1993. DO NOT include on this line any excluded benefits shown on line 19.	21	
22	Enter $2,400 ($4,800 if two or more qualifying persons).	22	
23	Enter the amount from line 19.	23	
24	Subtract line 23 from line 22. If zero or less, **STOP.** You cannot take the credit. **Exception.** If you paid 1992 expenses in 1993, see the line 10 instructions.	24	
25	Enter the **smaller** of line 21 or 24 here **and** on line 4 on the front of this schedule.	25	

1993 Schedule 2 (Form 1040A) page 2

Figure 1-10 (continued) Form 1040A

**Schedule 3
(Form 1040A)**

Department of the Treasury—Internal Revenue Service

**Credit for the Elderly or the Disabled
for Form 1040A Filers**

1993

OMB No. 1545-0085

Name(s) shown on Form 1040A

Your social security number

You may be able to use Schedule 3 to reduce your tax if by the end of 1993:

- You were age 65 or older, **OR**
- You were under age 65, you retired on **permanent and total** disability, and you received taxable disability income.

But you must also meet other tests. See the separate instructions for Schedule 3.

Note: *In most cases, the IRS can figure the credit for you. See page 38 of the Form 1040A instructions.*

Part I

Check the box for your filing status and age

If your filing status is:	And by the end of 1993:	Check only one box:
Single, Head of household, or Qualifying widow(er) with dependent child	1 You were 65 or older.	1 ☐
	2 You were under 65 and you retired on permanent and total disability	2 ☐
Married filing a joint return	3 Both spouses were 65 or older	3 ☐
	4 Both spouses were under 65, but only one spouse retired on permanent and total disability	4 ☐
	5 Both spouses were under 65, and both retired on permanent and total disability	5 ☐
	6 One spouse was 65 or older, and the other spouse was under 65 and retired on permanent and total disability	6 ☐
	7 One spouse was 65 or older, and the other spouse was under 65 and **NOT** retired on permanent and total disability	7 ☐
Married filing a separate return	8 You were 65 or older and you lived apart from your spouse for all of 1993	8 ☐
	9 You were under 65, you retired on permanent and total disability, and you lived apart from your spouse for all of 1993	9 ☐

If you checked box 1, 3, 7, or 8, skip Part II and complete Part III on the back. All others, complete Parts II and III.

Part II

Statement of permanent and total disability

Complete this part **only** if you checked box 2, 4, 5, 6, or 9 above.

IF: 1 You filed a physician's statement for this disability for 1983 or an earlier year, or you filed a statement for tax years after 1983 and your physician signed line B on the statement, **AND**

2 Due to your continued disabled condition, you were unable to engage in any substantial gainful activity in 1993, check this box . . . . ▶ ☐

- If you checked this box, you do not have to file another statement for 1993.
- If you **did not** check this box, have your physician complete the following statement:

Physician's statement (See instructions at bottom of page 2.)

I certify that _____
Name of disabled person

was permanently and totally disabled on January 1, 1976, or January 1, 1977, **OR** was permanently and totally disabled on the date he or she retired. If retired after December 31, 1976, enter the date retired ▶ _____

Physician: Sign your name on **either** line A or B below.

A The disability has lasted or can be expected to last continuously for at least a year . . . . . _____
Physician's signature   Date

B There is no reasonable probability that the disabled condition will ever improve . . . . . _____
Physician's signature   Date

Physician's name   Physician's address

For Paperwork Reduction Act Notice, see Form 1040A instructions.   Cat. No. 12064K   **1993 Schedule 3 (Form 1040A) page 1**

Figure 1-10 (continued)   Form 1040A

1993 Schedule 3 (Form 1040A) page 2

Name(s) shown on page 1 | Your social security number

Part III Figure your credit	10	If you checked (in Part I): Enter: Box 1, 2, 4, or 7 . . . . $5,000 Box 3, 5, or 6 . . . . $7,500 Box 8 or 9 . . . . $3,750	10	
		Caution: *If you checked box 2, 4, 5, 6, or 9 in Part I, you* **MUST** *complete line 11 below. All others, skip line 11 and enter the amount from line 10 on line 12.*		
	11	• If you checked box 6 in Part I, add $5,000 to the taxable disability income of the spouse who was under age 65. Enter the total. • If you checked box 2, 4, or 9 in Part I, enter your taxable disability income. • If you checked box 5 in Part I, add your taxable disability income to your spouse's taxable disability income. Enter the total. **TIP:** For more details on what to include on line 11, see the instructions.	11	
	12	• If you completed line 11, look at lines 10 and 11. Enter the **smaller** of the two amounts. • All others, enter the amount from line 10.	12	
	13	Enter the following pensions, annuities, or disability income that you (and your spouse if filing a joint return) received in 1993:		
	a	Nontaxable part of social security benefits, and Nontaxable part of railroad retirement benefits treated as social security. See instructions. 13a		
	b	Nontaxable veterans' pensions and any other pension, annuity, or disability benefit that is excluded from income under any other provision of law. See instructions. 13b		
	c	Add lines 13a and 13b. (Even though these income items are not taxable, they **must** be included here to figure your credit.) If you did not receive any of the types of nontaxable income listed on line 13a or 13b, enter -0- on line 13c. 13c		
	14	Enter the amount from Form 1040A, line 17. 14		
	15	If you checked (in Part I): Enter: Box 1 or 2 . . . . $7,500 Box 3, 4, 5, 6, or 7 . . . . $10,000 Box 8 or 9 . . . . $5,000	15	
	16	Subtract line 15 from line 14. If line 15 is more than line 14, enter -0-. 16		
	17	Divide line 16 above by 2. 17		
	18	Add lines 13c and 17.	18	
	19	Subtract line 18 from line 12. If line 18 is more than line 12, stop here; you **cannot** take the credit. Otherwise, go to line 21.	19	
	20	Decimal amount used to figure the credit.	20	× .15
	21	Multiply line 19 above by the decimal amount (.15) on line 20. Enter the result here and on Form 1040A, line 24b.	21	
Instructions for physician's statement		**Taxpayer.**—If you retired after December 31, 1976, enter the date you retired in the space provided in Part II. **Physician.**—A person is permanently and totally disabled if **both** of the following apply: 1. He or she cannot engage in any substantial gainful activity because of a physical or mental condition, and 2. A physician determines that the disability has lasted or can be expected to last continuously for at least a year or can lead to death.		

Figure 1-10 (continued)   Form 1040A

The addition of the three schedules to Form 1040A greatly increases the number of taxpayers who can use this form. However, note that any taxpayer who itemizes deductions or has taxable income of $50,000 or more cannot use Form 1040A.

Form 1040

Taxpayers who are not eligible to file Form 1040EZ or Form 1040A must file Form 1040. This includes all taxpayers who itemize deductions, claim adjustments to income other than contributions to individual retirement accounts, claim credits or report income sources other than those reported on Form 1040A, or simply have taxable income exceeding $50,000.

Figure 1-11 illustrates a filled-in Form 1040 for Henry and Marilyn Morgan, a married couple filing a joint return. Form 1040 provides for all possible filing statuses, as well as for reporting personal exemption deductions. The Morgans are claiming one exemption deduction for Mary Lou Morgan, a granddaughter. Therefore, their deduction for personal exemptions (line 36) is $7,050.

All sources of income are reportable in the income section of Form 1040. This includes the door prize, valued at $700, which is reported on line 22 ("Other income"). Any deductions *for* adjusted gross income (AGI) are reported on lines 24 through 30 as "Adjustments to Income." The Morgans qualify for one deduction for AGI, a $2,000 contribution to an individual retirement account.

Line 34 is used to report the larger of the standard deduction or itemized deductions. Since both spouses are age 65 or older in 1993, their normal standard deduction of $6,200 is increased by $1,400 (i.e., $700 for each instance of being age 65 or older). If the Morgans had elected to itemize deductions, they would be required to attach a Schedule A to the tax return. This form is illustrated in Chapter 4.

Since the Morgans' taxable income is less than $100,000, their gross tax liability must be computed from the tax tables. This tax is computed to be $13,508, according to the 1993 married filing jointly tax rate table. Assuming that they had income tax withholdings of $13,400, the Morgans owe a balance of $108, which they must pay when they file their tax return.

REVIEW V

1. Which of the following conditions would disqualify an individual from filing a Form 1040EZ?
    (a) Taxpayer has $320 of interest income.
    (b) Taxpayer has salary income exceeding $30,000.
    (c) Taxpayer has $380 of dividend income.
    (d) None of the above would disqualify the taxpayer.
2. Which of the following conditions would disqualify an individual from filing a Form 1040A?
    (a) Taxpayer has $800 of dividend income.
    (b) Taxpayer has an individual retirement account deduction.

1-50　Filing the Individual Tax Return

Form 1040 — U.S. Individual Income Tax Return — 1993

Department of the Treasury—Internal Revenue Service
For the year Jan. 1–Dec. 31, 1993, or other tax year beginning _____, 1993, ending _____, 19 ___
OMB No. 1545-0074

Label (See instructions on page 12.) Use the IRS label. Otherwise, please print or type.

- Your first name and initial / Last name: **Henry R. Morgan**
- Your social security number: **614 32 1126**
- If a joint return, spouse's first name and initial / Last name: **Marilyn M. Morgan**
- Spouse's social security number: **732 01 6464**
- Home address (number and street): **1120 Mamie Street**
- City, town or post office, state, and ZIP code: **Hattiesburg, MS 39401**

For Privacy Act and Paperwork Reduction Act Notice, see page 4.

Presidential Election Campaign (See page 12.)
- Do you want $3 to go to this fund? — **Yes: X**
- If a joint return, does your spouse want $3 to go to this fund? — **Yes: X**

Note: Checking "Yes" will not change your tax or reduce your refund.

Filing Status (See page 12.) Check only one box.

1. ☐ Single
2. ☒ Married filing joint return (even if only one had income)
3. ☐ Married filing separate return. Enter spouse's social security no. above and full name here. ▶ _____
4. ☐ Head of household (with qualifying person). (See page 13.) If the qualifying person is a child but not your dependent, enter this child's name here. ▶ _____
5. ☐ Qualifying widow(er) with dependent child (year spouse died ▶ 19 ___). (See page 13.)

Exemptions (See page 13.)

6a ☒ Yourself. If your parent (or someone else) can claim you as a dependent on his or her tax return, do not check box 6a. But be sure to check the box on line 33b on page 2.
b ☒ Spouse
No. of boxes checked on 6a and 6b: **2**

c Dependents:

(1) Name (first, initial, and last name)	(2) Check if under age 1	(3) If age 1 or older, dependent's social security number	(4) Dependent's relationship to you	(5) No. of months lived in your home in 1993
Mary Lou Morgan		212 60 4140	Granddaughter	12

No. of your children on 6c who:
- lived with you: _____
- didn't live with you due to divorce or separation (see page 15): **1**

Dependents on 6c not entered above: _____

d If your child didn't live with you but is claimed as your dependent under a pre-1985 agreement, check here ▶ ☐

e Total number of exemptions claimed.

Add numbers entered on lines above ▶ **3**

If more than six dependents, see page 14.

Income

Attach Copy B of your Forms W-2, W-2G, and 1099-R here.

If you did not get a W-2, see page 10.

If you are attaching a check or money order, put it on top of any Forms W-2, W-2G, or 1099-R.

7	Wages, salaries, tips, etc. Attach Form(s) W-2	80,800
8a	Taxable interest income (see page 16). Attach Schedule B if over $400	300
8b	Tax-exempt interest (see page 17). DON'T include on line 8a: 400	
9	Dividend income. Attach Schedule B if over $400	200
10	Taxable refunds, credits, or offsets of state and local income taxes (see page 17)	
11	Alimony received	
12	Business income or (loss). Attach Schedule C or C-EZ	
13	Capital gain or (loss). Attach Schedule D	
14	Capital gain distributions not reported on line 13 (see page 17)	
15	Other gains or (losses). Attach Form 4797	
16a	Total IRA distributions. 16a _____ b Taxable amount (see page 18)	16b
17a	Total pensions and annuities. 17a _____ b Taxable amount (see page 18)	17b
18	Rental real estate, royalties, partnerships, S corporations, trusts, etc. Attach Schedule E	
19	Farm income or (loss). Attach Schedule F	
20	Unemployment compensation (see page 19)	
21a	Social security benefits. 21a _____ b Taxable amount (see page 19)	21b
22	Other income. List type and amount—see page 20 — Door prize - TV	700
23	Add the amounts in the far right column for lines 7 through 22. This is your **total income** ▶	82,000

Adjustments to Income (See page 20.)

24a	Your IRA deduction (see page 20)	
24b	Spouse's IRA deduction (see page 20)	2,000
25	One-half of self-employment tax (see page 21)	
26	Self-employed health insurance deduction (see page 22)	
27	Keogh retirement plan and self-employed SEP deduction	
28	Penalty on early withdrawal of savings	
29	Alimony paid. Recipient's SSN ▶ _____	
30	Add lines 24a through 29. These are your **total adjustments** ▶	200

Adjusted Gross Income

31 Subtract line 30 from line 23. This is your **adjusted gross income**. If this amount is less than $23,050 and a child lived with you, see page EIC-1 to find out if you can claim the "Earned Income Credit" on line 56. ▶ **80,000**

Cat. No. 11320B   Form **1040** (1993)

Figure 1-11 Form 1040

Chapter Appendix: *Responsibilities of Taxpayers and Tax Preparers* 1-51

Form 1040 (1993) — Page 2

Tax Computation (See page 23.)	32	Amount from line 31 (adjusted gross income)	32	80,000
	33a	Check if: ☐ You were 65 or older, ☐ Blind; ☐ Spouse was 65 or older, ☐ Blind. Add the number of boxes checked above and enter the total here ▶ 33a	2	
	b	If your parent (or someone else) can claim you as a dependent, check here ▶ 33b ☐		
	c	If you are married filing separately and your spouse itemizes deductions or you are a dual-status alien, see page 24 and check here ▶ 33c ☐		
	34	Enter the larger of your: **Itemized deductions** from Schedule A, line 26, **OR** **Standard deduction** shown below for your filing status. **But if you checked any box on line 33a or b,** go to page 24 to find your standard deduction. If you checked **box 33c**, your standard deduction is zero. • Single—$3,700 • Head of household—$5,450 • Married filing jointly or Qualifying widow(er)—$6,200 + 700 + 700 • Married filing separately—$3,100	34	7,600
	35	Subtract line 34 from line 32	35	72,400
	36	If line 32 is $81,350 or less, multiply $2,350 by the total number of exemptions claimed on line 6e. If line 32 is over $81,350, (see the worksheet on page 25) for the amount to enter	36	7,050
If you want the IRS to figure your tax, see page 24.	37	**Taxable income.** Subtract line 36 from line 35. If line 36 is more than line 35, enter -0-	37	65,350
	38	Tax. Check if from **a** ☒ Tax Table, **b** ☐ Tax Rate Schedules, **c** ☐ Schedule D Tax Worksheet, or **d** ☐ Form 8615 (see page 25). Amount from Form(s) 8814 ▶ **e**	38	13,508
	39	Additional taxes (see page 25). Check if from **a** ☐ Form 4970 **b** ☐ Form 4972	39	
	40	Add lines 38 and 39 ▶	40	13,508
Credits (See page 25.)	41	Credit for child and dependent care expenses. Attach Form 2441 — 41		
	42	Credit for the elderly or the disabled. Attach Schedule R — 42		
	43	Foreign tax credit. Attach Form 1116 — 43		
	44	Other credits (see page 26). Check if from **a** ☐ Form 3800 **b** ☐ Form 8396 **c** ☐ Form 8801 **d** ☐ Form (specify) ___ — 44		
	45	Add lines 41 through 44	45	
	46	Subtract line 45 from line 40. If line 45 is more than line 40, enter -0- ▶	46	13,508
Other Taxes	47	Self-employment tax. Attach Schedule SE. Also, see line 25	47	
	48	Alternative minimum tax. Attach Form 6251	48	
	49	Recapture taxes (see page 26). Check if from **a** ☐ Form 4255 **b** ☐ Form 8611 **c** ☐ Form 8828	49	
	50	Social security and Medicare tax on tip income not reported to employer. Attach Form 4137	50	
	51	Tax on qualified retirement plans, including IRAs. If required, attach Form 5329	51	
	52	Advance earned income credit payments from Form W-2	52	
	53	Add lines 46 through 52. This is your **total tax** ▶	53	13,508
Payments Attach Forms W-2, W-2G, and 1099-R on the front.	54	Federal income tax withheld. If any is from Form(s) 1099, check ▶ ☐ — 54	13,400	
	55	1993 estimated tax payments and amount applied from 1992 return — 55		
	56	**Earned income credit.** Attach Schedule EIC — 56		
	57	Amount paid with Form 4868 (extension request) — 57		
	58a	Excess social security, Medicare, and RRTA tax withheld (see page 28) — 58a		
	b	Deferral of additional 1993 taxes. Attach Form 8841 — 58b		
	59	Other payments (see page 28). Check if from **a** ☐ Form 2439 **b** ☐ Form 4136 — 59		
	60	Add lines 54 through 59. These are your **total payments** ▶	60	13,400
Refund or Amount You Owe	61	If line 60 is more than line 53, subtract line 53 from line 60. This is the amount you OVERPAID. ▶	61	
	62	Amount of line 61 you want **REFUNDED TO YOU**. ▶	62	
	63	Amount of line 61 you want **APPLIED TO YOUR 1994 ESTIMATED TAX** ▶ 63		
	64	If line 53 is more than line 60, subtract line 60 from line 53. This is the **AMOUNT YOU OWE.** For details on how to pay, including what to write on your payment, see page 29	64	108
	65	Estimated tax penalty (see page 29). Also include on line 64 — 65		

Sign Here
Keep a copy of this return for your records.

Under penalties of perjury, I declare that I have examined this return and accompanying schedules and statements, and to the best of my knowledge and belief, they are true, correct, and complete. Declaration of preparer (other than taxpayer) is based on all information of which preparer has any knowledge.

Your signature	Date	Your occupation
Henry T. Morgan	4-15-94	Professor
Spouse's signature. If a joint return, BOTH must sign.	Date	Spouse's occupation
Marilyn M. Morgan	4-15-94	Professor

Paid Preparer's Use Only

Preparer's signature	Date	Check if self-employed ☐	Preparer's social security no.
Firm's name (or yours if self-employed) and address		E.I. No.	
		ZIP code	

Figure 1-11 (continued)   Form 1040

(c) Taxpayer has three qualifying dependents.
(d) Taxpayer's taxable income is $60,200.

3. During 1993 Chuck Windsor filed a married-filing separately tax return and itemized his deductions. Chuck's wife Ellen also filed a separate return for that year, and her itemized deductions totaled $1,200. Her only income was a $30,000 salary. Ellen must file
   (a) a Form 1040EZ.
   (b) a Form 1040A.
   (c) a Form 1040.
   (d) any of the forms listed above.

4. During 1993 Stephanie Mills received $24,000 of salary, $350 of interest income, and $890 of dividend income. What is the simplest tax form that she can file for 1993?
   (a) Form 1040EZ
   (b) Form 1040A
   (c) Form 1040
   (d) either Form 1040EZ or Form 1040A

Answers are on page 1-54.

CHAPTER APPENDIX: RESPONSIBILITIES OF TAXPAYERS AND TAX PREPARERS

(Code Sections 6651, 6662, 6663, 6694, 6695, 6701, 6702, 6713, and 7201)

In the final analysis, a taxpayer is responsible for all information shown on his or her tax return. It is often said that our tax system is a voluntary one; however, various penalty provisions have been included in the Code in order to "foster voluntary compliance." The major penalties applicable to taxpayers are summarized in this section.

Because of the complexity of our federal tax system, many taxpayers rely on other individuals to determine their tax liability, usually for a fee. Unfortunately, there is no assurance that all "paid preparers" are qualified to determine a person's tax liability and report it correctly. For this reason, the Code includes a number of penalty provisions applicable to certain actions of tax preparers. These provisions are also summarized in this Appendix.

PENALTY PROVISIONS APPLICABLE TO INDIVIDUAL TAXPAYERS

Table 1-5 summarizes the major Code penalty provisions applicable to individual taxpayers. Again, the point must be made that each taxpayer is responsible for his or her own return. The fact that a paid preparer completed the tax return does not excuse the taxpayer from the application of these penalties.

One other provision that may apply to individuals is the penalty for underpayment of tax liability. This penalty, which is in the form of an interest charge at a high rate (generally, a current interest rate *plus* 3%) is described in greater detail in Chapter 5. In addition, various other penalties, such as failure to include social security numbers on the tax return, may apply to individuals.

Table 1-5 Selected Penalty Provisions Applicable to Individual Taxpayers

Action of Taxpayer	Penalty
Failure to file a return by the due date (including legal extensions)	5% of tax liability for each month the return is late (25% maximum); 15% and 75% if fraud
Failure to pay a tax liability by the due date for payment	½% per month for each month (or portion of a month) that the payment is late. This penalty can offset any failure-to-file penalty.
Substantial understatement of tax liability (defined as exceeding the greater of $5,000 or 10% of the correct liability)	20% of the understated amount, unless "substantial authority" exists for the position taken on the tax return
Filing a "frivolous return" (one that does not have enough information to determine the tax liability or one that on its face is clearly incorrect)	$500 (includes any return filed for the purpose of delaying or interfering with the administration of the tax laws)
Negligence or intentional disregard of rules or regulations related to the income tax	20% of the underpayment of the portion of tax liability attributable to negligence
Fraudulent preparation of the tax return	75% of the underpayment due to fraud*

*Criminal penalties of fines of up to $100,000 and imprisonment for periods of up to one year may be assessed in lieu of the civil penalty described above.

Table 1-6 Selected Penalty Provisions Applicable to Tax Preparers

Action of Preparer	Penalty
Disclosure or use of information from a tax return by the preparer	$1,000 and/or imprisonment for up to one year
Failure to furnish a copy of the tax return to the taxpayer	$50 per failure (unless due to "reasonable cause")
Failure to sign the return as an income tax preparer	$50 per failure (unless due to "reasonable cause")
Failure to furnish identifying number on prepared returns	$50 per failure
Failure to retain a copy of each return prepared (or a list of such returns)	$50 per failure
Negotiation or endorsement of a check in respect to taxes that is issuable to a taxpayer	$500 for each such check
Understatement of tax liability due to an unrealistic position (a position not likely to be sustained on its own merits)	$250 for each return
Willful attempt to understate tax liability or reckless or intentional disregard of rules or regulations	$1,000 for each return
Aiding and abetting an understatement of tax liability on a tax return	$1,000 for each return
Willful preparation of a return in which material items are known to be incorrect	$100,000 fine and/or imprisonment for up to three years*

*This is a criminal penalty, not a civil penalty.

PENALTY PROVISIONS APPLICABLE TO TAX PREPARERS

In our society, almost anyone can hold himself or herself out as a "tax expert." In the case of tax return preparers, an Internal Revenue Service publication known as *Treasury Circular 230* specifies certain rules of conduct. In addition, it is necessary to have in place a series of penalties designed to "foster voluntary compliance" by tax professionals. Table 1-6 summarizes the major penalties applicable to tax preparers.

It is interesting to note that there is a penalty for failure to sign a return as a tax preparer. You may have noticed the space for this signature on the bottom of the Forms 1040A and 1040 illustrated in this chapter. In addition, the identification number of the preparer (usually a social security number) is required. This assists the IRS in uncovering unscrupulous preparers and locating returns that may contain similar errors.

Tables 1-5 and 1-6 offer only an overview of the penalty provisions applicable to taxpayers and tax preparers. There are many other legal and ethical considerations involved in determining and reporting an individual's tax liability. These topics are better left to a more advanced course in taxation.

CHAPTER PROBLEMS

PART

I   1. "Prior to 1913, all U.S. income tax laws were unconstitutional." Do you agree? Explain.

I   2. The Revenue Reconciliation Act of 1993 contained a number of tax changes. Nonetheless, it is viewed as simply an amendment of the Internal Revenue Code of 1986. Explain why such a tax act is not a new "code."

I   3. Trace the steps that a successful tax bill follows through the two houses of Congress, noting in your answer any points in the process where a vote is required.

I   4. What key factors must a taxpayer consider when choosing a court to hear a tax case?

II   5. During 1993 Allen Roe received $32,000 of salary, $2,000 of dividends, $1,000 of interest on a savings account, $600 of interest on state of Wisconsin bonds, and $3,000 of gross rent receipts (expenses related to the rents total $800). What is Allen Roe's gross income?

ANSWERS TO REVIEW V

1. (c) There is no provision on Form 1040EZ for reporting dividend income. Only salary income and interest income may be reported on this form.
2. (d) Taxpayers using Form 1040A must use the Form 1040A tax tables to compute tax liability, and these tables are limited to taxable incomes of less than $50,000.
3. (c) Since Chuck itemized deductions on a separate return, Ellen must do the same on her separate return. Thus, Ellen must use Form 1040 for 1993, since it is not possible to itemize deductions on Form 1040EZ or Form 1040A.
4. (b) Dividend income is not reportable on Form 1040EZ but can be reported on Form 1040A. Since Stephanie meets all of the other requirements, she can file a Form 1040A in 1993, rather than the more complicated Form 1040.

II 6. Determine the total deductions *from* adjusted gross income in 1993 for each of the following taxpayers:
   (a) Bob Allen, a single 62-year-old taxpayer, has $4,000 of legitimate itemized deductions.
   (b) Ron and Helen Wood, both age 43, provide all of the support of their twin daughters. Their legitimate itemized deductions total $6,250.
   (c) Hal Thomas, a single 60-year-old taxpayer, qualifies as a head of household because he provides all of the support of his 86-year-old mother. Hal's legitimate itemized deductions total $3,980.
   (d) Connie Swift, age 33, files married-filing separately. Her legitimate itemized deductions total $3,150. (Her husband filed a separate return and itemized.)

II 7. Ross and Mildred Allen, both age 45, have no dependents. Their taxable income in 1993 was $240,000. Determine their gross tax liability, assuming that a joint tax return is filed. How may they elect to pay the 1993 gross tax liability?

II 8. For the tax year 1993 Ryan Wilson (age 38 and divorced) qualifies as a head of household because he provides all of the support of his 11-year-old son Adam. Wilson's tax records disclose the following for 1993:

   Gross wages received $72,500
   Total interest income ($400 from Iowa bonds) 1,900
   Alimony paid to former spouse..3,300
   Local property taxes paid*...3,500
   Contributions to qualified charities*..2,000
   Qualified home mortgage interest paid*......................................4,300
   Federal income taxes withheld from salary...............................18,500
         *Qualified itemized deduction

   Calculate Wilson's 1993 taxable income and net tax liability (or refund due).

III 9. Hank and Nancy Arnold, ages 63 and 67, respectively, provide all of the support of Hank's 90-year-old mother Sue, who is legally blind. During 1993 Hank and Nancy had $44,000 of salary income and $800 of dividend income. Their legitimate itemized deductions total $6,300. Determine the Arnolds' 1993 taxable income, assuming that a joint return is filed.

III 10. Darlene Love, age 42, elects to file married-filing separately in 1993. Her only income was a $32,000 salary, and her legitimate itemized deductions total $2,250. Determine Darlene's 1993 taxable income, assuming that (a) her husband itemizes on a separate return and (b) her husband uses the standard deduction on a separate return.

III 11. Determine the total deductions *from* adjusted gross income for each of the following individuals. In each case, assume that the individual is claimed as an exemption on his or her parents' tax return and therefore cannot take a personal exemption deduction.
   (a) Melva Ames earned $600 from a paper route and received $1,200 of taxable dividends in 1993. Her legitimate itemized deductions total $420.
   (b) Same as (a), except Melva's legitimate itemized deductions total $680.
   (c) Dan Ack earned $1,460 as a summer lifeguard and received $900 of taxable interest income in 1993. His legitimate itemized deductions total $610.
   (d) Same as (c), except that Dan's lifeguard earnings for 1993 were $3,950.

III 12. Determine the taxpayer's filing status for each of the following situations:
   (a) Jill Abramson was divorced from her husband in December 1993. She retained custody of their six-year-old daughter Mary.
   (b) Alice Carroll's husband Tom died in February 1993. During the year, Alice provided all of the support of Tom's 86-year-old mother, who lived with her.
   (c) Same as (b), except the year is 1994 and Alice continued to provide all of the support of Tom's mother.
   (d) Tamara Russell provided over half of the support of her 23-year-old niece, Winnie Russell. Tamara cannot claim Winnie as a personal exemption deduction, since she had $2,500 of taxable income.
   (e) Tab Brando provides all of the support of his dependent parents, who reside in a nursing home.

III 13. Yolanda Moody is a single taxpayer of age 74. She is legally blind. What is the maximum amount of income that she may receive and yet not be required to file an income tax return in 1993?

IV 14. Determine the total number of exemption deductions allowed in each of the following cases:
   (a) Mark Wiedemier (age 68) provides over half of the support of his 80-year-old mother, who resides in a nursing home. His mother received $1,700 of interest on state of Ohio bonds and $1,300 of dividends on corporate stocks in 1993.
   (b) Janet Penn, a single 56-year-old taxpayer, provides over half of the support of her 30-year old son Ron, a full-time student who earned $2,600 of salary during the summer of 1993.
   (c) Larry and Donna Vaughn, both age 45, provide all of the support of their blind 22-year-old daughter Ann. They also provided $3,800 of the total support spent on their 19-year-old son Jeff. The remaining $5,600 of Jeff's support was provided by an academic scholarship he received from the university in 1993.
   (d) Same as (c), except that Larry Vaughn died on March 1, 1993.
   (e) Jane Mays provided over 80% of the support of her married 23-year-old daughter Miriam in 1993. Miriam filed a joint return with her husband Tolbert in order to recover $600 of tax withholdings on Tolbert's salary of $2,200 (Miriam had no income during the year).

IV 15. Henry and Wilma Rudolph are divorced taxpayers who have a 12-year-old daughter, Roxanne. Determine which taxpayer is entitled to claim a dependency deduction for Roxanne in 1993 under each of the following situations:
   (a) The taxpayers were divorced in 1993, and Wilma was granted custody of Roxanne. During the year, Henry contributed $1,300 toward Roxanne's support.
   (b) Same as (a), except that the divorce was granted in 1983, and the divorce decree specifies that Henry is entitled to the exemption deduction for Roxanne.
   (c) Same as (b), except that Henry contributed $540 to Roxanne's support in 1993.

IV 16. During 1993 Tom Randle's total support of $8,800 was provided by the following sources: $2,600 social security, $800 from his brother Allen, $2,100 from his sister Judy, $3,000 from his daughter Cynthia, and $300 from his own dividend income. Who is entitled to claim an exemption deduction for Tom, and what procedures must be followed in order to claim the deduction?

IV 17. Dick and Diedra Allen, both age 45, have $183,400 of adjusted gross income in 1993 and $20,000 of legitimate itemized deductions (after all appropriate reductions are reflected). Assuming that they have no dependents, determine their 1993 taxable income. (Hint: Do not forget to reflect the phaseout effects on the exemptions.)

IV 18. In each of the following cases, determine the final allowable deduction for personal exemptions after reflecting the phaseout computations (assume a 1993 year):
(a) A single taxpayer qualifies for one exemption and has adjusted gross income of $124,2000.
(b) A married couple qualifies for three exemptions and has adjusted gross income of $162,703.
(c) A married-filing separately individual qualifies for one exemption and has adjusted gross income of $85,400.
(d) A head of household qualifies for two exemptions and has adjusted gross income of $164,050.

V 19. John Smiley, age 16, is claimed as a dependency exemption on his parents' tax return. During 1993 John received $1,100 of interest on taxable corporate bonds, $300 of interest on tax-exempt municipal bonds, and $1,400 of dividends on corporate stocks. What is John's 1993 taxable income?

V 20. Sue Kane, age 68, had the following sources of income in 1993: $4,500 interest on a certificate of deposit at First Bank, $12,800 dividends on AB common stock, and $9,600 salary from a part-time job. She provides all of the support of her 87-year-old mother, who is legally blind. Compute Sue's 1993 taxable income and tax liability, assuming that she had $1,800 of income tax withholdings.

V 21. Marcello Brazzi, age 17, is claimed as an exemption on his parents' tax return in 1993. During 1993 Marcello received $1,600 interest from a savings account, $800 interest from taxable bonds, and $1,800 salary from a part-time job. His legitimate itemized deductions for 1993 total $400. Determine Marcello's 1993 taxable income and gross tax liability.

APX 22. Would a taxpayer save money by filing his tax return and deliberately paying the deficiency three months late, so that he can earn 10% interest on the tax due? Explain.

APX 23. Why is a tax return preparer required to sign all tax returns that he or she prepares? What is the penalty for failing to sign a return so prepared?

Tax Return Problems

(Use the appropriate blank forms located at the end of this chapter.)

24. [Form 1040EZ] Martha Goldstein (single, age 20) received wages of $18,450 in 1993. Her employer withheld total of $3,830 of federal income taxes from these wages. She also received $130 interest from a personal savings account. Prepare a 1993 Form 1040EZ for Martha.

25. [Form 1040A] Using the facts of Problem 20, prepare a Form 1040A for Sue Kane for 1993.

26. [Form 1040] Using the facts of Problem 8, prepare a Form 1040 for Ryan Wilson for 1993.

How Would You Rule?

27. During 1993 Mariann Beck's 18-year-old niece Jane, a full-time student, lived with her the entire year. Mariann can meet the 50% support test only if she can include the cost of a used car purchased for Jane in 1993. Jane uses the car to commute to school and for recreational purposes. Can Mariann include the cost of the automobile as an item of

support in meeting the support test for a dependency exemption? What is your opinion?

28. Bill and Charlotte Cridlin provide over half of the support of their 22-year-old daughter Ann, who has a full-time job and earned $13,000 in 1993. Ann takes four college courses at night, which qualifies her as a full-time student under the school's policies. May Bill and Charlotte claim a dependency exemption for Ann? What is your opinion?

Tax Return Portfolio Problem

You are now ready to begin preparation of the necessary tax returns for the Harold A. and Maude L. Neilson family. This "portfolio" problem is contained in Appendix A of this textbook, and portions of the returns will be completed at the end of each chapter. If this problem is assigned by your instructor, complete the instructions for the segment of the portfolio labeled "Chapter 1." These instructions involve

- the completion of a Form 1040EZ for Robert T. Neilson, and
- the completion of the personal information and exemption sections of Form 1040 for Harold and Maude Neilson.

All necessary forms for this problem appear in the appendix at the back of the book.

Chapter 1 Problem 24   Name _____   *1-59*

Form 1040EZ Department of the Treasury—Internal Revenue Service
Income Tax Return for Single and Joint Filers With No Dependents   **1993**

OMB No. 1545-0675

Use the IRS label (See page 10.) Otherwise, please print.

LABEL HERE

- Print your name (first, initial, last)
- If a joint return, print spouse's name (first, initial, last)
- Home address (number and street). If you have a P.O. box, see page 11. Apt. no.
- City, town or post office, state and ZIP code. If you have a foreign address, see page 11.

Your social security number

Spouse's social security number

See instructions on back and in Form 1040EZ booklet.

Presidential Election Campaign (See page 11.)

Note: *Checking "Yes" will not change your tax or reduce your refund.*
Do you want $3 to go to this fund? ▶
If a joint return, does your spouse want $3 to go to this fund? ▶

Yes No

Filing status

1 ☐ Single   ☐ Married filing joint return (even if only one had income)

Report your income

Attach Copy B of Form(s) W-2 here. Attach any tax payment on top of Form(s) W-2.

Note: *You must check Yes or No.*

2 Total wages, salaries, and tips. This should be shown in box 1 of your W-2 form(s). Attach your W-2 form(s).   2

3 Taxable interest income of $400 or less. If the total is over $400, you cannot use Form 1040EZ.   3

4 Add lines 2 and 3. This is your **adjusted gross income**.   4

5 Can your parents (or someone else) claim you on their return?
☐ Yes. Do worksheet on back; enter amount from line G here.
☐ No. If **single**, enter 6,050.00.
If **married**, enter 10,900.00.
For an explanation of these amounts, see back of form.   5

6 Subtract line 5 from line 4. If line 5 is larger than line 4, enter 0. This is your **taxable income**.   6

Dollars Cents

Figure your tax

7 Enter your Federal income tax withheld from box 2 of your W-2 form(s).   7

8 **Tax.** Look at line 6 above. Use the amount on **line 6** to find your tax in the tax table on pages 24–28 of the booklet. Then, enter the tax from the table on this line.   8

Refund or amount you owe

9 If line 7 is larger than line 8, subtract line 8 from line 7. This is your **refund**.   9

10 If line 8 is larger than line 7, subtract line 7 from line 8. This is the **amount you owe**. For details on how to pay, including what to write on your payment, see page 16.   10

Sign your return

Keep a copy of this form for your records.

I have read this return. Under penalties of perjury, I declare that to the best of my knowledge and belief, the return is true, correct, and accurately lists all amounts and sources of income I received during the tax year.

Your signature | Spouse's signature if joint return
Date | Your occupation | Date | Spouse's occupation

For IRS Use Only — Please do not write in boxes below.

Copyright © 1994 by Harcourt Brace & Company. All rights reserved.

1-60   Chapter 1 Problem 24

1993	**Instructions for Form 1040EZ**
Use this form if	• Your filing status is single or married filing jointly. • You do not claim any dependents. • You (and your spouse if married) were under 65 on January 1, 1994, and not blind at the end of 1993. • Your taxable income (line 6) is less than $50,000. • You had **only** wages, salaries, tips, and taxable scholarship or fellowship grants, and your taxable interest income was $400 or less. **But** if you earned tips, including allocated tips, that are not included in box 5 and box 7 of your W-2, you may not be able to use Form 1040EZ. See page 13. • You did not receive any advance earned income credit payments. **Caution:** *If married and either you or your spouse had total wages of over $57,600, you may not be able to use this form. See page 6.* If you are not sure about your filing status, see page 12. If you have questions about dependents, call Tele-Tax (see page 22) and listen to topic 354. If you **can't use this form**, call Tele-Tax (see page 22) and listen to topic 352.
Filling in your return	Because this form is read by a machine, please print your numbers inside the boxes like this: `9 8 7 6 5 4 3 2 1 0` Do not type your numbers. Do not use dollar signs. Most people can fill in the form by following the instructions on the front. But you will have to use the booklet if you received a scholarship or fellowship grant or tax-exempt interest income, such as on municipal bonds. Also, use the booklet if you received a Form 1099-INT showing income tax withheld (backup withholding). **Remember,** you must report all wages, salaries, and tips even if you don't get a W-2 form from your employer. You must also report all your taxable interest income, including interest from banks, savings and loans, credit unions, etc., even if you don't get a Form 1099-INT. If you paid someone to prepare your return, see page 17.

Worksheet for dependents who checked "Yes" on line 5	Use this worksheet to figure the amount to enter on line 5 if someone can claim you (or your spouse if married) as a dependent, even if that person chooses not to do so. To find out if someone can claim you as a dependent, call Tele-Tax (see page 22) and listen to topic 354.
	
	A. Enter the amount from line 2 on the front. A. _____
	B. Minimum standard deduction. B. _____600.00
	C. Enter the LARGER of line A or line B here. C. _____
	D. Maximum standard deduction. If single, enter 3,700.00; if married, enter 6,200.00. D. _____
	E. Enter the SMALLER of line C or line D here. This is your standard deduction. E. _____
	F. Exemption amount.
	  • If single, enter 0.
	  • If married and both you and your spouse can be claimed as dependents, enter 0.
	  • If married and only one of you can be claimed as a dependent, enter 2,350.00. F. _____
	G. Add lines E and F. Enter the total here and on line 5 on the front. G. _____
	
	If you checked "No" on line 5 because no one can claim you (or your spouse if married) as a dependent, enter on line 5 the amount shown below that applies to you.
	• Single, enter 6,050.00. This is the total of your standard deduction (3,700.00) and personal exemption (2,350.00).
	• Married, enter 10,900.00. This is the total of your standard deduction (6,200.00), exemption for yourself (2,350.00), and exemption for your spouse (2,350.00).

Avoid mistakes	Please see page 17 of the Form 1040EZ booklet for a list of common mistakes to avoid that will help you make sure your form is filled in correctly.
Mailing your return	Mail your return by **April 15, 1994.** Use the envelope that came with your booklet. If you don't have that envelope, see page 29 for the address to use.

Copyright © 1994 by Harcourt Brace & Company. All rights reserved.

Chapter 1 Problem 25   Name _____   1-61

Form 1040A Department of the Treasury—Internal Revenue Service
U.S. Individual Income Tax Return **1993**   IRS Use Only—Do not write or staple in this space.

OMB No. 1545-0085

Label (See page 15.)

L A B E L   H E R E

Your first name and initial | Last name

If a joint return, spouse's first name and initial | Last name

Home address (number and street). If you have a P.O. box, see page 16. | Apt. no.

City, town or post office, state, and ZIP code. If you have a foreign address, see page 16.

Use the IRS label. Otherwise, please print or type.

Your social security number

Spouse's social security number

For Privacy Act and Paperwork Reduction Act Notice, see page 4.

Presidential Election Campaign Fund (See page 16.)
Do you want $3 to go to this fund? . . . .
If a joint return, does your spouse want $3 to go to this fund?

Yes | No

Note: *Checking "Yes" will not change your tax or reduce your refund.*

Check the box for your filing status
(See page 16.)
Check only one box.

1 ☐ Single
2 ☐ Married filing joint return (even if only one had income)
3 ☐ Married filing separate return. Enter spouse's social security number above and full name here. ▶ _____
4 ☐ Head of household (with qualifying person). (See page 17.) If the qualifying person is a child but not your dependent, enter this child's name here. ▶ _____
5 ☐ Qualifying widow(er) with dependent child (year spouse died ▶ 19___). (See page 18.)

Figure your exemptions
(See page 19.)

If more than seven dependents, see page 22.

6a ☐ **Yourself.** If your parent (or someone else) can claim you as a dependent on his or her tax return, **do not** check box 6a. But be sure to check the box on line 18b on page 2.
b ☐ Spouse
c **Dependents:**

(1) Name (first, initial, and last name)	(2) Check if under age 1	(3) If age 1 or older, dependent's social security number	(4) Dependent's relationship to you	(5) No. of months lived in your home in 1993

d If your child didn't live with you but is claimed as your dependent under a pre-1985 agreement, check here . . . . ▶ ☐
e Total number of exemptions claimed.

No. of boxes checked on 6a and 6b ____
No. of your children on 6c who:
• lived with you ____
• didn't live with you due to divorce or separation (see page 22) ____
Dependents on 6c not entered above ____
Add numbers entered on lines above ____

Figure your total income

Attach Copy B of your Forms W-2 and 1099-R here.

If you didn't get a W-2, see page 24.

If you are attaching a check or money order, put it on top of any Forms W-2 or 1099-R.

7   Wages, salaries, tips, etc. This should be shown in box 1 of your W-2 form(s). Attach Form(s) W-2. | 7
8a **Taxable** interest income (see page 25). If over $400, also complete and attach Schedule 1, Part I. | 8a
 b Tax-exempt interest. DO NOT include on line 8a.   8b |
9   Dividends. If over $400, also complete and attach Schedule 1, Part II. | 9
10a Total IRA distributions.   10a | 10b Taxable amount (see page 26).   10b
11a Total pensions and annuities.   11a | 11b Taxable amount (see page 26).   11b
12 Unemployment compensation (see page 30). | 12
13a Social security benefits.   13a | 13b Taxable amount (see page 30).   13b
14 Add lines 7 through 13b (far right column). This is your **total income.** ▶ 14

Figure your adjusted gross income

15a Your IRA deduction (see page 32).   15a
 b Spouse's IRA deduction (see page 32).   15b
 c Add lines 15a and 15b. These are your **total adjustments.**   15c
16 Subtract line 15c from line 14. This is your **adjusted gross income.** If less than $23,050 and a child lived with you, see page 63 to find out if you can claim the "Earned income credit" on line 28c. ▶ 16

Cat. No. 11327A   1993 Form 1040A page 1

1993 Form 1040A page 2

Name(s) shown on page 1 | Your social security number

Figure your standard deduction, exemption amount, and taxable income	17	Enter the amount from line 16.	17
	18a	Check if: ☐ You were 65 or older ☐ Blind ☐ Spouse was 65 or older ☐ Blind **Enter number of boxes checked ▶ 18a** ☐	
	b	If your parent (or someone else) can claim you as a dependent, check here . . . . ▶ 18b ☐	
	c	If you are married filing separately and your spouse files Form 1040 and itemizes deductions, see page 36 and check here ▶ 18c ☐	
	19	Enter the **standard deduction** shown below for your filing status. **But if you checked any box on line 18a or b,** go to page 36 to find your standard deduction. **If you checked box 18c,** enter -0-. • Single—$3,700 • Head of household—$5,450 • Married filing jointly or Qualifying widow(er)—$6,200 • Married filing separately—$3,100	19
	20	Subtract line 19 from line 17. If line 19 is more than line 17, enter -0-.	20
	21	Multiply $2,350 by the total number of exemptions claimed on line 6e.	21
	22	Subtract line 21 from line 20. If line 21 is more than line 20, enter -0-. This is your **taxable income.** ▶	22
Figure your tax, credits, and payments *If you want the IRS to figure your tax, see the instructions for line 22 on page 37*	23	Find the tax on the amount on line 22. Check if from: ☐ Tax Table (pages 50–55) or ☐ Form 8615 (see page 38).	23
	24a	Credit for child and dependent care expenses. Complete and attach Schedule 2. 24a	
	b	Credit for the elderly or the disabled. Complete and attach Schedule 3. 24b	
	c	Add lines 24a and 24b. These are your **total credits.**	24c
	25	Subtract line 24c from line 23. If line 24c is more than line 23, enter -0-.	25
	26	Advance earned income credit payments from Form W-2.	26
	27	Add lines 25 and 26. This is your **total tax.** ▶	27
	28a	Total Federal income tax withheld. If any tax is from Form(s) 1099, check here. ▶ ☐ 28a	
	b	1993 estimated tax payments and amount applied from 1992 return. 28b	
	c	**Earned income credit.** Complete and attach Schedule EIC. 28c	
	d	Add lines 28a, 28b, and 28c. These are your **total payments.** ▶	28d
Figure your refund or amount you owe	29	If line 28d is more than line 27, subtract line 27 from line 28d. This is the amount you **overpaid.**	29
	30	Amount of line 29 you want **refunded to you.**	30
	31	Amount of line 29 you want **applied to your 1994 estimated tax.** 31	
	32	If line 27 is more than line 28d, subtract line 28d from line 27. This is the **amount you owe.** For details on how to pay, including what to write on your payment, see page 42.	32
	33	Estimated tax penalty (see page 43). Also, include on line 32. 33	

Sign your return

Under penalties of perjury, I declare that I have examined this return and accompanying schedules and statements, and to the best of my knowledge and belief, they are true, correct, and accurately list all amounts and sources of income I received during the tax year. Declaration of preparer (other than the taxpayer) is based on all information of which the preparer has any knowledge.

▶ Your signature | Date | Your occupation

Keep a copy of this return for your records.

▶ Spouse's signature. If joint return, BOTH must sign. | Date | Spouse's occupation

Paid preparer's use only

Preparer's signature ▶ | Date | Check if self-employed ☐ | Preparer's social security no.

Firm's name (or yours if self-employed) and address ▶ | E.I. No. ZIP code

Chapter 1 Problem 25   Name _____   *1-63*

**Schedule 1
(Form 1040A)**

Department of the Treasury—Internal Revenue Service

**Interest and Dividend Income
for Form 1040A Filers**

1993

OMB No 1545-0085

Name(s) shown on Form 1040A

Your social security number

Part I

Interest income

(See pages 25 and 56.)

Note: *If you received a Form 1099–INT, Form 1099–OID, or substitute statement from a brokerage firm, enter the firm's name and the total interest shown on that form.*

1 List name of payer. If any interest is from a seller-financed mortgage and the buyer used the property as a personal residence, see page 56 and list this interest first. Also, show that buyer's social security number and address.

	Amount
1	

2 Add the amounts on line 1.   **2**

3 Excludable interest on series EE U.S. savings bonds issued after 1989 from Form 8815, line 14. You MUST attach Form 8815 to Form 1040A.   **3**

4 Subtract line 3 from line 2. Enter the result here and on Form 1040A, line 8a.   **4**

Part II

Dividend income

(See pages 25 and 57.)

Note: *If you received a Form 1099–DIV or substitute statement from a brokerage firm, enter the firm's name and the total dividends shown on that form.*

5 List name of payer

	Amount
5	

6 Add the amounts on line 5. Enter the total here and on Form 1040A, line 9.   **6**

For Paperwork Reduction Act Notice, see Form 1040A instructions.   Cat. No. 12075R   1993 Schedule 1 (Form 1040A) page 1

Copyright © 1994 by Harcourt Brace & Company. All rights reserved.

Chapter 1 Problem 26   Name _____   1-65

Form 1040 — U.S. Individual Income Tax Return 1993

Department of the Treasury—Internal Revenue Service
For the year Jan. 1–Dec. 31, 1993, or other tax year beginning _____, 1993, ending _____, 19___
OMB No. 1545-0074
IRS Use Only—Do not write or staple in this space

Label (See instructions on page 12.) Use the IRS label. Otherwise, please print or type.

- Your first name and initial _____ Last name _____
- If a joint return, spouse's first name and initial _____ Last name _____
- Home address (number and street). If you have a P.O. box, see page 12. _____ Apt. no ____
- City, town or post office, state, and ZIP code. If you have a foreign address, see page 12. _____

Your social security number _____
Spouse's social security number _____

For Privacy Act and Paperwork Reduction Act Notice, see page 4.

Presidential Election Campaign (See page 12.)
- Do you want $3 to go to this fund? Yes ☐ No ☐
- If a joint return, does your spouse want $3 to go to this fund? Yes ☐ No ☐

Note: Checking "Yes" will not change your tax or reduce your refund.

Filing Status (See page 12.) Check only one box.

1. ☐ Single
2. ☐ Married filing joint return (even if only one had income)
3. ☐ Married filing separate return. Enter spouse's social security no. above and full name here. ▶ _____
4. ☐ Head of household (with qualifying person). (See page 13.) If the qualifying person is a child but not your dependent, enter this child's name here. ▶ _____
5. ☐ Qualifying widow(er) with dependent child (year spouse died ▶ 19___). (See page 13.)

Exemptions (See page 13.)

- 6a ☐ **Yourself.** If your parent (or someone else) can claim you as a dependent on his or her tax return, **do not** check box 6a. But be sure to check the box on line 33b on page 2
- b ☐ **Spouse**
- c **Dependents:**

(1) Name (first, initial, and last name)	(2) Check if under age 1	(3) If age 1 or older, dependent's social security number	(4) Dependent's relationship to you	(5) No. of months lived in your home in 1993

If more than six dependents, see page 14.

- No. of boxes checked on 6a and 6b ____
- No. of your children on 6c who:
  • lived with you ____
  • didn't live with you due to divorce or separation (see page 15) ____
- Dependents on 6c not entered above ____

- d If your child didn't live with you but is claimed as your dependent under a pre-1985 agreement, check here ▶ ☐
- e Total number of exemptions claimed

Add numbers entered on lines above ▶ ____

Income

Attach Copy B of your Forms W-2, W-2G, and 1099-R here.

If you did not get a W-2, see page 10.

If you are attaching a check or money order, put it on top of any Forms W-2, W-2G, or 1099-R.

7	Wages, salaries, tips, etc. Attach Form(s) W-2	
8a	Taxable interest income (see page 16). Attach Schedule B if over $400	
b	Tax-exempt interest (see page 17). DON'T include on line 8a 8b ____	
9	Dividend income. Attach Schedule B if over $400	
10	Taxable refunds, credits, or offsets of state and local income taxes (see page 17)	
11	Alimony received	
12	Business income or (loss). Attach Schedule C or C-EZ	
13	Capital gain or (loss). Attach Schedule D	
14	Capital gain distributions not reported on line 13 (see page 17)	
15	Other gains or (losses). Attach Form 4797	
16a	Total IRA distributions 16a ____ b Taxable amount (see page 18)	16b
17a	Total pensions and annuities 17a ____ b Taxable amount (see page 18)	17b
18	Rental real estate, royalties, partnerships, S corporations, trusts, etc. Attach Schedule E	
19	Farm income or (loss). Attach Schedule F	
20	Unemployment compensation (see page 19)	
21a	Social security benefits 21a ____ b Taxable amount (see page 19)	21b
22	Other income. List type and amount—see page 20 ____	
23	Add the amounts in the far right column for lines 7 through 22. This is your **total income** ▶	

Adjustments to Income (See page 20.)

24a	Your IRA deduction (see page 20)	
b	Spouse's IRA deduction (see page 20)	
25	One-half of self-employment tax (see page 21)	
26	Self-employed health insurance deduction (see page 22)	
27	Keogh retirement plan and self-employed SEP deduction	
28	Penalty on early withdrawal of savings	
29	Alimony paid. Recipient's SSN ▶ ____	
30	Add lines 24a through 29. These are your **total adjustments**	

Adjusted Gross Income

31. Subtract line 30 from line 23. This is your **adjusted gross income**. If this amount is less than $23,050 and a child lived with you, see page EIC-1 to find out if you can claim the "Earned Income Credit" on line 56 ▶

Cat. No. 11320B   Form **1040** (1993)

Copyright © 1994 by Harcourt Brace & Company. All rights reserved.

Form 1040 (1993)   Page **2**

Tax Computation (See page 23.)	32	Amount from line 31 (adjusted gross income)	32
	33a	Check if: ☐ **You** were 65 or older, ☐ Blind; ☐ **Spouse** was 65 or older, ☐ Blind. Add the number of boxes checked above and enter the total here ▶ 33a	
	b	If your parent (or someone else) can claim you as a dependent, check here ▶ 33b ☐	
	c	If you are married filing separately and your spouse itemizes deductions or you are a dual-status alien, see page 24 and check here ▶ 33c ☐	
	34	Enter the larger of your: **Itemized deductions** from Schedule A, line 26, OR **Standard deduction** shown below for your filing status. **But if you checked any box on line 33a or b,** go to page 24 to find your standard deduction. If you checked **box 33c**, your standard deduction is zero. • Single—$3,700 • Head of household—$5,450 • Married filing jointly or Qualifying widow(er)—$6,200 • Married filing separately—$3,100	34
	35	Subtract line 34 from line 32	35
	36	If line 32 is $81,350 or less, multiply $2,350 by the total number of exemptions claimed on line 6e. If line 32 is over $81,350, see the worksheet on page 25 for the amount to enter	36
If you want the IRS to figure your tax, see page 24.	37	**Taxable income.** Subtract line 36 from line 35. If line 36 is more than line 35, enter -0-	37
	38	Tax. Check if from **a** ☐ Tax Table, **b** ☐ Tax Rate Schedules, **c** ☐ Schedule D Tax Worksheet, or **d** ☐ Form 8615 (see page 25). Amount from Form(s) 8814 ▶ **e** _____	38
	39	Additional taxes (see page 25). Check if from **a** ☐ Form 4970 **b** ☐ Form 4972 ▶	39
	40	Add lines 38 and 39	40
Credits (See page 25.)	41	Credit for child and dependent care expenses. Attach Form 2441	41
	42	Credit for the elderly or the disabled. Attach Schedule R	42
	43	Foreign tax credit. Attach Form 1116	43
	44	Other credits (see page 26). Check if from **a** ☐ Form 3800 **b** ☐ Form 8396 **c** ☐ Form 8801 **d** ☐ Form (specify) _____	44
	45	Add lines 41 through 44	45
	46	Subtract line 45 from line 40. If line 45 is more than line 40, enter -0- ▶	46
Other Taxes	47	Self-employment tax. Attach Schedule SE. Also, see line 25	47
	48	Alternative minimum tax. Attach Form 6251	48
	49	Recapture taxes (see page 26). Check if from **a** ☐ Form 4255 **b** ☐ Form 8611 **c** ☐ Form 8828	49
	50	Social security and Medicare tax on tip income not reported to employer. Attach Form 4137	50
	51	Tax on qualified retirement plans, including IRAs. If required, attach Form 5329	51
	52	Advance earned income credit payments from Form W-2	52
	53	Add lines 46 through 52. This is your **total tax** ▶	53
Payments Attach Forms W-2, W-2G, and 1099-R on the front.	54	Federal income tax withheld. If any is from Form(s) 1099, check ▶ ☐	54
	55	1993 estimated tax payments and amount applied from 1992 return	55
	56	**Earned income credit.** Attach Schedule EIC	56
	57	Amount paid with Form 4868 (extension request)	57
	58a	Excess social security, Medicare, and RRTA tax withheld (see page 28)	58a
	b	Deferral of additional 1993 taxes. Attach Form 8841	58b
	59	Other payments (see page 28). Check if from **a** ☐ Form 2439 **b** ☐ Form 4136	59
	60	Add lines 54 through 59. These are your **total payments** ▶	60
Refund or Amount You Owe	61	If line 60 is more than line 53, subtract line 53 from line 60. This is the amount you **OVERPAID** ▶	61
	62	Amount of line 61 you want **REFUNDED TO YOU** ▶	62
	63	Amount of line 61 you want **APPLIED TO YOUR 1994 ESTIMATED TAX** ▶ 63	
	64	If line 53 is more than line 60, subtract line 60 from line 53. This is the **AMOUNT YOU OWE**. For details on how to pay, including what to write on your payment, see page 29	64
	65	Estimated tax penalty (see page 29). Also include on line 64	65

Sign Here
Keep a copy of this return for your records.

Under penalties of perjury, I declare that I have examined this return and accompanying schedules and statements, and to the best of my knowledge and belief, they are true, correct, and complete. Declaration of preparer (other than taxpayer) is based on all information of which preparer has any knowledge.

Your signature	Date	Your occupation
Spouse's signature. If a joint return, BOTH must sign.	Date	Spouse's occupation

Paid Preparer's Use Only

Preparer's signature	Date	Check if self-employed ☐	Preparer's social security no.
Firm's name (or yours if self-employed) and address		E.I. No.	
		ZIP code	

CHAPTER 2

Gross Income of Individuals: Inclusions

The starting point for calculating an individual's tax liability is to determine gross income, which represents total income less allowable exclusions. Unfortunately, the concept of "income" for tax purposes is somewhat hard to pin down, in that many economic, social, political, and revenue considerations have influenced this determination. The purpose of this chapter is to introduce the basic concepts used to determine which income items are subject to tax. Chapter 3 is devoted to an examination of those items that Congress has excluded from taxation.

I GROSS INCOME: GENERAL CONCEPTS AND METHODS OF REPORTING
(Code Sections 61, 441, 446, and 451)

DEFINITIONS OF INCOME

The term *income* has never been universally defined, and different segments of our society have developed their own views of what income is. For example, economists use an all-inclusive definition of income. They believe we should calculate income by determining an individual's net increase in wealth for the year (measured by comparing the fair market values of all properties owned at the beginning and end of the year) and adding consumption expenditures to this total. The amount spent on consumption is added to the increase in wealth because these amounts are presumed to have come from an income source, which is not reflected in the change in net wealth.

☑ **Example 1.** Apple owned properties worth $100,000 at the beginning of 1993 and $130,000 at the end of 1993. Apple also spent $12,000 on food, utilities, and other nondurable items in 1993. Apple's "economic income" for 1993 is $42,000 (the $30,000 increase in value of properties plus the $12,000 consumption expenditures).

Note that the economists' definition of income includes all increases and decreases in the value of property owned by the individual, regardless of whether the property was actually sold during the year. This is in contrast to the accountants' definition of income, commonly referred to as the *realization principle*, which includes only those increases and decreases in property values that come about, or are realized, in a market transaction.

✓ **Example 2.** Bittner purchased five acres of land for $10,000 on 1/6/93. The fair market value of this land on 12/31/93 is $11,500. This $1,500 appreciation in value is not considered to be income for accounting purposes (although it would be income under the economists' definition). The $1,500 appreciation will be recognized as accounting income only when the land is sold or exchanged in a verifiable market transaction and the gain or loss can be measured.

Many of our tax laws are based on a realization concept, in that most sources of taxable income must be realized in a verifiable transaction similar to that required by the accounting definition. It is interesting to note that the term *income* is used throughout our tax laws yet is never separately defined. Code Sec. 61, reprinted below, provides only a general statement regarding income.

THE LAW

Sec. 61—Except as otherwise provided in this subtitle, gross income means all income from whatever source derived, including (but not limited to) the following items:
  (1) Compensation for services, including fees, commissions, and similar items;
  (2) Gross income derived from business;
  (3) Gains derived from dealing in property;
  (4) Interest;
  (5) Rents;
  (6) Royalties;
  (7) Dividends;
  (8) Alimony and separate maintenance payments;
  (9) Annuities;
  (10) Income from life insurance and endowment contracts;
  (11) Pensions;
  (12) Income from discharge of indebtedness;
  (13) Distributive share of partnership income;
  (14) Income in respect of a decedent; and
  (15) Income from an interest in an estate or trust.

Note that Sec. 61 explicitly states that gross income includes all sources of income "... except as otherwise provided in this subtitle." As mentioned earlier, any exceptions to taxable sources must be provided by Congress as exclusions. The list of 15 items in the Code section quoted above is intended only to provide common examples of taxable sources of income and is by no means all-inclusive.

✓ **Example 3.** Crandall purchased a state lottery ticket for $1, and she learned a week later that she had won $20,000. Since Congress has never provided an exclusion for lottery winnings, Crandall must report the $20,000 as income on her tax return for the year in which she receives her winnings. The fact that lottery winnings are not specifically mentioned as being a taxable source of income in Code Sec. 61 is irrelevant.

Method of Payment

Any income realized during the year and not subject to an exclusion provision must be recognized, or reported, for tax purposes. Income does not necessarily have to be received in cash; for example, income may be realized through the receipt of property or services. In both cases, the income is measured by the fair market value (cash equivalent) of the property or services.

✓ **Example 4.** Ashton owns an apartment building. In lieu of paying Ashton the normal rent for March 1993, Baxter gave Ashton an oil painting worth $800. Baxter had purchased the painting five years ago for $300. Ashton must report the $800 fair market value of the painting as income in 1993. As we will see in Chapter 6, Baxter must also report a $500 gain on her 1993 return (i.e., the $800 value of the painting less her $300 cost). In effect, the transaction is treated as if Baxter had first sold the painting for $800 cash and then given the $800 to Ashton.

✓ **Example 5.** Assume that Davis, another tenant, agreed to perform legal services for Ashton in lieu of paying rent for June 1993. Davis, an attorney, would normally have charged $800 for such services. Ashton must report the $800 fair market value of the services as rent income in 1993. In addition, Davis must recognize the value of the rent, $800, as compensation for the services performed.

A sale of property also generates taxable income; however, the taxable gain is limited to the amount by which the total selling price of the property is greater than its tax basis (usually cost). Thus, a taxpayer who purchases securities for $8,000 and then sells them for $11,000 would report a $3,000 taxable gain; the other $8,000 represents a cost recovery. If the securities are classified as capital assets and are held longer than a year, the taxpayer would report the gain as a "long-term capital gain," described in Chapter 6.

On the other hand, if the securities were sold for $6,000, the taxpayer would recognize a $2,000 "long-term capital loss." As explained in Chapter 6, a maximum of $3,000 of such capital losses can offset ordinary (noncapital-gain) income in any one year.

Taxable income can be created in a variety of other situations. For example, assume that selected employees are given the opportunity to purchase expensive products from their employer at substantial discounts. Do the discounts constitute taxable income to the selected employees? The answer in most cases is yes, even though the parties may characterize the discount as a "gift" from the employer to the employees.

☑ **Example 6.** Fendrich works for Ace Automobile Sales. Because of Fendrich's exceptional sales performance in August, Ace offers her an opportunity to purchase a new automobile for $6,500. Ace had purchased this automobile for $8,000. Fendrich must report the $1,500 discount as taxable income. In this instance, the discount is viewed merely as additional compensation.

One of the frustrations encountered in the study of tax law is the inevitable number of exceptions that accompany a general rule. For example, note that the above discussion of selective employee discounts concludes that in "most cases" the discount is taxable income. Theoretically, income results in any situation where property (or services) is transferred to an employee for less than fair market value. However, as a practical matter, taxpayers are able to exclude certain "fringe benefits" if certain requirements are met. These exclusions are discussed in Chapter 3.

The Reporting Period

Our tax system is based on an annual reporting period. A taxpayer may never use a reporting period of longer than one year, although occasionally periods of less than one year are necessary (e.g., a taxpayer's first or last tax return).

A taxpayer may elect to use a calendar year or a fiscal year. Most individual taxpayers elect a calendar year, which is simply a tax year ending on December 31. A taxpayer may also elect a fiscal year, which is a tax year ending on the last day of a month other than December.

Once an accounting period is selected, a taxpayer must continue to use that reporting period in future years, unless the IRS gives permission to change the period. Generally, the IRS will grant permission to change accounting periods only when a valid business reason exists for the change. A change of accounting period will also create a "short" accounting period (less than 12 months), which requires special "annualization" tax calculations (not discussed in this textbook).

☑ **Example 7.** Beryl Robinson requests permission to change his accounting period in 1993 from a calendar year to a fiscal year ending March 31. If the IRS grants permission, Beryl will file his first fiscal-year return for the period April 1, 1993, to March 31, 1994. Beryl will also have to file a tax return for the short period January 1, 1993, to March 31, 1993.

ACCOUNTING METHODS

THE LAW

Sec. 446(c)—Permissible methods. Subject to the provisions of subsections (a) and (b), a taxpayer may compute taxable income under any of the following methods of accounting—
- *(1) the cash receipts and disbursements method;*
- *(2) an accrual method;*
- *(3) any other method permitted by this chapter; or*
- *(4) any combination of the foregoing methods permitted under regulations prescribed by the Secretary.*

A taxpayer must use an accounting method that clearly reflects income and must apply it on a consistent basis. An *accounting method* is the basis on which a taxpayer regularly computes his or her income. Although a few special accounting methods are provided for individual items in the tax law, as a practical matter a taxpayer uses one of three basic overall methods of accounting: the cash method, the accrual method, or a hybrid method.

Before we proceed with a discussion of these three accounting methods, a word of caution is in order. To illustrate the various accounting methods, we must necessarily mention a few concepts related to the recognition of business income. However, a detailed examination of business income, deduction, and credits is reserved for Chapters 8 and 9.

Under the *cash method*, revenue is recognized when actually received, and expenses when actually paid. This is the simplest accounting method, and it is used by the vast majority of individual taxpayers, who sometimes use a checkbook as their "accounting records." The cash method does not imply that income is recognized only when cash is received; the fair market value of property or services received must be recognized as income on a "cash equivalent" basis. As long as the property or services received can be valued, the income is recognized when received.

Example 8. Jane Gray, a cash-basis, calendar-year landscaper, completed two jobs in the last week of 1993. She was paid $300 cash for Job 1 and was given a 90-day negotiable note for $450 for Job 2 (the note has a current value of $400). Jane must recognize $700 gross income in 1993. The $300 cash is obviously income, and the fair market value of the note ($400) must also be recognized on a cash equivalent basis. If Jane collects the full $450 from the note in 1994, she must recognize $50 additional income in that year.

☑ **Example 9.** Assume the same facts in Example 8, except that Job 1 was done on credit, with a regular accounts receivable established for the customer. In this case, no income will be recognized in 1993 for Job 1 until the cash is collected, since an unsecured accounts receivable is not considered to have a fair market value capable of reasonable estimate. The $300 revenue will not be recognized until it is actually collected.

TAX TIP

The cash basis can offer tax savings opportunities for the sole proprietor who provides services. Since income is not recognized until cash is received, billings near the end of the year could be delayed so that income would be taxed in the following year when received. Likewise, expense payments could be accelerated near the end of a year to decrease the taxable income for that year.

Under the *accrual method*, revenues are recognized when they are earned, and expenses are recognized when they are incurred. In the case of services, income is earned when substantially all the work effort is completed: The actual payment date is irrelevant.

☑ **Example 10.** Martha's Company, an accrual-basis, calendar-year wholesale vegetable dealer, sells 300 cases of tomatoes on account to Eveready Supermarkets on December 18, 1993, for $800. Eveready pays for these cases on January 13, 1994. Martha's must recognize the $800 as sales revenue on its 1993 tax return.

A taxpayer may also elect a *hybrid method* of accounting. As the name implies, a hybrid method is a combination of two or more acceptable accounting methods. For example, the Code requires use of the accrual basis for reporting the gross profit (sales minus cost of goods sold) from sales of inventory items, when such gross profit is a significant portion of a taxpayer's income. This requirement is discussed in Chapter 8.

Although a taxpayer's choice of tax reporting is frequently referred to as an "accounting" method, the actual calculation of taxable income can differ significantly from the calculation of income for normal accounting purposes, such as financial statement presentations. It is important to remember that the primary objective of our income tax system is to raise revenues. In attempting to achieve this objective, Congress has established a number of tax principles that override the normal accounting conventions for cash-basis and accrual-basis determinations of income. Several of these important concepts are discussed in the following section.

The Wherewithal-to-Pay Principle

Quite simply, the wherewithal-to-pay principle states that income should be taxed when the taxpayer is best able to pay and the government is best able to collect. For example, prepayments of income received by a taxpayer are generally taxed immediately, although the income will not actually be earned until a future tax year. This tax result applies to both cash-basis and accrual-basis taxpayers.

☑ **Example 11.** Gregory Company, an accrual-basis, calendar-year taxpayer, leases a warehouse to Slay on 10/1/93. Slay pays two years' rent of $7,200. For accounting purposes, Gregory will recognize only $900 of this prepayment as income in 1993 (3/24s of $7,200) because this is the only amount earned as of the end of the year. Nevertheless, Gregory must report the entire $7,200 as income on its 1993 tax return. Under the wherewithal-to-pay concept, Gregory is best able to pay the tax in the year of receipt, and this is also the best time for the government to collect the tax.

Sometimes the wherewithal-to-pay principle can work in the taxpayer's favor. For example, certain exchanges of property by a taxpayer are not subject to tax, because the taxpayer has no wherewithal to pay the tax and is in the same economic position after the exchange. These nontaxable exchange rules are discussed in Chapter 9. However, the following example demonstrates the logic of these rules.

☑ **Example 12.** Harold Herrington's business warehouse was destroyed by a fire in March 1993. The warehouse had a tax basis of $20,000 at the time of the fire, but was insured for its current value of $32,000. Herrington used the $32,000 insurance proceeds to construct a new warehouse. Although Herrington has realized an "accounting" gain of $12,000 ($32,000 insurance less $20,000 basis), a special tax provision limits the taxable gain to any insurance proceeds not reinvested in a replacement property. Since Herrington has reinvested all the proceeds in the replacement warehouse, he has no taxable gain because he has no wherewithal to pay the tax and his economic position (i.e., owning a warehouse) has not changed.

The Constructive-Receipt Doctrine

The constructive-receipt doctrine is a variation of the wherewithal-to-pay principle. This doctrine states that a taxpayer must recognize an amount as income as soon as it can be reduced to his or her possession. The ability to receive income is in effect considered to be the equivalent of actual receipt; in both cases, the taxpayer is presumed to have a wherewithal to pay the tax.

Three conditions must be met before a taxpayer has constructive receipt: (1) the taxpayer must have access to the funds or property, (2) the funds or property must be available, and (3) withdrawal or use of the funds or property is not subject to significant restrictions. This principle can be illustrated by several examples.

☑ **Example 13.** Janet Miller has a passbook savings account that earned $420 interest in 1993. This amount is taxed to Janet in 1993, whether or not she withdrew the interest during the year. All three conditions for constructive receipt are satisfied: Janet can withdraw the interest at any time, the interest is available for withdrawal, and there are no significant restrictions on any withdrawal.

☑ **Example 14.** Bill Small, a sales manager for Purvis Company, receives a salary check every two weeks. Because of other large sources of income received in 1993, Bill asks his employer to delay mailing his last two salary checks for 1993 until January 1994. Bill will be taxed on these last two checks in 1993, because he could have actually received them that year.

☑ **Example 15.** Tedro Corporation mails its quarterly dividend to shareholders on December 30 of each year. Cynthia Allen, who owns 50 of Tedro's outstanding shares of stock, received her last quarterly dividend check for 1993 on January 2, 1994. Assuming that Cynthia is a calendar-year taxpayer, she will report this dividend as income on her 1994 tax return. She did not have constructive receipt until the check was actually received in 1994.

The Claim-of-Right Doctrine

The claim-of-right doctrine states that an amount of income that is unrestricted as to use is taxed *no later* than when received. This doctrine extends the constructive-receipt doctrine by requiring income recognition even where income has been received erroneously. If the income is available for unrestricted use at the end of the year, the amount must be reported as income for that year. In other words, each tax year stands alone for purposes of income recognition, and amounts received in error must be corrected with deductions in future tax years.

☑ **Example 16.** Robert Stevens is a commissioned sales agent with ABCO Corporation. At the end of each tax year, ABCO pays a special bonus to all its sales agents based on a productivity formula. Robert Stevens' bonus for 1993 was calculated to be $5,500, and he was paid this amount on December 29 of that year. Four months later ABCO informed Stevens that a mistake had been made in the calculation of his bonus, and that he would have to return $2,500 to ABCO. Despite the error, Stevens must report the entire $5,500 as income on his 1993 return, since he had an unrestricted right to this amount as of December 31, 1993. (Stevens will be allowed to take a $2,500 deduction on his 1994 return to compensate for the error.)

One exception to the claim-of-right doctrine is for prepayments received by accrual-basis services taxpayers. Prepayments for future services may be allocated to the period in which the services are performed; however, the services must be completed by the *end* of the tax year following the year of prepayment. In effect, a one-year deferral for a portion of the prepaid services is permitted. If the prepaid services cannot be completed by the end of the following tax year, the prepayment is taxed immediately in the year of receipt.

☑ **Example 17.** PEST, an accrual-basis, calendar-year exterminating company, offers one- and two-year contracts for monthly pest control services. On October 1, 1993, A company pays $1,200 to PEST for a one-year contract and Z Company pays $2,400 for a two-year contract. PEST will report $300 of the contract with A Company as income in 1993 (3/12 × $1,200); the remaining $900 of this contract may be deferred until 1994, since the services will be completed by the end of 1994. On the other hand, PEST must report the entire $2,400 of the two-year contract with Z Company in 1993, since the services will not be completed by the end of 1994.

A similar exception to the claim-of-right doctrine is made for accrual-basis taxpayers who receive advance payments of inventory. In general, this exception allows the taxpayer to postpone income recognition for the prepayment until delivery is made and the transaction is closed.

This concludes the discussion of accounting methods. The remainder of this chapter is devoted to an examination of various types of income that are subject to special inclusion rules.

REVIEW I

1. Billmore, an attorney, spent ten hours of his time filing a petition for the Tax Court on behalf of Bell Corporation. In return for his services, Bell Corporation issued Billmore 100 shares of its $100 par common stock. The stock was worth $12 a share on the date of issue. Billmore must report gross income from this transaction of
   (a) $0.
   (b) $200.
   (c) $1,000.
   (d) $1,200.
2. Mary Jill Meyers, an accrual-basis, calendar-year taxpayer, owns a ten-unit apartment complex. During 1993 she collected $80,000 for 1993 rental periods and $18,000 prepayments for 1994 rent. How much of the $98,000 is taxable to Mary Jill in 1993?
   (a) $0
   (b) $18,000
   (c) $80,000
   (d) $98,000
3. During 1993 Alex Hammer, a cash-basis taxpayer, earned interest of $430 on a savings account and $80 on a checking account. The $80 earned on the checking account was withdrawn in 1993, but the $430 was left in the savings account. How much interest income must Alex report on his 1993 return?
   (a) $0
   (b) $80
   (c) $430
   (d) $510

4. Mary Rydell, an accrual-basis, calendar-year taxpayer, owns and operates a lawn-care service. For $900 she offers customers a one-year contract, which provides monthly lawn maintenance and disease treatment. On June 1, 1993, she received a $900 prepayment for a one-year contract from Reliance Corporation. How much of this prepayment is taxable to Mary in 1993?
   (a) $0
   (b) $375
   (c) $525
   (d) $900

Answers are on page 2-12.

II SPECIAL INCLUSIONS: INTEREST, DIVIDENDS, AND ANNUITIES
(Code Sections 72, 103, 135, 301, 305, and 316)

If an item of income is not specifically excludable, it is usually taxable under the Code Sec. 61 phrase ". . . from whatever source derived." Chapter 3 of this textbook is devoted to detailed examination of the exclusion provisions enacted by Congress. However, certain income sources are subject to either inclusion or exclusion, depending on the particular circumstances of each situation. The following discussion highlights the special income-inclusion rules for interest, dividends, and annuities.

INTEREST INCOME

Interest income may be identified as compensation received for the use of money. Gross income generally includes any interest actually or constructively received during the tax year. However, exceptions are made for interest derived from state and local governmental obligations and for interest from United States savings bonds.

THE LAW

Sec. 103(a)—Except as provided in subsection (b), gross income does not include interest on any state or local bond.

Interest received from obligations of a state (or territory) or its localities is excludable from income. "Localities" include cities, towns, counties, and other political subdivisions. This exclusion provision for municipal bonds was enacted by Congress so that the federal government would not impinge on a state's ability to generate income. As a result, states and localities are able to offer investors an interest rate that is lower than the rate on taxable obligations. However, the exclusion does not apply to "arbitrage bonds" (where the proceeds are reinvested by the state for a higher interest return) or "private activity bonds" (where the bonds benefit nonpublic individuals or businesses).

TAX TIP

Municipal bonds may be attractive investments to taxpayers in the 31%, 36%, or 39.6% brackets, since the interest rate "spread" between taxable bonds and municipal bonds has narrowed over the years. This is especially true if the interest is also exempt from state taxation. This might be the case, for example, for interest on obligations of the state in which the taxpayer resides.

To illustrate, assume that a taxpayer has a 39.6% marginal federal income tax rate and a 5% marginal state income tax rate. If taxable corporate bond issues are currently paying 10% annual interest, the after-tax rate of return on such bonds would be 5.54% (i.e., 10% less 3.96% federal taxes [10% × .396] and .5% state taxes [10% × .05]). Thus, if municipal bonds issued by the taxpayer's state of residence are paying more than 5.54% annual interest, they will be a better buy.

Interest received from obligations of the United States and its agencies is subject to federal taxation. (However, interest on obligations of a territory, a possession, or the District of Columbia is exempt from taxation.) Even so, a special rule applies to Series E (issued before 1980) and Series EE (issued after 1979) savings bonds issued at a discount. No interest payments are made on these bonds; rather, the bond increases in value each year until maturity. Since the bond can be redeemed at any time, a constructive receipt of the income occurs each year. However, a special tax provision allows a cash-basis taxpayer to either (1) recognize the increase in value each year as income or (2) defer recognition until the bond is actually redeemed or sold. (Even at maturity, a taxpayer has the option of exchanging the E or EE bonds for Series HH bonds, which will defer the recognition of deferred interest on the E or EE bonds. However, interest on the HH bonds is reported on a semiannual basis.)

Example 18. Martha Graham, a cash-basis taxpayer, purchased a $1,000 face (maturity) value Series EE bond on January 1, 1993, for $750. On December 31, 1993, the bond has a redemption value of $778. Martha can either report the $28 increase in value of the bond as interest income on her 1993 return or wait until the bond is actually redeemed (or sold) and recognize all accrued interest at that time.

TAX TIP

In some cases, cash-basis taxpayers may choose to recognize the interest income on U.S. savings bonds on an annual basis. This eliminates the "bunching" of income in the year of sale or redemption, when tax rates could conceivably be higher. However, a major disadvantage of this election is that it is irrevocable; a taxpayer will have to continue recognizing the income on an annual basis for all such bonds. Under the deferral election, the taxpayer can control the year of recognition (up until maturity) by deciding in what tax year the bonds will be sold or redeemed.

For tax years after 1989, another special tax option with Series EE bonds is available. If certain requirements are met, a taxpayer who redeems such bonds to pay education costs related to attending college or a vocational school may exclude at redemption a portion or all of the interest income, which otherwise would be taxable. The exclusion is available for only those bonds purchased after 1989 by a taxpayer age 25 or older. The proceeds must be used for qualifying educational expenses of the taxpayer, the taxpayer's spouse, or a qualifying dependent.

There are two restrictions on the availability of the exclusion at redemption. First, the exclusion of interest is limited to that portion of the total redemption proceeds that is used for qualifying educational expenses. Second, the exclusion is uniformly phased out for the $15,000 adjusted gross income between $45,500 and $60,500 for single taxpayers, and for the $30,000 adjusted gross income between $68,250 and $98,250 for married taxpayers in 1993.

Example 19. In 1993 Jane and Henry Martin redeem several EE bonds to pay the college expenses of their son Kevin. They receive a total of $10,000 at redemption, of which $3,000 represents interest income. Education expenses paid from these proceeds total $8,000. The portion of the $3,000 interest excludable at various levels of adjusted gross income would be computed as follows (note that the fraction used in the computation is the portion of the $30,000 range not phased out by the taxpayer's AGI):

AGI	Computation	Exclusion
$58,000	($3,000 × 8/10) × 30/30	$2,400
78,250	($3,000 × 8/10) × 20/30	1,600
93,250	($3,000 × 8/10) × 5/30	400
98,250	($3,000 × 8/10) × 0/30	0

Form 8815 is used to compute this exclusion. This form is illustrated in Figure 2-1, using the facts of this example and assuming an AGI of $78,250.

ANSWERS TO REVIEW I

1. (d) The 100 shares of stock represent taxable compensation for the legal services Billmore performed. The amount of income is measured by the fair market value of the property received, or $12 per share.
2. (d) The wherewithal-to-pay concept generally requires immediate recognition of the 1994 prepayments, regardless of the reporting method used by the taxpayer.
3. (d) All interest income either actually or constructively received by Hammer during the tax year is taxable. He had unrestricted access to both amounts during 1993.
4. (c) Since the services will be completely performed by the end of the following tax year (1994), Rydell, an accrual-basis taxpayer, must report $525 (7/12 of $900) as income on her 1993 tax return.

Form **8815**	**Exclusion of Interest From Series EE U.S. Savings Bonds Issued After 1989** (For Filers With Qualified Higher Education Expenses) ▶ Attach to Form 1040 or Form 1040A. ▶ See instructions on back.	OMB No. 1545-1173 **1993** Attachment Sequence No. 57
Department of the Treasury Internal Revenue Service		

Caution: *If your filing status is married filing a separate return,* **do not** *file this form. You* **cannot** *take the exclusion even if you paid qualified higher education expenses in 1993.*

Name(s) shown on return	Your social security number
Jane & Henry Martin	644 : 10 : 2023

1	(a) Name of person (you, your spouse, or your dependent) who was enrolled at or attended an eligible educational institution	(b) Name and address of eligible educational institution
	Kevin Martin	Cleveland State University Cleveland, Ohio

If you need more space, attach a statement.

2	Enter the total qualified higher education expenses you paid in 1993 for the persons listed in column (a) of line 1. See the instructions to find out which expenses qualify	2	8,000
3	Enter the total of any nontaxable educational benefits (such as nontaxable scholarship or fellowship grants) received for 1993 for the persons listed in column (a) of line 1. See instructions	3	0
4	Subtract line 3 from line 2. If zero or less, **STOP**; you **cannot** take the exclusion	4	8,000
5	Enter the total proceeds (principal and interest) from all series EE U.S. savings bonds **issued after 1989** that you **cashed during 1993**	5	10,000
6	Enter the interest included on line 5. See instructions	6	3,000
7	Is line 4 less than line 5? • **No.** Enter "1.00." • **Yes.** Divide line 4 by line 5. Enter the result as a decimal (to at least two places).	7	x .80
8	Multiply line 6 by line 7	8	2,400
9	Enter your modified adjusted gross income. See instructions . . .	9	78,250
	Note: *If line 9 is $60,500 or more ($98,250 or more if married filing a joint return),* **STOP;** *you* **cannot** *take the exclusion.*		
10	Enter $45,500 ($68,250 if married filing a joint return)	10	68,250
11	Subtract line 10 from line 9. If zero or less, skip line 12, enter -0- on line 13, and go to line 14	11	10,000
12	Divide line 11 by $15,000 (by $30,000 if married filing a joint return). Enter the result as a decimal (to at least two places)	12	x .333
13	Multiply line 8 by line 12	13	800
14	**Excludable savings bond interest.** Subtract line 13 from line 8. Enter the result here and on Schedule B (Form 1040), line 3, or Schedule 1 (Form 1040A), line 3, whichever applies ▶	14	1,600

Paperwork Reduction Act Notice

We ask for the information on this form to carry out the Internal Revenue laws of the United States. You are required to give us the information. We need it to ensure that you are complying with these laws and to allow us to figure and collect the right amount of tax.

The time needed to complete and file this form will vary depending on individual circumstances. The estimated average time is: **Recordkeeping,** 53 min.; **Learning about the law or the form,** 11 min.; **Preparing the form,** 35 min.; and **Copying, assembling, and sending the form to the IRS,** 34 min.

If you have comments concerning the accuracy of these time estimates or suggestions for making this form more simple, we would be happy to hear from you. You can write to both the IRS and the Office of Management and Budget at the addresses listed in the instructions of the tax return with which this form is filed.

Cat. No. 10822S

Form **8815** (1993)

Figure 2-1 Form 8815

Form 8815 (1993) Page **2**

General Instructions

Purpose of Form
If you cashed series EE U.S. savings bonds in 1993 that were issued after 1989, you may be able to exclude from your income part or all of the interest on those bonds. Use Form 8815 to figure the amount of any interest you may exclude.

Who May Take the Exclusion
You may take the exclusion if **all four** of the following apply:

1. You cashed qualified U.S. savings bonds in 1993 that were issued after 1989.

2. You paid qualified higher education expenses in 1993 for yourself, your spouse, or your dependents.

3. Your filing status is single, married filing a joint return, head of household, or qualifying widow(er) with dependent child.

4. Your modified adjusted gross income is less than $60,500 (less than $98,250 if married filing a joint return). Use the line 9 worksheet on this page to figure your modified adjusted gross income.

Note: *If your filing status is married filing a separate return, you* **cannot** *take the exclusion.*

U.S. Savings Bonds That Qualify for Exclusion
To qualify for the exclusion, the bonds must be series EE U.S. savings bonds issued after 1989 in your name, or, if you are married, they may be issued in your name and your spouse's name. Also, you must have been age 24 or older before the bonds were issued. **Bond information will be verified with Department of the Treasury records.**

Note: *A bond bought by a parent and issued in the name of his or her child who is under age 24 will not qualify for the exclusion by the parent or child.*

Recordkeeping Requirements
To verify the amount of interest you exclude, you should keep the following records:

- A written record of each post-1989 series EE U.S. savings bond that you cash. Your written record must include the serial number, issue date, face value, and total redemption proceeds (principal and interest) of each bond. For this purpose, you may use **Form 8818**, Optional Form To Record Redemption of Series EE U.S. Savings Bonds Issued After 1989.

- Bills, receipts, canceled checks, or other documentation showing that you paid qualified higher education expenses during the year.

Specific Instructions

To figure the amount of interest you may exclude, you must complete the following lines on your tax return if they apply to you.

Form 1040 filers, complete lines 7, 8b, 9 through 22, and 24a through 30. Also, complete Schedule B (Form 1040) through line 2.

Form 1040A filers, complete lines 7, 8b, 9 through 13b, and 15a through 15c. Also, complete Schedule 1 (Form 1040A) through line 2.

But if you received social security benefits, use the worksheet in **Pub. 915**, Social Security Benefits and Equivalent Railroad Retirement Benefits, to figure the taxable amount, if any, of your benefits. **Do not** use the social security worksheet in the instructions for Form 1040 or Form 1040A. **Also,** if you made contributions to your IRA for 1993 and you were covered by a retirement plan at work or through self-employment, use the chart and worksheets in **Pub. 590**, Individual Retirement Arrangements (IRAs), to figure your IRA deduction. **Do not** use the chart or IRA worksheet in the instructions for Form 1040 or Form 1040A.

Line 1
Column (a).—Enter the name of the person who was enrolled at or attended an eligible educational institution. This person must be you, your spouse, or your dependent(s) whom you claim on line 6c of Form 1040 or Form 1040A.

Column (b).—Enter the name and address of the eligible educational institution. If the person was enrolled at or attended more than one institution, list the names and addresses of all institutions. An **eligible educational institution** is a college, university, or vocational education school.

Line 2
Enter the total **qualified higher education expenses** you paid in 1993. These include only tuition and fees required for the enrollment or attendance of the person(s) listed on line 1, column (a), at the eligible educational institution(s) listed on line 1, column (b). They **do not** include expenses for the following:

- Room and board.

- Courses involving sports, games, or hobbies that are not part of a degree or certificate granting program.

Do not include on line 2 expenses that were covered by nontaxable educational benefits paid directly to, or by, the educational institution.

Line 3
Enter on this line the total qualified higher education expenses included on line 2 that were covered by nontaxable educational benefits.

Example. You paid $10,000 of qualified higher education expenses in 1993 to the eligible educational institution your son attended. You claim your son as a dependent on line 6c of your 1993 tax return. Your son received a $2,000 nontaxable scholarship grant for 1993, which was paid directly to him. You would enter $10,000 on line 2 and $2,000 on line 3.

Nontaxable educational benefits include:

- Scholarship or fellowship grants excludable from income under Internal Revenue Code section 117.

- Veterans' educational assistance benefits.

- Employer-provided educational assistance benefits.

- Any other payments (but not gifts, bequests, or inheritances) for educational expenses that are exempt from income tax by any U.S. law.

Do not include on line 3 nontaxable educational benefits paid directly to, or by, the educational institution.

Line 6
If you used Form 8818 to record the bonds you cashed in 1993, enter on line 6 the amount from Form 8818, line 5. If you did not use Form 8818, use the worksheet below to figure the amount to enter on line 6.

Worksheet—Line 6 (keep for your records)

1. Enter the face value of all post-1989 bonds cashed in 1993 . . . . _____

2. Enter the amount from Form 8815, line 5 . . . . . . _____

3. Multiply line 1 above by 50% (.50) . . . . _____

4. Subtract line 3 from line 2. This is the interest on the bonds. Enter the result here and on Form 8815, line 6 . . . . _____

Line 9
Use the worksheet below to figure your modified adjusted gross income. But if any of the following apply, see **Pub. 550**, Investment Income and Expenses, before using the worksheet.

- You are filing **Form 2555**, Foreign Earned Income, **Form 2555-EZ**, Foreign Earned Income Exclusion, or **Form 4563**, Exclusion of Income for Bona Fide Residents of American Samoa.

- You are excluding income from Puerto Rico.

- You have investment interest expense attributable to royalty income.

Worksheet—Line 9 (keep for your records)

1. **Form 1040 filers,** enter the amount from Schedule B, line 2.

   Form 1040A filers, enter the amount from Schedule 1, line 2.   78,250

2. **Form 1040 filers,** add the amounts on lines 7, 9 through 15, 16b, 17b, 18 through 20, 21b, and 22. Enter the total.

   Form 1040A filers, add the amounts on lines 7, 9, 10b, 11b, 12, and 13b. Enter the total.   0

3. Add lines 1 and 2 . . .   78,250

4. **Form 1040 filers,** enter the amount from line 30.

   Form 1040A filers, enter the amount from line 15c.   0

5. Subtract line 4 from line 3. Enter the result here and on Form 8815, line 9 . . .   78,250

Figure 2-1 (continued) Form 8815

DIVIDEND INCOME

A dividend is a distribution of money or property made by a corporation to its shareholders. Some payments characterized as dividends in nonshareholder situations are not treated as dividends for tax purposes. For example, the "dividend" paid by a savings and loan company to its depositors is actually interest income. Also, the "dividend" paid by a life insurance company to its policyholders is actually a nontaxable refund of a portion of the premium paid by the policyholders.

THE LAW

Sec. 316(a)—General rule: For purposes of this subtitle, the term "dividend" means any distribution of property made by a corporation to its shareholders—
(1) out of its earnings and profits accumulated after February 28, 1913, or
(2) out of its earnings and profits of the taxable year.

A dividend payment to a shareholder may be characterized for tax purposes as ordinary dividend income, a nontaxable distribution, or a capital gain distribution. A distribution is treated as ordinary income to the extent of the corporation's current or accumulated "earnings and profits." The calculation of earnings and profits is rather complex, but basically a positive earnings and profits balance indicates that a corporation can pay a dividend from current (or past) earnings without having to return some or all of a shareholder's original investment.

Example 20. Bell Company has $80,000 total earnings and profits at the beginning of 1993. During 1993 Bell distributed a $50,000 cash dividend to its shareholders. Since this distribution is less than total earnings and profits, the dividend will be taxable to the shareholders. The ending earnings and profits balance would then be $30,000: the $80,000 beginning balance less the $50,000 distribution. (Any net income generated by Bell Company in 1993 would increase the earnings and profits balance.)

Any distribution exceeding the earnings and profits of the corporation is first presumed to be a tax-free recovery of investment cost by the shareholder. If the shareholder recovers his or her investment cost, any excess distribution is usually treated as a capital gain. In effect, the distribution is treated as though the shareholder had sold his or her stock at a gain.

Example 21. Mel Allen purchased 100 shares of Capra Corporation stock ten years ago for $4,000. Allen received a dividend distribution of $8,000 in 1993; however, only $3,000 represents dividend income because of Capra's low earnings and profits. The $3,000 will be taxed as ordinary dividend income, and $4,000 of the distribution will be a nontaxable return of investment cost. The $1,000 excess will be taxed as a capital gain, since Allen has recovered his original investment cost.

Taxing the shareholder on a dividend distribution creates a double tax on income, because the distributing corporation is also subject to a tax on its income. In 1954 Congress enacted a special $100 exclusion ($200 on a joint return) to provide some relief from this double taxation. However, this exclusion was repealed for tax years after 1986, primarily because of the lower individual and corporate tax rates enacted that year.

> **TAX TIP**
>
>
>
> With the repeal of the dividend exclusion, some small investors in the stock market may shift their stock investments to growth stocks that pay only a small dividend. The appreciation in value of the stock investment is not taxed until the shares are sold or exchanged in a market transaction. Furthermore, any gain at that time will be capital gain, which (as discussed in Chapter 6) can absorb capital losses or possibly qualify for a slightly lower tax rate.

Occasionally a company will issue a dividend in property rather than cash. Such distributions are taxable to the extent of the fair market value of the property (subject to the corporation's earnings and profits). However, a dividend paid in the stock of the issuing company is normally not taxable, because usually each shareholder has the same percentage of ownership in the corporation after the dividend as before the dividend.

Example 22. Bill Ryan owns 1% (100 shares) of Dell Corporation's 10,000 shares of common stock. In 1993 he received 10 shares of stock as part of a 10% stock dividend issued by the company. Bill now owns 110 shares of Dell Corporation stock, but this still represents only 1% of Dell's outstanding stock (110/11,000). This stock dividend is not taxable.

Recently a number of corporations have offered "dividend reinvestment plans," which provide their shareholders the option of receiving either cash or additional stock in the company. The ability to receive cash invokes the constructive-receipt doctrine, which makes such a distribution taxable to the shareholder, regardless of which option is chosen.

Example 23. Janet Kimberly (single) owns 1,000 shares of Iowa Power Company. During 1993 the utility offers her the choice of receiving a cash dividend of $950 or additional shares of company stock worth $950. Even if Janet elects to receive the stock, she must report the $950 as income.

REPORTING INTEREST AND DIVIDEND INCOME

Schedule B of Form 1040 is used to report interest and dividend income received during the year, if either amount exceeds $400. Figure 2-2 illustrates a filled-in Schedule B. Note that the dividend section of the form transfers any capital-gain distri-

Schedules A&B (Form 1040) 1993		OMB No 1545-0074	Page **2**

Name(s) shown on Form 1040. Do not enter name and social security number if shown on other side.

Richard & Patricia Nottingham

Your social security number: 412 : 06 : 1134

Schedule B—Interest and Dividend Income
Attachment Sequence No. 08

Part I Interest Income

(See pages 16 and B-1.)

Note: *If you had over $400 in taxable interest income, you must also complete Part III.*

	Interest Income		Amount
1	List name of payer. If any interest is from a seller-financed mortgage and the buyer used the property as a personal residence, see page B-1 and list this interest first. Also show that buyer's social security number and address ▶ Fox Valley Savings & Loan	1	752
2	Add the amounts on line 1	2	752
3	Excludable interest on series EE U.S. savings bonds issued after 1989 from Form 8815, line 14. You MUST attach Form 8815 to Form 1040	3	
4	Subtract line 3 from line 2. Enter the result here and on Form 1040, line 8a ▶	4	752

Note: If you received a Form 1099-INT, Form 1099-OID, or substitute statement from a brokerage firm, list the firm's name as the payer and enter the total interest shown on that form.

Part II Dividend Income

(See pages 17 and B-1.)

Note: *If you had over $400 in gross dividends and/or other distributions on stock, you must also complete Part III.*

	Dividend Income		Amount
5	List name of payer. Include gross dividends and/or other distributions on stock here. Any capital gain distributions and nontaxable distributions will be deducted on lines 7 and 8 ▶ IBM Common	5	623
6	Add the amounts on line 5	6	623
7	Capital gain distributions. Enter here and on Schedule D* .	7	
8	Nontaxable distributions. (See the inst. for Form 1040, line 9.)	8	
9	Add lines 7 and 8	9	
10	Subtract line 9 from line 6. Enter the result here and on Form 1040, line 9 ▶	10	623

*If you received capital gain distributions but do not need Schedule D to report any other gains or losses, see the instructions for Form 1040, lines 13 and 14.

Note: If you received a Form 1099-DIV or substitute statement from a brokerage firm, list the firm's name as the payer and enter the total dividends shown on that form.

Part III Foreign Accounts and Trusts

(See page B-2.)

If you had over $400 of interest or dividends OR had a foreign account or were a grantor of, or a transferor to, a foreign trust, you must complete this part.

		Yes	No
11a	At any time during 1993, did you have an interest in or a signature or other authority over a financial account in a foreign country, such as a bank account, securities account, or other financial account? See page B-2 for exceptions and filing requirements for Form TD F 90-22.1		X
b	If "Yes," enter the name of the foreign country ▶		
12	Were you the grantor of, or transferor to, a foreign trust that existed during 1993, whether or not you have any beneficial interest in it? If "Yes," you may have to file Form 3520, 3520-A, or 926		X

For Paperwork Reduction Act Notice, see Form 1040 instructions.

Schedule B (Form 1040) 1993

Figure 2-2 Form 1040, Schedule B

Income	7	Wages, salaries, tips, etc. Attach Form(s) W-2	7	
Attach Copy B of your Forms W-2, W-2G, and 1099-R here.	8a	Taxable interest income (see page 16). Attach Schedule B if over $400	8a	752
	b	Tax-exempt interest (see page 17). DON'T include on line 8a **8b** 100		
	9	Dividend income. Attach Schedule B if over $400	9	623
	10	Taxable refunds, credits, or offsets of state and local income taxes (see page 17)	10	
	11	Alimony received	11	
If you did not get a W-2, see page 10.	12	Business income or (loss). Attach Schedule C or C-EZ	12	
	13	Capital gain or (loss). Attach Schedule D	13	
	14	Capital gain distributions not reported on line 13 (see page 17)	14	
	15	Other gains or (losses). Attach Form 4797	15	
If you are attaching a check or money order, put it on top of any Forms W-2, W-2G, or 1099-R.	16a	Total IRA distributions **16a** b Taxable amount (see page 18)	16b	
	17a	Total pensions and annuities **17a** b Taxable amount (see page 18)	17b	
	18	Rental real estate, royalties, partnerships, S corporations, trusts, etc. Attach Schedule E	18	
	19	Farm income or (loss). Attach Schedule F	19	
	20	Unemployment compensation (see page 19)	20	
	21a	Social security benefits **21a** b Taxable amount (see page 19)	21b	
	22	Other income. List type and amount—see page 20	22	
	23	Add the amounts in the far right column for lines 7 through 22. This is your **total income** ▶	23	

Figure 2-3   Form 1040—Income Section

butions to Schedule D (Capital Gains and Losses). Total taxable dividends (line 10) are then transferred to Form 1040, line 9 (shown as Figure 2-3).

The taxpayer reports the amount of interest and dividend income reported by each financial institution on Forms 1099-INT (interest) and 1099-DIV (dividends). The financial institution forwards copies of these forms to the IRS, so that the government can compare these with amounts reported on the tax return. Figures 2-4 and 2-5 illustrate these two forms with information reported on the filled-in Schedule B of Figure 2-2.

ANNUITY INCOME

An annuity is a contractual arrangement to pay a designated sum to an individual at regular intervals, either for a fixed period of time or for life. The annuity is a form of investment, and the purchaser (owner) of the annuity obviously expects total payments to exceed the original cost of the annuity. This excess represents interest, which is subject to taxation.

THE LAW

Sec. 72—(a) General rule for annuities. Except as otherwise provided in this chapter, gross income includes any amount received as an annuity (whether for a period certain or during one or more lives) under an annuity, endowment, or life insurance contract.

(b) Exclusion ratio. In general. Gross income does not include that part of any amount received as an annuity . . . which bears the same ratio to such amount as the investment in the contract (as of the annuity starting date) bears to the expected return under the contract (as of such date).

Figure 2-4   Form 1099-Int

[ ] CORRECTED (if checked)

PAYER'S name, street address, city, state, and ZIP code	Payer's RTN (optional)	OMB No. 1545-0112	**Interest Income**
Fox Valley Savings & Loan 1239 Burk Road Fairfax, VA 22030		Statement for Recipients of	

PAYER'S Federal identification number	RECIPIENT'S identification number	1 Earnings from savings and loan associations, credit unions, bank deposits, bearer certificates of deposit, etc.		**Copy B For Recipient**
22-65654	412-06-1134	$ 752		This is important tax information and is being furnished to the Internal Revenue Service. If you are required to file a return, a negligence penalty or other sanction will be imposed on you if this income is taxable and the IRS determines that it has not been reported.
RECIPIENT'S name Patricia Nelson		2 Early withdrawal penalty $	3 U.S. Savings Bonds, etc. $	
Street address 1240 Sunnyvale Drive		4 Federal income tax withheld $		
City, state, and ZIP code Fairfax, VA 22030		5 Foreign tax paid	6 Foreign country or U.S. possession	
Account number (optional)		$		

Form **1099-INT**   Department of the Treasury - Internal Revenue Service

Figure 2-4   Form 1099-Int

[ ] VOID   [ ] CORRECTED

PAYER'S name, street address, city, state, and ZIP code	1a Gross dividends and other distributions on stock (Total of 1b, 1c, 1d, and 1e)	OMB No. 1545-0110	**Dividends and Distributions**
International Business Machines 1212 Avenue of the Americas New York, NY 10023	$ 623		
	1b Ordinary dividends $ 623	Statement for Recipients of	

PAYER'S Federal identification number	RECIPIENT'S identification number	1c Capital gain distributions	1d Nontaxable distributions	**Copy C For Payer**
54-66453	412-06-1134	$	$	
RECIPIENT'S name Patricia Nelson		1e Investment expenses $	2 Federal income tax withheld $	For Paperwork Reduction Act Notice and instructions for completing this form, see Instructions for Forms 1099, 1098, 5498, and W-2G.
Street address 1240 Sunnyvale Drive		3 Foreign tax paid $	4 Foreign country or U.S. possession	
City, state, and ZIP code Fairfax, VA 22030		**Liquidation Distributions**		
Account number (optional)		5 Cash $	6 Noncash (Fair market value) $	

Form **1099-DIV**   Department of the Treasury - Internal Revenue Service

Figure 2-5   Form 1099-Div

Annuity payments are generally taxed according to the assumption that a portion of each payment represents a return of investment cost, and the remaining portion represents income (interest). The portion representing a return of investment cost (called the *exclusion ratio*) is nontaxable and is calculated by the following formula:

$$\text{Exclusion Ratio} = \frac{\text{Investment in Contract}}{\text{Total Expected Return}}$$

The *investment in contract* is the total cost of the annuity less any nontaxable refunds of purchase price. The *total expected return* is the sum of all payments expected to be received under the annuity contract. For fixed-period ("term certain") annuities, the calculation of the exclusion ratio is relatively straightforward.

☑ **Example 24.**   Lawrence O'Brien purchases an annuity contract for $7,500 beginning on 1/1/93. The contract provides for ten annual $1,000 payments beginning on 6/1/93. Lawrence's exclusion ratio is 75%, calculated as follows:

$$\text{Exclusion Ratio} = \frac{\text{Investment in Contract}}{\text{Total Expected Return}}$$

$$= \frac{\$7,500}{(\$1,000 \times 10)} = \frac{\$7,500}{\$10,000} = \underline{\underline{.75}}$$

Thus, $750 of each $1,000 payment (.75 × $1,000) is a nontaxable return of investment cost, and $250 of each payment ($1,000 – $750) is taxable interest income. Note that over the ten-year period Lawrence will fully recover his $7,500 cost and will recognize the $2,500 excess as interest income.

The exclusion ratio calculation is more complex for annuities payable over one or more person's lifetime(s). Since the total expected return depends on the life expectancy of the annuitant, the Internal Revenue Service has provided tables of life expectancies in terms of number of years, so the taxpayer must convert annuity payments to an annual basis before calculating the total expected return.

✓ **Example 25.** Margaret Olsen, age 65, purchased an annuity contract on 1/1/93 for $30,000. The contract provides for quarterly payments of $600 for life beginning on 4/1/93. According to the IRS tables, a 65-year-old person is expected to live for 20 more years. Margaret's exclusion ratio would be 62.5 percent, calculated as

$$\text{Exclusion Ratio} = \frac{\text{Investment in Contract}}{\text{Total Expected Return}}$$

$$= \frac{\$30,000}{(\$600 \times 4 \times 20)} = \frac{\$30,000}{\$48,000} = \underline{\underline{.625}}$$

Thus, $375 of each quarterly payment ($600 × .625) will be a nontaxable return of investment cost, and $225 of each quarterly payment ($600 – $375) will be taxable interest. Note that the $600 quarterly payment is multiplied by 4 in the calculation; the payment must be converted to an equivalent annual payment (since the table mortality values are expressed in terms of *years* of remaining life expectancy).

Margaret will report the total pension payments received during the year and the taxable portion of these payments on line 17 of Form 1040 as follows:

If you are attaching a check or money order, put it on top of any Forms W-2, W-2G, or 1099-R.					
16a	Total IRA distributions	16a		b Taxable amount (see page 18)	16b
17a	Total pensions and annuities	17a	2,400	b Taxable amount (see page 18)	17b 900
18	Rental real estate, royalties, partnerships, S corporations, trusts, etc. Attach Schedule E				18
19	Farm income or (loss). Attach Schedule F				19
20	Unemployment compensation (see page 19)				20

THE LAW

Sec. 72—(b)(2). Exclusion limited to investment. The portion of any amount received as an annuity which is excluded from gross income under paragraph (1) shall not exceed the unrecovered investment in the contract immediately before the receipt of such amount.

> *(3). Deduction where annuity payments cease before entire investment recovered. (A) In general. If—*
> *(i) after the annuity starting date, payments as an annuity under the contract cease by reason of death of the annuitant, and*
> *(ii) as of the date of such cessation, there is unrecovered investment in the contract, the amount of such unrecovered investment . . . shall be allowed as a deduction to the annuitant for his last taxable year.*

If a taxpayer lives longer than the life expectancy used to compute his or her expected return, all annuity payments received after that time (i.e., after full cost recovery) are fully taxable. If a taxpayer dies before the contract cost is fully recovered, the unrecovered portion of the investment in the contract is deducted on his or her final income tax return, as an itemized deduction. This deduction is not subject to the 2% floor on miscellaneous itemized deductions discussed in Chapter 4. These two rules apply only to annuities with payments beginning after 1986; if payments began before that time, neither adjustment is made.

Example 26. Assume the same facts as Example 25. If Margaret were still alive on 4/1/13 (20 years after receiving the first quarterly payment), then she would have fully recovered her "investment in the contract" with the 1/1/13 payment. Therefore, the entire $600 payment received on 4/1/13, as well as all subsequent payments, would be fully taxable.

Example 27. Assume the same facts as Example 25, except that Margaret died on 2/1/94. Since she had recovered only $1,500 of her original cost of the annuity (four payments at $375 each), the unrecovered investment in the contract of $28,500 may be taken as an itemized deduction on her final income tax return filed for 1994.

Example 28. Assume the same facts as Example 25, except that the first annuity payment was received in 1985. In this case, the annuity exclusion ratio would not be changed after Margaret fully recovered her cost (as in Example 26), and no deduction would be available if she died before recovering her investment in the contract (as in Example 27).

The Appendix to this chapter examines in more detail the annuity calculations for payments based on life expectancies. Extracts from the IRS tables are illustrated in this discussion.

A special exception to the annuity rules pertains to "employee annuities," if payments began prior to July 2, 1986. An employee annuity is a retirement contract purchased jointly by an employer and an employee during the employee's working years. Frequently, the employee's contributions to the contract are relatively minor when compared to the benefits to be received. To simplify the reporting of such annuities, the employee can use a cost recovery method of reporting the annuity payments, if he or she can recover his or her total cost contributions during the first three years in which payments are made.

Under the cost recovery method, payments are excluded entirely from income until the payments equal the employee's cost contribution; payments received after that time are fully taxable. If the employee cannot fully recover his or her cost contribution within three years, then the regular annuity rules using the exclusion ratio calculation are applied. This cost recovery method was *repealed* for employee annuities with payments beginning after July 1, 1986; the normal exclusion rules for annuities are used for such contracts.

☑ **Example 29.** Sal O'Brien was a high school teacher in Texas. He retired on January 1, 1986, and on February 1, 1986, began receiving monthly payments of $500 for his remaining lifetime. Sal had contributed a total of $14,000 to the retirement plan during his working years. At the rate of $500 a month, Sal recovered his $14,000 investment in 28 months. Since this recovery period was less than three years, Sal would have reported the payments for tax purposes on a cost recovery basis as follows:

Year	Total Payments	Excludable	Taxable
1986	11 ($5,500)	$5,500	$ 0
1987	12 ($6,000)	6,000	0
1988	12 ($6,000)	2,500	3,500
1989 and later years	12 ($6,000)	0	6,000

☑ **Example 30.** Assume the same facts as Example 29, except that Sal had contributed $24,000 to the retirement plan. Since Sal would not have recovered his $24,000 contributions within three years of the first payment (the recovery at three years would be only $18,000, or 36 × $500), he would not use the cost recovery method to report his annuity income. Instead, he would compute an exclusion ratio using the $24,000 contributions as his investment in contract and using an expected return based on IRS life-expectancy tables.

☑ **Example 31.** Assume the same facts as Example 29, except that Sal received his first annuity payment on January 1, 1989. Sal may not use the cost recovery method, since payments began after July 1, 1986; he must use the regular exclusion rules to determine the taxable portion of each payment.

TAX TIP

Annuities are sometimes marketed as a tax-deferral device for retirement purposes. A person could purchase an annuity during working years and have the payments begin at retirement. The advantage of such an arrangement is that the income earned on such an investment is not taxed until the payments begin at retirement, a time when the taxpayer may be in a lower tax bracket. The disadvantage of such a plan is that the payments for the annuity are not deductible. As we will see in Chapters 4 and 8, contributions to several types of retirement plans that offer annuity payments at retirement will be deductible (or excludable) at the time such payments are made.

II. Special Inclusions: Interest, Dividends, and Annuities

1 Control number		OMB No. 1545-0008		
2 Payer's name, address, and ZIP code State of Texas 101 Capitol Austin, TX 78712		3 Payer's Federal identification number	4 Payer's state I.D. number	
		5 State income tax withheld	6 Name of state	
		7 Tax amt not determined / Deceased / Legal rep	Subtotal / IRA, SEP / Void	
8 Recipient's social security no. 120-61-4431	9 Gross annuity, pension, etc. 6,000	10 Taxable amount 6,000	11 Federal income tax withheld	
12 Recipient's name, address, and ZIP code Sal O'Brien 1101 West Main College Station, TX 78743		13	14 Distribution code	
		Copy B—File with recipient's FEDERAL tax return This information is being furnished to the Internal Revenue Service.		

Form **W-2P** — Statement for Recipients of Annuities, Pensions, Retired Pay, or IRA Payments — Department of the Treasury, Internal Revenue Service

Figure 2-6 Form W-2P

Employers are required to issue a Form W-2P to summarize annuity and pension payments to employees. A sample W-2P is shown in Figure 2-6, using the data of Example 29 above for payments received after 1989. Note the disclosure of the taxable amount on line 10 of the form.

REVIEW II

1. Which of the following amounts of interest income is subject to the federal income tax?
   (a) interest on state of New York bonds
   (b) interest on United States savings bonds
   (c) interest on Dover City municipal bonds
   (d) None of the above is subject to tax.
2. In 1993 Henry and Ginger Gomez received the following amounts, which were labeled as dividends in their records:

	Henry	Ginger	Jointly Held
Able Corporation (U.S.)	$ 90	$ 50	$ 0
State Savings & Loan (passbook savings account)	180	220	0
Brandon Corp. (U.S.)	0	0	50
Lincoln Insurance Co. (a refund of premium cost)	0	0	30

Assuming that Henry and Ginger file a joint return, what is the amount of actual "dividends" to be reported in 1993?
- (a) $140
- (b) $190
- (c) $590
- (d) $620

3. Ronald Hardin purchased an annuity contract for $15,000. The contract provides for semiannual payments of $500 beginning January 1, 1993, and lasting for the remainder of Ronald's lifetime. Mortality tables indicate that Ronald has a remaining life expectancy of 25 years. How much of each $500 payment is taxable to Ronald?
- (a) $0
- (b) $200
- (c) $300
- (d) $500

4. Assume the same facts as Problem 3. If Ronald Hardin dies on September 1, 2000, his final income tax return will include, related to the annuity, an itemized deduction of
- (a) $0.
- (b) $4,800.
- (c) $10,200.
- (d) $16,000.

Answers are on page 2-26.

III MISCELLANEOUS INCLUSIONS: RENTS AND ALIMONY
(Code Sections 66, 71, 107 and 109)

RENTS

Rent may be defined as a payment for the use of property. All rent payments are taxable, and any prepayments of rent received are immediately taxable under the constructive receipt doctrine. Prepaid rents normally do not qualify for the special one-year deferral available for prepaid services, discussed earlier in this chapter, because most rental agreements do not provide for significant services by the lessor.

The constructive-receipt doctrine does not apply to deposits collected at the inception of the lease, if such deposits are designed to secure performance from the lessee. A common example of such a deposit is an amount collected for potential damages to the leased property over the life of the lease. Since the deposit is refundable if no damage occurs, the lessor is not actually in constructive receipt of the sum. However, any amounts withheld for damages at the end of the lease are taxable to the lessor.

✓ **Example 32.** Sara Mills owns an apartment building composed of four rental units. In March 1993, she rented one of the apartments to Bob Salvo on a one-year contract that provided for a monthly rental of $450. Sara collected $1,200 at the inception of the lease, which represented payment of the first and last month's rent and a damage deposit of $300. The $900 of prepaid rent is taxable immediately; however, the deposit is not taxable.

✓ **Example 33.** Assume in Example 32 that Sara withheld $120 of the $300 damage deposit at the end of the lease for damage to the carpets. The remaining $180 was refunded to Bob Salvo. The $120 is taxable to Sara, regardless of whether or not she actually spends the amount on carpet repairs. (Any amount spent on repairs would be deductible, as discussed in Chapter 8.)

Occasionally a lessee makes an improvement to the rental property during a lease. Most rent contracts stipulate that such improvements remain with the property at the end of the lease. This raises the following question: Is the lessor taxed on the value of these improvements when the lease expires? The answer is no, although the lessor has a zero cost basis in the improvement when computing gain on a later sale of the property. However, the value of the improvement will be taxable to the lessor if it is in lieu of any rent otherwise owed by the lessee.

✓ **Example 34.** John Adams rents a business building to Bow Company under a five-year lease that states that any improvements made to the building during the lease revert to Adams at the end of the lease. In the second year of the lease, Bow Company constructs an addition to the building. At the end of the lease, the addition is worth $8,000. Adams is not taxed on the value of this improvement; however, his cost basis of the improvement for tax purposes is $0 for computing gain on a later sale of the building. In effect, the gain is just postponed, not eliminated.

✓ **Example 35.** Assume the same facts as Example 34, except that Adams and Bow Company agree that the improvement will be in lieu of any rent payments by Bow for the remainder of the lease. In this case, the value of the improvement will be taxable to Adams as additional rental income.

Code Sec. 107 provides a special exception to the taxability of rent payments. A "minister of the gospel" is not taxed on the rental value of a home furnished the minister as part of his or her compensation. This exemption from taxation also applies to payment of expenses related to providing the home, such as utilities. This special exclusion from taxation forms a valuable part of a minister's compensation package.

✓ **Example 36.** Ralph Jackson is a minister at First Methodist Church. During 1993 he received a salary of $45,000 and was allowed to live rent-free in a home owned by the church. The fair rental value of the home is $850 a month. In addition, the church paid $2,300 of utility expenses and $330 of repair expenses related to the home in 1993. Jackson is taxed only on the $45,000 of salary in 1993.

ALIMONY PAYMENTS

The tax treatment of alimony is based in part on the wherewithal-to-pay principle. Payments that meet the federal tax definition of alimony are taxed to the *recipient* spouse and are deductible (for adjusted gross income) by the *payor* spouse. The recipient spouse is taxed on the alimony because he or she has the wherewithal-to-pay tax on that amount. Additionally, allowing a deduction to the paying spouse removes this amount from that spouse's income, because he or she does not have the wherewithal to pay tax on this amount. The alimony includable in the income of the recipient spouse is the same as the amount deductible by the payor spouse.

Four conditions must be met in order for payments to be treated as alimony for tax purposes: (1) the payments must be *in cash* and made pursuant to a divorce decree or other separation instrument, (2) this written instrument does not designate such payments as *not* qualifying as alimony for tax purposes, (3) the spouses are not members of the same household, and (4) there is no liability for payment after the death of the payee spouse.

If these conditions are met, payments will be treated as alimony for tax purposes. It is important to note that payments designated as child support are not treated as alimony. Such payments are not deductible by the payor and are not taxable to the recipient spouse. If payments in any year are less then amounts specified in the divorce decree or written instruments, they are first treated as child support.

ANSWERS TO REVIEW II

1. (b) Interest on obligations of the United States is always subject to tax. (Note: Interest on U.S. savings bonds may be deferred temporarily, but it is eventually subject to taxation.)
2. (b) The interest on the passbook savings account and the refund of insurance premiums do not qualify as dividends.
3. (b) Ronald's exclusion ratio is 60%, calculated as follows:

$$\text{Exclusion Ratio} = \frac{\text{Investment in Contract}}{\text{Total Expected Return}}$$

$$= \frac{\$15,000}{(\$500 \times 2 \times 25)} = \underline{\underline{.60}}$$

Thus, $300 of each payment is excludable ($500 × .60), and $200 of each payment is taxable ($500 × .40).

4. (c) At the time of his death, Ronald had received 16 semiannual payments, of which the total cost recovery (at $300 per payment) was $4,800. Thus, the unrecovered investment in the contract of $10,200 ($15,000 − $4,800) is allowed as an itemized deduction on his final tax return.

☑ **Example 37.** Under the terms of their divorce decree, Bob Adams is to pay $1,000 per month alimony and $1,000 per month child support to his former spouse Ellen. If all payments are made as scheduled in 1993, Bob will deduct $12,000 as alimony and Ellen will recognize the same amount as gross income. If Bob pays a total of only $15,000 in 1993, the first $12,000 is treated as nondeductible child support, and the remaining $3,000 is treated as alimony (deductible by Bob and includable by Ellen).

Bob will report the $3,000 deductible alimony on line 29 of Form 1040 as follows (note that the recipient's social security number is required, so that the IRS can verify that the amount is reported as income by Ellen):

Adjustments to Income (See page 20.)	24a Your IRA deduction (see page 20)	24a		
	b Spouse's IRA deduction (see page 20)	24b		
	25 One-half of self-employment tax (see page 21)	25		
	26 Self-employed health insurance deduction (see page 22)	26		
	27 Keogh retirement plan and self-employed SEP deduction	27		
	28 Penalty on early withdrawal of savings	28		
	29 Alimony paid. Recipient's SSN ▶ 41 23 6643	29	3,000	
	30 Add lines 24a through 29. These are your **total adjustments** ▶			30 3,000
Adjusted Gross Income	31 Subtract line 30 from line 23. This is your **adjusted gross income**. If this amount is less than $23,050 and a child lived with you, see page EIC-1 to find out if you can claim the "Earned Income Credit" on line 56 ▶			31 57,000

Likewise, Ellen will report the $3,000 alimony as income on line 11 of Form 1040 as follows:

Income Attach Copy B of your Forms W-2, W-2G, and 1099-R here. If you did not get a W-2, see page 10. If you are attaching a check or money order, put it on top of any Forms W-2, W-2G, or 1099-R.	7 Wages, salaries, tips, etc. Attach Form(s) W-2		7 40,000
	8a Taxable interest income (see page 16). Attach Schedule B if over $400		8a
	b Tax-exempt interest (see page 17). DON'T include on line 8a	8b	
	9 Dividend income. Attach Schedule B if over $400		9
	10 Taxable refunds, credits, or offsets of state and local income taxes (see page 17)		10
	11 Alimony received		11 3,000
	12 Business income or (loss). Attach Schedule C or C-EZ		12
	13 Capital gain or (loss). Attach Schedule D		13
	14 Capital gain distributions not reported on line 13 (see page 17)		14
	15 Other gains or (losses). Attach Form 4797		15
	16a Total IRA distributions . 16a	b Taxable amount (see page 18)	16b
	17a Total pensions and annuities 17a	b Taxable amount (see page 18)	17b
	18 Rental real estate, royalties, partnerships, S corporations, trusts, etc. Attach Schedule E		18
	19 Farm income or (loss). Attach Schedule F		19
	20 Unemployment compensation (see page 19)		20
	21a Social security benefits 21a	b Taxable amount (see page 19)	21b
	22 Other income. List type and amount—see page 20		22
	23 Add the amounts in the far right column for lines 7 through 22. This is your **total income** ▶		23 43,000

Code Sec. 71(f) contains a special "recapture" rule to prevent excessive front-loading of alimony payments. Since the tax treatment of alimony is loosely based on a "sharing of income" assumption as reflected by the wherewithal-to-pay principle, Congress did not want to extend full deductibility to large front-end cash payments that are essentially similar to lump-sum property settlements.

> ## THE LAW
>
>
> *Sec. 71(f)—(1) In general. If there are excess alimony payments—*
> *(A) the payor spouse shall include the amount of such excess payments in gross income for the payor spouse's taxable year beginning in the 3rd post-separation year, and*
> *(B) the payee spouse shall be allowed a deduction in computing adjusted gross income for the amount of such excess payments for the payee's taxable year beginning in the 3rd post-separation year.*

The special recapture rule is applied in the third "postseparation year," or the third year that alimony payments are made. The recapture is determined for the first- and second-year alimony payments and is recognized in the third year by reversing the prior treatment (i.e., "recapturing" the deduction by increasing the income of the payor spouse and decreasing the income of the recipient spouse with a deduction *for* AGI).

The recapture amounts for the second postseparation year (Year 2) and the first postseparation year (Year 1) are computed as follows:

Year 2 Recapture = Year 2 Alimony Payments − (Year 3 Alimony Payments + $15,000)

Year 1 Recapture = Year 1 Alimony Payments − {[("Corrected" Year 2 Alimony Payments + Year 3 Alimony Payments)/2] + $15,000}

Two points should be noted when we are examining these recapture formulas. First, there is no Year 2 recapture unless the Year 3 payments decreased more than $15,000 compared to those of Year 2; Congress in effect considers such a decrease to be evidence of "front-loading." Second, if Year 2 recapture exists, then the Year 2 payment must be reduced by the recapture before Year 1 recapture is computed (hence the term "corrected" Year 2 in the Year 1 formula).

Example 38. Jack and Rita Hull were divorced in 1991. Under the terms of the divorce decree, Jack will pay Rita the following amounts of alimony during the first three years of their divorce: 1991 ($85,000), 1992 ($60,000), and 1993 ($40,000). Jack paid and deducted $85,000 in 1991 and $60,000 in 1992, and Rita included the same amounts as income on her return. The recaptures are computed as follows:

Year 2 (1992) = $60,000 − ($40,000 + $15,000) = $ 5,000

Year 1 (1991) = $85,000 − {[($55,000 + $40,000)/2] + $15,000} = $22,500

Note in the calculations above that the Year 2 figure used in the Year 1 recapture computation was the "corrected" number of $55,000 ($60,000 less the $5,000 recapture). Thus, the total recapture amount is $27,500. In addition to deducting the regular $40,000 Year 3 payment on his 1993 return, Jack will also have to include the $27,500 recapture in gross income. Likewise, Rita will recognize the regular $40,000 Year 3 payment as income in 1993 and deduct the $27,500 recapture in computing adjusted gross income.

Worksheet for Recapture of Alimony
(For instruments executed after 1986)

Note: Do not enter less than zero on any line.

1. Alimony paid in **2nd year**			$60,000
2. Alimony paid in **3rd year**		$40,000	
3. Floor		$15,000	
4. Add lines 2 and 3			55,000
5. Subtract line 4 from line 1				$5,000
6. Alimony paid in **1st year**			85,000
7. Adjusted alimony paid in **2nd year** (line 1 less line 5)		55,000	
8. Alimony paid in **3rd year**		40,000	
9. Add lines 7 and 8		95,000	
10. Divide line 9 by 2		47,500	
11. Floor		$15,000	
12. Add lines 10 and 11			62,500
13. Subtract line 12 from line 6				22,500
14. **Recaptured alimony.** Add lines 5 and 13				* $27,500

* **If you deducted alimony paid**, report this amount as income on line 11, Form 1040.

If you reported alimony received, deduct this amount on line 29, Form 1040.

Figure 2-7 Alimony Recapture Worksheet

The alimony rules discussed thus far apply only to divorce decrees and separation instruments executed after 1984. In addition, more stringent recapture rules apply for instruments executed in 1985 and 1986. Coverage of these earlier rules is beyond the scope of this course. For details on these rules, see IRS Publication 504, *Tax Information for Divorced or Separated Individuals*.

Finally, IRS Publication 17, *Your Federal Income Tax*, presents a worksheet for computing alimony recapture. This approach may help you understand these computations. A completed worksheet using the facts of Example 38 is shown in Figure 2-7.

TAX TIP

If both spouses agree, any payments that would otherwise qualify as alimony for tax purposes may be labeled in the divorce decree as *not* qualifying as alimony. A *recipient* spouse may insist on such a provision, since he or she would not want to pay taxes on any amounts received. On the other hand, the *payor* spouse would obviously want to treat such amounts as alimony in order to deduct the payments.

If there is a disparity between the two spouses' marginal tax brackets, it is possible that *both* spouses can realize savings by treating the payments as alimony. For example, assume that Al and Pam O'Neil are in the process of obtaining a divorce, and Al demands at least $1,000 per month of after-tax cash as part of the divorce settlement. Pam's marginal tax rate is 31%, and Al's marginal tax rate is 15%. If Pam pays Al $1,000 per month that is labeled "not alimony" in the divorce decree, her after-tax annual cash outlay is $12,000. On the other hand, if she agrees to pay $1,300 per month deductible alimony (i.e., without the "not alimony" label), her annual after-tax cost is only $10,764 ($15,600 × .69). Furthermore, Al's after-tax cash received each year is $13,260 ($15,600 × .85). Both parties benefit under this scenario.

REVIEW III

1. Ray Meyer owns a rental apartment complex. During December 1993, he collected $5,000 of prepaid rents and $2,000 of damage deposits for new leases. During this month, he also refunded $1,600 of $2,500 worth of damage deposits for leases expiring in December; the remaining $900 was withheld for actual damages to the apartments. Ray's gross income from the apartments for December is
   (a) $ 900.
   (b) $5,000.
   (c) $5,900.
   (d) $7,000.
2. Bee Company leased a factory building from Brenda Allen for ten years. During the lease, Bee Company added a room to the building, and under the terms of the lease, the building reverts to Allen at the end of the lease. The room addition was constructed for $2,200 and was worth $3,500 at the end of the lease. At the end of the lease, Allen must report gross income of
   (a) $ 0.
   (b) $1,300.
   (c) $2,200.
   (d) $3,500.
3. Under the terms of their divorce decree, Brian Parsons agrees to pay his former spouse Jennifer the following amounts during the first three postseparation years:
   1991—$40,000
   1992—$20,000
   1993—$ 5,000
   What portion of the alimony payments of 1991 and 1992 are recapturable in 1993 (i.e., added to Brian's gross income and deducted from Jennifer's gross income)?
   (a) $ 0
   (b) $15,000
   (c) $12,500
   (d) $60,000

4. Assume the same facts as Question 3, except that the 1991 payment was $27,000. In this case, the total recapture in 1993 would be
   (a) $ 0.
   (b) $2,000.
   (c) $2,500.
   (d) $7,500.

Answers are on page 2-32.

IV ASSIGNMENT OF INCOME AND THE ALLOCABLE PARENTAL ("KIDDIE") TAX
(Code Sections 1, 2, and 66)

ASSIGNMENT OF INCOME

The source of an income item generally determines who must report the income for tax purposes. For example, income from services is taxed to the person who actually performs the services. Without such a provision in our tax law, taxpayers would be encouraged to "assign away" income to other taxpayers in lower tax brackets in order to achieve significant tax savings.

Example 39. Sidney Mann, an attorney, earned $100,000 in 1993. At the beginning of 1993, Sidney agreed to assign half of his earnings to a savings account for the benefit of his 17-year-old daughter, Sharon. All $100,000 will be taxed to Sidney in 1993, since he cannot shift the liability for tax on this amount.

The tax treatment of income from property is somewhat different, since a person is not actively generating the income. Since the property generates the income, the logical conclusion is to tax the legal owner of the property.

Example 40. Refer to Example 39 above. Assuming that Mann legally transfers $50,000 to the savings account in 1993, any interest income generated by this account will be taxed to Sharon, since she is now the legal owner of the property. Even though she is a minor, Sharon (or her guardian) must file a tax return in 1993 and report the interest income.

An exception to the property income rule is made in the case of gifts of property from a parent to a minor child. Specifically, if any of the income from the property accruing after the date of the gift is used to pay for the support of the child, the income will be taxed to the parent. The parent is taxed in this case because he or she has a legal obligation to provide for the support of his or her child, and using the child's income to meet this obligation is treated the same as using the parent's income.

There are two important exceptions to the assignment of income concepts discussed above. These are the treatment of "community property income" and the treatment of unearned income of certain dependent children. Each is discussed in the following sections.

COMMUNITY PROPERTY INCOME

Nine states have *community property* laws that specify the rights of husband and wife in property acquired after marriage. These states are Louisiana, Texas, New Mexico, Arizona, Nevada, California, Washington, Wisconsin, and Idaho. Community property laws basically provide that all services income and income from property acquired after marriage are presumed to be earned one-half by each spouse. Of course, such distinctions are meaningful only if the couple files separate returns; on a joint return, all income is combined.

Property acquired before marriage is treated as *separate property* (with the exception of the three states noted below), and the related income is not split between the spouses. Property inherited or received as a gift after marriage is also treated as separate property.

State community property laws are followed for federal income tax purposes because they establish the legal ownership of property and income. All services income and income from community property in these nine states is split evenly between the two spouses for separate returns (of course, no allocation is necessary for a joint return). Thus, services income is not necessarily taxed to the person who performed the services. Furthermore, in three community property states (Texas, Louisiana, and Idaho), the *income* from separate property is considered to be community property and is also allocated between the two spouses.

✓ **Example 41.** Mike and Gloria Stevens are married residents of *California*. During 1993 they earned the following income:

ANSWERS TO REVIEW III

1. (c) The prepaid rent is always taxable, and the damage deposits that were not refunded are also taxable under the claim-of-right doctrine.
2. (a) The value of such improvements is specifically excluded from taxation. However, the lessor's tax (cost) basis in the improvements is $0.
3. (c) There is no recapture for 1992, since the payments did not decrease more than $15,000 in 1993. However, there is recapture for 1991 of $12,500, the excess of the $40,000 1991 payment over the sum of (1) the average of the 1992 and 1993 payments ($12,500) plus (2) $15,000.
4. (a) The decrease in the Year 2 alimony payment does not exceed $15,000, and the difference between the Year 1 payment and the average of the Year 2 and Year 3 payments is also less than $15,000.

	Mike	Gloria	Total
Salary	$20,000	$18,000	$38,000
Income from property acquired *after* marriage	1,000	3,000	4,000
Income from property acquired *before* marriage	2,000	6,000	8,000

The salaries and income from properties acquired after marriage are considered to be community properties. Assuming that Mike and Gloria file separate returns, Mike will report gross income of $23,000 (one-half of the total salary and income from community property plus the $2,000 income from his separate property). Gloria will report gross income of $27,000 (one-half of the total salary and income from community property plus the $6,000 income from her own separate property).

Example 42. Assume the same facts as Example 41, except that Mike and Gloria reside in *Texas*. In this case, the income from properties acquired before marriage will also be community property. Mike and Gloria would each report $25,000 of gross income on separate returns, which represents one-half of all income received in 1993.

THE ALLOCABLE PARENTAL ("KIDDIE") TAX ON MINORS

As a result of the Tax Reform Act of 1986, a portion of some children's income may be taxed at their parents' marginal tax rates. This provision is a third method of discouraging transfers of income-producing properties from high-tax-bracket parents to low-tax-bracket children. The other two provisions, the limited standard deduction on unearned income and the disallowed exemption of a dependent, were discussed earlier in Chapter 1.

THE LAW

Code Sec. 1(i). Certain unearned income of minor children taxed as if parent's income. (1) In general. In the case of any child to whom the subsection applies, the tax imposed by this section shall be equal to the greater of—
(A) the tax imposed by this section without regard to this subsection, or
(B) the sum of—
  (i) the tax which would be imposed by this section if the taxable income of such child for the taxable year were reduced by the net unearned income of of such child, plus
  (ii) such child's share of the allocable parental tax.

Children Subject to the Allocable Parental Tax

The portion of a child's tax liability that is computed using a parent(s)'s tax rate is referred to as the *allocable parental tax*. However, the popular press soon coined the term "kiddie" tax as a simpler substitute. There are two significant limitations on this provision: (1) it applies only to a child under the age of 14 at the end of the tax year and (2) it applies only to investment ("unearned") income that exceeded $1,200 during 1993. For purposes of requirement (2), investment income generally includes all income other than salaries, wages, tips, bonuses, and other amounts paid for work actually done. Thus, the most common investment incomes are interest, dividends, and royalties.

Example 43. Tom West, age 11, is claimed as an exemption on his parents' tax return. During 1993 Tom earned $1,200 from a paper route and $400 from mowing lawns and received $500 of interest and $350 of dividend income. Tom is not subject to the allocable parental tax, since his investment income ($850) is less than $1,200.

Example 44. Rita Jenkins, age 15, is claimed as an exemption on her parents' tax return. During 1993 she received $600 interest income and $2,200 dividend income. Rita is not subject to the allocable parental tax, since she is not less than 14 years of age.

THE LAW

Code Sec. 1(i)(3). For purposes of this subsection—
(A) In general. The term "allocable parental tax" means the excess of—
    (i) the tax which would be imposed by this section on the parent's taxable income if such income included the net unearned income of all children of the parent to whom this subsection applies, over
    (ii) the tax imposed by this section on the parent without regard to this subsection.

There are two reasons why the "allocable parental tax" applies only to the net investment income exceeding $1,200 in 1993. First, a child is always entitled to a minimum $600 standard deduction, even if that child is claimed as an exemption deduction by his or her parent(s). Second, Congress decided to tax an equivalent amount of taxable investment income ($600 in 1993) at the child's rate, so that the complicated allocation procedures would not apply to small amounts of investment income. In effect, the first $600 of *taxable* investment income in 1993—i.e., after the $600 minimum standard deduction is subtracted—is taxed at the child's normal rate.

☑ **Example 45.** Sue Markam, age 8, is claimed as an exemption deduction on her parents' return. During 1993 she received $1,050 of interest income. Her taxable income for 1993 is $450 ($1,050 less a $600 standard deduction and $0 exemption deduction, since she is claimed by her parents), and her tax liability is $68 ($450 × .15). She is not subject to the allocable parental tax, because her investment income is less than $1,200.

TAX TIP

When making investments for their children under age 14, parents may want to consider investments that generate little or no income during the years prior to the child's 14th birthday. One possibility would be an investment in tax-exempt municipal bonds, which could be switched over to taxable investments when the child reached age 14. Another possibility would be investments in corporate stocks with appreciation potential, as opposed to large annual dividend yields. Such appreciation is taxable only when the stock is sold, and this taxable event could be delayed until the child reaches age 14 or older. At that time, the gain would be taxed at the child's marginal tax rate. The same rationale applies to investments in "deep discount" bonds, since the discount (in reality, interest income) is not taxable until the bonds are redeemed or sold.

Computing the Allocable Parental Tax

Technically, the amount of investment income subject to taxation at the parents' marginal tax rate is the *net unearned income*, defined, in 1993, as the gross investment income less the $600 minimum standard deduction plus the *larger* of $600 or the itemized deductions directly related to producing such investment income. Since most children under age 14 will not have significant amounts of the latter types of expenses, the $600 amount is normally used. Thus, in most cases, the net unearned income is simply the excess of the total investment income over $1,200 in 1993.

Once determined, the amount of "net unearned income" is then added to the parent's taxable income and the tax on the parents' return is then recomputed. This total tax is then reduced by the original tax liability reported on the parents' return in order to determine the "marginal" tax attributable to the net unearned income of the child. This marginal tax, termed the *allocable parental tax*, is then added to the regular tax liability on the remaining taxable income of the child (i.e., total taxable income less the "net unearned income"). The latter tax is computed using the child's normal tax rates.

Whew! And some people thought they would take it easy on kids! A comprehensive example will help clarify this troublesome computation. Note that the tax year 1993 is used in the following example, in order to illustrate the use of appropriate tax forms later in this section.

✓ **Example 46.** James Pinson, age 12, is claimed as an exemption deduction on his parents' tax return. During 1993 he earned $1,800 interest and $1,000 dividends. Expenses directly related to the production of this income total $150. His parents filed a joint return in 1993, reporting taxable income of $80,000 and a gross tax liability (determined from the tax tables) of $17,610. James' 1993 taxable income is $2,200 ($2,800 gross income less a $600 standard deduction and $0 personal exemption deduction). His tax liability is $540, the sum of the following two amounts:

(a) Tax on net unearned income of $1,600 ($2,800 less a $600 standard deduction, since it exceeds the $150 itemized deductions, and an additional $600 taxed at the child's rate in the computations):

Tax on $81,600 using joint return rates (i.e., tax on sum of parents' taxable income plus the net unearned income)	$18,058
Tax on $80,000 using joint return rates (i.e., as reported by parents)	(17,610)
Allocable parental tax	$ 448

(b) Tax on remaining taxable income of $600 (i.e., $2,200 taxable income less $1,600 unearned) computed at the child's tax rate (15%) 92

Total tax liability (a + b) .... $ 540

We can illustrate the net effect of the allocable parental tax in Example 46 by comparing the $540 tax liability with the tax liability due without the allocable parental tax. According to the tax tables, for a single individual, the tax due on $2,200 of taxable income would be $332. Thus, the allocable parental tax generated $208 of additional tax, which equals the $1,600 of net unearned income multiplied by 13%, the difference in the marginal tax rates of the parents (28%) and the child (15%).

TAX TIP

There is another side to the allocable parental tax computation; the procedure does allow parents to achieve tax savings on the first dollars of investment income transferred to a child. In 1993 this could be as much as $295 (i.e., $1,200 times a 24.6% difference [39.6% − 15%] in marginal tax rates). Channeling investments to children under age 14 in amounts sufficient to generate approximately $1,200 of interest income per year may yield significant savings over a period of years. For example, if in 1993 a 39.6%-bracket parent transferred such amounts to four children, over ten years the tax savings could be as

> much as $11,800 ($295 tax savings per year × 4 × 10). If current interest rates are about 6%, the parent could transfer approximately $20,000 of investments to a child under age 14 and avoid the allocable parental tax.

Form 8615 is used to compute the allocable parental tax. A completed Form 8615 is illustrated in Figure 2-8, using the facts of Example 46. Note that this form is attached to the dependent child's tax return, and the computed tax liability is transferred to the appropriate line on the child's return.

Special Problems with the Allocable Parental Tax

In some circumstances, the allocable parental tax computation may result in *less* tax than would be due if the net unearned income were taxed at the child's rate (e.g., the parents' marginal tax rate is less than the child's marginal tax rate). If this occurs, the allocable parental tax computation is ignored, and the entire amount of taxable income is taxed at the child's rate. Note on the Form 8615 in Figure 2-8 that line 18 requires the use of the larger of the tax computed with the allocable parental tax (line 16) or the tax computed with the child's tax rate (line 17).

If the child's married parents file separate returns, then the parent with the greater taxable income will be used in the computations. For children of divorced parents, the taxable income of the custody parent is used for purposes of computing the allocable parental tax. And finally, if more than one child in a family has "net unearned income," then the allocable parental tax is computed using the net unearned income of all children and the tax so computed is then allocated to each child based on his or her share of the total net unearned income. (Line 12(b) of Form 8615 is used to make this computation.)

✓ Example 47. Bob and Jane Kenny (ages 5 and 9, respectively) are claimed as dependents on their parents' tax return in 1993. Bob had $1,000 of net unearned income and Jane had $2,000 of net unearned income in 1993. Assuming that the "allocable parental tax" computed with this $3,000 of unearned income was $930, Bob's share would be $310 ($930 × $1,000/$3,000), and Jane's share would be $620 ($930 × $2,000/$3,000). Each would report his or her respective share on line 13 of Form 8615.

Finally, in 1988 Congress responded to widespread criticism of the allocable parental tax reporting procedures by providing an election whereby the parents may claim the child's unearned income on their tax returns. This election is available only if (a) the child's gross income consists entirely of interest and/or dividends, (b) such gross income is more than $500 and less than $5,000, and (c) no estimated tax payments were made on behalf of the child. If these conditions are met, the child is treated as having no gross income for the year (and is not required to file a return), and the child's gross income exceeding $1,000 is reported on the parents' return. In addition, the parents must increase their tax liability by the lesser of $75 or 15% of the child's gross income exceeding $500. This requirement taxes the first $500 of taxable investment income at the child's 15% rate, rather than at the parents' rate.

Form 8615 — Tax for Children Under Age 14 Who Have Investment Income of More Than $1,200

Department of the Treasury — Internal Revenue Service

OMB No. 1545-0998

1992

Attachment Sequence No. 33

► See instructions below and on back.
► Attach ONLY to the child's Form 1040, Form 1040A, or Form 1040NR.

General Instructions

Purpose of Form. For children under age 14, investment income (such as taxable interest and dividends) over $1,200 is taxed at the parent's rate if the parent's rate is higher than the child's rate. If the child's investment income is more than $1,200, use this form to figure the child's tax.

Investment Income. As used on this form, "investment income" includes all taxable income other than earned income as defined on page 2. It includes income such as taxable interest, dividends, capital gains, rents, royalties, etc. It also includes pension and annuity income and income (other than earned income) received as the beneficiary of a trust.

Who Must File. Generally, Form 8615 must be filed for any child who was under age 14 on January 1, 1993, and who had more than $1,200 of investment income. If neither parent was alive on December 31, 1992, do not use Form 8615. Instead, figure the child's tax in the normal manner.

Note: *The parent may be able to elect to report the child's interest and dividends on his or her return. If the parent makes this election, the child will not have to file a return or Form 8615. For more details, see the instructions for Form 1040 or Form 1040A, or get* **Form 8814,** *Parents' Election To Report Child's Interest and Dividends.*

Additional Information. For more details, get **Pub. 929,** Tax Rules for Children and Dependents.

Incomplete Information for Parent. If a child's parent or guardian cannot obtain the information needed to complete Form 8615 before the due date of the child's return, reasonable estimates of the parent's taxable income or filing status and the net investment income of the parent's other children may be made. The appropriate line(s) of Form 8615 must be marked "Estimated." For more details, see Pub. 929.

(Instructions continue on back.)

	Child's name shown on return	Child's social security number
	James C. Pinson	633 : 01 : 2234
A	Parent's name (first, initial, and last). **Caution:** See instructions on back before completing. Vada R. & Helen C. Pinson	B Parent's social security number 420 : 11 : 6001
C	Parent's filing status (check one): ☐ Single ☐ Married filing jointly ☐ Married filing separately ☐ Head of household ☐ Qualifying widow(er)	

Step 1 — Figure child's net investment income

1	Enter child's investment income, such as taxable interest and dividend income. See instructions. If this amount is $1,200 or less, **stop here;** do not file this form	1	2,800
2	If the child DID NOT itemize deductions on Schedule A (Form 1040 or Form 1040NR), enter $1,200. If the child ITEMIZED deductions, see instructions	2	1,200
3	Subtract line 2 from line 1. If the result is zero or less, **stop here;** do not complete the rest of this form but ATTACH it to the child's return	3	1,600
4	Enter child's **taxable** income from Form 1040, line 37; Form 1040A, line 22; or Form 1040NR, line 35	4	2,200
5	Enter the **smaller** of line 3 or line 4 here ▶	5	1,600

Step 2 — Figure tentative tax based on the tax rate of the parent listed on line A

6	Enter parent's **taxable** income from Form 1040, line 37; Form 1040A, line 22; Form 1040EZ, line 5; or Form 1040NR, line 35. If the parent transferred property to a trust, see instructions	6	80,000
7	Enter the total, if any, of the net investment income from Forms 8615, line 5, of ALL OTHER children of the parent. **Do not** include the amount from line 5 above	7	0
8	Add lines 5, 6, and 7	8	81,600
9	Tax on line 8 based on the **parent's** filing status. See instructions. If from Schedule D, enter amount from line 22 of that Schedule here ▶ _____	9	18,058
10	Enter parent's tax from Form 1040, line 38; Form 1040A, line 23; Form 1040EZ, line 7; or Form 1040NR, line 36. If from Schedule D, enter amount from line 22 of that Schedule here ▶ _____	10	17,610
11	Subtract line 10 from line 9. If line 7 is blank, enter on line 13 the amount from line 11; skip lines 12a and 12b	11	448
12a	Add lines 5 and 7 . . . . 12a 1,600		
b	Divide line 5 by line 12a. Enter the result as a decimal (rounded to two places)	12b	× 1.00
13	Multiply line 11 by line 12b ▶	13	448

Step 3 — Figure child's tax

Note: *If lines 4 and 5 above are the same, go to line 16.*

14	Subtract line 5 from line 4 . . . . 14 600		
15	Tax on line 14 based on the **child's** filing status. See instructions. If from Schedule D, enter amount from line 22 of that Schedule here ▶ _____	15	92
16	Add lines 13 and 15	16	540
17	Tax on line 4 based on the **child's** filing status. See instructions. If from Schedule D, check here ▶ ☐	17	322
18	Enter the **larger** of line 16 or line 17 here and on Form 1040, line 38; Form 1040A, line 23; or Form 1040NR, line 36. Be sure to check the box for "Form 8615" even if line 17 is more than line 16 ▶	18	540

For Paperwork Reduction Act Notice, see back of form.   Cat. No. 64113U   Form **8615** (1992)

Figure 2-8   Form 8615

Example 48. Refer to Example 46. Since James' gross income for 1993 consisted entirely of dividends and interest totaling more than $500 (but less than $5,000), his parents may elect to increase their gross income by $1,800, James' gross income excluding $1,000. The parents must also increase their gross tax liability by $75, or 15% of the first $500 of taxable income that is not included in the $1,800 of additional gross income. James will not be required to file a tax return in 1993.

Form 8814 is used to report this election and must be attached to the parents' tax return. Figure 2-9 illustrates this form, using the data of Example 46. Note that the gross income exceeding $1,000 ($1,800 on line 5) is added to the parents' gross income on line 22 of Form 1040. Also note that the $75 tax on the first $500 of James' taxable gross income (line 8) is added to his parents' tax liability on line 38 of Form 1040.

TAX TIP

Wait a minute! If you examine the preceding discussion and Form 8814 closely, you will discover that this procedure taxes all the child's unearned income exceeding *$1,000* (not $1,200) at the parents' marginal tax rate with only *$500* (not $600) being taxed at the child's rate! As a result, the tax is actually a few dollars *higher* if the child does not file a return. Why? Because the $1,000 and $500 used on Form 8814 are the amounts that actually applied in 1990 before the two amounts were adjusted for inflation in the years following 1990 (as mandated by the Code). When Congress passed the legislation, they did *not* also index the numbers used in this special election to report the income on the parents' return. Therefore, the IRS cannot change these numbers on Form 8814 until Congress corrects this oversight.

Also, including a portion of the child's income in the parents' gross income increases the parents' adjusted gross income. This will reduce any itemized deductions that have floors based on a percentage of adjusted gross income, such as medical expenses, casualty and theft losses, and miscellaneous itemized deductions. The impact of these two factors should be considered when electing to use Form 8814.

REVIEW IV

 1. Because her husband Tom supported her financially through medical school, Mary Cannon signs an agreement that transfers 30% of her medical earnings to Tom for the next five years. Mary's total income in 1993, the first year of this arrangement, is $80,000. Mary must report gross income in 1993 of
    (a) $0.
    (b) $24,000.
    (c) $56,000.
    (d) $80,000.

2-40 *Gross Income of Individuals: Inclusions*

Form **8814**	**Parents' Election To Report Child's Interest and Dividends**	OMB No. 1545-1128
Department of the Treasury Internal Revenue Service	▶ See instructions below and on back. ▶ Attach to parents' Form 1040 or Form 1040NR.	**19****93** Attachment Sequence No. **40**

Name(s) shown on your return: Vada R. & Helen C. Pinson

Your social security number: 420 11 6001

A Child's name (first, initial, and last)

B Child's social security number: 633 01 2234

C If more than one Form 8814 is attached, check here . . . . ▶ ☐

Step 1 Figure amount of child's interest and dividend income to report on your return

1a Enter your child's **taxable** interest income. If this amount is different from the amounts shown on the child's Forms 1099-INT and 1099-OID, see the instructions . . . . | **1a** | 1,800 |

b Enter your child's **tax-exempt** interest income. **DO NOT** include this amount on line 1a . . . . | **1b** | |

2a Enter your child's gross dividends, including any Alaska Permanent Fund dividends. If none, enter -0- on line 2c and go to line 3. If your child received any capital gain distributions or dividends as a nominee, see the instructions . . . . | **2a** | 900 |

b Enter your child's nontaxable distributions that are included on line 2a. These should be shown in box 1d of Form 1099-DIV . . . . | **2b** | |

c Subtract line 2b from line 2a . . . . | **2c** | 900 |

3 Add lines 1a and 2c. If the total is $1,000 or less, skip lines 4 and 5 and go to line 6. If the total is $5,000 or more, **do not** file this form. Your child **must** file his or her own return to report the income . . . . | **3** | 2,700 |

4 Base amount . . . . | **4** | 1,000 00 |

5 Subtract line 4 from line 3. If you checked the box on line C above or if line 2a includes any capital gain distributions, see the instructions. Also, include this amount in the total on Form 1040, line 22, or Form 1040NR, line 22. In the space next to line 22, enter "Form 8814" and show the amount. Go to line 6 below . . . . ▶ | **5** | 1,700 |

Step 2 Figure your tax on the first $1,000 of child's interest and dividend income

6 Amount not taxed . . . . | **6** | 500 00 |

7 Subtract line 6 from line 3. If the result is zero or less, enter -0- . . . . | **7** | 2,200 |

8 Tax. Is the amount on line 7 less than $500?
  • **NO.** Enter $75 here and see the **Note** below.
  • **YES.** Multiply line 7 by 15% (.15). Enter the result here and see the **Note** below. | **8** | 75 |

Note: *If you checked the box on line C above, see the instructions. Otherwise, include the amount from line 8 in the tax you enter on Form 1040, line 38, or Form 1040NR, line 37. Also, enter the amount from line 8 in the space provided next to line 38 on Form 1040, or next to line 37 on Form 1040NR.*

General Instructions

Purpose of Form.—Use this form if you elect to report your child's income on your return. If you do, your child will not have to file a return. You can make this election if your child meets **all** of the following conditions:

• Was under age 14 on January 1, 1994.
• Is required to file a 1993 return.
• Had income only from interest and dividends, including Alaska Permanent Fund dividends.
• Had gross income for 1993 that was less than $5,000.

• Had no estimated tax payments for 1993.
• Did not have any overpayment of tax shown on his or her 1992 return applied to the 1993 return.
• Had no Federal income tax withheld from his or her income (backup withholding).

You must also qualify as explained on page 2 of these instructions.

Step 1 of the form is used to figure the amount of your child's income to report on your return. **Step 2** is used to figure an additional tax that must be added to your tax.

How To Make the Election.—To make the election, complete and attach Form 8814 to your tax return and file your return by the due date (including extensions). A separate Form 8814 must be filed for **each** child whose income you choose to report.

Caution: *The Federal income tax on your child's income may be less if you file a tax return for the child instead of making this election. This is because you cannot take certain deductions that your child would be entitled to on his or her own return. For details, see* **Deductions You May Not Take** *on page 2.*

For Paperwork Reduction Act Notice, see back of form. Cat. No. 10750J Form **8814** (1993)

Figure 2-9 Form 8814

2. What is the only type of income for a married couple filing separately that would be taxed differently in Texas and California (two community property states)?
   (a) salary income earned after marriage
   (b) salary income earned before marriage
   (c) income from property acquired by purchase after marriage
   (d) income from property acquired by purchase before marriage
3. During the year 1993, Annie Glidden, age 12, received $900 of dividends, $700 of interest from a savings account, and $500 of interest from a state of Kentucky bond. What portion of this income will be taxed at her parents' rate?
   (a) $ 0
   (b) $ 400
   (c) $ 500
   (d) $ 900
4. During 1993 Charles Windsor, age six, received $1,130 from a savings account. What portion of this income will be taxed at his parents' rate?
   (a) $ 0
   (b) $ 30
   (c) $ 530
   (d) $1,030

Answers are on page 2-42.

CHAPTER APPENDIX: ANNUITY CALCULATIONS BASED ON LIFE EXPECTANCIES

The annuity discussion in this chapter briefly mentioned the life expectancy tables provided by the Internal Revenue Service. The IRS provides several tables in the tax regulations to deal with various annuity arrangements based on one or more life expectancies. The purpose of this Appendix is to introduce three of these tables, portions of which are illustrated in Table 2-1.

Part A of Table 2-1 (Ordinary Life–One Life) is used to compute the expected return for an *ordinary life annuity* based on one life expectancy. The column labeled "Multiple" provides the life expectancies (in years) corresponding to the ages listed in the first column. In applying this table, we use the annuitant's age closest to the "annuity starting date" (the first day of the first payment period). (If annuity payments are not made more often than on a quarterly basis, another table must be used to adjust the multiple in Table 2-1. Because this adjustment is so small, this procedure is not covered in this text.)

✓ **Example 49.** Jean Logan, age 70, purchased for $9,000 an annuity that will pay her $250 quarterly for the remainder of her life. Assuming that Jean's 70th birthday is closest to the annuity starting date, the correct multiple to use in computing her expected return is 16.0 (Table 2-1, Part A). Her exclusion ratio would be computed as follows:

Table 2-1 Expected Return Multiples—Life Annuities

A. Ordinary Life—One Life

Age	Multiple	Age	Multiple
61	23.3	66	19.2
62	22.5	67	18.4
63	21.6	68	17.6
64	20.8	69	16.8
65	20.0	70	16.0

B. Joint Life—Two Lives

			Age		
Age	61	62	63	64	65
61	17.9	17.5	17.1	16.7	16.2
62	17.5	17.1	16.8	16.3	15.9
63	17.1	16.8	16.4	16.0	15.6
64	16.7	16.3	16.0	15.6	15.3
65	16.2	15.9	15.6	15.3	14.9

C. Joint and Survivor—Two Lives

			Age		
Age	61	62	63	64	65
61	28.7	28.3	27.8	27.4	27.1
62	28.3	27.8	27.3	26.9	26.5
63	27.8	27.3	26.9	26.4	26.0
64	27.4	26.9	26.4	25.9	25.5
65	27.1	26.5	26.0	25.5	25.0

ANSWERS TO REVIEW IV

1. (d) Income from services is always taxed to the person who performed the services. Since the $80,000 represents compensation for services performed by Mary, not Tom, the assignment of 30% of the earnings to Tom will not be recognized for tax purposes.

2. (d) The income is from *separate* property (property acquired prior to marriage). Texas is one of three states (Louisiana and Idaho are the others) that treats such income as community income (split evenly between the two spouses). The other six community property states (which include California) do not split income on such properties.

3. (b) The interest on state of Kentucky bonds would not be taxable; therefore, the gross income is only $1,600. Of this total, the amount in excess of $1,200, or $400, is subject to the allocable parental tax.

4. (a) Since the taxpayer's unearned income does not exceed $1,200, none of the total will be subject to the allocable parental tax. After a $600 standard deduction is subtracted, the remaining $530 will be taxed at the child's rate of 15%.

$$\text{Exclusion Ratio} = \frac{\text{Investment in Contract}}{\text{Total Expected Return}} = \frac{\$9{,}000}{(\$250 \times 4 \times 16.0)}$$

$$= .5625$$

Thus, Jean may exclude 56.25% of each $250 payment, or $140.62, and the remaining $109.38 will be taxable. (Note that we convert the quarterly payments to an annual return by multiplying by 4.)

A *joint annuity* is a contract providing for payments to two people as long as both of them live (with no payments to the survivor), and a *joint and survivor annuity* is a contract providing for payments to continue until both annuitants die. Part B of Table 2-1 is used to compute the expected return for a joint annuity. To locate the correct multiple, we find the intersection of the ages of the two annuitants closest to the annuity starting date. This multiple is based on both life expectancies and is used to compute the expected return.

✓ **Example 50.** Wes and Marva Kelley (ages 64 and 63, respectively) purchase a joint annuity for $11,520. The contract provides for $500 semiannual payments until either Wes or Marva dies; the survivor will not be entitled to any benefits. The correct multiple to use for their expected return is 16.0 (Table 2, Part B). This is an estimate of the number of years remaining until the *first* spouse dies. Their exclusion ratio would be computed as follows:

$$\text{Exclusion Ratio} = \frac{\text{Investment in Contract}}{\text{Total Expected Return}} = \frac{\$11{,}520}{(\$500 \times 2 \times 16.0)}$$

$$= .7200$$

Thus, Wes and Marva may exclude 72% of each payment, or $360, and the remaining $140 will be taxable. The payments end as soon as either spouse dies.

Part C of Table 2-1 is used to compute the expected return for a *joint and survivor annuity*. A joint and survivor annuity is structured so that a first (original) annuitant receives a certain benefit for life, and after the first annuitant's death, a second (survivor) annuitant begins to receive a benefit. If the benefit to both annuitants is the same, the multiple in Part C of Table 2-1 is used to compute one overall expected return. This expected return multiple is based on both life expectancies and is not adjusted after the first annuitant dies.

✓ **Example 51.** Curt and Cathy Norris (ages 63 and 65, respectively) purchased a joint and survivor annuity for $46,800. The annuity contract provides for payments of $200 a month to Curt for the rest of his life, and after his death, $200 per month to Cathy until she dies. The correct multiple to use for their expected return is 26.0 (Table 2-1, Part C), which represents an estimate of the remaining number of years until *both* spouses have died. Their exclusion ratio is computed as follows:

$$\text{Exclusion Ratio} = \frac{\text{Investment in Contract}}{\text{Total Expected Return}} = \frac{\$46{,}800}{(\$200 \times 12 \times 26.0)}$$

$$= .7500$$

Thus, 75% of each $200 monthly payment, or $150, will be excludable by *either* spouse until both spouses have died.

If the joint and survivor annuity provides for different benefits to the original annuitant and the surviving annuitant, an expected return calculation must be made for each annuitant (since Part C of Table 2-1 assumes that each annuitant receives the same benefit). First, we calculate an expected return for the original annuitant using Part A of Table 2-1 (ordinary annuity–one life). Then we compute an expected return for the surviving annuitant by using a multiple equal to the difference between the life expectancy of both annuitants combined (Part C of Table 2-1) and the life expectancy of the original annuitant (Part A of Table 2-1). This multiple represents the number of years that the survivor annuitant is expected to live *after* the original annuitant dies. Finally, the two expected return amounts are added together, and we use this total expected return to compute the exclusion ratio for the normal annuity calculations.

✓ **Example 52.** Assume the same facts as Example 51, except that the annuity contract provides for payments of $100 a month to Cathy after Curt dies. The total expected return for Curt and Cathy would be calculated as follows:

Curt's expected return ($200 × 12 × 21.6) $51,840
Cathy's expected return [$100 × 12 × (26.0 - 21.6)] 5,280
Total expected return $57,120

Note that the expected return multiple for Cathy (the survivor annuitant) is 4.4 years, which is the life expectancy for Curt and Cathy combined (26.0 years) less the life expectancy for Curt alone (21.6 years). The exclusion ratio would then be computed as follows:

$$\text{Exclusion Ratio} = \frac{\text{Investment in Contract}}{\text{Total Expected Return}} = \frac{\$46,800}{\$57,120}$$

$$= .8193$$

Thus, Curt will exclude 81.93% of each $200 payment, or $163.86, and after he dies, Cathy will exclude 81.93% of each $100 payment, or $81.93. (If Cathy dies first, Curt will continue to use the 81.93% exclusion ratio until he dies.)

This concludes a brief overview of annuity calculations based on life expectancy tables. One other point is worth noting: The mortality tables are "gender neutral," in that the same return multiple is used for both males and females. This has not always been the case in our tax law; the gender-neutral tables were added to the Regulations only in the early 1980s.

CHAPTER PROBLEMS

PART I

1. Richard Wilson purchased a personal residence in Woodland on February 2, 1991, for $60,000. In 1993 the city of Woodland announced that a new manufacturing operation would be located near Wilson's residence. In December 1993, Wilson's residence was appraised at a value of $105,000, and he promptly listed his house for sale at $110,000. The house was not sold at the end of 1993. How much income must Wilson report on his 1993 return?

I 2. In each of the following cases, determine when the income would be reported by the taxpayer in 1993:
  (a) Al Sharp earned $400 interest on a passbook savings account in 1993; he did not withdraw it until 1994.
  (b) Mary Allen received her semiannual dividend check from Boz Company on January 4, 1994.
  (c) Same as (b), except that the check arrived in Mary's post office box on December 26, 1993, but she chose not to pick it up until January 4, 1994.
  (d) Beth Wong, an accrual-basis taxpayer, sold an item of inventory in December 1993 for $450. This amount was collected in January 1994.

I 3. On December 15, 1993, Alice Camden performed legal services for Bill Robinson and established a normal 30-day accounts receivable for $800. On December 28, Alice agreed to accept ten shares of B Company stock as payment for half of the receivable balance. The stock was purchased by Robinson in 1990 for $250 and was worth $400 on December 28, 1993, the date of transfer. On January 8, 1994, Robinson paid off the $400 receivable balance in cash. Assuming that Alice is a calendar-year taxpayer, determine her gross income for 1993 and 1994 using (a) the cash basis and (b) the accrual basis.

I 4. Determine the amount of gross income to be reported for tax purposes in 1993 in each of the following circumstances (all taxpayers use a calendar year):
  (a) Bob Williams (cash basis), a bank employee, embezzeled $3,000 of bank funds in 1993. When the theft was discovered in 1994, he returned the funds.
  (b) Mary Watkins (accrual basis) rents her old residence on October 1, 1993, receiving one year's rent of $7,200 in advance at that time.
  (c) Wanda Bond (cash basis) received a $3,000 bonus in December 1993. In February 1994, an error was discovered in the bonus calculation, and Wanda was required to refund $1,000 of the bonus.
  (d) Craig Vardon earned $560 interest on a passbook savings account in 1993. He did not withdraw any of this interest in 1993.

I 5. Determine the amount of gross income reportable for 1993 for the following accrual-basis, calendar-year taxpayers:
  (a) David Gomez, a CPA, received a $12,000 retainer from Abbot Corporation on October 1, 1993. The retainer represents a one-year prepayment for monthly accounting and tax services to be performed by Gomez.
  (b) Same as (a), except that the $12,000 retainer represents a prepayment for two years of services.
  (c) Sylvia Weinhart, an antique furniture dealer, receives a $600 deposit for an antique cabinet on November 1, 1993. Sylvia had purchased the cabinet for $4,200, and delivered the cabinet on March 15, 1994. The sale price of the cabinet was $4,800.

II 6. On July 1, 1993, Greg Mason purchased a $10,000 face-value U.S. savings bond (Series EE) at its discount price of $7,500. As of December 31, 1993, the bond could be redeemed for $7,825. Assuming that Greg is a cash-basis taxpayer and chooses not to redeem the bond at year-end, what are his alternatives for reporting the interest income from this bond?

II 7. Jane Alexander, a single taxpayer, owns 100 shares of Computer Company stock, acquired in 1990 for $1,000. In August 1993, Computer Company issued a 10% stock dividend, at a time when the stock was selling for $120 a share. In December 1993,

Computer Company paid a $2 per share cash dividend; however, only $1.70 of the $2 was paid out of the company's earnings and profits. How much gross income must Alexander report in 1993 from these transactions?

II 8. Tom and Christine Kelly received the following payments during 1993:

Payor	Tom	Christine
First National Bank (savings accounts)	$150	$400
State of Delaware bonds (interest)	800	600
American Life Insurance (dividend representing a refund of premium cost)	—	200
ABC Corporation (dividends on common stock)	60	30
East Coast Utilities (dividend on common stock, which was reinvested in additional stock under the company's dividend reinvestment plan)	800	860
CDE Corporation (dividends on common stock):		
From earnings and profits	—	90
Return of capital	—	20

Determine the total taxable income realized by Tom and Christine Kelley from these payments, assuming that they file a joint return.

II 9. Determine the amount taxable in 1993 for each of the following annuity contracts:
   (a) For $6,600 Linda Grey purchased an annuity contract that provides for 20 semiannual installments of $1,000. She received two payments in 1993.
   (b) Terry Allison purchased an annuity contract for $60,000. The contract provides for annual payments of $6,000 for the remainder of his life. Allison's remaining life expectancy at the beginning of the first payment period is 25 years, and he received one payment in 1993.
   (c) Margaret Rushing purchased an annuity in 1993 for $20,736. The contract provides for monthly payments of $200 for the remainder of her life. Rushing's life expectancy at the beginning of the first payment period is 18 years, and she received six payments in 1993.

II 10. James Rogers retired in December 1991 from the city of New York public school system. In January 1992, he began receiving monthly payments of $700 from an employee annuity to which he had contributed a total of $15,600 during his working years (the balance of the investment premiums were contributed by the state of New York). Rogers' remaining life expectancy is 20 years.
   (a) Determine the gross income reportable by Rogers from this retirement plan in 1993.
   (b) Would your answer change if Rogers' monthly benefit were only $300? Explain.

III 11. Ronald and Catherine McDonald own a five-unit rental apartment complex. Determine the tax consequences of the following 1993 transactions, assuming that the McDonalds file a calendar-year, cash-basis return:
   (a) Received $28,050 of rental payments in 1993, of which $4,200 represents late payments of 1992 rent and $3,050 represents prepayments of 1994 rent;
   (b) Received $5,200 of damage deposits for new leases written in 1993, and withheld $2,000 from deposits of $6,300 related to leases expiring in 1993 (the remaining $4,300 was refunded to the tenants);
   (c) Received a new air conditioner worth $600 from a tenant whose lease expired in 1993 (the air conditioner was in lieu of the last month's rent);
   (d) Received a new set of storm windows and storm doors worth $850 from a tenant whose fully paid lease expired in 1993 (under the lease terms, any improvements revert to the McDonalds).

III 12. Determine the taxability of the described payments in each of the following independent cases (all payments are made in accordance with the terms of a written divorce decree, except for case c):
   (a) Sue Allen receives $400 a month alimony and $200 a month child support until she dies or remarries.
   (b) Nan Brown receives $15,000 of a principal alimony sum of $40,000 in 1993 (the first payment year); the balance is to be paid in ten annual installments of $2,500.
   (c) Dee Canton voluntarily pays her former spouse Larry $400 a month for six months in 1993 (the divorce decree, which requires alimony payments of $400 a month for Larry's life until he dies or remarries, does not take effect until January 1994).
   (d) Douglas Drewery pays his former spouse $500 per month alimony and $300 per month child support.

III 13. Under the terms of their divorce decree, Martha Plimpton will pay her former spouse George the following amounts of qualifying alimony in the first three postseparation years: 1991 ($70,000), 1992 ($50,000), and 1993 ($20,000). How much (if any) recapture of alimony must Martha and George report in 1993?

III 14. Refer to Problem 13. How would your answer change if the 1993 payment were $35,000 rather than $20,000?

IV 15. Who will be taxed on the income in the following cases?
   (a) Mary Allen earned $40,000 as a CPA in 1993 and assigned 1/10 of her earnings to her brother.
   (b) Bradley Wayne deposited $20,000 in a savings account for his 15-year-old daughter, Debra. The account was in Debra's name and earned $1,800 interest in 1993, which remained deposited in the account.
   (c) Same as (b), except that Bradley uses the $1,800 interest to pay Debra's tuition at a private school.

IV 16. Allen and Gloria Stephenson are married and are residents of California, a community property state. They elect to file married-filing separately in 1993, and their income that year consisted of the following:

	Allen	Gloria
Salaries	$16,000	$24,000
Interest income on properties acquired before marriage	3,000	4,000
Interest income on properties acquired after marriage	6,000	2,000
Prize won on game show	3,000	—

   (a) Determine the gross income reported by each spouse on married-filing separately returns in 1993.
   (b) Same as (a), except that Allen and Gloria are residents of New Jersey (a non-community property state).

IV 17. John Smiley, age 11, is claimed as a dependency exemption by his parents on a joint return. During 1993 John received $1,100 interest on taxable corporate bonds, $400 interest on tax-exempt municipal bonds, and $1,500 dividends on stocks. What is John's 1993 taxable income?

IV 18. Refer to Problem 17. Assuming that John's parents have a tax rate of 31% (based on $100,000 of taxable income), compute John's 1993 gross tax liability.

	19. Rico Brazzi, age 12, is claimed as an exemption on his parents' tax return in 1993. His parents reported taxable income of $90,000 for that year. During 1993 Rico received $1,700 interest from a savings account, $800 interest from taxable bonds, and $3,200 dividends on corporate stocks. His legitimate itemized deductions for 1993 total $400. What is Rico's 1993 gross tax?
IV	
APX	20. Gerald and Diane Metzer (ages 64 and 65, respectively) purchased a joint annuity in 1993 for $14,784. The annuity provides for quarterly payments of $600 for as long as both spouses live; when one spouse dies, the payments stop immediately. How much of each payment is taxable to Gerald and Diane on a joint return?
APX	21. Rhonda Craig purchased a joint and survivor annuity in 1993 for $13,330. The annuity contract provides for semiannual payments of $500 to Rhonda for life, and when she dies, semiannual payments of $400 to her husband Hal for life (if he outlives Rhonda). At the annuity starting date, Rhonda was 65 years old and Hal was 61 years old. How much of each $500 payment to Rhonda is taxable? Assuming that Hal outlives Rhonda, how much of each $400 payment will be taxable to Hal?

TAX RETURN PROBLEMS

22. [Form 1040, Schedule B] Using the information in Problem 8 above, prepare a 1993 Form 1040, Schedule B for Tom and Christine Kelley, assuming that they file a joint return.
23. [Form 8615] Using the facts of Problem 19, prepare a Form 8615 for Rico Brazzi for 1993.

HOW WOULD YOU RULE?

24. Max Baker received a $1,200 informant's fee from the Internal Revenue Service for disclosing information concerning a special fund kept by his former employer. The fee was calculated as 10% of the additional tax liability resulting from the audit of his former employer. Is this fee taxable to Baker? What is your opinion?
25. Sharon Landers purchased a new automobile for $9,000. Under a special rebate offer by the manufacturer, she received a rebate check for $600. Is this rebate taxable to Sharon? What is your opinion?

TAX RETURN PORTFOLIO PROBLEM

If this problem is assigned by your instructor, refer to Appendix A and complete the instructions for the segment labeled "Chapter 2." These instructions include salary information; the completion of Form 1040, Schedule B for Harold and Maude Neilson; and the partial completion of Form 1040A and related Form 8615 for Martha Neilson.

Chapter 2 Problem 22   Name _____   2-49

Schedules A&B (Form 1040) 1993 | OMB No 1545-0074 | Page 2

Name(s) shown on Form 1040. Do not enter name and social security number if shown on other side. | Your social security number

Schedule B—Interest and Dividend Income

Attachment Sequence No 08

Part I Interest Income

(See pages 16 and B-1.)

Note: If you had over $400 in taxable interest income, you must also complete Part III.

Interest Income	Amount

1 List name of payer. If any interest is from a seller-financed mortgage and the buyer used the property as a personal residence, see page B-1 and list this interest first. Also show that buyer's social security number and address ▶

Note: If you received a Form 1099-INT, Form 1099-OID, or substitute statement from a brokerage firm, list the firm's name as the payer and enter the total interest shown on that form.

2 Add the amounts on line 1 . . . . | **2** |
3 Excludable interest on series EE U.S. savings bonds issued after 1989 from Form 8815, line 14. You MUST attach Form 8815 to Form 1040 . . . . . . | **3** |
4 Subtract line 3 from line 2. Enter the result here and on Form 1040, line 8a ▶ | **4** |

Part II Dividend Income

(See pages 17 and B-1.)

Note: If you had over $400 in gross dividends and/or other distributions on stock, you must also complete Part III.

Dividend Income	Amount

5 List name of payer. Include gross dividends and/or other distributions on stock here. Any capital gain distributions and nontaxable distributions will be deducted on lines 7 and 8 ▶

Note: If you received a Form 1099-DIV or substitute statement from a brokerage firm, list the firm's name as the payer and enter the total dividends shown on that form.

6 Add the amounts on line 5 . . . . | **6** |
7 Capital gain distributions. Enter here and on Schedule D* . | **7** |
8 Nontaxable distributions. (See the inst. for Form 1040, line 9.) | **8** |
9 Add lines 7 and 8 . . . . | **9** |
10 Subtract line 9 from line 6. Enter the result here and on Form 1040, line 9 ▶ | **10** |

*If you received capital gain distributions but do not need Schedule D to report any other gains or losses, see the instructions for Form 1040, lines 13 and 14.

Part III Foreign Accounts and Trusts

(See page B-2.)

If you had over $400 of interest or dividends OR had a foreign account or were a grantor of, or a transferor to, a foreign trust, you must complete this part. | Yes | No |

11a At any time during 1993, did you have an interest in or a signature or other authority over a financial account in a foreign country, such as a bank account, securities account, or other financial account? See page B-2 for exceptions and filing requirements for Form TD F 90-22.1 . . . .
  b If "Yes," enter the name of the foreign country ▶ ....
12 Were you the grantor of, or transferor to, a foreign trust that existed during 1993, whether or not you have any beneficial interest in it? If "Yes," you may have to file Form 3520, 3520-A, or 926 .

For Paperwork Reduction Act Notice, see Form 1040 instructions.   Schedule B (Form 1040) 1993

Copyright © 1994 by Harcourt Brace & Company. All rights reserved.

Chapter 2 Problem 23   Name _____   2-51

Form 8615
Department of the Treasury
Internal Revenue Service

**Tax for Children Under Age 14
Who Have Investment Income of More Than $1,200**
▶ See instructions below and on back.
▶ Attach ONLY to the child's Form 1040, Form 1040A, or Form 1040NR.

OMB No. 1545-0998
1992
Attachment Sequence No. **33**

General Instructions

Purpose of Form. For children under age 14, investment income (such as taxable interest and dividends) over $1,200 is taxed at the parent's rate if the parent's rate is higher than the child's rate. If the child's investment income is more than $1,200, use this form to figure the child's tax.

Investment Income. As used on this form, "investment income" includes all taxable income other than earned income as defined on page 2. It includes income such as taxable interest, dividends, capital gains, rents, royalties, etc. It also includes pension and annuity income and income (other than earned income) received as the beneficiary of a trust.

Who Must File. Generally, Form 8615 must be filed for any child who was under age 14 on January 1, 1993, and who had more than $1,200 of investment income. If neither parent was alive on December 31, 1992, do not use Form 8615. Instead, figure the child's tax in the normal manner.

Note: *The parent may be able to elect to report the child's interest and dividends on his or her return. If the parent makes this election, the child will not have to file a return or Form 8615. For more details, see the instructions for Form 1040 or Form 1040A, or get* **Form 8814,** *Parents' Election To Report Child's Interest and Dividends.*

Additional Information. For more details, get **Pub. 929,** Tax Rules for Children and Dependents.

Incomplete Information for Parent. If a child's parent or guardian cannot obtain the information needed to complete Form 8615 before the due date of the child's return, reasonable estimates of the parent's taxable income or filing status and the net investment income of the parent's other children may be made. The appropriate line(s) of Form 8615 must be marked "Estimated." For more details, see Pub. 929.

(Instructions continue on back.)

	Child's name shown on return	Child's social security number
A	Parent's name (first, initial, and last). **Caution:** *See instructions on back before completing.*	B Parent's social security number
C	Parent's filing status (check one): ☐ Single ☐ Married filing jointly ☐ Married filing separately ☐ Head of household ☐ Qualifying widow(er)	

Step 1 Figure child's net investment income

1	Enter child's investment income, such as taxable interest and dividend income. See instructions. If this amount is $1,200 or less, **stop here;** do not file this form	1	
2	If the child DID NOT itemize deductions on Schedule A (Form 1040 or Form 1040NR), enter $1,200. If the child ITEMIZED deductions, see instructions	2	
3	Subtract line 2 from line 1. If the result is zero or less, **stop here;** do not complete the rest of this form but ATTACH it to the child's return	3	
4	Enter child's **taxable** income from Form 1040, line 37; Form 1040A, line 22; or Form 1040NR, line 35 .	4	
5	Enter the **smaller** of line 3 or line 4 here . . . . ▶	5	

Step 2 Figure tentative tax based on the tax rate of the parent listed on line A

6	Enter parent's **taxable** income from Form 1040, line 37; Form 1040A, line 22; Form 1040EZ, line 5; or Form 1040NR, line 35. If the parent transferred property to a trust, see instructions . .	6	
7	Enter the total, if any, of the net investment income from Forms 8615, line 5, of ALL OTHER children of the parent. **Do not** include the amount from line 5 above	7	
8	Add lines 5, 6, and 7	8	
9	Tax on line 8 based on the **parent's** filing status. See instructions. If from Schedule D, enter amount from line 22 of that Schedule D here ▶ _____	9	
10	Enter parent's tax from Form 1040, line 38; Form 1040A, line 23; Form 1040EZ, line 7; or Form 1040NR, line 36. If from Schedule D, enter amount from line 22 of that Schedule D here ▶ _____	10	
11	Subtract line 10 from line 9. If line 7 is blank, enter on line 13 the amount from line 11; skip lines 12a and 12b	11	
12a	Add lines 5 and 7	12a			
b	Divide line 5 by line 12a. Enter the result as a decimal (rounded to two places) . . . . . . ▶	12b	× .
13	Multiply line 11 by line 12b . . . . ▶	13	

Step 3 Figure child's tax

Note: *If lines 4 and 5 above are the same, go to line 16.*

14	Subtract line 5 from line 4	14		
15	Tax on line 14 based on the **child's** filing status. See instructions. If from Schedule D, enter amount from line 22 of that Schedule D here ▶ _____	15	
16	Add lines 13 and 15	16	
17	Tax on line 4 based on the **child's** filing status. See instructions. If from Schedule D, check here ▶ ☐	17	
18	Enter the **larger** of line 16 or line 17 here and on Form 1040, line 38; Form 1040A, line 23; or Form 1040NR, line 36. Be sure to check the box for "Form 8615" even if line 17 is more than line 16 . ▶	18	

For Paperwork Reduction Act Notice, see back of form.   Cat. No. 64113U   Form **8615** (1992)

Copyright © 1994 by Harcourt Brace & Company. All rights reserved.

Comprehensive Tax Return Problem 1

Form 1040A and Schedules 1 and 2

Howard and Jan Woodward, ages 41 and 43, plan to file a joint tax return in 1993. Howard's social security number is 343-67-1024, and Jan's is 455-78-9080. The Howards live at 2301 Presidents Drive in Fargo, North Dakota 58105. They both elect to contribute to the presidential election fund.

They provide all of the support of their 6-year-old son Hal (social security number 444-34-2331) and 80% of the support of their 19-year-old daughter Ellen (social security number 344-56-0904), a full-time student at North Dakota State University, who earned $2,650 from a summer job in 1993. They also provided 80% of the support of Howard's 69-year-old father William (social security number 233-67-9843), whose only sources of income in 1993 were $1,050 interest on certificates of deposit, $6,600 of social security, and $450 interest on State of North Dakota bonds. William lives in a nursing home.

Howard worked as a sales clerk for Super Electronics Store in 1993, receiving a salary of $24,000. His Form W-2 discloses that $4,850 of federal income taxes was withheld from his salary. Jan is legally blind and earned $13,200 from a part-time job in 1993 ($2,800 was withheld for federal income taxes). Jan also earned $850 on a savings account (none was withdrawn during the year) and $2,300 dividends on Dakota Power common stock.

During 1993 the Howards paid the Tiny Tot Childcare Agency $2,570 to care for Hal while Howard and Jan worked. Their legitimate itemized deductions for 1993 total $3,300.

REQUIRED: Prepare a Form 1040A for Howard and Jan Woodward for 1993, with accompanying Schedules 1 and 2.

Comprehensive Tax Return Problem 1   Name _____   2-55

Form 1040A Department of the Treasury—Internal Revenue Service
U.S. Individual Income Tax Return **1993**   IRS Use Only—Do not write or staple in this space.

OMB No. 1545-0085

Label (See page 15.)

Your first name and initial | Last name

If a joint return, spouse's first name and initial | Last name

Home address (number and street). If you have a P.O. box, see page 16. | Apt. no.

City, town or post office, state, and ZIP code. If you have a foreign address, see page 16.

Use the IRS label. Otherwise, please print or type.

Your social security number

Spouse's social security number

For Privacy Act and Paperwork Reduction Act Notice, see page 4.

Presidential Election Campaign Fund (See page 16.)
Do you want $3 to go to this fund?
If a joint return, does your spouse want $3 to go to this fund?

Yes | No

Note: Checking "Yes" will not change your tax or reduce your refund.

Check the box for your filing status
(See page 16.)
Check only one box.

1 ☐ Single
2 ☐ Married filing joint return (even if only one had income)
3 ☐ Married filing separate return. Enter spouse's social security number above and full name here. ▶ _____
4 ☐ Head of household (with qualifying person). (See page 17.) If the qualifying person is a child but not your dependent, enter this child's name here. ▶ _____
5 ☐ Qualifying widow(er) with dependent child (year spouse died ▶ 19___). (See page 18.)

Figure your exemptions
(See page 19.)

If more than seven dependents, see page 22.

6a ☐ **Yourself.** If your parent (or someone else) can claim you as a dependent on his or her tax return, **do not** check box 6a. But be sure to check the box on line 18b on page 2.
b ☐ **Spouse**
c **Dependents:**

(1) Name (first, initial, and last name)	(2) Check if under age 1	(3) If age 1 or older, dependent's social security number	(4) Dependent's relationship to you	(5) No. of months lived in your home in 1993

No. of boxes checked on 6a and 6b ____

No. of your children on 6c who:
• lived with you ____
• didn't live with you due to divorce or separation (see page 22) ____

Dependents on 6c not entered above ____

d If your child didn't live with you but is claimed as your dependent under a pre-1985 agreement, check here .... ▶ ☐
e Total number of exemptions claimed.

Add numbers entered on lines above ☐

Figure your total income

Attach Copy B of your Forms W-2 and 1099-R here.

If you didn't get a W-2, see page 24.

If you are attaching a check or money order, put it on top of any Forms W-2 or 1099-R.

7 Wages, salaries, tips, etc. This should be shown in box 1 of your W-2 form(s). Attach Form(s) W-2. | 7 |
8a **Taxable** interest income (see page 25). If over $400, also complete and attach Schedule 1, Part I. | 8a |
b **Tax-exempt** interest. DO NOT include on line 8a. 8b |
9 Dividends. If over $400, also complete and attach Schedule 1, Part II. | 9 |
10a Total IRA distributions. 10a | 10b Taxable amount (see page 26). 10b |
11a Total pensions and annuities. 11a | 11b Taxable amount (see page 26). 11b |
12 Unemployment compensation (see page 30). | 12 |
13a Social security benefits. 13a | 13b Taxable amount (see page 30). 13b |
14 Add lines 7 through 13b (far right column). This is your **total income.** ▶ 14 |

Figure your adjusted gross income

15a Your IRA deduction (see page 32). 15a
b Spouse's IRA deduction (see page 32). 15b
c Add lines 15a and 15b. These are your **total adjustments.** | 15c |
16 Subtract line 15c from line 14. This is your **adjusted gross income.** If less than $23,050 and a child lived with you, see page 63 to find out if you can claim the "Earned income credit" on line 28c. ▶ 16 |

Cat. No. 11327A   1993 Form 1040A page 1

Copyright © 1994 by Harcourt Brace & Company. All rights reserved.

1993 Form 1040A page 2

Name(s) shown on page 1 | Your social security number

Figure your standard deduction, exemption amount, and taxable income

17 Enter the amount from line 16. | 17

18a Check if: ☐ You were 65 or older ☐ Blind Enter number of boxes checked ▶ 18a
     ☐ Spouse was 65 or older ☐ Blind

  b If your parent (or someone else) can claim you as a dependent, check here . . . . ▶ 18b ☐

  c If you are married filing separately and your spouse files Form 1040 and itemizes deductions, see page 36 and check here ▶ 18c ☐

19 Enter the **standard deduction** shown below for your filing status. **But if you checked any box on line 18a or b,** go to page 36 to find your standard deduction. **If you checked box 18c,** enter -0-.
    • Single—$3,700   • Head of household—$5,450
    • Married filing jointly or Qualifying widow(er)—$6,200
    • Married filing separately—$3,100 | 19

20 Subtract line 19 from line 17. If line 19 is more than line 17, enter -0-. | 20

21 Multiply $2,350 by the total number of exemptions claimed on line 6e. | 21

22 Subtract line 21 from line 20. If line 21 is more than line 20, enter -0-. This is your **taxable income.** ▶ 22

Figure your tax, credits, and payments

If you want the IRS to figure your tax, see the instructions for line 22 on page 37.

23 Find the tax on the amount on line 22. Check if from:
    ☐ Tax Table (pages 50–55) or ☐ Form 8615 (see page 38). | 23

24a Credit for child and dependent care expenses. Complete and attach Schedule 2. | 24a

  b Credit for the elderly or the disabled. Complete and attach Schedule 3. | 24b

  c Add lines 24a and 24b. These are your **total credits.** | 24c

25 Subtract line 24c from line 23. If line 24c is more than line 23, enter -0-. | 25

26 Advance earned income credit payments from Form W-2. | 26

27 Add lines 25 and 26. This is your **total tax.** ▶ 27

28a Total Federal income tax withheld. If any tax is from Form(s) 1099, check here. ▶ ☐ | 28a

  b 1993 estimated tax payments and amount applied from 1992 return. | 28b

  c **Earned income credit.** Complete and attach Schedule EIC. | 28c

  d Add lines 28a, 28b, and 28c. These are your **total payments.** ▶ 28d

Figure your refund or amount you owe

29 If line 28d is more than line 27, subtract line 27 from line 28d. This is the amount you **overpaid.** | 29

30 Amount of line 29 you want **refunded to you.** | 30

31 Amount of line 29 you want **applied to your 1994 estimated tax.** | 31

32 If line 27 is more than line 28d, subtract line 28d from line 27. This is the **amount you owe.** For details on how to pay, including what to write on your payment, see page 42. | 32

33 Estimated tax penalty (see page 43). Also, include on line 32. | 33

Sign your return

Under penalties of perjury, I declare that I have examined this return and accompanying schedules and statements, and to the best of my knowledge and belief, they are true, correct, and accurately list all amounts and sources of income I received during the tax year. Declaration of preparer (other than the taxpayer) is based on all information of which the preparer has any knowledge.

Your signature | Date | Your occupation

Keep a copy of this return for your records.

Spouse's signature. If joint return, BOTH must sign. | Date | Spouse's occupation

Paid preparer's use only

Preparer's signature ▶ | Date | Check if self-employed ☐ | Preparer's social security no.

Firm's name (or yours if self-employed) and address ▶ | E.I. No.
 | ZIP code

Comprehensive Tax Return Problem 1   Name _____   2-57

Schedule 1
(Form 1040A)
Department of the Treasury—Internal Revenue Service
Interest and Dividend Income for Form 1040A Filers   **1993**
OMB No 1545-0085

Name(s) shown on Form 1040A | Your social security number

Part I
Interest income
(See pages 25 and 56.)

Note: *If you received a Form 1099–INT, Form 1099–OID, or substitute statement from a brokerage firm, enter the firm's name and the total interest shown on that form.*

1 List name of payer. If any interest is from a seller-financed mortgage and the buyer used the property as a personal residence, see page 56 and list this interest first. Also, show that buyer's social security number and address.

Amount

| | 1 | |

2 Add the amounts on line 1.   2
3 Excludable interest on series EE U.S. savings bonds issued after 1989 from Form 8815, line 14. You MUST attach Form 8815 to Form 1040A.   3
4 Subtract line 3 from line 2. Enter the result here and on Form 1040A, line 8a.   4

Part II
Dividend income
(See pages 25 and 57.)

Note: *If you received a Form 1099–DIV or substitute statement from a brokerage firm, enter the firm's name and the total dividends shown on that form.*

5 List name of payer

Amount

| | 5 | |

6 Add the amounts on line 5. Enter the total here and on Form 1040A, line 9.   6

For Paperwork Reduction Act Notice, see Form 1040A instructions.   Cat. No. 12075R   1993 Schedule 1 (Form 1040A) page 1

Copyright © 1994 by Harcourt Brace & Company. All rights reserved.

**Schedule 2
(Form 1040A)**

Department of the Treasury—Internal Revenue Service

Child and Dependent Care Expenses for Form 1040A Filers

1993

OMB No. 1545-0085

Name(s) shown on Form 1040A | Your social security number

You need to understand the following terms to complete this schedule: **Dependent care benefits, Earned income, Qualified expenses,** and **Qualifying person(s).** See **Important terms** on page 58. Also, if you had a child born in 1993 and line 17 of Form 1040A is less than $23,050, see **A change to note** on page 59.

Part I

Persons or organizations who provided the care

You MUST complete this part.

1 | (a) Care provider's name | (b) Address (number, street, apt. no., city, state, and ZIP code) | (c) Identifying number (SSN or EIN) | (d) Amount paid (see page 61)

(If you need more space, use the bottom of page 2.)

2 Add the amounts in column (d) of line 1. 2

3 Enter the number of **qualifying persons** cared for in 1993 ▶ ☐

Did you receive **dependent care benefits?**
— NO ⟶ Complete only Part II below.
— YES ⟶ Complete Part III on the back now.

Part II

Credit for child and dependent care expenses

4 Enter the amount of **qualified expenses** you incurred and paid in 1993. DO NOT enter more than $2,400 for one qualifying person or $4,800 for two or more persons. If you completed Part III, enter the amount from line 25. 4

5 Enter YOUR **earned income.** 5

6 If married filing a joint return, enter YOUR SPOUSE'S earned income (if student or disabled, see page 61); **all others,** enter the amount from line 5. 6

7 Enter the **smallest** of line 4, 5, or 6. 7

8 Enter the amount from Form 1040A, line 17. 8

9 Enter on line 9 the decimal amount shown below that applies to the amount on line 8.

If line 8 is—		Decimal amount is	If line 8 is—		Decimal amount is
Over	But not over		Over	But not over	
$0	10,000	.30	$20,000	22,000	.24
10,000	12,000	.29	22,000	24,000	.23
12,000	14,000	.28	24,000	26,000	.22
14,000	16,000	.27	26,000	28,000	.21
16,000	18,000	.26	28,000	No limit	.20
18,000	20,000	.25			

9 X .

10 Multiply **line 7** by the decimal amount on line 9. Enter the result. Then, see page 61 for the amount of credit to enter on Form 1040A, line 24a. 10 =

Caution: *If you paid $50 or more in a calendar quarter to a person who worked in your home, you must file an employment tax return. Get **Form 942** for details.*

For Paperwork Reduction Act Notice, see Form 1040A instructions.   Cat. No. 10749I   1993 Schedule 2 (Form 1040A) page 1

CHAPTER 3

Gross Income of Individuals: Exclusions

Items of income that Congress has specifically exempted from taxation are referred to as *exclusions*. Most exclusions are specifically enacted into the Code by Congress, but through various pronouncements and tax decisions, the Internal Revenue Service and the Courts have also established certain exclusion rules for a few items. This chapter reviews the various exclusion rules by grouping them into logical classifications. (Perhaps the term *logical* is an overstatement, because there is such a variety of exclusions that we must use a "miscellaneous" category in Part IV of this chapter!)

I DONATIVE TRANSFERS AND LIFE INSURANCE
(Code Sections 74, 101, 102, and 117)

GIFTS AND BEQUESTS

THE LAW

Sec. 102—(a) General rule. Gross income does not include the value of property acquired by gift, bequest, devise, or inheritance.
(b) Income. Subsection (a) shall not exclude from gross income—
(1) the income from any property referred to in subsection (a); or
(2) where the gift, bequest, devise, or inheritance is of income from property, the amount of such income.

Property acquired by either gift or inheritance is specifically excluded from *income* taxation. However, these transfers may be subject to a federal gift tax or a federal estate tax based on the fair market value of the property. (These taxes would be studied in an advanced course in taxation.) Although the value of the gift or inherited property is excluded from taxation, any income the property generates will be subject to the normal gross income rules.

☑ Example 1. Marsha Anton received 100 shares of Apple Corporation stock worth $3,000 as a gift from her mother on October 1, 1993. On December 15, Anton received a check for $195, which represented a quarterly dividend from Apple Corporation. The $3,000 value of the stock is not taxable to Anton; however, she must report the $195 dividend as income on her 1993 return.

Congress set up the exclusion for gifts and bequests because it wanted to exempt purely donative transfers from taxation. However, if the gift or bequest represents compensation for past, present, or future services, it will be taxable.

☑ Example 2. Jan Williamson was voted the top salesperson of the month at Malvern Products. The owners of Malvern Products decided to give Williamson new carpeting for her home as a gift for her contributions to the firm. Most likely, Williamson will be required to report the fair market value of the carpeting as income on her tax return. It would be very difficult for Williamson and her employer to convince the IRS that the carpeting was anything other than compensation for her sales performance.

THE LAW

Sec. 101(b)—Employee's death benefits. (1) General rule. Gross income does not include amounts received (whether in a single sum or otherwise) by the beneficiaries or the estate of an employee, if such amounts are paid by or on behalf of an employer and are paid by reason of the death of the employee.
(2) Special rules for paragraph (1). (A) $5,000 limitation. The aggregate amounts excludable under paragraph (1) with respect to the death of any employee shall not exceed $5,000.

An interesting example of the question of intent is the tax treatment of benefits an employer pays to a deceased employee's beneficiaries or estate. Do these death benefits represent a gift, or are they additional compensation for past services the employee performed? Obviously, the answer depends on the facts and circumstances of each particular case. In order to reduce the controversy in such cases, Congress enacted a special exclusion of $5,000 per employee for such death benefits. If there is more than one beneficiary, the $5,000 exclusion must be allocated among the beneficiaries according to the ratio of the amount received by each beneficiary compared to the total payments.

☑ **Example 3.** Orland Mills received an $8,000 death benefit check from his deceased father's employer. Orland will exclude $5,000 of the benefit and report the remaining $3,000 as gross income on his tax return.

☑ **Example 4.** Ranger Corporation paid death benefits of $4,000 to each of the four children of Julie Anders, a deceased employee. Since each child received 25% of the total $16,000 benefit paid, each child may exclude 25% of $5,000, or $1,250, of the death benefit received.

LIFE INSURANCE PROCEEDS

THE LAW

Sec. 101(a)(1)—General rule. Except as otherwise provided in paragraph (2) and in subsection (d), gross income does not include amounts received (whether in a single sum or otherwise) under a life insurance contract, if such amounts are paid by reason of the death of the insured.

Life insurance proceeds paid when the the insured person dies are generally treated as a donative item and are excluded from income. This exclusion does not apply to a beneficiary who acquires the policy for a valuable consideration. In this case, the consideration paid for the insurance policy is viewed as a speculative investment, and the insurance money received that exceeds the cost of the policy (including payments after purchase) is taxable.

☑ **Example 5.** Karen Allen purchased a $50,000 insurance policy on her own life, naming her husband Ralph as beneficiary. Karen died in 1993, and Ralph received the $50,000 face value of the policy. These insurance proceeds are not taxable, because they are paid by reason of death, and Ralph did not acquire the policy for a valuable consideration.

☑ **Example 6.** Assume the same facts as Example 5, except that before she died Karen sold the insurance policy for $6,000 to her sister Mary, who made herself the beneficiary. Before Karen's death in 1993, Mary made additional premium payments of $2,500 on the policy. Of the $50,000 insurance proceeds Mary received, she must include $41,500 in her 1993 gross income (the $50,000 proceeds minus the $6,000 paid for the policy and minus the $2,500 of additional premium payments).

If the owner of a life insurance policy sells or surrenders it before he or she dies, any realized gain must be recognized for tax purposes. A realized gain occurs when the sales price (or cash surrender value) of the policy is greater than the total net premiums paid on the policy.

☑ **Example 7.** Assume the same facts as Example 6, and assume that Karen had made $3,800 of premium payments on the policy before selling it to Mary for $6,000. Karen must recognize $2,200 of gross income from selling the policy ($6,000 minus $3,800).

☑ **Example 8.** After making premium payments of $6,300 on a $40,000 life insurance policy, Wendell Frame surrendered the policy to the insurance company, receiving $8,400 cash. Frame must report $2,100 of gross income ($8,400 minus $6,300) from canceling the policy.

An insurance contract frequently gives the beneficiary of a life insurance policy an option to receive the proceeds in installments, which also provides an interest return. If a taxpayer chooses to receive installment payments, the amounts received will be taxed much like an annuity, with the face value of the policy being recovered tax free over the life of the installments. In effect, the face value of the policy is treated as the "investment in the contract."

☑ **Example 9.** Nancy Wiederman, the beneficiary of a $100,000 life insurance policy on her brother Ross, chooses under the insurance contract to receive the proceeds in ten equal installments of $12,500. Wiederman may exclude $10,000 of each payment (an exclusion ratio of 80%, or the $100,000 face value divided by the $125,000 expected return). The remaining $2,500 of each payment is taxable as interest.

PRIZES AND AWARDS

THE LAW

Sec. 74—Prizes and Awards. (a) General rule. Except as otherwise provided in this section or in section 117 (relating to qualified scholarships), gross income includes amounts received as prizes and awards.

At one time, only prizes and awards that were "earned" were taxable, but this administrative guideline proved unworkable and led to many curious court cases. For example, if you walked into a store and won a prize for being the one-millionth customer, did you "earn" that prize? Because of such complexities, Congress has simply declared that virtually all prizes and awards are taxable. At one time, awards made for a religious, charitable, scientific, educational, artistic, literary, or civic achievement could be excluded. Examples of excludable awards included teaching awards, Nobel Prizes, and Pulitzer Prizes. Although this exclusion is no longer available, a taxpayer receiving such an award may exclude the amount if he or she donates it to a charity.

☑ **Example 10.** Harold Nickerson received a new automobile for being named the most valuable player in an all-star basketball game. The fair market value of this car is taxable to Nickerson, since there is no exclusion for such awards.

✓ **Example 11.** Margaret Regging received $1,000 for being named the outstanding educator in the state of Maryland. The state does not sponsor a formal contest for the award. Instead, nominations are solicited from the local boards of education. This award is taxable to Margaret; however, she may exclude the award if she donates it to a charity.

TAX TIP

Being able to exclude the value of a prize given to a charity may not, at first, seem to be particularly helpful to a taxpayer, since an itemized deduction is available for such contributions. However, as will be discussed in Chapter 4, charitable contributions for individuals are limited to 50% of adjusted gross income (AGI) in any year; therefore, the exclusion possibility avoids this limit.

For example, assume that a college professor with $50,000 AGI wins the Nobel Prize, valued at $400,000. By donating the entire amount to charity, the professor can exclude the $400,000 from her income. If this provision did not exist, she would be taxed on the entire $400,000, and the maximum deduction she could take for such a contribution would be limited to $225,000 in the year of receipt (50% of $450,000 AGI). (Of course, if the professor decides to keep the award—a likely possibility!—the entire amount is taxable in the year of receipt.)

There is still one type of award that is excludable: employee achievement awards for service or safety. Generally, the amount that can be excluded is the same amount allowed as a deduction to the employer. This can be from $400 (for "nonqualified plans") to $1,600 (for "qualified plans"). The details of such achievement programs are discussed in Chapter 8 in connection with the employer's deduction.

✓ **Example 12.** Mandy Illid retired in 1993 after 30 years of service with Bee Corporation. In recognition of her service accomplishment, Bee gave her a new watch worth $360. The value of the watch is not taxable to Mandy, and Bee Corporation will be able to deduct the $360.

SCHOLARSHIPS AND FELLOWSHIPS

THE LAW

Sec. 117(a)—General rule. Gross income does not include any amount received as a qualified scholarship by an individual who is a candidate for a degree at an educational organization described in section 170(b)(1)(A)(ii).

The tax treatment of scholarship income depends on several factors. A *candidate for a degree* may exclude the value of a scholarship or fellowship if two conditions are met: (1) the scholarship is not compensation for past, present, or future services and (2) the scholarship is not primarily for the benefit of the grantor. However, the exclusion is allowed only for amounts actually spent on tuition, fees, books, supplies, and equipment required for course work.

✓ **Example 13.** Morris Jenkins, an entering freshman at State University, is awarded a $1,000 merit scholarship from the general university funds. He spends the entire amount on books and tuition. The scholarship is nontaxable.

✓ **Example 14.** Linda Jennings, a graduate student at Southern University, is awarded a $2,000 fellowship grant for grading papers and supervising a study lab for students. This fellowship is taxable, since it represents compensation for services.

✓ **Example 15.** Dell Corporation awards a $5,000 scholarship grant to Glenn Hubbard, an employee, so that he can return to school for a master's degree. As a condition of receiving the award, Glenn is required to work for Dell Corporation for a minimum of two years after receiving the degree. The $5,000 award is taxable to Glenn, since it represents compensation for future services and also provides a significant benefit to the donor.

✓ **Example 16.** Bobby Schwer received a $5,000 scholarship from Lemmings University. Of this amount, he spent $2,000 for tuition, $500 for computer lab fees, $200 for books, $1,800 for room and board, and $500 for transportation. He can exclude only the $2,700 paid for tuition, fees, and books; the remaining $2,300 is taxable.

TAX TIP

Sometimes a scholarship or fellowship grant that involves some service may also have a pure scholarship element. In such cases, the recipient should try to determine the value of such services, so that the remaining portion of the scholarship can be excluded from income. For example, assume that Beth Crews, a graduate student, is given a $3,000 scholarship for a semester. Under the terms of the fellowship, she is required to grade papers for a faculty member for 20 hours a week during the 15-week semester. If the normal rate of pay for student assistants is $6 per hour, then she should report $1,800 of the fellowship as compensation for services ($6 × 20 × 15) and exclude the remaining $1,200 as qualifying scholarship income.

Code Sec. 117 also provides an exclusion for "qualified tuition reductions" that an employee of an educational institution receives. This exclusion is generally available only for courses below the graduate level; however, graduate students who are engaged in teaching or research activities will also qualify for the exclusion. Furthermore, such tuition reduction plans may not discriminate in favor of "highly compensated employees." The Code establishes a number of complex tests to ensure that the benefit is available to a broad range of employees.

☑ **Example 17.** Pat Cosentino, a secretary in the English Department at State University, enrolls in an undergraduate accounting course in 1993 under the university's policy of allowing all employees to take one course free of charge each semester. The normal tuition charged for this course is $560. Pat may exclude the value of this course.

REVIEW I

1. David Montoya, a calendar-year taxpayer, inherited $10,000 from his aunt's estate in May 1993. He invested the $10,000 in a one-year certificate of deposit, which accumulated $730 of interest by the end of 1993. In 1993, David is taxed on
    (a) $0.
    (b) $730.
    (c) $10,000.
    (d) $10,730.
2. Bill and Laura Meyers received from their father's employer death benefit payments of $6,000 and $4,000, respectively, in 1993. In 1993, Bill and Laura will report taxable benefit payments of
    (a) $0 for Bill and $0 for Laura.
    (b) $1,000 for Bill and $0 for Laura.
    (c) $3,000 for Bill and $2,000 for Laura.
    (d) $6,000 for Bill and $4,000 for Laura.
3. Janet Dole is the beneficiary of a $60,000 life insurance policy on the life of her husband Reginald. Under a provision of the policy, she elects to receive the proceeds in 20 equal installments of $5,000. For each $5,000 payment received, Janet can exclude a total of
    (a) $0.
    (b) $3,000.
    (c) $4,000.
    (d) $5,000.
4. Lawrence Faskowitz, a medical researcher, received a one-year $30,000 research grant from State University for postdoctoral research. The grant is payable in monthly amounts of $2,500, and Faskowitz received seven payments in 1993. Of the $17,500 received in 1993, Faskowitz may exclude
    (a) $0.
    (b) $300.
    (c) $2,100.
    (d) $17,500.

Answers are on page 3-8.

II ACCIDENT, HEALTH, AND OTHER COMPENSATION PAYMENTS
(Code Sections 85, 104, 105, and 106)

EMPLOYER PAYMENT OF ACCIDENT AND HEALTH-PLAN PREMIUMS

THE LAW

Sec. 106—Contributions by employer to accident and health plans. Gross income of an employee does not include employer-provided coverage under an accident or health plan.

It is not unusual for employers to provide accident and health care insurance for their employees. Sec. 106 specifically excludes these premium payments from being a taxable part of an employee's income. Although Congress occasionally considers taxing a portion or all of these payments, it is unlikely that this politically popular provision will be changed in the near future.

☑ **Example 18.** Hal Reneau is an employee of Ace Company. During 1993 Ace paid $980 of premiums on an accident and health policy for Hal. Hal will not be taxed on these premium payments.

ANSWERS TO REVIEW I

1. (b) The value of the inheritance is not taxable, but any income produced by the property is subject to the normal inclusion rules.
2. (c) Only one $5,000 death benefit exclusion is available for all beneficiaries. This exclusion is divided up according to the amount each beneficiary receives. Bill's exclusion will be $3,000 [$6,000/($6,000 + $4,000) × $5,000], and Laura's will be $2,000 [$4,000/($6,000 + $4,000) × $5,000].
3. (b) Janet may exclude $3,000 as a pro rata recovery of the face value of the insurance policy [($60,000/$100,000) × $5,000], or $3,000.
4. (a) The exclusion for scholarships and fellowships is available only for candidates for a degree. Since Faskowitz is not pursuing a degree, he would not qualify for an exclusion.

ACCIDENT AND HEALTH-PLAN BENEFITS

THE LAW

*Sec. 105—(a) Amounts attributable to employer contributions. Except as otherwise provided in this section, amounts received by an employee through accident or health insurance for personal injuries or sickness shall be included in gross income to the extent such amounts (1) are attributable to contributions by the employer which were not includable in the gross income of the employee, or (2) are paid by the employer.
(b) Amounts expended for medical care . . . gross income [do] not include amounts referred to in subsection (a) if such amounts are paid . . . to reimburse the taxpayer . . . for the medical care . . . of the taxpayer, his spouse, and his dependents. . . .*

The tax treatment of accident and health policy benefits depends on who has purchased the accident and health insurance policy. Benefits a taxpayer receives under a policy that he or she purchased are excludable from income. These excludable benefits include compensation for medical expenses, disability (income replacement) pay, and loss of limb or bodily function. The exclusion for these benefits is justified under the theory that the benefits represent a nontaxable recovery of premium payments on the policy.

Example 19. Al Michael missed five weeks of work in 1993 and received $11,000 reimbursement for medical expenses plus $125 a week under an insurance (income replacement) plan that he had purchased. These benefit payments may be excluded, since Alfred purchased the policy.

The employee can also exclude policy benefits received for medical expenses and loss of limb or bodily function, if the employer purchased the policy. However, disability benefits representing compensation for lost income are taxable. (Such payments may qualify for a special credit if the taxpayer is permanently disabled; see Chapter 5.)

Example 20. Assume the same facts as Example 19, except that it was Al Michael's employer who purchased the policy. Although the reimbursement for medical expenses is still excludable, the disability payments would be taxable, since they represent compensation for lost (taxable) income. As mentioned earlier, the premium payments that Michael's employer makes on the policy are specifically excluded from income.

The tax treatment of accident and health benefits is summarized in a flowchart in Figure 3-1.

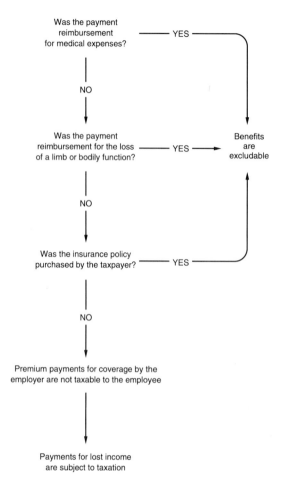

Figure 3-1 Taxability of Accident and Health-Plan Benefits

WORKER'S COMPENSATION

A taxpayer may also receive state compensation for his or her accident or sickness. Payments from state disability funds and from worker's compensation funds are excludable if the amounts are for compensation for personal injury or sickness. However, payments that are a substitute for lost wages are taxable. Generally, most worker's compensation payments are excludable.

UNEMPLOYMENT COMPENSATION

> **THE LAW**
>
>
>
> Sec. 85—(a) General rule. In the case of an individual, gross income includes unemployment compensation.

For many years, unemployment compensation paid under government programs was fully excludable from income. In 1978 Congress decided that a full exclusion was not warranted for taxpayers who have large amounts of income from other sources. Accordingly, Congress enacted a provision that taxed a portion of any unemployment compensation a person received if his or her income exceeded certain adjusted gross income levels.

As part of the general income-base broadening that was incorporated in the *Tax Reform Act of 1986,* Congress decided to tax *all* unemployment compensation an individual received. Thus, all such payments received are now fully taxable, regardless of the taxpayer's income level.

☑ **Example 21.** Bruce Thompson, a single taxpayer, received $2,200 of unemployment compensation in 1993. His only other source of income that year was a salary of $11,300. Thompson must include the $2,200 of unemployment compensation, as well as the salary, in his 1993 gross income.

LAWSUIT DAMAGES

Damage payments received from a lawsuit represent another type of compensation payment. Generally, these awards are nontaxable if they are compensation for an item that was not taxable in the first place (e.g., a person's health in a case related to personal injury or sickness). Any damages that compensate the taxpayer for lost income will generally be taxable, unless unrelated to a physical injury. Furthermore, punitive damages are taxable—under the theory that they represent a windfall profit.

☑ **Example 22.** Wanda Schwartz was involved in an auto accident in 1992. In 1993 she sued the other party and collected $20,000 for medical expense reimbursements and $30,000 for pain and emotional suffering. Both amounts are excludable, since they are replacing a nontaxable item (the taxpayer's health).

☑ **Example 23.** B Company owns a patent on an electroplating process. During 1993 B sued Clone Corporation for treble damages under federal laws for patent infringement. B won the case and received $1,800,000: $600,000 compensation for estimated lost profits due to the infringement, and $1,200,000 of punitive damages. B will be taxed on the entire $1,800,000; the first $600,000 is compensation for lost income, and the remaining $1,200,000 is for punitive damages.

TAX TIP

Taxpayers should be very careful when specifying desired damages in a lawsuit, because the tax treatment of any compensation payments received depends on these labels. For example, the courts have defined nontaxable damages for "personal injuries or sickness" to include emotional distress, libel, slander, and other nonphysical wrongs. On the other hand, the courts have said that compensation for damage to a taxpayer's business reputation is taxable. When lump-sum settlements include both taxable and nontaxable damages, the recipient must show how the money should be divided and must give good reasons for the division.

REVIEW II

1. Richard Bloom purchased an accident and health insurance policy with his own funds in 1993. Which of the following benefit payments under this policy are taxable to Bloom?
   (a) compensation for medical expenses due to illness
   (b) compensation for loss of an arm while at work
   (c) compensation for lost wages during a three-week absence
   (d) None of the above is taxable.
2. Nelson Fendrich is covered by an accident and health insurance policy purchased by his employer. Which of the following benefit payments under this policy are taxable?
   (a) compensation for medical expenses due to illness
   (b) compensation for loss of an arm while at work
   (c) compensation for lost wages during a three-week absence
   (d) All of the above are taxable.
3. Greta Nielson, a 50-year-old single taxpayer, was forced to permanently retire in March 1993 after suffering a job-related injury. She received weekly disability payments of $125 a week for 40 weeks in 1993 from an employer-financed policy. Of the $5,000 disability payments received in 1993, Nielson may exclude
   (a) $0.
   (b) $1,000.
   (c) $2,500.
   (d) $5,000.
4. Mark Hull, a single taxpayer, received $3,400 of unemployment compensation in 1993. His only other source of income in 1993 was a salary of $13,600. The amount of unemployment compensation taxable to Mark in 1993 is
   (a) $0.
   (b) $1,700.
   (c) $2,500.
   (d) $3,400.

Answers are on page 3-14.

III EMPLOYEE BENEFITS
(Code Sections 79, 105, 119, 120, 125, 127, 129, and 132)

Over the years, Congress has enacted a broad range of statutory exclusions for certain benefits paid to employees. One of these items, the exclusion for employer-financed premiums on accident and health policies, was discussed earlier in this chapter. The following discussion highlights the other major employment-related exclusions.

Before we discuss these exclusions, it is important to note that the benefit of the exclusion to an employee is worth more than merely receiving an equivalent amount of taxable compensation and purchasing the benefit. For example, assume that an employee in the 31% marginal income tax bracket receives an excludable benefit worth $300. To purchase the same benefit, the employee would need to receive $435 of taxable compensation, because $300 cash would be available to spend only after the employee has paid $135 ($435 × .31) in taxes to the government. An employee in the 39.6% marginal income tax bracket would need to receive $497 of taxable compensation for the same benefit.

Table 3-1 Uniform Group-Term Life Insurance Rates (per $1,000 of Coverage)

Age	Cost per $1,000 of Coverage	Age	Cost per $1,000 of Coverage
Under 30	$.08	50–54	$ .48
30–34	.09	55–59	.75
35–39	.11	60–64	1.17
40–44	.17	65–69	2.10
45–49	.29	70 and over	3.76

GROUP-TERM LIFE INSURANCE

THE LAW

Sec. 79(a)—General rule. There shall be included in the gross income of an employee for the taxable year an amount equal to the cost of group-term life insurance on his life provided it exceeds the sum of—
(1) the cost of $50,000 of such insurance, and
(2) the amount (if any) paid by the employee toward the purchase of such insurance.

A special exclusion is available for employer payments of premiums for group-term life insurance coverage for employees. The exclusion is limited to premiums on the first $50,000 of coverage. Premiums on coverage in excess of $50,000 are taxable to employees according to uniform premium rates provided in the Tax Regulations. These uniform rates are shown in Table 3-1. Employees who have more than one employer are entitled to exclude only the premiums on the first $50,000 of coverage. Any employee contributions to the premium costs reduce the taxable amount.

Example 24. Rebecca Smith, age 47, is provided with $80,000 of group-term life insurance coverage by her employer, Braxton Manufacturing, in 1993. Smith must include $104.40 in her 1993 gross income, which is the uniform annual premium cost for coverage in excess of $50,000 (i.e., 30 units of $1,000 coverage × $.29 monthly rate × 12 months).

The exclusion for premiums on the first $50,000 of coverage applies only to *group-term* life insurance. As discussed throughout this section, most statutory exclusions for fringe benefits must apply to a broad class of employees. Premium payments by employers for ordinary life insurance are normally taxable to the employee, unless a corporate employer is the beneficiary of the policy.

☑ **Example 25.** Richland Corporation covers each of its officers with $200,000 face-value ordinary life insurance policies. Richland is the beneficiary on each of the policies. The premium payments are not taxable to the employees, since no direct benefit accrues to them. However, if the employees could designate the beneficiary of the policy, the premiums would be taxed to the employees as additional compensation.

MEALS AND LODGING

Occasionally, an employee is furnished free meals and/or lodging as part of his or her job. These benefits may be excluded if certain conditions are met. In general, the exclusions are justified under the theory that the meals and lodging are primarily for the benefit of the *employer,* not the employee.

THE LAW

Sec. 119(a)—There shall be excluded from gross income of an employee the value of any meals or lodging furnished to him, his spouse, or any of his dependents by or on behalf of his employer for the convenience of the employer, but only if—
(1) in the case of meals, the meals are furnished on the business premises of the employer, or
(2) in the case of lodging, the employee is required to accept such lodging on the business premises of his employer as a condition of his employment.

The value of *meals* furnished by an employer may be excluded if (1) the meals are furnished on the employer's premises and (2) the meals are for the employer's convenience. These factors, taken together, indicate that meals are not furnished as compensation but are provided primarily to benefit the employer. However, if an employee is given an option to receive cash, the value of the meals is considered to be taxable compensation.

ANSWERS TO REVIEW II

1. (d) All benefits are considered to be a return of premium cost, since Bloom purchased the policy.
2. (c) Compensation for lost wages is taxable when the employer finances the insurance policy.
3. (a) Since her employer financed the policy, she cannot exclude the disability income payments.
4. (d) All unemployment compensation payments are now fully taxable.

☑ **Example 26.** Linda Young, a waitress at Mel's Diner, is given a free lunch while on duty so that she is available to assist during the lunchtime rush. The value of these lunches may be excluded, since the meals are furnished on the business premises and are for the convenience of the employer.

☑ **Example 27.** Robert Jensen, an orderly in the emergency room at State Hospital, is given a free dinner at the hospital cafeteria so that he is readily available for emergencies. The value of these dinners may be excluded; the meals are primarily for the benefit of the hospital.

☑ **Example 28.** Nancy Allen, a nurse at University Hospital, is provided free meals at the hospital while on duty; optionally, she may elect to receive a weekly cash allowance. Allen cannot exclude the value of the meals; the cash option indicates that the meals are primarily a form of compensation.

TAX TIP

Sometimes an employer will furnish "supper money" to employees who are working after normal hours. Based on the Sec. 119 rules discussed above, one would normally conclude that such payments represent taxable compensation. However, an obscure IRS ruling issued years ago states that such amounts are not taxable.

The value of lodging furnished by an employer is also excludable if (1) the lodging is on the business premises, (2) the lodging is for the employer's convenience, and (3) the employee is required to accept the lodging as a condition of employment. The last condition, which is not required for meals, indicates that lodging on the premises is necessary for the employee to perform adequately his or her duties. Consistent with this principle, an option to receive cash or an option to live elsewhere makes the value of the lodging taxable to the employee.

☑ **Example 29.** Hal Wedgeworth manages the Bayside Apartment complex. The owners require that he live in one of the apartments so that he is always available to handle any problems. The value of the lodging is not taxable to Wedgeworth.

Special exclusions are available for other types of lodging. For example, most quarters allowances (or cash allowances in lieu of quarters) for military and government employees are excludable from income. And, as mentioned in Chapter 2, a "parsonage allowance" paid to an ordained minister is excludable from income.

MEDICAL REIMBURSEMENT AND EDUCATIONAL ASSISTANCE PLANS

In 1978 Congress added two new categories of excludable employee fringe benefits. One of these exclusions is for employer reimbursement of employee medical expenses. Sec. 105(e) states that "... amounts received under an accident or health plan for employees... shall be treated as amounts received through accident or health insurance." This exclusion applies only if the reimbursement plan is available to all employees; for example, payments from a medical reimbursement plan that applies only to highly compensated employees (e.g., company officers) would not qualify for the exclusion.

☑ **Example 30.** Blanda Corporation has a plan that reimburses 100% of all medical expenses paid by employees for themselves, their spouses, and their dependents. During 1993 Allen Schwartz, an employee, paid $1,200 of hospital charges, $600 of physician fees, and $150 for medicines and drugs. Blanda reimbursed him the total of $1,950, and he can exclude the entire amount.

A second exclusion enacted in 1978 applies to the first $5,250 of employer reimbursement of employee educational expenses. To qualify, the educational assistance plan must be in writing and must be generally available to all employees (i.e., it must not discriminate in favor of highly compensated employees). The exclusion is limited to reimbursement for books, tuition, supplies, and fees for undergraduate or graduate courses. The courses do not necessarily have to be related to the employee's job, but purely recreational courses do not qualify for the exclusion.

This exclusion was scheduled to expire on July 1, 1992. However, Congress retroactively extended the exclusion through the end of 1994 as part of the 1993 Tax Act.

☑ **Example 31.** Under a written educational assistance plan available to all employees, Susan McCain received the following payments from her employer in May 1993: tuition for a data processing course, $250; lab fees, $75; textbook charges, $60; meals, $150; and transportation costs, $155. McCain may exclude the reimbursement for the tuition, lab fees, and textbooks. The remaining payments are taxable.

GROUP LEGAL SERVICES AND DEPENDENT CARE ASSISTANCE PLANS

Two other specific exclusions for employees were added to the Code in the late 1970s for qualified group legal service plans (Sec. 120) and qualified dependent care assistance plans (Sec. 129). The former exclusion applied to amounts contributed by an employer to a nondiscriminatory plan that provided specified personal legal services for employees and their dependents. The exclusion also applied to the value of the legal services provided to the employee; however, the exclusion was limited to $70 per employee per year. Congress has allowed this exclusion to expire for employer amounts contributed after June 30, 1992.

☑ **Example 32.** Rhonda Welch received free legal advice worth $120 from her employer's group legal service plan in 1993. She may not exclude any of the value of the legal services received, since the services were received after June 30, 1992.

The Sec. 129 exclusion for dependent care assistance programs is available when an employer provides employees with dependent care assistance payments under a nondiscriminatory plan. Such exclusion is limited to the *lesser* of (a) $5,000 ($2,500 for married-filing separately) and (b) in the case of a married employee, the lesser earned income of the two spouses. The latter limitation effectively eliminates the exclusion when one spouse does not work (e.g., has no earned income) and is theoretically available to care for the dependents. However, the earned income limitation does not apply for any month in which the nonworking spouse is disabled or is a full-time student.

No exclusion is available for employer reimbursement of payments to the provider of the dependent care if that person is either the employee's dependent or the employee's child under the age of 19 at the close of the taxable year. And finally, any amounts qualifying for the exclusion will not also qualify for the child and dependent care credit discussed in Chapters 1 and 5.

☑ **Example 33.** Allen and Helen Morris paid a neighbor $5,600 in 1993 to care for their three children while they worked. Allen's 1993 salary was $38,000, and Helen's 1993 salary was $46,000. The $5,600 was reimbursed by Helen's employer under a qualified dependent care assistance program. On their 1993 return, Allen and Helen may exclude $5,000 of the assistance payments.

☑ **Example 34.** Assume the same facts as Example 33, except that Allen worked part-time in 1993 and earned only $4,100, even though he also received $28,000 of interest income during the year. In this case, the exclusion is limited to Allen's *earned* income of $4,100.

☑ **Example 35.** Assume the same facts as Example 33, except that Allen was physically disabled for the entire year and had no income. In this case, the earned income limit does not apply, and the maximum $5,000 exclusion is allowed.

MISCELLANEOUS FRINGE BENEFITS

THE LAW

Sec. 132(a)—Gross income shall not include any fringe benefit which qualifies as a—
(1) no-additional-cost service,
(2) qualified employee discount,
(3) working condition fringe, or
(4) de minimus fringe.

Over the years, taxpayers and the IRS have been at odds over the taxability of a variety of fringe benefits. In order to resolve some of these controversies, Congress enacted legislation in 1984 that excluded four general types of fringe benefits, provided that certain conditions were met. Each of these is discussed briefly in this section.

No-Additional-Cost Service

Occasionally, employers will provide free of charge to employees a service similar to a service provided to a customer. If the service is of the same type sold to the public in the line of business in which the employee works, the value of the service is excludable from the employee's income, provided that the employer incurs no substantial cost in providing the service. For purposes of the latter requirement, the term *substantial cost* includes any forgone revenue. The exclusion also applies to retired employees and to the employee's spouse or dependent children.

Example 36. Mary Bittner is an employee of Earth Airline. Earth allows all of its employees to fly on a standby basis for one-eighth of the normal fare when they are off duty. During 1993 Mary spent $600 for such flights; the normal cost to customers would be $4,800. Since such tickets could be used only on a standby basis (i.e., when empty seats were available), there was no significant additional cost to the employer. Thus, Mary is not taxed on the $4,200 value of the fringe benefit.

Qualified Employee Discounts

Offering purchase discounts to employees has been a popular fringe benefit for many employers over the years. Because some of these price reductions can be quite substantial, Congress has established limits on the excludability of such discounts provided in a line of business in which the employee works. The discount exclusion on merchandise is limited to the employer's gross profit percentage, and the discount exclusion on services is limited to 20% of the normal selling price of such services to the general public.

This exclusion also applies to retired employees and to the employee's spouse and dependent children. However, the qualified discount exclusion does not apply to real property (e.g., land and buildings) or personal property that is commonly held for investment (e.g., securities).

Example 37. Gil Clancy is an employee of AB Department Store. During 1993 under AB's 40% employee discount policy, he purchased a $300 suit for $180. AB's gross profit percentage for 1993 was 25%. Since the maximum discount exclusion for employees of AB would be 25%, Gil is taxed on $45 (15% of $300) of the employee discount on the suit.

Example 38. Marsha Thompkins is an employee of Allen & Allen, a law firm. During 1993 Marsha paid a firm member $400 for legal advice on her divorce; the normal charge for such services to customers would be $500. Since the services discount is not greater than 20%, Marsha will exclude the $100 employee discount from income.

TAX TIP

In some lines of business, the employer's gross profit percentage on merchandise can be quite large. One example is the clothing industry, where profit margins can be 50% or greater. In such cases, an employee discount program can generate significant savings for an employee, since the exclusion is also available for the employee's spouse and dependents.

For example, assume that under the employee discount program Pam Spero, a salesperson with Ace Department Store, purchased $2,000 of clothing from her employer for $1,000. If Ace's gross profit percentage is 50% or greater, the entire $1,000 fringe benefit is excludable. If Pam's marginal income tax rate were 31% and the discount program were not available, she would have needed to receive $1,450 additional salary to have the $1,000 additional after-tax cash to purchase the clothing at retail value.

Working Condition Fringes

A special exclusion is available for goods and services furnished to an employee as a "working condition fringe" benefit. These goods and services qualify for exclusion if they otherwise would have been deductible if the employee had to pay for them.

Example 39. Rob Howard's employer gives him a company automobile to use during working hours. Rob's employer also pays the subscription fees for two professional journals Rob uses in his job. Since Rob would otherwise be able to deduct the subscription costs and the costs associated with the company car, neither payment by his employer is includable in Rob's income for tax purposes.

In the previous example, the employee was not taxed on the business use of the company automobile. But what about any personal use? The answer is simple: Any personal use of a company-provided car is a taxable noncash fringe benefit to an employee. The employer has the responsibility for determining the actual value of this benefit and reporting that amount to the employee. The Code provides several alternative methods of determining this value, including the use of an "annual lease value table."

Example 40. Sue Aka's employer, Bee Company, provides her with a car free of charge in 1993. The car is worth $12,000. According to the "annual lease value table" of Reg. 1.61-21(d), the annual lease value of such a car is $3,600, and this amount will be included in Sue's gross income reported by Bee Company. (However, as will be discussed in Chapter 8, if Sue used the car for business purposes, she would be entitled to a deduction for the business usage.)

De Minimus Fringe

De minimus fringe benefits include any employer-provided property or services that have relatively small value and that it would be administratively impractical for the employer to account for. Examples include typing of personal letters, use of a company copying machine, small holiday gifts, and occasional supper money or taxi fare for employees working overtime.

Example 41. Each Thanksgiving, Gun Company gives each of its employees a turkey. The value of each turkey is approximately $18. The employees may exclude the value of their turkey from their gross incomes each year.

MISCELLANEOUS EXCLUDABLE EMPLOYEE BENEFITS

In recent years Congress has added several new categories of nontaxable employee fringe benefits, including the following:

(1) the value of employer-provided athletic facilities located on the business premises;

(2) the value of meals purchased below fair market value at employer-provided eating facilities (provided that the yearly income of the facility equals or exceeds the cost of operating the facility);

(3) free parking spaces provided by the employer on or near the business premises;

(4) certain interest-free loans to employees (discussed in the next section).

Note that all of these benefits are services that should be available for most employees. Group coverage requirements are imposed to ensure that the benefit is not available only to highly compensated employees. Benefits that discriminate in favor of a particular class of employees, such as company officers, are usually treated as taxable compensation.

Example 42. Braddock Corporation provides group-term life insurance coverage for all its employees. The coverage is always twice the salary of the employee. In addition, the company provides a medical reimbursement plan for the corporate officers, with coverage equal to three times the salary of each employee. The premium payments on the first $50,000 of group-term life insurance coverage may be excluded by each employee; however, payments from the medical reimbursement plan will be taxable to the officers.

CAFETERIA PLANS

Many companies offer their employees flexible benefit plans, which are sometimes called "cafeteria plans." These plans allow employees to select the particular fringe benefits they want from a package of benefits offered by an employer. As long as the flexible benefit plan does not discriminate in favor of highly compensated employees, any noncash benefits may be excluded *if* they would otherwise be excludable on an individual basis. The exclusions are available even if the employee has the option of receiving cash. This is an important exception to the constructive-receipt doctrine.

✓ **Example 43**. Jennifer Warren, an employee at Bristow Company, is permitted to select $1,500 of benefits from a qualifying flexible benefits package. She selects the following: $800 of group health insurance coverage, $600 of child care services, and $100 cash. Of the three benefits selected, only the $100 cash is taxable.

REVIEW III

1. Bill Allen's employer provides him with $80,000 of group-term life insurance coverage. The employer's actual cost for this coverage is $160, and the uniform monthly rate per the tax regulations is $.09 per thousand. As a result of this insurance coverage, Allen must report gross income of
   (a) $32.40.
   (b) $60.00.
   (c) $86.40.
   (d) $160.00.
2. Ginger Rosema, a nurse at Highland Hospital, is provided a free lunch each workday in the hospital cafeteria so that she will be available for any emergency. The estimated value of the free meals she received in 1993 was $450, although the cost to the hospital for the meals was approximately $200. Rosema must report gross income from these meals of
   (a) $0.
   (b) $200.
   (c) $250.
   (d) $450.
3. Bradley Nix is the night manager at the Shady Arms motel. He is provided a room at the motel, free of charge, although he is not required to stay at the motel as a condition of employment. The fair rental value of this room in 1993 was $4,400. Nix estimates that living elsewhere would have cost at least $5,200. Nix must report 1993 gross income of
   (a) $0.
   (b) $800.
   (c) $4,400.
   (d) $5,200.
4. Folbert Company offers a written educational assistance plan for all of its corporate officers. During May 1993, Ellie Barber, the company treasurer, was reimbursed $175 for the tuition charge for an accounting course she took at a local university. She was also reimbursed $40 for textbook charges. These reimbursements will increase Barber's 1993 gross income by
   (a) $0.
   (b) $40.
   (c) $175.
   (d) $215.

Answers are on page 3-22.

IV MISCELLANEOUS EXCLUSIONS
(Code Sections 86, 108, 111, 911, and 1017)

SOCIAL SECURITY PAYMENTS

The Internal Revenue Service ruled in 1938 that social security benefits were excludable from income. This exclusion was justified on the grounds that contributions to the social security fund are made with after-tax dollars, and benefits represent a recovery of investment cost and/or a nontaxable government welfare payment. However, mounting budgetary problems forced Congress to tax a portion of such payments in 1983 and later years as a means of ensuring the future solvency of the trust fund.

THE LAW

Sec. 86(a)—In general. Gross income for the taxable year of any taxpayer . . . includes . . . social security benefits in an amount equal to the lesser of—
(1) one-half of the social security benefits received during the taxable year, or
(2) one-half of the excess described in subsection (b)(1).

Under current law, a portion of social security or railroad retirement payments is includable in gross income if an individual's "modified adjusted gross income" (e.g., AGI plus any tax-exempt interest and excludable foreign-earned income received) plus one-half of the benefits received exceed a base amount of $32,000 (married-filing jointly), $25,000 (single individuals), or $0 (married-filing separately). The amount taxable is the *lesser* of (1) one-half of this excess amount and (2) one-half of the actual social security benefits received.*

Example 44. Marilyn Andrews, a retired single taxpayer, received $4,200 of social security benefits in 1993. Her other 1993 income consisted of $14,000 of taxable

---

ANSWERS TO REVIEW III

1. (a) Premium payments for coverage in excess of $50,000 are taxable according to a uniform rate schedule. The coverage for the taxpayer is $.09 per $1,000 of coverage per month, so the total taxable amount is $32.40 (30 units of coverage × .09 × 12 months).
2. (a) The value of the meals is excludable, since they are furnished on the business premises and are for the convenience of the employer.
3. (c) The value of the room is taxable, because Nix was *not* required to accept the lodging as a condition of employment.
4. (d) The reimbursements are taxable, because the educational assistance plan discriminates in favor of the company officers.

---

*For changes in the tax law effective for tax years beginning in 1994, see Appendix J.

interest, $11,500 of taxable dividends, and $8,500 of tax-exempt interest. Andrews will be taxed on the lesser of

(a) One-half of excess income per formula:

Adjusted gross income (14,000 + 11,500)	$25,500
Tax-exempt interest received	8,500
"Modified adjusted gross income"	$34,000
One-half of social security received	2,100
Total	$36,100
Base amount (single taxpayer)	(25,000)
Excess income	$11,100
Portion potentially subject to tax	× .50
Taxable portion per formula	$ 5,550

(b) One-half of social security benefits:

($4,200 × .50) .... $ 2,100

Thus, Andrews will be taxed on $2,100 of social security income in 1993.

The instructions to Form 1040 provide a worksheet for determining the taxable portion of social security and railroad retirement benefits received. This is illustrated in Figure 3-2, using the facts of Example 44.

Social Security Benefits Worksheet—Lines 21a and 21b (keep for your records)

If you are married filing separately and you **lived apart** from your spouse for all of 1993, enter "D" to the left of line 21a.

1. Enter the total amount from **box 5** of **all** your Forms SSA-1099 and Forms RRB-1099 (if applicable) . . . . 1. __4,200__

   Note: If line 1 is zero or less, stop here; none of your social security benefits are taxable. Otherwise, go to line 2.

2. Divide line 1 above by 2 . . . . 2. __2,100__

3. Add the amounts on Form 1040, lines 7, 8a, 9 through 15, 16b, 17b, 18 through 20, and line 22. Do not include here any amounts from box 5 of Forms SSA-1099 or RRB-1099 . . . 3. __25,500__

4. Enter the amount from Form 1040, line 8b . . . . . . 4. __8,500__

5. Add lines 2, 3, and 4 . . . . 5. __36,100__

6. Enter the total adjustments from Form 1040, line 30 . . . 6. _____

7. Subtract line 6 from line 5 . . . . 7. __36,100__

8. Enter on line 8 the amount shown below for your filing status:
   - Single, Head of household, or Qualifying widow(er), enter $25,000
   - Married filing jointly, enter $32,000
   - Married filing separately, enter -0- ($25,000 if you **lived apart** from your spouse for all of 1993)

   8. __25,000__

9. Subtract line 8 from line 7. If zero or less, enter -0-. . . . 9. __11,100__
   - If line 9 is zero, stop here. None of your social security benefits are taxable. Do not enter any amounts on lines 21a or 21b. **But** if you are married filing separately and you **lived apart** from your spouse for all of 1993, enter -0- on line 21b. Be sure you entered "D" to the left of line 21a.
   - If line 9 is more than zero, go to line 10.

10. Divide line 9 above by 2 . . . . 10. __5,550__

11. **Taxable social security benefits.**
    - First, enter on Form 1040, line 21a, the amount from line 1.
    - Then, enter the **smaller** of line 2 or line 10 here and on Form 1040, line 21b . . . . 11. __2,100__

Note: If part of your benefits are taxable for 1993 **and** they include benefits paid in 1993 that were for an earlier year, you may be able to reduce the taxable amount shown on the worksheet. Get Pub. 915 for details.

Figure 3-2 Worksheet to Determine Taxable social security

TAX TIP

Social security recipients whose combinations of modified adjusted gross income and one-half of social security benefits received during a year are just below the base amounts should carefully evaluate the tax effects of generating additional income during that year. Such additional income may cause a portion of the social security benefits to be taxable, and this would increase the marginal tax rate applicable to such income by 50%.

For example, assume that during a year a single taxpayer receives $4,000 salary from a part-time job, $20,000 of taxable dividends, and $2,000 of social security benefits. Further assume that the taxpayer claims one exemption and uses the standard deduction. If the taxpayer has the opportunity to earn an additional $1,000 salary during the year, his tax liability will increase $225. In effect, the tax rate for this additional income is 22.5%, or 150% of the normal 15% rate for this level of income. The $225 increase in tax liability is computed as follows:

	Without Additional Salary	With Additional Salary	Difference
Salary	$ 4,000	$ 5,000	$1,000
Taxable interest and dividends	20,000	20,000	
Taxable social security	0 *	500 **	500
Adjusted gross income	$24,000	$25,500	$1,500
Standard deduction (1993)	(3,700)	(3,700)	
Exemption (1993)	(2,350)	(2,350)	
Taxable income	$17,950	$19,450	$1,500
Gross tax	$ 2,692	$ 2,917	$ 225

* Taxable = [$24,000 + (1/2 × $2,000) − $25,000] × 1/2 = $0
** Taxable = [$25,000 + (1/2 × $2,000) − $25,000] × 1/2 = $500

Note that the additional $1,000 of salary caused $500 of the social security to be taxed; in effect, a $1,000 increase in income caused a $1,500 (150%) increase in taxable income! Thus, the effective rate of tax on the $1,000 additional income is 22.5% ($225/$1,000), or 150% of the normal rate of 15%.

FOREIGN EARNED INCOME EXCLUSION

A U.S. citizen who earns income in a foreign country may be subject to an income tax in the foreign country. Generally, income earned in a foreign country is also subject to the U.S. income tax. Congress has provided some relief from this double taxation through a special exclusion. (Alternatively, a taxpayer may benefit from a foreign tax credit, which is discussed in Chapter 5.)

The foreign income exclusion is available for the services income of a taxpayer who either is a bona fide resident of the foreign country or was present in the country for at least 330 consecutive days during any 12-month period. The maximum exclusion is $70,000 per year. A taxpayer residing in the foreign country for less than a year must prorate the maximum exclusion based on total workdays.

☑ **Example 45.** Deborah Allison, a U.S. citizen, worked as an attorney in Brazil for the entire year 1993. She earned a total of $110,000 in legal fees during the year. She may exclude $70,000 of this income in 1993.

A special exclusion is also available for the excessive living expenses of an individual and his or her family while they are residing in the foreign country. The amount excludable from income is the excess of the actual housing costs over 16% of the pay scale for a government employee at Step 1 of Grade 14 (GS-14). Form 2555 is used to report this exclusion, as well as the regular exclusion for earned income from a foreign country.

PUBLIC ASSISTANCE PAYMENTS

Most forms of public assistance are excludable from income. These items are viewed as donative transfers, rather than as compensation. Excludable items include the following:

(1) Food stamps

(2) Aid to Families with Dependent Children

(3) Antipoverty program payments from the Office of Economic Opportunity

(4) Payments to the blind

(5) Restitution payments to crime victims

Medicare benefits and supplemental policy benefits are similarly excluded from income. These are considered to be social transfer payments.

MILITARY PAYMENTS

Although the basic salary paid to military personnel is taxable compensation, a number of other military-related payments are excludable from income. For example, retirement pay related to a disability is excludable (normal retirement pay is taxable). Other forms of excludable payments include the following:

(1) Quarters, subsistence, and uniform allowance

(2) Family separation allowances (because of overseas duty)

(3) Combat pay

(4) Veterans' education and training benefits (e.g., G.I. Bill benefits)

(5) Grants to disabled veterans for special automobiles and housing

(6) Overseas cost-of-living allowances

(7) Death gratuity pay

FORGIVENESS OF DEBT

Normally, the reduction by a lender of the amount of a borrower's outstanding debt will result in taxable income to the borrower, since the gratuitous forgiveness of the debt increases the borrower's net worth (i.e., decreases the liabilities without a corresponding increase in other liabilities or decrease in assets). However, under one of several provisions in the tax law, a borrower may be able to exclude a portion of or all of the forgiven debt. First, the borrower may be able to successfully contend that the forgiveness of debt is a gift from the lender. As discussed earlier, donative transfers for no consideration are excludable from income. A gift is more likely to be a nonbusiness item, such as a family loan. Usually, a forgiveness of debt in a business setting is motivated by a substantial business reason, and therefore is taxable.

Example 46. Bill McAllister is unable to pay the $110,000 balance he owes to his major supplier of spare parts, Bledsoe Supplies. Because of the volume of business McAllister has provided in the past, Bledsoe agrees to cancel $40,000 of this debt in an effort to help McAllister avoid bankruptcy. The forgiveness appears to be motivated by a business reason; the $40,000 is taxable to McAllister.

If the debt forgiveness does not qualify as a gift, a special tax provision for insolvent or bankrupt taxpayers is available that has the potential effect of postponing the recognition of gain. This provision allows the borrower to elect to reduce certain favorable "tax attributes" (e.g., net operating losses and credit carryovers) and/or the basis of depreciable property and real property held as inventory by the amount of the forgiven debt. (Tax attributes and depreciation methods are discussed later in the course.) By reducing future tax attributes and depreciation deductions, forgiving the debt gradually increases income in future years. In effect, a temporary exclusion is created.

Example 47. Jane Seymour is insolvent and unable to pay a $40,000 outstanding balance on business machinery and equipment that cost $100,000. She has no favorable tax attributes. The creditor forgives the debt. Rather than immediately recognize the $40,000 forgiven debt as income, she may elect to reduce her depreciable basis in the machinery to $60,000. Future depreciation (expense) deductions would then be $40,000 less than if the debt forgiveness had not occurred.

The 1993 act extends the basis reduction option to *nonbankrupt, solvent* taxpayers. However, the election is available only for debt on realty used in a trade or business.

INTEREST-FREE OR BELOW-MARKET LOANS

As a general rule, any interest-free or below-market rate loans made after June 6, 1984, will require the lender to treat the forgone interest as income and require the borrower to treat the same amount as interest expense. In effect, the transaction is treated as if the lender gave the amount of forgone interest to the borrower, and the borrower then paid the amount back to the lender as interest. However, there are two major exceptions to this rule; these imputed interest rules do not apply to (1) loans that do not exceed $10,000 or (2) gift loans that do not exceed $100,000 (where the imputed interest is limited to the lender's "net investment income").

☑ **Example 48.** Gina Law's employer loaned her $8,000 as an interest-free loan in 1993. The loan matures in two years. Since the loan is for less than $10,000, the forgone interest is ignored for tax purposes.

☑ **Example 49.** Assume the same facts as Example 48, except that the loan was for $100,000, and the forgone interest in 1993 at current interest rates was $9,000. Gina is treated as receiving $9,000 of additional taxable compensation in 1993 (the IRS would simply not permit such a loan to be characterized as a "gift"). Furthermore, the law assumes that she repaid the $9,000 as interest to her employer. Her employer then reports this amount as interest income and Gina may or may not deduct it under the rules discussed in Chapter 4. (Since the interest is most likely treated as compensation, Gina's employer would be able to deduct the $9,000.)

TAX BENEFIT RULE

In general, when a taxpayer recovers a portion or all of an expenditure that was fully deducted in a previous tax year, the recovery must be included in gross income in the year received. Although technically the prior year's return was in error, the recovery is taxed in the year received, because our tax system operates on an annual basis.

This strict adherence to an annual basis of accounting can create inequities for some taxpayers. Congress mitigated some of the potential inequities of an annual reporting requirement by enacting what is commonly referred to as the "tax benefit rule." This rule is similar to an exclusion provision, in that the recoveries of items that were previously deducted are limited to the amount of the tax benefit generated in the prior year. The remaining portion of the recovery may be excluded because it did not provide a tax benefit in the earlier years. This tax benefit rule can be illustrated by three examples.

☑ **Example 50.** Ben Hamlin incurred a $1,000 hospital bill in 1993 and deducted this amount as part of his itemized deductions. However, Hamlin could deduct only $250 of this payment because of the 7.5% floor on medical expenses (i.e., medical expenses are deductible only to the extent that they exceed 7.5% of a taxpayer's AGI). In 1994 Hamlin unexpectedly received a $1,000 reimbursement check from his insurance company for the 1993 expenditure. Hamlin will include only $250 of the reimbursement in his 1994 gross income, since this was the actual tax benefit (deduction) he received in 1993. The remaining $750 of reimbursement is excludable.

☑ **Example 51.** Rhonda Stivic, a single taxpayer, itemized her deductions in 1993, claiming $3,900 of itemized deductions, or $200 in excess of the normal standard deduction of $3,700. Included in the $3,900 total deductions was an $800 deduction for state income taxes paid, based on the amount of withholdings from her checks in 1993. In 1994 Stivic received a $375 refund on her 1993 state income tax return. Although technically in 1993 she deducted $375 of state income taxes that were never paid, the recovery (additional income) on her 1994 federal tax return will be limited to $200. The maximum benefit she received from the $375 deduction in 1993 was $200, and the 1994 income recovery is limited to $200.

✓ **Example 52.** Assume the same facts as Example 51, except that Stivic did not itemize her deductions in 1993, because they totaled less than $3,700. In this case, none of the $375 state tax refund received in 1994 will be included in 1994 income, since the $375 did not generate a tax benefit in 1993.

REVIEW IV

1. During 1993 Harold Henning, age 69, received $4,000 of social security payments, $20,000 of taxable interest, and $6,200 of tax-exempt interest. His gross income reportable on a single tax return for 1993 would be
   (a) $20,000.
   (b) $21,600.
   (c) $22,000.
   (d) $24,000.
2. Which of the following benefit payments received by an army officer will be taxable?
   (a) education benefits under the G.I. Bill
   (b) living allowances for family while stationed overseas
   (c) $1,050 monthly salary
   (d) $300-a-month combat pay
3. Teresa Maudlin recently had a $30,000 business debt forgiven by a creditor. She will be able to postpone recognition of the income from this forgiven debt only if she
   (a) does not itemize her deductions.
   (b) is bankrupt or insolvent, or the debt is on business realty.
   (c) switches from the cash basis to the accrual basis.
   (d) invests $30,000 in tax-exempt municipal bonds.
4. Harold Robinson deducted medical expenditures of $450 on his 1992 tax return; however, the "7.5% of adjusted gross income" floor on medical deductions limited the medical expense deduction to $190. If in 1993 Robinson receives reimbursement for the $450 expenditure, he must increase his 1993 gross income by
   (a) $0.
   (b) $190.
   (c) $260.
   (d) $450.

Answers are on page 3-30.

CHAPTER APPENDIX: MEASURING THE VALUE OF AN EXCLUSION

Tax considerations play an important part in evaluating different investment alternatives. When alternative investments are being compared, the projected incomes for each investment should be stated in after-tax dollars. This is especially critical when we are evaluating an investment that produces income that is partially or wholly exempt from taxation.

For example, assume that a taxpayer is given the opportunity to invest in either an 8% tax-exempt bond or a 10% taxable bond. Which investment offers the highest return? Of course, the answer depends on the taxpayer's *marginal income tax rate* (the rate applying to the additional income generated by the investment). If the taxpayer's marginal tax bracket is 15%, then she should invest in the taxable bond, because she will realize an 8.5% return on the bond after paying 15% of the interest return to the government in taxes. On the other hand, a 39.6%-bracket taxpayer would be better off to invest in the 8% nontaxable bond, since his after-tax rate of return would be only 6.04% after he pays 39.6% of the interest return as federal taxes.

Simple algebra can be used to determine what before-tax rate of return must be earned from a taxable investment to equal a given rate of return from a nontaxable investment. The formula to determine this "break-even" rate of return is as follows:

$$\text{Break-Even Rate of Return for a Taxable Investment} = \frac{\text{Rate of Return on Nontaxable Investment}}{(100\% - \text{Taxpayer's Marginal Tax Rate})}$$

For example, consider the two situations described above. For a 15%-bracket taxpayer, the necessary rate of return from a taxable bond would be 9.41%, computed as follows:

$$\text{Break-Even Rate of Return for a Taxable Investment} = \frac{\text{Rate of Return on Nontaxable Investment}}{(100\% - \text{Taxpayer's Marginal Tax Rate})}$$

$$= \frac{.08}{(1.00 - .15)} = \underline{.0941}$$

Thus, a taxable investment that returns 9.41% before taxes will return 8% after taxes when the taxpayer's marginal tax rate is 15% [i.e., .0941 × (1.00 − .15) = .08].

On the other hand, the necessary rate of return from a taxable bond for a 39.6% bracket taxpayer would be 13.25%, computed as follows:

$$\text{Break-Even Rate of Return for a Taxable Investment} = \frac{\text{Rate of Return on Nontaxable Investment}}{(100\% - \text{Taxpayer's Marginal Tax Rate})}$$

$$= \frac{.08}{(1.00 - .396)} = \underline{.1325}$$

Thus, a taxable investment that returns 13.25% before taxes will return 8% after taxes when the taxpayer's marginal tax rate is 39.6% [i.e., .1325 × (1.00 − .396) = .08].

These two examples help to illustrate why investments that offer tax-exempt income are usually favored by high-income (high-tax-bracket) taxpayers. And for much the same reasons, fringe benefit exclusions tend to be worth more to highly compensated employees, because they would otherwise require larger amounts of before-tax compensation to purchase the same benefits.

✓ **Example 53.** Belva Robinson's employer provides her with a nontaxable fringe benefit worth $2,000. If she has a marginal tax rate of 31%, she would have to receive $2,900 of additional salary to purchase the same benefit [$2,000/(1.0 − .31)]. If she has a marginal tax rate of 15%, she would have to receive only $2,353 of additional salary to purchase the same benefit [$2,000/(1.0 − .15)].

CHAPTER PROBLEMS

PART

I 1. On February 1, 1993, Bob Tanner, a single taxpayer, inherited $100,000 from his father's estate. Tanner immediately invested $50,000 in ABC Corporation common stock and $50,000 in state of New Mexico bonds. These two investments generated $1,220 dividends and $8,100 interest, respectively, in 1993. Determine Tanner's reportable gross income for 1993.

I 2. Wanda Stinson, an employee with Gilbert Company, died in March 1993. Gilbert Company paid death benefits of $6,000 to her husband Robert and $2,000 to each of her three children. How much of these payments is includable in the 1993 income of Robert and the children?

I 3. Determine the taxability of the following:
(a) Alex Apple receives $100,000 cash as the beneficiary of his father's life insurance policy.
(b) Same as (a), except that Apple elects to receive the insurance in 20 equal installments of $8,000.
(c) Bill Meyer surrenders a $50,000 policy on his own life to the insurer, receiving the cash surrender value of $8,500 (total premiums paid by Meyer were $4,900).
(d) Jean Benson received the $75,000 face value of a life insurance policy on the life of her brother James. Jean had purchased the policy from her brother six years ago for $12,000 and had named herself as the beneficiary. (Premiums paid by Jean totaled $7,500.)

I 4. Hal Wilson retired after 25 years of service. Under its qualified services award program, AZ Company gave Hal a watch that has a value of $370. Will Hal have to report the value of the watch as taxable income?

ANSWERS TO REVIEW IV

1. (b) The exclusion is limited to the lesser of one-half of the social security benefits received ($2,000) and one-half of the "excess amount" [$1,600, or 1/2 × ($20,000 + $6,200 + $2,000 − $25,000)].
2. (c) The normal salary received by military personnel is not exempt from taxation. The remaining benefits are excludable.
3. (b) The special election to reduce the depreciable basis of property is limited to insolvent or bankrupt taxpayers, unless the debt is on business realty.
4. (b) The amount of the recovery includable in 1993 gross income is limited to the amount of the actual tax benefit (deduction) received in 1992, or $190.

I 5. Determine the taxability of the following payments:
   (a) Janet Wilson won $5,000 in a contest to name a new product.
   (b) Rob Barlow received $3,000 for being selected Educator of the Year in Kentucky by the state legislature.
   (c) Barbara Brandon, a college freshman, received an academic scholarship from Woodson College for $4,000. Of this amount, she spent $3,400 for tuition, books, and fees.
   (d) For grading papers for a professor (12 hours a week), Hal Linden, a graduate student at Guilford University, received $50 a week from a school fund.

I 6. Jennifer Wells received a grant from the National Science Foundation to continue the chemotherapy research that was the subject of the dissertation she completed two years earlier. She will receive $450 a month for two years. How much (if any) of this grant is taxable to Jennifer?

II 7. During 1993 Joe Horvath was covered by an accident and health insurance policy furnished by his employer, Wayside Industries. Wayside paid the $640 of insurance premiums on the policy During 1993 and Horvath received the following benefit payments under the policy in 1993: $1,250 reimbursement for medical expenses associated with a five-week illness and $1,000 compensation for a portion of Horvath's lost wages during this five-week period.
   (a) How much gross income does Horvath realize from these payments in 1993?
   (b) Would your answer be different if Horvath himself had purchased the policy? Explain.

II 8. Ralph Anders, age 55, was forced to retire in 1993 because of a job-related injury. He immediately began receiving full disability income payments of $180 a week from an accident and health policy provided by his employer. Anders received 50 weekly payments in 1993. His only other income in 1993 was $13,500 of taxable interest. How much gross income did Anders realize in 1993 from the disability payments?

II 9. During 1993 Eleanor Watson, a single taxpayer, received $2,400 from a state unemployment compensation fund. Her only other income in 1993 was a salary of $11,500. How much of the unemployment compensation is taxable to Eleanor in 1993?

II 10. Determine the amount of gross income realized by the recipient from the following payments (treat each case independently):
   (a) Apple's employer pays the $420 premium on an accident and health insurance policy.
   (b) Brown received $3,000 compensation for lost wages from a wage continuation policy that he purchased with his own funds.
   (c) Jenkins received $10,000 from an employer-financed accident and health policy as compensation for the loss of his hand in a job-related accident.
   (d) During all of 1993, Davis received $300 of worker's compensation each week and $80 a week disability from an employer-financed accident and health policy. (Davis is permanently disabled and had no other income in 1993.)
   (e) Elam was injured in a car accident in 1993 and received $6,000 for medical expenses and $4,000 for pain and emotional suffering as part of a lawsuit related to the accident.

III 11. During 1993 Ellen Goodman, age 32, was covered by two insurance policies financed by her employer. One policy provided group-term life insurance coverage of $70,000, and the other (available only to corporate officers) provided ordinary whole life insurance coverage of $150,000. The employer payments on the policies were $195 for the group coverage (allocable to Ellen) and $850 for the ordinary life policy. How much gross income does Ellen recognize in 1993 from these payments?

III 12. Determine which of the following are excludable (treat each case separately):
   (a) meals furnished to a bank teller on the premises so that he is available to work over the noon hour
   (b) cash meal allowance to a highway patrolman who eats while on the road (no accounting for the expenses is required)
   (c) lodging furnished to an apartment manager (on the premises) as a condition of employment
   (d) lodging furnished to the maintenance superintendent of an apartment building (optionally, the superintendent may elect to receive a cash allowance)

III 13. Wrightman Company offers a written educational assistance plan for all its employees. During March 1993, Martha Vandella received reimbursement for the following expenditures she incurred in taking a management course at a local university: $280 for tuition, a $20 computer usage fee, $30 for textbooks, $150 for travel, and $20 for meals. Determine the gross income Vandella realized in 1993.

III 14. Boaters Incorporated offers its employees a flexible benefits package (a "cafeteria plan"). Employees may select benefits worth 5% of their gross salaries. Which of the following benefits would be taxable to an employee (assume that the plan does not discriminate in favor of highly compensated employees):
   (a) group-term life insurance coverage for twice the employee's salary of $45,000
   (b) group legal services worth $200
   (c) ordinary life insurance coverage (the employee names the beneficiary)
   (d) child and dependent care services worth $3,000
   (e) cash payments (up to $600 maximum)
   (f) medical reimbursement plans (maximum $1,000 reimbursement).

III 15. Which of the following benefits would be taxable to Ellen Oliver, an employee of Y Company, who received $45,000 salary in 1993?
   (a) $360 value of free parking provided by the company in a parking lot across the street from the company
   (b) $1,000 discount on company products sold to Ellen under the company's 40% discount policy for employees (the company's gross profit percentage for 1993 was 20%)
   (c) $20 value of personal copying that Ellen did on the company's copying machine
   (d) $5,200 value of child care services reimbursed by Y Company
   (e) $20 value of Christmas ham given to each employee

IV 16. Theresa Baylor, single, age 67, received $6,600 of social security payments in 1993. Her other income consisted of $11,000 taxable interest, $12,500 taxable dividends, and $8,000 tax-exempt interest. How are the social security payments reported for tax purposes?

IV 17. Nicholas Andropov, a U.S. citizen, worked as a scientist at a university in Greece for all of 1993. He received a salary of $93,500 for his period of employment. How is the $93,500 reported on Andropov's 1993 U.S. tax return?

IV 18. Which of the following benefit payments can the recipient exclude?
   (a) $480 tuition reimbursement received by a veteran under the G.I. Bill

(b) $600 value of interest forgone on an $8,000 interest-free loan from an employer
(c) $1,080 monthly salary of an army lieutenant
(d) $1,125 of Aid to Families with Dependent Children received by a divorced parent
(e) $840 worth of food stamps received by a family

IV 19. In 1993 Harold Feldman was unable to pay a $20,000 liability outstanding on equipment he purchased from Machines Incorporated. As part of a plan to help Feldman avoid bankruptcy, Machines Incorporated agreed to cancel $12,000 of the liability. Can Feldman exclude or postpone the recognition of income from this debt cancellation? Would your answer be different if the property is business realty?

IV 20. On her 1992 tax return, Jan Williams deducted the $2,000 cost of reconstructive surgery she had had performed that year. However, only $600 of this amount was actually deductible for tax purposes (i.e., the amount that exceeded 7.5% of adjusted gross income). Much to her surprise, the $2,000 payment was reimbursed by her personal health insurance policy in 1993. Does Williams recognize any taxable income from this $2,000 reimbursement? Explain.

APX 21. Alfred Smith's marginal income tax rate for 1993 is expected to be 31%. He is considering investing $10,000 in state of Michigan bonds, which pay an annual rate of 6.7%. What interest rate would Smith have to earn from a taxable investment to provide the same after-tax cash offered by the Michigan bonds?

TAX RETURN PROBLEM

22. [Form 1040] Using the information provided in Problem 16 above, complete a 1993 Form 1040 (front page only) and a social security worksheet for Theresa Baylor.

HOW WOULD YOU RULE?

23. During 1993 Alice Wakeman, the owner of TABCO Products, recommended Arrow Company, a raw materials supplier for her company, to several friends at a manufacturing convention. This recommendation generated $500,000 of sales for Arrow Company, and the company showed its appreciation to Wakeman by giving her a new automobile worth $11,000. Is the value of this automobile taxable to Wakeman? What is your opinion?

24. Katherine Grant won a $5,000 scholarship for being named Miss Florida in a statewide beauty contest. Can Grant exclude this scholarship? What is your opinion?

TAX PORTFOLIO PROBLEM FOR THE NEILSON FAMILY

If your instructor has assigned this problem, refer to Appendix A and complete the portion labeled "Chapter 3." This includes information on miscellaneous sources of income for the Neilsons.

Chapter 3 Problem 22   Name_____   3-35

Form 1040 — Department of the Treasury—Internal Revenue Service
U.S. Individual Income Tax Return 1993

For the year Jan. 1–Dec. 31, 1993, or other tax year beginning _____ 1993, ending _____ 19 ___
OMB No. 1545-0074
IRS Use Only—Do not write or staple in this space

Label (See instructions on page 12.) Use the IRS label. Otherwise, please print or type.

- Your first name and initial | Last name | Your social security number
- If a joint return, spouse's first name and initial | Last name | Spouse's social security number
- Home address (number and street). If you have a P.O. box, see page 12 | Apt. no
- City, town or post office, state, and ZIP code. If you have a foreign address, see page 12.

For Privacy Act and Paperwork Reduction Act Notice, see page 4.

Presidential Election Campaign (See page 12.)
- Do you want $3 to go to this fund? .... Yes / No
- If a joint return, does your spouse want $3 to go to this fund? ......

Note: Checking "Yes" will not change your tax or reduce your refund.

Filing Status (See page 12.) Check only one box.
1. Single
2. Married filing joint return (even if only one had income)
3. Married filing separate return. Enter spouse's social security no. above and full name here. ▶ _____
4. Head of household (with qualifying person). (See page 13.) If the qualifying person is a child but not your dependent, enter this child's name here. ▶ _____
5. Qualifying widow(er) with dependent child (year spouse died ▶ 19 ___). (See page 13.)

Exemptions (See page 13.)

6a ☐ **Yourself.** If your parent (or someone else) can claim you as a dependent on his or her tax return, **do not** check box 6a. But be sure to check the box on line 33b on page 2
b ☐ **Spouse**
c Dependents:

(1) Name (first, initial, and last name)	(2) Check if under age 1	(3) If age 1 or older, dependent's social security number	(4) Dependent's relationship to you	(5) No. of months lived in your home in 1993

If more than six dependents, see page 14.

- No. of boxes checked on 6a and 6b ____
- No. of your children on 6c who:
  - lived with you ____
  - didn't live with you due to divorce or separation (see page 15) ____
- Dependents on 6c not entered above ____

d If your child didn't live with you but is claimed as your dependent under a pre-1985 agreement, check here ▶ ☐
e Total number of exemptions claimed ....

Add numbers entered on lines above ▶ ____

Income

Attach Copy B of your Forms W-2, W-2G, and 1099-R here.

If you did not get a W-2, see page 10.

If you are attaching a check or money order, put it on top of any Forms W-2, W-2G, or 1099-R.

7	Wages, salaries, tips, etc. Attach Form(s) W-2	7
8a	Taxable interest income (see page 16). Attach Schedule B if over $400	8a
b	Tax-exempt interest (see page 17). DON'T include on line 8a	8b
9	Dividend income. Attach Schedule B if over $400	9
10	Taxable refunds, credits, or offsets of state and local income taxes (see page 17)	10
11	Alimony received	11
12	Business income or (loss). Attach Schedule C or C-EZ	12
13	Capital gain or (loss). Attach Schedule D	13
14	Capital gain distributions not reported on line 13 (see page 17)	14
15	Other gains or (losses). Attach Form 4797	15
16a	Total IRA distributions . 16a _____ b Taxable amount (see page 18)	16b
17a	Total pensions and annuities 17a _____ b Taxable amount (see page 18)	17b
18	Rental real estate, royalties, partnerships, S corporations, trusts, etc. Attach Schedule E	18
19	Farm income or (loss). Attach Schedule F	19
20	Unemployment compensation (see page 19)	20
21a	Social security benefits 21a _____ b Taxable amount (see page 19)	21b
22	Other income. List type and amount—see page 20 _____	22
23	Add the amounts in the far right column for lines 7 through 22. This is your **total income** ▶	23

Adjustments to Income (See page 20.)

24a	Your IRA deduction (see page 20)	24a	
b	Spouse's IRA deduction (see page 20)	24b	
25	One-half of self-employment tax (see page 21)	25	
26	Self-employed health insurance deduction (see page 22)	26	
27	Keogh retirement plan and self-employed SEP deduction	27	
28	Penalty on early withdrawal of savings	28	
29	Alimony paid. Recipient's SSN ▶ _____	29	
30	Add lines 24a through 29. These are your **total adjustments** ▶		30

Adjusted Gross Income

31 Subtract line 30 from line 23. This is your **adjusted gross income**. If this amount is less than $23,050 and a child lived with you, see page EIC-1 to find out if you can claim the "Earned Income Credit" on line 56 ▶ | 31 |

Cat. No. 11320B   Form **1040** (1993)

Copyright © 1994 by Harcourt Brace & Company. All rights reserved.

Social Security Benefits Worksheet—Lines 21a and 21b (keep for your records)

If you are married filing separately and you **lived apart** from your spouse for all of 1993, enter "D" to the left of line 21a.

1. Enter the total amount from **box 5** of **all** your **Forms SSA-1099** and **Forms RRB-1099** (if applicable) . . . . 1. _____

   Note: *If line 1 is zero or less, stop here; none of your social security benefits are taxable. Otherwise, go to line 2.*

2. Divide line 1 above by 2 . . . . 2. _____

3. Add the amounts on Form 1040, lines 7, 8a, 9 through 15, 16b, 17b, 18 through 20, and line 22. Do not include here any amounts from box 5 of Forms SSA-1099 or RRB-1099 . . 3. _____

4. Enter the amount from Form 1040, line 8b . . . . . . 4. _____

5. Add lines 2, 3, and 4 . . . . 5. _____

6. Enter the total adjustments from Form 1040, line 30 . . . 6. _____

7. Subtract line 6 from line 5 . . . . 7. _____

8. Enter on line 8 the amount shown below for your filing status:
   - Single, Head of household, or Qualifying widow(er), enter $25,000
   - Married filing jointly, enter $32,000
   - Married filing separately, enter -0- ($25,000 if you **lived apart** from your spouse for all of 1993)

   8. _____

9. Subtract line 8 from line 7. If zero or less, enter -0-. . . . 9. _____
   - If line 9 is zero, stop here. None of your social security benefits are taxable. Do not enter any amounts on lines 21a or 21b. **But** if you are married filing separately and you **lived apart** from your spouse for all of 1993, enter -0- on line 21b. Be sure you entered "D" to the left of line 21a.
   - If line 9 is more than zero, go to line 10.

10. Divide line 9 above by 2 . . . . 10. _____

11. **Taxable social security benefits.**
    - First, enter on Form 1040, line 21a, the amount from line 1.
    - Then, enter the **smaller** of line 2 or line 10 here and on Form 1040, line 21b . . . . 11. _____

Note: *If part of your benefits are taxable for 1993 **and** they include benefits paid in 1993 that were for an earlier year, you may be able to reduce the taxable amount shown on the worksheet. Get Pub. 915 for details.*

CHAPTER 4

Deductions for Personal Expenses of Individuals

In determining taxable income, no item may be subtracted unless the deduction for that item has been specifically authorized by Congress. Taxpayers are allowed deductions for certain expenses and losses related to business, investment, and personal activities. These deductible expenditures are classified into one of three major categories: (1) trade or business expenses and losses, (2) income-producing expenses and losses, and (3) personal expenses and losses. This chapter examines in detail the specific requirements for the most common deductible personal expenses. The tax treatments of business expenses and losses and of expenses and losses incurred in income-producing activities are covered in more detail in the later chapters of the book.

Code Sec. 212 authorizes a deduction for expenses paid or incurred in (a) the production of income, (b) the maintenance or conservation of income-producing property, and (c) the determination or litigation of a tax liability. Certain investment expenses (such as interest on a margin account and the rental fee for a safety deposit box) and expenses related to tax matters are itemized deductions for individual taxpayers. Other expenses (for example, expenses related to rental real estate) are reported on their own specific tax forms and become part of adjusted gross income. These expenses are discussed as part of either trade or business expenses or expenses incurred in the production of income.

Secs. 213 through 219 address other deductions for expenses that are primarily personal in nature. Most of these expenses are deductible *from* adjusted gross income as itemized deductions on Schedule A of Form 1040, but alimony and retirement savings deductions are "above-the-line" deductions (i.e., deductions *for* adjusted gross income). It is important to distinguish between these "above-the-line" deductions (deductions *for* AGI) and "below-the-line" deductions (deductions *from* AGI). Since a percentage of AGI is usually the limitation applied to certain itemized deductions, an error in determining AGI may affect many other entries on the tax return.

Part I introduces the medical expense itemized deduction. Personal medical expenses are deductible subject to certain limitations based on the taxpayer's adjusted gross income. Part II examines the deductibility of interest, and Part III discusses deductible taxes and charitable contributions. Only certain types of these expenses are deductible, and limitations may be placed on their degree of deductibility as well. Part

Table 4-1 Deductible Personal and Employee Expenses

I. Deductions *for* Adjusted Gross Income
   A. Reimbursed and substantiated employee business expenses
   B. Alimony payments
   C. IRA contributions within prescribed limitations
II. Deductions *from* Adjusted Gross Income (Itemized Deductions)
   A. Medical expenses in excess of 7 1/2% of AGI
      1. Doctors, dentists, and nurses
      2. Hospitals and medically required nursing home care
      3. Medical insurance premiums
      4. Prescription drugs and insulin
      5. Eyeglasses, hearing aids, and other prosthetic devices
      6. Necessary transportation and lodging for medical care
   B. Interest
      1. Qualified home mortgage interest
      2. Interest on home equity loans of less than $100,000
      3. Deductible investment interest
   C. Taxes
      1. State and local income taxes
      2. Real estate and personal property taxes
   D. Charitable contributions—Subject to 50%, 30%, and 20% of AGI limitations
      1. Cash and fair market value of property given to qualified charities within prescribed limits
      2. Ordinary income property (valued at basis)
      3. Capital-gain property (valued at basis) given to private nonoperating foundations
   E. Personal casualty and theft losses—in excess of 10% of AGI
      1. Losses exceeding $100 per occurrence from accidents, fires, tornadoes, hurricanes, embezzlement, theft, and other casualties
   F. Moving expenses
      1. Direct costs of moving household goods and family without limit
      2. Premove house-hunting trips, temporary living expenses, and costs of changing residences, within specific limits
   G. Miscellaneous expenses—in excess of 2% of AGI
      1. Unreimbursed employee business expenses, or expenses reimbursed under a nonaccountable plan
      2. Expenses to find a job in the same profession
      3. Professional dues, journal subscriptions, and professional education
      4. Tax preparation, consultation, and litigation
      5. Investment expenses

IV examines the personal casualty and theft loss deduction and the deductibility of moving expenses, and Part V presents several of the other, more commonly encountered miscellaneous itemized deductions, including unreimbursed employee business expenses and expenses related to the determination of taxes. The rules for the deductibility of alimony payments and individual retirement accounts (IRAs) are addressed in Part VI. Since most individuals are cash-basis, calendar-year taxpayers, the following discussions are based on that assumption. Any deviations from this will be specifically noted. Table 4-1 lists the most common deductions the taxpayer encounters.

I. THE MEDICAL EXPENSE DEDUCTION
(Code Section 213)

Congress permits itemized deductions for certain personal expenses and losses if they exceed certain limits. By not allowing deductions for small amounts, Congress has substantially lessened record-keeping for the taxpayer and the administrative burden on the IRS. Certain items, however, if they are very large in relation to income, could be an excessive financial burden on the taxpayer, so Congress has chosen to permit the taxpayer to deduct medical expenses that exceed a percentage of AGI as itemized deductions.

THE LAW

Sec. 213(a)—Allowance of Deduction.—There shall be allowed as a deduction the expenses paid during the taxable year, not compensated for by insurance or otherwise, for medical care of the taxpayer, his spouse, or a dependent (as defined in section 152), to the extent that such expenses exceed 7.5 percent of adjusted gross income.

☑ Example 1. Wilma Blount is a widow with two children. Her medical expenses in the current year were $3,500 and her AGI was $30,000. Wilma may deduct only $1,250 of medical expenses—the amount that exceeds $2,250 (.075 × $30,000).

Taxpayers are permitted deductions for medical expenses in excess of any insurance reimbursements that are paid during the taxable year for themselves, their spouse, and their dependents. To qualify a family member as a dependent for the medical expense deduction, both the joint return and gross-income tests are waived. If a taxpayer charges qualifying expenses on a credit card, they are considered paid when charged, regardless of when the credit card bill is paid.

Medical expenses allowed as deductions include the following:

1. Costs of diagnosis, cure, treatment, or prevention of disease;
2. Costs incurred to affect any structure or function of the body (except purely elective cosmetic surgery);
3. Costs of prescription drugs and insulin;
4. Costs of medical insurance, including supplementary medical insurance under Medicare;
5. Costs of transportation necessary to obtain medical care at 9 cents per mile; and
6. Costs of up to $50 per night for lodging away from home essential to obtaining medical care.

More specifically, the allowable medical costs include such expenses as

1. Doctors and dentists, including chiropractors, optometrists, psychologists, and Christian Science practitioners;

2. Hospitals, including nursing, therapy, laboratory, drugs, x-ray, and meals and lodging furnished as part of the medical treatment;

3. Ambulance and other transportation essential for medical care, including auto expenses, taxis, airplanes, and trains;

4. Medical, hospital, and dental insurance premiums;

5. Special appliances, such as artificial limbs, wheelchairs, eyeglasses, contact lenses, hearing aids, and false teeth;

6. Prescription medicine and drugs only, with the exception of insulin;

7. Special foods prescribed by a doctor for the treatment of a specific illness, guide dogs, and medically necessary expenditures for capital alterations to living quarters.

✓ **Example 2.** Joyce Smith became acutely ill and was rushed to the hospital for an emergency appendectomy. Her bills included $3,690 for the hospital, $2,000 for the surgeon, $400 for the anesthesiologist, and $100 for the ambulance that took her to the hospital. Joyce's AGI for the year is $20,000. All of Joyce's expenses qualify as medical expenses and may be deducted (if unreimbursed by insurance) to the extent they exceed 7.5% of her AGI. Following is an illustration of how these items would appear in the medical deduction section of Schedule A, Form 1040.

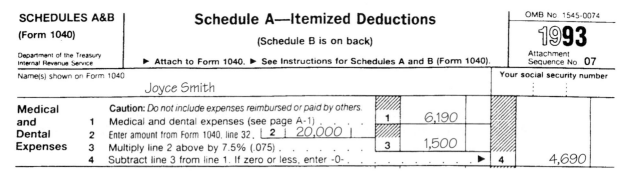

Several controversial items may come up in determining what expenses qualify as medical expenses. Expenses for items related to general health are not deductible; thus, fees for health club memberships, weight loss clinics, and smoking clinics are generally nondeductible, unless prescribed as treatment for a specific health condition. For example, an obese person may be required to lose weight before undergoing heart surgery. Cosmetic surgery that is not to correct a deformity arising from or directly related to a congenital disfigurement, personal injury, or disfiguring disease is not deductible. Only drugs prescribed by a doctor and insulin are deductible as medical expenses. Over-the-counter items such as aspirin, vitamins, cotton, bandages, and gauze are not deductible.

✓ **Example 3.** Willy Morton decided he needed to pay more attention to his general health. He joined Weight Watchers®, purchased a health club membership for $500, and started taking several types of vitamins daily. None of these items is allowed as a deduction since all are for general health only.

Transportation required for medical care—including such items as cab fare, parking, tolls, and actual auto expenses—is normally deductible. As an alternative to actual auto expense, a taxpayer may deduct 9 cents per mile. If the taxpayer travels to another locality for medical treatment, the costs of travel will be deductible if the primary purpose is to obtain medical care and if it is reasonable for the taxpayer to go to that location.

☑ **Example 4.** Troy Brown had to visit his doctor every other week to have his blood pressure and hemoglobin monitored. The distance was 20 miles round trip, he paid a $.60 toll, and parking was generally $1.00. Troy took the standard 9 cents per mile deduction. Troy's total deductible cost for 26 trips was $88.40 (26 × [(.09 × 20) + .60 + 1.00]).

Meals and lodging while a person is hospitalized are deductible as part of the costs of hospitalization, but meals the person eats during outpatient treatment are not. Lodging away from home for an outpatient is deductible up to $50 per night per person if the lodging is not extravagant and if there is no other personal nonmedical benefit involved. The lodging for a companion is also deductible if the companion is necessary to facilitate travel (e.g., a parent accompanying a child).

☑ **Example 5.** Wilson Morris took his dependent elderly father to a special Alzheimer's treatment center at the Mayo Clinic. The trip was 400 miles each way by auto, and during treatment they stayed 10 nights in a hotel that charged $75 per day for their double room. Their meals while at the clinic cost $530. Since Wilson's father is his dependent, Wilson may deduct $72 (.09 × 400 × 2) for the transportation to and from Rochester and $750 for the room since that is less than $50 per day per person for him and his father. The cost of meals is not deductible.

☑ **Example 6.** Augusta Allen decided to go to Arizona to visit friends. On her way there she became ill and was taken from the plane to the hospital. She stayed three days in the hospital, stayed another week with her friends, and returned home. Her plane fare was $425, her hospital bill was $3,250, and the ambulance was $150. Augusta may deduct the hospital and ambulance bills, but may not deduct the $425 plane fare since medical treatment was not the primary motivation for the trip.

If the taxpayer's home is remodeled or renovated for medical reasons, the expense may or may not be fully deductible. If the renovations are to a rental dwelling (i.e., one not owned by the taxpayer) or if the remodeling is to accommodate a physically handicapped individual (e.g., wheelchair ramps, widened doorways, flashing lights for deaf individuals), they are fully deductible. Other capital expenditures primarily for medical reasons (e.g., elevators, or a whirlpool for a severe arthritic) are deductible only to the extent that the cost exceeds the value added to the dwelling. If the capital item qualifies as a medical expense, the costs of operating and maintaining it are also deductible.

☑ **Example 7.** Maureen O'Riley had to use a wheelchair to get around due to a broken hip that would not heal properly. She had to remodel her bathroom, at a cost of $2,000, so that the shower and sink could accommodate a wheelchair. Maureen's doctor also directed her to install a spa, at a cost of $1,600, so that she could have therapy for her hip. The cost of the bathroom remodeling is fully deductible, but because the addition of the spa added $1,000 to the value of the house, only $600 of its cost ($1,600 cost − $1,000 increase in value) can be deducted.

All costs of maintaining a qualifying person in a nursing home or other institution are deductible if the primary purpose is for medical care, not for personal convenience. If the primary purpose is personal, only the separate costs for medical services are deductible; costs for meals and lodging are personal and not deductible.

☑ **Example 8.** Greg Lawrence convinced his mother to stay in an unskilled nursing facility while he went on an extended vacation. Although she was generally able to take care of herself, her home was in an area where there had been several robberies and he did not want to worry about her safety while he was gone. The nursing home cost $1,700 for the month ($1,300 for room and board and $400 for nursing and other medical services). Greg's mother is independently wealthy and pays all her own expenses. She may treat only the $400 as an allowable medical expense. If she could not care for herself, all $1,700 would be deductible as a medical expense.

If a taxpayer receives an insurance reimbursement for medical expenses incurred, the deduction is limited to the net unreimbursed amount. If the reimbursement is received in a year subsequent to the year in which the medical expense is paid, the taxpayer must look back to see how the medical expense was treated in the year of payment. If the taxpayer used the standard deduction in the year the expense was paid, no tax benefit was received from the medical expense and the reimbursement may be ignored; it is not income. If the taxpayer itemized deductions in the year the expense was paid, however, the taxpayer must declare income to the extent of the original tax benefit received—that is, the least of (1) the reimbursement amount, (2) the excess of itemized deductions over the standard deduction, or (3) the actual medical deduction. The application of the tax benefit rule was discussed more fully in Chapter 3.

☑ **Example 9.** Alice Gold paid $4,200 for allowable medical expenses last year. This year she received a reimbursement of $1,500 from her insurance company. Alice's total itemized deductions were $6,000, her deductible medical expenses were only $600, and her standard deduction was $3,700. Alice must declare $600 of the reimbursement as income on this year's return.

TAX TIP

By timing elective medical treatment and the payment of medical bills, taxpayers may "bunch" their medical expenses into a particular tax year to increase the likelihood that their total expenses will exceed 7.5% of AGI. By so doing, they may be able to deduct a portion of the total expense.

REVIEW I

1. During the current year William Ray had the following medical expenses: hospital, $3,200; doctor, $1,200; prescription drugs, $320; aspirin and vitamins, $90; eyeglasses and hearing aid, $750; transportation to Arizona for a rest, $450; and a tennis court for general exercise, $6,000. If the tennis court increased his home's value by $5,000 and Ray's AGI is $62,000, what is his allowable medical expense deduction?
   (a) $0
   (b) $820
   (c) $1,270
   (d) $2,270

2. Arlo was the sole support of his mother Esther. In the current year, because he didn't want her to stay alone in his home, Arlo paid $7,500 for nursing home care for Esther during the time he took an extended European tour. The costs were broken down as follows: meals, $1,250; room, $4,000; nursing care, $1,500; doctor's visits, $500; and prescription drugs, $250. Arlo also paid doctor and dentist bills of $6,700 for himself, for which his insurance company reimbursed him $3,200. What is Arlo's allowable medical deduction if his AGI is $36,000?
   (a) $14,200
   (b) $9,550
   (c) $6,350
   (d) $3,050

3. Mary Andrews is a single mother with two dependent daughters. One of the daughters was born with liver disease and needed a liver transplant. Mary took her daughter to Pittsburgh for the transplant. The cost of their transportation was $2,000. The daughter's hospital and doctor's bills were $125,000, of which $110,000 was paid by Mary's insurance. Mary also traveled between Pittsburgh and her home to visit with her other daughter briefly four times, at a total cost of $1,100. What is Mary's medical expense deduction if her adjusted gross income was $22,000?
   (a) $15,350
   (b) $26,350
   (c) $13,350
   (d) $18,350

4. Morgan Faircloth received a $3,000 reimbursement from his insurance company for doctor and hospital bills that he paid last year. Morgan's total itemized deductions were $4,700, of which $3,700 were for medical expenses. If Morgan's standard deduction was $3,600 last year, how much income must he report due to the $3,000 insurance reimbursement?
   (a) $3,000
   (b) $1,300
   (c) $3,700
   (d) $3,100

Answers are on page 4-8.

II INTEREST DEDUCTIONS

When Congress passed the Tax Reform Act of 1986, it repealed the deduction for personal (consumer) interest, subject to a four-year phaseout period. In doing so, Congress created several classes of interest, other than personal interest, that would be deductible subject to certain restrictions. Three of these classes are (1) interest incurred in a trade or business (but *not* as an employee), (2) investment interest, and (3) qualified residence interest. Business interest normally is fully deductible against the income from the business on Schedule C and is not discussed here. Investment interest and the interest on qualified residential property are deductible within certain limits as itemized deductions on Schedule A of Form 1040.

QUALIFIED RESIDENCE INTEREST

THE LAW

Sec. 163(h) Disallowance of Deduction for Personal Interest.—(1) In General.—In the case of a taxpayer other than a corporation, no deduction shall be allowed under this chapter for personal interest paid or accrued during the taxable year.
(2) Personal Interest.—For purposes of this subsection, the term "personal interest" means any interest allowable as a deduction under this chapter other than—
    (A) interest paid or accrued on indebtedness incurred or continued in connection with the conduct of a trade or business (other than the trade or business of performing services as an employee),
    (B) any investment interest . . .
    (D) any qualified residence interest (within the meaning of paragraph (3) . . .
(3) Qualified Residence Interest.—For purposes of this subsection—
    (A) In General.—The term "qualified residence interest" means any interest which is paid or accrued during the taxable year on—
        (i) acquisition indebtedness with respect to any qualified residence of the taxpayer, or
        (ii) home equity indebtedness with respect to any qualified residence of the taxpayer.

ANSWERS TO REVIEW I

1. (b) Ray's hospital, doctor, prescription drug, eyeglass, and hearing aid costs are his only deductible medical costs. Thus, his allowable deduction is $820 [$3,200 + $1,200 + $320 + $750 − .075(62,000)]. The transportation to Arizona and the tennis courts are for general health purposes and are not deductible.
2. (d) Since the use of the nursing home was for his convenience, Arlo may deduct only the medical costs related to his mother's stay in the nursing home; he is not permitted to deduct the costs of room and meals. His deduction is [$1,500 + $500 + $250 + $6,700 − $3,200 − .075($36,000)] = $3,050.
3. (a) Mary had $15,350 [$17,000 − .075($22,000)] of deductible medical expenses. The $1,100 for her own trips back home are not deductible.
4. (b) Of the reimbursement, $1,100 is income. This is the smallest of the reimbursement amount ($3,000), the medical deduction ($3,700), and the itemized deductions in excess of the standard deduction ($4,700 − $3,600 = $1,100).

> (B) *Acquisition Indebtedness.—*
>   (i) *In General.—*The term "acquisition indebtedness" means any indebtedness which—
>   (I) is incurred in acquiring, constructing, or substantially improving any qualified residence of the taxpayer, and
>   (II) is secured by such residence. . . .
> (4) (A)(i) *In General.—*The term "qualified residence" means—
>   (I) the principal residence . . . and
>   (II) 1 other residence of the taxpayer. . . .

Even though home mortgage interest is generally considered personal interest, the repeal of this particular itemized deduction has never been seriously considered. Thus, Congress excluded this interest from the general repeal of personal interest by designating it as "qualified residence" interest. The law provides reasonably generous limitations on its deductibility that are designed to curb excessive abuse of the residential interest deduction.

To be deductible, the interest must be qualified residence interest. Qualified residence interest may be either *acquisition indebtedness* or *home equity indebtedness* on the taxpayer's qualified residence(s). *Acquisition indebtedness* is any debt incurred to acquire, construct, or improve the taxpayer's principal residence and up to one secondary residence. For acquisitions after October 13, 1987, total acquisition indebtedness is limited to $1,000,000 ($500,000 for married-filing separately). Acquisition indebtedness incurred on or before October 13, 1987, is not subject to limitation. However, any pre-October 14, 1987, debt reduces the $1,000,000 limitation for determining qualifying post-October 13, 1987, debt. The amount of acquisition debt outstanding is determined for each year that interest is paid.

✓ **Example 10.** In 1975 Marlo White purchased a home for $3.5 million, on which she took out a $2.5 million mortgage. Marlo may deduct all the interest, since the $1,000,000 limit does not apply. If Marlo had purchased the home after October 13, 1987, she would be limited to interest deductions on only $1 million of the debt principal. Marlo's brother, John, however, purchased a home for $1,200,000 on December 15, 1985, financing $950,000 of the purchase price. On January 3, 1993, he purchased a condominium that cost $200,000, and took out a $150,000 mortgage on it. The balance on the mortgage on the first home is $920,000 in 1993. Thus, John can deduct the interest on only $80,000 of the condominium mortgage, since the $920,000 balance on the pre-1987 loan reduces the $1,000,000 limit.

TAX TIP

Taxpayers may want to limit the down payment and obtain as much financing as possible on the purchase of a residence to keep cash in reserve for future purchases, since the interest on the mortgage (of $1 million or less) is fully deductible.

Home equity indebtedness is defined as loans secured by the taxpayer's qualifying residence(s) that are *not* acquisition indebtedness. Home equity indebtedness cannot exceed the lesser of $100,000 or the difference between the fair market value of the qualifying residences and the acquisition indebtedness. This limit applies to post-October 13, 1987, indebtedness. Home equity loans taken out prior to October 14, 1987, are considered part of acquisition debt that is not subject to any limitation. The total post-October 13, 1987, qualified residence interest cannot exceed $1.1 million—$1 million in acquisition debt and $100,000 in home equity debt.

✓ **Example 11.** Joyce Smith purchased her home in 1970 for $120,000, secured by a $100,000 mortgage. The home has a current value of $300,000 and the mortgage balance is $20,000. In the current year, she paid $800 of interest on this loan balance. Joyce takes out a $150,000 home equity loan to purchase a Rolls Royce, on which she paid $15,000 of interest in the current year. Joyce is able to deduct interest on only $100,000 of the home equity loan—the lesser of $100,000 or $280,000 (the home's $300,000 fair market value less the remaining $20,000 acquisition mortgage). She must prorate the interest between the deductible and nondeductible portions, and as a result she may deduct only $10,000 of the home equity loan interest. Below we can see how this item would appear in the interest section of Schedule A, Form 1040.

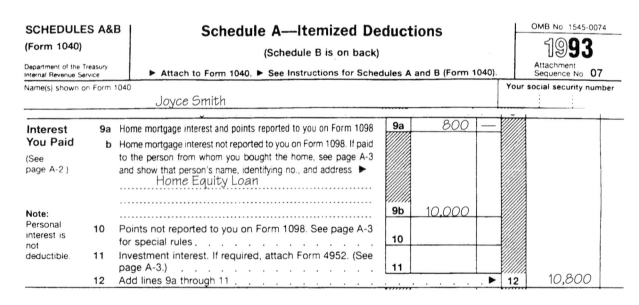

Note that the use to which the funds are put is irrelevant as long as the home equity loan is secured by a qualifying residence.

If a taxpayer refinances a home after October 13, 1987, the refinancing will be acquisition indebtedness to the extent that it does not exceed the principal of the refinanced debt. Additionally, the proceeds must be used to pay off the old debt directly.

TAX TIP

The taxpayer may use the proceeds of a home equity loan for purely personal purchases, such as an automobile, and thus deduct the interest up to the allowable limits.

A taxpayer may have two qualifying residences—one must be the taxpayer's principal residence and the second a residence designated by the taxpayer that meets ownership and use tests. To qualify as a residence, the property must provide sleeping, cooking, and bathing facilities. Thus, boats and motor homes may qualify as second residences if they are so equipped. Normally, the second residence must be used by the taxpayer for at least 14 days each year or 10% of its total usage, if longer, to be so designated. If, however, the taxpayer derives no rental income from the property, it may be designated as a second residence even if no personal use is made of the property.

Example 12. Myrna Collins lives in a home in North Dakota but keeps a Florida condominium for winter vacations. She normally uses the condominium three or four months per year. During the current year, she was unable to use the condominium due to an illness in the family. If she did not rent out the property at any time during the year, she may still designate the condominium as her second residence.

If the taxpayer is required to pay interest in advance (i.e., points) to secure a mortgage for the *purchase* of his or her principal residence, the points may be deducted in the year paid. Other prepaid interest, however, must generally be capitalized and amortized over the life of the loan.

Example 13. Jacob Wright purchased a new home for $150,000, secured by a $120,000 first mortgage. To obtain the best mortgage terms, Jacob had to pay 2 1/2 "points" ($3,000) up front on the mortgage. Jacob may deduct the $3,000 as points if the home qualifies as his principal residence.

Only points on the *purchase* of a principal residence qualify for an immediate deduction. Points paid to *refinance* a principal residence to take advantage of changes in interest rates generally must be amortized over the life of the loan. There is a possibility, however, that points incurred on the refinancing of a short-term balloon mortgage that was part of the original residence purchase may be deductible. Points paid for the purchaser of the residence by the seller are considered a cost of selling the property and reduce any gain (or increase any loss) realized on the sale. They may not be deducted as interest.

TAX TIP

A taxpayer purchasing a residence must be careful to pay the points separately rather than allowing the mortgage company to reduce the loan proceeds by the points. In this latter case, the taxpayer is denied a deduction for the points and *must* amortize them over the life of the mortgage, even if they were paid to purchase the principal residence.

INVESTMENT INTEREST LIMITATIONS

Taxpayers are permitted to deduct as an itemized deduction any interest incurred to purchase or carry investment property. Investment property is not the same as property used in a trade or business. Interest incurred in a trade or business is normally deductible from the income earned by the business. Though the holding of rental properties is generally not considered a trade or business, the interest on debt incurred to hold the rental property is treated as debt incurred in a trade or business and is deductible from the rental income.

THE LAW

Sec. 163(d)(1)—In General.—In the case of a taxpayer other than a corporation, the amount allowed as a deduction under this chapter for investment interest for any taxable year shall not exceed the net investment income of the taxpayer for the taxable year.

Investment interest does not include qualified residence interest, personal interest, interest on rental properties, which currently* are always deemed passive activities, or interest to purchase or carry tax-exempt securities. Interest incurred to purchase stocks or bonds (e.g., on margin accounts) or other investments, such as raw land, would qualify. Deductibility is limited, however, to net investment income. Net investment income is the excess of investment income over investment expenses. Qualifying investment income is the gross income from investment property plus the net gains from the sale of investment property, in excess of net capital gains from investment property. Taxpayers may include all or part of their net capital gain in net investment income if they exclude that amount from net capital gains subject to the 28% capital gains tax rate.

Investment expenses are the expense items, except interest, related to the investment income property. Any interest disallowed as a current deduction may be carried forward and deducted in the succeeding year(s) subject to the same limitations. Form 4952 is used to determine the investment interest deduction.

Example 14. Andrew Jones's income from investments for this year is as follows:

IBM stock	$ 2,000 dividends
GM bonds	1,000 interest
Gain on the sale of AT&T stock	10,000 net gain

Andrew has a margin account on which he paid $2,400 interest and several pieces of land on which he paid mortgage interest of $11,000. Andrew has $13,000 of net investment income this year but $13,400 of interest expense. Andrew's current deduction is limited to $13,000. The $400 interest deduction that is disallowed may be carried over to the succeeding year. If the $10,000 of net gain on the sale of AT & T stock were capital gain, Andrew would only be able to deduct $3,000 of interest expense unless he forgos the 28% capital gains tax rate on all or part of the $10,000 capital gain.

*For changes in the tax law effective for tax years beginning in 1994, see Appendix J.

✓ **Example 15.** In the current year, Joyce Smith has $30,000 of investment interest expense and only $14,000 of net investment income. Joyce has excess investment interest expense of $16,000, and she may deduct none of this in excess of the $14,000 regular deduction. The $16,000 excess is carried forward to the succeeding year. Below we see this information for Joyce, as it would appear on Schedule A, Form 1040, along with the information from Example 11.

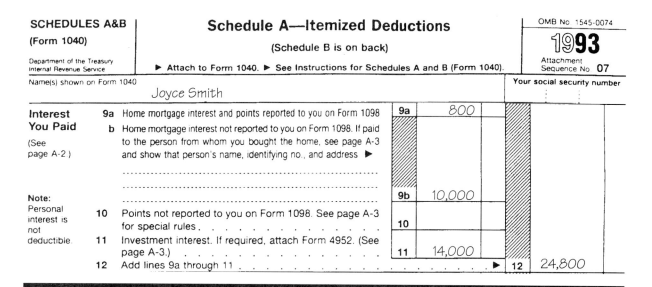

TAX TIP

A taxpayer who expects to sell some investment property at a gain taxed at ordinary income rates should consider accelerating the sale into the current tax year if he or she has excess investment interest expense. The otherwise disallowed excess investment interest expense can offset all or part of the recognized gain, relieving some or all of the tax due on the sale. Thus, the taxpayer has access to the sale proceeds at an earlier date without experiencing adverse tax consequences.

OTHER PERSONAL INTEREST

The Tax Reform Act of 1986 repealed the deduction for personal (consumer) interest for tax years beginning after 1990. Personal interest includes interest on loans to acquire personal autos, household furnishings, appliances, student loans, loans on life insurance policies, interest on the underpayment of taxes, and interest on credit cards. No personal interest is allowed as a deduction in 1991 and beyond.

✓ **Example 16.** In the current year John Allen paid $250 interest on a loan to purchase his personal auto, $190 in credit card interest, and $30 interest on a loan to purchase a television set. John may take no deduction for personal interest since it is after 1991 and all personal interest deductions are denied.

REVIEW II

1. In 1989 Reginald Trump purchased a home for $2,500,000. During the current year his average mortgage balance was $1,400,000. He also took out a $200,000 home equity loan to purchase a yacht. If Reginald paid $140,000 interest on the mortgage loan and $24,000 interest on the home equity loan, what is his qualified residence interest deduction?
   (a) $100,000
   (b) $112,000
   (c) $140,000
   (d) $164,000

2. Albert and Alberta Retiree own a home in Maine and a motor home that they use to travel and live in during the winter months. In the current year they paid $1,400 in interest on their home and $700 interest on the motor home. What is their qualified residence interest?
   (a) $0
   (b) $700
   (c) $1,400
   (d) $2,100

3. Ernie had a $6,000 noncapital gain on the sale of some securities, $20,200 income from investments with related expenses of $19,100, and interest expense related to all his investments of $16,200. How much may Ernie deduct as investment interest expense?
   (a) $0
   (b) $1,100
   (c) $7,100
   (d) $16,200

4. Joanna has the following interest expense for the current year: home mortgage, $1,200; auto loan, $425; student loan, $67; and credit card interest, $420. What is her interest deduction?
   (a) $0
   (b) $1,200
   (c) $1,382
   (d) $2,112

Answers are on page 4-16.

III DEDUCTIONS FOR TAXES AND CHARITABLE CONTRIBUTIONS
(Code Sections 164, and 170)

DEDUCTION FOR TAXES

Taxpayers may also deduct other specified expenditures as itemized deductions on Schedule A of Form 1040. One relief measure for taxpayers is the deduction provided for income and property taxes levied by another taxing jurisdiction. The Tax Reform Act of 1986 did away with the deduction for state and local sales taxes, however.

THE LAW

Sec. 164(a)—General Rule.—Except as otherwise provided in this section, the following taxes shall be allowed as a deduction for the taxable year within which paid or accrued:

(1) State and local, and foreign, real property taxes.

(2) State and local personal property taxes.

(3) State and local, and foreign, income, war profits, and excess profits taxes.

A taxpayer is permitted to deduct, as an itemized deduction, state and local income taxes and property taxes related to real or personal property, not held for business or income production, that are paid during the tax year. If property taxes are levied on business or certain investment-related assets, the taxpayer generally deducts them from the related income in arriving at adjusted gross income. Though foreign, state, and local *income* taxes may be related to business or investment *income,* a taxpayer may deduct only income taxes as an itemized deduction. (There are, however, provisions whereby a taxpayer may take a *credit* for foreign income taxes.) Note that personal property taxes levied on either tangible or intangible personal property are deductible only if they are levied by a state or local government. Foreign personal property taxes are not deductible.

☑ **Example 17.** Joyce Smith had $300 withheld from her wages for state income taxes; she paid property taxes of $575 on her home; she purchased a car, on which she paid $230 in sales tax; and she received dividends on foreign investments, on which $25 was withheld for taxes. Joyce may include in her itemized deductions $900 in taxes ($575 + $300 + $25). The sales tax is no longer deductible. These items would appear on Form 1040, Schedule A as follows:

SCHEDULES A&B (Form 1040) Department of the Treasury Internal Revenue Service	Schedule A—Itemized Deductions (Schedule B is on back) ▶ Attach to Form 1040. ▶ See Instructions for Schedules A and B (Form 1040).		OMB No 1545-0074 **1993** Attachment Sequence No 07
Name(s) shown on Form 1040 Joyce Smith			Your social security number
Taxes You Paid (See page A-1.)	5 State and local income taxes	5	300
	6 Real estate taxes (see page A-2)	6	575
	7 Other taxes. List—include personal property taxes ▶ Tax on foreign investment	7	25
	8 Add lines 5 through 7 . . . . ▶	8	900

In order for a property tax to be deductible, it must be levied on the *value* of the property. If the tax includes any amount characterized as a fee for services (e.g., garbage collection or sewer use), that portion is nondeductible. Special assessments on real property are deductible only if they do not increase the value of the property. Thus, assessments for repairs, maintenance, and interest would be deductible, while assessments for street lights or sidewalks would be nondeductible additions to the basis of the property.

☑ **Example 18.** Jeremy Allen's itemized property tax bill of $2,300 includes $500 for the cost of the sewer pipe extension that runs in front of his home and $200 for twice-weekly garbage collection. Jeremy also pays $125 to license his auto because it is a full-sized auto weighing 4,000 pounds. Jeremy may include only $1,600 of his property tax bill as an itemized deduction. The sewer assessment must be added to the basis of the house, and the garbage fee is for a service rendered. Auto license fees based on *weight* are not deductible; if a portion of the fee were based on the auto's *value,* that portion would be deductible as a tax.

TAX TIP

Often, cash-basis taxpayers can time the payment of their property tax so that they may deduct two years' taxes in one tax year; this is helpful if the taxpayer's total itemized deductions are very close to the amount of his or her standard deduction. By doing this, the taxpayer may benefit from itemizing one year and taking the standard deduction the next.

If a taxpayer sells or buys a residence during the year, property taxes must be prorated on a daily basis between the buyer and the seller, with the day of purchase allocated to the buyer. This allocation is required regardless of which party actually pays the taxes. An adjustment in the purchase price or selling price is required to achieve the proper allocation.

Example 19. Sally Withers purchased a home on December 1, 1993, for $175,000. She paid the entire annual property taxes of $3,650 as part of the purchase agreement. Sally is allowed to deduct only $310 [(31/365) × $3,650] as property tax. The $3,340 balance must be added to the purchase price of the house.

The Tax Reform Act of 1986 repealed the itemized deduction for state and local sales taxes. Sales taxes paid for business and investment property may be treated as part of the purchase price and included in the taxpayer's basis.

Cash-basis taxpayers normally deduct state and local income taxes in the year paid. Most taxpayers who are not self-employed have income taxes withheld from their wages and may treat the withholding as taxes paid, deducting them for the year in which they are withheld. Estimated tax payments made during the tax year and any tax deficiencies paid during the current year for a prior year's tax are also currently deductible. (Note that federal income taxes paid or withheld are not a deductible item on the federal income tax return.)

Example 20. Anna Ramirez had $500 of state taxes withheld from her wages, made an additional estimated tax payment of $200 due to self-employment income, and

---

ANSWERS TO REVIEW II

1. (b) Reginald's deduction is limited to the interest related to a $1,000,000 mortgage and a $100,000 home equity loan; thus, the deduction is limited to $100,000 plus $12,000 of interest.
2. (d) Albert and Alberta may deduct all $2,100 of interest since both items qualify as personal residences.
3. (c) Ernie has net investment income of $7,100 [6,000 + (20,200 − 19,100)].
4. (b) Joanna may deduct only her home mortgage interest.

paid a $250 state tax deficiency for a prior tax year. Anna may take an itemized deduction of $950 ($500 + $200 + $250) as taxes paid in the current year.

Many taxpayers have too much money withheld from their wages for state and local income taxes and receive a refund when they file their income tax returns. If the taxpayer used the standard deduction in the year the taxes were withheld, the refund is not income. If, however, the taxpayer itemized deductions, income is recognized in an amount equal to the lesser of the refund or the amount by which itemized deductions exceed the standard deduction. The amount of income recognized is another application of the tax benefit rule discussed in greater detail in Chapter 3.

☑ **Example 21.** Sheila Craft had $600 in state taxes withheld last year, and when she filed her state tax return for last year, she was entitled to a $75 refund. Sheila filed a Form 1040A for federal income tax purposes last year. Since she did not itemize last year, she may ignore the refund. If Sheila had itemized, she would have to recognize income based on the tax benefit rule (i.e., to the extent she benefited from the deduction for the taxes last year ($600) up to the refunded amount of $75).

CHARITABLE CONTRIBUTION DEDUCTIONS

The Tax Code gives taxpayers an incentive to support charitable organizations by allowing them to deduct, within certain limits, the contributions they make to qualifying organizations as itemized deductions.

THE LAW

Sec. 170(a)—Allowance of Deduction.—(1)—General Rule.—There shall be allowed as a deduction any charitable contribution (as defined in subsection (c)) payment of which is made within the taxable year. . . .

To be deductible, contributions must be made to qualifying charitable organizations, which include

1. A state, a United States possession, a political subdivision of a state or possession, the United States, or the District of Columbia;

2. Corporations, trusts, funds, or foundations organized under the laws of one of the states, the District of Columbia, the United States, or any United States possession, if the organization operates exclusively for religious, scientific, literary, or educational purposes or for the prevention of cruelty to children or animals;

3. A veteran's organization;

4. Nonprofit volunteer fire or civil defense organizations;

5. A fraternal society operating under the lodge system, if contributions are used for acceptable charitable purposes; and

6. Nonprofit cemeteries, if funds are used for general perpetual maintenance.

The IRS publishes a list of qualifying organizations in the *Cumulative List of Organizations,* although an organization is not required to be listed to qualify. Most charitable contributions are made to public charities, which include organizations such as churches, universities and other tax-exempt educational institutions, hospitals and other tax-exempt medical organizations, units of government, and private foundations that distribute their contributions to public charities. Veterans' and fraternal organizations, cemetery associations, and private nonoperating foundations (those that do not distribute all income to public charities) are private charities. Donations to public and private charities are deductible, although different limitations may apply. Deductions are not allowed, however, for contributions made directly or indirectly to or for the benefit of individuals.

✓ **Example 22.** Joyce Smith donated $300 to her church, $250 to United Way and $140 to the Kiwanis Club—$40 was designated for their shelter for battered children and $100 was designated for dialysis treatments for another member. Joyce may deduct $590 on her tax return ($300 + $250 + $40); the $100 designated for the other member is disallowed. These items would appear on Schedule A, Form 1040, as follows:

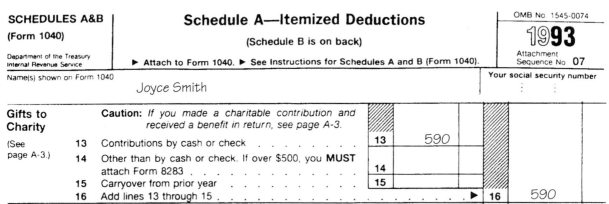

While donations of cash and property are the usual form of charitable contribution, out-of-pocket expenses incurred by the taxpayer in performing duties for qualifying charitable organizations are also deductible. These costs would include uniforms, uniform maintenance, transportation, and travel expenses incurred primarily for charitable purposes. A taxpayer who uses a personal vehicle for charitable purposes may deduct the actual costs incurred (limited to gas and oil) or a mileage rate of 12 cents per mile. Costs of parking and tolls may also be deducted under either method of determining auto expense.

✓ **Example 23.** Judy Golightly was a leader for a Brownie troop. She paid $75 for her uniform; drove a total of 500 miles during the year for troop activities (total gas cost was $40), and bought supplies costing $200 for the troop. She may deduct the following as a charitable contribution:

Cost of uniform	$ 75
Transportation (.12 × 500)	60
Supplies	200
	$335

> **THE LAW**
>
>
>
> Sec. 170(b) Percentage Limitations.—(1) Individuals.—In the case of an individual, the deduction provided in subsection (a) shall be limited as provided in the succeeding subparagraphs.
> (A) General Rule.—Any charitable contribution to—...
>   (i)   a church or a convention or association of churches...
>   (viii)   any organization described in section 509(a)(2) or (3),
> shall be allowed to the extent that the aggregate of such contributions does not exceed 50 percent of the taxpayer's contribution base for the taxable year,...

An individual is subject to a complex set of limitations, depending upon the type of property donated and the classification of the recipient. Overall, however, the individual taxpayer may not take a current deduction for cash and property that exceeds 50% of AGI. Any charitable contribution that exceeds the 50% limitation may be carried forward for five years.

The amount of a taxpayer's charitable contribution is usually measured by the fair market value of the property at the date of donation. There are several exceptions to this valuation, however:

1. If the taxpayer donates property that would yield ordinary income if the property were sold (e.g., inventory or capital assets held for one year or less), the donation's value is its fair market value reduced by this ordinary income potential.

2. If the taxpayer donates appreciated long-term capital-gain property (capital assets—for example, most personal and investment assets—held for more than one year) or Sec. 1231 property (discussed in a later chapter), the fair market value of the donation *must* be reduced by this appreciation if the property (a) is tangible personal property that is put to an unrelated use by the charity or (b) is donated to a private nonoperating foundation.

Example 24. Violet Spencer owns a clothing store and donates old stock to local charities several times a year. During the current year Violet donated clothing that cost $2,000 and had a fair market of $3,000. If Violet sold the clothing, she would have $1,000 of ordinary income. Thus, she must reduce the $3,000 fair market value of the donation by the $1,000 potential income. She may deduct only $2,000 as a charitable contribution. If the clothing had a fair market value of only $1,500, her deduction would have been limited to that amount.

Example 25. Ned Johnson donated to the Salvation Army a boat with a fair market value of $45,000 and a basis of $35,000. The boat was long-term capital-gain property, that is, a capital asset held longer than one year. The Salvation Army could not use the boat, so it was immediately sold. Ned must reduce his charitable contribution deduction by the $10,000 appreciation since the property was tangible personal property that the charity put to an unrelated use.

>
> ### TAX TIP
>
> Taxpayers can avoid gain recognition, and thus the corresponding taxes, on donations of appreciated property to qualifying charities. In doing so, they benefit from reduced taxes in two ways: They pay no tax on the appreciation of the property, and they take a deduction for the charitable contribution at fair market value.

>
> ### THE LAW
>
> *Sec. 170(b)(1)(B) Other Contributions.—Any charitable contribution other than a charitable contribution to which subparagraph (A) applies shall be allowed to the extent that the aggregate of such contributions does not exceed the lesser of*
> *(i) 30 percent of the taxpayer's contribution base for the taxable year, or*
> *(ii) the excess of 50 percent of the taxpayer's contribution base for the taxable year over the amount of charitable contributions allowable under subparagraph (A)....*

If a taxpayer makes a charitable contribution of capital-gain property to other than a private nonoperating foundation, the fair market value deduction is limited to no more than 30% of AGI. In the determination of this 30% limitation, however, property subject to the 50% limitation must be considered first. (Note that this 30% limitation does not apply to the long-term capital-gain property given to a public charity and put to an unrelated use. The fair market value of the deduction for this property *must* be reduced by the long-term capital gain as discussed above and illustrated in Example 25, and is subject to the 50% limitation as a result.)

Example 26. Wanda Adams gave the museum a painting that has a fair market value of $20,000 and a basis of $4,000. She also gave $10,000 cash to her church and $15,000 cash to the Heart Fund. Wanda's AGI is $60,000. She may deduct $30,000 (50% × $60,000) as follows:

$10,000 cash to the church
$15,000 cash to the Heart Fund
$5,000 of the $20,000 fair market value of the painting to the museum

The remaining $15,000 of the museum donation that could not be deducted in the current year may be carried forward for a maximum of five years. If Wanda had no cash contributions, she would be able to deduct only $18,000 of the painting's value (30% × $60,000) due to the 30% limitation on donations of capital-gain property. In this latter case, she could carry the $2,000 balance forward and deduct it in a subsequent year.

A taxpayer may substitute the 50% overall limitation for the 30% of AGI limitation imposed on appreciated capital-gain property if the fair market value of the property is reduced by the capital gain that would be recognized if the property were sold. If this alternative is chosen in a particular year, it applies to all capital-gain property donated in that year.

☑ **Example 27.** Jim Thomas has stock with a basis of $19,000 that he donates to a local university. Its fair market value is only $20,000, and Jim's AGI is $40,000. If Jim reduces the fair market value of the stock donation by the $1,000 appreciation, he may deduct the entire $19,000 currently since the 50% of AGI limitation is $20,000. If he does not reduce the value, he may deduct only $12,000 currently (30% × $40,000); he may, however, carry the $8,000 balance forward and deduct it in a subsequent year.

TAX TIP

If the taxpayer expects a higher tax rate in the next year, the carryforward could be preferable to the reduction in the value of the charitable contribution of capital-gain property subject to the 30% limitation.

Donations to private nonoperating foundations are restricted even further. Private nonoperating foundations are those that do not receive contributions from the general public and do not meet certain requirements regarding distribution of income and/or contributions. A 30% limit applies to cash and ordinary income property donated to a private nonoperating foundation. Additionally, contributions of capital-gain property (after the *required* reduction in value for any appreciation) are limited to the lesser of 20% of the taxpayer's AGI or 30% of AGI less all capital-gain property given to public charities and subject to the 30% of AGI limitation. This 20% limitation is applied *after* both the 50% and 30% limitations are considered. However, contributions in excess of the 20% and 30% limits may be carried forward for five years. Figure 4-1 is a diagram of the charitable contributions limitations and their priority of application.

☑ **Example 28.** Ted Alonzo, a retired stockbroker, has an AGI of $50,000. He donates $10,000 to a local college library and gives 200 shares of stock, worth $15,000 and with a basis of $12,000, to a private nonoperating foundation. Ted may deduct the $10,000 cash donation to the library and $10,000 of the $12,000 allowable donation to the private nonoperating foundation. In this situation, Ted's charitable contribution deduction is limited to $20,000 (rather than $25,000 [50% × $50,000 AGI]) due to the 20% limit imposed on capital-gain property donated to a private nonoperating foundation. The $2,000 balance may be carried forward for five years. (Note that Ted *must* reduce the fair market value of the stock by the capital gain since it is given to a private nonoperating foundation.) Information on the stock donation is shown on Form 8283 in Figure 4-2.

If a taxpayer claims property contributions with a total value exceeding $500, he or she must file Form 8283, giving details of the donated property. If the deduction claimed for one item, or a group of similar items (except publicly traded securities), has a value of more than $5,000, an appraisal summary must also be completed as part of Form 8283, as shown in Figure 4-2.

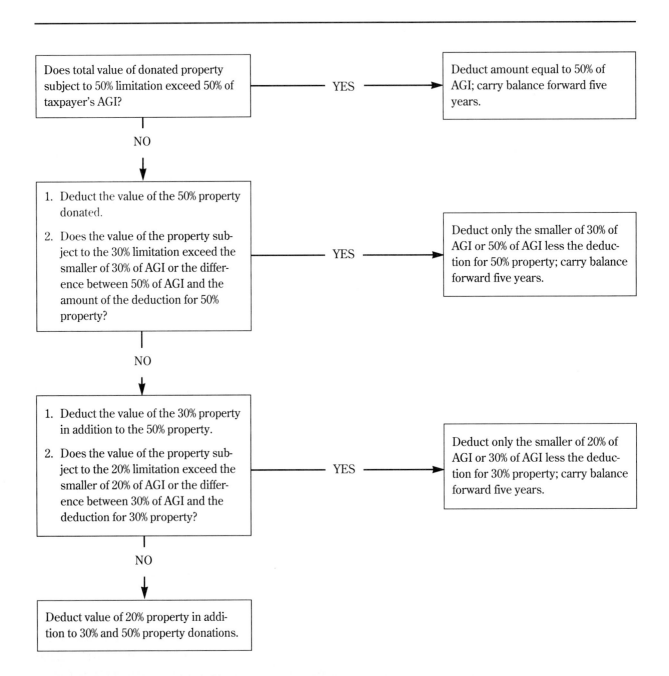

Figure 4-1 Charitable Contribution Limitations

Form **8283** (Rev. March 1990) Department of the Treasury Internal Revenue Service	**Noncash Charitable Contributions** ▶ Attach to your tax return if the total claimed deduction for all property contributed exceeds $500. ▶ See separate Instructions.	OMB No. 1545-0908 Expires 2-28-93 Attachment Sequence No. **55**
Name(s) shown on your income tax return Ted Alonzo		Identification number

Note: *Compute the amount of your contribution deduction before completing Form 8283. (See your tax return instructions.)*

Section A — Include in Section A **only** items (or groups of similar items) for which you claimed a deduction of $5,000 or less per item or group, and certain publicly traded securities (see Instructions).

Part I Information on Donated Property

1	(a) Name and address of the donee organization	(b) Description of donated property (attach a separate sheet if more space is needed)
A	Private Foundation	200 shares stock
B		
C		
D		
E		

Note: *If the amount you claimed as a deduction for the item is $500 or less, you do not have to complete columns (d), (e), and (f).*

	(c) Date of the contribution	(d) Date acquired by donor (mo., yr.)	(e) How acquired by donor	(f) Donor's cost or adjusted basis	(g) Fair market value	(h) Method used to determine the fair market value
A	1993	1987	Purchase	12,000	15,000	Stock Exchange Quotation
B						
C						
D						
E						

Part II Other Information—If you gave less than an entire interest in property listed in Part I, complete lines 2a–2e. If restrictions were attached to a contribution listed in Part I, complete lines 3a–3c.

2 If less than the entire interest in the property is contributed during the year, complete the following:

   a Enter letter from Part I that identifies the property _____. (If Part II applies to more than one property, attach a separate statement.)

   b Total amount claimed as a deduction for the property listed in Part I for this tax year _____; for any prior tax year(s) _____

   c Name and address of each organization to which any such contribution was made in a prior year (complete only if different than the donee organization above).

   Name of charitable organization (donee)

   Address (number and street)

   City or town, state, and ZIP code

   d The place where any tangible property is located or kept _____

   e Name of any person, other than the donee organization, having actual possession of the property _____

3 If conditions were attached to any contribution listed in Part I, answer the following questions and attach the required statement (see Instructions):   Yes   No

   a Is there a restriction, either temporary or permanent, on the donee's right to use or dispose of the donated property?

   b Did you give to anyone (other than the donee organization or another organization participating with the donee organization in cooperative fundraising) the right to the income from the donated property or to the possession of the property, including the right to vote donated securities, to acquire the property by purchase or otherwise, or to designate the person having such income, possession, or right to acquire?

   c Is there a restriction limiting the donated property for a particular use?

For Paperwork Reduction Act Notice, see separate Instructions.   Form **8283** (Rev. 3-90)

Figure 4-2   Form 8283

Form 8283 (Rev. 3-90)   Page **2**

Name(s) shown on your income tax return: Ted Alonzo   Identification number:

Section B — Appraisal Summary

Include in Section B only items (or groups of similar items) for which you claimed a deduction of more than $5,000 per item or group. *(Report contributions of certain publicly traded securities only in Section A.)*

If you donated art, you may have to attach the complete appraisal. See the **Note** in Part I below.

Part I — Information on Donated Property *(To be completed by the taxpayer and/or appraiser.)* — N/A

1 Check type of property:
- ☐ Art* (contribution of $20,000 or more)
- ☐ Art* (contribution of less than $20,000)
- ☐ Real Estate
- ☐ Coin Collections
- ☐ Gems/Jewelry
- ☐ Books
- ☐ Stamp Collections
- ☐ Other

*Art includes paintings, sculptures, watercolors, prints, drawings, ceramics, antique furniture, decorative arts, textiles, carpets, silver, rare manuscripts, historical memorabilia, and other similar objects. **Note:** If you donated art after December 31, 1987, and your total art contribution deduction was $20,000 or more, you must attach a complete copy of the signed appraisal. See Instructions.

2	(a) Description of donated property (attach a separate sheet if more space is needed)	(b) If tangible property was donated, give a brief summary of the overall physical condition at the time of the gift	(c) Appraised fair market value
A			
B	N/A		
C			
D			

	(d) Date acquired by donor (mo., yr.)	(e) How acquired by donor	(f) Donor's cost or adjusted basis	(g) For bargain sales after 6/6/88, enter amount received	See Instructions	
					(h) Amount claimed as a deduction	(i) Average trading price of securities
A						
B						
C						
D						

Part II — Taxpayer (Donor) Statement

List any item(s) included in Part I above that is (are) separately identified in the appraisal as having a value of $500 or less. See Instructions.

I declare that the following item(s) included in Part I above has (have) to the best of my knowledge and belief an appraised value of not more than $500 (per item). *(Enter identifying letter from Part I and describe the specific item):* _____

Signature of taxpayer (donor) ▶   Date ▶

Part III — Certification of Appraiser *(To be completed by the appraiser of the above donated property.)*

I declare that I am not the donor, the donee, a party to the transaction in which the donor acquired the property, employed by, married to, or related to any of the foregoing persons, or an appraiser regularly used by any of the foregoing persons and who does not perform a majority of appraisals during the taxable year for other persons.

Also, I declare that I hold myself out to the public as an appraiser or perform appraisals on a regular basis; and that because of my qualifications as described in the appraisal, I am qualified to make appraisals of the type of property being valued. I certify that the appraisal fees were not based upon a percentage of the appraised property value. Furthermore, I understand that a false or fraudulent overstatement of the property value as described in the qualified appraisal or this appraisal summary may subject me to the civil penalty under section 6701(a) (aiding and abetting the understatement of tax liability). I affirm that I have not been barred from presenting evidence or testimony by the Director of Practice.

Please Sign Here Signature ▶   Title ▶   Date of appraisal ▶

Business address   Identification number

City or town, state, and ZIP code

Part IV — Donee Acknowledgment *(To be completed by the charitable organization.)*

This charitable organization acknowledges that it is a qualified organization under section 170(c) and that it received the donated property as described in Part I on _____ (Date).

Furthermore, this organization affirms that in the event it sells, exchanges, or otherwise disposes of the property (or any portion thereof) within 2 years after the date of receipt, it will file an information return (**Form 8282**, Donee Information Return) with the IRS and furnish the donor a copy of that return. This acknowledgment does not represent concurrence in the claimed fair market value.

Name of charitable organization (donee)   Employer identification number

Address (number and street)   City or town, state, and ZIP code

Authorized signature   Title   Date

*U.S. Government Printing Office: 1990-262-151/00079

Figure 4-2 (continued)   Form 8283

REVIEW III

1. In the current year George paid the following taxes: withholding for federal taxes, $6,700; withholding for state income taxes, $2,300; state sales tax, $675; property tax, $1,600; and property tax assessment for street lights, $500. What is George's deduction for taxes?
   (a) $3,900
   (b) $4,575
   (c) $11,275
   (d) $11,775

2. Mary paid $225 to license her auto; $175 of this fee was based on its value of $17,500. She also paid an inheritance tax of $500 on property she inherited from her deceased uncle, $4,000 in state income taxes, $3,100 in social security taxes, and $200 for her fishing and hunting licenses. What is Mary's total itemized deduction for taxes?
   (a) $4,725
   (b) $4,675
   (c) $4,175
   (d) $4,925

3. Florence had $63,000 AGI this year and decided she wanted to give a substantial amount to charity. She donated a painting, which she had purchased many years ago for $5,000 and which was now worth $30,000, to a museum; a boat, which had cost her $4,500 and was now worth $6,000, to a private nonoperating foundation; and $10,000 cash to a local university. What is Florence's charitable contribution deduction?
   (a) $46,000
   (b) $33,400
   (c) $28,900
   (d) $19,500

4. Albert gave $6,000 to his church; donated clothes valued at $450 to Goodwill Industries; and gave stock worth $10,000, which had cost him $6,500, to a museum. If he has only $21,000 of AGI this year, what is his charitable contribution deduction?
   (a) $16,450
   (b) $12,950
   (c) $10,500
   (d) $12,750

Answers are on page 4-26.

IV. PERSONAL CASUALTY AND THEFT LOSSES AND THE MOVING EXPENSE DEDUCTION
(Code Sections 165, and 217)

PERSONAL CASUALTY AND THEFT LOSSES

Sections 165(a) and (c)(3) permit a taxpayer to deduct personal casualty and theft losses, subject to a $100 floor per occurrence, that in total exceed 10% of the taxpayer's AGI.

The deductible losses include those resulting from theft, storms, tornadoes, hurricanes, shipwreck, auto accidents, fires, and any other type of casualty that is sudden and unexpected. The loss must meet the test of *suddenness* and may not be the result of slow, progressive deterioration.

THE LAW

Sec. 165(a)—General Rule.—There shall be allowed as a deduction any loss sustained during the taxable year and not compensated for by insurance or otherwise.... (c) Limitation on Losses of Individuals.—In the case of an individual, the deduction under subsection (a) shall be limited to—... losses of property not connected with a trade or business or a transaction entered into for profit, if such losses arise from fire, storm, shipwreck, or other casualty, or from theft.

✓ **Example 29.** George Alexander's summer cottage was infested with termites, which slowly destroyed several beams in the foundation. Repairs were required that cost $2,300. George is not allowed a deduction for a casualty loss since damage by termites is normally slow and progressive and does not meet the suddenness test for casualty losses.

Personal casualty losses are normally deductible in the year of occurrence, and thefts are deductible in the year of discovery. The losses are reported on Form 4684. The amount of a personal casualty loss is measured by the difference in the property's fair market value before and after the casualty, or the property's adjusted basis, if less. If personal-use property is *totally* destroyed, the value of the loss is the *lesser* of the property's basis or its fair market value when destroyed. An alternative measure of loss is the cost of restoring the property to its former condition. Amounts that improve the property beyond its value at the time of the loss are not deductible, however. If the taxpayer receives an

ANSWERS TO REVIEW III

1. (a) George may not deduct payments for *federal* withholding taxes, state sales taxes, and the property tax assessment that increases the property's value.
2. (c) Only the $4,000 of state income taxes and $175 of the auto license fee (the portion based on value) are deductible.
3. (c) Florence may deduct the cash fully, but the deduction for the painting is limited to $18,900 (30% of $63,000). She must reduce the value of the deduction for the boat to $4,500 (and it is subject to a 20% limitation); she gets no current deduction, however, since she has already reached her 30% limit on capital-gain property with the donation of the painting. Her deduction, then, is $10,000 cash + $18,900 painting = $28,900. She may carry over to the next five years the $11,100 value of the painting and the $4,500 value of the boat not deducted currently.
4. (c) The total value of the cash and clothing ($6,450) may be deducted currently since it does not exceed 50% of AGI. Only $4,050 of the value of the stock can be deducted, however; this is the lesser of 30% of AGI (.3 × $21,000 = $6,300) or the balance of the 50% limitation after deduction for the cash and clothing [(.5 × $21,000) − $6,450 = $4,050]. Therefore, the total current deduction is $10,500, and the remaining value of the stock may be carried forward to the next five years as a charitable contribution deduction.

insurance reimbursement, the loss must be reduced by the insurance reimbursement. If the taxpayer has filed an insurance claim and *expects* a reimbursement, the deduction is reduced by the *expected* reimbursement. If the reimbursement is more or less than anticipated, income or additional loss is recognized in the year of reimbursement.

TAX TIP

If the taxpayer's loss is due to a casualty incurred in an area declared a disaster area by the President of the United States (e.g., Dade County, due to hurricane Andrew, and Des Moines, due to the flooding of the Mississippi River), the taxpayer may elect to deduct the loss in the year *prior* to its occurrence. This election is made on an amended return or the taxpayer's original return for the prior year (if it has not already been filed) and permits the taxpayer to receive a tax refund as soon as possible to aid in recovery from the casualty.

Example 30. Thad Tyler's house was destroyed by fire. The fair market value of the house at the time of the fire was $125,000. Its cost was $76,000. Thad filed for reimbursement from the insurance company and expected to receive $75,000. Thad has a unreimbursed loss of only $1,000 subject to the limits for deductibility. He must use the lesser of fair market value or adjusted basis to determine his loss. If Thad receives only $70,000 from the insurance company when it reimburses him in the next year, he will have an additional loss of $5,000 in the year of reimbursement, again subject to limitation.

THE LAW

Sec. 165(h)—Treatment of Casualty Gains and Losses.—(1) $100 Limitation per Casualty.—Any loss of an individual described in subsection (c)(3) shall be allowed only to the extent that the amount of the loss to such individual arising from each casualty, or from each theft, exceeds $100.
(2) Net Casualty Loss Allowed Only to the Extent It Exceeds 10 Percent of Adjusted Gross Income.
(A) In General.—If the personal casualty losses for any taxable year exceed the personal casualty gains for such taxable year, such losses shall be allowed for the taxable year only to the extent of the sum of—
(i) the amount of the personal casualty gains for the taxable year, plus
(ii) so much of such excess as exceeds 10 percent of the adjusted gross income of the individual.

To determine the amount deductible as a casualty loss, the taxpayer must complete several steps. First, the gains and losses, net of insurance reimbursements, must be determined from each of the casualty and theft losses occurring during a tax year. Second, each of the casualty or theft *losses* must then be reduced by a $100 floor. If a taxpayer has two or more casualty or theft losses, *each* loss must be reduced by the $100 floor. If there are several properties destroyed or stolen as part of a single casualty loss, however, only one $100 floor is applicable to that loss. Finally, all adjusted personal casualty and theft losses must be netted with the gains. If the result is a net casualty loss, the taxpayer may deduct the amount that exceeds 10% of AGI as an itemized deduction.

> **Example 31.** Carol Top's home and her antique auto were completely destroyed by a tornado. The house had a basis of $100,000 and a fair market value of $90,000. The auto had a basis of $7,000 but a fair market value of $14,000. After the tornado, someone entered Carol's house and stole a coin collection with a value and basis of $2,500. Later that year, Carol's boat was hit by another boat while docked and was totally destroyed. It had a basis of $40,000 and a fair market value of $65,000. Carol received insurance reimbursements as follows: house, $75,000; antique auto, $6,000; coin collection, $1,000; and boat, $50,000. Carol's AGI is $30,000. Carol has losses of $15,000 ($90,000 − $75,000) on the house and $1,000 ($7,000 − $6,000) on the antique auto; the combined loss of $16,000 must be reduced by a single $100 floor to $15,900. She had a loss of $1,500 ($2,500 − $1,000) on the coin collection; after applying the $100 floor, this becomes $1,400. She has a $10,000 ($50,000 − $40,000) gain on the boat. Netting her gains and losses yields a net loss of $7,300 ($15,900 + $1,400 − $10,000). Carol may deduct $4,300 as an itemized deduction, the amount by which the $7,300 net loss exceeds 10% of her $30,000 AGI.

If the personal casualty gains exceed the losses, then each gain or loss item is treated separately as a gain or loss from the sale or exchange of a capital asset as explained in Chapter 9. The details of the casualty and theft losses are reported on Form 4684, as illustrated in the following example.

> **Example 32.** Martin Warren, a retired salesman, has an AGI of $41,500 for the current year. During that year, he had the following medical expenses, primarily due to an auto accident: prescriptions, $400; doctors, $2,000; dentist, $600; medical insurance premiums, $2,300; hospitals, $250; eyeglasses, $200; transportation for medical treatment, $75; and wheelchair rental, $150. Additionally, Martin's auto was totally destroyed in the accident. It had a fair market value of $16,000 at the time of the accident and a basis of $21,000. Martin had forgotten to renew his auto insurance and so received no reimbursement for the auto. He may deduct $2,862.50 [($400 + 2,000 + 600 + 2,300 + 250 + 200 + 75 + 150) − (.075 × $41,500)] as a medical expense and $11,750 [$16,000 − 100 − (.10 × $41,500)] as a casualty loss deduction. We show how these items would appear on Schedule A and Form 4684 in Figure 4-3.

MOVING EXPENSE DEDUCTION

When a taxpayer moves from one location to another because of a change in employment, the costs of moving are permitted as an itemized deduction within limits. Prior to 1987, allowable moving expenses were deductible *for* AGI. The Tax Reform Act of 1986 reclassified them as an itemized deduction; they are not, however, subject to the 2% of AGI floor that applies to miscellaneous itemized deductions.

THE LAW

Sec. 217(a)—DEDUCTION ALLOWED.—There shall be allowed as a deduction moving expenses paid or incurred during the taxable year in connection with the commencement of work by the taxpayer as an employee or as a self-employed individual at a new principal place of work. . . .

(c) CONDITIONS FOR ALLOWANCE.—No deduction shall be allowed under this section unless—

(1) the taxpayer's new principal place of work—
  (A) is at least 35 miles farther from his former residence than was his former principal place of work, or
  (B) if he had no former principal place of work, is at least 35 miles from his former residence, and

(2) either—
  (A) during the 12-month period immediately following his arrival in the general location of his new principal place of work, the taxpayer is a full-time employee, in such general location, during at least 39 weeks, or
  (B) during the 24-month period immediately following his arrival in the general location of his new principal place of work, the taxpayer is a full-time employee or performs services as a self-employed individual on a full-time basis, in such general location, during at least 78 weeks, of which not less than 39 weeks are during the 12-month period referred to in subparagraph (A).

To qualify for the moving expense deduction, the taxpayer must meet employment, time, and distance requirements. First, the taxpayer must be either employed by another or self-employed at the new location on a full-time basis for a certain time period. If the taxpayer is an *employee,* the time test is satisfied by his being employed full-time for 39 weeks during the 12-month period immediately following the move. If the taxpayer is self-employed or an employee, the time test is satisfied by his working full-time for 78 weeks out of the 24 months following the move, with 39 of those weeks during the first 12 months. If the taxpayer is fired, is transferred, dies, or becomes disabled, the time tests are waived for deducting moving expenses.

✓ **Example 33.** Byron Grange moved from Miami to Dallas to accept a position with a new company. He arrived on January 2 and began work on Monday, January 4. He worked for six months (26 weeks) and quit. After two months he found a new job and worked throughout the rest of the year. Even though Byron worked for two different companies as an employee, he meets the 39-weeks test and may deduct his moving expenses.

✓ **Example 34.** Maureen Kelly moved to Miami to start her own business. She worked at the business for 14 months but could not make it profitable, so she decided to retire. Maureen was self-employed less than 78 weeks out of the 24 months after the move and so cannot deduct her moving expenses.

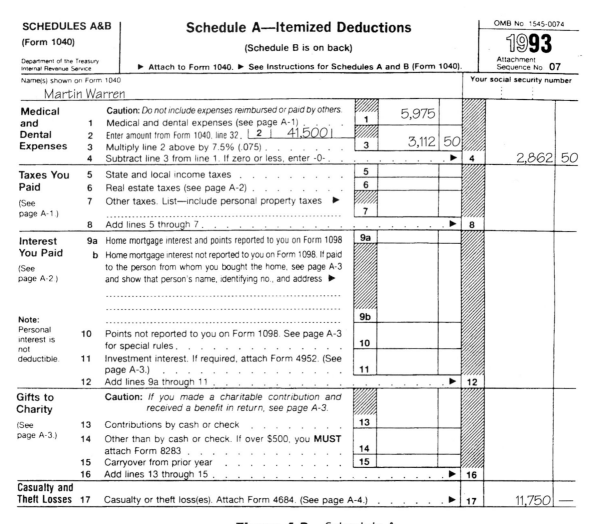

Figure 4-3 Schedule A

The law imposes a distance test to prevent taxpayers from changing employment in the same area, moving simultaneously, and deducting the expenses. The taxpayer is required to have a substantial increase in commuting distance in order to qualify. The commuting distance from his *old* home to his *new* job must be at least 35 miles more than the commuting distance from his *old* home to his *old* job using the most direct routes. Figure 4-4 illustrates this concept.

☑ **Example 35.** Charles English has lived and worked in Miami for three years. His employer transfers him to Dallas. He is allowed to deduct his moving expenses since the commuting distance from Miami to his job in Dallas is at least 35 miles farther than his commuting distance within Miami had been.

☑ **Example 36.** Jill Farley's old job was a ten-mile drive from her home. She changed jobs within the city and now must commute 40 miles to work. Jill is *not* allowed a moving expense deduction since her new commuting distance (40 miles) is not 35 miles farther than her old commuting distance (10 miles).

IV. *Personal Casualty and Theft Losses and the Moving Expense Deduction* 4-31

Form **4684**	**Casualties and Thefts**	OMB No. 1545-0177
Department of the Treasury Internal Revenue Service	▶ See separate instructions. ▶ Attach to your tax return. ▶ Use a separate Form 4684 for each different casualty or theft.	**1993** Attachment Sequence No. 26

Name(s) shown on tax return	Identifying number
Martin Warren	

SECTION A—Personal Use Property (Use this section to report casualties and thefts of property **not** used in a trade or business or for income-producing purposes.)

1 Description of properties (show type, location, and date acquired for each):
   Property A Automobile
   Property B ....
   Property C ....
   Property D ....

Properties (Use a separate column for each property lost or damaged from one casualty or theft.)

		A	B	C	D
2	Cost or other basis of each property	21,000	—		
3	Insurance or other reimbursement (whether or not you filed a claim). See instructions **Note:** *If line 2 is more than line 3, skip line 4.*	-0-			
4	Gain from casualty or theft. If line 3 is **more than** line 2, enter the difference here and skip lines 5 through 9 for that column. See instructions if line 3 includes insurance or other reimbursement you did not claim, or you received payment for your loss in a later tax year				
5	Fair market value **before** casualty or theft	16,000	—		
6	Fair market value **after** casualty or theft	-0-			
7	Subtract line 6 from line 5	16,000	—		
8	Enter the **smaller** of line 2 or line 7	16,000	—		
9	Subtract line 3 from line 8. If zero or less, enter -0-	16,000	—		

10	Casualty or theft loss. Add the amounts on line 9. Enter the total	10	16,000
11	Enter the amount from line 10 or $100, whichever is **smaller**	11	100
12	Subtract line 11 from line 10	12	15,900
	Caution: *Use only one Form 4684 for lines 13 through 18.*		
13	Add the amounts on line 12 of all Forms 4684	13	15,900
14	Combine the amounts from line 4 of all Forms 4684	14	-0-
15	• If line 14 is **more than** line 13, enter the difference here and on Schedule D. Do not complete the rest of this section (see instructions). • If line 14 is **less than** line 13, enter -0- here and continue with the form. • If line 14 is **equal to** line 13, enter -0- here. Do not complete the rest of this section.	15	-0-
16	If line 14 is **less than** line 13, enter the difference	16	15,900
17	Enter 10% of your adjusted gross income (Form 1040, line 32). Estates and trusts, see instructions	17	4,150
18	Subtract line 17 from line 16. If zero or less, enter -0-. Also enter result on Schedule A (Form 1040), line 17. Estates and trusts, enter on the "Other deductions" line of your tax return	18	11,750

For Paperwork Reduction Act Notice, see page 1 of separate instructions.   Cat. No. 129970   Form **4684** (1993)

Figure 4-3 (continued)   Form 4684

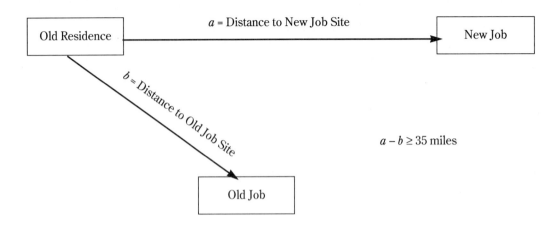

Note: Distance from *new* house to new job site is irrelevant.

Figure 4-4 Distance Test for Deductible Moving Expenses

Note that a taxpayer does not have to be employed at her old location to deduct moving expenses. Thus, a graduating student who accepts a job in a different location can deduct moving expenses. To do so, however, she must be able to show that the location of the new job is at least 35 miles from her current *residence* for tax years before 1994.*

THE LAW

Sec. 217(b) DEFINITION OF MOVING EXPENSES.—
(1) In General.—For purposes of this section, the term "moving expenses" means only the reasonable expenses—
  (A) of moving household goods and personal effects from the former residence to the new residence,
  (B) of traveling (including meals and lodging) from the former residence to the new place of residence,
  (C) of traveling (including meals and lodging), after obtaining employment, from the former residence to the general location of the new principal place of work and return, for the principal purpose of searching for a new residence,
  (D) of meals and lodging while occupying temporary quarters in the general location of the new principal place of work during any period of 30 consecutive days after obtaining employment, or
  (E) constituting qualified residence sale, purchase, or lease expenses. . . .

Even if the taxpayer meets the time and distance requirements, all moving expenses are not necessarily fully deductible. For tax years before 1994, the expenses must be

---

*For changes in the tax law effective for tax years beginning in 1994, see Appendix J.

categorized as either direct or indirect expenses.* *Direct expenses* include reasonable costs for moving the furniture, household goods, and other personal items, including automobiles, boats, and pets. Additionally, the costs of traveling by the most direct route from the old residence to the area of the new residence, including lodging and 80% of the cost of meals for tax years before 1994, are direct expenses. Note that the 80% limitation for tax years before 1994 on the deductibility of meals (discussed later in the chapter) is also imposed in all categories of moving expenses. Certain other items are included as direct expenses—such as packing, insurance, utility service charges, and storage for 30 days after the day the goods are moved from the residence.

There are three categories of *indirect expenses:* (1) pre-move house-hunting expenses, (2) temporary living expenses, and (3) qualifying expenses related to changing residences. *Premove house hunting* includes the cost of transportation, meals, and lodging to find a new residence *after* employment has been accepted. Temporary living expenses include meals and lodging at the new job location for up to 30 consecutive days *after* employment is obtained. The qualifying expenses related to changing residences include the costs of (a) buying a new residence, (b) selling an old residence, (c) obtaining a lease on a new residence, or (d) settling a lease on an old residence.

☑ **Example 37.** Sarah Nitrof went to Dallas to interview for a job; while there, she looked for an apartment. The trip cost $600. The next week she accepted the job and spent $400 on a return trip to apartment hunt. She also spent $300 on temporary living expenses and $1,000 moving her household goods. Sarah has $1,000 of direct and $700 of indirect moving expenses. The $600 for the first trip cannot be deducted as moving expense since she had not accepted the job. (The trip may, however, be deductible as a job-hunting expense.)

THE LAW

Sec. 217(c)(3) LIMITATIONS.—
(A) DOLLAR LIMITS.—The aggregate amount allowable as a deduction under subsection (a) in connection with a commencement of work which is attributable to expenses described in subparagraph (C) or (D) of paragraph (1) shall not exceed $1,500. The aggregate amount allowable as a deduction under subsection (a) which is attributable to qualified residence sale, purchase, or lease expenses shall not exceed $3,000, reduced by the aggregate amount so allowable which is attributable to expenses described in subparagraph (C) or (D) of paragraph (1).

Within each of these categories of indirect expenses, certain limitations are imposed. First, the deduction for expenses classified as pre-move house-hunting and temporary living expenses (categories (1) and (2)) is limited to $1,500—and again, the deductibility for meals is limited to 80% of costs incurred. Then, a second limitation of $3,000 is imposed on the deductibility of all three categories of *indirect* moving

*For changes in the tax law effective for tax years beginning in 1994, see Appendix J.

4-34 Deductions for Personal Expenses of Individuals

Table 4-2 Moving Expense Deductions

A.	Direct moving costs—		
	All costs for moving family members, pets, and household goods by the most direct route.		$xxxxxxxxxx
B.	Indirect moving expenses—		

First limitation:
1. Premove house hunting — xxxxxx
   plus
2. Temporary living expenses — xxxxxx
3. Total of 1 + 2 — xxxxxx
4. Compare (3) to $1,500 and include the smaller in second limitation

Second limitation:
4. Amount allowed from (4) — xxxxxx
   plus
5. Residence selling/leasing expenses — xxxxxx
6. Total of 4 + 5 — xxxxxx
7. Compare (6) to $3,000 and include the smaller amount as part of the moving expense deduction — xxxxxxxxxx

Total moving expenses allowed as an itemized deduction — $xxxxxxxxxx

expenses. Table 4-2 shows schematically the calculation of the moving expense deduction with these limitations. The taxpayer reports the details of his or her moving expense deduction on Form 3903.

✓ **Example 38.** Shirley North moved from New York to Pittsburgh. Her direct costs of moving included $2,000 for packing and shipping her household goods, $500 for her travel, and $60 for meals en route. She also incurred $300 in premove house-hunting expenses ($80 of which was for meals); $1,200 of temporary living expenses, which included $400 for meals; and $1,700 of expenses on the sale of her condominium in New York. Shirley may deduct $2,548 of direct moving expenses [$2,000 + 500 + .8 × 60]; $1,404 of the premove house-hunting and temporary living expenses [$220 + .8 × 80 + 800 + .8 × 400]; and $1,596 of the condominium selling expenses [$3,000 − 1,404]—for a total deduction of $5,548 for direct and indirect moving expenses. On Schedule A, Form 1040 below and Form 3903 in Figure 4-5, these items would appear as follows:

SCHEDULES A&B (Form 1040)
Department of the Treasury
Internal Revenue Service

Schedule A—Itemized Deductions
(Schedule B is on back)
▶ Attach to Form 1040. ▶ See Instructions for Schedules A and B (Form 1040).

OMB No 1545-0074
1993
Attachment Sequence No 07

Name(s) shown on Form 1040: *Shirley North*

Your social security number:

Casualty and Theft Losses	17	Casualty or theft loss(es). Attach Form 4684. (See page A-4.) ▶	17	
Moving Expenses	18	Moving expenses. Attach Form 3903 or 3903-F. (See page A-4.) ▶	18	5,548

✓ **Example 39.** Assume in the following example that Shirley's temporary living expenses were only $900 (including $400 for meals). She could deduct $1,104 of premove house-hunting and temporary living expenses and all $1,700 of the condominium sale expenses since the total does not exceed $3,000.

IV. Personal Casualty and Theft Losses and the Moving Expense Deduction 4-35

Form **3903**	**Moving Expenses**	OMB No. 1545-0062
Department of the Treasury Internal Revenue Service	▶ Attach to Form 1040. ▶ See separate instructions.	**1993** Attachment Sequence No. **62**

Name(s) shown on Form 1040: Shirley North   Your social security number:

Caution: *If you are a member of the armed forces, see the instructions before completing this form.*

1	Enter the number of miles from your **old home** to your **new workplace**	1	525
2	Enter the number of miles from your **old home** to your **old workplace**	2	25
3	Subtract line 2 from line 1. Enter the result but not less than zero ▶	3	500

If line 3 is 35 or more miles, complete the rest of this form. Also, see **Time Test** in the instructions. If line 3 is less than 35 miles, you may not deduct your moving expenses.

Part I Moving Expenses

Note: *Any payments your employer made for any part of your move (including the value of any services furnished in kind) should be included on your W-2 form. Report that amount on **Form 1040, line 7**. See **Reimbursements** in the instructions.*

Section A—Transportation of Household Goods

| 4 | Transportation and storage for household goods and personal effects | 4 | 2,000 |

Section B—Expenses of Moving From Old To New Home

5	Travel and lodging **not** including meals			5	500		
6	Total meals	6	60				
7	Multiply line 6 by 80% (.80)			7	48		
8	Add lines 5 and 7					8	548

Section C—Pre-move Househunting Expenses and Temporary Quarters
(for any 30 days in a row after getting your job)

9	Pre-move travel and lodging **not** including meals			9	220		
10	Temporary quarters expenses **not** including meals			10	800		
11	Total meal expenses for both pre-move househunting and temporary quarters	11	480				
12	Multiply line 11 by 80% (.80)			12	384		
13	Add lines 9, 10, and 12			13	1,404		

Section D—Qualified Real Estate Expenses

| 14 | Expenses of (check one) **a** ☒ selling or exchanging your old home, or **b** ☐ if renting, settling an unexpired lease. | 14 | 1,700 |
| 15 | Expenses of (check one) **a** ☐ buying your new home, or **b** ☐ if renting, getting a new lease. | 15 | -0- |

Part II Dollar Limits and Moving Expense Deduction

Note: *If you and your spouse moved to separate homes, see the instructions.*

16	Enter the **smaller** of: • The amount on line 13, or • $1,500 ($750 if married filing a separate return and at the end of 1993 you lived with your spouse who also started work in 1993).	16	1,404		
17	Add lines 14, 15, and 16	17	3,104		
18	Enter the **smaller** of: • The amount on line 17, or • $3,000 ($1,500 if married filing a separate return and at the end of 1993 you lived with your spouse who also started work in 1993).			18	3,000
19	Add lines 4, 8, and 18. Enter the total here and on Schedule A, line 18. This is your **moving expense deduction** ▶			19	5,548

For Paperwork Reduction Act Notice, see separate instructions.

Figure 4-5 Form 3903

REVIEW IV

1. During the current year a truck backed into Albert's personal auto and completely destroyed it. He had bought the car for $12,000; it had a fair market value of $7,500 when it was destroyed, and he received $5,000 for it from his insurance company. The same year Albert also lost an uninsured diamond ring, which had cost him $1,500 and was worth $2,000, and had his TV, video camera, and VCR stolen from his apartment. He had just pur-

chased these last three items for $1,800 and had not had time to insure them. If Albert's AGI is $27,000, what is his casualty and theft deduction for 1993?
   (a) $10,500
   (b) $7,800
   (c) $3,100
   (d) $1,400

2. Last year Wilma deducted only $10,000 of a casualty loss, since she expected a $20,000 reimbursement from her insurance company. Unfortunately, she received only $12,000 as the settlement in the current year. She also had a garage fire this year that totally destroyed her auto and garage. Fortunately, she had upgraded her insurance and so received $16,000 from the insurance company for both. The car had a fair market value of $9,200 and a basis of $10,500, and the garage had a fair market value of $6,800 and a basis of $3,200. If Wilma has $9,000 of AGI, how much may she deduct as a casualty loss in the current year?
   (a) $4,800
   (b) $7,000
   (c) $3,500
   (d) $19,300

3. In 1993 Aloysius Arnold moved from New York to Miami to take a new job. He incurred the following expenses, none of which were reimbursed by his new employer: premove house hunting, $1,700; cost of breaking the lease on his old apartment, $700; temporary living expenses after moving to Miami, $800; moving household goods, $1,800; and travel for himself and his family, $700. If Arnold's AGI is $45,000, how much may he deduct as moving expenses in 1993 if he meets both the time and distance requirements? Assume that the above items include only 80% of the cost of meals.
   (a) $2,500
   (b) $3,800
   (c) $4,700
   (d) $5,700

4. Wally Beaver moved to Atlanta from Miami on January 1, 1993, to find a new job. His direct moving expenses were $1,200, and he incurred $350 of indirect moving expenses. He worked as a waiter for six months and then moved back to Miami to return to college. How much may Wally deduct as moving expenses?
   (a) $0
   (b) $350
   (c) $1,200
   (d) $1,550

Answers are on page 4-38.

V EMPLOYEE BUSINESS EXPENSES AND OTHER MISCELLANEOUS DEDUCTIONS
(Code Sections 162, 212, 274, and 280A)

In the course of employment, the taxpayer may incur certain expenses that are directly related to his or her work. For most purposes, the taxpayer's status as an employee constitutes his or her trade or business. Thus, the taxpayer is permitted to deduct the ordinary and necessary expenses incurred as an employee. Whether an employee's business expenses are deductible *for* AGI or *from* AGI as an itemized deduction generally depends on whether the employer reimburses the employee for the expenses and what form the reimbursement takes. If the employee must account to the employer for the reimbursed expenses (an accountable plan), the reimbursed expenses are deductible *for* AGI. If the expenses either are unreimbursed or are reimbursed under a plan by which the employee does not have to account to the employer and return excess reimbursements (an unaccountable plan), the unreimbursed employee business expenses constitute a miscellaneous itemized deduction subject to the 2% of AGI floor.

Employee business expenses for which a deduction is allowed may take many forms. Expenses for such items as meals and an office in the home may be subject to limitations in addition to the 2% floor (e.g., only 80% of meal and entertainment costs are deductible). Other items, such as professional dues and transportation costs, are subject only to the 2% floor. The business expenses discussed below include travel, transportation, entertainment, home office expenses, and education expenses.

TRAVEL

THE LAW

Sec. 162(a) . . . including (2) traveling expenses (including amounts expended for meals and lodging other than amounts which are lavish or extravagant under the circumstances) while away from home in the pursuit of a trade or business . . .

Travel expenses include costs of transportation, lodging, incidental expenses, and, for tax years before 1994, 80% of the cost of meals* for travel "away from home." To be "away from home," the taxpayer (1) must have a tax home and (2) must be away for a sufficient period to require rest, usually overnight. As a general rule, a taxpayer's tax home is the regular place of employment; for most taxpayers, their regular place of employment is also in the vicinity of their place of residence. However, if a taxpayer conducted substantial business at a place that is not in the area of his or her residence, determining the tax home may be more difficult.

Taxpayers who are assigned to work temporarily (for a period of less than one year) away from their principal residences are allowed to deduct travel expenses (including lodging, 80% of meals, and incidentals such as tips and laundry). If the taxpayer has permanent employment in one location but chooses to live elsewhere, commuting on a regular basis, no deduction is permitted for the living expenses at either place—nor for the cost of transportation in traveling between the two locations.

Example 40. Alice Creer works for a large manufacturing firm in Chicago, for which she made several business trips during the year. Her plane and taxi fares were $1,200; meals, $600; and lodging, $1,400. All the expenses (with the exception of 20% of meal costs) constitute allowable travel expenses.

Example 41. Walter Johns is a baseball player who was recently traded to the San Diego Padres. Walter has always lived in Boston, and his children have attended school there all their lives. Walter rents a hotel room in San Diego during home games. He incurs meal and lodging costs of $1,700 during the season. John cannot deduct any of these expenses nor the expenses of traveling to and maintaining his home in Boston. San Diego is his tax home, and the costs of maintaining the two residences are nondeductible since they are the result of a personal decision.

*For changes in the tax law effective for tax years beginning in 1994, see Appendix J.

☑ **Example 42.** Bill Crown is a traveling salesman who works out of Dallas. He spends 90% of his time covering the southern half of the United States. During the past year, Bill incurred expenses of $6,400 for transportation, $2,000 for meals, and $15,000 for lodging. All of the expenses (with the exception of 20% of the meal costs) are allowable travel expenses. Even though Bill travels the majority of the time—he has no principal place of employment—he may consider his actual home in Dallas as his tax home.

If the taxpayer has neither a principal place of employment nor a personal residence, he may deduct no travel expenses.

☑ **Example 43.** Simon Lutz is an "over-the-road" driver. Because he is on the road almost 350 days a year, he does not maintain a permanent residence. Simon has no allowable travel expenses since he has no home from which to be away.

If a taxpayer's business travel has an element of personal pleasure involved, a deduction for a portion of the expenses is denied. If the principal purpose of the travel is business, all transportation expenses along with 80% of meal costs, lodging, and incidentals for the days spent on business are deductible. If the primary purpose is pleasure, however, the transportation costs are not deductible, and only 80% of meal costs, lodging, and incidental expenses related to business activities are deductible. In determining the principal purpose of the travel, the number of days spent on business relative to the number of days used for personal purposes is usually the determining factor. The taxpayer may count travel days as business days.

ANSWERS TO REVIEW IV

1. (d) Albert may deduct the losses on his auto and video equipment only. "Lost" items do not meet the requirements for deduction as casualties. Since the items are personal, the lesser of fair market value or basis is the measure of the loss, reduced by any insurance recovery loss; each separate event must be reduced by the $100 floor, and the total is subject to the 10% of AGI limitation. Therefore, Albert's deduction is $1,400 [(7,500 − 5,000 − 100) + (1,800 − 100) − (.10 × 27,000)].

2. (c) Wilma may deduct the $8,000 anticipated insurance recovery that is not realized in 1993. She does *not* reduce this by the $100 floor since that would have been done in the prior year. In the loss of her car and garage, Wilma has a gain of $3,600 [$16,000 − 9,200 − 3,200] using the lower of basis or fair market value to measure the loss. She must reduce her insurance loss by the net gain on the car and garage as well as by 10% of her AGI, for a deductible loss of $3,500 [$8,000 − $3,600 − (.10 × 9,000)].

3. (c) Arnold may deduct a total of $1,500 for premove house hunting and temporary living expenses; he may also deduct the full cost of breaking the lease, since it is less than the allowable limits, and the full cost of moving his family and household goods. There is no limit based on AGI for moving expenses.

4. (a) Wally cannot deduct any of his moving expenses since he does not meet the time test.

☑ **Example 44.** On Sunday afternoon John left New York for California. On Monday, Tuesday, and Wednesday he saw several customers; on Thursday he went to Disneyland; on Friday he visited friends; and on Saturday he returned to New York. His transportation cost $500; his meals, $350; his motel $350; his car rental for the period, $140. John spent a total of seven days away from home, five on business and two for personal reasons. He may deduct the entire $500 of transportation costs and five-sevenths of the other costs, or $550—5/7[(350 × .8) + 350 +140]—for a total of $1,050.

When members of a taxpayer's family accompany the taxpayer, the additional costs of their travel are not deductible unless the taxpayer can prove that the family member's presence has a *substantial* business purpose.

☑ **Example 45.** Stuart's wife, Ann, accompanied him to a convention. While there she entertained customers' wives, acted as a hostess in the hospitality suite, took telephone messages, and handled miscellaneous problems. For tax years before 1994, Stuart could deduct Ann's expenses since she performed substantial business services.*

TAX TIP

If the taxpayer's business requires that she stay over a weekend, she may count the weekend days as business days, even though she actually conducts no business then and spends that time in personal activities such as sightseeing.

The rules for the deductibility of foreign travel are more complex and are beyond the scope of this discussion. In addition, special limitations are applied to water travel, foreign conventions, and travel by cruise ship.

TRANSPORTATION EXPENSE

Transportation expense, or the cost of local travel, is not the same as travel expense. As described above, the latter includes the cost of meals, lodging, and incidentals, as well as transportation expense while the person is *away from home*. Also as a part of his or her job, an employee may incur the former: transportation expenses for travel in the general area of employment that do not meet the away-from-home test. A deduction for the expense of commuting to and from the taxpayer's regular place of work, however, is specifically denied. If a taxpayer is working on a *temporary* assignment away from the place where he or she normally works, the costs of going to and from the job are a deductible transportation expense. If the taxpayer has two jobs, the cost of going from one job to the other is deductible; however, going to the first job and returning home from the other constitute nondeductible commuting expenses. In situations where the employee works at several job sites, the cost of going *between* the sites is deductible. Finally, if the employee must transport bulky items to work and incurs additional costs to transport these items, the *additional* costs are deductible.

*For changes in the tax law effective for tax years beginning in 1994, see Appendix J.

✓ **Example 46.** Amy Peet works for an accountant whose offices are 18 miles from her home. Her employer assigns her to work at a client's office for two weeks on a special project. That office is 16 miles from her home. Amy may deduct the full cost of driving between her home and the client's office since it is not the place where she normally works.

✓ **Example 47.** Donald Glenn plays the tuba in the Milwaukee Symphony Orchestra. He lives only five blocks from the rehearsal and performance hall. The Symphony, however, does not provide a place for Donald to store his instrument between rehearsals and performances. Thus, he must carry the tuba back and forth. He would normally walk to the hall but must take a taxi to transport the tuba. During the year, he spent $250 on taxis. Donald would treat the $250 as a deductible transportation expense since he would incur no expense if he walked.

If a taxpayer has deductible transportation expense for use of a personal auto, the deduction may be based on actual costs or, alternatively, on the automatic mileage method, which permits a deduction of 28 cents per mile in 1993 for business miles driven. The taxpayer must use the automatic mileage method for the first year the car is put into service, since a switch from the actual cost method to the automatic mileage method on the same car is generally not permitted. Actual costs that the taxpayer can deduct include gas, oil, maintenance, insurance, depreciation, repairs, and interest. If the employee uses the auto for both business and pleasure, the costs must be allocated between business and personal usage. Regardless of the method chosen to determine deductible costs, the taxpayer may also deduct parking fees and tolls. If the taxpayer uses taxis or public transportation, the actual costs are deducted.

✓ **Example 48.** John Major uses his car to visit clients during the day; he normally checks into the office each morning and returns there at the end of the day. During 1993 John's automobile mileage was as follows:

Personal use	6,000 miles
Commuting from home to office	3,000 miles
Business use	9,000 miles

John's costs incurred for the entire 18,000 miles of use were

Gasoline	$ 900
Oil	50
Repairs and maintenance	225
Depreciation	2,000
Insurance	800
License	25
Business parking and tolls	400

John must apportion the costs other than parking and tolls among business use, personal use, and commuting use of the auto. His apportioned costs are $2,000 [(9,000/18,000) × (900 + 50 + 225 + 2,000 + 800 + 25)]. If he uses the automatic mileage method, however, he may deduct $2,520 (9,000 × $.28). He may deduct $2,920 (the $2,520 allowed under the automatic mileage method plus the $400 in tolls) since the parking and tolls are added to driving costs. Below we show how the above information is included in Schedule A, Form 1040 and Form 2106 in Figure 4-6.

ENTERTAINMENT EXPENSES

A taxpayer often incurs expenses for entertainment in the course of business for such things as meals, liquor, tickets to theaters and sporting events, golfing, and hunting and fishing trips.

THE LAW

Sec. 274(a)(1) In General.—No deduction otherwise allowable under this chapter shall be allowed for any item—(A) Activity.—with respect to an activity which is of the type generally considered to constitute entertainment, amusement, or recreation, unless the taxpayer establishes that the item was directly related to, or, in the case of an item directly preceding or following a substantial and bona fide business discussion (including business meetings at a convention or otherwise), that such item was associated with, the active conduct of the taxpayer's trade or business....

To be deductible, entertainment expenses must be directly related to or associated with the conduct of business. As is the case with business meals for tax years before 1994, however, only 80% of qualifying entertainment expenses are deductible.* Expenses qualify as *directly related* to business if the following conditions are met:

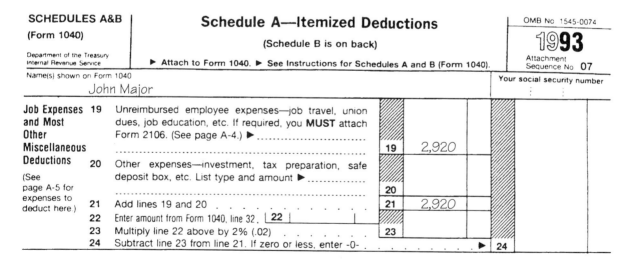

Figure 4-6 1040-Schedule A

---

*For changes in the tax law effective for tax years beginning in 1994, see Appendix J.

4-42   *Deductions for Personal Expenses of Individuals*

Form **2106**	**Employee Business Expenses**	OMB No 1545-0139
Department of the Treasury Internal Revenue Service	▶ See separate instructions. ▶ Attach to Form 1040.	**1993** Attachment Sequence No **54**
Your name John Major	Social security number	Occupation in which expenses were incurred

Part I — Employee Business Expenses and Reimbursements

STEP 1   Enter Your Expenses

		Column A Other Than Meals and Entertainment	Column B Meals and Entertainment
1	Vehicle expense from line 22 or line 29	2,520	
2	Parking fees, tolls, and transportation, including train, bus, etc., that **did not** involve overnight travel	400	
3	Travel expense while away from home overnight, including lodging, airplane, car rental, etc. **Do not** include meals and entertainment	1200 00	
4	Business expenses not included on lines 1 through 3. **Do not** include meals and entertainment	1100 00	
5	Meals and entertainment expenses (see instructions)		3000 00
6	**Total expenses.** In Column A, add lines 1 through 4 and enter the result. In Column B, enter the amount from line 5	5250 2,920	3000 0

Note: *If you were not reimbursed for any expenses in Step 1, skip line 7 and enter the amount from line 6 on line 8.*

STEP 2   Enter Amounts Your Employer Gave You for Expenses Listed in STEP 1

7	Enter amounts your employer gave you that were **not** reported to you in box 1 of Form W-2. Include any amount reported under code "L" in box 13 of your Form W-2 (see instructions)	1200 -0-	600

STEP 3   Figure Expenses To Deduct on Schedule A (Form 1040)

8	Subtract line 7 from line 6	4020 2,920	2400 —
	Note: *If **both columns** of line 8 are zero, **stop here.** If Column A is less than zero, report the amount as income on Form 1040, line 7, and enter -0- on line 10, Column A.*		
9	Enter 20% (.20) of line 8, Column B		480 —
10	In Column A, enter the amount from line 8. In Column B, subtract line 9 from line 8	2,920	1920 —
11	Add the amounts on line 10 of both columns and enter the total here. **Also, enter the total on Schedule A (Form 1040), line 19.** (Qualified performing artists and individuals with disabilities, see the instructions for special rules on where to enter the total.) ▶	11	8940 2,920

For Paperwork Reduction Act Notice, see instructions.   Cat. No. 11700N   Form **2106** (1993)

Figure 4-6 (continued)   Form 2106

Form 2106 (1993) Page **2**

Part II — Vehicle Expenses (See instructions to find out which sections to complete.)

Section A.—General Information

		(a) Vehicle 1	(b) Vehicle 2
12	Enter the date vehicle was placed in service	/ /	/ /
13	Total miles vehicle was driven during 1993	18,000 miles	miles
14	Business miles included on line 13	9,000 miles	miles
15	Percent of business use. Divide line 14 by line 13	50%	%
16	Average daily round trip commuting distance	miles	miles
17	Commuting miles included on line 13	3,000 miles	miles
18	Other personal miles. Add lines 14 and 17 and subtract the total from line 13	6,000 miles	miles

19 Do you (or your spouse) have another vehicle available for personal purposes? ☐ Yes ☐ No

20 If your employer provided you with a vehicle, is personal use during off duty hours permitted? ☐ Yes ☐ No ☒ Not applicable

21a Do you have evidence to support your deduction? ☐ Yes ☐ No

21b If "Yes," is the evidence written? ☐ Yes ☐ No

Section B.—Standard Mileage Rate (Use this section only if you own the vehicle.)

22 Multiply line 14 by 28¢ (.28). Enter the result here and on line 1. (Rural mail carriers, see instructions.) **22** 2,520

Section C.—Actual Expenses

		(a) Vehicle 1	(b) Vehicle 2
23	Gasoline, oil, repairs, vehicle insurance, etc.	2,000	
24a	Vehicle rentals		
b	Inclusion amount (see instructions)		
c	Subtract line 24b from line 24a		
25	Value of employer-provided vehicle (applies only if 100% of annual lease value was included on Form W-2—see instructions)		
26	Add lines 23, 24c, and 25	2,000	
27	Multiply line 26 by the percentage on line 15	1,000	
28	Depreciation. Enter amount from line 38 below	1,000	
29	Add lines 27 and 28. Enter total here and on line 1	2,000	

Section D.—Depreciation of Vehicles (Use this section only if you own the vehicle.)

		(a) Vehicle 1	(b) Vehicle 2
30	Enter cost or other basis (see instructions)		
31	Enter amount of section 179 deduction (see instructions)		
32	Multiply line 30 by line 15 (see instructions if you elected the section 179 deduction)		
33	Enter depreciation method and percentage (see instructions)		
34	Multiply line 32 by the percentage on line 33 (see instructions)	1,000	
35	Add lines 31 and 34	1,000	
36	Enter the limitation amount from the table in the line 36 instructions		
37	Multiply line 36 by the percentage on line 15		
38	Enter the **smaller** of line 35 or line 37. Also, enter this amount on line 28 above		

Figure 4-6 (continued) Form 2106

(1) the principal purpose for the entertainment is business; (2) the taxpayer expects a specific benefit or business result from the contact rather than simply "goodwill;" and (3) business discussions take place *during* the entertainment. If the entertainment takes place under circumstances that would make the conduct of business impossible or unlikely, the taxpayer must substantiate that business was actively conducted.

☑ **Example 49.** Mona took a customer to a Broadway play. During intermission they discussed at length an advertising campaign Mona had worked out for the customer's new product line. Mona may deduct 80% of the cost of the theater tickets as a directly related-to-business entertainment expense.

☑ **Example 50.** John gave his client tickets to a New York Islander game when he could not go with him at the last minute. The cost of tickets is not deductible as a directly related-to-business entertainment expense since no business could have been conducted. The tickets may qualify as a business gift, however.

Entertainment that does not qualify as a directly related-to-business expense may qualify as an *associated with* expense if business is conducted immediately before or after the entertainment. "Immediately before or after" normally means the entertainment takes place on the same day as the business discussions but the day before or after may be sufficient depending upon the circumstances.

☑ **Example 51.** Janet Deetz spent two full days in business meetings with a client, finishing late the second evening. The next morning Janet invited the client to play 18 holes of golf to relax. Janet would be able to deduct the cost as an entertainment expense associated with her business.

LIMITATION ON DEDUCTIBILITY OF MEALS AND ENTERTAINMENT

THE LAW

Sec. 274(n)(1) In General.—The amount allowable as a deduction under this chapter for (A) any expense for food or beverages, and (B) any item with respect to an activity which is of a type generally considered to constitute entertainment, amusement, or recreation, or with a facility used in connection with such activity, shall not exceed 80 percent of the amount of such expense. . . .

As mentioned earlier for tax years before 1994, taxpayers are allowed to deduct only 80% of the cost of their business meals and qualifying entertainment expenses.* There are certain exceptions to these rules, however. If the expenses are treated as compensation to the recipient or if the taxpayer is reimbursed for the expenses, the taxpayer

---
*For changes in the tax law effective for tax years beginning in 1994, see Appendix J.

may deduct 100% of the expense. Additionally, food and beverages furnished to employees on the business premises and recreational and social activities provided for employees are fully deductible.

✓ **Example 52.** After an afternoon business meeting, Willard Bryant took three clients out to dinner, at a cost of $140. Unless Willard is reimbursed by his employer, he may deduct only $112 as a meal expense (.80 × 140).

✓ **Example 53.** Karen Albert's consulting business incurred meal and entertainment expenses of $2,000 during July and paid $500 for a company picnic. The business may deduct $2,100 of meal and entertainment expense [(.8 × 2,000) + 500].

REIMBURSED EXPENSES

A taxpayer is permitted to take a deduction *for* AGI for employee business expenses for which he accounts to and is reimbursed by his employer, unless the reimbursement is made under a "nonaccountable plan." A nonaccountable plan is one that (1) does not require the employee to substantiate the expenses to the employer or (2) allows the employee to keep any reimbursements in excess of expenses incurred, whether substantiated or not. The employee's unreimbursed business expenses or those made under the nonaccountable plan are deductible only as a miscellaneous itemized deduction subject to the 2% of AGI floor.

Since reimbursements for expenses are often included in the taxpayer's income, permitting only an itemized deduction for such reimbursed expenses would prevent nonitemizers from getting any benefit from the deduction. In addition, the 2% of AGI floor affects itemizers whose itemized deductions are less than this floor amount. Thus, equity dictates that the reimbursed expenses should be deductible for adjusted gross income. However, the taxpayer who fails to substantiate these expenses or is allowed to keep excess reimbursements is allowed to deduct these expenses *only* as an itemized deduction.

The deductibility of substantiated reimbursed expenses specifically affects the deduction for meals and entertainment. If expenses are unreimbursed, the deduction is limited to 80% of the cost. If the substantiated expenses for meals and entertainment are reimbursed, however, the costs are fully deductible. The reimbursing employer in this case is limited to deducting only 80% of the costs.

✓ **Example 54.** Wilson Ward had the following business expenses, for which he made a full accounting to his employer. His AGI is $20,000.

Transportation	$ 2,000
Meals	950
Lodging	1,400
Entertainment	300

Wilson's employer reimburses him fully for his meals and lodging and pays $1,500 of his transportation costs but does not reimburse any amounts for entertainment. Wilson may take a $3,850 deduction for AGI (950 + 1,400 + 1,500); he may deduct $340 as an itemized deduction, determined as follows:

4-46   *Deductions for Personal Expenses of Individuals*

	$500	Unreimbursed transportation
plus	240	80% of the $300 unreimbursed entertainment expenses
	$740	
minus	(400)	2% of $20,000 AGI
	$340	Allowable deduction

Figure 4-7 illustrates Form 2106 with the above information entered.

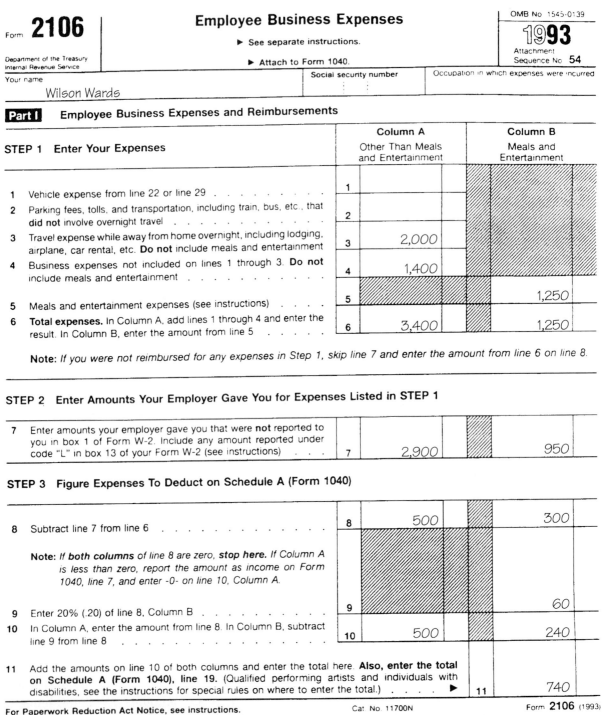

Figure 4-7   Form 2106

A taxpayer uses Form 2106 to report business expenses and reimbursements. There are certain circumstances under which the taxpayer may omit reporting expenses and reimbursements. If the employee's reimbursements equal the expenses and the employee adequately accounts to the employer, the employee may omit reporting the income *and* the expenses unless the employer has included the reimbursement in the employee's income. If the employer does not fully reimburse the employee for the expenses, then the employee must report *all* expenses and reimbursements. If the employer reimburses an amount in excess of expenses, the employee must include the reimbursements in income and is permitted only an itemized deduction for the expenses.

 Example 55. John was given a $600 monthly expense allowance when he was promoted to sales manager at the beginning of December. He is not required to make any accounting to his employer of how this allowance is spent. During December he incurred $500 in transportation expenses and $400 for meals and entertainment. John must include the $600 in income and is permitted to deduct only $820 [500 + (.8 × 400)] as an itemized deduction subject to the 2% floor. If John's expenses were less than $600, but his employer permitted him to keep the excess, he would have to treat the expenses as an itemized deduction regardless of whether or not he substantiated them.

TAX TIP

A taxpayer should negotiate with his employer to fully cover business expenses for which he provides a full accounting as part of his compensation package. He can then deduct all expenses for AGI rather than deducting them as itemized deductions subject to limitation.

HOME OFFICE EXPENSE

THE LAW

Sec. 280A(a) General Rule.—Except as otherwise provided...no deduction otherwise allowable under this chapter shall be allowed with respect to use of a dwelling unit which is used by the taxpayer during the taxable year as a residence...
(c)(1) Certain Business Use.—Subsection (a) shall not apply to any item to the extent such item is allocable to a portion of the dwelling unit which is exclusively used on a regular basis—
(A) [as] the principal place of business for any trade or business of the taxpayer,
(B) as a place of business which is used by patients, clients, or customers in meeting or dealing with the taxpayer in the normal course of his trade or business, or
(C) in the case of a separate structure which is not attached to the dwelling unit, in connection with the taxpayer's trade or business.
In the case of an employee, the preceding sentence shall apply only if the exclusive use referred to in the preceding sentence is for the convenience of his employer.

An employee must fulfill several specific requirements to deduct expenses of an office in the home. First, the office must be for the convenience of the employer. If the employer fails to provide adequate and appropriate work space for the employee, the taxpayer meets this requirement. Most employees, however, have a principal place of work outside their home and do not qualify. Next, the home office space must be used only for business—not for personal use—and it *must* be shown that it is for the convenience of the employer. The taxpayer *does not* have to have a separate room. Part of a room, if used exclusively for the taxpayer's business, will qualify. If the taxpayer uses the home office to meet customers, patients, or clients, the meetings must be in person (not solely by telephone) and they must take place on a regular and continuing basis.

Example 56. Mason Trip is a salesman who travels throughout Texas. His employer does not have any offices in the state so Mason works from his home. He uses one-half of his bedroom exclusively for storing his sales records, doing his paperwork, and making sales appointments. Mason qualifies to take a home office deduction for the expenses related to the portion of the bedroom he uses.

Example 57. Ellen Jackson is a teacher. Although she has an office at school, she prefers to work at home. She has a den she uses exclusively for class preparation and other school-related work. Ellen would not be allowed a deduction for a home office unless she could show that the office space provided at school was unsuitable for performing her duties.

If the taxpayer qualifies for a home office deduction, she may deduct an allocable portion of the expenses to the extent she has gross income less other allowable deductions from the activity. Typical expenses that must be allocated are rent, mortgage interest, taxes, depreciation, and utilities. Expenses *must* generally be allocated based on square footage. Since the deductible expenses are limited to gross income, expenses are deducted in a certain order: (1) business expenses other than those related to the home office (e.g., supplies and travel); (2) expenses that are otherwise deductible (e.g., mortgage interest and property taxes are deductible as itemized deductions); (3) other expenses, except depreciation, directly related to the home office (e.g., utilities and repairs); and (4) depreciation expense. Depreciation is deducted last since the taxpayer does not have to adjust the property's basis for the disallowed depreciation.

Example 58. In his home, Tom Freund has an office that qualifies for a home office deduction. He uses 300 of 1,500 available square feet for the office. The expenses associated with the entire home are

Taxes	$1,200
Interest	6,000
Depreciation	5,200
Electricity	1,800

Tom's income from his business is $4,200, and he has $2,000 of other expenses associated with it. Tom must first allocate the expenses to the home office:

Taxes   1200 × 1/5 = 240
  Interest   6,000 × 1/5 = 1,200
  Depreciation 5,200 × 1/5 = 1,040
  Electricity   1,800 × 1/5 = 360

Tom deducts the $1,440 in interest and taxes from the $2,200 gross income after the deduction for the $2,000 of other expenses associated with the business. Finally, he can deduct the $360 for electricity but only $400 of depreciation, for a maximum of $4,200 ($1,440 + 2,000 + 360 + 400 = $4,200). Additionally, Tom would reduce the basis of the home by only the $400 actual depreciation deduction. Figure 4-8 shows the home expenses as they would appear on Form 8829.

When an *employee* (rather than someone who is self-employed) incurs allowable home office expenses, the taxes and interest are deductible as itemized deductions under taxes and interest on Schedule A. The other home office expenses are deductible as miscellaneous itemized deductions subject to the floor of 2% of AGI.

TAX TIP

If a taxpayer has a second bona fide trade or business and her home is the principal place from which the business is conducted, office expenses may be deducted within the limits explained. For example, a CPA with a full-time position as a corporate controller may prepare tax returns for private clients during the year. This activity can constitute a second trade or business (other than as a corporate controller), allowing her to deduct qualifying home office expenses. Although a second trade or business does not require full-time activity, the taxpayer's activity must be significant for classification as a trade or business.

EDUCATIONAL EXPENSES

Employees may deduct expenses for education that are related to their work. To be deductible, the education must meet one of the two following requirements: (1) the education maintains or improves the skills required for the employee's current employment or (2) the education meets requirements of the employer or applicable law for the employee to maintain his or her position.

Example 59. Alexandra must complete 80 hours of continuing education every two years to maintain her certification as a CPA. She may deduct the cost of these continuing education courses.

Example 60. Joseph is a chemistry teacher. He decides, however, to enter law school at night. Joseph may not deduct the cost of these courses since they are not related to his current employment.

4-50 *Deductions for Personal Expenses of Individuals*

Form **8829**	**Expenses for Business Use of Your Home**	OMB No. 1545-1266
Department of the Treasury — Internal Revenue Service	▶ File only with Schedule C (Form 1040). Use a separate Form 8829 for each home you used for business during the year. ▶ See separate instructions.	**1993** Attachment Sequence No. **66**

Name(s) of proprietor(s): Tom Freund
Your social security number:

Part I — Part of Your Home Used for Business

1	Area used regularly and exclusively for business, regularly for day care, or for inventory storage. See instructions	1	300 sq. ft.
2	Total area of home	2	1,500 sq. ft.
3	Divide line 1 by line 2. Enter the result as a percentage	3	20 %
	• For day-care facilities not used exclusively for business, also complete lines 4–6.		
	• All others, skip lines 4–6 and enter the amount from line 3 on line 7.		
4	Multiply days used for day care during year by hours used per day	4	hr.
5	Total hours available for use during the year (365 days × 24 hours). See instructions	5	8,760 hr.
6	Divide line 4 by line 5. Enter the result as a decimal amount	6	.
7	Business percentage. For day-care facilities not used exclusively for business, multiply line 6 by line 3 (enter the result as a percentage). All others, enter the amount from line 3 ▶	7	20 %

Part II — Figure Your Allowable Deduction

		(a) Direct expenses	(b) Indirect expenses		
8	Enter the amount from Schedule C, line 29, **plus** any net gain or (loss) derived from the business use of your home and shown on Schedule D or Form 4797. If more than one place of business, see instructions			8	2,200
	See instructions for columns (a) and (b) before completing lines 9–20.				
9	Casualty losses. See instructions	9			
10	Deductible mortgage interest. See instructions	10	6,000		
11	Real estate taxes. See instructions	11	1,200		
12	Add lines 9, 10, and 11	12	7,200		
13	Multiply line 12, column (b) by line 7		13	1,440	
14	Add line 12, column (a) and line 13			14	1,440
15	Subtract line 14 from line 8. If zero or less, enter -0-			15	760
16	Excess mortgage interest. See instructions	16			
17	Insurance	17			
18	Repairs and maintenance	18			
19	Utilities	19	1,800		
20	Other expenses. See instructions	20			
21	Add lines 16 through 20	21	1,800		
22	Multiply line 21, column (b) by line 7		22	360	
23	Carryover of operating expenses from 1992 Form 8829, line 41		23		
24	Add line 21 in column (a), line 22, and line 23			24	360
25	Allowable operating expenses. Enter the **smaller** of line 15 or line 24			25	360
26	Limit on excess casualty losses and depreciation. Subtract line 25 from line 15			26	400
27	Excess casualty losses. See instructions		27		
28	Depreciation of your home from Part III below		28	1,040	
29	Carryover of excess casualty losses and depreciation from 1992 Form 8829, line 42		29		
30	Add lines 27 through 29			30	1,040
31	Allowable excess casualty losses and depreciation. Enter the **smaller** of line 26 or line 30			31	400
32	Add lines 14, 25, and 31			32	2,200
33	Casualty loss portion, if any, from lines 14 and 31. Carry amount to **Form 4684**, Section B			33	
34	Allowable expenses for business use of your home. Subtract line 33 from line 32. Enter here and on Schedule C, line 30. If your home was used for more than one business, see instructions ▶			34	2,200

Part III — Depreciation of Your Home

35	Enter the **smaller** of your home's adjusted basis or its fair market value. See instructions	35	
36	Value of land included on line 35	36	
37	Basis of building. Subtract line 36 from line 35	37	
38	Business basis of building. Multiply line 37 by line 7	38	
39	Depreciation percentage. See instructions	39	%
40	Depreciation allowable. Multiply line 38 by line 39. Enter here and on line 28 above. See instructions	40	1,040

Part IV — Carryover of Unallowed Expenses to 1994

41	Operating expenses. Subtract line 25 from line 24. If less than zero, enter -0-	41	-0-
42	Excess casualty losses and depreciation. Subtract line 31 from line 30. If less than zero, enter -0-	42	640

For Paperwork Reduction Act Notice, see page 1 of separate instructions.   Cat. No. 13232M   Form **8829** (1993)

Figure 4-8 Form 8829

If education is undertaken to qualify the taxpayer for a new trade or business or to meet the minimum requirements of the business, the expenses are not deductible. Often a fine line exists between education for a new trade or business and education to maintain or improve the taxpayer's current skills. A taxpayer may generally take courses that permit him or her to change duties within his employment; if, however, the education leads to a significant promotion and increase in pay, the educational expenses may be disallowed.

✓ Example 61. George Wilson has worked as janitor in a testing laboratory for the past ten years. During the last two years, he went to school on Saturdays to earn an MBA. When he completed the degree, he was named the manager of research and testing facilities at the laboratory. George's educational expenses would not be deductible since they qualified him for a significant promotion and pay increase.

OTHER MISCELLANEOUS ITEMIZED DEDUCTIONS

In addition to those previously discussed, there are many other expenses that taxpayers may deduct as miscellaneous itemized deductions. Expenses incurred as an employee for which the taxpayer may take a deduction include union dues, professional dues and licensing fees, business journals, small tools, supplies, special clothing and uniforms, and business gifts. To qualify as special clothing or uniforms, the clothes must *not* be suitable for everyday wear. The cost of maintaining special clothing is also deductible.

Taxpayers are permitted a deduction for business gifts of up to $25 in value per recipient. Only the actual gift cost is limited to this amount; wrapping and shipping costs may be paid in addition to the $25.

✓ Example 62. Paula Perry is a computer salesperson. Last year her unreimbursed expenses included $800 for business meals, $2,000 for business suits, and $1,500 for Christmas gifts for 30 clients. The gifts cost $50 apiece. Paula may deduct $640 (.8 × $800) for meals and $750 (30 × $25 limit per gift) for Christmas gifts. The cost of the business suits is not deductible.

A taxpayer may deduct job-hunting expenses incurred while looking for a new position in the *same* trade or business. If the trade or business of the taxpayer changes as a result of the new position, however, the costs are not deductible.

Costs associated with the determination or refund of any tax are also deductible under Sec. 212. Thus, a taxpayer may deduct personal tax return preparation fees, legal and accounting fees associated with personal tax planning and litigation, and appraisal fees for charitable contributions.

Finally, costs associated with investment income are deductible. These costs include the rental of safety deposit boxes to hold investment instruments, investment consulting fees, and subscriptions to investment journals. All of these miscellaneous itemized deductions as well as those discussed earlier are subject in the aggregate to the 2% of AGI floor.

Example 63. Everett Sloan has unreimbursed employee business expenses of $200, pays $150 for tax preparation, incurs investment expenses of $60, spent $1,500 trying to locate a better job in his field, and spent $200 for professional journal subscriptions. Everett's AGI is $32,000. The total eligible to be deducted is $2,110 (200 + 150 + 60 + 1,500 + 200). He may include $1,470 [$2,110 − (.02) × (32,000)] as miscellaneous itemized deductions—the amount in excess of 2% of his AGI. The above information would appear as follows on a Schedule A, Form 1040:

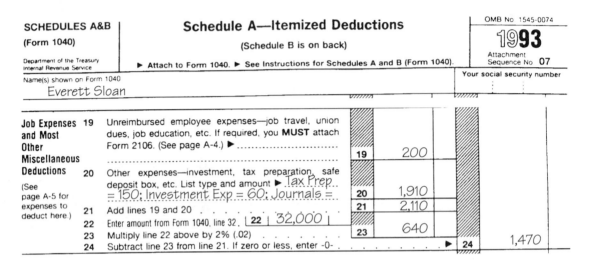

TAX TIP

To the extent possible, the taxpayer should "bunch" miscellaneous itemized deductions into one year to increase the likelihood of exceeding the 2% of AGI limit and benefit from their deductibility.

REDUCTION OF ITEMIZED DEDUCTIONS FOR HIGH-INCOME TAXPAYERS

For tax years beginning after December 31, 1990, individual taxpayers with adjusted gross incomes in excess of specified amounts must reduce certain itemized deductions by up to 80% of their total. This reduction applies to all allowable itemized deductions except medical expenses, casualty and theft losses, and investment interest expense. For each $100 that the taxpayer's AGI exceeds the specified limit, the total of the affected itemized deductions must be reduced by $3 (that is, a 3% reduction). The total reduction is not to exceed 80% of the total of itemized deductions, again excluding *medical, casualty* and *theft losses,* and *investment interest expense.* All other applicable limitations on the itemized deductions (for example, the 2% limit on miscellaneous itemized deductions) must be applied *before* this reduction is determined. The threshold amount for determining this adjustment was $100,000 ($50,000 for married individuals filing separately) for tax years beginning in 1991 and is adjusted annually for inflation. The threshold amount for 1993 is $108,450 ($54,225 for married individuals filing separately).

☑ **Example 64.** Sally Jones, a single individual, has AGI of $150,000 for the 1993 tax year. She itemized her deductions, which were medical expenses, $5,000; investment interest, $10,000; taxes, $20,000; miscellaneous deductions, $10,000. She must reduce her itemized deductions by $1,247 [.03 × ($150,000 – $108,450)]. Sally can deduct only $43,753 ($45,000 – $1,247) of itemized deductions. In no case could her itemized deductions be less than $21,000. She is allowed her medical expense and investment interest expense deductions in full and 20% of her other deductions, or $6,000 [.2 ($20,000 + $10,000)]. No more than $24,000 [.8 × ($20,000 + $10,000)] is disallowed due to this limitation.

☑ **Example 65.** Pierre Redux, a single man, had AGI of $185,000 and the following itemized deductions:

Medical expenses	$60,000
Taxes	20,000
Mortgage interest on residence	10,000

Pierre's itemized deductions after the reduction applicable to high-income taxpayers are $87,703, determined as follows: Pierre's excess AGI is $185,000 – $108,450 = $76,550. His reduction at 3% would be $2,297 (.03 × $76,550) unless the limitation on reductions applies; that is, his reduction in itemized deduction for taxes and mortgage interest could not exceed 80% of these items, or $24,000 (.8 × $30,000). His total itemized deductions are $60,000 for medical expenses and $27,703 for taxes and interest, for a total of $87,703. (The reduction is prorated—$1,531 to taxes and $766 to mortgage interest.) Schedule A and the itemized deduction worksheet with this information are shown in Figure 4-9.

REVIEW V

1. Jamie had to go to Los Angeles to attend a five-day seminar related to her job. She decided to leave four days early and spend those additional four days sightseeing. During the nine days in Los Angeles, she had the following expenses: lodging, $900; meals (at 80%), $315; seminar fee, $250; rental car for four days of sightseeing, $100; other sightseeing expenses, $75. How much of the above expenses qualifies as employee business expense?
   (a) $1,640
   (b) $1,465
   (c) $925
   (d) $911

2. Quentin used his personal auto extensively for business in the current year. By keeping a detailed diary, he knows he had 17,500 miles for business use and 5,000 miles for personal use. His expenses for the auto were as follows: gasoline, $2,300; oil, $100; repairs and maintenance, $500; insurance and license, $1,000; and depreciation, $3,000. How much may Quentin deduct for the business use of his auto?
   (a) $3,900
   (b) $4,200
   (c) $5,367
   (d) $6,900

3. Brian Bantrack often takes clients to dinner and sporting events to discuss continued purchases of items from the company he works for. Brian is careful to document these meetings and to discuss business specifically. During the current year Brian spent $3,800 on

Figure 4-9 Schedule A

Itemized Deductions Worksheet—Line 26 (keep for your records)

1. Add the amounts on Schedule A, lines 4, 8, 12, 16, 17, 18, 24, and 25 . . . . **1.** 90,000
2. Add the amounts on Schedule A, lines 4, 11, and 17, plus any gambling losses included on line 25 . . . . **2.** 60,000
   Caution: Be sure your total gambling losses are clearly identified on the dotted line next to line 25.
3. Subtract line 2 from line 1. If the result is zero, **stop here;** enter the amount from line 1 above on Schedule A, line 26, and see the **Note** below **3.** 30,000
4. Multiply line 3 above by 80% (.80) . . . **4.** 24,000
5. Enter the amount from Form 1040, line 32 **5.** 185,000
6. Enter $108,450 ($54,225 if married filing separately) **6.** 108,450
7. Subtract line 6 from line 5. If the result is zero or less, **stop here;** enter the amount from line 1 above on Schedule A, line 26, and see the **Note** below **7.** 76,550
8. Multiply line 7 above by 3% (.03) . . . **8.** 2,297
9. Enter the **smaller** of line 4 or line 8 . . . . **9.** 2,297
10. **Total itemized deductions.** Subtract line 9 from line 1. Enter the result here and on Schedule A, line 26, and see the **Note** below **10.** 87,703

*Note: Also enter on Form 1040, line 34, the **larger** of the amount you enter on Schedule A, line 26, or your standard deduction.*

Figure 4-9 (continued)

meals and $1,400 on tickets for football and basketball games. How much may he deduct if he receives no reimbursement from his employer and his AGI is $30,000?
   (a) $5,200
   (b) $4,160
   (c) $3,560
   (d) $1,400

4. Ellen White receives $3,600 annually as an expense allowance from her employer. She had the following business expenses: travel (other than meals), $3,000; meals, $800; and entertainment, $1,200. How much may she deduct as business expenses, both *for* AGI and *from* AGI, if her AGI is $25,000? She does not account to her employer for her expenses in order to receive the $300 per month allowance.

	FOR	FROM
(a)	$0	$4,100
(b)	$0	$4,600
(c)	$3,600	$0
(d)	$3,600	$1,400

5. Bernice Goldstein is self-employed and operates a dog training business out of her home. As an office she uses the den, which takes up 500 of the home's 2,500 total square feet of area. Bernice's income from the business is $8,000; she incurs the following expenses:

Utilities	$ 825
Taxes	$1,200
Interest	$ 700
Depreciation	$1,500

   She also has $1,200 of other business-related expenses. What is her allowable deduction?
   (a) $5,425
   (b) $4,225
   (c) $8,000
   (d) $2,045

6. Peter paid the following expenses during the current year: tax preparation fee, $250; safety deposit box rental for holding securities, $100; union dues, $500; uniforms, $400; and tools

for his job, $250. If his AGI is $15,200, how much of the above expenses may he deduct as an itemized deduction?
(a) $1,500
(b) $1,196
(c) $1,000
(d) $0

7. Bud Bundee is a CPA. He incurred the following educational expenses during the current year:

Tuition for law school	$4,500
Continuing education expenses	1,025
Tuition for daughter's college	6,000

How much may Bud deduct as educational expenses on his tax return?
(a) $5,525
(b) $11,525
(c) $1,025
(d) $7,025

8. Tina had the following itemized deductions in 1993:

Medical expenses	$1,200	(after 7.5% limitation)
Interest and taxes	3,250	
Miscellaneous	675	(after 2% floor)
Moving expenses	6,350	

If her AGI for 1993 was $170,000, what is the total of her itemized deductions?
(a) $11,475
(b) $9,628
(c) $9,532
(d) $9,600

Answers are on page 4-58.

VI MISCELLANEOUS DEDUCTIONS FOR ADJUSTED GROSS INCOME
(Code Section 215, and 219)

There are several personal items that taxpayers may deduct above the line (*for* AGI) in determining their tax liability. Those most commonly encountered are alimony payments and contributions to individual retirement accounts (IRAs).

ALIMONY PAID

THE LAW

Sec. 215—Alimony, etc., Payments.—(a) General Rule.—In the case of an individual, there shall be allowed as a deduction an amount equal to the alimony or separate maintenance payments paid during such individual's taxable year.
(b) Alimony or Separate Maintenance Payments Defined.—For purposes of this section, the term "alimony or separate maintenance payment" means any alimony or separate maintenance payment (as defined in section 71(b)) which is includable in the gross income of the recipient under section 71.

Transfers between spouses under a separate maintenance agreement or between ex-spouses as part of the divorce decree are considered alimony if they meet the following requirements:

1. the payments are in cash,
2. the payments are made pursuant to divorce or separation under a written decree of support,
3. the payments are required by the decree,
4. the spouses agree not to treat the payments as other than alimony,
5. the payments cease upon the death of the spouse *receiving* the alimony, and
6. the spouses do not file joint income tax returns and do not occupy the same household.

Qualifying alimony payments are deductible for AGI by the payor and must be included in the income of the payee. Alimony as income was discussed in Chapter 2.

Alimony payments must be for the support of the recipient-spouse. They must be either paid directly to the spouse or paid on the spouse's behalf for his or her legal obligations. Thus, rent, utilities, or mortgage payments made by one spouse for the support of the other normally constitute alimony. If, however, the payor-spouse owns the house in which the recipient-spouse lives, the payments on that home mortgage are not alimony since the mortgage is not the recipient-spouse's lawful obligation.

Example 66. Allen and Portia Counts were divorced last year. Allen pays Portia $200 per month and lets her live rent-free in one of the rental units he owns. Allen pays $600 per month on the mortgage and $750 annually for the property taxes. The only amount Allen may consider as alimony is the $200 monthly payment. If Portia lived in a rental unit that Allen did not own, he would be able to treat rent paid on her behalf as alimony.

Certain items are not alimony:

1. payments made for the support of minor children. Such payments, to be considered child support, must be (a) fixed or contingent on the child's status (such as age), (b) paid for the support of the child, and (c) set by decree.
2. payments made prior to the written divorce or separation agreement;
3. payments made voluntarily and not required by the decree;
4. nonsupport lump-sum payments and property settlements.

If a decree provides for both alimony and child support and the payor falls behind in payments, no payments are considered alimony until all child support in arrears is paid.

Example 67. William paid Toni $100,000 upon her agreeing to a divorce. He also gave her $3,000 per month for living expenses during the time they were waiting to go to court. The divorce decree provided that William would pay Toni $2,000 per month until she remarries for her support and $1,000 per month for the support of their 4-year-old daughter. William can deduct only the $2,000-per-month payment to Toni for her support as alimony *after* the divorce. The $100,000 is a property settlement; the $3,000-per-month payments made prior to the divorce are voluntary payments; and the $1,000-per-month payments are child support.

TAX TIP

Tax planning should be an integral part of any divorce settlement to minimize the overall tax burden. For example, if the parent paying the alimony and child support is in a much higher tax bracket than the custodial parent, the custodial parent could consider forgoing the dependency exemption in exchange for increased alimony payments. If the payor is in the 28% marginal tax bracket, a $2,000 dependency exemption will reduce taxes by $560. If the recipient is in the 15% marginal bracket, the deduction is worth only $300. If the payor increases alimony by $500 in exchange for the exemption, the custodial parent's net after-tax benefit is $125 {$500 −[(.15 × 500) + $300]}. The noncustodial parent's net after-tax benefit is $200 {$560 − [500 − .28(500)]}.

INDIVIDUAL RETIREMENT ACCOUNTS

Employee taxpayers may establish retirement accounts for themselves and their spouse. If certain requirements are met, the employee may also take a deduction *for* adjusted gross income of up to $2,000 ($2,250 on a spousal IRA) contributed to the IRA. These accounts permit the tax-free accumulation of income on amounts contributed to

ANSWERS TO REVIEW V

1. (c) The entire seminar fee and 5/9 of the meals and lodging qualify as employee business expenses.
2. (c) Quentin may deduct 17,500/22,500 of the $6,900 of expenses incurred, since this is greater than the automatic mileage method.
3. (c) Brian may deduct 80% of the meals and entertainment expenses incurred subject to the $600 AGI limitation.
4. (a) None of her expenses are deductible for AGI because her employer uses a nonaccountable plan. The meals and entertainment are subject to the 80% limitation, and the total amount is subject to the 2% floor.
5. (d) ($165 + $240 + $140 + $300)] + $1,200
6. (b) Peter may deduct all the expenses in excess of 2% of his AGI.
7. (c) Only the continuing education is deductible.
8. (b) .03 × ($170,000 − $108,450) = $1,847 reduction
$11,475 (total deductions) − $1,847 = $9,628

the plans as well as the possibility of deducting all or part of the principal contributed. Tax-free income accumulations and deductible contributions are not taxed until they are withdrawn.

THE LAW

Sec. 219(a)—Allowance of Deduction.—In the case of an individual, there shall be allowed as a deduction an amount equal to the qualified retirement contributions of the individual for the taxable year. (b) Maximum Amount of Deduction—
(1) In General.—The amount allowable as a deduction under subsection (a) to any individual for any taxable year shall not exceed the lesser of—
(A) $2,000, or
(B) an amount equal to the compensation in the individual's gross income for such taxable year.

Individual retirement accounts (IRAs) can be established by individuals for the benefit of themselves and their spouses. The annual allowable IRA *contribution* is the smaller of $2,000 or 100% of earned income. If the individual's spouse has little or no income, then the allowable IRA contribution is increased to $2,250. Up to $2,000 of the $2,250 may be directed to either spouse's accumulation in the IRA. If both spouses are employed, each may contribute the lesser of $2,000 or their earned income to their separate IRAs.

Example 68. Floyd and Myrtle Willets both work, and neither is covered by an employer-sponsored qualified retirement plan. Floyd earns $32,000 and Myrtle earns $42,000 annually. Each of them may put $2,000 into an IRA and deduct it on their tax return. If Myrtle does not work or has very little compensation income, Floyd may establish a spousal IRA contributing a maximum of $2,250 into their IRA. He may direct $2,000 of the $2,250 into either his or Myrtle's share of the account.

If the following requirements are met, all or a portion of the taxpayer's contribution to his or her IRA is deductible above the line (*for* adjusted gross income) in determining taxable income. If the taxpayer (or spouse, if married) is not covered by a qualified employer-sponsored retirement plan, the entire allowable contribution is deductible. If the taxpayer (or spouse, if married) is an active participant in a qualified employer-sponsored retirement plan, contributions may still be made to the retirement plan, but all or part of the contribution may not be deductible. If the taxpayer's AGI (without the IRA deduction) exceeds $25,000 ($40,000 on a joint return), the taxpayer's allowable deduction is phased out over the next $10,000 of AGI. The reduction in the deductible IRA contribution is $.20 (or $.225 for the spousal IRA of $2,250) for each dollar of AGI that exceeds the $25,000 (or $40,000) base amount. If the taxpayer's AGI is $35,000 or more ($50,000 or more on a joint return), no deduction is permitted. If a taxpayer's income is between $34,000 and $35,000 (or $49,000 and $50,000 on a joint return), he or she may make a minimum $200 deductible contribution. If the taxpayer deposits more than the $2,000 (or $2,250 with a spousal IRA) annual contribution limit, there is a 6%

penalty on excess contributions. This 6% penalty applies regardless of whether or not the $2,000 (or $2,250 on a spousal IRA) contribution to the IRA is deductible. In addition, there is a 10% penalty on premature withdrawals—that is, withdrawals made before the taxpayer reaches 59½ years of age.

The taxpayer has until the due date of his or her personal return (without extensions) to establish and/or make a contribution to an IRA. Thus, a calendar-year taxpayer has until April 15 of the following tax year to deposit funds into an IRA and, if eligible, take a deduction for the current tax year.

☑ **Example 69.** Morgan Stiles is single and has an AGI of $27,000 before his IRA contribution for 1993. Morgan is not covered by an employer-sponsored retirement plan. He has until April 15, 1994, to contribute up to $2,000 to his IRA and deduct it in determining his 1993 AGI.

☑ **Example 70.** If, in the preceding example, Morgan had been covered by an employer-sponsored retirement plan, his maximum deductible contribution would be $1,600 [$2,000 − (.2 × 2,000)].

☑ **Example 71.** If, in the previous examples, Morgan had an AGI of $34,900 before his IRA deduction, he would be allowed to deduct a minimum payment of $200 to his IRA.

When a taxpayer withdraws funds from an IRA at age 59½ or older, only those funds that have not been taxed previously will be taxed. If the taxpayer was permitted full deductions for amounts contributed to the IRA, all funds withdrawn represent untaxed interest and principal amounts and are fully taxable at time of withdrawal. Amounts in an IRA that were not deductible when contributed may be withdrawn without additional tax.

☑ **Example 72.** Jean Drury contributed $10,000 to her IRA over a ten-year period but was not permitted to take any deduction for these contributions since she was eligible to participate in an employer-sponsored qualified retirement plan. When she retired, she took all the money out of the plan in a lump-sum distribution of $25,000. Since $10,000 of the $25,000 represents a return of income already taxed, only $15,000 will be taxed as part of her income upon withdrawal.

TAX TIP

Since taxation of income from IRAs is postponed until the income is withdrawn, a taxpayer can shield the income earned on amounts contributed to an IRA from current taxation regardless of whether or not the annual contribution is deductible. If a taxpayer makes nondeductible contributions, *these* amounts may be withdrawn after age 59½ without additional taxation. Only the income on these contributions would be taxed when withdrawn.

REVIEW VI

1. Wanda and Wallace were divorced on February 1, 1993. Prior to the divorce, Wanda paid Wally $500 a month for six months for his support and $1,000 a month for the support of their two children. The divorce decree specified that Wanda must continue to pay Wally $500 per month per child until each reaches 18 years of age and $1,000 a month for Wally's support for two years only. How much may Wanda deduct as alimony in 1993?
   - (a) $0
   - (b) $11,000
   - (c) $11,500
   - (d) $22,000

2. Percy Wintree gave his wife their home as part of their divorce settlement. In addition, he is required to pay her utility bills and $500 per month for their two children. During the current year, Percy paid utility bills of $3,000. What is Percy's alimony deduction?
   - (a) $0
   - (b) $3,000
   - (c) $6,000
   - (d) $9,000

3. Jonah is a single taxpayer. His AGI before his IRA contribution is $32,500. If he is covered by an employer-sponsored retirement plan, what is his allowable IRA deduction?
   - (a) $0
   - (b) $500
   - (c) $750
   - (d) $1,500

4. John and Mary Cummings have AGI of $44,000. John puts $2,250 into an IRA for himself and Mary, splitting this equally between them. If John is covered by a qualified pension plan at his work, what is the deductible portion of the IRA?
   - (a) $0
   - (b) $1,125
   - (c) $1,350
   - (d) $1,450

Answers are on page 4-64.

CHAPTER PROBLEMS

PART

I

1. Sam had the following medically related expenses in the current year:
   - (a) Sam suffered a broken leg, for which he incurred a total of $1,500 in medical expenses for the doctor and hospital;
   - (b) Sam's wife made weekly trips to her allergist for allergy shots, driving a total of 1,000 miles;
   - (c) Sam bought his dependent daughter a pair of contact lenses for $120 and a wig for $60. She didn't like the color of her hair but was allergic to hair dyes.
   - (d) Sam installed a swimming pool in his backyard because he felt it would be good therapy for his broken leg. The pool cost him $5,000, but it increased the value of the home by only $2,600.

   Which of the above expenses are considered allowable medical expenses? If Sam's AGI is $32,000, what is his medical expense deduction?

I 2. Anna had the following medical expenses in the current year:
   (a) $400 for a back brace for her daughter to prevent curvature of the spine;
   (b) $300 for prescription drugs for herself and her daughter;
   (c) $6,000 for hospital and doctor while at a noted clinic specializing in the treatment of adolescent back deformities;
   (d) $100 a night for three nights for her and her daughter when they returned to the clinic for follow-up evaluation; meals during this time cost $120;
   (e) transportation costs of $600 for the two trips to the clinic;
   (f) $700 for a specially designed exercise machine for treatment of the daughter's back problem;
   (g) other doctor and dentist bills amounting to $1,500;
   (h) $1,500 for medical insurance.
   If Anna received $3,200 in reimbursement from her insurance and her AGI is $46,000, what is her medical expense deduction?

II 3. In 1986 Whit Meyer purchased a home for $1,400,000, on which he obtained a $1,200,000 mortgage. In the current year, when the mortgage balance was $925,000, he purchased a summer home for $325,000, securing it with a $275,000 mortgage. In order to obtain the down payment for this home and buy furniture and a boat, Whit took out a home equity loan on the first home for $250,000. How much interest may Whit deduct if his interest payments were $92,000 on the first home, $30,000 on the summer home, and $34,000 on the home equity loan?

II 4. Mary Lamb had a number of investments for the current year. She had income of $41,000 from several investments and had expenses of $32,500; additionally, she had a $6,000 capital gain from the sale of investment property. If Mary invested in an investment asset that had no income yet but that resulted in $21,000 of investment interest expense, how much interest expense could she deduct?

II 5. Nelson Brown liked to live beyond his means. As a result, during the current year he paid interest on personal debts as follows: credit cards, $920; auto loan, $680; home mortgage, $6,200; furniture purchase, $520; and guaranteed student loan, $260. What is Nelson's interest deduction?

III 6. During 1993 Jeremy had $2,400 withheld from his wages for federal taxes and $680 for state taxes. He made additional estimated tax payments of $600 and $200, respectively, to the federal and state governments. He received a federal refund of $320 and a state refund of $480 for the prior year. What is his itemized deduction for taxes for 1993 if he did not itemize his prior year's taxes?

III 7. George Jensen gave very generously to charities in the current year. With an AGI of $64,000, he gave $20,000 in cash to his church and its school; he gave some stock worth $9,000, which cost him $4,000, to a local college; and he gave some jewelry, which cost $5,000 but was now worth $12,000, to a private nonoperating foundation. What is George's charitable deduction? Explain any available carryovers.

IV 8. August Scott had a number of misfortunes during the current year. First, a thief stole his auto and totally wrecked it. The auto cost $12,000 and had a value of $8,000 when destroyed. August unfortunately had let his insurance lapse. Next, his wife lost a diamond ring while they were on vacation. The ring was worth $4,000, had cost only $3,000, and was insured for only $2,000. His summer home was damaged by a tornado. Its value before the tornado was $68,000; after, $42,000. He collected $20,000 from the insurance company. Finally, his home was broken into and his personal computer and computer game disks were stolen. He had a basis of $3,500 in this equipment, but its value at the time of the theft was only $1,400. If August's AGI is $46,000, how much is his casualty loss deduction on Schedule A?

I & IV 9. Bill Cole had the following items relevant to his current year's tax return:
(a) doctor bills, $3,000;
(b) hospital bills, $12,000;
(c) dentist, $2,000;
(d) eyeglasses and hearing aids, $725;
(e) medical insurance premiums, $1,100;
(f) reimbursements for medical expenses from insurance, $8,700;
(g) prescription drugs, $480;
(h) repair of home due to termite damage over five-year period, $6,200;
(i) fire damage (single occurrence):

Property	Cost	Fair Market Value
Garage	$8,200	$6,100
Auto	9,000	4,200
Homeowner's tools and equipment	2,000	700

insurance recovery on garage, $2,000;
insurance recovery on auto, $6,000;

If Bill's AGI is $32,500, what amounts may he deduct as itemized deductions?

IV 10. Bobby Martin moved from Fargo, North Dakota, to Wilmington, Delaware, to start a new job on April 1, 1993. He had the following moving expenses:

Cost of shipping household goods	$3,000
Transportation for himself and his family	680
Temporary living expenses:	
Meals	400
Lodging	600
Premove house hunting	800
Commission paid on sale of old residence	4,000

If Bobby received no reimbursements from his new employer, what is his moving expense deduction for 1993?

V 11. Donald Joker had the following business expenses during 1993:

Meals	$3,800
Lodging	6,200
Laundry	640
Transportation	4,600
Entertainment	2,100

Donald's employer gives him a $1,000-per-month expense allowance to cover his expenses. He is not required to make an accounting to the employer for this allowance. If his AGI is $37,000, excluding the reimbursement, explain in detail the effects of the above items on Donald's taxable income.

V   12. John was a self-employed manufacturer's representative for several hospital equipment suppliers. During the current year he used his converted detached garage as his office. Since he was new to this business, his commissions from sales were only $6,800. His expenses for the office were interest, $1,300; utilities, $600; telephone, $2,200; insurance, $300; taxes, $80; and depreciation, $3,200. Which of John's home office expenses are deductible? In what amounts?

V   13. Elizabeth Arden is a lawyer. Her employer requires her to take continuing professional education courses at a local law school. The courses cost her $1,250 during the current year. She also incurred the following other educational expenses: $750 for tuition to send her daughter to a private high school and $7,000 for law school tuition for her son. How much may Elizabeth deduct as education expenses on her tax return?

V   14. Mary Kay had the following itemized deductions during the current year:

Casualty losses (after limitations)	$2,750
Medical expenses (after 7.5% limitation)	6,825

If her AGI was $230,000, what amount may she take as itemized deductions?

VI   15. Which of the following are not necessary for a payment to be considered alimony?
    (a) Payments must be made in cash.
    (b) Payments are made pursuant to a divorce decree or decree of separate maintenance.
    (c) Payments continue after spouse's death.
    (d) A joint return is not filed by the divorcing spouses.

VI   16. Bill and Susan were divorced in May 1993. In February 1993 Susan gave Bill $50,000 to persuade him to agree to the divorce. In March and April 1993 Susan gave Bill $1,500 to pay for his living expenses. After the divorce, Susan continued to pay Bill $1,000 per month for his living expenses because she felt sorry for him. Classify the amounts and their deductibility for this case.

VI   17. As part of their divorce settlement, Sam transferred ownership of his boat to his ex-wife Julie. The boat had a fair market value of $75,000 and a basis of $45,000. What amount of gain or loss is recognized by Sam and/or Julie? What is Julie's basis in the boat?

VI   18. (a) Mary and Bob are married and have an AGI of $48,000. They are active participants in their qualified employee-sponsored retirement plans. If they contribute $4,000 to their IRAs, how much may they deduct?
    (b) If Mary were single and could not actively participate in an employer-sponsored plan, what amount would she be able to deduct if she contributed $2,000 to an IRA?

ANSWERS TO REVIEW VI

1. (b) Wanda may deduct only $11,000—$1,000 per month for February through December 1993—as alimony. She may not deduct any voluntary payments she made prior to the divorce decree.
2. (b) The $3,000 in utility bill payments may be deducted as support (alimony) payments.
3. (b) Jonah may deduct $500: $2,000 − (.2 × $7,500).
4. (c) $2,250 − [($44,000 − $40,000) × .225]

TAX RETURN PROBLEMS

19. [Form 4684; Form 1040 Schedule A] Using the information in Problem 9 above, complete Form 4684 and Form 1040 Schedule A for Bill Cole.
20. [Form 3903] Using the information in Problem 10 above, complete Form 3903 for Bobby Martin, assuming that he wants to take the maximum deduction allowed.

HOW WOULD YOU RULE?

21. Margaret Walsh had owned and lived in her home for 40 years. She wanted to keep the home in the family but knew that she could no longer maintain it properly. She decided to move into a retirement center and transferred title to the home to her daughter and son-in-law, who then moved in. She continued to pay the interest and principal on a home equity loan, which she had obtained to make substantial repairs two years ago, as well as the property taxes. How are these payments treated for income tax purposes?
22. Warren Allen was born and reared in England. Although he has lived in the United States for the last ten years, he feels strongly about his English roots. This current tax year, he donated a painting worth $10,000 (cost = $6,000) to the British Museum. May he deduct the gift as a charitable contribution?

TAX PORTFOLIO PROBLEM FOR THE NEILSON FAMILY

If your instructor has assigned this problem, refer to Appendix A and complete the portion labeled "Chapter 4." This includes the information on itemized deductions, employee expenses, moving expenses, and personal casualty losses. This information is used for the preparation of Schedule A and Forms 2106, 3903, and 4684 for Harold and Maude Neilson.

Chapter 4 Problem 19   Name_____   4-67

Form 4684
Department of the Treasury
Internal Revenue Service

Casualties and Thefts
▶ See separate instructions.
▶ Attach to your tax return.
▶ Use a separate Form 4684 for each different casualty or theft.

OMB No. 1545-0177
1993
Attachment Sequence No. 26

Name(s) shown on tax return | Identifying number

SECTION A—Personal Use Property (Use this section to report casualties and thefts of property **not** used in a trade or business or for income-producing purposes.)

1   Description of properties (show type, location, and date acquired for each):
    Property A ....
    Property B ....
    Property C ....
    Property D ....

	Properties (Use a separate column for each property lost or damaged from one casualty or theft.)			
	A	**B**	**C**	**D**
2 Cost or other basis of each property				
3 Insurance or other reimbursement (whether or not you filed a claim). See instructions				
Note: *If line 2 is more than line 3, skip line 4.*				
4 Gain from casualty or theft. If line 3 is **more than** line 2, enter the difference here and skip lines 5 through 9 for that column. See instructions if line 3 includes insurance or other reimbursement you did not claim, or you received payment for your loss in a later tax year				
5 Fair market value **before** casualty or theft				
6 Fair market value **after** casualty or theft				
7 Subtract line 6 from line 5				
8 Enter the **smaller** of line 2 or line 7				
9 Subtract line 3 from line 8. If zero or less, enter -0-				

10   Casualty or theft loss. Add the amounts on line 9. Enter the total **10**

11   Enter the amount from line 10 or $100, whichever is **smaller** **11**

12   Subtract line 11 from line 10 . . . .   **12**
     Caution: *Use only one Form 4684 for lines 13 through 18.*

13   Add the amounts on line 12 of all Forms 4684 . . . .   **13**

14   Combine the amounts from line 4 of all Forms 4684 . . . .   **14**

15   • If line 14 is **more than** line 13, enter the difference here and on Schedule D. Do not complete the rest of this section (see instructions).
     • If line 14 is **less than** line 13, enter -0- here and continue with the form.
     • If line 14 is **equal to** line 13, enter -0- here. Do not complete the rest of this section.   **15**

16   If line 14 **is less than** line 13, enter the difference **16**

17   Enter 10% of your adjusted gross income (Form 1040, line 32). Estates and trusts, see instructions **17**

18   Subtract line 17 from line 16. If zero or less, enter -0-. Also enter result on Schedule A (Form 1040), line 17. Estates and trusts, enter on the "Other deductions" line of your tax return **18**

For Paperwork Reduction Act Notice, see page 1 of separate instructions.   Cat. No. 129970   Form **4684** (1993)

Copyright © 1994 by Harcourt Brace & Company. All rights reserved.

4-68 Chapter 4 Problem 19

SCHEDULES A&B (Form 1040) Department of the Treasury Internal Revenue Service	Schedule A—Itemized Deductions (Schedule B is on back) ▶ Attach to Form 1040. ▶ See Instructions for Schedules A and B (Form 1040).	OMB No. 1545-0074 **1993** Attachment Sequence No **07**

Name(s) shown on Form 1040   Your social security number

Medical and Dental Expenses	1	Caution: *Do not include expenses reimbursed or paid by others.* Medical and dental expenses (see page A-1) . . .	1	
	2	Enter amount from Form 1040, line 32 . ┗ 2 ┛		
	3	Multiply line 2 above by 7.5% (.075)	3	
	4	Subtract line 3 from line 1. If zero or less, enter -0- . . . . ▶		4
Taxes You Paid (See page A-1.)	5	State and local income taxes	5	
	6	Real estate taxes (see page A-2)	6	
	7	Other taxes. List—include personal property taxes ▶	7	
	8	Add lines 5 through 7 . . . . ▶		8
Interest You Paid (See page A-2.) Note: Personal interest is not deductible.	9a	Home mortgage interest and points reported to you on Form 1098	9a	
	b	Home mortgage interest not reported to you on Form 1098. If paid to the person from whom you bought the home, see page A-3 and show that person's name, identifying no., and address ▶	9b	
	10	Points not reported to you on Form 1098. See page A-3 for special rules	10	
	11	Investment interest. If required, attach Form 4952. (See page A-3.)	11	
	12	Add lines 9a through 11 . . . . ▶		12
Gifts to Charity (See page A-3.)		Caution: *If you made a charitable contribution and received a benefit in return, see page A-3.*		
	13	Contributions by cash or check	13	
	14	Other than by cash or check. If over $500, you **MUST** attach Form 8283	14	
	15	Carryover from prior year	15	
	16	Add lines 13 through 15 . . . . ▶		16
Casualty and Theft Losses	17	Casualty or theft loss(es). Attach Form 4684. (See page A-4.) . . . . . . ▶		17
Moving Expenses	18	Moving expenses. Attach Form 3903 or 3903-F. (See page A-4.) . . . . ▶		18
Job Expenses and Most Other Miscellaneous Deductions (See page A-5 for expenses to deduct here.)	19	Unreimbursed employee expenses—job travel, union dues, job education, etc. If required, you **MUST** attach Form 2106. (See page A-4.) ▶	19	
	20	Other expenses—investment, tax preparation, safe deposit box, etc. List type and amount ▶	20	
	21	Add lines 19 and 20	21	
	22	Enter amount from Form 1040, line 32 . ┗ 22 ┛		
	23	Multiply line 22 above by 2% (.02)	23	
	24	Subtract line 23 from line 21. If zero or less, enter -0- . . . . ▶		24
Other Miscellaneous Deductions	25	Other—from list on page A-5. List type and amount ▶ .... ▶		25
Total Itemized Deductions	26	Is the amount on Form 1040, line 32, more than $108,450 (more than $54,225 if married filing separately)? • **NO.** Your deduction is not limited. Add lines 4, 8, 12, 16, 17, 18, 24, and 25 and enter the total here. Also enter on Form 1040, line 34, the **larger** of this amount or your standard deduction. • **YES.** Your deduction may be limited. See page A-5 for the amount to enter. ▶		26

For Paperwork Reduction Act Notice, see Form 1040 instructions.   Cat. No. 11330X   Schedule A (Form 1040) 1993

Copyright © 1994 by Harcourt Brace & Company. All rights reserved.

Chapter 4 Problem 20   Name_____   *4-69*

Form **3903**	**Moving Expenses**	OMB No. 1545-0062
Department of the Treasury Internal Revenue Service	▶ Attach to Form 1040. ▶ See separate instructions.	**1993** Attachment Sequence No. **62**

Name(s) shown on Form 1040   Your social security number

Caution: *If you are a member of the armed forces, see the instructions before completing this form.*

1 Enter the number of miles from your **old home** to your **new workplace** . . . . | 1 |
2 Enter the number of miles from your **old home** to your **old workplace** . . . . | 2 |
3 Subtract line 2 from line 1. Enter the result but not less than zero. . . . . ▶ | 3 |

If line 3 is 35 or more miles, complete the rest of this form. Also, see **Time Test** in the instructions. If line 3 is less than 35 miles, you may not deduct your moving expenses.

Part I   Moving Expenses

Note: *Any payments your employer made for any part of your move (including the value of any services furnished in kind) should be included on your W-2 form. Report that amount on **Form 1040, line 7**. See **Reimbursements** in the instructions.*

Section A—Transportation of Household Goods

4 Transportation and storage for household goods and personal effects . . . . | 4 |

Section B—Expenses of Moving From Old To New Home

5 Travel and lodging **not** including meals . . . . | 5 |
6 Total meals . . . . | 6 |
7 Multiply line 6 by 80% (.80) . . . . | 7 |
8 Add lines 5 and 7 . . . . | 8 |

Section C—Pre-move Househunting Expenses and Temporary Quarters
(for any 30 days in a row after getting your job)

9 Pre-move travel and lodging **not** including meals . . . . | 9 |
10 Temporary quarters expenses **not** including meals . . . . | 10 |
11 Total meal expenses for both pre-move househunting and temporary quarters . . . . | 11 |
12 Multiply line 11 by 80% (.80) . . . . | 12 |
13 Add lines 9, 10, and 12 . . . . | 13 |

Section D—Qualified Real Estate Expenses

14 Expenses of (check one) a ☐ selling or exchanging your old home, or
                              b ☐ if renting, settling an unexpired lease. | 14 |
15 Expenses of (check one) a ☐ buying your new home, or
                              b ☐ if renting, getting a new lease. | 15 |

Part II   Dollar Limits and Moving Expense Deduction

Note: *If you and your spouse moved to separate homes, see the instructions.*

16 Enter the **smaller** of:
   • The amount on line 13, or
   • $1,500 ($750 if married filing a separate return and at the end of
     1993 you lived with your spouse who also started work in 1993). | 16 |
17 Add lines 14, 15, and 16 . . . . | 17 |
18 Enter the **smaller** of:
   • The amount on line 17, or
   • $3,000 ($1,500 if married filing a separate return and at the end
     of 1993 you lived with your spouse who also started work in 1993). | 18 |
19 Add lines 4, 8, and 18. Enter the total here and on Schedule A, line 18. This is your **moving expense deduction** . . . . ▶ | 19 |

For Paperwork Reduction Act Notice, see separate instructions.   Cat. No. 12490K   Form **3903** (1993)

Printed on recycled paper

Copyright © 1994 by Harcourt Brace & Company. All rights reserved.

Comprehensive Tax Return Problem 2
Form 1040, Schedules A & B, Form 2106, Form 3903, and Form 4684

James and Kathleen Hethcox, both age 34, file a joint tax return for 1993. James's social security number is 332-10-4454, and Kathleen's is 434-22-1231. They reside at 1020 Butterfield Place, Ithaca, New York 14850. They provide over half the support of their 13-year-old son, Jason. Jason's social security number is 544-32-8902. Both James and Kathleen elect to contribute to the presidential election fund.

James is a community college instructor, and Kathleen is an advertising manager for a local company. Their Form W-2s for 1993 disclose the following:

	James	Kathleen
Gross salaries	$36,400	$53,200
Federal income tax withholdings	7,560	13,230
State income tax withholdings	1,040	2,450
FICA taxes paid	2,785	3,924

Their only other income in 1993 consisted of $820 interest on state of New York bonds, $1,200 interest on Best Corporation bonds, and $640 dividends on McGraw-Hill stock.

As an advertising manager with Singer Company, Kathleen incurs a substantial amount of employee business expenses. Most of these expenses are reimbursed by the company; however, during 1993 Kathleen incurred the following amounts, which were not reimbursed:

Parking and tolls on business trips	$ 102
Business miles driven to meetings (600 miles)	?
Hotel charges for out-of-town business meetings	1,862
Meals while out of town at business meetings	350
Professional journal subscriptions	420
Professional organization dues	540

James and Kathleen moved to Ithaca from Chicago, Illinois, in 1993 because of Kathleen's job transfer. Singer Company paid most of the moving expenses; however, the following amounts were not reimbursed:

Cost of driving cars to Ithaca (800 miles each car)	?
Meals incurred on trip from Chicago to Ithaca	$ 110
Temporary living expenses—Ithaca (without meals)	420
Meals during temporary living time in Ithaca	160
Cost of breaking apartment lease in Chicago	1,800
Premove house-hunting trip—lodging	652
Premove house-hunting trip—meals	250

James and Kathleen's personal records disclose the following personal expenses incurred during 1993:

Eyeglasses—Jason	$ 120
Home mortgage interest (qualifying residential)	6,230

Tax return preparation fee—1992 return	170
Veterinarian fees for family dog and cat	340
Contributions in cash to First Presbyterian Church	1,390
Interest charge on personal bank credit cards	420
Interest on personal boat loan (not secured by home)	880
Unreimbursed physician fees	730
Real estate taxes—personal residence	1,760
Utilities expense—Ithaca home	3,650
Contributions in cash to State University	940
Personal property taxes—autos (based on value)	670
Personal groceries purchased in 1993	5,852
Health insurance premiums paid	1,230
Life insurance premiums paid	3,420
Unreimbursed hospital charges	3,250
Investment advice fee on stock and bonds	300

Kathleen's diamond ring was stolen on March 1, 1993. She had originally purchased the ring for $11,200 in 1987, and it was worth $10,300 at the time of the theft. There was no insurance on the ring.

Singer Company does not offer a qualified retirement plan for its employees. However, Kathleen elects to contribute to an individual retirement account established in her own name. On December 28, 1993, she contributed $2,000 to the account.

REQUIRED: Prepare a Form 1040 for James and Kathleen Hethcox, with accompanying schedules A and B and Forms 2106, 3903, and 4684.

Comprehensive Tax Return Problem 2   Name _____ 4-73

Form 1040 — Department of the Treasury—Internal Revenue Service
U.S. Individual Income Tax Return 1993

IRS Use Only—Do not write or staple in this space

For the year Jan. 1–Dec. 31, 1993, or other tax year beginning _____ 1993, ending _____ 19___   OMB No. 1545-0074

Label (See instructions on page 12.)
Use the IRS label. Otherwise, please print or type.

- Your first name and initial | Last name | Your social security number
- If a joint return, spouse's first name and initial | Last name | Spouse's social security number
- Home address (number and street). If you have a P.O. box, see page 12 | Apt. no
- City, town or post office, state, and ZIP code. If you have a foreign address, see page 12.

For Privacy Act and Paperwork Reduction Act Notice, see page 4.

Presidential Election Campaign (See page 12.)
- Do you want $3 to go to this fund? .... Yes / No
- If a joint return, does your spouse want $3 to go to this fund? .... Yes / No

Note: Checking "Yes" will not change your tax or reduce your refund.

Filing Status (See page 12.) Check only one box.
1. ☐ Single
2. ☐ Married filing joint return (even if only one had income)
3. ☐ Married filing separate return. Enter spouse's social security no. above and full name here. ▶
4. ☐ Head of household (with qualifying person). (See page 13.) If the qualifying person is a child but not your dependent, enter this child's name here. ▶
5. ☐ Qualifying widow(er) with dependent child (year spouse died ▶ 19___). (See page 13.)

Exemptions (See page 13.)

6a ☐ **Yourself.** If your parent (or someone else) can claim you as a dependent on his or her tax return, **do not** check box 6a. But be sure to check the box on line 33b on page 2

b ☐ **Spouse**

c **Dependents:**
(1) Name (first, initial, and last name)	(2) Check if under age 1	(3) If age 1 or older, dependent's social security number	(4) Dependent's relationship to you	(5) No. of months lived in your home in 1993

If more than six dependents, see page 14.

- No. of boxes checked on 6a and 6b ____
- No. of your children on 6c who:
  • lived with you
  • didn't live with you due to divorce or separation (see page 15)
- Dependents on 6c not entered above
- Add numbers entered on lines above ▶

d If your child didn't live with you but is claimed as your dependent under a pre-1985 agreement, check here ▶ ☐
e Total number of exemptions claimed

Income

Attach Copy B of your Forms W-2, W-2G, and 1099-R here.

If you did not get a W-2, see page 10.

If you are attaching a check or money order, put it on top of any Forms W-2, W-2G, or 1099-R.

7   Wages, salaries, tips, etc. Attach Form(s) W-2 7
8a Taxable interest income (see page 16). Attach Schedule B if over $400 .... 8a
 b Tax-exempt interest (see page 17). DON'T include on line 8a 8b
9   Dividend income. Attach Schedule B if over $400 9
10 Taxable refunds, credits, or offsets of state and local income taxes (see page 17) .. 10
11 Alimony received 11
12 Business income or (loss). Attach Schedule C or C-EZ 12
13 Capital gain or (loss). Attach Schedule D 13
14 Capital gain distributions not reported on line 13 (see page 17) 14
15 Other gains or (losses). Attach Form 4797 15
16a Total IRA distributions . 16a   b Taxable amount (see page 18) 16b
17a Total pensions and annuities 17a   b Taxable amount (see page 18) 17b
18 Rental real estate, royalties, partnerships, S corporations, trusts, etc. Attach Schedule E .. 18
19 Farm income or (loss). Attach Schedule F 19
20 Unemployment compensation (see page 19) 20
21a Social security benefits 21a   b Taxable amount (see page 19) 21b
22 Other income. List type and amount—see page 20 22
23 Add the amounts in the far right column for lines 7 through 22. This is your **total income** ▶ 23

Adjustments to Income (See page 20.)

24a Your IRA deduction (see page 20) 24a
 b Spouse's IRA deduction (see page 20) 24b
25 One-half of self-employment tax (see page 21) 25
26 Self-employed health insurance deduction (see page 22) 26
27 Keogh retirement plan and self-employed SEP deduction 27
28 Penalty on early withdrawal of savings 28
29 Alimony paid. Recipient's SSN ▶ 29
30 Add lines 24a through 29. These are your **total adjustments** ▶ 30

Adjusted Gross Income

31 Subtract line 30 from line 23. This is your **adjusted gross income**. If this amount is less than $23,050 and a child lived with you, see page EIC-1 to find out if you can claim the "Earned Income Credit" on line 56 ▶ 31

Cat. No. 11320B   Form **1040** (1993)

Copyright © 1994 by Harcourt Brace & Company. All rights reserved.

Form 1040 (1993) Page 2

Tax Computation
(See page 23.)

32 Amount from line 31 (adjusted gross income) **32**

33a Check if: ☐ You were 65 or older, ☐ Blind; ☐ Spouse was 65 or older, ☐ Blind.
Add the number of boxes checked above and enter the total here ▶ **33a**

b If your parent (or someone else) can claim you as a dependent, check here ▶ **33b** ☐

c If you are married filing separately and your spouse itemizes deductions or you are a dual-status alien, see page 24 and check here .... ▶ **33c** ☐

34 Enter the larger of your:
- **Itemized deductions** from Schedule A, line 26, OR
- **Standard deduction** shown below for your filing status. But if you checked any box on line 33a or b, go to page 24 to find your standard deduction. If you checked **box 33c**, your standard deduction is zero.
  - Single—$3,700
  - Head of household—$5,450
  - Married filing jointly or Qualifying widow(er)—$6,200
  - Married filing separately—$3,100

34

35 Subtract line 34 from line 32 .... **35**

36 If line 32 is $81,350 or less, multiply $2,350 by the total number of exemptions claimed on line 6e. If line 32 is over $81,350, see the worksheet on page 25 for the amount to enter . **36**

37 Taxable income. Subtract line 36 from line 35. If line 36 is more than line 35, enter -0- **37**

If you want the IRS to figure your tax, see page 24.

38 Tax. Check if from **a** ☐ Tax Table, **b** ☐ Tax Rate Schedules, **c** ☐ Schedule D Tax Worksheet, or **d** ☐ Form 8615 (see page 25). Amount from Form(s) 8814 ▶ **e** _____ **38**

39 Additional taxes (see page 25). Check if from **a** ☐ Form 4970 **b** ☐ Form 4972 . **39**

40 Add lines 38 and 39 .... ▶ **40**

Credits
(See page 25.)

41 Credit for child and dependent care expenses. Attach Form 2441 . **41**

42 Credit for the elderly or the disabled. Attach Schedule R . **42**

43 Foreign tax credit. Attach Form 1116 .... **43**

44 Other credits (see page 26). Check if from **a** ☐ Form 3800 **b** ☐ Form 8396 **c** ☐ Form 8801 **d** ☐ Form (specify) _____ **44**

45 Add lines 41 through 44 .... **45**

46 Subtract line 45 from line 40. If line 45 is more than line 40, enter -0- . ▶ **46**

Other Taxes

47 Self-employment tax. Attach Schedule SE. Also, see line 25 . **47**

48 Alternative minimum tax. Attach Form 6251 .... **48**

49 Recapture taxes (see page 26). Check if from **a** ☐ Form 4255 **b** ☐ Form 8611 **c** ☐ Form 8828 **49**

50 Social security and Medicare tax on tip income not reported to employer. Attach Form 4137 . **50**

51 Tax on qualified retirement plans, including IRAs. If required, attach Form 5329 . **51**

52 Advance earned income credit payments from Form W-2 .... **52**

53 Add lines 46 through 52. This is your **total tax** .... ▶ **53**

Payments
Attach Forms W-2, W-2G, and 1099-R on the front.

54 Federal income tax withheld. If any is from Form(s) 1099, check ▶ ☐ **54**

55 1993 estimated tax payments and amount applied from 1992 return . **55**

56 Earned income credit. Attach Schedule EIC **56**

57 Amount paid with Form 4868 (extension request) **57**

58a Excess social security, Medicare, and RRTA tax withheld (see page 28) . **58a**

b Deferral of additional 1993 taxes. Attach Form 8841 ..... **58b**

59 Other payments (see page 28). Check if from **a** ☐ Form 2439 **b** ☐ Form 4136 ...... **59**

60 Add lines 54 through 59. These are your **total payments** .... ▶ **60**

Refund or Amount You Owe

61 If line 60 is more than line 53, subtract line 53 from line 60. This is the amount you **OVERPAID** . ▶ **61**

62 Amount of line 61 you want **REFUNDED TO YOU**. .... ▶ **62**

63 Amount of line 61 you want **APPLIED TO YOUR 1994 ESTIMATED TAX** ▶ **63**

64 If line 53 is more than line 60, subtract line 60 from line 53. This is the **AMOUNT YOU OWE**. For details on how to pay, including what to write on your payment, see page 29 . **64**

65 Estimated tax penalty (see page 29). Also include on line 64 **65**

Sign Here
Keep a copy of this return for your records.

Under penalties of perjury, I declare that I have examined this return and accompanying schedules and statements, and to the best of my knowledge and belief, they are true, correct, and complete. Declaration of preparer (other than taxpayer) is based on all information of which preparer has any knowledge.

Your signature	Date	Your occupation
Spouse's signature. If a joint return, BOTH must sign.	Date	Spouse's occupation

Paid Preparer's Use Only

Preparer's signature ▶	Date	Check if self-employed ☐	Preparer's social security no.
Firm's name (or yours if self-employed) and address ▶		E.I. No.	
		ZIP code	

Comprehensive Tax Return Problem 2   Name _____   4-75

SCHEDULES A&B
(Form 1040)
Department of the Treasury
Internal Revenue Service

Schedule A—Itemized Deductions
(Schedule B is on back)

▶ Attach to Form 1040. ▶ See Instructions for Schedules A and B (Form 1040).

OMB No. 1545-0074
1993
Attachment Sequence No. 07

Name(s) shown on Form 1040 | Your social security number

Medical and Dental Expenses		**Caution:** *Do not include expenses reimbursed or paid by others.*		
	1	Medical and dental expenses (see page A-1)	1	
	2	Enter amount from Form 1040, line 32.	2	
	3	Multiply line 2 above by 7.5% (.075)	3	
	4	Subtract line 3 from line 1. If zero or less, enter -0- ▶		4
Taxes You Paid (See page A-1.)	5	State and local income taxes	5	
	6	Real estate taxes (see page A-2)	6	
	7	Other taxes. List—include personal property taxes ▶	7	
	8	Add lines 5 through 7 ▶		8
Interest You Paid (See page A-2.) **Note:** Personal interest is not deductible.	9a	Home mortgage interest and points reported to you on Form 1098	9a	
	b	Home mortgage interest not reported to you on Form 1098. If paid to the person from whom you bought the home, see page A-3 and show that person's name, identifying no., and address ▶	9b	
	10	Points not reported to you on Form 1098. See page A-3 for special rules	10	
	11	Investment interest. If required, attach Form 4952. (See page A-3.)	11	
	12	Add lines 9a through 11 ▶		12
Gifts to Charity (See page A-3.)		**Caution:** *If you made a charitable contribution and received a benefit in return, see page A-3.*		
	13	Contributions by cash or check	13	
	14	Other than by cash or check. If over $500, you **MUST** attach Form 8283	14	
	15	Carryover from prior year	15	
	16	Add lines 13 through 15 ▶		16
Casualty and Theft Losses	17	Casualty or theft loss(es). Attach Form 4684. (See page A-4.) ▶		17
Moving Expenses	18	Moving expenses. Attach Form 3903 or 3903-F. (See page A-4.) ▶		18
Job Expenses and Most Other Miscellaneous Deductions (See page A-5 for expenses to deduct here.)	19	Unreimbursed employee expenses—job travel, union dues, job education, etc. If required, you **MUST** attach Form 2106. (See page A-4.) ▶	19	
	20	Other expenses—investment, tax preparation, safe deposit box, etc. List type and amount ▶	20	
	21	Add lines 19 and 20	21	
	22	Enter amount from Form 1040, line 32.	22	
	23	Multiply line 22 above by 2% (.02)	23	
	24	Subtract line 23 from line 21. If zero or less, enter -0- ▶		24
Other Miscellaneous Deductions	25	Other—from list on page A-5. List type and amount ▶ .... ▶		25
Total Itemized Deductions	26	Is the amount on Form 1040, line 32, more than $108,450 (more than $54,225 if married filing separately)? • **NO.** Your deduction is not limited. Add lines 4, 8, 12, 16, 17, 18, 24, and 25 and enter the total here. Also enter on Form 1040, line 34, the **larger** of this amount or your standard deduction. • **YES.** Your deduction may be limited. See page A-5 for the amount to enter. ▶		26

For Paperwork Reduction Act Notice, see Form 1040 instructions.   Cat. No. 11330X   Schedule A (Form 1040) 1993

Copyright © 1994 by Harcourt Brace & Company. All rights reserved.

Schedules A&B (Form 1040) 1993 — OMB No. 1545-0074 — Page **2**

Name(s) shown on Form 1040. Do not enter name and social security number if shown on other side. | Your social security number

Schedule B—Interest and Dividend Income

Attachment Sequence No. 08

Part I Interest Income

(See pages 16 and B-1.)

Note: If you received a Form 1099-INT, Form 1099-OID, or substitute statement from a brokerage firm, list the firm's name as the payer and enter the total interest shown on that form.

Note: *If you had over $400 in taxable interest income, you must also complete Part III.*

Interest Income | Amount

1. List name of payer. If any interest is from a seller-financed mortgage and the buyer used the property as a personal residence, see page B-1 and list this interest first. Also show that buyer's social security number and address ▶

2. Add the amounts on line 1 . . . . | 2
3. Excludable interest on series EE U.S. savings bonds issued after 1989 from Form 8815, line 14. You MUST attach Form 8815 to Form 1040 . . . . | 3
4. Subtract line 3 from line 2. Enter the result here and on Form 1040, line 8a ▶ | 4

Part II Dividend Income

(See pages 17 and B-1.)

Note: If you received a Form 1099-DIV or substitute statement from a brokerage firm, list the firm's name as the payer and enter the total dividends shown on that form.

Note: *If you had over $400 in gross dividends and/or other distributions on stock, you must also complete Part III.*

Dividend Income | Amount

5. List name of payer. Include gross dividends and/or other distributions on stock here. Any capital gain distributions and nontaxable distributions will be deducted on lines 7 and 8 ▶

6. Add the amounts on line 5 . . . . | 6
7. Capital gain distributions. Enter here and on Schedule D* . | 7
8. Nontaxable distributions. (See the inst. for Form 1040, line 9.) | 8
9. Add lines 7 and 8 . . . . | 9
10. Subtract line 9 from line 6. Enter the result here and on Form 1040, line 9 . ▶ | 10

*If you received capital gain distributions but do not need Schedule D to report any other gains or losses, see the instructions for Form 1040, lines 13 and 14.

Part III Foreign Accounts and Trusts

(See page B-2.)

If you had over $400 of interest or dividends OR had a foreign account or were a grantor of, or a transferor to, a foreign trust, you must complete this part. | Yes | No

11a. At any time during 1993, did you have an interest in or a signature or other authority over a financial account in a foreign country, such as a bank account, securities account, or other financial account? See page B-2 for exceptions and filing requirements for Form TD F 90-22.1 . . . .

b. If "Yes," enter the name of the foreign country ▶

12. Were you the grantor of, or transferor to, a foreign trust that existed during 1993, whether or not you have any beneficial interest in it? If "Yes," you may have to file Form 3520, 3520-A, or 926 .

For Paperwork Reduction Act Notice, see Form 1040 instructions.

Schedule B (Form 1040) 1993

Comprehensive Tax Return Problem 2   Name _____   4-77

Form **2106**	**Employee Business Expenses**	OMB No. 1545-0139
Department of the Treasury Internal Revenue Service	▶ See separate instructions. ▶ Attach to Form 1040.	**1993** Attachment Sequence No. 54

Your name	Social security number	Occupation in which expenses were incurred

Part I   Employee Business Expenses and Reimbursements

STEP 1 Enter Your Expenses		Column A Other Than Meals and Entertainment	Column B Meals and Entertainment
1	Vehicle expense from line 22 or line 29	1	/////
2	Parking fees, tolls, and transportation, including train, bus, etc., that did **not** involve overnight travel	2	/////
3	Travel expense while away from home overnight, including lodging, airplane, car rental, etc. **Do not** include meals and entertainment	3	/////
4	Business expenses not included on lines 1 through 3. **Do not** include meals and entertainment	4	/////
5	Meals and entertainment expenses (see instructions)	/////	5
6	**Total expenses.** In Column A, add lines 1 through 4 and enter the result. In Column B, enter the amount from line 5	6	

Note: If you were not reimbursed for any expenses in Step 1, skip line 7 and enter the amount from line 6 on line 8.

STEP 2   Enter Amounts Your Employer Gave You for Expenses Listed in STEP 1

7	Enter amounts your employer gave you that were **not** reported to you in box 1 of Form W-2. Include any amount reported under code "L" in box 13 of your Form W-2 (see instructions) . . .	7			

STEP 3   Figure Expenses To Deduct on Schedule A (Form 1040)

8	Subtract line 7 from line 6	8	
	Note: If **both columns** of line 8 are zero, **stop here.** If Column A is less than zero, report the amount as income on Form 1040, line 7, and enter -0- on line 10, Column A.		
9	Enter 20% (.20) of line 8, Column B	9	
10	In Column A, enter the amount from line 8. In Column B, subtract line 9 from line 8	10	
11	Add the amounts on line 10 of both columns and enter the total here. **Also, enter the total on Schedule A (Form 1040), line 19.** (Qualified performing artists and individuals with disabilities, see the instructions for special rules on where to enter the total.) . . . . . ▶	11	

For Paperwork Reduction Act Notice, see instructions.   Cat. No. 11700N   Form **2106** (1993)

Copyright © 1994 by Harcourt Brace & Company. All rights reserved.

Form 2106 (1993) Page **2**

Part II — Vehicle Expenses (See instructions to find out which sections to complete.)

Section A.—General Information

		(a) Vehicle 1	(b) Vehicle 2
12	Enter the date vehicle was placed in service	/ /	/ /
13	Total miles vehicle was driven during 1993	miles	miles
14	Business miles included on line 13	miles	miles
15	Percent of business use. Divide line 14 by line 13	%	%
16	Average daily round trip commuting distance	miles	miles
17	Commuting miles included on line 13	miles	miles
18	Other personal miles. Add lines 14 and 17 and subtract the total from line 13	miles	miles

19 Do you (or your spouse) have another vehicle available for personal purposes? ☐ Yes ☐ No

20 If your employer provided you with a vehicle, is personal use during off duty hours permitted? ☐ Yes ☐ No ☐ Not applicable

21a Do you have evidence to support your deduction? ☐ Yes ☐ No

21b If "Yes," is the evidence written? ☐ Yes ☐ No

Section B.—Standard Mileage Rate (Use this section only if you own the vehicle.)

22 Multiply line 14 by 28¢ (.28). Enter the result here and on line 1. (Rural mail carriers, see instructions.) **22**

Section C.—Actual Expenses

		(a) Vehicle 1	(b) Vehicle 2
23	Gasoline, oil, repairs, vehicle insurance, etc.		
24a	Vehicle rentals		
b	Inclusion amount (see instructions)		
c	Subtract line 24b from line 24a		
25	Value of employer-provided vehicle (applies only if 100% of annual lease value was included on Form W-2—see instructions)		
26	Add lines 23, 24c, and 25		
27	Multiply line 26 by the percentage on line 15		
28	Depreciation. Enter amount from line 38 below		
29	Add lines 27 and 28. Enter total here and on line 1		

Section D.—Depreciation of Vehicles (Use this section only if you own the vehicle.)

		(a) Vehicle 1	(b) Vehicle 2
30	Enter cost or other basis (see instructions)		
31	Enter amount of section 179 deduction (see instructions)		
32	Multiply line 30 by line 15 (see instructions if you elected the section 179 deduction)		
33	Enter depreciation method and percentage (see instructions)		
34	Multiply line 32 by the percentage on line 33 (see instructions)		
35	Add lines 31 and 34		
36	Enter the limitation amount from the table in the line 36 instructions		
37	Multiply line 36 by the percentage on line 15		
38	Enter the **smaller** of line 35 or line 37. Also, enter this amount on line 28 above		

Copyright © 1994 by Harcourt Brace & Company. All rights reserved.

Comprehensive Tax Return Problem 2   Name _____   4-79

Form **3903**
Department of the Treasury
Internal Revenue Service

Moving Expenses

▶ Attach to Form 1040.
▶ See separate instructions.

OMB No. 1545-0062

1993

Attachment Sequence No. **62**

Name(s) shown on Form 1040 | Your social security number

Caution: *If you are a member of the armed forces, see the instructions before completing this form.*

1. Enter the number of miles from your **old home** to your **new workplace** . . . . | 1 |
2. Enter the number of miles from your **old home** to your **old workplace** . . . . | 2 |
3. Subtract line 2 from line 1. Enter the result but not less than zero . . . . ▶ | 3 |

If line 3 is 35 or more miles, complete the rest of this form. Also, see **Time Test** in the instructions. If line 3 is less than 35 miles, you may not deduct your moving expenses.

Part I   Moving Expenses

Note: *Any payments your employer made for any part of your move (including the value of any services furnished in kind) should be included on your W-2 form. Report that amount on* **Form 1040, line 7.** *See* **Reimbursements** *in the instructions.*

Section A—Transportation of Household Goods

4. Transportation and storage for household goods and personal effects . . . . | 4 |

Section B—Expenses of Moving From Old To New Home

5. Travel and lodging **not** including meals . . . . | 5 |
6. Total meals . . . . | 6 |
7. Multiply line 6 by 80% (.80) . . . . | 7 |
8. Add lines 5 and 7 . . . . | 8 |

Section C—Pre-move Househunting Expenses and Temporary Quarters
(for any 30 days in a row after getting your job)

9. Pre-move travel and lodging **not** including meals . . . . | 9 |
10. Temporary quarters expenses **not** including meals . . . . | 10 |
11. Total meal expenses for both pre-move househunting and temporary quarters . . . . | 11 |
12. Multiply line 11 by 80% (.80) . . . . | 12 |
13. Add lines 9, 10, and 12 . . . . | 13 |

Section D—Qualified Real Estate Expenses

14. Expenses of (check one) **a** ☐ selling or exchanging your old home, or
    b ☐ if renting, settling an unexpired lease. | 14 |
15. Expenses of (check one) **a** ☐ buying your new home, or
    b ☐ if renting, getting a new lease. | 15 |

Part II   Dollar Limits and Moving Expense Deduction

Note: *If you and your spouse moved to separate homes, see the instructions.*

16. Enter the **smaller** of:
    - The amount on line 13, or
    - $1,500 ($750 if married filing a separate return and at the end of 1993 you lived with your spouse who also started work in 1993). | 16 |
17. Add lines 14, 15, and 16 . . . . | 17 |
18. Enter the **smaller** of:
    - The amount on line 17, or
    - $3,000 ($1,500 if married filing a separate return and at the end of 1993 you lived with your spouse who also started work in 1993). | 18 |
19. Add lines 4, 8, and 18. Enter the total here and on Schedule A, line 18. This is your **moving expense deduction** . . . . ▶ | 19 |

For Paperwork Reduction Act Notice, see separate instructions.   Cat. No. 12490K   Form **3903** (1993)

Printed on recycled paper

Copyright © 1994 by Harcourt Brace & Company. All rights reserved.

4-80   Comprehensive Tax Return Problem 2

Form **4684**	**Casualties and Thefts**	OMB No. 1545-0177
Department of the Treasury Internal Revenue Service	▶ See separate instructions. ▶ Attach to your tax return. ▶ Use a separate Form 4684 for each different casualty or theft.	**19**93 Attachment Sequence No. 26
Name(s) shown on tax return		Identifying number

SECTION A—Personal Use Property (Use this section to report casualties and thefts of property **not** used in a trade or business or for income-producing purposes.)

1   Description of properties (show type, location, and date acquired for each):
       Property **A** ....
       Property **B** ....
       Property **C** ....
       Property **D** ....

Properties (Use a separate column for each property lost or damaged from one casualty or theft.)

		A	B	C	D
2	Cost or other basis of each property				
3	Insurance or other reimbursement (whether or not you filed a claim). See instructions				
	Note: *If line 2 is **more than** line 3, skip line 4.*				
4	Gain from casualty or theft. If line 3 is **more than** line 2, enter the difference here and skip lines 5 through 9 for that column. See instructions if line 3 includes insurance or other reimbursement you did not claim, or you received payment for your loss in a later tax year				
5	Fair market value **before** casualty or theft . . .				
6	Fair market value **after** casualty or theft				
7	Subtract line 6 from line 5				
8	Enter the **smaller** of line 2 or line 7				
9	Subtract line 3 from line 8. If zero or less, enter -0-				

10	Casualty or theft loss. Add the amounts on line 9. Enter the total	10
11	Enter the amount from line 10 or $100, whichever is **smaller**	11
12	Subtract line 11 from line 10	12
	Caution: *Use only one Form 4684 for lines 13 through 18.*	
13	Add the amounts on line 12 of all Forms 4684	13
14	Combine the amounts from line 4 of all Forms 4684	14
15	• If line 14 is **more than** line 13, enter the difference here and on Schedule D. Do not complete the rest of this section (see instructions). • If line 14 is **less than** line 13, enter -0- here and continue with the form. • If line 14 is **equal to** line 13, enter -0- here. Do not complete the rest of this section.	15
16	If line 14 is **less than** line 13, enter the difference	16
17	Enter 10% of your adjusted gross income (Form 1040, line 32). Estates and trusts, see instructions	17
18	Subtract line 17 from line 16. If zero or less, enter -0-. Also enter result on Schedule A (Form 1040), line 17. Estates and trusts, enter on the "Other deductions" line of your tax return	18

For Paperwork Reduction Act Notice, see page 1 of separate instructions.   Cat. No. 12997O   Form **4684** (1993)

Copyright © 1994 by Harcourt Brace & Company. All rights reserved.

CHAPTER 5

Individual Tax Credits and Prepayments

In determining the final tax due, individual taxpayers are allowed a number of credits that directly reduce their tax liability. Several of these are *personal* credits, available to individual taxpayers only—for example, the child care credit and credit for the elderly. Other credits, available both to individuals and to other taxpayers as part of business or income-producing activities, include the credit for research activities and the low-income housing credit.

Most credits are allowed to offset only the taxpayer's actual tax liability; that is, the taxpayer cannot receive a refund if the available credit exceeds the tax he or she owes. Examples are the child care credit and the foreign tax credit. Several credits, such as the child care credit and the credit for the elderly, are simply lost if they exceed the tax liability. Other credits—for example, the foreign tax credit—have carryover provisions if they exceed the current usable limit. The taxpayer may carry them over and use them in subsequent tax years.

Finally, a few credits are refundable; that is, if the credit exceeds the tax liability, the taxpayer receives a payment from the government for the excess credit. The most common of the refundable credits is the earned-income credit. While the Internal Revenue Code identifies the taxes withheld on wages as refundable credits, withholding taxes are generally considered prepayments of taxes. The taxpayer is, however, entitled to a refund if withholding and other prepayments exceed the taxpayer's tax liability.

This chapter addresses the calculation of the more commonly encountered tax credits applicable to individuals. The business tax credits, which can apply to individuals who operate businesses or hold property to produce income, are explained in Chapter 9. Part I of Chapter 5 covers the earned-income credit and the credit for the elderly, Part II addresses the child and dependent care credit, and Part III explains several miscellaneous credits, including the foreign tax credit. Figure 5-1 presents the order in which individual taxpayers apply the credits (except the general business credit, discussed in Chapter 9) to their tax liability. Part IV details the payment of estimated taxes by individuals, while the Chapter Appendix provides a brief overview of the audit and appeals process for tax returns.

I. Nonrefundable Credits
- A. Child and Dependent Care Credit
- B. Credit for the Elderly or the Disabled
- C. Foreign Tax Credit

II. Refundable Credits
- D. Credit for All Taxes Paid
  1. Withholding Taxes
  2. Estimated Payments
  3. Application of Prior Refunds
- E. Earned Income Credit

Figure 5-1 Order of Deducting Tax Credits from Tax Liability (excludes General Business Credit—see Chapter 9)

I CREDITS AVAILABLE TO LOWER-INCOME TAXPAYERS
(Code Sections 22, and 32)

Several important personal credits applicable to lower-income taxpayers—the basic earned-income credit and its accompanying credit for a child born in 1993 and health insurance credit, and the credit for the elderly and permanently disabled—are explained here. The earned income credits are refundable credits and are applicable to a number of low-income taxpayers. The Revenue Reconciliation Act of 1990 made significant changes in the earned-income credit and the Revenue Reconciliation Act of 1993 will bring more changes for tax years *after* 1993.* The credit for the elderly and permanently disabled has limited applicability, and eligible individuals often overlook it.

EARNED-INCOME CREDIT

THE LAW

Sec. 32(a)—In the case of an eligible individual, there shall be allowed as a credit against the tax imposed by this subtitle for the taxable year an amount equal to the sum of—(1) the basic earned-income credit, and (2) the health insurance credit.

For tax years 1991 through 1993, the Revenue Reconciliation Act of 1990 made a number of modifications in the earned-income credit. This credit was retitled the "basic earned-income credit," and a supplemental young-child credit and health insurance credit were added. While all of these credits follow the basic format of the pre–1991 earned-income credit, the credit and phaseout percentages were changed, along with the eligibility requirements for claiming them.

---

*For changes in the tax law effective for tax years beginning in 1994, see Appendix J.

Eligibility Requirements

To claim the basic earned-income credit for tax years 1991, 1992, and 1993,* the taxpayer(s) must be either an individual or a married couple (filing a joint return) with whom one or more qualifying children live, and who have incomes of under a specified amount. If a married couple files separate returns, neither of them is eligible to claim this credit, nor is any taxpayer who claims the foreign earned-income exclusion.

Qualifying Child. To be a qualifying child, the child must meet relationship, principal abode, age, identification, and marital status tests as follows:

Relationship. The child must be either a natural child or an adopted child (or a descendent of the child) of the taxpayer. A stepchild of the taxpayer also qualifies, but not a descendent of the stepchild. A foster child qualifies if he or she lives with the taxpayer for the entire year and is cared for as a natural child.

Principal Abode. The qualifying child, if he or she is other than a foster child, must live with the taxpayer in the United States for more than one-half of the tax year. Foster children must live with the taxpayer for the entire year. A principal residence outside the United States will not qualify.

Age. The child must be under the age of 19 at the end of the calendar year unless he or she is a full-time student. In the case of a full-time student, the child must be under 24 at the end of the calendar year. If the child is permanently and totally disabled at any time during the year, the age limit is waived.

Identification. When filling out the appropriate tax forms, the taxpayer must include the name, age, and, for any child over the age of one at year end, social security number of the eligible child.

Marital Status. The child must not be married at year end, unless, if married, the taxpayer can claim a dependency exemption (or could claim one except for a divorce agreement surrendering this right) for the child.

If two or more taxpayers (other than a married couple filing jointly) are eligible individuals because of the same qualifying child, only the taxpayer with the greatest AGI may claim the credit. Moreover, a qualifying child of one eligible taxpayer may not also be an eligible taxpayer him- or herself and claim the earned-income credit. While these latter requirements may seem strange, they result from the qualifying child not having to be a dependent (except if married) of the eligible taxpayer.

☑ **Example 1.** Tina Godel's two children lived with her the entire tax year. Eric is 17 and has a full-time job at a fast food restaurant, so that he is self-supporting. Terri is 20, attends school part-time, and is supported by Tina. If Tina meets the income requirements for the basic earned-income credit, only Eric is a qualifying child. Terri exceeds the age limit and would have to attend school full-time to be a qualifying child. Whether Tina may claim a dependency exemption for one or both of the children is irrelevant (unless the child is married) for claiming the basic earned-income credit.

☑ **Example 2.** Sean (age 2) lives with his mother Alice (age 21) and grandmother Mary. Alice has a part-time job and had an AGI of $6,000 in 1993. Mary also works part-time and had an AGI of $9,000. Sean is a qualifying child for both Alice and Mary. Since Mary has the greater AGI she, rather than Alice, must claim the basic earned-income credit.

---

*For changes in the tax law effective for tax years beginning in 1994, see Appendix J.

THE EARNED-INCOME CREDIT FORMAT

The determination of the basic earned-income credit is a multistep (and sometimes confusing) process. The taxpayer must identify both his or her earned income and adjusted gross income. If either of these amounts is $23,050 or more for 1993, the taxpayer is not eligible for the earned-income credit. This income limitation has been adjusted annually for inflation.

Note that tables are available to assist in determining this credit along with a Schedule EIC. It is important to understand the theory and the calculations for this credit, however, for tax-planning purposes; for example, determining eligibility for advance payments is discussed later.

	1. (a)	Taxpayer's earned-income (up to a permitted maximum)
times	(b)	Credit rate
	(c)	Tentative earned-income credit
	2. (a)	Taxpayer's AGI
minus	(b)	Limitation amount
	(c)	Excess AGI
times	(d)	Phaseout percentage
	(e)	Credit reduction
	3. (a)	Maximum credit amount
minus	(b)	2(e) Credit reduction
	(c)	Adjusted tentative credit

4. Allowable credit = Smaller of 1(c) or 3(c)

Earned Income—1.(a). The taxpayer's earned income includes wages, salaries, tips, and earnings from self-employment. It does not include dividends, interest, or payments from pensions or annuities. There is a limit on the amount of the earned income that is eligible for the credit. This limit is adjusted annually for inflation. For 1993, the amount is $7,750.

Credit Percentage—1.(b). The Revenue Reconciliation Act of 1990 gradually increased the credit percentages from 16.7% to 18.5% for one qualifying child and from 17.3% to 19.5% for more than one qualifying child, as shown in Table 5-1. Multiplying the allowable earned income by the appropriate credit rate determines the taxpayer's tentative earned-income credit [1 (c)].

If the taxpayer's AGI exceeds a certain amount, the tentative credit is reduced by a percentage [the phaseout percentage—2 (d)] of the excess AGI [2 (c)]. Again, the phaseout percentage is different for one child than for more than one eligible child, and the AGI limit is adjusted annually for inflation. The AGI limitation amount is $12,200 for 1993.

If the taxpayer's AGI exceeds a certain amount, the tentative credit may be more than his or her allowable credit. For 1993, if the taxpayer's AGI exceeds $12,200, a second series of calculations is necessary. The taxpayer's excess AGI (the amount by which AGI exceeds $12,200 in 1993) is multiplied by a phaseout percentage to determine a credit reduction amount. Similar to the credit percentage, the phaseout percentage is different for one eligible child than for more than one eligible child. The AGI limitation amount also has been adjusted annually for inflation.

The credit reduction amount is subtracted from the maximum allowable credit [not the tentative-earned income credit 1(c)] to determine an adjusted tentative credit. (For 1993, the maximum allowable earned-income credit from the table for a taxpayer with one eligible child is $1,434.) The taxpayer's allowable credit is the lesser of the tentative earned-income credit [1(c)] and the adjusted tentative credit [3(c)]. (Now you know why tables are provided to assist taxpayers in this calculation.) If the taxpayer's earned income is equal to or greater than the maximum amount of earned income eligible for the credit ($7,750 in 1993), the calculations in Step 3 may be omitted and the allowable earned income credit is [1(c)] minus the credit reduction [2(e)].

Table 5-1 Earned-Income Credit and Phaseout Percentages

Tax Year	Number of Qualifying Children	Credit Percentage	Phaseout Percentage
1991	1	16.7	11.93
	2 or more	17.3	12.36
1992	1	17.6	12.57
	2 or more	18.4	13.14
1993	1	18.5	13.21
	2 or more	19.5	13.93

☑ **Example 3.** Using the $7,750 earned-income limit and $12,200 AGI limit for 1993, determine the earned-income credit for a taxpayer with one qualifying child, earned income of $6,500, and AGI of $12,500.

$ 6,500	Earned income	1(a)
× .185	Credit percentage (Table 5-1)	(b)
$ 1,203	Tentative credit	(c)
$ 12,500	AGI	2(a)
− 12,200	AGI limitation	(b)
$ 300		(c)
× .1321	Phaseout percentage (Table 5-1)	(d)
$ 40	Credit reduction	(e)
$ 1,434	Maximum allowable credit	3(a)
− 40	Credit reduction	(b)
$ 1,394	Adjusted tentative credit*	(c)

Allowable credit: $1,203 (the smaller of $1,394 and $1,203)

*Due to rounding, table amounts will differ slightly from calculated amounts.

✓ **Example 4.** Tim Garvin had earned income of $9,800 and AGI of $10,200. What is his earned-income credit for 1993 if he has three eligible children? Using the $7,750 earned-income limit, Tim would have a credit of

$7,750   Earned-income
× .195   Credit percentage
$1,511

Tim can use only the maximum allowable earned income to determine his tentative earned-income credit. Since Tim's AGI is less than the AGI limit, however, he does not have to calculate any possible reduction in this tentative credit.

The earned-income credit is a refundable credit. If the credit exceeds the taxpayer's tax liability, he will receive a payment from the government in the amount of the excess. Taxpayers eligible for the earned-income credit may also receive advance payments through their employers. Anyone who meets the eligibility requirements for the earned-income credit is eligible to receive these advance payments by filing a Form W-5, the Earned-Income Advance Payment Certificate, with his or her employer. A certificate can be filed with only one current employer at a time. Thus, a taxpayer holding two or more jobs should file the certificate with only one employer. For married couples eligible for the earned-income credit, each partner should file a certificate with his or her own employer, however. Taxpayers may receive advance payments of their earned-income credit from an employer. If they do receive advance payments, however, they must file an income tax return for the year in which advance payments are received—even though they otherwise would not be required to file a return. If their advance payments exceed their allowable credit, the excess increases the tax due for that year.

✓ **Example 5.** Toby Jones, a widower, lives in Mississippi and maintains a household for his 16-year-old son Bob. Toby has earned-income of $4,300 and dividend income of $1,100. His AGI is $5,400. Toby is eligible for a credit of $796 (.185 × $4,300) in 1993. With AGI of $5,400, Toby's taxable income is zero since his personal exemptions and standard deduction exceed his AGI. Toby will receive a payment from the government of $796 in addition to a refund of any tax withheld. Toby could have filed a Form W-5 as

---

Form W-5   **Earned Income Credit Advance Payment Certificate**   **1993**

Department of the Treasury
Internal Revenue Service

▶ This certificate expires on December 31, 1993.

Type or print your full name: *Toby Jones*

Your social security number:

Home address (number, street or rural route, apt. no.)

City, town or post office, state, and ZIP code: *Mississippi*

Note: *If you file Form W-5 with an employer to receive advance payments of the earned income credit for 1992, you must file Form 1040 or Form 1040A for 1992. If married, you must file a joint return, but see the instructions for an exception.*

		Yes	No
1	I expect to be eligible for the earned income credit for 1992, I have no other certificate in effect with any other current employer, and I choose to receive advance payment of the earned income credit	X	
2	Are you married?		X
3	If you are married, does your spouse have a certificate in effect for 1992 with any employer?		

Under penalties of perjury, I declare that the information I have furnished above is, to the best of my knowledge, true, correct, and complete.

Signature ▶ *Toby Jones*   Date ▶

shown abovej5-10 to receive advance payments of his earned-income credit from his employer during 1993.

☑ **Example 6.** Mary and Roger Witt have two qualifying children. Neither has been able to find full-time employment during 1993 and their earned income is only $7,800. They were forced to sell some stock during the year at a gain of $4,900. As a result, their AGI is $12,700. Their earned-income credit is calculated as follows:

Maximum earned income eligible for credit	$7,750
Credit rate	.195
	$1,511
Less reduction: (12,700 − 12,200) × .1393	70
Earned-income credit	$1,441

Since their standard deduction and four personal and dependency exemptions reduce their taxable income to zero, Mary and Roger would receive a $1,441 payment from the government in addition to a refund of all prepaid taxes. (Because their earned income exceeds the maximum eligible earned income, the adjusted tentative credit does not have to be calculated.)

TAX TIP

Some low-income taxpayers fail to claim their earned-income credit because they are not required to file a tax return. Since this is a *refundable* credit, it is important that eligible individuals file a return to claim the credit even if they have no tax liability.

Credit for a Child Born in 1993

The credit for a child born in 1993 (formerly the supplemental young-child credit) is a second part of the basic earned-income credit. The only difference in eligibility requirements between this and the basic earned-income credit is that the qualifying child must not be one year of age at the end of the calendar year. It thus provides an additional credit amount for the first year of a qualifying child's life. If the taxpayer has a child qualifying for this supplement to the earned-income credit, the taxpayer is eligible for an additional 5% credit. If the taxpayer has two or more qualifying children under one year of age, only one 5% additional credit is available.

Along with this added part of the earned-income credit of 5%, the taxpayer must phase out the credit using the phaseout percentage of 3.57%. As a result, this credit is phased out in the same manner as the basic earned-income credit.

☑ **Example 7.** Dora Lane had a baby on April 20 of the current tax year. She worked prior to the baby's birth and had earned income (and AGI) of $8,200. Using the

1993 earned-income limit of $7,750, Dora's basic earned-income credit and credit for a child born in 1993 are

	Earned-Income Basic Credit	Credit for Child Born in 1993
Earned-income limit	$7,750	$7,750
Credit percentage	$ .185	.05
Credit amount	$1,434	$ 388

Since Dora's AGI does not exceed the AGI limitation, there is no credit reduction required.

Although the earned-income credit is determined by a fairly complex series of calculations, the Service has provided relief by developing Schedule EIC and by providing tables (as shown in Appendix C) for credit determination. Additionally, the Serivce will calculate the credit for the taxpayer if the taxpayer requests this help on Forms 1040 or 1040A and provides the basic required information on Schedule EIC.

Note that if the taxpayer takes the credit for a child born in 1993 as part of the earned-income credit, no child or dependent care credit (explained in Part II) can be claimed for child care expenses related to that child. The child care credit may, however, be claimed for the child care expenses of other children. As part of the expanded earned-income credit, the credit for a child born in 1993 is also a refundable credit; that is, if the taxpayer's tax liability is less than the credit, the government will pay the taxpayer the difference.

HEALTH INSURANCE CREDIT

The health insurance credit is determined in the same manner as the earned-income credit and has the same eligibility requirements. The health insurance credit percentage is a fixed 6% and the phaseout percentage is a fixed 4.285%.

To claim this credit, the taxpayer may be required to report the insurance policy number or other proof of insurance along with all the other identifying information that must be reported for the earned-income credit. The taxpayer's credit cannot exceed the actual amount paid by the taxpayer for insurance coverage for medical care for the taxpayer and one or more qualifying children. The taxpayer must omit any costs that the government or a government agency reimburses, unless the reimbursement is included in income.

✓ **Example 8.** Jonah Whale paid $1,100 for a basic health insurance policy for himself and his qualifying child. Jonah's earned income and AGI were $11,500 for 1993. Using the $7,750 1993 limitation, his health insurance credit would be

$ 7,750	Earned-income maximum
x .06	Credit percentage
$ 465	(No phaseout required as AGI < $12,200)

✓ **Example 9.** Mary Jo Allen worked part-time as a cleaning lady before her second child was born on December 14 of the current year. She earned $8,500 during the year and paid $1,800 for basic health insurance for herself and her other child, age seven. She received $4,000 in alimony from her ex-husband, so her AGI was $12,500. She is entitled to the following credits:

Earned income and credit for a child born in 1993

$ 7,750	Earned-income maximum
× .245	(19.5 + 5) Credit percentages
$ 1,899	
$12,500	AGI
$12,200	AGI maximum
$ 300	
× .175	(13.93 + 3.57) Phaseout percentages
$ 53	

Net credit = $1,899 – $53 = $1,846

Health insurance credit

$ 7,750
× .06
$ 465
$ 300
× .04285
$ 13

Net credit = $465 – $13 = $452
Total net credits = $1,846 + $452 = $2,298

Figure 5-2 is a completed Schedule EIC for Mary Jo using the tables in Appendix C to determine the allowable credits. The health insurance credit is also refundable, as are the earned-income credit and the supplemental young-child credit.

CREDIT FOR THE ELDERLY AND PERMANENTLY DISABLED

Taxpayers who are over 65 years of age or are totally and permanently disabled are eligible for this credit if they meet certain income limitations.

THE LAW

Sec. 22(a)—In the case of a qualified individual, there shall be allowed as a credit against the tax imposed by this chapter for the taxable year an amount equal to 15 percent of such individual's section 22 amount for such taxable year.
(b)—For purposes of this section, the term "qualified individual" means any individual—
(1) who has attained age 65 before the close of the taxable year, or
(2) who retired on disability before the close of the taxable year and who, when he retired, was permanently and totally disabled.

SCHEDULE EIC
(Form 1040A or 1040)

Department of the Treasury
Internal Revenue Service

Earned Income Credit

▶ Attach to Form 1040A or 1040.
▶ See Instructions for Schedule EIC.

OMB No. 1545-0074

1993

Attachment Sequence No. **43**

Name(s) shown on return: Mary Jo Allen

Your social security number

Want the IRS to figure the credit for you? Just fill in this page. We'll do the rest.

General Information

To take this credit:
- You **must** have worked and earned **less** than $23,050, **and**
- Your adjusted gross income (Form 1040A, line 16, or Form 1040, line 31) must be less than $23,050, **and**
- Your filing status can be any status **except** married filing a separate return, **and**
- You **must** have at least one qualifying child (see boxes below), **and**
- You **cannot** be a qualifying child yourself.

A **qualifying child** is a child who:

is your:		was (at the end of 1993):		who:
son, daughter, adopted child, grandchild, stepchild, or foster child	**AND**	under age 19 **or** under age 24 and a full-time student **or** any age and permanently and totally disabled	**AND**	lived with you in the U.S. for more than half of 1993* (or all of 1993 if a foster child*)

*If the child didn't live with you for the required time (for example, was born in 1993), see the **Exception** on page 64 (1040A) or page EIC-2 (1040).

Do you have at least one qualifying child?	No ▶	You **cannot** take the credit. Enter "NO" next to line 28c of Form 1040A (or line 56 of Form 1040).
	Yes ▶	Go to line 1. But if the child was married or is also a qualifying child of another person (other than your spouse if filing a joint return), first see page 64 (1040A) or page EIC-2 (1040).

Information About Your Qualifying Child or Children

1(a) Child's name (first, initial, and last name) *If more than two qualifying children, see page 65 (1040A) or page EIC-2 (1040).*	(b) Child's year of birth	(c) a student under age 24 at end of 1993	(d) disabled (see booklet)	(e) If child was born before 1993, enter the child's social security number	(f) Child's relationship to you (for example, son, grandchild, etc.)	(g) Number of months child lived with you in the U.S. in 1993
Shelley	19 93				daughter	1
Martin	19 86			339 90 9999	son	12

Caution: If a child you listed above was born in 1993 **and** you chose to claim the credit or exclusion for child care expenses for this child on **Schedule 2** (Form 1040A) or **Form 2441** (Form 1040), check here ▶ ☐

Do you want the IRS to figure the credit for you?	Yes ▶	Fill in lines 2 and 3; **and** enter the amount from Form 1040A, line 16, or Form 1040, line 31, here. ▶ $
	No ▶	Go to page 2 on the back now.

Other Information

2	Enter any **nontaxable earned income** (see page 65 (1040A) or page EIC-2 (1040)) such as military housing and subsistence or contributions to a 401(k) plan. Also, list type and amount here. ▶	2	
3	Enter the total amount you paid in 1993 for health insurance that covered at least one qualifying child. See instructions	3	1,800

If you want the IRS to figure the credit for you:	**S T O P**	Attach this schedule to your return. • If filing Form 1040A, print "EIC" on the line next to line 28c. • If filing Form 1040, print "EIC" on the dotted line next to line 56.

For Paperwork Reduction Act Notice, see Form 1040A or 1040 instructions.   Cat. No. 13339M   Schedule EIC (Form 1040A or 1040) 1993

Figure 5-2 Schedule EIC

Schedule EIC (Form 1040A or 1040) 1993 — Page 2

Figure Your Basic Credit

4 Enter the amount from line 7 of Form 1040A or Form 1040. If you received a taxable scholarship or fellowship grant, see instructions .... **4** | 5,500

5 Enter any **nontaxable earned income** (see page 65 (1040A) or page EIC-2 (1040)) such as military housing and subsistence or contributions to a 401(k) plan. Also, list type and amount here. ▶ ....
.... **5** |

6 Form 1040 Filers Only: If you were self-employed **or** used Sch. C or C-EZ as a statutory employee, enter the amount from the worksheet on page EIC-3 .... **6** |

7 Earned income. Add lines 4, 5, and 6. If $23,050 or more, you **cannot** take the credit. Enter "NO" next to line 28c of Form 1040A (or line 56 of Form 1040) .... ▶ **7** | 5,500

8 Use **line 7** above to find your credit in **TABLE A** on pages **69 and 70** (1040A) or pages **EIC-4 and 5** (1040). Enter here .... **8** | 1,511

9 Adjusted gross income. Enter the amount from Form 1040A, line 16, or Form 1040, line 31 ▶ **9** | 12,500

10 Is line 9 $12,200 or more?

  YES. Use **line 9** to find your credit in **TABLE A** on pages **69 and 70** (1040A) or pages **EIC-4 and 5** (1040). Enter here ..... **10** | 1,460
  NO. Go to line 11.

11 Basic credit:
  • If you answered "YES" to line 10, enter the **smaller** of line 8 or line 10.
  • If you answered "NO" to line 10, enter the amount from line 8. **11** | 1,466

  Next: To take the health insurance credit, fill in lines 12–16. To take the extra credit for a child born in 1993, fill in lines 17–19. Otherwise, go to line 20 now.

Figure Your Health Insurance Credit

12 Use **line 7** above to find your credit in **TABLE B** on page **71** (1040A) or page **EIC-6** (1040). Enter here .... **12** | 465

13 Is line 9 above $12,200 or more?

  YES. Use **line 9** to find your credit in **TABLE B** on page **71** (1040A) or page **EIC-6** (1040). Enter here. .... **13** | 451
  NO. Go to line 14.

14 • If you answered "YES" to line 13, enter the **smaller** of line 12 or line 13.
  • If you answered "NO" to line 13, enter the amount from line 12. **14** | 451

15 Enter the total amount you paid in 1993 for health insurance that covered at least one qualifying child. See instructions .... **15** | 1,800

16 Health insurance credit. Enter the **smaller** of line 14 or line 15 .... **16** | 451

Figure Your Extra Credit for Child Born in 1993

Take this credit **only** if you did not take the credit or exclusion for child care expenses on **Schedule 2** or **Form 2441** for the same child.

TIP: You can take **both** the basic credit and the extra credit for your child born in 1993.

17 Use **line 7** above to find your credit in **TABLE C** on page **72** (1040A) or page **EIC-7** (1040). Enter here .... **17** | 388

18 Is line 9 above $12,200 or more?

  YES. Use **line 9** to find your credit in **TABLE C** on page **72** (1040A) or page **EIC-7** (1040). Enter here .... **18** | 376
  NO. Go to line 19.

19 Extra credit for child born in 1993:
  • If you answered "YES" to line 18, enter the **smaller** of line 17 or line 18.
  • If you answered "NO" to line 18, enter the amount from line 17. **19** | 376

Figure Your Total Earned Income Credit

20 Add lines 11, 16, and 19. Enter the total here and on Form 1040A, line 28c (or on Form 1040, line 56). This is your **total earned income credit** .... ▶ **20** | 2,293

TIP: Do you want the earned income credit added to your take-home pay in 1994? To see if you qualify, get **Form W-5** from your employer or by calling the IRS at 1-800-829-3676.

Figure 5-2 (continued) Schedule EIC

To be eligible for this credit, a married couple generally must file a joint return; the credit calculation will vary, however, depending whether one or both of the married persons are eligible individuals. Eligible individuals must be 65 or meet the requirements for permanent and total disability before the end of the tax year. Permanent and total disability requires a physical or mental impairment that is expected to result in death or that prevents employment. The condition must be continuous for no less than 12 months, and the taxpayer may be required to furnish proof of the disability.

To determine the credit, the 15% credit is multiplied by an initial amount, subject to income reductions, which are determined by the taxpayers' filing status. The initial amount is $5,000 for single individuals or for married couples if only one spouse is a qualified individual. The initial amount is increased to $7,500 for married couples if both spouses are qualified individuals. A married individual who has lived apart from his spouse the entire tax year may file a separate return using an initial amount of $3,750 to determine the credit. There are certain limitations on this initial amount based on disability income if the taxpayer(s) is not 65 years of age or over.

The initial amount must then be reduced for (a) social security benefits, railroad retirement benefits, certain veteran's benefits, and other pension and annuity payments that are excludable from income and (b) 50% of income in excess of the AGI limitation. The AGI limitation is $7,500 for a single individual, $10,000 for a married couple filing jointly, and $5,000 for a married individual filing separately. The initial amount is limited to disability income for a disabled taxpayer.

✓ **Example 10.** Joan and Maury Minor are 67 and 63, respectively. They receive $1,200 of social security benefits, have AGI of $11,200, and file a joint return. Joan and Maury determine their credit for the elderly as follows:

Initial amount—One eligible individual		$5,000
Less: Social security benefits	$1,200	
50% of AGI > $10,000	600	(1,800)
		$3,200
Credit percentage		.15
		$ 480

Figure 5-3 is a completed Schedule R for the Minors.

✓ **Example 11.** Mark Balaban was totally disabled in an automobile accident. He receives $6,500 in taxable disability income and $1,300 of nontaxable social security payments, and he has AGI of $9,100. Mark's credit is calculated as follows:

Initial amount—single individual		$5,000
Less: Excludable social security payment	$1,300	
50% of AGI > 7,500	800	(2,100)
		$2,900
Credit percentage		× .15
		$ 435

Since most elderly taxpayers receive substantial social security benefits, this credit has limited applicability. Monthly social security benefits of approximately $417 ($625) will reduce the initial amount of $5,000 ($7,500) to zero, eliminating the credit.

Schedule R (Form 1040)

Credit for the Elderly or the Disabled

Department of the Treasury
Internal Revenue Service

▶ Attach to Form 1040.   ▶ See separate instructions for Schedule R.

OMB No. 1545-0074

1993

Attachment Sequence No. **16**

Name(s) shown on Form 1040: Joan & Maury Minor

Your social security number:

You may be able to use Schedule R to reduce your tax if by the end of 1993:
- You were age 65 or older, **OR**
- You were under age 65, you retired on **permanent and total** disability, and you received taxable disability income.

But you must also meet other tests. See the separate instructions for Schedule R.

Note: *In most cases, the IRS can figure the credit for you. See page 25 of the Form 1040 instructions.*

Part I — Check the Box for Your Filing Status and Age

If your filing status is:	And by the end of 1993:	Check only one box:
Single, Head of household, or Qualifying widow(er) with dependent child	1 You were 65 or older	1 ☐
	2 You were under 65 and you retired on permanent and total disability	2 ☐
Married filing a joint return	3 Both spouses were 65 or older	3 ☐
	4 Both spouses were under 65, but only one spouse retired on permanent and total disability	4 ☐
	5 Both spouses were under 65, and both retired on permanent and total disability	5 ☐
	6 One spouse was 65 or older, and the other spouse was under 65 and retired on permanent and total disability	6 ☐
	7 One spouse was 65 or older, and the other spouse was under 65 and **NOT** retired on permanent and total disability	7 ☒
Married filing a separate return	8 You were 65 or older and you lived apart from your spouse for all of 1993	8 ☐
	9 You were under 65, you retired on permanent and total disability, and you lived apart from your spouse for all of 1993	9 ☐

If you checked box 1, 3, 7, or 8, skip Part II and complete Part III on the back. All others, complete Parts II and III.

Part II — Statement of Permanent and Total Disability (Complete **only** if you checked box 2, 4, 5, 6, or 9 above.)

IF: 1 You filed a physician's statement for this disability for 1983 or an earlier year, or you filed a statement for tax years after 1983 and your physician signed line B on the statement, **AND**

2 Due to your continued disabled condition, you were unable to engage in any substantial gainful activity in 1993, check this box ▶ ☐

- If you checked this box, you do not have to file another statement for 1993.
- If you **did not** check this box, have your physician complete the following statement.

Physician's Statement (See instructions at bottom of page 2.)

I certify that _____
Name of disabled person

was permanently and totally disabled on January 1, 1976, or January 1, 1977, **OR** was permanently and totally disabled on the date he or she retired. If retired after December 31, 1976, enter the date retired. ▶ _____

Physician: Sign your name on **either** line A or B below.

A The disability has lasted or can be expected to last continuously for at least a year

B There is no reasonable probability that the disabled condition will ever improve

Physician's signature _____ Date _____
Physician's signature _____ Date _____

Physician's name _____ Physician's address _____

For Paperwork Reduction Act Notice, see Form 1040 instructions.   Cat. No. 11359K   Schedule R (Form 1040) 1993

Figure 5-3 Schedule R

Schedule R (Form 1040) 1993   Page **2**

Part III   Figure Your Credit

10   If you checked (in Part I):   Enter:
       Box 1, 2, 4, or 7 . . . . $5,000
       Box 3, 5, or 6 . . . . $7,500   **10**   5,000
       Box 8 or 9 . . . . $3,750

       Caution: *If you checked box 2, 4, 5, 6, or 9 in Part I, you **MUST** complete line 11 below. All others, skip line 11 and enter the amount from line 10 on line 12.*

11   If you checked:
- Box 6 in Part I, add $5,000 to the taxable disability income of the spouse who was under age 65. Enter the total.
- Box 2, 4, or 9 in Part I, enter your taxable disability income.
- Box 5 in Part I, add your taxable disability income to your spouse's taxable disability income. Enter the total.

       TIP: *For more details on what to include on line 11, see the instructions.*

12   • If you completed line 11, look at lines 10 and 11. Enter the **smaller** of the two amounts.   **12**   5,000
       • All others, enter the amount from line 10.

13   Enter the following pensions, annuities, or disability income that you (and your spouse if filing a joint return) received in 1993:

    a   Nontaxable part of social security benefits, and Nontaxable part of railroad retirement benefits treated as social security. See instructions.   **13a**   1,200

    b   Nontaxable veterans' pensions, and Any other pension, annuity, or disability benefit that is excluded from income under any other provision of law. See instructions.   **13b**   1,200

    c   Add lines 13a and 13b. (Even though these income items are not taxable, they **must** be included here to figure your credit.) If you did not receive any of the types of nontaxable income listed on line 13a or 13b, enter -0- on line 13c **13c**   1,200

14   Enter the amount from Form 1040, line 32   **14**   11,200

15   If you checked (in Part I):   Enter:
       Box 1 or 2 . . . . $7,500
       Box 3, 4, 5, 6, or 7 . . . . $10,000   **15**   10,000
       Box 8 or 9 . . . . $5,000

16   Subtract line 15 from line 14. If line 15 is more than line 14, enter -0- **16**   1,200

17   Divide line 16 above by 2 . . . .   **17**   600

18   Add lines 13c and 17 . . . .   **18**   1,800

19   Subtract line 18 from line 12. If line 18 is more than line 12, stop here; you **cannot** take the credit. Otherwise, go to line 21 . . . .   **19**   3,200

20   Decimal amount used to figure the credit . . . .   **20**   × .15

21   Multiply line 19 above by the decimal amount (.15) on line 20. Enter the result here and on Form 1040, line 42. **Caution:** *If you file Schedule C, C-EZ, D, E, or F (Form 1040), your credit may be limited. See the instructions for line 21 for the amount of credit you can claim* **21**   480

Instructions for Physician's Statement

Taxpayer
If you retired after December 31, 1976, enter the date you retired in the space provided in Part II.

Physician
A person is permanently and totally disabled if **both** of the following apply:
    1. He or she cannot engage in any substantial gainful activity because of a physical or mental condition, and

    2. A physician determines that the disability has lasted or can be expected to last continuously for at least a year or can lead to death.

Figure 5-3 (continued)   Schedule R

Additionally, since determination of this credit is relatively complex, the IRS will compute the credit if the taxpayer supplies the required information on Schedule R. Alternatively, the taxpayer may use Schedule R to calculate the credit.

TAX TIP

A tax preparer should always ask what social security and other pension benefits a lower-income person receives. Since the taxpayer may not be aware of this credit for the elderly and permanently disabled, a preparer should take the time to determine whether the taxpayer is eligible.

REVIEW I

1. Which of the following is a refundable credit?
   (a) health insurance credit
   (b) basic earned-income credit
   (c) credit for a child born in 1993
   (d) All of the above.
2. Taxpayers eligible for the earned-income credit include
   (a) a married couple filing separately.
   (b) a surviving spouse.
   (c) a qualifying child.
   (d) none of the above.
3. The maximum basic earned-income credit percentage an eligible taxpayer with two children may claim in 1993 is
   (a) 13.21%.
   (b) 13.93%.
   (c) 18.5%.
   (d) 19.5%.
4. Donna Roy's baby is six months old at year end. Donna has been able to work only part-time during 1993, earning only $6,750. She has no other taxable income. What is her earned-income credit?
   (a) $0
   (b) $1,249
   (c) $1,586
   (d) $1,821
5. Susan and John Tuck are 63 and 67 years old, respectively, and file a joint return for the current year. Susan received $1,700 in social security benefits; they had earned income of $8,300 and dividend income of $2,250. Their AGI was $10,550. Determine their credit for the elderly and disabled.
   (a) $0
   (b) $750
   (c) $454
   (d) $495

Answers are on page 5-16.

II CHILD AND DEPENDENT CARE CREDIT
(Code Section 21)

Although most personal expenses the taxpayer incurs while working are not deductible, Congress encourages persons with dependents to work by providing a tax *credit* for child and dependent care. To be eligible for the credit, the taxpayer must maintain a home for a qualified dependent, incur expenses for care of the qualified dependent, and have earned income.

THE LAW

Sec. 21(a)(1)—In the case of an individual who maintains a household which includes as a member one or more qualifying individuals (as defined in subsection (b)(1)), there shall be allowed as a credit against the tax imposed by this chapter for the taxable year an amount equal to the applicable percentage of the employment-related expenses (as defined in subsection (b)(2)) paid by such individual during the taxable year.

A qualified dependent is a child of the taxpayer who is under 13 years of age, or a mentally or physically handicapped spouse or other dependent. If a child's parents are divorced, only the custodial parent qualifies for the credit, even though the noncustodial parent may be eligible to claim the dependency exemption.

The expenses qualifying for the child and dependent care credit must be incurred as a result of enabling the taxpayer to be employed. They include the costs of day care centers, nursery schools, and in-home care. If the cost of in-home care includes other housekeeping duties, such as cleaning and cooking, the entire cost will be eligible for the credit as long as the principal purpose is child care. The tuition for schools other than nursery schools and any transportation costs are not eligible for the child care credit. The costs of maintaining a child or other dependent (who spends at least eight hours per day in the taxpayer's home) in a dependent care center are eligible for the credit if the center (a) complies with all laws and regulations and (b) provides care for six or more individuals.

ANSWERS TO REVIEW I

1. (d)
2. (b)
3. (d)
4. (c) $6,750 × (.185 + .05) = $1,586
5. (c) $5,000

   − 1,700   Social Security

   − 275   .50($10,550 − $10,000) excess AGI

   $3,025

   ×   .15

   $453.75

If the payment for child care is made to a relative, the relative must not be a dependent of the taxpayer. If payment is made to another child of the taxpayer, that child cannot be a dependent *and* must be at least 19 years of age. If these conditions are not met, the child care payments are not eligible for the child care credit. If the taxpayer claims the supplemental young-child credit as part of the earned-income credit, the taxpayer may not claim the child and dependent care credit for any child care expenses for that child.

☑ **Example 12.** Tim Grant's wife died in 1991. So that he can go to work, Tim takes his daughter to a day care center. These expenses are eligible for the child care credit. If Tim paid his mother to care for his daughter, the expenses would be eligible for the credit only if his mother were not his dependent.

☑ **Example 13.** Gene and Kerry Lauden have two children. Gene is a partner in a local CPA firm. His wife Kerry is very active in volunteer work and spends several days a week helping at a local hospital. They have hired a woman to come into the home to care for the children when Kerry is at the hospital. None of these child care expenses are eligible for the child care credit since Kerry is not gainfully *employed*.

DETERMINING THE CHILD CARE CREDIT

THE LAW

Sec.21 (a)(2)—For purposes of paragraph (1), the term "applicable percentage" means 30 percent reduced (but not below 20 percent) by 1 percentage point for each $2,000 (or fraction thereof) by which the taxpayer's adjusted gross income for the taxable year exceeds $10,000. . . .

(c)—The amount of the employment-related expenses incurred during any taxable year which may be taken into account under subsection (a) shall not exceed—

(1) $2,400 if there is 1 qualifying individual with respect to the taxpayer for such taxable year, or

(2) $4,800 if there are 2 or more qualifying individuals with respect to the taxpayer for such taxable year.

First, the percentage of the expenses eligible for the child care credit is determined by the taxpayer's AGI. If the taxpayer's AGI is $10,000 or less, the percentage allowable is 30%. If the taxpayer's AGI is over $28,000, the percentage allowable is 20%. The allowable percentage must be reduced by 1% for each $2,000 (or part thereof) that the taxpayer's AGI exceeds $10,000. If a taxpayer's AGI is $14,300, he or she must reduce the credit percentage by 3%, from 30% to 27%. His or her AGI exceeds $10,000 by $4,300. Dividing this excess by $2,000 yields 2.15. This must be rounded *up* to a full 3% reduction in the allowable credit percentage. Completed Form 2441 provides a table that may be used as a quick reference to determine the credit percentage.

Next, the taxpayer may be permitted a child care credit for only a portion of the child care expenses incurred. If the taxpayer has only one dependent, dependent care expenses of no more than $2,400 per year are eligible for the child care credit. If the taxpayer has two or more dependents, the maximum amount eligible for the child care credit is increased to $4,800. In no case, however, may the eligible amount exceed the taxpayer's earned income. If the taxpayer is married, the maximum may not exceed the earned income of the spouse with the lower earned income, and the married couple *must* file a joint return to be eligible for any credit (unless the parent claiming the credit qualifies as single under the abandoned spouse provisions).

To determine the child care credit, the taxpayer multiplies the allowable credit percentage determined by his AGI by the maximum amount of expenses eligible for the credit, which is the least of (a) actual child care expenses, (b) $2,400 for one or $4,800 for more than one eligible dependent, or (c) the earned income (of the lower-earning spouse on a joint return). Taxpayers use Form 2441 to calculate and report the child care credit and are now required to report the Taxpayer Identification Number (TIN) of the person(s) to whom they make the child care payments.

Example 14. Cal Wofford spent $3,700 on daycare for his only daughter, Tiffany, during the current year when his earned income and adjusted gross income were $24,600. Cal's allowable credit percentage is 22%. Dividing the $14,600 excess over $10,000 by $2,000 yields 7.3. Rounding 7.3 up to 8% and subtracting from 30% yields an allowable credit of 22%. Since Cal has only one dependent, his expenses eligible for the child care credit are limited to $2,400. Thus, Cal's credit is $528 (.22 × $2,400). A completed Form 2441 is included as Figure 5-4.

Example 15. Bob and Joanne Sweet are both schoolteachers; since they have three children, Joanne substitutes only during emergencies in the local school system. Bob earned $28,400; Joanne earned $4,100; their combined AGI is $33,600. They paid Joanne's sister (not a dependent) $4,200 for child care. Since Bob's and Joanne's AGI exceeds $28,000, their allowable credit percentage is 20%. Their child care credit is limited to $820 (.20 × $4,100). The amount eligible for the child care is limited to Joanne's earned income since that is less than their child care expense.

Example 16. Al and Toni Rizzo separated shortly before the end of the tax year, and Toni refuses to file a joint return with Al, who has custody of the children. Even though they paid $4,200 for child care during the year, neither will be able to claim a child care credit on the "married-filing separately" tax returns. If Al qualified as unmarried under the abandoned spouse provisions, he would be able to claim a child care credit when filing as head of household.

TAX TIP

If the taxpayer's cost of child care is going to exceed the maximum amount on which the credit may be determined, the taxpayer loses nothing by paying a dependent for child care in excess of the allowable maximum. For example, if child care costs during the school year exceed the maximum, the taxpayer may pay an older sibling for child care during the summer without jeopardizing the credit.

Form 2441 — Child and Dependent Care Expenses (1993)

Form 2441
Department of the Treasury
Internal Revenue Service

Child and Dependent Care Expenses
▶ Attach to Form 1040.
▶ See separate instructions.

OMB No. 1545-0068
1993
Attachment Sequence No. 21

Name(s) shown on Form 1040: Cal Wofford
Your social security number:

You need to understand the following terms to complete this form: **Dependent Care Benefits, Earned Income, Qualified Expenses,** and **Qualifying Person(s).** See **Important Terms** on page 1 of the Form 2441 instructions. Also, if you had a child born in 1993 and line 32 of Form 1040 is less than $23,050, see **A Change To Note** on page 2 of the instructions.

Part I — Persons or Organizations Who Provided the Care
You **must** complete this part. (If you need more space, use the bottom of page 2.)

1	(a) Care provider's name	(b) Address (number, street, apt. no., city, state, and ZIP code)	(c) Identifying number (SSN or EIN)	(d) Amount paid (see instructions)
	Tiffany			

2 Add the amounts in column (d) of line 1 .... **2**
3 Enter the number of **qualifying persons** cared for in 1993 .... ▶ **1**

Did you receive **dependent care benefits?**
— NO ▶ Complete only Part II below.
— YES ▶ Complete Part III on the back now.

Part II — Credit for Child and Dependent Care Expenses

4 Enter the amount of **qualified expenses** you incurred and paid in 1993. DO NOT enter more than $2,400 for one qualifying person or $4,800 for two or more persons. If you completed Part III, enter the amount from line 25 .... **4** | 2,400

5 Enter YOUR earned income .... **5** | 24,600

6 If married filing a joint return, enter YOUR SPOUSE'S earned income (if student or disabled, see instructions); **all others,** enter the amount from line 5 .... **6** | 0

7 Enter the **smallest** of line 4, 5, or 6 .... **7** | 2,400

8 Enter the amount from Form 1040, line 32 ...... **8** | 24,600

9 Enter on line 9 the decimal amount shown below that applies to the amount on line 8

If line 8 is—		Decimal amount is	If line 8 is—		Decimal amount is
Over	But not over		Over	But not over	
$0	10,000	.30	$20,000	22,000	.24
10,000	12,000	.29	22,000	24,000	.23
12,000	14,000	.28	24,000	26,000	.22
14,000	16,000	.27	26,000	28,000	.21
16,000	18,000	.26	28,000	No limit	.20
18,000	20,000	.25			

9 | × .22

10 Multiply **line 7** by the decimal amount on line 9. Enter the result. Then, see the instructions for the amount of credit to enter on Form 1040, line 41 .... **10** | 528

Caution: If you paid $50 or more in a calendar quarter to a person who worked in your home, you must file an employment tax return. Get **Form 942** for details.

For Paperwork Reduction Act Notice, see separate instructions. Cat. No. 11862M Form **2441** (1993)

Figure 5-4 Form 2441

If the taxpayer's spouse is either disabled or a full-time student, special earned-income rules apply for determining the child care credit limitations. If the taxpayer has one dependent, the taxpayer's spouse is assumed to earn $200 per month while he or she is disabled or a full-time student. If the taxpayer has two or more dependents, the assumed earned income is increased to $400 per month. This assumed income has no effect on the couple's AGI, however.

Example 17. John Hanson is a full-time student during all of 1993. His wife earns $16,500 as a secretary and they incur $2,100 for child care during the year for their only child. John is assumed to earn $2,400 during the year ($200 per month × 12 months) and their allowable credit percentage is 26% (from Form 2441 in Figure 5-4). Their child care credit is only $546 (.26 × $2,100). The expenses eligible for the child care credit are limited to the actual expense incurred.

TAX TIP

Full-time students may assume the $200 or $400 monthly income only for each of the five or more months they must be in school to qualify as full-time students. Income earned during other months may be added to these assumed monthly income amounts, however, in determining the earned-income limitation.

Under current law, a taxpayer's employer may establish a qualified dependent care assistance plan. As discussed in Chapter 3, the taxpayer may exclude any payments of up to $5,000 ($2,500 for married filing separately) under such a plan from income as long as they are made for qualifying dependent care to permit the taxpayer to work. This type of fringe benefit is usually more valuable to an employee than the limited child care credit permitted under IRC Section 21; a taxpayer may not take a credit for amounts excluded from income under an employer-sponsored plan; note the reduction on line 23 of Form 2441 for these excluded benefits. As discussed earlier, a taxpayer may not claim the child care credit for a child for whom the taxpayer claims the credit for a child born in 1993.

REVIEW II

1. To be eligible for the child and dependent care credit, a taxpayer must
    (a) maintain a home for a qualified dependent.
    (b) incur expenses for care of the qualified dependent.
    (c) have earned income.
    (d) do all of the above.

2. Margo Lane is a single parent with one child who is eight years old. She pays a neighbor $360 to drive her child to school, pick her up afterwards, and drop her off at an after-school care center. She pays the center $900 during the school year for after-school care. She also paid her neighbor $2,800 to care for her child during the summer. If Margo's AGI is $23,450, what is her child care credit?
   (a) $480
   (b) $552
   (c) $851
   (d) $934

3. Joanne and Jimmy Perez have two children, ages 7 and 16. They pay a live-in housekeeper a $5,200 salary during the year for child care and household services. Additionally, they provide the housekeeper full room and board valued at $4,800 for the year. If the Perez's AGI is $57,000, what is their child care credit?
   (a) $1,040
   (b) $960
   (c) $720
   (d) $480

4. Gary Wilson's invalid mother lives with him. Although she receives a small amount of income from social security, Gary provides the majority of her support and claims her as a dependent. Last year, Gary found an adult day care center funded by the United Way. The day care center makes no charge for the care, but Gary paid $1,400 during the tax year for transportation for his mother to and from the day care center. Additionally, Gary gave the center $2,500 to purchase furniture and supplies. If Gary's AGI is $62,000, what is his dependent care credit?
   (a) $0
   (b) $280
   (c) $420
   (d) $480

5. Susan Chapman's husband, John, is a full-time candidate for a Ph.D. degree at a local university and does not have any income for the current year. Susan works as an accountant. They have two children, ages four and six. They paid Susan's sister-in-law $5,600 this tax year to take care of the children while Susan worked and John went to school. If their AGI is $26,400, what is their child care credit?
   (a) $0
   (b) $960
   (c) $1,008
   (d) $1,080

Answers are on page 5-22.

III MISCELLANEOUS CREDITS
(Code Section 27)

There are several additional credits that apply to individual taxpayers in limited and specific situations. Only one of these, the foreign tax credit, will be discussed at any length. A special residential mortgage interest credit expired at the end of 1987. Credit carryovers are still available, however. This credit was designed to assist first-time homebuyers who met certain requirements. A credit (the "orphan drug credit") is also available for costs incurred in testing drugs to treat rare diseases or conditions. Since drugs for rare conditions offer little profit potential to spur development, the credit is designed to make their development and testing more attractive. Finally, a credit is available for producing fuel from nonconventional sources, such as producing gas from geopressured brine or oil from shale and tar sands.

FOREIGN TAX CREDIT

To alleviate multiple taxation of a single income source, taxpayers have several alternatives for foreign source income. First, the taxpayer could take an itemized deduction for taxes paid on foreign income. Alternatively, the taxpayer could take a credit for foreign income taxes paid. Finally, a taxpayer who meets bona fide residency or physical presence tests may exclude all or part of foreign earned income. As discussed in Chapter 3, taxpayers qualifying for the foreign earned income exclusion may exclude a maximum of $70,000 of foreign earned income, as well as excluding housing costs that exceed a specific amount. Deductions are denied, however, for expenses related to the excluded income. Additionally, a taxpayer may not take a deduction or a credit for foreign income taxes paid on excluded income. Finally, anyone claiming the exclusion is denied all earned-income credits.

THE LAW

Sec. 27(a)—The amount of taxes imposed by foreign countries and possessions of the United States shall be allowed as a credit against the tax imposed by this chapter to the extent provided in section 901.

The foreign tax credit permits a direct reduction in the taxpayer's tax liability. Taking the tax credit is generally more advantageous to the taxpayer than taking an itemized deduction. Whether the foreign tax credit is more advantageous than the foreign income exclusion, however, depends on the relative income tax rates in the United States and the foreign country, and the taxpayer's other foreign income. Taxpayers may change from the credit or exclusion in one year to the exclusion or credit in the

---

ANSWERS TO REVIEW II

1. (d)
2. (b) $2,400 x .23 = $552. Transportation costs are not eligible for the child care credit.
3. (d) $2,400 x .20 = $480. The credit may be claimed for children under 13 only.
4. (a) None of Gary's outlays are eligible for the credit. He may, however, be able to deduct the $2,500 as a charitable contribution.
5. (c) $4,800 x .21 = $1,008. Since John is a full-time student, he is assumed to earn $400 per month (two eligible dependents).

next, respectively. If, however, the taxpayer changes from the exclusion to the credit, the exclusion may not be reelected for six tax years without permission from the Commissioner of the Internal Revenue Service.

The foreign tax credit a taxpayer is permitted to take in a particular tax year is the lesser of the actual foreign taxes paid or the portion of the U.S. tax attributable to foreign earned income. This limitation prevents the taxpayer from reducing current U.S. income taxes for foreign income taxes paid at higher effective rates than U.S. taxes. Unused foreign tax credits, however, may be carried back two years or forward five years to offset U.S. taxes in a year when the effective foreign income tax rate is lower than the U.S. rate.

To calculate the maximum foreign tax credit, the following formula may be used.

$$\frac{\text{Foreign Taxable Income}}{\text{All Taxable Income}} \times \text{U.S. Income Tax before Credits} = \text{Maximum Foreign Tax Credit}$$

✓ **Example 18.** Sally Church earned $45,000 of salary while she was on assignment in England. She is not eligible for the foreign income exclusion, however. She paid $18,000 of English taxes on this income. Her taxable income before exemptions for the year was $90,000, and her U.S. tax liability before any credits was $25,200. Sally may take a foreign credit of $12,600, which is the maximum credit allowed in the current year, determined as follows:

$$\frac{\$45,000}{\$90,000} \times 25,200 = \underline{\$12,600}$$

The $5,400 difference between the actual tax paid and the maximum allowable credit may be carried back two years or forward five years. Form 1116 with the above information is presented in Figure 5-5.

The taxpayer completes Form 1116 to claim the foreign tax credit. Separate forms must be completed for general types of foreign income as well as for certain other specific types of foreign income—for example, passive income, shipping income, and distributions from foreign sales corporations, since they are subject to separate limitations. Taxes paid on income from certain countries that support terrorism, do not have diplomatic relations with the United States, or whose governments are not recognized by the United States are not eligible for a tax credit.

REVIEW III

1. Which of the following is *not* true of the foreign earned-income exclusion?
    (a) Deductions are allowed for expenses related to excluded income.
    (b) A taxpayer may not take a deduction or a credit for foreign income taxes paid on excluded income.
    (c) Anyone claiming the exclusion is denied the earned-income credit.
    (d) A maximum of $70,000 of foreign earned income may be excluded.

Form 1116 — Foreign Tax Credit

Form 1116
Department of the Treasury
Internal Revenue Service

Foreign Tax Credit
Individual, Fiduciary, or Nonresident Alien Individual
▶ Attach to Form 1040, 1040NR, 1041, or 990-T.
▶ See separate instructions.

OMB No. 1545-0121
1992
Attachment Sequence No. 19

Name: Sally Church

Identifying number as shown on page 1 of your tax return

Report all amounts in U.S. dollars except where specified in Part II. Use a separate Form 1116 for each category of income listed below. Check only **one** box. Before you check a box, read **Categories of Income** on page 3 of the instructions. Complete this form for credit for taxes on:

- **a** ☐ Passive income
- **b** ☐ High withholding tax interest
- **c** ☐ Financial services income
- **d** ☐ Shipping income
- **e** ☐ Dividends from a DISC or former DISC
- **f** ☐ Certain distributions from a foreign sales corporation (FSC) or former FSC
- **g** ☒ Lump-sum distributions (see instructions before completing form)
- **h** ☐ General limitation income—all other income from sources outside the United States (including income from sources within U.S. possessions)

i Resident of (name of country) ▶

Note: If you paid taxes to one foreign country or U.S. possession, use column A in Part I and line A in Part II. If you paid taxes to **more than one** foreign country or U.S. possession, use a separate column and line for each country or possession.

Part I — Taxable Income or Loss From Sources Outside the United States for Separate Category Checked Above

		Foreign Country or U.S. Possession			Total
		A	B	C	(Add cols. A, B, and C.)
j	Enter the name of the foreign country or U.S. possession ▶	England			
1	Gross income from sources within country shown above and of the type checked above. (See instructions.):	45,000			**1** 45,000

Applicable deductions and losses. (See instructions.):

		A	B	C	Total
2	Expenses directly allocable to the income on line 1 (attach schedule).				
3	Pro rata share of other deductions not directly allocable:				
a	Certain itemized deductions or standard deduction. (See instructions.)				
b	Other deductions (attach schedule)				
c	Add lines 3a and 3b				
d	Total foreign source income. (See instructions.)				
e	Gross income from all sources. (See instructions.)				
f	Divide line 3d by line 3e				
g	Multiply line 3c by line 3f				
4	Pro rata share of interest expense. (See instructions.):				
a	Home mortgage interest from line 5 of the worksheet on page 6 of the instructions				
b	Other interest expense				
5	Losses from foreign sources.				
6	Add lines 2, 3g, 4a, 4b, and 5				**6**
7	Subtract line 6 from line 1. Enter the result here and on line 14. ▶				**7** 45,000

Part II — Foreign Taxes Paid or Accrued (See instructions.)

Country	Credit is claimed for taxes (you must check one)		Foreign taxes paid or accrued							
			In foreign currency			In U.S. dollars				
	(k) ☒ Paid (l) ☐ Accrued		Taxes withheld at source on:			Taxes withheld at source on:			(u) Other foreign taxes paid or accrued	(v) Total foreign taxes paid or accrued (add cols. (r) through (u))
	(m) Date paid or accrued		(n) Dividends	(o) Rents and royalties	(p) Interest	(q) Other foreign taxes paid or accrued	(r) Dividends	(s) Rents and royalties	(t) Interest		
A										18,000	18,000
B											
C											

8 Add lines A through C, column (v). Enter the total here and on line 9. ▶ **8**

For Paperwork Reduction Act Notice, see page 1 of separate instructions. Cat. No. 11440U Form **1116** (1992)

Figure 5-5 Form 1116

Form 1116 (1992) Page **2**

Part III — Figuring the Credit   Sally Church

Line	Description		Amount
9	Enter amount from line 8. This is the total foreign taxes paid or accrued for the category of income checked above Part I	9	18,000
10	Carryback or carryover (attach detailed computation)	10	
11	Add lines 9 and 10	11	18,000
12	Reduction in foreign taxes. (See instructions.)	12	—
13	Subtract line 12 from line 11. This is the total amount of foreign taxes available for credit	13	18,000
14	Enter amount from line 7. This is your taxable income or (loss) from sources outside the United States (before adjustments) for the category of income checked above Part I. (See instructions.)	14	45,000
15	Adjustments to line 14. (See instructions.)	15	
16	Combine the amounts on lines 14 and 15. This is your net foreign source taxable income. (If the result is zero or less, you have no foreign tax credit for the type of income you checked on page 1. Skip lines 17 through 21.)	16	45,000
17	**Individuals:** Enter amount from Form 1040, line 35. If you are a nonresident alien, enter amount from Form 1040NR, line 33. **Estates and trusts:** Enter your taxable income without the deduction for your exemption	17	90,000
	Caution: If you figured your tax using the maximum tax rate on capital gains, see instructions.		
18	Divide line 16 by line 17. (If line 16 is more than line 17, enter the figure "1.")	18	.50
19	**Individuals:** Enter amount from Form 1040, line 40, **less** any amounts on Form 1040, lines 41 and 42. If you are a nonresident alien, enter amount from Form 1040NR, line 38, less any amount on Form 1040NR, line 39. **Estates and trusts:** Enter amount from Form 1041, Schedule G, line 1c, or Form 990-T, line 8	19	25,200
20	Multiply line 19 by line 18. (Maximum amount of credit)	20	12,600
21	Enter the amount from line 13 or line 20, whichever is smaller. (If this is the only Form 1116 you are completing, skip lines 22 through 29 and enter this amount on line 30. Otherwise, complete the appropriate lines in Part IV.) ▶	21	12,600

Part IV — Summary of Credits From Separate Parts III (See instructions.)

22	Credit for taxes on passive income	22	
23	Credit for taxes on high withholding tax interest	23	
24	Credit for taxes on financial services income	24	
25	Credit for taxes on shipping income	25	
26	Credit for taxes on dividends from a DISC or former DISC	26	
27	Credit for taxes on certain distributions from a FSC or former FSC	27	
28	Credit for taxes on lump-sum distributions	28	
29	Credit for taxes on general limitation income (all other income from sources outside the United States)	29	
30	Add lines 22 through 29	30	
31	Reduction of credit for international boycott operations. (See instructions for line 12.)	31	
32	Subtract line 31 from line 30. This is your foreign tax credit. Enter here and on Form 1040, line 43; Form 1040NR, line 40; Form 1041, Schedule G, line 2a; or Form 990-T, line 9a ▶	32	

Figure 5-5 (continued)   Form 1116

2. Which of the following is *not* allowed?
   (a) changing from the foreign tax credit to the foreign earned-income exclusion
   (b) changing from the foreign tax exclusion to the foreign tax credit
   (c) changing from the foreign tax exclusion to the foreign tax credit and then back to the foreign tax exclusion in the next year
   (d) none of the above
3. Bill Jones earned $30,000 while on assignment in France. He paid $12,000 in French taxes on this income. His total income for the year was $55,000. His U.S. tax liability was $20,000. What is Bill's allowable foreign tax credit for this tax year?
   (a) $0
   (b) $6,000
   (c) $10,909
   (d) $12,000
4. Peter Taylor had $63,000 of foreign taxable income while working overseas this year and has $15,000 of other taxable income. He paid $18,400 in foreign taxes, and his U.S. tax is $17,160. What is his foreign tax credit?
   (a) $0
   (b) $13,860
   (c) $17,160
   (d) $18,400

Answers are on page 5-28.

IV ESTIMATED TAX PAYMENTS FOR INDIVIDUALS
(Code Sections 6621 and, 6654)

The federal tax system is a "pay-as-you-go" system; that is, taxpayers are required in most situations to make payments during the year based on their estimated tax liability at year-end.

THE LAW

Sec. 6654(a)—Except as otherwise provided in this section, in the case of any underpayment of estimated tax by an individual, there shall be added to the tax under Chapter 1 and the tax under Chapter 2 for the taxable year an amount determined by applying—
(1) the underpayment rate established under section 6621,
(2) to the amount of the underpayment,
(3) for the period of the underpayment. . . .
(c)(2)—In the case of the following installments:

Installment	The due date is:
1st	April 15
2nd	June 15
3rd	September 15
4th	January 15 of the following taxable year

Many taxpayers are excused from making estimated payments of taxes because their employers withhold taxes from their wages. If taxpayers have too little withholding from their salaries or have other income that is not subject to withholding, they may be required to make estimated tax payments in addition to their withholding. Generally, taxpayers must make estimated payments if their estimated unpaid taxes at year-end are $500 or more. If, however, their withholding is expected to equal 100% of their tax liability for the prior year or 90% of their actual tax liability for the current year, estimated payments are not required. Taxpayers may use the worksheet accompanying Form 1040ES to calculate their estimated unpaid tax due in order to determine whether estimated payments are required.

For tax years 1992 and 1993, taxpayers who have made estimated tax payments in any of the three previous years and whose current income is (1) more than $75,000 ($37,500 married filing separately) and (2) exceeds the prior year's income by more than $40,000 ($20,000 married-filing separately) may not use the exception for under-withholding penalties based on 100% of the prior year's tax liability. This rule has been eased for tax years after 1993.*

✓ **Example 19.** Alva and Eddy Trimble expect to have a tax liability of $11,000 for the current year. Last year they paid a total of $9,800 in income and self-employment taxes. Alva is self-employed while Eddy works for a corporation that withholds $450 per month for income taxes. Since Eddy's total withholding is only $5,400, they must make estimated payments. The minimum they would have to pay in estimated payments is $4,400—the lesser of $9,900 (90% of this year's expected tax liability of $11,000) or $9,800 (last year's tax liability) less the withholding of $5,400. The Trimbles would make four quarterly estimated tax payments of $1,100 each. Following is the above information as it would appear on Form 1040ES and the worksheet.

Form **1040-ES** | **1993 Payment Voucher 1**
Department of the Treasury
Internal Revenue Service

OMB No. 1545-0087

Return this voucher with check or money order payable to the **"Internal Revenue Service."** Please write your social security number and "1993 Form 1040-ES" on your check or money order. Please do not send cash. Enclose, but do not staple or attach, your payment with this voucher. File only if you are making a payment of estimated tax.

Calendar year—Due April 15, 1993

Amount of payment

$ 1,100

Your first name and initial: Eddy Trimble
Your last name:
Your social security number:

If joint payment, complete for spouse
Spouse's first name and initial: Alva Trimble
Spouse's last name:
Spouse's social security number:

Address (number, street, and apt. no.)
City, state, and ZIP code

For Paperwork Reduction Act Notice, see instructions on page 1. ☆ U.S. GOVERNMENT PRINTING OFFICE: 1992 315-197   Page 7

•
•
•

*For changes in the tax law effective for tax years beginning in 1994, see Appendix J.

1993 Estimated Tax Worksheet (keep for your records)

13a	Add lines 10 through 12 . . . . **13a**	
b	Earned income credit and credit from **Form 4136** **13b**	
c	Subtract line 13b from line 13a. Enter the result, but not less than zero. **THIS IS YOUR TOTAL 1993 ESTIMATED TAX** . . . . ▶ **13c**	11,000
14a	Multiply line 13c by 90% (66⅔% for farmers and fishermen) . . . **14a** 9,900	
b	Enter 100% of the tax shown on your 1992 tax return **14b** 9,800	
	Caution: If 14b is **smaller** than 14a **and** line 1 above is over $75,000 ($37,500 if married filing separately), stop here and see **Limit on Use of Prior Year's Tax** on page 1 before continuing.	
c	Enter the **smaller** of line 14a or 14b. **THIS IS YOUR REQUIRED ANNUAL PAYMENT TO AVOID A PENALTY** . . . . ▶ **14c**	9,800
	Caution: Generally, if you do not prepay at least the amount on line 14c, you may owe a penalty for not paying enough estimated tax. To avoid a penalty, make sure your estimate on line 13c is as accurate as possible. Even if you pay the required annual payment, you may still owe tax when you file your return. If you prefer, you may pay the amount shown on line 13c. For more details, get Pub. 505.	
15	Income tax withheld and estimated to be withheld during 1993 (including income tax withholding on pensions, annuities, certain deferred income, etc.) **15**	5,400
16	Subtract line 15 from line 14c. (**Note:** If zero or less, or line 13c minus line 15 is less than $500, stop here. You are not required to make estimated tax payments.) **16**	4,400
17	If the first payment you are required to make is due April 15, 1993, enter ¼ of line 16 (minus any 1992 overpayment that you are applying to this installment) here and on your payment voucher(s) **17**	1,100

Page 3

In determining the amount of estimated unpaid taxes, the taxpayers must consider all wages, salary, and other taxable income, adjustments and deductions to income, tax credits and withholding, and filing status and exemptions, as well as other taxes such as self-employment taxes and the alternative minimum tax. If taxpayers must make estimated payments, one-quarter of the estimated amount due must be paid by the 15th day of the fourth, sixth, and ninth months of the current tax year and the first month of the next tax year. The Form 1040ES outlines the steps a taxpayer should follow to determine the required estimated tax payments. The estimated tax form package contains deposit vouchers that taxpayers may use to make the estimated payments.

TAX TIP

If a taxpayer who does not experience a substantial increase in income adjusts his withholding to equal 100% of the prior year's tax liability, no estimated payments are required. The taxpayer, however, must have filed the prior year's return on a 12-month basis; that is, the prior year's return could not be a short period return.

ANSWERS TO REVIEW III

1. (a)
2. (c)
3. (c) ($30,000/$55,000) x ($20,000) = $10,909 allowable credit
4. (b) ($63,000/$78,000) x ($17,160) = $13,860 allowable credit

Taxpayers who make estimated payments are not relieved of the responsibility of filing tax returns after the close of the tax year. Estimated tax payments are credited against the actual tax due on the final return for the year. Husbands and wives may make separate or joint estimated tax payments without affecting their decision whether to file joint or separate tax returns. Separate estimated payments are simply credited to the joint return, while joint estimated payments may be credited against separate returns in any manner the taxpayers wish. Joint estimated payments may not be made by taxpayers not entitled to file joint returns—for example, spouses who have different tax years.

A taxpayer's estimated tax situation may change during the year. If so, the schedule for making estimated payments is adjusted based on the redetermination of estimated taxes payable. If the determination that estimated tax payments are required is made after the following dates, payments are made as follows:

Determination Date	Portion of Estimated Tax Due Each Due Date	Estimated Payment Dates
March 31–May 31	1/3	June 15, Sept. 15, Jan. 15
June 1–Aug. 31	1/2	Sept. 15, Jan. 15
Sept. 1–	all	Jan. 15

If the taxpayer does not meet the estimated payment requirement until September 1 or beyond, filing the return and paying the tax by January 31 relieves him of the requirement to make a January 15 estimated payment.

☑ **Example 20.** Due to a call of corporate bonds on September 10, Don Morgan now expects taxable income of $20,000, which will require him to make an estimated tax payment of $2,400 for the year. Don may make the estimated tax payment of $2,400 on January 15; alternatively, if he files his completed tax return by January 31, he may simply pay the tax due with this tax return.

A taxpayer who has a refund due for the prior tax year may credit that refund against the current year's estimated taxes. The taxpayer may credit it evenly to the four estimated payments or may credit it to the first installment(s) until it is exhausted.

☑ **Example 21.** Carolyn Taggart calculates an estimated tax payment of $2,000 paid in four installments. She has an $800 refund due from the prior year that she credits against this estimated tax, reducing the amount due to $1,200. Carolyn may make estimated payments as follows: four payments of $300 each or no payment on April 15, a $200 payment on June 15, and $500 payments on September 15 and January 15.

If taxpayers are already making estimated payments when their tax situation changes, any increases or decreases in the estimated taxes may be taken into consideration evenly over the remaining installments.

☑ **Example 22.** Nelson Brooke has made quarterly estimated tax payments of $750 on April 15 and June 15. Due to several stock transactions, he determines that his estimated tax payments must total $4,000 rather than $3,000. Nelson must increase his September 15 and January 15 payments by $500 each to $1,250 due to this increase.

UNDERPAYMENT PENALTIES

Taxpayers who fail to make the required estimated tax payments or who have insufficient withholding are subject to a penalty. To avoid the penalty, the taxpayer must make (a) prepayments equal to at least 90% of the amount due at any installment date, (b) prepayments equal to 100% of the tax due for the prior year's 12-month return, or (c) prepayments equal to 90% or more of the tax due by annualizing taxable income for the installment due dates. The penalties are determined in four increments for the tax year based on the estimated tax payment due dates. Taxpayers who are subject to withholding are considered to have had the payments withheld evenly during the year.

Although the underpayment penalty interest rate is adjusted quarterly based on the federal short-term interest rate, the penalty is not considered interest and the taxpayer cannot deduct it. The penalty is determined on Form 2210. A separate calculation is made based on each date the estimated tax payment is due. These calculations require multiplying the underpayment for that particular due date by the annual interest rate, prorated for the number of days from the date the payment was due to the date the tax liability was paid. Additionally, more than one calculation may be necessary for each estimated due date if the interest rate changes during that particular period, since these changes are not made to coincide with the payment due dates. A taxpayer preparing his or her own return may elect to have the IRS calculate the tax and bill him or her. A paid preparer must include Form 2210 to determine the penalty or subject himself or herself to penalty. Fortunately, many preparers use tax software for computer-generated tax returns that automatically calculates this penalty if all the necessary information regarding withholding and estimated payments is supplied.

Example 23. Albert Gonzales had $5,000 withheld from his paycheck for the 1992* tax year. He also had his own business, which increased his total tax liability from $5,200 to $9,400. Albert paid the balance of the tax due on April 15 when he filed his return. Albert would be subject to an underpayment penalty on $3,460 [(.90 × $9,400) − $5,000] of the balance due. Using the short method on page 1 of Form 2210, he determines that his penalty is $167.67. See Figure 5-6 for the calculation of the penalty.

*1993 form unavailable at date of publication.

REVIEW IV

1. Ginny Forbes has had a substantial increase in her income this year. Last year she paid $2,700 in taxes on income of $17,020. This year she expects to earn $42,000 and estimates that her tax liability will be $7,300. If she has $5,500 withheld, how much do her quarterly tax payments have to total if she is to avoid penalties for underpayment?
   (a) $0
   (b) $1,070
   (c) $1,800
   (d) $2,700
2. Ted Martin is now self-employed. Last year he worked for two companies, earning a total of $36,700, and paid taxes of $4,300. This year, he expects to owe only $2,850 in taxes due to the slow start of the business. What are his required total estimated tax payments if he wants to avoid any penalties?
   (a) $0
   (b) $2,565

Form 2210 — Underpayment of Estimated Tax by Individuals and Fiduciaries (1992)

OMB No. 1545-0140
Attachment Sequence No. 06
Department of the Treasury — Internal Revenue Service
▶ See separate instructions.
▶ Attach to Form 1040, Form 1040A, Form 1040NR, or Form 1041.

Name(s) shown on tax return: Albert Gonzales
Identifying number: _____

Part II — All Filers Must Complete This Part

Line	Description	Amount
2	Enter your 1992 tax after credits (see instructions)	9,400
3	Other taxes (see instructions)	
4	Add lines 2 and 3	9,400
5	Earned income credit	
6	Credit for Federal tax paid on fuels	
7	Add lines 5 and 6	
8	Current year tax. Subtract line 7 from line 4	9,400
9	Multiply line 8 by 90% (.90)	8,460
10	Withholding taxes. **Do not** include any estimated tax payments on this line (see instructions)	5,000
11	Subtract line 10 from line 8. If less than $500, stop here; **do not** complete or file this form. You do not owe the penalty	4,400
12	Prior year (1991) tax. (**Caution:** See instructions.)	
13	Enter the **smaller** of line 9 or line 12 (see instructions)	8,460

Part III — Short Method (Caution: Read the instructions to see if you can use the short method. If you checked box 1b, c, or d in Part I, skip this part and go to Part IV.)

Line	Description	Amount
14	Enter the amount, if any, from line 10 above	5,000
15	Enter the total amount, if any, of estimated tax payments you made	-0-
16	Add lines 14 and 15	5,000
17	**Total underpayment for year.** Subtract line 16 from line 13. (If zero or less, stop here; you do not owe the penalty. Do not file Form 2210 unless you checked box 1e or f above.)	3,460
18	Multiply line 17 by .04846	167.67
19	• If the amount on line 17 was paid **on or after** 4/15/93, enter -0-. • If the amount on line 17 was paid **before** 4/15/93, make the following computation to find the amount to enter on line 19. Amount on line 17 × Number of days paid before 4/15/93 × .00019	-0-
20	**PENALTY.** Subtract line 19 from line 18. Enter the result here and on Form 1040, line 65; Form 1040A, line 33; Form 1040NR, line 65; or Form 1041, line 26 ▶	167.67

For Paperwork Reduction Act Notice, see page 1 of separate instructions.   Cat. No. 11744P   Form **2210** (1992)

Figure 5-6 Form 2210

    (c) $2,850
    (d) $3,870

3. John Elder made $2,000 estimated tax payments on April 15, June 15, and September 15. In October, he sold a substantial amount of stock, which increased his estimated tax liability from $8,000 for the current year to $14,500. What is the minimum amount he must pay on his last tax deposit and by what date must it be made?
    (a) $7,500—January 15
    (b) $7,500—January 31
    (c) $7,050—January 15
    (d) $5,050—January 15

4. Wilma Randolf expects a $12,400 tax liability for the current year. She has $500 withheld from each monthly paycheck. What is the minimum estimated tax payment Wilma must make on April 15 for the current tax year?
    (a) $0
    (b) $100
    (c) $1,290
    (d) $1,500

5. Bob Gregory had a total tax liability of $16,000 for the past tax year and expects a $20,000 tax liability this year. Unfortunately, he made only $2,000 in estimated payments on April 15, June 15, September 15, and January 15. If the current interest rate is 10% for all underpayment penalties, what is his underpayment penalty assuming he files his return on April 15 of the current year and neither the past year nor the current year is a leap year?

(a) $0
(b) $400
(c) $532
(d) $800

Answers are on page 5-34.

CHAPTER APPENDIX: THE TAX RETURN AUDIT AND APPEALS PROCESS

The tax system of the United States is one of self-assessment. That is, taxpayers report their own income and deductions on returns prepared by themselves or other preparers. If the taxpayer hires a CPA or other tax return preparer to complete his or her return, the taxpayer must still file the return and is responsible for payment of all taxes, penalties, and interest. Unfortunately, not all taxpayers correctly report their amount of income and deductions—through error, ignorance, or deliberate evasion. As a result, the IRS systematically checks all returns to varying degrees.

First, the IRS checks all returns for the following items:

1. Business and individual returns are checked for the omission of signatures or taxpayer identification numbers. If omissions are found, the IRS will attempt to resolve the problem through the mail.

2. All returns are checked by computer for mathematical accuracy. If errors are found, the IRS recomputes the tax and either assesses an additional tax or recomputes the refund. Assessing additional tax in these circumstances does not require a formal notice of deficiency. Additionally, the taxpayer will not be charged interest if the deficiency is paid within ten days of the notice.

3. Returns are then checked manually or by computer for unallowable items; for example, a single taxpayer who uses the standard deduction for a married couple. Errors discovered in this manner are treated as mathematical errors; the assessment of additional tax does not require a formal notice of deficiency.

Only a portion of returns is selected for a more extensive audit. Certain returns will be identified by a computer program based on a number of characteristics. These characteristics are designed to select returns with a high probability of tax deficiency. The selected returns are then checked manually and those deemed appropriate are forwarded to the Examination division of the IRS. Other returns may be selected manually for audit for a variety of reasons. For example, if the IRS is auditing an S Corporation, it may also decide to audit the shareholders' returns. Finally, returns are selected at random for the Taxpayer Compliance Measurement Program (TCMP). These audits are comprehensive and require that the taxpayer substantiate all items. These audits are used to develop the computer program to select returns from the general population for audit.

If a return is selected for examination, it may be handled solely by letter or telephone if there are relatively few items in question. The taxpayer may, however, request an office or field examination. Returns with several or complex issues may be subject to office audit at the taxpayer's appropriate district office. The taxpayer is asked to bring documents supporting the items questioned, and the examination may not go beyond the items listed in the audit notification letter. Field audits, audits conducted at the taxpayer's location, are normally conducted for individual business and corporate returns. These audits involve complex issues and may require a complete review of the taxpayer's financial operation. In the field audit, unlike the office audit, the examiner may raise issues other than those set forth in the notification letter.

After an audit, the taxpayer receives an explanation of the proposed adjustment to his or her tax liability from the agent. If additional taxes are due and the taxpayer agrees to the adjustment, he or she may sign a waiver of restrictions on assessment. The service may then immediately assess the tax without sending the taxpayer the formal notice of deficiency. The taxpayer may prepay the additional tax with accrued interest or wait until he or she receives a formal payment request. Note, however, that the agreement must also be approved by the district office review staff.

If the taxpayer does not agree with the agent's adjustments, a supervisor or appeals officer will try to resolve the problem immediately. If this does not happen, the taxpayer is sent a "30-day letter" that formally notifies the taxpayer of the audit's outcome, the proposed tax adjustments, and his or her right of appeal. The taxpayer has 30 days to request a conference with an appeals officer. This "protest" must be in writing if the tax deficiency is more than $2,500 and the taxpayer must set forth specific reasons for disagreeing with the adjustment. The appeals officer has final and exclusive authority to resolve tax controversies prior to formal legal proceedings. The appeals division, under the supervision of the IRS's Chief Counsel, is specifically charged with settling taxpayer disputes in a fair and impartial manner.

If the taxpayer fails to respond to the 30-day letter, or if an agreement is not reached in an appeals conference, the taxpayer is sent a "90-day letter," the notice of deficiency. This letter must be sent by registered or certified mail and must be sent prior to the assessment of additional taxes. The taxpayer has 90 days within which to file a redetermination of deficiency with the Tax Court. If the taxpayer does not respond within the 90 days, the deficiency is assessed and the taxpayer *must* pay the deficiency before proceeding with any further litigation.

After paying the deficiency assessment, the taxpayer may sue for a refund of taxes in either the District Court or the Court of Federal Claims. Once the 90 days expire on the notice of deficiency, the taxpayer is barred from seeking redress in the Tax Court. In this case, the taxpayer must pay the tax and then sue for refund in one of the other two courts that hear tax matters.

The Small Claims Division of the Tax Court, which handles tax deficiencies of $10,000 or less, does not permit the taxpayer to appeal its decision. The taxpayer may appeal decisions in other courts. Decisions of the Tax Court and the District Court are appealed to the District Court of Appeals (Regional Circuit). Decisions of the Court of Federal Claims are appealed to the U.S. Court of Appeals for the Federal Circuit. Finally, all appellate decisions may be appealed to the Supreme Court. However, only a very limited number are granted "certiorari"—that is, will be heard by the Supreme Court. Figure 5-6 provides a schematic of the legal process from audit through appeal to the Supreme Court. A more complete discussion of the court system was presented in Chapter 1.

CHAPTER PROBLEMS

PART 1434

The tables in Appendix C or the formula method may be used to determine the earned-income credits for 1993; answers may differ slightly due to rounding.

I 1. John and Mary Wade support and maintain a home for their disabled son William. John earned $9,200 as a part-time auto mechanic and Mary received $2,100 in taxable pension benefits. Determine their basic earned-income credit for 1993.

I 2. Monica is a single parent who maintains a home for herself and her dependent 12-year-old daughter Josephine. During 1993 Monica earned $10,800 as a hotel housekeeper, had $900 in income taxes withheld, and received $800 of advanced payments on her earned-income credit. Monica also paid $900 in health insurance premiums for herself and her daughter. Calculate Monica's tax or refund due for 1993.

I 3. Joseph Going retired two years ago because of a permanent disability. This year Joseph's income consisted of $12,000 of taxable pension benefits, $600 of municipal bond interest, and $1,600 in social security payments. If Joseph is single, what is his credit for the elderly and disabled?

I 4. Lynn and Bill Stewart are 66 and 59, respectively. Bill is permanently and totally disabled. They receive $4,000 of social security benefits, have AGI of $11,500, and file a joint return. What is their credit for the elderly and disabled for the current year?

II 5. Lissette Barron pays her aunt (not her dependent) to come to her home five days per week to care for her young son while she works. The aunt also cleans and prepares meals for her. Lissette pays the aunt $80 per week for the babysitting and other services. Lissette files as head of household and has an AGI of $15,600 for the current year. Calculate Lissette's child care credit.

II 6. Mary supports her elderly mother. So that Mary can go to work, she takes her mother to a day care facility for Alzheimer's patients at a local hospital that meets the requirements of a dependent care center. The cost is partially subsidized, but Mary must pay $50 per week for a total of $2,600 per year. If Mary's AGI is $16,600, what is her dependent care credit?

ANSWERS TO REVIEW IV

1. (a) As long as her withholding exceeds last year's tax liability, no estimated payments are required.
2. (b) $2,850 × .9 = $2,565
3. (c) (.9 × $14,500) − $6,000 = $7,050
4. (c) [(.9 × $12,400) − $6,000]/4 = $5,160/4 = $1,290
5. (c) $2,000 × .1 × 365/365 = $200
       $2,000 × .1 × 304/365 = $167
       $2,000 × .1 × 212/365 = $116
       $2,000 × .1 × 90/365 = $ 49
                       Total $532

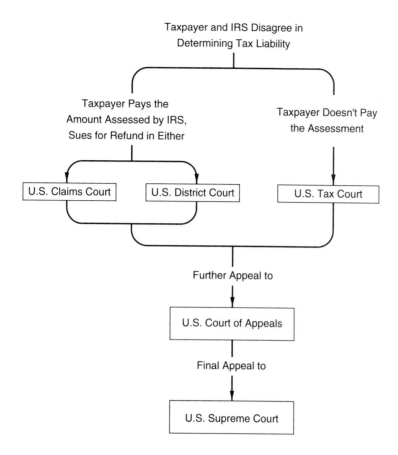

Figure 5-6 The Tax Appeals Process

II 7. Eliza and Roy have two daughters, Tiffany and Melody. Tiffany, four, is in Montessori preschool, which costs $4,200 per year, including $400 for transportation. Melody, nine, is in a boarding school that costs $9,000 per year. Eliza and Roy both work full-time and their AGI is $68,000. What is their allowable child care credit?

II 8. Mort and Mindy Grey have four children ages 7 through 16. They pay their 16-year-old, Joyce, $40 per week to watch the younger children after school and $100 per week for child care during the summer. During the current year, they paid Joyce $2,840 for child care. What is their child care credit if their AGI is $32,400? Would they be better off if they did not claim Joyce as a dependent?

II 9. Betty King is a full-time student and her husband, Bud, works part-time while rearing their two sons, Tom and Jerry. Bud's income for the current tax year was $3,950; their AGI was $11,200; and their child care expense was $3,210. Determine their child care credit.

III 10. What is the purpose of the orphan drug credit?

III 11. John Swintle has $100,000 of taxable earned income this year, on which he calculates he will owe $26,500 of federal income taxes. However, $60,000 of this income was earned while he worked overseas for part of the year. While there, he was required to pay $20,000 of income taxes on this income. What is his allowable foreign tax credit?

III 12. Marilyn Winslow has $4,000 of income from foreign sources on which $800 of foreign taxes are withheld. If her federal tax liability is $6,800 on $42,000 of taxable income, determine her allowable foreign tax credit.

III	13. Toby Moran is single and has $40,000 of taxable income; of this, $25,000 is foreign earned income. Toby is eligible for the foreign earned-income exclusion on this amount. If he paid $3,750 in foreign taxes, would Toby be better off taking the exclusion or the foreign tax credit? Use the tax rate tables in Appendix B to determine your answer, and omit apportionment of any deductions.
IV	14. Explain the different ways a taxpayer can avoid an underpayment penalty if her advance payments are less than the total tax due for 1993.
IV	15. Explain how the underpayment penalty is determined for a taxpayer who fails to make the required advance payments.
IV	16. Tom Bowen expects his tax liability to be $1,500 for the current tax year. He paid $8,800 in taxes last year. What are his required quarterly tax payments?
IV	17. Joseph White had made the required $3,000 estimated tax payments on April 15 and June 15 for the current tax year. Early in July, he realized that his total tax liability was going to be $10,000 more than expected. How does this change Joseph's estimated payments?
IV	18. George had $1,000 withheld each month from his paycheck. At the end of the year, his tax liability was $20,000. He is required to pay the underpayment penalty. Determine its amount if the applicable interest rate for the entire period is 12% and he paid his taxes on April 15 when due. (Assume a 365-day year.)
IV	19. George Wise did not expect to have any tax liability for the current year. In May, however, a company in which he owned a large block of stock was merged into another corporation in a taxable merger. George realized a gain of $85,000 on the stock and now expects a tax liability of $20,000 for the year. What should George do?
APX	20. What are the purposes of the 30-day letter and the 90-day letter?
APX	21. How many different ways may an examination of a tax return be conducted?
APX	22. What are the various courts to which a taxpayer may take a tax case?
APX	23. What are the appellate courts to which tax cases may be appealed?

TAX RETURN PROBLEMS

24. [Form 2441] Using the information in Problem 6 above, complete Form 2441 for Mary.
25. [Form 2210] Thomas and Carol Jensen needed to pay certain expenses during the tax year, so they decreased their withholding on their salaries by claiming several additional exemptions. When they filed their tax return, their tax liability was $16,200, but they had had only $11,050 withheld for payment of income taxes. If their liability for the prior year was $13,280, complete the short method of determining the underwithholding penalty on Form 2210 as provided.

HOW WOULD YOU RULE?

26. Janine Morgan's daughter Toni, age 18, married her high school boyfriend on March 12 of the current tax year. Unfortunately, the marriage was not happy from the beginning, and Toni returned to her mother's home to live on September 30. She remained

there the rest of the year and qualified as Janine's dependent. Is Toni a qualifying individual for purposes of Janine's claiming the earned-income credit?

27. Peter and Alice Trent both work full time. During the school year, Alice's mother provides after-school care for their two children at no cost to the Trents. During the summer, however, they send the children to summer camp for six weeks at a cost of $1,800 each. They pay a neighbor $1,600 to be responsible for the children when they are not at camp for the balance of summer vacation. How would you treat these payments in determining the amount eligible for the child and dependent care credit?

TAX PORTFOLIO PROBLEM FOR THE NEILSON FAMILY

If you instructor has assigned this problem, refer to Appendix A and complete the portion labeled "Chapter 5." This includes information on child care expenses used for completing Form 2441 for Harold and Maude Neilson and information necessary for computing the tax credit for the elderly and completing Schedule R for Harriet Neilson.

Chapter 5 Problem 24   Name _____   5-39

Form **2441**	**Child and Dependent Care Expenses**	OMB No. 1545-0068
Department of the Treasury Internal Revenue Service	▶ Attach to Form 1040. ▶ See separate instructions.	**1993** Attachment Sequence No. **21**
Name(s) shown on Form 1040		Your social security number

You need to understand the following terms to complete this form: **Dependent Care Benefits, Earned Income, Qualified Expenses,** and **Qualifying Person(s)**. See **Important Terms** on page 1 of the Form 2441 instructions. Also, if you had a child born in 1993 and line 32 of Form 1040 is less than $23,050, see **A Change To Note** on page 2 of the instructions.

Part I Persons or Organizations Who Provided the Care—You **must** complete this part.
(If you need more space, use the bottom of page 2.)

1	(a) Care provider's name	(b) Address (number, street, apt. no., city, state, and ZIP code)	(c) Identifying number (SSN or EIN)	(d) Amount paid (see instructions)

2 Add the amounts in column (d) of line 1 . . . . **2**

3 Enter the number of **qualifying persons** cared for in 1993 . . . . ▶ ☐

Did you receive **dependent care benefits?** — NO ⟶ Complete only Part II below.
— YES ⟶ Complete Part III on the back now.

Part II Credit for Child and Dependent Care Expenses

4 Enter the amount of **qualified expenses** you incurred and paid in 1993. DO NOT enter more than $2,400 for one qualifying person or $4,800 for two or more persons. If you completed Part III, enter the amount from line 25 . . . . **4**

5 Enter YOUR **earned income** **5**

6 If married filing a joint return, enter YOUR SPOUSE'S earned income (if student or disabled, see instructions); **all others,** enter the amount from line 5 . . . . **6**

7 Enter the **smallest** of line 4, 5, or 6 . . . . **7**

8 Enter the amount from Form 1040, line 32 . . . . **8**

9 Enter on line 9 the decimal amount shown below that applies to the amount on line 8

If line 8 is—		Decimal amount is	If line 8 is—		Decimal amount is
Over	But not over		Over	But not over	
$0	10,000	.30	$20,000	22,000	.24
10,000	12,000	.29	22,000	24,000	.23
12,000	14,000	.28	24,000	26,000	.22
14,000	16,000	.27	26,000	28,000	.21
16,000	18,000	.26	28,000	No limit	.20
18,000	20,000	.25			

9 X .

10 Multiply **line 7** by the decimal amount on line 9. Enter the result. Then, see the instructions for the amount of credit to enter on Form 1040, line 41 . . . . **10**

Caution: If you paid $50 or more in a calendar quarter to a person who worked in your home, you must file an employment tax return. Get **Form 942** for details.

For Paperwork Reduction Act Notice, see separate instructions.   Cat. No. 11862M   Form **2441** (1993)

Copyright © 1994 by Harcourt Brace & Company. All rights reserved.

Chapter 5 Problem 24   Name _____   5-40

Form 2441 (1993)   Page **2**

Part III   **Dependent Care Benefits**—Complete this part **only** if you received these benefits.

11   Enter the total amount of **dependent care benefits** you received for 1993. This amount should be shown in box 10 of your W-2 form(s). DO NOT include amounts that were reported to you as wages in box 1 of Form(s) W-2 . . . .   **11**

12   Enter the amount forfeited, if any. See the instructions **12**

13   Subtract line 12 from line 11 . . . .   **13**

14   Enter the total amount of **qualified expenses** incurred in 1993 for the care of the qualifying person(s) **14**

15   Enter the **smaller** of line 13 or 14 . . . .   **15**

16   Enter YOUR **earned income** **16**

17   If married filing a joint return, enter YOUR SPOUSE'S earned income (if student or disabled, see the line 6 instructions); if married filing a separate return, see the instructions for the amount to enter; **all others,** enter the amount from line 16 . .   **17**

18   Enter the **smallest** of line 15, 16, or 17 . . . .   **18**

19   **Excluded benefits.** Enter here the **smaller** of the following:
- The amount from line 18, or
- $5,000 ($2,500 if married filing a separate return **and** you were required to enter your spouse's earned income on line 17).

      . . . .   **19**

20   **Taxable benefits.** Subtract line 19 from line 13. Also, include this amount on Form 1040, line 7. On the dotted line next to line 7, write "DCB" **20**

To claim the child and dependent care credit, complete lines 21–25 below, and lines 4–10 on the front of this form.

21   Enter the amount of qualified expenses you incurred and paid in 1993. DO NOT include on this line any excluded benefits shown on line 19 . . . .   **21**

22   Enter $2,400 ($4,800 if two or more qualifying persons) . . .   **22**

23   Enter the amount from line 19 . . . .   **23**

24   Subtract line 23 from line 22. If zero or less, **STOP.** You cannot take the credit. **Exception.** If you paid 1992 expenses in 1993, see the line 10 instructions **24**

25   Enter the **smaller** of line 21 or 24 here **and** on line 4 on the front of this form **25**

Copyright © 1994 by Harcourt Brace & Company. All rights reserved.

Chapter 5 Problem 25   Name _____   5-41

Form 2210
Department of the Treasury
Internal Revenue Service

Underpayment of Estimated Tax by Individuals and Fiduciaries
▶ See separate instructions.
▶ Attach to Form 1040, Form 1040A, Form 1040NR, or Form 1041.

OMB No. 1545-0140
1992
Attachment Sequence No. 06

Name(s) shown on tax return | Identifying number

Note: *In most cases, you **do not** need to file Form 2210. The IRS will figure any penalty you owe and send you a bill. File Form 2210 **only** if one or more boxes in Part I apply to you. If you do not need to file Form 2210, you still may use it to figure your penalty. Enter the amount from line 20 or line 36 on the penalty line of your return, but do not attach Form 2210.*

Part I — Reasons For Filing
If 1a, b, c, or d below applies to you, you may be able to lower or eliminate your penalty. But you MUST check the boxes that apply and file Form 2210 with your tax return. If 1e or f below applies to you, check that box and file Form 2210 with your tax return.

1 Check whichever boxes apply (if none apply, see the **Note** above):

a ☐ You request a **waiver**. (In certain circumstances, the IRS will waive all or part of the penalty. See the instructions for **Waiver of Penalty**.)

b ☐ You use the **annualized income installment method**. (If your income varied during the year, this method may reduce the amount of one or more required installments. See **Instructions for Schedule B**.)

c ☐ You had Federal income tax withheld from wages and you treat it as paid for estimated tax purposes when it was **actually** withheld instead of in equal amounts on the payment due dates. (See the instructions for line 22.)

d ☐ (1) You made estimated tax payments for 1989, 1990, or 1991 (or were charged an estimated tax penalty for any of those years), **AND**
(2) Your adjusted gross income (AGI) is more than $75,000 (more than $37,500 if married filing separately), **AND**
(3) Your 1992 **modified** AGI exceeds your 1991 AGI by more than $40,000 (more than $20,000 if married filing separately), **AND**
(4) Your 2nd, 3rd, or 4th required installment (column (b), (c), or (d) of line 21) is based on **either** your 1991 tax **or** 90% of your 1992 **modified** tax.

See **Instructions for Schedule A** for more information.

e ☐ Conditions (1), (2), and (4) (but not condition (3)) in box 1d apply to you, and your 1992 AGI exceeds your 1991 AGI by more than $40,000 (more than $20,000 if married filing separately). If you check this box, you must also attach a computation of your 1992 modified AGI.

f ☐ One or more of your required installments (line 21) are based on your 1991 tax and you filed or are filing a joint return for either 1991 or 1992 but not for both years.

Part II — All Filers Must Complete This Part

2	Enter your 1992 tax after credits (see instructions)	2
3	Other taxes (see instructions)	3
4	Add lines 2 and 3	4
5	Earned income credit **5**	
6	Credit for Federal tax paid on fuels **6**	
7	Add lines 5 and 6	7
8	Current year tax. Subtract line 7 from line 4	8
9	Multiply line 8 by 90% (.90) **9**	
10	Withholding taxes. **Do not** include any estimated tax payments on this line (see instructions) .	10
11	Subtract line 10 from line 8. If less than $500, stop here; **do not** complete or file this form. You do not owe the penalty	11
12	Prior year (1991) tax. (**Caution:** *See instructions.*)	12
13	Enter the **smaller** of line 9 or line 12 (see instructions)	13

Part III — Short Method
(**Caution:** *Read the instructions to see if you can use the short method. If you checked box **1b, c,** or **d** in Part I, skip this part and go to Part IV.*)

14	Enter the amount, if any, from line 10 above **14**	
15	Enter the total amount, if any, of estimated tax payments you made **15**	
16	Add lines 14 and 15	16
17	**Total underpayment for year.** Subtract line 16 from line 13. (If zero or less, stop here; you do not owe the penalty. Do not file Form 2210 unless you checked box 1e or f above.)	17
18	Multiply line 17 by .04846	18
19	• If the amount on line 17 was paid **on or after** 4/15/93, enter -0-.	
	• If the amount on line 17 was paid **before** 4/15/93, make the following computation to find the amount to enter on line 19. Amount on line 17 × Number of days paid before 4/15/93 × .00019	19
20	**PENALTY.** Subtract line 19 from line 18. Enter the result here and on Form 1040, line 65; Form 1040A, line 33; Form 1040NR, line 65; or Form 1041, line 26 . . . . ▶	20

For Paperwork Reduction Act Notice, see page 1 of separate instructions.   Cat. No. 11744P   Form **2210** (1992)

Copyright © 1994 by Harcourt Brace & Company. All rights reserved.

CHAPTER 6

Gain and Loss Recognition: An Introduction

The taxation of property transactions is one of the most important parts of the Internal Revenue Code. To do effective tax reporting and planning, you must know the tax implications associated with property sales or exchanges. Unfortunately, some of these provisions are among the most complex in the tax law.

Congress did simplify the reporting of such gains and losses in the Tax Reform Act of 1986. However, the tax provisions, including the special rules for capital losses and long-term capital gains, are still quite complex.

Part I of this chapter reviews the fundamental concepts of property taxation and introduces one of the two parts of the gain and loss computation: the determination of the amount realized. Part II introduces the other basic part of property gain and loss calculations: the adjusted basis of the property sold or exchanged. Part III discusses the capital asset definition and describes the capital gain and loss netting process for individuals. And finally, Parts IV and V of the chapter discuss two special gain and loss computations involving installment sales and personal residence sales.

This chapter introduces the basic gain and loss calculations. Over the years, Congress, the IRS, and the courts have been very active in developing interpretations, modifications, and exceptions to the basic calculations. Some of the more important modifications are discussed in the Appendix to this chapter and in Chapter 9.

I CONCEPTS OF GAIN, LOSS, AND AMOUNT REALIZED
(Code Sections 165 and 1001)

Since the very first income tax laws, the gain or loss realized on the disposition—the selling or exchanging—of property has been treated differently than the income produced by the property. Early English common law taxed only the income produced by an asset; any gain or loss on the sale or exchange of the asset itself was exempted from taxation. This concept was carried over into the early versions of the U.S. tax laws. However, pressing revenue needs soon dictated that other sources of increase in individual wealth should be subject to taxation. The provisions have changed over the years, but most property transactions are taxed in some way, although special tax treatments are accorded to gains and losses related to "capital assets."

THE REALIZATION CRITERION

THE LAW

Sec. 1001(c)—*Recognition of Gain or Loss.*—Except as otherwise provided in this subtitle, the entire amount of the gain or loss, determined under this section, on the sale or exchange of property shall be recognized.

One of the fundamental requirements of property taxation is that a gain or loss must be *realized* in a verifiable transaction. Until the gain or loss can be measured with reasonable certainty through an arm's-length transaction, any increases or decreases in the value of an asset are not subject to taxation. To tax a gain or loss before it has been realized would involve the use of subjective estimates of value. Obviously, this would place a tremendous administrative burden on the IRS.

Example 1. Sue Adam owns a rental duplex located five miles from the site of a new nuclear plant under construction. Because of this location, a realtor appraised the duplex at a value of $15,000 less than its original cost two years ago. Sue may not deduct this loss in value on her tax return, because it was not realized in a market transaction. Such a loss is potentially deductible only when Sue sells or otherwise disposes of the property. (Recall also that a decline in value does not qualify as a casualty loss under the rules discussed in Chapter 4.)

Example 2. Bo Bar purchased 1,000 shares of BC Corporation stock in January 1993 for $5,000. Stock market quotations indicate that the stock is worth $6,500 at the end of the year. Bo does not recognize this $1,500 increase in value as income in 1993 because he has not realized the wealth increase in a market transaction.

DEDUCTIBILITY OF LOSSES

THE LAW

Sec. 165(c)—*Limitation on Losses of Individuals.*—In the case of an individual, the deduction under subsection (a) shall be limited to—
(1) losses incurred in a trade or business:
(2) losses incurred in any transaction entered into for profit, though not connected with a trade or business; and
(3) except as provided in subsection (h), losses of property not connected with a trade or business or a transaction entered into for profit, if such losses arise from fire, storm, shipwreck, or other casualty, or from theft.

In general, most realized gains are subject to taxation through the Code's all-inclusive definition of income. These include all gains on sales or exchanges of both business and personal assets, though some gains on business or income-producing assets may be postponed under the "nontaxable exchange" provisions discussed in Chapter 9. The same cannot be said for losses; the Code provides for the deductibility of only three types of losses. These are (1) trade or business losses, (2) income-producing losses, and (3) casualty or theft losses. The practical effect of this rule is to disallow loss deductions on the sale or exchange of personal properties (i.e., nonbusiness or nonincome-producing assets).

 Example 3. Carol Carson sold her personal automobile for $3,500. She purchased the car for $4,800 two years ago. Carson cannot deduct the loss on her tax return because the automobile is a personal asset.

 Example 4. Assume the same facts as in Example 3, except that Carson used the automobile for business purposes 60% of the time. In this case, the sale price and cost of the car must be allocated between the business and personal portions. Any loss on the 60% business portion (after the cost basis is adjusted for depreciation allowed) would be deductible, and any loss on the 40% personal portion would not be deductible.

TAX TIP

Taxpayers planning to sell their residence at a loss may want to consider converting the property to a rental property for a period of time. If the house can be considered an "income-producing" property, any loss on a later sale of it may be deductible. However, case law should be consulted when considering such a strategy. If the rental period is very short, the IRS may maintain that the rental was merely a sham to generate a loss deduction on the subsequent sale.

Once realization occurs, the taxable gain or loss must be computed. This involves a comparison of two amounts: the amount realized on the sale or exchange, and the adjusted cost basis of the property. The determination of the amount realized is discussed below, and the adjusted basis is discussed in Part II of this chapter.

MEASURING THE AMOUNT REALIZED

THE LAW

Sec. 1001(a)—Computation of gain or loss.—The gain from sale or other disposition of property shall be the excess of the amount realized therefrom over the adjusted basis provided in section 1011 for determining gain, and the loss shall be the excess of the adjusted basis provided in such section for determining loss over the amount realized. (b) Amount realized.—The amount realized from the sale or other disposition of property shall be the sum of any money received plus the fair market value of the property (other than money) received.

The concept of "amount realized" is much broader in scope than the commonly used definition of selling price. The amount realized is determined as follows:

Cash received	$X,XXX
+ Fair market value of property received	X,XXX
+ Fair market value of services received	X,XXX
+ Liabilities assumed by the purchaser	X,XXX
– Selling expenses	(X,XXX)
Amount realized	$X,XXX

Obviously, any cash received by the seller will be part of the amount realized for purposes of determining gain or loss. When property or services are received as part of the sales price, the amount realized is always measured by the fair market value of the property or services. The fair market value is the only true measure of increase in wealth. In effect, the transaction is usually treated as if the seller had converted the property received to cash. This parallels the "cash equivalent" doctrine discussed in Chapter 2.

☑ **Example 5.** Jan Bell purchased several gold coins in 1990 for $300. In 1993 he gives the coins to a plumber in exchange for extensive repairs to his residence. Ordinarily, the plumber would have charged $750 for his services. Bell must report a $450 gain on his 1993 return. The exchange is treated no differently than if Bell sold the coins for $750 and used the cash to pay the plumber. (The plumber would also be required to recognize $750 of services income from the transaction.)

Note that an exchange of services can create taxable income. Obviously, such exchanges cause administrative problems for the IRS, because no cash changes hands. Much has been written about the growing popularity of this "underground economy," and especially about the development of "clearing houses" for exchanges of services and products.

☑ **Example 6.** Mary Anderson, an attorney, agrees to act as a contractor's legal representative for certain business matters in exchange for some construction work on her personal residence. The value of the construction work is $3,600, which is also the value of the legal work. Anderson must report the $3,600 as income, and the contractor must report the $3,600 value of the legal services as income (although some or all of the amount may be deductible as a business expense).

The amount realized always includes any liabilities assumed by another party. In general, the tax law treats the assumed debt as though the seller had actually received cash and had used this cash to retire the debt. Also, inclusion of the assumed debt in the amount realized is consistent with the tax-basis rules for property, which include such liabilities in the basis of financed property.

☑ **Example 7.** Ralph Prizler purchased an antique cabinet in 1990 for $10,000, paying $3,000 down and financing the balance. In 1993 he sold the cabinet for $6,000 cash, and the purchaser assumed the remaining outstanding debt of $5,000. Prizler's amount realized on the sale is $11,000 (the $6,000 cash plus the $5,000 remaining debt assumed), his adjusted basis is the $10,000 cost, and his taxable gain on the sale is $1,000.

TAX TIP

A sale or an exchange involving one or more payments to be received in future years may be reported on an installment basis, whereby gain is recognized as cash or other consideration received. Because of the definition of "total contract price" used in these calculations, a seller may be able to shift tax liabilities into a later year if the seller finances a portion of the sales price, as opposed to allowing the purchaser to assume an existing mortgage. These possibilities are discussed in more detail in Part IV of this chapter.

Selling expenses are reductions in the amount realized and include all legitimate commissions and other costs incurred by the seller, such as advertising, legal fees, and transfer taxes. This reduction in the amount realized reflects the fact that the seller's wherewithal to pay tax has decreased because of the outlays for such expenditures.

REVIEW I

1. Bill Winkle purchased a two-apartment building in 1987 for $60,000. He lived in one apartment and rented the other for five years. In 1993 he sold the building for $42,000. He had deducted $8,000 of allowable depreciation on the rental portion of the building. Winkle may deduct a loss on his 1993 return of
   (a) $0.
   (b) $1,000.
   (c) $9,000.
   (d) $18,000.
2. In exchange for some dental work, Beth Akers transfers a sofa from her furniture dealership. The sofa cost $350 wholesale, and Akers normally sells it for $500. The value of the dental work Akers received was approximately $500. As a result of this transaction, she must recognize gross income of
   (a) $0.
   (b) $150.
   (c) $350.
   (d) $500.
3. In 1988 Mel Matusak bought five acres of land for $20,000, paying $5,000 down and financing the balance with a five-year mortgage. In 1993 Matusak sold the land for $18,000 cash, and the purchaser assumed the outstanding mortgage balance of $6,000. Matusak incurred $50 in selling costs and $30 in transfer fees in closing the sale. The amount realized by Matusak on the sale was
   (a) $17,920.
   (b) $18,000.
   (c) $23,920.
   (d) $24,000.

4. Assume the same facts as in Question 3. What was Matusak's tax basis in the property at the time of sale?
   (a) $5,000
   (b) $6,000
   (c) $17,000
   (d) $20,000

Answers are on page 6-8.

II DETERMINING THE ADJUSTED BASIS OF PROPERTY

(Code Sections 1011, 1012, 1014, 1015, and 1016)

The determination of adjusted basis can be much more difficult than the determination of the amount realized. The original basis of property depends on the method of acquisition, and certain events after acquisition can increase or decrease this figure (resulting in an "adjusted basis"). Four methods of acquisition are discussed in the following sections.

ORIGINAL COST BASIS

Before we turn to the alternative methods of determining basis, it is important to note the relationship between these calculations and the determination of a property's holding period. The concept of a holding period is used to distinguish short-term assets (those held for one year or less) from long-term assets (those held for longer than one year). For most properties, the holding period begins on the date of acquisition. However, if the determination of the adjusted basis of a particular property depends in whole or in part on the adjusted basis of a prior owner (or a prior property), the property's holding period includes the holding period of the prior owner (or prior property). This is called a *tacking* of holding periods, and it usually occurs when tax recognition is deferred through a "nontaxable" transaction.

✓ **Example 8.** In 1990 Kay Karrol purchased 100 shares of X Corporation stock for $1,100. In 1993 she received a ten-share nontaxable stock dividend. Tax regulations require that Karrol allocate a portion of the $1,100 cost of the 100 original shares to the 10 new shares; therefore, her new tax basis is now $10 per share (rather than $11). Because the cost basis of the new shares is determined by reference to the old shares, the holding period of the new shares includes the holding period of the old shares (back to 1990). Thus, if Karrol immediately sells the stock dividend shares, any capital gain or loss will be long term.

THE LAW

Sec. 1012—Basis of Property—Cost. The basis of property shall be the cost of such property, except as otherwise provided in this subchapter and . . . [other subchapters]. . . .

Purchased Property

In an arm's-length transaction, the original basis of purchased property is its initial cost. This includes cash, the adjusted basis of any property given up, and the amount of any liabilities assumed by the purchaser. The cost of the property also includes such incidental outlays as shipping, installation, and property transfer taxes. If several assets are acquired for one lump sum, the total cost is allocated based on the relative fair market values of the properties. This method is used for bargain purchases of several properties.

Example 9. Helen Brandon acquired a lathe and a drill press from a bankrupt company for $7,000. The lathe and the drill press have fair market values of $6,000 and $4,000, respectively. Brandon will allocate $4,200 of the cost to the lathe ($7,000 × 60%) and $2,800 of the cost to the drill press ($7,000 × 40%).

A taxpayer is entitled to increase the cost basis for any gain recognized in the acquisition of a property. This increase in basis eliminates the double taxation possibility on a later sale or exchange of the property. In an arm's-length fully taxable exchange of properties, the practical effect of this addition is to assign the fair market value of the property surrendered as the basis of the new property, assuming that the relative fair market values of the two properties are equal.

Example 10. In a fully taxable exchange, Bob Wills trades a personal boat ($4,000 adjusted basis, $5,500 fair market value) for a business automobile worth $5,500. Wills must report a $1,500 taxable gain on the exchange, and his basis in the automobile will be $5,500 ($4,000 + $1,500).

Example 11. Ann Benson works as a salesperson for an auto dealership. As a year-end bonus, she is allowed to purchase a new automobile from inventory for $5,000. The auto had an invoice cost to the dealer of $5,950. Because Benson is taxed on the $950 bargain purchase as additional compensation, her tax basis in the automobile will be $5,950 (the $5,000 cost plus the $950 recognized gain.)

THE LAW

Sec. 1014(a)—Except as otherwise provided in this section, the basis of property in the hands of a person acquiring the property from a decedent . . . shall be—
(1) the fair market value of the property at the date of the decedent's death, or
(2) in the case of an election under section 2032 . . . its value at the applicable valuation date. . . .

Inherited Property

The adjusted basis of inherited property is its fair market value on the date of the decedent's death, or, if the decedent's estate so chooses, its fair market value on the "alternate valuation date." The alternate valuation date, which is exactly six months after the date of death, is sometimes elected by the executor or the executrix of an estate to value the decedent's property for federal estate tax purposes. (The federal estate tax is a tax on the fair market value of property owned by an individual at death.) In effect, the beneficiary's basis is the same as the value used for federal estate tax purposes. If the alternate valuation date is selected and if the property is sold before this date, the sale price of the property is assumed to be its adjusted basis.

The use of fair market values to determine the basis of inherited property permanently exempts some increases in value from income taxation. To prevent schemes that would further maximize the potential tax savings, Congress has added two special provisions to the rules. First, the alternate valuation date may be elected only when the value of the gross estate and the gross estate tax *decreases;* otherwise, such an election could be made without any tax cost by estates not subject to the federal estate tax (generally, those of less than $600,000 total value). Second, no "step up" in basis is allowed for property given to the decedent within one year of his or her death when the property is inherited by the original donor. Otherwise, taxpayers might be encouraged to make "gifts in contemplation of death" to terminally ill relatives so that a higher tax basis would be provided through inheritance.

☑ **Example 12.** Fran Juarez inherited 1,000 shares of Z Company stock in 1993 from her father's estate. Her father had purchased the stock in 1990 for $60,000, and the stock was worth $85,000 on the date of his death. Juarez's tax basis in the stock is the $85,000 value on the date of death. Note that the $25,000 increase in value is permanently exempted from income taxation, though it may be subject to the federal estate tax.

☑ **Example 13.** Assume the same facts as in Example 12, except that it was Fran who originally purchased the stock for $60,000 in 1990, and she had made a gift of the stock to her father three months before he died. In this case, Fran's adjusted basis in the inherited stock is $60,000, her original tax basis; no step up in basis is permitted because her father died within one year of the original gift.

A special rule in the Code provides that the holding period for any inherited property is automatically presumed to be long term. Thus, a beneficiary who sells inherited property a few days after receiving it would report any gain or loss as long term in nature.

ANSWERS TO REVIEW I

1. (b) Only the $1,000 loss on the business portion is deductible. This is the $21,000 sales price allocable to the rental portion less the $22,000 adjusted basis for the rental portion ($30,000 less the $8,000 of allowable depreciation).
2. (b) The value of the dental work must be reported as the gross receipts, and this amount is reduced by the cost of the sofa.
3. (c) The amount realized includes the assumed mortgage, and this total is reduced by the selling expenses.
4. (d) The cost basis is unaffected by the method of financing the property.

GIFT PROPERTY

THE LAW

Sec. 1015(a)—Gifts After December 31, 1920.—If the property was acquired by gift after December 31, 1920, the basis shall be the same as it would be in the hands of the donor or the last preceding owner by whom it was not acquired as a gift, except that if such basis . . . is greater than the fair market value of the property at the time of the gift, then for the purpose of determining loss the basis shall be such fair market value.

Depending on the situation, gift property may have an adjusted basis for determining loss that is different than the adjusted basis for determining gain. This "dual basis" possibility exists for all gifts received after 1920 (any gift received prior to 1921 has an adjusted basis equal to its fair market value). The basis for calculating *gain* is always the adjusted basis of the gift to the donor (i.e., the person making the gift). As a result of this carryover of basis, the gift recipient may have to pay tax on an increase in value of the property that occurred when it was held by the donor. As mentioned earlier, a carryover of basis also results in a carryover of holding period; therefore, the beneficiary's holding period includes the donor's holding period.

Example 14. On March 1, 1993, Mel Morris received 500 shares of Tex stock from his aunt. She had purchased the stock on May 1, 1990, for $5,000, and it was worth $6,800 on the date of the gift. If Morris sells the stock on June 1, 1993, for $7,000, he will report a $2,000 long-term gain. The donor's basis is always used for purposes of determining gain, and Morris' holding period is assumed to begin on May 1, 1990—the date his aunt acquired the stock.

The adjusted basis for determining *loss* is defined as the *lesser* of the donor's adjusted basis or the fair market value of the gift on the date of the gift. Essentially, this rule prevents a taxpayer from deducting a loss in value that occurred when the property was held by the donor (although, as mentioned earlier, the same logic does not apply to gains). If the fair market value is less than the donor's basis and the amount realized on the sale is between the two possible bases, then *no* gain or loss is recognized on the sale or the exchange.

Example 15. Marge Stein received a gift of 50 shares of stock from her mother on January 1, 1993. The stock was worth $20,000 on that date, and it had originally cost $26,000 when her mother purchased it in 1989. If Stein sells the stock for $18,000 on November 1, 1993, she will recognize a $2,000 short-term loss. There is no tacking of holding periods, because Stein is not using her mother's basis for determining gain or loss.

Example 16. Assume the same facts as in Example 15, except that Stein sells the stock for $24,000. No gain or loss is recognized in this case, since the amount realized is between the two possible bases of $20,000 and $26,000.

In some instances, a donor may have to pay a federal gift tax on the transfer of property. In order to reduce the double taxation on a later sale by the donee, the donor's adjusted basis may be increased by a fraction of the gift tax paid by the donor. For gifts made prior to 1977, the addition to basis is 100% of the gift tax paid by the donor. For gifts made after 1976, the addition is limited to that fraction of the gift tax related to the appreciation in value of the gift occurring during the time it was held by the donor. This is computed by the following formula:

$$\text{Addition} = \frac{\text{Appreciation in Value}}{\text{Fair Market Value of Gift}} \times \text{Gift Tax Paid}$$

In no case can the sum of the donor's adjusted basis and the gift tax addition exceed the fair market value of the gift on the date of the gift. Thus, these computations are irrelevant if the fair market value of the gift is *less* than the donor's basis.

Example 17. Sid Schroeder received a gift of bonds from his sister in 1972. His sister purchased the bonds in 1970 for $6,000, and they were worth $8,000 on the date of the gift. Schroeder's sister paid $1,000 of federal gift tax on the transfer. Since 1972 was a year prior to 1977, Schroeder's adjusted basis in the bonds would be $7,000 (donor's basis of $6,000 plus 100% of the $1,000 gift tax paid by the donor). If Sid had received the gift in a year after 1976, his adjusted basis in the bonds would be $6,250 (donor's basis of $6,000 plus two-eighths of the $1,000 gift tax paid that relates to the $2,000 appreciation in value).

Table 6-1 presents a comprehensive set of calculations for the various basis rules relating to gift property. The examples assume that the gift occurs after 1976, so the fractional gift tax addition rules are used to increase the donor's adjusted basis, where appropriate. The various examples also demonstrate the consistency between a substituted basis and a holding period.

TAX TIP

When a taxpayer desires to transfer eventually all of his or her property to another person or persons, the relative adjusted bases and fair market values of the properties may dictate the method of transfer. For example, the taxpayer may decide to transfer high-basis property as lifetime gifts, because the beneficiary will use the donor's basis for gain computations on a subsequent sale. On the other hand, assets with a relatively low basis and a high market value may be transferred at death, because the beneficiary will use the fair market value as the basis for such inherited property. Of course, potential federal gift and estate taxes would also figure into such a decision.

Personal Property Converted to a Business Use

The basis for loss on the sale or exchange of personal property converted to a business use is the lesser of the taxpayer's adjusted basis in the property or the fair market value of the property on the date of conversion to business use. The purpose of this provision

Table 6-1 Examples of Gift Asset Sales

FACTS:
- Taxpayer receives 100 shares of stock as a gift on 4/1/93.
- Cost of stock to donor on 1/1/85 was $10,000.
- Donor paid a gift tax of $1,200 on the transfer.

Assuming a $15,000 Fair Market Value of Gift on the Date of Transfer	Assuming an $8,000 Fair Market Value of Gift on the Date of Transfer
If sold on 9/1/93 for $18,000:	**If sold on 9/1/93 for $18,000:**
Gain = $18,000 − [$10,000 + (5,000/15,000 × 1,200)] = $18,000 − $10,400 = $7,600 long-term gain*	Gain = $18,000 − $10,000 = $8,000 long-term gain*
If sold on 9/1/93 for $6,000:	**If sold on 9/1/93 for $6,000:**
Loss = $6,000 − $10,400 = $4,400 long-term loss*	Loss = $6,000 − $8,000 = $2,000 short-term loss†
If sold on 9/1/93 for $12,000:	**If sold on 9/1/93 for $8,500:**
Gain = $12,000 − $10,400 = $1,600 long-term gain*	Gain (or Loss) = $0‡

*Holding period begins 1/1/85 (since donor's basis is used)
†Holding period begins 4/1/93 (because fair market value is used as basis)
‡Selling price is between the two bases; thus, no gain or loss.

is to disallow the indirect deduction of a decline in value that occurred when the property was held for personal use. As discussed in Part I of this chapter, purely personal losses (other than casualty or theft losses) are not deductible for tax purposes.

☑ Example 18. Marla Cronin purchased a personal residence in 1990 for $70,000, and in 1993, when the property was worth $64,000, converted the residence into rental property. Cronin's basis for loss on a later sale or exchange is $64,000; to allow $70,000 as the tax basis would permit a $6,000 deduction for a personal loss.

BASIS ADJUSTMENTS SUBSEQUENT TO ACQUISITION

Several events occurring after the original acquisition of property can change its adjusted basis. Capital improvements generally increase the adjusted basis of property, and certain capital recoveries decrease the adjusted basis.

Capital improvements to an asset are generally defined as those expenditures that (1) significantly increase the value of an asset, (2) prolong the useful life of the asset, or (3) create a different use for the asset. Ordinary repairs that merely maintain the present operating condition of the asset are usually deductible immediately as expenses.

☑ Example 19. Bart Black owns a five-unit rental apartment building. During 1993 he spent $8,500 to install a new roof on the building and $600 to paint eight rooms. The cost of the roof would be added to the adjusted basis of the property, while the cost of painting would probably be deductible as an expense.

The adjusted basis of a property is reduced by any item that is considered to be a return of capital, as reflected by a deduction on the tax return. The three most common capital recoveries (discussed in Chapter 8) are depreciation, amortization, and depletion. Less obvious capital recoveries include casualty or theft losses (for property that is not completely destroyed) and nontaxable cash dividends (due to a lack of corporation "earnings and profits").

The adjusted basis of property is reduced by the depreciation allowed or allowable. If a taxpayer fails to take a depreciation deduction, the basis of the property is still reduced by the amount of depreciation that would have been allowed on a straight-line basis (unless the taxpayer elected accelerated recovery in earlier years when depreciation was taken on the asset).

TAX TIP

A taxpayer who fails to take depreciation deductions for certain years may be able to file amended returns and retroactively claim the deductions for all prior years still open under the statute of limitations (generally the three preceding tax years).

REVIEW II

1. Paul Pink inherited a boat from his father's estate in 1993. The boat cost $8,000 in 1980 and was worth $12,000 on the date of his father's death. An average of $3,000 of estate taxes was paid on the boat. Pink sold the boat four months after his father's death for $12,200. Pink must recognize
   (a) $0 gain or loss.
   (b) a $200 long-term gain.
   (c) a $1,200 short-term gain.
   (d) a $2,800 long-term loss.
2. Sue Akron purchased a personal residence in 1984 for $48,000, paying $16,000 down and financing the balance. In 1986, when the property was worth $42,000, she converted the residence to rental property. In 1988 the property was damaged by a storm and Akron deducted a $1,500 uninsured casualty loss. In 1993 she added a new garage to the property ($2,500 cost) and had one room wallpapered for $100. As of 1/1/93, Akron had properly deducted $8,000 of depreciation. Her adjusted basis for a sale of the property for $32,500 would be
   (a) $9,000.
   (b) $32,500.
   (c) $41,000.
   (d) $35,000.
3. Ike Hayes received 100 shares of stock as a gift from his mother on March 15, 1993. His mother had purchased the stock in 1990 for $8,000, and it was worth $6,500 on the date of the gift. Hayes's mother paid an $800 gift tax on the transfer. If Hayes sells the stock on July 3, 1993, for $9,000, he must recognize a
   (a) short-term gain of $1,850.
   (b) short-term gain of $2,500.
   (c) long-term gain of $1,000.
   (d) long-term gain of $1,850.

4. Assume the same facts as in Problem 3, except that Hayes sells the stock for $6,000. He must recognize a
   (a) short-term loss of $500.
   (b) short-term loss of $3,000.
   (c) long-term loss of $500.
   (d) long-term loss of $1,150.

Answers are on page 6-14.

III CAPITAL ASSETS AND THE NETTING PROCESS
(Code Sections 1211, 1212, 1221, 1222, and 1223)

Earlier in this chapter, we mentioned that gains and losses on the sale or exchange of "capital assets" are generally given special tax recognition. In tax years prior to 1988, Congress had chosen to tax long-term capital gains at significantly lower effective tax rates under the theory that mobility of capital should be encouraged and that several years of appreciation in value should not be taxed all at once. Currently, a small preferential treatment is available for long-term capital gains for most taxpayers, with somewhat larger benefits for high-income taxpayers. Congress has also generally limited the deductibility of capital losses against noncapital gains income. For these reasons, it is important to first know which properties qualify as capital assets.

CAPITAL ASSETS DEFINED

THE LAW

Sec. 1221—Capital Asset Defined.—For purposes of this subtitle, the term "capital asset" means property held by the taxpayer . . . but does not include—
(1) stock in trade of the taxpayer or other property of a kind which would properly be included in inventory;
(2) property . . . used in his trade or business . . .
(3) a copyright, a literary, musical, or artistic composition, a letter or memorandum, or similar property;
(4) accounts or notes receivable acquired in the ordinary course of a trade or business;
(5) a publication of the United States government . . . other than by a purchase at the price . . . offered for sale to the public.

Unfortunately, the Internal Revenue Code does not provide a definition of capital assets; rather, it lists several properties that will *never* be treated as capital assets (Sec. 1221, as shown above). All of these exceptions were originally based on the theory that none should be entitled to favorable capital gains treatment. Obviously, the sale of inventories will always generate ordinary (fully taxable) income. The same can be said for copyrights and other artistic compositions, which are similar in nature to inventories. Interestingly, the same rules apply to a person for whom the composition is intended, as well as any "carryover basis" recipient, such as a gift recipient.

In evaluating the exception for properties used in a trade or business, it is important to distinguish between productive business assets and investment assets. Not all of the assets of a business are productive (noncapital) assets. For example, the land on which a business is located is not a capital asset, but other land held by the company for investment purposes would be a capital asset. Obviously, the original intent at the time of acquiring the asset is an important factor in making such determinations.

☑ **Example 20.** Apple Corporation owns a 60% stock interest in B Company, which supplies a part used in Apple's manufacturing process. If the stock were acquired primarily to ensure a supply of parts inventory for Apple, the stock would probably be considered a "productive" business asset, not a capital asset. Apple could have difficulty convincing the government that the stock is held strictly for investment purposes.

The exception from capital-gains treatment for ordinary accounts and notes receivables is based on the fact that such receivables were generated in the ordinary course of business and represent nothing more than deferred ordinary income. Finally, the exception for certain government publications issued at a discount is designed to limit the charitable deductions for such properties by essentially classifying them as "ordinary income properties," subject to the restrictive rules discussed in Chapter 4.

If these properties never qualify as capital assets, then exactly what *does* qualify as a capital asset? Generally, any asset owned by an individual for personal or investment purposes is a capital asset. This would include such items as an individual's personal automobile, residence, furniture, land, and stock or bond investments. However, many assets have both capital and noncapital characteristics, and Congress, the IRS, and the courts have found it necessary to provide some rather arbitrary distinctions. Several of these special cases are discussed in the Appendix to this chapter.

ANSWERS TO REVIEW II

1. (b) The fair market value at the date of death is used as the adjusted basis of inherited property, and the property is presumed to be held on a long-term basis.
2. (d) For loss purposes, the fair market value of the property at the date of conversion is used as the initial basis. This basis is increased for the cost of the garage and it is decreased by the casualty loss and depreciation.
3. (c) The donor's cost is always used to calculate gain; therefore, the donor's holding period "tacks" to the holding period of Hayes. No gift tax addition is permitted, because the value on the date of the gift was less than the donor's cost.
4. (a) The lesser of the donor's cost or the fair market value on the date of the gift is used for losses, and no tacking of holding periods occurs.

THE CAPITAL-GAIN AND LOSS-NETTING PROCESS

THE LAW

Sec. 1222(3)—Long-term Capital Gain.—The term "long-term capital gain" means gain from the sale or exchange of a capital asset held for more than one year. . . .

The final taxable capital gain (or deductible capital loss) of a taxpayer depends on the number and type of capital transactions that occur during the year. The first step in the capital-gain and loss-netting process is to separate all capital transactions into one of two categories: either *short-term* capital gains and losses or *long-term* capital gains and losses. If the capital asset has a holding period of longer than one full year (including any "tacking" of holding periods as described earlier), then the gain or loss is long term; if the asset has a holding period of exactly one year or less, then the gain or loss is short term. For example, if an asset is purchased on January 12, 1993, the first day that the asset can be sold and receive long-term capital gains treatment would be January 13, 1994.

Example 21. Hal Brook purchased asset A on December 21, 1992, and asset B on January 31, 1993. Assuming that both properties are capital assets, asset A will achieve long-term status on December 22, 1993, and asset B will achieve long-term status on February 1, 1994.

Generally, the holding period of an asset begins on the day after the asset is acquired, unless a tacking of holding periods is appropriate under the rules discussed earlier in this chapter. The holding period ends on the date of disposal. Thus, the holding period does not include the day of acquisition but does include the date of disposal.

In netting capital gains and losses, it is important to understand the four possible tax treatments of a single capital asset transaction. Knowledge of these four possibilities is a prequisite to determining the final taxable result of a number of capital transactions. The four possible results for individual taxpayers are as follows:

1. *Short-term capital gain.* If a taxpayer's only capital transaction for the year is a short-term capital gain, the entire gain is fully included in ordinary taxable income. In this respect, the short-term gain is taxed no differently than other sources of income.

THE LAW

Sec. 1211(b)—Other Taxpayers.—In the case of a taxpayer other than a corporation, losses from sales or exchanges of capital assets shall be allowed only to the extent of gains from such sales or exchanges, plus (if such losses exceed gains) the lower of —
(1) $3,000 ($1,500 in the case of a married individual filing a separate return), or
(2) the excess of such losses over gains.

2. *Short-term capital loss.* If a taxpayer's only capital transaction for the year is a short-term capital loss, a maximum of $3,000 ($1,500 for married-filing separately) of the net loss can be taken as a deduction *for* adjusted gross income to offset any other sources of income. Any unused short-term loss can be carried forward indefinitely to future years and treated as a short-term capital loss in the carryover year.

✓ **Example 22.** Bruce Wills' only capital transaction in 1993 was a $4,200 net short-term capital loss. Assuming that Wills has at least $3,000 of other taxable income in 1993, a $3,000 deduction for AGI may be taken for the loss. The $1,200 excess loss will be carried over to 1994, where it will be treated as a short-term loss incurred in 1994.

3. *Long-term capital gain.* If a taxpayer's only capital transaction for the year is a long-term capital gain, the entire gain is included in taxable income. For tax years after 1986, any net long-term capital gain is taxed at a maximum rate of 28%. This means that the net long-term capital gain is taxed in the same manner as ordinary (noncapital-gains) income if the taxpayer's total taxable income (including the long-term capital gain) does not exceed the maximum income level of the 28% bracket for the taxpayer's filing status.

✓ **Example 23.** Assume that single taxpayer Martha Hyer's 1993 taxable income of $53,000 includes a $10,000 long-term capital gain. In this case, the $10,000 gain will be taxed the same as the $43,000 regular income, since Martha's total taxable income does not exceed $53,500, the upper income limit for the 28% rate bracket in the Single Rate Schedule (See Appendix B-1).

In 1993 and later years, the highest nominal tax rate applicable to individuals is 39.6%. Because Congress did not change the statutory language on the 28% maximum capital-gains rate as part of the 1990 tax legislation, a resulting preferential rate (ranging from 3 percentage points to 11.6 percentage points) may apply to such gains.

Thus, in computing an individual's tax liability for 1993, the taxpayer should never tax a net long-term capital gain at a rate that exceeds 28%. This is accomplished by treating any long-term capital gain as the *last* increment of income subject to tax. To the extent that any of this gain would have been taxed at a 31% or higher rate, a 28% maximum rate applies.

✓ **Example 24.** Assume the same facts as in Example 23, except Martha's taxable income is $70,000, including the $10,000 long-term gain. Since Martha is a single taxpayer, the 31% rate bracket is applicable to any income exceeding $53,500. Because her noncapital-gains income ($60,000) exceeds this amount, the entire $10,000 long-term capital gain is taxed at a flat 28% rate. Her 1993 tax liability is $16,922.00, computed as follows (using the tax rate schedule):

Tax on $60,000 ordinary income at normal rates:

[$12,107.50 + ($60,000 − $53,500) × .31] $14,122.00
Tax on $10,000 long-term capital gain:

($10,000 × .28) 2,800.00
Total 1991 tax liability $16,922.00

Note in this example that the 28% maximum rate resulted in $300 of tax savings (i.e., $10,000 × .03 rate differential).

✓ **Example 25.** Assume the same facts as in Example 24, except that Martha's 1993 taxable income is $54,200, including the $10,000 long-term capital gain. In this case, the first $53,500 of taxable income ($44,200 ordinary income and $9,300 of the capital gain) is taxed at normal rates, because the tax rate does not exceed 28%. The remaining $700 of capital gain would then be taxed at the maximum 28% rate. Martha's 1993 tax liability would be $12,303.00, computed as follows:

Tax on $53,500 ordinary income $12,107.00
Tax on $700 remaining capital gain (@ 28%) 196.00
Total 1993 tax liability $12,303.00

Note in this example that the 28% maximum rate resulted in $21 of tax savings (i.e., $700 × .03 rate differential).

TAX TIP

For taxpayers in the 36% or 39.6% tax brackets, the tax savings associated with long-term capital gains income are even greater. For example, a taxpayer with $300,000 of noncapital gains income and a $100,000 long-term capital gain will pay a flat $28,000 tax on the long-term capital gain ($100,000 × .28), as opposed to a $39,600 additional tax ($100,000 × .396) if the $100,000 were a short-term capital gain or ordinary income. Because of this strong incentive for high-income taxpayers to create long-term capital gains, Congress legislated several special safeguards into the law in 1993 to prevent the conversion of ordinary income into capital gain. One of these provisions, applicable to "conversion transactions," is described briefly in the appendix to this chapter.

4. *Long-term capital loss.* If a taxpayer's only capital transaction during the year is a long-term capital loss, up to $3,000 of the loss may be deducted for AGI (the same treatment as for short-term capital losses). Any excess loss can be carried forward indefinitely and retains its long-term character. A taxpayer is entitled to only one $3,000 maximum deduction for capital losses in one tax year; if both short-term and long-term transactions net to losses, the short-term losses are deducted first in determining taxable income.

☑ **Example 26.** Don Diego's only two capital transactions in 1993 were a $2,200 short-term capital loss and an $1,800 long-term loss. Diego will first deduct the short-term loss of $2,200, and then he will deduct $800 of the long-term loss, both as deductions for AGI. The $1,000 excess long-term loss is carried over to 1994 as a long-term loss.

Determining the net capital result for several transactions in the same year involves extending the four basic results within the framework of three basic steps. First, all short-term capital gains and losses are combined to determine a net short-term result. Second, all long-term gains and losses are combined to determine a net long-term result. Finally, the short-term and long-term results are compared to determine if the two results have the same signs (both are gains or both are losses) or opposite signs (one gain and one loss). If the results have the same sign, they are *not* combined; rather, each enters ordinary income separately and retains its short-term or long-term treatment according to the four basic rules. If the results have opposite signs, they are combined and the net difference is given the tax treatment of the larger sign (gain or loss, short-term or long-term) when it enters income. This three-step process is summarized in flowchart form in Figure 6-1.

Figure 6-2 presents a matrix summary of all capital-gain and -loss possibilities for individuals. To verify these results, apply the three-step procedure described earlier.

☑ **Example 27.** During 1993 Eddy Moore had $80,000 of ordinary income and the following capital transactions:

Short-term gains—$9,000   Long-term gains—$7,500
Short-term losses—($10,000)   Long-term losses—($10,000)

Moore's net short-term result is a $1,000 loss, and his net long-term result is a $2,500 loss. Because the two results have the same sign, they cannot be combined; instead, each enters taxable income separately under the basic rules. First, the $1,000 short-term loss offsets $1,000 of ordinary income, and then $2,000 of the long-term loss may also be used to offset ordinary income. The remaining $500 of long-term loss is carried forward indefinitely as long-term capital loss.

☑ **Example 28.** Assume the same facts as in Example 27, and assume that in 1994 Moore had $85,000 of ordinary taxable income and the following capital transactions:

Short-term gains—$4,200   Long-term gains—$300
Short-term losses—($3,000)   Long-term losses—($4,600)*

*Includes the $500 carryover from 1993.

The 1994 short-term transactions result in a $1,200 gain, and the long-term transactions result in a $4,300 loss. Because the short-term and long-term results have opposite signs, the two are combined, resulting in a $3,100 net loss. This loss is treated as a long-term capital loss (the larger sign), with $3,000 deducted for AGI in 1994 and a $100 long-term loss carryover to 1995.

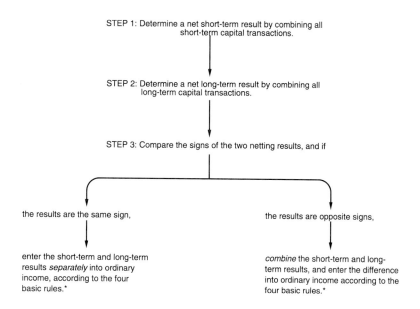

STEP 1: Determine a net short-term result by combining all short-term capital transactions.

STEP 2: Determine a net long-term result by combining all long-term capital transactions.

STEP 3: Compare the signs of the two netting results, and if

the results are the same sign,

enter the short-term and long-term results *separately* into ordinary income, according to the four basic rules.*

the results are opposite signs,

combine the short-term and long-term results, and enter the difference into ordinary income according to the four basic rules.*

*The four basic rules are

1. Short-term gains are fully taxable as ordinary income.

2. Short-term losses may offset a maximum $3,000 of ordinary income, with any excess losses carried over indefinitely as short-term losses.

3. Long-term gains are fully taxable, subject to a maximum tax rate of 28%.

4. Long-term losses may offset a maximum $3,000 of ordinary income (after reduction for short-term losses), with any excess losses carried over indefinitely as long-term losses.

Figure 6-1

	Net Short-Term Capital Gain	Net Short-Term Capital Loss
Net Long-Term Gain	Both gains are fully includable in income; however, the maximum tax rate applicable to the long-term gains only is 28%.	**If ST loss > LT gain:** Net difference offsets ordinary income $1 for $1 (up to a $3,000 maximum); excess is carried over indefinitely as ST. **If LT gain > ST loss:** Net difference is added to taxable income and is subject to a maximum tax rate of 28%.
Net Long-Term Capital Loss	**If ST gain > LT loss:** Net difference added to taxable income and is fully taxable. **If LT loss > ST gain:** Net difference offsets ordinary income $1 for $1 (up to a $3.00 maximum); excess is carried over indefinitely as LT.	Short-term loss offsets up to $3,000 of ordinary income first, $1 for $1, and then long-term loss offsets any remainder $1 for $1; excess losses are carried over indefinitely and retain their ST or LT character.

Figure 6-2

TABLE 6-2 Examples of Individual Capital Gain and Loss Nettings

	1993	1994	1995	1996	1997
Current-year capital transactions (before carryovers):					
ST gains	$16,000	$18,000	$ 3,000	$ 2,000	$ 9,000
ST losses	(18,000)	(26,000)	(2,000)	(6,000)	(1,000)
LT gains	24,000	2,000	8,000	4,000	8,000
LT losses	(12,000)	(1,000)	(2,000)	(8,000)	(6,000)
Net capital result (after carryovers):					
Net ST gain (Loss)	(2,000)	(8,000)	(3,000)	(4,000)	7,000
Net LT gain (Loss)	12,000	1,000	6,000	(4,000)	(2,000)
Taxable income:					
Salary	$70,000	$70,000	$70,000	$70,000	$70,000
Capital result	10,000*	(3,000)	3,000*	(3,000)	5,000
AGI	80,000	67,000	73,000	67,000	75,000
Deductions	(10,000)	(10,000)	(10,000)	(10,000)	(10,000)
Taxable	$70,000	$57,000	$63,000	$57,000	$65,000
Capital-loss Carryover:					
Short-term	0	(4,000)	0	(1,000)	0
Long-term	0	0	0	(4,000)	0

* Qualifies for 28% maximum rate.

Table 6-2 contains a more comprehensive example of the capital transactions netting process and illustrates the effects of capital-loss carryovers on the following year's computations. Notice that the final capital result each year affects the determination of adjusted gross income; this is because the capital-loss deduction is a deduction for AGI.

TAX TIP

Although capital gains are subject to minimal preferential treatment for the vast majority of taxpayers under current law, the designation as capital gain is still important. This is because such gains can absorb an equal amount of capital losses in the year, thus increasing the utilization of losses over $3,000. For example, a taxpayer with $14,000 of capital gains would be able to deduct a maximum of $17,000 of capital losses during the year (the capital gains absorb $14,000 of the losses in the nettings process, and the remaining $3,000 of losses can offset ordinary income). If the $14,000 income was ordinary noncapital-gain income, then the taxpayer would be able to deduct only $3,000 of capital losses.

REPORTING CAPITAL GAINS AND LOSSES

Schedule D of Form 1040 is used to report capital gains and losses for individual taxpayers. Figures 6-3 and 6-4 illustrate completed Schedule Ds for the 1993 and 1994 tax years of the comprehensive example in Table 6-2, assuming a single taxpayer.

Note that Parts I and II of Schedule D are used for the first two steps of the capital-gain and loss-netting process: determining the net short-term result and determining the net long-term result. Step 3, combining the two results, is accomplished in Part III (lines 18 and 19).

A special Schedule D tax worksheet is used to apply the 28% maximum tax rate for long-term capital gains. For the year 1993 illustrated in Figure 6-4, the entire $10,000 net long-term capital gain qualifies for the 28% rate, because the remaining portion of the taxable income ($60,000) exceeds the lower amount in the 31% tax bracket ($53,500 for a single individual). The final tax liability on line 13 is then transferred to Form 1040, line 38, as the gross tax liability.

Another Schedule D worksheet (not shown) is used to determine any capital-loss carryovers (both short and long term) into the next tax year. Figure 6-5 indicates that the 1994 netting results in a $7,000 short-term capital loss (line 18), of which $3,000 is deductible in 1994 (line 19). The unused short-term loss of $4,000 is carried forward to 1995.

Page 2 of Schedule D is a continuation page for additional capital transactions when a taxpayer has numerous gains and losses during a year. This page is illustrated as part of Figure 6-5. Finally, note in lines 3d and 11d the required listing of total sales prices reported by brokers to the taxpayer (Form 1099B, illustrated in Figure 6-6). The IRS uses this form to verify taxpayer reporting of the transaction.

SCHEDULE D (Form 1040)
Department of the Treasury
Internal Revenue Service

Capital Gains and Losses

▶ Attach to Form 1040. ▶ See Instructions for Schedule D (Form 1040).
▶ Use lines 20 and 22 for more space to list transactions for lines 1 and 9.

OMB No. 1545-0074

1993

Attachment Sequence No. **12**

Name(s) shown on Form 1040: Andrea North (1993)

Your social security number: 670 : 44 : 1010

Part I — Short-Term Capital Gains and Losses—Assets Held One Year or Less

(a) Description of property (Example: 100 sh. XYZ Co.)	(b) Date acquired (Mo., day, yr.)	(c) Date sold (Mo., day, yr.)	(d) Sales price (see page D-3)	(e) Cost or other basis (see page D-3)	(f) LOSS If (e) is more than (d), subtract (d) from (e)	(g) GAIN If (d) is more than (e), subtract (e) from (d)
1 500 sh. ABC	1-6-93	5-12-93	37,000	21,000		16,000
500 sh. DEF	3-2-93	6-3-93	82,000	100,000	18,000	

2 Enter your short-term totals, if any, from line 21 . . . . **2**

3 Total short-term sales price amounts. Add column (d) of lines 1 and 2 . . . **3** 119,000

4 Short-term gain from Forms 2119 and 6252, and short-term gain or (loss) from Forms 4684, 6781, and 8824 . . . **4**

5 Net short-term gain or (loss) from partnerships, S corporations, and fiduciaries from Schedule(s) K-1 . . . . **5**

6 Short-term capital loss carryover from 1992 Schedule D, line 38 . . . . **6**

7 Add lines 1, 2, and 4 through 6, in columns (f) and (g) **7** (18,000) 16,000

8 Net short-term capital gain or (loss). Combine columns (f) and (g) of line 7 . . . . **8** (2,000)

Part II — Long-Term Capital Gains and Losses—Assets Held More Than One Year

9 300 AT&T Bonds	4-3-83	7-1-93	37,300	13,300		24,000
500 sh. DEF	3-6-80	8-3-93	75,000	87,000	12,000	

10 Enter your long-term totals, if any, from line 23 . . . . **10**

11 Total long-term sales price amounts. Add column (d) of lines 9 and 10 . . . **11** 112,300

12 Gain from Form 4797; long-term gain from Forms 2119, 2439, and 6252; and long-term gain or (loss) from Forms 4684, 6781, and 8824 . . . . **12**

13 Net long-term gain or (loss) from partnerships, S corporations, and fiduciaries from Schedule(s) K-1 . . . . **13**

14 Capital gain distributions **14**

15 Long-term capital loss carryover from 1992 Schedule D, line 45 . . . . **15**

16 Add lines 9, 10, and 12 through 15, in columns (f) and (g) **16** (12,000) 24,000

17 Net long-term capital gain or (loss). Combine columns (f) and (g) of line 16 . . . . **17** 12,000

Part III — Summary of Parts I and II

18 Combine lines 8 and 17. If a loss, go to line 19. If a gain, enter the gain on Form 1040, line 13.
Note: *If both lines 17 and 18 are gains, see the **Schedule D Tax Worksheet** on page D-4* . . **18** 10,000

19 If line 18 is a (loss), enter here and as a (loss) on Form 1040, line 13, the **smaller** of these losses:
 a The (loss) on line 18; **or**
 b ($3,000) or, if married filing separately, ($1,500) . . . . **19** (   )
 Note: *See the **Capital Loss Carryover Worksheet** on page D-4 if the loss on line 18 exceeds the loss on line 19 **or** if Form 1040, line 35, is a loss.*

For Paperwork Reduction Act Notice, see Form 1040 instructions. Cat. No. 11338H Schedule D (Form 1040) 1993

Figure 6-3 Schedule D—Year 1993

Schedule D Tax Worksheet (keep for your records)

Use this worksheet to figure your tax **only** if both lines 17 and 18 of Schedule D are gains, **and:**			
Your filing status is: AND	Form 1040, line 37, is over:	Your filing status is: AND	Form 1040, line 37, is over:
Single	$53,500	Married filing separately	$44,575
Married filing jointly or qualifying widow(er)	$89,150	Head of household	$76,400

1. Enter the amount from Form 1040, line 37 . . .	1.	70,000
2. **Net capital gain.** Enter the **smaller** of Schedule D, line 17 or line 18 . . .	2.	10,000
3. If you are filing Form 4952, enter the amount from Form 4952, line 4e	3.	
4. Subtract line 3 from line 2. If zero or less, stop here; you cannot use this worksheet to figure your tax. Instead, use the Tax Table or Tax Rate Schedules	4.	10,000
5. Subtract line 4 from line 1	5.	60,000
6. Enter: $22,100 if single; $36,900 if married filing jointly or qualifying widow(er); $18,450 if married filing separately; or $29,600 if head of household	6.	22,100
7. Enter the **greater** of line 5 or line 6	7.	60,000
8. Subtract line 7 from line 1	8.	10,000
9. Figure the tax on the amount on line 7. Use the Tax Table or Tax Rate Schedules, whichever applies	9.	14,130
10. Multiply line 8 by 28% (.28)	10.	2,800
11. Add lines 9 and 10	11.	16,930
12. Figure the tax on the amount on line 1. Use the Tax Table or Tax Rate Schedules, whichever applies	12.	17,230
13. **Tax.** Enter the **smaller** of line 11 or line 12 here and on Form 1040, line 38. Check the box for Schedule D Tax Worksheet	13.	16,930

Figure 6-4 Schedule D Tax Worksheet

6-24 *Gain and Loss Recognition: An Introduction*

SCHEDULE D (Form 1040) Department of the Treasury Internal Revenue Service	**Capital Gains and Losses** ► Attach to Form 1040. ► See Instructions for Schedule D (Form 1040). ► Use lines 20 and 22 for more space to list transactions for lines 1 and 9.				OMB No. 1545-0074 **1993** Attachment Sequence No. **12**	
Name(s) shown on Form 1040 Andrea North (1994)					Your social security number 670 : 44 : 1010	

Part I Short-Term Capital Gains and Losses—Assets Held One Year or Less

(a) Description of property (Example: 100 sh. XYZ Co.)	(b) Date acquired (Mo., day, yr.)	(c) Date sold (Mo., day, yr.)	(d) Sales price (see page D-3)	(e) Cost or other basis (see page D-3)	(f) LOSS If (e) is more than (d), subtract (d) from (e)	(g) GAIN If (d) is more than (e), subtract (e) from (d)
1 10 sh. Alcoa	6-3-94	8-2-94	16,200	15,200		1,000
500 sh. IBM	1-4-94	8-8-94	52,000	61,000	9,000	
10 sh. Able	3-6-94	9-3-94	7,000	4,000		3,000
2 Enter your short-term totals, if any, from line 21		**2**	50,000		17,000	14,000
3 Total short-term sales price amounts. Add column (d) of lines 1 and 2 . . .		**3**	125,200			
4 Short-term gain from Forms 2119 and 6252, and short-term gain or (loss) from Forms 4684, 6781, and 8824				**4**		
5 Net short-term gain or (loss) from partnerships, S corporations, and fiduciaries from Schedule(s) K-1				**5**		
6 Short-term capital loss carryover from 1992 Schedule D, line 38				**6**		
7 Add lines 1, 2, and 4 through 6, in columns (f) and (g)				**7**	(26,000)	18,000
8 Net short-term capital gain or (loss). Combine columns (f) and (g) of line 7				**8**	(8,000)	

Part II Long-Term Capital Gains and Losses—Assets Held More Than One Year

9 60 sh. Bally	3-1-86	12-6-94	9,100	7,100		2,000
20 sh. Xerox	4-1-79	12-8-94	17,000	16,000	1,000	
10 Enter your long-term totals, if any, from line 23		**10**				
11 Total long-term sales price amounts. Add column (d) of lines 9 and 10 . . .		**11**	26,100			
12 Gain from Form 4797; long-term gain from Forms 2119, 2439, and 6252; and long-term gain or (loss) from Forms 4684, 6781, and 8824				**12**		
13 Net long-term gain or (loss) from partnerships, S corporations, and fiduciaries from Schedule(s) K-1				**13**		
14 Capital gain distributions				**14**		
15 Long-term capital loss carryover from 1992 Schedule D, line 45				**15**		
16 Add lines 9, 10, and 12 through 15, in columns (f) and (g)				**16**	(1,000)	2,000
17 Net long-term capital gain or (loss). Combine columns (f) and (g) of line 16				**17**		1,000

Part III Summary of Parts I and II

18 Combine lines 8 and 17. If a loss, go to line 19. If a gain, enter the gain on Form 1040, line 13. **Note:** *If both lines 17 and 18 are gains, see the Schedule D Tax Worksheet on page D-4* . . **18** (7,000)

19 If line 18 is a (loss), enter here and as a (loss) on Form 1040, line 13, the **smaller** of these losses:
  a The (loss) on line 18; **or**
  b ($3,000) or, if married filing separately, ($1,500) **19** (3,000)
  Note: *See the Capital Loss Carryover Worksheet on page D-4 if the loss on line 18 exceeds the loss on line 19 or if Form 1040, line 35, is a loss.*

For Paperwork Reduction Act Notice, see Form 1040 instructions. Cat. No. 11338H Schedule D (Form 1040) 1993

Figure 6-5 Schedule D—Year 1993

Schedule D (Form 1040) 1993 — Attachment Sequence No. 12 — Page 2

Name(s) shown on Form 1040. Do not enter name and social security number if shown on other side. (1994)

Part IV — Short-Term Capital Gains and Losses—Assets Held One Year or Less (Continuation of Part I)

(a) Description of property (Example: 100 sh. XYZ Co.)	(b) Date acquired (Mo., day, yr.)	(c) Date sold (Mo., day, yr.)	(d) Sales price (see page D-3)	(e) Cost or other basis (see page D-3)	(f) LOSS If (e) is more than (d), subtract (d) from (e)	(g) GAIN If (d) is more than (e), subtract (e) from (d)
20 11 sh. Bee	3-2-94	9-10-94	21,000	7,000		14,000
100 sh. Cane	4-1-94	4-18-94	39,000	56,000	17,000	
21 Short-term totals. Add columns (d), (f), and (g) of line 20. Enter here and on line 2			50,000		17,000	14,000

Part V — Long-Term Capital Gains and Losses—Assets Held More Than One Year (Continuation of Part II)

(a)	(b)	(c)	(d)	(e)	(f)	(g)
22						
23 Long-term totals. Add columns (d), (f), and (g) of line 22. Enter here and on line 10						

Figure 6-5 (continued) Schedule D—Year 1993

Figure 6-6 Form 1099B (1994)

Form 1099-B fields:
- PAYER'S name, street address, city, state, and ZIP code: Bradley Investing, 603 Matter, DeKalb, IL 60115
- 1a Date of sale: 6-3-94
- OMB No. 1545-0715
- Proceeds From Broker and Barter Exchange Transactions
- 2 Stocks, bonds, etc.: $16,200 (Reported to IRS)
- PAYER'S Federal identification number: 34-66412
- RECIPIENT'S identification number: 670-44-1010
- RECIPIENT'S name: Andrea North
- Street address: 1101 Annie Glidden Road
- City, state, and ZIP code: DeKalb, IL 60115
- 5 Description: 10 shares Alcoa Co.

REVIEW III

1. Which of the following items is not a capital asset?
   - (a) a personal automobile
   - (b) shares of stock held as an investment
   - (c) a delivery truck used in a sole proprietorship business
   - (d) antique furniture held as an investment

2. Bill Winchell had $90,000 of taxable income in 1993, which included $5,000 of short-term capital gains and $15,000 of long-term capital gains. What marginal tax rates will apply to the $5,000 and $15,000 gains, respectively (assuming that Bill is a single taxpayer)?
   - (a) 28% and 28%
   - (b) 31% and 31%
   - (c) 28% and 31%
   - (d) 31% and 28%

3. Susan Bond's 1993 capital transactions were as follows:
   LT capital gain—$6,000   ST capital gain—$5,000
   LT capital loss—($5,000)   ST capital loss—($8,500)
   The effect of these transactions on her 1993 AGI is
   - (a) a $1,000 decrease.
   - (b) a $2,500 decrease.
   - (c) a $3,000 decrease.
   - (d) a $3,500 decrease.

4. Hal Andre's 1993 capital transactions were as follows:
   LT capital gain—$3,000   ST capital gain—$2,500
   LT capital loss—($7,300)   ST capital loss—($4,600)
   Andre's capital loss carryover to 1994 will be
   - (a) $0.
   - (b) $2,500 long term.
   - (c) $3,400 long term.
   - (d) $600 short term and $2,800 long term.

Answers are on page 6-28.

IV. INSTALLMENT SALES
(Code Sections 453, 453A, and 453B)

When a person purchases an expensive object from another party, he or she may not have enough cash (or other property) on hand to pay for the item. The buyer could go to a commercial lending institution to obtain a loan, perhaps using the item to be purchased as collateral. He or she would then be able to pay the seller the agreed price in cash.

Alternately, the seller could help finance the purchase by accepting a note in exchange for all or a part of the purchase price. In this situation, however, the seller has a completed sale yet may have received little or no cash with which to pay the tax on any gain realized. The installment sale rules of Sec. 453 provide relief to the seller if certain specific requirements are met.

Under the installment sale provisions, the seller is permitted to defer recognition of any realized gain on the sale until the proceeds are actually received. As a result, the seller pays tax on the gain as the buyer pays for the item sold. This is one more application of the wherewithal-to-pay principle.

Deferral of recognition under the installment sale rules applies only to a realized *gain*. If a taxpayer has a loss on the sale of property, the installment rules do not apply, and the entire loss is recognized in the year of sale (unless some other Code provision prevents recognition).

THE LAW

Sec. 453(a)—Except as otherwise provided in this section, income from an installment sale shall be taken into account for purposes of this title under the installment method.

(b)(1)—The term "installment sale" means a disposition of property where at least 1 payment is to be received after the close of the taxable year in which the disposition occurs.

(b)(2)—The term "installment sale" does not include—(A) any dealer disposition [as defined in subsection (1)], or (B) a disposition of personal property of a kind which is required to be included in the inventory of the taxpayer if on hand at the close of the taxable year.

In order for income to qualify for installment treatment, several requirements must be met. First, the buyer must make at least one payment to the seller in a tax year after the year of sale. (No payments are required to be received in the year of sale.) Typically in an installment sale, the buyer gives the seller a cash down payment at the time of the sale and a note for the balance. The note is a written agreement that specifies the payment of the balance due with interest over a period of time. The rate of interest must meet certain guidelines (described below), or the taxpayer is required to make an adjustment in the selling price to reflect the proper rate.

☑ **Example 29.** Nancy Dowling sold her pleasure boat to John for $2,900, generating a $400 gain. John gave Nancy $500 cash and a note for the $2,400 balance. John is to pay Nancy $100 amonth for two years plus interest of 9% on the unpaid balance. Because Nancy will receive payments beyond the tax year of the sale, the transaction qualifies as an installment sale. The sale would also qualify if John promised to pay her the entire $2,900 plus interest any time after the end of the current tax year. The sale would not qualify, however, if Nancy had a realized loss on the transaction.

Not all sales or sellers are eligible to use the installment sale provisions. Any taxpayer who is classified as a "dealer" may not use the installment sale rules. A dealer is any person who sells personal property (such as furniture or appliances) and certain realty on a regular basis under the installment method. The "regular basis" requirement essentially means that such property would be considered to be inventory in the taxpayer's hands. Thus, the installment method would not be available for a business that sells a substantial portion of its normal inventory to one buyer on an installment plan. The installment method is also not available for sales of stocks and securities or for any sale under a revolving credit plan.

THE LAW

Sec. 453(d)(1)—Subsection (a) shall not apply to any disposition if the taxpayer elects to have subsection (a) not apply to such disposition.

(d)(2)—Except as otherwise provided by regulations, an election under paragraph (1) with respect to a disposition may be made only on or before the due date prescribed by law (including extensions) for filing the taxpayer's return of the tax imposed by this chapter for the taxable year in which the disposition occurs. Such an election shall be made in the manner prescribed by regulations.

When originally enacted, the use of the installment sale provisions had to be elected by the taxpayer. This is no longer the case, because the seller, if eligible, must now elect out of the installment method. If a taxpayer meets the requirements of Sec. 453,

ANSWERS TO REVIEW III

1. (c) Property used productively in a trade or business is never considered to be a capital asset.
2. (d) Only the long-term capital gain is eligible for special tax treatment in 1993 (a 28% maximum tax rate); the short-term gain is taxed as ordinary income.
3. (b) The capital transactions net to a $2,500 short-term capital loss, which is fully deductible against ordinary income.
4. (c) The short-term transactions net to a $2,100 loss, which is first deducted from AGI. The long-term transactions net to a $4,300 loss, of which $900 is deducted from AGI (to give the $3,000 maximum total deduction), and the $3,400 excess is carried forward to 1994.

reporting on an installment basis is mandatory unless this election is made. Taxpayers who have a tax rate that is lower than the rate they expect in the future may make this election, as may taxpayers who have unused capital or net operating losses. Generally, the taxpayer elects out of the installment method by appropriately recognizing all gains in the year of sale and noting this on the form (usually Schedule D) on which the gains are reported.

TAX TIP

Sellers who are willing to finance a purchase for a buyer must realize that they are accepting the risk that the buyer will not pay as required and that they may be forced to repossess the property. The seller should require a reasonable down payment as well as a fair rate of interest to compensate for this risk. Sales of personal property are particularly vulnerable to these risks, because the buyer may destroy or move the property so that repossession is impossible.

CALCULATIONS REQUIRED WITH THE INSTALLMENT METHOD

The calculations necessary to determine gain recognition under the installment method may be fairly complex in the year of sale. However, once a "gross profit percentage" is determined, the recognized gain in subsequent years is readily determined. In making these computations, the seller must be familiar with several terms:

1. The *selling price* is the gross sales price of the property, agreed upon by the buyer and the seller.

2. The *gross profit* is the selling price less the seller's adjusted basis in the property sold.

3. The *adjusted basis* of the property is the tax basis of the property to the owner plus any selling expenses incurred.

4. The *total contract price* is the total consideration that the seller is to receive. This is basically the total selling price less any liabilities of the seller that are transferred to (or assumed by) the buyer as part of the sale. However, if the liabilities assumed by the buyer exceed the seller's adjusted basis in the property (as determined above), the total contract price is increased by the excess liabilities. In effect, liabilities assumed in excess of the seller's basis are treated as cash received by the seller in the year of sale.

5. The *gross profit percentage* is the seller's gross profit divided by the total contract price. If the liabilities assumed by the buyer exceed the seller's adjusted basis (which includes any selling expenses), the gross profit percentage is always 100%.

THE LAW

Sec. 453(c)—For purposes of this section, the term "installment method" means a method under which the income recognized for any taxable year from a disposition is that proportion of the payments received in that year which the gross profit (realized or to be realized when payment is completed) bears to the total contract price.

☑ **Example 30.** Tom White sold an old computer for $2,000 through a newspaper ad. Tom's adjusted basis in the computer was $200, and the cost of the ad was $50. Tom's selling price is $2,000, and his gross profit is $1,750 [$2,000 − ($200 + $50)]. Because the buyer assumed no liabilities, Tom's total contract price equals the selling price of $2,000, and his gross profit percentage is 87.5% ($1,750/$2,000).

☑ **Example 31.** Meeghan Ryan sold a tractor-trailer, which had a basis of $10,000, for $17,500. The buyer assumed the outstanding balance of $8,000 on her loan and gave her a $9,500 installment note for the balance. A broker charged Meeghan $800 commission on the sale. Meeghan's gross profit is $6,700 [$17,500 − ($10,000 + $800)], and her contract price is $9,500 ($17,500 − $8,000). Meeghan's gross profit percentage is 70.52% ($6,700/$9,500). Thus, if Meeghan collected $3,000 cash in the year of sale, her taxable gain that year would be $2,115.60 ($3,000 × .7052).

☑ **Example 32.** Assume the same facts as in Example 31, except that Meeghan's adjusted basis is $6,000 ($5,200 tax basis plus $800 selling expenses). In this case, her gross profit would be $11,500 ($17,500 − $6,000), the total contract price would be $11,500 [$9,500 installment note plus the $2,000 excess of liabilities assumed ($8,000) over the adjusted basis of the property ($6,000)], and her gross profit percentage would be 100% ($11,500/$11,500). In addition, the $2,000 excess of liabilities over basis is treated as cash received in the year of sale. Thus, Meeghan's taxable gain in the year of sale (again assuming a first-year payment of $3,000) would be $5,000 [($3,000 + $2,000) × 1.00].

TAX TIP

It is not uncommon for individuals to take out second mortgages on real estate, because the value of the real estate generally appreciates and lenders are willing to accept such real estate as collateral. Individuals who sell such mortgaged property on an installment basis should pay particular attention to the tax implications of such sales, because the outstanding mortgage may be much larger than the basis of the property. As demonstrated above, this excess is treated as cash received in the year of sale. Thus, the taxpayer may unexpectedly have to pay tax on a significant portion of gain in the year of sale, even though little or no cash is received in that year.

Once a gross profit percentage is determined on an installment sale, the same percentage is used in all future years in which payments are received. The percentage is simply multiplied by the payment each year to determine the taxable gain. The taxpayer reports all details of an installment sale each year on Form 6252. This form is illustrated in Figure 6-7, using the facts of the following example.

Example 33. Toby Wallace sold 500 acres of land for a total consideration of $450,000. His adjusted basis in the property was $205,000, and his selling expenses were $12,500. The purchaser assumed a mortgage of $150,000 on the sale. Toby received a $50,000 cash down payment in the year of sale and accepted a ten-year installment note for the balance, which provided for $25,000 payments each year (beginning next year) plus 10% interest on the unpaid balance. The taxable gain recognized by Tony each year is determined as follows:

Selling price	$450,000
Adjusted basis ($205,000 + $12,500)	(217,500)
Gross profit	$232,500
Total contract price ($450,000 − $150,000)	$300,000
Gross profit percentage ($232,500/$300,000)	77.5%
Taxable in the year of sale ($50,000 × .775)	$ 38,750
Taxable in each later year ($25,000 × .775)	$ 19,375

The final recognized gain on Form 6252 ($38,750) on line 26 is transferred to Schedule D, line 11. Additionally, any interest income recognized in future years would simply be reported as ordinary income on Schedule B; this has no effect on the gross profit computations.

The relevant section of Schedule D for the facts of Example 33 would appear as follows:

Part II	Long-Term Capital Gains and Losses—Assets Held More Than One Year		
9			
10	Enter your long-term totals, if any, from line 23	10	
11	Total long-term sales price amounts. Add column (d) of lines 9 and 10	11	
12	Gain from Form 4797; long-term gain from Forms 2119, 2439, and 6252; and long-term gain or (loss) from Forms 4684, 6781, and 8824	12	38,750
13	Net long-term gain or (loss) from partnerships, S corporations, and fiduciaries from Schedule(s) K-1	13	
14	Capital gain distributions	14	
15	Long-term capital loss carryover from 1992 Schedule D, line 45	15	
16	Add lines 9, 10, and 12 through 15, in columns (f) and (g)	16	38,750
17	**Net long-term capital gain or (loss).** Combine columns (f) and (g) of line 16	17	38,750

6-32 Gain and Loss Recognition: An Introduction

Form **6252**	**Installment Sale Income**	OMB No. 1545-0228
Department of the Treasury Internal Revenue Service	▶ See separate instructions. ▶ Attach to your tax return. Use a separate form for each sale or other disposition of property on the installment method.	**19**92 Attachment Sequence No. **79**

Name(s) shown on return	Identifying number
Toby Wallace	462-11-3072

1 Description of property ▶ ....
2a Date acquired (month, day, and year) ▶ |____/____/____| b Date sold (month, day, and year) ▶ | 6 / 3 / 93 |
3 Was the property sold to a related party after May 14, 1980? See instructions . . . . ☐ Yes ☒ No
4 If the answer to question 3 is "Yes," was the property a marketable security? If "Yes," complete Part III. If
   "No," complete Part III for the year of sale and for 2 years after the year of sale. . . . . ☐ Yes ☐ No

Part I   **Gross Profit and Contract Price.** Complete this part for the year of sale only.

5	Selling price including mortgages and other debts. Do not include interest whether stated or unstated	5	450,000
6	Mortgages and other debts the buyer assumed or took the property subject to, but not new mortgages the buyer got from a bank or other source .	6	150,000
7	Subtract line 6 from line 5	7	300,000
8	Cost or other basis of property sold	8	205,000
9	Depreciation allowed or allowable	9	—
10	Adjusted basis. Subtract line 9 from line 8	10	205,000
11	Commissions and other expenses of sale	11	12,500
12	Income recapture from Form 4797, Part III. See instructions . .	12	—
13	Add lines 10, 11, and 12	13	217,500
14	Subtract line 13 from line 5. If zero or less, do not complete the rest of this form	14	232,500
15	If the property described on line 1 above was your main home, enter the total of lines 16 and 24 from Form 2119. Otherwise, enter -0-	15	0
16	**Gross profit.** Subtract line 15 from line 14	16	232,500
17	Subtract line 13 from line 6. If zero or less, enter -0-	17	0
18	**Contract price.** Add line 7 and line 17	18	300,000

Part II   **Installment Sale Income.** Complete this part for the year of sale and any year you receive a payment or have certain debts you must treat as a payment on installment obligations.

19	Gross profit percentage. Divide line 16 by line 18. For years after the year of sale, see instructions	19	.775
20	**For year of sale only**—Enter amount from line 17 above; otherwise, enter -0-	20	0
21	Payments received during year. See instructions. Do not include interest whether stated or unstated	21	50,000
22	Add lines 20 and 21	22	50,000
23	Payments received in prior years. See instructions. Do not include interest whether stated or unstated	23	
24	**Installment sale income.** Multiply line 22 by line 19	24	38,750
25	Part of line 24 that is ordinary income under recapture rules. See instructions	25	0
26	Subtract line 25 from line 24. Enter here and on Schedule D or Form 4797. See instructions	26	38,750

Part III   **Related Party Installment Sale Income.** Do not complete if you received the final payment this tax year.

27 Name, address, and taxpayer identifying number of related party ....
    ....
28 Did the related party, during this tax year, resell or dispose of the property ("second disposition")? . . . . ☐ Yes ☐ No
29 If the answer to question 28 is "Yes," complete lines 30 through 37 below unless one of the following conditions is met. Check only the box that applies.
  a ☐ The second disposition was more than 2 years after the first disposition (other than dispositions of marketable securities). If this box is checked, enter the date of disposition (month, day, year) ▶ |____/____/____|
  b ☐ The first disposition was a sale or exchange of stock to the issuing corporation.
  c ☐ The second disposition was an involuntary conversion where the threat of conversion occurred after the first disposition.
  d ☐ The second disposition occurred after the death of the original seller or buyer.
  e ☐ It can be established to the satisfaction of the Internal Revenue Service that tax avoidance was not a principal purpose for either of the dispositions. If this box is checked, attach an explanation. See instructions.

30	Selling price of property sold by related party	30	
31	Enter contract price from line 18 for year of first sale	31	
32	Enter the **smaller** of line 30 or line 31	32	
33	Total payments received by the end of your 1992 tax year. Add lines 22 and 23	33	
34	Subtract line 33 from line 32. If zero or less, enter -0-	34	
35	Multiply line 34 by the gross profit percentage on line 19 for year of first sale	35	
36	Part of line 35 that is ordinary income under recapture rules. See instructions	36	
37	Subtract line 36 from line 35. Enter here and on Schedule D or Form 4797. See instructions	37	

For Paperwork Reduction Act Notice, see separate instructions.   Cat. No. 13601R   Form **6252** (1992)

1993 form not available at press time.

Figure 6-7   Form 6252

> **TAX TIP**
>
>
>
> If very little gain is realized on a sale, a taxpayer may want to elect out of the installment method in order to avoid the required annual reporting. Form 6252 must be filed not only in the year of sale but in every year that payments are received under the installment sale contract.

CHARACTER OF THE GAIN

In general, the character of any installment gain depends on the character of the property sold. For most investment properties or personal assets, the gain will be capital gain. In other cases, special Code rules may apply. For example, a special provision applies to sales of time shares and residential lots, which, though sold by dealers and thus yielding ordinary income, are eligible for installment treatment.

Another special rule applies to "depreciation recapture" property. In general, the installment sale rules require the recognition of *all* ordinary recapture income in the year of sale. The depreciation recapture rules are discussed in Chapter 9.

INTEREST INCOME

If the installment receivable does not provide for an appropriate rate of interest, the buyer and seller may have to adjust the selling price of the asset to reflect the rate as specified by the Internal Revenue Code. This adjustment is designed to "filter out" any unstated interest income using present value principles.

For example, if a sale is made for $100,000 on terms of $10,000 annually for ten years without any interest specified, the taxpayer is required to use an appropriate rate of interest (generally the lesser of a current rate of interest or 9%) to determine the present value of the ten payments. The present value will be less than $100,000, and this present value represents the recomputed selling price of the property. The difference between the $100,000 and the recomputed selling price is unstated interest, to be recognized as interest income over the life of the installment note. We leave details of these intricate computations for a more advanced course in taxation.

OPTING OUT OF THE INSTALLMENT METHOD

If the taxpayer elects out of the installment method, income is recognized under the taxpayer's normal method of accounting. An accrual-basis taxpayer would recognize income based on the value of cash and property received in the year of sale plus the face amount of the installment receivable (assuming that a fair rate of interest is charged). A cash-basis taxpayer, on the other hand, would recognize income based on the value of the cash, property, or cash equivalents received in the year of sale.

OTHER CONSIDERATIONS

On certain installment sales, numerous complications can arise, including dispositions of installment notes, repossessions of installment sale property, and special "interest charge" rules applicable to certain sales of realty. These provisions affect only a small number of individuals and are not discussed further in this text.

One complication that can affect a much larger number of individuals is the treatment of certain installment sales to related parties. A *related party* is defined as a blood relative (other than a cousin) or an entity (e.g., partnership or corporation) in which the seller owns a controlling interest. In general, if the related-party buyer resells the property within two years of the original installment sale, any unrecognized gain on the original sale is reported immediately by the original seller. In effect, the tax law treats such circumstances as though the "family" (the two related parties) has "cashed in" the installment note.

✓ **Example 34.** Bob James sold ten acres of land to his sister Beth based on a ten-year installment note that will involve a total $50,000 gain. If Beth resells the property within two years of the original sale, Bob will be required to recognize any remaining deferred gain immediately. In effect, the family (Bob and Beth) has cashed in the installment note. Beth may also have taxable gain.

REVIEW IV

1. Barbara Hale is moving to Europe and has decided to sell most of her personal property, including her home. She sold her auto (original cost, $8,000) to a friend for $5,000 (payable with a $2,500 down payment and a one-year note for the balance). She also sold her home (original cost, $65,000) for $80,000, payable at $10,000 down with a 15-year note for the balance. She sold her furniture for $5,000 cash. Which of these sales qualifies for installment treatment for tax purposes?
   (a) all of the sales
   (b) none of the sales
   (c) the car and home only
   (d) the home only
2. Georgia O'Shea sold a painting (original cost, $3,000) for $18,000 at an auction. She received $5,000 down and took a one-year note for the balance. She paid the auction house a 10% commission. What is her gross profit percentage?
   (a) 88.00%
   (b) 83.33%
   (c) 73.33%
   (d) 70.00%
3. John Wagner sold land on December 30 for $100,000 cash and a ten-year $900,000 note with interest. In addition, the buyer assumed a $500,000 mortgage on the property. John paid a $120,000 commission on the sale. His adjusted basis in the land was $750,000. If John is a calendar-year taxpayer, how much income must he recognize in the year of sale under the installment method, assuming that only the $100,000 down payment is collected?
   (a) $63,000
   (b) $75,000
   (c) $100,000
   (d) $378,000
4. In 1993 Walter Scott sold farmland to a neighbor for a down payment of $50,000 and an installment note that provided for payments of $40,000 per year for four years beginning in 1994, plus 12% annual interest. Walter had paid $20,000 for the land 30 years ago. He paid an $11,000 commission on the sale. How much gain does Walter recognize in 1993 and in 1994 under the installment method?

(a) $179,000; $0
(b) $42,235; $36,188
(c) $42,615; $34,092
(d) $40,000; $34,750

Answers are on page 6-37.

V. SALE OF A PERSONAL RESIDENCE
(Code Sections 1034 and 121)

Two provisions in the Code provide tax relief to individuals on the sale or exchange of their personal residences. The first provision, Sec. 1034, is a nonelective provision applicable to the sale of the primary residence of any taxpayer who meets the stated requirements. The second provision, Sec. 121, is a once-only elective provision applicable to qualifying taxpayers age 55 and over. Taxpayers age 55 or older in certain cases may be able to utilize both provisions.

SEC. 1034 MANDATORY DEFERRAL PROVISION

THE LAW

Sec. 1034(a)—Nonrecognition of Gain. If property (in this section called "old residence") used by the taxpayer as his principal residence is sold by him and, within a period beginning 2 years before the date of such sale and ending 2 years after such date, property (in this section called "new residence") is purchased and used by the taxpayer as his principal residence, gain (if any) from such sale shall be recognized only to the extent that the taxpayer's adjusted sales price (as defined in subsection (b)) of the old residence exceeds the taxpayer's cost of purchasing the new residence.

In general, Sec. 1034 permits nonrecognition of *gain* only. This provision does not apply to losses on the sale of a personal residence, which are never deductible. Additionally, the provision applies only to specific property—the taxpayer's principal residence—which must be replaced within a specific time period with another principal residence. If all of the requirements of Sec. 1034 are met, a wherewithal-to-pay principle applies: any realized ("accounting") gain is recognized for tax purposes only to the extent that the "adjusted sales price" of the old residence is *not* reinvested in a new residence. Any realized gain that is not currently taxed will in turn reduce the cost basis of the new home. In this respect, Sec. 1034 operates in a fashion similar to two other nonrecognition provisions in the Code that are discussed in Chapter 9 (Sec. 1031 like-kind exchanges and Sec. 1033 involuntary conversions).

The taxpayer's principal residence is the place where the taxpayer actually lives for the greatest period of time during the tax year. The taxpayer can have only one principal residence. If the taxpayer converts a residence to rental property, it ceases to be his or her principal residence. If, however, a taxpayer rents the residence for a relatively short period (such as less than one year) due to an inability to sell it and continues to try to sell the property, the residence will still be considered the principal residence when the sale is finally consummated. Similarly, the taxpayer may rent the new residence for a short period prior to occupying it without tainting its status as a personal residence.

✓ **Example 35.** George Allen tried to sell his home for six months prior to moving to another city. He purchased and occupied a new home, renting his old residence for seven months before securing a buyer. George's sale of the old residence will qualify for Sec. 1034 nonrecognition of gain.

Under Sec. 1034, the taxpayer has a limited period in which to replace the old residence. He or she has from two years before the date of the sale of the old residence to two years after the sale of the old residence to occupy the new residence. Note, however, that the taxpayer must in fact occupy the new residence. The taxpayer also has the same period to build and occupy a newly constructed residence.

✓ **Example 36.** Sally James sold her old residence on January 20, 1993. She contracted to have a new residence built by February 15, 1994. Due to bad weather, strikes, and several other delays, Sally still could not occupy the residence by January 20, 1995. Sally is unable to use the nonrecognition provisions of Sec. 1034 on the sale of the old residence; if she postponed the gain recognition on her 1993 tax return, she must file an amended return and pay any tax, penalties, and interest due.

TAX TIP

In periods of economic slowdown, many taxpayers who relocate are forced to buy a replacement residence before selling their old residence. In such cases, the taxpayer may eventually have to accept a below-market offer on the old residence in order to ensure that the residence is sold within the two-year time frame of Sec. 1034. The reduced selling price may be more than offset by the tax savings of being able to use Sec. 1034 to postpone gain.

The special nonrecognition treatment of Sec. 1034 does not apply to a replacement residence that is subsequently sold during the two-year replacement period applicable to the old residence. However, if a second replacement residence is acquired during the replacement period, *that* residence will be considered the relevant replacement residence. If the sale of the first replacement residence is due to a job-related move for which a moving expense deduction would be allowed under Sec. 217(c), then nonrecognition will be available for that residence as well.

✓ **Example 37.** Jimmy Talbot sold his old residence on June 30, 1993, and purchased a new residence on the same day, occupying it immediately. Jimmy decided that he did not like his access to major highways from his new residence, and on March 15, 1994, sold the house and purchased another one closer to the highway. The first residence, purchased on June 30, 1993, does not qualify as a replacement residence under Sec. 1034, and any gain on its sale does not qualify for nonrecognition under Sec. 1034. However, the second residence, purchased on March 15, 1994, *will* qualify as a replacement residence under Sec. 1034 (assuming that Jimmy does not sell that home until after June 30, 1994).

The taxpayer is allowed to defer the entire gain on the sale of a personal residence if an amount equal to the "adjusted sales price" of the old residence is reinvested in the new residence. The adjusted sales price is the "amount realized" on the sale, less any "fixing-up" expenses.

The amount realized on the sale is the selling price, less the costs of selling the old residence, such as advertising, real estate commissions, legal fees, and title fees. Fixing-up expenses are those noncapital expenditures incurred within the 90-day period before the contract for sale is obtained, which are paid no later than 30 days after the date of sale. Such items as painting, wallpapering, and cleaning would qualify as fixing-up expenses.

✓ **Example 38.** Clyde Darwin sold his house for a gross sales price of $100,000. He paid a $6,000 real estate commission, $700 for a title policy, $300 for legal fees, and $500 to paint and clean the interior immediately prior to the sale. The amount realized on the sale is $93,000 ($100,000 − [$6,000 + $700 + $300]). His adjusted sales price is $92,500 ($93,000 − $500).

The adjusted sales price is used only to determine the amount that must be reinvested in the replacement residence in order to avoid gain recognition. The actual real-

---

ANSWERS TO REVIEW IV

1. (d) The car was sold at a loss, and there are no payments to be made beyond the year of sale for the furniture.
2. (c) The gross profit is $13,200 ($18,000 − $4,800), and the total contract price is $18,000. Therefore, the gross profit percentage is 73.33% ($13,200/$18,000).
3. (a) The gross profit is $630,000 ($1,500,000 less the adjusted basis of $870,000, which includes the 8% selling expenses). The total contract price is $1,000,000; thus, the gross profit percentage is 63% ($630,000/$1,000,000), and 63% of the $100,000 received in the year of sale, or $63,000, is taxable.
4. (c) The gross profit is $179,000 ($210,000 − $31,000), and the total contract price is $210,000. The gross profit percentage is 85.23% ($179,000/$210,000). The amount taxable in 1993 is $42,615 ($50,000 × .8523), and the amount taxable in 1994 is $34,092 ($40,000 × .8523).

ized gain on the sale is determined by comparing the amount realized with the adjusted basis of the residence.

☑ **Example 39.** In the preceding example, if Clyde had an adjusted basis in the residence of $67,000, he would have had a realized gain of $26,000 ($93,000 − $67,000). However, he would need to reinvest only $92,500 (the adjusted sales price) in his replacement residence to postpone recognition of the entire $26,000 realized gain.

If a taxpayer fails to reinvest the entire adjusted sales price in the replacement residence, all or part of the gain will have to be recognized. The gain recognized is the *lesser* of the realized gain or the amount by which the adjusted sales price exceeds the cost of the new residence. The latter amount represents the taxpayer's wherewithal to pay tax, in that this amount was not reinvested in the replacement residence. If a taxpayer purchases an existing home or constructs a new home, all capital expenditures made within the qualified replacement period may be included as part of the cost of the replacement residence.

☑ **Example 40.** Using the data from Examples 38 and 39, assume that Clyde purchased a replacement residence for a gross purchase price of $78,500, and that he spent $10,000 on a family room addition before the expiration of the two-year replacement period. Thus, the total qualifying replacement cost of the new residence is $88,500.

Because the adjusted basis of his old residence was $67,000, his realized gain on the sale was $26,000 ($93,000 − $67,000). However, his gain reportable for tax purposes is limited to that portion of the $92,500 adjusted sales price not reinvested in the new residence (total cost, $88,500). Thus, Clyde will report a taxable gain of $4,000 in the year of sale ($92,500 − $88,500).

The "price" for nonrecognition of a portion or all of a realized gain under Sec. 1034 is a reduction in the tax basis of the new residence. Specifically, the basis of the replacement residence is its cost less the *unrecognized* gain on the sale of the old residence. In effect, the taxpayer has not "paid" for this portion of basis by reporting this amount as taxable gain.

☑ **Example 41.** In the previous example, Clyde was able to postpone gain recognition on $22,000 (i.e., the $26,000 realized gain less the $4,000 recognized taxable gain). The basis of the new residence will be $66,500 [the $88,500 cost less the $22,000 of unrecognized (postponed) gain].

Figure 6-8 illustrates a simple format for calculating the taxable gain and basis of the replacement residence under Sec. 1034. If the reinvestment computation is used, the difference in the two gains ($22,000) reduces the basis of the replacement residence.

Joint or separate ownership by a husband and wife usually does not complicate the sale of a personal residence as long as the couple remains married. The sale of a personal residence pursuant to a divorce, or the purchase of a single residence by a newly married couple where both previously owned residences, complicates the nonrecognition provisions, and both topics are beyond the scope of this discussion.

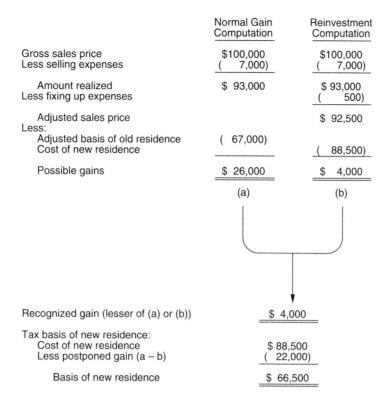

Figure 6-8 Format for Computing Gain on the Sale of a Personal Residence

Form 2119 is used to report the sale of a principal residence. Figure 6-9 illustrates this form, using the facts of Examples 38–41 (which are summarized in Figure 6-8). If a taxpayer does not replace the residence within the required time period, an amended form must be filed to report the gain. The net gain reported on Line 21 of Form 2119 is transferred to Schedule D. Using the facts of Figure 6-8, Schedule D would appear as follows:

Part II	Long-Term Capital Gains and Losses—Assets Held More Than One Year						
9							
10	Enter your long-term totals, if any, from line 23.	10					
11	**Total long-term sales price amounts.** Add column (d) of lines 9 and 10.	11					
12	Gain from Form 4797; long-term gain from Forms 2119, 2439, and 6252; and long-term gain or (loss) from Forms 4684, 6781, and 8824			12			4,000
13	Net long-term gain or (loss) from partnerships, S corporations, and fiduciaries from Schedule(s) K-1.			13			
14	Capital gain distributions			14			
15	Long-term capital loss carryover from 1992 Schedule D, line 45			15			
16	Add lines 9, 10, and 12 through 15, in columns (f) and (g)			16	(	)	4,000
17	**Net long-term capital gain or (loss).** Combine columns (f) and (g) of line 16			17			4,000

Form 2119 — Sale of Your Home — OMB No. 1545-0072 — **1993**
Department of the Treasury / Internal Revenue Service
Attach to Form 1040 for year of sale. ► See separate instructions. ► Please print or type.
Attachment Sequence No. 20

Your first name and initial. If a joint return, also give spouse's name and initial: **Clyde Darwin**
Your social security number: 612:44:7070

Fill in Your Address Only If You Are Filing This Form by Itself and Not With Your Tax Return

Part I — General Information

1. Date your former main home was sold (month, day, year) ▶ **1 / 5 / 93**
2. Have you bought or built a new main home? **☒ Yes ☐ No**
3. Is or was any part of either main home rented out or used for business? If "Yes," see instructions. **☐ Yes ☒ No**

Part II — Gain on Sale — Do not include amounts you deduct as moving expenses.

Line	Description	Amount
4	Selling price of home. Do not include personal property items you sold with your home	100,000
5	Expense of sale (see instructions)	7,000
6	Amount realized. Subtract line 5 from line 4	93,000
7	Adjusted basis of home sold (see instructions)	67,000
8	Gain on sale. Subtract line 7 from line 6	26,000

Is line 8 more than zero?
— Yes ▶ If line 2 is "Yes," you **must** go to Part III or Part IV, whichever applies. If line 2 is "No," go to line 9.
— No ▶ **Stop** and attach this form to your return.

9. If you haven't replaced your home, do you plan to do so within the **replacement period** (see instructions)? ☐ Yes ☐ No
   - If line 9 is "Yes," stop here, attach this form to your return, and see **Additional Filing Requirements** in the instructions.
   - If line 9 is "No," you **must** go to Part III or Part IV, whichever applies.

Part III — One-Time Exclusion of Gain for People Age 55 or Older
By completing this part, you are electing to take the one-time exclusion (see instructions). If you are not electing to take the exclusion, go to Part IV now.

10. Who was age 55 or older on the date of sale? ☐ You ☐ Your spouse ☐ Both of you
11. Did the person who was age 55 or older own and use the property as his or her main home for a total of at least 3 years (except for short absences) of the 5-year period before the sale? If "No," go to Part IV now. ☐ Yes ☐ No
12. At the time of sale, who owned the home? ☐ You ☐ Your spouse ☐ Both of you
13. Social security number of spouse at the time of sale if you had a different spouse from the one above. If you were not married at the time of sale, enter "None" ▶
14. **Exclusion.** Enter the **smaller** of line 8 or $125,000 ($62,500 if married filing separate return). Then, go to line 15.

Part IV — Adjusted Sales Price, Taxable Gain, and Adjusted Basis of New Home

Line	Description	Amount
15	If line 14 is blank, enter the amount from line 8. Otherwise, subtract line 14 from line 8	26,000
16	Fixing-up expenses (see instructions for time limits)	500
17	If line 14 is blank, enter amount from line 16. Otherwise, add lines 14 and 16	500
18	**Adjusted sales price.** Subtract line 17 from line 6	92,500
19b	Cost of new home (19a Date you moved into new home: **2 / 5 / 93**)	88,500
20	Subtract line 19b from line 18. If zero or less, enter -0-	4,000
21	**Taxable gain.** Enter the **smaller** of line 15 or line 20	4,000
22	**Postponed gain.** Subtract line 21 from line 15	22,000
23	**Adjusted basis of new home.** Subtract line 22 from line 19b	66,500

- If line 15 is zero, stop and attach this form to your return.
- If line 15 is more than zero and line 2 is "Yes," go to line 16 now.
- If you are reporting this sale on the installment method, stop and see the instructions.
- All others, stop and **enter the amount from line 15 on Schedule D, col. (g), line 4 or line 12.**

- If line 21 is zero, go to line 22 and attach this form to your return.
- If you are reporting this sale on the installment method, see the line 15 instructions and go to line 22.
- All others, **enter the amount from line 21 on Schedule D, col. (g), line 4 or line 12**, and go to line 22.

Sign Here Only If You Are Filing This Form by Itself and Not With Your Tax Return
Under penalties of perjury, I declare that I have examined this form, including attachments, and to the best of my knowledge and belief, it is true, correct, and complete.

Your signature: **Clyde Darwin** — Date: **4-1-94**

For Paperwork Reduction Act Notice, see separate instructions. Cat. No. 11710J Form **2119** (1993)

Figure 6-9 Form 2119

TAX TIP

The date of sale or purchase of a personal residence is the *closing date* of the sale, not the date of entering into an offer to purchase or sell the residence. Since closing dates are normally included in offers to purchase, the taxpayer should carefully select this date if meeting the two-year replacement period is in jeopardy.

SEC. 121 ONE-TIME ELECTIVE EXCLUSION

Sec. 121 of the Code permits a once-in-a-lifetime total forgiveness of gain of not more than $125,000 ($62,500 for married-filing separately) on the sale of a personal residence for a person who is 55 years of age or older on the date of sale. Because many elderly people have a major portion of their retirement assets in their home, Congress permits that home to be sold with no tax consequences if the realized gain is no more than $125,000 and the taxpayer otherwise qualifies. Any gain exceeding $125,000 is subject to taxation. A taxpayer does not have to purchase a new residence to elect this provision. However, if a new residence is repurchased, the taxpayer may be able to use Sec. 1034 to postpone any gain in excess of $125,000.

THE LAW

Sec. 121(a)—General Rule. At the election of the taxpayer, gross income does not include gain from the sale or exchange of property if (1) the taxpayer has attained the age of 55 before the date of such sale or exchange, and (2) during the 5-year period ending on the date of the sale or exchange, such property has been owned and used by the taxpayer as his principal residence for periods aggregating 3 years or more.
(b). Limitations. (1) Dollar limitation—The amount of the gain excluded from gross income under subsection (a) shall not exceed $125,000 ($62,500 in the case of a separate return by a married individual). (2) Application to Only One Sale or Exchange—Subsection (a) shall not apply to any sale or exchange by the taxpayer if an election by the taxpayer or his spouse under subsection (a) with respect to any other sale or exchange is in effect.

The taxpayer must own and use the home as his or her principal place of residence for at least three years during the five-year period immediately preceeding its sale. If the taxpayer becomes incapacitated, the three years will be satisfied by actually living in the home for at least one year and living an additional period in a nursing facility for a combined period of three years. The taxpayer must be age 55 or older when the sale is completed, although the contract may be entered into before the taxpayer's 55th birthday. A married couple may use the election if only one spouse meets the age, ownership, and use requirements.

> **TAX TIP**
>
>
>
> While either husband or wife may meet the age, ownership, and use requirements, the restrictions must be met by the same person. Thus, if only spouse A meets the age requirements and only spouse B meets the ownership requirements, the election would not be available. However, a deceased spouse who met the requirements before death will permit the surviving spouse to use this provision on the sale of their residence.

Unlike Sec. 1034, this section is an elective provision that is available only once in the taxpayer's lifetime. If the taxpayer is married and the election is made, both spouses must consent to the election and neither may use the provision again, regardless of the circumstances. This prohibition is enforced even if one spouse dies and the other remarries a person who has never used the election. The election may be revoked prior to the running of the statute of limitations for the return on which the election is made. If the election is made by a husband and wife, both spouses must consent to the revocation.

☑ **Example 42.** John and Mary Smith have owned and lived in their home for 35 years but can no longer maintain the property. John is 73 years old and Mary is 54 but in poor health. They purchased the home for $28,000 in 1955 and received $118,000 on its sale. They have a realized gain of $90,000 on the sale, which is not recognized if they use their Sec. 121 election.

The Sec. 121 exclusion provision can be used in conjunction with other nonrecognition provisions of the Code, such as the Sec. 1034 deferral rules discussed earlier. Thus, a person who elects Sec. 121 and purchases a replacement residence within the two-year replacement period may be able to defer a portion or all of the realized gain exceeding the $125,000 exclusion.

In applying Sec. 121 and Sec. 1034 to the same residence sale, the Sec. 121 exclusion provision is applied first. Because this is an *exclusion* provision, not a deferral provision, the exclusion (up to $125,000) reduces *both* the realized gain and the adjusted sales price used in the Sec. 1034 computation. The latter reduction lowers the minimum amount that the taxpayer has to invest in the new residence in order to defer additional gain.

☑ **Example 43.** Mike Sweeney purchased his home near downtown Atlanta 27 years ago for $41,000. The area has been redeveloped as a commercial area, and Mike has been offered $340,000 for the property. Mike is only 56 years old and plans to purchase a new residence. He buys one in an Atlanta surburb for $138,000 and plans to use both Secs. 121 and 1034 to avoid as much gain recognition as possible. He incurs selling expenses of $15,000 and no fixing-up expenses.

Figure 6-10 discloses the computation of Mike's realized gain, excluded gain, taxable gain, and basis of the new residence. This figure closely follows the format used in Figure 6-8. Note particularly that the $125,000 exclusion reduces *both* the realized gain and the adjusted sales price. Note also that the basis of the new residence is reduced only by the deferred gain, not by the excluded gain.

Form 2119 is also used to elect the Sec. 121 exclusion on the sale of a personal residence. Figure 6-11 illustrates a Form 2119 with this election, using the facts from Example 43 and Figure 6-10.

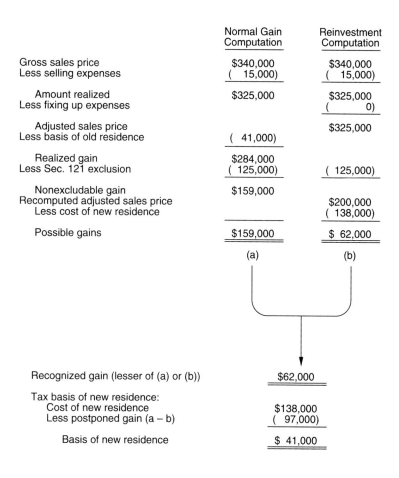

Figure 6-10 Format for Simultaneous Application of Secs. 121 and 1034

TAX TIP

In some cases, taxpayers age 55 or older who sell a personal residence and buy a replacement residence may not elect Sec. 121. This is because the deferral computation of Sec. 1034 may eliminate most, if not all, of the realized gain on the sale. In such a case, it may be unwise for the taxpayer to use his or her one-time election for very little tax savings. Instead, the taxpayer could save the Sec. 121 election for a later sale of the replacement residence, which may involve a much larger gain.

Form **2119**	**Sale of Your Home**	OMB No. 1545-0072
Department of the Treasury Internal Revenue Service	▶ Attach to Form 1040 for year of sale. ▶ See separate instructions. ▶ Please print or type.	**1993** Attachment Sequence No. 20

Your first name and initial. If a joint return, also give spouse's name and initial.	Last name	Your social security number
Mike Sweeney		420 : 11 : 6063

Fill in Your Address Only If You Are Filing This Form by Itself and Not With Your Tax Return	Present address (no., street, and apt. no., rural route, or P.O. box no. if mail is not delivered to street address)	Spouse's social security number
	1115 Marnie Street	: :
	City, town or post office, state, and ZIP code Atlanta, Georgia 30308	

Part I   General Information

1. Date your former main home was sold (month, day, year) ▶ **1** 6 / 2 / 93
2. Have you bought or built a new main home? .... ☒ Yes ☐ No
3. Is or was any part of either main home rented out or used for business? If "Yes," see instructions ☐ Yes ☒ No

Part II   Gain on Sale—Do not include amounts you deduct as moving expenses.

4. Selling price of home. Do not include personal property items you sold with your home .. **4** 340,000
5. Expense of sale (see instructions) **5** 15,000
6. Amount realized. Subtract line 5 from line 4 .... **6** 325,000
7. Adjusted basis of home sold (see instructions) **7** 41,000
8. Gain on sale. Subtract line 7 from line 6 .... **8** 284,000

Is line 8 more than zero?
— Yes ▶ If line 2 is "Yes," you **must** go to Part III or Part IV, whichever applies. If line 2 is "No," go to line 9.
— No ▶ **Stop** and attach this form to your return.

9. If you haven't replaced your home, do you plan to do so within the **replacement period** (see instructions)? ☐ Yes ☐ No
   - If line 9 is "Yes," stop here, attach this form to your return, and see **Additional Filing Requirements** in the instructions.
   - If line 9 is "No," you **must** go to Part III or Part IV, whichever applies.

Part III   One-Time Exclusion of Gain for People Age 55 or Older—By completing this part, you are electing to take the one-time exclusion (see instructions). If you are not electing to take the exclusion, go to Part IV now.

10. Who was age 55 or older on the date of sale? .... ☒ You ☐ Your spouse ☐ Both of you
11. Did the person who was age 55 or older own and use the property as his or her main home for a total of at least 3 years (except for short absences) of the 5-year period before the sale? If "No," go to Part IV now . . ☒ Yes ☐ No
12. At the time of sale, who owned the home? .... ☒ You ☐ Your spouse ☐ Both of you
13. Social security number of spouse at the time of sale if you had a different spouse from the one above. If you were not married at the time of sale, enter "None" ...... ▶ **13** : :
14. Exclusion. Enter the **smaller** of line 8 or $125,000 ($62,500 if married filing separate return). Then, go to line 15 .... **14** 125,000

Part IV   Adjusted Sales Price, Taxable Gain, and Adjusted Basis of New Home

15. If line 14 is blank, enter the amount from line 8. Otherwise, subtract line 14 from line 8 .. **15** 159,000
    - If line 15 is zero, stop and attach this form to your return.
    - If line 15 is more than zero and line 2 is "Yes," go to line 16 now.
    - If you are reporting this sale on the installment method, stop and see the instructions.
    - All others, stop and **enter the amount from line 15 on Schedule D, col. (g), line 4 or line 12.**
16. Fixing-up expenses (see instructions for time limits) **16** 0
17. If line 14 is blank, enter amount from line 16. Otherwise, add lines 14 and 16 . **17** 125,000
18. **Adjusted sales price.** Subtract line 17 from line 6 ...... **18** 200,000
19a. Date you moved into new home (month, day, year) ▶ 6 / 3 / 93   b Cost of new home **19b** 138,000
20. Subtract line 19b from line 18. If zero or less, enter -0- **20** 62,000
21. **Taxable gain.** Enter the **smaller** of line 15 or line 20 ..... **21** 62,000
    - If line 21 is zero, go to line 22 and attach this form to your return.
    - If you are reporting this sale on the installment method, see the line 15 instructions and go to line 22.
    - All others, **enter the amount from line 21 on Schedule D, col. (g), line 4 or line 12, and go to line 22.**
22. **Postponed gain.** Subtract line 21 from line 15 .... **22** 97,000
23. **Adjusted basis of new home.** Subtract line 22 from line 19b .. **23** 41,000

Sign Here Only If You Are Filing This Form by Itself and Not With Your Tax Return

Under penalties of perjury, I declare that I have examined this form, including attachments, and to the best of my knowledge and belief, it is true, correct, and complete.

Your signature	Date	Spouse's signature	Date
▶ Mike Sweeney	4-15-94	▶	
If a joint return, both must sign.			

For Paperwork Reduction Act Notice, see separate instructions.   Cat. No. 11710J   Form **2119** (1993)

Figure 6-11   Form 2119 with a Sec. 121 Election

REVIEW V

1. Walter and Nancy, both age 42, sold their personal residence for $185,000. They purchased it ten years ago for $80,000. Within three weeks they purchased a new home for $165,000. They paid $9,250 commission on the sale of their old home, incurred $1,000 in other expenses related to the sale, and had $2,000 in fixing-up expenses. What are their realized (accounting) gain and their recognized (taxable) gains?
   (a) $105,000 realized gain; $20,000 recognized gain
   (b) $ 94,750 realized gain; $20,000 recognized gain
   (c) $ 92,750 realized gain; $ 7,750 recognized gain
   (d) $94,750 realized gain; $7,750 recognized gain
2. After his wife died, Charles Wood sold his home for $110,000. The home originally cost $30,000, and he had added $25,000 in improvements over the years. Because he is not yet 55, Charles invested in an $85,000 condominium. If he incurred $6,000 in expenses in selling his home, what is his tax basis in the new condominium?
   (a) $49,000
   (b) $55,000
   (c) $19,000
   (d) $30,000
3. Martha Wilson, age 67, sold the home she had lived in for 45 years for $93,000 and moved into a rental congregate living facility for senior citizens. If her basis in the home was $12,000, what is her minimum recognized gain?
   (a) $0
   (b) $12,000
   (c) $81,000
   (d) $93,000
4. Willard Wellty, age 62, sold his home for $625,000 and purchased a smaller home for $425,000. Willard incurred $30,000 in selling expenses. Assuming that his basis in the old home was $430,000, his minimum gain to be recognized would be
   (a) $200,000.
   (b) $170,000.
   (c) $165,000.
   (d) $40,000.

Answers are on page 6-47.

CHAPTER APPENDIX: CAPITAL ASSET STATUS—SPECIAL CLASSIFICATIONS AND REPORTING
(Code Sections 165, 1235, 1236, 1237, and 1244)

The lack of a concrete definition of capital assets has plagued taxpayers, the IRS, and the courts for a number of years. In some cases, Congress has taken action to remove some of the uncertainty from a few of the more troublesome classification problems. We will discuss several of these provisions. Also, Congress has enacted two special capital asset reporting provisions for certain transactions in 1993 and later years.

WORTHLESS SECURITIES

One of the prerequisites for deducting a loss is that the loss has to be recognized in a market transaction. But what happens if a taxpayer owns worthless securities that no one will buy? Congress recognized that this would unduly penalize taxpayers, so a special rule was enacted that assumes that worthless securities are, in effect, sold for $0 on the last day of the tax year. The date is specified so that the loss may be labeled as either short term or long term.

✓ **Example 44.** Hank Ruth owns 1,000 shares of B Co. stock, which became worthless in 1993. Hank had originally purchased the stock on December 3, 1992, for $2,600. Hank will report a $2,600 long-term capital loss in 1993, because the stock was held longer than a year by December 31, 1993.

SECTION 1244 STOCK

In order to encourage investment in small business corporations, Congress enacted a special tax treatment for "Section 1244 Stock" (of course, defined in Code Sec. 1244!). Such stock basically represents the first $1,000,000 of original issue stock of a corporation. If a taxpayer owns such stock and it becomes worthless or is sold at a loss, the first $50,000 of loss each year ($100,000 on a joint return) can be reported as a fully deductible *ordinary* loss. Any excess loss is capital loss. The ordinary loss is thus not subject to the normal $3,000 capital loss limit.

✓ **Example 45.** Betty Adams sold 3,000 shares of Sec. 1244 stock in 1993 at a $63,000 loss. Assuming that she filed as a single individual, she may deduct $50,000 of the loss as an ordinary loss and $13,000 as a capital loss (with the latter subject to the possible $3,000 limit, depending on her other 1993 capital transactions).

SECURITIES OWNED BY SECURITIES DEALERS

A person in the trade or business of selling securities may also own some securities as a personal investment. Had Congress not drafted a special rule for such taxpayers, a dealer would be tempted to label all gain sales as "investments" (to obtain capital gains treatment, which could absorb capital losses) and to label all loss sales as "securities inventory" (to obtain ordinary loss deductions not subject to the $3,000 annual limit applicable to capital losses). To prevent such potential abuses, Congress requires all dealers to identify personal investment properties in their records on the date of purchase.*

SALES OF SUBDIVIDED REALTY

When a taxpayer divides realty held as an investment into several lots for sale, he or she may begin to take on the appearance of a real estate dealer. This is especially true if significant improvements have been made to the lots. As a dealer, the lots would be considered to be inventory, subject to ordinary income or loss treatment.

Congress has attempted to provide some guidance in this area by allowing the taxpayer to sell up to five lots (if held for at least five years, unless inherited) as capital

---

*For changes in the tax law effective for tax years beginning in 1994, see Appendix J.

assets. For these purposes, adjoining lots sold to the same purchaser are treated as one lot sale. However, in the year that the sixth lot is sold, 5% of the sales price of all lots sold in that year (which may include some of the first five lots) is taxed as ordinary income, with any remaining gain taxed as capital gain. Any selling expenses may first offset the ordinary income portion of the gain. Finally, if the taxpayer makes improvements to the property (e.g., roads, sewage) that exceed 10% of the value of the property, the taxpayer is treated as a dealer, with the entire gain (or loss) treated as ordinary in nature.

☑ **Example 46.** Bill Mason divided 20 acres of land held as an investment into ten 1-acre plots. During 1993 he sold seven lots to seven different buyers for $5,000 each (the adjusted basis of each lot was $3,000). Since 1993 is the year in which the sixth lot was sold, all seven lot sales are subject to the 5% rule. Thus, $250 must be reported as ordinary income (5% of $5,000), and the remaining $1,750 is reported as capital gain on each sale. Any selling expenses incurred would first offset the $250.

PATENTS, FRANCHISES, TRADEMARKS, AND TRADENAMES

As mentioned earlier in this chapter, copyrights are never considered capital assets in the hands of the creator. However, the same is not true for patents. In an effort to encourage inventive activity, Congress has provided capital asset status to patents, as long as all substantial rights to the patent are transferred in a sale or exchange. If the taxpayer limits the use of the patent to a period of time or a certain geographic area, the transaction will be treated as a lease (rental), not a sale or exchange. A similar rule applies to franchises, trademarks, and tradenames.

☑ **Example 47.** Judy Graham has a $4,000 investment in a patent that she developed. She sold rights to use the patent in a four-state area to Will Watson for $36,000. Because she has limited the use of the patent geographically, the $36,000 will be treated as rental income, and no basis recovery of the $4,000 is permitted (because a

---

ANSWERS TO REVIEW V

1. (d) The realized gain is $94,750 ($174,750 amount realized less $80,000 basis). However, the recognized gain is limited to $7,750 of the adjusted sales price of $172,750 that is not reinvested in the $165,000 cost of the new residence.
2. (b) The cost basis of the new residence of $85,000 is reduced by the $30,000 of gain not recognized due to Sec. 1034. The $30,000 of postponed gain is the difference between the $49,000 realized gain ($104,000 − $55,000) and the $19,000 recognized gain ($104,000 − $85,000).
3. (a) By using her Sec. 121 exclusion, Martha recognizes no gain on the sale.
4. (d) Willard will recognize the $40,000 realized gain remaining after using his $125,000 exclusion. He does not benefit from Sec. 1034, because he reinvested $45,000 less than the recomputed adjusted sales price of $470,000 ($595,000 − $125,000).

sale or exchange did not occur). The same result would have occurred if Judy had sold the rights for a limited time period (i.e., a time period less than the estimated useful life of the patent).

INVESTMENTS IN SMALL BUSINESS STOCK

Several provisions of the Revenue Reconciliation Act of 1993 were designed to encourage investments in small businesses. For example, new Sec. 1202 states that noncorporate taxpayers who hold qualified small business stock for more than five years may exclude 50% of any gain on the sale or exchange of the stock. The gain eligible for exclusion is limited to the greater of (1) ten times the investor's basis in the stock, or (2) $10 million less any previous dispositions of that stock.

This new provision applies to qualifying stock issued after August 10, 1993, so the first gains eligible for the exclusion will not occur until on or after August 11, 1998. However, it is important for investors to know now what stock qualifies for this exclusion. In general, a qualifying small business must meet four requirements:

1. The corporation must be a regular corporation; specialized corporations such as regulated investment companies and real estate investment trusts will not qualify;

2. The corporation must use at least 80% of its assets in the active conduct of a trade or business other than those based principally on services, such as accounting, health, and law;

3. The corporation must not be in the business of banking, leasing, insurance, financing, investing, farming, oil and gas, mining, or any activity that involves the operation of a hotel, motel, restaurant, or similar business; and

4. The corporation must have gross assets with an adjusted basis of $50 million or less on the day that the stock is issued; however, exceeding this limit on a later date will not disqualify any original qualifying issues.

The 50% exclusion means that the capital gain on the sale or exchange of such qualifying stock will be taxed at a maximum effective rate of 14% (28% × .50). However, one-half of any qualifying gain will be a "tax preference item" for purposes of the alternative minimum tax (as discussed in Chapter 7).

Example 48. X Corporation, a qualifying small business, issued $100,000 of stock in November 1993. In May 1994, X Corporations's adjusted basis in its gross assets exceeded $50 million for the first time. Any stock issued after that date by X will not qualify as small business stock; however, the $100,000 issue in 1993 will retain its status as qualifying stock for purposes of the exclusion.

ORDINARY INCOME CONVERSION TRANSACTIONS

The increased differential between ordinary income and capital gains rates in 1993 and later years caused Congress to enact several measures to prevent taxpayers from converting ordinary income into capital gain. One of these is new Sec. 1258, which recharacterizes a portion of or all capital gain from a conversion transaction as ordinary income for transactions entered into after April 30, 1993. A conversion transaction is defined as any transaction where substantially all of the taxpayer's expected return is risk-free and is merely attributable to the time value of money (i.e., the expected gain is the equivalent of interest income).

The computations under Sec. 1258 can be quite complex and the details are beyond the scope of this text. In general, the gain recharacterized as ordinary income is limited to the interest that would have accrued on the net investment at a yield of 120% of the applicable federal rate. The following example provides an overview of the scope of this provision.

Example 49. Bob Robinson purchased 100 shares of Tee Corporation stock on August 1, 1993 for $5,000. On the same date, Bob entered into a contract to sell the same 100 shares on December 1, 1994 for $5,800. It is clear from these two transactions that Bob is not at risk on the stock investment, since he has a guaranteed return of $800 that is the equivalent of interest. The stock purchase and sale are covered by the conversion transaction rules, and a portion of the gain on the sale (a computed interest return) must be reported as ordinary income. Any remaining gain will be reported as capital gain.

CHAPTER PROBLEMS

PART

I   1. Which of the following gains and losses will never be recognized for tax purposes?
   (a) a personal residence sold at a gain
   (b) corporate stock that has declined $4,000 in value
   (c) a business automobile sold at a loss
   (d) a condemned rental building sold at a loss
   (e) a vacation cabin sold at a gain

I   2. Julia Dole's automobile was used for business purposes 40% of the time and for personal use 60% of the time. The auto originally cost $8,000 in 1989, and $2,500 of legitimate depreciation deductions have been taken since acquisition. If Dole sells the auto in 1993 for $1,000, what amount of loss may she deduct on her 1993 return?

I   3. In 1983 Cal Smith purchased land for $80,000, paying $8,000 down and giving a 20-year note for the balance. In 1993 Smith sells the property for $25,000 cash plus an oil painting worth $30,000 (the painting had cost the purchaser $20,000 in 1988). In addition, the purchaser agreed to assume the outstanding liability of $68,000. What is Smith's basis in the property on the date of sale? What is Smith's amount realized on the sale?

I   4. In exchange for preparing her 1993 tax return, Wanda Wallace, a dentist, performed $200 of dental services for Helen Johnson, who prepared the return. What, if any, are the tax consequences of these transactions?

II   5. In 1990 Garson Greer purchased a delivery truck and a special trailer at an auction for a $24,000 lump-sum price. The truck was appraised at $20,000 and the trailer at $10,000. Greer spent an additional $500 fixing up the truck for his business. In 1993 a fire resulted in a $1,000 uninsured loss on the truck. If Greer had taken a total of $3,500 depreciation on the truck, what is its current adjusted basis?

II 6. In exchange for legal services performed in organizing a corporation, Ann Kennedy received 1,000 shares of Bee Company stock. The stock had a par value of $6 a share and was worth $8 a share when received. Two months later, Kennedy sells the shares for $8,700. What is her gain on the sale of the stock?

II 7. On June 1, 1993, Oliver Orange inherited an office building from his uncle's estate. His uncle had purchased the building in 1983 for $35,000 and had taken $6,000 of depreciation deductions before his death. The building was worth $48,000 on the date of his death. On November 15, 1993, Orange sold the building for $49,200. How much gain must Orange recognize on the sale? Is the result short term or long term?

II 8. On May 1, 1993, Martha News received a gift of 1,000 shares of AB stock from her brother. The stock cost her brother $4,000 in 1986, and it was worth $2,800 on the date of the gift. No gift tax was paid. Describe the amount and character of the gain or loss if News sells the stock on December 1, 1993, for (a) $5,200, (b) $2,900, or (c) $2,100.

II 9. On May 1, 1992, Babbs Hartley received a gift of 1,000 shares of CD stock from her father. Her father paid $20 a share for the stock in 1987, and it was worth $24 a share on the date of the gift. Hartley's father paid $1,200 gift tax on the transfer. If Hartley sells the stock on April 15, 1993, for $23 a share, how much gain or loss should she recognize?

II 10. In 1990 Ivan Morazova purchased a personal automobile for $7,000. In 1993 he started his own business and began using the automobile for business purposes 100% of the time. The value of the automobile at this time was $5,500. What is Morazova's adjusted basis for gain purposes? For loss purposes? Explain.

III 11. Which of the following assets would *never* be considered capital assets?
(a) a tractor used in a farming business
(b) stocks and bonds owned by a stock broker (held as a personal investment)
(c) a painting (not her own work) owned by an artist
(d) a Series HH savings bond owned by an investor
(e) a copyright to a book written by the taxpayer

III 12. During 1993 Sam Jacobs had $30,000 of adjusted gross income (other than capital transactions), $1,600 of short-term capital losses, and $2,500 of long-term losses. Determine Jacobs's capital loss deduction for 1993 and the carryover (if any) to 1994.

III 13. Assuming that a taxpayer had $40,000 of salary in 1993 and the following capital transactions, determine his adjusted gross income for 1993 and his capital loss carryover (if any) to 1994, noting any special treatments:
ST gains—$4,500   LT gains—$9,300
ST losses—($3,800) LT losses—($7,500)

III 14. Assuming that a taxpayer had $30,000 salary in 1993 and the following capital transactions, determine her adjusted gross income for 1993 and her capital loss carryover (if any) to 1994:
ST gains—$18,000   LT gains—$7,000
ST losses—($20,000) LT losses—($2,000)
LT loss carryover from 1992—($5,700)

III 15. During 1993 Linda Beech had a $10,000 short-term capital gain and a $20,000 long-term capital gain. Assuming that she files as a single individual, determine her tax liability, assuming that her only other 1993 income was a salary of (a) $15,000, (b) $25,000, or (c) $60,000.

IV 16. Harold Barnes sold five acres of land in 1993 for a total price of $100,000, payable as follows: $10,000 down payment in the year of sale, assumption of a $20,000 mortgage on the property by the purchaser, and a $70,000 12% installment note, payable in seven equal $10,000 installments beginning in 1994. Harold originally bought the land ten years ago for $22,000, and he incurred $2,000 of selling expenses on the sale. Determine Harold's taxable gain for (a) 1993 and (b) 1994.

IV 17. Assume the same facts as in Problem 16, except that Harold's basis in the land was $14,000 (not including the $2,000 of selling expenses). Redetermine the taxable gain reportable by Harold in (a) 1993 and (b) 1994.

IV 18. Marge Haddox sold a land investment in 1993 on an installment basis. The land was originally purchased in 1988 for $67,000. The total consideration to be received was $88,000, which consisted of a $10,000 down payment received on June 30, 1993, the assumption of an $18,000 mortgage by the purchaser, and a five-year installment note that provides for ten semiannual payments of $6,000 plus simple interest computed at an annual rate of 10%. (There were no selling expenses.) The first installment payment was received on December 31, 1993. How would Marge report the total consideration (payments and interest) of $19,000 received in the year of sale (1993)?

V 19. James and Rhonda Flemming sold their personal residence in 1993. The residence originally cost $40,000 in 1980, and they had added a garage at a cost of $5,000 in 1984. They spent $1,000 to have the house painted two weeks prior to the sale, and they incurred $5,000 in selling expenses associated with the sale. The total sales price of the home was $150,000. Determine their taxable gain and basis of the new home (if purchased), assuming that
(a) they did not buy a replacement residence.
(b) they spent $40,000 on a new residence.
(c) they spent $85,000 on a new residence.
(d) they spent $146,000 on a new residence.

V 20. Cynthia Matherly (single, age 52) sold her personal residence in 1993 for $380,000. She had originally purchased the residence 20 years ago for $50,000. She paid $2,000 to have the house cleaned and painted two weeks prior to the sale, and she incurred $15,000 in selling expenses related to the sale. Assuming that Cynthia purchased a new residence in 1993 for $175,000, determine her recognized gain on the sale and the basis of her new home.

V 21. Assume the same facts as in Problem 20, except that Cynthia is 62 years of age and she elects to exclude as much gain as possible under the tax law. Redetermine her recognized gain in the year of sale and the basis of her new home.

APX 22. On April 5, 1993, Ray McClary, a single taxpayer, purchased 1,000 shares of Bee Company stock for $54,500. On November 14, 1993, Bee Company was declared totally bankrupt, and the stock was judged to be completely worthless. Assuming that the shares were part of the $800,000 original issue of stock by Bee Company, how will McClary report these transactions for the tax year? Explain.

APX 23. Melva Rushing has held 20 acres of land as an investment for 12 years. In 1993 she divided the land into ten 2-acre lots, and she sold four of these lots to four different buyers in 1993 for $4,000 a lot. In 1994 she sold five more lots to five different buyers for $4,500 a lot. Assuming that Rushing had paid $10,000 for the land, how will she report the 1993 sales? The 1994 sales?

APX 24. William Tell developed a special motorboat fuel mixture in 1990 and immediately received a patent for his efforts. His total costs of developing the mixture were $6,500. In 1993 Tell sells the right to market the mixture to Bell Company for a period of five years. The total sales price is $100,000. How will Tell report this sale?

TAX RETURN PROBLEMS

25. [Schedule D] Janis Johnson, a single individual with taxable income of $36,000 in 1993, exclusive of capital transactions, had the following additional transactions during the year. Using this information, complete the Form 1040 Schedule D that follows.
    (a) AB stock (bought for $4,000 on 1/1/89) was sold on 4/2/93 for $6,000; CD stock (bought for $5,000 on 11/14/92) was sold on 5/3/93 for $4,500; and EF bonds (bought for $6,000 on 3/4/90) were sold on 7/3/93 for $6,400.
    (b) Johnson sold her personal automobile on 3/12/93 for $3,500 cash. The car had cost $4,800 on 4/15/89.
    (c) Johnson sold an antique vase that she had inherited from her mother's estate on 1/1/89. Her mother paid $6,000 for the vase in 1982, and it was worth $9,000 on the date of her death and $9,500 on the date that the estate distributed the asset to Johnson. The vase was sold on 9/1/93 for $10,200.
    (d) On 12/2/93 Johnson sold her personal boat for $7,800 cash. She had received the boat as a gift from her uncle in 1990 when it was worth $6,400. Her uncle had purchased the boat in 1985 for $4,800. A gift tax of $800 was paid on the transfer.
    (e) On 12/16/93 Johnson sold two acres of land for $3,000, for which the purchaser also assumed a $3,500 liability. Johnson paid $500 selling expenses. She had purchased the land in 1987 for $2,200.
    (f) On 4/10/93 Johnson exchanged some gold coins (purchased on 3/1/84 for $1,300) for a personal automobile worth $2,800.
    (g) Johnson sold 50 shares of Z Corporation stock for $8,200 on 12/28/93. She had received the shares as a gift from her mother in 1986, when they were worth $5,000. Her mother had originally purchased the shares for $6,000 in 1984, and she paid a gift tax of $600 on the transfer.
    (h) A real estate agent appraised Johnson's personal residence at $62,500 on 12/30/93. Johnson had purchased the residence on 1/12/92 for $64,000.
26. [Form 6252] Refer to Problem 16. Prepare a Form 6252 for Harold Barnes for the year of sale, 1993.
27. [Form 2119] Refer to Problem 21. Prepare a Form 2119 for Cynthia Matherly for the year of sale of the personal residence.

HOW WOULD YOU RULE?

28. Barbara Backhand is a professional tennis player. In 1993 she was ranked number one in the world and received numerous offers to endorse products. After months of negotiations, she signed a lifetime agreement with Duffer Products for $1 million. The con-

tract allows Duffer to use and exploit her name, signature, and portrait in any way the company chooses in connection with the sale, manufacture, and advertising of its product. Barbara contends that the sale of rights to her name, signature, and portrait should be taxed as a capital gain. What is your opinion?

29. Bob Marley owns an office building. During 1993 one of the tenants pays Bob $12,000 to cancel the lease, which still has 12 years of remaining life. Bob has computed the present value of the rents lost due to cancellation as $20,000, and he wants to report an $8,000 loss on his tax return. He contends that he "sold" the rights to $20,000 of future income for $12,000. What is your opinion?

TAX RETURN PORTFOLIO PROBLEM

If this problem in Appendix A to this text is assigned by your instructor, complete the instructions for the segment labeled "Chapter 6." This includes partial preparation of Schedule D and completion of Forms 2119 and 6252.

Chapter 6 Problem 25   Name _____   6-55

SCHEDULE D (Form 1040)
Department of the Treasury
Internal Revenue Service

Capital Gains and Losses

▶ Attach to Form 1040.   ▶ See Instructions for Schedule D (Form 1040).
▶ Use lines 20 and 22 for more space to list transactions for lines 1 and 9.

OMB No. 1545-0074

1993

Attachment Sequence No. **12**

Name(s) shown on Form 1040

Your social security number

Part I — Short-Term Capital Gains and Losses—Assets Held One Year or Less

(a) Description of property (Example: 100 sh. XYZ Co.)	(b) Date acquired (Mo., day, yr.)	(c) Date sold (Mo., day, yr.)	(d) Sales price (see page D-3)	(e) Cost or other basis (see page D-3)	(f) LOSS If (e) is more than (d), subtract (d) from (e)	(g) GAIN If (d) is more than (e), subtract (e) from (d)
1						

2 Enter your short-term totals, if any, from line 21. . . . .   **2**

3 **Total short-term sales price amounts.** Add column (d) of lines 1 and 2 . . .   **3**

4 Short-term gain from Forms 2119 and 6252, and short-term gain or (loss) from Forms 4684, 6781, and 8824 . . . .   **4**

5 Net short-term gain or (loss) from partnerships, S corporations, and fiduciaries from Schedule(s) K-1 . . . .   **5**

6 Short-term capital loss carryover from 1992 Schedule D, line 38 . . . . .   **6**

7 Add lines 1, 2, and 4 through 6, in columns (f) and (g). . . . .   **7** (   )

8 **Net short-term capital gain or (loss).** Combine columns (f) and (g) of line 7 . . . . . .   **8**

Part II — Long-Term Capital Gains and Losses—Assets Held More Than One Year

9						

10 Enter your long-term totals, if any, from line 23. . . . .   **10**

11 **Total long-term sales price amounts.** Add column (d) of lines 9 and 10 . . .   **11**

12 Gain from Form 4797; long-term gain from Forms 2119, 2439, and 6252; and long-term gain or (loss) from Forms 4684, 6781, and 8824 . . . .   **12**

13 Net long-term gain or (loss) from partnerships, S corporations, and fiduciaries from Schedule(s) K-1 . . . .   **13**

14 Capital gain distributions **14**

15 Long-term capital loss carryover from 1992 Schedule D, line 45 . . . .   **15**

16 Add lines 9, 10, and 12 through 15, in columns (f) and (g) . . . .   **16** (   )

17 **Net long-term capital gain or (loss).** Combine columns (f) and (g) of line 16 . . . . . .   **17**

Part III — Summary of Parts I and II

18 Combine lines 8 and 17. If a loss, go to line 19. If a gain, enter the gain on Form 1040, line 13.
    Note: *If both lines 17 and 18 are gains, see the* **Schedule D Tax Worksheet** *on page D-4* . .   **18**

19 If line 18 is a (loss), enter here and as a (loss) on Form 1040, line 13, the **smaller** of these losses:
  a The (loss) on line 18; **or**
  b ($3,000) or, if married filing separately, ($1,500) . . . .   **19** (   )

  Note: *See the* **Capital Loss Carryover Worksheet** *on page D-4 if the loss on line 18 exceeds the loss on line 19 or if Form 1040, line 35, is a loss.*

For Paperwork Reduction Act Notice, see Form 1040 instructions.   Cat. No. 11338H   Schedule D (Form 1040) 1993

Copyright © 1994 by Harcourt Brace & Company. All rights reserved.

Schedule D (Form 1040) 1993 Attachment Sequence No. **12** Page

Name(s) shown on Form 1040. Do not enter name and social security number if shown on other side. | Your social security number

Part IV — Short-Term Capital Gains and Losses—Assets Held One Year or Less *(Continuation of Part I)*

(a) Description of property (Example: 100 sh. XYZ Co.)	(b) Date acquired (Mo., day, yr.)	(c) Date sold (Mo., day, yr.)	(d) Sales price (see page D-3)	(e) Cost or other basis (see page D-3)	(f) LOSS If (e) is more than (d), subtract (d) from (e)	(g) GAIN If (d) is more than (e), subtract (e) from (d)
20						

21 Short-term totals. Add columns (d), (f), and (g) of line 20. Enter here and on line 2 . **21**

Part V — Long-Term Capital Gains and Losses—Assets Held More Than One Year *(Continuation of Part II)*

(a) Description of property	(b) Date acquired	(c) Date sold	(d) Sales price	(e) Cost or other basis	(f) LOSS	(g) GAIN
22						

23 Long-term totals. Add columns (d), (f), and (g) of line 22. Enter here and on line 10 . **23**

Copyright © 1994 by Harcourt Brace & Company. All rights reserved.

Chapter 6 Problem 26   Name _____   6-57

Form 6252
Department of the Treasury
Internal Revenue Service

Installment Sale Income
▶ See separate instructions.   ▶ Attach to your tax return.
Use a separate form for each sale or other disposition of property on the installment method.

OMB No. 1545-0228
1992
Attachment Sequence No. **79**

Name(s) shown on return

Identifying number

1   Description of property ▶ ....
2a Date acquired (month, day, and year) ▶ [__/__/__]   b Date sold (month, day, and year) ▶ [__/__/__]
3   Was the property sold to a related party after May 14, 1980? See instructions . . . . ☐ Yes ☐ No
4   If the answer to question 3 is "Yes," was the property a marketable security? If "Yes," complete Part III. If "No," complete Part III for the year of sale and for 2 years after the year of sale. . . . . ☐ Yes ☐ No

Part I   Gross Profit and Contract Price. Complete this part for the year of sale only.

5	Selling price including mortgages and other debts. Do not include interest whether stated or unstated	5
6	Mortgages and other debts the buyer assumed or took the property subject to, but not new mortgages the buyer got from a bank or other source . . . . [6 ___]	
7	Subtract line 6 from line 5 . . . . [7 ___]	
8	Cost or other basis of property sold . . . . [8 ___]	
9	Depreciation allowed or allowable . . . . [9 ___]	
10	Adjusted basis. Subtract line 9 from line 8 . . . . [10 ___]	
11	Commissions and other expenses of sale . . . . [11 ___]	
12	Income recapture from Form 4797, Part III. See instructions . . [12 ___]	
13	Add lines 10, 11, and 12	13
14	Subtract line 13 from line 5. If zero or less, do not complete the rest of this form	14
15	If the property described on line 1 above was your main home, enter the total of lines 16 and 24 from Form 2119. Otherwise, enter -0-	15
16	**Gross profit.** Subtract line 15 from line 14	16
17	Subtract line 13 from line 6. If zero or less, enter -0-	17
18	**Contract price.** Add line 7 and line 17	18

Part II   Installment Sale Income. Complete this part for the year of sale and any year you receive a payment or have certain debts you must treat as a payment on installment obligations.

19	Gross profit percentage. Divide line 16 by line 18. For years after the year of sale, see instructions	19
20	**For year of sale only**—Enter amount from line 17 above; otherwise, enter -0-	20
21	Payments received during year. See instructions. Do not include interest whether stated or unstated	21
22	Add lines 20 and 21	22
23	Payments received in prior years. See instructions. Do not include interest whether stated or unstated . . . . [23 ___]	
24	**Installment sale income.** Multiply line 22 by line 19	24
25	Part of line 24 that is ordinary income under recapture rules. See instructions	25
26	Subtract line 25 from line 24. Enter here and on Schedule D or Form 4797. See instructions	26

Part III   Related Party Installment Sale Income. Do not complete if you received the final payment this tax year.

27 Name, address, and taxpayer identifying number of related party ....
28 Did the related party, during this tax year, resell or dispose of the property ("second disposition")? . . . ☐ Yes ☐ No
29 If the answer to question 28 is "Yes," complete lines 30 through 37 below unless one of the following conditions is met. Check only the box that applies.
  a ☐ The second disposition was more than 2 years after the first disposition (other than dispositions of marketable securities). If this box is checked, enter the date of disposition (month, day, year) ▶ [__/__/__]
  b ☐ The first disposition was a sale or exchange of stock to the issuing corporation.
  c ☐ The second disposition was an involuntary conversion where the threat of conversion occurred after the first disposition.
  d ☐ The second disposition occurred after the death of the original seller or buyer.
  e ☐ It can be established to the satisfaction of the Internal Revenue Service that tax avoidance was not a principal purpose for either of the dispositions. If this box is checked, attach an explanation. See instructions.

30	Selling price of property sold by related party	30
31	Enter contract price from line 18 for year of first sale	31
32	Enter the **smaller** of line 30 or line 31	32
33	Total payments received by the end of your 1992 tax year. Add lines 22 and 23	33
34	Subtract line 33 from line 32. If zero or less, enter -0-	34
35	Multiply line 34 by the gross profit percentage on line 19 for year of first sale	35
36	Part of line 35 that is ordinary income under recapture rules. See instructions	36
37	Subtract line 36 from line 35. Enter here and on Schedule D or Form 4797. See instructions	37

For Paperwork Reduction Act Notice, see separate instructions.   Cat. No. 13601R   Form **6252** (1992)

1993 form not available at press time.

Copyright © 1994 by Harcourt Brace & Company. All rights reserved.

Chapter 6 Problem 27   Name _____   6-59

Form 2119
Department of the Treasury
Internal Revenue Service

Sale of Your Home
▶ Attach to Form 1040 for year of sale.
▶ See separate instructions.   ▶ Please print or type.

OMB No. 1545-0072
1993
Attachment Sequence No. 20

Your first name and initial. If a joint return, also give spouse's name and initial.   Last name | Your social security number

Fill in Your Address Only If You Are Filing This Form by Itself and Not With Your Tax Return
Present address (no., street, and apt. no., rural route, or P.O. box no. if mail is not delivered to street address) | Spouse's social security number
City, town or post office, state, and ZIP code

Part I   General Information

1. Date your former main home was sold (month, day, year) .... ▶   1 ___/___/___
2. Have you bought or built a new main home? ....   ☐ Yes ☐ No
3. Is or was any part of either main home rented out or used for business? If "Yes," see instructions   ☐ Yes ☐ No

Part II   Gain on Sale—Do not include amounts you deduct as moving expenses.

4. Selling price of home. Do not include personal property items you sold with your home ..   4
5. Expense of sale (see instructions)   5
6. Amount realized. Subtract line 5 from line 4   6
7. Adjusted basis of home sold (see instructions)   7
8. Gain on sale. Subtract line 7 from line 6   8

Is line 8 more than zero?
— Yes ▶ If line 2 is "Yes," you **must** go to Part III or Part IV, whichever applies. If line 2 is "No," go to line 9.
— No ▶ **Stop** and attach this form to your return.

9. If you haven't replaced your home, do you plan to do so within the **replacement period** (see instructions)? ☐ Yes ☐ No
   - If line 9 is "Yes," stop here, attach this form to your return, and see **Additional Filing Requirements** in the instructions.
   - If line 9 is "No," you **must** go to Part III or Part IV, whichever applies.

Part III   One-Time Exclusion of Gain for People Age 55 or Older—By completing this part, you are electing to take the one-time exclusion (see instructions). If you are not electing to take the exclusion, go to Part IV now.

10. Who was age 55 or older on the date of sale? .... ☐ You ☐ Your spouse ☐ Both of you
11. Did the person who was age 55 or older own and use the property as his or her main home for a total of at least 3 years (except for short absences) of the 5-year period before the sale? If "No," go to Part IV now .. ☐ Yes ☐ No
12. At the time of sale, who owned the home? .... ☐ You ☐ Your spouse ☐ Both of you
13. Social security number of spouse at the time of sale if you had a different spouse from the one above. If you were not married at the time of sale, enter "None" ....▶   13
14. **Exclusion.** Enter the **smaller** of line 8 or $125,000 ($62,500 if married filing separate return). Then, go to line 15   14

Part IV   Adjusted Sales Price, Taxable Gain, and Adjusted Basis of New Home

15. If line 14 is blank, enter the amount from line 8. Otherwise, subtract line 14 from line 8 ..   15
    - If line 15 is zero, stop and attach this form to your return.
    - If line 15 is more than zero and line 2 is "Yes," go to line 16 now.
    - If you are reporting this sale on the installment method, stop and see the instructions.
    - All others, stop and **enter the amount from line 15 on Schedule D, col. (g), line 4 or line 12.**
16. Fixing-up expenses (see instructions for time limits)   16
17. If line 14 is blank, enter amount from line 16. Otherwise, add lines 14 and 16   17
18. **Adjusted sales price.** Subtract line 17 from line 6   18
19a. Date you moved into new home (month, day, year) ▶ ___/___/___ b Cost of new home   19b
20. Subtract line 19b from line 18. If zero or less, enter -0-   20
21. **Taxable gain.** Enter the **smaller** of line 15 or line 20   21
    - If line 21 is zero, go to line 22 and attach this form to your return.
    - If you are reporting this sale on the installment method, see the line 15 instructions and go to line 22.
    - All others, **enter the amount from line 21 on Schedule D, col. (g), line 4 or line 12, and go to line 22.**
22. **Postponed gain.** Subtract line 21 from line 15   22
23. **Adjusted basis of new home.** Subtract line 22 from line 19b   23

Sign Here Only If You Are Filing This Form by Itself and Not With Your Tax Return
Under penalties of perjury, I declare that I have examined this form, including attachments, and to the best of my knowledge and belief, it is true, correct, and complete.
▶ Your signature _____ Date _____ ▶ Spouse's signature _____ Date _____
If a joint return, both must sign.

For Paperwork Reduction Act Notice, see separate instructions.   Cat. No. 11710J   Form **2119** (1993)

Printed on recycled paper

Copyright © 1994 by Harcourt Brace & Company. All rights reserved.

Comprehensive Tax Return Problem 3
Form 1040, Schedules B & D, Form 2119, Form 2441, and Form 6252

Myra S. Granger, age 32, is a widow who provides all of the support of her five-year-old son Kevin. Myra and Kevin live at 1108 Wintergreen Street, Cheney, Washington 99004. Myra's social security number is 501-65-4432, and Kevin's is 455-98-9098. Myra's husband Al died in 1992, and Myra will file her 1993 return as a qualifying widow. She does not elect to contribute to the presidential election campaign fund.

Myra is an office manager with Hecht's Department Stores. Her 1993 Form W-2 disclosed the following:

Gross salary	$44,700
Federal income tax withholdings	7,105
State income tax witholdings	946
FICA taxes paid	3,420

In addition to her salary, Myra had several property transactions during 1993. Statements from her broker indicate that she sold the following stock and bond investments in 1993:

- 100 shares of Wilson Company common stock were sold on 3/2/93 for $4,300. Myra had originally purchased the shares on 2/12/92 for $6,400.

- 50 shares of Buy Common preferred stock were sold on 3/4/93 for $8,950. Myra's late husband Al had purchased the shares on 4/1/78 for $1,350, and he willed the shares to Myra. The shares were worth $6,340 on 11/2/92, the date of Al's death.

- 60 shares of Sears, Inc., common stock were sold on 6/3/93 for $8,600. Myra had received the shares as a gift from her father on 8/1/92, when they were worth $11,240. Her father had originally paid $10,100 for the shares on 4/3/88.

In addition, Myra sold three other assets in 1993. On 7/2/93, she sold one of the two family automobiles for $6,500. The car was originally purchased on 3/4/87 for $11,200.

On 11/4/93, Myra sold her personal residence for $172,400. She had originally acquired the residence in 1978 (prior to her marriage to Al) for $64,000. Myra paid $600 to have the house cleaned two weeks prior to the sale, and she paid a $3,840 commission on the sale. Myra purchased a smaller residence on 11/6/93 for $138,600, and she occupied the new residence on the same day.

Myra also separately sold ten acres of land on a five-year installment contract on 6/1/93. The land was originally acquired as an investment on 8/7/81 for $20,000, and she sold land for a total consideration of $33,000, payable as follows: $3,000 down payment on 6/1/93, and the balance to be paid in ten semiannual payments of $3,000 plus 10% simple interest on the unpaid balance, beginning on 12/1/93. Myra incurred $460 of selling expenses on the sale. She received the down payment of $3,000 on 6/1/93 and the first payment of $4,500 ($3,000 principal and $1,500 interest) on 12/1/93.

Other than the state income tax withholdings, Myra's only itemized deductions for 1993 consist of $1,200 in property taxes, $830 in mortgage interest, and $300 of contributions. During 1993 she paid Helen Trough, a neighbor, a total of $2,740 to care for her son Kevin while she worked. Helen lives at 1105 Wintergreen in Cheney, and her social security number is 362-32-1244.

REQUIRED: Prepare a Form 1040 for Myra S. Granger, with accompanying Schedules B and D and Forms 2119, 2441, and 6252.

Comprehensive Tax Return Problem 3   Name _____   6-63

Form 1040 — Department of the Treasury—Internal Revenue Service
U.S. Individual Income Tax Return 1993
IRS Use Only—Do not write or staple in this space
For the year Jan. 1–Dec. 31, 1993, or other tax year beginning _____, 1993, ending _____, 19___
OMB No. 1545-0074

Label (See instructions on page 12.) Use the IRS label. Otherwise, please print or type.

- Your first name and initial | Last name | Your social security number
- If a joint return, spouse's first name and initial | Last name | Spouse's social security number
- Home address (number and street). If you have a P.O. box, see page 12. | Apt. no.
- City, town or post office, state, and ZIP code. If you have a foreign address, see page 12.

For Privacy Act and Paperwork Reduction Act Notice, see page 4.

Presidential Election Campaign (See page 12.)
- Do you want $3 to go to this fund? .... Yes / No
- If a joint return, does your spouse want $3 to go to this fund? .... Yes / No

Note: Checking "Yes" will not change your tax or reduce your refund.

Filing Status (See page 12.) Check only one box.

1. ☐ Single
2. ☐ Married filing joint return (even if only one had income)
3. ☐ Married filing separate return. Enter spouse's social security no. above and full name here. ▶ _____
4. ☐ Head of household (with qualifying person). (See page 13.) If the qualifying person is a child but not your dependent, enter this child's name here. ▶ _____
5. ☐ Qualifying widow(er) with dependent child (year spouse died ▶ 19___). (See page 13.)

Exemptions (See page 13.)

6a ☐ **Yourself.** If your parent (or someone else) can claim you as a dependent on his or her tax return, **do not** check box 6a. But be sure to check the box on line 33b on page 2.
No. of boxes checked on 6a and 6b ____

b ☐ **Spouse** ....

c **Dependents:**

(1) Name (first, initial, and last name)	(2) Check if under age 1	(3) If age 1 or older, dependent's social security number	(4) Dependent's relationship to you	(5) No. of months lived in your home in 1993

If more than six dependents, see page 14.

No. of your children on 6c who:
- lived with you ____
- didn't live with you due to divorce or separation (see page 15) ____

Dependents on 6c not entered above ____

d If your child didn't live with you but is claimed as your dependent under a pre-1985 agreement, check here ▶ ☐
e Total number of exemptions claimed

Add numbers entered on lines above ▶ ____

Income

Attach Copy B of your Forms W-2, W-2G, and 1099-R here.

If you did not get a W-2, see page 10.

If you are attaching a check or money order, put it on top of any Forms W-2, W-2G, or 1099-R.

7   Wages, salaries, tips, etc. Attach Form(s) W-2 .... **7**
8a Taxable interest income (see page 16). Attach Schedule B if over $400 .... **8a**
 b Tax-exempt interest (see page 17). DON'T include on line 8a **8b** |____|
9   Dividend income. Attach Schedule B if over $400 .... **9**
10 Taxable refunds, credits, or offsets of state and local income taxes (see page 17) . **10**
11 Alimony received **11**
12 Business income or (loss). Attach Schedule C or C-EZ **12**
13 Capital gain or (loss). Attach Schedule D **13**
14 Capital gain distributions not reported on line 13 (see page 17) **14**
15 Other gains or (losses). Attach Form 4797 .... **15**
16a Total IRA distributions . **16a** |____| b Taxable amount (see page 18) **16b**
17a Total pensions and annuities **17a** |____| b Taxable amount (see page 18) **17b**
18 Rental real estate, royalties, partnerships, S corporations, trusts, etc. Attach Schedule E **18**
19 Farm income or (loss). Attach Schedule F **19**
20 Unemployment compensation (see page 19) **20**
21a Social security benefits **21a** |____| b Taxable amount (see page 19) **21b**
22 Other income. List type and amount—see page 20 .... **22**
23 Add the amounts in the far right column for lines 7 through 22. This is your **total income** ▶ **23**

Adjustments to Income (See page 20.)

24a Your IRA deduction (see page 20) **24a**
 b Spouse's IRA deduction (see page 20) **24b**
25 One-half of self-employment tax (see page 21) ... **25**
26 Self-employed health insurance deduction (see page 22) **26**
27 Keogh retirement plan and self-employed SEP deduction **27**
28 Penalty on early withdrawal of savings **28**
29 Alimony paid. Recipient's SSN ▶ _____   **29**
30 Add lines 24a through 29. These are your **total adjustments** .... ▶ **30**

Adjusted Gross Income

31 Subtract line 30 from line 23. This is your **adjusted gross income**. If this amount is less than $23,050 and a child lived with you, see page EIC-1 to find out if you can claim the "Earned Income Credit" on line 56 .... ▶ **31**

Cat. No. 11320B   Form **1040** (1993)

Copyright © 1994 by Harcourt Brace & Company. All rights reserved.

Form 1040 (1993) Page 2

Tax Computation (See page 23.)	32	Amount from line 31 (adjusted gross income)	32
	33a	Check if: ☐ **You** were 65 or older, ☐ Blind; ☐ **Spouse** was 65 or older, ☐ Blind. Add the number of boxes checked above and enter the total here ▶ 33a	
	b	If your parent (or someone else) can claim you as a dependent, check here ▶ 33b ☐	
	c	If you are married filing separately and your spouse itemizes deductions or you are a dual-status alien, see page 24 and check here . . . . . . ▶ 33c ☐	
	34	Enter the larger of your: **Itemized deductions** from Schedule A, line 26, **OR** **Standard deduction** shown below for your filing status. **But if you checked any box on line 33a or b**, go to page 24 to find your standard deduction. If you checked **box 33c,** your standard deduction is zero. • Single—$3,700 • Head of household—$5,450 • Married filing jointly or Qualifying widow(er)—$6,200 • Married filing separately—$3,100	34
	35	Subtract line 34 from line 32	35
	36	If line 32 is $81,350 or less, multiply $2,350 by the total number of exemptions claimed on line 6e. If line 32 is over $81,350, see the worksheet on page 25 for the amount to enter	36
If you want the IRS to figure your tax, see page 24.	37	**Taxable income.** Subtract line 36 from line 35. If line 36 is more than line 35, enter -0-	37
	38	Tax. Check if from **a** ☐ Tax Table, **b** ☐ Tax Rate Schedules, **c** ☐ Schedule D Tax Worksheet, or **d** ☐ Form 8615 (see page 25). Amount from Form(s) 8814 ▶ **e** _____	38
	39	Additional taxes (see page 25). Check if from **a** ☐ Form 4970 **b** ☐ Form 4972	39
	40	Add lines 38 and 39 ▶	40
Credits (See page 25.)	41	Credit for child and dependent care expenses. Attach Form 2441 — 41	
	42	Credit for the elderly or the disabled. Attach Schedule R . — 42	
	43	Foreign tax credit. Attach Form 1116 — 43	
	44	Other credits (see page 26). Check if from **a** ☐ Form 3800 **b** ☐ Form 8396 **c** ☐ Form 8801 **d** ☐ Form (specify) _____ — 44	
	45	Add lines 41 through 44	45
	46	Subtract line 45 from line 40. If line 45 is more than line 40, enter -0- ▶	46
Other Taxes	47	Self-employment tax. Attach Schedule SE. Also, see line 25	47
	48	Alternative minimum tax. Attach Form 6251	48
	49	Recapture taxes (see page 26). Check if from **a** ☐ Form 4255 **b** ☐ Form 8611 **c** ☐ Form 8828	49
	50	Social security and Medicare tax on tip income not reported to employer. Attach Form 4137	50
	51	Tax on qualified retirement plans, including IRAs. If required, attach Form 5329	51
	52	Advance earned income credit payments from Form W-2	52
	53	Add lines 46 through 52. This is your **total tax** ▶	53
Payments Attach Forms W-2, W-2G, and 1099-R on the front.	54	Federal income tax withheld. If any is from Form(s) 1099, check ▶ ☐ — 54	
	55	1993 estimated tax payments and amount applied from 1992 return . — 55	
	56	**Earned income credit.** Attach Schedule EIC — 56	
	57	Amount paid with Form 4868 (extension request) — 57	
	58a	Excess social security, Medicare, and RRTA tax withheld (see page 28) . — 58a	
	b	Deferral of additional 1993 taxes. Attach Form 8841 — 58b	
	59	Other payments (see page 28). Check if from **a** ☐ Form 2439 **b** ☐ Form 4136 — 59	
	60	Add lines 54 through 59. These are your **total payments** ▶	60
Refund or Amount You Owe	61	If line 60 is more than line 53, subtract line 53 from line 60. This is the amount you **OVERPAID** ▶	61
	62	Amount of line 61 you want **REFUNDED TO YOU** ▶	62
	63	Amount of line 61 you want **APPLIED TO YOUR 1994 ESTIMATED TAX** ▶ 63	
	64	If line 53 is more than line 60, subtract line 60 from line 53. This is the **AMOUNT YOU OWE.** For details on how to pay, including what to write on your payment, see page 29	64
	65	Estimated tax penalty (see page 29). Also include on line 64 — 65	

Sign Here
Keep a copy of this return for your records.

Under penalties of perjury, I declare that I have examined this return and accompanying schedules and statements, and to the best of my knowledge and belief, they are true, correct, and complete. Declaration of preparer (other than taxpayer) is based on all information of which preparer has any knowledge

▶ Your signature | Date | Your occupation

▶ Spouse's signature. If a joint return, BOTH must sign. | Date | Spouse's occupation

Paid Preparer's Use Only

Preparer's signature ▶	Date	Check if self-employed ☐	Preparer's social security no.
Firm's name (or yours if self-employed) and address ▶		E.I. No.	
		ZIP code	

Comprehensive Tax Return Problem 3 Name _____ 6-65

Schedules A&B (Form 1040) 1993
OMB No. 1545-0074 Page **2**

Name(s) shown on Form 1040. Do not enter name and social security number if shown on other side.
Your social security number

Schedule B—Interest and Dividend Income

Attachment Sequence No **08**

Part I
Interest Income

(See pages 16 and B-1.)

Note: If you received a Form 1099-INT, Form 1099-OID, or substitute statement from a brokerage firm, list the firm's name as the payer and enter the total interest shown on that form.

Note: *If you had over $400 in taxable interest income, you must also complete Part III.*

Interest Income	Amount
1 List name of payer. If any interest is from a seller-financed mortgage and the buyer used the property as a personal residence, see page B-1 and list this interest first. Also show that buyer's social security number and address ▶	1

2 Add the amounts on line 1	2
3 Excludable interest on series EE U.S. savings bonds issued after 1989 from Form 8815, line 14. You MUST attach Form 8815 to Form 1040	3
4 Subtract line 3 from line 2. Enter the result here and on Form 1040, line 8a ▶	4

Part II
Dividend Income

(See pages 17 and B-1.)

Note: If you received a Form 1099-DIV or substitute statement from a brokerage firm, list the firm's name as the payer and enter the total dividends shown on that form.

Note: *If you had over $400 in gross dividends and/or other distributions on stock, you must also complete Part III.*

Dividend Income	Amount
5 List name of payer. Include gross dividends and/or other distributions on stock here. Any capital gain distributions and nontaxable distributions will be deducted on lines 7 and 8 ▶	5

6 Add the amounts on line 5		6
7 Capital gain distributions. Enter here and on Schedule D* .	7	
8 Nontaxable distributions. (See the inst. for Form 1040, line 9.)	8	
9 Add lines 7 and 8		9
10 Subtract line 9 from line 6. Enter the result here and on Form 1040, line 9 ▶		10

If you received capital gain distributions but do not need Schedule D to report any other gains or losses, see the instructions for Form 1040, lines 13 and 14.

Part III
Foreign Accounts and Trusts

(See page B-2.)

If you had over $400 of interest or dividends OR had a foreign account or were a grantor of, or a transferor to, a foreign trust, you must complete this part.

	Yes	No
11a At any time during 1993, did you have an interest in or a signature or other authority over a financial account in a foreign country, such as a bank account, securities account, or other financial account? See page B-2 for exceptions and filing requirements for Form TD F 90-22.1 . . .		
b If "Yes," enter the name of the foreign country ▶		
12 Were you the grantor of, or transferor to, a foreign trust that existed during 1993, whether or not you have any beneficial interest in it? If "Yes," you may have to file Form 3520, 3520-A, or 926 .		

For Paperwork Reduction Act Notice, see Form 1040 instructions.
Schedule B (Form 1040) 1993

Copyright © 1994 by Harcourt Brace & Company. All rights reserved.

Comprehensive Tax Return Problem 3   Name_____   6-67

SCHEDULE D (Form 1040)	Capital Gains and Losses	OMB No. 1545-0074
Department of the Treasury Internal Revenue Service	▶ Attach to Form 1040. ▶ See Instructions for Schedule D (Form 1040). ▶ Use lines 20 and 22 for more space to list transactions for lines 1 and 9.	**1993** Attachment Sequence No. **12**

Name(s) shown on Form 1040 | Your social security number

Part I — Short-Term Capital Gains and Losses—Assets Held One Year or Less

(a) Description of property (Example: 100 sh. XYZ Co.)	(b) Date acquired (Mo., day, yr.)	(c) Date sold (Mo., day, yr.)	(d) Sales price (see page D-3)	(e) Cost or other basis (see page D-3)	(f) LOSS If (e) is more than (d), subtract (d) from (e)	(g) GAIN If (d) is more than (e), subtract (e) from (d)
1						

2 Enter your short-term totals, if any, from line 21 . . . . **2**
3 **Total short-term sales price amounts.** Add column (d) of lines 1 and 2 . . . **3**
4 Short-term gain from Forms 2119 and 6252, and short-term gain or (loss) from Forms 4684, 6781, and 8824 . . . . **4**
5 Net short-term gain or (loss) from partnerships, S corporations, and fiduciaries from Schedule(s) K-1 . . . . **5**
6 Short-term capital loss carryover from 1992 Schedule D, line 38 . . . . **6**
7 Add lines 1, 2, and 4 through 6, in columns (f) and (g) . . . . **7** (|)
8 **Net short-term capital gain or (loss).** Combine columns (f) and (g) of line 7 . . . . **8**

Part II — Long-Term Capital Gains and Losses—Assets Held More Than One Year

9						

10 Enter your long-term totals, if any, from line 23 . . . . **10**
11 **Total long-term sales price amounts.** Add column (d) of lines 9 and 10 . . . **11**
12 Gain from Form 4797; long-term gain from Forms 2119, 2439, and 6252; and long-term gain or (loss) from Forms 4684, 6781, and 8824 . . . . **12**
13 Net long-term gain or (loss) from partnerships, S corporations, and fiduciaries from Schedule(s) K-1 . . . . **13**
14 Capital gain distributions **14**
15 Long-term capital loss carryover from 1992 Schedule D, line 45 . . . . **15**
16 Add lines 9, 10, and 12 through 15, in columns (f) and (g) . . . . **16** (|)
17 **Net long-term capital gain or (loss).** Combine columns (f) and (g) of line 16 . . . . **17**

Part III — Summary of Parts I and II

18 Combine lines 8 and 17. If a loss, go to line 19. If a gain, enter the gain on Form 1040, line 13.
Note: *If both lines 17 and 18 are gains, see the **Schedule D Tax Worksheet** on page D-4* . . **18**
19 If line 18 is a (loss), enter here and as a (loss) on Form 1040, line 13, the **smaller** of these losses:
  a The (loss) on line 18; **or**
  b ($3,000) or, if married filing separately, ($1,500) . . . . **19** (|)
Note: *See the **Capital Loss Carryover Worksheet** on page D-4 if the loss on line 18 exceeds the loss on line 19 **or** if Form 1040, line 35, is a loss.*

For Paperwork Reduction Act Notice, see Form 1040 instructions.   Cat. No. 11338H   Schedule D (Form 1040) 1993

Copyright © 1994 by Harcourt Brace & Company. All rights reserved.

Schedule D (Form 1040) 1993   Attachment Sequence No. **12**   Page **2**

Name(s) shown on Form 1040. Do not enter name and social security number if shown on other side.   Your social security number

Part IV — Short-Term Capital Gains and Losses—Assets Held One Year or Less (Continuation of Part I)

(a) Description of property (Example: 100 sh. XYZ Co.)	(b) Date acquired (Mo., day, yr.)	(c) Date sold (Mo., day, yr.)	(d) Sales price (see page D-3)	(e) Cost or other basis (see page D-3)	(f) LOSS If (e) is more than (d), subtract (d) from (e)	(g) GAIN If (d) is more than (e), subtract (e) from (d)
20						
21 Short-term totals. Add columns (d), (f), and (g) of line 20. Enter here and on line 2 . **21**						

Part V — Long-Term Capital Gains and Losses—Assets Held More Than One Year (Continuation of Part II)

(a) Description of property	(b) Date acquired	(c) Date sold	(d) Sales price	(e) Cost or other basis	(f) LOSS	(g) GAIN
22						
23 Long-term totals. Add columns (d), (f), and (g) of line 22. Enter here and on line 10 . **23**						

Copyright © 1994 by Harcourt Brace & Company. All rights reserved.

Comprehensive Tax Return Problem 3   Name_____   6-69

Form 2119
Department of the Treasury
Internal Revenue Service

Sale of Your Home

▶ Attach to Form 1040 for year of sale.
▶ See separate instructions.   ▶ Please print or type.

OMB No. 1545-0072

1993

Attachment Sequence No. 20

Your first name and initial. If a joint return, also give spouse's name and initial.   Last name   Your social security number

Fill in Your Address Only If You Are Filing This Form by Itself and Not With Your Tax Return

Present address (no., street, and apt. no., rural route, or P.O. box no. if mail is not delivered to street address)   Spouse's social security number

City, town or post office, state, and ZIP code

Part I General Information

1 Date your former main home was sold (month, day, year) . . . . ▶ **1** __/__/__
2 Have you bought or built a new main home? . . . . ☐ Yes ☐ No
3 Is or was any part of either main home rented out or used for business? If "Yes," see instructions . . ☐ Yes ☐ No

Part II Gain on Sale—Do not include amounts you deduct as moving expenses.

4 Selling price of home. Do not include personal property items you sold with your home . . **4**
5 Expense of sale (see instructions) **5**
6 Amount realized. Subtract line 5 from line 4 . . . . **6**
7 Adjusted basis of home sold (see instructions) **7**
8 **Gain on sale.** Subtract line 7 from line 6 . . . . **8**

Is line 8 more than zero?

— **Yes** ▶ If line 2 is "Yes," you **must** go to Part III or Part IV, whichever applies. If line 2 is "No," go to line 9.

— **No** ▶ **Stop** and attach this form to your return.

9 If you haven't replaced your home, do you plan to do so within the **replacement period** (see instructions)? ☐ Yes ☐ No
 • If line 9 is "Yes," stop here, attach this form to your return, and see **Additional Filing Requirements** in the instructions.
 • If line 9 is "No," you **must** go to Part III or Part IV, whichever applies.

Part III One-Time Exclusion of Gain for People Age 55 or Older—By completing this part, you are electing to take the one-time exclusion (see instructions). If you are not electing to take the exclusion, go to Part IV now.

10 Who was age 55 or older on the date of sale? . . . . ☐ You ☐ Your spouse ☐ Both of you
11 Did the person who was age 55 or older own and use the property as his or her main home for a total of at least 3 years (except for short absences) of the 5-year period before the sale? If "No," go to Part IV now . . ☐ Yes ☐ No
12 At the time of sale, who owned the home? . . . . ☐ You ☐ Your spouse ☐ Both of you
13 Social security number of spouse at the time of sale if you had a different spouse from the one above. If you were not married at the time of sale, enter "None" . . . . ▶ **13**
14 **Exclusion.** Enter the **smaller** of line 8 or $125,000 ($62,500 if married filing separate return). Then, go to line 15 . . . . **14**

Part IV Adjusted Sales Price, Taxable Gain, and Adjusted Basis of New Home

15 If line 14 is blank, enter the amount from line 8. Otherwise, subtract line 14 from line 8 . . **15**
 • If line 15 is zero, stop and attach this form to your return.
 • If line 15 is more than zero and line 2 is "Yes," go to line 16 now.
 • If you are reporting this sale on the installment method, stop and see the instructions.
 • All others, stop and **enter the amount from line 15 on Schedule D, col. (g), line 4 or line 12.**
16 Fixing-up expenses (see instructions for time limits) **16**
17 If line 14 is blank, enter amount from line 16. Otherwise, add lines 14 and 16 . . . . . **17**
18 **Adjusted sales price.** Subtract line 17 from line 6 . . . . **18**
19a Date you moved into new home (month, day, year) ▶ __/__/__ b Cost of new home **19b**
20 Subtract line 19b from line 18. If zero or less, enter -0- **20**
21 **Taxable gain.** Enter the **smaller** of line 15 or line 20 . . . . **21**
 • If line 21 is zero, go to line 22 and attach this form to your return.
 • If you are reporting this sale on the installment method, see the line 15 instructions and go to line 22.
 • All others, **enter the amount from line 21 on Schedule D, col. (g), line 4 or line 12,** and go to line 22.
22 Postponed gain. Subtract line 21 from line 15 . . . . **22**
23 **Adjusted basis of new home.** Subtract line 22 from line 19b **23**

Sign Here Only If You Are Filing This Form by Itself and Not With Your Tax Return

Under penalties of perjury, I declare that I have examined this form, including attachments, and to the best of my knowledge and belief, it is true, correct, and complete.

Your signature   Date   Spouse's signature   Date

▶ _____   ▶ _____

If a joint return, both must sign.

For Paperwork Reduction Act Notice, see separate instructions.   Cat. No. 11710J   Form **2119** (1993)

Printed on recycled paper

Copyright © 1994 by Harcourt Brace & Company. All rights reserved.

6-70 Name _____ Comprehensive Tax Return Problem 3

Form 2441
Department of the Treasury
Internal Revenue Service

Child and Dependent Care Expenses

▶ Attach to Form 1040.
▶ See separate instructions.

OMB No. 1545-0068

1993

Attachment Sequence No. **21**

Name(s) shown on Form 1040 | Your social security number

You need to understand the following terms to complete this form: **Dependent Care Benefits, Earned Income, Qualified Expenses,** and **Qualifying Person(s)**. See **Important Terms** on page 1 of the Form 2441 instructions. Also, if you had a child born in 1993 and line 32 of Form 1040 is less than $23,050, see **A Change To Note** on page 2 of the instructions.

Part I — Persons or Organizations Who Provided the Care—You must complete this part.
(If you need more space, use the bottom of page 2.)

1	(a) Care provider's name	(b) Address (number, street, apt. no., city, state, and ZIP code)	(c) Identifying number (SSN or EIN)	(d) Amount paid (see instructions)

2 Add the amounts in column (d) of line 1 . . . . **2** ☐

3 Enter the number of **qualifying persons** cared for in 1993 . . . . ▶ ☐

Did you receive **dependent care benefits?**
— **NO** ▶ Complete only Part II below.
— **YES** ▶ Complete Part III on the back now.

Part II — Credit for Child and Dependent Care Expenses

4 Enter the amount of **qualified expenses** you incurred and paid in 1993. DO NOT enter more than $2,400 for one qualifying person or $4,800 for two or more persons. If you completed Part III, enter the amount from line 25 . . . . **4**

5 Enter YOUR **earned income** **5**

6 If married filing a joint return, enter YOUR SPOUSE'S earned income (if student or disabled, see instructions); **all others,** enter the amount from line 5 . . . . **6**

7 Enter the **smallest** of line 4, 5, or 6 . . . . **7**

8 Enter the amount from Form 1040, line 32 . . . . **8**

9 Enter on line 9 the decimal amount shown below that applies to the amount on line 8

If line 8 is—		Decimal amount is	If line 8 is—		Decimal amount is
Over	But not over		Over	But not over	
$0	10,000	.30	$20,000	22,000	.24
10,000	12,000	.29	22,000	24,000	.23
12,000	14,000	.28	24,000	26,000	.22
14,000	16,000	.27	26,000	28,000	.21
16,000	18,000	.26	28,000	No limit	.20
18,000	20,000	.25			

9 X .

10 Multiply **line 7** by the decimal amount on line 9. Enter the result. Then, see the instructions for the amount of credit to enter on Form 1040, line 41 . . . . **10**

Caution: *If you paid $50 or more in a calendar quarter to a person who worked in your home, you must file an employment tax return. Get* **Form 942** *for details.*

For Paperwork Reduction Act Notice, see separate instructions. Cat. No. 11862M Form **2441** (1993)

Copyright © 1994 by Harcourt Brace & Company. All rights reserved.

Comprehensive Tax Return Problem 3 Name _____ 6-71

Form 6252
Department of the Treasury
Internal Revenue Service

Installment Sale Income
► See separate instructions. ► Attach to your tax return.
Use a separate form for each sale or other disposition of property on the installment method.

OMB No. 1545-0228
1992
Attachment Sequence No. 79

Name(s) shown on return

Identifying number

1 Description of property ► ....
2a Date acquired (month, day, and year) ► __/__/__ b Date sold (month, day, and year) ► __/__/__
3 Was the property sold to a related party after May 14, 1980? See instructions . . . . ☐ Yes ☐ No
4 If the answer to question 3 is "Yes," was the property a marketable security? If "Yes," complete Part III. If "No," complete Part III for the year of sale and for 2 years after the year of sale . . . . ☐ Yes ☐ No

Part I Gross Profit and Contract Price. Complete this part for the year of sale only.

5	Selling price including mortgages and other debts. Do not include interest whether stated or unstated	5	
6	Mortgages and other debts the buyer assumed or took the property subject to, but not new mortgages the buyer got from a bank or other source	6	
7	Subtract line 6 from line 5	7	
8	Cost or other basis of property sold	8	
9	Depreciation allowed or allowable	9	
10	Adjusted basis. Subtract line 9 from line 8 .	10	
11	Commissions and other expenses of sale . .	11	
12	Income recapture from Form 4797, Part III. See instructions	12	
13	Add lines 10, 11, and 12	13	
14	Subtract line 13 from line 5. If zero or less, do not complete the rest of this form	14	
15	If the property described on line 1 above was your main home, enter the total of lines 16 and 24 from Form 2119. Otherwise, enter -0-	15	
16	**Gross profit.** Subtract line 15 from line 14	16	
17	Subtract line 13 from line 6. If zero or less, enter -0-	17	
18	**Contract price.** Add line 7 and line 17	18	

Part II Installment Sale Income. Complete this part for the year of sale and any year you receive a payment or have certain debts you must treat as a payment on installment obligations.

19	Gross profit percentage. Divide line 16 by line 18. For years after the year of sale, see instructions	19	
20	**For year of sale only**—Enter amount from line 17 above; otherwise, enter -0-	20	
21	Payments received during year. See instructions. Do not include interest whether stated or unstated	21	
22	Add lines 20 and 21	22	
23	Payments received in prior years. See instructions. Do not include interest whether stated or unstated	23	
24	**Installment sale income.** Multiply line 22 by line 19	24	
25	Part of line 24 that is ordinary income under recapture rules. See instructions	25	
26	Subtract line 25 from line 24. Enter here and on Schedule D or Form 4797. See instructions	26	

Part III Related Party Installment Sale Income. Do not complete if you received the final payment this tax year.

27 Name, address, and taxpayer identifying number of related party ....
....
28 Did the related party, during this tax year, resell or dispose of the property ("second disposition")? . . . . ☐ Yes ☐ No
29 If the answer to question 28 is "Yes," complete lines 30 through 37 below unless one of the following conditions is met. Check only the box that applies.
  a ☐ The second disposition was more than 2 years after the first disposition (other than dispositions of marketable securities). If this box is checked, enter the date of disposition (month, day, year) ► __/__/__
  b ☐ The first disposition was a sale or exchange of stock to the issuing corporation.
  c ☐ The second disposition was an involuntary conversion where the threat of conversion occurred after the first disposition.
  d ☐ The second disposition occurred after the death of the original seller or buyer.
  e ☐ It can be established to the satisfaction of the Internal Revenue Service that tax avoidance was not a principal purpose for either of the dispositions. If this box is checked, attach an explanation. See instructions.

30	Selling price of property sold by related party	30	
31	Enter contract price from line 18 for year of first sale	31	
32	Enter the **smaller** of line 30 or line 31	32	
33	Total payments received by the end of your 1992 tax year. Add lines 22 and 23	33	
34	Subtract line 33 from line 32. If zero or less, enter -0-	34	
35	Multiply line 34 by the gross profit percentage on line 19 for year of first sale	35	
36	Part of line 35 that is ordinary income under recapture rules. See instructions	36	
37	Subtract line 36 from line 35. Enter here and on Schedule D or Form 4797. See instructions	37	

For Paperwork Reduction Act Notice, see separate instructions. Cat. No. 13601R Form **6252** (1992)
1993 form not available at press time.

Copyright © 1994 by Harcourt Brace & Company. All rights reserved.

CHAPTER 7

Special Tax Computations for Individuals

Over the years, some taxpayers have reduced their tax burden by using the tax laws to their advantage, while others have paid larger amounts due to certain features within these laws. Taxpayers were able to invest in assets known as "tax shelters," which enabled them to deduct losses for tax purposes when they experienced no real economic losses, thereby reducing the amount of tax owed. Other taxpayers would occasionally receive inordinately large amounts of income in a particular year. Since the tax rates increase as taxable income increases, these taxpayers would pay a larger tax than they would normally pay if this income had been spread over a number of years. For a number of years, such taxpayers were permitted to calculate the tax due under specific income-averaging provisions. Although these provisions were eliminated by the Tax Reform Act of 1986, Congress enacted other provisions designed to make the tax laws more equitable.

Several alternatives for computing taxable income and the tax due were included in the Tax Reform Act of 1986. Several of these alternatives are addressed in this chapter. Part I of the chapter deals with an alternative tax calculation—the alternative minimum tax, or AMT—which exacts a tax from taxpayers who pay little or no regular tax while having substantial amounts of economic income. This tax is based on a broader definition of taxable income to which an alternate tax rate structure is applied. While the AMT has been around for a number of years, the Tax Reform Act of 1986 made a number of changes in its structure, the Revenue Reconciliation Act of 1990 increased the AMT rate for individuals from 21 to 24%, and the Revenue Reconciliation Act of 1993 increased rates to 26% and 28% for individual taxpayers..

Part II of the chapter presents a special tax calculation used for lump-sum distributions from pension and profit-sharing plans, called five-year forward averaging. The main feature of this provision is that it permits taxpayers to calculate the tax *as if* one-fifth of the lump-sum distribution was received in each of five years instead of all being received in one year. However, the total tax, which is five times the tax on one-fifth the distribution, must be paid as part of the tax for the year in which the entire distribution is received.

Part III briefly describes the limitations on the deductibility of certain losses that affect individual taxpayers due to the passive loss rules. Taxpayers who do not materially participate in trades or businesses that incur losses may not be able to deduct the losses currently. Taxpayers with losses from rental properties are also subject to complex limitations on their deductibility.

Part IV discusses the various forms and procedures for obtaining extensions of time to file tax returns and for filing amended returns. In many instances, taxpayers may not have sufficient information to file the required tax returns by the due date, or they may have simply run out of time. Individual taxpayers can receive automatic four-month extensions to file their tax returns; they may also obtain an additional two months with sufficient reason. These extensions do not, however, permit an extension of time to pay the tax due. Also, if taxpayers discover an error or omission from a prior tax return, they can file an amended return within the statute of limitations to correct the error or omission.

Finally, the appendix to the chapter outlines some of the more common charges for interest and other penalties taxpayers may incur for underpayments of taxes and the interest the IRS must pay on monies owed the taxpayers.

I THE ALTERNATIVE MINIMUM TAX
(Code Sections 55, 56, 57, and 58)

For many social and economic reasons, certain items of income have been excluded and certain beneficial deductions included in the determination of taxable income. For some taxpayers, these tax benefits have greatly reduced the amount of tax due. To ensure that taxpayers, with substantial amounts of economic income pay some tax, Congress enacted the alternative minimum tax (AMT). The purpose of the AMT is to exact tax from persons who pay little or no regular tax. This tax is calculated using a broadly based concept of taxable income by omitting or modifying many of the tax benefits included in the determination of regular taxable income. This concept of alternative minimum taxable income (AMTI) is coupled with rates of 26% and 28% for individuals and 20% for corporations.

THE LAW

Sec. 55(a)—There is hereby imposed (in addition to any other tax imposed by the subtitle) a tax equal to the excess (if any) of—(1) the tentative minimum tax for the taxable years, over (2) the regular tax for the taxable year.
55(b)(1)(A)(i)—In the case of a taxpayer other than a corporation, the tentative minimum tax for the taxable year is the sum of—
   (I) 26 percent of so much of the taxable excess as does not exceed $175,000, plus
   (II) 28 percent of so much of the taxable excess as exceeds $175,000 . . .
(ii)—For purposes of clause (i), the term 'taxable excess' means so much of the alternative minimum taxable income for the taxable year as exceeds the exemption amount.

The AMT has taken a number of turns over the years and, in its present form, is generally effective in taxing individuals who might escape taxation. It does, however, require a number of complex calculations to convert regular taxable income to AMTI. The basic format for this conversion for either individuals or corporations is

	Regular taxable income
plus	Positive adjustments
less	Negative adjustments
plus	Tax preferences
	Tentative AMTI
less	Allowable exemption
	AMTI
times	AMTI tax rate
	Tentative minimum tax
less	Regular tax
	AMT

The adjustments, preferences, and exemptions will be discussed in that order at length in the following sections, using Example 1, presented below to illustrate many of the items.

One item that causes substantial confusion is the exact definition of the alternative minimum tax. Taxpayers who have relevant amounts of AMT adjustments and preferences must make two separate tax calculations—one for the regular tax and one for the AMT. Taxpayers will *always* pay the regular tax. If, however, the AMT calculation yields a tentative tax greater than the regular tax, only the amount in excess of the regular tax is defined as the AMT. If the tentative AMT is less than the regular tax, taxpayers must still pay the full regular tax. Thus, the AMT is paid only by taxpayers whose tentative AMT is greater than their regular tax. (See Figure 7-1.)

To determine AMTI, taxpayers must understand an extensive list of positive and negative adjustments to regular taxable income as well as the additions to regular taxable income for tax preferences. There are a number of adjustments that apply to non-corporate taxpayers only, while others apply to all taxpayers. One item, the accumulated current earnings adjustment (or the now-repealed book income adjustment) applies solely to corporate taxpayers, and will not be discussed here.

☑ **Example 1.** We will use the following example throughout the remaining discussion of the AMTI to illustrate the adjustments, preference items, and the exemptions that are calculated to convert regular taxable income to AMTI and to calculate the AMT.

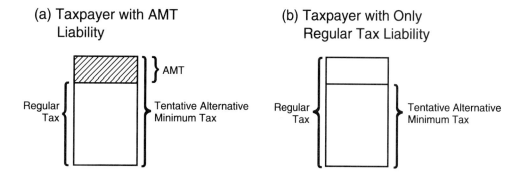

Figure 7-1 Alternative Minimum Tax

Completed Form 6251 presented in Figure 7-2 uses this information. However, we will also include additional examples to illustrate points not covered by this example.

Howard and Martha Jones have the following items of income and deduction for determining their tax for 1993:

Income

Salaries	
Martha	$ 65,000
Howard	135,000
Interest	23,000
Short-term capital gain	19,000
Sole proprietorship income	58,000

Deductions

Medical expense	$25,000
Interest—Qualified residential mortgage	7,700
Taxes—state and local	44,000
Contributions	
Cash	34,000
Tangible property	8,600
Miscellaneous	11,000

Neither Howard nor Martha is blind or 65 years of age. They have no dependents. The sole proprietorship income includes the following depreciation deductions:

    $20,000 ACRS on post-1986 property (ADS would be $8,000)
    $15,000 ACRS on pre-1987 realty (SL would be $5,000)*

The Jones' regular taxable income would be determined in the following manner:

Income Items

Salaries		$200,000
Interest income		23,000
Short-term capital gain		19,000
Sole proprietorship income		58,000
Adjusted gross income		$300,000
Itemized deductions		
Medical ($25,000 – 7.5% of AGI)	$ 2,500	
Qualified mortgage interest	7,700	
Taxes—state and local	44,000	
Contributions	42,600	
Miscellaneous ($11,000 – 2% of AGI)	5,000	
Total itemized deductions		($96,053) [1]
Personal exemptions		(0) [1]
TAXABLE INCOME		$203,947
REGULAR TAX LIABILITY (1993 joint rates)		$ 58,950

[1] Note: This calculation includes the limitation on itemized deductions for high-income taxpayers. Their itemized deductions are reduced by $5,747 [.03 (300,000 AGI – 108,450 MIN)]. Personal exemptions are completely phased out.

A completed Form 6251 calculating AMTI and the Jones' AMT is presented in Figure 7-2. It will be referred to throughout the following discussions.

---

*The alternative cost recovery system (ACRS), the alternative depreciation system (ADS) and straight-line (SL) depreciation are discussed in Chapter 8. They are included here for illustrative purposes only.

Form 6251 — Alternative Minimum Tax—Individuals

Form 6251
Department of the Treasury
Internal Revenue Service

Alternative Minimum Tax—Individuals
► See separate instructions.
► Attach to Form 1040 or Form 1040NR.

OMB No. 1545-0227
1993
Attachment Sequence No. 32

Name(s) shown on Form 1040: Howard & Martha Jones
Your social security number:

Part I — Adjustments and Preferences

#	Description	Amount
1	If you itemized deductions on Schedule A (Form 1040), go to line 2. If you did not itemize deductions, enter your standard deduction from Form 1040, line 34, and skip to line 6	
2	Medical and dental expenses. See instructions	2,500
3	Taxes. Enter the amount from Schedule A, line 8	44,000
4	Certain interest on a home mortgage not used to buy, build, or improve your home	
5	Miscellaneous itemized deductions. Enter the amount from Schedule A, line 24	5,000
6	Refund of taxes. Enter any tax refund from Form 1040, line 10 or 22	( )
7	Investment interest. Enter difference between regular tax and AMT deduction	
8	Post-1986 depreciation. Enter difference between regular tax and AMT depreciation	12,000
9	Adjusted gain or loss. Enter difference between AMT and regular tax gain or loss	
10	Incentive stock options. Enter excess of AMT income over regular tax income	
11	Passive activities. Enter difference between AMT and regular tax income or loss	
12	Beneficiaries of estates and trusts. Enter the amount from Schedule K-1 (Form 1041), line 8	
13	Tax-exempt interest from private activity bonds issued after 8/7/86	
14	Other. Enter the amount, if any, for each item and enter the total on line 14.	
	a Charitable contributions g Long-term contracts	
	b Circulation expenditures h Loss limitations	
	c Depletion i Mining costs	
	d Depreciation (pre-1987) 10,000 j Pollution control facilities	
	e Installment sales k Research and experimental	
	f Intangible drilling costs l Tax shelter farm activities	
	m Related adjustments	10,000
15	**Total Adjustments and Preferences.** Combine lines 1 through 14	73,500

Part II — Alternative Minimum Taxable Income

#	Description	Amount
16	Enter the amount from **Form 1040, line 35.** If less than zero, enter as a (loss)	203,947
17	Net operating loss deduction, if any, from Form 1040, line 22. Enter as a positive amount	
18	If Form 1040, line 32, is over $108,450 (over $54,225 if married filing separately), enter your itemized deductions limitation, if any, from line 9 of the worksheet for Schedule A, line 26	(5,747)
19	Combine lines 15 through 18	271,700
20	Alternative tax net operating loss deduction. See instructions	
21	**Alternative Minimum Taxable Income.** Subtract line 20 from line 19. (If married filing separately and line 21 is more than $165,000, see instructions.)	271,700

Part III — Exemption Amount and Alternative Minimum Tax

22 **Exemption Amount.** (If this form is for a child under age 14, see instructions.)

If your filing status is:	And line 21 is not over:	Enter on line 22:
Single or head of household	$112,500	$33,750
Married filing jointly or qualifying widow(er)	150,000	45,000
Married filing separately	75,000	22,500

If line 21 is **over** the amount shown above for your filing status, see instructions.

#	Description	Amount
22		14,575
23	Subtract line 22 from line 21. If zero or less, enter -0- here and on lines 26 and 28	257,125
24	If line 23 is $175,000 or less ($87,500 or less if married filing separately), multiply line 23 by 26% (.26). Otherwise, see instructions	68,495
25	Alternative minimum tax foreign tax credit. See instructions	—
26	Tentative minimum tax. Subtract line 25 from line 24	68,495
27	Enter your tax from Form 1040, line 38 (plus any amount from Form 4970 included on Form 1040, line 39), minus any foreign tax credit from Form 1040, line 43	58,950
28	**Alternative Minimum Tax.** (If this form is for a child under age 14, see instructions.) Subtract line 27 from line 26. If zero or less, enter -0-. Enter here and on Form 1040, line 48	9,545

For Paperwork Reduction Act Notice, see separate instructions.   Cat. No. 13600G   Form **6251** (1993)

*Taxable income *before* personal exemptions.

Figure 7-2 Form 6251

ADJUSTMENTS

Adjustments to regular taxable income to determine AMTI may be both positive and negative; that is, in one year a positive adjustment may be required, while in a later year the effect may reverse and require a negative adjustment. *Adjustments* differ from *preferences* in this regard since preference items are only additions to regular income. A preference item never results in a deduction from regular income to determine AMTI.

Note that adjustments made to regular taxable income in the determination of AMTI are often confusing. For example, many items are *not* allowed as deductions in determining AMTI but are deducted in determining regular taxable income. To convert regular taxable income to AMTI, the amount of the deduction is *added back* to regular taxable income. In making adjustments, the following should be kept in mind: (1) If the allowable deduction for AMTI is *less* than the deduction for regular taxable income, the *difference* is *added back* to regular taxable income. (2) If the deduction is *greater* for AMTI than the deduction for regular taxable income, the *difference* is *subtracted* to determine AMTI.

☑ **Example 2.** Howard and Martha Jones' regular taxable income includes a $20,000 deduction for post-1986 ACRS depreciation on property. Only an $8,000 depreciation deduction is permitted in determining AMTI. They must *add* the $12,000 difference to their regular taxable income to determine AMTI.

(1) *Personal Exemptions*

No deduction is permitted for personal or dependency exemptions in determining AMTI; thus, the amount entered on line 16 of Form 6251 is taxable income *before* the personal exemptions (from line 35 of Form 1040).

(2) *Standard Deduction*

(Line 1 Form 6251). A standard deduction is not allowed in determining AMTI; if the taxpayer claimed the standard deduction, it must be added back to regular taxable income to determine AMTI. The Jones' itemized their deductions, so no adjustment is necessary on Line 1 of Form 6251 in Figure 7-2.

☑ **Example 3.** Taylor and Mary Calderone claimed a standard deduction of $6,200 and $9,400 of exemptions in arriving at $62,000 of regular taxable income. Taylor's AMTI before any other adjustments is $77,600 since neither exemptions nor a standard deduction is allowed when determining AMTI.

(3) *Itemized Deductions*

Several itemized deductions are either limited further or omitted entirely in determining AMTI. The itemized deductions fully deductible in determining AMTI are charitable contributions, casualty and theft losses, and moving expenses. No adjustment is required for these. Those *disallowed* in their entirety are the deductions for taxes paid and for miscellaneous deductions subject to the 2% of AGI limitation. The total amount of these deductions must be added back to regular taxable income to determine AMTI.

☑ **Example 4.** Walter Adler had deducted $12,000 of property taxes, $6,000 of state income taxes, and $600 of intangible taxes in determining his regular taxable income of $87,000. Since no deduction for taxes is permitted in determining AMTI, Walter must add $18,600 to regular taxable income to determine AMTI.

☑ **Example 5.** Howard and Martha Jones deducted $44,000 of state and local taxes and miscellaneous itemized deductions of $5,000 on their tax return. Neither of these deductions is permitted in determining AMTI. Lines 3 and 5 on Form 6251 in Figure 7-2 reflect these additions to regular taxable income to determine AMTI.

(a) *Medical Expenses.* (Line 2, Form 6251) Taxpayers are permitted to deduct only medical expenses in excess of 10% of AGI* in determining AMTI rather than the excess over 7½% of AGI, which is permitted in determining regular taxable income; that is, an additional amount of medical expense equal to 2½% of AGI is disallowed as a deduction and must be added back to regular taxable income to determine AMTI. If the taxpayer's allowable medical expense deduction is less than 2½% of AGI, the adjustment is limited to this lesser amount.

☑ **Example 6.** In determining her regular taxable income, Cary Hunter was permitted to deduct $12,000 of medical expenses for the current year when her AGI was $60,000. Cary must reduce this deduction by $1,500 (.025 × $60,000) and add this amount back to regular taxable income to calculate AMTI.

☑ **Example 7.** Howard and Martha Jones deducted $2,500 of medical expenses in determining their regular taxable income. The $2,500 represented the excess of their total medical expenses ($25,000) over 7.5% of their AGI (7.5% × $300,000 = $22,500). For AMTI purposes, they can deduct only medical expenses that exceed 10% of AGI. Since their medical expenses do not exceed $30,000 (10% of $300,000), they have no medical expense deduction in determining AMTI and must add back the $2,500 deduction taken for regular tax purposes on Line 2 of Form 6251 in Figure 7-2.

(b) *Interest Expense.* (Lines 4 and 7, Form 6251) Only the portion of itemized interest deductions for qualified housing interest and points and investment interest expense are deductible in determining AMTI. An adjustment must be made for the amount of nonqualifying home mortgage interest that was claimed as an itemized deduction. Qualifying home mortgage interest must be one of the following:
　(i) For mortgages entered into before July 1, 1982: interest for debt secured by the taxpayer's principal home or by a residence used on a permanent basis by the taxpayer or a member of the taxpayer's family.
　(ii) For mortgages entered into after June 30, 1982: interest for debt undertaken to purchase, construct, or substantially rehabilitate the taxpayer's principal residence.
　Under this second qualification, the proceeds of a second mortgage on the taxpayer's principal residence undertaken after June 30, 1982, must be used to substantially improve that residence. Additionally, the interest on any mortgage for *other than the taxpayer's principal residence* after that date is not qualified home mortgage interest.

*Technically, the taxpayer is permitted a deduction for medical expenses in excess of 10% of ATAGI (alternative tax AGI); however, a discussion of ATAGI is beyond the scope of this text.

A positive adjustment (add-back) must be made for any nonqualifying home mortgage interest that the taxpayer included in itemized deductions.

☑ Example 8. Perry Allen has two homes, one in New York, his principal residence, and one in Florida, where he spends several months during the winter. In determining his regular taxable income of $127,000, Perry deducted $25,000 and $18,000 of mortgage interest, respectively, on the homes. Only the $25,000 of interest on Perry's principal residence is deductible in determining AMTI. Perry must add $18,000 to his regular taxable income to determine AMTI.

☑ Example 9. Howard and Martha Jones had no interest expense other than for their qualified mortgage and have no adjustments on either lines 4 or 7 of Form 6251 in Figure 7-2.

(c) *Other Miscellaneous Deductions.* (Line 5, Form 6251) A few other miscellaneous itemized deductions are not subject to the 2% AGI limitation; generally these are deductible for AMTI calculations and, therefore, do *not* require an adjustment (add-back) to regular income to determine AMTI.

(4) Business Income and Expense Adjustments

Several adjustments are made to determine AMTI by taxpayers who own sole proprietorships or hold interests in partnerships and certain corporations. Business income and expenses are presented later in Chapter 8, and the taxation of partnerships and corporations is presented in Chapter 10. The business adjustments introduced here are mentioned only to complete the discussion of AMTI and the placement of adjustment items on Form 6251. Extensive computations to calculate these adjustments will not have to be made at this point and should not be of concern to the student when determining AMTI.

(a) *Depreciation.* (Line 8, Form 6251) For property placed in service after 1986, the taxpayer who uses the modified accelerated cost recovery system (MACRS) method of depreciation must recalculate depreciation expense using the alternative depreciation system (ADS). That is, if the taxpayer uses MACRS depreciation for post-1986 assets, a second depreciation schedule must be maintained for those assets for the purpose of making adjustments to determine AMTI. The alternative depreciation system generally requires 150% declining-balance depreciation over a life that is somewhat longer than the MACRS life for most personal property and straight-line depreciation over 40 years for real property. Since ADS reduces the depreciation expense in the earlier years (relative to the MACRS depreciation expense for regular tax purposes) and extends the depreciable life, the taxpayer makes positive adjustments to regular taxable income in determining AMTI in these early years. The adjustments will then reverse in later years.

☑ Example 10. Howard and Martha Jones had $20,000 of depreciation expense for post-1986 tangible property in determining regular taxable income. The allowable ADS depreciation deduction is only $8,000. The $12,000 difference is a positive adjustment as shown on Line 8 of Form 6251 in Figure 7-2.

(b) *Circulation, Research and Experimental, and Mine Exploration and Development Expenditures.* (Lines 14(b), (i), and (k), Form 6251) Circulation, research and experimental, and mine exploration and development expenditures may be deducted in their entirety in the year incurred by taxpayers in determining regular taxable income. These expenses must be capitalized and deducted ratably over three years (circulation) or ten years (research and mine) for AMTI purposes, however. Thus, large positive adjustments are made in the first year that reverse as negative adjustments in subsequent years.

(c) *Pollution Control Facilities.* (Line 14(j), Form 6251) Taxpayers are required to depreciate pollution control facilities using a longer ADS depreciable life rather than the five years permitted for regular tax purposes. Positive adjustments must be made in early years that then reverse in later years similar to the post-1986 depreciation adjustments.

(d) *Completed Contract and Installment Sales Methods.* (Lines 14(e) and (g), Form 6251) The completed contract and installment sales methods of recognizing income permit taxpayers to postpone income recognition for determining regular taxable income. Taxpayers must recognize income by the percentage of completion method and at the time of sale, respectively, when determining AMTI. Thus, positive adjustments are required initially that reverse in later years.

(5) Disposition Gains and Losses

When taxpayers are required to use a depreciation schedule for AMTI purposes that is different than the one used for regular tax purposes, they must also keep separate records of the adjusted bases of the assets. When the assets are disposed of, taxpayers use the appropriate adjusted basis to determine the gain or loss on disposition; that is, the regular tax adjusted basis is used to determine gain or loss for regular income determination, while the AMTI adjusted basis is used to determine gain or loss for AMTI. These differences require an adjustment to regular taxable income (line 9 of Form 6251) for determination of AMTI.

Example 11. Brian Donohue sold a building for $200,000 that cost him $185,000. He had deducted $120,000 of depreciation for regular tax purposes, but his deduction for AMTI was only $90,000. Brian has a gain of $135,000 ($200,000 – $65,000 regular tax basis) for regular tax purposes, but his gain is only $105,000 ($200,000 – $95,000 AMTI basis) for AMTI. Brian reduces regular taxable income by the $30,000 difference to determine AMTI. This adjustment would appear on Line 9 of Form 6251. (Note that Example 1 does not contain any gain or loss adjustments.)

(6) *Incentive Stock Options*

When a taxpayer exercises an incentive stock option, no income is recognized for regular tax purposes until the stock is sold; that is, neither the granting nor the exercise of the option is a taxable event when determining regular taxable income. The difference between the exercise price and the fair market value of the stock when the option is exercised, however, is income for AMTI purposes and requires a positive adjustment to regular income (line 10 of Form 6251) to determine AMTI.

Example 12. Five years ago, Howard Jones was granted an incentive stock option to purchase 1,000 shares of stock at $5 per share. If Howard exercises the option in the current year when the stock is selling for $15 per share, he would have no income for regular tax purposes, but his income for AMTI purposes would be $10,000 (1,000 × [$15 − $5]) of income for AMTI. Howard would make a $10,000 positive adjustment to regular taxable income. (Note that Howard Jones in Example 1 did *not* exercise any options.)

TAX PREFERENCE ITEMS

After taxpayers have made the proper adjustments to regular taxable income to determine AMTI, items of tax preference must also be added. Tax preference items are positive adjustments. Though they may reverse in future years, the reversal is ignored. The most common tax preference items an individual taxpayer will encounter are as follows.

(1) Charitable Contribution of Appreciated Property

If a taxpayer makes a donation of appreciated property to a charitable institution and deducts the full fair market value of that property, the taxpayer escapes taxation on the appreciation for regular tax purposes in addition to getting a charitable contribution deduction in excess of basis. Prior to 1991, the untaxed portion of capital gains was a tax preference item. The Revenue Reconciliation Act of 1990 gave a one-year break (for the 1991 tax year) from the inclusion of untaxed capital gains on contributions of *tangible* personal property in AMTI. This break was subsequently extended to donations of tangible personal property made before July 1, 1992. The Revenue Reconciliation Act of 1993 made permanent the exclusion of the capital gain on donations of tangible personal property retroactive to July 1, 1992; furthermore, for donations in tax years beginning in 1993, the untaxed capital gains on *all* personal property is no longer a preference item for AMTI determination. Note, however, that appreciation on donated nonpersonal property is a preference item reported on line 14(a), Form 6251.

Example 13. Abby Laughlin took a $50,000 charitable contribution deduction in 1990 for a donation of a painting that cost $10,000 to the museum at University of Miami. The $40,000 untaxed capital gain appreciation was a preference item that was added to regular taxable income to determine AMTI. If the painting had been donated in 1991, or later, the appreciation would not be a preference item.

(2) Tax-Exempt Interest

A few tax-exempt bonds are defined as private activity bonds. The interest on these bonds is tax exempt for regular tax purposes but not for AMTI; the interest on these bonds is a tax preference item and appears on line 13 of Form 6251.

(3) Business Preferences

Several preference items affect only businesses. The most commonly encountered ones are percentage depletion, accelerated depreciation on real property, and intangible drilling costs. These items are presented here briefly to complete the AMTI preference discussion. Business expenses are discussed at length in Chapter 8.

(a) *Percentage Depletion.* (Line 14(c), Form 6251) Taxpayers with investments in certain minerals are allowed to use percentage depletion instead of cost depletion. Percentage depletion allows the taxpayer to take a depletion deduction even though the entire basis has already been recovered through prior deductions. The percentage depletion deduction taken after the taxpayer's adjusted basis in the property is zero, however, is considered a tax preference item.

✓ **Example 14.** Peter Lance bought a gold mine many years ago that only recently has extracted ore. His adjusted basis in the property at the beginning of the current tax year is $24,000. His percentage depletion allowance is $84,000. Peter is permitted to deduct the $84,000 depletion allowance in determining regular taxable income. Peter's basis in the property is reduced to zero by $24,000 of this depletion deduction. The $60,000 excess is a preference item that is added to regular taxable income to determine AMTI.

(b) *Accelerated Depreciation.* (Line 14(d), Form 6251) Excess depreciation on real property and leased personal property put in service *before 1987* is considered a preference item. Excess depreciation is defined as the difference between the depreciation deduction using an accelerated method of depreciation and the alternative straight-line depreciation deduction. If the accelerated method provides a greater depreciation deduction than the straight-line alternative, the excess is a preference item. The largest category of excess depreciation—accelerated depreciation on personal property owned and used by the taxpayer (rather than leased to another party)—is not considered a preference item. Unlike the *adjustment* for property put in service *after 1986,* no adjustment is permitted in later years for preference items.

Not all excess depreciation on pre-1987 property is considered a preference item. Only excess depreciation on real property and *leased* personal property put in service before 1987 is considered a preference item. Note, however, that excess depreciation on personal property owned and used by the taxpayer is not a preference item.

✓ **Example 15.** Myrtle Crook took $15,000 of accelerated ACRS depreciation on a building she purchased in 1984. The alternative straight-line depreciation would have been $13,000. The $2,000 excess depreciation is a preference item that Myrtle must add to regular taxable income to determine AMTI.

✓ **Example 16.** Howard and Martha Jones took a deduction of $15,000 for ACRS depreciation on pre-1987 realty. The straight-line depreciation would have been $5,000. They have a $10,000 preference item as shown on Line 14(d) of Form 6251 in Figure 7-2.

(4) Intangible Drilling Costs

A portion of the intangible drilling and development costs (IDCs) for productive oil, gas, and geothermal wells that is expensed is considered a preference item. If the taxpayer chooses to capitalize and amortize the IDCs over the ten-year period rather than expensing them, no preference item exists.

AMTI EXEMPTION

THE LAW

Sec. 55(d)—For purposes of this section (1)—In the case of a taxpayer other than a corporation, the term "exemption amount" means (A) $45,000 in the case of (i) a joint return, or (ii) a surviving spouse, (B) $33,750 in the case of an individual who (i) is not a married individual, and (ii) is not a surviving spouse, and (C) $22,500 in the case of (i) a married individual who files a separate return, or (ii) an estate or trust. . . . (3) The exemption amount of any taxpayer shall be reduced (but not below zero) by an amount equal to 25 percent of the amount by which the alternative minimum taxable income of the taxpayer exceeds (A) $150,000 in the case of a taxpayer described in paragraph (1)(A) or (2), (B) $112,500 in the case of a taxpayer described in paragraph (1)(B), and (C) $75,000 in the case of taxpayer described in paragraph (1)(C).

After the taxpayer makes all positive and negative adjustments and adds the preference items to regular taxable income, the exemption amount must be determined. Unfortunately, the exemption amount is not simply a flat amount. First, the initial exemption amount varies with the taxpayer's filing status. Then this initial amount is reduced proportionately as the taxpayer's AMTI before exemption exceeds some base amount. For every one dollar that the taxpayer's AMTI before the exemption exceeds the base amount, the exemption is reduced by 25 cents; that is, the exemption amount is reduced (but not below zero) by one-fourth the amount AMTI exceeds the base amount. If the taxpayer's AMTI before exemption is sufficiently large, the exemption will be wiped out completely by the proportionate reduction and the exemption will be zero. Table 7-1 highlights these items.

Example 17. Howard and Martha Jones have an AMTI before exemption of $271,700. Their exemption is limited to $14,575 determined as follows:

```
                                  $45,000   Base
less 1/4 ($271,700 − $150,000) =   30,425
                                  $14,575
```

(Line 22, Form 6251 in Figure 7-2.)

Table 7-1 AMTI Exemption and Base Amounts

Filing Status	Initial Exemption Amount	Base AMTI	Income at Which Exemption = 0
Married-filing jointly	$45,000	$150,000	$330,000
Single or head of household	$33,750	$112,500	$247,500
Married-filing separately	$22,500	$ 75,000	$165,000

CALCULATING THE ALTERNATIVE MINIMUM TAX

The most difficult part of calculating the alternative minimum tax is determining AMTI. Once that is determined, the tax rate to be applied to AMTI is 26% of AMTI to $175,000 and 28% of AMTI in excess of $175,000 for tax years beginning after December 31, 1992. Prior to 1991, the tax rate was a flat 21% for individuals and for 1991 and 1992 tax years the tax rate was a flat 24% for individuals. The taxpayer is not permitted to use any tax credits to offset the AMT except the foreign tax credit. Deducting the foreign tax credit from this calculation yields the taxpayer's *tentative* alternative minimum tax. To determine whether the AMT is in fact due, the taxpayer must subtract the regular tax due before tax credits (other than the foreign tax credit). If this calculation results in a negative amount, no AMT will be paid. If the calculation yields a positive amount, the excess of the tentative AMT over the regular tax is the AMT that the taxpayer will pay. This amount is reported on the taxpayer's Form 1040 and increases the total tax the taxpayer pays with the return.

✓ **Example 18.** Howard and Martha Jones have an AMTI after their exemption of $257,125. Their regular tax liability is $58,950 and their AMT is determine as follows:

			AMT Calculations	
	$257,125	AMTI	$175,000	$82,125
	× AMT Rate		× .26	× .28
less Tentative AMT	$ 68,495		$ 45,500	$22,995
less Regular tax liability	58,950			
	$ 9,545	AMT		

(See lines 23–28, Form 6251 in Figure 7-2.)

TAX TIP

Taxpayers with substantial preference items and positive adjustments who expect to pay the alternative minimum tax in the current year should consider postponing deductions to the extent possible. If these deductions are used currently against AMTI, they will offset only income taxed at 26% or 28%. By postponing them to a year in which the regular tax applies, they can offset income taxes at a rate of up to 39.6%.

THE AMT CREDIT

Some of the AMT adjustments and preference items are due to "timing differences" in that recognition of income is accelerated (for incentive stock options) or recognition of expenses is postponed (for depreciation). In later years, these items will "turn around" for regular tax purposes. For example, the entire gain on an incentive stock option is recognized for regular tax purposes when the stock is actually sold, and depreciation deductions will be smaller in the later years of an asset's life.

Due to these timing differences, a taxpayer could be taxed on the same amount twice—once as part of AMTI and again as part of regular taxable income. To alleviate this possibility, Congress enacted an AMT credit. This credit is the difference between the computed AMT and a modified AMT calculated by including only the following *permanent* (nontiming) adjustments and preferences: itemized deduction adjustments, personal exemption deduction adjustment, charitable contribution preferences, and tax-exempt interest preferences. The difference in these two AMT tax computations is the AMT credit. This credit may offset any *regular* tax liability in a future year. It may not offset the AMT in any year, however.

✓ **Example 19.** Using the data from Example 1, the computed AMT for Howard and Martha Jones using only permanent adjustments and preferences would be $1,845, computed as follows:

Taxable income before exemptions			$203,947
Less itemized deduction limitation			(5,747)
Adjustments for itemized deductions			
($2,500 + $44,000 + $5,000)			51,500
Charitable contribution preference			0
Tax-exempt interest preference			0
AMTI exemption [$45,000 − (($249,700 − $150,000) × .25)]			(20,075)

	AMT Calculation		
Net AMTI	$175,000	$54,625	$229,625
	× .26	× .28	× AMT rate
AMT	$ 45,500	$15,295	$ 60,795
less regular tax			(58,950)
Modified AMT Excess			$ 1,845

Thus, $7,700 of the $9,545 total 1993 AMT ($9,545 − $1,845) was caused by timing differences. This amount may be carried forward to future tax years as a credit against future regular tax liabilities.

REVIEW I

1. Marty Dennis has regular taxable income of $41,450 after claiming two exemptions of $2,350 each and a standard deduction of $5,450. If Marty has no other adjustments, what is his AMTI before the AMT exemption?
   (a) $42,300
   (b) $47,300
   (c) $49,450
   (d) $51,600
2. Shirley Thomas' AGI is $67,000. She has deductible medical expenses of $24,000 and a personal exemption of $2,350. Given this information only, what is Shirley's regular taxable income and AMTI before the AMT exemption?
   (a) $45,675; $49,700
   (b) $45,675; $47,600
   (c) $40,650; $43,000
   (d) $40,650; $40,900

3. Whit Lowell paid $38,000 interest on his first mortgage and $8,000 interest on a home equity loan on his principal residence; he also paid $10,200 of mortgage interest on his summer home. Whit took out the home equity loan two years ago to buy a Mercedes convertible. If Whit's regular taxable income is $102,000 before his personal exemption, what is his AMTI before the AMT exemption?
   (a) $158,000
   (b) $120,200
   (c) $102,000
   (d) $83,800

4. Winfred Coronado had regular taxable income of $200,000 before his personal exemption but after equipment depreciation of $40,000, a deduction for depletion of $140,000 (cost basis before depletion = $14,000), and a deduction of $30,000 for pollution control facilities. If ADS depreciation is $25,000 for the equipment and $15,000 for the pollution control facilities, what is Winfred's AMTI before the AMT exemption?
   (a) $230,000
   (b) $300,000
   (c) $356,000
   (d) $370,000

5. Alana West has $63,000 in regular taxable income (before her personal exemption) after a $20,000 percentage depletion deduction on mineral property and excess depreciation on pre-1987 real property of $12,000. Alana recovered her basis in the mineral property two years ago. What is Alana's AMT exemption if she is married but files separately?
   (a) $45,000
   (b) $40,000
   (c) $22,500
   (d) $17,500

6. Warren Oak has regular taxable income (before his personal exemption) of $12,200. He has $82,000 of preference items and $143,000 of positive adjustments. What is Warren's AMT if he is a single individual with no dependents?
   (a) $237,200
   (b) $234,625
   (c) $62,195
   (d) $61,002

Answers are on page 7-16.

II LUMP-SUM DISTRIBUTIONS FROM RETIREMENT PLANS

(Code Sections 401, 402, and 403)

Taxpayers who receive large distributions from qualified pension or profit-sharing plans could face a substantial tax liability if the taxable portion of the distribution is added to the taxpayers' other income for that year and taxes are determined under the usual graduated rate system. As a result, lump-sum distributions from qualified pension and profit-sharing plans are eligible to be taxed using a special tax computation called five-year forward averaging. A qualfiied retirement plan is one that meets specific requirements for tax-favored treatment. These requirements are beyond the scope of this discussion.

THE LAW

Sec. 402(d) (4) (A)—For purposes of this section and section 403, the term "lump-sum distribution" means the distribution or payment within one taxable year of the recipient of the balance to the credit of an employee which becomes payable to the recipient . . . (ii) after the employee attains age 59½, ...

To be eligible for this special tax computation, a taxpayer must receive the distribution within one tax year. This does not mean that only one payment can be received, but if several payments are received, they cannot be spread over more than one tax year. The amount received in the distribution must be the entire balance in all qualified pension plans or all qualified profit-sharing plans that the employer has for that employee. Thus, if the taxpayer's employer has established two or more pension (or profit-sharing) plans on behalf of the employee, the proceeds from all plans must be distributed during the tax year. If the employer has both pension *and* profit-sharing plans for the employee, the distribution may be limited to *either* the pension or the profit-sharing plan.

Example 20. Joseph Parks retired on August 31 at age 63 from the company for which he had worked for 40 years. He was a participant in two different company pension plans and in the current profit-sharing plan. To qualify for special tax treatment as a lump-sum distribution, Joseph must choose one of the following alternatives:

ANSWERS TO REVIEW I

1. (d) $41,450 + $4,700 + $5,450 = $51,600
2. (a) Reg. tax. inc.   AMTI
       $67,000 $45,675
       – 2,350   + 2,350
       –18,975   (24,000 – [.075 × 67,000])   + 1,675 (.025 × 67,000)
       $45,675 $49,700
3. (b) $102,000
       +10,200   Mortgages on second homes and home
       + 8,000   equity loans not used to improve the
       $120,200   residence may not be deducted for AMTI.
4. (c) $200,000   AMTI
       + 15,000   Equipment depreciation adjustment
       +126,000   Depletion in excess of basis
       + 15,000   Pollution control facilities adjustment
5. (d) $22,500 – ($63,000 + $20,000 + $12,000 – $75,000) × .25
6. (c) $12,200 + $82,000 + $143,000 = $237,200 AMTI before exemption
       $33,750 – [($237,200 – $112,500) × .25] = $2,575 Exemption
       $237,200 – $2,575 = $234,625 AMTI
       ($175,000 × .26) + [($234,625 – $175,000) × .28] = $62,195

(a) Take all the money in both pension plans only in one year;

(b) Take all the money in the profit-sharing plan only in one year; or

(c) Take all the money in all three plans in the one tax year.

The lump-sum distribution from a pension or profit-sharing plan must meet certain criteria to qualify for special tax treatment. To be eligible for the special tax treatment under five-year forward averaging, the lump-sum distribution must be made after the employee reaches the age of 59½ and has a minimum of five tax years of participation in the plan. A beneficiary may waive this latter requirement and elect lump-sum treatment if the participant has died.

Example 21. Joseph Parks, from the previous example, qualifies for the special lump-sum distribution provisions since he is past age 59½ and, due to his long years of service, he most likely meets the minimum five-year participation requirements.

TAX TIP

Taxpayers should be careful that they qualify for forward averaging. Nonqualifying distributions from pension or profit-sharing plans not only subject the taxpayer to tax determined by including the entire taxable portion in taxable income but may also subject the taxpayer to penalties. For example, this extra income could result in a penalty for failing to have sufficient amounts withheld or paid in as estimated tax payments.

ONE-TIME ELECTION

THE LAW

Sec. 402(d)(4)(B)—Not more than 1 election may be made under this subparagraph by any taxpayer with respect to any employee. No election may be made under this subparagraph by any taxpayer other than an individual, an estate, or a trust.

The election to have the taxable portion of a lump-sum distribution taxed under the five-year forward averaging provisions is a once-only election. If the taxpayer receives a lump-sum distribution in one year and elects to use five-year forward averaging, the taxable portion of all future lump-sum distributions is ineligible for averaging and must be added to taxable income in the year received to determine the taxpayer's regular tax due. If the taxpayer receives two or more lump-sum distributions in one tax year, the tax on the taxable portion of all distributions must be determined under the five-year forward averaging method if the taxpayer elects forward averaging for any distribution. The taxpayer cannot apply five-year forward averaging to less than all eligible distributions received in that year. Thus, a taxpayer cannot roll over any part of one or more distributions into an individual retirement account (IRA) and still use five-year forward averaging for the retained portion. This once-only election applies to an individual, to that person's estate, and to any trust to which the distribution is made. If the taxpayer elects to use the five-year forward averaging method during his or her lifetime, the estate may not make another election if it receives a lump-sum distribution upon his or her death.

TAX TIP

Because five-year forward averaging is a once-only election, taxpayers may want to forgo it if a second qualifying lump-sum distribution is expected in a later year. If the second distribution has a substantially greater amount of taxable income, then using the five-year forward averaging at that time may substantially reduce the overall tax liability.

FIVE-YEAR AVERAGING

THE LAW

Sec. 402(d)(1)(A)—There is hereby imposed a tax (in the amount determined under subparagraph (B)) on the lump-sum distribution. (B) The amount of tax imposed by subparagraph (A) for any taxable year is an amount equal to 5 times the tax which would be imposed by subsection (c) of section 1 if the recipient were an individual referred to in such subsection and the taxable income were an amount equal to 1/5 of the excess of (i) the total taxable amount of the lump-sum distribution for the taxable year, over (ii) the minimum distribution allowance.

When this special five-year forward averaging tax computation is elected, no part of a lump-sum distribution is added to the taxpayer's regular taxable income for the year. Instead, a totally separate calculation is made, and the tax determined in this separate calculation is added to the tax due on taxable income determined in the usual manner but excluding the lump-sum distribution. The taxpayer uses Form 4972 to determine this tax.

Essentially, five-year forward averaging requires the taxpayer to divide the taxable portion of the lump-sum distribution by five; a tax is calculated on this amount using the rate schedule for single individuals; then this tax is multiplied by five to determine the total tax due on the lump-sum distribution. This tax is then added to the tax determined on the taxpayer's taxable income calculated without the lump-sum distribution.

Example 22. Mary Austin received a $90,000 taxable distribution from her pension plan, which is eligible for five-year forward averaging, when she retired. To calculate the tax due, Mary divides the $90,000 by 5 and, using the tax rate schedule for single individuals, determines the tax on $18,000. The tax at the 15% rate is $2,700. Multiplying $2,700 by 5 yields a total tax due for the lump-sum distribution of $13,500. Mary adds this tax to the tax due on her regular taxable income that excludes this distribution. Figure 7-3 shows a completed Form 4972 with the above information.

Form 4972
Department of the Treasury
Internal Revenue Service

Tax on Lump-Sum Distributions
(Use This Form Only for Lump-Sum Distributions From Qualified Retirement Plans)
▶ Attach to Form 1040 or Form 1041. ▶ See separate instructions.

OMB No. 1545-0193
1993
Attachment Sequence No. **28**

Name of recipient of distribution: Mary Austin

Identifying number

Part I — Complete this part to see if you qualify to use Form 4972.

		Yes	No
1	Did you roll over any part of the distribution? If "Yes," do not complete the rest of this form		
2	Was the retirement plan participant born before 1936? If "No," do not complete the rest of this form		
3	Was this a lump-sum distribution from a qualified pension, profit-sharing, or stock bonus plan? (See **Distributions That Qualify for the 20% Capital Gain Election or for 5- or 10-Year Averaging** in the instructions.) If "No," do not complete the rest of this form		
4	Was the participant in the plan for at least 5 years before the year of the distribution?		
5	Was this distribution paid to you as a beneficiary of a plan participant who died?		

If you answered "No" to both questions **4** and **5**, do not complete the rest of this form.

6 Was the plan participant:
 a An employee who received the distribution because he or she quit, retired, was laid off, or was fired? **6a**
 b Self-employed or an owner-employee who became permanently and totally disabled before the distribution? **6b**
 c Age 59½ or older at the time of the distribution? **6c**

If you answered "No" to question **5** and **all** parts of question **6**, do not complete the rest of this form.

7 Did you use Form 4972 in a prior year for any distribution received after 1986 for the same plan participant, including you, for whom the 1992 distribution was made? If "Yes," do not complete the rest of this form. **7**

If you qualify to use this form, you may choose to use Part II, Part III, or Part IV; **or** Part II and Part III; **or** Part II and Part IV.

Part II — Complete this part to choose the 20% capital gain election. (See instructions.)

8	Capital gain part from box 3 of Form 1099-R. (See instructions.)	8	
9	Multiply line 8 by 20% (.20) and enter here. If you do not choose to use Part III or Part IV, also enter the amount on Form 1040, line 39, or Form 1041, Schedule G, line 1b	9	

Part III — Complete this part to choose the 5-year averaging method. (See instructions.)

10	Ordinary income from Form 1099-R, box 2a minus box 3. If you did not complete Part II, enter the taxable amount from box 2a of Form 1099-R. (See instructions.)	10	90,000
11	Death benefit exclusion. (See instructions.)	11	
12	Total taxable amount—Subtract line 11 from line 10	12	90,000
13	Current actuarial value of annuity, if applicable (from Form 1099-R, box 8)	13	
14	Adjusted total taxable amount—Add lines 12 and 13. If this amount is $70,000 or more, skip lines 15 through 18, and enter this amount on line 19	14	90,000
15	Multiply line 14 by 50% (.50), but **do not** enter more than $10,000 . **15**		
16	Subtract $20,000 from line 14. If line 14 is $20,000 or less, enter -0- . **16**		
17	Multiply line 16 by 20% (.20) . **17**		
18	Minimum distribution allowance—Subtract line 17 from line 15	18	
19	Subtract line 18 from line 14	19	90,000
20	Federal estate tax attributable to lump-sum distribution. Do not deduct on Form 1040 or Form 1041 the amount attributable to the ordinary income entered on line 10. (See instructions.)	20	—
21	Subtract line 20 from line 19	21	90,000
22	Multiply line 21 by 20% (.20)	22	18,000
23	Tax on amount on line 22. See instructions for Tax Rate Schedule	23	2,700
24	Multiply line 23 by five (5). If line 13 is blank, skip lines 25 through 30, and enter this amount on line 31	24	13,500
25	Divide line 13 by line 14 and enter the result as a decimal. (See instructions.)	25	
26	Multiply line 18 by the decimal amount on line 25	26	
27	Subtract line 26 from line 13	27	
28	Multiply line 27 by 20% (.20)	28	
29	Tax on amount on line 28. See instructions for Tax Rate Schedule	29	
30	Multiply line 29 by five (5)	30	
31	Subtract line 30 from line 24. (Multiple recipients, see instructions.)	31	13,500
32	Tax on lump-sum distribution—Add Part II, line 9, and Part III, line 31. Enter on Form 1040, line 39, or Form 1041, Schedule G, line 1b ▶	32	13,500

For Paperwork Reduction Act Notice, see separate instructions. Cat. No. 13187U Form **4972** (1992)

Figure 7-3 Form 4972

> **TAX TIP**
>
>
>
> Because five-year forward averaging requires an entirely separate calculation, the taxpayer's other taxable income is irrelevant in determining whether to elect its provisions. Thus, a taxpayer could elect five-year forward averaging in a high income year as well as a low income year without penalty.

Not all amounts distributed from a pension and profit-sharing plan will necessarily be taxable to the employee. If the employee contributed amounts to the plan on which taxes had already been paid, the employee is not required to pay taxes when this sum is returned because it is considered a return of the taxpayer's basis.

Example 23. Margaret Olson received $68,000 in a lump-sum distribution from her pension plan when she retired. Over the years, Margaret had made contributions of $8,000 to the plan from her after-tax income; that is, she had paid taxes on the $8,000 as it was earned. Only $60,000 of the lump-sum distribution is taxable. The other $8,000 represents a return of basis.

Some pension and profit-sharing plans are set up so that only the employer makes contributions to the plan. Others are set up so that the employee may make "tax sheltered" contributions; that is, the employee's taxable income is reduced by the contributions the employee makes to the plan. These contributions are made on a before-tax basis and *do not* give the taxpayer basis. All employer contributions and employee before-tax contributions will constitute taxable income as part of a lump-sum distribution.

Example 24. Walter Bird received a $30,000 lump-sum distribution from his pension plan when he reached age 60. He had contributed $5,000 on a before-tax basis; the balance represented employer contributions and pension plan earnings. All $30,000 is taxable income to Walter when he receives the lump-sum distribution.

MINIMUM DISTRIBUTION ALLOWANCES

Taxpayers who receive lump-sum distributions of less than $70,000 may exclude a portion of the distribution, termed the *minimum distribution allowance*, from taxable income when making the five-year forward averaging calculation. This minimum distribution allowance is calculated as follows:

Step 1: Compare 1/2 of the taxable portion of the lump-sum distribution to $10,000; use the lesser amount in Step 2.

Step 2: Subtract 20% of the taxable portion of the lump-sum distribution in excess of $20,000 from the amount determined in Step 1. This is the minimum distribution allowance.

Example 25. Al Trader received a $38,000 taxable lump-sum distribution that is eligible for five-year forward averaging. His minimum distribution allowance is determined as follows:

Step 1: 1/2 ($38,000) = $19,000 which is > $10,000;
Use $10,000 in Step 2.

Step 2:
$10,000
less .20 ($38,000 − $20,000) =   3,600
Minimum distribution allowance = $ 6,400

Because the minimum distribution allowance is a deduction from the taxable portion of the lump-sum distribution, only $31,600 constitutes taxable income for the five-year forward averaging calculation.

TAX TIP

Taxpayers with taxable lump-sum distributions in excess of $70,000 have no minimum distribution allowance. This allowance, however, is available only when electing forward averaging. A taxpayer who does not elect forward averaging must add the entire taxable portion of the distribution to taxable income and may not exclude any as a minimum distribution allowance.

PRIOR LAW TEN-YEAR AVERAGING COMPUTATION

Taxpayers who were age 50 before January 1, 1986, are still eligible to elect a ten-year forward averaging provision of pre-1987 law instead of the current five-year forward averaging provision. The calculation of the tax under ten-year forward averaging is similar to that for five-year averaging; that is, the taxpayer divides the taxable portion of the lump-sum distribution by 10 and pays 10 times the tax determined on this amount. In determining the tax, however, the taxpayer must use the income tax rate for single individuals that was in effect in 1986. Because current rates are somewhat lower than those in effect in 1986, ten-year averaging does not yield a lower tax than five-year averaging when the lump-sum distribution becomes large. Ten-year averaging is computed on the second page of Form 4972 shown in Figure 7-4, but the computation is beyond the scope of the text.

An additional provision that only affects taxpayers who were 50 prior to January 1, 1986, is the capital-gain relief provision. These taxpayers can also elect to have a portion of their pre-1974 pension plan contributions taxed at a flat 20% rate, with the balance treated under the five- or ten-year forward averaging provisions.

REVIEW II

1. Edna Murray, age 54, withdrew $25,000 of the $75,000 in her pension plan when she fell and broke her hip and was unable to work for eight months. Why is the distribution not eligible for five-year forward averaging?

Form 4972 (1993) Page **2**

Part IV Complete this part to choose the 10-year averaging method. (See instructions.)

33	Ordinary income part from Form 1099-R, box 2a minus box 3. If you did not complete Part II, enter the taxable amount from box 2a of Form 1099-R. (See instructions.)	33
34	Death benefit exclusion. (See instructions.)	34
35	Total taxable amount—Subtract line 34 from line 33	35
36	Current actuarial value of annuity, if applicable (from Form 1099-R, box 8)	36
37	Adjusted total taxable amount—Add lines 35 and 36. If this amount is $70,000 or more, skip lines 38 through 41, and enter this amount on line 42	37
38	Multiply line 37 by 50% (.50), but **do not** enter more than $10,000 . | 38 |	
39	Subtract $20,000 from line 37. If line 37 is $20,000 or less, enter -0- . . . . | 39 |	
40	Multiply line 39 by 20% (.20) . . . . | 40 |	
41	Minimum distribution allowance—Subtract line 40 from line 38	41
42	Subtract line 41 from line 37	42
43	Federal estate tax attributable to lump-sum distribution. Do not deduct on Form 1040 or Form 1041 the amount attributable to the ordinary income entered on line 33. (See instructions.) . .	43
44	Subtract line 43 from line 42	44
45	Multiply line 44 by 10% (.10)	45
46	Tax on amount on line 45. See instructions for Tax Rate Schedule	46
47	Multiply line 46 by ten (10). If line 36 is blank, skip lines 48 through 53, and enter this amount on line 54	47
48	Divide line 36 by line 37 and enter the result as a decimal. (See instructions.)	48
49	Multiply line 41 by the decimal amount on line 48	49
50	Subtract line 49 from line 36	50
51	Multiply line 50 by 10% (.10)	51
52	Tax on amount on line 51. See instructions for Tax Rate Schedule	52
53	Multiply line 52 by ten (10)	53
54	Subtract line 53 from line 47. (Multiple recipients, see instructions.)	54
55	Tax on lump-sum distribution—Add Part II, line 9, and Part IV, line 54. Enter on Form 1040, line 39, or Form 1041, Schedule G, line 1b . . . . ▶	55

Figure 7-4   Ten-Year Averaging Calculation (Form 4972)

(a) The entire balance is paid out.
(b) Edna is not over 59½.
(c) Edna is permanently disabled.
(d) Edna is eligible for ten-year forward averaging.

2. Stan Tilley has retirement funds in a pension plan with Company ABC, a former employer, and retirement funds in a pension plan and a separate profit-sharing plan with Company XYZ. If Stan takes all of the funds from the pension plan of Company XYZ, from what other plan(s) must he have lump-sum distributions in the same year to qualify for five-year forward averaging?
(a) none
(b) pension plan of company ABC
(c) profit-sharing plan of company XYZ
(d) pension plan of ABC and profit-sharing plan of XYZ

3. Barry Bard received a $48,000 taxable distribution from his profit-sharing plan after the minimum distribution allowance and elects to use five-year forward averaging. What is the tax due on this distribution?
(a) $9,600
(b) $7,200
(c) $6,000
(d) $41,440

4. Allison Nelson received a $16,500 lump-sum distribution from a pension plan that qualifies for five-year forward averaging. What is her minimum distribution allowance?
(a) $0
(b) $5,650
(c) $8,250
(d) $10,000

5. George Morgan received a $69,000 distribution from his profit-sharing plan. He had contributed $12,000 to the plan on an after-tax basis. Determine George's total tax due if his regular income tax liability without the lump-sum distribution is $6,800.
(a) $1,632
(b) $8,432
(c) $14,960
(d) $17,120

Answers are on page 7-24.

III PASSIVE LOSS LIMITATIONS
(Code Section 469)

To discourage the creation of "tax shelters"—investment vehicles that had allowed taxpayers to deduct losses that had little economic substance from other sources of real economic income—IRC Sec. 469 with its concept of passive activities was created. Under current law, if an individual taxpayer invests in activities classified as passive, the deductibility of losses incurred is limited by a complex set of passive loss limitation rules. Form 8582 and its accompanying directions and worksheets enable the taxpayer to determine the deductibility of passive losses for a particular year.

Passive activities are defined as any trade or business activity in which the taxpayer does not materially participate, or any rental activity that does not meet specific exclusion criteria. To materially participate in a trade or business, a taxpayer must meet one of seven tests—four based on current activity, two based on prior years' activity, and the seventh one based on all relevant facts and circumstances. The four current activity tests are (1) the individual's participation is greater than 500 hours, (2) the individual's participation constitutes the major portion of participation by all individuals, (3) the individual participates more than 100 hours and no other person participates more, and (4) the individual's activity is greater than 100 hours and he or she meets an aggregate of 500 hours for activities in which he or she significantly participates over 100 hours. If the taxpayer has one or more activities in this latter category in which he or she participates over 100 hours each, but the total is less than 500 hours for all, the gains and losses from these activities must be netted. If the result is a net loss, the gains and losses are considered passive. If, however, the result is a net *gain,* this net gain is considered to be only from an activity that is *not* passive.

Prior years' activities will qualify for current material participation if (1) the individual has materially participated in any five of the preceding ten years or (2) the individual materially participated in *any* three prior years and it is a personal service activity. The requirements for material participation are summarized in Table 7-2.

✓ **Example 26.** Michael Peters spent 220 hours in his attempt to start and operate a small tax service last year. He did all the work himself and his net income from the business was $2,100. Michael materially participated in the business since he provided the major portion of all activity. The $2,100 constitutes active income.

ANSWERS TO REVIEW II

1. (b)
2. (a) Only a pension plan of the same employer would be required to be distributed in the same tax year.
3. (b) $48,000/5 = $9,600
   $\times$ .15
   $1,440
   $\times$ 5
   $7,200 Total tax due
4. (c) Step 1: 1/2 $\times$ ($16,500) = $8,250 < $10,000
   Use $8,250 in Step 2.
   Step 2: Since the distribution does not exceed $20,000, the $8,250 does not have to be reduced and the minimum distribution allowance is $8,250.
5. (c) Step 1: 1/2 $\times$ ($57,000) = $28,500 > $10,000
   Use $10,000 in Step 2.
   Step 2: $10,000
   .20 $\times$ ($57,000 − $20,000) = (7,400)
   Minimum distribution allowance = $ 2,600
   ($57,000 − $2,600)/5 = $10,880
   $\times$ .15   Tax rate
   $ 1,632
   $\times$ 5
   Tax on lump-sum distribution $ 8,160
   plus   6,800   Regular tax
   $14,960

Table 7-2 Requirements for Material Participation in an Activity

A. Current activity basis
1. Greater than 500 hours
2. Provides major portion of activity
3. Greater than 100 hours participation exceeds participation by any other person
4. Greater than 100 hours participation and aggregate "significant" participation equals 500 hours or more. (Note that special gain/loss recognition rules apply if aggregate significant participation is less than 500 hours.)

B. Prior years' activity basis
1. Material participation in any five of ten preceding years
2. Material participation in any three years of a personal service activity

C. Facts and circumstances—Taxpayer must consider all relevant facts and circumstances

✓ **Example 27.** Marjorie Black participated 320 hours in Activity A, which had a $2,700 loss, and 110 hours in Activity B, which had $1,400 of net income. Marjorie must aggregate these activities; because she participated a total of only 430 hours in both, she must net the income against the loss. The $1,300 resulting net loss causes the $2,700 loss and $1,400 income to be considered passive. If a net gain had resulted, the net gain would have been active income.

DEFINITIONS

By definition, rental activities are considered passive activities.* This blanket rule would be grossly unfair to many rental activities that constitute active businesses such as auto rental companies and motels. In general, rental businesses that have average rentals of (1) less than 8 days or (2) less than 30 days, but provide significant services as part of the rental, are not considered passive. Additionally, passive losses from rental real estate may be deductible within certain limits as discussed below.

Due to the nature of limited partnerships, a limited partner's activities are considered passive. On the other hand, any working interest in an oil or gas property is *not* passive if the taxpayer does not have limited liability.

GENERAL REPORTING RULES

Taxpayers may deduct losses from passive activities to the extent that they have income from passive activities. Passive losses, except those subject to the rental real estate exception, may not offset income from salary, wages, or other activities in which the taxpayer does materially participate. If taxpayers have nondeductible passive losses in excess of passive income, these losses are carried over to the subsequent years and are deductible in the carryover year subject to the limitations in that year. There is no limit to the number of years to which these losses may be carried. Finally, in the year that taxpayers dispose of the activity, they may deduct any current or prior disallowed losses against (1) income from or gain on the disposition of the activity, (2) income from other passive activities, and (3) any other income including active and investment income, in that order.

*For changes in the tax law effective for years beginning in 1994, see Appendix J.

☑ **Example 28.** George Watson had two passive activities. Activity A has a $1,200 gain and Activity B has a $2,400 loss. George may deduct only $1,200 of the loss from B against A's passive income. He may carry the remaining $1,200 loss from B to future years when it can be deducted against additional passive income or when the activity is disposed of.

RENTAL REAL ESTATE ACTIVITY EXCEPTION

Taxpayers who own 10% or more in a rental real estate activity and actively participate in the management of the project may be allowed to deduct up to $25,000 of passive losses in excess of passive income. This exception, however, is phased out proportionately for taxpayers with AGI between $100,000 and $150,000. The $25,000 deduction is reduced 50 cents for each $1 when income exceeds $100,000. Thus, it is eliminated completely for taxpayers with AGI of $150,000 or more.

☑ **Example 29.** John and Mary have AGI of $120,000. They have losses from their rental apartment building of $23,000. Since their income exceeds $100,000 by $20,000, the maximum $25,000 passive deduction is reduced by $10,000 to $15,000. Thus, after deducting the $15,000 of passive losses, the taxpayers have income of $105,000. The $8,000 of disallowed passive losses may be carried forward and deducted in future years against other passive income or when the rental property is disposed of. Deductible passive losses on rental real estate are entered on Schedule E, discussed in Chapter 8.

☑ **Example 30.** Marjorie Morningsun had the following results from her investment in two real estate activities: Activity A had a net loss of $20,000 and Activity B had net income of $6,000. Even though Marjorie's modified adjusted gross income of $110,000 exceeds the threshold $100,000, she is still able to deduct all $20,000 of the passive real estate loss as shown in Figure 7-5, which presents this information on Form 8582.

TAX TIP

Taxpayers cannot circumvent the passive loss rules by deducting passive losses against investment income. Taxpayers must separate their income into three "baskets"—active, passive, and investment. Strict limits are placed on the deductibility of losses from passive or investment activities against income from any source other than another passive or investment activity, respectively.

REVIEW III

1. During the current year George Alto participated for 600 hours in Activity A, an S Corporation for which he performs geological surveys; 280 hours in Activity B, which is his sole proprietorship with no employees; and 55 hours in Activity C, his brother's business, taking inventory counts. Which activities are active and which are passive?

Form **8582**	**Passive Activity Loss Limitations**	OMB No. 1545-1008
Department of the Treasury Internal Revenue Service	▶ See separate instructions. ▶ Attach to Form 1040 or Form 1041.	**1993** Attachment Sequence No. **88**

Name(s) shown on return: Marjorie Morningsun

Identifying number:

Part I — 1992 Passive Activity Loss

Caution: *See the instructions for Worksheets 1 and 2 on page 7 before completing Part I.*

Rental Real Estate Activities With Active Participation (For the definition of active participation see **Active Participation in a Rental Real Estate Activity** on page 3 of the instructions.)

1a Activities with net income (from Worksheet 1, column (a))	1a	6,000
b Activities with net loss (from Worksheet 1, column (b))	1b	(20,000)
c Prior year unallowed losses (from Worksheet 1, column (c))	1c	( )
d Combine lines 1a, 1b, and 1c	1d	(14,000)

All Other Passive Activities

2a Activities with net income (from Worksheet 2, column (a))	2a	
b Activities with net loss (from Worksheet 2, column (b))	2b	( )
c Prior year unallowed losses (from Worksheet 2, column (c))	2c	( )
d Combine lines 2a, 2b, and 2c	2d	

3 Combine lines 1d and 2d. If the result is net income or zero, see the instructions for line 3. If this line and line 1d are losses, go to line 4. Otherwise, enter -0- on line 9 and go to line 10 . . | **3** | (14,000) |

Part II — Special Allowance for Rental Real Estate With Active Participation

Note: *Enter all numbers in Part II as positive amounts. (See instructions on page 7 for examples.)*

4	Enter the **smaller** of the loss on line 1d or the loss on line 3	**4**	14,000
5	Enter $150,000. If married filing separately, see the instructions	5	150,000
6	Enter modified adjusted gross income, but not less than zero (see instructions)	6	100,000
	Note: *If line 6 is equal to or greater than line 5, skip lines 7 and 8, enter -0- on line 9, and then go to line 10. Otherwise, go to line 7.*		
7	Subtract line 6 from line 5	7	40,000
8	Multiply line 7 by 50% (.5). **Do not** enter more than $25,000. If married filing separately, see instructions	**8**	20,000
9	Enter the **smaller** of line 4 or line 8	**9**	14,000

Part III — Total Losses Allowed

10	Add the income, if any, on lines 1a and 2a and enter the total	**10**	6,000
11	Total losses allowed from all passive activities for **1992.** Add lines 9 and 10. See the instructions to find out how to report the losses on your tax return	**11**	20,000*

For Paperwork Reduction Act Notice, see separate instructions. Cat. No. 63704F Form **8582** (1992)

*The $20,000 passive loss is carried to Schedule E where $6,000 will offset the $6,000 of passive income and the $14,000 balance will be deducted (due to the real estate exception) on the taxpayer's Form 1040.

Figure 7-5 Form 8582

(a) All are active.
(b) All are passive.
(c) Activity A is active; B and C are passive.
(d) Activities A and B are active; C is passive.

2. Mary Barnes has $60,000 of passive income from one activity and $45,000 and $90,000 of losses from two other passive activities. How much may Mary deduct in the current year and what are her carryovers?
    (a) All losses are deductible.
    (b) Mary may deduct $60,000 of losses; she may carry over $75,000 of losses from the other loss activities.
    (c) Mary may deduct $60,000 of losses but may only deduct the remaining losses when the activities are sold.
    (d) Mary may deduct $60,000 of losses but no carryovers are permitted.

3. Alton Lamb has $140,000 of AGI and a $75,000 loss from a very large rental complex. How much of this loss may Alton deduct in the current year?
    (a) $75,000
    (b) $25,000
    (c) $5,000
    (d) $0

4. John Williams has $84,000 of passive losses from activity A, $8,000 of passive income from Activity B, and $20,000 of passive income from Activity C. None of the activities are rental real estate. How much of the passive loss may be deducted in the current year?
    (a) $0
    (b) $8,000
    (c) $28,000
    (d) $84,000

Answers are on page 7-30.

IV EXTENSIONS AND AMENDED RETURNS
(Code Sections 6071, 6072, and 6081)

Often taxpayers are unable to meet filing deadlines for their returns. For example, an individual may be ill and unable to get all the necessary materials ready to prepare the return by April 15. Instead of filing the return, the individual may file for an automatic four-month extension for filing the return. This extension should give the taxpayer sufficient time to gather the data for filing the return by the extended due date. Corporations and partnerships may also file for extensions for filing their returns; corporations, however, are given an automatic six-month extension; partnerships are given a three-month extension. Table 7-3 details the normal due dates for calendar-year and fiscal-year taxpayers, the extensions available, and the forms on which they are requested. If a due date falls on a Saturday, Sunday, or holiday, the due date is extended to the first working day after the scheduled due date.

An individual may also receive an additional two-month extension and a partnership an additional three-month extension so that each may have six months in total beyond the original due date for filing their returns. There are several things that must be noted about these additional extensions. First, the taxpayer generally must have made a timely application for the automatic extension. The taxpayer must file the application in duplicate and state a valid reason why the taxpayer is unable to meet the deadline as permitted by the automatic extension. The IRS is not required to approve this applica-

Table 7-3 Filing Requirements

	Individuals	Partnerships*	Corporations*
Unextended due date for calendar-year filers	April 15	April 15	March 15
Unextended due date for fiscal-year filers	15th day of fourth month following end of tax year	15th day of fourth month following end of tax year	15th day of third month following end of tax year
Automatic extension period	4 months	3 months	6 months
Extension form to be filed	Form 4868	Form 8736	Form 7004
Additional extension available	2 months	3 months	None
Extension form to be filed	Form 2688	Form 8800	N/A

*Partnership taxation and corporate taxation are discussed in Chapter 10. The filing requirements for these entities are included here for information purposes only.

tion for a second extension. If the application is not approved, the IRS will notify the taxpayer, in which case the IRS will normally give the taxpayer a ten-day grace period for filing the return.

Although taxpayers may file for an automatic extension to file their returns, they get no extension of time to pay the tax owed. Individuals who fail to pay a sufficient amount to cover their tax liability with Form 4868 will be assessed interest on the balance due, regardless of the reason. Taxpayers may also be assessed a late payment penalty of .5% per month if the IRS fails to accept the reason for the failure to pay. Note that these interest and penalty charges are in addition to the penalty for failure to pay sufficient amounts as estimated taxes. None of the penalties are deductible by the taxpayers; the interest payment constitutes personal interest and is nondeductible.

Individuals are assessed penalties if they fail to *file* their returns by their due date plus extensions. The penalty for individuals for failure to file is 5% of the tax due per month up to a maximum of 25%.

AMENDING RETURNS

Taxpayers may discover new facts, errors, or omissions on previously filed tax returns. When items come to light that alter the information on the taxpayers' original return, then they can file an amended return. An individual files an amended return using Form 1040X; a corporation files an 1120X. In general, an amended return must be filed before the expiration of the statute of limitations for the return; that is, within three years of the date the return was filed, or two years from the date the tax was paid, whichever is later. If the return was filed prior to its due date, the amended return must be filed within three years of the due date.

Form 1040X provides a relatively simple format for making changes in a prior year's return. It is necessary to list only certain items as originally reported, the changes in these items, and their corrected amounts. A space is provided for the taxpayer to provide an explanation for the changes to income, deductions, and/or credits that are reported on the form. The taxpayer must then recompute the tax with these changes and determine whether an additional tax is owed or a refund is due. If there is additional tax due because of the amended return, the IRS will send the taxpayer a bill for the interest due on the additional tax.

STATUTE OF LIMITATIONS

To provide for the orderly administration of the tax laws and a measure of certainty regarding tax assessments, both taxpayers filing corrected tax returns and the Internal Revenue Service making additional assessments of taxes must do so within time limits. These time limit restrictions are called the *statute of limitations.*

For taxpayers, the statute of limitations provides the time limit in which they must file an amended return to correct an error in the return originally filed. Taxpayers have three years from the date the return was filed or two years from the date the tax was paid (if later) in which to file an amended return. If the taxpayer files a return prior to its due date, then the statute of limitations is three years from the due date of the return.

Example 31. Mary Donohue filed her 1990 tax return on January 25, 1991, and her 1991 tax return on July 10, 1993, without having filed a request for an extension of time to file. Mary has until April 15, 1994, to amend her 1990 tax return (three years from its due date) and until July 10, 1995, to amend her 1991 return (three years from the date the return was filed). If Mary had failed to pay her tax due for 1991 until August 1, 1993, she would have until August 1, 1995, to amend the return (two years from the date the tax was paid).

Similar rules apply to the Internal Revenue Service, but in certain instances, the statute of limitations is extended to aid in enforcement of the tax laws. Under normal circumstances, the IRS cannot assess additional tax if more than three years has passed since the date the return was filed (or its due date if filed early), or, if later, two years after the tax was paid. This statute is extended, however, to six years from the date the return was filed if the taxpayer has omitted items from gross income that exceed 25% of the gross income reported on the return. If the IRS can show that the return filed was fraudulent, there is no statute of limitations and the IRS may assess additional tax, penalties, and interest at any time. It is, however, the IRS's responsibility to prove fraud; the taxpayer is not required to prove that fraud did not exist.

These limitations have the following practical consequences. The IRS generally starts an audit of a return to determine if additional tax is due during the first two years after the return is filed. This allows a full year to complete the audit and assess an addi-

---

ANSWERS TO REVIEW III

1. (d) Activity A is active since George participates more than 500 hours; Activity B is active since George provides over 100 hours that constitute the major portion of total activity.
2. (b) Mary may deduct $60,000 of losses against the $60,000 of passive income; she may carry over a total of $75,000 in losses prorated to each of the loss activities.
3. (c) Of the $25,000 rental activity exception, Alton is entitled to only $5,000 since he must phase out the $25,000 on the basis of 50 cents for each dollar that his AGI exceeds $100,000.
4. (c) He may deduct passive losses equal to passive income.

tional tax before the statute of limitation runs out. If, however, the taxpayer's return currently under audit appears suspicious, then prior and subsequent returns may also be audited. It is in these cases that the IRS will generally invoke the six-year statute for understatement of gross revenue or the unlimited statute for fraudulent returns.

✓ **Example 32.** On November 15, 1994, Donna Ferrara was assessed an additional tax of $2,000 for her 1991 tax return filed on April 15, 1993. In the process of auditing this return, the agent discovered a $62,000 deposit to Donna's checking account on January 12, 1990. Donna could not substantiate that this money was a gift, an inheritance, or other nontaxable sum. The agent then assessed $27,000 in additional taxes for this income for the 1990 tax year since Donna had reported income of only $53,000 for her 1990 tax return filed on June 20, 1991. The assessment of the $2,000 for Donna's 1993 tax year was within the normal three-year statute of limitations, which extends to April 15, 1995. The $27,000 assessment falls within the six-year statute of limitations, which extends to June 20, 1997, because there was a greater than 25% understatement of gross revenues.

The IRS could also initiate an audit outside the normal time frame if it receives information that fraud or material understatements of revenue are involved. This information could be obtained through audits of other taxpayers or possibly from information obtained from third parties, such as financial institutions, disgruntled employees, or informants. There is a "bounty" of up to 10% of the additional tax collected for identifying suspected tax evaders.

TAX TIP

If a taxpayer fails to file a tax return for any year, there is no statute of limitations applicable to the assessment of tax. Since all the statutes of limitation are based on either the filing of the return or the payment of taxes, no limitation can be invoked if no return is filed.

REVIEW IV

1. Julia Tuggle, an individual, has a fiscal year end of March 31 for her individual tax return. By what date must she file her request for an automatic extension and what is her extended due due?
   (a) June 15; October 15
   (b) June 15; December 15
   (c) July 15; November 15
   (d) July 15; January 15
2. What is the maximum date the IRS can extend the due date for the return of an individual who has a June 30, 1992, fiscal year end?
   (a) April 15, 1993
   (b) October 15, 1992
   (c) November 15, 1992
   (d) December 15, 1992

3. A taxpayer who discovers an error in his 1989 calendar-year tax return filed on January 30, 1990, has until what date to file an amended return?
   (a) April 15, 1992
   (b) April 15, 1993
   (c) April 15, 1994
   (d) August 15, 1993

Answers are on page 7-34.

CHAPTER APPENDIX: INTEREST CHARGES AND PENALTIES

Taxpayers who fail to have sufficient taxes withheld or fail to make appropriate estimated tax payments are subject to penalties for underwithholding as explained in Chapter 5. Taxpayers who fail to pay the actual tax on a timely basis can also be charged interest on these underpayments. These charges are true interest charges—as opposed to penalties—for failing to remit to the government the taxes owed. Prior to the repeal of the deduction for personal interest expense, these interest charges were deductible as an itemized deductions; the charges characterized as penalties were never deductible.

The interest rate that has been charged has varied over the years. Prior to 1987, the interest rate was pegged at 100% of the prime lending rate charged by banks and was adjusted semiannually. Since the beginning of 1987, the interest rate charged taxpayers is the current interest rate for short-term federal obligations plus 3%. This rate is adjusted four times per year and is compounded on a daily basis. The regulations provide tables for calculating the interest due.

The taxpayer's tax payment is due with the return filed on April 15 (for a calendar-year taxpayer) or with a request for extension of time to file filed by that same date. An extension of time to file is *not* an extension of time to pay the tax. The taxpayer is expected to estimate the tax due and pay that amount with the extension form. The IRS does not have to accept the extension (although it is normally an automatic extension for four months for individual taxpayers) if the taxpayer fails to make a "good faith" estimate of the taxes due, although a failure to *pay* will not invalidate the extension. If the taxpayer deliberately underestimates the tax due with the filing of the extension, the IRS can assess an additional penalty for failure-to-pay along with the interest charge for underpayment of taxes. The failure-to-pay penalty is .5% per month (or part of a month) up to a total of 25%. It is assessed if the taxpayer fails to pay the tax due by August 15, or if the amount of tax due is more than 10% of the total tax liability shown on the tax return. The taxpayer can avoid this penalty by showing reasonable cause for the failure to pay the tax on a timely basis.

✓ **Example 33.** Jeremy Icon failed to pay his $2,000 tax balance due April 15, 1993, until May 17, 1993. Assuming the rate for tax underpayments is 11%, Jeremy owes $19.37 ($2,000 × .009688978) interest on the underpayment since he was 32 days late. (The .0009688978 factor was obtained from the tables in the regulations for 32 days at 11% interest). If Jeremy's total tax shown on the return was less than $20,000, he could be assessed an additional penalty of $20 (1% × $2,000) for failure to pay the tax on a timely basis.

The IRS automatically assesses these interest and penalty charges when tax payments are not paid on a timely basis. They will also assess interest on these interest and penalty charges as part of the assessment for the period of time it took to make the assessment. The taxpayer has ten days to make the payment or additional interest will be charged. In general, if the taxpayer is notified of an assessment for additional *taxes and interest,* interest will be charged on the added taxes and interest to the date of the assessment. If the taxpayer responds by paying the tax and interest within ten days, no additional interest is charged.

Example 34. Tina Renaldi was assessed an additional $800 in taxes and interest of $40 on this deficiency through July 10 of the current year, when she received the deficiency notice. If Tina pays the $840 by July 20, no additional interest will be owed. If Tina fails to pay within the required 10-day period, the IRS can charge interest until the deficiency is paid. If, however, Tina proves that the additional assessment is incorrect, *no* taxes or interest would be owed.

If a taxpayer has an net operating loss or business credit in a future year that is carried back to a year in which taxes were not paid on a timely basis, *no* adjustment is made for the interest and penalties owed. The taxpayer is still responsible for interest and penalties on underpayments, even though a refund is obtained in a future year due to the carryback provisions.

Taxpayers who fail to file their tax returns are subject to a penalty for the failure to file a return. This penalty is 5% per month (or part of a month) with a maximum penalty of 25%. A minimum penalty of $100 or the amount of tax shown on the return applies if the return is filed more than 60 days after the due date. If the taxpayer is subject to the failure-to-pay penalty in the same month, this penalty is reduced by the .5% failure-to-pay penalty. The failure-to-file penalty may also be abated by showing reasonable cause for the failure to file the return.

Example 35. Joan Bowers has invested heavily in real estate, depleting her available cash. Since she had no money, she failed to file her tax return to 1992 until June 30, 1993. She paid the $15,000 total tax due with the return. She was required to pay a failure-to-file penalty of $2,025 ([.15 − .015] × $15,000) and a $225 (.015 × $15,000) penalty for failure to pay the tax in addition to interest on the unpaid taxes. The failure-to-file penalty would normally be $2,250 (.15 × 15,000) for the over-two-months that the return was late. Since the failure-to-pay penalty of $225 was assessed for that period, the failure-to-pay penalty was reduced by that amount.

Taxpayers who overpay their taxes may also receive interest payments from the government under certain circumstances. If the taxpayer files a timely return and does not receive a refund within 45 days of the due date for the return, the taxpayer is entitled to receive interest for the delay beyond the 45-day period. The interest that is paid is based on the current rate for short-term government securities plus 2%. Prior to 1987, the interest charged taxpayers on underpayments was the same as the interest paid on overpayments, but now a 1% differential exists.

7-34 Special Tax Computations for Individuals

> ✓ **Example 36.** Olga Tinette filed her tax return on January 30, 1993, for the 1992 tax year. Due to an inadvertent error, she did not receive her $1,000 refund until July 15, 1993. The government must pay Olga interest on the refund from 45 days after April 15. Although Olga filed her return early, she is not entitled to interest until 45 days after the April 15 due date for the return.

If a taxpayer files an amended return in which a refund of prior taxes is claimed, the taxpayer is entitled to interest on this refund. The taxpayer is not entitled to receive interest if a refund is claimed due to a carryback to a prior year of a current net operating loss or business credit.

Numerous other penalties can be imposed on the taxpayer and, possibly, the tax preparer for negligence, intentional disregard of rules, substantial valuation errors, and fraud. These are beyond the scope of this text; however, they are mentioned briefly in Chapter 1.

CHAPTER PROBLEMS

PART
I 1. Winnie and Wally Jones had $43,000 of taxable income after their standard deduction of $6,200 and their personal and dependency exemptions of $14,100. What is their AMTI if they have $60,000 of tax preferences?

I 2. Bobby Nailor, a head of household, had $72,000 of taxable income after he deducted the following itemized deductions:

   $8,000   Medical expenses
   $4,000   Charitable contributions
   $12,000 Casualty loss
   $12,000 Qualified home mortgage interest
   $8,000   State and local taxes

   He also had $4,700 of personal exemptions. What is Bobby's AMTI if he has $10,000 of positive adjustments and $30,000 of positive preference items?

I 3. Aldo Domenique, a single individual, had $40,000 of depreciation expense on post-1986 ACRS assets and $27,000 of accelerated depreciation on pre-1987 real property. The ADS depreciation and straight-line depreciation would have been $23,000 and $22,000 respectively. If Aldo had AMTI of $78,000 before his depreciation adjustments and preferences, what would his final AMTI be?

I 4. Tory Long has $287,000 of taxable income before exemptions on which she owes a tax of $78,360 after her child care credit. She has $86,000 of preference items, $76,000 of

---

ANSWERS TO REVIEW IV

1. (c)
2. (a)
3. (b)

positive adjustments, and $12,000 of negative adjustments. What is her AMT if she is head of household?

I   5. During the current year, Anna Chang donated to a museum a painting that was valued at $750,000. She had paid only $5,000 for this painting many year ago on a trip to China. Anna also had an interest in a silver mine and took a $25,000 percentage depletion allowance even though her basis in the mine was zero. If Anna's tax was $24,000 (after credits) on taxable income of $121,000 in 1993, what is her AMTI if she is single, has no dependents, and does not itemize her deductions?

II   6. Phyllis Lory retired from her job after 30 years of service. Because of her long service, she participated in both the original pension plan and the company's current profit sharing plan. She can take the money from both plans as lump-sum distributions or she can set up regular payments. What are the tax alternatives that apply to the payment options available to her?

II   7. Willy August decided to take a $75,000 lump-sum distribution from his pension plan in the current year. He has taxable income for the year of $19,000 excluding the distribution. If Willy is married, filing jointly, how much tax will he save by using the five-year averaging method of determining the tax. (Use the tax rate schedule for 1993.)

II   8. Marc Bono took a $60,000 lump-sum distribution from his pension plan in 1993. Although he contributed to the plan, each dollar he put in is matched by his employer's contribution or interest earned of $5. Marc's contributions were made from his after-tax income. How much of the lump-sum distribution is taxable to him? What is his minimum distribution allowance and his tax due if he uses five-year averaging?

II   9. Nancy Softheart, a calendar year taxpayer, received a distribution of $40,000 on December 13, 1992, and an $80,000 distribution on January 4, 1993, from her profit-sharing plan to close out her entire balance. What is her minimum distribution allowance and what is her tax using five-year forward averaging if she is a calendar-year taxpayer?

III   10. Jorge Ramirez owns a small restaurant about five miles from his home. He generally works at the restaurant from 6 AM until 3 PM since it is open weekdays only for breakfast and lunch. He employs three other people in the restaurant on a part-time basis. Jorge also is an accomplished guitarist and occasionally plays on weekends for weddings and parties. Last year he spent 80 hours doing this and earned $1,500. The restaurant lost $2,000, however. Are these activities active or passive? Explain your answer.

III   11. Myra Adams has a regular full-time job in addition to owning two different businesses in which she employs qualified full-time personnel. Business A required 125 hours of her time last year and she had $3,000 of income. Business B required 60 hours of her time, and had a loss of $5,000. How does Myra treat these items of income and loss?

III   12. Ward Clevenger is a bookkeeper and had his own full-time business for seven years. He had only one other employee, a part-time secretary. This year, however, he took a full-time position with another firm and kept only a few clients from the business on whom he spent only 75 hours during the year. A former client of Ward's sued him for a fall on his premises, and due to the settlement, the business lost $15,000. How should Ward treat the loss?

III   13. Alice O'Day has a $22,000 loss for the current year from the apartment complex she owns. Her active income from other sources is $132,000. Can Alice deduct any of the $22,000 loss on her tax return?

IV   14. By what date must a June 30 partnership file its return if it does not have an extension? If it has an automatic extension? What is the last date a timely filed return can be filed?

IV 15. How long is the automatic extension for an individual? What is the last date that a January 31 fiscal year end individual can file a timely return?

IV 16. George Ellis, a calendar year taxpayer, had an automatic extension to file his individual tax return for 1992. He filed the return on June 2, 1993. What is the last date on which he can file an amended return?

IV 17. Ellen Thompson filed her tax return on April 14, 1993, but she was unable to pay the tax due until December of that year. What is the last date that she can file an amended return?

IV 18. (a) Willy Newman had a $37,000 tax liability for the 1992 tax year when he filed his return on April 15, 1993. He was able to pay only $10,000 in addition to the $5,000 he had had withheld during the tax year. What types of penalties may Willy be assessed if he does not pay the balance until June 10, 1993?

(b) What are the consequences if he files an automatic extension that includes the $10,000 payment but does not file and pay the balance due until August 15, 1993?

(c) What are the consequences if he does not obtain an extension and does not file the return and pay the balance due until June 10, 1993?

TAX RETURN PROBLEMS

19. [Form 6251] Using the information in Problem 1, complete Form 6251 for Winnie and Wally Jones.

20. [Form 4972] Portland Wylie took a $52,000 fully taxable lump-sum distribution from her pension plan in the current tax year when she retired at age 63. Complete Form 4972 for Portland since she is eligible to use five-year forward averaging.

HOW WOULD YOU RULE?

21. Matty and Leland Hayward separated in March of the current tax year and are planning to file for divorce when they reach agreement on the division of properties. Because of their joint and separate liabilities on a joint return, they will file separate tax returns. Matty remained in the family home and had custody of their only child, Amanda. If both Matty and Leland will be subject to the alternative minimum tax, what is their exemption amount and at what level of alternative minimum taxable income must each of them be concerned about the phasing out of their exemption amount?

22. Bob Farrell worked two jobs for two employers during the last 12 years prior to his retirement last year at age 66. He decided to take an immediate $22,000 lump-sum distribution from the pension plan of Employer A but took nothing from the profit sharing plan of Employer B. Bob elected to use the five-year forward averaging provision for the pension plan distribution because he was going to start receiving the income from the profit sharing plan in the form of an annuity starting in two years. Bob, however, was killed in an auto accident during the current tax year and his estate received a $40,000 lump-sum distribution from the profit sharing plan of Employer B. What special tax treatments would be available to the estate for this lump-sum distribution?

TAX PORTFOLIO PROBLEM FOR THE NEILSON FAMILY

If your instructor has assigned this optional extension to the portfolio problem, refer to Appendix A and complete the portion labeled "Chapter 7." This refers to "Optional Extension I" which includes additional information necessary to compute the alternative minimum tax and prepare Form 6251 for Harold and Maude Adams.

Chapter 7 Problem 19 Name _____ 7-37

Form **6251**	**Alternative Minimum Tax—Individuals**	OMB No. 1545-0227
Department of the Treasury Internal Revenue Service	▶ See separate instructions. ▶ Attach to Form 1040 or Form 1040NR.	**1993** Attachment Sequence No. **32**

Name(s) shown on Form 1040 | Your social security number

Part I — Adjustments and Preferences

1	If you itemized deductions on Schedule A (Form 1040), go to line 2. If you did not itemize deductions, enter your standard deduction from Form 1040, line 34, and skip to line 6 . .	1
2	Medical and dental expenses. See instructions	2
3	Taxes. Enter the amount from Schedule A, line 8	3
4	Certain interest on a home mortgage not used to buy, build, or improve your home . .	4
5	Miscellaneous itemized deductions. Enter the amount from Schedule A, line 24	5
6	Refund of taxes. Enter any tax refund from Form 1040, line 10 or 22	6 ( )
7	Investment interest. Enter difference between regular tax and AMT deduction	7
8	Post-1986 depreciation. Enter difference between regular tax and AMT depreciation . . .	8
9	Adjusted gain or loss. Enter difference between AMT and regular tax gain or loss . . .	9
10	Incentive stock options. Enter excess of AMT income over regular tax income	10
11	Passive activities. Enter difference between AMT and regular tax income or loss . . .	11
12	Beneficiaries of estates and trusts. Enter the amount from Schedule K-1 (Form 1041), line 8	12
13	Tax-exempt interest from private activity bonds issued after 8/7/86	13
14	Other. Enter the amount, if any, for each item and enter the total on line 14.	
	a Charitable contributions . [ ] g Long-term contracts . . [ ]	
	b Circulation expenditures . [ ] h Loss limitations . . . . [ ]	
	c Depletion . . . . . [ ] i Mining costs . . . . [ ]	
	d Depreciation (pre-1987) . [ ] j Pollution control facilities . [ ]	
	e Installment sales . . . [ ] k Research and experimental [ ]	
	f Intangible drilling costs . [ ] l Tax shelter farm activities . [ ]	
	m Related adjustments . . [ ]	14
15	**Total Adjustments and Preferences.** Combine lines 1 through 14 . . . . ▶	15

Part II — Alternative Minimum Taxable Income

16	Enter the amount from **Form 1040, line 35.** If less than zero, enter as a (loss) . . . ▶	16
17	Net operating loss deduction, if any, from Form 1040, line 22. Enter as a positive amount .	17
18	If Form 1040, line 32, is over $108,450 (over $54,225 if married filing separately), enter your itemized deductions limitation, if any, from line 9 of the worksheet for Schedule A, line 26	18 ( )
19	Combine lines 15 through 18 . . . . ▶	19
20	Alternative tax net operating loss deduction. See instructions	20
21	**Alternative Minimum Taxable Income.** Subtract line 20 from line 19. (If married filing separately and line 21 is more than $165,000, see instructions.) . . . . ▶	21

Part III — Exemption Amount and Alternative Minimum Tax

22	**Exemption Amount.** (If this form is for a child under age 14, see instructions.)			
	If your filing status is:	**And line 21 is not over:**	**Enter on line 22:**	
	Single or head of household	$112,500	$33,750	
	Married filing jointly or qualifying widow(er)	150,000	45,000	22
	Married filing separately	75,000	22,500	
	If line 21 is **over** the amount shown above for your filing status, see instructions.			
23	Subtract line 22 from line 21. If zero or less, enter -0- here and on lines 26 and 28 . ▶			23
24	If line 23 is $175,000 or less ($87,500 or less if married filing separately), multiply line 23 by 26% (.26). Otherwise, see instructions			24
25	Alternative minimum tax foreign tax credit. See instructions			25
26	Tentative minimum tax. Subtract line 25 from line 24 . . . . ▶			26
27	Enter your tax from Form 1040, line 38 (plus any amount from Form 4970 included on Form 1040, line 39), minus any foreign tax credit from Form 1040, line 43			27
28	**Alternative Minimum Tax.** (If this form is for a child under age 14, see instructions.) Subtract line 27 from line 26. If zero or less, enter -0-. Enter here and on Form 1040, line 48 ▶			28

For Paperwork Reduction Act Notice, see separate instructions.   Cat. No. 13600G   Form **6251** (1993)

Copyright © 1994 by Harcourt Brace & Company. All rights reserved.

Chapter 7 Problem 20   Name _____   7-39

Form 4972
Department of the Treasury
Internal Revenue Service

Tax on Lump-Sum Distributions
(Use This Form Only for Lump-Sum Distributions From Qualified Retirement Plans)
▶ Attach to Form 1040 or Form 1041.   ▶ See separate instructions.

OMB No. 1545-0193
1993
Attachment Sequence No. **28**

Name of recipient of distribution

Identifying number

Part I — Complete this part to see if you qualify to use Form 4972.

		Yes	No
1	Did you roll over any part of the distribution? If "Yes," do not complete the rest of this form		
2	Was the retirement plan participant born before 1936? If "No," do not complete the rest of this form		
3	Was this a lump-sum distribution from a qualified pension, profit-sharing, or stock bonus plan? (See **Distributions That Qualify for the 20% Capital Gain Election or for 5- or 10-Year Averaging** in the instructions.) If "No," do not complete the rest of this form		
4	Was the participant in the plan for at least 5 years before the year of the distribution?		
5	Was this distribution paid to you as a beneficiary of a plan participant who died?		

If you answered "No" to both questions 4 and 5, do not complete the rest of this form.

6 Was the plan participant:

		Yes	No
a	An employee who received the distribution because he or she quit, retired, was laid off, or was fired?		
b	Self-employed or an owner-employee who became permanently and totally disabled before the distribution?		
c	Age 59½ or older at the time of the distribution?		

If you answered "No" to question 5 and **all** parts of question 6, do not complete the rest of this form.

7 Did you use Form 4972 in a prior year for any distribution received after 1986 for the same plan participant, including you, for whom the 1992 distribution was made? If "Yes," do not complete the rest of this form

If you qualify to use this form, you may choose to use Part II, Part III, or Part IV; **or** Part II and Part III; **or** Part II and Part IV.

Part II — Complete this part to choose the 20% capital gain election. (See instructions.)

8	Capital gain part from box 3 of Form 1099-R. (See instructions.)	8	
9	Multiply line 8 by 20% (.20) and enter here. If you do not choose to use Part III or Part IV, also enter the amount on Form 1040, line 39, or Form 1041, Schedule G, line 1b	9	

Part III — Complete this part to choose the 5-year averaging method. (See instructions.)

10	Ordinary income from Form 1099-R, box 2a minus box 3. If you did not complete Part II, enter the taxable amount from box 2a of Form 1099-R. (See instructions.)	10	
11	Death benefit exclusion. (See instructions.)	11	
12	Total taxable amount—Subtract line 11 from line 10	12	
13	Current actuarial value of annuity, if applicable (from Form 1099-R, box 8)	13	
14	Adjusted total taxable amount—Add lines 12 and 13. If this amount is $70,000 or more, skip lines 15 through 18, and enter this amount on line 19	14	
15	Multiply line 14 by 50% (.50), but **do not** enter more than $10,000 . . 15		
16	Subtract $20,000 from line 14. If line 14 is $20,000 or less, enter -0- 16		
17	Multiply line 16 by 20% (.20) 17		
18	Minimum distribution allowance—Subtract line 17 from line 15	18	
19	Subtract line 18 from line 14	19	
20	Federal estate tax attributable to lump-sum distribution. Do not deduct on Form 1040 or Form 1041 the amount attributable to the ordinary income entered on line 10. (See instructions.)	20	
21	Subtract line 20 from line 19	21	
22	Multiply line 21 by 20% (.20)	22	
23	Tax on amount on line 22. See instructions for Tax Rate Schedule	23	
24	Multiply line 23 by five (5). If line 13 is blank, skip lines 25 through 30, and enter this amount on line 31	24	
25	Divide line 13 by line 14 and enter the result as a decimal. (See instructions.)	25	
26	Multiply line 18 by the decimal amount on line 25	26	
27	Subtract line 26 from line 13	27	
28	Multiply line 27 by 20% (.20)	28	
29	Tax on amount on line 28. See instructions for Tax Rate Schedule	29	
30	Multiply line 29 by five (5)	30	
31	Subtract line 30 from line 24. (Multiple recipients, see instructions.)	31	
32	Tax on lump-sum distribution—Add Part II, line 9, and Part III, line 31. Enter on Form 1040, line 39, or Form 1041, Schedule G, line 1b . . . . ▶	32	

For Paperwork Reduction Act Notice, see separate instructions.   Cat. No. 13187U   Form **4972** (1992)

Form 4972 (1993) Page **2**

Part IV   Complete this part to choose the 10-year averaging method. (See instructions.)

33	Ordinary income part from Form 1099-R, box 2a minus box 3. If you did not complete Part II, enter the taxable amount from box 2a of Form 1099-R. (See instructions.)	33	
34	Death benefit exclusion. (See instructions.)	34	
35	Total taxable amount—Subtract line 34 from line 33	35	
36	Current actuarial value of annuity, if applicable (from Form 1099-R, box 8)	36	
37	Adjusted total taxable amount—Add lines 35 and 36. If this amount is $70,000 or more, skip lines 38 through 41, and enter this amount on line 42	37	
38	Multiply line 37 by 50% (.50), but **do not** enter more than $10,000 38		
39	Subtract $20,000 from line 37. If line 37 is $20,000 or less, enter -0- 39		
40	Multiply line 39 by 20% (.20) 40		
41	Minimum distribution allowance—Subtract line 40 from line 38	41	
42	Subtract line 41 from line 37	42	
43	Federal estate tax attributable to lump-sum distribution. Do not deduct on Form 1040 or Form 1041 the amount attributable to the ordinary income entered on line 33. (See instructions.)	43	
44	Subtract line 43 from line 42	44	
45	Multiply line 44 by 10% (.10)	45	
46	Tax on amount on line 45. See instructions for Tax Rate Schedule	46	
47	Multiply line 46 by ten (10). If line 36 is blank, skip lines 48 through 53, and enter this amount on line 54	47	
48	Divide line 36 by line 37 and enter the result as a decimal. (See instructions.)	48	
49	Multiply line 41 by the decimal amount on line 48	49	
50	Subtract line 49 from line 36	50	
51	Multiply line 50 by 10% (.10)	51	
52	Tax on amount on line 51. See instructions for Tax Rate Schedule	52	
53	Multiply line 52 by ten (10)	53	
54	Subtract line 53 from line 47. (Multiple recipients, see instructions.)	54	
55	Tax on lump-sum distribution—Add Part II, line 9, and Part IV, line 54. Enter on Form 1040, line 39, or Form 1041, Schedule G, line 1b ▶	55	

CHAPTER 8

Deductions: Income-Producing Activities and Trades or Businesses

Deductions are matters of legislative grace, in that no item may be subtracted in determining taxable income unless that item is specifically authorized by Congress. Deductible expenditures are classified into one of three major categories: (1) trade or business expenses, (2) income-producing expenses, and (3) personal expenses. The purpose of this chapter is to examine the specific requirements for the most common expenses in the first two categories (trade or business expenses and income-producing expenses). The tax treatments of various personal expenses reportable as itemized deductions were previously discussed in Chapter 4.

I. REQUIREMENTS OF A DEDUCTION
(Code Sections 162, 212, and 262)

In the earlier discussions of gross income, we noted that all sources of income are presumed to be taxable unless specifically excluded by law. It is interesting to note that Congress applies the *opposite* logic to deductions: all expenditures are presumed to be *nondeductible* unless specifically authorized by law. A taxpayer who wishes to deduct a specific expenditure must be able to identify a specific provision of the Internal Revenue Code granting such a deduction. Fortunately, Congress has simplified this search for authority by enacting two "umbrella" provisions, Code Secs. 162 and 212, that grant deductions for a variety of common expenditures.

THE LAW

Sec. 162(a)—There shall be allowed as a deduction all the ordinary and necessary expenses paid or incurred during the taxable year in carrying on any trade or business...

Code Sec. 162 authorizes a deduction for all ordinary and necessary expenses incurred in carrying on a business. This provision grants the authority for deducting literally hundreds of items related to operating an active business, such as salaries, cost of goods sold, supplies, depreciation, and so on.

THE LAW

Sec. 212—In the case of an individual, there shall be allowed as a deduction all the ordinary and necessary expenses paid or incurred during the taxable year -
(1) for the production or collection of income;
(2) for the management, conservation, or maintenance of property held for the production of income; or
(3) in connection with the determination, collection, or refund of any tax.

Code Sec. 212 authorizes a deduction for any expenses paid or incurred in (1) the production of income, (2) the maintenance or conservation of income-producing property, or (3) the determination or litigation of a tax liability. This provision grants the authority for deducting expenditures associated with passive income-producing activities that do not qualify as trade or businesses (e.g., a rental fee for a safety deposit box used to store investment securities).

Any expenditure not qualifying under either Sec. 162 or Sec 212 is treated as a nondeductible personal expenditure, unless a specific Code section provides for its deductibility. The most common examples of these deductible expenses were discussed in Chapter 4.

CRITERIA FOR DEDUCTIBILITY

To be deductible, an income-producing or a trade or business expense must be ordinary, necessary, and reasonable in amount. The "ordinary" requirement is satisfied when an expense would be reasonably expected to occur in similar activities or businesses with similar circumstances. The "necessary" requirement is satisfied when an expenditure is appropriate and helpful to the activity or business. And finally, the "reasonableness" requirement is met if the expenditure is not extravagant or unnecessarily large under the circumstances.

Example 1. Jane Watson manufactures draperies for mobile homes and pays a percentage of sales to the officers of mobile home manufacturers. Watson soon became the largest supplier of draperies in the industry. Though such expenditures were perhaps "necessary" for the taxpayer to become successful, they were not "ordinary" if the practice of making such payments was not widespread.

Example 2. A corporation paid all of the expenses of converting the president's farm into a "unique horticultural showplace." The purpose of the expenditure was to provide a location where the president could leisurely entertain customers. This expenditure would probably not be deductible, because it is not a "necessary" promotion expense.

Example 3. Bob and Mary Chambliss own all of the stock of C Corporation. During the year, Mary managed the company full-time and received a salary of $40,000. Bob had another full-time job with Blue Company; however, he was paid a $30,000 salary by C Corporation for consulting services (one day a month). Most likely, the IRS would disallow Bob's salary deduction as "unreasonable." If the fair value of the consulting services was $6,000, then the other $24,000 of Bob's salary would be reclassified as dividend income.

TIMING OF DEDUCTIBILITY

One other requirement for expenses is that they must be paid or incurred during the taxable year. It is very important to note that the normal cash versus accrual basis distinctions are not always followed for tax purposes. The tax law requires deferral of any expenditure that creates an asset with a useful life extending materially into the next year. This is true regardless of whether the taxpayer is on the cash or accrual basis.

Example 4. Margaret Hall, a cash-basis calendar-year taxpayer, prepays $12,000 for two years' rent on an office building on October 1, 1993. She may deduct only $1,500 of this prepayment on her 1993 return (3/24 × $12,000), which represents the amount of rental expense actually *incurred* in 1993. The remaining $10,500 represents prepayment for 21 months of rent that will not be incurred until 1994 and a portion of 1995.

The tax treatment of expenses creates an interesting paradox for prepaid expenses. Prepayments of expenses are immediately taxable to the recipient (regardless of basis) under the wherewithal-to-pay principle; however, such prepayments are *not* immediately deductible by the payer (regardless of basis) because the expenditure must be incurred (i.e., used up) before being deductible.

Example 5. John Davis, a calendar-year taxpayer, borrowed $10,000 on a 12-month, 6% note for his sole proprietorship business on October 1, 1993. The note plus interest is repayable in full on October 1, 1994. If Davis is a cash-basis taxpayer, no interest expense will be deductible until 1994, when the loan is repaid. Although three months of interest expense were incurred as of the end of 1993, a cash-basis taxpayer cannot deduct an expense until it is actually paid. If Davis were an accrual-basis taxpayer, the three months of interest ($300) that were incurred in 1993 would be deductible.

DISALLOWED DEDUCTIONS

In light of the previous discussion, we may be somewhat surprised to discover that Congress has enacted several provisions that specifically *disallow* certain types of expenditures as deductions. Given that *no* item is deductible unless specifically allowed by Congress, it is natural to question why Congress felt the need to enact specific disallowance provisions. The answer is simple: Congress wanted to state unequivocally that certain expenditures will never be deductible, even though they might otherwise appear to meet the criteria for deductibility under either Sec. 162 or Sec. 212.

Expenditures Frustrating Public Policy

Any payment that violates public policy is not deductible. Examples of the prohibited deductions include fines, bribes, penalties, and kickbacks. Obviously, Congress felt that the effects of violating a law should not be mitigated by allowing a deduction for such payments, even when the violation was unintentional.

Example 6. A trucking company deliberately incurred several fines in a state for operating trucks over weight limits. The company could justify these violations as being economically feasible, because it would cost the company more to circumvent the state or carry lighter loads, which was also more dangerous. Although the company can make persuasive arguments that the fines are ordinary and necessary business expenses, the fines violate public policy and are not deductible.

Because of potential abuses, Congress has also specifically disallowed deductions for political contributions. Lobbying expenses are deductible only if they relate to written or oral testimony regarding proposed legislation by local councils or similar governing bodies that will directly affect the business interests of the taxpayer. For example, the expenses incurred by company officers in testifying before the city council on legislation that will regulate their business operations is deductible.

Expenses Related to Tax-Exempt Income

Any expenses incurred in producing tax-exempt income are not deductible. Congress believes that it is inconsistent to reward taxpayers with a deduction when the income generated by the expenditure is excludable. This disallowance provision is most commonly encountered with investments in state or municipal securities.

Example 7. Bradley Thornton paid $1,200 of interest expense in 1993 on a $10,000 loan obtained from First National Bank in January of that year. Thornton invested $5,000 of the loan proceeds in state of Massachusetts bonds and $5,000 in ABC Corporation bonds. One-half of the interest expense paid by Thornton is not deductible, because half of the loan proceeds was invested in securities that produce tax-exempt income (the Massachusetts bonds).

Personal (Hobby) Expenditures versus Business Expenditures

The distinction between business and personal expenses is not always clearly defined. For example, assume that Byron Thames, a successful business executive, earns $300,000 salary a year. Thames also owns a farm located 40 miles from his primary residence. During the current year, the farm generated $3,000 revenues and $25,000 expenses. Are all these expenses deductible as business expenses, or will they be disallowed as personal expenses, under the assumption that the farming activity is a hobby?

THE LAW

Sec. 183(d)—If the gross income from an activity for 3 or more of the taxable years in the period of 5 consecutive taxable years which ends with the taxable year exceeds the deductions attributable to such activity . . . then, unless the Secretary establishes to the contrary, such activity shall be presumed . . . to be an activity engaged in for profit.

Obviously, the answer to this question depends on the facts and circumstances of the case. Congress certainly does not want to subsidize the personal hobbies of taxpayers. In an effort to reduce the controversies between taxpayers and the IRS on this issue, Congress enacted a special *hobby loss rule*.

In essence, the hobby loss rule states that an activity will be presumed to be hobby if it fails to produce a profit in at least three of five consecutive years. If the activity fails this test, then any expenses incurred in the activity are deductible only to the extent of the gross income from the activity. In the above example, Thames could deduct only $3,000 of expenses if he fails the three-out-of-five-year test. The excess expenses are disallowed as personal expenditures (although they may be carried forward to offset income in future years). In applying this rule, any casualty losses, interest, and taxes incurred in the activity *must* be deducted first, because these items may otherwise be deductible as itemized deductions.

TAX TIP

If taxpayers have been engaged in an activity for less than five years and are audited by the IRS, they can elect to postpone the determination of business or hobby status if it is still possible to meet the three-out-of-five-year test. This is done by filing a request with the IRS at the time of the audit. However, one disadvantage of filing such a request is that the normal three-year statute of limitations is also extended for the year in question.

For tax years beginning after 1986, the IRS has one additional weapon to use in dealing with hobby losses: the Sec. 469 passive loss rules. In general, these rules limit deductions from "passive activities" to the incomes from such activities. These rules were discussed in Chapter 7.

Deductibility of Losses

The term *loss* generally refers to a realized decrease in wealth of an individual or business. A loss implies that a taxpayer did not fully realize the full benefits of an expenditure; examples include property destroyed by a natural disaster and a sale of property for less than its adjusted basis.

THE LAW

Sec. 165(a)—General Rule. There shall be allowed as a deduction any loss sustained during the taxable year and not compensated for by insurance or otherwise . . .
(c) Limitation on Losses of Individuals.—In the case of an individual, the deduction under subsection (a) shall be limited to—
(1) losses incurred in a trade or business;
(2) losses incurred in any transaction entered into for profit, though not connected with a trade or business; and
(3) except as provided in subsection (h), losses of property not connected with a trade or business or a transaction entered into for profit, if such losses arise from fire, storm, shipwreck, or other casualty, or from theft.

An individual may deduct only three types of losses: (1) losses incurred in a trade or business, (2) losses incurred in an income-producing activity, and (3) personal casualty and theft losses. Note that the three categories of loss deductions parallel the three categories of expense deductions (Sec. 162 expenses, Sec. 212 expenses, and personal itemized deductions). One practical effect of this rule is to disallow losses on the sale or exchange of personal properties.

Example 8. Donna Reed sold her personal automobile in 1993 for $2,400. The automobile was originally purchased in 1988 for $5,500. The $3,100 loss realized by Reed is not deductible, because the automobile is personal property.

EXPENSES RELATED TO INCOME-PRODUCING ACTIVITIES

Under Sec. 162, an individual engaged in a trade or business is permitted to deduct losses and expenses that are ordinary and necessary for that trade or business and that are reasonable in nature. Individuals, however, often have other activities in which they invest with the intent of earning a profit. If they do not devote sufficient time on a regular and continuous basis to the activity, however, it cannot be considered a trade or business.

For an individual, the deductions for expenses and losses incurred in a trade or business are reported on Schedule C (discussed later in this chapter). However, expenses related to a taxpayer's trade or business of being an *employee* are not included in that category. As discussed in Chapter 4, most unreimbursed expenses incurred by an employee are generally subject to limited deductibility as miscellaneous itemized deductions on Schedule A.

An individual taxpayer is also permitted a deduction for adjusted gross income (AGI) for expenses related to two other types of income: rents and royalties. Rental income is derived from the use of a taxpayer's property by others. Royalty income may be derived from the extraction of minerals from property or from a licensing arrangement for an intangible asset such as a patent or copyright. Ownership of rental properties by a taxpayer does not normally qualify as a trade or business. If, however, the taxpayer provides substantial services along with the rental (e.g., a hotel or motel), then the activity may constitute a trade or business.

Amounts that constitute rental payments must be included in income when the payments are received regardless of the taxpayer's method of accounting. Amounts that constitute refundable deposits are not income until the deposit is forfeited.

TAX TIP

Prepaid rents are generally taxable when received, regardless of the period to which they relate. By requiring a larger security deposit rather than collecting the last month's rent at the beginning of a rental period, a landlord may postpone the recognition of income.

Income and expenses from rents and royalties are reported on Schedule E (illustrated in Figure 8-1, using the facts of Examples 9, 10, and 11). Note that the deductible

I. Requirements of a Deduction   8-7

SCHEDULE E (Form 1040) Department of the Treasury Internal Revenue Service	**Supplemental Income and Loss** (From rental real estate, royalties, partnerships, S corporations, estates, trusts, REMICs, etc.) ▶ Attach to Form 1040 or Form 1041. ▶ See Instructions for Schedule E (Form 1040).	OMB No. 1545-0074 **1993** Attachment Sequence No. **13**
Name(s) shown on return Anthony Rossi		Your social security number 621 : 30 : 4465

Part I   Income or Loss From Rental Real Estate and Royalties   Note: *Report income and expenses from your business of renting personal property on **Schedule C** or **C-EZ** (see page E-1). Report farm rental income or loss from **Form 4835** on page 2, line 39.*

1 Show the kind and location of each **rental real estate property**:	2 For each rental real estate property listed on line 1, did you or your family use it for personal purposes for more than the greater of 14 days or 10% of the total days rented at fair rental value during the tax year? (See page E-1.)		Yes	No
A 1211 Harmon Street (duplex) Jackson, MS 39205		A		X
B 1910 Harmon Street (5-acre oil lease) Jackson, MS 39205		B		X
C		C		

			Properties			Totals
Income:			A	B	C	(Add columns A, B, and C.)
3 Rents received	3	24,000			3	
4 Royalties received	4		40,000		4	
Expenses:						
5 Advertising	5					
6 Auto and travel (see page E-2)	6					
7 Cleaning and maintenance	7	400				
8 Commissions	8	750				
9 Insurance	9	1,200				
10 Legal and other professional fees	10					
11 Management fees	11					
12 Mortgage interest paid to banks, etc. (see page E-2)	12	4,000			12	
13 Other interest	13					
14 Repairs	14					
15 Supplies	15	725				
16 Taxes	16	3,200				
17 Utilities	17					
18 Other (list) ▶	18					
19 Add lines 5 through 18	19	10,275			19	
20 Depreciation expense or depletion (see page E-2)	20	12,500	6,000		20	
21 Total expenses. Add lines 19 and 20	21	22,775				
22 Income or (loss) from rental real estate or royalty properties. Subtract line 21 from line 3 (rents) or line 4 (royalties). If the result is a (loss), see page E-2 to find out if you must file **Form 6198**.	22	1,225	34,000			
23 Deductible rental real estate loss. **Caution:** *Your rental real estate loss on line 22 may be limited. See page E-3 to find out if you must file **Form 8582**.*	23	( )	( )	( )		
24 **Income.** Add positive amounts shown on line 22. **Do not** include any losses					24	35,225
25 **Losses.** Add royalty losses from line 22 and rental real estate losses from line 23. Enter the total losses here					25	( )
26 **Total rental real estate and royalty income or (loss).** Combine lines 24 and 25. Enter the result here. If Parts II, III, IV, and line 39 on page 2 do not apply to you, also enter this amount on Form 1040, line 18. Otherwise, include this amount in the total on line 40 on page 2					26	35,225

For Paperwork Reduction Act Notice, see Form 1040 instructions.   Cat. No. 11344L   Schedule E (Form 1040) 1993

Figure 8-1   Schedule E

Schedule E (Form 1040) 1993 — Attachment Sequence No. 13 — Page 2

Name(s) shown on return. Do not enter name and social security number if shown on other side. — Your social security number

Note: *If you report amounts from farming or fishing on Schedule E, you must enter your gross income from those activities on line 41 below.*

Part II — Income or Loss From Partnerships and S Corporations

If you report a loss from an at-risk activity, you MUST check either column (e) or (f) of line 27 to describe your investment in the activity. See page E-4. If you check column (f), you must attach **Form 6198**.

27	(a) Name	(b) Enter P for partnership; S for S corporation	(c) Check if foreign partnership	(d) Employer identification number	(e) All is at risk	(f) Some is not at risk
A	Alpha Company	S		44-7063122	X	
B	Public Partners	P		16-3744221	X	
C						
D						
E						

	Passive Income and Loss		Nonpassive Income and Loss		
	(g) Passive loss allowed (attach Form 8582 if required)	(h) Passive income from Schedule K-1	(i) Nonpassive loss from Schedule K-1	(j) Section 179 expense deduction from Form 4562	(k) Nonpassive income from Schedule K-1
A		400			
B		13,000			
C					
D					
E					
28a Totals		13,400			
b Totals					

29 Add columns (h) and (k) of line 28a 29   13,400
30 Add columns (g), (i), and (j) of line 28b 30 (13,400)
31 Total partnership and S corporation income or (loss). Combine lines 29 and 30. Enter the result here and include in the total on line 40 below 31

Part III — Income or Loss From Estates and Trusts

32	(a) Name	(b) Employer identification number
A		
B		
C		

	Passive Income and Loss		Nonpassive Income and Loss	
	(c) Passive deduction or loss allowed (attach Form 8582 if required)	(d) Passive income from Schedule K-1	(e) Deduction or loss from Schedule K-1	(f) Other income from Schedule K-1
A				
B				
C				
33a Totals				
b Totals				

34 Add columns (d) and (f) of line 33a 34
35 Add columns (c) and (e) of line 33b . . . . 35 ( )
36 Total estate and trust income or (loss). Combine lines 34 and 35. Enter the result here and include in the total on line 40 below 36

Part IV — Income or Loss From Real Estate Mortgage Investment Conduits (REMICs)—Residual Holder

37	(a) Name	(b) Employer identification number	(c) Excess inclusion from Schedules Q, line 2c (see page E-4)	(d) Taxable income (net loss) from Schedules Q, line 1b	(e) Income from Schedules Q, line 3b

38 Combine columns (d) and (e) only. Enter the result here and include in the total on line 40 below   38

Part V — Summary

39 Net farm rental income or (loss) from **Form 4835**. Also, complete line 41 below 39
40 TOTAL income or (loss). Combine lines 26, 31, 36, 38, and 39. Enter the result here and on Form 1040, line 18 . . . . ▶ 40   48,625
41 **Reconciliation of Farming and Fishing Income:** Enter your **gross** farming and fishing income reported in Parts II and III and on line 39 (see page E-4) 41

Figure 8-1 (continued) Schedule E

items related to rent and royalty income include expenditures such as advertising, automobile and travel, insurance, mortgage interest, repairs, taxes, utilities, wages, depreciation, and depletion.

☑ Example 9. Anthony Rossi has a piece of rental property on which he received gross rents of $24,000. The expenses he incurred were interest ($4,000), taxes ($3,200), cleaning ($400), commissions ($750), depreciation ($12,500), insurance ($1,200), and miscellaneous supplies ($725). Anthony is able to deduct the expenses against the gross rents in determining AGI, leaving a net income of $1,225 reportable on Schedule E (see Figure 8-1).

☑ Example 10. Anthony Rossi also owns some land on which an oil company is drilling for oil and gas. Anthony received $40,000 in royalty income from this activity and qualifies for a depletion deduction of $6,000. The depletion expense is a deduction for AGI, leaving net Schedule E royalty income of $34,000 (see Figure 8-1).

An individual may also be a partner in a partnership or a shareholder in an S corporation. The ordinary income or loss items (e.g., the individual's share of receipts less expenses) from these "pass through" entities are also reported on Schedule E. Income is taxed fully to the partner or shareholder as part of his or her AGI, while losses would be deductible *for* AGI subject to certain limitations. An introduction to the tax consequences of partnerships and S corporations is included in Chapter 10.

☑ Example 11. Anthony Rossi also owns a 10% interest in Alpha Company (an S corporation) and a 50% partnership interest in Public Partners. His share of the ordinary incomes from these two entities was $400 and $13,000, respectively. Anthony will report these net amounts on Part II, page 2 of Schedule E, which results in additional gross income (see Figure 8-1).

The Schedule E total income (or loss) is transferred to Form 1040, line 18. Effectively, this means that all deductions taken on Schedule E are deductions *for* AGI, since line 18 of Form 1040 is part of "gross income." The net income of $48,625 shown on Schedule E in Figure 8-1 would be shown on Form 1040 as follows:

Income	7	Wages, salaries, tips, etc. Attach Form(s) W-2	7	
Attach Copy B of your Forms W-2, W-2G, and 1099-R here.	8a	Taxable interest income (see page 16). Attach Schedule B if over $400	8a	
	b	Tax-exempt interest (see page 17). DON'T include on line 8a 8b		
	9	Dividend income. Attach Schedule B if over $400	9	
	10	Taxable refunds, credits, or offsets of state and local income taxes (see page 17)	10	
	11	Alimony received	11	
If you did not get a W-2, see page 10.	12	Business income or (loss). Attach Schedule C or C-EZ	12	
	13	Capital gain or (loss). Attach Schedule D	13	
	14	Capital gain distributions not reported on line 13 (see page 17)	14	
	15	Other gains or (losses). Attach Form 4797	15	
If you are attaching a check or money order, put it on top of any Forms W-2, W-2G, or 1099-R.	16a	Total IRA distributions . 16a b Taxable amount (see page 18)	16b	
	17a	Total pensions and annuities 17a b Taxable amount (see page 18)	17b	
	18	Rental real estate, royalties, partnerships, S corporations, trusts, etc. Attach Schedule E	18	48,625
	19	Farm income or (loss). Attach Schedule F	19	
	20	Unemployment compensation (see page 19)	20	
	21a	Social security benefits 21a b Taxable amount (see page 19)	21b	
	22	Other income. List type and amount—see page 20	22	
	23	Add the amounts in the far right column for lines 7 through 22. This is your **total income** ▶	23	

The range of possible income-producing activities is not just limited to rents and royalties. For example, an individual who invests in stocks and bonds may deduct all ordinary and necessary expenses associated with this activity. However, such deductions are allowed only as miscellaneous itemized deductions (*from* AGI), because rents and royalties are the only two income-producing activities for which expenses are allowed as deductions *for* AGI.

✓ **Example 12.** Marjorie Wilkes pays $200 a year rent for a safety deposit box, which is used to store her stock and bond investments. Since the investments constitute an income-producing activity, the $200 is a deductible expense under Sec. 212. However, the $200 must be reported as a miscellaneous itemized deduction, on Schedule A, subject to the 2% floor.

REVIEW I

1. Maude Macy, a calendar-year, cash-basis taxpayer, paid $21,600 in advance for three years rent on a business building. The prepayment was made on August 1, 1993. On her 1993 tax return, Macy may deduct rent expense of
   (a) $ 0.
   (b) $ 3,000.
   (c) $18,600.
   (d) $21,600.
2. Which of the following expenditures are deductible by an individual taxpayer?
   (a) a $30 speeding ticket incurred on the way to work
   (b) interest expense of $100 on a $1,000 loan used to purchase U.S. Savings Bonds
   (c) a $400 penalty for failing to file a tax return
   (d) None of the above are deductible.
3. Lance Wetzel, a neurosurgeon, raced miniature cars several weekends during 1993. He won $600 from these races In 1993 and incurred $19,000 of expenses. Wetzel has raced cars for five years and has shown a profit only in 1990. On his 1993 tax return, Wetzel can deduct racing expenses of
   (a) $ 0.
   (b) $ 600.
   (c) $18,400.
   (d) $19,000.
4. Which of the following items is not allowed as a deduction for AGI in computing an individual's taxable income?
   (a) a $500 repair to a rental property owned by the taxpayer
   (b) a $700 payment for legal advice on royalty income
   (c) a $300 subscription to a stock market service by an investor
   (d) a $500 rent payment by a sole proprietor

Answers are on page 8-12.

II BUSINESS EXPENSES: INVENTORIES AND COST OF GOODS SOLD
(Code Sections 453, 471, 472, 474)

The term *inventory* refers to goods held primarily for resale by business taxpayers. Taxpayers are permitted to recover their cost of inventory sold when computing gross income. This "cost of goods sold" represents a major deduction for many business taxpayers. The following discussion highlights the primary tax considerations inherent in cost of goods sold calculations.

THE INVENTORY REQUIREMENT

Any changes in the beginning and ending inventories of a taxpayer must be reflected in gross income when such inventories are a significant factor in producing income. These inventory changes are automatically reflected when a taxpayer uses a *perpetual* inventory system. In a perpetual system, the actual cost of each inventory item sold can be determined from the taxpayer's accounting records at any time.

Changes in beginning and ending inventory values are necessary to determine cost of goods sold when a taxpayer is unable to identify exactly which inventory items were sold. A taxpayer cannot simply deduct the net cost of purchases for the year, because some of these purchases may be unsold at the end of the year. Likewise, some of the inventory items sold during the year may have actually been purchased in a prior year. To compensate for these possibilities, a taxpayer determining cost of goods sold must adjust purchases for the beginning and ending inventory values in the following manner:

Beginning inventory cost	$ XX,XXX
plus: Net purchases for the year	XXX,XXX
Cost of goods available for sale	$XXX,XXX
minus: Ending inventory cost	(XX,XXX)
Cost of goods sold	$XXX,XXX

The net effect of this *periodic* inventory system is to assume that any inventory available for sale during the year and not on hand at the end of the year was sold during the year. Therefore, any inventory items withdrawn from the business by the owner for personal usage and not recorded as sales must be *subtracted* from purchases in the cost of goods sold calculations. Otherwise, the periodic computation would provide a deduction for an otherwise nondeductible personal expenditure.

☑ **Example 13.** Renee Williams owns and operates a neighborhood grocery store. Each week she withdraws approximately $60 (original purchase cost) of food for her family's use. She must decrease the net purchases figure used in the cost of goods sold computation by the total cost of the withdrawn items.

We mentioned one other requirement for inventories briefly in Chapter 2. In determining gross income, the accrual basis must be used for gross profit computations when inventories are a significant component of income. Specifically, a cash-basis taxpayer must convert sales and purchases to an accrual basis in computing cost of goods sold. Recall that under the accrual basis, revenues are recognized when earned (date of sale) and expenses are recognized when incurred (date of purchase).

The cash-basis sales and purchases figures can be easily converted to the accrual basis by adding the *ending* receivables and payables balances to cash-basis sales and purchases, respectively, and then subtracting the *beginning* receivables and payables balances from the resulting totals. Recall that all sales and purchases on account were originally recorded in the receivables and payables accounts.

✓ **Example 14.** Ralph Teague is a cash-basis, calendar-year sporting goods dealer. During 1993 he collected $320,000 from cash sales and sales on account, and paid $210,000 for cash purchases and payments on account for credit purchases. A check of Teague's accounting records revealed the following account balances:

	January 1, 1993	December 31, 1993
Accounts receivable	$30,000	$32,300
Accounts payable	24,000	21,000

Additionally, records of Teague's year-end physical inventory counts disclosed that the beginning inventory balance was $38,000 and the ending inventory balance was $43,000. Teague's gross profit on the *accrual* basis for 1993 would be $120,300, computed as follows:

Gross sales ($320,000 + $32,300 − $30,000)		$322,300
Cost of goods sold:		
Beginning inventory	$ 38,000	
Purchases ($210,000 + $21,000 − $24,000)	207,000	
Goods available for sale	$245,000	
Ending inventory	(43,000)	
Cost of goods sold		(202,000)
Gross profit (accrual basis)		$120,300

The increase in gross sales of $2,300 caused by the conversion simply represents the net increase in accounts receivable that was not collected in cash as of the end of 1993 (but nevertheless was *earned* on the accrual basis). Similarly, the decrease in purchases of $3,000 caused by the net decrease in accounts payable indicates that $3,000 of the payments on account in 1993 were actually for purchases incurred in prior years.

ANSWERS TO REVIEW I

1. (b) An expense can never be deducted before it is incurred. Therefore, Macy can deduct only that portion of the rent covering the period August 1, 1993, to December 31, 1993. The deduction is $3,000 (5/36 × $21,600).
2. (b) The interest income from U.S. Savings Bonds is taxable. Therefore, the $100 of interest expense is an allowable deduction (i.e., an expense incurred in the production of income under Sec. 212).
3. (b) Since the taxpayer fails the three-out-of-five-year presumptive test, the expense deductions are limited to the income from the activity, which is presumed to be a hobby.
4. (c) Expenses related to income-producing activities other than rents and royalties are deductions from AGI, subject to the 2% of AGI floor.

TAX TIP

Knowledge of this technique for converting from the cash to the accrual basis is important for cash-basis taxpayers, because accounting records can be simplified by using the cash basis throughout the year and converting these totals to the accrual basis at the end of the year. Reference need only be made to the receivables and payables records at the end of the year to make this conversion. Obviously, the ending balances for one year are the beginning balances for the next year. Thus, many small businesses can reduce their tax records to a checkbook and simple files for accounts receivable and accounts payable.

INVENTORY COSTING METHODS

Goods Included in Inventory

For income tax purposes, inventory includes all finished goods, partially finished goods, and raw materials. The ending inventory value should include only merchandise in which title has actually passed to the taxpayer; for example, items held on consignment are not included in the inventory of the consignee, because title to the goods rests with the consignor.

Ending inventories can be valued under either of two methods: (1) cost or (2) lower of cost or market. Once adopted, this overall method of valuing inventories cannot be changed without the permission of the IRS. The inventory method should be consistently applied for all tax years.

Under the *cost* method, inventories are valued at the actual purchases prices, plus any freight-in charges, and less any cash discounts. For manufactured goods, the cost includes all necessary factory costs, such as direct materials, direct labor, and factory overhead. Factory overhead refers to all nonmaterial and nonlabor costs incurred in the manufacture of a product, such as factory supplies, factory utilities, and rent on the factory building. Overhead does not include purely selling and administrative expenses, which may be deducted in full as ordinary and necessary business expenses.

Example 15. During 1993 Binswanger Company incurred the following costs in producing 10,000 items of inventory:

Raw materials for inventory	$ 40,000
Salaries—factory labor	80,000
Factory supplies	10,000
Factory utilities	20,000
Salaries—sales personnel	40,000
Total factory costs	$190,000

All of the above costs are inventoriable except the $40,000 salaries of the sales personnel, which can be deducted in full. The inventory cost of each item would be $15

($150,000/10,000). If Binswanger sells 9,000 of these items in 1993 its cost of goods sold would be $135,000 (9,000 × $15), and its ending inventory would be $15,000 (1,000 × $15).

Instead of the cost method, a taxpayer may elect to value ending inventories using a *lower of cost or market method.* "Market" refers to the current price of the item on the inventory date. In applying the lower of cost or market rule, the cost and market price of *each* inventory item are compared; the total cost and total market values of all items combined are irrelevant.

Example 16. Jane Allison operates a motorcycle dealership and uses lower of cost or market inventory procedures. Her inventory consists of five different models of cycles, and relevant cost and market prices of each model are

Model	Cost	Market	Lower of Cost or Market
A	$24,000	$27,000	$24,000
B	16,000	14,000	14,000
C	9,000	10,000	9,000
D	17,000	18,000	17,000
E	32,000	25,000	25,000
Total	$98,000	$94,000	$89,000

Allison's ending inventory will be valued at $89,000. The $98,000 total cost and $94,000 total market value figures are irrelevant.

For a variety of reasons, inventory goods sometimes cannot be sold at normal prices. Imperfections, style changes, and excessive quantities are just a few of the factors that may reduce the estimated selling price of inventories. Regardless of whether a taxpayer uses a cost or lower of cost or market procedure, these goods may be valued at a "bona fide selling price," defined as an actual offering price for the goods no later than 30 days after the inventory date. Only an actual offer to sell the goods at the reduced price will justify a write-down in the recorded value of the inventory.

Example 17. Tolbert Blake, a farm equipment manufacturer, has a large inventory of spare parts for regular equipment inventory. Blake believes that the cost of 25% of these spare parts should be reduced from $100 each to $30 each, because it is doubtful that this portion of the spare parts inventory will ever be sold. However, Blake refuses to offer these parts for sale for less than $100 each for fear that a competitor would purchase the parts. Blake cannot write-down the value of this excess inventory of spare parts unless he actually offers the parts for sale at the reduced price within 30 days of the inventory date.

Inventory Cost-Flow Assumptions

As mentioned earlier, many businesses cannot identify from their purchase records exactly which inventory items were sold during a given tax year. These taxpayers must use a *periodic* inventory system, which indirectly estimates the cost of goods sold. Using this method requires use of the following formula, mentioned earlier, which is illustrated with hypothetical numbers:

Beginning inventory	$ 30,000
Net purchases	260,000
Goods available for sale	$290,000
Ending inventory	(42,000)
Cost of goods sold	$248,000

In making this cost of goods sold computation, the taxpayer would obtain the net purchases figure ($260,000) from his or her purchase records for the year. Also, the beginning inventory figure would simply be last year's ending inventory figure. But one important question remains: Given that the taxpayer is unable to identify which items of inventory were sold during the year, how can he or she derive an ending inventory figure?

Obviously, an assumption concerning the *order* of goods sold must be made. The three most common cost-flow assumptions are average cost; first-in, first-out (FIFO); and last-in, first-out (LIFO). Each of these cost-flow assumptions can be illustrated by means of a simple example.

☑ **Example 18.** Ann McClary is a retail dealer of Product A. Her 1993 inventory and purchase records for Product A disclose the following:

1/1/93	Beginning inventory (6,000 units @ $6)	$ 36,000
2/3/93	Purchases (2,000 units @ $8)	16,000
4/5/93	Purchases (4,000 units @ $9)	36,000
8/1/93	Purchases (3,000 units @ $11)	33,000
11/2/93	Purchases (5,000 units @ $13)	65,000
	Goods available (20,000 units)	$186,000

A physical count of goods on hand on December 31, 1993, revealed that 7,000 units of Product A were still on hand.

The ending inventory determined under various methods is

Average cost (7,000 × $9.30)	$ 65,100
First-in, first-out [(5,000 × $13) + (2,000 × $11)]	$ 87,000
Last-in, first-out [(6,000 × $6) + (1,000 × $8)]	$ 44,000

The *average cost* method does not assume a particular order of cost flow. Rather, the assumption is made that goods were sold from all purchased lots and the beginning inventory, and that an average cost based on total goods available for sale would be a representative ending inventory cost. In Example 18, the average cost per unit is $9.30 ($186,000/20,000), and the ending inventory would be valued at $65,100 (7,000 units @ $9.30).

The *first-in, first-out* (FIFO) method assumes that the *earliest* purchases were the first items sold; therefore, the ending inventory would be composed of the most *recently purchased* items. The ending inventory cost is determined by using the most recently purchased layers, up to the quantity of the ending inventory. In Example 18, the ending inventory would be presumed to consist of the 5,000 units acquired on 11/2/93 and the 2,000 units acquired on 8/1/93. Therefore, the ending inventory under FIFO would be $87,000 (5,000 units @ $13 plus 2,000 units @ $11).

The *last-in, first-out* (LIFO) method assumes that the *latest* purchases were the first items sold. Therefore, the ending inventory would be composed of the *earliest* purchases. The ending inventory cost is determined by using the earliest purchased layers (including the beginning inventory), up to the quantity of the ending inventory. In Example 18, the ending inventory using LIFO would be presumed to consist of the 6,000 units in the beginning inventory and 1,000 of the units acquired on 2/3/93. Therefore, the ending inventory under LIFO would be $44,000 (6,000 units @ $6 plus 1,000 units @ $8).

In comparing these three cost-flow assumptions, we must emphasize one important point: neither the IRS nor the Internal Revenue Code requires taxpayers to use a cost-flow assumption that most closely follows the actual physical flow of their inventories. This factor has encouraged many taxpayers to elect the LIFO method, which produces the largest cost of goods sold (and smallest taxable income) of the three methods during periods of rising prices. Reference to the three examples above discloses cost of goods sold figures of $120,900 (average cost), $99,000 (FIFO), and $142,000 (LIFO), computed as follows:

	Avg. Cost	FIFO	LIFO
Beginning inventory	$ 36,000	$ 36,000	$ 36,000
Purchases	150,000	150,000	150,000
Goods available for sale	$186,000	$186,000	$186,000
Ending inventory	(65,100)	(87,000)	(44,000)
Cost of goods sold	$120,900	$ 99,000	$142,000

Note that the cost of goods sold is much higher (and taxable income is lower) for LIFO because prices were rising during the year (from $6 to $13 per unit).

This economic incentive for electing LIFO has caused Congress to establish specific requirements for its usage. Taxpayers elect LIFO by completing Form 970 for the tax year in which LIFO is adopted. Once elected, the LIFO method may not be discontinued unless permission to do so is received from the IRS.

TAX TIP

In some businesses, the general price levels of their inventories may be decreasing, rather than increasing. A good example is the electronics industry, in which prices of transistors and computer chips have fallen rapidly over the years. For these taxpayers, it may make sense to elect a FIFO inventory system, where the earlier, higher-priced purchases are used in computing cost of goods sold. In addition, manufacturers that use such products as raw materials may elect FIFO for their raw material inventory and LIFO for their finished goods inventory.

The LIFO method cannot be used in conjunction with the lower of cost or market procedure. If a lower of cost or market method were used prior to the adoption of LIFO, any previous write-downs in inventory values to market must be restored to income in three equal amounts in the year of change and the following two years.

✓ **Example 19.** Paul Prince adopts the LIFO method in 1993. In years prior to 1993, Prince had used lower of cost or market procedures to write down the value of his inventory a total of $9,300. (The goods in his 1993 beginning inventory had cost $100,000 but were valued under lower of cost or market procedures at $90,700.) Prince must recognize $3,100 of additional income ($9,300/3) on his 1993, 1994, and 1995 tax returns.

TAX TIP

The possible tax costs of switching to LIFO, as illustrated by the preceding example, may be more than offset by the tax savings generated by LIFO during times of rising prices. For example, assume in the previous example that at the end of the following year (1994) the taxpayer had exactly the same quantity in ending inventory; however, prices had increased 10% during the year. With LIFO, the ending inventory would be the same ($100,000), and the cost of goods sold would be 10% higher because the inventory purchased during the current year is presumed to have been sold first. With FIFO, those higher-priced goods would still be in the ending inventory.

REVIEW II

1. During 1993 Tom Innis, an accrual-basis taxpayer, had $180,000 of inventory purchases, $6,000 of which were used for personal consumption. Those items withdrawn for personal use were not recorded as sales. Physical counts disclosed ending inventories of $30,000 in 1992 and $34,000 in 1993. On his 1993 return, Innis will report cost of goods sold of
   (a) $180,000.
   (b) $178,000.
   (c) $174,000.
   (d) $170,000.
2. During 1993 William Graves, a cash-basis taxpayer, furnishes the following information from business records:

	1/1/93 Balance	12/31/93 Balance
Merchandise inventory	$60,000	$55,000
Accounts payable	46,000	58,000

Graves' inventory records also indicate that 1993 cash purchases and payments on account for credit purchases totaled $420,000. Assuming that inventories are a significant component of income, Graves will report cost of goods sold in 1993 of
   (a) $437,000.
   (b) $425,000.

(c) $420,000.
(d) $413,000.

3. Barbara Patterson's ending inventory consists of four products. The original costs and market value of each of these products on December 31, 1993, were as follows:

	Cost	Market
Product 1	$80,000	$86,000
Product 2	24,000	17,000
Product 3	18,000	13,000
Product 4	56,000	57,000

Using lower of cost or market procedures, Patterson's ending inventory would be valued at
(a) $178,000.
(b) $173,000.
(c) $166,000.
(d) $160,000.

4. As a result of applying lower of cost or market procedures, Raphael Ortiz has written down the cost of his beginning 1993 inventory a total of $12,000 in prior years. If Ortiz adopts the LIFO method In 1993 he must increase his 1993 income by
(a) $0.
(b) $3,000.
(c) $4,000.
(d) $12,000.

Answers are on page 8-20.

III DEPRECIATION, MACRS, AND ACRS DEDUCTIONS
(Code Sections 167, 168, 179)

Depreciation, MACRS, and ACRS deductions represent logical applications of the basic principle that an expenditure can never be deducted before it is actually incurred (i.e., "used up"). The cost of a tangible asset used in a trade or business is usually recovered over several tax years, which represent either (1) the estimated useful life of the property (for assets acquired *before* 1981) or (2) an arbitrary class life for the property (for assets acquired *after* 1980).

The cost recovery process for assets acquired before 1981 is known as *depreciation*, and the cost recovery process for assets acquired after 1980 is known as the Accelerated Cost Recovery System (ACRS). The ACRS rules were substantially modified for properties acquired after 1986, and these rules are commonly referred to as *modified ACRS* (MACRS).

THE LAW

Sec. 167(a)—There shall be allowed as a depreciation deduction a reasonable allowance for the exhaustion, wear and tear (including a reasonable allowance for obsolescence)—

(1) of property used in the trade or business, or
(2) of property held for the production of income.

The only properties qualifying for depreciation or ACRS deductions are properties used in a trade or business or properties held for the production of income. Assets that are personal in nature do not qualify for cost recovery. In addition, property subject to cost recovery must have a limited useful life.

✓ **Example 20.** Rebecca Grey purchased one acre of vacant downtown property to use as a city parking lot. She installed fences and a pay booth, and she paved the entire area. The cost of the fences, booth, and paving would be subject to cost recovery, since these properties normally have limited useful lives. However, the land is not eligible for cost recovery.

Generally, the depreciable cost of a property includes all acquisition costs, commissions, and fees, as well as any installation costs. A special rule applies when personal property is converted to a business or income-producing use. The cost recovery basis of such property is the *lesser* of the original cost of the property or its fair market value at the time of conversion. This provision is necessary to prevent the deduction of a loss that is personal in nature.

✓ **Example 21.** Jim Holden purchased a new personal residence in 1981 for $60,000. In 1993 when the property was worth $49,000, Holden converted the residence to rental property. Holden's basis for cost recovery purposes is $49,000. To allow a $60,000 cost recovery basis would permit Holden to deduct an $11,000 personal loss.

The following discussion of cost recovery deductions is devoted primarily to the MACRS procedure, which applies to depreciable assets acquired after 1986. However, much of the MACRS and ACRS procedures are based on depreciation principles, which apply to assets acquired before 1981. For this reason, the basic rules of depreciation are discussed first in the following section, followed by a detailed examination of the MACRS procedure. Finally, a brief summary of the ACRS procedure, applicable to assets acquired after 1980 and before 1987, is provided because some of these assets are still in use.

DEPRECIATION (ASSETS ACQUIRED BEFORE 1981)

Depreciation is defined as a reasonable allowance for the exhaustion, wear, and tear (and obsolescence) of trade or business or income-producing properties. For assets acquired prior to 1981, the depreciation calculation is a function of three factors: salvage value, useful life, and depreciation method.

Subject to certain de minimis rules, assets acquired before 1981 can never be depreciated below a reasonable *salvage value,* which is the estimated value of the asset at the end of its useful life. Since this salvage value is expected to be recovered ultimately in cash or property, this portion of the asset's cost should not be recovered prior to disposal.

A second factor necessary to calculate depreciation is an estimate of the property's *useful life.* In general, an asset must be depreciated over its expected useful life. The IRS has published guideline lives by type of asset to assist a taxpayer in assigning a useful life to an asset. Taxpayers could not use useful lives shorter than these guideline lives unless they could demonstrate unusual "facts and circumstances" when audited by the IRS.

The final factor necessary to calculate depreciation is the *depreciation method*. The tax law permits a taxpayer to use any consistent method of depreciation, subject to certain limitations. As a practical matter, however, the three most common depreciation methods are the straight-line, sum-of-the-years' digits, and declining-balance methods. Each of these methods is specifically sanctioned by the Code.

Allowable Depreciation Methods

The *straight-line method* is the simplest depreciation method, with the total cost spread evenly over the useful life of the asset. As with all depreciation methods, the asset is not depreciated below a reasonable salvage value.

The *sum-of-the-years' digits method* is an accelerated depreciation method, in that larger depreciation deductions are taken in the earlier years of the asset's life, with smaller deductions in later years. The sum-of-the-years' digits method applies a decreasing fraction each year to the depreciable cost of the asset. The numerator of the fraction is the remaining useful life of the asset at the beginning of the year, and the denominator is the sum of the numbers representing each year of the useful life of the asset.

The *declining-balance method,* another accelerated depreciation procedure, applies a constant fraction to a decreasing dollar amount each year. The fraction is expressed as a percentage of the straight-line depreciation rate, and the dollar amount is the remaining undepreciated cost ("book value") of the asset at the beginning of the year. The initial cost of the asset for the first-year calculation is not reduced for salvage value; rather, the asset cannot be depreciated below a reasonable salvage value at the end of its useful life.

ANSWERS TO REVIEW II

1. (d) The net purchases must be reduced by the cost of the items withdrawn for personal use ($6,000). Thus, the cost of goods sold is $170,000, computed as follows: $30,000 (beginning inventory) plus $174,000 (net purchases) less $34,000 (ending inventory).
2. (a) In computing cost of goods sold, net purchases must be converted to the accrual basis figure of $432,000 ($420,000 + 58,000 − 46,000). Cost of goods sold is $437,000 ($60,000 + 432,000 − 55,000).
3. (c) The lower of cost or market procedure is applied on an item-by-item basis. Thus, the final inventory value of $166,000 is composed of the $80,000 cost for Product 1, the $17,000 market value of Product 2, the $13,000 market value of Product 3, and the $56,000 cost of Product 4.
4. (c) A taxpayer electing LIFO must restore all previous write-downs of inventory to income in three equal installments, beginning with the year of change. Therefore, Ortiz will recognize $4,000 additional income ($12,000/3) in 1993 (the year of change), 1994, and 1995.

These three basic depreciation methods can be illustrated by means of a simple example.

☑ **Example 22.** Ann Borsch purchased new office furniture for her business on 1/1/80. The furniture cost $4,200 and had useful life of ten years and a negligible salvage value. Ann's depreciation deduction for the first two years of the asset's useful life under the three methods would be:

Year	Straight-Line	Sum-of-the-Years' Digits	200% Declining Balance
1	$420 (a)	$764 (b)	$840 (d)
2	420 (a)	687 (c)	672 (e)

(a) $4,200 / 10 (depreciable cost / useful life)

(b) $4,200 × 10/55 (10/55 = remaining life/(1 + 2 + 3 + ... + 10))

(c) $4,200 × 9/55 (9/55 = remaining life/(1 + 2 + 3 + ... + 10))

(d) $4,200 × .20 (.20 = 200% of the 10% per year straight-line rate)

(e) $3,360 × .20 ($3,360 = $4,200 cost − $840 total depr.)

If the taxpayer in the preceding example elected to use a declining-balance method of depreciation for the entire life of the asset, she will not completely recover the cost of the asset after ten years. To adjust for this discrepancy, the IRS allows a taxpayer to switch to the straight-line method at any time without prior permission.

In 1969 Congress established the following maximum depreciation rates for all properties by distinguishing rates applicable to realty (buildings and permanent building attachments) and personalty (all other tangible properties):

Maximum Depreciation Rates
(by Asset Classification)

Type of Asset	Maximum Rate (% of Straight-Line)
New personalty	200%
Used personalty	150%
New residential realty	200%
Used residential realty*	125%
New commercial realty	150%
Used commercial realty	100%

*Must be at least 20 years old

Note that the higher recovery rates are available for new property, rather than used property, and that preferential treatment is given to "residential" realty. In order to qualify as residential realty, at least 80% of gross income from the property must be from dwelling units rented to nontransients. Rental properties that do not meet this 80% test, as well as all nonrental properties, will be classified as commercial realty.

> **TAX TIP**
>
>
>
> Because taxpayers can automatically switch to the straight-line method at any time, it becomes relevant to ask the question as to when this should be done. As a rule, the optimum point to switch methods is the either the middle year of the asset's life, or one year later. This option of converting to the straight-line method is still relevant, particularly for real estate acquired prior to 1981 (since the useful life for such real estate was usually 30 or 40 years).

Many other factors affect these calculations. For example, what if a calendar-year taxpayer purchased an asset on October 1? In this case, the taxpayer would take 3/12 of the annual depreciation deduction for the first year of asset use and take 9/12 of the annual depreciation for the last year of use.

Some of the depreciation calculations for pre-1981 asset acquisitions may involve the use of the Asset Depreciation Range (ADR) system. Under this system, assets were depreciated over useful life categories of up to 20% more or 20% less than the guideline lives. The 20% boundaries were known as the "range" of possible recovery periods, and the guideline life was known as the "midpoint life." For example, a taxpayer who purchases a machine with a guideline life of ten years could choose a recovery period of as little as 8 years (20% less than the guideline life) or as much as 12 years (20% more than the guideline life). The guideline life of ten years is also the midpoint life. As described below, the ADR "midpoint" lives are still used for classification purposes under the ACRS and MACRS rules.

Other complexities of the pre-1981 depreciation calculations are of diminished importance with the advent of the Accelerated Cost Recovery System. However, the depreciation calculations must still be made for assets acquired prior to 1981 that have useful lives extending into years after 1980.

MODIFIED ACCELERATED COST RECOVERY SYSTEM (FOR ASSETS ACQUIRED AFTER 1986)

The Accelerated Cost Recovery System (ACRS), introduced by the Economic Recovery Tax Act of 1981, was designed to simplify depreciation calculations and to stimulate investment by offering greatly accelerated rates of recovery for business assets. These procedures apply to most tangible assets acquired after 1980, with special modifications for assets acquired after 1986.

The ACRS procedure greatly simplified cost recovery calculations by eliminating such subjective factors as "salvage value" and "useful life." The entire cost of an asset is now recovered over an arbitrary number of years that is generally shorter than the expected useful life of the asset. Depreciation calculations are greatly simplified by multiplying the original depreciable cost of the asset by a statutory percentage from tables furnished by the IRS.

As mentioned earlier, the original 1981 ACRS provisions were substantially modified by the Tax Reform Act of 1986. The revised system is commonly referred to as MACRS (shorthand for "modified ACRS"). Since these modified rules apply to all property

TABLE 8-1 MACRS Class Life Categories and Recovery Methods for Personalty

Class Life (Years)	Description of Property	Recovery Method
3	Property with ADR midpoint lives of 4 years or less (except automobiles, lightweight trucks, and certain horses)	200% DB
5	Automobiles, lightweight trucks, R&D equipment, and property with ADR midpoint lives of more than 4 but less than 10 years	200% DB
7	Single-purpose agricultural facilities, office furniture, fixtures and equipment, and any personalty having no ADR midpoint life specified, and property with ADR midpoint lives of at least 10 but less than 16 years	200% DB
10	Property with ADR midpoint lives of at least 16 but less than 20 years	200% DB
15	Wastewater treatment plants, telephone distribution equipment, and property with ADR midpoint lives of at least 20 but less than 25 years	150% DB
20	Sewer pipes, property with ADR midpoint lives of at least 25 years (other than realty with an ADR midpoint of 27.5 years or more)	150% DB

acquisitions after 1986, the following discussion is devoted to these provisions. However, because many properties acquired after 1980 and before 1987 are still in service use, a brief mention of the rules applicable to these "ACRS" properties follows the MACRS discussion.

THE LAW

Sec. 168(a)—General Rule. Except as otherwise provided in this section, the depreciation deduction provided by section 167(a) for any tangible property shall be determining using—
(1) the applicable depreciation method,
(2) the applicable recovery period, and
(3) the applicable convention.

Personalty under MACRS

As mentioned earlier, the term *personalty* refers to all tangible property other than land, buildings, and permanent building components. Under MACRS, all personalty is grouped into one of the six class life categories described in Table 8-1. These class life categories represent the MACRS recovery periods, using the declining-balance method disclosed for each asset category.

Generally, the entire cost of personalty acquired after 1986 is eligible for cost recovery deductions. However, Congress enacted a special election in Sec. 179 designed to aid small business. This provision allows a taxpayer to expense up to $17,500 of the cost of personalty in the year of acquisition. Any amount so expensed is not eligible for cost recovery deductions in future years. The full $17,500 deduction is allowed only to taxpayers who acquire $200,000 or less personalty in total during the tax year; any personalty acquisitions exceeding $200,000 reduce the Sec. 179 maximum deduction of $17,500 on a dollar-for-dollar basis. (The deduction is further limited to the taxable income of the business; however, any unused qualifying amount may be carried over to succeeding years as a deduction.)

✓ **Example 23.** Marilyn Wallace acquired $180,000 of personalty during 1993. She elects to immediately expense $17,500 of the total cost of such properties under Sec. 179. Thus, on her 1993 return, she will deduct $17,500 as an expense, and compute her regular MACRS deduction on a cost basis of $162,500 ($180,000 − $17,500).

✓ **Example 24.** Assume the same facts as Example 23, except that the total acquisitions of personalty in 1993 were $206,500. If Marilyn elects Sec. 179 expensing, her maximum expense deduction will be $11,000 (i.e., $17,500 less the $6,500 of personalty acquisitions which exceed $200,000). If the total personalty acquisitions during the year were $217,500 or more, no Sec. 179 deduction would be allowed.

Once the cost basis is adjusted for any Sec. 179 expensing, the MACRS computations are relatively simple. Each year's MACRS deduction is determined by multiplying the cost basis by a recovery table factor. The recovery table to be used depends on whether the "mid-year" or the "mid-quarter" convention applies.

The *mid-year* convention is used in years when 40% or less of the acquisitions of personalty are placed into service during the last three months of the tax year. As the name implies, the "mid-year" convention treats all personalty acquisitions as though they were purchased in the middle of the year. Thus, a half-year's cost recovery deduction is allowed in the year of acquisition, and another half-year's deduction is allowed in the year following the end of the asset's class life (or the year of disposition, if earlier). The mid-year recovery table is reproduced in Appendix E-1 of this text.

In examining the mid-year recovery table in Appendix E-1, several observations regarding MACRS recovery in general should be noted. First, the recovery factors of each class life total 100%; any salvage value is ignored under MACRS. Second, the recovery method used in developing the factors depends on the class life, as disclosed in Table 8-1. Note that the first four classes of personalty (3-, 5-, 7-, and 10-year classes) use the 200% declining-balance method, and the other two classes (15- and 20-year classes) use the 150% declining-balance method. In each case, a conversion to the straight-line method is automatically made at the optimum point.

✓ **Example 25.** Helen Trough purchased two items of personalty: a business van costing $20,000 in May and a plating machine costing $90,000 in June. She elects to expense $17,500 of the cost of the plating machine under Sec. 179. The machinery has no ADR mid-point life specified and therefore must be assigned a class life of seven years under MACRS (see Table 8-1). The van (a "lightweight" truck) is five-year property. Assuming that these were Helen's only acquisitions of personalty during the year, her total cost recovery deduction would be computed as follows:

Van—MACRS ($20,000 × .20*)	$ 4,000
Machinery—Sec. 179 ($17,500 maximum)	17,500
Machinery—MACRS ($72,500 × .1429**)	10,360
Total MACRS deduction	$31,860

* Mid-year MACRS, Year 1, five-year class (Table E-1)
** Mid-year MACRS, Year 1, seven-year class (Table E-1)

The *mid-quarter* convention is required when more than 40% of all personalty acquired during the year was placed into service during the last quarter (i.e., three months) of the year. When this rule applies, the cost recovery deduction for each item of personalty acquired during the year is based on the assumption that the property was acquired in the middle of the actual quarter of purchase. For example, an asset acquired on January 13 would be presumed to have been placed into service on February 15, the middle of the first quarter. Tables E-2 through E-5 of the Appendix to this book disclose the MACRS factors for each of the four possible quarters of the year.

Example 26. Assume the same facts as Example 25, except that the machinery was acquired in October. Because the personalty acquisitions in the last quarter of the year ($90,000) exceed 40% of the total personalty acquisitions during the year ($110,000), Helen's MACRS deductions will be computed using the mid-quarter convention as follows:

Van—MACRS ($20,000 × .25*)	$ 5,000
Machinery—Sec. 179 ($17,500 maximum)	17,500
Machinery—MACRS ($72,500 × .0357**)	2,588
Total MACRS deduction	$25,088

* Second quarter MACRS, Year 1, five-year class (Table E-3)
** Fourth quarter MACRS, Year 1, seven-year class (Table E-5)

TAX TIP

A comparison of the computed cost recovery deductions in Examples 25 and 26 reveals why Congress requires the mid-quarter rule in certain situations. If not for this rule, taxpayers could "load up" personalty purchases near the end of the year and still receive a half-year's cost recovery deduction.

However, in some cases, the mid-quarter rule may actually work to the taxpayer's advantage if acquisitions are made only in the first and last quarter. For example, if a taxpayer purchases $119,000 of personalty in January and $81,000 of personalty in December, the mid-quarter rule applies, and yet the total deduction under the mid-quarter rule is *larger* than the a deduction allowed under the mid-year rule! To illustrate, if the properties were five-year properties, the mid-year deduction would be $40,000 ($119,000 × 20%, plus $81,000 × 20%), and the mid-quarter deduction would be $45,700 ($119,000 × 35%, plus $81,000 × 5%).

The MACRS rules provide for a special election whereby taxpayers may choose straight-line recovery methods for assets. There are actually two methods for accomplishing this purpose. First, the taxpayer may simply elect to use straight-line recovery over the MACRS life of the asset. Any such election is binding on all personalty acquired during that year in the same class life category. All other conventions of MACRS apply in conjunction with such a straight-line election, including the Sec. 179 expensing election and the mid-year or mid-quarter conventions.

THE LAW

Sec. 168(b)(5)—Election. A [straight-line] election . . . may be made with respect to 1 or more classes of property for any taxable year and once made with respect to any class shall apply to all property in such class placed in service during such taxable year. Such an election, once made, shall be irrevocable.

Example 27. Assume the same facts as Example 25, except that Helen Trough elected straight line recovery for the two assets. In this case, her cost recovery deduction would be computed as follows:

Van—Cost recovery ($20,000/5 × 1/2)	$ 2,000
Machinery—Sec. 179 ($17,500 maximum)	17,500
Machinery—Cost recovery ($72,500/7 × 1/2)	5,179
Total deduction	$24,679

THE LAW

Sec. 168(g)(2)—Alternative depreciation system. For purposes of paragraph (1), the alternative depreciation system is depreciation determined by using—
(A) the straight-line method (without regard to salvage value),
(B) the applicable convention determined under subsection (d), and
(C) a recovery period determined under the following . . .

A second straight-line recovery election is also available to taxpayers. Under Sec. 168(g), a taxpayer may elect a special "alternative depreciation system (ADS)." Under this method, straight-line recovery deductions are also computed using the applicable conventions and Sec. 179 expensing elections. Likewise, there is the same straight-line consistency requirement (i.e., any ADS election applies to all properties in the same class acquired during the year). However, in a major departure from the other elective straight-line method, the recovery period used is generally the *mid-point ADR class life*, unless otherwise specified.

☑ **Example 28.** Assume that Roy Rogers purchased a new machine in 1993 that has a mid-point ADR life of ten years. If Rogers elects to use normal MACRS procedures or elects to use straight-line recovery under the method described earlier, he will use a seven-year recovery period. This is because any personalty with an ADR mid-point life of ten years is in the seven-year MACRS class. However, if Rogers elects the *alternative depreciation system,* he must assign the property to a ten-year class (the ADR mid-point life).

The major exceptions to this rule for personalty, where arbitrary ADS recovery periods are assigned, are automobiles (5 years, the same as the MACRS life) and any personalty with no class life (12 years rather than 7 years under MACRS). The IRS has released tables with straight-line recovery factors for the various "ADS" recovery periods, and these are disclosed in Appendix E-6.

☑ **Example 29.** Assume the same facts as Example 25, except that Helen Trough elected the alternative depreciation system for the two assets. Her cost recovery deduction would be computed as follows:

Van—Cost recovery ($20,000 × .10*)	$ 2,000
Machinery—Sec. 179 ($17,500 maximum)	17,500
Machinery—Cost recovery ($72,500 × .0417**)	3,023
Total deduction	$22,523

*Mid-year ADS, 5-year class, Year 1 factor (Appendix E-6)
** Mid-year ADS, 12-year class, Year 1 factor (Appendix E-6)

Note that the van always has an ADS class life of 5 years and that the machinery has an ADS class life of 12 years, since no ADR mid-point life is given for the asset.

TAX TIP

There may be a number of reasons that a taxpayer would elect one of the two straight-line recovery methods for acquisitions. First, the taxpayer may have just begun business and expects little or no income in the early years. By electing a straight-line recovery method, larger deductions will be available in later years, when marginal tax rates may be higher. Second, a taxpayer may prefer straight-line recovery because it simplifies computations and is consistent with the normal accounting records. And finally, as discussed in Chapter 7, the ADS method (with some modifications) is required for alternative minimum tax purposes, and using this method avoids two sets of records.

There are two other provisions related to MACRS deductions for personalty worth noting. These are the Sec. 280F special rules for "listed properties" and "luxury automobiles." In both cases, the intent of the rules is to limit deductions for certain properties that may have significant personal usage.

THE LAW

Sec. 280F(b)(2)—Depreciation. If any listed property is not predominantly used in a qualified business use for any taxable year, the deduction allowed under section 168 . . . shall be determined under section 168(g) (relating to alternative depreciation system).

The "listed property" rules apply to passenger automobiles, computers, amusement properties, and other properties specified in the Regulations. If a taxpayer uses the listed property more than 50% of the time for business purposes, there are no special restrictions on the use of any of the MACRS elections discussed above. However, failure to meet the business usage test means that the taxpayer is *required* to use the alternative depreciation system described above. In effect, the taxpayer must use straight-line recovery over the ADR mid-point lives (unless one of the special arbitrary ADS recovery periods for autos or property with no ADR mid-point life applies).

Example 30. Beth Williams purchased a personal computer in 1993 for $10,000. The computer has an ADR mid-point of ten years. If she uses the equipment 80% of the time in her sole proprietorship business, she may use the MACRS life and recovery method in computing her cost recovery deduction. If she elects MACRS, the deduction for the asset (a seven-year property under MACRS) will be $1,143 ($10,000 × .1429 MACRS factor × 80% business usage).

Example 31. Assume the same facts as in Example 30, except that the computer is used only 40% of the time in Williams' business. Since the greater than 50% business usage test is not met, she must use straight-line ADS recovery on the 40% business usage portion. Furthermore, she must use a recovery period of ten years, the ADR mid-point life of the computer. Therefore, her 1993 deduction will be $200, or $4,000 × .05 (40% business usage × the ten-year ADS factor from Appendix E-6).

The luxury auto limitations restrict any cost recovery deduction on passenger automobiles to the following amounts: $2,860 for the first year, $4,600 for the second year, $2,750 for the third year, and $1,675 for each succeeding year. (These are the 1993 amounts; each amount is adjusted for inflation on an annual basis.) Three observations are important in regard to these limits. First, the limits apply only when the cost of the auto exceeds $14,300; otherwise, the normal MACRS calculations would provide a smaller deduction than the limit. Second, a taxpayer may continue to take MACRS deductions beyond the fourth year (at a maximum of $1,675 a year) until the entire cost of the automobile is recovered. Finally, if the auto is used less than 100% of the time for business purposes, the annual dollar limits are proportionately reduced.

Example 32. Ray Holmes purchased a new auto in 1993 for $15,000, which will be used 80% of the time in his business. His cost recovery deductions for the $12,000 depreciable portion of the cost ($15,000 × .80) would be as follows (note that the normal MACRS deduction is less than the limit in the sixth year, 1998):

1993	($2,860 × .80)	$ 2,288
1994	($4,600 × .80)	3,680
1995	($2,750 × .80)	2,200
1996	($1,675 × .80)	1,340
1997	($1,675 × .80)	1,340
1998	($15,000 × .80 × .0576)	691
1999	(Remaining amount)	461
Total cost recovery		$12,000

Both the listed property rules and the luxury automobile rules may apply at the same time, since an automobile is "listed property." The Sec. 179 expensing election is also subject to the listed property and luxury auto limitations; thus, the $17,500 maximum deduction is reduced to $2,860 for autos.

TAX TIP

At first glance, it may appear that one way to get around the luxury auto and listed property limits would be to lease the auto, rather than purchase it, and deduct the lease payments. However, a special "income inclusion" rule of Sec. 280F requires the taxpayer to increase gross income by an amount (computed from a table) that puts the taxpayer in the same economic position as if he or she had purchased the auto and was subject to the limits. For the gruesome details, see Regs.Sec.1.280F-5T.

Realty under MACRS

Several of the MACRS principles discussed thus far are modified when applied to realty. First, there are only two classes of realty: residential and nonresidential (commercial) realty. Residential realty is defined as before, that is, at least 80% of rental receipts are from dwelling units. Any realty that does not meet this test is classified as commercial realty. This would include any realty used in a trade or business and any rental realty that does not meet the 80% test.

The cost of residential realty is recovered over a 27.5-year period, and commercial realty is recovered either over a 31.5-year period (for properties acquired before May 13, 1993) or a 39-year period (for properties acquired on or after May 13, 1993). In contrast to personalty, only the straight-line recovery method is available for such real estate. Furthermore, cost recovery deductions are based on the "mid-month" convention, an assumption that the realty was placed into service in the middle of the month. Appendices F-1 and F-2 reproduce the realty recovery tables for 27.5-year residential and 31.5-year nonresidential realty acquired after 1986. (As we go to press, the IRS has not issued recovery tables for 39-year commercial realty.) As with personalty under MACRS, the recovery deduction is computed simply by multiplying the cost of the property by the appropriate cost recovery factor (depending on the month of the tax year that the property is placed into service).

✓ **Example 33.** Maria Perez acquired two buildings during 1993: a residential rental duplex on 4/1/93 for $100,000 and an office building for her sole proprietorship business on 9/1/93 for $200,000. Her cost recovery deduction for these two properties would be

Rental duplex ($100,000 × .02576 *)	$2,576
Office building ($200,000 × .00748 **)	1,496
Total deduction	$4,072

*MACRS factor, Month 4, residential realty (Appendix F-1)
**MACRS factor, Month 9, 39-year nonresidential realty, approximated by authors (1/39 × 3.5/12)

Since MACRS for post-86 acquisitions of realty is based on the straight-line method, there is no need for an optional straight-line method. However, the Alternative Depreciation System (ADS) described earlier can also be elected for realty. If ADS is elected for realty, a *40-year* straight-line recovery rate is required for both residential and nonresidential realty (including both 31.5-year and 39-year properties). ADS is elected on a property by property basis for realty; there is no consistency requirement as exists for personalty. The ADS recovery tables for realty are reproduced in Appendix F-3.

✓ **Example 34.** Assume the same facts as Example 33, except that Perez elects ADS recovery for both buildings. In this case, her cost recovery deduction would be

Rental duplex ($100,000 × .01771 *)	$1,771
Office building ($200,000 × .00729 **)	1,458
Total deduction	$3,229

*ADS factor, Month 4, realty (Appendix F-3)
**ADS factor, Month 9, realty (Appendix F-3)

MACRS AND THE ALTERNATIVE MINIMUM TAX

As discussed in Chapter 7, taxpayers must use the alternative depreciation system (ADS) for purposes of the alternative minimum tax (AMT). For realty, this means 40-year, straight-line recovery using Appendix F-3 as described above. However, for personalty, taxpayers are permitted to use a special ADS recovery table (*solely* for purposes of the AMT) based on the 150% declining-balance method (rather than the usual straight-line ADS method). This table is reproduced in Appendix I.

For example, if a taxpayer acquired a new machine (ten-year ADR mid-point life) for $10,000 in 1993 the regular tax MACRS deduction would be $1,429 ($10,000 × .1429 MACRS factor, seven-year property, Appendix E-1). The AMT deduction under 150% ADS would be $750 ($10,000 × .075 ADS factor, ten-year, mid-point life property, Appendix I). The difference of $679 ($1,429 − $750) is a positive adjustment for depreciation in the AMT calculation, as previously discussed in Chapter 7.

ACCELERATED COST RECOVERY SYSTEM (FOR ASSETS ACQUIRED AFTER 1980 AND BEFORE 1987)

As mentioned earlier, the original ACRS rules applied to depreciable assets acquired after 1980 and before 1987. Because some of these properties may still be in service use, it is appropriate to mention briefly some of the key differences between MACRS and ACRS for both personalty and realty.

Personalty under ACRS

The key features of the original ACRS rules as they relate to personalty include the following:

1. There were only four classes of personalty under the ACRS rules: 3-year, 5-year, 10-year, and 15-year classes. Under the original system, automobiles were in the three-year class, and most other personalty (other than that used by public utilities) was in the five-year class.

2. For any properties acquired after 1982, the depreciable basis was reduced for one-half of any "investment credit" claimed by the taxpayer. This credit was repealed for years after 1985.

3. ACRS recovery tables for personalty were all based on the mid-year convention and the 150% declining-balance method, with a switch to straight-line at the optimum point. Although the mid-year convention was used, the additional half-year of cost recovery was built into the ACRS recovery period; in other words, the cost recovery was not extended an additional half year. Appendix G-1 reproduces the original ACRS personalty recovery tables.

4. The taxpayer could elect straight-line recovery over one of three possible recovery periods for each asset. The ADS method was not available under the original ACRS.

5. The Sec. 179 immediate expensing election was limited to a maximum of $5,000; however, there was no phaseout of the limit for excessive personalty acquisitions.

6. The listed property rules applied under ACRS (with special restrictions on the investment credit), and the luxury auto rules also applied (at different amounts).

☑ **Example 35.** Al Waxman acquired $15,000 of personalty on 11/1/86 and elected Sec. 179 expensing. His Sec. 179 deduction would be $5,000 in 1986, and his cost recovery deduction for 1986 would have been $1,500 ($10,000 × .15, the Year 1 ACRS factor for five-year property from Appendix G-1). Note that the mid-quarter rule did not apply under ACRS.

Realty under ACRS

The key features of the original ACRS rules as they relate to realty include the following:

1. Realty was divided into two classes: low-income housing and other realty. Low-income housing qualified for 200% declining-balance recovery, and other realty qualified for 175% declining-balance recovery. Low-income housing Code requirements are not discussed here.

2. Congress kept changing its mind about the appropriate recovery period for realty. Although the recovery period for low-income housing remained at 15 years, the recovery period for other realty depended on the date of acquisition. The possible recovery periods were 15 years (acquisitions after 12/31/80 and before 3/16/84), 18 years (acquisitions after 3/15/84 and before 5/9/85), and 19 years (acquisitions after 5/8/85 and before 1/1/87).

3. The 15-year recovery tables were based on a full-month convention (an assumption that properties were placed into service on the first day of the month), and the 18- and 19-year properties were based on a mid-month convention (described earlier for MACRS properties). All three recovery tables are included in Appendix H.

4. Taxpayers could choose from three optional straight-line recovery periods for each class of realty. This election was made on a property-by-property basis.

✓ **Example 36.** Henry Stein purchased an office building on 6/1/83 for $100,000 and a company warehouse on 4/3/86 for $300,000. His 1993 ACRS deductions for these two properties would be computed as follows:

Office building ($100,000 × .05 *)	$ 5,000
Company warehouse ($300,000 × .048 **)	14,400
Total deduction	$19,400

*ACRS factor, Month 6, Year 11, 15-year realty (Appendix H-1)
**ACRS factor, Month 4, Year 8, 19-year realty (Appendix H-3)

SUMMARY

Form 4562 is used to report all depreciation and cost recovery deductions. This form is illustrated in Figure 8-2. Note particularly the special reporting requirements for listed properties and luxury autos on page 2 of the form. The total deduction is carried forward to the appropriate form, such as Schedule C for businesses and Schedule E for rental properties. Finally, Table 8-2 summarizes the major components of the MACRS procedure.

III. Depreciation, MACRS, and ACRS Deductions   8-33

Form **4562**	**Depreciation and Amortization**	OMB No. 1545-0172
Department of the Treasury Internal Revenue Service	(Including Information on Listed Property) ▶ See separate instructions. ▶ Attach this form to your return.	**1993** Attachment Sequence No. **67**

Name(s) shown on return: Doug Anders
Identifying number: 402-63-1140

Business or activity to which this form relates: Anders Consulting

Part I — Election To Expense Certain Tangible Property (Section 179) (Note: If you have any "Listed Property," complete Part V before you complete Part I.)

1	Maximum dollar limitation (If an enterprise zone business, see instructions.)	**1** $17,500
2	Total cost of section 179 property placed in service during the tax year (see instructions)	**2** 19,500
3	Threshold cost of section 179 property before reduction in limitation	**3** $200,000
4	Reduction in limitation. Subtract line 3 from line 2, but do not enter less than -0-	**4** 0
5	Dollar limitation for tax year. Subtract line 4 from line 1, but do not enter less than -0-. (If married filing separately, see instructions.)	**5** 17,500

(a) Description of property	(b) Cost	(c) Elected cost
6 Duplicating machine	19,500	17,500

7	Listed property. Enter amount from line 26.	**7**
8	Total elected cost of section 179 property. Add amounts in column (c), lines 6 and 7	**8** 17,500
9	Tentative deduction. Enter the smaller of line 5 or line 8	**9** 17,500
10	Carryover of disallowed deduction from 1992 (see instructions)	**10**
11	Taxable income limitation. Enter the smaller of taxable income or line 5 (see instructions)	**11** 17,500
12	Section 179 expense deduction. Add lines 9 and 10, but do not enter more than line 11	**12** 17,500
13	Carryover of disallowed deduction to 1994. Add lines 9 and 10, less line 12 ▶ **13** 0	

Note: *Do not use Part II or Part III below for listed property (automobiles, certain other vehicles, cellular telephones, certain computers, or property used for entertainment, recreation, or amusement). Instead, use Part V for listed property.*

Part II — MACRS Depreciation For Assets Placed in Service ONLY During Your 1993 Tax Year (Do Not Include Listed Property)

(a) Classification of property	(b) Month and year placed in service	(c) Basis for depreciation (business/investment use only—see instructions)	(d) Recovery period	(e) Convention	(f) Method	(g) Depreciation deduction
14 General Depreciation System (GDS) (see instructions):						
a 3-year property						
b 5-year property						
c 7-year property		2,000*	7	MY	200%DB	286
d 10-year property						
e 15-year property						
f 20-year property						
g Residential rental property			27.5 yrs. 27.5 yrs.	MM MM	S/L S/L	
h Nonresidential real property	3-1-93	200,000		MM MM	S/L S/L	5,026
15 Alternative Depreciation System (ADS) (see instructions):						
a Class life					S/L	
b 12-year			12 yrs.		S/L	
c 40-year			40 yrs.	MM	S/L	

Part III — Other Depreciation (Do Not Include Listed Property)

16	GDS and ADS deductions for assets placed in service in tax years beginning before 1993 (see instructions)	**16**
17	Property subject to section 168(f)(1) election (see instructions)	**17**
18	ACRS and other depreciation (see instructions)	**18** 4,020

Part IV — Summary

19	Listed property. Enter amount from line 25.	**19** 3,143
20	Total. Add deductions on line 12, lines 14 and 15 in column (g), and lines 16 through 19. Enter here and on the appropriate lines of your return. (Partnerships and S corporations—see instructions)	**20** 29,975
21	For assets shown above and placed in service during the current year, enter the portion of the basis attributable to section 263A costs (see instructions) **21** 0	

For Paperwork Reduction Act Notice, see page 1 of the separate instructions.   Cat. No. 12906N   Form **4562** (1993)

*Remaining cost of duplicating machine not expensed.

Figure 8-2 Form 4562

Form 4562 (1993) Page 2

Part V — Listed Property—Automobiles, Certain Other Vehicles, Cellular Telephones, Certain Computers, and Property Used for Entertainment, Recreation, or Amusement

For any vehicle for which you are using the standard mileage rate or deducting lease expense, complete only 22a, 22b, columns (a) through (c) of Section A, all of Section B, and Section C if applicable.

Section A—Depreciation and Other Information (Caution: *See instructions for limitations for automobiles.*)

22a Do you have evidence to support the business/investment use claimed? ☐ Yes ☐ No   22b If "Yes," is the evidence written? ☐ Yes ☐ No

(a) Type of property (list vehicles first)	(b) Date placed in service	(c) Business/ investment use percentage	(d) Cost or other basis	(e) Basis for depreciation (business/investment use only)	(f) Recovery period	(g) Method/ Convention	(h) Depreciation deduction	(i) Elected section 179 cost
23 Property used more than 50% in a qualified business use (see instructions):								
Computer	1-5-93	100 %	8,000	8,000	7	GDS-MY	1,143	0
Delivery Auto	1-12-93	100 %	10,000	10,000	5	GDS-MY	2,000	0
		%						
24 Property used 50% or less in a qualified business use (see instructions):								
		%				S/L –		
		%				S/L –		
		%				S/L –		

25 Add amounts in column (h). Enter the total here and on line 19, page 1 . . . . . . **25** 3,143
26 Add amounts in column (i). Enter the total here and on line 7, page 1 . . . . **26** 0

Section B—Information Regarding Use of Vehicles—*If you deduct expenses for vehicles:*
- Always complete this section for vehicles used by a sole proprietor, partner, or other "more than 5% owner," or related person.
- If you provided vehicles to your employees, first answer the questions in Section C to see if you meet an exception to completing this section for those vehicles.

	(a) Vehicle 1	(b) Vehicle 2	(c) Vehicle 3	(d) Vehicle 4	(e) Vehicle 5	(f) Vehicle 6
27 Total business/investment miles driven during the year (DO NOT include commuting miles)	13,100					
28 Total commuting miles driven during the year	0					
29 Total other personal (noncommuting) miles driven	0					
30 Total miles driven during the year. Add lines 27 through 29.	13,100					
	Yes No	Yes No	Yes No	Yes No	Yes No	Yes No
31 Was the vehicle available for personal use during off-duty hours?	X					
32 Was the vehicle used primarily by a more than 5% owner or related person?	X					
33 Is another vehicle available for personal use?	X					

Section C—Questions for Employers Who Provide Vehicles for Use by Their Employees
Answer these questions to determine if you meet an exception to completing Section B. **Note:** *Section B must always be completed for vehicles used by sole proprietors, partners, or other more than 5% owners or related persons.*

	Yes	No
34 Do you maintain a written policy statement that prohibits all personal use of vehicles, including commuting, by your employees?		
35 Do you maintain a written policy statement that prohibits personal use of vehicles, except commuting, by your employees? (See instructions for vehicles used by corporate officers, directors, or 1% or more owners.)		
36 Do you treat all use of vehicles by employees as personal use?		
37 Do you provide more than five vehicles to your employees and retain the information received from your employees concerning the use of the vehicles?		
38 Do you meet the requirements concerning qualified automobile demonstration use (see instructions)?		

Note: *If your answer to 34, 35, 36, 37, or 38 is "Yes," you need not complete Section B for the covered vehicles.*

Part VI Amortization

(a) Description of costs	(b) Date amortization begins	(c) Amortizable amount	(d) Code section	(e) Amortization period or percentage	(f) Amortization for this year
39 Amortization of costs that begins during your 1993 tax year:					

40 Amortization of costs that began before 1993 . . . . **40**
41 Total. Enter here and on "Other Deductions" or "Other Expenses" line of your return . . **41**

Figure 8-2 (continued)   Form 4562

Table 8-2 Summary of the Modified Accelerated Cost Recovery System

Characteristic	Personalty	Realty
Recovery classes	Six (3-, 5-, 7-, 10-, 15-, and 20-year classes)	Two (27.5-year for residential and 31.5-year or 39-year for commercial)
Acquisition-year assumption	Mid-year (mid-quarter if more than 40% acquired in last quarter)	Mid-month
Recovery method	200% declining balance for first four classes, 150% for others	Straight-line
Immediate expense option (Sec. 179)	Maximum of $10,000, with $1 for $1 phaseout for acquisitions exceeding $200,000	None available
Non-ADS straight-line election	Straight-line recovery over class life	Not applicable
ADS (Alternative Depreciation System)	Straight-line recovery over mid-point ADR lives (with a few exceptions)	Straight-line recovery over a 40-year life
Listed property limitations	ADS required if business use does not exceed 50%	Not applicable
Luxury auto limitations	Limited ACRS deductions for autos exceeding certain cost (approximately $13,800 in 1993)	Not applicable

REVIEW III

1. Which of the following properties is not eligible for depreciation or cost recovery deductions?
   (a) a four-apartment building rented out as dwelling units
   (b) a drill press used by a construction company
   (c) a personal automobile owned by an individual
   (d) a microcomputer used by a stock brokerage firm
2. Mel Wilson purchased $210,900 of personalty during 1993. His maximum Sec. 179 (immediate expensing) deduction for this property would be
   (a) $ 0.
   (b) $ 3,400.
   (c) $ 6,600.
   (d) $10,000.
3. Hal Wilson acquired a new duplicating machine in 1993. The asset has an ADR mid-point (guideline) life of ten years. In computing cost recovery deductions, Wilson would use lives of
   (a) five years for MACRS and seven years for ADS.
   (b) seven years for MACRS and ten years for ADS.
   (c) seven years for both MACRS and ADS.
   (d) ten years for both MACRS and ADS.
4. Wendy Allison purchased a new office building in October, 1993. She will rent the offices exclusively to commercial (business) clients. In computing cost recovery deductions, Allison would use lives of
   (a) 27.5 years for MACRS and 39 years for ADS.
   (b) 27.5 years for MACRS and 40 years for ADS.
   (c) 39 years for MACRS and 40 years for ADS.
   (d) 40 years for both MACRS and ADS.

Answers are on page 8-36.

IV RETIREMENT PLANS FOR SELF-EMPLOYED INDIVIDUALS
(Code Sections 401, 403, 415)

Congress has traditionally offered various tax incentives for businesses and individuals to establish private retirement plans. With the budget deficit crisis and mushrooming social security commitments, businesses are increasingly encouraged to assist employees in providing for their own retirement. In the case of self-employed individuals, the tax incentive is known as a Keogh (or "H.R. 10") plan. (The name "Keogh" refers to the member of Congress who introduced the idea as House of Representatives Bill No. 10.)

There are three primary tax incentives associated with "qualified retirement plans" (e.g., those plans such as Keoghs), which receive preferential tax treatment. First, the employer who makes the contribution obtains an immediate tax deduction, subject to certain limitations. Second, the contributions, which are made to an independent trusteed account through a bank or other fiduciary, earn income on a tax-free basis; in other words, the retirement trust is tax exempt. And third, the covered employees (or, as described below, the self-employed person) are not taxed on either the contributions or their earnings until they actually receive the benefits, which usually occurs at retirement.

Example 37. Wanda Rawles' employer, Bill Ace Construction, contributed 8% of her $30,000 salary to a qualified retirement plan. Assuming that certain limitations are met, Bill Ace will deduct the $2,400 as a business expense, any earnings on the contributions in future years will be exempt from tax, and Wanda will not be taxed on any of the accumulation on her behalf in the retirement trust until she begins to receive distributions later.

ANSWERS TO REVIEW III

1. (c) Only properties used in a trade or business or income-producing activities are depreciable. A personal automobile would not qualify for cost recovery.
2. (c) The $10,000 maximum is reduced $1 for $1 for any personalty acquisitions exceeding $200,000 during the year. Thus, the reduction is $10,900, and the maximum Sec. 179 deduction is $6,600.
3. (b) Property with an ADR mid-point of ten years or more is in the seven-year MACRS class; however, the mid-point life of ten years is used for ADS election purposes.
4. (c) Since the property is commercial realty (more than 20% of the rents are from nonresidential tenants), *and* was acquired on or after May 13, 1993, the MACRS recovery period is 39 years. Under ADS, all realty is recovered over a 40-year period.

Any Keogh plan established by a self-employed individual must meet a number of coverage and vesting rules under the Code. For example, the plan must allow all employees age 21 or older with at least one year of service (defined as 1,000 hours) to participate in the plan. Furthermore, the plan must meet certain comparison tests to ensure that the plan does not discriminate in favor of highly compensated employees. And finally, the plan must have a reasonable vesting schedule for employees, that is, a reasonably short waiting period before the employee has a nonforfeitable right to contributions made on his or her behalf. For example, an employee must vest under one of two schedules: 100% after five years, or 20% after three years, with 20% increases in Years 4 through 7 (when 100% vesting occurs).

TAX TIP

Because a qualified Keogh plan must cover all eligible employees, some self-employed individuals are hesitant to establish such plans because of the potential costs. Instead, they establish their own Individual Retirement Accounts (IRAs), which allow deductible contributions of up to $2,000 a year by any individual who is not covered by any other type of qualified retirement plan. (The specific rules for IRAs are discussed in Chapter 4.) Although the deduction is smaller for an IRA, the self-employed individual is *not* required to cover employees.

A self-employed individual who establishes a qualified retirement plan for employees is technically not an employee. However, assuming that the various coverage and vesting requirements are met, a self-employed individual may deduct limited amounts of contributions to a Keogh plan on his or her own behalf. This account works in a fashion similar to the accounts for employees, in that the self-employed individual may deduct the contributions (subject to certain limitations). The contributions are generally made to a trust organization that manages the funds, and earnings on these contributions are exempt from tax. Like employees, the self-employed individual is not taxed on contributions or earnings until they are withdrawn.

It is important to point out where the two expense deductions are reported by the self-employed individual. Deductible contributions on behalf of *employees* are reported as ordinary business deductions on Schedule C of Form 1040 (illustrated in the next section of this chapter). Deductible contributions on behalf of the *self-employed individual* are reported as deductions FOR adjusted gross income on line 27 of the front page of Form 1040.

In computing the allowable deductions for Keogh plans, it is important to distinguish "defined benefit" plans from "defined contribution" plans. Each is discussed briefly below.

DEFINED BENEFIT PLANS

A *defined benefit* plan provides for specific dollar payments to employees at retirement (i.e., the "benefit" is defined in advance). Such plans are sometimes called *pension plans* because they are based on the expected employee pension at retirement.

Because the projected benefit is stated in terms of future dollars, the allowable contribution and deduction amounts must be determined actuarially through the use of present value computations. The complexity of such plans generally calls for professional actuarial assistance each year, and this factor alone has made defined contribution plans (described below) the more popular Keogh vehicle. Discussion of the computational details for defined benefit plans is beyond the scope of this text.

> ## TAX TIP
>
>
>
> Although defined benefit plans are not used often for Keogh purposes, such plans may offer substantial tax advantages for the business owner who is near retirement age. For example, under current law, a self-employed individual using a defined benefit plan may contribute and deduct the present value of an amount that would generate an annual benefit at retirement of up to approximately $115,000. Thus, a sole proprietor who establishes a Keogh plan near retirement could contribute relatively large amounts to the plan during the final working years.

DEFINED CONTRIBUTION PLANS

A *defined contribution* plan provides for a predetermined contribution rate to the retirement plan (i.e., the "contribution" is defined in advance). In a sole proprietorship setting, the defined contribution plan is either a profit-sharing plan or a money purchase plan. A *profit-sharing* plan allows employees (or their beneficiaries) to share in the profits of the business according to an annually specified formula. For example, the plan might provide that 10% of the business profits will be contributed to the retirement plan, with the contribution to each employee's account based on his or her salary relative to total employee salaries. On the other hand, a *money purchase* plan is a plan where contributions are based on a stated formula. For example, the plan might require annual contributions of 8% of each participating employee's salary. In either type of plan, the contribution formula must be definite and not left to the discretion of the sole proprietor.

> ## TAX TIP
>
>
>
> It is extremely important for a sole proprietor to comply with the various coverage and contribution requirements once a qualified plan is established. If these requirements are not met, the plan loses its "qualified" status, and all of the invested earnings are taxable. Furthermore, no deduction would be allowed for contributions to the plan unless the employees had an immediate claim of right to the contribution (which, of course, would mean that the amount would be taxable to the employee once the claim of right is established).
>
> Self-employed individuals who are concerned about the potential costs of a Keogh plan may want to consider establishing a profit-sharing plan. This would ensure that contributions would be required only when the business shows a profit.

The following discussion highlights the aggregate amount that is *deductible* for contributions on behalf of all employees. However, it is important to note that there is a separate limit on the amount *contributable* on behalf of any one employee, regardless of the overall deduction limitation. For defined contribution plans, this is the smaller of $30,000 or 25% of the employee's annual earnings.

THE LAW

Sec. 404(a)(3)—Limit on deductible contributions. In general. In the taxable year when paid, if the contributions are paid into a stock bonus or profit-sharing trust ... in an amount not in excess of 15 percent of the compensation otherwise paid or accrued during the taxable year ... to the beneficiaries under the plan.

Deduction for Contributions on Behalf of Employees

In the case of both profit-sharing and money-purchase plans, the maximum deduction for contributions on behalf of employees is 15% of the aggregate compensation of all covered employees. Any contributions in excess of the 15% limit may be carried forward to future years and utilized whenever contributions are less than the 15% limit in those years. As mentioned earlier, this amount is deducted as a business expense of the sole proprietor on Schedule C.

Example 38. Ace Graham owns and operates a retail store. Several years ago, he established a profit-sharing retirement plan for his employees. During 1993 and 1994, the total compensation of all covered employees was $300,000 and $320,000, respectively. Contributions to the retirement plan totaled $48,000 in 1993 and $41,000 in 1994. Ace's 1993 deduction for contributions to the plan on behalf of his employees is limited to $45,000 ($300,000 × .15). However, in 1994 he can deduct $44,000 (the $41,000 actual contribution plus the $3,000 excess carryover from 1993), since the total is less than 15% of the 1994 compensation.

TAX TIP

Recall from the earlier discussion that once contributions are invested in a qualified retirement account, the earnings on the contributions are tax exempt. Given this fact, an employer may be tempted to deliberately overcontribute to a plan to generate tax-free income that might ultimately revert to the employer. To prevent this scenario, Congress established a special 10% excise tax on any "excess" contributions (i.e., above the deductible limit).

The excise tax applies until the excess is either withdrawn or used up correctly in a carryover year. For instance, in Example 38, Ace would have to pay a 10% excise tax on the $3,000 excess contribution in 1993. However, the penalty would cease to apply after 1994, when the excess is used up as a carryover.

Deductions for Contributions on Behalf of the Owner

The maximum amount deductible as a contribution on behalf of the business owner depends on whether the Keogh is a profit-sharing plan or a money purchase plan. In either case, the contribution is limited to the lesser of $30,000 or a percentage of the "earned income" from the business. (Incidentally, the maximum deduction is also the maximum amount that the self-employed individual may contribute on his or her own behalf.) The "earned income" is the net income from the sole proprietorship business, as determined on Schedule C (which takes into account the deduction for contributions to the plan on behalf of employees). As mentioned earlier, the deduction is taken *for* AGI on Form 1040 (line 27), not on Schedule C.

The self-employed individual must be able to demonstrate that personal services were a definite factor in producing the "earned income." Thus, a person who owns a business but contributes no services of any kind could not make a Keogh contribution on his or her own behalf.

For a *profit-sharing plan,* the maximum deduction is the *lesser* of $30,000 or 13.043% of the self-employment income. Why such an uneven percentage as 13.043? The answer lies in the typical legalese used in the Code, which states that the deduction is 15% of the net income *after* deducting the contribution on behalf of the self-employed individual. Mathematically, this works out to be .13043 (.15/1.15) of the self-employment income *before* deducting the contribution. This is the easier rule to apply, because it does not involve a trial-and-error process.

✓ **Example 39.** Norma Kelly owns and operates a computer service bureau and maintains a profit-sharing Keogh plan for her employees. Her self-employment (Schedule C) income for 1993 was $100,000. The maximum amount that she may contribute and deduct to the Keogh plan on her own behalf is $13,043 ($100,000 × .13043), since this is less than $30,000. (Note that the $13,043 is also 15% of $86,957, the $100,000 income less the $13,043 deduction.)

For a *money-purchase* plan, the maximum deduction is the *lesser* of $30,000 or 20% of the self-employment income. Once again, the Code uses the mental gymnastic language of 25% of the self-employment income *after* deducting the contribution on behalf of the owner. This is equivalent to deducting .20 (.25/1.25) of the self-employment income shown on Schedule C.

✓ **Example 40.** Assume the same facts as Example 39, except that Norma's Keogh plan is a money-purchase plan. In this case, her contribution on her own behalf is limited to $20,000 ($100,000 × .20), because this is less than $30,000. (Note that $20,000 is also 25% of $80,000, the $100,000 income less the $20,000 deduction.)

MISCELLANEOUS REQUIREMENTS

In order to deduct contributions to a Keogh plan, the actual plan must be established before the end of the tax year. However, once the plan is established, deductible contributions may be made up to the due date of the tax return, including extensions. This

TABLE 8-3 Defined Contribution Keogh Plan Limits

Contributions on Behalf of	Maximum Allowable Contribution	Maximum Allowable Deduction
Employees:		
Profit-sharing plans or money-purchase plans	Lesser of $30,000 or 25% of compensation for each employee	15% of total compensation of all covered employees
Self-Employed Business owner:		
Profit-sharing plans	Lesser of $30,000 or 13.043% of Schedule C self-employed income	Same as maximum contribution
Money-purchase plans	Lesser of $30,000 or 20% of Schedule C self-employed income	Same as maximum contribution

provides the business owner with a grace period of three and a half months to determine the required contribution.

☑ **Example 41.** Jill Tredgar established a qualified Keogh plan for her employees on December 17, 1993. Assuming that she is a calendar-year taxpayer, she has until April 15, 1994, to contribute to the plan, and she may deduct these contributions on her 1993 return.

Once an employee or business owner retires, he or she usually begins to receive retirement benefits. If an employee or owner elects to receive the benefits as an annuity, each payment is taxed according to the annuity rules described in Chapter 2. In most cases, each payment is fully taxable, since the employee (or business owner) was not taxed on the original contributions or earnings on the contributions. If the employee or owner elects to receive the accumulated benefit as a lump sum upon retirement, he or she may elect the special five-year averaging computations described in Chapter 7. And finally, an employer or employee may elect to "roll over" the lump sum into an Individual Retirement Account (IRA), which postpones the tax incidence until distributions are made from the IRA.

There are strict penalties for premature distributions from a Keogh plan. In general, the distribution is immediately taxable and is also subject to a 10% excise tax. The 10% excise tax does not apply to distributions made on or after age 59 1/2 or to distributions for a variety of other reasons (e.g., death of the employee or business owner).

The preceding discussion has only touched the surface of the complex topic of qualified retirement plans. For example, there is also a special Simplified Employee Pension Plan (SEPP), whereby the employer can simply establish IRAs for each of his or her employees (as well as for himself or herself) and make deductible contributions to these accounts, subject to certain limits. The details concerning SEPPs and other qualified retirement plans are beyond the scope of this text.

Table 8-3 summarizes the primary tax rules regarding defined contribution Keogh plans. Again, it is important to note the difference between the maximum allowable *contribution* and the maximum allowable *deduction*. For contributions on behalf of employees, these amounts are quite different; however, for the self-employed business owner, the two amounts are the same.

REVIEW IV

1. Gail May owns and operates her own electronics store. During 1993 she established a profit-sharing Keogh plan. Total compensation paid to employees during 1993 was $200,000. During 1993 she contributed $29,200 to the Keogh plan on behalf of her employees. Her allowable Schedule C *deduction* for these contributions would be
   (a) $20,000.
   (b) $29,200.
   (c) $30,000.
   (d) $50,000.
2. Refer to Question 1. Assume that Ruth Domlevy is an employee of Gail's business and that she received a salary of $40,000 in 1993. The maximum contribution that Gail could make on behalf of Ruth to the Keogh plan in 1993 would be
   (a) $ 6,000.
   (b) $ 8,000.
   (c) $10,000.
   (d) $30,000.
3. Refer to Question 1. Assume that Gail's Schedule C self-employment income for 1993 (after deducting contributions on behalf of employees) was $160,000. The maximum amount that she can contribute and deduct on her own behalf in 1993 is
   (a) $16,420.
   (b) $20,869.
   (c) $30,000.
   (d) $32,000.
4. Assume the same facts as Question 3, except that the plan is a money-purchase pension plan. The maximum amount that Gail can contribute and deduct on her own behalf in 1993 is
   (a) $16,420.
   (b) $20,869.
   (c) $30,000.
   (d) $32,000.

Answers are on page 8-44.

V MISCELLANEOUS BUSINESS EXPENSES
(Code Sections 162, 164, 166, 174, and 611-613)

Our discussion so far has focused on three major business expense deductions: cost of goods sold, depreciation, and Keogh retirement plans. The deductibility of most other business expenses is usually determined by referring to the requirements of Sec. 162 (e.g., ordinary, necessary, and paid or incurred). However, special tax rules apply to certain expenditures, and the remainder of this chapter examines a few of these requirements.

AMORTIZATION

The term *amortization* refers to cost recovery procedures applicable to intangible assets. Intangible assets are those properties that do not have a physical existence. These include such properties as leaseholds, patents, copyrights, trademarks, and franchises.

Generally, the cost of an intangible asset must be recovered on a *straight-line* basis over the estimated useful life of the asset to the taxpayer. This economic useful life may be established by law (e.g., patents and copyrights) or by contractual agreements (e.g., leases). In other cases, special rules may apply. For example, Sec. 197, as added by the 1993 Act, permits taxpayers who acquire businesses to amortize such purchased intangibles as goodwill over a 15-year period.

Perhaps the most commonly encountered special amortization rules relate to research and experimentation expenditures. Research and experimentation expenditures (R&E) are defined as all costs incident to the development or improvement of an experimental model, plant process, product, formula, invention, or similar property. Taxpayers can choose one of three amortization methods for such expenditures: (1) expense the costs immediately as incurred, (2) amortize the costs over a period of not less than five years, or (3) defer cost recovery until the project is either sold or abandoned. Regardless of the cost recovery method chosen, any expenditures for *tangible* properties such as machinery and buildings must be recovered under normal MACRS rules. The annual MACRS deduction is then treated as a qualifying R&E expenditure.

Example 42. Paula Jensen incurred the following expenses in 1993 for experimental designs for her company's product: $60,000 salaries of research personnel, $30,000 utilities, and $10,000 MACRS current year deductions for research lab equipment. Jensen may report these expenses in one of three ways: (1) deduct the entire $100,000 in 1993 (2) amortize the $100,000 on a straight-line basis over a period of not less than five years, or (3) defer any deductions until the product is sold or the process is abandoned.

DEPLETION

Depletion is a term used to refer to cost recovery deduction procedures for such natural resources as oil, gas, geothermal wells, and timber. The deduction is available to anyone who has an "economic interest" in the natural resource. Generally, this means that the deduction is available to an *operator* (the person who has paid an amount to lease the property and extract the natural resource) and the *property owner* (who generally has a profits interest in the production, usually referred to as a royalty interest).

THE LAW

Sec. 611(a)—General Rule. In the case of mines, oil and gas wells, other natural deposits, and timber, there shall be allowed as a deduction in computing taxable income a reasonable allowance for depletion ... according to the peculiar conditions in each case ...

There are two basic methods of computing depletion, the cost method and the percentage method. The owner or operator may choose the method that yields the larger deduction each year on each property. However, the percentage method is not available for timber and for large oil and gas operators (as explained below).

The *cost method* of depletion is applied by dividing the adjusted basis of the natural resource (i.e., the undepleted cost) by an estimate of the number of remaining recoverable units, and then multiplying the rate per unit by the number of units sold during the year. Once the cost of the resource is fully recovered, no deductions are allowed beyond that point.

> **Example 43.** Bill Wilson, an independent oil and gas operator, paid $400,000 to Vicki Thompson for rights to drill for oil on her property in 1993. At that time, it was estimated that total production from the property would be 50,000 barrels of oil. During 1993 Wilson produced and sold 15,000 barrels of oil. The allowable depletion deduction using the cost method would be $120,000, or the 15,000 barrels sold times the depletable rate per unit of $8 per barrel ($400,000/50,000). The depletion deduction for 1994 will be based on an undepleted cost of $280,000 ($400,000 less the $120,000 depletion deduction for 1993).

The *percentage method* of depletion does not depend on the cost of the natural resource. Rather, an arbitrary percentage rate (established by the Code for the particular natural resource) is multiplied times the gross income from the property. The "gross income" from the property for an operator is the total revenue less any royalty payments to the landowner.

There are two limits applicable to the percentage method of depletion. First, the depletion deduction may not exceed 50% of the taxable income from the property (i.e., gross income less expenses directly attributable to the property). A 100% of taxable income limit applies to oil and gas properties. Second, in the case of oil and gas properties, the deduction is also limited to 65% of the operator's overall taxable income on the return (with some modifications).

The percentage rate applicable to a resource is defined in the Code. For example, for oil and gas properties, the rate is 15%. However, the percentage method is available

---

ANSWERS TO REVIEW IV

1. (b) The maximum *deduction* for contributions to a defined-contribution plan such as a profit-sharing plan is 15% of total compensation. Since the $29,200 actual contribution is less than the 15% limit of $30,000 (15% of $200,000), the deduction is the actual amount paid.
2. (c) The maximum *contribution* to a defined-contribution plan on behalf of any one employee is limited to the lesser of $30,000 or 25% of the employee's compensation. In this case, 25% of the $40,000 compensation, or $10,000, would be the maximum allowable contribution.
3. (b) The maximum *contribution* and *deduction* on behalf of the business owner to a profit-sharing Keogh plan is the lesser of $30,000 or 13.043% of the self-employment income, which in this case would be $20,869.
4. (c) The maximum *contribution* and *deduction* on behalf of the business owner to a money-purchase Keogh plan is the lesser of $30,000 or 20% of the self-employment income ($32,000 in this case). Thus, $30,000 is the limit.

only for "small independent producers," defined as those operators who produce less than 1,000 barrels of oil or 6,000,000 cubic feet of gas per day.

☑ **Example 44.** Assume the same facts as in Example 43, with the assumption that Wilson pays a 1/8 royalty (based on gross sales revenue) to Thompson, the land owner. Furthermore, assume that Thompson's direct expenses applicable to the property in 1993 were $226,250, and that each barrel of oil was sold for $20. Based on these assumptions, Wilson's 1993 results before considering depletion were as follows:

Sales revenue (15,000 x $20)	$300,000
minus Royalty payment ($300,000 x 1/8)	(37,500)
Gross income from property	$262,500 × .15 = $39,375
minus Direct expenses related to property	(226,250)
Taxable income from property	$ 36,250 × 1.00 = $36,250

In this case, Thompson's depletion deduction using the percentage method would be limited to $36,250, or 100% of the $36,250 *taxable* income from the property, because this is less than $39,375, or 15% of the $262,500 *gross* income from the property. If 65% of Thompson's overall taxable income reported on his return was less than $36,250, the depletion deduction would be further limited to this amount.

What about the owner of the property? He or she also has an "economic interest" in the property and is allowed to compute depletion deductions. Normally, this will be done with the percentage method, because the owner will have little if any cost to recover. The appropriate percentage would be multiplied times any lease bonuses and royalty payments received during the year, assuming that production has begun.

☑ **Example 45.** Assume the same facts as in Examples 43 and 44. Vicki Thompson will be entitled to a percentage depletion deduction in 1993 of $65,625, or 15% of the sum of her $400,000 lease bonus payment and the $37,500 royalty payment based on production.

Because percentage depletion is not a cost-based method, an operator or land owner may continue to deduct depletion as long as the property is generating gross income. Thus, it is possible for depletion deductions to eventually exceed the total cost of the property when the percentage method is used.

TAX TIP

The ability to deduct cost recovery beyond the original cost of the property with percentage depletion sounds almost too good to be true, and it is! Congress felt that this was a benefit not available to most taxpayers, so they defined the depletion deductions in excess of the original cost of the property as a "tax preference item" for purposes of the alternative minimum tax discussed in Chapter 7. In effect, these excess deductions are not allowed in the alternative minimum tax computation.

BAD DEBT DEDUCTIONS

Taxpayers are allowed a deduction for any debt obligation (business or nonbusiness) that becomes worthless during the tax year. Bad debts are deductible only if the worthlessness can be proven, either by bankruptcy proceedings, court action, or evidence that legal action would likely prove fruitless. In addition, a bad business debt is deductible only if it has been previously included in income. This effectively limits bad debt deductions to accrual basis business taxpayers (or those cash basis business taxpayers who must report gross profit on the accrual basis because inventories are a significant component of income).

THE LAW

Sec. 166(a)—(1) Wholly worthless debts. There shall be allowed as a deduction any debt which becomes worthless within the taxable year.
(2) Partially worthless debts. When satisfied that a debt is recoverable only in part, the Secretary may allow such debt, in an amount not in excess of the part charged off within the taxable year, as a deduction.

Example 46. Mary Freeman, a cash-basis sole proprietor, performed legal services of $300 on account for Rice Company. Rice subsequently failed to pay the amount due. Freeman is not entitled to a bad debt deduction because the $300 was never included in income on the cash basis.

Business bad debts may be deducted only through the use of the *direct writeoff* method. Under this method, a deduction is taken when the debt is judged to be worthless. A deduction may also be taken for the partial worthlessness of a debt. If the amount of the bad debt is subsequently recovered, then the recovery must be included in income in that year under the tax benefit rule.

Example 47. Bradley Stokes, an accrual basis sole proprietor, performs accounting services worth $600 in 1992 for Balboa Company on account. In 1993 Stokes judged this debt to be worthless and deducted the $600 as an ordinary and necessary business expense on his Schedule C. In 1994 Balboa Company unexpectedly paid the $600 balance. Stokes must include the $600 as income on his 1994 return, since he received a $600 benefit from the 1993 deduction.

Taxpayers may also deduct nonbusiness debts that are judged to be worthless during the tax year. However, these personal bad debts must be reported for tax purposes as *short-term capital losses*. As explained in Chapter 6, capital loss treatment may limit the deductions to a maximum of $3,000 in any one tax year, unless other capital gains are present. However, any excess capital losses may be deducted in future years, subject again to the potential $3,000 limit.

☑ **Example 48.** Beverly Simon loaned $600 to her neighbor in 1991. The neighbor was unable to repay the loan on its due date in 1993. Simon may report the $600 as a short-term capital loss in 1993 to be combined with other capital gains and losses.

Sometimes it is difficult to distinguish between a business and a nonbusiness debt. In general, the Courts and the IRS have narrowly defined a "business debt." For example, a loan from a shareholder to a corporation is generally treated as a nonbusiness bad debt, unless the loan had a substantial employment-related purpose (e.g., preserving the job of the shareholder/employee).

TAX TIP

Taxpayers who loan money to relatives or close friends should be sure to structure the loan in the same manner as a loan to unrelated parties (i.e., reasonable rate of interest, reasonable due date, collateral, etc.). Otherwise, if the debt proves to be uncollectible, the IRS may deny a deduction on the grounds that the original loan was a gift and it was never intended that the amount would be repaid. Evidence of legal action against the borrower may also help the taxpayer's case.

REPAIR EXPENSES

Taxpayers may deduct all ordinary and necessary expenses of repairing property that is either used in a trade or business or held for the production of income. Expenditures incurred in repairing purely personal properties are not deductible.

Repair expenses must be distinguishable from capital expenditures, the cost of which must be capitalized and recovered through depreciation or ACRS procedures. The distinction between repair expenses and capital expenditures is not always a clear one. Generally, an expenditure must be capitalized and depreciated if it (1) significantly increases the value of the property, (2) prolongs the property's useful life, or (3) creates a different use for the property.

☑ **Example 49.** Apple Company spent $380 to repair the roof of its warehouse. This expenditure would most likely be classified as a deductible repair expense. On the other hand, the cost of a new roof would probably be a capital expenditure because it would significantly increase the useful life and value of the building.

SPECIAL PARTIAL DEDUCTION FOR HEALTH INSURANCE PREMIUMS PAID BY SELF-EMPLOYED INDIVIDUALS

In 1986 Congress instituted a special deduction *for* AGI for self-employed individuals. This deduction is for 25% of the amount paid during the year for insurance that constitutes medical care for the taxpayer, his or her spouse, and dependents. This special provision for self-employed individuals allows a partial deduction on line 26 of Form 1040 without regard to whether the taxpayer itemizes or has enough medical expenses to exceed the AGI floor. This deduction is scheduled to expire for years after 1993.

✓ **Example 50.** Alice Cramden, a self-employed individual, paid $880 for health insurance coverage for her family in 1993. She may deduct 25% of this amount, or $220, for AGI. The remaining $660 of premiums is combined with other medical expenses as a potential itemized deduction from AGI (subject to a 7.5% of AGI floor).

SPECIAL PARTIAL DEDUCTION FOR SELF-EMPLOYMENT TAX PAID BY SELF-EMPLOYED INDIVIDUALS

For tax years after 1989, a self-employed person is allowed a deduction for one-half of the self-employment liability for the year. As explained later in this section, this tax is the means by which a self-employed person contributes to the Social Security System each year. Because the self-employment tax rate is twice the rate that an employer pays (and deducts) when matching employee social security withholding, Congress felt that it was only fair to allow the sole proprietor to deduct half of this tax as well. The tax is computed on Schedule SE, which is also illustrated in this section. This amount is also a deduction *for* AGI on line 25 of Form 1040.

✓ **Example 51.** Martha Wills has $40,000 of net income from her sole proprietorship business In 1993 and her self-employment tax on this amount is $5,652. One half of this amount, or $2,826, is allowed as a deduction *for* AGI.

TAX COLLECTIONS

One of the most common business deductions is for salaries and wages of employees. It is important to note that the tax deduction is for the *gross* amount of wages; withholdings for payroll taxes, insurance, union dues, and other items do not change the fact that the employer is initially paying the gross amount to employees and then is acting as a collection agent for the various withholdings.

✓ **Example 52.** Belva Cooley, an employee of Jackson Company, receives a net paycheck of $480 a week. Her weekly gross pay is $650, and Jackson Company withholds $100 for federal income taxes, $40 for state income taxes, and $30 for health insurance coverage. Jackson will deduct $650 salary expense for each weekly check issued to Cooley.

We should note that any amounts withheld from an employee's check are considered to be paid by the employee, not the employer. Therefore, the employer is not entitled to deduct such items as income and social security taxes collected on behalf of the federal and state governments, as well as state and local sales taxes. However, any taxes actually imposed on and *paid* by the employer are deductible. As explained in the Appendix to this chapter, employers can deduct the federal unemployment tax, the state unemployment tax, and the employer's share of the social security tax (which generally matches the employee's contribution).

TAX-REPORTING PROCEDURES FOR SOLE PROPRIETORS

Individuals who own a business or practice a trade or profession must file a Schedule C, Profit or Loss From Business, with their regular Form 1040 tax return. This form summarizes all income and expenses for a trade or business and resembles the traditional income statement used for financial accounting purposes. This form is illustrated in Figure 8-3 for the same hypothetical taxpayer (Douglas Anders) used to illustrate the depreciation form earlier in this chapter (Figure 8-2). Page 2 of Schedule C is used to disclose the detailed computation of cost of goods sold shown on line 4 of page 1. Note also that the deduction for depreciation cost recovery on line 13 is supported by the detailed calculations on Form 4562.

Figure 8-4 illustrates a Form 1040 that discloses the carryover of amounts from Schedule C. Note on the 1040 that Anders' contributions to the Keogh plan on his own behalf (assumed to be 10% of profits) are deducted on line 27 of the 1040, while contributions to the plan on behalf of his employees (assumed to be $9,462) are reported on line 19 of Schedule C as business expenses. Also note that lines 25 and 26 of Form 1040 are used to report the deductions for one-half of the self-employment tax and 25% of the health insurance premiums paid by the self-employed individual.

The final Schedule C net income or loss figure is carried over to line 12 of Form 1040 as an addition to gross income. In effect, this means that all business expenses of the sole proprietor are allowed as deductions *for* AGI. It is important to note that the owner of the business does not deduct a salary paid to himself or herself; such a salary is merely a distribution of the net income and does not affect the tax return.

Because a sole proprietor does not have an employer to withhold FICA (social security) taxes, he or she must also pay social security tax with the federal income tax return. This taxed is based on the earnings from self-employment, which includes the Schedule C net income. This tax is calculated on Schedule SE, illustrated in Figure 8-5.

For 1993 the self-employment tax consists of two components: a social security tax (12.4% on the first $57,600 of Schedule C self-employment income) and a medicare tax (2.9% on the first $135,000 of self-employment income).* Thus, the first $57,600 of self-employment income is subject to a combined rate of 15.3%. Sole proprietors who have no wages from other employment during the year generally complete page 1 of Schedule SE (the "short schedule"), as illustrated in Figure 8-5.

Note that the net effect of the multiplication by .9235 on line 4 of the "short schedule" is to allow a deduction for 7.65% of the self-employment income in computing the tax; this amount is half of the combined 15.3% rate. This "deduction" was added to the tax law concurrently with the special deduction for one-half of the Social Security tax discussed earlier in the chapter.

If the sole proprietor receives wages subject to FICA withholding during the year *and* the sum of the wages and self-employment income exceeds $57,600, page 2 of the Schedule SE (the "long schedule") must be completed. This is because any salary

---

*For changes in the tax law effective for tax years beginning in 1994, see Appendix J.

SCHEDULE C (Form 1040)

Profit or Loss From Business
(Sole Proprietorship)

Department of the Treasury
Internal Revenue Service

▶ Partnerships, joint ventures, etc., must file Form 1065.
▶ Attach to Form 1040 or Form 1041. ▶ See Instructions for Schedule C (Form 1040).

OMB No. 1545-0074

1993

Attachment Sequence No. 09

Name of proprietor: Douglas Anders

Social security number (SSN): 402 63 1140

A Principal business or profession, including product or service (see page C-1): Anders Consulting

B Enter principal business code (see page C-6) ▶ 7 1 2 8 6

C Business name. If no separate business name, leave blank.: Anders Consulting

D Employer ID number (EIN), if any: 9 1 4 4 6 6 8 8 0

E Business address (including suite or room no.) ▶ 146 Jasper Street
City, town or post office, state, and ZIP code: Greensboro, NC 27410

F Accounting method: (1) ☐ Cash (2) ☐ Accrual (3) ☐ Other (specify) ▶

G Method(s) used to value closing inventory: (1) ☐ Cost (2) ☐ Lower of cost or market (3) ☐ Other (attach explanation) (4) ☐ Does not apply (if checked, skip line H)

	Yes	No
H Was there any change in determining quantities, costs, or valuations between opening and closing inventory? If "Yes," attach explanation		X
I Did you "materially participate" in the operation of this business during 1993? If "No," see page C-2 for limit on losses . . .	X	

J If you started or acquired this business during 1993, check here ▶ ☐

Part I Income

1 Gross receipts or sales. **Caution:** If this income was reported to you on Form W-2 and the "Statutory employee" box on that form was checked, see page C-2 and check here ▶ ☐	1	304,482
2 Returns and allowances	2	
3 Subtract line 2 from line 1	3	304,482
4 Cost of goods sold (from line 40 on page 2)	4	42,610
5 **Gross profit.** Subtract line 4 from line 3	5	261,872
6 Other income, including Federal and state gasoline or fuel tax credit or refund (see page C-2) ▶	6	
7 **Gross income.** Add lines 5 and 6	7	261,872

Part II Expenses. Caution: Do not enter expenses for business use of your home on lines 8–27. Instead, see line 30.

8 Advertising	8	12,320	19 Pension and profit-sharing plans	19	733
9 Bad debts from sales or services (see page C-3)	9	2,140	20 Rent or lease (see page C-4): a Vehicles, machinery, and equipment	20a	653
10 Car and truck expenses (see page C-3)	10		b Other business property	20b	11,150
11 Commissions and fees	11		21 Repairs and maintenance	21	
12 Depletion	12		22 Supplies (not included in Part III)	22	
13 Depreciation and section 179 expense deduction (not included in Part III) (see page C-3)	13	29,975	23 Taxes and licenses	23	
			24 Travel, meals, and entertainment: a Travel	24a	
14 Employee benefit programs (other than on line 19)	14		b Meals and entertainment		
15 Insurance (other than health)	15	3,020	c Enter 20% of line 24b subject to limitations (see page C-4)		
16 Interest: a Mortgage (paid to banks, etc.)	16a	9,462	d Subtract line 24c from line 24b	24d	
b Other	16b		25 Utilities	25	
17 Legal and professional services	17		26 Wages (less jobs credit)	26	134,580
18 Office expense	18		27 Other expenses (from line 46 on page 2)	27	
28 **Total expenses** before expenses for business use of home. Add lines 8 through 27 in columns				28	204,033
29 Tentative profit (loss). Subtract line 28 from line 7				29	57,839
30 Expenses for business use of your home. Attach **Form 8829**				30	
31 **Net profit or (loss).** Subtract line 30 from line 29. • If a profit, enter on **Form 1040, line 12,** and ALSO on **Schedule SE, line 2** (statutory employees, see page C-5). Fiduciaries, enter on Form 1041, line 3. • If a loss, you MUST go on to line 32.				31	57,839

32 If you have a loss, check the box that describes your investment in this activity (see page C-5).
• If you checked 32a, enter the loss on **Form 1040, line 12,** and ALSO on **Schedule SE, line 2** (statutory employees, see page C-5). Fiduciaries, enter on Form 1041, line 3.
• If you checked 32b, you MUST attach **Form 6198.**

32a ☐ All investment is at risk.
32b ☐ Some investment is not at risk.

For Paperwork Reduction Act Notice, see Form 1040 instructions.   Cat. No. 11334P   Schedule C (Form 1040) 1993

Figure 8-3 Schedule C

Schedule C (Form 1040) 1993 — Page 2

Part III — Cost of Goods Sold (see page C-5)

33	Inventory at beginning of year. If different from last year's closing inventory, attach explanation	8,020
34	Purchases less cost of items withdrawn for personal use (51,650 − 350)	51,300
35	Cost of labor. Do not include salary paid to yourself	
36	Materials and supplies	
37	Other costs	
38	Add lines 33 through 37	59,320
39	Inventory at end of year	16,710
40	**Cost of goods sold.** Subtract line 39 from line 38. Enter the result here and on page 1, line 4	42,610

Part IV — Information on Your Vehicle.
Complete this part **ONLY** if you are claiming car or truck expenses on line 10 and are not required to file Form 4562 for this business.

41 When did you place your vehicle in service for business purposes? (month, day, year) ▶ ...../...../.....

42 Of the total number of miles you drove your vehicle during 1993, enter the number of miles you used your vehicle for:

  a Business .... b Commuting .... c Other ....

43 Do you (or your spouse) have another vehicle available for personal use? ☐ Yes ☐ No

44 Was your vehicle available for use during off-duty hours? ☐ Yes ☐ No

45a Do you have evidence to support your deduction? ☐ Yes ☐ No
  b If "Yes," is the evidence written? ☐ Yes ☐ No

Part V — Other Expenses.
List below business expenses not included on lines 8–26 or line 30.

46 Total other expenses. Enter here and on page 1, line 27	

Figure 8-3 (continued) Schedule C

Form 1040 — U.S. Individual Income Tax Return (1993)

Department of the Treasury—Internal Revenue Service
For the year Jan. 1–Dec. 31, 1993, or other tax year beginning _____, 1993, ending _____, 19 ___
OMB No. 1545-0074

Label (See instructions on page 12.) Use the IRS label. Otherwise, please print or type.

- Your first name and initial: **Douglas**   Last name: **Anders**
- Home address (number and street): **146 Jasper Street**
- City, town or post office, state, and ZIP code: **Greensboro, NC 27410**
- Your social security number: **402:63:1140**

Presidential Election Campaign (See page 12.)
- Do you want $3 to go to this fund? — No: **X**
- If a joint return, does your spouse want $3 to go to this fund?

Note: Checking "Yes" will not change your tax or reduce your refund.

Filing Status (See page 12.) Check only one box.

1. **X** Single
2. ☐ Married filing joint return (even if only one had income)
3. ☐ Married filing separate return. Enter spouse's social security no. above and full name here. ▶
4. ☐ Head of household (with qualifying person). (See page 13.) If the qualifying person is a child but not your dependent, enter this child's name here. ▶
5. ☐ Qualifying widow(er) with dependent child (year spouse died ▶ 19 ___). (See page 13.)

Exemptions (See page 13.)

- 6a ☐ Yourself. If your parent (or someone else) can claim you as a dependent on his or her tax return, do not check box 6a. But be sure to check the box on line 33b on page 2.
- b ☐ Spouse
- c Dependents:

(1) Name (first, initial, and last name)	(2) Check if under age 1	(3) If age 1 or older, dependent's social security number	(4) Dependent's relationship to you	(5) No. of months lived in your home in 1993

If more than six dependents, see page 14.

- d If your child didn't live with you but is claimed as your dependent under a pre-1985 agreement, check here ▶ ☐
- e Total number of exemptions claimed

No. of boxes checked on 6a and 6b: **1**
No. of your children on 6c who:
 • lived with you
 • didn't live with you due to divorce or separation (see page 15)
Dependents on 6c not entered above
Add numbers entered on lines above ▶ **1**

Income

Attach Copy B of your Forms W-2, W-2G, and 1099-R here.

7	Wages, salaries, tips, etc. Attach Form(s) W-2	
8a	Taxable interest income (see page 16). Attach Schedule B if over $400	
b	Tax-exempt interest (see page 17). DON'T include on line 8a [8b]	
9	Dividend income. Attach Schedule B if over $400	
10	Taxable refunds, credits, or offsets of state and local income taxes (see page 17)	
11	Alimony received	
12	Business income or (loss). Attach Schedule C or C-EZ	57,839
13	Capital gain or (loss). Attach Schedule D	
14	Capital gain distributions not reported on line 13 (see page 17)	
15	Other gains or (losses). Attach Form 4797	
16a	Total IRA distributions [16a] ___ b Taxable amount (see page 18)	
17a	Total pensions and annuities [17a] ___ b Taxable amount (see page 18)	
18	Rental real estate, royalties, partnerships, S corporations, trusts, etc. Attach Schedule E	
19	Farm income or (loss). Attach Schedule F	
20	Unemployment compensation (see page 19)	
21a	Social security benefits [21a] ___ b Taxable amount (see page 19)	
22	Other income. List type and amount—see page 20	
23	Add the amounts in the far right column for lines 7 through 22. This is your **total income** ▶	57,839

Adjustments to Income (See page 20.)

24a	Your IRA deduction (see page 20)	
b	Spouse's IRA deduction (see page 20)	
25	One-half of self-employment tax (see page 21) (8172/2)	4,086
26	Self-employed health insurance deduction (see page 22)	220
27	Keogh retirement plan and self-employed SEP deduction	5,784
28	Penalty on early withdrawal of savings	
29	Alimony paid. Recipient's SSN ▶	
30	Add lines 24a through 29. These are your **total adjustments** ▶	10,090

Adjusted Gross Income

31. Subtract line 30 from line 23. This is your **adjusted gross income**. If this amount is less than $23,050 and a child lived with you, see page EIC-1 to find out if you can claim the "Earned Income Credit" on line 56 ▶ **47,749**

Cat. No. 11320B   Form **1040** (1993)

Figure 8-4 Form 1040 (Reflecting Schedule C Carryovers)

SCHEDULE SE
(Form 1040)

Department of the Treasury
Internal Revenue Service

Self-Employment Tax

▶ See Instructions for Schedule SE (Form 1040).

▶ Attach to Form 1040.

OMB No. 1545-0074

1993

Attachment
Sequence No. **17**

Name of person with **self-employment** income (as shown on Form 1040)
Douglas Anders

Social security number of person with **self-employment** income ▶ 402 63 1140

Who Must File Schedule SE

You must file Schedule SE if:

- Your wages (and tips) subject to social security AND Medicare tax (or railroad retirement tax) were less than $135,000; **AND**
- Your net earnings from self-employment from other than church employee income (line 4 of Short Schedule SE or line 4c of Long Schedule SE) were $400 or more; **OR**
- You had church employee income of $108.28 or more. Income from services you performed as a minister or a member of a religious order **is not** church employee income. See page SE-1.

Note: *Even if you have a loss or a small amount of income from self-employment, it may be to your benefit to file Schedule SE and use either "optional method" in Part II of Long Schedule SE. See page SE-3.*

Exception. If your only self-employment income was from earnings as a minister, member of a religious order, or Christian Science practitioner, **AND** you filed Form 4361 and received IRS approval not to be taxed on those earnings, **DO NOT** file Schedule SE. Instead, write "Exempt–Form 4361" on Form 1040, line 47.

May I Use Short Schedule SE or MUST I Use Long Schedule SE?

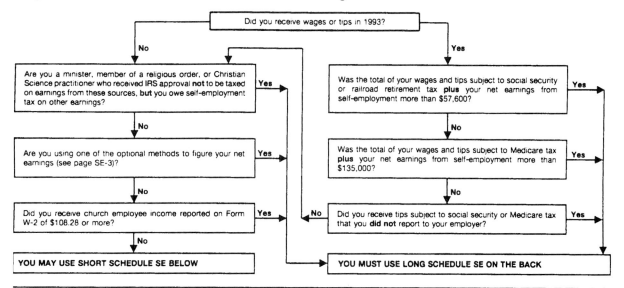

Section A—Short Schedule SE. Caution: *Read above to see if you can use Short Schedule SE.*

1	Net farm profit or (loss) from Schedule F, line 36, and farm partnerships, Schedule K-1 (Form 1065), line 15a	1	
2	Net profit or (loss) from Schedule C, line 31; Schedule C-EZ, line 3; and Schedule K-1 (Form 1065), line 15a (other than farming). Ministers and members of religious orders see page SE-1 for amounts to report on this line. See page SE-2 for other income to report	2	57,839
3	Combine lines 1 and 2	3	57,839
4	**Net earnings from self-employment.** Multiply line 3 by 92.35% (.9235). If less than $400, **do not** file this schedule; you do not owe self-employment tax . . . . ▶	4	53,414
5	**Self-employment tax.** If the amount on line 4 is: • $57,600 or less, multiply line 4 by 15.3% (.153) and enter the result. • More than $57,600 but less than $135,000, multiply the amount in excess of $57,600 by 2.9% (.029). Then, add $8,812.80 to the result and enter the total. • $135,000 or more, enter $11,057.40. Also enter on **Form 1040, line 47. (Important:** You are allowed a deduction for **one-half** of this amount. Multiply line 5 by 50% (.5) and enter the result on **Form 1040, line 25.)**	5	8,172

For Paperwork Reduction Act Notice, see Form 1040 instructions.   Cat. No. 11358Z   Schedule SE (Form 1040) 1993

Figure 8-5 Schedule SE

Schedule SE (Form 1040) 1993	Attachment Sequence No. 17	Page 2
Name of person with **self-employment** income (as shown on Form 1040)	Social security number of person with **self-employment** income ▶	

Section B—Long Schedule SE

Part I Self-Employment Tax

Note: *If your only income subject to self-employment tax is church employee income, skip lines 1 through 4b. Enter -0- on line 4c and go to line 5a. Income from services you performed as a minister or a member of a religious order* **is not** *church employee income. See page SE-1.*

A If you are a minister, member of a religious order, or Christian Science practitioner **AND** you filed Form 4361, but you had $400 or more of **other** net earnings from self-employment, check here and continue with Part I . . . . ▶ ☐

1	Net farm profit or (loss) from Schedule F, line 36, and farm partnerships, Schedule K-1 (Form 1065), line 15a. **Note:** *Skip this line if you use the farm optional method. See page SE-3*	**1**	
2	Net profit or (loss) from Schedule C, line 31; Schedule C-EZ, line 3; and Schedule K-1 (Form 1065), line 15a (other than farming). Ministers and members of religious orders see page SE-1 for amounts to report on this line. See page SE-2 for other income to report. **Note:** *Skip this line if you use the nonfarm optional method. See page SE-3*	**2**	
3	Combine lines 1 and 2	**3**	
4a	If line 3 is more than zero, multiply line 3 by 92.35% (.9235). Otherwise, enter amount from line 3	**4a**	
b	If you elected one or both of the optional methods, enter the total of lines 17 and 19 here	**4b**	
c	Combine lines 4a and 4b. If less than $400, **do not** file this schedule; you do not owe self-employment tax. **Exception.** If less than $400 and you had church employee income, enter -0- and continue . ▶	**4c**	
5a	Enter your church employee income from Form W-2. **Caution:** *See page SE-1 for definition of church employee income* **5a**		
b	Multiply line 5a by 92.35% (.9235). If less than $100, enter -0-	**5b**	
6	**Net earnings from self-employment.** Add lines 4c and 5b	**6**	
7	Maximum amount of combined wages and self-employment earnings subject to social security tax or the 6.2% portion of the 7.65% railroad retirement (tier 1) tax for 1993	**7**	57,600 00
8a	Total social security wages and tips (from Form(s) W-2) and railroad retirement (tier 1) compensation **8a**		
b	Unreported tips subject to social security tax (from Form 4137, line 9) **8b**		
c	Add lines 8a and 8b	**8c**	
9	Subtract line 8c from line 7. If zero or less, enter -0- here and on line 10 and go to line 12a ▶	**9**	
10	Multiply the **smaller** of line 6 or line 9 by 12.4% (.124)	**10**	
11	Maximum amount of combined wages and self-employment earnings subject to Medicare tax or the 1.45% portion of the 7.65% railroad retirement (tier 1) tax for 1993	**11**	135,000 00
12a	Total Medicare wages and tips (from Form(s) W-2) and railroad retirement (tier 1) compensation **12a**		
b	Unreported tips subject to Medicare tax (from Form 4137, line 14) . **12b**		
c	Add lines 12a and 12b	**12c**	
13	Subtract line 12c from line 11. If zero or less, enter -0- here and on line 14 and go to line 15	**13**	
14	Multiply the **smaller** of line 6 or line 13 by 2.9% (.029)	**14**	
15	**Self-employment tax.** Add lines 10 and 14. Enter here and on **Form 1040, line 47. (Important:** You are allowed a deduction for **one-half** of this amount. Multiply line 15 by 50% (.5) and enter the result on **Form 1040, line 25.)**	**15**	

Part II Optional Methods To Figure Net Earnings (See page SE-3.)

Farm Optional Method. You may use this method **only** if **(a)** Your gross farm income[1] was not more than $2,400 **or (b)** Your gross farm income[1] was more than $2,400 and your net farm profits[2] were less than $1,733.

16	Maximum income for optional methods	**16**	1,600 00
17	Enter the **smaller** of: two-thirds (⅔) of gross farm income[1] (not less than zero) **or** $1,600. Also, include this amount on line 4b above	**17**	

Nonfarm Optional Method. You may use this method **only** if **(a)** Your net nonfarm profits[3] were less than $1,733 and also less than 72.189% of your gross nonfarm income,[4] **and (b)** You had net earnings from self-employment of at least $400 in 2 of the prior 3 years. **Caution:** *You may use this method no more than five times.*

18	Subtract line 17 from line 16	**18**	
19	Enter the **smaller** of: two-thirds (⅔) of gross nonfarm income[4] (not less than zero) **or** the amount on line 18. Also, include this amount on line 4b above	**19**	

[1] From Schedule F, line 11, and Schedule K-1 (Form 1065), line 15b.
[2] From Schedule F, line 36, and Schedule K-1 (Form 1065), line 15a.
[3] From Schedule C, line 31; Schedule C-EZ, line 3; and Schedule K-1 (Form 1065), line 15a.
[4] From Schedule C, line 7; Schedule C-EZ, line 1; and Schedule K-1 (Form 1065), line 15c.

Figure 8-5 (continued) Schedule SE

received by the taxpayer that was subject to FICA withholding by an employer reduces the base amounts dollar for dollar (lines 8a and 12a of the long schedule).

> ✓ **Example 53.** Bob Astin's net income from his sole proprietorship in 1993 was $20,000. Astin also earned a salary of $50,000 from Ace Corporation in 1993. Since Astin has already paid social security tax through withholdings on $50,000 of income during the year, only $7,600 of the proprietorship income is subject to the 12.4% Social Security tax. However, 92.35% of the entire $20,000 is subject to the medicare tax, since total wages plus self-employment income was less than $135,000. Thus, page 2 of Astin's 1993 Schedule SE will show a self-employment tax of $1,478 ($7,600 × .124 plus $20,000 × .9235 × .029).

The net self-employment tax shown on line 5 of the short form (or line 15 of the long form) is added to the total tax liability of the taxpayer on line 47 of page 2 of Form 1040, as illustrated here:

Other Taxes	47	Self-employment tax. Attach Schedule SE. Also, see line 25.	47	8,172
	48	Alternative minimum tax. Attach Form 6251	48	
	49	Recapture taxes (see page 26). Check if from a ☐ Form 4255 b ☐ Form 8611 c ☐ Form 8828	49	
	50	Social security and Medicare tax on tip income not reported to employer. Attach Form 4137	50	
	51	Tax on qualified retirement plans, including IRAs. If required, attach Form 5329	51	
	52	Advance earned income credit payments from Form W-2	52	
	53	Add lines 46 through 52. This is your **total tax**. ▶	53	

Finally, for 1993 and later years, a special Schedule C-EZ may be used in lieu of Schedule C for cash-basis service sole proprietors with gross receipts of $25,000 or less. This form is illustrated in Figure 8-6.

REVIEW V

1. Broome Company incurred the following research and experimentation expenditures in 1993: $40,000 salaries, $5,000 supplies, and $15,000 utilities. Assuming that Broome elects to take the maximum deduction possible for these expenses In 1993 the total deduction would be
   (a) $ 0.
   (b) $ 6,000.
   (c) $12,000.
   (d) $60,000.

2. During 1993 Bill Blass, a small oil and gas operator, incurred the following results on the leasehold of Property A:

Sales revenue (20,000 barrels @ $20)	$400,000
Royalty paid to landowner (1/8)	(50,000)
Gross income from property A	$350,000
Direct expenses of property A	(305,000)
Net income before depletion deduction	$ 45,000

   At the beginning of 1993, Blass's undepleted cost in Property A was $120,000, and it was estimated that there were still 60,000 barrels to recover. Blass's overall personal taxable income on his return before considering depletion is $240,000. Blass's maximum depletion deduction for 1993 using the cost method is
   (a) $ 40,000.
   (b) $ 45,000.
   (c) $ 52,500.
   (d) $120,000.

SCHEDULE C-EZ
(Form 1040)
Department of the Treasury
Internal Revenue Service

Net Profit From Business
(Sole Proprietorship)
▶ Partnerships, joint ventures, etc., must file Form 1065.
▶ Attach to Form 1040 or Form 1041. ▶ See instructions on back.

OMB No. 1545-0074

1993

Attachment Sequence No. **09A**

Name of proprietor: Judy Graham

Social security number (SSN): 416 40 3321

Part I — General Information

You May Use This Form If You:
- Had gross receipts from your business of $25,000 or less.
- Had business expenses of $2,000 or less.
- Use the cash method of accounting.
- Did not have an inventory at any time during the year.
- Did not have a net loss from your business.
- Had only one business as a sole proprietor.

And You:
- Had no employees during the year.
- Are not required to file **Form 4562**, Depreciation and Amortization, for this business. See the instructions for Schedule C, line 13, on page C-3 to find out if you must file.
- Do not deduct expenses for business use of your home.
- Do not have prior year unallowed passive activity losses from this business.

A Principal business or profession, including product or service: Word Processing Service

B Enter principal business code (see page C-6) ▶ 7 8 7 2

C Business name. If no separate business name, leave blank.: Graham's WordPerfect

D Employer ID number (EIN), if any

E Business address (including suite or room no.). Address not required if same as on Form 1040, page 1.
806 Main Street
City, town or post office, state, and ZIP code
Petal, MS 39465

Part II — Figure Your Net Profit

1	**Gross receipts.** If more than $25,000, you **must** use Schedule C. **Caution:** If this income was reported to you on Form W-2 and the "Statutory employee" box on that form was checked, see **Statutory Employees** in the instructions for Schedule C, line 1, on page C-2 and check here ▶ ☐	1	23,860
2	**Total expenses.** If more than $2,000, you **must** use Schedule C. See instructions	2	1,800
3	**Net profit.** Subtract line 2 from line 1. Enter on **Form 1040, line 12,** and ALSO on **Schedule SE, line 2.** (Statutory employees **do not** report this amount on Schedule SE, line 2. Fiduciaries, enter on Form 1041, line 3.) If less than zero, you **must** use Schedule C	3	22,060

Part III — Information on Your Vehicle. Complete this part ONLY if you are claiming car or truck expenses on line 2.

4 When did you place your vehicle in service for business purposes? (month, day, year) ▶ ...... / ...... / ......

5 Of the total number of miles you drove your vehicle during 1993, enter the number of miles you used your vehicle for:

a Business .... b Commuting .... c Other ....

6 Do you (or your spouse) have another vehicle available for personal use? ☐ Yes ☐ No

7 Was your vehicle available for use during off-duty hours? ☐ Yes ☐ No

8a Do you have evidence to support your deduction? ☐ Yes ☐ No

b If "Yes," is the evidence written? ☐ Yes ☐ No

For Paperwork Reduction Act Notice, see Form 1040 instructions.   Cat. No. 14374D   Schedule C-EZ (Form 1040) 1993

Figure 8-6   Schedule C-EZ Form 1040

3. Assume the same facts as Question 2. Blass's maximum depletion deduction for 1993 using the percentage method is
   (a) $ 40,000.
   (b) $ 45,000.
   (c) $ 52,500.
   (d) $120,000.
4. A self-employed individual may take a deduction for AGI for
   (a) 25% of health insurance and 25% of self-employment tax.
   (b) 25% of health insurance and 50% of self-employment tax.
   (c) 50% of health insurance and 25% of self-employment tax.
   (d) 50% of health insurance and 50% of self-employment tax.

Answers are on page 8-59.

CHAPTER APPENDIX: EMPLOYMENT TAXES— AN INTRODUCTION

(Code Sections 3101–3113 and 3301–3306)

If a sole proprietor has one or more employees, he or she will probably be required to withhold federal income tax and social security taxes from their wages. In addition, the business owner will be subject to payment of matching shares of the employees' social security taxes under the Federal Insurance Contributions Act (FICA), as well as payment of the entire amount of federal unemployment tax under the Federal Unemployment Tax Act (FUTA). Every employer subject to these requirements must have an employer identification number, obtained by filing Form SS-4. This form is illustrated in Figure 8-7.

Obviously, it becomes very important in such cases to determine exactly who is an employee. In general, if a person's services are subject to the will and control of others, both as to *what* shall be done and *how* it should be done, then he or she is classified as an employee. Two other characteristics of an employer-employee relationship are the right to discharge an individual and the furnishing of supplies, tools, and/or a place to work.

If a sole proprietor (or any other type of entity, for that matter) has employees, he or she must be concerned with the strict reporting requirements for the tax withholdings and the payroll taxes imposed on the employer. The primary tax forms used for these purposes are Forms 941 (Employer's Quarterly Federal Tax Return) and Form 940 (Employers Annual Federal Unemployment [FUTA] Tax Return). Each of these returns is discussed briefly in the following section. For additional details on employment taxes, refer to Circular E, Employer's Tax Guide, which is published by the IRS.

FORM 941

THE LAW

Sec. 3102(a)—The tax imposed by section 3101 [social security tax on employees] shall be collected by the employer of the taxpayer, by deducting the amount of the tax from the wages as and when paid.

Form SS-4 (Rev. August 1989)
Department of the Treasury
Internal Revenue Service

Application for Employer Identification Number
(For use by employers and others. Please read the attached instructions before completing this form.) Please type or print clearly.

EIN
OMB No. 1545-0003
Expires 7-31-91

1. Name of applicant (True legal name) (See instructions.)
   Ann Landers

2. Trade name of business, if different from name in line 1

3. Executor, trustee, "care of name"

4a. Mailing address (street address) (room, apt., or suite no.)
    604 Addison

4b. City, state, and ZIP code
    Spokane, Washington 99258

5a. Address of business. (See instructions.)
    same

5b. City, state, and ZIP code
    same

6. County and state where principal business is located
   Spokane, Washington

7. Name of principal officer, grantor, or general partner. (See instructions.) ▶
   Ann Landers

8a. Type of entity (Check only one box.) (See instructions.)
    ☒ Individual SSN 582 31 6144
    ☐ REMIC
    ☐ State/local government
    ☐ Other nonprofit organization (specify)
    ☐ Other (specify) ▶
    ☐ Estate
    ☐ Plan administrator SSN
    ☐ Personal service corp.
    ☐ National guard
    ☐ Other corporation (specify)
    ☐ Federal government/military
    If nonprofit organization enter GEN (if applicable)
    ☐ Trust
    ☐ Partnership
    ☐ Farmers' cooperative
    ☐ Church or church controlled organization

8b. If a corporation, give name of foreign country (if applicable) or state in the U.S. where incorporated ▶
    Foreign country
    State

9. Reason for applying (Check only one box)
   ☐ Started new business
   ☒ Hired employees
   ☐ Created a pension plan (specify type) ▶
   ☐ Banking purpose (specify) ▶
   ☐ Changed type of organization (specify) ▶
   ☐ Purchased going business
   ☐ Created a trust (specify) ▶
   ☐ Other (specify) ▶

10. Date business started or acquired (Mo., day, year) (See instructions.)
    1-6-93

11. Enter closing month of accounting year. (See instructions.)
    12-93

12. First date wages or annuities were paid or will be paid (Mo., day, year). **Note:** *If applicant is a withholding agent, enter date income will first be paid to nonresident alien. (Mo., day, year).*

13. Enter highest number of employees expected in the next 12 months. **Note:** *If the applicant does not expect to have any employees during the period, enter "0."* ▶
    Nonagricultural: 8 Agricultural: Household:

14. Does the applicant operate more than one place of business? ☐ Yes ☒ No
    If "Yes," enter name of business. ▶

15. Principal activity or service (See instructions.) ▶ consulting

16. Is the principal business activity manufacturing? ☐ Yes ☒ No
    If "Yes," principal product and raw material used ▶

17. To whom are most of the products or services sold? Please check the appropriate box.
    ☒ Public (retail) ☐ Other (specify) ▶ ☐ Business (wholesale) ☐ N/A

18a. Has the applicant ever applied for an identification number for this or any other business? ☐ Yes ☒ No
     Note: *If "Yes," please complete lines 18b and 18c.*

18b. If you checked the "Yes" box in line 18a, give applicant's true name and trade name, if different than name shown on prior application.
     True name ▶   Trade name ▶

18c. Enter approximate date, city, and state where the application was filed and the previous employer identification number if known.
     Approximate date when filed (Mo., day, year) | City and state where filed | Previous EIN

Under penalties of perjury, I declare that I have examined this application, and to the best of my knowledge and belief, it is true, correct, and complete.

Name and title (Please type or print clearly.) ▶ Ann Landers

Signature ▶ *Ann Landers*

Telephone number (include area code)
509-555-1212

Date ▶ 1-6-93

Note: Do not write below this line. For official use only.

Please leave blank ▶ | Geo. | Ind. | Class | Size | Reason for applying

For Paperwork Reduction Act Notice, see attached instructions.   ☆U.S. Government Printing Office: 1989-262-151/80163   Form **SS-4** (Rev. 8-89)

Figure 8-7 Form SS-4

Withheld income taxes and social security taxes are reported together on Form 941, although special forms exist for agricultural employees (Form 943), household employees (Form 942), and noncovered employees (941E). Form 941 is a quarterly return and is due one month after the end of each quarter. However, ten extra days are allowed if the employer must deposit the tax (under the rules described below), and such tax is deposited in full on a timely basis.

Each month of a return period is divided into eight deposit periods (called "eighth monthly periods") ending on the 3rd, 7th, 11th, 15th, 19th, 22nd, 25th, and last day of each month. A deposit is required when the total FICA and withheld income taxes exceed one of three threshholds:

1. If the tax owed is $3,000 or more for an "eighth monthly period," at least 95% of the amount due must be deposited within three banking days (one day if the amount exceeds $100,000).

2. If the tax owed is $500 or more but less than $3,000 at the end of a month, the entire amount must be deposited by the 15th of the next month.

3. If the tax owed is less than $500, the amount must be deposited by the end of the month following the end of the quarterly return period.

A deposit is made by sending a single check or postal money order to an authorized financial institution or a Federal Reserve Bank. Each deposit must be accompanied by a Form 8109, Federal Deposit Coupon (a book of such coupons is mailed to an employer at the time of applying for an identification number). This form is illustrated in Figure 8-8. Penalties are imposed for a failure to make timely deposits.

In determining the total income tax withheld from wages, an employer generally uses either a percentage method or a wage-bracket method. Under the *percentage method*, an employer will compute withholding for each employee by first multiplying a special "allowance amount" (depending on the type of pay period) by the number of allowances claimed by an employee. Generally, the number of such allowances equals the number of personal exemptions claimed by the employee on his or her federal tax return, although additional allowances may be available if the employee is paying alimony, has a large amount of itemized deductions or tax credits, or simply chooses to have extra withholdings for the year. Each employee is required to file a form W-4 with

---

ANSWERS TO REVIEW V

1. (d) One of the three optional tax treatments for such expenditures is simply to deduct all qualifying expenses in the year of incurrence.
2. (a) The depletion rate per unit is $2 ($120,000/60,000), and when multiplied times the 20,000 barrels sold during the year yields a deduction of $40,000.
3. (b) Normally, the percentage deduction would be 15% of the gross income from the property, or $52,500. However, the percentage deduction is further limited to 100% of the $45,000 taxable income from the property, or $45,000. (The other limit, 65% of the taxpayer's overall taxable income, would not apply in this case.)
4. (b) Both items are allowed as deductions for AGI in the tax year.

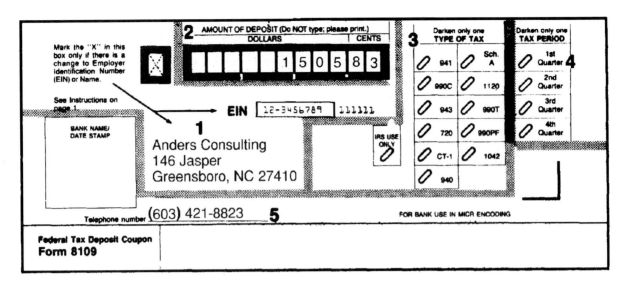

Figure 8-8 Form 8109

his or her employer indicating the number of allowances claimed for income tax withholding purposes. A filled-in Form W-4 is illustrated in Figure 8-9.

For 1993 the "withholding allowance" for each exemption claimed by the taxpayer on the Form W-4 is determined according to the payroll period from the following table (based on a $2,350 exemption for 1993):

Payroll Period	Amount of One W/H Exemption
Weekly	$ 45.19
Biweekly	90.38
Semimonthly	97.92
Monthly	195.83
Quarterly	587.50
Semiannual	1,175.00
Annual	2,350.00
Daily or miscellaneous (per day)	9.04

After subtracting the total amount of allowances, the final withholding is determined from a rate table (for both single and married persons) furnished by the IRS in Circular E. A portion of the semimonthly table is reproduced in Figure 8-10.

✓ **Example 54.** Anders Consulting employs the following five individuals, all of whom are paid on a semimonthly basis in 1993:

Name	Marital Status	No. of Exemptions	Semimonthly Salary
Alvin Thomas	Married	2	$1,200
Judy Graham	Single	1	1,100
Thomas Fairley	Single	1	970
Jenny Hethcox	Married	3	1,300
Robert Cuevas	Married	4	1,350
		Total salary	$5,920

1993 Form W-4

Department of the Treasury
Internal Revenue Service

Purpose. Complete Form W-4 so that your employer can withhold the correct amount of Federal income tax from your pay.

Exemption From Withholding. Read line 7 of the certificate below to see if you can claim exempt status. *If exempt, complete line 7; but do not complete lines 5 and 6.* No Federal income tax will be withheld from your pay. Your exemption is good for one year only. It expires February 15, 1994.

Basic Instructions. Employees who are not exempt should complete the Personal Allowances Worksheet. Additional worksheets are provided on page 2 for employees to adjust their withholding allowances based on itemized deductions, adjustments to income, or two-earner/two-job situations. Complete all worksheets that apply to your situation. The worksheets will help you figure the number of withholding allowances you are entitled to claim. However, you may claim fewer allowances than this.

Head of Household. Generally, you may claim head of household filing status on your tax return only if you are unmarried and pay more than 50% of the costs of keeping up a home for yourself and your dependent(s) or other qualifying individuals.

Nonwage Income. If you have a large amount of nonwage income, such as interest or dividends, you should consider making estimated tax payments using Form 1040-ES. Otherwise, you may find that you owe additional tax at the end of the year.

Two-Earner/Two-Jobs. If you have a working spouse or more than one job, figure the total number of allowances you are entitled to claim on all jobs using worksheets from only one Form W-4. This total should be divided among all jobs. Your withholding will usually be most accurate when all allowances are claimed on the W-4 filed for the highest paying job and zero allowances are claimed for the others.

Advance Earned Income Credit. If you are eligible for this credit, you can receive it added to your paycheck throughout the year. For details, get Form W-5 from your employer.

Check Your Withholding. After your W-4 takes effect, you can use **Pub. 919**, Is My Withholding Correct for 1993?, to see how the dollar amount you are having withheld compares to your estimated total annual tax. Call 1-800-829-3676 to order this publication. Check your local telephone directory for the IRS assistance number if you need further help.

Personal Allowances Worksheet

For 1993, the value of your personal exemption(s) is reduced if your income is over $108,450 ($162,700 if married filing jointly, $135,600 if head of household, or $81,350 if married filing separately). Get Pub. 919 for details.

- **A** Enter "1" for **yourself** if no one else can claim you as a dependent . . . . **A** _____
- **B** Enter "1" if:
  - You are single and have only one job; or
  - You are married, have only one job, and your spouse does not work; or
  - Your wages from a second job or your spouse's wages (or the total of both) are $1,000 or less.
  . . **B** _____
- **C** Enter "1" for your **spouse.** But, you may choose to enter -0- if you are married and have either a working spouse or more than one job (this may help you avoid having too little tax withheld) . . . . **C** _____
- **D** Enter number of **dependents** (other than your spouse or yourself) whom you will claim on your tax return . . . . **D** _____
- **E** Enter "1" if you will file as **head of household** on your tax return (see conditions under **Head of Household,** above) . **E** _____
- **F** Enter "1" if you have at least $1,500 of **child or dependent care expenses** for which you plan to claim a credit . . **F** _____
- **G** Add lines A through F and enter total here. Note: *This amount may be different from the number of exemptions you claim on your return* ▶ **G** _____

For accuracy, do all worksheets that apply.
- If you plan to **itemize or claim adjustments to income** and want to reduce your withholding, see the Deductions and Adjustments Worksheet on page 2.
- If you are **single** and have **more than one job** and your combined earnings from all jobs exceed $30,000 OR if you are **married** and have a **working spouse or more than one job,** and the combined earnings from all jobs exceed $50,000, see the Two-Earner/Two-Job Worksheet on page 2 if you want to avoid having too little tax withheld.
- If **neither** of the above situations applies, **stop here** and enter the number from line G on line 5 of Form W-4 below.

---- Cut here and give the certificate to your employer. Keep the top portion for your records. ----

Form W-4
Department of the Treasury
Internal Revenue Service

Employee's Withholding Allowance Certificate
▶ For Privacy Act and Paperwork Reduction Act Notice, see reverse.

OMB No. 1545-0010
1993

1	Type or print your first name and middle initial	Last name	2	Your social security number
	Alvin Thomas			321-44-0162

Home address (number and street or rural route)
101 Main

3 ☐ Single ☐ Married ☐ Married, but withhold at higher Single rate.
Note: *If married, but legally separated, or spouse is a nonresident alien, check the Single box.*

City or town, state, and ZIP code
Greensboro, NC 27410

4 If your last name differs from that on your social security card, check here and call 1-800-772-1213 for more information . . . . ▶ ☐

5	Total number of allowances you are claiming (from line G above or from the worksheets on page 2 if they apply) .	5	2
6	Additional amount, if any, you want withheld from each paycheck	6 $	1

7 I claim exemption from withholding for 1993 and I certify that I meet **ALL** of the following conditions for exemption:
- Last year I had a right to a refund of **ALL** Federal income tax withheld because I had **NO** tax liability; **AND**
- This year I expect a refund of **ALL** Federal income tax withheld because I expect to have **NO** tax liability; **AND**
- This year if my income exceeds $600 and includes nonwage income, another person cannot claim me as a dependent.

If you meet all of the above conditions, enter "EXEMPT" here . . . . ▶ | 7 |

Under penalties of perjury, I certify that I am entitled to the number of withholding allowances claimed on this certificate or entitled to claim exempt status.

Employee's signature ▶ Alvin Thomas   Date ▶ January 3, 19 93

8	Employer's name and address (Employer: Complete 8 and 10 only if sending to the IRS)	9	Office code (optional)	10	Employer identification number
	Anders Consulting 146 Jasper Street Greensboroo, NC 27410				

Cat. No. 10220Q

Figure 8-9 Form W-4

Form W-4 (1993) Page **2**

Deductions and Adjustments Worksheet

Note: *Use this worksheet only if you plan to itemize deductions or claim adjustments to income on your 1993 tax return.*

1. Enter an estimate of your 1993 itemized deductions. These include: qualifying home mortgage interest, charitable contributions, state and local taxes (but not sales taxes), medical expenses in excess of 7.5% of your income, and miscellaneous deductions. (For 1993, you may have to reduce your itemized deductions if your income is over $108,450 ($54,225 if married filing separately). Get Pub. 919 for details.) .... **1** $ _____

2. Enter:
   - $6,200 if married filing jointly or qualifying widow(er)
   - $5,450 if head of household
   - $3,700 if single
   - $3,100 if married filing separately
   .... **2** $ _____

3. **Subtract** line 2 from line 1. If line 2 is greater than line 1, enter -0- .... **3** $ _____
4. Enter an estimate of your 1993 adjustments to income. These include alimony paid and deductible IRA contributions **4** $ _____
5. **Add** lines 3 and 4 and enter the total .... **5** $ _____
6. Enter an estimate of your 1993 nonwage income (such as dividends or interest income) ..... **6** $ _____
7. **Subtract** line 6 from line 5. Enter the result, but not less than -0- . ... **7** $ _____
8. **Divide** the amount on line 7 by $2,500 and enter the result here. Drop any fraction ...... **8** _____
9. Enter the number from Personal Allowances Worksheet, line G, on page 1 .... **9** _____
10. **Add** lines 8 and 9 and enter the total here. If you plan to use the Two-Earner/Two-Job Worksheet, also enter the total on line 1, below. Otherwise, **stop here** and enter this total on Form W-4, line 5, on page 1. .... **10** _____

Two-Earner/Two-Job Worksheet

Note: *Use this worksheet only if the instructions for line G on page 1 direct you here.*

1. Enter the number from line G on page 1 (or from line 10 above if you used the Deductions and Adjustments Worksheet) **1** _____
2. Find the number in **Table 1** below that applies to the **LOWEST** paying job and enter it here .... **2** _____
3. If line 1 is **GREATER THAN OR EQUAL TO** line 2, subtract line 2 from line 1. Enter the result here (if zero, enter -0-) and on Form W-4, line 5, on page 1. **DO NOT** use the rest of this worksheet .... **3** _____

Note: *If line 1 is **LESS THAN** line 2, enter -0- on Form W-4, line 5, on page 1. Complete lines 4–9 to calculate the additional withholding amount necessary to avoid a year-end tax bill.*

4. Enter the number from line 2 of this worksheet .... **4** _____
5. Enter the number from line 1 of this worksheet .... **5** _____
6. **Subtract** line 5 from line 4 .... **6** _____
7. Find the amount in **Table 2** below that applies to the **HIGHEST** paying job and enter it here .... **7** $ _____
8. **Multiply** line 7 by line 6 and enter the result here. This is the additional annual withholding amount needed **8** $ _____
9. Divide line 8 by the number of pay periods remaining in 1993. (For example, divide by 26 if you are paid every other week and you complete this form in December 1992.) Enter the result here and on Form W-4, line 6, page 1. This is the additional amount to be withheld from each paycheck .... **9** $ _____

Table 1: Two-Earner/Two-Job Worksheet

Married Filing Jointly		All Others	
If wages from **LOWEST** paying job are—	Enter on line 2 above	If wages from **LOWEST** paying job are—	Enter on line 2 above
0 - $3,000	0	0 - $6,000	0
3,001 - 8,000	1	6,001 - 11,000	1
8,001 - 13,000	2	11,001 - 15,000	2
13,001 - 18,000	3	15,001 - 19,000	3
18,001 - 22,000	4	19,001 - 24,000	4
22,001 - 27,000	5	24,001 - 50,000	5
27,001 - 31,000	6	50,001 and over	6
31,001 - 35,000	7		
35,001 - 40,000	8		
40,001 - 60,000	9		
60,001 - 85,000	10		
85,001 and over	11		

Table 2: Two-Earner/Two-Job Worksheet

Married Filing Jointly		All Others	
If wages from **HIGHEST** paying job are—	Enter on line 7 above	If wages from **HIGHEST** paying job are—	Enter on line 7 above
0 - $50,000	$350	0 - $30,000	$350
50,001 - 100,000	660	30,001 - 60,000	660
100,001 and over	730	60,001 and over	730

Privacy Act and Paperwork Reduction Act Notice.—We ask for the information on this form to carry out the Internal Revenue laws of the United States. The Internal Revenue Code requires this information under sections 3402(f)(2)(A) and 6109 and their regulations. Failure to provide a completed form will result in your being treated as a single person who claims no withholding allowances. Routine uses of this information include giving it to the Department of Justice for civil and criminal litigation and to cities, states, and the District of Columbia for use in administering their tax laws.

The time needed to complete this form will vary depending on individual circumstances. The estimated average time is: **Recordkeeping** 46 min., **Learning about the law or the form** 10 min., **Preparing the form** 69 min. If you have comments concerning the accuracy of these time estimates or suggestions for making this form more simple, we would be happy to hear from you. You can write to both the **Internal Revenue Service**, Washington, DC 20224, Attention: IRS Reports Clearance Officer, T:FP; and the **Office of Management and Budget,** Paperwork Reduction Project (1545-0010), Washington, DC 20503. **DO NOT** send the tax form to either of these offices. Instead, give it to your employer.

Figure 8-9 (continued) Form W-4

Figure 8-10 — Percentage Withholding Tables (1993)

TABLE 1—WEEKLY Payroll Period

(a) SINGLE person (including head of household)—

If the amount of wages (after subtracting withholding allowances) is: The amount of income tax to withhold is:

Not over $49 . . . . . $0

Over—	But not over—		of excess over—
$49	—$451 . . .	15%	—$49
$451	—$942 . . .	$60.30 plus 28%	—$451
$942	. . . .	$197.78 plus 31%	—$942

(b) MARRIED person—

If the amount of wages (after subtracting withholding allowances) is: The amount of income tax to withhold is:

Not over $119 . . . . $0

Over—	But not over—		of excess over—
$119	—$784 . . .	15%	—$119
$784	—$1,563 . . .	$99.75 plus 28%	—$784
$1,563	. . . .	$317.87 plus 31%	—$1,563

TABLE 2—BIWEEKLY Payroll Period

(a) SINGLE person (including head of household)—

Not over $97 . . . . . $0

Over—	But not over—		of excess over—
$97	—$902 . . .	15%	—$97
$902	—$1,884 . .	$120.75 plus 28%	—$902
$1,884	. . . . . .	$395.71 plus 31%	—$1,884

(b) MARRIED person—

Not over $238 . . . . $0

Over—	But not over—		of excess over—
$238	—$1,567 . . .	15%	—$238
$1,567	—$3,125 . . .	$199.35 plus 28%	—$1,567
$3,125	. . . .	$635.59 plus 31%	—$3,125

TABLE 3—SEMIMONTHLY Payroll Period

(a) SINGLE person (including head of household)—

Not over $105 . . . . $0

Over—	But not over—		of excess over—
$105	—$977 . . .	15%	—$105
$977	—$2,041 . .	$130.80 plus 28%	—$977
$2,041	. . . . . .	$428.72 plus 31%	—$2,041

(b) MARRIED person—

Not over $258 . . . . $0

Over—	But not over—		of excess over—
$258	—$1,698 . . .	15%	—$258
$1,698	—$3,385 . . .	$216.00 plus 28%	—$1,698
$3,385	. . . .	$688.36 plus 31%	—$3,385

TABLE 4—MONTHLY Payroll Period

(a) SINGLE person (including head of household)—

Not over $210 . . . . $0

Over—	But not over—		of excess over—
$210	—$1,954 . .	15%	—$210
$1,954	—$4,081 . .	$261.60 plus 28%	—$1,954
$4,081	. . . . . .	$857.16 plus 31%	—$4,081

(b) MARRIED person—

Not over $517 . . . . $0

Over—	But not over—		of excess over—
$517	—$3,396 . . .	15%	—$517
$3,396	—$6,771 . . .	$431.85 plus 28%	—$3,396
$6,771	. . . .	$1,376.85 plus 31%	—$6,771

Using the percentage method of withholding, Anders Consulting would withhold the following from each employee's semimonthly paycheck (determined from Figure 8-10):

Name	Salary	E/M*	W/H Allow.	Salary Net of Allow.	Computed Withholding
Alvin Thomas	$1,200	(2M)	$195.84	$1,004.16	$111.92
Judy Graham	1,100	(1S)	97.92	1,002.08	137.82
Thomas Fairley	970	(1S)	97.92	872.08	115.06
Jenny Hethcox	1,300	(3M)	293.76	1,006.24	112.24
Robert Cuevas	1,350	(4M)	391.68	958.32	105.05
				Total withholding	$582.09

*Exemptions/Marital status

Under the *wage-bracket method*, the employer will determine the total withholding from a table provided in Circular E by using the appropriate payroll period (daily, weekly, biweekly, semimonthly, or monthly), total wages, and the number of total withholding allowances. A portion of this table for semimonthly pay periods is reproduced in Figure 8-11.

☑ **Example 55.** Assume the same facts as in Example 54, except that Anders uses the wage-bracket method for withholding. The amounts to be withheld from each employee's semimonthly paycheck, using Figure 8-11, would be

Name	Salary	Marital Status	W/H Allow.	Computed Withholding
Alvin Thomas	$1,200	Married	2	$113
Judy Graham	1,100	Single	1	141
Thomas Fairley	970	Single	1	115
Jenny Hethcox	1,300	Married	3	114
Robert Cuevas	1,350	Married	4	105
			Total withholding	$588

Social security taxes withheld and the employer's share of social security taxes due for employees are also reported on Form 941. A filled-in Form 941, using the data of the previous examples converted to a quarterly basis, is illustrated in Figure 8-12. Note that the income taxes withheld are reported on line 3, and the combined employer and employee contribution on social security taxes (at a 15.3% rate) is reported on line 8. The 15.3% combined rate is composed of 7.65% withheld from employees' pay and another 7.65% contributed ("matched") by the employer. As mentioned earlier, only the 7.65% actually paid by the employer is deductible on Schedule C as a business expense.

The 15.3% combined rate applicable to employees and employers is a combination of a 12.4% social security tax (line 6a) and a 2.9% medicare tax (line 7). The 12.4% social security tax applies to the first *$57,600* of each employee's wages, and the medicare tax applies to the first *$135,000* of wages.*

In addition to filing Form 941, an employer must furnish to each employee a Form W-2, Wage and Tax Statement, by January 31 of each year. This statement summarizes total salary payments, tax withholdings, and FICA withholdings for the previous year. This form is illustrated in Figure 8-13, using the data for Alvin Thomas in the previous example (converted to an annual basis). State income tax withholdings are assumed to be 2% of salary.

In addition, Form W-3, Transmittal of Income Tax Statements, is filed for the calendar year with the Social Security Administration. This document summarizes totals for all Form W-2s for the year and is transmitted with copies of all W-2s, and the totals must reconcile. Figure 8-14 illustrates a completed Form W-3 for the previous examples.

As mentioned earlier in this chapter, the sole proprietor pays his or her share of social security taxes by filing Schedule SE with Form 1040. Also, a sole proprietor is liable for estimated income taxes, which must be paid in quarterly installments. For these reasons, any income or "salary" of a sole proprietor is ignored when completing Form 941.

---

*For changes in the tax law effective for tax years beginning in 1994, see Appendix J.

SINGLE Persons—SEMIMONTHLY Payroll Period
(For Wages Paid in 1993)

If the wages are—		And the number of withholding allowances claimed is—										
At least	But less than	0	1	2	3	4	5	6	7	8	9	10
		The amount of income tax to be withheld is—										
$820	$840	$109	$94	$79	$65	$50	$35	$21	$6	$0	$0	$0
840	860	112	97	82	68	53	38	24	9	0	0	0
860	880	115	100	85	71	56	41	27	12	0	0	0
880	900	118	103	88	74	59	44	30	15	0	0	0
900	920	121	106	91	77	62	47	33	18	3	0	0
920	940	124	109	94	80	65	50	36	21	6	0	0
940	960	127	112	97	83	68	53	39	24	9	0	0
960	980	130	115	100	86	71	56	42	27	12	0	0
980	1,000	134	118	103	89	74	59	45	30	15	1	0
1,000	1,020	140	121	106	92	77	62	48	33	18	4	0
1,020	1,040	146	124	109	95	80	65	51	36	21	7	0
1,040	1,060	151	127	112	98	83	68	54	39	24	10	0
1,060	1,080	157	130	115	101	86	71	57	42	27	13	0
1,080	1,100	162	135	118	104	89	74	60	45	30	16	1
1,100	1,120	168	141	121	107	92	77	63	48	33	19	4
1,120	1,140	174	146	124	110	95	80	66	51	36	22	7
1,140	1,160	179	152	127	113	98	83	69	54	39	25	10
1,160	1,180	185	157	130	116	101	86	72	57	42	28	13
1,180	1,200	190	163	136	119	104	89	75	60	45	31	16
1,200	1,220	196	169	141	122	107	92	78	63	48	34	19
1,220	1,240	202	174	147	125	110	95	81	66	51	37	22
1,240	1,260	207	180	152	128	113	98	84	69	54	40	25
1,260	1,280	213	185	158	131	116	101	87	72	57	43	28
1,280	1,300	218	191	164	136	119	104	90	75	60	46	31
1,300	1,320	224	197	169	142	122	107	93	78	63	49	34
1,320	1,340	230	202	175	147	125	110	96	81	66	52	37
1,340	1,360	235	208	180	153	128	113	99	84	69	55	40
1,360	1,380	241	213	186	159	131	116	102	87	72	58	43
1,380	1,400	246	219	192	164	137	119	105	90	75	61	46
1,400	1,420	252	225	197	170	142	122	108	93	78	64	49

MARRIED Persons—SEMIMONTHLY Payroll Period
(For Wages Paid in 1993)

If the wages are—		And the number of withholding allowances claimed is—										
At least	But less than	0	1	2	3	4	5	6	7	8	9	10
		The amount of income tax to be withheld is—										
700	720	68	53	38	24	9	0	0	0	0	0	0
720	740	71	56	41	27	12	0	0	0	0	0	0
740	760	74	59	44	30	15	0	0	0	0	0	0
760	780	77	62	47	33	18	3	0	0	0	0	0
780	800	80	65	50	36	21	6	0	0	0	0	0
800	820	83	68	53	39	24	9	0	0	0	0	0
820	840	86	71	56	42	27	12	0	0	0	0	0
840	860	89	74	59	45	30	15	1	0	0	0	0
860	880	92	77	62	48	33	18	4	0	0	0	0
880	900	95	80	65	51	36	21	7	0	0	0	0
900	920	98	83	68	54	39	24	10	0	0	0	0
920	940	101	86	71	57	42	27	13	0	0	0	0
940	960	104	89	74	60	45	30	16	1	0	0	0
960	980	107	92	77	63	48	33	19	4	0	0	0
980	1,000	110	95	80	66	51	36	22	7	0	0	0
1,000	1,020	113	98	83	69	54	39	25	10	0	0	0
1,020	1,040	116	101	86	72	57	42	28	13	0	0	0
1,040	1,060	119	104	89	75	60	45	31	16	1	0	0
1,060	1,080	122	107	92	78	63	48	34	19	4	0	0
1,080	1,100	125	110	95	81	66	51	37	22	7	0	0
1,100	1,120	128	113	98	84	69	54	40	25	10	0	0
1,120	1,140	131	116	101	87	72	57	43	28	13	0	0
1,140	1,160	134	119	104	90	75	60	46	31	16	2	0
1,160	1,180	137	122	107	93	78	63	49	34	19	5	0
1,180	1,200	140	125	110	96	81	66	52	37	22	8	0
1,200	1,220	143	128	113	99	84	69	55	40	25	11	0
1,220	1,240	146	131	116	102	87	72	58	43	28	14	0
1,240	1,260	149	134	119	105	90	75	61	46	31	17	2
1,260	1,280	152	137	122	108	93	78	64	49	34	20	5
1,280	1,300	155	140	125	111	96	81	67	52	37	23	8
1,300	1,320	158	143	128	114	99	84	70	55	40	26	11
1,320	1,340	161	146	131	117	102	87	73	58	43	29	14
1,340	1,360	164	149	134	120	105	90	76	61	46	32	17
1,360	1,380	167	152	137	123	108	93	79	64	49	35	20
1,380	1,400	170	155	140	126	111	96	82	67	52	38	23

Figure 8-11 Partial Withholding Tables (Wage Bracket Method)

Form 941 (Rev. January 1994) — Department of the Treasury, Internal Revenue Service

Employer's Quarterly Federal Tax Return

► See separate instructions for information on completing this return. Please type or print.

4141

OMB No. 1545-0029

Enter state code for state in which deposits made (see page 2 of instructions).

Name (as distinguished from trade name): Douglas Anders
Trade name, if any: Anders Consulting
Address (number and street): 146 Jasper, Greensboro NC 27410
Date quarter ended: 3-31-93
Employer identification number: 91-4466880

Proof as of August 1993 (subject to change)

If address is different from prior return, check here ►

If you do not have to file returns in the future, check here ► ☐ (and enter) date final wages paid ► 3-31-93

If you are a seasonal employer, see **Seasonal employers** on page 2 and check here (see instructions) ►

Line	Description	Amount
1	Number of employees (except household) employed in the pay period that includes March 12th ►	5
2	Total wages and tips subject to withholding, plus other compensation ($5,920 semi-mo x6)	35,520
3	Total income tax withheld from wages, tips, and sick pay ('588 x 6)	3,528
4	Adjustment of withheld income tax for preceding quarters of calendar year	
5	Adjusted total of income tax withheld (line 3 as adjusted by line 4—see instructions)	3,528
6a	Taxable social security wages . . . $35,520 × 12.4% (.124) =	4,404
6b	Taxable social security tips . . . $ × 12.4% (.124) =	
7	Taxable Medicare wages and tips . . . $35,520 × 2.9% (.029) =	1,031
8	Total social security and Medicare taxes (add lines 6a, 6b, and 7). Check here if wages are not subject to social security and/or Medicare tax ► ☐	5,435
9	Adjustment of social security and Medicare taxes (see instructions for required explanation) Sick Pay $ ___ ± Fractions of Cents $ ___ ± Other $ ___ =	
10	Adjusted total of social security and Medicare taxes (line 8 as adjusted by line 9—see instructions)	5,435
11	**Total taxes** (add lines 5 and 10)	8,963
12	Advance earned income credit (EIC) payments made to employees, if any	
13	Net taxes (subtract line 12 from line 11). **This should equal line 17, column (d) below** (or line D of Schedule B (Form 941))	8,963
14	Total deposits for quarter, including overpayment applied from a prior quarter	8,963
15	**Balance due** (subtract line 14 from line 13). Pay to Internal Revenue Service	0
16	Overpayment, if line 14 is more than line 13, enter excess ► $ ___ and check if to be: ☐ Applied to next return OR ☐ Refunded.	

- **Monthly depositors:** Complete line 17, columns (a) through (d) and check here . . . ► ☐
- **Semiweekly depositors:** Complete Schedule B and check here . . . ► ☐
- **All filers:** If line 13 is less than $500, you need not complete line 17 or Schedule B.

17 Monthly Summary of Federal Tax Liability.

(a) First month liability	(b) Second month liability	(c) Third month liability	(d) Total liability for quarter

Sign Here — Under penalties of perjury, I declare that I have examined this return, including accompanying schedules and statements, and to the best of my knowledge and belief, it is true, correct, and complete.

Signature ► Douglas Anders   Print Your Name and Title ► Owner   Date ► 4-6-93

For Paperwork Reduction Act Notice, see page 1 of separate instructions.   Cat. No. 17001Z   Form 941 (Rev. 1-94)

Figure 8-12 Form 941

1 Control number						
		OMB No. 1545-0008				
2 Employer's name, address, and ZIP code Anders Consulting 146 Jasper Greensboro, NC 27410			6 Statutory employee [X] / Deceased ☐ / Pension plan ☐ / Legal rep. ☐ / 942 emp. ☐ / Subtotal ☐ / Deferred compensation ☐ / Void ☐			
			7 Allocated tips		8 Advance EIC payment	
			9 Federal income tax withheld 2,760		10 Wages, tips, other compensation 28,800	
3 Employer's identification number 91-4466880		4 Employer's state I.D. number	11 Social security tax withheld 2,203.20		12 Social security wages 28,800	
5 Employee's social security number 321-44-0162			13 Social security tips		14 Nonqualified plans	
19 Employee's name, address and ZIP code Alvin Thomas 101 Main Greensboro, NC 27410			15 Dependent care benefits		16 Fringe benefits incl. in Box 10	
			17		18 Other	
20	21		22		23	
24 State income tax 576	25 State wages, tips, etc. 28,800	26 Name of state NC	27 Local income tax —	28 Local wages, tips, etc. —	29 Name of locality —	

Copy 1 For State, City, or Local Tax Department   Dept. of the Treasury—Internal Revenue Service

form W-2 Wage and Tax Statement

Employee's and employer's copy compared ☐

Figure 8-13   Form W-2

---

1 Control number	33333	For Official Use Only ▶ OMB No. 1545-0008			
☐ Kind of Payer ▶	2 941/941E [X] Military ☐ 943 ☐ CT-1 ☐ 942 ☐ Medicare gov't. emp. ☐		3 Employer's state I.D. number 91-4466880		5 Total number of statements
			4		
6 Establishment number	7. Allocated tips			8 Advance EIC payments	
9 Federal income tax withheld 14,112	10 Wages, tips, and other compensation 142,080			11 Social security tax withheld 10,870	
12 Social security wages 142,080	13 Social security tips			14 Nonqualified plans	
15 Dependent care benefits	16 Adjusted total social security wages and tips 142,080			17 Deferred compensation	
18 Employer's identification number 91-4466880				19 Other EIN used this year	
20 Employer's name Anders Consulting 146 Jasper Greensboro, NC 27410				21 Gross annuity, pension, etc. (Form W-2P)	
				23 Taxable amount (Form W 2P)	
				24 Income tax withheld by third-party payer	
22 Employer's address and ZIP code (If available, place label over boxes 18 and 20)					

Under penalties of perjury, I declare that I have examined this return and accompanying documents, and to the best of my knowledge and belief, they are true, correct, and complete.

Signature ▶ Douglas Anders   Title ▶ owner   Date ▶ 1-10-94

Telephone number (optional) _____

Figure 8-14   Form W-3

FORM 940

The federal unemployment system and state unemployment systems provide payments to workers who have lost their jobs. Most employers pay both a state and a federal unemployment tax. For federal purposes, the tax is generally due when either (1) employee wages for the quarter total $1,500 or more or (2) in at least 20 different calendar weeks, there was at least part of a day in which an individual was an employee.

THE LAW

Sec. 3301—There is hereby imposed on every employer (as defined in section 3306(a)) for each calendar year an excise tax, with respect to having individuals in his employee, equal to—
(1) 6.2 percent in case the case of calendar years 1988 through 1995; or
(2) 6.0 percent in the case of calendar year 1996 and each calendar year thereafter; of the total wages (as defined in section 3306(b)) paid by him during the calendar year with respect to employment . . .

The federal unemployment tax is reported on Form 940, Employer's Annual Federal Unemployment (FUTA) Tax Return. The return covers one calendar year and is generally due one month after the year ends, although deposits are required within one month of the end of a quarter if the total undeposited tax exceeds $100.

The federal unemployment tax is figured on the first $7,000 of wages paid to each employee during the year. The tax is imposed only on the employer; it is not withheld from employee wages. The FUTA rate is nominally 6.2% for years through 1995; however, an employer is usually given a credit for up to 5.4% of the state unemployment tax he or she pays. If the employer's state experience rate is less than 5.4%, the full 5.4% credit may still be taken. Thus, the FUTA rate can be as low as 0.8% of the first $7,000 of each employee's wages.

Figure 8-15 illustrates a filled-in Form 940 for Anders Consulting, using the data for the five employees described earlier. Note that this form also includes a record of deposits made during the year.

TAX TIP

This Appendix has only touched the surface of the many employment tax issues confronting an employer. It is imperative that employers, particularly sole proprietors, be aware of these requirements. Many small businesses have incurred unnecessary penalty and interest assessments because they were lax in reporting employment taxes. In many cases, they encountered business difficulties because they had to use otherwise needed cash for the deficiencies, interest, and penalties associated with failure to determine the correct employment tax liabilities.

Form **940**	**Employer's Annual Federal Unemployment (FUTA) Tax Return**	OMB No. 1545-0028
Department of the Treasury Internal Revenue Service	▶ For Paperwork Reduction Act Notice, see separate instructions.	19**92**

If incorrect, make any necessary change. ▶	Name (as distinguished from trade name) — Douglas Anders Calendar year 1992	T / FF / FD / FP / I / T
	Trade name, if any — Anders Consulting	
	Address and ZIP code — 146 Jasper, Greensboro, NC 27410 Employer identification number 91-4466880	

A Are you required to pay unemployment contributions to only one state? . . . . ☒ Yes ☐ No
B Did you pay all state unemployment contributions by February 1, 1993? (If a 0% experience rate is granted check "Yes.") . . . . ☒ Yes ☐ No
C Were all wages that were taxable for FUTA tax also taxable for your state's unemployment tax? . . . . ☒ Yes ☐ No
D Did you pay all wages in a state other than Michigan? . . . . ☒ Yes ☐ No

If you answered "No" to any of these questions, you must file Form 940. If you answered "Yes" to all the questions, you may file Form 940-EZ which is a simplified version of Form 940. You can get Form 940-EZ by calling 1-800-TAX-FORM (1-800-829-3676).

If you will not have to file returns in the future, check here, complete, and sign the return . . . . ▶ ☐
If this is an Amended Return, check here . . . . ▶ ☐

Part I Computation of Taxable Wages

1	Total payments (including exempt payments) during the calendar year for services of employees.	1	142,080
2	Exempt payments. (Explain each exemption shown, attach additional sheets if necessary.) ▶	2 (Amount paid)	
3	Payments of more than $7,000 for services. Enter only amounts over the first $7,000 paid to each employee. Do not include payments from line 2. The $7,000 amount is the Federal wage base. Your state wage base may be different. **Do not use the state wage limitation**	3	
4	Total exempt payments (add lines 2 and 3)	4	107,080
5	**Total taxable wages** (subtract line 4 from line 1) . . . . ▶	5	35,000
6	Additional tax resulting from credit reduction for unpaid advances to the State of Michigan. Enter the wages included on line 5 for Michigan and multiply by .011. (See the separate Instructions for Form 940.) Enter the credit reduction amount here and in Part II, line 5: Michigan wages × .011 = ... ▶	6	0

Part II Tax Due or Refund

1	Gross FUTA tax. Multiply the wages in Part I, line 5, by .062		1	2,170
2	Maximum credit. Multiply the wages in Part I, line 5, by .054 . . .	2	1,890	
3	**Computation of tentative credit:**			

(a) Name of state	(b) State reporting number(s) as shown on employer's state contribution returns	(c) Taxable payroll (as defined in state act)	(d) State experience rate From / To	(e) State experience rate	(f) Contributions if rate had been 5.4% (col. (c) × .054)	(g) Contributions payable at experience rate (col. (c) × col. (e))	(h) Additional credit (col. (f) minus col.(g)). If 0 or less, enter 0.	(i) Contributions actually paid to state

3a	Totals . . . ▶			
3b	**Total tentative credit** (add line 3a, columns (h) and (i) only—see instructions for limitations on late payments) ▶			
4	**Credit:** Enter the smaller of the amount in Part II, line 2, or line 3b .	4	1,890	
5	Enter the amount from Part I, line 6		5	0
6	**Credit allowable** (subtract line 5 from line 4). (If zero or less, enter 0.)		6	1,890
7	**Total FUTA tax** (subtract line 6 from line 1)		7	280
8	Total FUTA tax deposited for the year, including any overpayment applied from a prior year . .		8	280
9	**Balance due** (subtract line 8 from line 7). This should be $100 or less. Pay to the Internal Revenue Service . . . . ▶		9	0
10	**Overpayment** (subtract line 7 from line 8). Check if it is to be: ☐ **Applied** to next return, or ☐ **Refunded** . . . . ▶		10	

Part III Record of Quarterly Federal Tax Liability for Unemployment Tax (Do not include state liability)

Quarter	First	Second	Third	Fourth	Total for year
Liability for quarter	200	80	0	0	280

Under penalties of perjury, I declare that I have examined this return, including accompanying schedules and statements, and to the best of my knowledge and belief, it is true, correct, and complete, and that no part of any payment made to a state unemployment fund claimed as a credit was or is to be deducted from the payments to employees.

Signature ▶ Douglas Anders   Title (Owner, etc.) ▶ owner   Date ▶ 2-1-94

Figure 8-15   Form 940

CHAPTER PROBLEMS

PART

I   1. Classify each of the following expenditures as either (1) deductible for AGI, (2) deductible from AGI (but not subject to the 2% floor), or (3) deductible from AGI and subject to the 2% floor.
       (a) repairs to a rental duplex paid for by the owner
       (b) interest expense paid on a business loan by the sole proprietor of a business
       (c) safety deposit box rental for securities of a self-employed stockbroker (used for business records of sales)
       (d) real estate taxes paid on a personal residence by the owner
       (e) subscription to *Stock Line Review* by an investor
       (f) legal fees relating to royalty income

I   2. Which of the following items is deductible by Sally Kramer, a cash-basis, calendar-year taxpayer who owns and operates a sporting goods store?
       (a) interest expense on a loan to purchase State of South Carolina bonds
       (b) gas and oil expenditures for her automobile (used 60% for business purposes)
       (c) a $35 expenditure for a speeding ticket incurred on the way to a customer's location
       (d) a $100 contribution to a candidate for sheriff

I   3. Bob Andrews borrowed $10,000 from First National Bank on July 1, 1993. The loan proceeds were used to purchase additional equipment that will be used in his business. The loan is repayable on July 1, 1994, along with $1,800 interest. What is the interest expense deduction for Andrews on his 1993 calendar-year return, assuming that Andrews uses the (a) cash-basis? (b) accrual basis?

I   4. Helen Anderson, a cash-basis, calendar-year taxpayer, is a successful physician who also owns a farm. Helen devotes much of her spare time to the farming operation, which has not shown a profit in two of the last four years. As of December 15, 1993, the farm results were:

Gross receipts (crop sales)		$10,200
Interest expense (farm loans)	$6,800	
Utilities expense	5,200	
Supplies expense	8,100	
Taxes on farm properties	4,100	
MACRS deductions—farm property	6,000	
Total expenses		(30,200)
Net loss from farming		($20,000)

Assuming than no other farm revenues or expenses are incurred as of the end of 1993, how would Anderson report the farming activity on her 1993 return?

II   5. An examination of the accounting records of Bob Young, a cash-basis sole proprietor, disclosed the following results for 1993:

Cash sales and collections on account	$640,000
Goods purchased and payments on account	410,000
Accounts receivable balance, 1/1/93	32,000
Accounts receivable balance, 12/31/93	38,400
Accounts payable balance, 1/1/93	26,000
Accounts payable balance, 12/31/93	24,500

Goods inventory, 1/1/93   50,300
Goods inventory, 12/31/93   46,200

The records also indicate that Bob Young withdrew $3,600 (cost) of inventory for personal use (no adjustment was made in the accounting records). Assuming that inventories are a significant income component, determine the correct 1993 gross income after accrual conversions.

II 6. Yolanda Yale uses lower of cost or market procedures in valuing its ending inventory. Based on the following facts, determine Yale's 1993 ending inventory value:

Product	Cost	12/31/93 Market
A	$ 82,000	$ 86,000
B	33,000	31,000
C	105,000	82,000
D	98,000	101,000

II 7. Thomas Willard's inventory records for 1993 disclose the following information:

Beginning inventory (10,000 @ $18) $180,000
2/6/93 purchase (5,000 @ $20)   100,000
6/3/93 purchase (8,000 @ $24)   192,000
9/4/93 purchase (10,000 @ $27)   270,000
12/6/93 purchase (12,000 @ $32)   384,000

The records also indicate that 40,000 units of inventory were sold in 1993 for a total of $1,320,000.

(a) Determine the 1993 ending inventory, cost of goods sold, and gross profit for Willard, using
  (1) average cost
  (2) first-in, first-out (FIFO)
  (3) last-in, first-out (LIFO)
(b) Assuming that Willard is in the 31% tax bracket, how much income taxes would he save in 1993 if he used the LIFO method as compared to the FIFO method?

II 8. Sandra Lockett has used the lower of cost or market method to value her business inventories for the last five years. On 12/31/92, her ending inventory was valued at $84,000 using this method; however, the actual cost of this inventory was $99,000. If Barnett elects to switch to the LIFO method in 1993 what tax adjustments must be made in 1993 and future years? Explain.

III 9. Which of the following assets are eligible for cost recovery deductions (i.e., depreciation, ACRS, or MACRS):
(a) rental duplex (owner lives in half, rents one half)
(b) chain-link fences surrounding a manufacturing plant
(c) ten acres of land used as a business parking lot
(d) an earthen dam constructed on farm property
(e) new personal residence

III 10. During 1993 Norma Ray purchased $213,500 of business machinery and equipment. All purchases were in March, and all assets had ADR mid-point lives of ten years.
(a) Assuming that Norma elects to expense as much of the cost of the assets as possible under Sec. 179, what would be her total cost recovery deduction for the 1993 purchases (Sec. 179 and MACRS)?

(b) How would your answer change if all personalty was acquired in November (assuming that Norma uses a calendar year for tax purposes)?

III 11. During the year 1993, Abe Johnson acquired the following assets to use in his sole proprietorship business:

Date	Asset	Cost
3-1-93	Office equipment	$20,000
4-6-93	Delivery truck	15,000
4-3-93	Plating machine*	30,000
4-3-93	Factory warehouse	90,000

*ADR mid-point life is ten years.

Assuming that Johnson elects to expense as much of the cost of the office equipment as possible under Sec. 179, determine his total 1993 MACRS cost recovery deduction.

III 12. Assume the same facts as Question 11, except that the plating machine was acquired on 11/4/93. Redetermine the 1993 MACRS cost recovery deduction.

III 13. Determine the appropriate depreciation, ACRS, or MACRS deduction for the following assets of Sue Clark (assume a 1993 current year and that Clark does not elect Sec. 179 expensing):

Date Acquired	Asset	Cost	Recovery Method
1-1-80	Office building	$200,000	Depr.*
6-1-86	Factory warehouse	100,000	ACRS
2-1-93	Office typewriter	5,000	MACRS
3-3-93	Factory warehouse	90,000	MACRS
12-1-93	Rental apt. building	300,000	MACRS

*Straight-line method with a $40,000 salvage value and a 40-year useful life

III 14. Determine the appropriate cost recovery deductions for the following assets (treat each case independently):
   (a) a business machine with a ten-year ADR mid-point life is acquired on 1/1/93 for $10,000, and the taxpayer elects the Alternative Depreciation System for the asset
   (b) an automobile to be used 90% of the time for business purposes is acquired on 1/1/93 for $20,000
   (c) a factory building acquired on 1/1/93 for $400,000, and the taxpayer elects the Alternative Depreciation System
   (d) a computer with a ten-year ADR midpoint life (cost of $5,000 on 1/1/93) is to be used 40% of the time for business and 60% of the time for personal use

IV 15. Bill Allen established a defined contribution profit-sharing retirement plan in 1993. During 1993 he contributed $64,000 to the plan on behalf of employees. The total compensation of all employees covered by the plan was $410,000. How much of this total may Allen deduct as a business expense in 1993? Are there any other tax consequences associated with the contribution?

IV 16. Alice Cambden has provided a defined contribution profit-sharing plan for her employees. During 1993 her Schedule C self-employment earnings were $80,000.
   (a) What is the maximum amount that she may contribute and deduct on her own behalf to the Keogh in 1993?

(b) How would your answer change if her Schedule C self-employment earnings were $180,000?

IV 17. Assume the same facts as Question 16, except that the plan is a money-purchase plan. How would your answers to parts (a) and (b) change?

IV 18. Flora Winger is an employee of B Company, which has a defined benefit money purchase Keogh retirement plan. During 1993 Flora was paid a total salary of $80,000. Ignoring the potential deduction, what is the maximum amount that B Company can contribute to the plan on Flora's behalf in 1993? Would your answer change if Flora's salary was $160,000?

V 19. Melissa Bland incurred the following research and experimentation expenditures in 1993: $80,000 salaries of research personnel, $20,000 of MACRS deductions on R&E equipment, and $40,000 miscellaneous cash expenses. Explain the tax options available to Bland in reporting these expenditures.

V 20. Gina Mitchell, an independent oil and gas operator, incurred the following results in 1993 related to her production from Hal Smith's property:

Sales revenues (10,000 barrels @ $32)	$320,000
minus royalty to Smith (1/8 × $320,000)	(40,000)
Gross income	$280,000
minus direct expenses	(240,000)
Taxable income from property	$ 40,000

At the beginning of 1993, Gina's undepleted cost in the Smith project was $60,000, and it was estimated that 20,000 barrels of oil remained on the property.
(a) What would Gina's 1993 depletion deduction be using the cost method?
(b) What would Gina's 1993 depletion deduction be using the percentage method?
(c) What would be the allowable depletion deduction for Smith, the property owner?

V 21. Melvin Zorba uses the direct method of reporting business bad debts. In 1993 the $2,000 accounts receivable balance of Allen Bell, a customer, was judged to be uncollectible, and the account was written off. In 1994 Bell unexpectedly repaid the balance. Explain how these transactions should be reported for tax purposes.

V 22. Label each of the following expenditures as either (1) a nondepreciable capital expenditure, (2) a depreciable capital expenditure, or (3) a repair expense.
(a) $400 paid to a contractor to paint a rental duplex
(b) $600 paid to overhaul the engine in a 1975 truck used for business deliveries
(c) $1,200 for annual inspection on a $150,000 oil well
(d) $1,800 for a new roof on a portable company building
(e) $1,200 for a color monitor for a business computer
(f) $80,000 for 40 acres to be used as a business parking lot

V 23. During the year 1993 Sam Dell's company payroll records revealed the following information:
Sam Dell—$40,000 withdrawal for his personal use
Other employees—$180,000 gross salary, with withholdings of $40,000 federal income taxes, $4,000 state income taxes, and $18,000 FICA (social security) taxes
The records also disclose that as an employer, Dell paid $18,000 of matching FICA taxes, $7,000 of federal unemployment (FUTA) taxes, and $1,000 state unemployment (SUTA) taxes. In addition, he paid in $12,000 of estimated federal income

taxes on his own behalf as an individual. How much of these payments are deductible by Dell as business expenses on his 1993 income tax return?

V   24. During 1993 Linda Staniszewski, a sole proprietor, paid $1,240 for health insurance coverage for herself and her family and paid $5,200 of self-employment tax. Assuming that Linda does not itemize her deductions In 1993 how much (if any) of these amounts may she deduct?

APX   25. Sandra Riggins owns and operates her own business and employs the following three individuals in 1993:

Employee	Annual Salary	Marital Status	Exemptions
Sue Cain	$24,000	Married	2
Al Adams	$30,000	Married	2
Nan Wood	$21,000	Single	1

Assuming that Sue pays her employees on a semimonthly basis (24 equal checks), determine the appropriate federal withholding for each employee for one paycheck using (a) the percentage method and (b) the wage-bracket method.

APX   26. Assume the same facts as in Problem 25. Determine the total amount of (1) FICA taxes that would be due each quarter on a Form 941 and (2) the amount of federal unemployment (FUTA) taxes due for the year on Form 940.

TAX RETURN PROBLEMS

27. [Form 4562] Using the data in Problem 11, complete a current Form 4562 (Cost Recovery) for the taxpayer.

28. [Schedules C and SE] Based on the following information, prepare a current Schedule C and SE for Wanda Wallace, a self-employed hardware store owner who uses the accrual basis of accounting and the cost method for inventories:

Sales revenue	746,520
Repairs to store equipment	1,220
Supplies expense	680
Building insurance (4 years, beginning in January, this year)	7,200
Depreciation (from Form 4562)	82,600
Salaries of sales employees	130,000
Gross purchases of merchandise	410,000
Utilities expense	7,300
Rent on store location	24,000
State & federal unemployment taxes paid	6,200
Delivery expenses	8,100
Merchandise inventory, January 1	26,000
Merchandise inventory, December 31	34,000
Merchandise withdrawn for personal use	6,200
Cash withdrawn from business for personal use	30,000

29. [Form 941] Based on the information given in Problem 25, prepare a Form 941 for the first quarter of the year.

30. [Form 940] Based on the information given in Problem 25, prepare a Form 940 for the year.

HOW WOULD YOU RULE?

31. May Roulette owns and operates a gambling casino. During 1993 May spent $9,000 for limousine, hotel, and meal charges for six of her "best" customers who make annual visits to her casino. May contends that these expenditures are ordinary and necessary expenses of "carrying on" a gambling business and are therefore deductible under Sec. 162. What is your opinion?
32. Shane Moriarity acquired five acres of land to use as a landfill to bury trash collected by his disposal business. Since he will dig huge holes to bury the trash, and the land will be worth a great deal less after the holes are filled, he wants to know if he can allocate part of the cost of the land to the hole and depreciate it. What is your opinion?

TAX RETURN PORTFOLIO PROBLEM

If this problem was assigned by your instructor, refer to Appendix A and complete the instructions for the segment labeled "Chapter 8." These instructions include the completion of Form 1040, Schedules C and SE, and Form 4562 for Harold J. and Maude B. Neilson, as well as a Schedule E for Harriet Neilson.

Chapter 8 Problem 28   Name_____8-77

Form 4562
Department of the Treasury
Internal Revenue Service

Depreciation and Amortization
(Including Information on Listed Property)

▶ See separate instructions.   ▶ Attach this form to your return.

OMB No. 1545-0172
1993
Attachment Sequence No. 67

Name(s) shown on return

Identifying number

Business or activity to which this form relates

Part I — Election To Expense Certain Tangible Property (Section 179) (Note: If you have any "Listed Property," complete Part V before you complete Part I.)

1	Maximum dollar limitation (If an enterprise zone business, see instructions.) **1**	$17,500
2	Total cost of section 179 property placed in service during the tax year (see instructions) . . **2**	
3	Threshold cost of section 179 property before reduction in limitation **3**	$200,000
4	Reduction in limitation. Subtract line 3 from line 2, but do not enter less than -0- **4**	
5	Dollar limitation for tax year. Subtract line 4 from line 1, but do not enter less than -0-. (If married filing separately, see instructions.) **5**	

(a) Description of property	(b) Cost	(c) Elected cost
6		

7	Listed property. Enter amount from line 26. . . . . **7**	
8	Total elected cost of section 179 property. Add amounts in column (c), lines 6 and 7 . . . **8**	
9	Tentative deduction. Enter the smaller of line 5 or line 8 . . . . **9**	
10	Carryover of disallowed deduction from 1992 (see instructions). **10**	
11	Taxable income limitation. Enter the smaller of taxable income or line 5 (see instructions) . **11**	
12	Section 179 expense deduction. Add lines 9 and 10, but do not enter more than line 11 . . **12**	
13	Carryover of disallowed deduction to 1994. Add lines 9 and 10, less line 12 ▶ **13**	

Note: *Do not use Part II or Part III below for listed property (automobiles, certain other vehicles, cellular telephones, certain computers, or property used for entertainment, recreation, or amusement). Instead, use Part V for listed property.*

Part II — MACRS Depreciation For Assets Placed in Service ONLY During Your 1993 Tax Year (Do Not Include Listed Property)

(a) Classification of property	(b) Month and year placed in service	(c) Basis for depreciation (business/investment use only—see instructions)	(d) Recovery period	(e) Convention	(f) Method	(g) Depreciation deduction
14 General Depreciation System (GDS) (see instructions):						
a 3-year property						
b 5-year property						
c 7-year property						
d 10-year property						
e 15-year property						
f 20-year property						
g Residential rental property			27.5 yrs.	MM	S/L	
			27.5 yrs.	MM	S/L	
h Nonresidential real property				MM	S/L	
				MM	S/L	
15 Alternative Depreciation System (ADS) (see instructions):						
a Class life					S/L	
b 12-year			12 yrs.		S/L	
c 40-year			40 yrs.	MM	S/L	

Part III — Other Depreciation (Do Not Include Listed Property)

16	GDS and ADS deductions for assets placed in service in tax years beginning before 1993 (see instructions) **16**	
17	Property subject to section 168(f)(1) election (see instructions) **17**	
18	ACRS and other depreciation (see instructions) **18**	

Part IV — Summary

19	Listed property. Enter amount from line 25. . . . . **19**	
20	**Total.** Add deductions on line 12, lines 14 and 15 in column (g), and lines 16 through 19. Enter here and on the appropriate lines of your return. (Partnerships and S corporations—see instructions) **20**	
21	For assets shown above and placed in service during the current year, enter the portion of the basis attributable to section 263A costs (see instructions) **21**	

For Paperwork Reduction Act Notice, see page 1 of the separate instructions.   Cat. No. 12906N   Form **4562** (1993)

Form 4562 (1993) — Page 2

Part V — Listed Property—Automobiles, Certain Other Vehicles, Cellular Telephones, Certain Computers, and Property Used for Entertainment, Recreation, or Amusement

For any vehicle for which you are using the standard mileage rate or deducting lease expense, complete only 22a, 22b, columns (a) through (c) of Section A, all of Section B, and Section C if applicable.

Section A—Depreciation and Other Information (Caution: See instructions for limitations for automobiles.)

22a Do you have evidence to support the business/investment use claimed? ☐ Yes ☐ No   22b If "Yes," is the evidence written? ☐ Yes ☐ No

(a) Type of property (list vehicles first)	(b) Date placed in service	(c) Business/ investment use percentage	(d) Cost or other basis	(e) Basis for depreciation (business/investment use only)	(f) Recovery period	(g) Method/ Convention	(h) Depreciation deduction	(i) Elected section 179 cost
23 Property used more than 50% in a qualified business use (see instructions):								
		%						
		%						
		%						
24 Property used 50% or less in a qualified business use (see instructions):								
		%				S/L –		/////
		%				S/L –		/////
		%				S/L –		/////

25 Add amounts in column (h). Enter the total here and on line 19, page 1 . . . . . . **25** _____

26 Add amounts in column (i). Enter the total here and on line 7, page 1 . . . . **26** _____

Section B—Information Regarding Use of Vehicles—If you deduct expenses for vehicles:

- Always complete this section for vehicles used by a sole proprietor, partner, or other "more than 5% owner," or related person.
- If you provided vehicles to your employees, first answer the questions in Section C to see if you meet an exception to completing this section for those vehicles.

	(a) Vehicle 1		(b) Vehicle 2		(c) Vehicle 3		(d) Vehicle 4		(e) Vehicle 5		(f) Vehicle 6	
27 Total business/investment miles driven during the year (DO NOT include commuting miles)												
28 Total commuting miles driven during the year												
29 Total other personal (noncommuting) miles driven												
30 Total miles driven during the year. Add lines 27 through 29												
	Yes	No	Yes	No	Yes	No	Yes	No	Yes	No	Yes	No
31 Was the vehicle available for personal use during off-duty hours?												
32 Was the vehicle used primarily by a more than 5% owner or related person?												
33 Is another vehicle available for personal use?												

Section C—Questions for Employers Who Provide Vehicles for Use by Their Employees

Answer these questions to determine if you meet an exception to completing Section B. Note: Section B must always be completed for vehicles used by sole proprietors, partners, or other more than 5% owners or related persons.

	Yes	No
34 Do you maintain a written policy statement that prohibits all personal use of vehicles, including commuting, by your employees?		
35 Do you maintain a written policy statement that prohibits personal use of vehicles, except commuting, by your employees? (See instructions for vehicles used by corporate officers, directors, or 1% or more owners.)		
36 Do you treat all use of vehicles by employees as personal use?		
37 Do you provide more than five vehicles to your employees and retain the information received from your employees concerning the use of the vehicles?		
38 Do you meet the requirements concerning qualified automobile demonstration use (see instructions)? . .	/////	/////

Note: If your answer to 34, 35, 36, 37, or 38 is "Yes," you need not complete Section B for the covered vehicles.

Part VI — Amortization

(a) Description of costs	(b) Date amortization begins	(c) Amortizable amount	(d) Code section	(e) Amortization period or percentage	(f) Amortization for this year
39 Amortization of costs that begins during your 1993 tax year:			/////	/////	/////

40 Amortization of costs that began before 1993 . . . . **40** _____

41 Total. Enter here and on "Other Deductions" or "Other Expenses" line of your return . . . **41** _____

Copyright © 1994 by Harcourt Brace & Company. All rights reserved.

Chapter 8 Problem 28   Name _____   8-79

SCHEDULE C (Form 1040)
Department of the Treasury
Internal Revenue Service

Profit or Loss From Business
(Sole Proprietorship)
▶ Partnerships, joint ventures, etc., must file Form 1065.
▶ Attach to Form 1040 or Form 1041.   ▶ See Instructions for Schedule C (Form 1040).

OMB No. 1545-0074

1993

Attachment Sequence No. 09

Name of proprietor

Social security number (SSN)

A Principal business or profession, including product or service (see page C-1)

B Enter principal business code (see page C-6) ▶

C Business name. If no separate business name, leave blank.

D Employer ID number (EIN), if any

E Business address (including suite or room no.) ▶ ....
City, town or post office, state, and ZIP code

F Accounting method: (1) ☐ Cash   (2) ☐ Accrual   (3) ☐ Other (specify) ▶ ....

G Method(s) used to value closing inventory: (1) ☐ Cost   (2) ☐ Lower of cost or market   (3) ☐ Other (attach explanation)   (4) ☐ Does not apply (if checked, skip line H) | Yes | No |

H Was there any change in determining quantities, costs, or valuations between opening and closing inventory? If "Yes," attach explanation . . . .

I Did you "materially participate" in the operation of this business during 1993? If "No," see page C-2 for limit on losses. . .

J If you started or acquired this business during 1993, check here . . . . ▶ ☐

Part I Income

1	Gross receipts or sales. **Caution:** If this income was reported to you on Form W-2 and the "Statutory employee" box on that form was checked, see page C-2 and check here . . . . ▶ ☐	1	
2	Returns and allowances	2	
3	Subtract line 2 from line 1	3	
4	Cost of goods sold (from line 40 on page 2)	4	
5	**Gross profit.** Subtract line 4 from line 3	5	
6	Other income, including Federal and state gasoline or fuel tax credit or refund (see page C-2) . .	6	
7	**Gross income.** Add lines 5 and 6 . . . . ▶	7	

Part II Expenses. Caution: Do not enter expenses for business use of your home on lines 8–27. Instead, see line 30.

8	Advertising	8		19	Pension and profit-sharing plans	19
9	Bad debts from sales or services (see page C-3)	9		20	Rent or lease (see page C-4):	
10	Car and truck expenses (see page C-3)	10			a Vehicles, machinery, and equipment .	20a
					b Other business property . .	20b
11	Commissions and fees. . .	11		21	Repairs and maintenance . .	21
12	Depletion.	12		22	Supplies (not included in Part III) .	22
13	Depreciation and section 179 expense deduction (not included in Part III) (see page C-3)	13		23	Taxes and licenses	23
				24	Travel, meals, and entertainment:	
					a Travel	24a
					b Meals and entertainment .	
14	Employee benefit programs (other than on line 19) . .	14			c Enter 20% of line 24b subject to limitations (see page C-4) .	
15	Insurance (other than health) .	15				
16	Interest:					
a	Mortgage (paid to banks, etc.) .	16a			d Subtract line 24c from line 24b .	24d
b	Other	16b		25	Utilities	25
17	Legal and professional services	17		26	Wages (less jobs credit) . . .	26
18	Office expense	18		27	Other expenses (from line 46 on page 2)	27
28	**Total expenses** before expenses for business use of home. Add lines 8 through 27 in columns. . ▶	28				
29	Tentative profit (loss). Subtract line 28 from line 7	29				
30	Expenses for business use of your home. Attach **Form 8829**	30				
31	**Net profit or (loss).** Subtract line 30 from line 29.					
	• If a profit, enter on **Form 1040, line 12,** and ALSO on **Schedule SE, line 2** (statutory employees, see page C-5). Fiduciaries, enter on Form 1041, line 3.					31
	• If a loss, you MUST go on to line 32.					
32	If you have a loss, check the box that describes your investment in this activity (see page C-5).					
	• If you checked 32a, enter the loss on **Form 1040, line 12,** and ALSO on **Schedule SE, line 2** (statutory employees, see page C-5). Fiduciaries, enter on Form 1041, line 3.			32a ☐ All investment is at risk.		
	• If you checked 32b, you MUST attach **Form 6198.**			32b ☐ Some investment is not at risk.		

For Paperwork Reduction Act Notice, see Form 1040 instructions.   Cat. No. 11334P   Schedule C (Form 1040) 1993

Copyright © 1994 by Harcourt Brace & Company. All rights reserved.

8-80   Chapter 8 Problem 28

Schedule C (Form 1040) 1993   Page **2**

Part III — Cost of Goods Sold (see page C-5)

33 Inventory at beginning of year. If different from last year's closing inventory, attach explanation	33	
34 Purchases less cost of items withdrawn for personal use	34	
35 Cost of labor. Do not include salary paid to yourself	35	
36 Materials and supplies	36	
37 Other costs	37	
38 Add lines 33 through 37	38	
39 Inventory at end of year	39	
40 **Cost of goods sold.** Subtract line 39 from line 38. Enter the result here and on page 1, line 4	40	

Part IV — Information on Your Vehicle. Complete this part **ONLY** if you are claiming car or truck expenses on line 10 and are not required to file Form 4562 for this business.

41 When did you place your vehicle in service for business purposes? (month, day, year) ▶ ..../......../........

42 Of the total number of miles you drove your vehicle during 1993, enter the number of miles you used your vehicle for:

    a Business .... **b** Commuting .... **c** Other ....

43 Do you (or your spouse) have another vehicle available for personal use? .... ☐ Yes   ☐ No

44 Was your vehicle available for use during off-duty hours? .... ☐ Yes   ☐ No

45a Do you have evidence to support your deduction? .... ☐ Yes   ☐ No
   b If "Yes," is the evidence written? .... ☐ Yes   ☐ No

Part V — Other Expenses. List below business expenses not included on lines 8–26 or line 30.

....		
....		
....		
....		
....		
....		
....		
....		
46 **Total other expenses.** Enter here and on page 1, line 27	46	

✰ Printed on recycled paper

Copyright © 1994 by Harcourt Brace & Company. All rights reserved.

Chapter 8 Problem 28   Name _____   *8-81*

SCHEDULE SE
(Form 1040)
Department of the Treasury
Internal Revenue Service

Self-Employment Tax

▶ See Instructions for Schedule SE (Form 1040).

▶ Attach to Form 1040.

OMB No. 1545-0074

1993

Attachment
Sequence No. **17**

Name of person with **self-employment** income (as shown on Form 1040)	Social security number of person with **self-employment** income ▶	

Who Must File Schedule SE

You must file Schedule SE if:

- Your wages (and tips) subject to social security AND Medicare tax (or railroad retirement tax) were less than $135,000; **AND**
- Your net earnings from self-employment from other than church employee income (line 4 of Short Schedule SE or line 4c of Long Schedule SE) were $400 or more; **OR**
- You had church employee income of $108.28 or more. Income from services you performed as a minister or a member of a religious order **is not** church employee income. See page SE-1.

Note: Even if you have a loss or a small amount of income from self-employment, it may be to your benefit to file Schedule SE and use either "optional method" in Part II of Long Schedule SE. See page SE-3.

Exception. If your only self-employment income was from earnings as a minister, member of a religious order, or Christian Science practitioner, **AND** you filed Form 4361 and received IRS approval not to be taxed on those earnings, **DO NOT** file Schedule SE. Instead, write "Exempt–Form 4361" on Form 1040, line 47.

May I Use Short Schedule SE or MUST I Use Long Schedule SE?

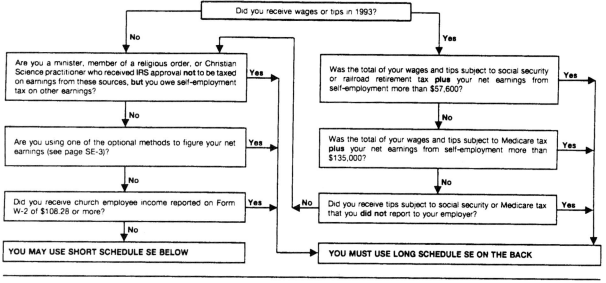

Section A—Short Schedule SE. Caution: *Read above to see if you can use Short Schedule SE.*

1	Net farm profit or (loss) from Schedule F, line 36, and farm partnerships, Schedule K-1 (Form 1065), line 15a	1	
2	Net profit or (loss) from Schedule C, line 31; Schedule C-EZ, line 3; and Schedule K-1 (Form 1065), line 15a (other than farming). Ministers and members of religious orders see page SE-1 for amounts to report on this line. See page SE-2 for other income to report	2	
3	Combine lines 1 and 2	3	
4	**Net earnings from self-employment.** Multiply line 3 by 92.35% (.9235). If less than $400, **do not** file this schedule; you do not owe self-employment tax . . . . ▶	4	
5	**Self-employment tax.** If the amount on line 4 is: • $57,600 or less, multiply line 4 by 15.3% (.153) and enter the result. • More than $57,600 but less than $135,000, multiply the amount in excess of $57,600 by 2.9% (.029). Then, add $8,812.80 to the result and enter the total. • $135,000 or more, enter $11,057.40. Also enter on **Form 1040, line 47.** (**Important:** You are allowed a deduction for **one-half** of this amount. Multiply line 5 by 50% (.5) and enter the result on **Form 1040, line 25.**)	5	

For Paperwork Reduction Act Notice, see Form 1040 instructions.   Cat. No. 11358Z   Schedule SE (Form 1040) 1993

Copyright © 1994 by Harcourt Brace & Company. All rights reserved.

Chapter 8 Problem 29   Name_____   8-83

Form **941**
(Rev. January 1994)
Department of the Treasury
Internal Revenue Service

4141

Employer's Quarterly Federal Tax Return
▶ See separate instructions for information on completing this return.
Please type or print.

Proof as of August 1993 (subject to change)

OMB No. 1545-0029

T	
FF	
FD	
FP	
I	
T	

Enter state code for state in which deposits made ▶ ☐ (see page 2 of instructions).

Name (as distinguished from trade name)

Date quarter ended

Trade name, if any

Employer identification number

Address (number and street)

City, state, and ZIP code

If address is different from prior return, check here ▶ ☐

IRS Use

If you do not have to file returns in the future, check here ▶ ☐ and enter date final wages paid ▶
If you are a seasonal employer, see **Seasonal employers** on page 2 and check here (see instructions) ▶ ☐

1 Number of employees (except household) employed in the pay period that includes March 12th ▶
2 Total wages and tips subject to withholding, plus other compensation **2**
3 Total income tax withheld from wages, tips, and sick pay **3**
4 Adjustment of withheld income tax for preceding quarters of calendar year **4**

5 Adjusted total of income tax withheld (line 3 as adjusted by line 4—see instructions) . . . **5**
6a Taxable social security wages . . . . $_____ × 12.4% (.124) = **6a**
  b Taxable social security tips . . . . $_____ × 12.4% (.124) = **6b**
7 Taxable Medicare wages and tips . . . . . $_____ × 2.9% (.029) =   **7**
8 Total social security and Medicare taxes (add lines 6a, 6b, and 7). Check here if wages are not subject to social security and/or Medicare tax . . . . ▶ ☐ **8**
9 Adjustment of social security and Medicare taxes (see instructions for required explanation)
   Sick Pay $_____ ± Fractions of Cents $_____ ± Other $_____ = **9**
10 Adjusted total of social security and Medicare taxes (line 8 as adjusted by line 9—see instructions) **10**

11 **Total taxes** (add lines 5 and 10) **11**

12 Advance earned income credit (EIC) payments made to employees, if any **12**
13 Net taxes (subtract line 12 from line 11). **This should equal line 17, column (d) below (or line D of Schedule B (Form 941))** **13**

14 Total deposits for quarter, including overpayment applied from a prior quarter **14**

15 Balance due (subtract line 14 from line 13). Pay to Internal Revenue Service **15**
16 Overpayment, if line 14 is more than line 13, enter excess here ▶ $_____
   and check if to be: ☐ Applied to next return   **OR**   ☐ Refunded.

- **Monthly depositors:** Complete line 17, columns (a) through (d) and check here . . . . ▶ ☐
- **Semiweekly depositors:** Complete Schedule B and check here . . . . ▶ ☐
- **All filers:** If line 13 is less than $500, you need not complete line 17 or Schedule B.

17 Monthly Summary of Federal Tax Liability.

(a) First month liability	(b) Second month liability	(c) Third month liability	(d) Total liability for quarter

Sign Here
Under penalties of perjury, I declare that I have examined this return, including accompanying schedules and statements, and to the best of my knowledge and belief, it is true, correct, and complete.

Signature ▶   Print Your Name and Title ▶   Date ▶

For Paperwork Reduction Act Notice, see page 1 of separate instructions.   Cat. No. 17001Z   Form **941** (Rev. 1-94)

Copyright © 1994 by Harcourt Brace & Company. All rights reserved.

Chapter 8 Problem 30   Name _____   8-85

Form 940
Department of the Treasury
Internal Revenue Service

Employer's Annual Federal Unemployment (FUTA) Tax Return

▶ For Paperwork Reduction Act Notice, see separate instructions.

OMB No. 1545-0028

1992

T	
FF	
FD	
FP	
I	
T	

If incorrect, make any necessary change. ▶

Name (as distinguished from trade name)   Calendar year

Trade name, if any

Address and ZIP code   Employer identification number

A   Are you required to pay unemployment contributions to only one state? . . . . ☐ Yes ☐ No
B   Did you pay all state unemployment contributions by February 1, 1993? (If a 0% experience rate is granted check "Yes.") . . . . ☐ Yes ☐ No
C   Were all wages that were taxable for FUTA tax also taxable for your state's unemployment tax? . . . . . ☐ Yes ☐ No
D   Did you pay all wages in a state other than Michigan? . . . . ☐ Yes ☐ No

If you answered "No" to any of these questions, you must file Form 940. If you answered "Yes" to all the questions, you may file Form 940-EZ which is a simplified version of Form 940. You can get Form 940-EZ by calling 1-800-TAX-FORM (1-800-829-3676).

If you will not have to file returns in the future, check here, complete, and sign the return . . . . ▶ ☐
If this is an Amended Return, check here . . . . ▶ ☐

Part I   Computation of Taxable Wages

1   Total payments (including exempt payments) during the calendar year for services of employees . **1**

2   Exempt payments. (Explain each exemption shown, attach additional sheets if necessary.) ▶ ....
   Amount paid
   2

3   Payments of more than $7,000 for services. Enter only amounts over the first $7,000 paid to each employee. Do not include payments from line 2. The $7,000 amount is the Federal wage base. Your state wage base may be different. **Do not use the state wage limitation**   **3**

4   Total exempt payments (add lines 2 and 3) **4**
5   **Total taxable wages** (subtract line 4 from line 1) . . . . ▶ **5**
6   Additional tax resulting from credit reduction for unpaid advances to the State of Michigan. Enter the wages included on line 5 for Michigan and multiply by .011. (See the separate Instructions for Form 940.) Enter the credit reduction amount here and in Part II, line 5: Michigan wages _____ × .011 = ... ▶ **6**

Be sure to complete both sides of this return and sign in the space provided on the back.   Cat. No. 112340   Form **940** (1992)

Copyright © 1994 by Harcourt Brace & Company. All rights reserved.

Part II Tax Due or Refund

1. Gross FUTA tax. Multiply the wages in Part I, line 5, by .062 . . . . **1**
2. Maximum credit. Multiply the wages in Part I, line 5, by .054 . . . **2**
3. **Computation of tentative credit:**

(a) Name of state	(b) State reporting number(s) as shown on employer's state contribution returns	(c) Taxable payroll (as defined in state act)	(d) State experience rate		(e) State experience rate	(f) Contributions if rate had been 5.4% (col. (c) x .054)	(g) Contributions payable at experience rate (col. (c) x col. (e))	(h) Additional credit (col. (f) minus col.(g)). If 0 or less, enter 0.	(i) Contributions actually paid to state
			From	To					

3a. Totals . . . ▶

3b. **Total tentative credit** (add line 3a, columns (h) and (i) only—see instructions for limitations on late payments) ▶

4. **Credit:** Enter the smaller of the amount in Part II, line 2, or line 3b . **4**
5. Enter the amount from Part I, line 6 . . . . **5**
6. **Credit allowable** (subtract line 5 from line 4). (If zero or less, enter 0.) **6**
7. **Total FUTA tax** (subtract line 6 from line 1) **7**
8. Total FUTA tax deposited for the year, including any overpayment applied from a prior year . . **8**
9. **Balance due** (subtract line 8 from line 7). This should be $100 or less. Pay to the Internal Revenue Service . . . . ▶ **9**
10. **Overpayment** (subtract line 7 from line 8). Check if it is to be: ☐ **Applied to next return,** or ☐ **Refunded** . . . . ▶ **10**

Part III Record of Quarterly Federal Tax Liability for Unemployment Tax *(Do not include state liability)*

Quarter	First	Second	Third	Fourth	Total for year
Liability for quarter					

Under penalties of perjury, I declare that I have examined this return, including accompanying schedules and statements, and to the best of my knowledge and belief, it is true, correct, and complete, and that no part of any payment made to a state unemployment fund claimed as a credit was or is to be deducted from the payments to employees.

Signature ▶   Title (Owner, etc.) ▶   Date ▶

Comprehensive Tax Return Problem 4
Form 1040, Schedules A, C, E, and SE, Form 4562

Allen B. Ward, age 38, is a divorced taxpayer who provides 80% of the support of his 15-year-old daughter Patricia. Allen and Patricia live at 1106 Cumberland Lane, Huntington, West Virginia 25701. Allen's social security number is 611-34-6576, and Patricia's is 455-43-0989. Allen elects to contribute to the presidential election campaign fund. Patricia worked during the summer at a local fast-food restaurant, earning $2,345.

Allen began his own plumbing business in January 1993. Prior to this time, he was an employee of Dunderson Co. The cash-basis records for his plumbing business (Ward's Plumbing) disclosed the following results (EI #43-3243256):

Cash sales and collections on account	$238,450
Cash purchases and payments on account	89,340
Expenses:	
Utilities	4,920
Legal and accounting fees	3,600
Bad debts written off as uncollectible	4,200
Gross wages paid (two employees)	56,300
Supplies expense	975
Insurance (expires 1/1/94)	6,450
Property taxes paid	2,123
Advertising (newspaper ads)	3,200
Mortgage interest on building loan	12,360
Repair expenses	1,240
FICA taxes paid (employees' share collected)	4,307
FICA taxes paid (employer's share paid)	4,307
FUTA (federal unemployment taxes) paid	453
SUTA (state unemployment taxes) paid	640

Allen's accounting records also disclose the following account balances, which are necessary to convert cash-basis gross profit to the accrual basis, since inventories are significant:

Account	12/31/92 Balance	12/31/93 Balance
Accounts receivable	$18,650	$20,380
Accounts payable	14,330	9,450
Merchandise inventory	26,700	21,340

Allen acquired the following assets in January 1993 for his business and elected the following cost recovery methods:

Asset	Cost	Recovery Method	Mid-point Life
Welding equipment	$ 32,300*	MACRS (200% DB)	10 years
Shop building	142,000	MACRS (SL)	—
Pipe cutters	12,400	MACRS (200% DB)	None given
Delivery truck	11,300	MACRS (200% DB)	5 years

*Allen elects to expense as much of this cost as possible under Sec. 179.

On February 5, 1993, Allen acquired a rental house at 403 Daley Street in Huntington. He paid $60,000 for the house, and immediately paid $8,000 for furniture and fixtures for the property (mid-point life of ten years). During 1993 he collected $9,000 of rents and had the following expenses: $2,750 mortgage interest, $300 repairs, $820 property taxes, and $120 legal fees.

Allen's personal records disclose the following expenditures in 1993 (no attempt has been made to separate the personal from business items, or the deductible from the nondeductible items):

Property taxes on personal residence	$1,740
Interest on personal automobile loan	620
State sales taxes paid on 1993 personal purchases	564
Cash contributions to church	1,060
Mortgage interest on personal residence	4,206
Unreimbursed hospital costs	2,300
Dues paid to professional plumbing association	820
Fee paid for preparation of 1992 tax return	140
Cash contribution to Marshall University	1,000
Business luncheons with customers (total)	450
Notepad gifts given to customers (worth $10 each)	830
Contribution to an Individual Retirement Account (Allen does not have a Keogh plan)	2,000
Alimony paid to first wife (divorce decree provides for payments of $100 per month until she dies or remarries)	1,200
Child support paid to first wife (decree requires $200 per month)	2,400

REQUIRED: Prepare a Form 1040 for Allen B. Ward, with accompanying Schedules A, C, E, SE, and two Forms 4562 (one for the business and one for the rental property). Assume that Ward made $5,000 of estimated federal income tax payments in 1993.

Comprehensive Tax Return Problem 4   Name _____   8-89

Form 1040 U.S. Individual Income Tax Return 1993

Department of the Treasury—Internal Revenue Service

For the year Jan. 1–Dec. 31, 1993, or other tax year beginning _____, 1993, ending _____, 19 ___   OMB No. 1545-0074

IRS Use Only—Do not write or staple in this space

Label
(See instructions on page 12.)
Use the IRS label. Otherwise, please print or type.

- Your first name and initial | Last name | Your social security number
- If a joint return, spouse's first name and initial | Last name | Spouse's social security number
- Home address (number and street). If you have a P.O. box, see page 12. | Apt. no.
- City, town or post office, state, and ZIP code. If you have a foreign address, see page 12.

For Privacy Act and Paperwork Reduction Act Notice, see page 4.

Presidential Election Campaign
(See page 12.)

Do you want $3 to go to this fund? ....   Yes [ ]   No [ ]
If a joint return, does your spouse want $3 to go to this fund? ....   Yes [ ]   No [ ]

Note: Checking "Yes" will not change your tax or reduce your refund.

Filing Status
(See page 12.)
Check only one box.

1 [ ] Single
2 [ ] Married filing joint return (even if only one had income)
3 [ ] Married filing separate return. Enter spouse's social security no. above and full name here. ▶ _____
4 [ ] Head of household (with qualifying person). (See page 13.) If the qualifying person is a child but not your dependent, enter this child's name here. ▶ _____
5 [ ] Qualifying widow(er) with dependent child (year spouse died ▶ 19 ___). (See page 13.)

Exemptions
(See page 13.)

6a [ ] **Yourself.** If your parent (or someone else) can claim you as a dependent on his or her tax return, **do not** check box 6a. But be sure to check the box on line 33b on page 2

 b [ ] **Spouse**

 c **Dependents:**

(1) Name (first, initial, and last name)	(2) Check if under age 1	(3) If age 1 or older, dependent's social security number	(4) Dependent's relationship to you	(5) No. of months lived in your home in 1993

If more than six dependents, see page 14.

No. of boxes checked on 6a and 6b ____
No. of your children on 6c who:
• lived with you ____
• didn't live with you due to divorce or separation (see page 15) ____
Dependents on 6c not entered above ____

d If your child didn't live with you but is claimed as your dependent under a pre-1985 agreement, check here ▶ [ ]
e Total number of exemptions claimed ....

Add numbers entered on lines above ▶ ____

Income

Attach Copy B of your Forms W-2, W-2G, and 1099-R here.

If you did not get a W-2, see page 10.

If you are attaching a check or money order, put it on top of any Forms W-2, W-2G, or 1099-R.

7	Wages, salaries, tips, etc. Attach Form(s) W-2	7	
8a	Taxable interest income (see page 16). Attach Schedule B if over $400	8a	
b	Tax-exempt interest (see page 17). DON'T include on line 8a	8b	
9	Dividend income. Attach Schedule B if over $400	9	
10	Taxable refunds, credits, or offsets of state and local income taxes (see page 17)	10	
11	Alimony received	11	
12	Business income or (loss). Attach Schedule C or C-EZ	12	
13	Capital gain or (loss). Attach Schedule D	13	
14	Capital gain distributions not reported on line 13 (see page 17)	14	
15	Other gains or (losses). Attach Form 4797	15	
16a	Total IRA distributions . [16a]____ b Taxable amount (see page 18)	16b	
17a	Total pensions and annuities [17a]____ b Taxable amount (see page 18)	17b	
18	Rental real estate, royalties, partnerships, S corporations, trusts, etc. Attach Schedule E	18	
19	Farm income or (loss). Attach Schedule F	19	
20	Unemployment compensation (see page 19)	20	
21a	Social security benefits [21a]____ b Taxable amount (see page 19)	21b	
22	Other income. List type and amount—see page 20 _____	22	
23	Add the amounts in the far right column for lines 7 through 22. This is your **total income** ▶	23	

Adjustments to Income
(See page 20.)

24a	Your IRA deduction (see page 20)	24a	
b	Spouse's IRA deduction (see page 20)	24b	
25	One-half of self-employment tax (see page 21)	25	
26	Self-employed health insurance deduction (see page 22)	26	
27	Keogh retirement plan and self-employed SEP deduction	27	
28	Penalty on early withdrawal of savings	28	
29	Alimony paid. Recipient's SSN ▶ _____	29	
30	Add lines 24a through 29. These are your **total adjustments** .... ▶	30	

Adjusted Gross Income

| 31 | Subtract line 30 from line 23. This is your **adjusted gross income**. If this amount is less than $23,050 and a child lived with you, see page EIC-1 to find out if you can claim the "Earned Income Credit" on line 56 .... ▶ | 31 | |

Cat. No. 11320B   Form **1040** (1993)

Copyright © 1994 by Harcourt Brace & Company. All rights reserved.

Form 1040 (1993) Page 2

Tax Computation
(See page 23.)

- **32** Amount from line 31 (adjusted gross income) **32**
- **33a** Check if: ☐ **You** were 65 or older, ☐ Blind; ☐ **Spouse** was 65 or older, ☐ Blind.
  Add the number of boxes checked above and enter the total here . . . . ▶ **33a**
- **b** If your parent (or someone else) can claim you as a dependent, check here . ▶ **33b** ☐
- **c** If you are married filing separately and your spouse itemizes deductions or you are a dual-status alien, see page 24 and check here . . . . ▶ **33c** ☐
- **34** Enter the larger of your:
  - **Itemized deductions** from Schedule A, line 26, **OR**
  - **Standard deduction** shown below for your filing status. **But if you checked any box on line 33a or b**, go to page 24 to find your standard deduction. If you checked **box 33c**, your standard deduction is zero.
    - Single—$3,700
    - Head of household—$5,450
    - Married filing jointly or Qualifying widow(er)—$6,200
    - Married filing separately—$3,100

  34
- **35** Subtract line 34 from line 32 . . . . **35**
- **36** If line 32 is $81,350 or less, multiply $2,350 by the total number of exemptions claimed on line 6e. If line 32 is over $81,350, see the worksheet on page 25 for the amount to enter . **36**
- **37** **Taxable income.** Subtract line 36 from line 35. If line 36 is more than line 35, enter -0-. **37**

If you want the IRS to figure your tax, see page 24.

- **38** Tax. Check if from **a** ☐ Tax Table, **b** ☐ Tax Rate Schedules, **c** ☐ Schedule D Tax Worksheet, or **d** ☐ Form 8615 (see page 25). Amount from Form(s) 8814 ▶ **e** _____ **38**
- **39** Additional taxes (see page 25). Check if from **a** ☐ Form 4970 **b** ☐ Form 4972 . . **39**
- **40** Add lines 38 and 39 . . . . ▶ **40**

Credits
(See page 25.)

- **41** Credit for child and dependent care expenses. Attach Form 2441 **41**
- **42** Credit for the elderly or the disabled. Attach Schedule R . **42**
- **43** Foreign tax credit. Attach Form 1116 . . . . **43**
- **44** Other credits (see page 26). Check if from **a** ☐ Form 3800
  b ☐ Form 8396 **c** ☐ Form 8801 **d** ☐ Form (specify) _____ **44**
- **45** Add lines 41 through 44 . . . . **45**
- **46** Subtract line 45 from line 40. If line 45 is more than line 40, enter -0- . . . . . ▶ **46**

Other Taxes

- **47** Self-employment tax. Attach Schedule SE. Also, see line 25 . . . . **47**
- **48** Alternative minimum tax. Attach Form 6251 . . . . **48**
- **49** Recapture taxes (see page 26). Check if from **a** ☐ Form 4255 **b** ☐ Form 8611 **c** ☐ Form 8828 **49**
- **50** Social security and Medicare tax on tip income not reported to employer. Attach Form 4137 **50**
- **51** Tax on qualified retirement plans, including IRAs. If required, attach Form 5329 . **51**
- **52** Advance earned income credit payments from Form W-2 . . . . **52**
- **53** Add lines 46 through 52. This is your **total tax** . . . . ▶ **53**

Payments
Attach Forms W-2, W-2G, and 1099-R on the front.

- **54** Federal income tax withheld. If any is from Form(s) 1099, check ▶ ☐ **54**
- **55** 1993 estimated tax payments and amount applied from 1992 return . **55**
- **56** **Earned income credit.** Attach Schedule EIC **56**
- **57** Amount paid with Form 4868 (extension request) . . . **57**
- **58a** Excess social security, Medicare, and RRTA tax withheld (see page 28) . **58a**
- **b** Deferral of additional 1993 taxes. Attach Form 8841 . . . **58b**
- **59** Other payments (see page 28). Check if from **a** ☐ Form 2439
  b ☐ Form 4136 . . . . **59**
- **60** Add lines 54 through 59. These are your **total payments** . . . . ▶ **60**

Refund or Amount You Owe

- **61** If line 60 is more than line 53, subtract line 53 from line 60. This is the amount you **OVERPAID**. ▶ **61**
- **62** Amount of line 61 you want **REFUNDED TO YOU**. . . . . ▶ **62**
- **63** Amount of line 61 you want **APPLIED TO YOUR 1994 ESTIMATED TAX** ▶ **63**
- **64** If line 53 is more than line 60, subtract line 60 from line 53. This is the **AMOUNT YOU OWE**. For details on how to pay, including what to write on your payment, see page 29 . . **64**
- **65** Estimated tax penalty (see page 29). Also include on line 64 **65**

Sign Here
Keep a copy of this return for your records.

Under penalties of perjury, I declare that I have examined this return and accompanying schedules and statements, and to the best of my knowledge and belief, they are true, correct, and complete. Declaration of preparer (other than taxpayer) is based on all information of which preparer has any knowledge.

▶ Your signature | Date | Your occupation

▶ Spouse's signature. If a joint return, BOTH must sign. | Date | Spouse's occupation

Paid Preparer's Use Only

Preparer's signature ▶ | Date | Check if self-employed ☐ | Preparer's social security no.

Firm's name (or yours if self-employed) and address ▶ | E.I. No. | ZIP code

Comprehensive Tax Return Problem 4 Name_____ 8-91

SCHEDULES A&B
(Form 1040)
Department of the Treasury
Internal Revenue Service

Schedule A—Itemized Deductions
(Schedule B is on back)
▶ Attach to Form 1040. ▶ See Instructions for Schedules A and B (Form 1040).

OMB No. 1545-0074
1993
Attachment Sequence No. 07

Name(s) shown on Form 1040 | Your social security number

Medical and Dental Expenses		**Caution:** *Do not include expenses reimbursed or paid by others.*		
	1	Medical and dental expenses (see page A-1)	1	
	2	Enter amount from Form 1040, line 32. ⌊2⌋		
	3	Multiply line 2 above by 7.5% (.075)	3	
	4	Subtract line 3 from line 1. If zero or less, enter -0- ▶		4
Taxes You Paid (See page A-1.)	5	State and local income taxes	5	
	6	Real estate taxes (see page A-2)	6	
	7	Other taxes. List—include personal property taxes ▶	7	
	8	Add lines 5 through 7 ▶		8
Interest You Paid (See page A-2.) **Note:** Personal interest is not deductible.	9a	Home mortgage interest and points reported to you on Form 1098	9a	
	b	Home mortgage interest not reported to you on Form 1098. If paid to the person from whom you bought the home, see page A-3 and show that person's name, identifying no., and address ▶	9b	
	10	Points not reported to you on Form 1098. See page A-3 for special rules	10	
	11	Investment interest. If required, attach Form 4952. (See page A-3.)	11	
	12	Add lines 9a through 11 ▶		12
Gifts to Charity (See page A-3.)		**Caution:** *If you made a charitable contribution and received a benefit in return, see page A-3.*		
	13	Contributions by cash or check	13	
	14	Other than by cash or check. If over $500, you **MUST** attach Form 8283	14	
	15	Carryover from prior year	15	
	16	Add lines 13 through 15 ▶		16
Casualty and Theft Losses	17	Casualty or theft loss(es). Attach Form 4684. (See page A-4.) ▶		17
Moving Expenses	18	Moving expenses. Attach Form 3903 or 3903-F. (See page A-4.) ▶		18
Job Expenses and Most Other Miscellaneous Deductions (See page A-5 for expenses to deduct here.)	19	Unreimbursed employee expenses—job travel, union dues, job education, etc. If required, you **MUST** attach Form 2106. (See page A-4.) ▶	19	
	20	Other expenses—investment, tax preparation, safe deposit box, etc. List type and amount ▶	20	
	21	Add lines 19 and 20	21	
	22	Enter amount from Form 1040, line 32. ⌊22⌋		
	23	Multiply line 22 above by 2% (.02)	23	
	24	Subtract line 23 from line 21. If zero or less, enter -0- ▶		24
Other Miscellaneous Deductions	25	Other—from list on page A-5. List type and amount ▶ .... ▶		25
Total Itemized Deductions	26	Is the amount on Form 1040, line 32, more than $108,450 (more than $54,225 if married filing separately)? • **NO.** Your deduction is not limited. Add lines 4, 8, 12, 16, 17, 18, 24, and 25 and enter the total here. Also enter on Form 1040, line 34, the **larger** of this amount or your standard deduction. • **YES.** Your deduction may be limited. See page A-5 for the amount to enter. ▶		26

For Paperwork Reduction Act Notice, see Form 1040 instructions.   Cat. No. 11330X   Schedule A (Form 1040) 1993

Copyright © 1994 by Harcourt Brace & Company, Inc. All rights reserved.

Comprehensive Tax Return Problem 4   Name _____   8-93

| SCHEDULE C
(Form 1040)
Department of the Treasury
Internal Revenue Service | **Profit or Loss From Business**
(Sole Proprietorship)
▶ Partnerships, joint ventures, etc., must file Form 1065.
▶ Attach to Form 1040 or Form 1041. ▶ See Instructions for Schedule C (Form 1040). | OMB No. 1545-0074
1993
Attachment
Sequence No. 09 |

Name of proprietor   Social security number (SSN)

A	Principal business or profession, including product or service (see page C-1)	B Enter principal business code (see page C-6) ▶
C	Business name. If no separate business name, leave blank.	D Employer ID number (EIN), if any

E Business address (including suite or room no.) ▶ ....
   City, town or post office, state, and ZIP code

F Accounting method: (1) ☐ Cash   (2) ☐ Accrual   (3) ☐ Other (specify) ▶ ....

G Method(s) used to   Lower of cost   Other (attach   Does not apply (if
   value closing inventory: (1) ☐ Cost (2) ☐ or market (3) ☐ explanation) (4) ☐ checked, skip line H)   Yes | No

H Was there any change in determining quantities, costs, or valuations between opening and closing inventory? If "Yes," attach
   explanation . . . .
I Did you "materially participate" in the operation of this business during 1993? If "No," see page C-2 for limit on losses. . .
J If you started or acquired this business during 1993, check here . . . . ▶ ☐

Part I Income

1	Gross receipts or sales. **Caution:** If this income was reported to you on Form W-2 and the "Statutory employee" box on that form was checked, see page C-2 and check here . . . . . . ▶ ☐	1	
2	Returns and allowances	2	
3	Subtract line 2 from line 1	3	
4	Cost of goods sold (from line 40 on page 2)	4	
5	**Gross profit.** Subtract line 4 from line 3	5	
6	Other income, including Federal and state gasoline or fuel tax credit or refund (see page C-2) . .	6	
7	**Gross income.** Add lines 5 and 6 . . . . ▶	7	

Part II Expenses. Caution: Do not enter expenses for business use of your home on lines 8–27. Instead, see line 30.

8	Advertising	8		19	Pension and profit-sharing plans	19	
9	Bad debts from sales or services (see page C-3) . .	9		20	Rent or lease (see page C-4):		
				a	Vehicles, machinery, and equipment .	20a	
10	Car and truck expenses (see page C-3)	10		b	Other business property . .	20b	
				21	Repairs and maintenance . .	21	
11	Commissions and fees. . .	11		22	Supplies (not included in Part III) .	22	
12	Depletion	12		23	Taxes and licenses . . .	23	
13	Depreciation and section 179 expense deduction (not included in Part III) (see page C-3) .	13		24	Travel, meals, and entertainment:		
				a	Travel	24a	
				b	Meals and entertainment .		
14	Employee benefit programs (other than on line 19) . . .	14		c	Enter 20% of line 24b subject to limitations (see page C-4) .		
15	Insurance (other than health) .	15					
16	Interest:						
a	Mortgage (paid to banks, etc.) .	16a		d	Subtract line 24c from line 24b .	24d	
b	Other	16b		25	Utilities	25	
17	Legal and professional services	17		26	Wages (less jobs credit) . .	26	
				27	Other expenses (from line 46 on page 2)	27	
18	Office expense	18					

28	**Total expenses** before expenses for business use of home. Add lines 8 through 27 in columns . . ▶	28	
29	Tentative profit (loss). Subtract line 28 from line 7	29	
30	Expenses for business use of your home. Attach **Form 8829**	30	
31	**Net profit or (loss).** Subtract line 30 from line 29. • If a profit, enter on **Form 1040, line 12,** and ALSO on **Schedule SE, line 2** (statutory employees, see page C-5). Fiduciaries, enter on Form 1041, line 3. • If a loss, you MUST go on to line 32.	31	
32	If you have a loss, check the box that describes your investment in this activity (see page C-5). • If you checked 32a, enter the loss on **Form 1040, line 12,** and ALSO on **Schedule SE, line 2** (statutory employees, see page C-5). Fiduciaries, enter on Form 1041, line 3. • If you checked 32b, you MUST attach **Form 6198.**	32a ☐ All investment is at risk. 32b ☐ Some investment is not at risk.	

For Paperwork Reduction Act Notice, see Form 1040 instructions.   Cat. No. 11334P   Schedule C (Form 1040) 1993

Copyright © 1994 by Harcourt Brace & Company. All rights reserved.

Schedule C (Form 1040) 1993 Page **2**

Part III Cost of Goods Sold (see page C-5)

33 Inventory at beginning of year. If different from last year's closing inventory, attach explanation	33
34 Purchases less cost of items withdrawn for personal use	34
35 Cost of labor. Do not include salary paid to yourself	35
36 Materials and supplies	36
37 Other costs	37
38 Add lines 33 through 37	38
39 Inventory at end of year	39
40 **Cost of goods sold.** Subtract line 39 from line 38. Enter the result here and on page 1, line 4	40

Part IV Information on Your Vehicle. Complete this part **ONLY** if you are claiming car or truck expenses on line 10 and are not required to file Form 4562 for this business.

41 When did you place your vehicle in service for business purposes? (month, day, year) ▶ ..../......../........

42 Of the total number of miles you drove your vehicle during 1993, enter the number of miles you used your vehicle for:

   a Business .... **b** Commuting .... **c** Other ....

43 Do you (or your spouse) have another vehicle available for personal use? . . . . ☐ Yes ☐ No

44 Was your vehicle available for use during off-duty hours? . . . . ☐ Yes ☐ No

45a Do you have evidence to support your deduction? . . . . ☐ Yes ☐ No
   b If "Yes," is the evidence written? . . . . ☐ Yes ☐ No

Part V Other Expenses. List below business expenses not included on lines 8–26 or line 30.

....	
....	
....	
....	
....	
....	
....	
....	
....	
46 **Total other expenses.** Enter here and on page 1, line 27	46

Printed on recycled paper

Comprehensive Tax Return Problem 4 Name_____ 8-95

SCHEDULE E (Form 1040)
Department of the Treasury
Internal Revenue Service

Supplemental Income and Loss
(From rental real estate, royalties, partnerships, S corporations, estates, trusts, REMICs, etc.)
▶ Attach to Form 1040 or Form 1041. ▶ See Instructions for Schedule E (Form 1040).

OMB No. 1545-0074

1993

Attachment Sequence No. 13

Name(s) shown on return

Your social security number

Part I — Income or Loss From Rental Real Estate and Royalties
Note: *Report income and expenses from your business of renting personal property on* **Schedule C** *or* **C-EZ** *(see page E-1). Report farm rental income or loss from* **Form 4835** *on page 2, line 39.*

1 Show the kind and location of each **rental real estate property**:	2 For each rental real estate property listed on line 1, did you or your family use it for personal purposes for more than the greater of 14 days or 10% of the total days rented at fair rental value during the tax year? (See page E-1.)	Yes	No
A	A		
B	B		
C	C		

Income:		Properties			Totals
		A	B	C	(Add columns A, B, and C.)
3 Rents received	3				3
4 Royalties received	4				4
Expenses:					
5 Advertising	5				
6 Auto and travel (see page E-2) .	6				
7 Cleaning and maintenance . .	7				
8 Commissions	8				
9 Insurance	9				
10 Legal and other professional fees	10				
11 Management fees	11				
12 Mortgage interest paid to banks, etc. (see page E-2)	12				12
13 Other interest	13				
14 Repairs	14				
15 Supplies	15				
16 Taxes	16				
17 Utilities	17				
18 Other (list) ▶	18				
19 Add lines 5 through 18 . . .	19				19
20 Depreciation expense or depletion (see page E-2)	20				20
21 Total expenses. Add lines 19 and 20	21				
22 Income or (loss) from rental real estate or royalty properties. Subtract line 21 from line 3 (rents) or line 4 (royalties). If the result is a (loss), see page E-2 to find out if you must file **Form 6198**. . .	22				
23 Deductible rental real estate loss. **Caution:** *Your rental real estate loss on line 22 may be limited. See page E-3 to find out if you must file* **Form 8582**	23	( )	( )	( )	
24 **Income.** Add positive amounts shown on line 22. **Do not** include any losses					24
25 **Losses.** Add royalty losses from line 22 and rental real estate losses from line 23. Enter the total losses here					25 ( )
26 **Total rental real estate and royalty income or (loss).** Combine lines 24 and 25. Enter the result here. If Parts II, III, IV, and line 39 on page 2 do not apply to you, also enter this amount on Form 1040, line 18. Otherwise, include this amount in the total on line 40 on page 2					26

For Paperwork Reduction Act Notice, see Form 1040 instructions.   Cat. No. 11344L   Schedule E (Form 1040) 1993

Copyright © 1994 by Harcourt Brace & Company. All rights reserved.

SCHEDULE SE
(Form 1040)

Department of the Treasury
Internal Revenue Service

Self-Employment Tax

▶ See Instructions for Schedule SE (Form 1040).
▶ Attach to Form 1040.

OMB No. 1545-0074

1993

Attachment
Sequence No. **17**

Name of person with **self-employment** income (as shown on Form 1040)	Social security number of person with **self-employment** income ▶	

Who Must File Schedule SE
You must file Schedule SE if:
- Your wages (and tips) subject to social security AND Medicare tax (or railroad retirement tax) were less than $135,000; **AND**
- Your net earnings from self-employment from other than church employee income (line 4 of Short Schedule SE or line 4c of Long Schedule SE) were $400 or more; **OR**
- You had church employee income of $108.28 or more. Income from services you performed as a minister or a member of a religious order **is not** church employee income. See page SE-1.

Note: *Even if you have a loss or a small amount of income from self-employment, it may be to your benefit to file Schedule SE and use either "optional method" in Part II of Long Schedule SE. See page SE-3.*

Exception. If your only self-employment income was from earnings as a minister, member of a religious order, or Christian Science practitioner, **AND** you filed Form 4361 and received IRS approval not to be taxed on those earnings, **DO NOT** file Schedule SE. Instead, write "Exempt–Form 4361" on Form 1040, line 47.

May I Use Short Schedule SE or MUST I Use Long Schedule SE?

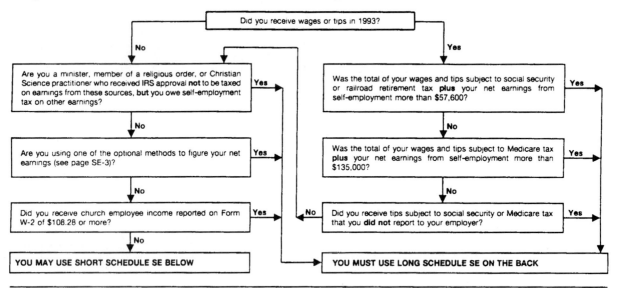

Section A—Short Schedule SE. Caution: *Read above to see if you can use Short Schedule SE.*

1	Net farm profit or (loss) from Schedule F, line 36, and farm partnerships, Schedule K-1 (Form 1065), line 15a	1
2	Net profit or (loss) from Schedule C, line 31; Schedule C-EZ, line 3; and Schedule K-1 (Form 1065), line 15a (other than farming). Ministers and members of religious orders see page SE-1 for amounts to report on this line. See page SE-2 for other income to report	2
3	Combine lines 1 and 2	3
4	**Net earnings from self-employment.** Multiply line 3 by 92.35% (.9235). If less than $400, **do not** file this schedule; you do not owe self-employment tax . . . . ▶	4
5	**Self-employment tax.** If the amount on line 4 is: • $57,600 or less, multiply line 4 by 15.3% (.153) and enter the result. • More than $57,600 but less than $135,000, multiply the amount in excess of $57,600 by 2.9% (.029). Then, add $8,812.80 to the result and enter the total. • $135,000 or more, enter $11,057.40. Also enter on **Form 1040, line 47. (Important:** You are allowed a deduction for **one-half** of this amount. Multiply line 5 by 50% (.5) and enter the result on **Form 1040, line 25.**)	5

For Paperwork Reduction Act Notice, see Form 1040 instructions.   Cat. No. 11358Z   Schedule SE (Form 1040) 1993

Comprehensive Tax Return Problem 4   Name _____   8-97

Form 4562
Department of the Treasury
Internal Revenue Service

Depreciation and Amortization
(Including Information on Listed Property)

▶ See separate instructions.   ▶ Attach this form to your return.

OMB No. 1545-0172
1993
Attachment Sequence No. **67**

Name(s) shown on return | Identifying number

Business or activity to which this form relates

Part I — Election To Expense Certain Tangible Property (Section 179) (Note: If you have any "Listed Property," complete Part V before you complete Part I.)

1	Maximum dollar limitation (If an enterprise zone business, see instructions.) **1**	$17,500
2	Total cost of section 179 property placed in service during the tax year (see instructions) .. **2**	
3	Threshold cost of section 179 property before reduction in limitation **3**	$200,000
4	Reduction in limitation. Subtract line 3 from line 2, but do not enter less than -0- **4**	
5	Dollar limitation for tax year. Subtract line 4 from line 1, but do not enter less than -0-. (If married filing separately, see instructions.) **5**	

(a) Description of property	(b) Cost	(c) Elected cost
6		

7	Listed property. Enter amount from line 26 .... **7**	
8	Total elected cost of section 179 property. Add amounts in column (c), lines 6 and 7 ... **8**	
9	Tentative deduction. Enter the smaller of line 5 or line 8 .... **9**	
10	Carryover of disallowed deduction from 1992 (see instructions) **10**	
11	Taxable income limitation. Enter the smaller of taxable income or line 5 (see instructions) .. **11**	
12	Section 179 expense deduction. Add lines 9 and 10, but do not enter more than line 11 ... **12**	
13	Carryover of disallowed deduction to 1994. Add lines 9 and 10, less line 12 ▶ **13**	

Note: *Do not use Part II or Part III below for listed property (automobiles, certain other vehicles, cellular telephones, certain computers, or property used for entertainment, recreation, or amusement). Instead, use Part V for listed property.*

Part II — MACRS Depreciation For Assets Placed in Service ONLY During Your 1993 Tax Year (Do Not Include Listed Property)

(a) Classification of property	(b) Month and year placed in service	(c) Basis for depreciation (business/investment use only—see instructions)	(d) Recovery period	(e) Convention	(f) Method	(g) Depreciation deduction
14 General Depreciation System (GDS) (see instructions):						
a 3-year property						
b 5-year property						
c 7-year property						
d 10-year property						
e 15-year property						
f 20-year property						
g Residential rental property			27.5 yrs.	MM	S/L	
			27.5 yrs.	MM	S/L	
h Nonresidential real property				MM	S/L	
				MM	S/L	
15 Alternative Depreciation System (ADS) (see instructions):						
a Class life					S/L	
b 12-year			12 yrs.		S/L	
c 40-year			40 yrs.	MM	S/L	

Part III — Other Depreciation (Do Not Include Listed Property)

16	GDS and ADS deductions for assets placed in service in tax years beginning before 1993 (see instructions)	**16**
17	Property subject to section 168(f)(1) election (see instructions)	**17**
18	ACRS and other depreciation (see instructions)	**18**

Part IV — Summary

19	Listed property. Enter amount from line 25	**19**
20	Total. Add deductions on line 12, lines 14 and 15 in column (g), and lines 16 through 19. Enter here and on the appropriate lines of your return. (Partnerships and S corporations—see instructions)	**20**
21	For assets shown above and placed in service during the current year, enter the portion of the basis attributable to section 263A costs (see instructions)	**21**

For Paperwork Reduction Act Notice, see page 1 of the separate instructions.   Cat. No. 12906N   Form **4562** (1993)

Copyright © 1994 by Harcourt Brace & Company. All rights reserved.

Form 4562 (1993) Page **2**

Part V — Listed Property—Automobiles, Certain Other Vehicles, Cellular Telephones, Certain Computers, and Property Used for Entertainment, Recreation, or Amusement

*For any vehicle for which you are using the standard mileage rate or deducting lease expense, complete **only** 22a, 22b, columns (a) through (c) of Section A, all of Section B, and Section C if applicable.*

Section A—Depreciation and Other Information (Caution: See instructions for limitations for automobiles.)

22a Do you have evidence to support the business/investment use claimed? ☐ Yes ☐ No 22b If "Yes," is the evidence written? ☐ Yes ☐ No

(a) Type of property (list vehicles first)	(b) Date placed in service	(c) Business/investment use percentage	(d) Cost or other basis	(e) Basis for depreciation (business/investment use only)	(f) Recovery period	(g) Method/Convention	(h) Depreciation deduction	(i) Elected section 179 cost
23 Property used more than 50% in a qualified business use (see instructions):								
		%						
		%						
		%						
24 Property used 50% or less in a qualified business use (see instructions):								
		%				S/L –		
		%				S/L –		
		%				S/L –		

25 Add amounts in column (h). Enter the total here and on line 19, page 1. . . . . . . **25**
26 Add amounts in column (i). Enter the total here and on line 7, page 1 . . . . **26**

Section B—Information Regarding Use of Vehicles—If you deduct expenses for vehicles:

- Always complete this section for vehicles used by a sole proprietor, partner, or other "more than 5% owner," or related person.
- If you provided vehicles to your employees, first answer the questions in Section C to see if you meet an exception to completing this section for those vehicles.

	(a) Vehicle 1		(b) Vehicle 2		(c) Vehicle 3		(d) Vehicle 4		(e) Vehicle 5		(f) Vehicle 6	
27 Total business/investment miles driven during the year (DO NOT include commuting miles)												
28 Total commuting miles driven during the year												
29 Total other personal (noncommuting) miles driven												
30 Total miles driven during the year. Add lines 27 through 29.												
	Yes	No	Yes	No	Yes	No	Yes	No	Yes	No	Yes	No
31 Was the vehicle available for personal use during off-duty hours?												
32 Was the vehicle used primarily by a more than 5% owner or related person?												
33 Is another vehicle available for personal use?												

Section C—Questions for Employers Who Provide Vehicles for Use by Their Employees

*Answer these questions to determine if you meet an exception to completing Section B. **Note:** Section B must always be completed for vehicles used by sole proprietors, partners, or other more than 5% owners or related persons.*

	Yes	No
34 Do you maintain a written policy statement that prohibits all personal use of vehicles, including commuting, by your employees?		
35 Do you maintain a written policy statement that prohibits personal use of vehicles, except commuting, by your employees? (See instructions for vehicles used by corporate officers, directors, or 1% or more owners.)		
36 Do you treat all use of vehicles by employees as personal use?		
37 Do you provide more than five vehicles to your employees and retain the information received from your employees concerning the use of the vehicles?		
38 Do you meet the requirements concerning qualified automobile demonstration use (see instructions)? . .		

Note: *If your answer to 34, 35, 36, 37, or 38 is "Yes," you need not complete Section B for the covered vehicles.*

Part VI — Amortization

(a) Description of costs	(b) Date amortization begins	(c) Amortizable amount	(d) Code section	(e) Amortization period or percentage	(f) Amortization for this year
39 Amortization of costs that begins during your 1993 tax year:					

40 Amortization of costs that began before 1993 . . . . **40**
41 **Total.** Enter here and on "Other Deductions" or "Other Expenses" line of your return . . . **41**

Comprehensive Tax Return Problem 4   Name_____8-99

Form 4562
Department of the Treasury
Internal Revenue Service

Depreciation and Amortization
(Including Information on Listed Property)

▶ See separate instructions.   ▶ Attach this form to your return.

OMB No. 1545-0172
1993
Attachment Sequence No. 67

Name(s) shown on return | Identifying number

Business or activity to which this form relates

Part I — Election To Expense Certain Tangible Property (Section 179) (Note: *If you have any "Listed Property," complete Part V before you complete Part I.*)

1	Maximum dollar limitation (If an enterprise zone business, see instructions.) **1**	$17,500
2	Total cost of section 179 property placed in service during the tax year (see instructions) .. **2**	
3	Threshold cost of section 179 property before reduction in limitation **3**	$200,000
4	Reduction in limitation. Subtract line 3 from line 2, but do not enter less than -0- **4**	
5	Dollar limitation for tax year. Subtract line 4 from line 1, but do not enter less than -0-. (If married filing separately, see instructions.) **5**	

(a) Description of property	(b) Cost	(c) Elected cost
6		

7	Listed property. Enter amount from line 26. ...... **7**	
8	Total elected cost of section 179 property. Add amounts in column (c), lines 6 and 7 ... **8**	
9	Tentative deduction. Enter the smaller of line 5 or line 8 .... **9**	
10	Carryover of disallowed deduction from 1992 (see instructions). **10**	
11	Taxable income limitation. Enter the smaller of taxable income or line 5 (see instructions) .. **11**	
12	Section 179 expense deduction. Add lines 9 and 10, but do not enter more than line 11 .. **12**	
13	Carryover of disallowed deduction to 1994. Add lines 9 and 10, less line 12 ▶ **13**	

Note: *Do not use Part II or Part III below for listed property (automobiles, certain other vehicles, cellular telephones, certain computers, or property used for entertainment, recreation, or amusement). Instead, use Part V for listed property.*

Part II — MACRS Depreciation For Assets Placed in Service ONLY During Your 1993 Tax Year (Do Not Include Listed Property)

(a) Classification of property	(b) Month and year placed in service	(c) Basis for depreciation (business/investment use only—see instructions)	(d) Recovery period	(e) Convention	(f) Method	(g) Depreciation deduction
14 General Depreciation System (GDS) (see instructions):						
a 3-year property						
b 5-year property						
c 7-year property						
d 10-year property						
e 15-year property						
f 20-year property						
g Residential rental property			27.5 yrs.	MM	S/L	
			27.5 yrs.	MM	S/L	
h Nonresidential real property				MM	S/L	
				MM	S/L	
15 Alternative Depreciation System (ADS) (see instructions):						
a Class life					S/L	
b 12-year			12 yrs.		S/L	
c 40-year			40 yrs.	MM	S/L	

Part III — Other Depreciation (Do Not Include Listed Property)

16	GDS and ADS deductions for assets placed in service in tax years beginning before 1993 (see instructions) **16**	
17	Property subject to section 168(f)(1) election (see instructions) **17**	
18	ACRS and other depreciation (see instructions) **18**	

Part IV — Summary

19	Listed property. Enter amount from line 25. .... **19**	
20	Total. Add deductions on line 12, lines 14 and 15 in column (g), and lines 16 through 19. Enter here and on the appropriate lines of your return. (Partnerships and S corporations—see instructions) **20**	
21	For assets shown above and placed in service during the current year, enter the portion of the basis attributable to section 263A costs (see instructions) **21**	

For Paperwork Reduction Act Notice, see page 1 of the separate instructions.   Cat. No. 12906N   Form **4562** (1993)

Copyright © 1994 by Harcourt Brace & Company. All rights reserved.

Form 4562 (1993) Page 2

Part V — Listed Property—Automobiles, Certain Other Vehicles, Cellular Telephones, Certain Computers, and Property Used for Entertainment, Recreation, or Amusement

For any vehicle for which you are using the standard mileage rate or deducting lease expense, complete only 22a, 22b, columns (a) through (c) of Section A, all of Section B, and Section C if applicable.

Section A—Depreciation and Other Information (Caution: See instructions for limitations for automobiles.)

22a Do you have evidence to support the business/investment use claimed? ☐ Yes ☐ No   22b If "Yes," is the evidence written? ☐ Yes ☐ No

(a) Type of property (list vehicles first)	(b) Date placed in service	(c) Business/investment use percentage	(d) Cost or other basis	(e) Basis for depreciation (business/investment use only)	(f) Recovery period	(g) Method/ Convention	(h) Depreciation deduction	(i) Elected section 179 cost
23 Property used more than 50% in a qualified business use (see instructions):								
		%						
		%						
		%						
24 Property used 50% or less in a qualified business use (see instructions):								
		%				S/L –		
		%				S/L –		
		%				S/L –		

25 Add amounts in column (h). Enter the total here and on line 19, page 1 . . . . . . | 25 |
26 Add amounts in column (i). Enter the total here and on line 7, page 1 . . . . | 26 |

Section B—Information Regarding Use of Vehicles—If you deduct expenses for vehicles:

- Always complete this section for vehicles used by a sole proprietor, partner, or other "more than 5% owner," or related person.
- If you provided vehicles to your employees, first answer the questions in Section C to see if you meet an exception to completing this section for those vehicles.

	(a) Vehicle 1		(b) Vehicle 2		(c) Vehicle 3		(d) Vehicle 4		(e) Vehicle 5		(f) Vehicle 6	
27 Total business/investment miles driven during the year (DO NOT include commuting miles)												
28 Total commuting miles driven during the year												
29 Total other personal (noncommuting) miles driven												
30 Total miles driven during the year. Add lines 27 through 29												
	Yes	No	Yes	No	Yes	No	Yes	No	Yes	No	Yes	No
31 Was the vehicle available for personal use during off-duty hours?												
32 Was the vehicle used primarily by a more than 5% owner or related person?												
33 Is another vehicle available for personal use?												

Section C—Questions for Employers Who Provide Vehicles for Use by Their Employees

Answer these questions to determine if you meet an exception to completing Section B. Note: Section B must always be completed for vehicles used by sole proprietors, partners, or other more than 5% owners or related persons.

	Yes	No
34 Do you maintain a written policy statement that prohibits all personal use of vehicles, including commuting, by your employees?		
35 Do you maintain a written policy statement that prohibits personal use of vehicles, except commuting, by your employees? (See instructions for vehicles used by corporate officers, directors, or 1% or more owners.)		
36 Do you treat all use of vehicles by employees as personal use?		
37 Do you provide more than five vehicles to your employees and retain the information received from your employees concerning the use of the vehicles?		
38 Do you meet the requirements concerning qualified automobile demonstration use (see instructions)? . .		

Note: *If your answer to 34, 35, 36, 37, or 38 is "Yes," you need not complete Section B for the covered vehicles.*

Part VI — Amortization

(a) Description of costs	(b) Date amortization begins	(c) Amortizable amount	(d) Code section	(e) Amortization period or percentage	(f) Amortization for this year
39 Amortization of costs that begins during your 1993 tax year:					
40 Amortization of costs that began before 1993				40	
41 **Total.** Enter here and on "Other Deductions" or "Other Expenses" line of your return . . .				41	

CHAPTER 9

Special Computations and Credits for Business Taxpayers

Under an all-inclusive concept of gross income, property transactions that result in increases or decreases in the wealth of a business would all have tax implications. Congress has provided, however, for certain specific exceptions to income and loss recognition for certain business transactions.

To understand the concept of nonrecognition, we must first review the difference between income realization and income recognition. Income realization is a transactions-based concept (i.e., if there is a transaction or event that results in a change in a business's wealth, then there is realization as measured by this change). For example, when a sole proprietor sells land purchased ten years ago and used in the business, there is a market transaction. The change in wealth is measured by the difference between the selling price and the original purchase price. Although the price of the land most probably has either increased or decreased gradually over the ten years it was owned, this increase or decrease in wealth is realized and measured only at the time of the sale transaction.

Whether that income or loss is recognized for tax purposes is a function of the tax laws. Due to the all-inclusive concept of income, unless a specific provision permits a realized gain or loss to go unrecognized, recognition is triggered by a realization transaction. And while the most familiar realization transaction is a sale, several other occurrences, such as exchanges, abandonments, condemnations, and casualties, are considered realization events as well.

Many nonrecognition provisions for realized gains take into consideration the taxpayer's economic status or ability to pay. For example, if a taxpayer sells a personal residence and invests an equal or greater amount in a new residence, gain is not recognized because the taxpayer's economic status has not improved as discussed in Chapter 6. If a sole proprietor exchanges one piece of equipment for another, his or her economic status may not have changed. However, if taxes must be paid because of the gain on the exchange of the equipment, the sole proprietor would be worse off economically. When the taxpayer makes an exchange of business property that meets certain conditions, the law permits nonrecognition of gain. Because the taxpayer doesn't recognize gain, no taxes need be paid, and the taxpayer is in the same economic condition as before.

Other provisions in the law require recognition of specific types of income (e.g., the sale of a capital asset at a gain gives rise to capital gain rather than ordinary income). The sale of business-use property results in either Sec. 1231 gain or loss, which may be treated as a capital gain or ordinary loss, due to some complex rules that apply to business property. While the distinction between capital and ordinary income has been blurred with the prior repeal of favorable capital gains treatment (a reduced capital gains tax rate for individuals has crept back into the law, however), it is still essential to distinguish between capital and ordinary income and losses, because the deductibility of capital losses is limited.

Finally, the tax laws are often used to encourage certain taxpayer behaviors. Often this encouragement is provided through a system of tax credits. For example, credits are provided for the use of alternative fuel sources, for rehabilitating certain structures, and for employing persons who may have difficulty finding jobs.

This chapter deals with some of the more important nonrecognition provisions, as well as some other specialized recognition provisions applicable to businesses. Parts I and II examine the provisions covering like-kind exchanges and involuntary conversions. Parts III and IV explore the details of the types of income recognition required on the sale of depreciable business and investment property. Part V examines the various business credits available to taxpayers. The Appendices present the concept of net operating losses for individual taxpayers and briefly review the now-expired provisions of the regular investment tax credit.

I LIKE-KIND EXCHANGES
(Code Sections 1031 and 1044)

When taxpayers trade one piece of property for another, has there been a change in economic status? Are the taxpayers in a position to pay taxes on a realized gain? Similarly, should a realized loss give rise to a recognized loss? The like-kind exchange provisions of Section 1031 answer these questions by providing for nonrecognition of *gain* and *loss* on exchange transactions meeting certain specified criteria.

THE LAW

Sec. 1031(a)(1)—Nonrecognition of Gain or Loss from Exchanges Solely in Kind—No gain or loss shall be recognized on the exchange of property held for productive use in a trade or business or for investment if such property is exchanged solely for property of a like kind which is to be held either for productive use in a trade or business or for investment.

The first requirement of the like-kind exchange provision is that the property exchanged must be business or investment property and the property received in the exchange must subsequently be held for business or investment purposes. No personal use property qualifies for this nonrecognition provision.

 Example 1. Winston Quick exchanges his family automobile for a truck that he will use in a messenger business he is starting. This transaction will not qualify for nonrecognition because the property exchanged is personal use property and has not been used in a trade or business.

Although the properties exchanged must be business or investment properties, business property may be exchanged for investment property and investment property may be exchanged for business property.

☑ **Example 2.** Amy Clarke exchanges a piece of undeveloped land she held as an investment for a building located in a shopping center in which she plans to relocate her restaurant. This exchange qualifies for nonrecognition treatment.

Prior to the issuance of regulations in 1991, the definition of property eligible for the like-kind recognition provisions was very broad; that is, as long as the properties were business or investment assets, any piece of realty could be exchanged for any other piece of realty. Any piece of personalty could be exchanged for any other piece of personalty. *Personalty* is a term that encompasses all other property not defined as realty (real property). The 1991 regulations greatly limit this flexibility for personalty, however, because like-kind now refers to property "of the same class." While all real property is considered "of the same class," personalty is divided into classes that are used to determine the depreciation deductions for tangible depreciable property. As a result, computers cannot be exchanged for trucks, automobiles for light trucks, nor office furniture and equipment for computers, since each of these items falls into a separate class for depreciation purposes—and thus are not of like kind. If the tangible depreciable property does not have a specific class assigned for depreciation purposes, then the SIC (Standard Industrial Classification) Code is used to determine classes.

Intangible assets, nondepreciable personalty, and personalty held for investment purposes are not assigned to classes. They pose particular problems when determining their eligibility for like-kind exchange nonrecognition, which are beyond the scope of this discussion.

☑ **Example 3.** Simeon Walsh exchanges typewriters used in his insurance business for a duplicating machine. Assuming the equipment will be used in his trade or business, the exchange qualifies as a like-kind exchange since all properties are in the office equipment class.

EXCEPTIONS TO NONRECOGNITION

In addition to the above restrictions, Sec. 1031(a)(2) sets forth several specific types of property that are not eligible for nonrecognition treatment. These exceptions include

1. stock in trade or other property held primarily for sale
2. stock, bonds, or notes (except as noted later)
3. other securities or evidences of indebtedness or interest
4. interests in a partnership

If a taxpayer wants to enter into an exchange involving inventory or investment securities, the above exceptions would force recognition of any realized gain or loss (unless unrecognized because of another provision). While there had been much controversy over the exchange of partnership interests, the law is now clear; it does not permit the exchange of limited or general partnership interests, regardless of the nature of the properties held by the partnership. Sec. 1031(e) provides one other exception to nonrecognition property—cattle of the opposite sex are not like-kind property. Thus, a cow may not be exchanged for a bull.

☑ **Example 4.** Margo White exchanged a block of 1,000 shares of IBM stock that she purchased 12 years ago at $12,000 for a block of 1,000 shares of Xerox stock currently selling at $21,000. Although the shares are similar, Margo must recognize the $9,000 gain on the exchange because exchanges of stock are ineligible for like-kind exchange treatment.

TAX TIP

A taxpayer should generally avoid a like-kind exchange if loss property is involved. If the property is *sold* rather than exchanged, the realized loss can be recognized (unless some other nonrecognition provision applies).

REALIZED GAINS AND LOSSES

Although gains and losses are not *recognized* on exchanges solely of qualifying like-kind property, taxpayers must be aware of any gain or loss if the basis of the property surrendered is different than the fair market value of the property received. Regardless of any nonrecognition provision, if the fair market value of property received is greater than the surrendered property's basis, gain is realized. If the fair market value is less than the basis, loss is realized.

Cash and Fair Market Value of Property Received
– Basis of Property Surrendered
Gain (Loss) Realized

☑ **Example 5.** Jim Pruitt exchanged office furniture (fair market value = $2,000; basis = $1,000) for a used computer (fair market value = $2,000; basis = $2,500) that Nancy Peal used in her business. Since only like-kind property is exchanged, neither Jim nor Nancy will recognize the gain or loss. Jim has a realized but unrecognized gain of $1,000 ($2,000 fair market value of the computer less $1,000 basis in furniture). Nancy has a $500 realized but unrecognized loss ($2,000 fair market value of furniture less the $2,500 basis in the computer).

There are two primary reasons for determining realized gains and losses on like-kind exchanges: (1) the basis of the property received must be adjusted due to the nonrecognition, as discussed later and (2) if some of the property exchanged is not qualified property (boot), then all or a portion of the realized gain may have to be recognized. In no instance, however, can the *recognized* gain exceed the *realized* gain.

EFFECT OF BOOT

Sec. 1031(a) provides nonrecognition only if business or investment property is exchanged *solely* for qualified like-kind property. Sec. 1031(b), however, permits the receipt of other property in addition to the like-kind property without making the whole transaction taxable.

This is the typical "boot" provision found in this and many other nonrecognition provisions. As long as all of the property exchanged qualifies for nonrecognition, no problems arise. As soon as any money or other nonqualifying property is exchanged, the

THE LAW

Sec. 1031(b)—Gain from Exchanges Not Solely In Kind—If an exchange would be within the provisions of subsection (a),... if it were not for the fact that the property received in exchange consists not only of property permitted by such provisions to be received without the recognition of gain, but also of other property or money, then the gain, if any, to the recipient shall be recognized, but in an amount not in excess of the sum of such money and the fair market value of such other property.

party who *receives* this "boot" may have to recognize all or part of the realized gain. Boot is any property that does not qualify as like-kind property or that is not the requisite business or investment property. Boot represents something of value with which the taxpayer can pay taxes. We must stress, however, that no gain can be recognized if there is no gain realized, nor will the gain recognized exceed the value of the boot received. Thus, to determine the amount of gain recognized, both the value of the boot and the amount of the realized gain must be determined. The gain recognized is the *lesser* of the fair market value of boot received or the realized gain.

Example 6. Myron Davidson exchanged a rental apartment building for a piece of land in Arizona and cash of $40,000. The building has a basis of $356,000 and a fair market value of $520,000. The land is appraised at $480,000, so Myron insisted on $40,000 cash to conclude the transaction. Myron's realized gain on the transaction is $164,000 ($520,000 − $356,000). Myron received only $40,000 of boot, however. He must recognize $40,000 of the $164,000 realized gain. The result would be the same if Myron had received any property other than business or investment real property valued at $40,000. Form 8824 reflecting this information is shown in Figure 9-1.

Example 7. Brad Jones has six old light delivery trucks that he exchanges for three newer light trucks and an automobile. He gives the auto to his wife for her personal use. The old delivery trucks have a basis of $23,000 and the three trucks and auto have a fair market value of $38,000. Brad has a realized gain of $15,000. If the auto has a fair market value of more than $15,000, Brad will recognize a maximum of $15,000 gain. If the auto is worth less than $15,000, then the value of the auto (boot) is the maximum amount of gain that Brad will have to recognize.

Any liabilities of the taxpayer assumed by the other party to the transaction are to be considered money received by the taxpayer, and, as a result, are considered boot. If, however, the taxpayer also assumes liabilities of the other party, this represents boot given. Liabilities exchanged on a like-kind exchange may offset one another, yielding either a net liability (boot) received or a net liability (boot) given. If the taxpayer has net boot received (the other party assumes the greater amount of liabilities), the taxpayer is considered to have received money in the amount of this excess net boot, causing gain recognition. Net boot given does not give rise to gain recognition, however.

Example 8. Felix Jones and Maria Smith exchanged some business realty, each assuming the other's mortgage on the transaction. Felix's property had a basis of $100,000, a fair market value of $125,000, and a mortgage of $50,000. Maria's property had a basis of $130,000, a fair market value of $150,000, and a mortgage of $75,000.

Form 8824 — Like-Kind Exchanges (and nonrecognition of gain from conflict-of-interest sales)

OMB No. 1545-1190
1992
Attachment Sequence No. 49

Department of the Treasury — Internal Revenue Service
► See separate instructions.   ► Attach to your tax return.
► Use a separate form for each like-kind exchange.

Name(s) shown on tax return: Myron Davidson
Identifying number:

Part I — Information on the Like-Kind Exchange

Note: If the property described on line 1 or line 2 is real property located outside the United States, indicate the country.

1. Description of like-kind property given up ► Rental Apartment Building
2. Description of like-kind property received ► Land in Arizona

Part II — Realized Gain or (Loss), Recognized Gain, and Basis of Like-Kind Property Received

Caution: If you transferred and received (a) more than one group of like-kind properties, or (b) cash or other (not like-kind) property, see instructions under Multi-Asset Exchanges.

Note: Complete lines 12 through 14 ONLY if you gave up property that was not like-kind. Otherwise, go to line 15.

12	Fair market value (FMV) of other property given up	
13	Adjusted basis of other property given up	
14	Gain or (loss) recognized on other property given up. Subtract line 13 from line 12. Report the gain or (loss) in the same manner as if the exchange had been a sale	
15	Cash received, FMV of other property received, plus net liabilities assumed by other party, reduced (but not below zero) by any exchange expenses you incurred. See instructions	40,000
16	FMV of like-kind property you received	480,000
17	Add lines 15 and 16	520,000
18	Adjusted basis of like-kind property you gave up, net amounts paid to other party, plus any exchange expenses not used on line 15. See instructions	356,000
19	**Realized gain or (loss).** Subtract line 18 from line 17	164,000
20	Enter the smaller of line 15 or line 19, but not less than zero	40,000
21	Ordinary income under recapture rules. Enter here and on Form 4797, line 17. See instructions	
22	Subtract line 21 from line 20. If zero or less, enter -0-. If more than zero, enter here and on Schedule D or Form 4797, unless the installment method applies. See instructions	40,000
23	**Recognized gain.** Add lines 21 and 22	40,000
24	Deferred gain or (loss). Subtract line 23 from line 19. If a related party exchange, see instructions	124,000
25	Basis of like-kind property received. Subtract line 15 from the sum of lines 18 and 23	356,000

For Paperwork Reduction Act Notice, see separate instructions.   Cat. No. 12311A   Form **8824** (1992)

1993 form not available at press time.

Figure 9-1   Form 8824

Felix's gain on the transaction is $25,000 (amount realized of $125,000 [$150,000 + $50,000 liability surrendered − $75,000 liability assumed] less the basis of $100,000).

Since Felix assumed Maria's mortgage in excess of the mortgage assumed *by* Maria, he receives no money (boot) on the transaction and recognizes no gain. Maria, on the other hand, has a realized gain of $20,000 (amount realized of $150,000 [$125,000 + $75,000 liability surrendered − $50,000 liability assumed] less the basis of $130,000). Felix assumed Maria's mortgage of $75,000 while Maria assumed Felix's $50,000 mortgage. Maria is considered to have received the excess, $25,000, as cash (boot). Maria must recognize a gain of $20,000—the lesser of the boot received ($25,000) or the realized gain ($20,000)—on the transaction.

TAX TIP

A taxpayer who needs cash should complete a contemplated exchange first and then obtain a mortgage on the newly exchanged property. If the taxpayer obtained a mortgage on the old property, the assumption of the mortgage by the other party to the exchange could trigger gain recognition.

Only boot in the form of *liabilities assumed* by the parties to a like-kind exchange may be offset against one another to determine a net amount. Other forms of boot given and received do *not* offset one another. The total *boot* received must be considered in gain recognition. Moreover, any boot given by the taxpayer (that is, property that does not qualify for like-kind exchange treatment) is considered *sold* and could result in gain or loss recognition generally for that property.

Sec. 1031(c) specifically provides that if there is a loss realized on a like-kind exchange involving boot, no loss will be recognized. The receipt of boot can trigger only gain recognition. If there is a loss on a qualifying like-kind exchange, it is never recognized.

☑ **Example 9.** Willard Andrews trades office furniture with a basis of $4,000 for office equipment worth $2,000 and $1,000 cash. Willard has a realized loss on the transaction of $1,000. Even though he received boot of $1,000, *no loss is recognized*.

BASIS

Because property, other than boot, received in a like-kind exchange must be business or investment property, it is necessary to determine its basis. If it is depreciable property, the basis must be known for future depreciation deductions. This would also be true for property subject to depletion or amortization. In addition, it is necessary to establish basis so that the gain or loss can be determined on any subsequent disposition.

THE LAW

Sec. 1031(d)—Basis—If property was acquired on an exchange described in this section, . . . then the basis shall be the same as that of the property exchanged, decreased in the amount of any money received by the taxpayer and increased in the amount of gain or decreased in the amount of loss to the taxpayer that was recognized on such exchange. If the property so acquired consisted in part of the type of property permitted by this section, . . . to be received without the recognition of gain or loss, and in part of other property, the basis provided in this subsection shall be allocated between the properties (other than money) received, and for the purpose of the allocation there shall be assigned to such other property an amount equivalent to its fair market value at the date of the exchange.

The basis of like-kind property received in a like-kind exchange is a carryover basis (i.e., the basis of the property surrendered carries over in whole or in part to the property received). This carryover basis must be adjusted to reflect the other characteristics of the transaction, however. In determining the basis of the property received, the basis of the property surrendered must be *increased* by any gain recognized on the transaction and the fair market value of boot *paid* and *decreased* by the fair market value of boot *received*. In this calculation, *all* liabilities are treated as boot.

    Basis of Like-Kind Property Surrendered
    + Fair Market Value of Nonlike-Kind Property Surrendered (Boot Given)
    + Liabilities Assumed by Seller (Treated as Cash Given)

+ Gain Recognized on Like-Kind Property
　　− Fair Market Value of Nonlike-Kind Property Received (Boot Received)
　　− Liabilities Assumed by Buyer (Treated as Cash Received)
　　Basis of Like-Kind Property Received

> ✓ **Example 10.** Angela Rossi exchanged two computers with a basis of $5,000 for a new computer system worth $8,000, which was subject to a loan of $2,000 that she assumed, and $1,000 in cash. Angela's realized gain is $2,000 (amount realized of $7,000 [$8,000 − $2,000 liability assumed + $1,000 cash] less basis of $5,000). Her recognized gain is only $1,000. Angela's basis in the computer system is $7,000 ($5,000 carryover basis + $2,000 liability assumed + $1,000 gain recognized − $1,000 cash received).

There is a short-cut method to determine the basis of the like-kind property received in a qualifying exchange. The basis is the fair market value of the property received, decreased by the unrecognized gain or increased by the unrecognized loss.

　　Fair Market Value of Property Received in Exchange
　　− Unrecognized Gain or
　　+ Unrecognized Loss
　　Basis of Like-Kind Property Received

Applying this short-cut method to the preceding example yields the same basis of $7,000 ($8,000 fair market value of the truck decreased by the $1,000 of realized but unrecognized gain).

Money received in an exchange always has its face value as basis. All other nonqualifying property (boot) in a like-kind exchange takes its fair market value as its basis.

THREE-PARTY AND DEFERRED EXCHANGES

If two taxpayers can agree to a direct and simultaneous exchange of business or investment properties, the use of the like-kind exchange provisions poses little difficulty. Often, however, it may be necessary for more than two parties to become involved in an exchange of properties. For example, A and B may both wish to exchange their business or investment assets rather than selling them; unfortunately, although B would like A's property, A does not want B's property. C, however, would like B's property and C has a property that A finds attractive. As a result, a "three-corner" simultaneous exchange occurs as follows: A transfers his property to B, B transfers his property to C, and C transfers his property to A. Each party qualifies for like-kind exchange treatment if the properties meet the above like-kind requirements. Each party determines the realized gain, recognized gain, and basis in the property received in the same manner as detailed for the direct two-party exchange.

Nonsimultaneous exchanges may also qualify for the like-kind exchange treatment if certain specific conditions are met:

1. The property to be acquired must be identified within 45 days of the disposition of the unwanted property.

2. The property must actually be acquired within 180 days (or by the due date of the taxpayer's return, if earlier).

3. The taxpayer must not have access to the proceeds from the disposition of the unwanted property.

✓ **Example 11.** Janice Slow has a building that is no longer used in her business. She knows there is land available outside the city on which she can relocate the business. She finds a buyer for her building but she would prefer not to recognize the gain by using the like-kind exchange rules. The buyer wants the building immediately, however, so Janice sells the building on April 1. All of the proceeds are placed with an escrow agent, out of Janice's reach, while she locates a suitable piece of land. If Janice identifies the land by May 16 (45 days) and actually acquires it by September 28 (180 days) with the funds held in escrow, the nonsimultaneous transfer qualifies as a like-kind exchange.

INVESTMENT IN SPECIALIZED SMALL BUSINESS INVESTMENT COMPANIES

THE LAW

Sec. 1044 (a)—Nonrecognition of Gain—In the case of the sale of any publicly traded securities . . . , gain from such a sale shall be recognized only to the extent that the amount realized on such sale exceeds (1) the cost of any common stock or partnership interest in a specialized small business investment company purchased by the taxpayer during the 60-day period beginning on the day of such sale, reduced by (2) any portion of such cost previously taken into account under this section. This section shall not apply to any gain which is treated as ordinary income for the purposes of this subtitle.

The Revenue Reconciliation Act of 1993 added Sec. 1044 which provides for the limited tax-free exchange of certain investments. To encourage investment in small businesses, individuals and C corporations may defer recognition of *capital* gain on the sale of publicly-traded securities to the extent the proceeds are reinvested in specialized small business investment companies (SSBIC) within 60 days of the date of sale. An SSBIC is a partnership or corporation licensed by the Small Business Administration Act of 1958 as effective on May 13, 1993. The amount of gain eligible to be rolled over by an individual is the lesser of $50,000 or $500,000 less any gain previously excluded. If the individual is married filing separately, the eligible gain is the lesser of $25,000 or $250,000 less any previously excluded gain. A corporation may exclude the lesser of $250,000 or $1,000,000 less any previously excluded gain. This provision does not apply to partnerships, S corporations, or estates of trusts. It only applies to gain realized on or after August 10, 1993.

REVIEW I

1. Albert Allen exchanged 100 shares of Alco stock (valued at $4,000) for 50 shares of Stevens Corporation (also valued at $4,000), both publicly traded stocks. He then exchanged a building that he used in his business for land to be used as a future plant site worth $250,000. Albert had a $2,500 basis in the Alco stock and a $125,000 basis in the building. What is his realized and recognized gain on these two exchanges?

(a) $0
(b) $125,000 realized and recognized gain
(c) $126,500 realized gain; $1,500 recognized gain
(d) $126,500 realized gain; $126,500 recognized gain

2. Jeremy Sludge exchanged a tractor and trailer that had a basis of $6,800 for some machinery worth $10,000 and $2,000 cash. What is his recognized gain on the exchange?
(a) $0
(b) $2,000
(c) $5,200
(d) $12,000

3. Margaret Walsh exchanged three old computers and $500 cash for a new computer worth $7,000 for use in her business. She had a $1,500 basis in the computers. What is her recognized gain on the exchange?
(a) $0
(b) $500
(c) $5,000
(d) $5,500

4. Donald Dull exchanged an apartment building with a $200,000 mortgage and a basis of $300,000 for a tract of land on which he planned to develop a shopping center. The land was worth $800,000, and he assumed a $300,000 mortgage. What is his realized and recognized gain?
(a) $400,000 realized; $0 recognized
(b) $700,000 realized; $0 recognized
(c) $400,000 realized; $400,000 recognized
(d) $700,000 realized; $300,000 recognized

Answers are on page 9-12.

II INVOLUNTARY CONVERSIONS
(Code Section 1033)

Certain events not under a taxpayer's control may result in the disposition of one piece of property and replacement with another. While these events may lead to realization of gain, the taxpayer's economic condition may be such that paying taxes on the gain would be a hardship. Recognizing this, Congress has defined certain events as involuntary conversions and permits the taxpayer to elect nonrecognition of *gain* if certain requirements are met. *Losses* on involuntary conversions are recognized, however, unless some other law prohibits or limits the deduction. Sec. 1033 provides for the elective nonrecognition of *gain* only.

THE LAW

Sec. 1033(a)—General Rule—If property (as a result of its destruction in whole or in part, theft, seizure, or requisition or condemnation or threat or imminence thereof) is compulsorily or involuntarily converted—(1) Into property similar or related in service or use to the property so converted, no gain shall be recognized. (2) Into money or into property not similar or related in service or use to the converted property, the gain (if any) shall be recognized except to the extent hereinafter provided. . . .

Involuntary conversions encompass a number of events including destruction, theft, requisition, and condemnation. In the context of an involuntary conversion, destruction has the same meaning it has under casualty and theft losses except that the suddenness test does not have to be met. Thus, while "slow" damage from termites does not qualify for the casualty loss deduction, the replacement of property due to the termite damage would qualify for nonrecognition of gain as an involuntary conversion. In order to be considered a seizure, requisition, or condemnation, property must be taken without the taxpayer's consent by an agency authorized to so seize property, it must be taken for the public good, and the taxpayer must be compensated for the seizure.

☑ **Example 12.** A 50-foot-wide frontage strip along a narrow highway was condemned so that the highway could be widened into six lanes. Each of the property owners was compensated by the highway department that had the authority to so condemn. This constitutes a condemnation eligible for nonrecognition by those taxpayers who meet the replacement requirements.

Because involuntary conversions cover a broad range of events, it is not uncommon to have realized gain. For casualties and thefts, the proceeds from insurance coverage generally constitute the amount realized for the determination of gain. If the amount of the loss, as measured for tax purposes, on the converted property is less than the insurance settlement, then gain is realized. In condemnation proceedings, payment by the governmental agency is the amount realized. Again, if the payment is greater than the amount of the loss, gain is realized. Several rules must be followed in measuring the amount of the loss:

1. The loss on property that is not completely destroyed is measured by the *lesser* of the difference in the property's fair market value of the property before and after the involuntary conversion or the property's adjusted basis.

2. If business property is entirely destroyed or condemned, the loss is *always* the property's adjusted basis.

3. If personal use property is entirely destroyed or condemned, loss is measured by the *lesser* of the property's adjusted basis or the its fair market value just prior to the loss.

If the insurance payment or other payments received as compensation for an involuntary conversion are less than the measure of the loss, then the taxpayer has a realized loss. Losses, however, would be recognized under this provision unless some other nonrecognition provision is encountered. Gains and losses from casualties and thefts are reported on Form 4684; gains and losses from involuntary conversions other than casualties and thefts are reported on Form 4797. Only gains that do not qualify for nonrecognition would be reported, however.

Involuntary conversions are normally reported in the year they occur and thefts in the year of discovery. If, however, the loss is from a casualty in an area designated by the President as a disaster area, the taxpayer electively may deduct the loss in the tax year immediately preceding the year of actual loss. This permits the taxpayer to reduce the prior year's income (and thus taxes) for the loss, allowing some measure of immediate relief.

☑ **Example 13.** Joe Black's bulldozer was stolen. He had acquired the bulldozer several years ago for $20,000, depreciating it so that its basis and value were only $11,000. Fortunately, Joe had replacement cost coverage on his insurance policy and was compensated for the loss based on its current replacement price of $23,000. Joe has a realized gain of $12,000 on the theft. He will not have to recognize the gain if he invests the proceeds in similar replacement property. If Joe received less than $11,000 from the insurance company, he would have a loss on the property that would be recognized, even though he invests in similar use property.

If only part of a piece of property is condemned but the whole piece constitutes a single economic unit, the taxpayer may voluntarily sell the rest of the property and apply the nonrecognition provisions to the whole unit to the extent the taxpayer invests in replacement property.

✓ **Example 14.** After a partial strip of land constituting a major portion of a parking lot was condemned, Sandra Block decided to sell the remaining portion, because she no longer had enough land to profitably operate the parking lot. Sandra received $15,000 for the condemned strip and $10,000 for the rest of the land. Her basis in the property was $8,500, so she had a realized gain on the two transactions of $16,500. If she meets the replacement property requirements, she will not have to recognize any of the gain.

A taxpayer may also be eligible to use this provision if the property is voluntarily sold under the threat of condemnation. To qualify, the taxpayer must have received notification of the condemnation and must believe that the property will in fact be condemned. It is not necessary for the actual condemnation proceedings to have taken place prior to the property's sale.

A special relief provision was included in the Revenue Reconciliation Act of 1993 (and made retroactive to federal disaster areas declared on or after September 1, 1991). It permits taxpayers whose principal residences were involuntarily converted in a presidentially-declared federal disaster area to avoid the recognition of gain realized on the involuntary conversion. The insurance proceeds on the home and contents (that were not scheduled property) may be commingled and treated as one common pool of funds. Thus, no separate gain is recognized on the contents of the home (which are personal use property) and gain recognized is limited to funds that are not reinvested in a personal residence and contents similar in use to those destroyed.

ANSWERS TO REVIEW I

1. (c) Albert realized $125,000 of gain on the building and $1,500 gain on the stock. The stock does *not* qualify for nonrecognition as a like-kind exchange, however.
2. (b) Jeremy must recognize the lesser of gain realized ($5,200) because this is not a like-kind exchange of personalty.
3. (a) Margaret recognized no gain since she did not *receive* any boot.
4. (a) $800,000 land
        + 200,000 liability surrendered
        − 300,000 liability assumed
        $700,000
        − 300,000 basis
        $400,000 gain realized

   No gain is recognized because liabilities assumed exceed the liabilities surrendered.

REPLACEMENT PROPERTY

To use the nonrecognition provisions for involuntary conversions, the taxpayer must obtain replacement property that meets the specific requirement of being similar or related in service or use. For property that is *used* by the taxpayer, the replacement property must meet a "functional use" test (i.e., the use of the replacement property must be the same as the converted property). The courts have held that a billiard center was not a replacement for a bowling alley because it did not meet the functional use test.

☑ **Example 15.** Conrad Bullard's shoe manufacturing plant was destroyed by a tornado. With the insurance proceeds, Conrad purchased a new building in an industrial development area, purchased new equipment, and continued manufacturing shoes. Conrad has met the functional use test and is eligible for nonrecognition of gain.

☑ **Example 16.** Marilyn Nadell owned a preschool day care center that was destroyed by a flood. She used the insurance proceeds to replace the building and opened a much-needed hospice for terminally ill cancer patients. Marilyn would not be able to invoke the nonrecognition provision because the hospice does not meet the functional use test.

A taxpayer may acquire an 80% or more interest in a corporation that owns property which meets this similar or related use test and qualify for nonrecognition of gain.

If the taxpayer has *rental* property that is subject to an involuntary conversion, only a "taxpayer use" test must be met (i.e., the rental property must be replaced only by other rental property). The use to which the lessees put the property is irrelevant.

☑ **Example 17.** Peter Tong owned a building that he rented to a clothing manufacturer. When the building was destroyed by fire, Peter built a complex of smaller units that he rented to various businesses. Peter may use the nonrecognition provision for the realized gain because he meets the "taxpayer use" test for rental property.

If real property used by the taxpayer in his or her business or held for the production of income is condemned by an outside authority, the taxpayer may use the more liberal like-kind exchange rules (i.e., he or she need only replace the property with other real property). This relaxed replacement rule does not apply to any other involuntary conversions other than *condemnations* of real business or investment property.

☑ **Example 18.** Amy Sach's six-unit apartment building was condemned to facilitate a major urban renewal project. Amy used the proceeds of the condemnation to purchase a tract of vacant land in an unincorporated area for a future apartment complex. Amy had a $150,000 gain that is unrecognized because she replaced the condemned investment realty with other investment realty. If Amy's rental property had been destroyed by fire, she would have had to meet the "taxpayer use" test by replacing it with other rental property to be eligible for nonrecognition of gain.

OTHER REQUIREMENTS

Use of the nonrecognition provisions under Sec. 1033 requires replacement property to be acquired within a specified period. For involuntary conversions of property other than a personal residence in a presidentially-declared federal disaster area and condemnations of real property used in a business or held for the production of income, the replacement period extends from the date of the conversion until the last day of the *second* taxable year after the year in which the gain is realized. For *condemnations* of real property used in business or held for investment, this period is extended one year (i.e., it extends from the date of threat or imminence of condemnation until the last day of the *third* taxable year after the first year in which gain is realized). The replacement period for a taxpayer's principal residence damaged or destroyed due to a natural disaster in a presidentially-declared federal disaster area (e.g., the areas in south Florida and Louisiana hit by Hurricane Andrew and the parts of the midwestern states flooded by the Mississippi River) is extended to four years following the end of the first year of gain realization. This latter provision was added by the Revenue Reconciliation Act of 1993 and was made retroactive to disaster areas so designated by the President on or after September 1, 1991.

Example 19. Sophie Wild's business auto with a $9,000 basis was stolen and wrecked on June 15, 1992. The insurance company paid $15,000 as its replacement value. Sophie has until December 31, 1994 (assuming she is a calendar-year taxpayer), to replace the auto and qualify for nonrecognition under Sec. 1033. If Sophie received $250,000 for a *condemned* business warehouse on January 21, 1992, she would have until December 31, 1995, to invest in qualifying replacement property. If Sophie's home had been destroyed by the Mississippi floods in 1993, but she did not receive the insurance proceeds until 1994, she would have until the end of 1998 to invest in a qualified replacement residence, assuming she had a realized gain on the insurance settlement.

If the taxpayer's replacement property is acquired directly in an involuntary conversion, the nonrecognition of gain is mandatory. For example, if a city condemns a taxpayer's property and simply transfers title to another piece of qualifying property as compensation, the taxpayer *cannot* recognize gain on the transaction.

Example 20. Wallace Warren's business auto was stolen while he was on a business trip. His insurance company found a nearly identical auto to replace the one stolen. Although Wallace's adjusted basis in the stolen auto was $4,000 and the fair market value of the replacement auto was $8,000, he cannot recognize gain since he received the replacement auto directly.

If, however, the taxpayer receives money or other nonqualifying property and then uses the money to acquire *qualifying* property, the nonrecognition provisions of Sec. 1033 are elective. The election is made by simply not reporting any of the gain on the tax return for the year in which the gain is realized. If actual replacement has not been made by the time the tax return is filed, the taxpayer must notify the IRS when replacement property is obtained. An amended return must be filed if no replacement property is obtained within the required time.

When the taxpayer obtains replacement property directly (and no gain is permitted to be recognized), the basis of the old property carries over to the new property without any adjustment. If the taxpayer receives money or other property for the converted property first and then replaces it with qualifying property, no gain is recognized as long as the amount reinvested in the replacement property equals or exceeds the proceeds from the conversion. If the taxpayer fails to reinvest the entire amount, gain is recognized to the extent of the lesser of the gain realized or the balance of the unreinvested proceeds. The basis of the property in this latter case is the cost of the property acquired, decreased by any unrecognized gain.

✓ **Example 21.** Carol Jones's six-unit apartment building, which had a basis of $250,000, was destroyed by fire. The insurance company paid Carol the $350,000 replacement value for the building. Carol could not find any suitable apartments but she was able to purchase several warehouse buildings that she could rent to several tenants. These buildings cost $328,000. Carol qualifies for nonrecognition under Sec. 1033 because she meets the taxpayer use test for replacement of rental property. Her realized gain is $100,000 ($350,000 – $250,000). Because she reinvested all but $22,000 ($350,000 – $328,000) of the proceeds from the conversion, that is the extent of the gain she must recognize. The basis of the new property is its cost of $328,000 reduced by the unrecognized gain of $78,000, or $250,000.

TAX TIP

A taxpayer may want to recognize gain on an involuntary conversion if the taxpayer's marginal tax rate is lower at the time of the conversion than the expected future marginal tax rate. By recognizing gain, the taxpayer would have a higher basis in the replacement property, and that would mean larger depreciation deductions in future years.

REVIEW II

1. Nancy Delano owned a restaurant that was condemned to make way for an interstate highway. She received $500,000 in 1992 for the restaurant and land that had a basis of $324,000. What is her gain realized and what is the last year in which she can invest in replacement property to avoid gain recognition?
   (a) $176,000 gain realized; 1994
   (b) $176,000 gain realized; 1995
   (c) $324,000 gain realized; 1993
   (d) $500,000 gain realized; 1994
2. Xelia Jones' secretarial business was completely destroyed by fire. The equipment, machines, and furniture had a value of $210,000 and basis of $160,000. Xelia received a $200,000 settlement from the insurance company for her loss. Xelia reinvested all the proceeds in replacement equipment, machines, and furniture. What are the tax consequences of this involuntary conversion?
   (a) $10,000 recognized loss
   (b) $40,000 recognized gain
   (c) no recognized gain
   (d) $200,000 recognized loss
3. Bruce Wills owned a bowling alley that was destroyed by a tornado; the bowling alley had a basis of $80,000, and he received $200,000 from the insurance company as a settlement. Because bowling was losing popularity as a sport, Bruce invested the $200,000 in a miniature golf course. What are Bruce's tax consequences?
   (a) $0
   (b) $120,000 gain realized; no gain recognized

(c) $120,000 gain realized and recognized
(d) $200,000 gain realized and recognized

4. Jon Quinn used the entire $450,000 insurance settlement he received for his condemned rental warehouse with a basis of $350,000 to purchase a rental office building. The building's cost was $950,000, so he took out a mortgage of $500,000. What is his basis in this new building?
   (a) $450,000
   (b) $800,000
   (c) $850,000
   (d) $950,000

Answers are on page 9-18.

III SECTION 1231 TREATMENT
(Code Section 1231)

Business assets held more than one year are given special treatment on dispositions by the Internal Revenue Code. These assets, called *Sec. 1231 assets*, are given ordinary loss treatment if their dispositions in a tax year result in a net loss. If their dispositions result in a net gain, the net gain is reclassified as a long-term capital gain. Since the repeal of the capital gains deduction for individuals and the alternative capital gains rate for corporations, this special treatment has lost much of its effect. Note, however, that the maximum capital gains rate is 28% for individual taxpayers only. The major benefit is still that a net Sec. 1231 loss is fully deductible as ordinary income. If the loss were treated as a capital loss, its deductibility for individuals would be limited to $3,000 in excess of capital gains (or would be deductible only against capital gains by corporations). Gains and losses on the sale or exchange of business assets are reported on Form 4797.

THE LAW

Sec. 1231(b)—Definition of Property Used in the Trade or Business—For purposes of this section—(1) General Rule—The term "property used in the trade or business" means property used in the trade or business, of a character which is subject to the allowance for depreciation provided in section 167, held for more than 1 year, and real property used in the trade or business held for more than 1 year, which is not—

(A) property of a kind which would properly be includible in the inventory of the taxpayer...

(B) property held by the taxpayer primarily for sale to customers in the ordinary course of his trade or business,

(C) a copyright, a literary, musical, or artistic composition, a letter or memorandum, or similar property, held by a taxpayer... or

(D) a publication of the United States Government....

Sec. 1231(b) defines fairly explicitly what properties constitute Sec. 1231 property. Sec. 1231 assets specifically include depreciable and real property used in the taxpayer's trade or business that has been held for more than one year and specifically excludes inventory and stock in trade. Rental property held by the taxpayer for more than one year also constitutes Sec. 1231 property. Copyrights, artistic compositions, letters, etc., are excluded if held by the creator, because they constitute a form of inventory. Government publications are excluded unless purchased by the holder at the normal selling price. Business property held for one year or less is also excluded. The section also lists several other types of property that are considered Sec. 1231 property:

1. timber, coal, or domestic iron ore
2. cattle and horses held for more than 24 months for breeding, draft, dairy, or sporting purposes
3. other livestock held for more that 12 months for breeding, draft, dairy, or sporting purposes, excluding poultry
4. unharvested crops on land held for more than one year if the land and the crops are sold at the same time to the same person

Example 22. Alice Dunn has a manufacturing business, owns several pieces of rental real estate, owns and operates a dairy farm, and has composed several musical compositions that have been performed by a local band. All of the depreciable and real property *used* in the manufacturing business; the rental properties; and the land, buildings, equipment, and cows (held over 24 months) used in the dairy business are Sec. 1231 assets. The inventories of the manufacturing business and the musical compositions are not Sec. 1231 assets.

Example 23. Walter Lenox started a small manufacturing business. He bought a building, machinery, office furniture and equipment, and raw materials for the manufacturing process. All of the items except the raw materials are Sec. 1231 assets if they are held for more than one year. The raw materials are inventory and are specifically excluded from the Sec. 1231 asset category.

RECOGNITION OF SECTION 1231 GAINS AND LOSSES

THE LAW

Sec. 1231(a)—General Rule—(1) Gains Exceed Losses—If—
  (A) the section 1231 gains for any taxable year, exceed
  (B) the 1231 losses for such taxable year, such gains and losses shall be treated as long-term capital gains or long-term capital losses, as the case may be.
(2) Gains Do Not Exceed Losses—If—
  (A) the section 1231 gains for any taxable year, do not exceed
  (B) the section 1231 losses for such taxable year, such gains and losses shall not be treated as gains and losses from sales or exchanges of capital assets.

Sec. 1231 requires the netting of gains and losses against one another. If the outcome is a net loss, the gains and losses are all treated as ordinary income and loss items. The specification that the gains and losses that make up the net Sec. 1231 loss cannot be treated as gains or losses from sales or exchanges of capital assets prohibits capital treatment. The only alternative to capital treatment is ordinary income or loss treatment.

> ✓ **Example 24.** Don Eisner sold a business machine, an auto, and some office equipment at a $12,000 Sec. 1231 loss, a $4,500 Sec. 1231 gain, and a $5,300 Sec. 1231 gain, respectively. John has a Sec. 1231 net loss of $2,200 on these transactions. Each of the items will be treated as an ordinary income and loss item, allowing the losses to be deducted in full.

If the netting process yields a net Sec. 1231 gain, then a different treatment results—the net Sec. 1231 gain is treated as a long-term capital gain. A five-year lookback rule, however, requires a taxpayer to *recapture* net Sec. 1231 gains as ordinary income to the extent Sec. 1231 losses that remain unrecaptured were deducted within the last five years. If the taxpayer had no deductible net Sec. 1231 losses within the last five tax years, the net gain is treated as a long-term capital gain. Otherwise, the taxpayer must reduce the net Sec. 1231 gain for these unrecaptured Sec. 1231 losses from the five prior years; only the excess net Sec. 1231 gain is then treated as a capital gain. This net Sec. 1231 gain is then netted with all other long-term capital gains and losses as part of the capital gain netting process discussed in Chapter 6.

> ✓ **Example 25.** Ike Towne's company sold three business assets that had been used for several years; this year asset A was sold at a gain of $2,000; asset B was sold at a loss of $3,000; and asset C was sold at a $15,000 gain. Ike has a net Sec. 1231 gain of $14,000. The gains and losses are treated as long term capital gains and losses as long as Ike has no Sec. 1231 losses deducted within the last five years. If Ike had deducted a $6,000 Sec. 1231 loss two years ago, then $6,000 of this gain would be treated as ordinary income and only the balance of $8,000 would be treated as long-term capital gain. Figure 9-2 shows the latter information entered on Form 4797 and Schedule D.

ANSWERS TO REVIEW II

1. (b) Because this was a condemnation, Nancy has until the end of the third tax year following the involuntary conversion to invest in replacement property.
2. (c) Xelia has a realized $40,000 gain on the equipment, machines, and furniture. Because she reinvested the entire proceeds in qualifying property, no gain is recognized.
3. (c) The replacement property does not meet the functional use test, and Bruce must recognize all the gain realized.
4. (c)

Total purchase price	$950,000
less: Unrecognized gain on condemnation	(100,000)
Basis in office building	$850,000

III. Section 1231 Treatment 9-19

Form **4797**	**Sales of Business Property**	OMB No. 1545-0184
Department of the Treasury Internal Revenue Service	(Also Involuntary Conversions and Recapture Amounts Under Sections 179 and 280F(b)(2)) ▶ Attach to your tax return. ▶ See separate instructions.	**1993** Attachment Sequence No. **27**

Name(s) shown on return: Ike Towne

Identifying number:

1. Enter here the gross proceeds from the sale or exchange of real estate reported to you for 1993 on Form(s) 1099-S (or a substitute statement) that you will be including on line 2, 11, or 22 . . . . **1**

Part I — Sales or Exchanges of Property Used in a Trade or Business and Involuntary Conversions From Other Than Casualty or Theft—Property Held More Than 1 Year

(a) Description of property	(b) Date acquired (mo., day, yr.)	(c) Date sold (mo., day, yr.)	(d) Gross sales price	(e) Depreciation allowed or allowable since acquisition	(f) Cost or other basis, plus improvements and expense of sale	(g) LOSS ((f) minus the sum of (d) and (e))	(h) GAIN ((d) plus (e) minus (f))
2 A							2,000
B						3,000	
C							15,000

3. Gain, if any, from Form 4684, line 39 . . . . **3**
4. Section 1231 gain from installment sales from Form 6252, line 26 or 37 . . . . . . **4**
5. Section 1231 gain or (loss) from like-kind exchanges from Form 8824 . . . . **5**
6. Gain, if any, from line 34, from other than casualty or theft **6**
7. Add lines 2 through 6 in columns (g) and (h) **7** (3,000)   17,000
8. Combine columns (g) and (h) of line 7. Enter gain or (loss) here, and on the appropriate line as follows: . . . **8**   14,000

   Partnerships—Enter the gain or (loss) on Form 1065, Schedule K, line 6. Skip lines 9, 10, 12, and 13 below.

   S corporations—Report the gain or (loss) following the instructions for Form 1120S, Schedule K, lines 5 and 6. Skip lines 9, 10, 12, and 13 below, unless line 8 is a gain and the S corporation is subject to the capital gains tax.

   All others—If line 8 is zero or a loss, enter the amount on line 12 below and skip lines 9 and 10. If line 8 is a gain and you did not have any prior year section 1231 losses, or they were recaptured in an earlier year, enter the gain as a long-term capital gain on Schedule D and skip lines 9, 10, and 13 below.

9. Nonrecaptured net section 1231 losses from prior years (see instructions) **9**   6,000
10. Subtract line 9 from line 8. If zero or less, enter -0-. Also enter on the appropriate line as follows (see instructions): **10**   8,000

    S corporations—Enter this amount (if more than zero) on Schedule D (Form 1120S), line 13, and skip lines 12 and 13 below.

    All others—If line 10 is zero, enter the amount from line 8 on line 13 below. If line 10 is more than zero, enter the amount from line 9 on line 13 below, and enter the amount from line 10 as a long-term capital gain on Schedule D.

Part II — Ordinary Gains and Losses

11. Ordinary gains and losses not included on lines 12 through 18 (include property held 1 year or less):

12. Loss, if any, from line 8 . . . . **12**
13. Gain, if any, from line 8, or amount from line 9 if applicable **13**   6,000
14. Gain, if any, from line 33 . . . . **14**
15. Net gain or (loss) from Form 4684, lines 31 and 38a **15**
16. Ordinary gain from installment sales from Form 6252, line 25 or 36 . . . . **16**
17. Ordinary gain or (loss) from like-kind exchanges from Form 8824 . . . . **17**
18. Recapture of section 179 expense deduction for partners and S corporation shareholders from property dispositions by partnerships and S corporations (see instructions) **18**
19. Add lines 11 through 18 in columns (g) and (h) . . . . **19** (   )   6,000
20. Combine columns (g) and (h) of line 19. Enter gain or (loss) here, and on the appropriate line as follows: . . . **20**   6,000

    a. For all except individual returns: Enter the gain or (loss) from line 20 on the return being filed.
    b. For individual returns:
       (1) If the loss on line 12 includes a loss from Form 4684, line 35, column (b)(ii), enter that part of the loss here and on line 20 of Schedule A (Form 1040). Identify as from "Form 4797, line 20b(1)." See instructions . . . **20b(1)**
       (2) Redetermine the gain or (loss) on line 20, excluding the loss, if any, on line 20b(1). Enter here and on Form 1040, line 15 . **20b(2)**

For Paperwork Reduction Act Notice, see page 1 of separate instructions.   Cat. No. 130861   Form **4797** (1993)

Figure 9-2   Form 4797

**SCHEDULE D
(Form 1040)**

Department of the Treasury
Internal Revenue Service

Capital Gains and Losses

▶ Attach to Form 1040. ▶ See Instructions for Schedule D (Form 1040).
▶ Use lines 20 and 22 for more space to list transactions for lines 1 and 9.

OMB No. 1545-0074

1993

Attachment Sequence No. **12**

Name(s) shown on Form 1040: Ike Towne

Your social security number

Part II Long-Term Capital Gains and Losses—Assets Held More Than One Year

9

10 Enter your long-term totals, if any, from line 23 . . . . | 10 |

11 **Total long-term sales price amounts.** Add column (d) of lines 9 and 10 . . . | 11 |

12 Gain from Form 4797; long-term gain from Forms 2119, 2439, and 6252; and long-term gain or (loss) from Forms 4684, 6781, and 8824 . . . . | 12 | 8,000

13 Net long-term gain or (loss) from partnerships, S corporations, and fiduciaries from Schedule(s) K-1 . . . . | 13 |

14 Capital gain distributions . . . . | 14 |

15 Long-term capital loss carryover from 1992 Schedule D, line 45 . . . . | 15 |

16 Add lines 9, 10, and 12 through 15, in columns (f) and (g) . . . . . . | 16 |(   ) | 8,000

17 **Net long-term capital gain or (loss).** Combine columns (f) and (g) of line 16 . . . . . . | 17 | 8,000

Figure 9-2 (continued)   Schedule D

THE LAW

Sec. 1231(a)(3)—Section 1231 Gains and Losses—For purposes of this subsection—
(A) Sec. 1231 Gain—The term "section 1231 gain" means—
  (i) any recognized gain on the sale or exchange of property used in the trade or business, and
  (ii) any recognized gain from the compulsory or involuntary conversion (as a result of destruction in whole or in part, theft, or seizure, or an exercise of the power or requisition or condemnation or the threat or imminence thereof) into other property or money of—
    (I) property used in the trade or business, or
    (II) any capital asset which is held for more than 1 year and is held in connection with a trade or business or a transaction entered into for profit.
(B) Section 1231 Loss—The term "section 1231 loss" means any recognized loss from a sale or exchange or conversion described in subparagraph (A). . . .

This section, in addition to stating that the Sec. 1231 gains include the *recognized* gain on the sale or exchange of business property, specifies that certain property subject to an involuntary conversion is Sec. 1231 property. This section extends the definition of gains from Sec. 1231 assets to include the gains from *any* trade or business property and business or investment capital assets held more than one year, which are subject to certain involuntary conversions. Involuntary conversions include thefts, seizures, condemnations, and casualties. A similar rule applies to *losses* from involuntary conversions, except for property subject to casualty and theft losses.

THE LAW

Sec. 1231(a)(4)(C)—In the case of any involuntary conversion...arising from fire, storm, shipwreck, or other casualty, or from theft, of any
(i) property used in the trade or business, or
(ii) any capital asset which is held for more than 1 year and is held in connection with a trade or business or a transaction entered into for profit,
this subsection shall not apply to such conversion (whether resulting in gain or loss) if during the taxable year the recognized losses from such conversions exceed the recognized gains from such conversions.

This section sets apart the treatment of casualty and theft gains and losses on business and investment assets from the gains and losses resulting from other involuntary conversions, and adds another step to the Sec. 1231 netting process. All casualty and theft gains and losses from productive business assets and business and investment capital assets held more than one year must be netted against one another. If the net result is a gain, then these assets are considered Sec. 1231 assets, and the gains and losses are netted with the gains and losses on all other Sec. 1231 property, including business and capital assets subject to other types of involuntary conversions. If the result is a net casualty loss, however, then the individual gains and losses are treated separately. The losses on the productive business assets are ordinary losses (i.e., deductible *for* adjusted gross income); the losses on the investment property are itemized deductions (i.e., deductible *from* adjusted gross income).

The complete netting process for Sec. 1231 assets requires three steps as illustrated in the Figure 9-3.

Step 1: Net casualty and theft gains and losses on productive business assets and business and investment capital assets. If a *net gain* results, proceed to Step 2.

Step 2: Net gains and losses from Step 1, with other gains and losses from (1) involuntary conversions of productive business assets and business and investment capital assets and (2) sales and exchanges of all other Sec. 1231 assets. If a *net gain* results, proceed to Step 3.

Step 3: The net gain is treated as a long-term capital gain (less the amount subject to the five-year look-back rule illustrated in Figure 9-4) and is netted with the gains and losses from the sales or exchanges of all other long-term capital assets. (Because all the Sec. 1231 gains and losses are converted to long-term capital assets, only the net amount has to be used in this final netting process.)

If results at the end of Step 1 are a net loss, the items do not continue in the netting process. All gains and losses receive ordinary income treatment except the casualty losses on the investment assets; these losses are treated as itemized deductions.

If the results of Step 2 are a net loss, the results are similar (i.e., the netting process stops). All gains and losses except losses on investment assets are treated as ordinary income items. The investment property casualty losses are itemized deductions.

Example 26. Simon Wolf had the following items of gain and loss on productive business assets held more than one year during the tax year:

1.	Machine	Destroyed by fire	$5,000	loss
2.	Typewriter	Stolen	800	gain
3.	Machine	Sold	4,000	gain
4.	Building	Sold	20,000	gain
5.	Furniture	Sold	6,000	loss
6.	Land	Condemned	12,000	loss

Simon must first net items (1) and (2), which are theft and casualty losses:

$5,000 Loss + $800 Gain = $4,200 Net Loss.

Because the result is a net loss, each item is treated separately as an item of ordinary income and loss. Simon then nets the other gains against the losses:

$4,000 Gain + $20,000 Gain − $6,000 Loss − $12,000 = $6,000 Net Gain

This $6,000 net gain enters the capital gain and loss netting process as a long-term capital gain (assuming the five-year look-back rule does not apply). The above information

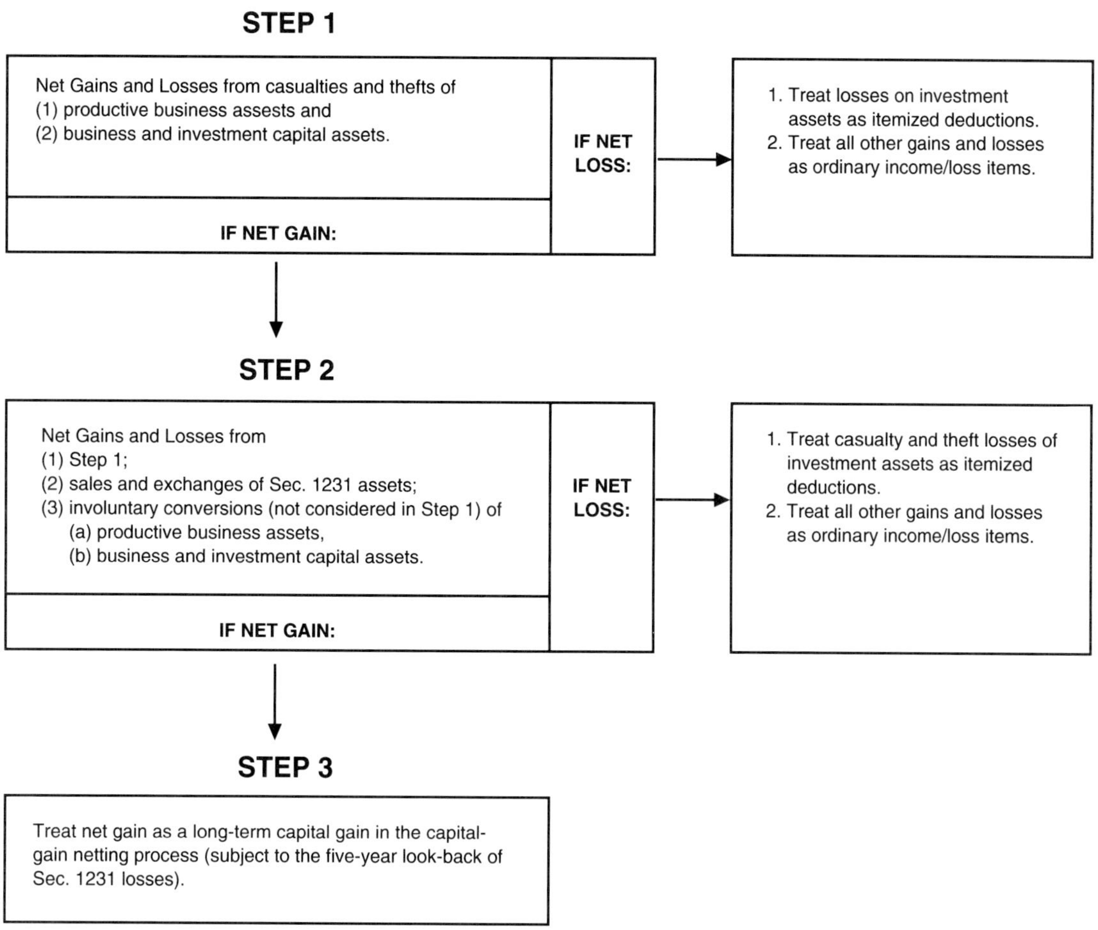

STEP 1

Net Gains and Losses from casualties and thefts of (1) productive business assests and (2) business and investment capital assets.	**IF NET LOSS:** →	1. Treat losses on investment assets as itemized deductions. 2. Treat all other gains and losses as ordinary income/loss items.
IF NET GAIN: ↓		

STEP 2

Net Gains and Losses from
(1) Step 1;
(2) sales and exchanges of Sec. 1231 assets;
(3) involuntary conversions (not considered in Step 1) of
   (a) productive business assets,
   (b) business and investment capital assets.
	IF NET LOSS: →	1. Treat casualty and theft losses of investment assets as itemized deductions.
		2. Treat all other gains and losses as ordinary income/loss items.

IF NET GAIN: ↓		

STEP 3

Treat net gain as a long-term capital gain in the capital-gain netting process (subject to the five-year look-back of Sec. 1231 losses).

Figure 9-3 Asset Netting Process

Step 1

        Current Year's Net Section-1231 Gain
less Unrecaptured Section 1231 Losses from Five Prior Years

equals Net Section-1231 Gains Treated as Capital Gain

Step 2

        Current Years Net Section-1231 Gain
less Amount Treated as Capital Gain from Step 1

equals Amount Recaptured in Current Year as Ordinary Gain

Figure 9-4 Five-Year Look-Back for Section 1231 Gains

is entered on Forms 4797 and 4684 (Section B) in Figure 9-5. If Simon had also lost investment securities worth $5,000 in the fire, his net loss would increase to $9,200; the $5,000 loss on the securities would have to be treated as an itemized deduction, however. Note that casualty and theft losses on business and income-producing property are reported on page 2 of Form 4684; casualty and theft losses on personal use property are reported on page 1 of Form 4684 as illustrated previously in Chapter 4.

REVIEW III

1. Yolanda Casey had the following long-term property sales from her business during the current year:

	Basis	Selling Price
Machines	$ 20,000	$ 18,000
Building	100,000	135,000
Equipment	35,000	30,000

   Additionally, she sold some securities at a $12,000 gain. What gain must be included in her income and what is its character, assuming she had no prior capital losses?
   (a) $28,000 Sec. 1231 gain; $12,000 capital gain
   (b) $40,000 capital gain
   (c) $7,000 capital loss; $47,000 Sec. 1231 gain
   (d) $40,000 Sec. 1231 gain

2. Terri Walsh had a $6,000 Sec. 1231 loss four years ago and a Sec. 1231 gain in the current year of $16,000. What will be the final tax treatment if she had no other property transactions?
   (a) $16,000 Sec. 1231 gain
   (b) $16,000 capital gain
   (c) $10,000 Sec. 1231 gain; $6,000 ordinary income
   (d) $10,000 capital gain; $6,000 ordinary income

3. Louann Mason lost her garage and several autos in a fire at her rental car business. She also sold some other business properties. The details follow:

Asset	Basis	Selling Price or FMV	Insurance Recovery
Garage	$14,000	$18,000	$12,000
Autos	70,000	74,000	80,000
Machines	4,000	9,000	N/A
Furniture	8,000	7,000	N/A

   How are these items finally taxed to Louann if she had no prior Sec. 1231 losses?
   (a) $8,000 capital gain; $4,000 Sec. 1231 gain
   (b) $12,000 Sec. 1231 gain
   (c) $12,000 capital gain
   (d) $3,000 Sec. 1231 loss; $15,000 capital gain

4. George Andrews has the following equipment sales from his business:

Asset	Basis	Selling Price
10 Typewriters	$ 4,000	$2,000
2 Computers	12,000	8,000
1 Postage machine	500	750

III. Section 1231 Treatment 9-25

Form **4797**	**Sales of Business Property**	OMB No. 1545-0184
Department of the Treasury Internal Revenue Service	(Also Involuntary Conversions and Recapture Amounts Under Sections 179 and 280F(b)(2)) ▶ Attach to your tax return. ▶ See separate instructions.	**1993** Attachment Sequence No. **27**

Name(s) shown on return: Simon Wolf

Identifying number:

1 Enter here the gross proceeds from the sale or exchange of real estate reported to you for 1993 on Form(s) 1099-S (or a substitute statement) that you will be including on line 2, 11, or 22 . . . . | 1 |

Part I — Sales or Exchanges of Property Used in a Trade or Business and Involuntary Conversions From Other Than Casualty or Theft—Property Held More Than 1 Year

(a) Description of property	(b) Date acquired (mo., day, yr.)	(c) Date sold (mo., day, yr.)	(d) Gross sales price	(e) Depreciation allowed or allowable since acquisition	(f) Cost or other basis, plus improvements and expense of sale	(g) LOSS ((f) minus the sum of (d) and (e))	(h) GAIN ((d) plus (e) minus (f))
2 Machine (3)							4,000
Building							20,000
Furniture						6,000	
Land						12,000	

3 Gain, if any, from Form 4684, line 39 . . . . | 3 |
4 Section 1231 gain from installment sales from Form 6252, line 26 or 37 . . . . . . | 4 |
5 Section 1231 gain or (loss) from like-kind exchanges from Form 8824 . . . . . . | 5 |
6 Gain, if any, from line 34, from other than casualty or theft . . . . | 6 |
7 Add lines 2 through 6 in columns (g) and (h) . . . . | 7 | (18,000) | 24,000
8 Combine columns (g) and (h) of line 7. Enter gain or (loss) here, and on the appropriate line as follows: . . . | 8 | 6,000

 Partnerships—Enter the gain or (loss) on Form 1065, Schedule K, line 6. Skip lines 9, 10, 12, and 13 below.
 S corporations—Report the gain or (loss) following the instructions for Form 1120S, Schedule K, lines 5 and 6. Skip lines 9, 10, 12, and 13 below, unless line 8 is a gain and the S corporation is subject to the capital gains tax.
 All others—If line 8 is zero or a loss, enter the amount on line 12 below and skip lines 9 and 10. If line 8 is a gain and you did not have any prior year section 1231 losses, or they were recaptured in an earlier year, enter the gain as a long-term capital gain on Schedule D and skip lines 9, 10, and 13 below.

9 Nonrecaptured net section 1231 losses from prior years (see instructions) . . . . | 9 | 0
10 Subtract line 9 from line 8. If zero or less, enter -0-. Also enter on the appropriate line as follows (see instructions): | 10 | 6,000
 S corporations—Enter this amount (if more than zero) on Schedule D (Form 1120S), line 13, and skip lines 12 and 13 below.
 All others—If line 10 is zero, enter the amount from line 8 on line 13 below. If line 10 is more than zero, enter the amount from line 9 on line 13 below, and enter the amount from line 10 as a long-term capital gain on Schedule D.

Part II — Ordinary Gains and Losses

11 Ordinary gains and losses not included on lines 12 through 18 (include property held 1 year or less):

12 Loss, if any, from line 8 . . . . | 12 |
13 Gain, if any, from line 8, or amount from line 9 if applicable . . . . | 13 | | 0
14 Gain, if any, from line 33 . . . . | 14 |
15 Net gain or (loss) from Form 4684, lines 31 and 38a . . . . | 15 | 4,200
16 Ordinary gain from installment sales from Form 6252, line 25 or 36 . . . . | 16 |
17 Ordinary gain or (loss) from like-kind exchanges from Form 8824 . . . . | 17 |
18 Recapture of section 179 expense deduction for partners and S corporation shareholders from property dispositions by partnerships and S corporations (see instructions) . . . . . | 18 |
19 Add lines 11 through 18 in columns (g) and (h) . . . . | 19 | (4,200)
20 Combine columns (g) and (h) of line 19. Enter gain or (loss) here, and on the appropriate line as follows: . . . | 20 | (4,200)
 a For all except individual returns: Enter the gain or (loss) from line 20 on the return being filed.
 b For individual returns:
  (1) If the loss on line 12 includes a loss from Form 4684, line 35, column (b)(ii), enter that part of the loss here and on line 20 of Schedule A (Form 1040). Identify as from "Form 4797, line 20b(1)." See instructions . . . . | 20b(1) |
  (2) Redetermine the gain or (loss) on line 20, excluding the loss, if any, on line 20b(1). Enter here and on Form 1040, line 15 . | 20b(2) |

For Paperwork Reduction Act Notice, see page 1 of separate instructions. Cat. No. 130861 Form **4797** (1993)

Figure 9-5 Form 4797

9-26 Special Computations and Credits for Business Taxpayers

Form 4684 (1993)   Attachment Sequence No. **26**   Page **2**

Name(s) shown on tax return. Do not enter name and identifying number if shown on other side. | Identifying number

Simon Wolf

SECTION B—Business and Income-Producing Property (Use this section to report casualties and thefts of property used in a trade or business or for income-producing purposes.)

Part I Casualty or Theft Gain or Loss (Use a separate Part I for each casualty or theft.)

19 Description of properties (show type, location, and date acquired for each):
- Property A Machine (1)
- Property B Typewriter
- Property C ____
- Property D ____

Properties (Use a separate column for each property lost or damaged from one casualty or theft.)

	A	B	C	D
20 Cost or adjusted basis of each property	5,000			
21 Insurance or other reimbursement (whether or not you filed a claim). See the instructions for line 3. *Note: If line 20 is more than line 21, skip line 22.*				
22 Gain from casualty or theft. If line 21 is **more than** line 20, enter the difference here and on line 29 or line 34, column (c), except as provided in the instructions for line 33. Also, skip lines 23 through 27 for that column. See the instructions for line 4 if line 21 includes insurance or other reimbursement you did not claim, or you received payment for your loss in a later tax year		800		
23 Fair market value **before** casualty or theft				
24 Fair market value **after** casualty or theft				
25 Subtract line 24 from line 23				
26 Enter the **smaller** of line 20 or line 25	5,000			
Note: If the property was totally destroyed by casualty or lost from theft, enter on line 26 the amount from line 20.				
27 Subtract line 21 from line 26. If zero or less, enter -0-	5,000	800		

28 Casualty or theft loss. Add the amounts on line 27. Enter the total here and on line 29 or line 34 (see instructions).   **28** 5,000

Part II Summary of Gains and Losses (from separate Parts I)

(a) Identify casualty or theft	(b) Losses from casualties or thefts		(c) Gains from casualties or thefts includible in income
	(i) Trade, business, rental or royalty property	(ii) Income-producing property	

Casualty or Theft of Property Held One Year or Less

29	( )	( )	
	( )	( )	
30 Totals. Add the amounts on line 29	( )	( )	

31 Combine line 30, columns (b)(i) and (c). Enter the net gain or (loss) here and on Form 4797, line 15. If Form 4797 is not otherwise required, see instructions   **31**

32 Enter the amount from line 30, column (b)(ii) here and on Schedule A (Form 1040), line 20. Partnerships, S corporations, estates and trusts, see instructions   **32**

Casualty or Theft of Property Held More Than One Year

33 Casualty or theft gains from Form 4797, line 34   **33**

| 34 | (5,000) | ( ) | 800 |
| 35 Total losses. Add amounts on line 34, columns (b)(i) and (b)(ii) | (5,000) | ( ) | |

36 Total gains. Add lines 33 and 34, column (c)   **36** 800
37 Add amounts on line 35, columns (b)(i) and (b)(ii)   **37** (5,000)
38 If the loss on line 37 is **more than** the gain on line 36:
- a Combine line 35, column (b)(i) and line 36, and enter the net gain or (loss) here. Partnerships and S corporations see the note below. All others enter this amount on Form 4797, line 15. If Form 4797 is not otherwise required, see instructions   **38a** (4,200)
- b Enter the amount from line 35, column (b)(ii) here. Partnerships and S corporations see the note below. Individuals enter this amount on Schedule A (Form 1040), line 20. Estates and trusts, enter on the "Other deductions" line of your tax return   **38b**

39 If the loss on line 37 **is equal to** or **less than** the gain on line 36, combine these lines and enter here. Partnerships, see the note below. All others, enter this amount on Form 4797, line 3   **39**

Note: Partnerships, enter the amount from line 38a, 38b, or line 39 on Form 1065, Schedule K, line 7. S corporations, enter the amount from line 38a or 38b on Form 1120S, Schedule K, line 6.

Figure 9-5 (continued)   Form 4684

If George had no prior Sec. 1231 losses, how are these transactions taxed?
(a) $6,250 Sec. 1231 loss
(b) $6,000 Sec. 1231 loss
(c) $5,750 Capital loss
(d) $5,750 Ordinary loss

Answers are on page 9-28.

IV. DEPRECIATION RECAPTURE
(Code Sections 1245 and 1250)

Business assets are given favorable tax treatment by their designation as Sec. 1231 assets. If the Sec. 1231 assets disposed of in a tax year yield a net loss, the loss is treated as an ordinary loss fully deductible against other income items. If, however, the disposition of the Sec. 1231 assets yields a net gain, the net gain is treated as a long-term capital gain (to the extent it exceeds unrecaptured Sec. 1231 losses from the five prior years). In this way, the net Sec. 1231 gain can be used to offset capital losses that might otherwise be nondeductible due to the capital loss limitation rules. Congress did not, however, believe that a taxpayer should be able to take depreciation deductions—which offset ordinary income—and then sell the business assets at a gain, benefiting from the tax-favored status of capital gains.

To rectify this situation, several recapture provisions were enacted. Simply stated, the recapture provisions require that all, or a part of, the gain on the disposition of business property on which prior depreciation deductions had been taken will be recaptured as ordinary income. Recapture, however, does not affect property sold at a loss. Because recapture applies only to business property, it is reported on Form 4797 along with Sec. 1231 gains and losses.

THE LAW

Sec. 1245(a)—General Rule—(1) Ordinary income—Except as otherwise provided in this section, if section 1245 property is disposed of the amount by which the....fair market value of such property exceeds the adjusted basis of such property shall be treated as ordinary income....

(3) Section 1245 Property—For purposes of this section, the term "section 1245 property" means any property which is or has been property of a character subject to the allowance for depreciation provided in section 167 (or subject to the allowance of amortization provided in section 185) and is ...

(A) personal property,

(B) other property (not including a building or its structural components)...

(D) single purpose agricultural or horticultural structure...

(E) a storage facility...used in connection with the distribution of petroleum or any primary product of petroleum.

Under the above definition, Sec. 1245 property includes all depreciable personal property owned by taxpayers. Under the Modified Accelerated Cost Recovery System (MACRS), the nonrealty asset classes are generally Sec. 1245 assets. A major departure from this generalization occurred under the Accelerated Cost Recovery System (ACRS), which applied to assets put in service between January 1, 1981, and December 31, 1986. If a taxpayer used an accelerated method of depreciation rather than a straight-line alternative for *nonresidential* real property, the nonresidential real property was reclassified and made subject to the Sec. 1245 recapture rules.

✓ **Example 27.** Madge Muldoon sold a factory building for $125,000 that she purchased in 1983 for $130,000. She used ACRS depreciation and her basis at the date of sale was $50,000. Madge has a gain of $75,000 on the sale, all of which is Sec. 1245 gain. If the building had been *residential* rental property, the gain would not have been Sec. 1245 gain.

Sec. 1245 recapture requires recognizing as ordinary income an amount of gain not to exceed the previous depreciation deductions. Using a simple rule of thumb, all gain realized on a Sec. 1245 asset that is sold *below* its original cost will be recaptured as ordinary income. Any gain in excess of the Sec. 1245 recapture amount (for example, when the selling price exceeds the asset's original cost) is treated as Sec. 1231 gain.

✓ **Example 28.** Sylvia Black has a dump truck that cost her $105,000 at acquisition. She depreciates the asset under MACRS and its adjusted basis is now $63,000. She has a buyer for the truck who is willing to pay $68,000. If Sylvia sells the truck, she will have to recognize $5,000 of Sec. 1245 recapture as ordinary income.

ANSWERS TO REVIEW III

1. (b) Machine $ (2,000)   Sec. 1231 loss
       Building   35,000   Sec. 1231 gain
       Equipment   (5,000)   Sec. 1231 loss
                       $28,000   Sec. 1231 net gain (treated as capital gain)
   $28,000 + $12,000 = $40,000 capital gain
2. (d) Terri must recapture $6,000 as ordinary income; the balance of $10,000 is taxed as a capital gain.
3. (c) Garage $ (2,000)   casualty loss
       Autos   10,000   casualty gain
                     $ 8,000   net casualty gain
                     $ 8,000   net casualty gain
       + Machines   5,000   Sec. 1231 gain
       – Furniture   (1,000)   Sec. 1231 loss
                     $12,000   net Sec. 1231 gain taxed as a capital gain
4. (d) Typewriters $(2,000)   Sec. 1231 loss
       Computers   (4,000)   Sec. 1231 loss
       Postage machine   250   Sec. 1231 gain
                       ($5,750) net Sec. 1231 loss taxed as an ordinary loss

✓ **Example 29.** Maury Wold has a factory building that he purchased in 1982 for $220,000. He used an accelerated method of depreciation under ACRS and its basis is now $140,000. He has a buyer for the property who will pay $320,000. Even though the property is realty, it is subject to Sec. 1245 recapture because it is nonresidential realty depreciated under an accelerated ACRS method. Maury has a realized gain of $180,000. Only $80,000 of the gain, however, is Sec. 1245 recapture because that is the amount of the prior depreciation deductions. The rest of the gain, $100,000, is treated as Sec. 1231 gain. Form 4797 reflecting the above transaction is shown in Figure 9-6 along with the information from Example 31.

SECTION 1250 RECAPTURE

THE LAW

Sec. 1250(a)—General Rule—Except as otherwise provided in this section—(1) Additional Depreciation After December 31, 1975—
(A) In General—If section 1250 property is disposed of after December 31, 1975, then the applicable percentage of the lower of—
(i) that portion of the additional depreciation (as defined in subsection (b)(1) or (4)) attributable to periods after December 31, 1975, in respect of the property, or
(ii) the excess of the amount realized (in the case of a sale, exchange, or involuntary conversion), or the fair market value of such property (in the case of any other disposition), over the adjusted basis of such property, shall be treated as gain which is ordinary income. Such gain shall be recognized notwithstanding any other provision of this subtitle.
(B) Applicable Percentage—For purposes of subparagraph (A), the term "applicable percentage" means—...(v) in the case of all other section 1250 property, 100 percent.

Recapture under Sec. 1250 requires recognition of only a portion of the gain on the sale of certain Sec. 1231 assets as ordinary income. Sec. 1250 property is depreciable *real* property that is not Sec. 1245 property. *Nonresidential* real property placed in service from 1981 through 1986 that has been depreciated under an ACRS accelerated method of depreciation is defined as Sec. 1245 property, however. *Residential* real property placed in service in 1981 through 1986 and depreciated under an ACRS accelerated method, however, *is* subject to the Sec. 1250 recapture rules.

The recapture potential of Sec. 1250 property is limited to its *excess depreciation*. Excess depreciation is defined as the amount by which the actual depreciation deductions (or allowable depreciation deductions if the taxpayer fails to take a full depreciation deduction in any year) exceeds the allowable depreciation under the straight-line alternative. Similar to the Sec. 1245 rules, any gain in excess of the recapture potential is treated as Sec. 1231 gain. If the property is held for one year or less, all depreciation is recaptured.

9-30 *Special Computations and Credits for Business Taxpayers*

Form **4797**	**Sales of Business Property**	OMB No. 1545-0184
Department of the Treasury Internal Revenue Service	(Also Involuntary Conversions and Recapture Amounts Under Sections 179 and 280F(b)(2)) ▶ Attach to your tax return. ▶ See separate instructions.	**1993** Attachment Sequence No. 27

Name(s) shown on return: Maury Wold   Identifying number:

1 Enter here the gross proceeds from the sale or exchange of real estate reported to you for 1993 on Form(s) 1099-S (or a substitute statement) that you will be including on line 2, 11, or 22 . . . . | 1 |

Part I Sales or Exchanges of Property Used in a Trade or Business and Involuntary Conversions From Other Than Casualty or Theft—Property Held More Than 1 Year

(a) Description of property	(b) Date acquired (mo., day, yr.)	(c) Date sold (mo., day, yr.)	(d) Gross sales price	(e) Depreciation allowed or allowable since acquisition	(f) Cost or other basis, plus improvements and expense of sale	(g) LOSS ((f) minus the sum of (d) and (e))	(h) GAIN ((d) plus (e) minus (f))
2							

3 Gain, if any, from Form 4684, line 39 . . . . | 3 | | |
4 Section 1231 gain from installment sales from Form 6252, line 26 or 37 . . . . | 4 | | |
5 Section 1231 gain or (loss) from like-kind exchanges from Form 8824 . . . . | 5 | | |
6 Gain, if any, from line 34, from other than casualty or theft . . . . | 6 | | 185,000 |
7 Add lines 2 through 6 in columns (g) and (h) . . . . | 7 | ( ) | 185,000 |
8 Combine columns (g) and (h) of line 7. Enter gain or (loss) here, and on the appropriate line as follows: . . . | 8 | | 185,000 |

  Partnerships—Enter the gain or (loss) on Form 1065, Schedule K, line 6. Skip lines 9, 10, 12, and 13 below.

  S corporations—Report the gain or (loss) following the instructions for Form 1120S, Schedule K, lines 5 and 6. Skip lines 9, 10, 12, and 13 below, unless line 8 is a gain and the S corporation is subject to the capital gains tax.

  All others—If line 8 is zero or a loss, enter the amount on line 12 below and skip lines 9 and 10. If line 8 is a gain and you did not have any prior year section 1231 losses, or they were recaptured in an earlier year, enter the gain as a long-term capital gain on Schedule D and skip lines 9, 10, and 13 below.

9 Nonrecaptured net section 1231 losses from prior years (see instructions) . . . . | 9 |
10 Subtract line 9 from line 8. If zero or less, enter -0-. Also enter on the appropriate line as follows (see instructions): | 10 |

  S corporations—Enter this amount (if more than zero) on Schedule D (Form 1120S), line 13, and skip lines 12 and 13 below.

  All others—If line 10 is zero, enter the amount from line 8 on line 13 below. If line 10 is more than zero, enter the amount from line 9 on line 13 below, and enter the amount from line 10 as a long-term capital gain on Schedule D.

Part II Ordinary Gains and Losses

11 Ordinary gains and losses not included on lines 12 through 18 (include property held 1 year or less):

12 Loss, if any, from line 8 . . . . | 12 | | |
13 Gain, if any, from line 8, or amount from line 9 if applicable . . . . | 13 | | 140,000 |
14 Gain, if any, from line 33 . . . . | 14 | | |
15 Net gain or (loss) from Form 4684, lines 31 and 38a . . . . | 15 | | |
16 Ordinary gain from installment sales from Form 6252, line 25 or 36 . . . . | 16 | | |
17 Ordinary gain or (loss) from like-kind exchanges from Form 8824 . . . . | 17 | | |
18 Recapture of section 179 expense deduction for partners and S corporation shareholders from property dispositions by partnerships and S corporations (see instructions) . . . . | 18 | | |
19 Add lines 11 through 18 in columns (g) and (h) . . . . | 19 | ( ) | 140,000 |
20 Combine columns (g) and (h) of line 19. Enter gain or (loss) here, and on the appropriate line as follows: . . . | 20 | | 140,000 |

  a For all except individual returns: Enter the gain or (loss) from line 20 on the return being filed.

  b For individual returns:

    (1) If the loss on line 12 includes a loss from Form 4684, line 35, column (b)(ii), enter that part of the loss here and on line 20 of Schedule A (Form 1040). Identify as from "Form 4797, line 20b(1)." See instructions . . . . | 20b(1) |

    (2) Redetermine the gain or (loss) on line 20, excluding the loss, if any, on line 20b(1). Enter here and on Form 1040, line 15 . . | 20b(2) | 140,000 |

For Paperwork Reduction Act Notice, see page 1 of separate instructions. Cat. No. 13086I Form **4797** (1993)

Figure 9-6 Form 4797

IV. Depreciation Recapture 9-31

Form 4797 (1993) Page 2

Part III Gain From Disposition of Property Under Sections 1245, 1250, 1252, 1254, and 1255

21	(a) Description of section 1245, 1250, 1252, 1254, or 1255 property:			(b) Date acquired (mo., day, yr.)	(c) Date sold (mo., day, yr.)
A	Factory building (ex. 29)			1982	1991
B	Building (ex. 31)				
C					
D					

	Relate lines 21A through 21D to these columns	▶	Property A	Property B	Property C	Property D
22	Gross sales price (Note: See line 1 before completing.)	22	320,000	285,000		
23	Cost or other basis plus expense of sale	23	220,000	300,000		
24	Depreciation (or depletion) allowed or allowable	24	80,000	160,000		
25	Adjusted basis. Subtract line 24 from line 23	25	140,000	140,000		
26	Total gain. Subtract line 25 from line 22	26	180,000	145,000		
27	**If section 1245 property:**					
a	Depreciation allowed or allowable from line 24	27a	80,000			
b	Enter the **smaller** of line 26 or 27a	27b	80,000			
28	**If section 1250 property:** If straight line depreciation was used, enter -0- on line 28g, except for a corporation subject to section 291.					
a	Additional depreciation after 1975 (see instructions)	28a		60,000		
b	Applicable percentage multiplied by the **smaller** of line 26 or line 28a (see instructions)	28b		60,000		
c	Subtract line 28a from line 26. If residential rental property or line 26 is not more than line 28a, skip lines 28d and 28e	28c		85,000		
d	Additional depreciation after 1969 and before 1976	28d				
e	Enter the **smaller** of line 28c or 28d	28e				
f	Section 291 amount (corporations only)	28f				
g	Add lines 28b, 28e, and 28f	28g		60,000		
29	**If section 1252 property:** Skip this section if you did not dispose of farmland or if this form is being completed for a partnership.					
a	Soil, water, and land clearing expenses	29a				
b	Line 29a multiplied by applicable percentage (see instructions)	29b				
c	Enter the **smaller** of line 26 or 29b	29c				
30	**If section 1254 property:**					
a	Intangible drilling and development costs, expenditures for development of mines and other natural deposits, and mining exploration costs (see instructions)	30a				
b	Enter the **smaller** of line 26 or 30a	30b				
31	**If section 1255 property:**					
a	Applicable percentage of payments excluded from income under section 126 (see instructions)	31a				
b	Enter the **smaller** of line 26 or 31a	31b				

Summary of Part III Gains. Complete property columns A through D, through line 31b before going to line 32.

32	Total gains for all properties. Add columns A through D, line 26	32	325,000
33	Add columns A through D, lines 27b, 28g, 29c, 30b, and 31b. Enter here and on line 14	33	140,000
34	Subtract line 33 from line 32. Enter the portion from casualty or theft on Form 4684, line 33. Enter the portion from other than casualty or theft on Form 4797, line 6	34	185,000

Part IV Recapture Amounts Under Sections 179 and 280F(b)(2) When Business Use Drops to 50% or Less See instructions for Part IV.

			(a) Section 179	(b) Section 280F(b)(2)
35	Section 179 expense deduction or depreciation allowable in prior years	35		
36	Recomputed depreciation (see instructions)	36		
37	Recapture amount. Subtract line 36 from line 35. See instructions for where to report	37		

Figure 9-6 Form 4797 (continued)

☑ **Example 30.** John White was depreciating an apartment building under the ACRS accelerated method. The actual depreciation deducted over the six years John held the building was $125,000. Straight-line depreciation would have been $75,000. The building has a $50,000 Sec. 1250 recapture potential. If the property had been *nonresidential* property, it would have been Sec. 1245 property and all $125,000 of depreciation deductions would be subject to recapture.

☑ **Example 31.** Maury Wold sold a building for $285,000 that had a basis of $140,000. The building originally cost $300,000 and had been depreciated under a pre-ACRS accelerated method. Straight-line depreciation would have been $100,000. Maury must recognize $60,000 Sec. 1250 recapture as ordinary income and $85,000 Sec. 1231 gain on the sale:

Original cost	$300,000	Selling price	$285,000
– Accel. deprec.	160,000	– Adj. basis	140,000
Adj. basis	$140,000	Total gain	$125,000
Accel. deprec.	$160,000	Total gain	$125,000
– St.-line dep.	100,000	– Sec. 1250 recap.	60,000
Excess deprec.	$ 60,000	Sec. 1231 gain	$ 85,000
(Sec. 1251 recapture)			

The above information is included in Form 4797 in Figure 9-6.

The Sec. 1250 recapture provisions are ineffective for property placed in service after 1986 and depreciated under MACRS. Because MACRS allows only straight-line depreciation for real property, there is no excess depreciation to be recaptured.

There have been several changes in the recapture rules over the years. For property placed in service prior to 1976, Sec. 1250 requires recapture of only a portion of the excess depreciation. A complete discussion of these pre-1976 rules is beyond the scope of this text.

TAX TIP

As long as there is little or no preferential treatment for net Sec. 1231 gains taxed as capital gains, a taxpayer is generally better off using accelerated MACRS depreciation methods for personalty rather than the alternative straight-line method. The greater amount of Sec. 1245 recapture taxed as ordinary income (rather than as capital gains) will have little effect on the taxpayer's tax liability unless there is an excess of capital losses realized in that year.

REVIEW IV

1. William Waters sold an auto and a truck used in his business. The truck was purchased in 1984 for $50,000, and William used ACRS depreciation; its basis when it was sold for

$24,000 was $16,000; the auto was acquired in 1987 for $12,000 and had a $9,000 basis when sold for $8,000. What is William's gain or loss on the transactions and its character?
   (a) $7,000 Sec. 1231 gain
   (b) $7,000 Sec. 1245 recapture
   (c) $8,000 Sec. 1245 recapture; $1,000 Sec. 1231 loss
   (d) $8,000 Sec. 1231 gain; $1,000 ordinary loss
2. Jason Allen acquired a rental office building in 1983 for $275,000. Accelerated depreciation taken was $125,000 while straight-line depreciation would have been $70,000 up to the date of sale at a price of $320,000. What is Jason's gain or loss on the sale and what is its character?
   (a) $ 70,000 Sec. 1250 recapture; $100,000 Sec. 1231 gain
   (b) $125,000 Sec. 1245 recapture; $ 45,000 Sec. 1231 gain
   (c) $170,000 Sec. 1231 gain
   (d) $170,000 capital gain
3. Aimee Martin purchased a warehouse in 1979 for $400,000. Using accelerated depreciation she claimed $200,000 of deductions up to the sale date in the current year for a selling price of $325,000. Straight-line depreciation would have been $105,000. What is Aimee's gain or loss on the sale and what is its character?
   (a) $125,000 capital gain
   (b) $125,000 Sec. 1231 gain
   (c) $125,000 Sec. 1245 recapture
   (d) $ 95,000 Sec. 1250 recapture; $30,000 Sec. 1231 gain
4. Portia Porter sold the following items in the current year:

Asset	Orig. Cost	Dep.Taken	Method	Sale Price
Equipment	$ 20,000	$ 15,000	MACRS	$ 10,000
Furniture	10,000	5,000	MACRS	4,000
Retail offices	175,000	55,000	ACRS	210,000
Warehouse	300,000	140,000	SL	150,000

What is Portia's gain or loss on the sale of all of these assets and what is its character?
   (a) $84,000 capital gain
   (b) $84,000 Sec. 1231 gain
   (c) $60,000 Sec. 1245 recapture; $24,000 Sec. 1231 gain
   (d) $84,000 Sec. 1245 recapture

Answers are on page 9-34.

GENERAL BUSINESS TAX CREDITS
(Code Sections 38–48, and 51)

The general business credit is made up of eight separate credits—the investment tax credit, the targeted jobs credit, the alcohol fuels credit, the research expenditures credit, the low-income housing credit, the enhanced oil recovery credit, the disabled access credit, and the renewable electricity production credit.* Additionally, the investment tax credit is actually made up of three distinct credits—the rehabilitation credit, the business energy credit, and the reforestation credit. Several of these credits have

*For a discussion of a ninth credit effective for tax years beginning in 1994, see Appendix J.

been modified a number of times since their initial enactment; new credits have been added; and other credits have been repealed. The business energy credit and the rehabilitation credit are two that have been modified over the years. Other business credits, such as the targeted jobs credit and the research expenditure credit, were set to expire in 1992. Many of these credits had been set to expire at earlier dates. However, Congress previously extended their expiration dates a number of times and the Revenue Reconciliation Act of 1993 extended the credits again—and made these extensions retroactive to the earlier expiration dates.

Off and on over the past 30 years, taxpayers were able to take a credit for investments in tangible personal property used in their businesses. The Tax Reform Act of 1986 repealed this regular investment tax credit for all but certain transition property placed in service after December 31, 1985. Although this credit has little relevancy today, Congress may reinstate it at some time in the future to stimulate investment in new equipment, and thus it will be briefly reviewed in the Appendix.

THE GENERAL BUSINESS CREDIT FORMAT

The general business credit—which is made up of the investment credit, the targeted jobs credit, the alcohol fuels credit, the research expenditures credit, the low-income housing credits, the enhanced oil recovery credit, the disabled access credit, and the renewable electricity production credit*—is subject to a set of limitations on its use and the carryover of excess credits. Additionally, if the taxpayer has other nonrefundable credits, the general business credit is last in priority in offsetting the taxpayer's tax liability. For an individual, the nonrefundable personal credits, such as the child care credit and the credit for the elderly, offset the tax liability before the general business credit is considered. The foreign tax credit, the "orphan" drug testing credit, and the nonconventional fuel source credit are also deducted before the general business credit.

ANSWERS TO REVIEW IV

1. (c) $8,000 Sec. 1245 recapture on the truck and $1,000 Sec. 1231 loss on the auto
2. (b) Total gain = $170,000
    $125,000 = Sec. 1245 recapture
    45,000 = Sec. 1231 gain
3. (d) Gain realized = $125,000
    Excess depreciation taken = $95,000
    Therefore: $95,000 = Sec. 1250 recapture
    30,000 = Sec. 1231 gain
4. (c) Equipment $5,000   Sec. 1245 recapture
    Furniture   1,000   Sec. 1231 loss
    Offices   55,000   Sec. 1245 recapture
                   35,000   Sec. 1231 gain
    Warehouse   10,000   Sec. 1231 loss
    There is a total of $60,000 Sec. 1245 recapture taxed as ordinary income and a net $24,000 Sec. 1231 gain that would be taxed as capital gains.

---

*For changes in the tax law effective for years beginning in 1994, see Appendix J.

☑ **Example 32.** Joanna Allen has a tax liability of $22,000 before credits. She is eligible for a $1,000 child care credit, a $3,000 foreign tax credit, and a $16,000 general business credit. Her net tax liability is determined as follows:

Gross tax liability	$22,000
less: Nonrefundable personal credit for child care	1,000
	$21,000
less: Foreign tax credit	3,000
Net tax liability before general business credit	$18,000
less: General business credit	$16,000
Net tax due	$ 2,000

The general business credit a taxpayer may use in a tax year to offset net tax liability (after considering the other priority nonrefundable credits) is limited to $25,000 plus 75% of the tax liability in excess of $25,000.

☑ **Example 33.** Al Rivera has a net tax liability of $89,000. He has an $82,000 general business credit. He may use only $73,000 of the general business credit to offset the tax liability, due to the limitation, determined as follows:

$$\$25,000 + .75(\$89,000 - \$25,000)$$
$$\$25,000 + \$48,000 = \$73,000$$

The taxpayer does not, however, lose the benefit of the credits in excess of the allowable amounts. Unused general business tax credits may be carried back 3 years and then carried forward 15 years. The taxpayer *must* carry the credit back before it may be carried forward. If the taxpayer has unused credits available from several years, including the current year, the FIFO (first-in, first out) method is used to determine carryover priority. This method is most favorable to him or her because a carryover provision expires after a particular time period.

☑ **Example 34.** Peter Thomas has a net tax liability of $41,000 after credits other than the general business credit. He has a general business credit of $4,000 generated in the current tax year, a $27,000 credit from the first preceding tax year, and a $19,000 credit from the second preceding tax year. Peter will use the credits as follows:

Allowable tax credit:	
$25,000 + .75 ($41,000 - $25,000)	$37,000
Using FIFO:	
Second preceding year	<19,000>
First preceding year	<18,000>
	$37,000
Available carryovers:	
First preceding year ($27,000 - $18,000)	$ 9,000
Current year	$ 4,000

☑ **Example 35.** Walter Stiles has a net tax liability of $45,000 before his general business credit of $52,000 for 1993. Walter had a net tax liability of $4,000 in 1990, $1,000 in 1991, and 0 in 1992. In 1993 Walter may use $40,000 [$25,000 + .75 × ($45,000 − 25,000)] of his general business credit against his $45,000 tax liability paying only $5,000 tax. The $12,000 unused general business credit must first be carried back to offset the $4,000 tax liability from 1990. The $8,000 credit remaining is then carried forward to offset the $1,000 tax liability in 1991. The $7,000 remaining unused credit must be held for carryover to 1994. Walter will use this carryover credit to offset the 1994 tax liability before any general business credit arising in that year.

The various elements of the general business credit are combined on Form 3800 for determining the applicable limitations. If the taxpayer is eligible to use only one of the business credits, the taxpayer does not have to use Form 3800 but may determine the allowable credit using the separate reporting form for that particular credit.

☑ **Example 36.** Jason Blankenstein has a net tax liability of $85,000. He is eligible for a $60,000 rehabilitation credit and a $30,000 targeted jobs credit. Jason may use a total of $70,000 of the credits to offset the tax liability determined as follows:

$$\$25,000 + .75(\$85,000 - \$25,000)$$
$$\$25,000 + \$45,000 = \$70,000$$

He uses a proportionate amount of each of the credits:

$$\text{Targeted Jobs Credit} - \$70,000 \times (\$30,000/\$90,000) = \$23,333$$
$$\text{Rehabilitation Credit} - \$70,000 \times (\$60,000/\$90,000) = \$46,667$$

TAX TIP

If general business credit carryovers are about to expire, the taxpayer should consider accelerating income recognition so that there are current tax liabilities against which the credits may be applied before expiration.

INVESTMENT TAX CREDIT

The Investment Tax Credit (ITC) is actually three separate credits that are applicable to different types of property.

> # THE LAW
>
>
> *Sec. 46(a) Amount of the Investment Credit—For purposes of section 38, the amount of the investment credit determined under this section for any taxable year shall be the sum of—*
> *(1) the rehabilitation credit,*
> *(2) the energy credit, and*
> *(3) the reforestation credit.*

The business energy credit and the rehabilitation credit have been part of the investment tax credit for a number of years, while the reforestation credit was added as part of the Revenue Reconciliation Act of 1990. The available investment credits are reported on Form 3468. These credits are then combined with the other general business credits and are subject to the general business credit limitations and carryover provisions explained above.

To continue to encourage certain activities on the part of taxpayers, Congress left intact the business energy investment credit and the credit for qualified rehabilitation expenditures when it repealed the regular ITC. With the repeal of the regular ITC percentage except for transition property, the only credits that remain for property investments are generally the energy, rehabilitation, and reforestation credits. If a taxpayer has property eligible for both the energy credit and the rehabilitation credit, he or she must choose between the two as the energy credit and the rehabilitation credit may not be taken on the same property.

REHABILITATION CREDIT

To encourage updating of older industrial and commercial buildings and the preservation of certified historical structures, Congress enacted the rehabilitation credit in 1981 as part of the investment credit. The credit was modified rather than repealed by the Tax Reform Act of 1986. There are two types of qualifying property: (1) buildings built before 1936 are eligible for a 10% credit and (2) certified historical structures are eligible for a 20% credit as shown in Table 9-1.

Table 9-1

Type of Building	Rate
Pre-1936 Buildings	10%
Certified historical structures	20%

The 10% credit applies to rehabilitation expenses incurred for nonresidential real property or residential rental property placed in service prior to 1936. To qualify as a certified historic structure and the 20% credit on rehabilitation expenditures, a building must be listed on the National Register or located in a registered historic district and certified as having historic significance.

Because the purpose of the credit is to use existing buildings, certain criteria must be met to qualify:

1. 50% or more of the external walls must be retained as external walls.
2. 75% or more of the external walls and internal structural framework must be retained.

Additionally, rehabilitation expenditures must equal the adjusted basis of the building or $5,000, if greater, within a 24-month rehabilitation period selected by the taxpayer.

The taxpayer must reduce the property's basis by the full amount of the credit, and depreciation is restricted to the straight-line method. If the taxpayer disposes of the property before the end of five years, part or all of the credit must be recaptured; that is, the "recapture" amount must be added back to the current year's tax liability. The credit is reported on Form 3468 along with any business energy credit for which the taxpayer is eligible. If the taxpayer has no other general business credits, only Form 3468 must be filed. If there are other general business credits, they are combined on Form 3800.

Example 37. Maurice White spent $50,000 rehabilitating a pre-1936 office building that cost him $25,000 to purchase, and $125,000 rehabilitating a small bed and breakfast inn listed on the National Register that he purchased for $40,000. Maurice is eligible for the following credits:

Office building	10% × ($50,000)	$ 5,000
Inn	20% × ($125,000)	25,000
	Total	$30,000

The above information is included on Form 3468 shown in Figure 9-7.

TAX TIP

To take advantage of the rehabilitation credit, a taxpayer should consider spending additional amounts on rehabilitation to meet the $5,000 or adjusted basis requirement to take the rehabilitation credit if that is the only requirement not met. For example, if an historic structure has a $40,000 basis and the taxpayer has spent $38,000 in rehabilitating the building, an additional $2,001 in expenditures will result in the taxpayer obtaining an $8,000 (.20 × $40,001) credit.

BUSINESS ENERGY CREDIT

The business energy credit applies to investments in certain types of energy resources. The creditable property and the credit percentages are as follows:

Property	Credit
Solar energy	10%
Geothermal equipment	10%

Form **3468**	**Investment Credit**	OMB No. 1545-0155
Department of the Treasury Internal Revenue Service	▶ Attach to your return. ▶ See separate instructions.	**1992** Attachment Sequence No. **52**
Name(s) as shown on return: Maurice White		Identifying number

Part I — Current Year Investment Credit

Note: *Generally, you cannot claim the regular investment credit for property placed in service after December 31, 1985 (see instructions).*

1. Rehabilitation credit. Enter the amount of qualified rehabilitation expenditures and multiply by the percentage shown:
   - **a** Pre-1936 buildings . . . . _50,000_ × 10% (.10) **1a** 5,000
   - **b** Certified historic structures (attach NPS certificate) . . . . _125,000_ × 20% (.20) **1b** 25,000

     Enter NPS number assigned or the flow-through entity's identifying number (see instructions) . . . . _____

     Transition property:
   - **c** 30-year-old buildings . . . . _____ × 10% (.10) **1c**
   - **d** 40-year-old buildings . . . . _____ × 13% (.13) **1d**
   - **e** Certified historic structures (attach NPS certificate) . . . . _____ × 25% (.25) **1e**

     Enter NPS number assigned or the flow-through entity's identifying number (see instructions) . . . . _____

2. **a** Energy credit. Enter the basis of energy property placed in service during the tax year (see instructions) . . . . _____ × 10% (.10) **2a**
   - **b** Transition property. Attach computation (see instructions). . . **2b**

3. Reforestation credit. Enter the amortizable basis of qualified timber property acquired during the taxable year (see instructions for limitations) . . . . _____ × 10% (.10) **3**

4. Regular investment credit for transition property. Enter qualified investment (see instructions) . . . . _____ × 6.5% (.065) **4**

5. Credit from cooperatives. Enter the unused regular investment credit for transition property and the unused energy credit from cooperatives **5**

6. **Current year investment credit.** Add lines 1a through 5 . . . . **6** 30,000

1993 form not available at press time.

Figure 9-7 Form 3468

A 15% credit for investment in ocean thermal property expired at the end of 1989, and the above credits were to expire on December 31, 1991. In the latter part of 1991, Congress extended the expiration date for credits on these energy properties for six months; the Comprehensive National Energy Policy Act of 1993 extends this credit permanently. These credits are reported and calculated on Form 3468 and become a part of the general business credit. They are subject to the income limitations and carryover rules that apply to all general business credits.

Taxpayers who claim the energy credit must reduce the property's basis by one-half of the credit for depreciation purposes. Additionally, the recapture of all or part of the credit is required if the property is not held for a full five years. The rate of recapture is 20% for each full or part year that the property is held less than the five full years.

☑ **Example 38.** James Swan invests $200,000 in a solar energy system for his plant. He is entitled to a $20,000 energy tax credit (.10 × $200,000) for this investment. For depreciation purposes, James must reduce the property's basis by $10,000. If he disposes of the property at the *beginning* of the fourth year of use (that is, he holds the property for only three full years, two years less than the required five years), he must recapture 40% ($8,000) of the credit.

TAX TIP

Both the energy credit and the rehabilitation credit can substantially reduce the costs of investing in the qualifying property. The taxpayer must be careful that the property meets the specific requirements of each credit, however, and that the holding periods are met; otherwise, credit recapture will be triggered.

THE REFORESTATION CREDIT

Taxpayers are allowed a tax credit of 10% of up to $10,000 ($5,000 married filing separately) invested in reforestation of qualified timber property. Qualified timber property is property located within the United States that the taxpayer holds for the cultivating and planting of trees. The trees must be cut for sale or used in the production of wood products. Eligible costs for the credit include

1. site preparation

2. seeds or seedlings

3. labor, equipment depreciation, and tools incurred in the planting process

☑ **Example 39.** Martha Mullins owns 2,000 acres of property in Minnesota. She decided to plant half of the acreage in pine trees for sale to local industries. She spent $20,000 for the seedlings and labor to have them planted. Martha would be entitled to a $1,000 (10% of the maximum $10,000) reforestation credit.

OTHER GENERAL BUSINESS CREDITS

The Targeted Jobs Credit

The targeted jobs credit is designed to encourage taxpayers to employ certain disadvantaged persons. These targeted groups include

1. vocational rehabilitation referrals
2. economically disadvantaged youths
3. economically disadvantaged Vietnam-era veterans
4. Social Security Supplementary Income recipients
5. general assistance recipients
6. youths participating in cooperative education programs
7. economically disadvantaged ex-convicts
8. eligible work incentive employees
9. members of economically disadvantaged families
10. qualified summer youth employees

THE LAW

Sec. 51(a)—For purposes of section 38, the amount of the targeted jobs credit determined under this section for the taxable year shall be equal to 40 percent of the qualified first-year wages for such year....

(b)(1)—The term "qualified wages" means the wages paid or incurred by the employer during the taxable year to individuals who are members of a targeted group. (2)—The term "qualified first-year wages" means, with respect to any individual, qualified wages attributable to service rendered during the 1-year period beginning with the day the individual begins work for the employer.
(3)—The amount of the qualified first-year wages, which may be taken into account with respect to any individual shall not exceed $6,000 per year.

Individuals must be certified by an appropriate local agency as a member of one of the above targeted groups for the employer to claim the credit. IRC Section 51(d) further defines the requirements for membership in each of these groups.

There are two differing computations for the targeted jobs credit. One formula applies solely to qualified summer youth employees and a second formula applies to all other targeted groups. The general targeted jobs credits that apply to categories (1) through (8) provide a maximum credit of 40% for the first $6,000 of first-year wages paid to qualifying individuals. The employer is required to reduce wage expense by the amount of the credit, however.

Example 40. Charles Lane hires an economically disadvantaged Vietnam-era veteran as certified by a local social welfare agency on March 1, 1992. During 1992 Charles pays the man $5,200 for part-time work. Charles may claim a targeted jobs credit of $2,080 (.40 × $5,200), but he must reduce his wage expense to $3,120 ($5,200 − $2,080).

Form 5884 — Jobs Credit (1992)

Name(s) as shown on return: Charles Lane

Part I — Current Year Jobs Credit

1. Enter the total qualified wages paid or incurred during the tax year for services of employees who are certified as members of a targeted group ... **1** | 800
2. Enter 40% (.40) of line 1 here. You must subtract this amount from the deduction on your return for salaries and wages. (Members of a group of trades or businesses under common control, see instructions.) ... **2** | 320
3. Flow-through jobs credits from other entities —
   - a Shareholder — Schedule K-1 (Form 1120S), lines 12d, 12e, or 13
   - b Partner — Schedule K-1 (Form 1065), lines 13d, 13e, or 14
   - c Beneficiary — Schedule K-1 (Form 1041), line 13
   - d Patron — Written statement from cooperative ... **3** | —
4. **Current year jobs credit.** Add lines 2 and 3. (S corporations, partnerships, estates, trusts, and cooperatives, see instructions.) ... **4** | 320

1993 form not available at press time.

Figure 9-8 Form 5884

✓ **Example 41.** Charles continues to employ the man throughout 1993, paying him $7,800 in wages ($650 per month). Charles may take an additional credit of $320 (.40 × $800) and he must reduce his wage expense to $7,480 ($7,800 − $320). Since the veteran exceeded $6,000 wages in his first 12 months of employment, the credit is limited to a total of $2,400 (.40 × $6,000) during this period. The information in this example is shown on Form 5884 in Figure 9-8.

An alternative calculation is required to determine the credit for employing certified qualifying summer youths. The credit for youths hired is similar to the general targeted jobs credit explained previously, except that only $3,000 of wages is eligible for the 40% credit.

For the employer of certified summer youths to be eligible for the credit, the following requirements must be met:

1. The youths must be 16 or 17 years of age when hired.
2. They may not have worked for the employer previously.
3. The services must be performed over a 90-day period from May 1 through September 15.

✓ **Example 42.** During the summer of 1993, Nancy Taylor hired two 17-year-old qualified summer youths as lifeguards during July and August. Nancy paid one youth $3,400 and the other $2,300 during the two-month period. Nancy may claim a credit of $2,120 [.40 × ($3,000 maximum + $2,300)]. Nancy must reduce the $5,700 of wage expense by the $2,120 credit.

✓ **Example 43.** Marcy Walker hired Tom, a qualified youth, in May 1993, as a general helper. During the summer Tom worked for Marcy, he earned $4,300. Marcy is

Form 5884 — Jobs Credit (1992)

Form **5884**	**Jobs Credit**	OMB No. 1545-0219 **1992** Attachment Sequence No. 77
Department of the Treasury Internal Revenue Service	▶ Attach to your return.	
Name(s) as shown on return: Marcy Walker		Identifying number

Part I — Current Year Jobs Credit

1	Enter the total qualified wages paid or incurred during the tax year for services of employees who are certified as members of a targeted group	1	3,000
2	Enter 40% (.40) of line 1 here. You must subtract this amount from the deduction on your return for salaries and wages. (Members of a group of trades or businesses under common control, see instructions.)	2	1,200
3	Flow-through jobs credits from other entities — If you are a— Shareholder / Partner / Beneficiary / Patron — Then enter total of current year jobs credit(s) from— Schedule K-1 (Form 1120S), lines 12d, 12e, or 13; Schedule K-1 (Form 1065), lines 13d, 13e, or 14; Schedule K-1 (Form 1041), line 13; Written statement from cooperative	3	—
4	**Current year jobs credit.** Add lines 2 and 3. (S corporations, partnerships, estates, trusts, and cooperatives, see instructions.)	4	1,200

1993 form not available at press time.

Figure 9-9 Form 5884

eligible for a $1,200 credit (.40 × $3,000). Marcy must reduce her wage expense by the credit to $3,100 ($4,300 – $1,200). This information is shown on Form 5884 in Figure 9-9.

A qualified summer youth may be eligible for the general targeted jobs credit if he or she continues to work beyond the allowable 90-day period. To qualify, however, the individual must be recertified as eligible and the $6,000 general jobs credit wage limit must be reduced by the wages on which the summer youth credit was calculated.

✓ **Example 44.** If, in the preceding example, Tom was recertified and continued to work for Marcy earning an additional $4,200 during 1993, Marcy would be able to claim another $1,200 (.40 × $3,000) general jobs credit. Marcy would also have to reduce her wage expense by this $1,200 credit.

The targeted jobs credit was set to expire for all categories of employees hired after 1991. Congress first extended this credit for six months and has now extended it through December 31, 1994 as part of the Revenue Reconciliation Act of 1993. These targeted jobs tax credits are reported on Form 5884. If the taxpayer has no other business credits, Form 5884 alone may be used. If other business credits are claimed, Form 3800 must also be filed in order to summarize the reporting of all business credits.

TAX TIP

Taxpayers who hire individuals qualifying for the targeted jobs credit and then let them go when the credit maximum is reached may be making unsound business decisions. The value of the trained employee should not be underestimated when considering hiring another new employee simply to receive the credit.

Research Expenditures Credit

>
> # THE LAW
>
> *Sec. 41(a)*—*For purposes of section 38, the research credit determined under this section for the taxable year shall be an amount equal to the sum of—*
> *(1) 20 percent of the excess (if any) of—*
> *(A) the qualified research expenses for the taxable year, over*
> *(B) the base period research expenses, and*
> *(2) 20 percent of the basic research payments determined under subsection (e)(1)(A).*

Research payments eligible for the 20% credit are divided into two categories:

1. qualified research expenditures in excess of a base period amount
2. payments for basic research made to qualified organizations under a written agreement.

The first category includes both in-house research expenses and 65% of the research expenses paid to third parties for qualified research. Eligible in-house expenses include employee wages, cost of supplies, and third-party computer expense for qualified research. Qualifying research must be related to a current trade or business of the taxpayer. Eligible activities include the development of experimental models, plant processes, new formulas, inventions, or improvements to existing processes or property.

Not all qualifying expenses are eligible for the credit. Only those "excess expenditures"—research expenses in excess of a base amount—are eligible for the 20% credit. Determination of the base amount requires calculating (1) a fixed-base percentage, which is the ratio of qualified research expenditures to total gross receipts using data from tax years beginning in 1984 through 1988 and multiplying that number by the average annual gross receipts for the four years prior to the current year. Businesses with research expenditures and gross receipts in fewer than three tax years from 1984 through 1988 are permitted a fixed-base percentage of 3%,* with a maximum of 16% allowed any business. To prevent "loading" research expenditures into one year for credit purposes, the base amount cannot be less than 50% of the current year's research expenditures.

Example 45. John Forte's company manufactures heavy-duty truck washers. Qualifying research expenses and gross receipts for 1986 through 1993 are as follows:

Tax Year	Research Expense	Annual Gross Receipts
1986	$ 23,000	$272,000
1987	74,000	408,000
1988	62,000	425,000
1989	46,000	315,000

*For changes in the tax law effective for years after 1998, see Appendix J.

1990	32,000	391,000
1991	48,000	400,000
1992	60,000	433,000
1993	119,000	682,000

John's fixed-base percentage is 14.39% ([$23,000 + $74,000 + $62,000]/[$272,000 + $408,000 + $425,000]). His calculated base amount is $55,366 (.1439 × $384,750; $384,750 = [$433,000 + $400,000 + $391,000 + $315,000]/4). Since this base amount is less than $59,500 (.5 × $119,000), John must use this as his base amount. The excess expenditures eligible for the credit are $59,500 ($119,000 − $59,500) and the credit then is $11,900 (.2 × $59,500). If the calculated base amount had been greater than $59,500, that amount would have been used to determine the excess expenditures and the research credit. Form 6765, Figure 9-10, illustrates this example.

Example 46. Julia Morgan's company began operations in 1992. It spent $42,000 on qualifying research that year. During 1993 Julia contracted with an outside firm to do research at a cost of $50,000. Because it is contract research, however, only $32,500 (65% × $50,000) is eligible for the research credit.

Form 6765 — Credit for Increasing Research Activities (or for claiming the orphan drug credit)
OMB No. 1545-0619
1992
Attachment Sequence No. 81
Department of the Treasury, Internal Revenue Service
► See separate Instructions.
► Attach to your return.

Name(s) as shown on return: John Forte
Identifying number:

Part III — Current Year Credit for Increasing Research Activities

11	Basic research payments paid or incurred to qualified organizations	
12	Base period amount	
13	Subtract line 12 from line 11. If less than zero, enter -0-	-0-
	Qualified research expenses paid or incurred (lines 14–17):	
14	Wages for qualified services (do not include wages used in figuring the jobs credit)	
15	Cost of supplies	
16	Rental or lease costs of computers	
17	65% (.65) of contract expenses	
18	Total qualified research expenses. Add lines 14 through 17	119,000
19	Enter fixed-base percentage, but not more than 16% (see instructions)	.1439 %
20	Enter average annual gross receipts (see instructions)	384,750
21	Base amount. Multiply line 20 by the percentage on line 19 (see instructions)	55,366
22	Subtract line 21 from line 18	63,634
23	Multiply line 18 by 50% (.50)	59,500
24	Enter smaller of line 22 or 23	59,500
25	Add lines 13 and 24	59,500
26	Tentative credit. Multiply line 25 by 20% (.20). If you do not elect the reduced credit under Section 280C(c), enter the result and see the instructions. If you do elect the reduced credit, multiply the result by 66% (.66) and enter that amount instead. Also write "Sec. 280C" in the margin to the right of the entry space.	11,900
27	Flow-through research credit(s) from a partnership, S corporation, estate, or trust	
28	Current year credit for increasing research activities. Add lines 26 and 27. Enter here and see Claiming the Credit on page 2 to see if you have to file Form 3800	11,900

See Paperwork Reduction Act Notice on page 2.   Cat. No. 13700H   Form **6765** (1991)
1993 form not available at press time.

Figure 9-10 Form 6765

To be eligible for the 20% research credit, basic research payments must be made in cash to a qualifying organization such as a university, a scientific research or tax-exempt organization, or a grant organization. The research must either be performed or controlled by the organization. Only basic research payments in excess of the qualified organization base-period amount are eligible for this portion of the credit. Determination of the qualified organization base-period amount is beyond the scope of this text, however. The basic research payments that do not exceed this qualified base-period amount (and thus are not eligible for the credit as basic research payments) may be eligible for the qualified research expenditure credit under the first category, as explained previously.

☑ **Example 47.** Walter Black's company made a cash payment of $100,000 to a local university to aid in its basic research efforts in biomedical engineering. The company's qualified base period amount is $20,000. The company may claim a $16,000 credit [.20 ($100,000 − $20,000)] for basic research. The excluded $20,000 may be eligible for a credit, however, as part of the company's qualifying research credit category.

The taxpayer may either expense currently or capitalize research expenditures electively. For tax years beginning after 1988, the taxpayer must reduce the amount expensed or capitalized by 50% of the credit claimed for qualified research expenses or basic research payments. The taxpayer is not required to claim the full amount of the research credit, but this election is beyond the scope of this text.

☑ **Example 48.** Thomas Crane is eligible for a $40,000 research credit for basic research payments of $200,000 in excess of the base amount of $20,000. If Thomas takes the full $40,000 credit, he must reduce the research expenditure either expensed or capitalized to $200,000 [220,000 − (.50 × 40,000)].

The research credit is now in effect through the middle of 1995. This credit had been extended several times in the past and a three-year extension to the current mid-1995 date was included in the Revenue Reconciliation Act of 1993. The taxpayer claims the credit for research activities on Form 6765, and it is combined with the other general business credits on Form 3800.

Low-Income Housing Credit

The credit for the construction, rehabilitation, or acquisition of low-income housing was added to the general business credits as part of Tax Reform Act of 1986.

THE LAW

Sec. 42(a)—For purposes, of section 38, the amount of the low-income housing credit determined under this section for any taxable year in the credit period shall be an amount equal to—
(1) the applicable percentage of
(2) the qualified basis of each qualified low-income building....
(b)(2)(A)—In the case of any qualified low-income building placed in service by the taxpayer after 1987, the term "applicable percentage" means the appropriate percentage prescribed by the Secretary....
(B) The percentages prescribed ... will yield over a 10-year period amounts of credit under subsection (a) which have present value equal to—
(i) 70 percent of the qualified basis of a building described in paragraph (1)(A), and
(ii) 30 percent of the qualified basis of a building described in paragraph (1)(B).

This credit is subject to a series of complex requirements for eligibility. First, each state is allotted a portion of the maximum national annual low-income housing credit. The state must then allocate a portion of this credit to the property owner.

There are two different credit percentages prescribed monthly by the Secretary based on the type of low-income housing property. The credit percentage allowed for new unsubsidized buildings is prescribed to provide a present-value credit amount over ten years equal to 70% of the building's qualified basis. The credit percentage for federally subsidized new buildings or existing buildings is prescribed by the Secretary to provide a present-value credit amount equal to 30% of the building's qualified basis. To be part of a low-income housing project, a certain portion of the units must have occupants who meet limited income requirements and the required rental payments are restricted. The project must meet these requirements within a certain period after being placed in service. (For single buildings this is 12 months.)

Example 49. Sara Major places $100,000 of qualified basis new low-income property in service in 1991. If she is allowed a 9% credit as prescribed by the Secretary and she meets all other eligibility requirements, Sara may take a $9,000 credit in 1991 and each of the following nine years. (Note that a building placed in service *during* a tax year requires an adjustment to the first year's credit.)

This credit was made permanent by the Revenue Reconciliation Act of 1993 and has no scheduled expiration date. The taxpayer reports the total of the low-income housing credits on Form 8586. Form 8609, however, must be completed for each of the projects eligible for this credit. These totals are then combined with other credits on Form 3800. The credit is spread over ten years beginning with the year the project is placed in service, or, electively, the following year. If the project fails to meet qualified basis requirements during the 15-year compliance period, recapture of prior credits is required.

> **TAX TIP**
>
>
>
> If the taxpayer can obtain either subsidized or nonsubsidized financing for the low-income housing, the credit percentage should be carefully weighed in determining the form of financing chosen because the difference can have a dramatic effect on the low-income housing's overall return to the owner.

Disabled Access Credit

To encourage small businesses to make their premises accessible to disabled individuals, the Revenue Reconciliation Act of 1990 provides a credit equal to 50% of the expenditures in the tax year in excess of $250 to $10,250 for modifications to the workplace. A small business is defined as one that has gross receipts of no more than $1 million or had no more than 30 full-time employees during the preceding tax year. Costs eligible for the credit include

1. costs of removing architectural, communication, physical, or transportation barriers
2. costs to accommodate the hearing impaired
3. costs to accommodate the visually impaired
4. costs to acquire or modify equipment for the disabled
5. costs to provide other similar services or equipment

The costs incurred in connection with new construction are not eligible for the credit. Moreover, the taxpayer may not take a deduction or increase the basis of property for the amount of the credit taken.

Example 50. Allen Morgan hired several persons to build ramps at his retail store to accommodate persons in wheelchairs. He spent $9,550 for the material and labor. Allen may take a 50% credit of $4,650 [.50 × ($9,550 − $250)] for these expenditures. He must, however, reduce the basis of these improvements by the $4,650 credit for depreciation purposes.

The Alcohol Fuels Credit

The alcohol fuels credit is another credit that is a combination of several credits related to the production and use of alcohol as an alternative fuel source. The amount of the credit is either 54 or 40 cents per gallon (depending on the proof of the alcohol) for

1. alcohol mix fuels produced and either used or sold by the taxpayer in his or her business
2. alcohol fuel sold or used by the taxpayer in his or her business

The Revenue Reconciliation Act of 1990 added a 10 cents per gallon credit for the production of ethanol by taxpayers qualifying as small producers with production not exceeding 15,000,000 gallons annually. The credit is generally applicable until the year 2001.

Enhanced Oil Recovery Credit

The Revenue Reconciliation Act of 1990 added a 15% credit for qualified enhanced oil recovery costs incurred by the taxpayer. The costs must relate to a certified qualified enhanced oil recovery project located within the United States. Costs eligible for the credit include depreciable tangible property used in the project and intangible drilling and development costs incurred in connection with the project. The credit is subject to reduction as the price of crude oil increases. Additionally, the deductibility of expenses and the basis of property must be reduced by the amount of the credit taken.

Renewable Electricity Production Credit

For tax years after 1992, a producer of electricity is eligible for a credit of 1.5 cents per kilowatt hour of electricity sold to an unrelated person and produced from a qualified energy resource at a qualified facility during the ten-year period following the date the qualified facility is put into service. This credit is subject to certain limitations and adjustments, as well as an inflation adjustment for the 1.5 cents per kilowatt hour credit. It also has a number of technical details and definitions as part of the statute.

REVIEW V

1. Which of the following credits is *not* part of the general business credit?
   (a) targeted jobs credit
   (b) low-income housing credit
   (c) rehabilitation credit
   (d) foreign tax credit
2. If Barbara Reyes has a tax liability of $124,000, what is the maximum amount that can be offset by the general business credit?
   (a) $25,000
   (b) $93,000
   (c) $99,250
   (d) $124,000
3. Which of the following persons are not eligible to be certified for the targeted jobs credit?
   (a) economically disadvantaged Vietnam veterans
   (b) college work-study employees
   (c) general assistance recipients
   (d) qualified summer youth employees
4. Walter Ainsborough has been eligible for business credits for several years. His credits and tax liabilities for the years at issue are

Year	General Business Credit	Tax Liability
1984	0	$ 8,000
1985	0	6,000
1986	0	24,000
1987	$31,000	35,000
1988	0	0
1989	69,000	46,500
1990	28,000	7,500

What is Walter's credit carryover from 1990 available for use in future years?
(a) $0
(b) $1,125
(c) $3,750
(d) $8,875

5. Troy Bancroft had the following items pertaining to his business:
   (1) employed a qualified summer youth, paying him $3,800 during the summer.
   (2) invested $27,000 in solar energy equipment to help meet his energy needs.
   (3) rehabilitated a qualifying certified historic structure at a cost of $275,000.
   (4) paid a social security supplementary income recipient $7,200 during his first year of employment.

   Troy's general business credit for the current year is (assuming all other requirements are met)
   (a) $6,300.
   (b) $33,800.
   (c) $61,300.
   (d) $62,100.

6. The low-income housing credit percentage allowed for federally subsidized new or existing buildings is prescribed to provide a present-value credit amount over ten years equal to
   (a) 70% of the building's qualified basis.
   (b) 50% of the building's qualified basis.
   (c) 30% of the building's qualified basis.
   (d) None of the above.

Answers are on page 9-52.

CHAPTER APPENDIX: NET OPERATING LOSS DEDUCTIONS
(Code Section 172)

To make the income tax somewhat more equitable, Congress has written into the tax laws certain alternatives for computing taxable income and taxes due. One of these, the net operating loss carryover, provides a limited amount of relief from the annual system of taxation. If Taxpayer A has $100,000 of business income in one tax year and a $50,000 business loss in the next tax year while Taxpayer B has $25,000 of business income in the same two consecutive tax years, the tax laws would require the payment of a greater amount of taxes by Taxpayer A because of the structure of the tax system. If both Taxpayer A and Taxpayer B could report their income over the two-year period, they would report $50,000 of total business income and would pay the same amount of tax. This is not the case, however, due to the annual system of reporting on which our tax system is founded.

There is, however, relief for those taxpayers who have business income in some years while reporting losses in others. This relief comes in the form of a net operating loss (NOL) deduction. Basically, the taxpayer is permitted to carry the loss from a loss year to a year in which taxable income was reported, deducting the loss against this income in determining the tax due.

THE LAW

Sec. 172(a)—There shall be allowed as a deduction for the taxable year an amount equal to the aggregate of (1) the net operating loss carryovers to such year plus (2) the net operating loss carrybacks to such year. For purposes of this subtitle, the term "net operating loss deduction" means the deduction allowed by this subsection.

(b)(1)(A)—Except as otherwise provided in this paragraph, a net operating loss for any taxable year shall be a net operating loss carryback to each of the 3 taxable years preceding the taxable year of such loss. (B)—Except as otherwise provided in this paragraph, a net operating loss for any taxable year ending after December 31, 1975, shall be a net operating loss carryover to each of the 15 taxable years following the taxable year of the loss.

A taxpayer is permitted to carry back a net operating loss 3 years and/or carry forward the net operating loss for 15 years. The taxpayer is not required to carry back a net operating loss; the taxpayer can elect to carry the loss forward only. If the taxpayer chooses to carry the net operating loss back, it *must* be carried back first to the third preceding tax year and then to the second preceding tax year before it can be carried back to the tax year immediately preceding the current tax year. If the taxpayer had taxable income in one or more of the preceding three years, the advantage of using the carryback feature is that the taxpayer can obtain a refund of taxes from one or more prior years. The disadvantage is that the carryback requires an almost complete redetermination of the carryback year's taxable income, tax due, allowable credits and carryovers. It could also place the taxpayer in the situation of having to pay an alternative minimum tax in place of the regular tax. For these and other reasons, it is not uncommon for taxpayers to forgo the carryback provision and wait until a future year to carry over a prior year's loss against that year's income.

Example 51. Morgan Wolf has had income in each of the last five years but in 1993 he has a net operating loss of $15,000. If Morgan uses the NOL carryback provision, he must first carry the loss back to 1990; if any part of the loss remains, it can be carried to 1991 and then to 1992.

Taxpayers are also permitted to carry NOLs forward for 15 years, either after they use the 3-year carryback provision or as an alternative to carrying the loss back. When they carry NOLs forward, they must carry them to the first year in which they have income, and then to each subsequent income year in turn, until the NOL is exhausted (or the 15th year is reached). Figure 9-11 illustrates these carryover provisions for the NOLs.

Example 52. Portia Thomas reported an enormous net operating loss in 1991, her only loss year. Portia can carry the loss back to 1988, 1989, and 1990, in sequence, and then forward 15 years starting with 1992, 1993, 1994, etc., until it is totally used up or the final carryover year of 2006 is reached. Alternatively, Portia can carry the loss forward only for 15 years starting with 1992 and continuing until 2006 or the loss is exhausted.

Carryback/Carryforward	Carryforward Only
1988	1991 Loss Year
1989	
1990	1992
	1993
1991 Loss year	1994
	·
1992	·
1993	2006
·	
·	
2006	

Figure 9-11   NOL Carryovers

Taxpayers do not have to file any special forms to forgo the carryback provision of the NOL. Because they normally have only three years from the due date of their return to file an amended return for a prior year on which they take the NOL deduction, the passage of time will prevent them from using the carryback. If they choose to carry forward a net operating loss before the statute of limitations runs out for making a carryback, however, the taxpayer simply attaches a statement to the return indicating the intention to forgo the carryback of the NOL.

☑   **Example 53.**   Tina Yale had an unused net operating loss from her 1987 return, filed April 15, 1988. In 1993 she has substantial income against which this prior loss can be offset. Because more than three years have passed since Tina filed her 1987

ANSWERS TO REVIEW V

1. (d) The foreign tax credit is a separate credit.
2. (c) $25,000 + .75 ($124,000 − $25,000)
3. (b) College work-study employees are not part of the targeted groups.
4. (d) The $31,000 business credit from 1987 first offsets the $8,000, 1984 tax liability and then it offsets $6,000 of the 1985 liability and $17,000 of the $24,000, 1986 tax liability. The $69,000 business credit from 1989 first offsets the $7,000 tax liability from 1986; then it offsets $32,500 [$25,000 + .75($35,000 − $25,000)] of the 1987 liability and finally $29,500 of the 1989 tax liability. The $28,000 credit from 1990 first offsets $11,625 {[$25,000 + .75 × (46,500 − $25,000)] − $29,500} of the balance of the 1989 tax liability eligible for the credit; then it offsets the $7,500 of the 1990 tax liability, leaving $8,875 to be carried forward.
5. (c)

Qualified summer youth credit	$3,000 × .40 =	$ 1,200
Solar energy credit	$27,000 × .10 =	2,700
Rehabilitation credit	$275,000 × .20 =	55,000
Targeted jobs credit	6,000 × .40 =	2,400
		$61,300

6. (c)

return, she can no longer carry the net operating loss back to a prior year; she can, however, carry it forward to 1993 (after first carrying it forward to any income years between 1987 and 1993).

If an individual taxpayer chooses to claim a net operating loss carryback, Form 1045 may be filed after the tax return for the loss year is filed but within one year of the close of the tax year of the loss to obtain a "quick" refund. A corporate taxpayer would make the same claim for a "quick" refund by filing Form 1139. If the taxpayer fails to file the claim for the quick refund within the permitted time, an amended return may be filed for the year to which the loss is to be carried within the time limits prescribed for filing amended returns—usually three years from the due date of the return. Chapter 7 provides more detail on the filing of amended returns by a taxpayer.

TAX TIP

A taxpayer should carefully examine whether the NOL should be carried back or carried forward only. In most instances, using the quick refund provision for the NOL carryback puts money most quickly into the taxpayer's hands. There have been, however, certain quirks in the tax law that gave the taxpayer no refund of prior taxes in spite of an NOL carryback.

CALCULATING THE NET OPERATING LOSS

The purpose of the NOL deduction is, unfortunately, far easier to understand for the individual taxpayer than the process required to calculate it. This loss deduction is designed to reflect the taxpayer's real loss in an economic sense and it is solely an *operating* loss; that is, it is a loss related to trade or business operations. Note, however, that the taxpayer's deduction for personal casualty and theft losses is treated as a business loss in determining the NOL deduction. Thus, a taxpayer whose only trade or business is as an employee will not have an NOL deduction (unless the taxpayer has a large casualty or theft loss) regardless of the negative amount reported as taxable income on the Form 1040.

To have a NOL, an individual taxpayer must have trade or business (or casualty and theft) losses. Additionally, individual taxpayers are required to make certain adjustments to their business operating losses to determine the NOL deduction because individual taxpayers have many transactions and artificial deductions that are unrelated to business operations. If the taxpayer has income from nonbusiness transactions that exceeds nonbusiness losses and deductions, the excess must be used to reduce the NOL.

On the other hand, the NOL deduction for a corporate taxpayer is generally its reported taxable loss for the year. This is the result of the basic assumption that a corporation's sole existence is business motivated. The same simplicity does not follow individual taxpayers, however, due to the complex structure of the individual tax formula.

THE LAW

Sec. 172(c)—For purposes of this section, the term "net operating loss" means the excess of the deductions allowed by this chapter over the gross income. Such excess shall be computed with the modifications specified in subsection (d).

Sec. 172(d)(1)—No net operating loss deduction shall be allowed. (2)—In the case of a taxpayer other than a corporation, the amount deductible on account of losses from sales or exchanges of capital assets shall not exceed the amount includable on account of gains from sales or exchanges of capital assets. (3)—No deduction shall be allowed under section 151 (relating to personal exemptions)....(4)—In the case of a taxpayer other than a corporation, the deductions allowable by this chapter which are not attributable to a taxpayer's trade or business shall be allowed only to the extent of the amount of the gross income not derived from such trade or business....(C) any deduction allowable under section 165(c)(3) (relating to casualty losses) shall not be taken into account.

To calculate the allowable NOL deduction, the taxpayer starts with the negative amount reported on the taxable income line of the Form 1040. The taxpayer must then make certain adjustments or "add-backs" that will, in effect, lessen this negative amount. If at any time during this adjustment process the amount becomes positive, the taxpayer simply will have no NOL deduction.

Taxable Loss as Reported on Form 1040 (negative number)
+ NOLs Carried from Other Tax Years
+ Personal and Dependency Exemptions
+ Adjustments Required for Capital and Nonbusiness Items

Net Operating Loss (NOL)—must be a negative number

The first adjustment the taxpayer must make is to remove (add back) any NOL deductions carried forward from a prior year or back from a subsequent year. The taxpayer then adds back the amounts allowed as personal and dependency exemption deductions because these are purely artificial deductions permitted by the tax code. Finally, the taxpayer makes a complex adjustment that takes into consideration capital gains and losses and nonbusiness income and deductions. This adjustment entails the following steps:

1. Nonbusiness capital gains and losses: If the taxpayer has nonbusiness capital losses in excess of nonbusiness capital gains, the excess is added back to the reported loss. Net nonbusiness capital gains are considered in Step 2.

2. Nonbusiness income and expenses: If the taxpayer has nonbusiness expenses in excess of nonbusiness income plus net nonbusiness capital gains from Step 1, this excess is added back to the reported loss. Net nonbusiness capital gains in excess of net nonbusiness expenses are considered in Step 3.

3. Business capital gains and losses: If the taxpayer has business capital losses in excess of business capital gains plus the excess net nonbusiness capital gains

over net nonbusiness expenses from Step 2, this excess must be added back to the reported loss.

Example 54. Joseph Parker has the following income and losses:

Nonbusiness income	$3,000
Nonbusiness expenses	8,000
Nonbusiness capital gains	4,000
Nonbusiness capital losses	2,500
Business capital gains	2,500
Business capital losses	4,000

Joseph's adjustment for the above items is determined as follows:

Step 1:	Nonbusiness capital losses	$2,500	
	Nonbusiness capital gains	4,000	
	Net nonbusiness capital gains	$1,500	
	(No adjustment—carry $1,500 to Step 2.)		
Step 2:	Nonbusiness expenses	$8,000	
	Nonbusiness income	3,000	
	plus: Net nonbusiness capital gain	1,500	(from Step 1)
	Adjustment		$3,500
Step 3:	Business capital losses	$4,000	
	Business capital gains	2,500	
	Adjustment		$1,500
	Total adjustment		$5,000

In making the above calculation, we must understand several issues and definitions, including the treatment of casualty and theft losses of personal property as business losses. First, business income includes salary and wages as an employee and is not limited to income from self-employment. Second, contributions to retirement plans, IRAs, and Keoghs are *not* allowed to be treated as business deductions. Third, the major nonbusiness deductions are the standard deduction or itemized deductions. Itemized deductions must be reduced, however, for those deductions that *are* treated as business losses or expenses, such as the casualty or theft losses and other deductible business items such as union dues, uniforms, tools, and qualifying educational expenses.

Example 55. Maury Willems had $17,500 of itemized deductions that included a $7,000 deductible theft loss for an automobile and $1,200 of deductible qualifying educational expenses. Maury's itemized deductions, considered nonbusiness expenses, are $9,300 ($17,500 – $7,000 – $1,200).

Example 56. Kay Rizzo opened a dress shop at the beginning of 1992. Because this was her first year of operation, she reported a $40,000 loss for this sole proprietorship on her Schedule C and Form 1040. Kay also had $5,000 of dividend and interest income, a $7,000 long-term capital gain on the sale of a lot, and a $9,000 long-term loss on the sale of some stock. Kay is single with no dependents and does not itemize. Assume that Kay's standard deduction is $3,600 and exemption is $2,300. Kay has an NOL deduction from this year of $38,400 determined as follows:

Kay's total income (loss) (reported on Form 1040)

	$ 5,000	Div./Int. income
	(40,000)	Business loss
	(2,000)	Net cap. loss
	($37,000)	AGI
less	3,600	Std. ded.
less	2,300	Pers. exemp.
	($42,900)	Taxable income (Loss)

Net operating loss deduction

	($42,900)	Taxable income
Adjustments (add-backs):		
NOL deductions	0	
Personal exemption	2,300	
(1) Excess nonbusiness capital losses	2,000	
(2) Excess nonbusiness expenses	0	
(3) Excess business capital losses	0	
	($38,600)	

This NOL can be carried back to Kay's third preceding tax year or carried forward 15 years. A Form 1045, Schedule A, page 2, reflecting the above information and required calculations, is shown in Figure 9-12.

TAX TIP

If a taxpayer has an NOL that is about to expire, alternatives that provide smaller deductions (for example, straight-line versus modified ACRS depreciation) or accelerate income (using percentage of completion rather than the completed contract method of income recognition) should be used to determine taxable income. Thus, there will be greater taxable income with which to offset the NOL carryforward.

An individual taxpayer who carries an NOL to another year in which taxable income is reduced to a negative amount may not simply carry this number to another carryover year. Instead, a separate calculation must again be made to determine the amount of the NOL carryover that is available to offset income in another carryover year. While this calculation is similar to that made to determine the NOL deduction in the loss year, its exact determination is beyond the scope of this text.

THE REGULAR INVESTMENT TAX CREDIT

The regular investment tax credit applies with certain limitations to a taxpayer's investment in qualifying property. The Tax Reform Act of 1986 repealed the regular

Chapter Appendix: Net Operating Loss Deductions 9-57

Form **1045**	**Application for Tentative Refund**	OMB No. 1545-0098
Department of the Treasury Internal Revenue Service	▶ Before you fill out this form, read the instructions on page 3. ▶ Do not attach to your income tax return—mail in a separate envelope. ▶ For use by individuals, estates, or trusts.	**1992**

	Name — Kay Rizzo	Social security or employer identification number
Please type or print	Number, street, and apt. or suite no. (if P.O. box or foreign address, see instructions)	Spouse's social security number
	City, town or post office, state, and ZIP code	Telephone no. (optional) ( )

1 This application is filed to carry back: (a) Net operating loss (from Schedule A, page 2, line 21) **$ 38,400**   (b) Unused general business credit $

Schedule A—Net Operating Loss (NOL) (See instructions.)

1	Adjusted gross income from 1991 Form 1040, line 32. Estates and trusts, skip lines 1 and 2		1	<37,000>
2	Deductions (individuals only):			
a	Enter amount from your 1991 Form 1040, line 34	2a 3,600		
b	Multiply $2,150 by the total number of exemptions on your 1991 Form 1040, line 6e	2b 2,300		
c	Add lines 2a and 2b		2c	(5,900)
3	Combine lines 1 and 2c. Estates and trusts, enter your taxable income		3	<42,900>
	Note: If line 3 is zero or more, do not complete rest of schedule. You do not have a net operating loss.			
	Adjustments:			
4	Exemptions from line 2b above. Estates and trusts, enter exemption from your tax return		4	2,300
5	Nonbusiness capital losses (enter as a positive number)	5 9,000		
6	Nonbusiness capital gains	6 7,000		
7	If line 5 is more than line 6, enter difference; otherwise, enter -0-.	7 2,000		
8	If line 6 is more than line 5, enter difference; otherwise, enter -0-.	8 -0-		
9	Nonbusiness deductions (see instructions)	9 3,400		
10	Nonbusiness income (other than capital gains) (see instructions)	10 5,000		
11	Add lines 8 and 10	11 5,000		
12	If line 9 is more than line 11, enter difference; otherwise, enter -0-		12	-0-
13	If line 11 is more than line 9, enter difference (but do not enter more than line 8); otherwise, enter -0-	13 -0-		
14	Business capital losses (enter as a positive number)	14 —		
15	Business capital gains	15 —		
16	Add lines 13 and 15	16 —		
17	If line 14 is more than line 16, enter difference; otherwise, enter -0-.	17 -0-		
18	Add lines 7 and 17	18 2,000		
19	Enter the loss, if any, from line 17 of Schedule D (Form 1040). (Estates and trusts, enter the loss, if any, from line 17, column (c), of Schedule D (Form 1041).) Enter as a positive number. (If you do not have a loss on that line, skip lines 19 through 21 and enter on line 22 the amount from line 18.)	19 2,000		
20	Enter the loss from line 18 of Schedule D (Form 1040). (Estates and trusts, enter the loss from line 18 of Schedule D (Form 1041).) Enter as a positive number	20 2,000		
21	Subtract line 20 from line 19	21 -0-		
22	Subtract line 21 from line 18		22	2,000
23	Net operating loss deduction for losses from other years (enter as a positive number)		23	-0-
24	Add lines 4, 12, 22, and 23		24	4,300
25	**Net Operating Loss.**—Combine lines 3 and 24. If the combined amount is less than zero, enter it here and on page 1, line 1a. **Note:** If the combined amount is zero or more, you **do** not have a net operating loss		25	38,600

1993 form not available at press time.

Figure 9-12   Form 1045

investment tax credit (ITC) for property put in service after December 31, 1985, except for certain transition property. The regular ITC in one of its various forms had been used by Congress as a stimulus to investment almost continuously since its introduction in 1961. The regular ITC was available for investment in new and a portion of used tangible personal property that the taxpayer used in his trade or business. Land, buildings, and their structural components were specifically excluded from eligibility for the ITC. The most recent (1981) version of the ITC permitted either a 6 or 10% credit, depending upon the property's recovery period under ACRS. Three-year property was eligible for a 6% credit; five-year or longer property was eligible for a 10% credit. Taxpayers were required to reduce the depreciable basis of the regular ITC property by one-half of the ITC taken or, alternatively, they had to reduce the 6 or 10% credit by two percentage points to 4 or 8%, respectively.

Example 57. Marjorie Martin put a $10,000 truck and a $50,000 machine into service in 1985. The truck was three-year ACRS property and the machine was five-year property. In 1985 Marjorie could have claimed regular investment tax credits on the property as follows

With basis reduction:
Truck: 6% × $10,000	$ 600
Machine: 10% × $50,000	5,000
Total	$ 5,600
Truck basis: $10,000 – 1/2 ($600)	$ 9,700
Machine basis: $50,000 – 1/2 ($5000)	$47,500

Without basis reduction:
Truck: 4% × $10,000	$ 400
Machine: 8% × $50,000	4,000
Total	$ 5,600
Truck basis = $10,000	
Machine basis = $50,000	

Although the credit itself has been repealed, taxpayers were generally subject to the ITC recapture provisions for the regular ITC for up to five years after 1985. If a taxpayer disposed of the regular ITC property prematurely, all or a portion of the original credit taken had to be recaptured as an addition to the tax liability. Taxpayers "earned" one-third or one-fifth of their ITC, for three- and five-year property, respectively, for each full year they held the property prior to disposition. Thus, after three or five full years, no credit recapture was required. If the taxpayer reduced the property's basis rather than using the reduced ITC, a portion of the reduced basis was restored on a premature disposition.

Example 58. Albert Feine put $200,000 of five-year ACRS property in service on December 1, 1985, on which he took a $20,000 ITC (10%). For depreciation purposes, he reduced the property's basis to $190,000 (one-half of the $20,000 ITC). In mid-1988, he disposed of part of the property that had an original cost of $100,000. Because Albert had held the property only two *full* years, he is entitled to only 40% of the ITC on that portion of the property. He is allowed an ITC of only $4,000 [.40 × .10 × $100,000] instead of the $10,000 [.10 × $100,000] claimed. He must recapture $6,000 in 1988 as a direct addition to his tax liability. He may, however, increase the property's basis for determining gain or loss on disposal by $3,000; that is, one-half of the recaptured credit.

REVIEW APPENDIX

1. Abraham Toller had a $70,000 NOL in 1992. Assuming all other tax years have income, what is the first year to which the loss must be carried?
   (a) 1988
   (b) 1989
   (c) 1989 or 1993
   (d) 1993
2. Cheryl Lux had a $21,000 NOL in calendar year 1993. If 1990 is the earliest year to which the NOL can be carried, by what date must she file to claim her refund of 1990 taxes paid?
   (a) December 31, 1994
   (b) April 15, 1995
   (c) April 15, 1997
   (d) Both (a) and (c)
3. Shawn Taylor had the following business income and losses during the eight-year period the business has been operating. If all losses constitute NOLs that may be carried to other years, in what year will all losses be absorbed? What is the amount of income remaining in that year, assuming a schedule most advantageous to the taxpayer?

Year	Amount	Year	Amount
1986	($2,000)	1990	$2,000
1987	6,000	1991	4,000
1988	(3,000)	1992	3,000
1989	(6,000)	1993	6,000

   (a) 1990; $2,000
   (b) 1991; $1,000
   (c) 1991; $2,000
   (d) 1992; $0
4. Janine Davis reported a taxable loss of $27,300 on her Form 1040. Included in this loss were $4,600 for exemptions, $9,300 for itemized deductions, and a business capital loss of $2,200. What is Janine's NOL deduction assuming no nonbusiness income?
   (a) $27,000
   (b) $17,700
   (c) $13,400
   (d) $11,200
5. Alex Thames had a $39,200 taxable loss on his Form 1040. The following items were included: $2,700 of nonbusiness capital gains, a $5,000 business capital loss, itemized deductions of $21,000 including a $15,000 loss from a fire at his personal residence, salary of $5,000, dividends of $2,000, and $9,200 in exemptions. What is his NOL deduction?
   (a) $38,600
   (b) 28,700
   (c) $23,700
   (d) $18,700

Answers are on page 9-60.

CHAPTER PROBLEMS

PART
I
1. Susan exchanges an apartment building for raw land that Bill has held as an investment. The apartment building's fair market value is $100,000, its basis is $50,000, and there is a $20,000 mortgage outstanding that Bill assumes. The land is worth $110,000 and there is a $30,000 mortgage outstanding that Susan assumes.
   (a) What is Susan's realized gain or loss on the exchange?
   (b) What is her recognized gain or loss?
   (c) What is Susan's basis in the land?

I
2. Using the data from Problem 1, if Bill's basis in the land was $40,000
   (a) What is Bill's realized gain or loss on the exchange?
   (b) What is Bill's recognized gain or loss?
   (c) What is Bill's basis in the apartment building?

I
3. Paul exchanges 1,000 shares of stock in Albatuna Corporation that he purchased four years ago for $10,000 for two trucks Sean had used in his delivery business. The trucks have a basis of $10,000; the fair market value of the stock is $25,000. What are Paul's and Sean's realized and recognized gains or losses on the exchange?

I
4. Mandy exchanged several pieces of office equipment with a fair market value of $15,000 and a basis of $12,000 for some office furniture worth $8,000, a computer worth

---

ANSWERS TO REVIEW APPENDIX

1. (c) Abraham has the option of carrying the loss back three years to 1989 or forward only to 1993 and subsequent years.

2. (d) Cheryl may file for a quick refund by the end of the tax year immediately following the loss year (that is, by December 31, 1994) or by the date for a amended return, usually three years after the original due date for the loss year's return (that is, April 15, 1997).

3. (b) $2,000 1986 loss carried to 1987; $4,000 income remains.
   $3,000 1988 loss carried to 1987; $1,000 income remains.
   $6,000 1989 loss; $1,000 carried to 1987; $2,000 carried to 1990; $3,000 balance carried to 1991; $1,000 income remains.

4. (d) ($27,300) + $4,600 + $9,300 + $2,200. All items constitute positive adjustments to the loss.

5. (c) Income (Loss) from Form 1040   ($39,200) Taxable loss
   Additions: Exemptions   + 9,200
   Step 1: No adjustment
   Step 2: $6,000   Nonbusiness expense (21,000 – 15,000)
           (2,000)   Nonbusiness income (dividend)
           (2,700)   Net nonbusiness capital gains
                                                      + 1,300
   Step 3: Business capital loss   + 5,000
                                                             $23,700 NOL

$2,000 that she is going to give to her daughter for personal use, and $5,000 cash. What are Mandy's tax consequences on this exchange? If the office equipment's basis is $17,000, what are the tax consequences?

I   5. Winter Corporation exchanges several pieces of machinery worth $50,000, which are subject to a $10,000 mortgage and have a basis of $30,000, for land that has a fair market value of $60,000 and is subject to a $20,000 mortgage. Winter Corporation plans to use the land to build an addition to its plant. What are the tax consequences to Winter on this exchange and what is its basis in the land?

II   6. What is the amount of the loss in each of the following situations for tax purposes?
(a) William's barn was partially destroyed by a tornado. The barn, which had an adjusted basis of $10,000, had a fair market value of $40,000 before and $15,000 after the tornado.
(b) Margie owned an apartment house that burned to the ground. The apartment house had a fair market value of $70,000 and an adjusted basis of $20,000. Margie had no insurance.

II   7. Jake Ball's personal auto was totally destroyed when a truck's brakes failed and the truck crashed into the auto. The car had cost $16,500 and had a basis and fair market value of $11,000 at the time of the accident. Jake received a settlement of $10,000 from his insurance company. Jake purchased a replacement auto for $9,000. What is Jake's realized and recognized gain or loss?

II   8. Rob's apartment house was condemned to make way for a highway. The building had an adjusted basis of $120,000 and a fair market value of $200,000 at the time of the condemnation. If Rob was paid $175,000 compensation for the apartment building, what is his realized gain? If he purchases a new apartment building 26 months later for $165,000, what is his recognized gain?

II   9. Marjorie White operated a tool and die manufacturing plant that was destroyed when a natural gas pipeline ruptured, resulting in a devastating explosion. Marjorie had been anxious to invest in a less time-consuming business, so she took the $875,000 insurance settlement and purchased a motel for $1,250,000 in the Florida Keys. If the plant and equipment that were destroyed had a fair market value of $900,000 and a basis of $450,000, what is Marjorie's realized and recognized gain?

II   10. Allen Taylor owned a restaurant that had had numerous sanitation violations and was ordered closed by the Health Department. Allen then sold the restaurant, which had a basis of $150,000, for $240,000. Several months later, Allen took $50,000 of the proceeds and invested in a new restaurant, financing the balance of the $300,000 purchase price. The remaining $190,000 was used to invest in stocks, buy personal items, and take an extended vacation. What is Allen's realized and recognized gain?

III   11. Charles sold four assets that he had held for more than one year during the current tax year: a delivery truck used in his dry cleaning business at a loss of $1,000, some land he had used for a parking lot at a gain of $1,500, some obsolete inventory from his gift shop at a gain of $600, and a mare that he owned for 28 months at a gain of $2,200. What are the types of Charles's gains? Explain how they would be treated for reporting on a tax return.

III   12. Using the information from Problem 11, explain how your answer would change if Charles had deducted $450 of Sec. 1231 losses in the prior tax year.

III   13. Ellen had the following gains and losses on productive business assets held for more than one year this tax year:

Assets	Event	Gain(Loss)
Land	Sold	$25,000
Computer	Stolen	(2,000)
Building	Sold	20,000
Furniture	Fire	(3,000)
Typewriter	Stolen	(500)

Using the netting process described in this section, determine the treatment of each of the above gains and losses and the amount and treatment of the net gain or loss.

III   14. Walter Crane had the following recognized gains and losses on qualifying Sec. 1231 properties from the specified events:

Asset	Event	Gain(Loss)
Truck	Sale	$ 2,500
Land	Condemnation	20,000
Building	Tornado	(12,000)
Equipment	Theft	1,000
Machinery	Sale	(5,000)
Auto	Accident	(1,000)

Explain how each of these items enters the netting process and what the final result will be for tax purposes.

III   15. How would your answer to Problem 14 change if Walter Crane had deducted $7,000 of Sec. 1231 losses in the previous year?

IV   16. Whit Morrisson sold (a) a factory building for $150,000 that had an original cost of $125,000 and had $60,000 of ACRS depreciation taken, (b) machines that cost $75,000 for $140,000 (straight-line depreciation taken on the machines was $40,000), and (c) a building for $320,000 that cost $280,000 and had $120,000 of straight-line depreciation taken. What are the amount and type of Whit's gain if all of the properties qualify as Sec. 1231 assets?

IV   17. Steve has a computer that cost him $10,000 three years ago. He has depreciated it on a straight-line basis so that its adjusted basis is now $5,000. Larry is willing to pay $7,500 for the computer. If Steve sells the computer, what would be his Sec. 1245 recapture and his Sec. 1231 gain?

IV   18. Dave owns a factory building that he bought on January 1, 1983, for $150,000. He used the ACRS method of depreciation and his adjusted basis is presently $65,000. Under the straight-line method, his adjusted basis would be been $90,000. What is the amount and type of Dave's recapture potential if he sells the building?

IV   19. Using the data from Problem 18, if Dave sells the building to Bill for $350,000, what is the amount and type of his recognized gain?

IV   20. Luis sells an office building for $375,000 when his basis is $125,000. The building originally cost $300,000 and had been depreciated under a pre–ACRS accelerated method. Straight-line depreciation would have been $105,000. What is the amount and type of Luis's recognized gain?

IV 21. Imelda Lui sold the following assets from her business during the current tax year:

Asset	Original Cost	Depreciation Method	Depreciation Taken	Selling Price
Machine 1	$ 25,000	MACRS	$ 15,000	$ 8,000
Machine 2	80,000	ACRS	50,000	20,000
Building 1	250,000	ACRS	130,000	260,000
(Straight-line depreciation would have been $70,000)				
Land	75,000	N/A		110,000
Building 2	50,000	SL	25,000	35,000

Imelda deducted a $14,000 Sec. 1231 loss three years ago. Determine the amount and character of the recognized gains and losses on each of the above items. Determine how they would be treated on the taxpayer's return.

V 22. Jeremy and Sonja Johnson, a married couple with two dependent children, have a taxable income of $29,000 for 1993. Determine their net tax due if they are eligible for a $960 child care credit, a $250 foreign tax credit, and a $6,400 general business credit. Use the 1993 tax rate tables provided in Appendix C.

V 23. Erica Minor, a single taxpayer with no dependents, has taxable income of $43,000 for 1993. If she is eligible for a $13,000 general business credit, what is her tax liability? What is the amount of any general business credit carryover? What is her net tax due and or credit carryover if her taxable income is $97,000? Use the 1993 tax rate schedules/tables provided in Appendices B and C.

V 24. Rick Rack has a tax liability of $60,000 for 1993 and is eligible for a $68,000 general business credit. He paid income taxes of $6,000 in 1992, $3,500 in 1991, $2,000 in 1990 and $20,000 in 1989. What is Rick's net tax liability for 1993? What refunds of prior years' taxes will Rick receive by using the general business credit carryovers for which he is eligible?

V 25. Renata Seybold bought $25,000 of geothermal equipment and $8,000 of solar energy panels during the current tax year. Determine Renata's business energy credit and the properties' depreciable bases. What is Renata's energy credit recapture potential if she plans to dispose of the geothermal property at the end of three years?

V 26. Joseph Trump purchased a pre-1936 warehouse for $87,000 and spent $34,000 rehabilitating it to rent as a storage facility. What is the amount of Trump's rehabilitation credit and the warehouse's basis? If Trump spent $105,000 rehabilitating the building, what is his credit and basis in the property?

V 27. Jason Howe hired four certified disadvantaged Vietnam veterans as laborers in his contracting business in the fall of 1992. The wages paid each man during fall of 1992 and spring of 1993 are as follows:

Veteran	Wages in 1992	Wages in 1993
Tom	$3,200	$ 1,800
Dick	3,400	9,600
Harry	8,400	2,100
John	2,000	16,000

Determine Jason's 1992 and 1993 targeted jobs credit and deductible wage expense for these men.

V 28. In 1993 Will Run hired two certified summer youths as groundskeepers for a golf course for the months of June, July, and August. Will paid one youth $4,700 and the other $2,600 during this period. How much is Will's targeted job's credit for 1993 and what amount of wage expense may he deduct?

V 29. Steve Viceroy's company had qualifying research expenditures as follows during the specified years:

Year	Research Expenditures	Annual Gross Receipts
1985	$10,000	$ 500,000
1986	50,000	1,500,000
1987	45,000	2,000,000
1988	20,000	2,900,000
1989	25,000	2,700,000
1990	30,000	2,400,000
1991	75,000	2,700,000
1992	80,000	2,700,000
1993	75,000	2,900,000

In 1993 the company also made a cash payment of $80,000 to a local university for help in designing a prototype model of a laser cutting tool for packaging products. Determine the company's research credit for 1993.

V 30. Amelia Rush constructed a $350,000 low-rise rental complex using federally subsidized low-interest financing. The federally prescribed rates are 12% and 5% for the 70% and 30% present value, respectively. Determine Amelia's credit for low income housing assuming the entire complex is a qualified facility.

APX 31. Taylor James had a $72,000 NOL in 1993. To what years is he entitled to carry this loss?

APX 32. What are the advantages and disadvantages of carrying a NOL back to a prior year?

APX 33. Bud Cole had the following income/loss history for his business since it began operations in 1988. Ignoring redeterminations of income to carryover years, how would Bud treat the income/loss years?

1988 ($10,000)   1992 $ 9,000
1989 ($ 6,000)   1993 ($ 5,000)
1990 $ 2,000   1994 ($ 6,000)
1991 $18,000   1995 $12,000

APX 34. Todd Warren had salary and dividend income of only $12,000 during the current year. He was in a serious auto accident and had $24,000 of deductible medical expenses. What is Todd's NOL?

APX 35. Aileen Rodgers had a small business that had a $15,000 operating loss during the current year. She had $5,000 of investment income and $11,000 of itemized deductions, including a $5,000 deductible personal casualty loss. What is Aileen's NOL that may be carried to and deducted in another year?

APX 36. Warren Myers had the following income (loss) and deductions for the current year:

Dividends	$ 3,000
Loss from business	($63,000)
Medical expense	$10,000
Charitable contributions	$ 2,000

Warren is married with two dependent children. He files a joint return with his wife. What is Warren's allowable NOL deduction? (Assume personal and dependency exemptions are $2,350 each.)

APX 37. Wilma Breakstone had the following income and loss items.

Dividend income	$ 3,000
Standard deduction	$ 6,000
Personal capital gain	$10,000
Personal capital loss	($ 8,000)
Business capital gain	$ 6,000
Loss from business operations	($92,000)

Determine Wilma's allowable NOL deduction if she is married, files a joint return, has four dependent children, and each personal and dependency exemption is $2,350.

APX 38. On January 1, 1984, Jeff purchased a five-year property for $75,000. He took the full 10% investment tax credit. He sold the machine when he had used it for 26 months. What was Jeff's ITC recapture?

APX 39. Sam purchased $60,000 of eligible five-year property and $30,000 of three-year property, placing them in service on August 1, 1985. He sold the five-year property on September 15, 1988. Compute Sam's investment tax credit for 1985, recapture amount in 1988, and the basis of the property sold if (a) Sam elected the reduced property basis or (b) Sam elected the reduced investment tax credit.

TAX RETURN PROBLEMS

40. [Form 4684; Form 4797] Using the information from Problem 13, enter the gain and loss amounts on Forms 4684 and 4797 and complete them to the extent possible, assuming that all assets were acquired after 1986.

41. [Form 4797; Form 1040 Schedule D] Use the following information to complete Forms 4797 and 1040 Schedule D. Joe Robbins sold the following properties used in his sole proprietorship on June 6, 1993:

Date Acquired	Item	Cost	Method of Depreciation	Adj. Basis	Selling Price
8/10/92	Auto	$14,000	MACRS	$12,700	$11,000
6/7/89	Computer	6,000	MACRS	1,000	3,000
5/5/84	Building	125,000	ACRS	54,000	142,000

Joe also sold the following investments on June 6, 1993:

a. 10,000 shares of AEC stock for $100,000; the stock was purchased on 11/1/90 for $92,000.

b. 5,000 shares of FIG stock for $20,000; the stock was purchased on 12/5/92 for $32,000.

HOW WOULD YOU RULE?

42. Paul Jergens bought a new automobile for his personal use for $18,000 on 6/9/92. At the beginning of 1993, he decided to let one of the salesmen employed by his sole proprietorship have the auto for business use. At the time, the auto was worth $13,000. The salesman did not like the auto. He returned it to the business and Paul then sold it for $13,200 on 8/8/93, because he had purchased another personal auto and had no further use for this particular car. If Paul took a depreciation deduction on the auto for the period of its business use of $1,700, how would he handle the sale of the auto for tax purposes?

43. Mary and Joe Myers ran a small appliance repair shop in the converted garage attached to their home. During the winter, they had a number of very heavy snowfalls. Snow and ice built up on the roof of the garage over several months. Their neighbor (who was also their insurance agent) told them that they should get up on the roof and get the snow and ice off before the weight damaged the roof. Unfortunately, they did not heed their neighbor's advice, and in early March, an additional 4-inch snowfall caused one area of the roof to collapse. The roof sustained $3,000 damage and tools and equipment inside worth $890 had to be replaced due to water damage. Their insurance policy did not cover the damage since the insurance company claimed the Myers were negligent by not removing the snow and ice from the roof between snowfalls. Would they be allowed any deduction for their sustained loss for tax purposes?

TAX PORTFOLIO PROBLEM FOR THE NEILSON FAMILY

If your instructor has assigned this problem, refer to Appendix A and complete the portion labeled "Chapter 9." This includes the information on sales of business assets which is necessary to complete Form 4797 for Harold and Maude Neilson.

Chapter 9 Problem 40   Name _____   9-67

Form 4684
Department of the Treasury
Internal Revenue Service

Casualties and Thefts
▶ See separate instructions.
▶ Attach to your tax return.
▶ Use a separate Form 4684 for each different casualty or theft.

OMB No. 1545-0177

1993

Attachment Sequence No. 26

Name(s) shown on tax return

Identifying number

SECTION A—Personal Use Property (Use this section to report casualties and thefts of property **not** used in a trade or business or for income-producing purposes.)

1 Description of properties (show type, location, and date acquired for each):
   Property **A** ....
   Property **B** ....
   Property **C** ....
   Property **D** ....

Properties (Use a separate column for each property lost or damaged from one casualty or theft.)

	A	B	C	D
2 Cost or other basis of each property				
3 Insurance or other reimbursement (whether or not you filed a claim). See instructions				
Note: If line 2 is **more than** line 3, skip line 4.				
4 Gain from casualty or theft. If line 3 is **more than** line 2, enter the difference here and skip lines 5 through 9 for that column. See instructions if line 3 includes insurance or other reimbursement you did not claim, or you received payment for your loss in a later tax year				
5 Fair market value **before** casualty or theft				
6 Fair market value **after** casualty or theft				
7 Subtract line 6 from line 5				
8 Enter the **smaller** of line 2 or line 7				
9 Subtract line 3 from line 8. If zero or less, enter -0-				

10	Casualty or theft loss. Add the amounts on line 9. Enter the total	10
11	Enter the amount from line 10 or $100, whichever is **smaller**	11
12	Subtract line 11 from line 10	12
	Caution: Use only one Form 4684 for lines 13 through 18.	
13	Add the amounts on line 12 of all Forms 4684	13
14	Combine the amounts from line 4 of all Forms 4684	14
15	• If line 14 is **more than** line 13, enter the difference here and on Schedule D. Do not complete the rest of this section (see instructions). • If line 14 is **less than** line 13, enter -0- here and continue with the form. • If line 14 is **equal to** line 13, enter -0- here. Do not complete the rest of this section.	15
16	If line 14 is **less than** line 13, enter the difference	16
17	Enter 10% of your adjusted gross income (Form 1040, line 32). Estates and trusts, see instructions	17
18	Subtract line 17 from line 16. If zero or less, enter -0-. Also enter result on Schedule A (Form 1040), line 17. Estates and trusts, enter on the "Other deductions" line of your tax return	18

For Paperwork Reduction Act Notice, see page 1 of separate instructions.   Cat. No. 12997O   Form **4684** (1993)

Copyright © 1994 by Harcourt Brace & Company. All rights reserved.

Form 4684 (1993) Attachment Sequence No. **26** Page **2**

Name(s) shown on tax return. Do not enter name and identifying number if shown on other side. | Identifying number

SECTION B—Business and Income-Producing Property (Use this section to report casualties and thefts of property used in a trade or business or for income-producing purposes.)

Part I Casualty or Theft Gain or Loss (Use a separate Part I for each casualty or theft.)

19 Description of properties (show type, location, and date acquired for each):
  Property A ....
  Property B ....
  Property C ....
  Property D ....

Properties (Use a separate column for each property lost or damaged from one casualty or theft.)

	A	B	C	D
20 Cost or adjusted basis of each property				
21 Insurance or other reimbursement (whether or not you filed a claim). See the instructions for line 3. **Note:** *If line 20 is more than line 21, skip line 22.*				
22 Gain from casualty or theft. If line 21 is **more than** line 20, enter the difference here and on line 29 or line 34, column (c), except as provided in the instructions for line 33. Also, skip lines 23 through 27 for that column. See the instructions for line 4 if line 21 includes insurance or other reimbursement you did not claim, or you received payment for your loss in a later tax year				
23 Fair market value **before** casualty or theft				
24 Fair market value **after** casualty or theft				
25 Subtract line 24 from line 23				
26 Enter the **smaller** of line 20 or line 25 **Note:** *If the property was totally destroyed by casualty or lost from theft, enter on line 26 the amount from line 20.*				
27 Subtract line 21 from line 26. If zero or less, enter -0-				

28 Casualty or theft loss. Add the amounts on line 27. Enter the total here and on line 29 or line 34 (see instructions). | **28** |

Part II Summary of Gains and Losses (from separate Parts I)

(a) Identify casualty or theft	(b) Losses from casualties or thefts		(c) Gains from casualties or thefts includible in income
	(i) Trade, business, rental or royalty property	(ii) Income-producing property	

Casualty or Theft of Property Held One Year or Less

29	(	)(	)	
	(	)(	)	
30 Totals. Add the amounts on line 29	**30** (	)(	)	

31 Combine line 30, columns (b)(i) and (c). Enter the net gain or (loss) here and on Form 4797, line 15. If Form 4797 is not otherwise required, see instructions | **31** |

32 Enter the amount from line 30, column (b)(ii) here and on Schedule A (Form 1040), line 20. Partnerships, S corporations, estates and trusts, see instructions | **32** |

Casualty or Theft of Property Held More Than One Year

33 Casualty or theft gains from Form 4797, line 34			**33**	
34	(	)(	)	
	(	)(	)	
35 Total losses. Add amounts on line 34, columns (b)(i) and (b)(ii)	**35** (	)(	)	/////
36 Total gains. Add lines 33 and 34, column (c)			**36**	
37 Add amounts on line 35, columns (b)(i) and (b)(ii)			**37**	

38 If the loss on line 37 is **more than** the gain on line 36:
  a Combine line 35, column (b)(i) and line 36, and enter the net gain or (loss) here. Partnerships and S corporations see the note below. All others enter this amount on Form 4797, line 15. If Form 4797 is not otherwise required, see instructions | **38a** |
  b Enter the amount from line 35, column (b)(ii) here. Partnerships and S corporations see the note below. Individuals enter this amount on Schedule A (Form 1040), line 20. Estates and trusts, enter on the "Other deductions" line of your tax return | **38b** |

39 If the loss on line 37 is **equal to** or **less than** the gain on line 36, combine these lines and enter here. Partnerships, see the note below. All others, enter this amount on Form 4797, line 3 | **39** |

Note: *Partnerships, enter the amount from line 38a, 38b, or line 39 on Form 1065, Schedule K, line 7. S corporations, enter the amount from line 38a or 38b on Form 1120S, Schedule K, line 6.*

Chapter 9 Problem 40   Name _____   9-69

Form 4797
Department of the Treasury
Internal Revenue Service

Sales of Business Property
(Also Involuntary Conversions and Recapture Amounts Under Sections 179 and 280F(b)(2))
▶ Attach to your tax return.   ▶ See separate instructions.

OMB No. 1545-0184
1993
Attachment Sequence No. **27**

Name(s) shown on return | Identifying number

1   Enter here the gross proceeds from the sale or exchange of real estate reported to you for 1993 on Form(s) 1099-S (or a substitute statement) that you will be including on line 2, 11, or 22 . . . . | 1 |

Part I   Sales or Exchanges of Property Used in a Trade or Business and Involuntary Conversions From Other Than Casualty or Theft—Property Held More Than 1 Year

(a) Description of property	(b) Date acquired (mo., day, yr.)	(c) Date sold (mo., day, yr.)	(d) Gross sales price	(e) Depreciation allowed or allowable since acquisition	(f) Cost or other basis, plus improvements and expense of sale	(g) LOSS ((f) minus the sum of (d) and (e))	(h) GAIN ((d) plus (e) minus (f))
2							

3   Gain, if any, from Form 4684, line 39 . . . .   **3**
4   Section 1231 gain from installment sales from Form 6252, line 26 or 37 . . . .   **4**
5   Section 1231 gain or (loss) from like-kind exchanges from Form 8824 . . . .   **5**
6   Gain, if any, from line 34, from other than casualty or theft **6**
7   Add lines 2 through 6 in columns (g) and (h) . . . .   **7** (   )
8   Combine columns (g) and (h) of line 7. Enter gain or (loss) here, and on the appropriate line as follows: **8**
    Partnerships—Enter the gain or (loss) on Form 1065, Schedule K, line 6. Skip lines 9, 10, 12, and 13 below.
    S corporations—Report the gain or (loss) following the instructions for Form 1120S, Schedule K, lines 5 and 6. Skip lines 9, 10, 12, and 13 below, unless line 8 is a gain and the S corporation is subject to the capital gains tax.
    All others—If line 8 is zero or a loss, enter the amount on line 12 below and skip lines 9 and 10. If line 8 is a gain and you did not have any prior year section 1231 losses, or they were recaptured in an earlier year, enter the gain as a long-term capital gain on Schedule D and skip lines 9, 10, and 13 below.
9   Nonrecaptured net section 1231 losses from prior years (see instructions) **9**
10 Subtract line 9 from line 8. If zero or less, enter -0-. Also enter on the appropriate line as follows (see instructions):   **10**
    S corporations—Enter this amount (if more than zero) on Schedule D (Form 1120S), line 13, and skip lines 12 and 13 below.
    All others—If line 10 is zero, enter the amount from line 8 on line 13 below. If line 10 is more than zero, enter the amount from line 9 on line 13 below, and enter the amount from line 10 as a long-term capital gain on Schedule D.

Part II   Ordinary Gains and Losses

11 Ordinary gains and losses not included on lines 12 through 18 (include property held 1 year or less):

12 Loss, if any, from line 8 . . . .   **12**
13 Gain, if any, from line 8, or amount from line 9 if applicable **13**
14 Gain, if any, from line 33 . . . .   **14**
15 Net gain or (loss) from Form 4684, lines 31 and 38a **15**
16 Ordinary gain from installment sales from Form 6252, line 25 or 36 . . . .   **16**
17 Ordinary gain or (loss) from like-kind exchanges from Form 8824 . . . .   **17**
18 Recapture of section 179 expense deduction for partners and S corporation shareholders from property dispositions by partnerships and S corporations (see instructions) **18**
19 Add lines 11 through 18 in columns (g) and (h) . . . .   **19** (   )
20 Combine columns (g) and (h) of line 19. Enter gain or (loss) here, and on the appropriate line as follows: **20**
    a   For all except individual returns: Enter the gain or (loss) from line 20 on the return being filed.
    b   For individual returns:
    (1)   If the loss on line 12 includes a loss from Form 4684, line 35, column (b)(ii), enter that part of the loss here and on line 20 of Schedule A (Form 1040). Identify as from "Form 4797, line 20b(1)." See instructions . . . .   **20b(1)**
    (2)   Redetermine the gain or (loss) on line 20, excluding the loss, if any, on line 20b(1). Enter here and on Form 1040, line 15 .   **20b(2)**

For Paperwork Reduction Act Notice, see page 1 of separate instructions.   Cat. No. 13086I   Form **4797** (1993)

Copyright © 1994 by Harcourt Brace & Company. All rights reserved.

Form 4797 (1993) Page 2

Part III — Gain From Disposition of Property Under Sections 1245, 1250, 1252, 1254, and 1255

21	(a) Description of section 1245, 1250, 1252, 1254, or 1255 property:	(b) Date acquired (mo., day, yr.)	(c) Date sold (mo., day, yr.)
A			
B			
C			
D			

	Relate lines 21A through 21D to these columns ▶		Property A	Property B	Property C	Property D
22	Gross sales price (Note: See line 1 before completing).	22				
23	Cost or other basis plus expense of sale	23				
24	Depreciation (or depletion) allowed or allowable	24				
25	Adjusted basis. Subtract line 24 from line 23	25				
26	Total gain. Subtract line 25 from line 22	26				
27	**If section 1245 property:**					
a	Depreciation allowed or allowable from line 24	27a				
b	Enter the **smaller** of line 26 or 27a	27b				
28	**If section 1250 property:** If straight line depreciation was used, enter -0- on line 28g, except for a corporation subject to section 291.					
a	Additional depreciation after 1975 (see instructions)	28a				
b	Applicable percentage multiplied by the **smaller** of line 26 or line 28a (see instructions)	28b				
c	Subtract line 28a from line 26. If residential rental property or line 26 is not more than line 28a, skip lines 28d and 28e	28c				
d	Additional depreciation after 1969 and before 1976	28d				
e	Enter the **smaller** of line 28c or 28d	28e				
f	Section 291 amount (corporations only)	28f				
g	Add lines 28b, 28e, and 28f	28g				
29	**If section 1252 property:** Skip this section if you did not dispose of farmland or if this form is being completed for a partnership.					
a	Soil, water, and land clearing expenses	29a				
b	Line 29a multiplied by applicable percentage (see instructions)	29b				
c	Enter the **smaller** of line 26 or 29b	29c				
30	**If section 1254 property:**					
a	Intangible drilling and development costs, expenditures for development of mines and other natural deposits, and mining exploration costs (see instructions)	30a				
b	Enter the **smaller** of line 26 or 30a	30b				
31	**If section 1255 property:**					
a	Applicable percentage of payments excluded from income under section 126 (see instructions)	31a				
b	Enter the **smaller** of line 26 or 31a	31b				

Summary of Part III Gains. Complete property columns A through D, through line 31b before going to line 32.

32	Total gains for all properties. Add columns A through D, line 26	32	
33	Add columns A through D, lines 27b, 28g, 29c, 30b, and 31b. Enter here and on line 14	33	
34	Subtract line 33 from line 32. Enter the portion from casualty or theft on Form 4684, line 33. Enter the portion from other than casualty or theft on Form 4797, line 6	34	

Part IV — Recapture Amounts Under Sections 179 and 280F(b)(2) When Business Use Drops to 50% or Less
See instructions for Part IV.

			(a) Section 179	(b) Section 280F(b)(2)
35	Section 179 expense deduction or depreciation allowable in prior years	35		
36	Recomputed depreciation (see instructions)	36		
37	Recapture amount. Subtract line 36 from line 35. See instructions for where to report	37		

Chapter 9 Problem 41   Name _____   9-71

Form 4797
Department of the Treasury
Internal Revenue Service

Sales of Business Property
(Also Involuntary Conversions and Recapture Amounts Under Sections 179 and 280F(b)(2))
▶ Attach to your tax return.   ▶ See separate instructions.

OMB No. 1545-0184
1993
Attachment Sequence No. 27

Name(s) shown on return | Identifying number

1 Enter here the gross proceeds from the sale or exchange of real estate reported to you for 1993 on Form(s) 1099-S (or a substitute statement) that you will be including on line 2, 11, or 22 . . . . | 1 |

Part I — Sales or Exchanges of Property Used in a Trade or Business and Involuntary Conversions From Other Than Casualty or Theft—Property Held More Than 1 Year

(a) Description of property	(b) Date acquired (mo., day, yr.)	(c) Date sold (mo., day, yr.)	(d) Gross sales price	(e) Depreciation allowed or allowable since acquisition	(f) Cost or other basis, plus improvements and expense of sale	(g) LOSS ((f) minus the sum of (d) and (e))	(h) GAIN ((d) plus (e) minus (f))
2							

3   Gain, if any, from Form 4684, line 39 . . . . | 3 |
4   Section 1231 gain from installment sales from Form 6252, line 26 or 37 . . . . | 4 |
5   Section 1231 gain or (loss) from like-kind exchanges from Form 8824 . . . . | 5 |
6   Gain, if any, from line 34, from other than casualty or theft . . . . | 6 |
7   Add lines 2 through 6 in columns (g) and (h) . . . . | 7 | (|) |
8   Combine columns (g) and (h) of line 7. Enter gain or (loss) here, and on the appropriate line as follows: . . . . | 8 |
   Partnerships—Enter the gain or (loss) on Form 1065, Schedule K, line 6. Skip lines 9, 10, 12, and 13 below.
   S corporations—Report the gain or (loss) following the instructions for Form 1120S, Schedule K, lines 5 and 6. Skip lines 9, 10, 12, and 13 below, unless line 8 is a gain and the S corporation is subject to the capital gains tax.
   All others—If line 8 is zero or a loss, enter the amount on line 12 below and skip lines 9 and 10. If line 8 is a gain and you did not have any prior year section 1231 losses, or they were recaptured in an earlier year, enter the gain as a long-term capital gain on Schedule D and skip lines 9, 10, and 13 below.
9   Nonrecaptured net section 1231 losses from prior years (see instructions) . . . . | 9 |
10 Subtract line 9 from line 8. If zero or less, enter -0-. Also enter on the appropriate line as follows (see instructions): | 10 |
   S corporations—Enter this amount (if more than zero) on Schedule D (Form 1120S), line 13, and skip lines 12 and 13 below.
   All others—If line 10 is zero, enter the amount from line 8 on line 13 below. If line 10 is more than zero, enter the amount from line 9 on line 13 below, and enter the amount from line 10 as a long-term capital gain on Schedule D.

Part II   Ordinary Gains and Losses

11 Ordinary gains and losses not included on lines 12 through 18 (include property held 1 year or less):

12 Loss, if any, from line 8 . . . . | 12 |
13 Gain, if any, from line 8, or amount from line 9 if applicable . . . . | 13 |
14 Gain, if any, from line 33 . . . . | 14 |
15 Net gain or (loss) from Form 4684, lines 31 and 38a . . . . | 15 |
16 Ordinary gain from installment sales from Form 6252, line 25 or 36 . . . . | 16 |
17 Ordinary gain or (loss) from like-kind exchanges from Form 8824 . . . . | 17 |
18 Recapture of section 179 expense deduction for partners and S corporation shareholders from property dispositions by partnerships and S corporations (see instructions) . . . . . . | 18 |
19 Add lines 11 through 18 in columns (g) and (h) . . . . | 19 | (|) |
20 Combine columns (g) and (h) of line 19. Enter gain or (loss) here, and on the appropriate line as follows: . . . | 20 |
   a For all except individual returns: Enter the gain or (loss) from line 20 on the return being filed.
   b For individual returns:
     (1) If the loss on line 12 includes a loss from Form 4684, line 35, column (b)(ii), enter that part of the loss here and on line 20 of Schedule A (Form 1040). Identify as from "Form 4797, line 20b(1)." See instructions . . . . | 20b(1) |
     (2) Redetermine the gain or (loss) on line 20, excluding the loss, if any, on line 20b(1). Enter here and on Form 1040, line 15 . | 20b(2) |

For Paperwork Reduction Act Notice, see page 1 of separate instructions.   Cat. No. 13086I   Form **4797** (1993)

Form 4797 (1993) Page **2**

Part III Gain From Disposition of Property Under Sections 1245, 1250, 1252, 1254, and 1255

21 (a) Description of section 1245, 1250, 1252, 1254, or 1255 property:	(b) Date acquired (mo., day, yr.)	(c) Date sold (mo., day, yr.)
A		
B		
C		
D		

	Relate lines 21A through 21D to these columns ▶		Property A	Property B	Property C	Property D
22	Gross sales price (**Note:** *See line 1 before completing.*)	22				
23	Cost or other basis plus expense of sale	23				
24	Depreciation (or depletion) allowed or allowable	24				
25	Adjusted basis. Subtract line 24 from line 23	25				
26	Total gain. Subtract line 25 from line 22	26				
27	**If section 1245 property:**					
a	Depreciation allowed or allowable from line 24	27a				
b	Enter the **smaller** of line 26 or 27a	27b				
28	**If section 1250 property:** If straight line depreciation was used, enter -0- on line 28g, except for a corporation subject to section 291.					
a	Additional depreciation after 1975 (see instructions)	28a				
b	Applicable percentage multiplied by the **smaller** of line 26 or line 28a (see instructions)	28b				
c	Subtract line 28a from line 26. If residential rental property or line 26 is not more than line 28a, skip lines 28d and 28e	28c				
d	Additional depreciation after 1969 and before 1976	28d				
e	Enter the **smaller** of line 28c or 28d	28e				
f	Section 291 amount (corporations only)	28f				
g	Add lines 28b, 28e, and 28f	28g				
29	**If section 1252 property:** Skip this section if you did not dispose of farmland or if this form is being completed for a partnership.					
a	Soil, water, and land clearing expenses	29a				
b	Line 29a multiplied by applicable percentage (see instructions)	29b				
c	Enter the **smaller** of line 26 or 29b	29c				
30	**If section 1254 property:**					
a	Intangible drilling and development costs, expenditures for development of mines and other natural deposits, and mining exploration costs (see instructions)	30a				
b	Enter the **smaller** of line 26 or 30a	30b				
31	**If section 1255 property:**					
a	Applicable percentage of payments excluded from income under section 126 (see instructions)	31a				
b	Enter the **smaller** of line 26 or 31a	31b				

Summary of Part III Gains. Complete property columns A through D, through line 31b before going to line 32.

32	Total gains for all properties. Add columns A through D, line 26	32	
33	Add columns A through D, lines 27b, 28g, 29c, 30b, and 31b. Enter here and on line 14	33	
34	Subtract line 33 from line 32. Enter the portion from casualty or theft on Form 4684, line 33. Enter the portion from other than casualty or theft on Form 4797, line 6	34	

Part IV Recapture Amounts Under Sections 179 and 280F(b)(2) When Business Use Drops to 50% or Less
See instructions for Part IV.

			(a) Section 179	(b) Section 280F(b)(2)
35	Section 179 expense deduction or depreciation allowable in prior years	35		
36	Recomputed depreciation (see instructions)	36		
37	Recapture amount. Subtract line 36 from line 35. See instructions for where to report	37		

Chapter 9 Problem 41   Name _____   9-73

SCHEDULE D
(Form 1040)
Department of the Treasury
Internal Revenue Service

Capital Gains and Losses

▶ Attach to Form 1040.   ▶ See Instructions for Schedule D (Form 1040).
▶ Use lines 20 and 22 for more space to list transactions for lines 1 and 9.

OMB No. 1545-0074

1993

Attachment
Sequence No. **12**

Name(s) shown on Form 1040

Your social security number

Part I — Short-Term Capital Gains and Losses—Assets Held One Year or Less

(a) Description of property (Example: 100 sh. XYZ Co.)	(b) Date acquired (Mo., day, yr.)	(c) Date sold (Mo., day, yr.)	(d) Sales price (see page D-3)	(e) Cost or other basis (see page D-3)	(f) LOSS If (e) is more than (d), subtract (d) from (e)	(g) GAIN If (d) is more than (e), subtract (e) from (d)
1						

2 Enter your short-term totals, if any, from line 21 . . . . **2**

3 **Total short-term sales price amounts.** Add column (d) of lines 1 and 2 . . **3**

4 Short-term gain from Forms 2119 and 6252, and short-term gain or (loss) from Forms 4684, 6781, and 8824 . . . . **4**

5 Net short-term gain or (loss) from partnerships, S corporations, and fiduciaries from Schedule(s) K-1 . . . . **5**

6 Short-term capital loss carryover from 1992 Schedule D, line 38 . . . . **6**

7 Add lines 1, 2, and 4 through 6, in columns (f) and (g) . . . . **7** ( )

8 **Net short-term capital gain or (loss).** Combine columns (f) and (g) of line 7 . . . . . . **8**

Part II — Long-Term Capital Gains and Losses—Assets Held More Than One Year

9						

10 Enter your long-term totals, if any, from line 23 . . . . **10**

11 **Total long-term sales price amounts.** Add column (d) of lines 9 and 10 . . **11**

12 Gain from Form 4797; long-term gain from Forms 2119, 2439, and 6252; and long-term gain or (loss) from Forms 4684, 6781, and 8824 . . . . **12**

13 Net long-term gain or (loss) from partnerships, S corporations, and fiduciaries from Schedule(s) K-1 . . . . **13**

14 Capital gain distributions **14**

15 Long-term capital loss carryover from 1992 Schedule D, line 45 . . . . **15**

16 Add lines 9, 10, and 12 through 15, in columns (f) and (g) . . . . . . **16** ( )

17 **Net long-term capital gain or (loss).** Combine columns (f) and (g) of line 16 . . . . . **17**

Part III — Summary of Parts I and II

18 Combine lines 8 and 17. If a loss, go to line 19. If a gain, enter the gain on Form 1040, line 13.
Note: *If both lines 17 and 18 are gains, see the Schedule D Tax Worksheet on page D-4* . . **18**

19 If line 18 is a (loss), enter here and as a (loss) on Form 1040, line 13, the **smaller** of these losses:
   a The (loss) on line 18; **or**
   b ($3,000) or, if married filing separately, ($1,500) . . . . **19** ( )
   Note: *See the Capital Loss Carryover Worksheet on page D-4 if the loss on line 18 exceeds the loss on line 19 or if Form 1040, line 35, is a loss.*

For Paperwork Reduction Act Notice, see Form 1040 instructions.   Cat. No. 11338H   Schedule D (Form 1040) 1993

Copyright © 1994 by Harcourt Brace & Company. All rights reserved.

Schedule D Tax Worksheet (keep for your records)

Use this worksheet to figure your tax **only** if both lines 17 and 18 of Schedule D are gains, **and:**			
Your filing status is: AND	Form 1040, line 37, is over:	Your filing status is: AND	Form 1040, line 37, is over:
Single.	$53,500	Married filing separately.	$44,575
Married filing jointly or qualifying widow(er) . . .	$89,150	Head of household . . .	$76,400

1. Enter the amount from Form 1040, line 37 . . . . . . 1. _____
2. **Net capital gain.** Enter the **smaller** of Schedule D, line 17 or line 18 . . . . 2. _____
3. If you are filing Form 4952, enter the amount from Form 4952, line 4e . . . . 3. _____
4. Subtract line 3 from line 2. If zero or less, stop here; you cannot use this worksheet to figure your tax. Instead, use the Tax Table or Tax Rate Schedules, whichever applies . . . . 4. _____
5. Subtract line 4 from line 1 . . . . 5. _____
6. Enter: $22,100 if single; $36,900 if married filing jointly or qualifying widow(er); $18,450 if married filing separately; or $29,600 if head of household. . . . . 6. _____
7. Enter the **greater** of line 5 or line 6 . . . . 7. _____
8. Subtract line 7 from line 1 . . . . 8. _____
9. Figure the tax on the amount on line 7. Use the Tax Table or Tax Rate Schedules, whichever applies . . . . 9. _____
10. Multiply line 8 by 28% (.28) . . . . 10. _____
11. Add lines 9 and 10 . . . . 11. _____
12. Figure the tax on the amount on line 1. Use the Tax Table or Tax Rate Schedules, whichever applies . . . . 12. _____
13. **Tax.** Enter the **smaller** of line 11 or line 12 here and on Form 1040, line 38. Check the box for Schedule D Tax Worksheet. 13. _____

Comprehensive Tax Return Problem 5
Form 1040, Schedules, C, D, SE, and Forms 4562 and 4797

Katherine H. Ransone, age 34, is a single taxpayer who owns and operates Ransone Consulting, a systems consulting firm. Katherine's social security number is 432-54-7862, and her employer identification number (for employment tax purposes) is 61-3425432. Katherine lives at 1031 Westwood Boulevard, Sacramento, California 95819. Her business is located at 1221 Capital Street in Sacramento. Katherine elects to contribute to the presidential election fund.

Katherine's accrual basis accounting records for the consulting business disclose the following results for 1993:

Consulting fee income	$312,400
Insurance expense	$ 8,400
Fees paid to subcontract programmers	36,240
Building rent	18,000
Salaries paid to employees	112,500
Payroll taxes (imposed on employer)	13,400
Utilities	4,930
Business meals with customers	230
Advertising	12,300
Supplies	1,653
Legal and accounting services	4,800

In January 1993 Katherine sold her former office building and land, furniture, and equipment. The sales prices of the assets (all originally acquired in 1985) were $140,000 (building), $36,000 (land), $2,600 (furniture), and $10,200 (equipment). She then rented new office space and acquired new furniture and equipment. Details regarding both the old and new assets are as follows:

Asset	Date Acq.	Cost	Recovery Class	Recovery Method	Total Recoveries in Prior Years
Land	1/1/85	$ 30,000	N.A.	N.A.	N.A.
Building	1/1/85	180,000	18 yrs.	SL	$80,000
Furniture	1/1/85	7,400	5 yrs.	ACRS	7,400
Equipment	3/1/85	10,000	5 yrs.	ACRS	10,000
Furniture*	1/3/93	12,000	7 yrs.	MACRS	—
Equipment *	1/4/93	20,000	5 yrs.	MACRS	—

*Katherine elects to expense $17,500 of the cost under Sec. 179.

Katherine's only other source of income in 1993 was $14,600 from the 6/12/93 sale of 100 shares of Reynolds Metals common stock. Katherine had originally purchased the shares for $19,000 on 8/13/92.

Katherine does not have enough deductions to itemize in 1993. During the year, she made estimated federal tax payments of $28,000 ($7,000 per quarter).

REQUIRED: Prepare a Form 1040 for Katherine H. Ransone for 1993, with accompanying Schedules C, D, SE, and Forms 4562 and 4797.

Comprehensive Tax Return Problem 5 Name_____ 9-77

Form 1040 — U.S. Individual Income Tax Return 1993

Department of the Treasury—Internal Revenue Service

For the year Jan. 1–Dec. 31, 1993, or other tax year beginning _____, 1993, ending _____, 19__ OMB No. 1545-0074

IRS Use Only—Do not write or staple in this space.

Label (See instructions on page 12.) Use the IRS label. Otherwise, please print or type.

- Your first name and initial / Last name / Your social security number
- If a joint return, spouse's first name and initial / Last name / Spouse's social security number
- Home address (number and street). If you have a P.O. box, see page 12. / Apt. no.
- City, town or post office, state, and ZIP code. If you have a foreign address, see page 12.

For Privacy Act and Paperwork Reduction Act Notice, see page 4.

Presidential Election Campaign (See page 12.)
- Do you want $3 to go to this fund? .... Yes / No
- If a joint return, does your spouse want $3 to go to this fund? .... Yes / No

Note: Checking "Yes" will not change your tax or reduce your refund.

Filing Status (See page 12.) Check only one box.
1. ☐ Single
2. ☐ Married filing joint return (even if only one had income)
3. ☐ Married filing separate return. Enter spouse's social security no. above and full name here. ▶ ____
4. ☐ Head of household (with qualifying person). (See page 13.) If the qualifying person is a child but not your dependent, enter this child's name here. ▶ ____
5. ☐ Qualifying widow(er) with dependent child (year spouse died ▶ 19__). (See page 13.)

Exemptions (See page 13.)

6a ☐ **Yourself.** If your parent (or someone else) can claim you as a dependent on his or her tax return, **do not** check box 6a. But be sure to check the box on line 33b on page 2

b ☐ **Spouse**

c **Dependents:**
(1) Name (first, initial, and last name)	(2) Check if under age 1	(3) If age 1 or older, dependent's social security number	(4) Dependent's relationship to you	(5) No. of months lived in your home in 1993

If more than six dependents, see page 14.

- No. of boxes checked on 6a and 6b ____
- No. of your children on 6c who:
  - lived with you ____
  - didn't live with you due to divorce or separation (see page 15) ____
- Dependents on 6c not entered above ____
- Add numbers entered on lines above ▶ ____

d If your child didn't live with you but is claimed as your dependent under a pre-1985 agreement, check here ▶ ☐

e Total number of exemptions claimed

Income

Attach Copy B of your Forms W-2, W-2G, and 1099-R here.

If you did not get a W-2, see page 10.

If you are attaching a check or money order, put it on top of any Forms W-2, W-2G, or 1099-R.

7	Wages, salaries, tips, etc. Attach Form(s) W-2	7	
8a	Taxable interest income (see page 16). Attach Schedule B if over $400	8a	
b	Tax-exempt interest (see page 17). DON'T include on line 8a	8b	
9	Dividend income. Attach Schedule B if over $400	9	
10	Taxable refunds, credits, or offsets of state and local income taxes (see page 17)	10	
11	Alimony received	11	
12	Business income or (loss). Attach Schedule C or C-EZ	12	
13	Capital gain or (loss). Attach Schedule D	13	
14	Capital gain distributions not reported on line 13 (see page 17)	14	
15	Other gains or (losses). Attach Form 4797	15	
16a	Total IRA distributions. 16a ____ b Taxable amount (see page 18)	16b	
17a	Total pensions and annuities 17a ____ b Taxable amount (see page 18)	17b	
18	Rental real estate, royalties, partnerships, S corporations, trusts, etc. Attach Schedule E	18	
19	Farm income or (loss). Attach Schedule F	19	
20	Unemployment compensation (see page 19)	20	
21a	Social security benefits 21a ____ b Taxable amount (see page 19)	21b	
22	Other income. List type and amount—see page 20 ____	22	
23	Add the amounts in the far right column for lines 7 through 22. This is your **total income** ▶	23	

Adjustments to Income (See page 20.)

24a	Your IRA deduction (see page 20)	24a	
b	Spouse's IRA deduction (see page 20)	24b	
25	One-half of self-employment tax (see page 21)	25	
26	Self-employed health insurance deduction (see page 22)	26	
27	Keogh retirement plan and self-employed SEP deduction	27	
28	Penalty on early withdrawal of savings	28	
29	Alimony paid. Recipient's SSN ▶ ____	29	
30	Add lines 24a through 29. These are your **total adjustments** ▶	30	

Adjusted Gross Income

31 Subtract line 30 from line 23. This is your **adjusted gross income**. If this amount is less than $23,050 and a child lived with you, see page EIC-1 to find out if you can claim the "Earned Income Credit" on line 56 ▶ | 31 | |

Cat. No. 11320B   Form **1040** (1993)

Copyright © 1994 by Harcourt Brace & Company. All rights reserved.

Form 1040 (1993)   Page 2

Tax Computation

(See page 23.)

32. Amount from line 31 (adjusted gross income)

33a. Check if: ☐ **You** were 65 or older, ☐ Blind; ☐ **Spouse** was 65 or older, ☐ Blind.
Add the number of boxes checked above and enter the total here ▶ 33a

b. If your parent (or someone else) can claim you as a dependent, check here ▶ 33b ☐

c. If you are married filing separately and your spouse itemizes deductions or you are a dual-status alien, see page 24 and check here ▶ 33c ☐

34. Enter the larger of your:
{ **Itemized deductions** from Schedule A, line 26, **OR**
Standard deduction shown below for your filing status. **But if you checked any box on line 33a or b**, go to page 24 to find your standard deduction.
If you checked **box 33c**, your standard deduction is zero.
- Single—$3,700
- Head of household—$5,450
- Married filing jointly or Qualifying widow(er)—$6,200
- Married filing separately—$3,100 }

35. Subtract line 34 from line 32

36. If line 32 is $81,350 or less, multiply $2,350 by the total number of exemptions claimed on line 6e. If line 32 is over $81,350, see the worksheet on page 25 for the amount to enter

37. **Taxable income.** Subtract line 36 from line 35. If line 36 is more than line 35, enter -0-

If you want the IRS to figure your tax, see page 24.

38. Tax. Check if from **a** ☐ Tax Table, **b** ☐ Tax Rate Schedules, **c** ☐ Schedule D Tax Worksheet, or **d** ☐ Form 8615 (see page 25). Amount from Form(s) 8814 ▶ **e** _____

39. Additional taxes (see page 25). Check if from **a** ☐ Form 4970 **b** ☐ Form 4972

40. Add lines 38 and 39

Credits

(See page 25.)

41. Credit for child and dependent care expenses. Attach Form 2441

42. Credit for the elderly or the disabled. Attach Schedule R

43. Foreign tax credit. Attach Form 1116

44. Other credits (see page 26). Check if from **a** ☐ Form 3800
b ☐ Form 8396 **c** ☐ Form 8801 **d** ☐ Form (specify) _____

45. Add lines 41 through 44

46. Subtract line 45 from line 40. If line 45 is more than line 40, enter -0-

Other Taxes

47. Self-employment tax. Attach Schedule SE. Also, see line 25

48. Alternative minimum tax. Attach Form 6251

49. Recapture taxes (see page 26). Check if from **a** ☐ Form 4255 **b** ☐ Form 8611 **c** ☐ Form 8828

50. Social security and Medicare tax on tip income not reported to employer. Attach Form 4137

51. Tax on qualified retirement plans, including IRAs. If required, attach Form 5329

52. Advance earned income credit payments from Form W-2

53. Add lines 46 through 52. This is your **total tax**

Payments

Attach Forms W-2, W-2G, and 1099-R on the front.

54. Federal income tax withheld. If any is from Form(s) 1099, check ▶ ☐

55. 1993 estimated tax payments and amount applied from 1992 return

56. **Earned income credit.** Attach Schedule EIC

57. Amount paid with Form 4868 (extension request)

58a. Excess social security, Medicare, and RRTA tax withheld (see page 28)

b. Deferral of additional 1993 taxes. Attach Form 8841

59. Other payments (see page 28). Check if from **a** ☐ Form 2439
b ☐ Form 4136

60. Add lines 54 through 59. These are your **total payments** ▶

Refund or Amount You Owe

61. If line 60 is more than line 53, subtract line 53 from line 60. This is the amount you **OVERPAID** ▶

62. Amount of line 61 you want **REFUNDED TO YOU** ▶

63. Amount of line 61 you want **APPLIED TO YOUR 1994 ESTIMATED TAX** ▶

64. If line 53 is more than line 60, subtract line 60 from line 53. This is the **AMOUNT YOU OWE.** For details on how to pay, including what to write on your payment, see page 29

65. Estimated tax penalty (see page 29). Also include on line 64

Sign Here

Keep a copy of this return for your records.

Under penalties of perjury, I declare that I have examined this return and accompanying schedules and statements, and to the best of my knowledge and belief, they are true, correct, and complete. Declaration of preparer (other than taxpayer) is based on all information of which preparer has any knowledge.

Your signature   Date   Your occupation

Spouse's signature. If a joint return, BOTH must sign.   Date   Spouse's occupation

Paid Preparer's Use Only

Preparer's signature   Date   Check if self-employed ☐   Preparer's social security no.

Firm's name (or yours if self-employed) and address   E.I. No.   ZIP code

Comprehensive Tax Return Problem 5 Name_____ 9-79

SCHEDULE C
(Form 1040)

Department of the Treasury
Internal Revenue Service

Profit or Loss From Business
(Sole Proprietorship)
▶ Partnerships, joint ventures, etc., must file Form 1065.
▶ Attach to Form 1040 or Form 1041. ▶ See Instructions for Schedule C (Form 1040).

OMB No. 1545-0074

1993

Attachment Sequence No. 09

Name of proprietor	Social security number (SSN)

A	Principal business or profession, including product or service (see page C-1)	**B** Enter principal business code (see page C-6) ▶
C	Business name. If no separate business name, leave blank.	**D** Employer ID number (EIN), if any

E Business address (including suite or room no.) ▶ ....
City, town or post office, state, and ZIP code

F Accounting method: (1) ☐ Cash   (2) ☐ Accrual   (3) ☐ Other (specify) ▶ ....

G Method(s) used to value closing inventory: (1) ☐ Cost (2) ☐ Lower of cost or market (3) ☐ Other (attach explanation) (4) ☐ Does not apply (if checked, skip line H) | Yes | No

H Was there any change in determining quantities, costs, or valuations between opening and closing inventory? If "Yes," attach explanation . . . .

I Did you "materially participate" in the operation of this business during 1993? If "No," see page C-2 for limit on losses. . . .

J If you started or acquired this business during 1993, check here . . . . ▶ ☐

Part I Income

1	Gross receipts or sales. **Caution:** *If this income was reported to you on Form W-2 and the "Statutory employee" box on that form was checked, see page C-2 and check here* . . . . . . ▶ ☐	1	
2	Returns and allowances	2	
3	Subtract line 2 from line 1	3	
4	Cost of goods sold (from line 40 on page 2)	4	
5	**Gross profit.** Subtract line 4 from line 3	5	
6	Other income, including Federal and state gasoline or fuel tax credit or refund (see page C-2) . . ▶	6	
7	**Gross income.** Add lines 5 and 6 . . . . ▶	7	

Part II Expenses. Caution: Do not enter expenses for business use of your home on lines 8–27. Instead, see line 30.

8	Advertising	8		19	Pension and profit-sharing plans	19
9	Bad debts from sales or services (see page C-3) . .	9		20	Rent or lease (see page C-4):	
				a	Vehicles, machinery, and equipment .	20a
10	Car and truck expenses (see page C-3) . . .	10		b	Other business property . .	20b
				21	Repairs and maintenance . .	21
11	Commissions and fees . . .	11		22	Supplies (not included in Part III) .	22
12	Depletion	12		23	Taxes and licenses	23
13	Depreciation and section 179 expense deduction (not included in Part III) (see page C-3) . .	13		24	Travel, meals, and entertainment:	
				a	Travel	24a
				b	Meals and entertainment .	
14	Employee benefit programs (other than on line 19) . . .	14		c	Enter 20% of line 24b subject to limitations (see page C-4) .	
15	Insurance (other than health) .	15				
16	Interest:					
a	Mortgage (paid to banks, etc.) .	16a		d	Subtract line 24c from line 24b .	24d
b	Other	16b		25	Utilities	25
17	Legal and professional services	17		26	Wages (less jobs credit) . .	26
				27	Other expenses (from line 46 on page 2)	27
18	Office expense	18				

28	**Total expenses** before expenses for business use of home. Add lines 8 through 27 in columns . . ▶	28	
29	Tentative profit (loss). Subtract line 28 from line 7	29	
30	Expenses for business use of your home. Attach **Form 8829**	30	
31	**Net profit or (loss).** Subtract line 30 from line 29.		
	• If a profit, enter on **Form 1040, line 12,** and ALSO on **Schedule SE, line 2** (statutory employees, see page C-5). Fiduciaries, enter on Form 1041, line 3.	31	
	• If a loss, you MUST go on to line 32.		
32	If you have a loss, check the box that describes your investment in this activity (see page C-5).		
	• If you checked 32a, enter the loss on **Form 1040, line 12,** and ALSO on **Schedule SE, line 2** (statutory employees, see page C-5). Fiduciaries, enter on Form 1041, line 3.	32a ☐ All investment is at risk.	
	• If you checked 32b, you MUST attach **Form 6198.**	32b ☐ Some investment is not at risk.	

For Paperwork Reduction Act Notice, see Form 1040 instructions.   Cat. No. 11334P   Schedule C (Form 1040) 1993

Copyright © 1994 by Harcourt Brace & Company. All rights reserved.

Schedule C (Form 1040) 1993 Page **2**

Part III — Cost of Goods Sold (see page C-5)

33	Inventory at beginning of year. If different from last year's closing inventory, attach explanation	33
34	Purchases less cost of items withdrawn for personal use	34
35	Cost of labor. Do not include salary paid to yourself	35
36	Materials and supplies	36
37	Other costs	37
38	Add lines 33 through 37	38
39	Inventory at end of year	39
40	**Cost of goods sold.** Subtract line 39 from line 38. Enter the result here and on page 1, line 4	40

Part IV — Information on Your Vehicle. Complete this part ONLY if you are claiming car or truck expenses on line 10 and are not required to file Form 4562 for this business.

41 When did you place your vehicle in service for business purposes? (month, day, year) ▶ ....../....../......

42 Of the total number of miles you drove your vehicle during 1993, enter the number of miles you used your vehicle for:

a Business .... b Commuting .... c Other ....

43 Do you (or your spouse) have another vehicle available for personal use? .... ☐ Yes ☐ No

44 Was your vehicle available for use during off-duty hours? .... ☐ Yes ☐ No

45a Do you have evidence to support your deduction? .... ☐ Yes ☐ No
  b If "Yes," is the evidence written? .... ☐ Yes ☐ No

Part V — Other Expenses. List below business expenses not included on lines 8–26 or line 30.

	....	
	....	
	....	
	....	
	....	
	....	
	....	
	....	
	....	
46	**Total other expenses.** Enter here and on page 1, line 27	46

Printed on recycled paper

Comprehensive Tax Return Problem 5   Name_____   9-81

SCHEDULE D
(Form 1040)
Department of the Treasury
Internal Revenue Service

Capital Gains and Losses

▶ Attach to Form 1040.   ▶ See Instructions for Schedule D (Form 1040).
▶ Use lines 20 and 22 for more space to list transactions for lines 1 and 9.

OMB No. 1545-0074

1993

Attachment Sequence No. **12**

Name(s) shown on Form 1040 | Your social security number

Part I — Short-Term Capital Gains and Losses—Assets Held One Year or Less

(a) Description of property (Example: 100 sh. XYZ Co.)	(b) Date acquired (Mo., day, yr.)	(c) Date sold (Mo., day, yr.)	(d) Sales price (see page D-3)	(e) Cost or other basis (see page D-3)	(f) LOSS If (e) is more than (d), subtract (d) from (e)	(g) GAIN If (d) is more than (e), subtract (e) from (d)
1						

2 Enter your short-term totals, if any, from line 21 . . . . **2**

3 **Total short-term sales price amounts.** Add column (d) of lines 1 and 2 . . . **3**

4 Short-term gain from Forms 2119 and 6252, and short-term gain or (loss) from Forms 4684, 6781, and 8824 . . . . **4**

5 Net short-term gain or (loss) from partnerships, S corporations, and fiduciaries from Schedule(s) K-1 . . . . **5**

6 Short-term capital loss carryover from 1992 Schedule D, line 38 . . . . . **6**

7 Add lines 1, 2, and 4 through 6, in columns (f) and (g). . . . . **7** (	)

8 **Net short-term capital gain or (loss).** Combine columns (f) and (g) of line 7 . . . . **8**

Part II — Long-Term Capital Gains and Losses—Assets Held More Than One Year

9						

10 Enter your long-term totals, if any, from line 23 . . . . **10**

11 **Total long-term sales price amounts.** Add column (d) of lines 9 and 10 . . . **11**

12 Gain from Form 4797; long-term gain from Forms 2119, 2439, and 6252; and long-term gain or (loss) from Forms 4684, 6781, and 8824 . . . . **12**

13 Net long-term gain or (loss) from partnerships, S corporations, and fiduciaries from Schedule(s) K-1 . . . . **13**

14 Capital gain distributions **14**

15 Long-term capital loss carryover from 1992 Schedule D, line 45 . . . . **15**

16 Add lines 9, 10, and 12 through 15, in columns (f) and (g) . . . . . . **16** (	)

17 **Net long-term capital gain or (loss).** Combine columns (f) and (g) of line 16 . . . . . . **17**

Part III — Summary of Parts I and II

18 Combine lines 8 and 17. If a loss, go to line 19. If a gain, enter the gain on Form 1040, line 13. **Note:** If both lines 17 and 18 are gains, see the **Schedule D Tax Worksheet** on page D-4 . . **18**

19 If line 18 is a (loss), enter here and as a (loss) on Form 1040, line 13, the **smaller** of these losses:
  a The (loss) on line 18; **or**
  b ($3,000) or, if married filing separately, ($1,500) . . . . **19** (	)
  Note: See the **Capital Loss Carryover Worksheet** on page D-4 if the loss on line 18 exceeds the loss on line 19 **or** if Form 1040, line 35, is a loss.

For Paperwork Reduction Act Notice, see Form 1040 Instructions.   Cat. No. 11338H   Schedule D (Form 1040) 1993

Copyright © 1994 by Harcourt Brace & Company. All rights reserved.

Schedule D Tax Worksheet (keep for your records)

Use this worksheet to figure your tax **only** if both lines 17 and 18 of Schedule D are gains, **and:**

Your filing status is:	AND	Form 1040, line 37, is over:	Your filing status is:	AND	Form 1040, line 37, is over:
Single.		$53,500	Married filing separately.		$44,575
Married filing jointly or qualifying widow(er)		$89,150	Head of household		$76,400

1. Enter the amount from Form 1040, line 37 . . . . . . 1. _____
2. **Net capital gain.** Enter the **smaller** of Schedule D, line 17 or line 18 . . . . 2. _____
3. If you are filing Form 4952, enter the amount from Form 4952, line 4e . . . . . . 3. _____
4. Subtract line 3 from line 2. If zero or less, stop here; you cannot use this worksheet to figure your tax. Instead, use the Tax Table or Tax Rate Schedules, whichever applies . . . . . . 4. _____
5. Subtract line 4 from line 1 . . . . 5. _____
6. Enter: $22,100 if single; $36,900 if married filing jointly or qualifying widow(er); $18,450 if married filing separately; or $29,600 if head of household. . . . . 6. _____
7. Enter the **greater** of line 5 or line 6 . . . . 7. _____
8. Subtract line 7 from line 1 . . . . 8. _____
9. Figure the tax on the amount on line 7. Use the Tax Table or Tax Rate Schedules, whichever applies . . . . . . 9. _____
10. Multiply line 8 by 28% (.28) . . . . 10. _____
11. Add lines 9 and 10 . . . . 11. _____
12. Figure the tax on the amount on line 1. Use the Tax Table or Tax Rate Schedules, whichever applies . . . . . . 12. _____
13. **Tax.** Enter the **smaller** of line 11 or line 12 here and on Form 1040, line 38. Check the box for Schedule D Tax Worksheet. 13. _____

Comprehensive Tax Return Problem 5   Name_____   9-83

SCHEDULE SE
(Form 1040)
Department of the Treasury
Internal Revenue Service

Self-Employment Tax

► See Instructions for Schedule SE (Form 1040).
► Attach to Form 1040.

OMB No. 1545-0074

1993

Attachment
Sequence No. 17

Name of person with **self-employment** income (as shown on Form 1040)	Social security number of person with **self-employment** income ►	

Who Must File Schedule SE

You must file Schedule SE if:

- Your wages (and tips) subject to social security AND Medicare tax (or railroad retirement tax) were less than $135,000; **AND**
- Your net earnings from self-employment from other than church employee income (line 4 of Short Schedule SE or line 4c of Long Schedule SE) were $400 or more; **OR**
- You had church employee income of $108.28 or more. Income from services you performed as a minister or a member of a religious order **is not** church employee income. See page SE-1.

Note: *Even if you have a loss or a small amount of income from self-employment, it may be to your benefit to file Schedule SE and use either "optional method" in Part II of Long Schedule SE. See page SE-3.*

Exception. If your only self-employment income was from earnings as a minister, member of a religious order, or Christian Science practitioner, **AND** you filed Form 4361 and received IRS approval not to be taxed on those earnings, **DO NOT** file Schedule SE. Instead, write "Exempt–Form 4361" on Form 1040, line 47.

May I Use Short Schedule SE or MUST I Use Long Schedule SE?

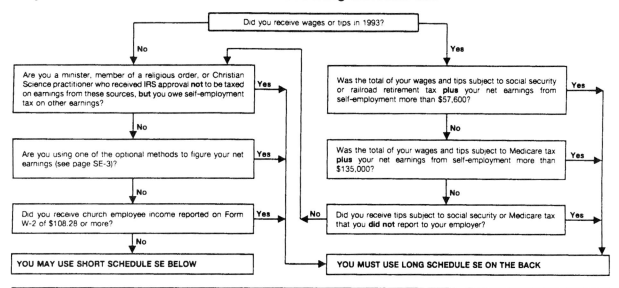

Section A—Short Schedule SE. Caution: *Read above to see if you can use Short Schedule SE.*

1	Net farm profit or (loss) from Schedule F, line 36, and farm partnerships, Schedule K-1 (Form 1065), line 15a	1	
2	Net profit or (loss) from Schedule C, line 31; Schedule C-EZ, line 3; and Schedule K-1 (Form 1065), line 15a (other than farming). Ministers and members of religious orders see page SE-1 for amounts to report on this line. See page SE-2 for other income to report	2	
3	Combine lines 1 and 2	3	
4	**Net earnings from self-employment.** Multiply line 3 by 92.35% (.9235). If less than $400, **do not** file this schedule; you do not owe self-employment tax . . . . ►	4	
5	**Self-employment tax.** If the amount on line 4 is: • $57,600 or less, multiply line 4 by 15.3% (.153) and enter the result. • More than $57,600 but less than $135,000, multiply the amount in excess of $57,600 by 2.9% (.029). Then, add $8,812.80 to the result and enter the total. • $135,000 or more, enter $11,057.40. Also enter on **Form 1040, line 47. (Important:** You are allowed a deduction for **one-half** of this amount. Multiply line 5 by 50% (.5) and enter the result on **Form 1040, line 25.)**	5	

For Paperwork Reduction Act Notice, see Form 1040 instructions.   Cat. No. 11358Z   Schedule SE (Form 1040) 1993

Copyright © 1994 by Harcourt Brace & Company. All rights reserved.

Schedule SE (Form 1040) 1993 — Attachment Sequence No. **17** — Page **2**

| Name of person with **self-employment** income (as shown on Form 1040) | Social security number of person with **self-employment** income ▶ | | |

Section B—Long Schedule SE

Part I Self-Employment Tax

Note: *If your only income subject to self-employment tax is church employee income, skip lines 1 through 4b. Enter -0- on line 4c and go to line 5a. Income from services you performed as a minister or a member of a religious order is not church employee income. See page SE-1.*

A If you are a minister, member of a religious order, or Christian Science practitioner **AND** you filed Form 4361, but you had $400 or more of **other** net earnings from self-employment, check here and continue with Part I . . . . . ▶ ☐

1. Net farm profit or (loss) from Schedule F, line 36, and farm partnerships, Schedule K-1 (Form 1065), line 15a. **Note:** *Skip this line if you use the farm optional method. See page SE-3* . . **1**
2. Net profit or (loss) from Schedule C, line 31; Schedule C-EZ, line 3; and Schedule K-1 (Form 1065), line 15a (other than farming). Ministers and members of religious orders see page SE-1 for amounts to report on this line. See page SE-2 for other income to report. **Note:** *Skip this line if you use the nonfarm optional method. See page SE-3* **2**
3. Combine lines 1 and 2 . . . . **3**
4. a If line 3 is more than zero, multiply line 3 by 92.35% (.9235). Otherwise, enter amount from line 3 **4a**
   b If you elected one or both of the optional methods, enter the total of lines 17 and 19 here . . **4b**
   c Combine lines 4a and 4b. If less than $400, **do not** file this schedule; you do not owe self-employment tax. **Exception.** If less than $400 and you had church employee income, enter -0- and continue . ▶ **4c**
5. a Enter your church employee income from Form W-2. **Caution:** *See page SE-1 for definition of church employee income* **5a**
   b Multiply line 5a by 92.35% (.9235). If less than $100, enter -0- . . **5b**
6. **Net earnings from self-employment.** Add lines 4c and 5b **6**
7. Maximum amount of combined wages and self-employment earnings subject to social security tax or the 6.2% portion of the 7.65% railroad retirement (tier 1) tax for 1993 . . . . . . **7** | 57,600 | 00
8. a Total social security wages and tips (from Form(s) W-2) and railroad retirement (tier 1) compensation **8a**
   b Unreported tips subject to social security tax (from Form 4137, line 9) **8b**
   c Add lines 8a and 8b **8c**
9. Subtract line 8c from line 7. If zero or less, enter -0- here and on line 10 and go to line 12a ▶ **9**
10. Multiply the **smaller** of line 6 or line 9 by 12.4% (.124) **10**
11. Maximum amount of combined wages and self-employment earnings subject to Medicare tax or the 1.45% portion of the 7.65% railroad retirement (tier 1) tax for 1993 . . . . . . **11** | 135,000 | 00
12. a Total Medicare wages and tips (from Form(s) W-2) and railroad retirement (tier 1) compensation **12a**
    b Unreported tips subject to Medicare tax (from Form 4137, line 14) . **12b**
    c Add lines 12a and 12b **12c**
13. Subtract line 12c from line 11. If zero or less, enter -0- here and on line 14 and go to line 15 . **13**
14. Multiply the **smaller** of line 6 or line 13 by 2.9% (.029) **14**
15. **Self-employment tax.** Add lines 10 and 14. Enter here and on **Form 1040, line 47. (Important:** You are allowed a deduction for **one-half** of this amount. Multiply line 15 by 50% (.5) and enter the result on **Form 1040, line 25.)** **15**

Part II Optional Methods To Figure Net Earnings (See page SE-3.)

Farm Optional Method. You may use this method **only** if **(a)** Your gross farm income[1] was not more than $2,400 **or (b)** Your gross farm income[1] was more than $2,400 and your net farm profits[2] were less than $1,733.

16. Maximum income for optional methods . . . . **16** | 1,600 | 00
17. Enter the **smaller** of: two-thirds (⅔) of gross farm income[1] (not less than zero) **or** $1,600. Also, include this amount on line 4b above **17**

Nonfarm Optional Method. You may use this method **only** if **(a)** Your net nonfarm profits[3] were less than $1,733 and also less than 72.189% of your gross nonfarm income,[4] **and (b)** You had net earnings from self-employment of at least $400 in 2 of the prior 3 years. **Caution:** *You may use this method no more than five times.*

18. Subtract line 17 from line 16 . . . . **18**
19. Enter the **smaller** of: two-thirds (⅔) of gross nonfarm income[4] (not less than zero) **or** the amount on line 18. Also, include this amount on line 4b above **19**

[1] From Schedule F, line 11, and Schedule K-1 (Form 1065), line 15b.
[2] From Schedule F, line 36, and Schedule K-1 (Form 1065), line 15a.
[3] From Schedule C, line 31; Schedule C-EZ, line 3; and Schedule K-1 (Form 1065), line 15a.
[4] From Schedule C, line 7; Schedule C-EZ, line 1; and Schedule K-1 (Form 1065), line 15c.

Comprehensive Tax Return Problem 5   Name_____   9-85

Form **4562**	**Depreciation and Amortization**	OMB No. 1545-0172
Department of the Treasury Internal Revenue Service	(Including Information on Listed Property) ▶ See separate instructions. ▶ Attach this form to your return.	**19**`93` Attachment Sequence No. 67
Name(s) shown on return		Identifying number

Business or activity to which this form relates

Part I — Election To Expense Certain Tangible Property (Section 179) (Note: If you have any "Listed Property," complete Part V before you complete Part I.)

1	Maximum dollar limitation (If an enterprise zone business, see instructions.)	1	$17,500
2	Total cost of section 179 property placed in service during the tax year (see instructions)	2	
3	Threshold cost of section 179 property before reduction in limitation	3	$200,000
4	Reduction in limitation. Subtract line 3 from line 2, but do not enter less than -0-	4	
5	Dollar limitation for tax year. Subtract line 4 from line 1, but do not enter less than -0-. (If married filing separately, see instructions.)	5	

(a) Description of property	(b) Cost	(c) Elected cost
6		

7	Listed property. Enter amount from line 26.	7	
8	Total elected cost of section 179 property. Add amounts in column (c), lines 6 and 7	8	
9	Tentative deduction. Enter the smaller of line 5 or line 8	9	
10	Carryover of disallowed deduction from 1992 (see instructions)	10	
11	Taxable income limitation. Enter the smaller of taxable income or line 5 (see instructions)	11	
12	Section 179 expense deduction. Add lines 9 and 10, but do not enter more than line 11	12	
13	Carryover of disallowed deduction to 1994. Add lines 9 and 10, less line 12 ▶	13	

Note: *Do not use Part II or Part III below for listed property (automobiles, certain other vehicles, cellular telephones, certain computers, or property used for entertainment, recreation, or amusement). Instead, use Part V for listed property.*

Part II — MACRS Depreciation For Assets Placed in Service ONLY During Your 1993 Tax Year (Do Not Include Listed Property)

(a) Classification of property	(b) Month and year placed in service	(c) Basis for depreciation (business/investment use only—see instructions)	(d) Recovery period	(e) Convention	(f) Method	(g) Depreciation deduction
14 General Depreciation System (GDS) (see instructions):						
a 3-year property						
b 5-year property						
c 7-year property						
d 10-year property						
e 15-year property						
f 20-year property						
g Residential rental property			27.5 yrs.	MM	S/L	
			27.5 yrs.	MM	S/L	
h Nonresidential real property				MM	S/L	
				MM	S/L	
15 Alternative Depreciation System (ADS) (see instructions):						
a Class life					S/L	
b 12-year			12 yrs.		S/L	
c 40-year			40 yrs.	MM	S/L	

Part III — Other Depreciation (Do Not Include Listed Property)

16	GDS and ADS deductions for assets placed in service in tax years beginning before 1993 (see instructions)	16	
17	Property subject to section 168(f)(1) election (see instructions)	17	
18	ACRS and other depreciation (see instructions)	18	

Part IV — Summary

19	Listed property. Enter amount from line 25.	19	
20	**Total.** Add deductions on line 12, lines 14 and 15 in column (g), and lines 16 through 19. Enter here and on the appropriate lines of your return. (Partnerships and S corporations—see instructions)	20	
21	For assets shown above and placed in service during the current year, enter the portion of the basis attributable to section 263A costs (see instructions)	21	

For Paperwork Reduction Act Notice, see page 1 of the separate instructions.   Cat. No. 12906N   Form **4562** (1993)

Copyright © 1994 by Harcourt Brace & Company. All rights reserved.

Form 4562 (1993) Page 2

Part V — Listed Property—Automobiles, Certain Other Vehicles, Cellular Telephones, Certain Computers, and Property Used for Entertainment, Recreation, or Amusement

For any vehicle for which you are using the standard mileage rate or deducting lease expense, complete only 22a, 22b, columns (a) through (c) of Section A, all of Section B, and Section C if applicable.

Section A—Depreciation and Other Information (Caution: See instructions for limitations for automobiles.)

22a Do you have evidence to support the business/investment use claimed? ☐ Yes ☐ No   22b If "Yes," is the evidence written? ☐ Yes ☐ No

(a) Type of property (list vehicles first)	(b) Date placed in service	(c) Business/ investment use percentage	(d) Cost or other basis	(e) Basis for depreciation (business/investment use only)	(f) Recovery period	(g) Method/ Convention	(h) Depreciation deduction	(i) Elected section 179 cost
23 Property used more than 50% in a qualified business use (see instructions):								
		%						
		%						
		%						
24 Property used 50% or less in a qualified business use (see instructions):								
		%			S/L –			
		%			S/L –			
		%			S/L –			

25 Add amounts in column (h). Enter the total here and on line 19, page 1. . . . . . | 25 |
26 Add amounts in column (i). Enter the total here and on line 7, page 1 . . . . | | 26 |

Section B—Information Regarding Use of Vehicles—If you deduct expenses for vehicles:

- Always complete this section for vehicles used by a sole proprietor, partner, or other "more than 5% owner," or related person.
- If you provided vehicles to your employees, first answer the questions in Section C to see if you meet an exception to completing this section for those vehicles.

	(a) Vehicle 1	(b) Vehicle 2	(c) Vehicle 3	(d) Vehicle 4	(e) Vehicle 5	(f) Vehicle 6
27 Total business/investment miles driven during the year (DO NOT include commuting miles)						
28 Total commuting miles driven during the year						
29 Total other personal (noncommuting) miles driven						
30 Total miles driven during the year. Add lines 27 through 29.						
	Yes No	Yes No	Yes No	Yes No	Yes No	Yes No
31 Was the vehicle available for personal use during off-duty hours?						
32 Was the vehicle used primarily by a more than 5% owner or related person?						
33 Is another vehicle available for personal use?						

Section C—Questions for Employers Who Provide Vehicles for Use by Their Employees

*Answer these questions to determine if you meet an exception to completing Section B. **Note:** Section B must always be completed for vehicles used by sole proprietors, partners, or other more than 5% owners or related persons.*

	Yes	No
34 Do you maintain a written policy statement that prohibits all personal use of vehicles, including commuting, by your employees?		
35 Do you maintain a written policy statement that prohibits personal use of vehicles, except commuting, by your employees? (See instructions for vehicles used by corporate officers, directors, or 1% or more owners.)		
36 Do you treat all use of vehicles by employees as personal use?		
37 Do you provide more than five vehicles to your employees and retain the information received from your employees concerning the use of the vehicles?		
38 Do you meet the requirements concerning qualified automobile demonstration use (see instructions)? . .		

Note: If your answer to 34, 35, 36, 37, or 38 is "Yes," you need not complete Section B for the covered vehicles.

Part VI — Amortization

(a) Description of costs	(b) Date amortization begins	(c) Amortizable amount	(d) Code section	(e) Amortization period or percentage	(f) Amortization for this year
39 Amortization of costs that begins during your 1993 tax year:					

40 Amortization of costs that began before 1993 . . . . | 40 |
41 Total. Enter here and on "Other Deductions" or "Other Expenses" line of your return . . . | 41 |

Copyright © 1994 by Harcourt Brace & Company. All rights reserved.

Comprehensive Tax Return Problem 5   Name_____ 9-87

Form **4797**	**Sales of Business Property**	OMB No. 1545-0184
Department of the Treasury Internal Revenue Service	(Also Involuntary Conversions and Recapture Amounts Under Sections 179 and 280F(b)(2)) ▶ Attach to your tax return. ▶ See separate instructions.	**1993** Attachment Sequence No. 27

Name(s) shown on return   Identifying number

1   Enter here the gross proceeds from the sale or exchange of real estate reported to you for 1993 on Form(s) 1099-S (or a substitute statement) that you will be including on line 2, 11, or 22 . . . . **1**

Part I — Sales or Exchanges of Property Used in a Trade or Business and Involuntary Conversions From Other Than Casualty or Theft—Property Held More Than 1 Year

(a) Description of property	(b) Date acquired (mo., day, yr.)	(c) Date sold (mo., day, yr.)	(d) Gross sales price	(e) Depreciation allowed or allowable since acquisition	(f) Cost or other basis, plus improvements and expense of sale	(g) LOSS ((f) minus the sum of (d) and (e))	(h) GAIN ((d) plus (e) minus (f))
2							

3   Gain, if any, from Form 4684, line 39 . . . . **3**
4   Section 1231 gain from installment sales from Form 6252, line 26 or 37 . . . . **4**
5   Section 1231 gain or (loss) from like-kind exchanges from Form 8824 . . . . **5**
6   Gain, if any, from line 34, from other than casualty or theft **6**
7   Add lines 2 through 6 in columns (g) and (h) . . . . **7** (   )
8   Combine columns (g) and (h) of line 7. Enter gain or (loss) here, and on the appropriate line as follows: **8**
   Partnerships—Enter the gain or (loss) on Form 1065, Schedule K, line 6. Skip lines 9, 10, 12, and 13 below.
   S corporations—Report the gain or (loss) following the instructions for Form 1120S, Schedule K, lines 5 and 6. Skip lines 9, 10, 12, and 13 below, unless line 8 is a gain and the S corporation is subject to the capital gains tax.
   All others—If line 8 is zero or a loss, enter the amount on line 12 below and skip lines 9 and 10. If line 8 is a gain and you did not have any prior year section 1231 losses, or they were recaptured in an earlier year, enter the gain as a long-term capital gain on Schedule D and skip lines 9, 10, and 13 below.
9   Nonrecaptured net section 1231 losses from prior years (see instructions) **9**
10 Subtract line 9 from line 8. If zero or less, enter -0-. Also enter on the appropriate line as follows (see instructions): **10**
   S corporations—Enter this amount (if more than zero) on Schedule D (Form 1120S), line 13, and skip lines 12 and 13 below.
   All others—If line 10 is zero, enter the amount from line 8 on line 13 below. If line 10 is more than zero, enter the amount from line 9 on line 13 below, and enter the amount from line 10 as a long-term capital gain on Schedule D.

Part II — Ordinary Gains and Losses

11 Ordinary gains and losses not included on lines 12 through 18 (include property held 1 year or less):

12 Loss, if any, from line 8 . . . . **12**
13 Gain, if any, from line 8, or amount from line 9 if applicable **13**
14 Gain, if any, from line 33 . . . . **14**
15 Net gain or (loss) from Form 4684, lines 31 and 38a **15**
16 Ordinary gain from installment sales from Form 6252, line 25 or 36 . . . . **16**
17 Ordinary gain or (loss) from like-kind exchanges from Form 8824 . . . . **17**
18 Recapture of section 179 expense deduction for partners and S corporation shareholders from property dispositions by partnerships and S corporations (see instructions) **18**
19 Add lines 11 through 18 in columns (g) and (h) . . . . **19** (   )
20 Combine columns (g) and (h) of line 19. Enter gain or (loss) here, and on the appropriate line as follows: **20**
 a For all except individual returns: Enter the gain or (loss) from line 20 on the return being filed.
 b For individual returns:
   (1) If the loss on line 12 includes a loss from Form 4684, line 35, column (b)(ii), enter that part of the loss here and on line 20 of Schedule A (Form 1040). Identify as from "Form 4797, line 20b(1)." See instructions . . . **20b(1)**
   (2) Redetermine the gain or (loss) on line 20, excluding the loss, if any, on line 20b(1). Enter here and on Form 1040, line 15 . **20b(2)**

For Paperwork Reduction Act Notice, see page 1 of separate instructions.   Cat. No. 130861   Form **4797** (1993)

Copyright © 1994 by Harcourt Brace & Company. All rights reserved.

Form 4797 (1993)   Page **2**

Part III — Gain From Disposition of Property Under Sections 1245, 1250, 1252, 1254, and 1255

21	(a) Description of section 1245, 1250, 1252, 1254, or 1255 property:	(b) Date acquired (mo., day, yr.)	(c) Date sold (mo., day, yr.)
A			
B			
C			
D			

	Relate lines 21A through 21D to these columns ▶		Property A	Property B	Property C	Property D
22	Gross sales price (**Note:** See line 1 before completing.)	22				
23	Cost or other basis plus expense of sale	23				
24	Depreciation (or depletion) allowed or allowable	24				
25	Adjusted basis. Subtract line 24 from line 23	25				
26	Total gain. Subtract line 25 from line 22	26				
27	**If section 1245 property:**					
a	Depreciation allowed or allowable from line 24	27a				
b	Enter the **smaller** of line 26 or 27a	27b				
28	**If section 1250 property:** If straight line depreciation was used, enter -0- on line 28g, except for a corporation subject to section 291.					
a	Additional depreciation after 1975 (see instructions)	28a				
b	Applicable percentage multiplied by the **smaller** of line 26 or line 28a (see instructions)	28b				
c	Subtract line 28a from line 26. If residential rental property or line 26 is not more than line 28a, skip lines 28d and 28e	28c				
d	Additional depreciation after 1969 and before 1976	28d				
e	Enter the **smaller** of line 28c or 28d	28e				
f	Section 291 amount (corporations only)	28f				
g	Add lines 28b, 28e, and 28f	28g				
29	**If section 1252 property:** Skip this section if you did not dispose of farmland or if this form is being completed for a partnership.					
a	Soil, water, and land clearing expenses	29a				
b	Line 29a multiplied by applicable percentage (see instructions)	29b				
c	Enter the **smaller** of line 26 or 29b	29c				
30	**If section 1254 property:**					
a	Intangible drilling and development costs, expenditures for development of mines and other natural deposits, and mining exploration costs (see instructions)	30a				
b	Enter the **smaller** of line 26 or 30a	30b				
31	**If section 1255 property:**					
a	Applicable percentage of payments excluded from income under section 126 (see instructions)	31a				
b	Enter the **smaller** of line 26 or 31a	31b				

Summary of Part III Gains. Complete property columns A through D, through line 31b before going to line 32.

32	Total gains for all properties. Add columns A through D, line 26	32	
33	Add columns A through D, lines 27b, 28g, 29c, 30b, and 31b. Enter here and on line 14	33	
34	Subtract line 33 from line 32. Enter the portion from casualty or theft on Form 4684, line 33. Enter the portion from other than casualty or theft on Form 4797, line 6	34	

Part IV — Recapture Amounts Under Sections 179 and 280F(b)(2) When Business Use Drops to 50% or Less
See instructions for Part IV.

			(a) Section 179	(b) Section 280F(b)(2)
35	Section 179 expense deduction or depreciation allowable in prior years	35		
36	Recomputed depreciation (see instructions)	36		
37	Recapture amount. Subtract line 36 from line 35. See instructions for where to report	37		

CHAPTER 10

Formation and Taxation of Business Entities

Taxpayers who wish to operate a business have several alternative forms in which they can conduct operations. The most common of these are the sole proprietorship, the partnership, and the corporation. Each of these forms has a differing level of complexity for its formation and different tax consequences for its operations.

The opening of a sole proprietorship often requires no more than simply providing the service or selling the product for which the taxpayer receives payment. No formal declaration of a business is necessary. For example, a corporate accountant prepares a few tax returns for her neighbors for which she is paid a total of $600. The taxpayer did nothing extraordinary—yet to the extent she earned money for this service, the taxpayer has a sole proprietorship.

The sole proprietorship cannot be separated from the sole proprietor (owner), who must be an individual for legal purposes, nor can the income and expenses of the sole proprietorship be separated from the taxpayer/owner for federal tax purposes. The income and expenses of the sole proprietorship are reported on Schedule C (or, if eligible, Schedule C-EZ) and form a part of the individual taxpayer's tax return as illustrated in Chapter 8.

A partnership requires two or more taxpayers who join together as co-owners of a business with the intent to share the profits of the business. Partners are not required to be individuals but may be corporations, other partnerships, estates, and trusts.

Most states have adopted all or a major portion of the Uniform Partnership Act, which provides that partners share equally in profits and losses and own an equal interest in partnership capital. Thus, in a two-person partnership, the partners share everything 50–50; while in a four-person partnership, each would have a 25% interest. Because partners may desire to share profits on some other basis, such as time spent on partnership activities, a partnership should not be formed without adequate preparation and documentation, usually in consultation with both a lawyer and an accountant skilled in the partnership area.

Partnerships are recognized as legal entities. They are tax-*reporting* entities, but not taxpaying entities. The total income or loss of a partnership is reported to the Internal Revenue Service although the partnership is not required to pay any tax on its income. Instead, the partnership allocates to each partner a share of the income or loss based on the partners' profit or loss sharing ratios. The partners then report individually their share of income or loss on their separate tax returns. Because of this feature, a partnership is termed a "conduit" or "pass-through" entity. The partnership income is subject to tax only once—at the individual partner's tax rate.

Corporations are quite different from partnerships and sole proprietorships both in formation and taxation. First, a corporation must meet certain formalities of the state in which it is incorporated to become a recognized corporation. Corporations issue stock to the owner(s) who are shareholders. A corporation may have one or many shareholders, and generally the shareholders may buy and sell their shares freely. There are no restrictions on who may be a shareholder.

The corporate form of organization has the disadvantage of being subject to double taxation (unless an election is made to be treated as an S corporation as explained later). Corporations are taxpayers. They report their income and pay taxes based on a corporate rate schedule that differs from the rate schedule for individual taxpayers. When the corporation makes distributions of this income to its shareholders in the form of dividends, the shareholders must treat the dividends as taxable income and pay taxes a second time.

A type of corporation known as an S corporation, described in subchapter S of the Code, can be used to avoid this double taxation. If a corporation meets certain requirements, it can elect to be an S corporation. The income and losses of an S corporation are passed through to its shareholders at the end of the tax year in which it is earned in a manner similar to that of a partnership to its partners. The S corporation is also a "conduit," and the income passed through to the shareholders is taxed on their individual tax returns.

This chapter presents an overview of the tax consequences of the formation and operation of both partnerships and corporations. Part I concentrates on the formation of the partnership, and Part II discusses the operation of the partnership and the effects operations have on the partners. Part III emphasizes the corporate and shareholder effects resulting from the formation of the corporation. Part IV addresses the actual taxation of the corporation as a separate taxable entity; Part V introduces the basic concepts of the S corporation—a restricted form of corporation that avoids double taxation. An appendix to this chapter presents a tabular comparison of the major characteristics between a sole proprietorship, a partnership, a C corporation, and an S corporation.

TAX TIP

While tax consequences usually figure prominently in determining the form in which a business is operated, other factors should not be ignored such as the problems encountered in buying and selling interests and complications upon the death of an owner.

I INTRODUCTION TO PARTNERSHIP TAXATION
(Code Sections 721, 722, 723, and 761)

THE LAW

Sec. 761(a)—For purposes of this subtitle, the term "partnership" includes a syndicate, group, pool, joint venture, or other unincorporated organization through or by means of which any business, financial operation, or venture is carried on, and which is not, within the meaning of this title, a corporation or a trust or estate.

In general, an active trade or business that has more than one owner and is not incorporated is a partnership for tax purposes. Persons sharing expenses only—on a piece of land, for example—do not have a partnership because profit sharing is required for partnership status.

There are two types of partnerships that may be established, general and limited partnerships. A general partnership is owned solely by general partners; a limited partnership is owned by at least one general partner and one or more limited partners.

General and limited partners differ in the following ways:

1. A general partner has unlimited liability for partnership debt; the limited partners' liability is limited to their contributions to the partnership capital.

2. A general partner can participate in the management of the partnership whereas limited partners may not.

3. General partners are subject to self-employment taxes on partnership income, but limited partners are not.

Limited partnership interests in a limited partnership are often sold by syndicators in a manner similar to corporate stock. The syndicator often is the general partner in the partnership as well. At one time, limited partnerships were sold extensively as tax shelters and many had no real economic substance. Congress instituted a number of provisions to curb the perceived abuses. These provisions include the at-risk rules, which prevent the deduction of losses unless the partners have an economic risk of loss, and the passive loss rules, which disallow the deduction of passive losses from a limited partnership unless the taxpayer has passive income from other sources. Then in 1987, Congress designated certain partnerships as publicly traded partnerships (PTPs) that are treated as corporations for tax purposes.

PARTNERSHIP FORMATION

The formation of a partnership is, in most cases, a nontaxable event to both the partners and the partnership.

THE LAW

Sec. 721(a)—No gain or loss shall be recognized to a partnership or to any of its partners in the case of a contribution of property to the partnership in exchange for an interest in the partnership.

A partner normally may contribute property, including cash, in exchange for a partnership interest without incurring any tax consequences. This tax-free treatment applies to any type of property transferred—even to the accounts receivable of a cash basis taxpayer or installment receivables—on which income has not yet been recognized. If a partner contributes services for an interest in the partnership, however, the partner recognizes income in the value of the services rendered.

✓ **Example 1.** Joseph White and William Brown form J & W Enterprises as a partnership. Joseph contributes real property worth $100,000 in which he has a $50,000 basis and William contributes equipment and material worth $80,000 (basis to him of $60,000) and labor worth $20,000 to remodel the facilities for the business. Joseph and William each receive a 50% interest in the partnership. Joseph recognizes no gain or loss on the creation of the partnership and the contribution of the real property for his partnership interest. William must recognize $20,000 of income for the labor performed in exchange for that portion of his partnership interest. The partnership either expenses or capitalizes the value of the services as appropriate. William does not, however, recognize any income for the contribution of the equipment and materials.

These results are more readily visualized if William is first assumed to contribute $20,000 cash to the partnership. The partnership then pays William for the services performed for the remodeling work. In this case, the partnership would most likely capitalize the $20,000 in remodeling expense as part of the cost of the building because it pertains to preparation of the realty for use by the partnership. Because the partner recognizes income, his basis in the partnership interest received includes an amount equal to the income recognized.

Basis of Partnership Interest

When forming a partnership, the basis of the property contributed is the starting point for determining each partner's basis in the partnership interest. This basis, determined by referring to the basis of the other property, is generally referred to as a *substituted basis*.

THE LAW

Sec. 722—The basis of an interest in a partnership acquired by a contribution of property, including money, to the partnership shall be the amount of such money and the adjusted basis of such property to the contributing partner at the time of the contribution....

One situation in which this substituted basis rule is altered occurs if a partner contributes personal use property to the partnership and the fair market value of the property is *less* than its basis in the partner's hands. In this case, the lower fair market value is used as the partner's basis in the partnership interest and as the partnership's basis in the property.

Partnership's Basis in Contributed Property

When property is transferred to a partnership in exchange for a partnership interest, the partnership recognizes neither gain nor loss. The partnership takes the same basis (a carryover basis) in the property that the partner had.

THE LAW

Sec. 723—The basis of property contributed to a partnership by a partner shall be the adjusted basis of such property to the contributing partner at the time of the contribution....

An exception similar to that for the partner's basis applies here; that is, if the partner contributes personal-use property to the partnership, the basis cannot be greater than the fair market value at the time of the contribution.

☑ **Example 2.** Using the information from Example 1, Joseph has a substituted basis in his partnership interest of $50,000, and the partnership has a carryover basis in the real property of $50,000. William has a basis of $80,000 ($60,000 substituted basis plus the $20,000 of recognized income) in his partnership interest. If the value of William's services are all capitalized, the partnership has a basis of $80,000 in the equipment and building improvements. If the partnership expenses $5,000 of the cost of William's labor, the basis in the improvements will be $5,000 less. If the real property that Joseph contributed was his personal residence with a basis of $110,000 but a fair market value of only $100,000, his partnership interest basis and the partnership's basis in the real property would be limited the the lower fair market value of $100,000.

Effect of Liabilities on Partner's Basis in Partnership Interest

A unique feature of the partnership form for tax purposes is the effect liabilities have on a partner's basis in the partnership interest. If a partnership undertakes a liability, it is treated as if the partners borrowed the money personally in proportion to their partnership interests and then contributed that money to the partnership. If the partnership pays off a liability, the partnership is assumed to make a proportionate cash distribution to each of the partners that they, in turn, use to pay off the liability. Because of these assumed cash contributions and distributions relating to partnership liabilities, the partners increase their bases for their proportionate share of liabilities undertaken by the partnership, and they decrease their bases when the partnership pays off the liabilities. The basis in each partner's interest in the partnership is determined by adding that partner's share of partnership liabilities to the carryover basis from the property contributed by the partner to the partnership.

☑ **Example 3.** Tammy White received a 30% interest in a partnership in exchange for property valued at $30,000 in which she had a $20,000 basis. Shortly thereafter, the partnership borrowed $20,000 from a bank for working capital. Tammy's share of the partnership liability is $6,000. Her basis in her partnership interest is $26,000, determined as follows:

```
          $20,000   (substituted from property contributed)
plus        6,000   (share of partnership liability)
          $26,000
```

Tammy is assumed to have borrowed $6,000 of the $20,000 partnership loan personally and to have contributed that to the partnership along with the other property.

Exactly which partners are assumed to borrow money and in what amount is dependent on two factors: (1) the type of debt the partnership undertakes and (2) the date the liabilities are undertaken. There are two types of debt—recourse and nonrecourse. If the debt is recourse debt, the lender has the right to seize the partners' personal assets as well as the assets of the partnership to satisfy the debt. If the debt is nonrecourse, the lender can only seize the specific property to satisfy the debt, not the general assets of the partnership or the personal assets of any of the partners.

If the debt was created before January 30, 1989, only the general partners share in recourse liabilities according to their loss-sharing ratio. All partners, both general and limited, share in the nonrecourse liabilities in proportion to their profit-sharing ratios, however. If the debt was created after January 29, 1989, the liability-sharing rules become far more complex and a complete discussion of liability sharing is beyond the scope of this text. Basically, to determine the liability-sharing amounts for recourse debt, partnership assets are assumed to be worthless and the partnership is constructively liquidated. The amount that partners would be required to contribute on the assumed liquidation determines the partners' share of liabilities. Nonrecourse debt is generally shared in the same manner as the partners' deductions relative to that debt. There are several complex exceptions to this basic rule for minimum gains and pre-contribution gain and loss, however.

✓ **Example 4.** Amy Levander is a 50% general partner in a partnership that has two 25% limited partners. The partnership borrows $50,000 on December 20, 1988, from a bank on its general line of credit. Because this type of debt is recourse debt, Amy alone would increase her partnership basis for the entire $50,000 debt. If the $50,000 were borrowed as a nonrecourse mortgage on a piece of land the partnership owns, Amy would be entitled to increase her basis by $25,000 only, and each of the limited partners would increase their basis by $12,500. If the debt had been incurred after January 29, 1989, the answers could be substantially different and their determination would be beyond the scope of this discussion.

When a partnership assumes a liability from a partner on the contribution of property, the partners—including the contributing partner—again are assumed to personally borrow an appropriate share of money and give it to the partnership. Moreover, the partnership then is assumed to take that money and pay it to the contributing partner; the partner then pays off the liability with the money from the partnership and is relieved of the liability. Because the partner is assumed to receive a distribution equal to the assumed debt, the partner's basis in the partnership interest must be reduced for this distribution. Thus, a partner's basis in the partnership interest requires *two* adjustments when the partnership assumes a liability of that partner:

1. The partner's basis must be increased for the appropriate share of the liability assumed (the appropriate share assumed borrowed as a partner).

2. The partner's basis must be decreased by the entire liability assumed (the assumed cash distribution to pay off the entire liability).

✓ **Example 5.** In November 1988, James Thurmond transfered a building with a fair market value of $200,000, a basis of $100,000, and a nonrecourse mortgage of $50,000 that the partnership assumed in exchange for a 20% partnership and profits interest. James' basis in his partnership interest is $60,000 determined as follows:

	$100,000	Substituted basis in property contributed
plus	10,000	(.2 × $50,000) Proportionate share of liability assumed
less	50,000	Assumed cash distribution for liability assumed by partnership
	$ 60,000	Basis in partnership interest

Because the debt was undertaken prior to January 30, 1989, all partners share in the nonrecourse liability according to their profits interest.

We can summarize the procedures to determine a partner's initial basis in the partnership interest:

	XXX	Basis of cash and property contributed
plus	XXX	Partner's appropriate share of partnership liabilities
less	XXX	Partner's liability assumed by the partnership
plus	XXX	Income recognized by partner for services performed in exchange for partnership interest
equals	XXX	Partner's basis in partnership interest

Holding Period

A partner's holding period in the partnership interest "tacks on" to the partner's holding period for those assets contributed that are capital assets or Sec. 1231 business property in the hands of the contributing partner. A partnership interest received in exchange for ordinary income assets, such as accounts receivable or inventory, begins on the date the partnership interest is acquired. The partnership's holding period in the assets acquired includes the partner's holding period regardless of the type of assets acquired.

Depreciation Recapture

When partners transfer property that they have been depreciating to a partnership, the depreciation recapture normally transfers to the partnership along with the property. Recognition of the recapture is deferred until the partnership sells the property.

Sales of Contributed Assets by the Partnership

When a partner contributes property to a partnership, the partnership not only takes a carryover basis but its holding period also includes the time held by the partner. The character of the asset, however, in the hands of the partnership is determined by the use to which the partnership puts the property. A personal use asset of a partner becomes Sec. 1231 business property if used in the partnership business operations. The type of gain or loss on any subsequent disposition of these properties is normally determined by the character of the property in the hands of the partnership with certain modifications. Special rules must be followed for gain and loss recognition on the subsequent disposition of accounts receivable, inventory, and capital loss property, but these rules are beyond the scope of the text.

Partner-Partnership Transactions

A partner is treated as a nonpartner for most transactions with the partnership. The partner is able to transact business as if this relationship simply did not exist. If, in transferring property to a partnership in exchange for a partnership interest, the partner receives some other property in addition to the partnership interest, this exchange is treated as a sale. Unlike certain other exchange transactions, this other property that the partner receives is not treated as boot. Rather, the partner must divide the property transfer into two parts—one part is in exchange for the partnership interest and the other part is a sale.

Example 6. Joyce Kilman exchanged a building worth $300,000 in which she had a $150,000 basis for a 50% interest in a partnership that was worth $200,000 and $100,000 cash. Joyce must treat this as a contribution of 2/3 ($200,000) of the building in exchange for the partnership interest and a sale of 1/3 for the $100,000 cash received. She must recognize gain of $50,000 on this sale portion ($100,000 − $50,000 basis on 1/3 of the property). Additionally, if the partnership exchanged an asset other than cash that had a basis of other than $100,000, the partnership would also recognize gain or loss on the transaction.

If a partner owns more than a 50% interest in the partnership, there are some situations in which modifications must be made to gain and loss recognition. The most common modification is that losses are disallowed on sales of property. A gain on the subsequent sale of the property is reduced by the previously disallowed loss, however. This rule also applies to transactions between partnerships in which the same partners have greater than 50% interests in each partnership.

TAX TIP

A partner who is not more than a 50% partner can sell loss property to the partnership at any time, including partnership formation, and recognize the loss. As discussed later, a shareholder, regardless of percentage ownership, cannot receive sale treatment and recognize a loss if the transfer of property is part of a nontaxable corporate formation.

REVIEW 1

Use the following data to answer Questions 1 through 4:
George Taylor transferred a truck and some machinery from his business to a partnership in exchange for a 20% interest. The truck had a $2,000 basis and a fair market value of $5,000; the machinery had a $25,000 basis and a fair market value of $20,000.

1. What is George's recognized gain or loss?
   - (a) $0 gain and loss
   - (b) $3,000 gain, no loss
   - (c) $0 gain, $5,000 loss
   - (d) $3,000 gain and $5,000 loss

2. What is George's basis in his partnership interest?
   (a) $7,000
   (b) $22,000
   (c) $27,000
   (d) $30,000
3. What is the partnership's basis in the assets transferred?
   (a) $2,000 and $20,000
   (b) $2,000 and $25,000
   (c) $5,000 and $20,000
   (d) $5,000 and $25,000
4. If the machinery had been George's personal use property rather than a business asset, what would his basis be in his partnership interest?
   (a) $7,000
   (b) $22,000
   (c) $27,000
   (d) $30,000
5. What is Todd Walton's basis in his 30% capital and profits interest in T & T partnership if he contributes property worth $80,000, a basis of $30,000, and a nonrecourse mortgage of $25,000 that is assumed by the partnership? (Assume this is a pre-January 30, 1989 transfer.)
   (a) $80,000
   (b) $30,000
   (c) $12,500
   (d) $5,000
6. Agnes Holt, a 20% partner in Zippy partnership, purchased some used equipment from the partnership for another business. She paid $20,000 for the equipment, and its basis to the partnership was $25,000. What gain or loss does the partnership recognize and what is Agnes's basis in the property?
   (a) $0, $20,000
   (b) $0, $25,000
   (c) $5,000 loss, $20,000
   (d) $5,000 loss, $25,000

Answers are on page 10-10.

II PARTNERSHIP INCOME—PARTNERSHIP TAXATION
(Code Sections 701–709)

Partnerships do not pay taxes on income earned by the partnership. The partnership is a conduit only for taxation purposes. The partnership reports the appropriate income share to each partner at the end of its tax year. The partners include their income shares in their own tax returns.

THE LAW

Sec. 702(b)—The character of any item of income, gain, loss, deduction, or credit included in a partner's distributive share under Paragraphs (1) through (7)...shall be determined as if such item were realized directly from the source... (c)—...the gross income of a partner... shall include his distributive share of the gross income of the partnership.

☑ **Example 7.** Maureen Malloy owns a 20% interest in a partnership that has a regular taxable income of $200,000. Maureen includes 20% of the $200,000 or $40,000 in her taxable income for the current year.

The ratio by which the partners share in the income and loss items is dictated by the partnership agreement. A partner can have both an income interest and a capital interest in the partnership. The income interest relates to the profit and loss sharing ratio; the capital interest relates to the partner's interest in the partnership assets. While these items are not necessarily the same, they will, for all discussions in this text, be considered identical. Moreover, a partner's income-sharing ratio does not have to be the same as his or her ratio for sharing losses. Unless otherwise specified, they are again assumed to be the same.

PARTNERSHIP INCOME

A partnership determines its income in a similar manner as would an individual.

THE LAW

Sec. 703(a)—The taxable income of a partnership shall be computed in the same manner as in the case of an individual except that—(1) the items described in Section 702(a) shall be separately stated, and (2) the following deductions shall not be allowed...(A) the deductions for personal exemptions...(B) the deduction for taxes...paid or accrued to foreign countries and to possessions of the United States, (C) the deduction for charitable contributions...(D) the net operating loss deduction...(E) the additional itemized deductions for individuals...(F) the deduction for depletion...with respect to oil and gas wells.

This Code section may seem confusing, but there is a basic theory underlying the conduit theory of the partnership's reporting of income for partner taxation:

1. The ultimate taxpayer for partnership income is assumed to be an individual.
2. There are many items that receive special treatment when determining an individual's income tax liability such as capital gains and losses and itemized deductions.

ANSWERS TO REVIEW I

1. (a) No gain or loss is recognized.
2. (c) George has a substituted basis from the property transferred.
3. (b) The partnership takes George's basis in the assets.
4. (b) George would have to use the lower fair market value as basis for the machinery.
5. (c) $30,000 − $25,000 + $7,500 (.30 × $25,000)
6. (c) The partnership recognizes the $5,000 loss on the equipment and Agnes takes the purchase price of $20,000 as her basis.

3. These special items must be reported separately by the partnership to the partner so that they can be treated appropriately at the individual partner level.

4. All items that do not receive special treatment are passed through in one lump sum to the partner as partnership regular or ordinary taxable income or loss.

Table 10-1 Separately Stated Items on Partnership Tax Return

Charitable contributions

Dividends

Foreign taxes paid

Capital gains and losses

Sec. 1231 gains and losses

Tax-exempt interest

Recoveries of prior expenses paid or bad debts

Special allocation items

It is essential to understand the taxation of an individual to accurately determine which items of partnership income must be reported separately and which are combined to form partnership taxable "ordinary" income. Table 10-1 lists some of the more commonly encountered items of partnership income/expense that must be separately stated.

☑ **Example 8.** Partnership XYZ had sales revenue of $200,000, cost of goods sold of $90,000, dividend income of $20,000, operating expenses of $120,000, and made cash charitable contributions of $15,000 to a qualifying charity. An individual is subject to a limitation on the deductibility of investment (portfolio) expenses equal to investment income. Dividends constitute investment income; in applying this limitation, the individual partner must take into consideration investment income and expenses passed through by the partnership. Thus, the dividends are reported as a separate income item. Moreover, an individual is subject to limitations on the deductibility of charitable contributions as itemized deductions. Charitable contributions made by the partnership must also be reported to the partners separately so they can determine their eligibility to deduct their share on their individual tax returns. Sales revenue, cost of goods sold, and operating expenses remain and are lumped together to determine partnership taxable income (loss), because these receive no special treatment at the partner level.

If Mark is a 50% partner in Partnership XYZ, he would include in his individual tax return $10,000 of dividend income (Schedule B, Form 1040), a $7,500 charitable contribution (Schedule A, Form 1040), and a $5,000 loss (Schedule E, Form 1040) from partnership operations.

TAX TIP

One advantage to using the partnership form for business rather than the S corporation (discussed later) form is that many states treat an S corporation as a regular corporation for state income tax purposes. Thus, the partnership may be the only form in which double taxation can be avoided at both the federal and state income tax levels.

PARTNERSHIP ORGANIZATIONAL EXPENSES

THE LAW

Sec. 709(b)(1)—Amounts paid or incurred to organize a partnership may, at the election of the partnership...be treated as deferred expenses. Such deferred expenses shall be allowed as a deduction ratably over such period of not less than 60 months as may be selected by the partnership (beginning with the month in which the partnership begins business)....

Legal and accounting fees form a major part of the costs of forming a partnership, and they are capitalized by the partnership. The partnership can then elect to amortize them over a period of no less than 60 months. The amortization begins in the month that the partnership begins business.

Any costs associated with the syndication or sale of partnership interests may not be included in the above, however. These costs are principally encountered on the formation and sale of limited partnerships, although a general partnership may also incur them in certain situations. These sales and syndication fees are capitalized and may not be deducted by either the partnership or the partners.

Example 9. Ben and Jerry formed a partnership to sell Italian ices from street vendors in Miami. Ben and Jerry had several meetings with their attorney and accountant as well as a meeting in which they laid out all their plans for the partnership. The lawyer charged $1,500 for her services and the accountant charged $1,000. The formation meeting between Ben and Jerry cost $250. They spent another $400 in advertising and solicitation expense to find limited partners for the additional capital. Ben and Jerry's partnership incurred a total of $2,750 in organizational expenses that can be capitalized and amortized over a 60-month or longer period. The $400 spent to find the limited partners is a nondeductible capital item.

If the partnership is a calendar-year partnership that begins operations in April, it may amortize $412.50 ($2,750 × [9/60]) in the first year of operation. It may amortize $550 in Years 2 through 5, and the final $137.50 in Year 6. The partnership may amortize a smaller amount each year by selecting an amortization period of longer than 60 months. If a partnership ceases operations before the organizational expenses have been completely amortized, the balance remaining may be expensed in the final year of operation.

GUARANTEED PAYMENTS TO PARTNERS

If one or more partners provides something of particular value to the partnership, such as special business skills or needed capital, the partner(s) can be compensated for these before the partnership taxable income is determined. Any amount that is clearly designated as a specific payment to a partner without any consideration of the partnership income is designated a *guaranteed payment*. The partnership takes a deduction for guaranteed payments before determining taxable income. The partner must include this guaranteed payment in income in addition to the appropriate share of partnership income or loss.

✓ **Example 10.** Mary Wall and Karen James form a catering partnership. Mary is a gourmet cook and brings ten years of food service experience to the partnership while Karen puts up $50,000 capital. Mary and Karen are to share profits equally after Mary takes a $20,000 annual salary and Karen is paid 10% annual interest based on her beginning capital balance. In their first year of business, the partnership has taxable income (before the guaranteed payments) of $24,000. The taxable income after the guaranteed payments is

	$24,000	
less	20,000	Salary to Mary
less	5,000	(.10 × $50,000) Interest to Karen
	($1,000)	Partnership Loss

Mary must include the $20,000 salary and her $500 portion of the partnership loss in her income. Karen includes $5,000 interest and her $500 portion of the partnership loss in her income. Both treat the guaranteed payments as ordinary income, and they are subject to self-employment taxes.

Note that any payments that are determined by reference to the partnership income are treated as distributive share payments—not as guaranteed payments.

✓ **Example 11.** In the preceding example, Mary is to receive a salary equal to taxable income (after Karen's guaranteed interest payment) up to $20,000. If taxable income exceeds $20,000, the excess is to be split equally between Mary and Karen. With taxable income of $24,000 before Karen's interest and Mary's salary, only $19,000 is available as a salary payment to Mary ($24,000 − $5,000). The $19,000 is considered a distributive income share, not a guaranteed payment because it is determined by reference to partnership income. There would be no taxable income or loss remaining to allocate to Mary and Karen.

SPECIAL ALLOCATIONS

When partners contribute property to a partnership that has a fair market value different than its basis, the contributing partner would be able to shift gain or loss to the other partners if special allocations were not required for certain items of gain, loss, income, and expense.

The special allocation procedures require the allocation of any gain (or loss) that was unrecognized at the time the property was contributed to the partnership, to the contributing partner at the time the property is sold. This allocation cannot, however, exceed the actual amount of gain (or loss) recognized at the time the property is sold by the partnership. Details related to these computations are beyond the scope of this course, however.

TAX TIP

Selling or leasing the property to the partnership rather than contributing it can avoid these special allocation procedures. Greater-than-50% partners must remember that loss recognition on a sale would be disallowed.

FILING PARTNERSHIP RETURNS

Partnerships file Form 1065, the partnership information reporting form, with the IRS. This form includes Schedule K, which details all the separately stated items of income and loss along with the residual taxable income on a summary basis. Schedule K-1s are also completed for each partner. The K-1 shows each partner's distributive share of all items of gain and loss. The partnership must provide a copy of the appropriate K-1 to each partner from which he or she can then file his or her own tax return.

Partnerships are required to file Form 1065 by the 15th day of the fourth month after the close of the tax year. They may file Form 8736 to obtain an automatic three-month extension to file the partnership tax return. Partnerships do not pay taxes, but they may be liable for a late filing penalty of up to $250 per partner if they fail to timely file the tax return.

Example 12. FEV Partnership has the following items that affect income:

Gross sales	$225,000
Sales returns	5,000
Cost of goods sold	80,000
Dividend income	10,000
Interest on municipal bonds	20,000
Guaranteed payments to partners	45,000
Salaries	30,000
Taxes	10,000
Depreciation	20,000
Interest expense (business loan)	2,000
Charitable contribution	5,000
Travel expense	3,000
Meals & entertainment	6,000

FEV's taxable income and separately stated items are determined as follows:

Gross sales	$225,000	
less Sales returns	5,000	
Net sales	$220,000	
less Cost of goods sold	80,000	
Gross profit on sales		$140,000

less Expenses:
Guaranteed payments	$ 45,000	
Salaries	30,000	
Taxes	10,000	
Interest	2,000	
Depreciation	20,000	
Travel	3,000	
Meals & entertainment (80%)	4,800	
		$114,800
Partnership ordinary taxable income		$ 25,200
Separately stated items:		
Dividends	$ 10,000	
Charitable contributions	5,000	
Interest on municipal bonds	20,000	

Completed Form 1065 is presented in Figure 10-1 using the information in this example. A Schedule K-1 (Form 1065) for 30% partner, James Favel, is shown in Figure 10-4. James also receives a $20,000 guaranteed payment.

PARTNERS' BASES ADJUSTMENTS

Partners must continually keep track of their bases in their partnership interests after the initial determination at the time the partnership is formed. (If the partner purchases the partnership interest from another partner, the beginning basis is the purchase price.) Partners increase bases for their proportionate share of any increase in liabilities undertaken by the partnership and by their allocated share of any income and gain items arising from partnership operations. Their bases are decreased for their allocated share of losses and deductions, their share of liabilities discharged by the partnership, and by partnership distributions (discussed later).

☑ **Example 13.** Jordan March had a $40,000 beginning basis in his partnership that included $20,000 as his proportionate share of partnership liabilities. The partnership paid off $100,000 of liabilities, $8,000 of which were allocated to Jordan. Jordan must reduce his partnership basis to $32,000 because the discharge of the liability is treated as a cash distribution to him.

If a partnership passes through losses or deductions in excess of a partner's basis, the partner may not deduct these on his or her tax return. A pro rata share of these disallowed losses and expenses must be held in suspense until such time as the partner has positive basis in the partnership interest.

☑ **Example 14.** Toni Moran has a $5,000 basis in her partnership interest at the beginning of the year. At the end of the year, the partnership reported to Toni that she had a $4,000 share of partnership income and a $15,000 share of Sec. 1231 losses. Toni's basis is increased by the $4,000 income share and decreased to zero by $9,000 of the $15,000 Sec. 1231 losses. The $6,000 balance is held in suspense until Toni has a positive basis in the partnership interest.

Figure 10-1 Form 1065

Form 1065 (1993) Page **3**

Schedule K — Partners' Shares of Income, Credits, Deductions, Etc.

		(a) Distributive share items		(b) Total amount
Income (Loss)	1	Ordinary income (loss) from trade or business activities (page 1, line 22)	1	25,200
	2	Net income (loss) from rental real estate activities *(attach Form 8825)*	2	
	3a	Gross income from other rental activities	3a	
	b	Expenses from other rental activities *(attach schedule)*	3b	
	c	Net income (loss) from other rental activities. Subtract line 3b from line 3a	3c	
	4	Portfolio income (loss) (see instructions): a Interest income (Tax exempt = 20,000)	4a	
	b	Dividend income	4b	10,000
	c	Royalty income	4c	
	d	Net short-term capital gain (loss) *(attach Schedule D (Form 1065))*	4d	
	e	Net long-term capital gain (loss) *(attach Schedule D (Form 1065))*	4e	
	f	Other portfolio income (loss) *(attach schedule)*	4f	
	5	Guaranteed payments to partners	5	
	6	Net gain (loss) under section 1231 (other than due to casualty or theft) *(attach Form 4797)*	6	
	7	Other income (loss) *(attach schedule)*	7	
Deductions	8	Charitable contributions (see instructions) *(attach schedule)*	8	5,000
	9	Section 179 expense deduction *(attach Form 4562)*	9	
	10	Deductions related to portfolio income (see instructions) (itemize)	10	
	11	Other deductions *(attach schedule)*	11	
Investment Interest	12a	Interest expense on investment debts	12a	
	b (1)	Investment income included on lines 4a through 4f above	12b(1)	10,000
	(2)	Investment expenses included on line 10 above	12b(2)	
Credits	13a	Credit for income tax withheld	13a	
	b	Low-income housing credit (see instructions):		
	(1)	From partnerships to which section 42(j)(5) applies for property placed in service before 1990	13b(1)	
	(2)	Other than on line 13b(1) for property placed in service before 1990	13b(2)	
	(3)	From partnerships to which section 42(j)(5) applies for property placed in service after 1989	13b(3)	
	(4)	Other than on line 13b(3) for property placed in service after 1989	13b(4)	
	c	Qualified rehabilitation expenditures related to rental real estate activities *(attach Form 3468)*	13c	
	d	Credits (other than credits shown on lines 13b and 13c) related to rental real estate activities (see instructions)	13d	
	e	Credits related to other rental activities (see instructions)	13e	
	14	Other credits (see instructions)	14	
Self-Employment	15a	Net earnings (loss) from self-employment	15a	70,200
	b	Gross farming or fishing income	15b	
	c	Gross nonfarm income	15c	
Adjustments and Tax Preference Items	16a	Depreciation adjustment on property placed in service after 1986	16a	
	b	Adjusted gain or loss	16b	
	c	Depletion (other than oil and gas)	16c	
	d (1)	Gross income from oil, gas, and geothermal properties	16d(1)	
	(2)	Deductions allocable to oil, gas, and geothermal properties	16d(2)	
	e	Other adjustments and tax preference items *(attach schedule)*	16e	
Foreign Taxes	17a	Type of income ▶ .... b Foreign country or U.S. possession ▶		
	c	Total gross income from sources outside the United States *(attach schedule)*	17c	
	d	Total applicable deductions and losses *(attach schedule)*	17d	
	e	Total foreign taxes (check one): ▶ ☐ Paid ☐ Accrued	17e	
	f	Reduction in taxes available for credit *(attach schedule)*	17f	
	g	Other foreign tax information *(attach schedule)*	17g	
Other	18a	Total expenditures to which a section 59(e) election may apply	18a	
	b	Type of expenditures ▶		
	19	Tax-exempt interest income	19	
	20	Other tax-exempt income	20	
	21	Nondeductible expenses	21	
	22	Other items and amounts required to be reported separately to partners (see instructions) *(attach schedule)*		
Analysis	23a	Income (loss). Combine lines 1 through 7 in column (b). From the result, subtract the sum of lines 8 through 12a, 17e, and 18a	23a	

b Analysis by type of partner:	(a) Corporate	(b) Individual		(c) Partnership	(d) Exempt organization	(e) Nominee/Other
		i. Active	ii. Passive			
(1) General partners						
(2) Limited partners						

Figure 10-1 (continued) Form 1065

PARTNERSHIP TAXABLE YEAR

There are complex restrictions on the tax years that partnerships may adopt. In general, a partnership must use either the same tax year as the majority of its partners or the same year as all of its principal (5% or more) partners. If the majority of principal partners have different tax years, the partnership uses a tax year that allows the "least aggregate deferral" of income and loss items. The tax year restrictions are designed to prevent deferral of income on the part of the partners because their partnership income is passed through to them as of the last day of the partnership tax year.

PARTNERSHIP DISTRIBUTIONS

Partners, in general, may receive cash distributions from the partnerships in which they have an interest tax free as long as they have bases in their partnership interests. If a partner receives a cash distribution in excess of basis, regardless of whether the distribution is from a continuing or a liquidating partnership, the partner must recognize gain to the extent the cash exceeds the basis of the partnership interest.

If the partnership discharges liabilities, each partner must treat his or her proportionate share of the discharge as a distribution of money that reduces his or her basis in the partnership interest. If this "distribution" exceeds the partner's basis, it is treated in the same manner as an actual cash distribution; that is, gain is recognized to the extent the share of the liabilities discharged exceeds the partner's basis in the partnership interest.

Loss Recognition

Partners who receive distributions of property other than cash may face some complex problems. Because a capital interest in a partnership is interpreted as an interest in each of the assets of the partnership equal to the partner's capital interest, a distribution of assets other than in proportion to the partner's interest is called a *disproportionate distribution*. These distributions require a complex analysis that is beyond the scope of this brief discussion.

If a partner receives a pro rata (proportionate) distribution of assets, however, gain or loss is recognized in only a few limited circumstances. If the partnership is not liquidating or is not making the final liquidating distribution, the partner receiving the distribution *never* recognizes loss. If the partnership is making the final liquidating distribution and the partner receives *only* cash, accounts receivable, and inventory (but no other property), the partner recognizes loss only to the extent the basis of the property received is less than the partner's basis in the partnership interest. If the partner receives property other than cash, accounts receivables, and inventory, no loss is recognized.

✓ **Example 15.** John Williams received $4,000 cash and accounts receivable with a zero basis from a partnership in which he had a $10,000 basis in a nonliquidating pro rata distribution. John does not recognize any loss because the distribution is not the final liquidating distribution. He would have a $6,000 basis remaining in his partnership interest. If it were the final liquidating distribution, John would recognize a loss of $6,000 on the distribution and would take the same basis in the assets that the partnership had as explained below.

Gain Recognition

If the partner receives cash and other property, and the basis in the partnership interest is less than the total basis of the cash and property received, gain is recognized only if the amount of cash alone received exceeds the partner's basis in the partnership interest. This applies regardless of whether the distribution is liquidating or nonliquidating. No gain is recognized if the amount of cash received is less than the basis of the partnership interest. If only property other than cash is received, no gain is recognized as well.

All of these rules follow from the principle that a partner who receives a pro rata distribution from a partnership takes a carryover basis in the property received. At the same time, the partner reduces the basis in the partnership interest for the basis of the property received. On a liquidating distribution, any basis remaining after cash distributions attaches to the other property received in the distribution.

☑ **Example 16.** Marjorie received cash of $5,000 and property with a basis to the partnership of $4,000 in a pro rata liquidating distribution. She exchanged her partnership interest that had a $6,000 basis remaining. Marjorie recognizes neither gain nor loss on the distribution. She takes a $5,000 basis in the cash that reduces the basis in her partnership interest to $1,000. The property she receives takes this remaining $1,000 as its basis.

☑ **Example 17.** Assume the same facts as the preceding example except that Marjorie had a $15,000 basis in her partnership interest before the distribution. The cash still takes a $5,000 basis and reduces the basis in her partnership interest to $10,000. The property received in the distribution takes this $10,000 as its basis. Marjorie recognizes neither gain nor loss.

TAX TIP

When property distributions, other than cash, are made from a partnership to the partners, they should take care with the asset proportions distributed. The partners could have some very unpleasant tax consequences if the distribution is determined to be disproportionate.

SALE OF A PARTNERSHIP INTEREST

When a partner sells his or her partnership interest, he or she is presumed to first sell a share of the partnership's ordinary income assets and then the remaining interest in the partnership as a capital asset. This peculiar two-step sale procedure is required so that the partner cannot avoid ordinary income recognition by selling the partnership interest. The ordinary income assets are unrealized receivables (receivables on which income has not been recognized), depreciation recapture, and substantially appreciated inventory. Once the partner determines the ordinary income to be recognized on the sale of these ordinary income assets at their fair market value, the remaining proceeds of the partnership sale are used to determine capital gain or loss on the remaining partnership interest.

✓ **Example 18.** Sol Alonzo sold his 1/3 interest in the Italy Travel partnership (Basis = $20,000) for $25,000. The partnership had $30,000 in unrealized receivables (Basis = 0). Sol must recognize $10,000 of ordinary income of the sale of his share of the receivables first. He then has a $5,000 capital loss on his remaining interest in the partnership ($25,000 proceeds − $10,000 for his share of the receivables − $20,000 basis in partnership interest).

If the partner is relieved of partnership liabilities as part of the sale of the partnership interest, the liabilities are treated as part of the cash proceeds on the sale. The results would be the same for the above example if the purchaser of Sol's interest had paid only $20,000 for the interest but Sol had been relieved of his share of the partnership liabilities in the amount of $5,000.

RETIRING A PARTNER

A partnership may buy out a partner's interest, retiring him or her as a partner, rather than the partner selling the interest to an outside party. The payments to the partner must be broken into income payments and property payments. In this case, however, only payments for unrealized receivables, depreciation recapture, and goodwill are defined as income payments. All other payments (property payments) are treated as payments for the partner's interest in partnership property; that is, capital gains or losses. Income payments made by the partnership to the partner are ordinary income to the partner and are a deductible expense of the partnership. Details of these complex computations are beyond the scope of this course.

REVIEW II

1. John Mayberry is a 45% partner in an electrical contracting business. During the current year, the business had the following items of income and expense.

Gross sales	$2,500,000
Material used	750,000
Salaries and wages	700,000
Interest on municipal bonds	5,000
Charitable contributions	10,000
Interest on accounts payable	3,000

    What amount of partnership income must John report on his tax return, excluding all separately stated items?
    (a) $466,650
    (b) $468,900
    (c) $471,150
    (d) $472,500

2. P & T Partnership had $1,400 of accounting fees, $2,800 of legal fees, and $6,000 of sales fees incurred in organizing and selling interests in a limited partnership formed to build a small shopping complex in the Everglades. The partnership is a calendar-year taxpayer and began operations in September of the current year. What is the maximum deduction the partnership may take in this first year for formation expenses?
    (a) $280
    (b) $840
    (c) $680
    (d) $4,200

3. Pauline owns a 50% interest in ABD Partnership. She is to receive all partnership income up to $25,000 and one-half of all separately stated items and income in excess of $25,000. If the partnership has $75,000 of income and separately stated dividend income of $5,000, what is Pauline's guaranteed payment from the partnership?
   (a) $0
   (b) $2,500
   (c) $25,000
   (d) $50,000

4. Allen Layton received a cash distribution of $15,000 and his share of Sec. 1231 assets valued at $50,000 in a pro rata distribution when the partnership in which he was a 50% partner dissolved. The basis of the Sec. 1231 assets was $30,000 and Allen's basis in his partnership interest was $60,000. What was Allen's recognized gain or loss on the distribution?
   (a) $0
   (b) $5,000 gain
   (c) $5,000 loss
   (d) $15,000 loss

5. Using the information from Question 5, what is Allen's basis in the Sec. 1231 property?
   (a) $0
   (b) $30,000
   (c) $45,000
   (d) $50,000

Answers are on page 10-22.

III. INTRODUCTION TO C CORPORATION TAXATION

(Code Sections 351, 357, 362, and 1032)

The corporate form of operating a business offers one very distinct advantage—the shareholders' liability is limited to their investment in the corporation. The personal assets of shareholders cannot be seized to satisfy a judgment against the corporation. While there are other advantages and disadvantages, this is usually the single overriding feature in selecting the corporate form.

FORMING OF CORPORATION

Shareholder Tax Consequences

The formation of a corporation can normally be accomplished without tax consequences.

THE LAW

Sec. 351(a)—No gain or loss shall be recognized if property is transferred to a corporation by one or more persons solely in exchange for stock in such corporation and immediately after the exchange such person or persons are in control (as defined in section 368(c)) of the corporation.

Note that Sec. 351 quoted here applies not only to the formation of a new corporation but also to the transfer of property to an *existing* corporation that meets the requirements of Sec. 351. The provisions of Sec. 351 must be met exactly and several of the terms used need additional explanation.

Property: The transfer of property to a corporation includes cash as well as tangible and intangible, real and personal, property. If a taxpayer performs services for the corporation in exchange for stock, the taxpayer must recognize compensation income equal to the value of the stock received (or services rendered if that value is more readily determinable), because services are not considered property.

☑ **Example 19.** John Jones contributes $10,000 and Bill White contributes property worth $9,000 and his legal services valued at $1,000 in exchange for 50 shares each of stock in a new corporation. Bill must recognize $1,000 income on the receipt of the stock for his legal services. The other transfers of property, however, result in no gain or loss being recognized.

Transfer: The transfer may be by one person or by any number of persons as long as the 80% control requirement is met. The transfers do not have to be made at the exact same time. They must, however, be made as part of the same plan to transfer the property to the corporation, and these transfers must take place over a reasonable time period.

☑ **Example 20.** Tony Maples agrees to form a corporation with his three brothers to make and deliver pizza. Tony has $20,000 cash; one brother has a building, another has equipment, and the third has several delivery vehicles and office furniture. It takes three months to move all the assets to the building and for the corporation to begin operations. The transfers all qualify as part of the original plan to form the corporation and will result in no gain or loss being recognized by the brothers.

Persons: Persons is used in its broadest sense. Thus, individuals, partnerships, other corporations, estates, and trusts may own stock in corporations.

ANSWERS TO REVIEW II

1. (c) .45 × ($2,500,000 − $750,000 − $700,000 − $3,000) Interest on accounts payable is a business expense included in partnership income. Municipal bond interest is nontaxable income.
2. (a) $4,200 × (4/60)
3. (a) Because her salary is dependent on partnership income, it is not considered a guaranteed payment.
4. (a) As long as Sec. 1231 property is received, Allen recognizes no gain or loss on a pro rata distribution.
5. (c) Allen has a $15,000 basis in the cash; the remaining $45,000 partnership basis is assigned to the Sec. 1231 property regardless of its basis to the partnership or its fair market value.

Stock: The persons making property transfers to a corporation can receive only stock in that corporation if the exchange is to be totally tax free. They cannot receive cash, any other type of property, short-term notes, or debt securities, from the corporation without the possibility of incurring tax consequences. If anything other than stock is received, but the other requirements are met, the other property will be treated as boot. To the extent that stock is received, however, the transfer will have no tax consequences. If *no* stock is received, the transfers do not meet the requirements of Sec. 351 and will be treated under other provisions of the tax law—generally as either sales of property to the corporation or as contributions to the corporation's capital.

Example 21. Marge Tyler has a wholly owned corporation. (a) She transfers some equipment with a $20,000 basis to the corporation for 500 additional shares of stock worth $30,000. Because Marge received only stock, she recognizes no gain or loss on the transfer of the equipment to the corporation.

(b) Marge transfers the equipment to the corporation for 400 shares of stock worth $24,000 and a $6,000 note. Marge must treat the note as boot and will have to recognize a $6,000 gain on the transfer of the property (because the $6,000 boot received is less than the $10,000 accounting gain).

(c) Marge transfers the equipment to the corporation and receives only a long-term note for $30,000. The transfer does not qualify under Sec. 351, and Marge must treat the transfer as a sale of the equipment to the corporation, and report a $10,000 gain.

Control: The transferors under Sec. 351 must control the corporation immediately after the transfer. Control requires ownership of at least 80% of the combined voting power of all classes of stock entitled to vote *and* 80% of the total number of shares of all other (nonvoting) classes of stock. Note that the transferors do not have to *acquire* control as a result of the transfer; they must simply have control *after* the transfer. This permits a transfer to an existing corporation to qualify under Sec. 351. The persons considered transferors must transfer property to the corporation. If a person performs only services for the corporation in exchange for stock, the stock that that person receives cannot be included in determining whether the transferors meet the control requirement. If this control requirement is not met, none of the transferors of property qualify under Sec. 351 for nonrecognition treatment. They must treat the transfers under other applicable provisions such as the sale or exchange of property.

Example 22. Five shareholders make the following transfers to a new corporation in exchange for stock:

Shareholder	Property Transferred	Value	Shares Received
Mary	Equipment	$20,000	1,000
John	Real estate	100,000	5,000
George	Cash	40,000	2,000
Allen	Services only	10,000	500
Alice	Equipment	30,000	1,500

In determining if the control requirement is met, the 500 shares that Allen received for services only cannot be counted. Mary, John, George, and Alice transferred property to the corporation and hold 9,500 of the 10,000 outstanding shares of stock after the transfer. Thus, the transferors own 95% of the corporation and are in control for purposes of Sec. 351. If Allen had received more than 2,000 of the 10,000 outstanding shares solely for services rendered, the control requirement could not be met.

TAX TIP

A sole proprietor can avoid current recognition of gain on the sale of business assets to another business by structuring the asset transfer as part of a qualifying Sec. 351 transaction. By having the sole proprietor and the acquiring business transfer all of the assets of both to a third corporate business in exchange solely for stock, gain is unrecognized. The new shareholder could then sell a small portion of stock, recognizing a minimum amount of gain, if some cash is needed.

BOOT

If a taxpayer receives something other than stock of the corporation in a transfer qualifying under Sec. 351, this "something" is considered boot. While the receipt of boot does not disqualify the transfer under Sec. 351, the nonrecognition provisions must be modified in a manner similar to other "boot" receipt provisions.

THE LAW

Sec. 351(b)—If...there is received, in addition to the stock permitted to be received under subsection (a), other property or money, then (1) gain (if any) to such recipient shall be recognized, but not in excess of (A) the amount of money received, plus (B) the fair market value of such other property received; and (2) no loss to such recipient shall be recognized.

The transferor who receives boot, in addition to stock, in a Sec. 351 transfer must follow the typical gain recognition rules for boot received; that is, the transferor recognizes gain to the extent of the *lesser* of the value of the boot received or gain realized. No *loss* is ever recognized, however, regardless of the amount of boot received.

Example 23. Tom Smith transfers a building with a fair market value of $100,000 and an adjusted basis of $40,000 to a corporation in exchange for $70,000 of stock and a $30,000 note as part of a qualifying Sec. 351 transaction. Tom has a realized gain on the transfer of $60,000 ($100,000 − $40,000). The boot, however, has a value of only $30,000. Thus, Tom's recognized gain is limited to the lesser amount of $30,000.

✓ **Example 24.** Marlene Pituro transferred some equipment to a corporation in a qualifying Sec. 351 transaction. The equipment had a basis of $75,000, and Marlene received stock worth $30,000 and $30,000 cash. Marlene has a realized loss of $15,000 ($60,000 – $75,000) on the transfer that is not recognized regardless of having received boot.

A major complication of this boot rule arises when the taxpayer transfers two or more properties in exchange for stock and boot under Sec. 351. The taxpayer must determine the realized gain or loss on each property separately. To do this, the stock and boot received must be apportioned pro rata to each of the properties transferred based on their relative fair market values. Gain only would be recognized on those properties with realized gains, but the realized losses on loss properties would not be recognized.

ASSUMPTION OF LIABILITIES

If the corporation assumes liabilities of the taxpayer on the transfer of property in a Sec. 351 transaction, the liabilities assumed do not normally constitute boot for gain recognition purposes. The assumption of liabilities is considered cash received, however, in determining the amount of realized gain or loss on the properties transferred. This "cash" can trigger gain recognition as boot in only two limited circumstances—liabilities assumed in excess of basis and liabilities assumed with no business purpose. Details of these exceptions are beyond the scope of this text.

CHARACTER OF GAIN RECOGNIZED

Taxpayers who are required to recognize gain on a Sec. 351 transaction generally look to the type of property transferred to determine the type of gain recognized. For example, long-term capital gain property gives rise to long-term capital gain, Sec. 1231 property yields Sec. 1231 gain, and inventory and other ordinary income property give rise to ordinary income.

SHAREHOLDER BASIS IN STOCK AND PROPERTY

If a shareholder receives only stock in a Sec. 351 transaction, his or her basis in the property transferred is substituted for the stock received in the transaction.

✓ **Example 25.** Marlo Gwinn received 2,000 shares of stock in a qualifying Sec. 351 transaction in exchange for land currently worth $100,000. She had purchased the land five years earlier for $35,000 and had made no improvements to it. Marlo's stock will have a substituted basis of $35,000—her basis in the land transferred.

There is only one situation in which this substituted basis rule must be modified. If the property transferred by the shareholder was personal use property, the basis cannot exceed the property's fair market value at the time of the transfer. Thus, on personal use property with a basis greater than its fair market value, the shareholder-transferor has an unrecognized loss.

If a shareholder receives property other than stock in a Sec. 351 transaction, determining the basis in the stock becomes more complex. The shareholder who receives other property (boot) must first determine if there is any gain that must be recognized on the transaction. The other property received has a basis of fair market value. The stock basis can then be calculated from the following formula and is considered a substituted basis:

	Basis Formulation
	Adjusted Basis of Property Transferred
plus	Gain Recognized by Transferor
less	Fair Market Value of Boot Received (including Liabilities Assumed by the Corporation)
	Stock Basis

Note that *all liabilities* assumed by the corporation must be treated as boot even though they are not considered boot for gain recognition purposes.

✓ **Example 26.** George Tiger transferred some property with a basis of $200,000 to his controlled corporation in exchange for $175,000 in stock and $75,000 cash. George has a realized gain of $50,000 ($250,000 – $200,000). He also recognized a $50,000 gain because this is the lesser of the gain realized or the boot ($75,000) received. George's basis in the stock is determined as follows:

	$200,000	Adjusted basis in property transferred
plus	50,000	Gain recognized
less	75,000	Boot received
	$175,000	Stock basis

✓ **Example 27.** Arleta Thompson transferred equipment with a basis of $50,000 to her controlled corporation in exchange for $30,000 in stock and the assumption of the $40,000 mortgage on the equipment. Arleta has a realized but *unrecognized* gain of $20,000 ($70,000 – $50,000) on the transfer since the assumption of the liability is not considered boot for gain recognition. Arleta's basis in the stock received is determined as follows:

	$50,000	Adjusted basis of property transferred
plus	0	Gain recognized
less	40,000	Liability assumed (treated as boot in the basis calculation)
	$10,000	Stock basis

If a shareholder-taxpayer receives more than one class of stock in a Sec. 351 transaction, the basis of the stock calculated by the basis formula must be apportioned between these classes by their relative fair market values. The fair market values used are those at the date of the transfer.

HOLDING PERIOD

Because the shareholder's basis in the stock received in a Sec. 351 transaction is determined by referring to the basis of the property transferred, the taxpayer normally adds (tacks on) the holding period of the property to the holding period of the stock. This rule holds true for all capital and Sec. 1231 property, but not for ordinary income property, transferred for stock. The holding period for stock exchanged for ordinary income property begins at the date of transfer.

All property other than the stock received by the transferor-shareholder in a Sec. 351 transaction is considered to have been purchased from the corporation at its fair market value. As in other purchases, the holding period begins on the date the property is acquired.

DEPRECIATION RECAPTURE

When a shareholder transfers property that would be subject to depreciation recapture on its sale to a corporation in a Sec. 351 transaction, this recapture is avoided. Instead, the recapture potential carries over to the corporation. On a subsequent disposition of the property by the corporation, all depreciation would be recaptured by the corporation, including that related to the shareholder's prior depreciation.

TAX TIP

Even though the shareholder transfers ordinary income assets to a corporation in a Sec. 351 transaction, the stock received will normally be a capital asset in the shareholder's hands. Thus, a Sec. 351 transaction does permit a shareholder to convert ordinary income (on the sale of ordinary income assets) to capital gain (on the sale of the corporate stock).

CORPORATE TAX CONSEQUENCES FOR SECTION 351 TRANSFERS

When a corporation issues stock in exchange for property, no gain or loss is ever recognized by the corporation.

THE LAW

Sec. 1032(a)—No gain or loss shall be recognized to a corporation on the receipt of money or other property in exchange for stock (including treasury stock) of such corporation.

This nonrecognition provision applies both when the corporation is a party to a Sec. 351 transfer and when the stock is sold to a shareholder. A corporation simply does not recognize gain or loss on transactions involving solely its own stock. Similarly, a corporation does not recognize gain or loss on the *issuance* of its debt instruments, although gain or loss may be recognized when the debt is retired.

If the corporation transfers any property other than stock or securities in a Sec. 351 transaction, that property is considered sold by the corporation to the shareholder. The corporation must recognize gain or loss on this sale unless some other provision prevents recognition. For example, if there is a realized loss on the property transferred, and the recipient shareholder is a related party as defined by Sec. 267, the corporation will not recognize the loss. However, the transfer of property by a corporation to a shareholder as part of a Sec. 351 exchange happens in only a small percentage of transactions, because most Sec. 351 transactions occur at the formation of a new corporation.

BASIS IN PROPERTY RECEIVED

In most cases, the corporation takes a carryover basis; that is, the same basis that the property received had in the hands of the transferor-shareholder. If the property was personal use property in the hands of the transferor-shareholder, the corporation's basis in the property cannot exceed its fair market value. If the transferor-shareholder recognized gain on the transaction because of boot received, the *corporation* increases the basis of the property received by the gain recognized by the shareholder.

✓ **Example 28.** Amy Blank transferred land with a $40,000 basis to a corporation in a Sec. 351 transaction in exchange for stock and cash. She recognized $20,000 gain on the transfer. The corporation has a $60,000 ($40,000 + $20,000) basis in the land because it adds the $20,000 gain recognized by Amy to the $40,000 carryover basis.

REVIEW III

Answer Questions 1 through 3 using the following information:
Moe, Curly, and Larry decide to form a corporation to operate a celebrity look-alike business called Impostors, Inc. Moe contributes $60,000 cash; Curly contributes real property worth $100,000 with a $50,000 basis and a $40,000 mortgage that is assumed by the corporation; and Larry contributes equipment, costumes, and makeup worth $50,000 (basis = $30,000), in addition to performing all the necessary legal and accounting services incident to organizing the corporation. Moe, Curly, and Larry each receive 100 shares of stock worth $60,000 in the exchange.

1. How much gain do Moe, Curly, and Larry, recognize, respectively, on their contributions to the corporation?
   (a) $0, $0, $0
   (b) $0, $0, $10,000
   (c) $0, $10,000, $30,000
   (d) $0, $50,000, $30,000
2. What are Curly's and Larry's bases in the stock received?
   (a) $10,000, $30,000
   (b) $10,000, $40,000
   (c) $50,000, $40,000
   (d) $100,000, $30,000
3. What is the corporation's basis in the real property and the equipment, costumes, and makeup?

(a) $50,000, $30,000
(b) $50,000, $40,000
(c) $60,000, $40,000
(d) $100,000, $30,000

Use the following information to answer Questions 4 through 6:

May Tip transferred an apartment complex to her controlled corporation in a qualifying Sec. 351 transaction. The complex had a value of $2,000,000, a basis of $1,200,000, and a mortgage of $400,000 that the corporation assumed. In addition, May received $400,000 cash from the corporation.

4. What is May's recognized gain on the transfer of the apartment complex to the corporation?
   (a) $0
   (b) $400,000
   (c) $800,000
   (d) $1,200,000

5. What is May's basis in the stock received?
   (a) $2,000,000
   (b) $1,200,000
   (c) $800,000
   (d) $0

6. What is the corporation's basis in the apartment complex?
   (a) $2,000,000
   (b) $1,600,000
   (c) $1,200,000
   (d) $800,000

Answers are on page 10-31.

IV TAXATION OF CORPORATE INCOME
(Code Sections 11, 55, 170, 243, and 248)

Corporations, other than those that make a valid S election, are separate taxable entities. The formula by which their tax is determined is much simpler than the tax formula for individuals:

```
        Income (from whatever source)
less    Exclusions from Gross Income
        Gross Income
less    Deductions
        Taxable Income
times   Applicable Tax Rates
        Gross Tax
less    Tax Credits & Prepayments
        Tax Owed or Refund Due
```

The primary difference between this tax formula and that for individuals is that there is no adjusted gross income. Due to the nature of the corporation, the intermediate calculation of the adjusted gross income is unnecessary. There are, however, many similarities in the taxation of individuals and corporations. If an item is income to an individual, it is generally income to the corporation also. If an item is excluded from taxation by the individual, it is generally excluded by the corporation. The rules determining the taxability or nontaxability of income items are not affected by the nature of the taxpaying entity.

Corporations differ, however, in that they have only business deductions. They have no standard deduction, itemized deductions, or personal or dependency exemptions. They are permitted to deduct all expenses that qualify as ordinary and necessary business expenses from gross income. A corporation is assumed to have a business purpose for its existence; thus, all expenditures that are reasonable and meet the ordinary and necessary criteria are legitimate business expenses and are deductible. There are, however, certain additions and modifications to these business deductions when determining corporate income.

Corporations also have a different tax rate schedule than do individuals, as explained below. Finally, because many of the tax credits are personal in nature—for example, the child care credit—far fewer credits are applicable to corporations than to individuals.

CORPORATE TAX RATE SCHEDULE

The corporate tax rates on the first $100,000 of taxable income effective July 1, 1987, are as follows:

0 – $ 50,000	15%
$50,001 – 75,000	25%
75,001 – 100,000	34%

✓ **Example 29.** ABC Corporation has taxable income of $67,000. Its tax is

$50,000 × .15 = $ 7,500
17,000 × .25 =   4,250
Total tax $11,750

Corporations are subject to a surtax of 5% on income between $100,000 and $335,000 to phase out the benefit of the lower 15% and 25% tax rates. This surtax adds the following to the tax rate schedule:

$100,000 – 335,000   39%

If the corporation's taxable income is over $100,000 but less than $335,000, the tax can be determined by adding $22,250 (the tax on $100,000) to the 39% tax on income in excess of $100,000.

✓ **Example 30.** Corporation XYZ has $221,000 of taxable income. Its tax is

$22,250   (tax on $100,000)
plus $121,000 × .39 = 47,190
                     $69,440

The Revenue Reconciliation Act of 1993 added another layer to the corporate tax rate schedule by increasing the tax rate on taxable income in excess of $10,000,000 to 35% and incorporating a second surtax on incomes in excess of $15,000,000. This surtax is 3% of income in excess of $15,000,000 or $100,000 of additional tax, if smaller. This latter provision effectively recaptures the benefit of the lower maximum tax rate on incomes below $10,000,000 ($10,000,000 × .01 = $100,000). Thus, the marginal tax rate on incomes from $15,000,000 to $18,333,333 is 38%. When the corporate taxable income reaches $18,333,333, the rate then returns to 35% since the $100,000 will have been recaptured [($18,333,333 − $15,000,000) × .03 = $100,000]. The complete corporate tax rate schedule is

$ 0	−$	50,000	15%
50,000	−	75,000	25%
75,000	−	100,000	34%
100,000	−	335,000	39%
335,000	−	10,000,000	34%
10,000,000	−	15,000,000	35%
15,000,000	−	18,333,333	38%
over		18,333,333	35%

The tax on corporate taxable income of $335,000 to $10,000,000 can be determined using a flat rax rate of 34%; the tax on corporate taxable income of $10,000,000 to $15,000,000, can be determined by adding $3,400,000 (the tax on $10,000,000) to the 35% tax on income in excess of $10,000,000 (but below $15,000,001); and the tax on corporate taxable income over $18,333,333 can be determined using a flat tax rate of 35%.

ANSWERS TO REVIEW III

1. (b) Neither Moe nor Curly recognize gain or income. Larry must recognize $10,000 income for the legal and accounting services performed. He received stock worth $60,000, but the property transferred was only worth $50,000. The services had a value of $10,000.
2. (b) Curly has a substituted basis of $50,000 less $40,000 for the liability assumed, which is treated as boot for the basis calculation. Larry has a $30,000 substituted basis that is increased by $10,000 to $40,000 because of the $10,000 of income recognized.
3. (a) The corporation takes carryover bases in the properties transferred. The $10,000 services performed by Larry are expensed or capitalized as appropriate by the corporation.
4. (b) May must recognize $400,000 gain—the lesser of the gain realized ($800,000) or the amount of the boot received of $400,000 (excluding the assumed liability).
5. (c) $1,200,000 substituted basis + $400,000 gain recognized − $800,000 boot received.
6. (b) The corporation has a carryover basis ($1,200,000) increased by the gain recognized ($400,000) by the shareholder.

☑ **Example 31.** If ABC Corporation has income of $467,000, its tax is

$$
\begin{aligned}
\$\ 50{,}000 \times .15 &= \$\ \ 7{,}500 \\
25{,}000 \times .25 &= \ \ \ 6{,}250 \\
25{,}000 \times .34 &= \ \ \ 8{,}500 \\
235{,}000 \times .39 &= \ \ 91{,}650 \\
132{,}000 \times .34 &= \ \underline{\ 44{,}880} \\
&\ \ \ \$158{,}780
\end{aligned}
$$

or more simply, $467{,}000 \times .34 = \$158{,}780$.

☑ **Example 32.** Megabucks Corporation has taxable income of $12,500,000. Its tax is $4,275,000, determined as follows:

$$
\begin{aligned}
\$10{,}000{,}000 \times .34 &= \$3{,}400{,}000 \\
\text{plus}\quad 2{,}500{,}000 \times .35 &= \ \ \ \underline{875{,}000} \\
&\ \ \$4{,}275{,}000
\end{aligned}
$$

If Megabucks has taxable income of $16,000,000, its tax is $5,530,000, determined as follows:

$$
\begin{aligned}
\$10{,}000{,}000 \times .34 &= \$3{,}400{,}000 \\
5{,}000{,}000 \times .35 &= \ \ 1{,}750{,}000 \\
1{,}000{,}000 \times .38 &= \ \ \ \underline{\ 380{,}000} \\
&\ \ \$5{,}530{,}000
\end{aligned}
$$

If Megabucks has taxable income of $20,000,000, its tax is $7,000,000 ($20,000,000 × .35).

CORPORATE TAXABLE INCOME

As previously mentioned, most income items, exclusions, and business deductions are included or excluded from corporate taxable income using the same principles that applied to determine an individual's taxable income. There are, however, four differences commonly encountered in this determination of corporate taxable income:

1. The charitable contribution deduction is limited to 10% of corporate taxable income before certain deductions.

2. A corporation is permitted a 70, 80, or 100% dividend received deduction on dividends received from another corporation, depending on its percentage ownership in the corporation.

3. Corporations are not permitted to deduct any capital losses from ordinary income.

4. Corporations can amortize organizational expenditures.

CHARITABLE CONTRIBUTION DEDUCTIONS

Corporations are limited to a charitable contribution deduction equal to 10% of taxable income before the charitable contribution deduction and any net operating or capital loss carrybacks. These exclusions from taxable income in determining the limitation are logical. If the charitable contribution itself was not omitted, the determination of the limitation would be circular, requiring several mathematical iterations to arrive at a solution. If the net operating and capital loss carry*backs* were not omitted, the charitable contribution deduction would have to be redetermined whenever a net operating or capital loss was carried back to a prior year. However, the net operating and capital losses from earlier years are known when the current year's taxable income is determined. Thus, net operating and capital loss carry*forwards* are included in taxable income when calculating the charitable contribution deduction limitation.

✓ **Example 33.** Durbin Corporation has $120,000 of taxable income before its charitable contribution deduction and the $20,000 net operating loss carryover from last year. Durbin gave $30,000 to eligible charities this year. Durbin is entitled to a charitable contribution deduction of $10,000, determined as follows:

	$120,000	
less	20,000	NOL carry*forward*
	$100,000	
times	.10	Limitation percentage
	$ 10,000	Charitable contribution deduction

Durbin's charitable contribution deduction of $10,000 will not change if, in a later year, it has a NOL that it carries *back* to this year.

Any charitable contributions that cannot be deducted in the current year due to the charitable contribution limitation can be carried forward for five tax years. In any contribution carryover year, the corporation is still subject to the 10% limitation. Moreover, current charitable contributions are deducted first before any contribution carryovers. Any charitable contribution carryovers that remain at the end of the five-year carryover period simply expire.

A corporation generally uses the same values for charitable contributions of property as an individual. Refer to Chapter 4 for a review of the rules for contributions of ordinary income and capital gain properties.

DIVIDEND RECEIVED DEDUCTION

Corporations that own stock in other corporations are permitted a dividend received deduction that is related to its ownership percentage in that corporation. If the corporation receiving the dividend owns less than 20% of all outstanding stock by value and by voting power of the payor corporation, the dividend received deduction is 70%. If the dividend is received from an affiliated corporation (that is, both corporations are part of an affiliated group meeting minimum 80% ownership by value and voting power requirements), a 100% dividend received deduction is permitted. If the corporation receiving the dividend owns 20% or more (by vote and value) of the payor corporation but is not an affiliated corporation, the dividend received deduction is 80%.

✓ **Example 34.** Corporation A is owned 5% by Corporation M and 40% by Corporation N. Corporation M received a $2,000 dividend and Corporation N a $16,000 dividend in the current year. Corporation M is entitled to a $1,400 (.7 × $2,000) dividend received deduction and Corporation N a $12,800 (.8 × $16,000) deduction.

Income Limitations

A corporation's dividend received deduction may be limited to 70 or 80% (depending upon the ownership percentage) of taxable income under certain circumstances. If 70% of taxable income before the dividend received deduction, NOL carryovers, and capital loss carrybacks is less than the tentative 70% dividend received deduction, the dividend received deduction is limited to 70% of taxable income. This exception will be overridden, however, if a net operating loss is created or increased for the current year by using the full 70% dividend received deduction. (For a corporation entitled to an 80% dividend received deduction, the limitation is 80% of taxable income).

Example 35. Corporation D has the following income/expense items:

A. Operating revenue $100,000
    Operating expenses 80,000
    Dividends received (from 10% owned corporation) 40,000

Corporation D's taxable income before the dividend received deduction is $60,000 ($100,000 − $80,000 + $40,000); it may take the full $28,000 dividend received deduction because that is less than 70% of $60,000 ($42,000).

B. Same as A, except operating expenses are $108,000. Corporations D's taxable income before its dividend received deduction is $32,000. Its dividend received deduction is limited to $22,400 (.7 × $32,000) because this is less than $28,000. This limit applies because the full $28,000 dividend received deduction would not result in the corporation having a net operating loss ($100,000 − $108,000 + $40,000 − $28,000 = $4,000).

C. Same as A except operating expenses are $130,000. Taxable income before the dividend received deduction is $10,000. Because Corporation D's full dividend received deduction creates an $18,000 net operating loss, the taxable income limitation is overridden and its dividend received deduction is not limited to 70% of taxable income.

TAX TIP

Corporations that may be subject to the income limitation on the dividend received deduction should accelerate expenses (or postpone income recognition) to the current year to the extent possible. By doing so, they may be able to put the corporation into an NOL position when the full dividend received deduction is taken. If the corporation is subject to the income limitation, the balance of the dividend received deduction is simply lost. It may not be carried to any other year.

CORPORATE CAPITAL LOSSES

Unlike individuals, corporations are not allowed to offset any current ordinary income with capital losses. Corporations may offset capital losses against capital gains only.

They can, however, carry back capital losses three years and carry them forward for five years. All capital losses carried over to other years are treated as short-term capital losses regardless of whether they were short- or long-term in the year of origin. Losses that remain unused at the end of the five-year carryforward period are lost.

Corporations cannot elect to carry capital losses forward only; they must first carry the capital losses back to the third preceding tax year and then bring the losses forward to the succeeding two tax years in turn before they can be carried forward. Fortunately, however, capital losses are used on a first-incurred, first-used basis. Thus, if a loss from 1988 is about to expire at the end of 1993, it will be used to offset any 1993 capital gains before the losses from 1989 through 1992 are used.

Example 36. Corporation L had the following capital-gain and -loss history:

Year 1	$10,000	Year 4	($45,000)
Year 2	25,000	Year 5	(20,000)
Year 3	15,000	Year 6	25,000

Corporation L first carries the $45,000 capital loss from Year 4 back to Year 1 offsetting the $10,000 gain. The $35,000 loss remaining offsets the $25,000 gain in Year 2 and $10,000 of the $15,000 in Year 3. Then $5,000 of the $20,000 loss from Year 5 offsets the remaining $5,000 Year 3 gain; the balance is carried forward to Year 6 leaving a net gain of $10,000.

ORGANIZATION EXPENSES

There are certain costs, such as state filing fees and fees for the professional services of lawyers and accountants, incurred during corporate formation. These expenditures constitute an asset that benefits the corporation throughout its entire life. The Code, however, permits the corporation to amortize certain organization expenses over a five-year or longer period.

THE LAW

Sec. 248(a)—The organizational expenditures of a corporation may, at the election of the corporation..., be treated as deferred expenses. In computing taxable income, such expenses shall be allowed as a deduction ratably over such period of not less than 60 months as may be selected by the corporation (beginning with the month in which the corporation begins business).

Only those expenses incurred before the end of the corporation's first taxable year are eligible to be amortized under this provision. Organization expenses incurred after the end of this first tax year must be capitalized and cannot be amortized. They remain on the books of the corporation until it ceases to exist.

The expenses do not, however, have to be paid by the end of the first tax year, regardless of the method of accounting used by the corporation, whether cash or accrual basis. Organization expenses must simply be *incurred* prior to the end of the first tax year to be eligible for amortization.

The corporation amortizes the eligible organization expenses over a 60-month or longer period. To minimize taxes, most corporations choose the 60-month period. Amortization must begin with the month in which the corporation begins business operations.

☑ **Example 37.** Towne Corporation, a calendar-year corporation, was formed by three individuals in March 19X1 and began operations in July of that same year. In forming the business, the following expenses were incurred;

3/15	$200	State filing fee
3/15	500	Legal fee to draft articles of incorporation and bylaws
3/31	300	Accounting fees to set up computerized ledger system
3/31	200	Expenses of organizational meeting for directors and stockholders
4/1	100	Issuance of stock certificates

All expenses, except the cost of issuing the stock certificates, are organizational expenses incurred before the end of the first tax year. The cost of issuing the stock certificates is not an organizational expense but is treated as a reduction in the proceeds from the sale of stock. The $1,200 of eligible expenses may be amortized over 60 or more months beginning with the month of July. The corporation can amortize $20 per month ($1,200/60). Six months' amortization is permitted in 19X1 for a total of $120. The corporation can amortize $240 each year for years 19X2 through 19X5 and the final $120 in 19X6.

TAX TIP

Because corporations are generally free to select fiscal or calendar years as their tax year, they can select a tax year that allows them to include as many organizational expenses incurred as possible to maximize their allowable amortization expense.

FILING REQUIREMENTS

Corporations are required to file their tax returns by the 15th day of the third month following the close of the taxable year. For calendar-year corporations, this is March 15. C corporations are generally permitted to have either fiscal or calendar years for tax purposes.

Corporations are permitted an automatic six-month extension for filing their returns. They request the extension by filing Form 7004 by the due date for their tax return. They are required to pay the balance of their estimated tax due at that time.

Corporations file their tax information on either Form 1120 or the relatively new corporate short form, Form 1120A. To be eligible to use Form 1120A, the corporation's gross receipts, total income, and total assets must all be less than $250,000. The first pages of both Forms 1120 and 1120A are quite similar. Form 1120 is four pages long and 1120A only two pages; as a result, additional information is required to be provided by larger corporations not eligible to file Form 1120A.

☑ **Example 38.** FEV Corporation has the following items that affect income:

Gross sales	$225,000
Sales returns	5,000
Cost of goods sold	80,000
Dividend income (10% owned corporation)	10,000
Interest on municipal bonds	20,000
Salaries (officers)	45,000
Other salaries	30,000
Taxes	10,000
Depreciation	20,000
Interest expense	2,000
Charitable contributions	5,000
Travel expenses (excluding meals)	3,000
Meals & entertainment	6,000
NOL deduction—prior year	15,000

FEV's taxable income is determined as follows:

Income:

Gross sales		$225,000
Returns		(5,000)
Net sales		$220,000
Cost of goods sold		(80,000)
Gross profit on sales		$140,000
Dividend income		10,000
Total income		$150,000

Deductions:

Officers salaries	$ 45,000	
Other salaries	30,000	
Taxes	10,000	
Interest	2,000	
Depreciation	20,000	
Travel	3,000	
Meals & entertainment @ 80%	4,800	
NOL carryforward	15,000	
Total deductions before charitable cont. & div. rec. ded.		($129,800)
Net income before charitable cont. & div. rec. ded.		$ 20,200
Charitable contribution		(2,020)
(limited to 10%)		
Income before div. red. ded.		$ 18,180
Dividend received deduction		(7,000)
Taxable income		$ 11,180

Completed Forms 1120 (pages 1 and 2) and 1120A (page 1) are shown in Figure 10-2.

10-38 Formation and Taxation of Business Entities

Form 1120 — U.S. Corporation Income Tax Return (1993)

OMB No. 1545-0123

Department of the Treasury — Internal Revenue Service

For calendar year 1993 or tax year beginning ...., 1993, ending ...., 19 ...
► Instructions are separate. See page 1 for Paperwork Reduction Act Notice.

A Check if a:
1. Consolidated return (attach Form 851)
2. Personal holding co. (attach Sch. PH)
3. Personal service corp. (as defined in Temporary Regs. sec. 1.441-4T—see instructions)

Use IRS label. Otherwise, please print or type.

Name: **FEV Corporation**
Number, street, and room or suite no. (If a P.O. box, see page 6 of instructions.)
City or town, state, and ZIP code

B Employer identification number
C Date incorporated
D Total assets (see Specific Instructions) $

E Check applicable boxes: (1) ☐ Initial return (2) ☐ Final return (3) ☐ Change of address

Income

Line	Description	Amount	Line	Amount
1a	Gross receipts or sales	225,000		
1b	Less returns and allowances	5,000	1c	220,000
2	Cost of goods sold (Schedule A, line 8)		2	80,000
3	Gross profit. Subtract line 2 from line 1c		3	140,000
4	Dividends (Schedule C, line 19)		4	10,000
5	Interest		5	
6	Gross rents		6	
7	Gross royalties		7	
8	Capital gain net income (attach Schedule D (Form 1120))		8	
9	Net gain or (loss) from Form 4797, Part II, line 20 (attach Form 4797)		9	
10	Other income (see instructions—attach schedule)		10	
11	**Total income.** Add lines 3 through 10 ►		11	150,000

Deductions (See instructions for limitations on deductions.)

Line	Description	Amount	Line	Amount
12	Compensation of officers (Schedule E, line 4)		12	45,000
13a	Salaries and wages	30,000		
13b	Less jobs credit		13c	30,000
14	Repairs and maintenance		14	
15	Bad debts		15	
16	Rents		16	
17	Taxes and licenses		17	10,000
18	Interest		18	2,000
19	Charitable contributions (see instructions for 10% limitation)		19	2,020
20	Depreciation (attach Form 4562)	20,000		
21	Less depreciation claimed on Schedule A and elsewhere on return		21b	20,000
22	Depletion		22	
23	Advertising		23	
24	Pension, profit-sharing, etc. plans		24	
25	Employee benefit programs		25	
26	Other deductions (attach schedule) — Travel = 3,000; M&E @ 80% = 4,800		26	7,800
27	**Total deductions.** Add lines 12 through 26 ►		27	116,820
28	Taxable income before net operating loss deduction and special deductions. Subtract line 27 from line 11		28	33,180
29a	Less: Net operating loss deduction (see instructions)	15,000		
29b	Special deductions (Schedule C, line 20)	7,000	29c	22,000
30	**Taxable income.** Subtract line 29c from line 28		30	11,180
31	Total tax (Schedule J, line 10)		31	1,677

Tax and Payments

32. Payments:
  a. 1992 overpayment credited to 1993 — 32a
  b. 1993 estimated tax payments — 32b
  c. Less 1993 refund applied for on Form 4466 — 32c ( ) d Bal ► 32d
  e. Tax deposited with Form 7004 — 32e
  f. Credit from regulated investment companies (attach Form 2439) — 32f
  g. Credit for Federal tax on fuels (attach Form 4136). See instructions — 32g   32h
33. Estimated tax penalty (see instructions). Check if Form 2220 is attached ► ☐   33
34. **Tax due.** If line 32h is smaller than the total of lines 31 and 33, enter amount owed   34
35. **Overpayment.** If line 32h is larger than the total of lines 31 and 33, enter amount overpaid   35
36. Enter amount of line 35 you want: Credited to 1994 estimated tax ► .... Refunded ► 36

Please Sign Here — Under penalties of perjury, I declare that I have examined this return, including accompanying schedules and statements, and to the best of my knowledge and belief, it is true, correct, and complete. Declaration of preparer (other than taxpayer) is based on all information of which preparer has any knowledge.

Signature of officer — Date — Title

Paid Preparer's Use Only — Preparer's signature — Date — Check if self-employed ☐ — Preparer's social security number
Firm's name (or yours if self-employed) and address — E.I. No. ► — ZIP code ►

Cat. No. 11450Q

(Proof as of September 1993 — subject to change)

Figure 10-2 Form 1120

Form 1120 (1993) FEV Corp. Page **2**

Schedule A — Cost of Goods Sold (See instructions.)

1	Inventory at beginning of year	
2	Purchases	
3	Cost of labor	
4	Additional section 263A costs (attach schedule)	
5	Other costs (attach schedule)	
6	**Total.** Add lines 1 through 5	
7	Inventory at end of year	
8	**Cost of goods sold.** Subtract line 7 from line 6. Enter here and on page 1, line 2	80,000

9a Check all methods used for valuing closing inventory:
  ☐ Cost
  ☐ Lower of cost or market as described in Regulations section 1.471-4
  ☐ Writedown of subnormal goods as described in Regulations section 1.471-2(c)
  ☐ Other (Specify method used and attach explanation.) ▶ ....

 b Check if the LIFO inventory method was adopted this tax year for any goods (if checked, attach Form 970) ▶ ☐

 c If the LIFO inventory method was used for this tax year, enter percentage (or amounts) of closing inventory computed under LIFO 9c

 d Do the rules of section 263A (for property produced or acquired for resale) apply to the corporation? ... ☐ Yes ☐ No

 e Was there any change in determining quantities, cost, or valuations between opening and closing inventory? If "Yes," attach explanation .... ☐ Yes ☐ No

Schedule C — Dividends and Special Deductions (See instructions.)

		(a) Dividends received	(b) %	(c) Special deductions (a) × (b)
1	Dividends from less-than-20%-owned domestic corporations that are subject to the 70% deduction (other than debt-financed stock)	10,000	70	7,000
2	Dividends from 20%-or-more-owned domestic corporations that are subject to the 80% deduction (other than debt-financed stock)		80	
3	Dividends on debt-financed stock of domestic and foreign corporations (section 246A)		see instructions	
4	Dividends on certain preferred stock of less-than-20%-owned public utilities		42	
5	Dividends on certain preferred stock of 20%-or-more-owned public utilities		48	
6	Dividends from less-than-20%-owned foreign corporations and certain FSCs that are subject to the 70% deduction		70	
7	Dividends from 20%-or-more-owned foreign corporations and certain FSCs that are subject to the 80% deduction		80	
8	Dividends from wholly owned foreign subsidiaries subject to the 100% deduction (section 245(b))		100	
9	**Total.** Add lines 1 through 8. See instructions for limitation			
10	Dividends from domestic corporations received by a small business investment company operating under the Small Business Investment Act of 1958		100	
11	Dividends from certain FSCs that are subject to the 100% deduction (section 245(c)(1))		100	
12	Dividends from affiliated group members subject to the 100% deduction (section 243(a)(3))		100	
13	Other dividends from foreign corporations not included on lines 3, 6, 7, 8, or 11			
14	Income from controlled foreign corporations under subpart F (attach Form(s) 5471)			
15	Foreign dividend gross-up (section 78)			
16	IC-DISC and former DISC dividends not included on lines 1, 2, or 3 (section 246(d))			
17	Other dividends			
18	Deduction for dividends paid on certain preferred stock of public utilities (see instructions)			
19	**Total dividends.** Add lines 1 through 17. Enter here and on line 4, page 1 ▶	10,000		
20	**Total special deductions.** Add lines 9, 10, 11, 12, and 18. Enter here and on line 29b, page 1 ▶			7,000

Schedule E — Compensation of Officers (See instructions for line 12, page 1.)

Complete Schedule E only if total receipts (line 1a plus lines 4 through 10 on page 1, Form 1120) are $500,000 or more

(a) Name of officer	(b) Social security number	(c) Percent of time devoted to business	Percent of corporation stock owned		(f) Amount of compensation
			(d) Common	(e) Preferred	
1		%	%	%	
		%	%	%	
		%	%	%	
		%	%	%	
		%	%	%	

2	Total compensation of officers	45,000
3	Compensation of officers claimed on Schedule A and elsewhere on return	
4	Subtract line 3 from line 2. Enter the result here and on line 12, page 1	45,000

Figure 10-2 (continued)   Form 1120

10-40 Formation and Taxation of Business Entities

Form 1120-A — U.S. Corporation Short-Form Income Tax Return (1993)

OMB No. 1545-0890

Department of the Treasury / Internal Revenue Service

See separate instructions to make sure the corporation qualifies to file Form 1120-A.
For calendar year 1993 or tax year beginning ...., 1993, ending ...., 19.....

A Check this box if the corp. is a personal service corp. (as defined in Temporary Regs. section 1.441-4T—see instructions) ▶ ☐

Use IRS label. Otherwise, please print or type.

Name: **FEV Corporation**
Number, street, and room or suite no. (If a P.O. box, see page 6 of instructions.)
City or town, state, and ZIP code

B Employer identification number
C Date incorporated
D Total assets (see Specific Instructions) $

E Check applicable boxes: (1) ☐ Initial return (2) ☐ Change of address
F Check method of accounting: (1) ☐ Cash (2) ☐ Accrual (3) ☐ Other (specify)

Income

1a	Gross receipts or sales	225,000
1b	Less returns and allowances	5,000
1c	Balance	220,000
2	Cost of goods sold (see instructions)	80,000
3	Gross profit. Subtract line 2 from line 1c	140,000
4	Domestic corporation dividends subject to the 70% deduction	10,000
5	Interest	
6	Gross rents	
7	Gross royalties	
8	Capital gain net income (attach Schedule D (Form 1120))	
9	Net gain or (loss) from Form 4797, Part II, line 20 (attach Form 4797)	
10	Other income (see instructions)	
11	Total income. Add lines 3 through 10	150,000

Deductions

12	Compensation of officers (see instructions)	45,000
13a	Salaries and wages 225,000 b Less jobs credit c Balance	30,000
14	Repairs and maintenance	
15	Bad debts	
16	Rents	
17	Taxes and licenses	10,000
18	Interest	2,000
19	Charitable contributions (see instructions for 10% limitation)	2,020
20	Depreciation (attach Form 4562)	20,000
21a	Less depreciation claimed elsewhere on return	
21b		20,000
22	Other deductions (attach schedule) — Travel = 3,000; M&E @80% = 4,800	7,800
23	Total deductions. Add lines 12 through 22	116,820
24	Taxable income before net operating loss deduction and special deductions. Subtract line 23 from line 11	33,180
25a	Less: a Net operating loss deduction (see instructions)	15,000
25b	b Special deductions (see instructions)	7,000
25c		22,000
26	Taxable income. Subtract line 25c from line 24	11,180
27	Total tax (from page 2, Part I, line 7)	1,677

Tax and Payments

28 Payments:
- a 1992 overpayment credited to 1993 — 28a
- b 1993 estimated tax payments — 28b
- c Less 1993 refund applied for on Form 4466 — 28c (   ) Bal ▶ 28d
- e Tax deposited with Form 7004 — 28e
- f Credit from regulated investment companies (attach Form 2439) — 28f
- g Credit for Federal tax on fuels (attach Form 4136). See instructions — 28g
- h Total payments. Add lines 28d through 28g — 28h

29 Estimated tax penalty (see instructions). Check if Form 2220 is attached ▶ ☐
30 Tax due. If line 28h is smaller than the total of lines 27 and 29, enter amount owed
31 Overpayment. If line 28h is larger than the total of lines 27 and 29, enter amount overpaid
32 Enter amount of line 31 you want: Credited to 1994 estimated tax ▶   Refunded ▶

Please Sign Here — Under penalties of perjury, I declare that I have examined this return, including accompanying schedules and statements, and to the best of my knowledge and belief, it is true, correct, and complete. Declaration of preparer (other than taxpayer) is based on all information of which preparer has any knowledge.

Signature of officer / Date / Title

Paid Preparer's Use Only — Preparer's signature / Date / Check if self-employed ☐ / Preparer's social security number / Firm's name (or yours if self-employed) and address / E.I. No. / ZIP code

For Paperwork Reduction Act Notice, see page 1 of the instructions. Cat. No. 11456E Form 1120-A (1993)

Proof as of August 1993 (subject to change)

Figure 10-2 (continued) Form 1120-A

Although this is a relatively straightforward example, several points are worth noting. First, the corporation can deduct only 80% of the cost of meals and entertainment expenses. This limitation on the deductibility of meals and entertainment applies to all persons. Next, an intermediate taxable income must be calculated in order to determine the charitable contribution deduction. This intermediate income figure includes the NOL carryover. It is only an NOL *carryback* that is not included. Finally, because there is positive net income of $11,180 ($18,180 − $7,000 dividend income) when the full dividend received deduction is included, the income limitation on the dividend received deduction does not apply.

ALTERNATIVE MINIMUM TAX

Corporations are subject to an alternative minimum tax (AMT) of 20% of alternative minimum taxable income (AMTI). The format of the AMT as well as most of the adjustments and preference items are identical to those discussed for individuals in Chapter 7. The AMT rate for corporations is 20% and the corporate exemption is $40,000, however, this exemption is phased out at the rate of 25 cents for each dollar the AMTI, before the exemption, exceeds $150,000. Thus the exemption is zero at an AMTI of $310,000 or more.

	Corporate AMT Format
	Regular Taxable Income
plus/less	Adjustments
plus	Preferences
	AMTI before Exemption
less	Exemption
	AMTI
times	Tax Rate
	Tentative AMT before Credits
less	Credits
	Tentative AMT
less	Regular Tax
	AMT

The most common adjustments and tax preferences were discussed in Chapter 7 and will not be repeated here. Remember, however, that adjustments may be both positive and negative while preferences only increase regular taxable income when determining AMTI. There is one adjustment that applies to corporations only—the ACE (adjusted current earnings) adjustment. This adjustment is equal to 75% of the difference between ACE and the AMTI determined without the ACE adjustment. Determining ACE requires separate calculations and is a concept of income that is more like accounting or economic income than taxable income. Its calculation is beyond the scope of this text.

Once the ACE is determined, the tax rate is applied to AMTI. Allowable credits are then deducted and a tentative AMT determined. As it is for individuals, the AMT is formally defined as the excess of tentative AMT over the regular tax. The corporation pays an AMT only if its tentative AMT is greater than the regular tax. Otherwise, the corporation pays the regular tax only.

If the corporation pays the regular tax in some years and an AMT in others, an alternative minimum tax credit can offset the regular tax in future years. For tax years beginning after 1989, the alternative minimum tax credit for corporations is equal to the alternative minimum tax liability without adjustment. The AMT credit can be carried forward to a year in which only the regular tax is paid. It cannot be carried forward to any year in which an AMT is due. The AMT credit does not expire and may be carried forward to any future regular tax year.

A corporation files Form 4626 to report its AMT liability.

✓ **Example 39.** Z Corporation had $400,000 of regular taxable income. It had the following adjustments and preference items:

Positive adjustments—	
Depreciation	$ 30,000
Installment sales	200,000
Amortization of pollution control facilities	10,000
Negative adjustments—	
Long-term contracts	120,000
Tax Preferences—	
Depletion	50,000
Accelerated depreciation	20,000

The corporation's adjusted current earnings are $730,000. Z's AMT is

Regular taxable income	$400,000
Adjustments	+ 30,000
	+200,000
	+ 10,000
	−120,000
Preferences	+ 50,000
	+ 20,000
AMTI before ACE adjustment	$590,000
ACE adj. (.75 × [$730,000 − $590,000])	105,000
AMTI	$695,000
	× .20
Tentative AMT	$139,000
Regular tax = $400,000 × .34	$136,000
AMT	$ 3,000

A completed Form 4626 reflecting the above information is shown in Figure 10-3. Note that the $3,000 alternative minimum tax liability is the corporation's AMT credit and may be used to offset the regular tax in a future year in which only the regular tax liability is due.

Form **4626**	**Alternative Minimum Tax—Corporations** (including environmental tax) ▶ See separate instructions. ▶ Attach to the corporation's tax return.	OMB No. 1545-0175 **1992**
Department of the Treasury Internal Revenue Service		

Name	Employer identification number
Z Corporation	

1	Taxable income or (loss) before net operating loss deduction. (Important: See instructions if the corporation is subject to the environmental tax.)		**1**	400,000
2	**Adjustments:**			
a	Depreciation of tangible property placed in service after 1986	2a 30,000		
b	Amortization of certified pollution control facilities placed in service after 1986	2b 10,000		
c	Amortization of mining exploration and development costs paid or incurred after 1986	2c		
d	Amortization of circulation expenditures paid or incurred after 1986 (personal holding companies only)	2d		
e	Basis adjustments in determining gain or loss from sale or exchange of property	2e		
f	Long-term contracts entered into after February 28, 1986	2f (120,000)		
g	Installment sales of certain property	2g 200,000		
h	Merchant marine capital construction funds	2h		
i	Section 833(b) deduction (Blue Cross, Blue Shield, and similar type organizations only)	2i		
j	Tax shelter farm activities (personal service corporations only)	2j		
k	Passive activities (closely held corporations and personal service corporations only)	2k		
l	Certain loss limitations	2l		
m	Other adjustments	2m		
n	Combine lines 2a through 2m		**2n**	120,000
3	**Tax preference items:**			
a	Depletion	3a 50,000		
b	Tax-exempt interest from private activity bonds issued after August 7, 1986	3b		
c	Appreciated property charitable deduction	3c		
d	Intangible drilling costs	3d		
e	Reserves for losses on bad debts of financial institutions	3e		
f	Accelerated depreciation of real property placed in service before 1987	3f 20,000		
g	Accelerated depreciation of leased personal property placed in service before 1987 (personal holding companies only)	3g		
h	Amortization of certified pollution control facilities placed in service before 1987	3h		
i	Add lines 3a through 3h		**3i**	70,000
4	Pre-adjustment alternative minimum taxable income (AMTI). Combine lines 1, 2n, and 3i		**4**	590,000
5	**Adjusted current earnings (ACE) adjustment:**			
a	Enter the corporation's ACE from line 10 of the worksheet on page 7 of the instructions	5a 730,000		
b	Subtract line 4 from line 5a. If line 4 exceeds line 5a, enter the difference as a negative number (see instructions for examples)	5b 140,000		
c	Multiply line 5b by 75% and enter the result as a positive number	5c 105,000		
d	Enter the excess, if any, of the corporation's total increases in AMTI from prior year ACE adjustments over its total reductions in AMTI from prior year ACE adjustments (see instructions). Note: *You must enter an amount on line 5d (even if line 5b is positive).*	5d -0-		
e	ACE adjustment: • If you entered a positive number or zero on line 5b, enter the amount from line 5c on line 5e as a positive amount. • If you entered a negative number on line 5b, enter the smaller of line 5c or line 5d on line 5e as a negative amount.		**5e**	105,000
6	Combine lines 4 and 5e. If zero or less, stop here (the corporation is not subject to the alternative minimum tax)		**6**	695,000
7	Adjustment based on energy preferences. (Do not enter more than 40% of line 6.)		**7**	-0-
8	Alternative tax net operating loss deduction. (Do not enter more than the excess, if any, of: (a) 90% of line 6, over (b) line 7.)		**8**	-0-
9	**Alternative minimum taxable income.** Subtract the sum of lines 7 and 8 from line 6		**9**	695,000

For Paperwork Reduction Act Notice, see separate instructions. Cat No. 129651 Form **4626** (1992)

10	Enter the amount from line 9 (alternative minimum taxable income)	**10**	695,000
11	Exemption phase-out computation (if line 10 is $310,000 or more, skip lines 11a and 11b and enter -0- on line 11c):		
a	Subtract $150,000 from line 10 (if you are completing this line for a member of a controlled group of corporations, see instructions). If the result is zero or less, enter -0-	11a	
b	Multiply line 11a by 25%	11b	
c	Exemption. Subtract line 11b from $40,000 (if you are completing this line for a member of a controlled group of corporations, see instructions). If the result is zero or less, enter -0-	**11c**	-0-
12	Subtract line 11c from line 10. If the result is zero or less, enter -0-	**12**	695,000
13	Multiply line 12 by 20%	**13**	139,000
14	Alternative minimum tax foreign tax credit. (See instructions for limitations.)	**14**	-0-
15	Tentative minimum tax. Subtract line 14 from line 13	**15**	139,000
16	Regular tax liability before all credits except the foreign tax credit and possessions tax credit	**16**	136,000
17	**Alternative minimum tax.** Subtract line 16 from line 15. If the result is zero or less, enter -0-. Also enter the result on the line provided on the corporation's income tax return (e.g., if you are filing Form 1120 for 1992, enter this amount on line 9a, Schedule J)	**17**	3,000

1993 form not available at press time.

Figure 10-3 Form 4626

> **TAX TIP**
>
> Corporations that have large amounts of preference items or positive adjustments and know they will pay the AMT should accelerate as much regular taxable income (or postpone deductions) into the current year as is possible because the AMT rate is only 20% while the regular corporate tax rate can be as high as 35%.

DISTRIBUTIONS TO SHAREHOLDERS— AN OVERVIEW

One of the major drawbacks to the corporate form of business is the double taxation of corporate income. The corporation pays tax on income when it is earned, and the shareholder pays a second tax when the corporation distributes this after-tax income in the form of dividends.

Example 40. Todd Wills is the sole shareholder of See Corporation. During the last tax year, See Corporation had taxable income of $500,000 on which it paid a tax of $170,000. It had $330,000 of net after-tax earnings from which it could distribute dividends. Todd Wills pays taxes at the rate of 28%. If See Corporation distributes the $330,000 of net after-tax income to Todd, he will pay a second tax of $92,400. The total tax on the corporation's $500,000 of pretax income is $262,400—a combined tax rate in excess of 50%.

There are a number of reasons for the corporate form flourishing in spite of this tax burden. The limited liability afforded the shareholders is one of the primary reasons. As will be discussed in Part V, the S corporation provides limited liability while eliminating this double tax burden. Not all corporations can be S corporations, however, because there are a number of restrictions on eligible corporations. Those corporations that cannot elect S status could become partnerships—but large corporations simply do not find this alternative practical.

Prior to 1987 the corporate tax rate was lower than the maximum individual tax rate, and capital gains were given substantial preferential treatment. Corporations could reinvest their earnings—rather than pay dividends—causing their values to increase. At some future time, the shareholders could dispose of the shares at the favorable capital gains rate—thus minimizing the effects of double taxation.

The Revenue Reconciliation Act of 1993 again increased the maximum individual tax rate to a level greater than the maximum corporate tax rate for tax years beginning in 1993. This increase in the maximum individual tax rate also makes the 28% maximum tax rate on capital gains for individuals relatively more attractive.

Corporations can also include debt in their capital structure. Interest payments on debt are deductible by the corporation, and the repayment of principal has no tax consequences to either the corporation or the lender. Corporations must make sure that the debt is legitimate debt rather than disguised stock. Reasonable interest rates and maturity dates are two indications of legitimate debt. Corporate debt can be recharacterized as equity (stock) if it does not have substantial debt characteristics. If this happens, interest payments are not deductible by the corporation and both interest and principal payments can be taxed as dividends to the recipient-shareholder.

Although there is a general rule that all distributions to shareholders are dividends to the extent of the corporation's earnings and profits, a shareholder can receive sale treatment for certain distributions from the corporation. If certain complex requirements are met, a redemption of stock by the corporation from the shareholder will in fact be treated as a sale of the stock. Moreover, if the corporation is liquidating completely, the shareholders can treat the liquidating distributions as payment for their stock, generally resulting in capital gain. A complete discussion of dividend, redemptive, and liquidating distributions is beyond the scope of this brief introduction to corporate taxation. Shareholders must remember, however, that a corporate distribution to shareholders is treated as a dividend unless if can be shown that some other treatment is appropriate.

REVIEW IV

1. Loren Corporation had $308,000 of taxable income during the current year. Its regular tax due is
   (a) $77,000.
   (b) $92,970.
   (c) $103,370.
   (d) $120,120.

2. PDQ Corporation had the following items of income and expense during the current year:
   Sales revenue $1000
   Cost of sales 400
   Sales & administration 375
   Dividend income (25% owned corporation) 50
   Charitable contribution 50
   What is its taxable income?
   (a) $207.50
   (b) $202.50
   (c) $185.00
   (d) $180.00

3. Xanadu Co. had the following items pertaining to its current year's operations:
   Sales $862,000
   Cost of sales 443,000
   Operating expenses 269,000
   Capital loss 50,000
   What is its regular tax due?
   (a) $61,250
   (b) $41,750
   (c) $37,599
   (d) $22,250

4. Lamb Corporation had $360,000 of sales revenue, $200,000 cost of sales, $50,000 of dividend income from a 35% owned corporation, and $170,000 of operating expenses. What is Lamb's dividend received deduction?
   (a) $40,000
   (b) $35,000
   (c) $32,000
   (d) $28,000

5. Aubergon Corporation, a June 30 fiscal year-end corporation, incurred the following expenses when it was formed:
   1/15 State filing fees $200
   3/30 Legal expenses 900
   5/20 Stock issue expense 200
   6/10 Director's meetings 500
   7/5 Accountant's fees 800

The corporation began operations in April. What is Aubergon's amortization expense for its first tax year ending June 30, assuming it wants to minimize taxes?
(a) $16
(b) $13
(c) $120
(d) $80

6. Wander Dust Co. had $74,000 of taxable income in the current year. In determining its AMT, it has $194,000 of positive adjustments excluding its ACE, $38,000 of negative adjustments, $168,000 of preference items, and adjusted current earnings of $428,000. What is Wander Dust's AMT?
(a) $70,600
(b) $84,100
(c) $72,100
(d) $85,600

Answers are on page 10-48.

V S CORPORATIONS
(Code Sections 1361, 1362, 1363, 1366, 1367, 1368, 1372, 1377, and 1378)

S corporations are business entities that resemble both regular C corporations and partnerships, as well as having some of their own unique characteristics. They are corporations in the legal sense, offering the shareholders the protection of limited liability. They are hybrid entities for tax purposes. They have the same tax consequences on formation as a C corporation but their income is passed through to and taxed at the shareholder level in a manner almost identical to that of partnerships. They are unique in their treatment of distributions to shareholders and the determination of the shareholders' taxability on these distributions.

FORMATION OF S CORPORATIONS

An S corporation is formed under Sec. 351 in the same manner, and with the same tax consequences, as a C corporation as explained in detail previously. No gain or loss is recognized by either the corporation or the shareholders if the shareholders transfer property in exchange solely for stock of the S corporation in a qualifying Sec. 351 transfer. The shareholders take a carryover basis in their stock from the property transferred. The corporation has a carryover basis in the property transferred. The effects of boot on the transfer are also the same as described previously in Part III.

MAKING AN S ELECTION

THE LAW

Sec. 1361(b) (1)—For purposes of this subchapter, the term "small business corporation" means a domestic corporation which is not an ineligible corporation and which does not —(A) have more than 35 shareholders, (B) have as a shareholder a person (other than an estate and other than a trust described in subsection (c) (2)) who is not an individual, (C) have a nonresident alien as a shareholder, and (D) have more than 1 class of stock.

Corporations that want to be treated as S corporations for tax purposes must meet certain requirements and make a timely S election. To be an S corporation, the following must be met:

1. The corporation must be a domestic corporation. The corporation is incorporated in the United States or one of its territories. It cannot be incorporated in a foreign country.

2. It must be an eligible corporation. The corporation cannot be part of an affiliated group though it may own an *inactive* subsidiary; that is, a subsidiary that is completely nonoperating. The corporation cannot be a financial institution, insurance company, or a corporation electing to use the Puerto Rico and possessions tax credit.

3. The number of shareholders cannot exceed 35. In determining the number of shareholders, husband and wife are considered one shareholder regardless of whether they own the stock jointly or separately. If one spouse dies, the decedent's estate and the surviving spouse are still counted as one shareholder. If shareholders divorce, then they become two shareholders.

4. There can be only one class of stock outstanding. The corporation may have two or more issues of common stock that differ solely in the voting rights attaching to the stock. No preferred stock can be outstanding nor can the common stock have differences other than in voting rights. The corporation can have other classes of stock *authorized,* but they must remain unissued.

5. All shareholders must be eligible shareholders. No corporations, partnerships, or nonresident aliens may own stock in an S corporation. Only certain trusts are eligible shareholders. Except for voting trusts, eligible trusts have only one individual identified as the shareholder of the S corporation for determining the total number of S corporation shareholders.

Example 41. The Blinder Corporation has 42 shareholders, 5 of whom are married to 5 other shareholders, and 2 of whom are English citizens residing in the United States. The corporation cannot make an S election because it has too many shareholders (42 − 5 = 37). Note: the English citizens are residents of the United States and are eligible shareholders.

THE LAW

Sec. 1362(b)(1)—An election under subsection (a) may be made by a small business corporation for any taxable year—(A) at any time during the preceding taxable year, or (B) at any time during the taxable year and on or before the 15th day of the 3rd month of the taxable year.

An eligible corporation makes an S election by filing Form 2553 by the 15th day of the third month of the corporation's tax year to be effective for that year. An election to be effective for the following tax year may be made at any time after the first 2 ½ months of the tax year. Form 2553 requires the consent of all current shareholders and any former shareholders of the S corporation who would be affected by the S election for the current tax year.

An S corporation can revoke its election for the current year if shareholders owning more than 50% of the stock file the revocation before the 15th day of the third month of the current tax year. A revocation can be filed at any time during the tax year to be effective on or after the date of filing the revocation. If any date before the last day of the tax year is specified, the corporation will have two short tax years—the first part of the year as an S corporation and the balance as a C corporation.

If at any time during the year the S corporation does not meet all the requirements necessary to be an S corporation, its election terminates as of the day the disqualifying event occurs. If the disqualifying event is *inadvertent,* the IRS can permit the corporation to continue as an S corporation without a break if the event is corrected as soon as discovered.

Once an S election terminates, the corporation must usually wait until the fifth tax year after the termination to make a new election. The full five-year waiting period may be waived by the IRS if (1) the ownership of the corporation changes by more than 50% or (2) the termination was not the result of an act by the corporation.

SHAREHOLDERS' STOCK BASES

Each shareholder must continually track his or her basis in the stock starting at the time the stock is acquired. Income and loss items are passed through to the S corporation shareholders, and the stock basis is increased and decreased in a manner similar to that for the partnership. If the shareholder's basis is reduced to zero, however, no further losses can be passed through for use on the shareholder's personal tax return. These losses are held in suspense until the shareholder again has basis. Moreover, as

---

ANSWERS TO REVIEW IV

1. (c) $22,250 + .39($208,000) = $103,370
2. (a) The charitable contribution deduction is limited to $27.50 (.10 [$1000 − $400 − $375 + $50])
3. (b) The tax is based on taxable income of $150,000; the capital loss is not deductible against ordinary income.
4. (c) 80% of $40,000 taxable income before the dividend received deduction.
5. (d) ($200 + $900 + $500) × 3/60
6. (a) AMTI before the ACE is $398,000; the ACE is $22,500 (.75 × $30,000); the tentative AMT is $84,100 ($420,500 × .20); the regular tax on taxable income of $74,000 is $13,500; thus, the AMT is $70,600.

long as the shareholder has positive basis in the stock, distributions from the corporation to the shareholder are generally tax free.

Unlike partners in a partnership, S corporation shareholders do not increase their bases in stock for debt undertaken by the corporation, even if the shareholder personally guarantees the loan. If the shareholders make direct loans to the corporation, however, these loans have bases and the S corporation losses may be passed through and reported by the shareholders on their return to the extent they have bases in debt.

Example 42. Tony Wall owns 20% of an S corporation. He has a $25,000 basis in his stock, and the corporation owes him $10,000 on open account. The corporation has a very poor year and Tony's share of losses is $28,000. Tony reduces his stock basis to zero for $25,000 of the loss; the other $3,000 loss reduces his basis in the debt to $7,000.

S CORPORATION INCOME

The pass through of income and loss items to shareholders mimics that of a partnership to its partners. The S corporation's income or loss and each of the separable items are passed through to each shareholder based on his or her ownership percentage in the S corporation. If there has been a change in ownership during the year, these items will be allocated first on a daily basis, and then to each shareholder based on the ownership percentage for each day.

Example 43. Joe Simmons purchases a 30% interest in an S corporation for the last 120 days of the tax year. The S corporation reports $36,500 of income for the year. Joe will be allocated $3,600 of income as follows:

Daily income: $36,500/365 = $100 per day
Joe's share: $100 × 120 days × .30 ownership = $3,600

A comparison of Form K-1 for partnerships and Form K-1 for S corporations shown in Figure 10-4 highlights these similarities. Most of the differences appear in the types of questions asked and other information required. The same types of income, expense, gain, and loss that must be presented separately for partners must be presented separately for the S corporation shareholders. These are the same items that specifically affect the determination of an individual's income tax liability.

There are several S corporation items that differ in their treatment from that of partnerships. First, the S corporation amortizes organizational expenses over a 60-month or longer period in the same manner a C corporation does. (Syndication fees are not a factor here.) Second, the ordinary income passed through to the S corporation shareholder is not an item subject to self-employment taxes. Finally, regardless of ownership percentage, a shareholder of the S corporation can be an employee except for participation in certain fringe benefits. If the shareholder-employee owns more than a 2% interest in the corporation, health insurance, group term life insurance, and certain other fringe benefits provided are not deductible by the corporation.

10-50 Formation and Taxation of Business Entities

SCHEDULE K-1 (Form 1065)	Partner's Share of Income, Credits, Deductions, Etc.	OMB No. 1545-0099
Department of the Treasury Internal Revenue Service	▶ See separate instructions. For calendar year 1993 or tax year beginning , 1993, and ending , 19	1993

Partner's identifying number ▶   Partnership's identifying number ▶

Partner's name, address, and ZIP code   Partnership's name, address, and ZIP code

    James Favel   FEV Partnership

A This partner is a ☐ general partner ☐ limited partner
   ☐ limited liability company member
B What type of entity is this partner? ▶ ....
C Is this partner a ☐ domestic or a ☐ foreign partner?
D Enter partner's percentage of: (I) Before change or termination   (II) End of year
   Profit sharing . . . .% ....%
   Loss sharing . . . .% ....%
   Ownership of capital . . . .% ....%
E IRS Center where partnership filed return: ....

F Partner's share of liabilities (see instructions):
   Nonrecourse . . . . $ ....
   Qualified nonrecourse financing . $ ....
   Other . . . . $ ....
G Tax shelter registration number . ▶ ....
H Check here if this partnership is a publicly traded partnership as defined in section 469(k)(2) . . . . ☐
I Check applicable boxes: (1) ☐ Final K-1 (2) ☐ Amended K-1

J Analysis of partner's capital account:

(a) Capital account at beginning of year	(b) Capital contributed during year	(c) Partner's share of lines 3, 4, and 7, Form 1065, Schedule M-2	(d) Withdrawals and distributions	(e) Capital account at end of year (combine columns (a) through (d))
			( )	

	(a) Distributive share item		(b) Amount	(c) 1040 filers enter the amount in column (b) on:
Income (Loss)	1 Ordinary income (loss) from trade or business activities	1	7,560	See Partner's Instructions for Schedule K-1 (Form 1065).
	2 Net income (loss) from rental real estate activities	2		
	3 Net income (loss) from other rental activities	3		
	4 Portfolio income (loss):			
	a Interest (tax exempt = $6,000)	4a	3,000	Sch. B, Part I, line 1
	b Dividends	4b		Sch. B, Part II, line 5
	c Royalties	4c		Sch. E, Part I, line 4
	d Net short-term capital gain (loss)	4d		Sch. D, line 5, col. (f) or (g)
	e Net long-term capital gain (loss)	4e		Sch. D, line 13, col. (f) or (g)
	f Other portfolio income (loss) (attach schedule)	4f		Enter on applicable line of your return.
	5 Guaranteed payments to partner	5		See Partner's Instructions for Schedule K-1 (Form 1065).
	6 Net gain (loss) under section 1231 (other than due to casualty or theft)	6		
	7 Other income (loss) (attach schedule)	7		Enter on applicable line of your return.
Deductions	8 Charitable contributions (see instructions) (attach schedule)	8	1,500	Sch. A, line 13 or 14
	9 Section 179 expense deduction	9		See Partner's Instructions for Schedule K-1 (Form 1065).
	10 Deductions related to portfolio income (attach schedule)	10		
	11 Other deductions (attach schedule)	11		
Investment Interest	12a Interest expense on investment debts	12a		Form 4952, line 1
	b (1) Investment income included on lines 4a through 4f above	b(1)	3,000	See Partner's Instructions for Schedule K-1 (Form 1065).
	(2) Investment expenses included on line 10 above	b(2)		
Credits	13a Credit for income tax withheld	13a		See Partner's Instructions for Schedule K-1 (Form 1065).
	b Low-income housing credit:			
	(1) From section 42(j)(5) partnerships for property placed in service before 1990	b(1)		Form 8586, line 5
	(2) Other than on line 13b(1) for property placed in service before 1990	b(2)		
	(3) From section 42(j)(5) partnerships for property placed in service after 1989	b(3)		
	(4) Other than on line 13b(3) for property placed in service after 1989	b(4)		
	c Qualified rehabilitation expenditures related to rental real estate activities (see instructions)	13c		See Partner's Instructions for Schedule K-1 (Form 1065).
	d Credits (other than credits shown on lines 13b and 13c) related to rental real estate activities (see instructions)	13d		
	e Credits related to other rental activities (see instructions)	13e		
	14 Other credits (see instructions)	14		

For Paperwork Reduction Act Notice, see Instructions for Form 1065.   Cat. No. 11394R   Schedule K-1 (Form 1065) 1993

Figure 10-4   Schedule K-1, Form 1065

Schedule K-1 (Form 1065) 1993

	(a) Distributive share item		(b) Amount	(c) 1040 filers enter the amount in column (b) on:
Self-employment	15a Net earnings (loss) from self-employment	15a		Sch. SE, Section A or B
	b Gross farming or fishing income	15b	27,560	See Partner's Instructions for Schedule K-1 (Form 1065).
	c Gross nonfarm income	15c		
Adjustments and Tax Preference Items	16a Depreciation adjustment on property placed in service after 1986	16a		See Partner's Instructions for Schedule K-1 (Form 1065) and Instructions for Form 6251.
	b Adjusted gain or loss	16b		
	c Depletion (other than oil and gas)	16c		
	d (1) Gross income from oil, gas, and geothermal properties	d(1)		
	(2) Deductions allocable to oil, gas, and geothermal properties	d(2)		
	e Other adjustments and tax preference items (attach schedule)	16e		
Foreign Taxes	17a Type of income ▶			Form 1116, check boxes
	b Name of foreign country or U.S. possession ▶			
	c Total gross income from sources outside the United States (attach schedule)	17c		Form 1116, Part I
	d Total applicable deductions and losses (attach schedule)	17d		
	e Total foreign taxes (check one): ▶ ☐ Paid ☐ Accrued	17e		Form 1116, Part II
	f Reduction in taxes available for credit (attach schedule)	17f		Form 1116, Part III
	g Other foreign tax information (attach schedule)	17g		See Instructions for Form 1116.
Other	18a Total expenditures to which a section 59(e) election may apply	18a		See Partner's Instructions for Schedule K-1 (Form 1065).
	b Type of expenditures ▶			
	19 Tax-exempt interest income	19		Form 1040, line 8b
	20 Other tax-exempt income	20		See Partner's Instructions for Schedule K-1 (Form 1065).
	21 Nondeductible expenses	21		
	22 Recapture of low-income housing credit:			
	a From section 42(j)(5) partnerships	22a		Form 8611, line 8
	b Other than on line 22a	22b		

Supplemental Information

23 Supplemental information required to be reported separately to each partner (attach additional schedules if more space is needed):

Figure 10-4 (continued) Schedule K-1, Form 1065

SCHEDULE K-1
(Form 1120S)
Department of the Treasury
Internal Revenue Service

Shareholder's Share of Income, Credits, Deductions, etc.
▶ See separate instructions.
For calendar year 1993 or tax year
beginning   , 1993, and ending   , 19

OMB No. 1545-0130

1993

Shareholder's identifying number ▶   Corporation's identifying number ▶

Shareholder's name, address, and ZIP code   Corporation's name, address, and ZIP code

James Favel   FEV Corporation

A Shareholder's percentage of stock ownership for tax year (see Instructions for Schedule K-1) . . . . . ▶ 30 %
B Internal Revenue Service Center where corporation filed its return ▶
C Tax shelter registration number (see Instructions for Schedule K-1) . . . . . ▶
D Check applicable boxes: (1) ☐ Final K-1   (2) ☐ Amended K-1

	(a) Pro rata share items		(b) Amount	(c) Form 1040 filers enter the amount in column (b) on:
Income (Loss)	1 Ordinary income (loss) from trade or business activities	1	7,560	See Shareholder's Instructions for Schedule K-1 (Form 1120S)
	2 Net income (loss) from rental real estate activities	2		
	3 Net income (loss) from other rental activities	3		
	4 Portfolio income (loss):			
	a Interest	4a		Sch. B, Part I, line 1
	b Dividends	4b	3,000	Sch. B, Part II, line 5
	c Royalties	4c		Sch. E, Part I, line 4
	d Net short-term capital gain (loss)	4d		Sch. D, line 5, col. (f) or (g)
	e Net long-term capital gain (loss)	4e		Sch. D, line 13, col. (f) or (g)
	f Other portfolio income (loss) (attach schedule)	4f		(Enter on applicable line of your return.)
	5 Net gain (loss) under section 1231 (other than due to casualty or theft)	5		See Shareholder's Instructions for Schedule K-1 (Form 1120S)
	6 Other income (loss) (attach schedule)	6		(Enter on applicable line of your return.)
Deductions	7 Charitable contributions (see instructions) (attach schedule)	7	1,500	Sch. A, line 13 or 14
	8 Section 179 expense deduction	8		See Shareholder's Instructions for Schedule K-1 (Form 1120S)
	9 Deductions related to portfolio income (loss) (attach schedule)	9		
	10 Other deductions (attach schedule)	10		
Investment Interest	11a Interest expense on investment debts	11a		Form 4952, line 1
	b (1) Investment income included on lines 4a through 4f above	b(1)	3,000	See Shareholder's Instructions for Schedule K-1 (Form 1120S)
	(2) Investment expenses included on line 9 above	b(2)		
Credits	12a Credit for alcohol used as fuel	12a		Form 6478, line 10
	b Low-income housing credit:			
	(1) From section 42(j)(5) partnerships for property placed in service before 1990	b(1)		Form 8586, line 5
	(2) Other than on line 12b(1) for property placed in service before 1990	b(2)		
	(3) From section 42(j)(5) partnerships for property placed in service after 1989	b(3)		
	(4) Other than on line 12b(3) for property placed in service after 1989	b(4)		
	c Qualified rehabilitation expenditures related to rental real estate activities (see instructions)	12c		See Shareholder's Instructions for Schedule K-1 (Form 1120S).
	d Credits (other than credits shown on lines 12b and 12c) related to rental real estate activities (see instructions)	12d		
	e Credits related to other rental activities (see instructions)	12e		
	13 Other credits (see instructions)	13		
Adjustments and Tax Preference Items	14a Depreciation adjustment on property placed in service after 1986	14a		See Shareholder's Instructions for Schedule K-1 (Form 1120S) and Instructions for Form 6251
	b Adjusted gain or loss	14b		
	c Depletion (other than oil and gas)	14c		
	d (1) Gross income from oil, gas, or geothermal properties	d(1)		
	(2) Deductions allocable to oil, gas, or geothermal properties	d(2)		
	e Other adjustments and tax preference items (attach schedule)	14e		

For Paperwork Reduction Act Notice, see page 1 of Instructions for Form 1120S.   Cat. No. 11520D   Schedule K-1 (Form 1120S) 1993

Figure 10-4 (continued)   Schedule K-1, Form 1120S

Schedule K-1 (Form 1120S) (1993)   Page **2**

	(a) Pro rata share items	(b) Amount	(c) Form 1040 filers enter the amount in column (b) on:
Foreign Taxes	**15a** Type of income ▶		Form 1116, Check boxes
	b Name of foreign country or U.S. possession ▶		
	c Total gross income from sources outside the United States *(attach schedule)*	15c	Form 1116, Part I
	d Total applicable deductions and losses *(attach schedule)*	15d	
	e Total foreign taxes (check one): ▶ ☐ Paid ☐ Accrued	15e	Form 1116, Part II
	f Reduction in taxes available for credit *(attach schedule)*	15f	Form 1116, Part III
	g Other foreign tax information *(attach schedule)*	15g	See Instructions for Form 1116
Other	**16a** Total expenditures to which a section 59(e) election may apply	16a	See Shareholder's Instructions for Schedule K-1 (Form 1120S).
	b Type of expenditures ▶		
	17 Tax-exempt interest income	17	Form 1040, line 8b
	18 Other tax-exempt income	18	See Shareholder's Instructions for Schedule K-1 (Form 1120S)
	19 Nondeductible expenses	19	
	20 Property distributions (including cash) other than dividend distributions reported to you on Form 1099-DIV	20	
	21 Amount of loan repayments for "Loans From Shareholders"	21	
	22 Recapture of low-income housing credit:		
	a From section 42(j)(5) partnerships	22a	Form 8611, line 8
	b Other than on line 22a	22b	
Supplemental Information	**23** Supplemental information required to be reported separately to each shareholder *(attach additional schedules if more space is needed)*:		

(Proofs as of August 1993 – subject to change)

Figure 10-4 (continued)   Schedule K-1, Form 1120S

REPORTING REQUIREMENTS

S corporations must file Form 1120S by the 15th day of the third month following the end of their tax years. Most S corporations are calendar-year entities with a March 15 due date. S corporations are also allowed an automatic six-month extension by filing Form 7004.

Example 44. FEV Corporation, an S corporation, has the following items that affect income:

Gross sales	$225,000
Sales returns	5,000
Cost of goods sold	80,000
Dividend income	10,000
Interest on municipal bonds	20,000
Salaries (officers)	45,000
Other salaries	30,000
Taxes	10,000
Depreciation	20,000
Interest expense	2,000
Charitable contributions	5,000
Travel expenses (excluding meals)	3,000
Meals & entertainment	6,000

FEV's taxable income is determined as follows:

Income:		
Gross sales		$225,000
Returns		(5,000)
Net sales		$220,000
Cost of goods sold		(80,000)
Gross profit on sales		$140,000
Income before deductions		$140,000
Deductions:		
Officer salaries	$ 45,000	
Other salaries	30,000	
Taxes	10,000	
Interest	2,000	
Depreciation	20,000	
Travel	3,000	
Meals & entertainment @ 80%	4,800	
Total deductions		($114,800)
Net income excluding separable items		$ 25,200
Separable items:		
Dividends		$ 10,000
Charitable contributions		5,000
Municipal bond iinterest		20,000

A completed Form 1120S is included in Figure 10-5 using the information in this example. A Schedule K-1 (Form 1120S) for 30% shareholder, James Favel, is shown in Figure 10-4. James is an officer and receives a $20,000 salary.

Form 1120S — U.S. Income Tax Return for an S Corporation
Department of the Treasury / Internal Revenue Service
For calendar year 1993, or tax year beginning ...., 1993, and ending ...., 19 .....
▶ See separate instructions.
OMB No. 1545-0130
1993

- **A** Date of election as an S corporation
- **B** Business code no. (see Specific Instructions)
- Use IRS label. Otherwise, please print or type.
  - Name: **FEV Corporation**
  - Number, street, and room or suite no. (If a P.O. box, see page 8 of the instructions.)
  - City or town, state, and ZIP code
- **C** Employer identification number
- **D** Date incorporated
- **E** Total assets (see Specific Instructions) $

F Check applicable boxes: (1) ☐ Initial return (2) ☐ Final return (3) ☐ Change in address (4) ☐ Amended return
G Check this box if this S corporation is subject to the consolidated audit procedures of sections 6241 through 6245 (see instructions before checking this box) ▶ ☐
H Enter number of shareholders in the corporation at end of the tax year . . . . ▶

Caution: Include **only** trade or business income and expenses on lines 1a through 21. See the instructions for more information.

Income

1a	Gross receipts or sales	225,000	
1b	Less returns and allowances	5,000	
1c	Bal ▶		220,000
2	Cost of goods sold (Schedule A, line 8)		80,000
3	Gross profit. Subtract line 2 from line 1c		140,000
4	Net gain (loss) from Form 4797, Part II, line 20 (attach Form 4797)		
5	Other income (loss) (see instructions) (attach schedule)		
6	**Total income (loss).** Combine lines 3 through 5 ▶		140,000

Deductions (See instructions for limitations.)

7	Compensation of officers		45,000
8a	Salaries and wages	30,000	
8b	Less jobs credit		
8c	Bal		30,000
9	Repairs and maintenance		
10	Bad debts		
11	Rents		
12	Taxes and licenses		10,000
13	Interest		2,000
14a	Depreciation (see instructions)	20,000	
14b	Depreciation claimed on Schedule A and elsewhere on return		
14c	Subtract line 14b from line 14a		20,000
15	Depletion (**Do not deduct oil and gas depletion.**)		
16	Advertising		
17	Pension, profit-sharing, etc., plans		
18	Employee benefit programs		
19	Other deductions (see instructions) (attach schedule) Travel = 3,000; M&E = 4,800		7,800
20	**Total deductions.** Add lines 7 through 19 ▶		114,800
21	**Ordinary income (loss)** from trade or business activities. Subtract line 20 from line 6		25,200

Tax and Payments

- **22 Tax:**
  - a Excess net passive income tax (attach schedule) — 22a
  - b Tax from Schedule D (Form 1120S) — 22b
  - c Add lines 22a and 22b (see instructions for additional taxes) — 22c
- **23 Payments:**
  - a 1993 estimated tax payments — 23a
  - b Tax deposited with Form 7004 — 23b
  - c Credit for Federal tax paid on fuels (attach Form 4136) — 23c
  - d Add lines 23a through 23c — 23d
- **24** Estimated tax penalty (see instructions). Check if Form 2220 is attached. ▶ ☐
- **25 Tax due.** If the total of lines 22c and 24 is larger than line 23d, enter amount owed. See instructions for depositary method of payment ▶
- **26 Overpayment.** If line 23d is larger than the total of lines 22c and 24, enter amount overpaid ▶
- **27** Enter amount of line 26 you want: **Credited to 1994 estimated tax** ▶ | **Refunded** ▶

Please Sign Here: Under penalties of perjury, I declare that I have examined this return, including accompanying schedules and statements, and to the best of my knowledge and belief, it is true, correct, and complete. Declaration of preparer (other than taxpayer) is based on all information of which preparer has any knowledge.

▶ Signature of officer Date ▶ Title

Paid Preparer's Use Only: Preparer's signature / Date / Check if self-employed ☐ / Preparer's social security number / Firm's name (or yours if self-employed) and address / E.I. No. ▶ / ZIP code ▶

For Paperwork Reduction Act Notice, see page 1 of separate instructions. Cat. No. 11510H Form **1120S** (1993)

(Watermark: Proof as of August 1993 (subject to change))

Figure 10-5 Form 1120S

10-56 *Formation and Taxation of Business Entities*

Form 1120S (1993)   FEV Corporation   Page **2**

Schedule A	**Cost of Goods Sold** (See instructions.)	
1	Inventory at beginning of year	
2	Purchases	
3	Cost of labor	
4	Additional section 263A costs (see instructions) *(attach schedule)*	
5	Other costs *(attach schedule)*	
6	**Total.** Add lines 1 through 5	
7	Inventory at end of year	
8	**Cost of goods sold.** Subtract line 7 from line 6. Enter here and on page 1, line 2	80,000

9a Check all methods used for valuing closing inventory:
   (i)   ☐ Cost
   (ii) ☐ Lower of cost or market as described in Regulations section 1.471-4
   (iii) ☐ Writedown of "subnormal" goods as described in Regulations section 1.471-2(c)
   (iv) ☐ Other (specify method used and attach explanation) ▶ ....
 b Check if the LIFO inventory method was adopted this tax year for any goods (if checked, attach Form 970) . . . . . ▶ ☐
 c If the LIFO inventory method was used for this tax year, enter percentage (or amounts) of closing inventory computed under LIFO . . . . | 9c |
 d Do the rules of section 263A (for property produced or acquired for resale) apply to the corporation? . . . . ☐ Yes ☐ No
 e Was there any change in determining quantities, cost, or valuations between opening and closing inventory? . . ☐ Yes ☐ No
   If "Yes," attach explanation.

Schedule B Other Information   Yes | No

1 Check method of accounting: **(a)** ☐ Cash **(b)** ☐ Accrual **(c)** ☐ Other (specify) ▶ ....
2 Refer to the list in the instructions and state the corporation's principal:
  (a) Business activity ▶ .... **(b)** Product or service ▶ ....
3 Did the corporation at the end of the tax year own, directly or indirectly, 50% or more of the voting stock of a domestic corporation? (For rules of attribution, see section 267(c).) If "Yes," attach a schedule showing: **(a)** name, address, and employer identification number and **(b)** percentage owned . . . .
4 Was the corporation a member of a controlled group subject to the provisions of section 1561? . . . .
5 At any time during calendar year 1993, did the corporation have an interest in or a signature or other authority over a financial account in a foreign country (such as a bank account, securities account, or other financial account)? (See instructions for exceptions and filing requirements for form TD F 90-22.1.) . . . .
  If "Yes," enter the name of the foreign country ▶ ....
6 Was the corporation the grantor of, or transferor to, a foreign trust that existed during the current tax year, whether or not the corporation has any beneficial interest in it? If "Yes," the corporation may have to file Forms 3520, 3520-A, or 926 . . . .
7 Check this box if the corporation has filed or is required to file **Form 8264**, Application for Registration of a Tax Shelter . . . . ▶ ☐
8 Check this box if the corporation issued publicly offered debt instruments with original issue discount . . ▶ ☐
  If so, the corporation may have to file **Form 8281**, Information Return for Publicly Offered Original Issue Discount Instruments.
9 If the corporation: **(a)** filed its election to be an S corporation after 1986, **(b)** was a C corporation before it elected to be an S corporation **or** the corporation acquired an asset with a basis determined by reference to its basis (or the basis of any other property) in the hands of a C corporation, and **(c)** has net unrealized built-in gain (defined in section 1374(d)(1) in excess of the net recognized built-in gain from prior years, enter the net unrealized built-in gain reduced by net recognized built-in gain from prior years (see instructions) . . . . . . ▶ $ ....
10 Check this box if the corporation had subchapter C earnings and profits at the close of the tax year (see instructions) . . . . ▶ ☐

Designation of Tax Matters Person (See instructions.)
Enter below the shareholder designated as the tax matters person (TMP) for the tax year of this return:

Name of designated TMP ▶ ....   Identifying number of TMP ▶ ....

Address of designated TMP ▶ ....

Figure 10-5 (continued)   Form 1120S

SCHEDULE K-1 | Shareholder's Share of Income, Credits, Deductions, etc.
OMB No. 1545-0130

	(a) Pro rata share items		(b) Amount	(c) Form 1040 filers enter the amount in column (b) on:
Income (Loss)	1	Ordinary income (loss) from trade or business activities	1 25,200	See Shareholder's Instructions for Schedule K-1 (Form 1120S).
	2	Net income (loss) from rental real estate activities	2	
	3	Net income (loss) from other rental activities	3	
	4	Portfolio income (loss):		
	a	Interest . . . . . . Tax exempt int = 20,000	4a	Sch. B, Part I, line 1
	b	Dividends	4b 10,000	Sch. B, Part II, line 5
	c	Royalties	4c	Sch. E, Part I, line 4
	d	Net short-term capital gain (loss)	4d	Sch. D, line 5, col. (f) or (g)
	e	Net long-term capital gain (loss)	4e	Sch. D, line 13, col. (f) or (g)
	f	Other portfolio income (loss) *(attach schedule)*	4f	(Enter on applicable line of your return.)
	5	Net gain (loss) under section 1231 (other than due to casualty or theft)	5	See Shareholder's Instructions for Schedule K-1 (Form 1120S).
	6	Other income (loss) *(attach schedule)*	6	(Enter on applicable line of your return.)
Deductions	7	Charitable contributions (see instructions) *(attach schedule)* . .	7 5,000	Sch. A, line 13 or 14
	8	Section 179 expense deduction	8	See Shareholder's Instructions for Schedule K-1 (Form 1120S).
	9	Deductions related to portfolio income (loss) *(attach schedule)*	9	
	10	Other deductions *(attach schedule)*	10	
Investment Interest	11a	Interest expense on investment debts	11a	Form 4952, line 1
	b	(1) Investment income included on lines 4a through 4f above .	b(1) 10,000	See Shareholder's Instructions for Schedule K-1 (Form 1120S).
		(2) Investment expenses included on line 9 above	b(2)	

Figure 10-5 (continued) Form 1120S

S corporations may use a fiscal year-end that coincides with the tax year of a majority of the shareholders. If the shareholders have different tax years, the corporation will normally use a calendar tax year. S corporations that can establish a natural business cycle can use a tax year other than a calendar year.

S corporations are normally not taxpaying entities—but they are tax-reporting entities like partnerships. However, two situations may occur in which an S corporation itself may be required to pay a tax. Both of these taxes are generally applicable to S corporations that were, at one time, C (regular) corporations. If a corporation is and always has been an S corporation, these taxes ordinarily do not apply:

1. If the S corporation has earnings and profits from a year in which it was a C corporation, it could be subject to the tax on excess net passive income. To be subject to the tax, passive income such as dividend and interest must exceed 25% of its gross receipts. If the S corporation (with accumulated earnings and profits) is taxed on excess net passive income for three consecutive years, its S election terminates at the beginning of the fourth year.

2. If a C corporation makes a valid S election, it could be subject to the Sec. 1374 built-in gains tax. At the time of the S election, the S corporation must compare the bases of its assets to their fair market value. The excess of fair market value over the aggregate bases is the built-in gain. If any of these assets are sold within 10 years of the S election, the corporation must determine the amount of recognized built-in gain and pay a tax at the highest corporate rate using a relatively complex set of rules.

A complete discussion of these taxes is beyond the scope of this text, however.

SHAREHOLDER DISTRIBUTIONS

Distributions to shareholders of S corporations that have always been S corporations and that were established after the Subchapter S Revision Act of 1984 (SRA) are generally tax free. The S corporation keeps a summary record of all taxable income, gain, loss, and expense items in an account unique to S corporations called the *accumulated adjustments account* (AAA). From the S corporation's view, all distributions that do not exceed the positive balance in the AAA are a tax-free return of income that has already been taxed to the shareholders. Distributions that exceed the positive balance in the AAA cannot reduce the AAA below zero. Although the AAA can have a negative balance, only losses and expenses of the corporation in excess of income items can cause it to be negative—distributions cannot.

The shareholder can receive distributions tax free from the corporation as long as the shareholder has stock basis. If the distribution exceeds the shareholder's basis in the stock, the shareholder recognizes capital gain (assuming the stock is a capital asset) as if the stock were sold for the excess distribution.

✓ **Example 45.** Zephyr Corporation, an S corporation, has $70,000 of gross income and $60,000 of business expenses during the current tax year. It also has $1,000 of dividend income and $500 of charitable contributions in its first year of operation. John and Toby each own 50% of the stock with a $5,000 beginning basis. Zephyr Corporation's AAA and John's basis are affected by these items as follows:

	Zephyr's AAA	John's Basis
Beginning balance	0	$ 5,000
Corporate income	+ $10,000	+ 5,000
Dividend income	+ 1,000	+ 500
Charitable contribution	− 500	− 250
Ending balance	$10,500	$10,250

For the most part, the AAA does not affect the taxability of distributions to shareholder for these post-1984 S corporations that have always been and remain S corporations. If the S election terminates, however, shareholders may receive cash distributions tax free up to the amount of AAA (assuming they have adequate basis) during the post-termination period (which is at least one year in length). When the S election terminates, the corporation becomes a C corporation. Normally, a distribution from a C corporation is taxed as a dividend unless it can be shown that the distribution should be treated otherwise. The AAA allows the shareholder to avoid dividend treatment on cash distributions during this post-termination period.

The AAA's primary use is to determine the taxability or nontaxability of distributions from S corporations that were previously C corporations with positive earnings and profits or were S corporations prior to the SRA. A complete discussion of distributions from these corporations is beyond the scope of the text.

REVIEW V

1. TipTop Corporation began business on March 1 of the current year. It wants to make a timely election to be an S corporation. If it is a fiscal-year corporation with a January 31 year-end, by what date must its S election be made for the current year?
   (a) March 15
   (b) April 15

(c) May 15
(d) It can't make a valid election for the current year.

2. Window Washers is an S corporation with five shareholders each owning 20% of the stock. How many of the shareholders must consent to the revocation of its S election?
   (a) only one shareholder
   (b) any two shareholders
   (c) any three shareholders
   (d) all five shareholders

3. Violet Corporation's S election was terminated on March 22, 1988, when another corporation bought 10% of its stock. On January 2, 1991, the corporation sold Violet's stock. What is the first year for which Violet Corporation, a calendar corporation, can make a new S election?
   (a) 1991
   (b) 1992
   (c) 1993
   (d) 1994

4. Alice Payton contributed $10,000 to an S corporation when it was formed and received 10% of its stock. During its first year of operation, the corporation had income of $21,000, and it made a total pro rata distribution of $10,000 to its shareholders. This year it has a loss of $18,000. What is Alice's basis in her stock at the end of the current year?
   (a) $9,300
   (b) $10,000
   (c) $10,300
   (d) $10,400

5. An S corporation has the following items of income and expense:

Gross sales	$100,000
Cost of goods sold	40,000
Other operating expenses	32,000
Charitable contributions	2,000
Long-term capital gains	10,000
Sec. 1231 loss	5,000

   What is the corporation's taxable income exclusive of the separately stated items and what is its year-end balance in its AAA if its beginning balance was $87,000?
   (a) 28,000, 118,000
   (b) 23,000, 118,000
   (c) 28,000, 115,000
   (d) 23,000, 110,000

Answers follow on page 10-61.

CHAPTER APPENDIX: COMPARISON OF TAX CONSEQUENCES OF BUSINESS FORMS

	Sole Proprietorship	Partnership	C Corporation	S Corporation
Formation	No legal requirements	No legal requirements	Must follow state incorporation procedures	Must follow state incorporation procedures
Tax Consequences of Formation				
Owner	No gain or loss recognized	No gain or loss recognized	Gain recognized for boot and excess liabilities	Gain recognized for boot and excess liabilities
Business	No gain or loss recognized	No gain or loss recognized	Gain generally not recognized	Gain generally not recognized
Tax year	Same as sole proprietor	Same as majority or principal partners or "least aggregate deferral" year	Fiscal or calendar year	Calendar year or tax year of a majority of shareholders
Tax form	Schedule C, Form 1040	Form 1065	Form 1120 or 1120A	Form 1120S
Taxation of Nonliquidating Distributions				
Owner	Tax free	Generally tax free unless money received in excess of basis (recognize gain)	Dividends taxed to extent corporation has earnings and profits	Generally tax free to shareholders with basis in stock
Business	Tax free	Partnership recognizes no gain or loss, generally	Property distributed treated as sold by corporation; gain only recognized	Property distributed treated as sold by corporation; gain only recognized
Taxation of Liquidation Distributions				
Owner	Tax free	Tax free unless money received in excess of basis (recognize gain); loss recognized if only money, A/R, and inventory received	Shareholder generally receives sale or exchange treatment	Tax free to extent shareholder has basis in stock
Business	Tax free	Partnership recognizes no gain or loss, generally	Property distributed treated as sold by corporation	Property distributed treated as sold by corporation

CHAPTER PROBLEMS

PART I

1. (a) What form(s) of organization may a sole owner use to operate a business?
   (b) What form(s) of organization may two or more owners use to operate a business?

I 2. (a) What legal steps are required to form a sole proprietorship?
     (b) Partnership?
     (c) Corporation?
I 3. What are the differences between a limited and a general partnership for tax purposes?
I 4. Two bothers, Jeb and Zeb, join together as equal partners to sell custom boots that they manufacture. Jeb contributes $20,000 and several pieces of equipment worth $30,000. The equipment has a basis of $10,000. Zeb contributes the land and building in which he lived, moving to an apartment. The property has a fair market value of $50,000. Zeb paid $60,000 two years ago before the area was rezoned for commercial uses.
     (a) What are Jeb's and Zeb's realized gains or losses?
     (b) What are their recognized gains or losses?
     (c) What are their bases in their partnership interests?
     (d) What gain or loss does the partnership recognize?
     (e) What basis does the partnership have in the properties?

   For Problems 5, 6, and 7, assume that all debt is pre–January 30, 1989 debt and that the partners' profits and loss interests are the same as their partnership interests.

I 5. Ariel joins with three other persons to form a new partnership as a 25% partner. She contributes from her sole proprietorship the equipment worth $43,000 that she purchased two years ago. The equipment has a $30,000 basis and has a $10,000 nonrecourse mortgage that the partnership assumes. What is Ariel's basis in the partnership interest and her holding period? What is the partnership's basis in the property and its holding period?
I 6. Joe Jones receives a 40% interest in a new partnership in exchange for real property worth $250,000. His basis in the property is $160,000 and it is subject to a $75,000 nonrecourse mortgage that the partnership assumes. What is Joe's recognized gain or loss and what is his basis in the partnership interest?
I 7. Margo is a 35% partner in a partnership. She has a basis in the partnership of $21,000. The partnership borrows $100,000 from a bank.
     (a) If Margo is a limited partner, what is her basis in her partnership interest if the debt is recourse? Nonrecourse?

ANSWERS TO REVIEW V

1. (c) May 15 is the 15th day of the third month of its first tax year that begins on March 1.
2. (c) Any three shareholders together own a majority of the stock.
3. (b) The corporation has a short tax year in 1988 after it loses its S election. Thus, 1992 is its fifth tax year.
4. (a) $10,000 + .10 [$21,000 – $10,000 – $18,000] = $9,300
5. (a) The corporation has $28,000 of income; charitable contributions, capital gains, and Sec. 1231 losses are all separately stated items. All of these items, however, either increase or decrease the AAA (87,000 + 28,000 – 2,000 + 10,000 – 5,000 = 118,000).

(b) If Margo is a general partner, what is her basis in her partnership interest if the debt is recourse? Nonrecourse?

I 8. A partnership sold some accounts receivable that were contributed by a partner when the partnership was formed six months earlier. The partnership received $22,000 for the cash-basis receivables that had a face value of $40,000. How much and what type of income does the partnership recognize?

I 9. ABD Partnership sold a truck to a 60% partner for $8,000. The partnership had purchased the truck two years ago for $23,000 and had taken $11,000 of depreciation expense. What is the effect of the transaction on the partnership and what is the partner's basis in the truck?

II 10. A partnership had $327,000 in gross sales, $12,000 of dividend income, and $8,000 bond interest income ($5,000 from state of New York bonds); the partnership's expenses were cost of goods sold of $169,000, depreciation expense of $40,000, taxes of $9,000, interest expense of $40,000, advertising of $28,000, professional fees of $4,000, and charitable contributions of $8,000. How would a 20% partner report the above on his or her tax return?

II 11. What is a partnership's taxable income if Josie is to receive $25,000 salary and Terri is to receive a $10,000 salary regardless of operating results, and the partnership has $221,000 of revenue and $204,000 of expenses (without the partners' salaries), all from nonseparately stated items? How much income do Josie and Terri each report on their individual tax returns?

II 12. Trish joined in an equal partnership with two other persons by contributing land with a $75,000 basis and a fair market value of $120,000. The partnership sells the land several years later for $160,000. How much gain must Trish recognize?

II 13. When the partnership dissolved, Mary received a pro rata distribution of $20,000 of accounts receivable and $30,000 of inventory with bases of zero and $20,000, respectively, for her partnership interest with a $25,000 basis. What are the tax consequences for Mary?

II 14. Paul had a basis of $10,000 in his 20% partnership interest when the partnership paid off a $100,000 liability. Does the transaction affect Paul in any way? Explain.

III 15. Tom, Dick, and Harry formed a corporation. Tom contributed $10,000 cash and equipment worth $35,000 that had a basis of $20,000 in exchange for 30% of the corporate stock. Dick contributed a building worth $100,000, which had a basis of $20,000, in exchange for 40% of the stock and the corporation's assumption of the $40,000 mortgage on the building. Harry provided legal and accounting services valued at $14,000, a personal auto worth $10,000 (basis of $20,000), and business furniture and fixtures worth $21,000 that had a $25,000 basis. For Tom, Dick, and Harry, determine the following:
(a) gain realized
(b) gain recognized
(c) basis in stock received

III 16. Using the information in Problem 15, determine
(a) the gain or loss recognized by the corporation
(b) the corporation's bases in the properties received

III 17. George and Albert decided to consolidate their businesses into one new corporation. They transferred the following to the new corporation:

	George		Albert	
Asset	Real Estate	Equipment	Equipment	Cash
Basis	$400,000	$400,000	$250,000	$300,000
FMV	500,000	300,000	300,000	300,000

George and Albert each received 50% of the stock, but George also received $200,000 in cash. How much gain must George and Albert recognize? What are their bases in the stock received?

III 18. John transfers a building to his 60% owned corporation for its use. The building has a $300,000 basis and a fair market value of $250,000. The corporation has had some financial difficulties and gives John only $150,000 in the exchange. What are the tax consequences for John and the corporation?

IV 19. The Bright Company has $226,000 of taxable income before its $2,000 targeted jobs credit. What is Bright's tax liability?

IV 20. Peter Piper Corporation has sales of $328,000, operating expenses of $310,000, dividend income of $30,000 from AT&T stock, and charitable contributions of $5,000. What is its taxable income and income tax liability?

IV 21. Bauble Corporation had $124,000 of operating revenue and $126,000 of operating expenses. It also received a $20,000 dividend from a 30% owned corporation. What is Bauble's dividend received deduction?

IV 22. DDY Corporation had the following earnings history before any NOL carryovers:
Year 1 ($5,000)   Year 4 $12,000
Year 2 ($10,000) Year 5   ($3,000)
Year 3 $8,000   Year 6 $7,000
How would it use the NOLs to offset income?

IV 23. Jackson Company began business in April of the current year. It incurred expenses as follows:

Expense	Incurred	Amount
Initial organization meeting	March	$ 500
Legal fees	April	4,000
Stock issue costs	August	600
Temporary directors' meeting	September	1,000
Accounting set-up fee	January	1,200

How much can Jackson expense in its first year of operation if it has a calendar year-end? A March 31 year-end?

IV 24. Apollo Corporation has regular taxable income of $3,229,000 for the current tax year. It has $1,000,000 of tax preferences, $329,000 of positive adjustments, and $68,000 of negative adjustments pertaining to the AMT exclusive of the ACE adjustment. Its adjusted current earnings are $5,790,000. Does Apollo have to pay the AMT? If yes, what are the AMT and AMT credit?

V 25. What requirements must a corporation meet to be an S corporation?

V 26. Describe the various ways an S election can terminate.

V   27. If an S corporation election terminates, when may the corporation make another election to be an S corporation?

V   28. An S corporation has $20,000 of dividend income, gross profit on sales of $120,000, operating expenses of $90,000, and makes a charitable contribution of $10,000. John owns one-half of the stock for the last 200 days of the tax year. What effect do these items have on John's personal tax return?

V   29. If, in the preceding example, the corporation has a balance of $120,000 in its AAA at the beginning of the year and John paid $120,000 for his stock, what are the corporation's AAA and John's basis at year-end? How much cash can the corporation distribute to John before the distribution is taxable?

TAX RETURN PROBLEMS

30. (Form 1065; Schedule K-1) Using the information from Problem 10, complete Form 1065 for the partnership and the K-1 for the 20% partner to the extent possible from the information given.

31. (Form 1120) Bally Dance Togs, a corporation, had sales revenues of $3,450,000 during the past year. Its other items of income and expense were

    Income
        Dividends $ 20,000
        Interest on accounts receivable   2,000
        Interest on bond investment   30,000

Income	
Dividends	$ 20,000
Interest on accounts receivable	2,000
Interest on bond investment	30,000
Expense	
Cost of goods sold	$1,525,000
Salary and wages	560,000
($300,000 to officers)	
Insurance	200,000
Utilities	225,000
Travel (excluding meals)	175,000
Meals and entertainment	120,000
Commissions	600,000
Miscellaneous	45,000
Charitable contribution	40,000

Complete pages 1 and 2 of Form 1120 for the corporation.

HOW WOULD YOU RULE?

32. Amy Marchant was a 30% partner in XZB Partnership. She owned some machinery used in her sole proprietorship that the partnership could use. Since Amy was gradually shutting down her business, she decided to sell the machinery to the partnership. Unfortunately, the partnership was short of cash, so it was able to pay Amy only $60,000 for the machinery, which had a fair market value of $100,000, and a basis to Amy of $40,000. Amy accepted the $60,000 as full payment, however. How would Amy treat this transaction for tax purposes?

33. James Bumstead owned 100% of the stock of Dagwood Corporation, a regular C corporation. James had had some financial reversals in another business venture and needed cash quickly. He had Dagwood Corporation redeem 50% of his stock for $2,000,000.

The basis of the stock redeemed by the corporation was $500,000. How should James treat this redemption?

TAX RETURN PORTFOLIO PROBLEM

If your instructor has assigned this problem, refer to Appendix A and complete the portion labeled "Chapter 10." This includes information on the completion of all tax returns used in the portfolio problem.

Chapter 10 Problem 30   Name _____   10-67

Form **1065** Department of the Treasury Internal Revenue Service	**U.S. Partnership Return of Income** For calendar year 1993, or tax year beginning ...., 1993, and ending ...., 19 ..... ▶ See separate instructions.	OMB No. 1545-0099 **1993**

A Principal business activity	Use the IRS label. Other- wise, please print or type.	Name of partnership	**D** Employer identification number
B Principal product or service		Number, street, and room or suite no. (If a P.O. box, see page 9 of the instructions.)	**E** Date business started
C Business code number		City or town, state, and ZIP code	**F** Total assets (see Specific Instructions) $

G Check applicable boxes: (1) ☐ Initial return   (2) ☐ Final return   (3) ☐ Change in address   (4) ☐ Amended return
H Check accounting method: (1) ☐ Cash   (2) ☐ Accrual   (3) ☐ Other (specify) ▶ ....
I Number of Schedules K-1. Attach one for each person who was a partner at any time during the tax year ▶ ....

Caution: *Include only trade or business income and expenses on lines 1a through 22 below. See the instructions for more information.*

Income

1a	Gross receipts or sales	1a	
b	Less returns and allowances	1b	1c
2	Cost of goods sold (Schedule A, line 8)		2
3	Gross profit. Subtract line 2 from line 1c		3
4	Ordinary income (loss) from other partnerships and fiduciaries *(attach schedule)*		4
5	Net farm profit (loss) *(attach Schedule F (Form 1040))*		5
6	Net gain (loss) from Form 4797, Part II, line 20		6
7	Other income (loss) (see instructions) *(attach schedule)*		7
8	**Total income (loss).** Combine lines 3 through 7		8

Deductions (see instructions for limitations)

9a	Salaries and wages (other than to partners)	9a	
b	Less jobs credit	9b	9c
10	Guaranteed payments to partners		10
11	Repairs and maintenance		11
12	Bad debts		12
13	Rent		13
14	Taxes and licenses		14
15	Interest		15
16a	Depreciation (see instructions)	16a	
b	Less depreciation reported on Schedule A and elsewhere on return	16b	16c
17	Depletion (**Do not deduct oil and gas depletion.**)		17
18	Retirement plans, etc.		18
19	Employee benefit programs		19
20	Other deductions *(attach schedule)*		20
21	**Total deductions.** Add the amounts shown in the far right column for lines 9c through 20		21
22	**Ordinary income (loss)** from trade or business activities. Subtract line 21 from line 8		22

Please Sign Here

Under penalties of perjury, I declare that I have examined this return, including accompanying schedules and statements, and to the best of my knowledge and belief, it is true, correct, and complete. Declaration of preparer (other than general partner) is based on all information of which preparer has any knowledge.

▶ Signature of general partner   ▶ Date

Paid Preparer's Use Only

Preparer's signature ▶	Date	Check if self-employed ▶ ☐	Preparer's social security no.
Firm's name (or yours if self-employed) and address ▶		E.I. No. ▶	
		ZIP code ▶	

For Paperwork Reduction Act Notice, see page 1 of separate instructions.   Cat. No. 11390Z   Form **1065** (1993)

(Proof as of August 1993 (subject to change))

Copyright © 1994 by Harcourt Brace & Company. All rights reserved.

Form 1065 (1993) Page **2**

Schedule A — Cost of Goods Sold

1	Inventory at beginning of year	**1**
2	Purchases less cost of items withdrawn for personal use	**2**
3	Cost of labor	**3**
4	Additional section 263A costs (see instructions) (attach schedule)	**4**
5	Other costs (attach schedule)	**5**
6	**Total.** Add lines 1 through 5	**6**
7	Inventory at end of year	**7**
8	**Cost of goods sold.** Subtract line 7 from line 6. Enter here and on page 1, line 2	**8**

9a Check all methods used for valuing closing inventory:
  (i) ☐ Cost
  (ii) ☐ Lower of cost or market as described in Regulations section 1.471-4
  (iii) ☐ Writedown of "subnormal" goods as described in Regulations section 1.471-2(c)
  (iv) ☐ Other (specify method used and attach explanation) ▶ ....
 b Check this box if the LIFO inventory method was adopted this tax year for any goods (if checked, attach Form 970) . ▶ ☐
 c Do the rules of section 263A (for property produced or acquired for resale) apply to the partnership? . . ☐ Yes ☐ No
 d Was there any change in determining quantities, cost, or valuations between opening and closing inventory? ☐ Yes ☐ No
  If "Yes," attach explanation.

Schedule B — Other Information

		Yes	No
1	What type of entity is filing this return? Check the applicable box ▶ ☐ General partnership ☐ Limited partnership ☐ Limited liability company		
2	Are any partners in this partnership also partnerships?		
3	Is this partnership a partner in another partnership?		
4	Is this partnership subject to the consolidated audit procedures of sections 6221 through 6233? If "Yes," see **Designation of Tax Matters Partner** below		
5	Does this partnership meet **ALL THREE** of the following requirements?		
a	The partnership's total receipts for the tax year were less than $250,000;		
b	The partnership's total assets at the end of the tax year were less than $600,000; AND		
c	Schedules K-1 are filed with the return and furnished to the partners on or before the due date (including extensions) for the partnership return. If "Yes," the partnership is not required to complete Schedules L, M-1, and M-2; Item F on page 1 of Form 1065; or Item J on Schedule K-1		
6	Does this partnership have any foreign partners?		
7	Is this partnership a publicly traded partnership as defined in section 469(k)(2)?		
8	Has this partnership filed, or is it required to file, **Form 8264**, Application for Registration of a Tax Shelter? . .		
9	At any time during calendar year 1993, did the partnership have an interest in or a signature or other authority over a financial account in a foreign country (such as a bank account, securities account, or other financial account)? (See the instructions for exceptions and filing requirements for form TD F 90-22.1.) If "Yes," enter the name of the foreign country. ▶		
10	Was the partnership the grantor of, or transferor to, a foreign trust that existed during the current tax year, whether or not the partnership or any partner has any beneficial interest in it? If "Yes," you may have to file Forms 3520, 3520-A, or 926		
11	Was there a distribution of property or a transfer (e.g., by sale or death) of a partnership interest during the tax year? If "Yes," you may elect to adjust the basis of the partnership's assets under section 754 by attaching the statement described on page 4 of the instructions under **Elections Made By the Partnership**		

Designation of Tax Matters Partner (See instructions.)
Enter below the general partner designated as the tax matters partner (TMP) for the tax year of this return:

Name of designated TMP ▶ ....   Identifying number of TMP ▶ ....

Address of designated TMP ▶ ....

Chapter 10 Problem 30 10-69

Form 1065 (1993) Page **3**

Schedule K — Partners' Shares of Income, Credits, Deductions, Etc.

		(a) Distributive share items		(b) Total amount	
Income (Loss)	1	Ordinary income (loss) from trade or business activities (page 1, line 22)	1		
	2	Net income (loss) from rental real estate activities *(attach Form 8825)*	2		
	3a	Gross income from other rental activities	3a		
	b	Expenses from other rental activities *(attach schedule)*	3b		
	c	Net income (loss) from other rental activities. Subtract line 3b from line 3a	3c		
	4	Portfolio income (loss) (see instructions): **a** Interest income	4a		
	b	Dividend income	4b		
	c	Royalty income	4c		
	d	Net short-term capital gain (loss) *(attach Schedule D (Form 1065))*	4d		
	e	Net long-term capital gain (loss) *(attach Schedule D (Form 1065))*	4e		
	f	Other portfolio income (loss) *(attach schedule)*	4f		
	5	Guaranteed payments to partners	5		
	6	Net gain (loss) under section 1231 (other than due to casualty or theft) *(attach Form 4797)*	6		
	7	Other income (loss) *(attach schedule)*	7		
Deductions	8	Charitable contributions (see instructions) *(attach schedule)*	8		
	9	Section 179 expense deduction *(attach Form 4562)*	9		
	10	Deductions related to portfolio income (see instructions) (itemize) . .	10		
	11	Other deductions *(attach schedule)*	11		
Investment Interest	12a	Interest expense on investment debts	12a		
	b	(1) Investment income included on lines 4a through 4f above . . .	12b(1)		
		(2) Investment expenses included on line 10 above	12b(2)		
Credits	13a	Credit for income tax withheld	13a		
	b	Low-income housing credit (see instructions):			
		(1) From partnerships to which section 42(j)(5) applies for property placed in service before 1990	13b(1)		
		(2) Other than on line 13b(1) for property placed in service before 1990	13b(2)		
		(3) From partnerships to which section 42(j)(5) applies for property placed in service after 1989	13b(3)		
		(4) Other than on line 13b(3) for property placed in service after 1989	13b(4)		
	c	Qualified rehabilitation expenditures related to rental real estate activities *(attach Form 3468)*	13c		
	d	Credits (other than credits shown on lines 13b and 13c) related to rental real estate activities (see instructions)	13d		
	e	Credits related to other rental activities (see instructions)	13e		
	14	Other credits (see instructions)	14		
Self-Employment	15a	Net earnings (loss) from self-employment	15a		
	b	Gross farming or fishing income	15b		
	c	Gross nonfarm income	15c		
Adjustments and Tax Preference Items	16a	Depreciation adjustment on property placed in service after 1986	16a		
	b	Adjusted gain or loss	16b		
	c	Depletion (other than oil and gas)	16c		
	d	(1) Gross income from oil, gas, and geothermal properties	16d(1)		
		(2) Deductions allocable to oil, gas, and geothermal properties . .	16d(2)		
	e	Other adjustments and tax preference items *(attach schedule)* . .	16e		
Foreign Taxes	17a	Type of income ▶ .... **b** Foreign country or U.S. possession ▶			
	c	Total gross income from sources outside the United States *(attach schedule)*	17c		
	d	Total applicable deductions and losses *(attach schedule)*	17d		
	e	Total foreign taxes (check one): ▶ ☐ Paid ☐ Accrued	17e		
	f	Reduction in taxes available for credit *(attach schedule)*	17f		
	g	Other foreign tax information *(attach schedule)*	17g		
Other	18a	Total expenditures to which a section 59(e) election may apply . .	18a		
	b	Type of expenditures ▶..			
	19	Tax-exempt interest income	19		
	20	Other tax-exempt income	20		
	21	Nondeductible expenses	21		
	22	Other items and amounts required to be reported separately to partners (see instructions) *(attach schedule)*			
Analysis	23a	Income (loss). Combine lines 1 through 7 in column (b). From the result, subtract the sum of lines 8 through 12a, 17e, and 18a	23a		

		(a) Corporate	(b) Individual		(c) Partnership	(d) Exempt organization	(e) Nominee/Other
			i. Active	ii. Passive			
b Analysis by type of partner: (1) General partners							
(2) Limited partners							

Form 1065 (1993) Page **4**

Note: *If Question 5 of Schedule B is answered "Yes," the partnership is not required to complete Schedules L, M-1, and M-2.*

Schedule L — Balance Sheets

	Beginning of tax year		End of tax year	
Assets	(a)	(b)	(c)	(d)
1 Cash				
2a Trade notes and accounts receivable				
b Less allowance for bad debts				
3 Inventories				
4 U.S. government obligations				
5 Tax-exempt securities				
6 Other current assets (attach schedule)				
7 Mortgage and real estate loans				
8 Other investments (attach schedule)				
9a Buildings and other depreciable assets				
b Less accumulated depreciation				
10a Depletable assets				
b Less accumulated depletion				
11 Land (net of any amortization)				
12a Intangible assets (amortizable only)				
b Less accumulated amortization				
13 Other assets (attach schedule)				
14 Total assets				
Liabilities and Capital				
15 Accounts payable				
16 Mortgages, notes, bonds payable in less than 1 year				
17 Other current liabilities (attach schedule)				
18 All nonrecourse loans				
19 Mortgages, notes, bonds payable in 1 year or more				
20 Other liabilities (attach schedule)				
21 Partners' capital accounts				
22 Total liabilities and capital				

Schedule M-1 — Reconciliation of Income (Loss) per Books With Income (Loss) per Return (see instructions)

1 Net income (loss) per books		6 Income recorded on books this year not included on Schedule K, lines 1 through 7 (itemize): a Tax-exempt interest $	
2 Income included on Schedule K, lines 1 through 4, 6, and 7, not recorded on books this year (itemize):			
3 Guaranteed payments (other than health insurance)		7 Deductions included on Schedule K, lines 1 through 12a, 17e, and 18a, not charged against book income this year (itemize): a Depreciation $	
4 Expenses recorded on books this year not included on Schedule K, lines 1 through 12a, 17e, and 18a (itemize): a Depreciation $ .... b Travel and entertainment $			
		8 Add lines 6 and 7	
5 Add lines 1 through 4		9 Income (loss) (Schedule K, line 23a). Subtract line 8 from line 5	

Schedule M-2 — Analysis of Partners' Capital Accounts

1 Balance at beginning of year		6 Distributions: a Cash	
2 Capital contributed during year		b Property	
3 Net income (loss) per books		7 Other decreases (itemize):	
4 Other increases (itemize):			
		8 Add lines 6 and 7	
5 Add lines 1 through 4		9 Balance at end of year. Subtract line 8 from line 5	

Chapter 10 Problem 30   Name _____   *10-71*

SCHEDULE K-1
(Form 1065)
Department of the Treasury
Internal Revenue Service

Partner's Share of Income, Credits, Deductions, Etc.
▶ See separate instructions.
For calendar year 1993 or tax year beginning _____ , 1993, and ending _____ , 19 ___

OMB No. 1545-0099

1993

Partner's identifying number ▶   Partnership's identifying number ▶

Partner's name, address, and ZIP code   Partnership's name, address, and ZIP code

A This partner is a ☐ general partner ☐ limited partner
    ☐ limited liability company member
B What type of entity is this partner? ▶ ....
C Is this partner a ☐ domestic or a ☐ foreign partner?
D Enter partner's percentage of: (I) Before change   (II) End of
                                       or termination   year
    Profit sharing . . . . %   .... %
    Loss sharing . . . . %   .... %
    Ownership of capital . . .   . %   .... %
E IRS Center where partnership filed return: ....

F Partner's share of liabilities (see instructions):
    Nonrecourse . . . . $ ....
    Qualified nonrecourse financing . $ ....
    Other . . . . $ ....
G Tax shelter registration number . ▶ ....
H Check here if this partnership is a publicly traded
    partnership as defined in section 469(k)(2) . . . . ☐
I Check applicable boxes: **(1)** ☐ Final K-1 **(2)** ☐ Amended K-1

J Analysis of partner's capital account:

(a) Capital account at beginning of year	(b) Capital contributed during year	(c) Partner's share of lines 3, 4, and 7, Form 1065, Schedule M-2	(d) Withdrawals and distributions	(e) Capital account at end of year (combine columns (a) through (d))
			( )	

		(a) Distributive share item		(b) Amount	(c) 1040 filers enter the amount in column (b) on:
Income (Loss)	1	Ordinary income (loss) from trade or business activities . . .	1		⎫ See Partner's Instructions for Schedule K-1 (Form 1065).
	2	Net income (loss) from rental real estate activities	2		
	3	Net income (loss) from other rental activities	3		⎭
	4	Portfolio income (loss):			
	a	Interest	4a		Sch. B, Part I, line 1
	b	Dividends	4b		Sch. B, Part II, line 5
	c	Royalties	4c		Sch. E, Part I, line 4
	d	Net short-term capital gain (loss)	4d		Sch. D, line 5, col. (f) or (g)
	e	Net long-term capital gain (loss)	4e		Sch. D, line 13, col. (f) or (g)
	f	Other portfolio income (loss) *(attach schedule)* . . .	4f		Enter on applicable line of your return.
	5	Guaranteed payments to partner	5		See Partner's Instructions for Schedule K-1 (Form 1065).
	6	Net gain (loss) under section 1231 (other than due to casualty or theft)	6		
	7	Other income (loss) *(attach schedule)*	7		Enter on applicable line of your return.
Deductions	8	Charitable contributions (see instructions) *(attach schedule)*	8		Sch. A, line 13 or 14
	9	Section 179 expense deduction	9		⎫ See Partner's Instructions for Schedule K-1 (Form 1065).
	10	Deductions related to portfolio income *(attach schedule)* . .	10		
	11	Other deductions *(attach schedule)*	11		⎭
Investment Interest	12a	Interest expense on investment debts	12a		Form 4952, line 1
	b	**(1)** Investment income included on lines 4a through 4f above .	b(1)		⎫ See Partner's Instructions for Schedule K-1 (Form 1065).
		(2) Investment expenses included on line 10 above	b(2)		⎭
Credits	13a	Credit for income tax withheld	13a		See Partner's Instructions for Schedule K-1 (Form 1065).
	b	Low-income housing credit:			
		(1) From section 42(j)(5) partnerships for property placed in service before 1990	b(1)		⎫
		(2) Other than on line 13b(1) for property placed in service before 1990	b(2)		
		(3) From section 42(j)(5) partnerships for property placed in service after 1989	b(3)		Form 8586, line 5
		(4) Other than on line 13b(3) for property placed in service after 1989	b(4)		⎭
	c	Qualified rehabilitation expenditures related to rental real estate activities (see instructions)	13c		⎫
	d	Credits (other than credits shown on lines 13b and 13c) related to rental real estate activities (see instructions)	13d		See Partner's Instructions for Schedule K-1 (Form 1065).
	e	Credits related to other rental activities (see instructions) . . .	13e		
	14	Other credits (see instructions)	14		⎭

For Paperwork Reduction Act Notice, see Instructions for Form 1065.   Cat. No. 11394R   Schedule K-1 (Form 1065) 1993

Copyright © 1994 by Harcourt Brace & Company. All rights reserved.

Schedule K-1 (Form 1065) 1993 — Page 2

	(a) Distributive share item	(b) Amount	(c) 1040 filers enter the amount in column (b) on:
Self-employment	15a Net earnings (loss) from self-employment	15a	Sch. SE, Section A or B
	b Gross farming or fishing income	15b	See Partner's Instructions for Schedule K-1 (Form 1065).
	c Gross nonfarm income	15c	
Adjustments and Tax Preference Items	16a Depreciation adjustment on property placed in service after 1986	16a	See Partner's Instructions for Schedule K-1 (Form 1065) and Instructions for Form 6251.
	b Adjusted gain or loss	16b	
	c Depletion (other than oil and gas)	16c	
	d (1) Gross income from oil, gas, and geothermal properties	d(1)	
	(2) Deductions allocable to oil, gas, and geothermal properties	d(2)	
	e Other adjustments and tax preference items (attach schedule)	16e	
Foreign Taxes	17a Type of income ▶		Form 1116, check boxes
	b Name of foreign country or U.S. possession ▶		
	c Total gross income from sources outside the United States (attach schedule)	17c	Form 1116, Part I
	d Total applicable deductions and losses (attach schedule)	17d	
	e Total foreign taxes (check one): ▶ ☐ Paid ☐ Accrued	17e	Form 1116, Part II
	f Reduction in taxes available for credit (attach schedule)	17f	Form 1116, Part III
	g Other foreign tax information (attach schedule)	17g	See Instructions for Form 1116.
Other	18a Total expenditures to which a section 59(e) election may apply	18a	See Partner's Instructions for Schedule K-1 (Form 1065).
	b Type of expenditures ▶		
	19 Tax-exempt interest income	19	Form 1040, line 8b
	20 Other tax-exempt income	20	See Partner's Instructions for Schedule K-1 (Form 1065).
	21 Nondeductible expenses	21	
	22 Recapture of low-income housing credit:		
	a From section 42(j)(5) partnerships	22a	Form 8611, line 8
	b Other than on line 22a	22b	

Supplemental Information

23 Supplemental information required to be reported separately to each partner (attach additional schedules if more space is needed):

Proof as of August 1/93 (subject to change)

Chapter 10 Problem 31   Name _____   *10-73*

Form 1120 — U.S. Corporation Income Tax Return (1993)

Department of the Treasury — Internal Revenue Service
OMB No. 1545-0123

For calendar year 1993 or tax year beginning ...., 1993, ending ...., 19 ...
► Instructions are separate. See page 1 for Paperwork Reduction Act Notice.

A Check if a:
1. Consolidated return (attach Form 851) ☐
2. Personal holding co. (attach Sch. PH) ☐
3. Personal service corp. (as defined in Temporary Regs. sec. 1.441-4T—see instructions) ☐

Use IRS label. Otherwise, please print or type.
- Name
- Number, street, and room or suite no. (If a P.O. box, see page 6 of instructions.)
- City or town, state, and ZIP code

B Employer identification number
C Date incorporated
D Total assets (see Specific Instructions) $

E Check applicable boxes: (1) ☐ Initial return (2) ☐ Final return (3) ☐ Change of address

Income

1a	Gross receipts or sales _____ b Less returns and allowances _____ c Bal ►	1c
2	Cost of goods sold (Schedule A, line 8)	2
3	Gross profit. Subtract line 2 from line 1c	3
4	Dividends (Schedule C, line 19)	4
5	Interest	5
6	Gross rents	6
7	Gross royalties	7
8	Capital gain net income (attach Schedule D (Form 1120))	8
9	Net gain or (loss) from Form 4797, Part II, line 20 (attach Form 4797)	9
10	Other income (see instructions—attach schedule)	10
11	**Total income.** Add lines 3 through 10 ►	11

Deductions (See instructions for limitations on deductions.)

12	Compensation of officers (Schedule E, line 4)	12
13a	Salaries and wages _____ b Less jobs credit _____ c Balance ►	13c
14	Repairs and maintenance	14
15	Bad debts	15
16	Rents	16
17	Taxes and licenses	17
18	Interest	18
19	Charitable contributions (see instructions for 10% limitation)	19
20	Depreciation (attach Form 4562)	20
21	Less depreciation claimed on Schedule A and elsewhere on return	21a / 21b
22	Depletion	22
23	Advertising	23
24	Pension, profit-sharing, etc., plans	24
25	Employee benefit programs	25
26	Other deductions (attach schedule)	26
27	**Total deductions.** Add lines 12 through 26 ►	27
28	Taxable income before net operating loss deduction and special deductions. Subtract line 27 from line 11	28
29	Less: a Net operating loss deduction (see instructions)	29a
	b Special deductions (Schedule C, line 20)	29b / 29c
30	**Taxable income.** Subtract line 29c from line 28	30
31	**Total tax** (Schedule J, line 10)	31

Tax and Payments

32	Payments: a 1992 overpayment credited to 1993	32a
b	1993 estimated tax payments	32b
c	Less 1993 refund applied for on Form 4466	32c ( ) d Bal ► 32d
e	Tax deposited with Form 7004	32e
f	Credit from regulated investment companies (attach Form 2439)	32f
g	Credit for Federal tax on fuels (attach Form 4136). See instructions	32g / 32h
33	Estimated tax penalty (see instructions). Check if Form 2220 is attached ► ☐	33
34	**Tax due.** If line 32h is smaller than the total of lines 31 and 33, enter amount owed	34
35	**Overpayment.** If line 32h is larger than the total of lines 31 and 33, enter amount overpaid	35
36	Enter amount of line 35 you want: Credited to 1994 estimated tax ► Refunded ►	36

Please Sign Here

Under penalties of perjury, I declare that I have examined this return, including accompanying schedules and statements, and to the best of my knowledge and belief, it is true, correct, and complete. Declaration of preparer (other than taxpayer) is based on all information of which preparer has any knowledge.

► Signature of officer   Date   ► Title

Paid Preparer's Use Only

- Preparer's signature ►   Date   Check if self-employed ☐   Preparer's social security number
- Firm's name (or yours if self-employed) and address ►   E.I. No. ►   ZIP code ►

Cat. No. 11450Q

(Proof as of September 1993 — subject to change)

Copyright © 1994 by Harcourt Brace & Company. All rights reserved.

Form 1120 (1993) Page **2**

Schedule A — Cost of Goods Sold (See instructions.)

1	Inventory at beginning of year	1
2	Purchases	2
3	Cost of labor	3
4	Additional section 263A costs (attach schedule)	4
5	Other costs (attach schedule)	5
6	**Total.** Add lines 1 through 5	6
7	Inventory at end of year	7
8	**Cost of goods sold.** Subtract line 7 from line 6. Enter here and on page 1, line 2	8

9a Check all methods used for valuing closing inventory:
  ☐ Cost
  ☐ Lower of cost or market as described in Regulations section 1.471-4
  ☐ Writedown of subnormal goods as described in Regulations section 1.471-2(c)
  ☐ Other (Specify method used and attach explanation.) ▶ ....

b Check if the LIFO inventory method was adopted this tax year for any goods (if checked, attach Form 970) ... ▶ ☐

c If the LIFO inventory method was used for this tax year, enter percentage (or amounts) of closing inventory computed under LIFO ... | 9c |

d Do the rules of section 263A (for property produced or acquired for resale) apply to the corporation? ... ☐ Yes ☐ No

e Was there any change in determining quantities, cost, or valuations between opening and closing inventory? If "Yes," attach explanation ... ☐ Yes ☐ No

Schedule C — Dividends and Special Deductions (See instructions.)

		(a) Dividends received	(b) %	(c) Special deductions (a) × (b)
1	Dividends from less-than-20%-owned domestic corporations that are subject to the 70% deduction (other than debt-financed stock)		70	
2	Dividends from 20%-or-more-owned domestic corporations that are subject to the 80% deduction (other than debt-financed stock)		80	
3	Dividends on debt-financed stock of domestic and foreign corporations (section 246A)		see instructions	
4	Dividends on certain preferred stock of less-than-20%-owned public utilities		42	
5	Dividends on certain preferred stock of 20%-or-more-owned public utilities		48	
6	Dividends from less-than-20%-owned foreign corporations and certain FSCs that are subject to the 70% deduction		70	
7	Dividends from 20%-or-more-owned foreign corporations and certain FSCs that are subject to the 80% deduction		80	
8	Dividends from wholly owned foreign subsidiaries subject to the 100% deduction (section 245(b))		100	
9	**Total.** Add lines 1 through 8. See instructions for limitation			
10	Dividends from domestic corporations received by a small business investment company operating under the Small Business Investment Act of 1958		100	
11	Dividends from certain FSCs that are subject to the 100% deduction (section 245(c)(1))		100	
12	Dividends from affiliated group members subject to the 100% deduction (section 243(a)(3))		100	
13	Other dividends from foreign corporations not included on lines 3, 6, 7, 8, or 11			
14	Income from controlled foreign corporations under subpart F (attach Form(s) 5471)			
15	Foreign dividend gross-up (section 78)			
16	IC-DISC and former DISC dividends not included on lines 1, 2, or 3 (section 246(d))			
17	Other dividends			
18	Deduction for dividends paid on certain preferred stock of public utilities (see instructions)			
19	**Total dividends.** Add lines 1 through 17. Enter here and on line 4, page 1 ▶			
20	**Total special deductions.** Add lines 9, 10, 11, 12, and 18. Enter here and on line 29b, page 1 ▶			

Schedule E — Compensation of Officers (See instructions for line 12, page 1.)

Complete Schedule E only if total receipts (line 1a plus lines 4 through 10 on page 1, Form 1120) are $500,000 or more.

(a) Name of officer	(b) Social security number	(c) Percent of time devoted to business	Percent of corporation stock owned		(f) Amount of compensation
			(d) Common	(e) Preferred	
1		%	%	%	
		%	%	%	
		%	%	%	
		%	%	%	
		%	%	%	

2 Total compensation of officers ....
3 Compensation of officers claimed on Schedule A and elsewhere on return ....
4 Subtract line 3 from line 2. Enter the result here and on line 12, page 1 ....

APPENDIX A

Portfolio Problem

INTRODUCTION

The portfolio problem represents a continuing set of tax return preparation information for the Neilson family. The information presented below corresponds with each of the first nine chapters in the text. If your instructor assigns this problem, you should complete a portion of the various returns at the end of each chapter. Forms used in each chapter are summarized on the next page.

The purpose of the portfolio problem is to review the reporting procedures for the information provided in each chapter. This set of tax returns reviews the major concepts of individual taxation discussed in the text and should serve as a useful overview of the course.

THE NEILSON FAMILY

Harold A. and Maude L. Neilson are married taxpayers who live at 1211 Shelley Drive, Richmond, Virginia 23229. Both are 39 years old, and their social security numbers are 212-40-7070 (Harold) and 424-20-6868 (Maude). They plan to file a joint return for 1993.

Harold and Maude have three children who live with them. Their oldest son, Henry S. Neilson, is 19 years old, and his social security number is 412-60-4511. He provides over half of his own support and is not claimed as an exemption by Harold and Maude. Their daughter, Martha P. Neilson, is 11 years old, and her social security number is 382-10-4050. Although she is claimed as a dependent by Harold and Maude, she must file a Form 1040A due to interest and dividend income earned during the year. And finally, their youngest son, Allen T. Neilson, is five years old, and his social security number is 430-11-6062. He is claimed as a dependent by Harold and Maude, and he had no income in 1993.

Harriet T. Neilson (age 66), Harold's mother, also lives with the Neilsons. Her social security number is 641-80-7472. Because she received several sources of income in 1993, she must file a Form 1040. She is not claimed as a dependent by Harold and Maude.

All taxpayers elect to contribute to the election campaign.

CHAPTER ASSIGNMENTS

If you have not already done so, complete the taxpayer identification information at the top of each tax return, based on the information given in The Neilson Family section of

Portfolio Problem Tax Forms Utilized in Each Chapter

Form	1	2	3	4	5	6	7	8	9	10
Harold & Maude:										
1040	x	x	x	x				x	x	x
Sch A				x						x
Sch B		x								
Sch C								x		
Sch. D						x			x	x
Sch SE								x		
2106				x						
2119						x				
2441					x					
3903				x						
4562								x		
4684				x						x
4797									x	
6252						x				
Henry:										
1040EZ	x									
Martha:										
1040A		x								x
Sch. 1		x								
8615		x								x
Harriet:										
1040	x	x	x							x
Sch. B		x								
Sch. E								x		
Sch. R						x		x		x
4562								x		
Optional Extensions:										
6251							x			x
940								x		
941								x		

this problem on the previous page. Then, complete each of the chapter assignments described in the following sections.

CHAPTER 1

Harold A. and Maude L. Neilson

Harold and Maude elect to file a joint return in 1993. In addition to claiming exemptions for themselves, they will also claim exemptions for their daughter Martha and their youngest son Allen.

Harold is a salaried sales representative of Robert Shaw Company in Richmond. Following is his Form W-2 summarizing his annual salary, federal income tax withholdings, and state income tax withholdings. At this point, enter the gross salary in the gross income section of Form 1040 and the federal tax withholdings in the payments section of Form 1040.

Form W-2 Wage and Tax Statement

1	Control number	
	OMB No. 1545-0008	
2	Employer's name, address, and ZIP code	Robert Shaw Company, 1211 Glenside Drive, Richmond, VA 23228
3	Employer's identification number	60-4532112
4	Employer's state I.D. number	60-4532112
5	Employee's social security number	212-40-7070
19	Employee's name, address and ZIP code	Harold A. Neilson, 1211 Shelley Drive, Richmond, VA 23229
9	Federal income tax withheld	$13,980.00
10	Wages, tips, other compensation	$72,340.00
11	Social security tax withheld	$4,620.83
12	Social security wages	$57,600.00
24	State income tax	$4,894.00
25	State wages, tips, etc.	$72,340.00
26	Name of state	Virginia

Maude owns and operates her own engineering consulting and design business. Information regarding this business is in the Chapter 8 summary.

Henry S. Neilson

Henry Neilson, Harold and Maude's oldest son, is 19 years old. He graduated from high school in 1993 and accepted a job with Virginia Power as a line repairperson. His Form W-2 is illustrated on this page. His only other income for 1993 was $90 interest on a savings account at Heritage Savings and Loan. Henry is not claimed as an exemption by his parents. Complete a Form 1040EZ for Henry S. Neilson.

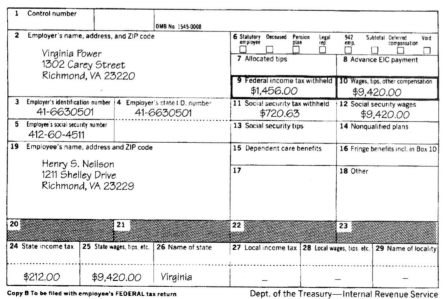

Form W-2 Wage and Tax Statement

2	Employer's name, address, and ZIP code	Virginia Power, 1302 Carey Street, Richmond, VA 23220
3	Employer's identification number	41-6630501
4	Employer's state I.D. number	41-6630501
5	Employee's social security number	412-60-4511
19	Employee's name, address and ZIP code	Henry S. Neilson, 1211 Shelley Drive, Richmond, VA 23229
9	Federal income tax withheld	$1,456.00
10	Wages, tips, other compensation	$9,420.00
11	Social security tax withheld	$720.63
12	Social security wages	$9,420.00
24	State income tax	$212.00
25	State wages, tips, etc.	$9,420.00
26	Name of state	Virginia

CHAPTER 2

Harold A. and Maude L. Neilson

During 1993 Harold and Maude received interest and dividend income from several institutions. This information is summarized on the Forms 1099-DIV and 1099-INT shown below and should be entered on Schedule B and carried over to Form 1040. In addition, Maude received $810 interest on City of Richmond bonds.

Form 1099-INT — Interest Income

- PAYER: Investors Savings & Loan, 1023 W. Franklin Street, Richmond, VA 23220
- PAYER'S Federal identification number: 41-6630523
- RECIPIENT'S identification number: 424-20-6868
- RECIPIENT: Maude L. Neilson, 1211 Shelley Drive, Richmond, VA 23229
- Box 1 Earnings from savings and loan associations, credit unions, bank deposits, bearer certificates of deposit, etc.: $2,810.00

Form 1099-DIV — Dividends and Distributions

- PAYER: Best Company, 1214 Monument Avenue, Richmond, VA 23220
- PAYER'S Federal identification number: 60-1126413
- RECIPIENT'S identification number: 212-40-7070
- RECIPIENT: Harold A. Neilson, 1211 Shelley Drive, Richmond, VA 23229
- Box 1a Gross dividends and other distributions on stock (Total of 1b, 1c, 1d, and 1e): $3,030.00
- Box 1b Ordinary dividends: $3,030.00

Martha P. Neilson

Martha Neilson, age 11, received interest and dividend income in 1993 (see Forms 1099-INT and 1099-DIV). These were her only sources of income in 1993. She has no itemized deductions, and she is claimed as a exemption by her parents Harold and Maude. Enter this information on Schedule 1 and Form 1040A and begin preparation of a Form 8615 by completing lines 1 through 5.

Harriet T. Neilson

Harriet T. Neilson, Harold's mother, lives with the Neilsons. During 1993 she received interest and dividend income from the sources disclosed on the Forms 1099-INT and 1099-DIV below. In addition, she received $340 of interest income from state of Virginia bonds. Enter this information on a Form 1040 and Schedule B for Harriet. Harriet is 66 years old.

Form 1099-INT — Interest Income

PAYER: First Trust Company, 11502 Broad Street, Richmond, VA 23220
PAYER'S Federal identification number: 61-3340216
RECIPIENT'S identification number: 382-10-4050
RECIPIENT: Martha P. Neilson, 1211 Shelley Drive, Richmond, VA 23229

- Box 1 Earnings from savings and loan associations, credit unions, bank deposits, bearer certificates of deposit, etc.: $782.00
- Box 2 Early withdrawal penalty: —
- Box 3 U.S. Savings Bonds, etc.: —
- Box 4 Federal income tax withheld: —
- Box 5 Foreign tax paid: —
- Box 6 Foreign country or U.S. possession: —

Copy B — For Recipient

Form 1099-DIV — Dividends and Distributions

PAYER: Helig Myers, Inc., 1631 Staples Mill Road, Richmond, VA 23228
PAYER'S Federal identification number: 44-6011234
RECIPIENT'S identification number: 382-10-4050
RECIPIENT: Martha P. Neilson, 1211 Shelley Drive, Richmond, VA 23229

- Box 1a Gross dividends and other distributions on stock (Total of 1b, 1c, 1d, and 1e): $548.00
- Box 1b Ordinary dividends: $548.00
- Box 1c Capital gain distributions: —
- Box 1d Nontaxable distributions: —
- Box 1e Investment expenses: —
- Box 2 Federal income tax withheld: —
- Box 3 Foreign tax paid: —
- Box 4 Foreign country or U.S. possession: —
- Liquidation Distributions — Box 5 Cash: —; Box 6 Noncash (Fair market value): —

Copy C — For Payer

Form 1099-INT — Interest Income

PAYER: First National Bank, 2051 Libbie Avenue, Richmond, VA 23228
PAYER'S Federal identification number: 71-2230406
RECIPIENT'S identification number: 641-80-7572
RECIPIENT: Harriet T. Neilson, 1211 Shelley Drive, Richmond, VA 23229

- Box 1 Earnings from savings and loan associations, credit unions, bank deposits, bearer certificates of deposit, etc.: $3,420.00
- Box 2 Early withdrawal penalty: —
- Box 3 U.S. Savings Bonds, etc.: —
- Box 4 Federal income tax withheld: —
- Box 5 Foreign tax paid: —
- Box 6 Foreign country or U.S. possession: —

Copy B — For Recipient

Form 1099-DIV — Dividends and Distributions

PAYER: Virginia Power, Dominion Resources, Inc., 1120 Byrd Street, Richmond, VA 23220
PAYER'S Federal identification number: 31-2060411
RECIPIENT'S identification number: 641-80-7472
RECIPIENT: Harriet T. Neilson, 1211 Shelley Drive, Richmond, VA 23229

- Box 1a Gross dividends and other distributions on stock (Total of 1b, 1c, 1d, and 1e): $4,970.00
- Box 1b Ordinary dividends: $4,970.00
- Box 1c Capital gain distributions: —
- Box 1d Nontaxable distributions: —
- Box 1e Investment expenses: —
- Box 2 Federal income tax withheld: —
- Box 3 Foreign tax paid: —
- Box 4 Foreign country or U.S. possession: —
- Liquidation Distributions — Box 5 Cash: —; Box 6 Noncash (Fair market value): —

Copy C — For Payer

CHAPTER 3

Harold A. and Maude L. Neilson

In March 1993, Harold won $1,660 from the state of Virginia lottery by correctly picking 5 of the 6 numbers in the weekly lotto game. The Form 1099-MISC shown below summarizes these winnings. Enter this information on the Form 1040.

In May 1993, Harold and Maude received a $650 refund from their 1992 state of Virginia income tax return. This information is disclosed on the Form 1099-G below. Harold and Maude had itemized their deductions in 1992. Enter this information on Form 1040.

PAYER'S name, street address, city, state, and ZIP code	1 Rents	OMB No. 1545-0115	Miscellaneous Income
State Lottery Commonwealth of Virginia 1202 Broad Street Richmond, VA 23222	2 Royalties 3 Prizes, awards, etc. $ 1,660.00	Statement for Recipients of	
PAYER'S Federal identification number: 62-4030112	RECIPIENT'S identification number: 212-40-7070	4 Federal income tax withheld	5 Fishing boat proceeds
RECIPIENT'S name: Harold A. Neilson Street address: 1211 Shelley Drive City, state, and ZIP code: Richmond, VA 23229	6 Medical and health care payments 8 Substitute payments in lieu of dividends or interest 10 Crop insurance proceeds	7 Nonemployee compensation 9 Payer made direct sales of $5,000 or more of consumer products to a buyer (recipient) for resale ▶ 11 State income tax withheld	Copy 1 For State Tax Department
Account number (optional)	12 State/Payer's state number		

Form **1099-MISC** — Department of the Treasury - Internal Revenue Service

PAYER'S name, street address, city, state, and ZIP code	1 Unemployment compensation	OMB No. 1545-0120	Certain Government Payments
Commonwealth of Virginia 1202 Broad Street Richmond, VA 23222	2 State or local income tax refunds, credits, or offsets $ 650.00		
PAYER'S Federal identification number: 62-4030112	RECIPIENT'S identification number: 212-40-7070	3 Box 2 amount is for tax year	4 Federal income tax withheld
RECIPIENT'S name: Harold A. Neilson, Maude L. Neilson Street address (including apt. no.): 1211 Shelley Drive City, state, and ZIP code: Richmond, VA 23229	5 Discharge of indebtedness 7 Agriculture payments	6 Taxable grants 8 The amount in Box 2 applies to income from a trade or business ▶	Copy B For Recipient This is important tax information and is being furnished to the Internal Revenue Service. If you are required to file a return, a negligence penalty or other sanction may be imposed on you if this income is taxable and the IRS determines that it has not been reported.
Account number (optional)			

Form **1099-G** — Department of the Treasury - Internal Revenue Service

Harriet T. Neilson

Harriet T. Neilson, age 66, began receiving social security benefits in October 1993. She received $622 a month, or a total of $1,866, which was disclosed on the Form SSA-1099 she received from the federal government. Enter this information on Form 1040, line 21a. (The taxable portion will be determined later after other income information is furnished.)

CHAPTER 4

Harold A. and Maude L. Neilson

Harold and Maude moved to Richmond on January 12, 1993. Prior to this time, they lived in DeKalb, Illinois, which is 980 miles from Richmond. Harold was transferred by his employer to Richmond; prior to the move, Harold commuted six miles from his home in DeKalb to the office. Harold's employer reimbursed some of his moving expenses; however, the following expenses were not reimbursed (and should be recorded on Form 3903):

Fee charged by movers for moving furniture	$ 2,840
Travel costs of moving family (without meals)	116
Meal expenses incurred en route by family	55
Commissions paid on sale of old residence	12,700
Premove house-hunting trip (without meals)	324
Meal expenses incurred in house-hunting trip	220

In his job as a sales representative, most of Harold's expenses are reimbursed by his employer. However, the following expenses incurred in 1993 were not reimbursed (and should be recorded on Form 2106):

Auto expenses (2,200 miles driven)	$?
Parking fees and tolls on business trips	178
Entertainment expenses and business meals	630
Travel expenses on business trips (without meals)	980
Professional dues	300
Professional journal and trade subscriptions	480

Harold and Maude's personal records indicate that the following personal expenses were incurred in 1993. Relevant information should be recorded on Schedule A.

Preparation fee for 1992 return (paid in 1993)	$ 220
Unreimbursed physician charges	840
Property taxes on personal residence	2,780
Contributions made in cash	4,300
Home mortgage interest (qualifying residential)	8,492
Personal property tax on value of personal autos	830
Estimated state income taxes paid by Maude	4,400
Contributions of capital-gain property (value)	500
State income tax withholdings—Harold (see W-2)	?

During the move to Richmond, the Neilson's recreational vehicle (RV) was destroyed by fire. The RV originally cost $32,300 in 1986 and was worth $18,200 at the time of the fire. After the fire, the value of the RV was estimated to be only $2,500. Unfortunately, Harold and Maude had allowed the insurance to lapse on the RV, and no reimbursement was received. This information should be entered on Form 4684; however, the final loss on line 18 cannot be determined until adjusted gross income is computed later in this problem. (Also, Schedule A cannot be completed at this time because adjusted gross income is not known.)

CHAPTER 5

Harold A. and Maude L. Neilson

During 1993 Harold and Maude paid Tiny Tot Nursery a total of $2,200 to care for their five-year-old son Allen while they worked. The nursery is located at 1015 Floyd Avenue, Richmond, Virginia 23284. Record this information on Form 2441; however, the form cannot be completed until the earned income of both spouses is determined. Therefore, complete only lines 1 through 8 at this time.

As a self-employed person, Maude Neilson made four estimated federal income tax payments in 1993 of $4,000 each. These amounts represent prepayments of estimated taxes for 1993 and should be recorded in the payments section of Form 1040.

Harriet T. Neilson

During 1993 Harriet Neilson made four quarterly estimated tax payments of $155 each to the federal government. This information should be recorded in the payments section of Form 1040.

Harriet potentially qualifies for the tax credit for the elderly. At this point, complete lines 10 through 13 of Schedule R. (The form will be completed later when other income information is given.)

CHAPTER 6

Harold A. and Maude L. Neilson

Harold and Maude incurred the following transactions involving capital assets in 1993, which should be recorded on Schedule D (note the Form 1099-B on the next page, which was furnished to the Neilsons by their broker):

- On September 3, 1993, the Neilsons sold an oil painting to Merrill Chase Galleries for $8,640. Harold had inherited the painting from his father in 1985. His father had originally purchased the painting in June 1982 for $2,300 and the painting was worth $5,570 on June 1, 1985, the date of his death.

- The Neilsons sold 100 shares of James River Company common on March 2, 1993, for $3,250. The shares were originally purchased on August 13, 1992, for $2,920.

- The Neilsons sold 40 shares of Circuit City stock on August 12, 1993, for $1,380. The shares were originally purchased on January 3, 1993, for $2,080.

	☐ CORRECTED (if checked)		
PAYER'S name, street address, city, state, and ZIP code Wheat First Securities 1301 W. Franklin Richmond, VA 23220	1a Date of sale 3-2-92, 8-12-92	OMB No. 1545-0715	**Proceeds From Broker and Barter Exchange Transactions**
	1b CUSIP No.		
	2 Stocks, bonds, etc. $ 4,630.00	Reported to IRS ☐ Gross proceeds ☐ Gross proceeds less commissions and option premiums	
PAYER'S Federal identification number 66-4122301	RECIPIENT'S identification number 212-40-7070	3 Bartering $	4 Federal income tax withheld $	**Copy B For Recipient**
RECIPIENT'S name Harold A. Neilson Maude L. Neilson		5 Description		This is important tax information and is being furnished to the Internal Revenue Service. If you are required to file a return, a negligence penalty or other sanction may be imposed on you if this income is taxable and the IRS determines that it has not been reported.
		Regulated Futures Contracts		
Street address (including apt. no.) 1211 Shelley Drive		6 Profit or (loss) realized in 1991 $	7 Unrealized profit or (loss) on open contracts—12/31/90 $	
City, state, and ZIP code Richmond, VA 23229		8 Unrealized profit or (loss) on open contracts—12/31/91 $	9 Aggregate profit or (loss) $	
Account number (optional)				

Form **1099-B**   Department of the Treasury - Internal Revenue Service

- The Neilsons sold a 19th century print on October 1, 1993, for $6,200. The print was received as a gift from Maude's mother on April 3, 1978. Her mother originally paid $9,700 for the print on March 3, 1972, and the print was worth $8,800 on the date of the gift. Her mother did not pay any gift tax.

On January 4, 1993, Harold and Maude sold their old residence in DeKalb, Illinois, for $178,500. They had originally acquired the home in 1978 for $103,200. Selling expenses were $12,700 (however, recall that some of this amount was deducted in determining moving expenses on Form 3903, and amounts reported there are not allowed as expenses on Form 2119). The Neilsons paid $300 to have two rooms painted two weeks prior to the sale. On January 6, 1993, Harold and Maude purchased their new residence in Richmond for a total of $164,500. Record this information on Form 2119, and enter the final gain on Schedule D.

On December 10, 1993, the Neilsons also sold 20 acres of land that they owned as a capital investment in DeKalb, Illinois. They had originally purchased the land on March 12, 1980, for $26,000, and they sold the land for $40,000, payable as follows: $8,000 down payment on December 10, 1993, and four annual installment payments of $8,000 plus 10% simple interest, to begin on December 10, 1994. The Neilsons paid $2,000 commissions on the sale. Record this information on Form 6252, and enter the final taxable gain on Schedule D.

(Note—Schedule D cannot be completed at this time, since Maude sold some business properties during 1993 that potentially affect the Schedule D result. This information is given in the Chapter 9 summary.)

CHAPTER 7

This portfolio problem has two optional extensions that may be assigned by your instructor. The first extension involves the preparation of Form 6251, the alternative minimum tax, for Harold and Maude Neilson. If your instructor assigns this extension, refer to "Optional Extension I," which follows the information for Chapter 10. (Note—the following assignments for Chapters 8, 9, and 10 must be completed before preparing Form 6251).

CHAPTER 8

Harold A. and Maude L. Neilson

Maude Neilson owns and operates her own engineering consulting and design firm, Neilson Design and Consulting, which is located at 800 Main, Suite B, Richmond, Virginia 23220. Her employer ID number is 31-6640532. She uses the accrual method for tax purposes and reports her small inventory of engineering instruments on the cost basis. Her accounting records disclose the following for 1993, which should be recorded on Schedule C:

Gross receipts (consulting and design fees)	$211,655
Gross receipts (sales of engineering instruments)	82,505
Sales returns and allowances	6,820
Purchases of engineering instruments	71,306
Physical inventory, instruments, 12/31/93	28,030
Physical inventory, instruments, 12/31/92	18,642
Gross wages paid to three employees	72,000
Fire insurance premiums paid (expired during 1993)	4,630
Office expense	626
Taxes and licenses expenses	11,865
Bad debts proven uncollectible	7,938
Business meals and entertainment (gross)	220
Legal and professional services expense	3,600
Mortgage interest paid on building	18,362
Commissions and fees paid subcontractors	2,380
Advertising expenses	8,425
Supplies (not included in inventories)	932
Utilities expense	3,420
Repairs and other maintenance expenses	1,826
Employee pension plan contribution (10% of wages)	7,200
Miscellaneous expenses (contract deliveries)	9,440

During 1993 Maude used the following assets in her business:

- A delivery automobile, which was originally acquired on 1/18/92 (last year) for $12,300. Maude elected MACRS recovery on the auto (five-year property). The car was used 100% for business purposes in 1993, when it was driven 12,600 miles. (Maude did not elect Sec. 179 expensing on the auto in 1992.)

- New display counters were acquired on January 12, 1993, for $18,600. Maude elects Sec. 179 expensing on the maximum possible cost in 1993, with the balance subject to seven-year MACRS recovery.

- Maude acquired an office building for her business on January 10, 1993, for $186,300. She elects MACRS recovery over a 31.5-year period.

This information should be recorded on Form 4562, with the net result transferred to Schedule C. The Schedule C result should then be carried forward to Form 1040, and the net income from Schedule C should be used to complete Schedule SE, which involves computation of the self-employment tax. (Recall that one-half of the self-employment tax is also deductible for adjusted gross income on Form 1040.)

Finally, Maude has established a Keogh retirement plan. As mentioned above, she contributed $7,200 to the retirement plan on behalf of her employees. Maude also contributes 10% of her net Schedule C income to the Keogh plan on her own behalf; record this contribution as a deduction for adjusted gross income on Form 1040 as well.

This portfolio problem has a second optional extension that involves preparation of a fourth-quarter Form 941 and a 1993 Form 940 for Maude's consulting business. If your instructor assigns this extension, refer to "Optional Extension II," which follows the information for Chapter 10.

Harriet T. Neilson

Harriet owns a rental duplex at 8040 Three Chopt Road, Richmond, Virginia 23220. The duplex was acquired in January, 1991, for $62,000 (27.5-year MACRS property), and she immediately furnished the duplex with furniture and appliances costing $9,000 (7-year MACRS property). Depreciation for these two assets should be recorded on Form 4562, with the net result transferred to Schedule E.

During 1993 Harriet collected $11,800 of rents from the tenants. She also incurred expenses for repairs ($430), cleaning ($150), taxes ($860), legal fees ($300), and mortgage interest ($2,850). These amounts should also be recorded on Schedule E, and the net result should be transferred to Form 1040.

CHAPTER 9

When Harold and Maude moved to Richmond in January 1993, Maude sold three assets that were used in her old consulting business in Geneva, Illinois. Details on these three asset sales, which should be recorded on Form 4797, are

- Five display counters were sold on January 10, 1993, for a total of $3,071. These counters were originally acquired on January 3, 1986, for $12,000, and a total of $12,000 had been deducted as depreciation in the years 1986–1990.

- Office furniture was sold on January 10, 1993, for $5,016. The furniture was originally acquired on January 6, 1986, for $4,416, and a total of $4,416 had been deducted as depreciation in the years 1986–1990.

- Five acres of business land was sold on January 10, 1993, for $8,000. The land was originally acquired on January 6, 1986, for $8,300.

The display counters and office furniture are both Sec. 1245 properties (reportable on page 2 of Form 4797), since both were sold at gains. The land is Sec. 1231 property (reportable on page 1 of Form 4797) since it was sold at a loss.

Once Form 4797 is completed, the totals should be carried forward to the appropriate location (either Schedule D for net Sec. 1231 gains or Form 1040 for ordinary income). Once the carryovers are made, Schedule D may then be completed, and the net gain or loss transferred to Form 1040.

CHAPTER 10

Harold A. and Maude L. Neilson

You are now ready to complete the Form 1040 for all the Neilsons by determining adjusted gross income, once all carryovers from Schedule D are complete. Then Form 4684 and Schedule A can be completed by computing the various floors based on adjusted gross income, and Form 2441 (dependent care credit) can also be completed. The final tax due (or refund) can now be computed.

Martha P. Neilson

Once Harold and Maude's taxable income is known, Form 8615 for Martha, which involves computation of the allocable parental tax, can be completed. Then Martha's Form 1040A can be completed once the tax liability is determined.

Harriet T. Neilson

Harriet's Form 1040 can now be completed by determining her gross income without the social security and then determining how much, if any, of the social security is taxable. Once the final gross income is determined, Harriet's standard deduction must be determined and entered on the Form 1040. Then her tax liability and tax credit for the elderly (Schedule R) may be computed.

PORTFOLIO PROBLEM OPTIONAL EXTENSION I FORM 6251

If your instructor assigns this optional extension of the portfolio problem, complete a Form 6251 to determine if Harold and Maude would be subject to the alternative minimum tax, based on the following additional information:

- Adjustments need to be made for taxes (line 3) and miscellaneous itemized deductions (line 5), and taxes (line 5d). Additionally, the refund of state taxes ($650) should be entered on line 6.

- The depreciation adjustment for property placed into service after 1986 (line 8) is based on a comparison of MACRS deductions and Alternative Depreciation System (ADS) deductions for the display counters, the building, and the auto. For these purposes, MACRS is the actual deduction taken on Form 4562, and ADS is based on the following for each asset: counters (10-year 150% ADS recovery, Year 1 factor), building (40-year straight-line ADS recovery, Year 1 factor), and the auto (5-year 150% ADS recovery, Year 2 factor). Note—on the counters, the Sec. 179 deduction is ignored in the adjustment; just compare MACRS and ADS on the amount that was not expensed.

- Harold and Maude had one preference item: $6,800 of tax-exempt interest from private activity bonds that was not taxable for regular tax purposes but is taxable for the alternative minimum tax.

If the tentative minimum tax (line 26) is greater than the regular tax liability (line 27), then Harold and Maude will have to pay the difference as an "alternative minimum tax" in 1993.

PORTFOLIO PROBLEM OPTIONAL EXTENSION II FORMS 941 AND 940

If your instructor assigns this optional extension of the portfolio problem, prepare a fourth quarter Form 941 and a 1993 Form 940 for Neilson Design and Consulting. Use the following information in preparing the problem:

Maude had three employees during the year 1993, and their names, marital status, withholding allowances, and semimonthly salaries were as follows:

Name	Marital Status	Withholding Allowances	Semimonthly Salaries
William Allen	S	1	$ 820
Barbara Brandon	S	2	900
Cheryl Craft	M	3	1,280

Maude uses the wage-bracket method in computing federal tax withholdings each paycheck; refer to Figure 8-11 in Chapter 8 to determine these amounts. Note that the Form 941 is for a quarter, which covers six pay periods (a total of $18,000). Maude always deposits the withholdings and FICA tax on each payday; therefore, she had made five of the six deposits for the last quarter (three on the 15th of each month, and two on the last day of each month), and will make the final deposit for the last pay period with the Form 941.

When completing the Form 940, remember that this is an annual return and only the first $7,000 wages of each employee is subject to the tax. Also, assume that Maude paid $1,134 of state unemployment taxes and will owe federal taxes only at the .008 rate shown on Part II, line 1. And finally, assume that Maude has deposited a total of $126 of FUTA taxes thus far in 1993 ($42 each quarter).

PORTFOLIO PROBLEM

Harold A. and Maude L. Neilson

CHECKLIST
Form 1040 .... _____
Schedule A .... _____
Schedule B .... _____
Schedule C .... _____
Schedule D .... _____
Schedule SE .... _____
Form 2106 .... _____
Form 2119 .... _____
Form 2441 .... _____
Form 3903 .... _____
Form 4562 .... _____
Form 4684 .... _____
Form 4797 .... _____
Form 6252 .... _____

Henry S. Neilson

CHECKLIST
Form 1040EZ .... _____

Martha P. Neilson

CHECKLIST
Form 1040A .... _____
Schedule 1 .... _____
Form 8615 .... _____

Harriet T. Neilson

CHECKLIST
Form 1040 .... _____
Schedule B .... _____
Schedule E .... _____
Schedule R .... _____
Form 4562 .... _____

PORTFOLIO PROBLEM OPTIONAL EXTENSION #1

Harold A and Maude L. Neilson
Alternative Minimum Tax

CHECKLIST
Form 6251 .... _____

PORTFOLIO PROBLEM OPTIONAL EXTENSION #2

Harold A. and Maude L. Neilson
Employment Tax Returns

CHECKLIST
Form 941 .... _____
Form 940 .... _____

Portfolio Problem (Harold A. and Maude L.)   Name _____   A-17

Form 1040

Department of the Treasury—Internal Revenue Service
U.S. Individual Income Tax Return 1993

For the year Jan. 1–Dec. 31, 1993, or other tax year beginning _____, 1993, ending _____, 19___ | OMB No. 1545-0074

IRS Use Only—Do not write or staple in this space

Label (See instructions on page 12.) Use the IRS label. Otherwise, please print or type.

L A B E L   H E R E

Your first name and initial | Last name | Your social security number

If a joint return, spouse's first name and initial | Last name | Spouse's social security number

Home address (number and street). If you have a P.O. box, see page 12. | Apt. no.

City, town or post office, state, and ZIP code. If you have a foreign address, see page 12.

For Privacy Act and Paperwork Reduction Act Notice, see page 4.

Presidential Election Campaign (See page 12.)

Do you want $3 to go to this fund? . . . . | Yes | No
If a joint return, does your spouse want $3 to go to this fund? . . . | |

Note: Checking "Yes" will not change your tax or reduce your refund.

Filing Status
(See page 12.)
Check only one box.

1. ☐ Single
2. ☐ Married filing joint return (even if only one had income)
3. ☐ Married filing separate return. Enter spouse's social security no. above and full name here. ▶ _____
4. ☐ Head of household (with qualifying person). (See page 13.) If the qualifying person is a child but not your dependent, enter this child's name here. ▶ _____
5. ☐ Qualifying widow(er) with dependent child (year spouse died ▶ 19___). (See page 13.)

Exemptions (See page 13.)

6a ☐ **Yourself.** If your parent (or someone else) can claim you as a dependent on his or her tax return, **do not** check box 6a. But be sure to check the box on line 33b on page 2
b ☐ **Spouse**
c **Dependents:**

(1) Name (first, initial, and last name)	(2) Check if under age 1	(3) If age 1 or older, dependent's social security number	(4) Dependent's relationship to you	(5) No. of months lived in your home in 1993

If more than six dependents, see page 14.

No. of boxes checked on 6a and 6b _____
No. of your children on 6c who:
• lived with you _____
• didn't live with you due to divorce or separation (see page 15) _____
Dependents on 6c not entered above _____

d If your child didn't live with you but is claimed as your dependent under a pre-1985 agreement, check here ▶ ☐
e Total number of exemptions claimed . . . .

Add numbers entered on lines above ▶ _____

Income

Attach Copy B of your Forms W-2, W-2G, and 1099-R here.

If you did not get a W-2, see page 10.

If you are attaching a check or money order, put it on top of any Forms W-2, W-2G, or 1099-R.

7 Wages, salaries, tips, etc. Attach Form(s) W-2 . . . . | 7
8a Taxable interest income (see page 16). Attach Schedule B if over $400 . . . | 8a
b Tax-exempt interest (see page 17). DON'T include on line 8a | 8b |
9 Dividend income. Attach Schedule B if over $400 . . . . | 9
10 Taxable refunds, credits, or offsets of state and local income taxes (see page 17) . . | 10
11 Alimony received . . . . | 11
12 Business income or (loss). Attach Schedule C or C-EZ . . . . | 12
13 Capital gain or (loss). Attach Schedule D . . . . | 13
14 Capital gain distributions not reported on line 13 (see page 17) . . . . . | 14
15 Other gains or (losses). Attach Form 4797 . . . . | 15
16a Total IRA distributions . | 16a | | b Taxable amount (see page 18) | 16b
17a Total pensions and annuities | 17a | | b Taxable amount (see page 18) | 17b
18 Rental real estate, royalties, partnerships, S corporations, trusts, etc. Attach Schedule E | 18
19 Farm income or (loss). Attach Schedule F . . . . | 19
20 Unemployment compensation (see page 19) . . . . | 20
21a Social security benefits | 21a | | b Taxable amount (see page 19) | 21b
22 Other income. List type and amount—see page 20 .... | 22
23 Add the amounts in the far right column for lines 7 through 22. This is your **total income** ▶ | 23

Adjustments to Income
(See page 20.)

24a Your IRA deduction (see page 20) . . . . | 24a
b Spouse's IRA deduction (see page 20) . . . . | 24b
25 One-half of self-employment tax (see page 21) . . . . | 25
26 Self-employed health insurance deduction (see page 22) | 26
27 Keogh retirement plan and self-employed SEP deduction | 27
28 Penalty on early withdrawal of savings . . . . | 28
29 Alimony paid. Recipient's SSN ▶ | 29
30 Add lines 24a through 29. These are your **total adjustments** . . . . ▶ | 30

Adjusted Gross Income

31 Subtract line 30 from line 23. This is your **adjusted gross income.** If this amount is less than $23,050 and a child lived with you, see page EIC-1 to find out if you can claim the "Earned Income Credit" on line 56 . . . . ▶ | 31

Cat. No. 11320B   Form **1040** (1993)

Copyright © 1994 by Harcourt Brace & Company. All rights reserved.

Form 1040 (1993) Page 2

Tax Computation (See page 23.)	32	Amount from line 31 (adjusted gross income)	32
	33a	Check if: ☐ **You** were 65 or older, ☐ Blind; ☐ **Spouse** was 65 or older, ☐ Blind. Add the number of boxes checked above and enter the total here . . . ▶ 33a	
	b	If your parent (or someone else) can claim you as a dependent, check here . ▶ 33b ☐	
	c	If you are married filing separately and your spouse itemizes deductions or you are a dual-status alien, see page 24 and check here . . . . ▶ 33c ☐	
	34	Enter the larger of your: { **Itemized deductions** from Schedule A, line 26, **OR** **Standard deduction** shown below for your filing status. **But if you checked any box on line 33a or b,** go to page 24 to find your standard deduction. If you checked **box 33c,** your standard deduction is zero. • Single—$3,700 • Head of household—$5,450 • Married filing jointly or Qualifying widow(er)—$6,200 • Married filing separately—$3,100 }	34
	35	Subtract line 34 from line 32	35
	36	If line 32 is $81,350 or less, multiply $2,350 by the total number of exemptions claimed on line 6e. If line 32 is over $81,350, see the worksheet on page 25 for the amount to enter .	36
	37	**Taxable income.** Subtract line 36 from line 35. If line 36 is more than line 35, enter -0- .	37
If you want the IRS to figure your tax, see page 24.	38	Tax. Check if from **a** ☐ Tax Table, **b** ☐ Tax Rate Schedules, **c** ☐ Schedule D Tax Worksheet, or **d** ☐ Form 8615 (see page 25). Amount from Form(s) 8814 ▶ **e** _____	38
	39	Additional taxes (see page 25). Check if from **a** ☐ Form 4970 **b** ☐ Form 4972 . . ▶	39
	40	Add lines 38 and 39	40
Credits (See page 25.)	41	Credit for child and dependent care expenses. Attach Form 2441	41	
	42	Credit for the elderly or the disabled. Attach Schedule R .	42	
	43	Foreign tax credit. Attach Form 1116	43	
	44	Other credits (see page 26). Check if from **a** ☐ Form 3800 **b** ☐ Form 8396 **c** ☐ Form 8801 **d** ☐ Form (specify) ___	44	
	45	Add lines 41 through 44	45
	46	Subtract line 45 from line 40. If line 45 is more than line 40, enter -0- . . . . . . ▶	46
Other Taxes	47	Self-employment tax. Attach Schedule SE. Also, see line 25	47
	48	Alternative minimum tax. Attach Form 6251	48
	49	Recapture taxes (see page 26). Check if from **a** ☐ Form 4255 **b** ☐ Form 8611 **c** ☐ Form 8828	49
	50	Social security and Medicare tax on tip income not reported to employer. Attach Form 4137	50
	51	Tax on qualified retirement plans, including IRAs. If required, attach Form 5329 . . .	51
	52	Advance earned income credit payments from Form W-2	52
	53	Add lines 46 through 52. This is your **total tax** . . . . ▶	53
Payments Attach Forms W-2, W-2G, and 1099-R on the front.	54	Federal income tax withheld. If any is from Form(s) 1099, check ▶ ☐	54	
	55	1993 estimated tax payments and amount applied from 1992 return .	55	
	56	**Earned income credit.** Attach Schedule EIC	56	
	57	Amount paid with Form 4868 (extension request) . . .	57	
	58a	Excess social security, Medicare, and RRTA tax withheld (see page 28) .	58a	
	b	Deferral of additional 1993 taxes. Attach Form 8841	58b	
	59	Other payments (see page 28). Check if from **a** ☐ Form 2439 **b** ☐ Form 4136	59	
	60	Add lines 54 through 59. These are your **total payments** . . . . ▶	60
Refund or Amount You Owe	61	If line 60 is more than line 53, subtract line 53 from line 60. This is the amount you **OVERPAID** . ▶	61
	62	Amount of line 61 you want **REFUNDED TO YOU** . . . . ▶	62
	63	Amount of line 61 you want **APPLIED TO YOUR 1994 ESTIMATED TAX** ▶	63	
	64	If line 53 is more than line 60, subtract line 60 from line 53. This is the **AMOUNT YOU OWE.** For details on how to pay, including what to write on your payment, see page 29 . . .	64
	65	Estimated tax penalty (see page 29). Also include on line 64	65	

Sign Here
Keep a copy of this return for your records.

Under penalties of perjury, I declare that I have examined this return and accompanying schedules and statements, and to the best of my knowledge and belief, they are true, correct, and complete. Declaration of preparer (other than taxpayer) is based on all information of which preparer has any knowledge.

▶ Your signature   Date   Your occupation

▶ Spouse's signature. If a joint return, BOTH must sign.   Date   Spouse's occupation

Paid Preparer's Use Only

Preparer's signature ▶   Date   Check if self-employed ☐   Preparer's social security no.

Firm's name (or yours if self-employed) and address   E.I. No.   ZIP code

Portfolio Problem (Harold A. and Maude L.)   Name _____   A-19

SCHEDULES A&B
(Form 1040)
Department of the Treasury
Internal Revenue Service

Schedule A—Itemized Deductions
(Schedule B is on back)
▶ Attach to Form 1040. ▶ See Instructions for Schedules A and B (Form 1040).

OMB No. 1545-0074
1993
Attachment Sequence No. 07

Name(s) shown on Form 1040 | Your social security number

Medical and Dental Expenses	1	Medical and dental expenses (see page A-1)	1	
	2	Enter amount from Form 1040, line 32 . ⌊2⌋		
	3	Multiply line 2 above by 7.5% (.075)	3	
	4	Subtract line 3 from line 1. If zero or less, enter -0-. . . . . ▶		4
Taxes You Paid (See page A-1.)	5	State and local income taxes	5	
	6	Real estate taxes (see page A-2)	6	
	7	Other taxes. List—include personal property taxes ▶	7	
	8	Add lines 5 through 7 . . . . ▶		8
Interest You Paid (See page A-2.) **Note:** Personal interest is not deductible.	9a	Home mortgage interest and points reported to you on Form 1098	9a	
	b	Home mortgage interest not reported to you on Form 1098. If paid to the person from whom you bought the home, see page A-3 and show that person's name, identifying no., and address ▶	9b	
	10	Points not reported to you on Form 1098. See page A-3 for special rules	10	
	11	Investment interest. If required, attach Form 4952. (See page A-3.)	11	
	12	Add lines 9a through 11 . . . . ▶		12
Gifts to Charity (See page A-3.)		**Caution:** *If you made a charitable contribution and received a benefit in return, see page A-3.*		
	13	Contributions by cash or check	13	
	14	Other than by cash or check. If over $500, you **MUST** attach Form 8283	14	
	15	Carryover from prior year	15	
	16	Add lines 13 through 15 . . . . ▶		16
Casualty and Theft Losses	17	Casualty or theft loss(es). Attach Form 4684. (See page A-4.) . . . . . ▶		17
Moving Expenses	18	Moving expenses. Attach Form 3903 or 3903-F. (See page A-4.) . . . . . ▶		18
Job Expenses and Most Other Miscellaneous Deductions (See page A-5 for expenses to deduct here.)	19	Unreimbursed employee expenses—job travel, union dues, job education, etc. If required, you **MUST** attach Form 2106. (See page A-4.) ▶	19	
	20	Other expenses—investment, tax preparation, safe deposit box, etc. List type and amount ▶	20	
	21	Add lines 19 and 20	21	
	22	Enter amount from Form 1040, line 32 . ⌊22⌋		
	23	Multiply line 22 above by 2% (.02)	23	
	24	Subtract line 23 from line 21. If zero or less, enter -0-. . . . . ▶		24
Other Miscellaneous Deductions	25	Other—from list on page A-5. List type and amount ▶ .... ▶		25
Total Itemized Deductions	26	Is the amount on Form 1040, line 32, more than $108,450 (more than $54,225 if married filing separately)? • **NO.** Your deduction is not limited. Add lines 4, 8, 12, 16, 17, 18, 24, and 25 and enter the total here. Also enter on Form 1040, line 34, the **larger** of this amount or your standard deduction. • **YES.** Your deduction may be limited. See page A-5 for the amount to enter. ▶		26

For Paperwork Reduction Act Notice, see Form 1040 instructions.   Cat. No. 11330X   Schedule A (Form 1040) 1993

Copyright © 1994 by Harcourt Brace & Company. All rights reserved.

A-20 Portfolio Problem (Harold A. and Maude L.)

Schedules A&B (Form 1040) 1993 OMB No. 1545-0074 Page **2**

Name(s) shown on Form 1040. Do not enter name and social security number if shown on other side. | Your social security number

Schedule B—Interest and Dividend Income
Attachment Sequence No. 08

Part I Interest Income

(See pages 16 and B-1.)

Note: *If you had over $400 in taxable interest income, you must also complete Part III.*

Interest Income	Amount

1. List name of payer. If any interest is from a seller-financed mortgage and the buyer used the property as a personal residence, see page B-1 and list this interest first. Also show that buyer's social security number and address ▶

Note: If you received a Form 1099-INT, Form 1099-OID, or substitute statement from a brokerage firm, list the firm's name as the payer and enter the total interest shown on that form.

2. Add the amounts on line 1 . . . . **2**
3. Excludable interest on series EE U.S. savings bonds issued after 1989 from Form 8815, line 14. You MUST attach Form 8815 to Form 1040 . . . . **3**
4. Subtract line 3 from line 2. Enter the result here and on Form 1040, line 8a ▶ **4**

Part II Dividend Income

(See pages 17 and B-1.)

Note: *If you had over $400 in gross dividends and/or other distributions on stock, you must also complete Part III.*

Dividend Income	Amount

5. List name of payer. Include gross dividends and/or other distributions on stock here. Any capital gain distributions and nontaxable distributions will be deducted on lines 7 and 8 ▶

Note: If you received a Form 1099-DIV or substitute statement from a brokerage firm, list the firm's name as the payer and enter the total dividends shown on that form.

6. Add the amounts on line 5 . . . . **6**
7. Capital gain distributions. Enter here and on Schedule D* . | **7**
8. Nontaxable distributions. (See the inst. for Form 1040, line 9.) | **8**
9. Add lines 7 and 8 . . . . **9**
10. Subtract line 9 from line 6. Enter the result here and on Form 1040, line 9 . ▶ **10**

*If you received capital gain distributions but do not need Schedule D to report any other gains or losses, see the instructions for Form 1040, lines 13 and 14.

Part III Foreign Accounts and Trusts

(See page B-2.)

If you had over $400 of interest or dividends OR had a foreign account or were a grantor of, or a transferor to, a foreign trust, you must complete this part. | Yes | No

11a. At any time during 1993, did you have an interest in or a signature or other authority over a financial account in a foreign country, such as a bank account, securities account, or other financial account? See page B-2 for exceptions and filing requirements for Form TD F 90-22.1 . . . .

  b. If "Yes," enter the name of the foreign country ▶ ....

12. Were you the grantor of, or transferor to, a foreign trust that existed during 1993, whether or not you have any beneficial interest in it? If "Yes," you may have to file Form 3520, 3520-A, or 926 .

For Paperwork Reduction Act Notice, see Form 1040 instructions. Schedule B (Form 1040) 1993

Copyright © 1994 by Harcourt Brace & Company. All rights reserved.

Portfolio Problem (Harold A. and Maude L.)   Name _____   A-21

SCHEDULE C
(Form 1040)

Department of the Treasury
Internal Revenue Service

Profit or Loss From Business
(Sole Proprietorship)
▶ Partnerships, joint ventures, etc., must file Form 1065.
▶ Attach to Form 1040 or Form 1041.   ▶ See Instructions for Schedule C (Form 1040).

OMB No. 1545-0074

1993

Attachment Sequence No. 09

Name of proprietor | Social security number (SSN)

A	Principal business or profession, including product or service (see page C-1)	B Enter principal business code (see page C-6) ▶
C	Business name. If no separate business name, leave blank.	D Employer ID number (EIN), if any
E	Business address (including suite or room no.) ▶ .... City, town or post office, state, and ZIP code	
F	Accounting method: (1) ☐ Cash (2) ☐ Accrual (3) ☐ Other (specify) ▶	
G	Method(s) used to value closing inventory: (1) ☐ Cost (2) ☐ Lower of cost or market (3) ☐ Other (attach explanation) (4) ☐ Does not apply (if checked, skip line H)	Yes / No
H	Was there any change in determining quantities, costs, or valuations between opening and closing inventory? If "Yes," attach explanation	
I	Did you "materially participate" in the operation of this business during 1993? If "No," see page C-2 for limit on losses.	
J	If you started or acquired this business during 1993, check here . . . . ▶ ☐	

Part I Income

1	Gross receipts or sales. **Caution:** *If this income was reported to you on Form W-2 and the "Statutory employee" box on that form was checked, see page C-2 and check here* . . . . ▶ ☐	1	
2	Returns and allowances	2	
3	Subtract line 2 from line 1	3	
4	Cost of goods sold (from line 40 on page 2)	4	
5	**Gross profit.** Subtract line 4 from line 3	5	
6	Other income, including Federal and state gasoline or fuel tax credit or refund (see page C-2) . . ▶	6	
7	**Gross income.** Add lines 5 and 6	7	

Part II Expenses. Caution: *Do not enter expenses for business use of your home on lines 8–27. Instead, see line 30.*

8	Advertising	8		19	Pension and profit-sharing plans	19
9	Bad debts from sales or services (see page C-3)	9		20	Rent or lease (see page C-4):	
				a	Vehicles, machinery, and equipment	20a
10	Car and truck expenses (see page C-3)	10		b	Other business property	20b
				21	Repairs and maintenance .	21
11	Commissions and fees .	11		22	Supplies (not included in Part III)	22
12	Depletion	12		23	Taxes and licenses . . .	23
13	Depreciation and section 179 expense deduction (not included in Part III) (see page C-3)	13		24	Travel, meals, and entertainment:	
				a	Travel	24a
				b	Meals and entertainment .	
14	Employee benefit programs (other than on line 19) . .	14		c	Enter 20% of line 24b subject to limitations (see page C-4)	
15	Insurance (other than health) .	15				
16	Interest:					
a	Mortgage (paid to banks, etc.)	16a		d	Subtract line 24c from line 24b	24d
b	Other	16b		25	Utilities	25
17	Legal and professional services	17		26	Wages (less jobs credit) .	26
				27	Other expenses (from line 46 on page 2)	
18	Office expense	18				27

28	**Total expenses** before expenses for business use of home. Add lines 8 through 27 in columns . . ▶	28
29	Tentative profit (loss). Subtract line 28 from line 7	29
30	Expenses for business use of your home. Attach **Form 8829**	30
31	**Net profit or (loss).** Subtract line 30 from line 29.	
	• If a profit, enter on **Form 1040, line 12,** and ALSO on **Schedule SE, line 2** (statutory employees, see page C-5). Fiduciaries, enter on Form 1041, line 3.	31
	• If a loss, you MUST go on to line 32.	
32	If you have a loss, check the box that describes your investment in this activity (see page C-5).	
	• If you checked 32a, enter the loss on **Form 1040, line 12,** and ALSO on **Schedule SE, line 2** (statutory employees, see page C-5). Fiduciaries, enter on Form 1041, line 3.	32a ☐ All investment is at risk. 32b ☐ Some investment is not at risk.
	• If you checked 32b, you MUST attach **Form 6198.**	

For Paperwork Reduction Act Notice, see Form 1040 instructions.   Cat. No. 11334P   Schedule C (Form 1040) 1993

Copyright © 1994 by Harcourt Brace & Company. All rights reserved.

Schedule C (Form 1040) 1993   Page **2**

Part III   Cost of Goods Sold (see page C-5)

33	Inventory at beginning of year. If different from last year's closing inventory, attach explanation	33	
34	Purchases less cost of items withdrawn for personal use	34	
35	Cost of labor. Do not include salary paid to yourself	35	
36	Materials and supplies	36	
37	Other costs	37	
38	Add lines 33 through 37	38	
39	Inventory at end of year	39	
40	**Cost of goods sold.** Subtract line 39 from line 38. Enter the result here and on page 1, line 4	40	

Part IV   Information on Your Vehicle. Complete this part **ONLY** if you are claiming car or truck expenses on line 10 and are not required to file Form 4562 for this business.

41   When did you place your vehicle in service for business purposes? (month, day, year) ▶ ..../......./........

42   Of the total number of miles you drove your vehicle during 1993, enter the number of miles you used your vehicle for:

    a Business .... **b** Commuting .... **c** Other ....

43   Do you (or your spouse) have another vehicle available for personal use? . . . . ☐ Yes   ☐ No

44   Was your vehicle available for use during off-duty hours? . . . . ☐ Yes   ☐ No

45a   Do you have evidence to support your deduction? . . . . ☐ Yes   ☐ No
   b   If "Yes," is the evidence written? . . . . ☐ Yes   ☐ No

Part V   Other Expenses. List below business expenses not included on lines 8–26 or line 30.

....		
....		
....		
....		
....		
....		
....		
....		
46 **Total other expenses.** Enter here and on page 1, line 27	46	

Portfolio Problem (Harold A. and Maude L.) Name _____ A-23

SCHEDULE D (Form 1040)
Department of the Treasury
Internal Revenue Service

Capital Gains and Losses

▶ Attach to Form 1040. ▶ See Instructions for Schedule D (Form 1040).
▶ Use lines 20 and 22 for more space to list transactions for lines 1 and 9.

OMB No. 1545-0074
1993
Attachment Sequence No. **12**

Name(s) shown on Form 1040

Your social security number

Part I — Short-Term Capital Gains and Losses—Assets Held One Year or Less

(a) Description of property (Example: 100 sh. XYZ Co.)	(b) Date acquired (Mo., day, yr.)	(c) Date sold (Mo., day, yr.)	(d) Sales price (see page D-3)	(e) Cost or other basis (see page D-3)	(f) LOSS If (e) is more than (d), subtract (d) from (e)	(g) GAIN If (d) is more than (e), subtract (e) from (d)
1						

2 Enter your short-term totals, if any, from line 21 . . . . **2**

3 **Total short-term sales price amounts.** Add column (d) of lines 1 and 2 . . . **3**

4 Short-term gain from Forms 2119 and 6252, and short-term gain or (loss) from Forms 4684, 6781, and 8824 . . . . **4**

5 Net short-term gain or (loss) from partnerships, S corporations, and fiduciaries from Schedule(s) K-1 . . . . **5**

6 Short-term capital loss carryover from 1992 Schedule D, line 38 . . . . . **6**

7 Add lines 1, 2, and 4 through 6, in columns (f) and (g) . . . . **7** ( )

8 **Net short-term capital gain or (loss).** Combine columns (f) and (g) of line 7 . . . . . . **8**

Part II — Long-Term Capital Gains and Losses—Assets Held More Than One Year

9						

10 Enter your long-term totals, if any, from line 23 . . . . **10**

11 **Total long-term sales price amounts.** Add column (d) of lines 9 and 10 . . . **11**

12 Gain from Form 4797; long-term gain from Forms 2119, 2439, and 6252; and long-term gain or (loss) from Forms 4684, 6781, and 8824 . . . . **12**

13 Net long-term gain or (loss) from partnerships, S corporations, and fiduciaries from Schedule(s) K-1 . . . . **13**

14 Capital gain distributions **14**

15 Long-term capital loss carryover from 1992 Schedule D, line 45 . . . . **15**

16 Add lines 9, 10, and 12 through 15, in columns (f) and (g) . . . . . . **16** ( )

17 **Net long-term capital gain or (loss).** Combine columns (f) and (g) of line 16 . . . . . . **17**

Part III — Summary of Parts I and II

18 Combine lines 8 and 17. If a loss, go to line 19. If a gain, enter the gain on Form 1040, line 13.
Note: *If both lines 17 and 18 are gains, see the Schedule D Tax Worksheet on page D-4* . . **18**

19 If line 18 is a (loss), enter here and as a (loss) on Form 1040, line 13, the **smaller** of these losses:
  a The (loss) on line 18; **or**
  b ($3,000) or, if married filing separately, ($1,500) . . . . **19** ( )
  Note: *See the Capital Loss Carryover Worksheet on page D-4 if the loss on line 18 exceeds the loss on line 19 or if Form 1040, line 35, is a loss.*

For Paperwork Reduction Act Notice, see Form 1040 instructions. Cat. No. 11338H Schedule D (Form 1040) 1993

Copyright © 1994 by Harcourt Brace & Company. All rights reserved.

Schedule D (Form 1040) 1993 — Attachment Sequence No. 12 — Page 2

Name(s) shown on Form 1040. Do not enter name and social security number if shown on other side.

Your social security number

Part IV — Short-Term Capital Gains and Losses—Assets Held One Year or Less (Continuation of Part I)

(a) Description of property (Example: 100 sh. XYZ Co.)	(b) Date acquired (Mo., day, yr.)	(c) Date sold (Mo., day, yr.)	(d) Sales price (see page D-3)	(e) Cost or other basis (see page D-3)	(f) LOSS If (e) is more than (d), subtract (d) from (e)	(g) GAIN If (d) is more than (e), subtract (e) from (d)
20						

21 Short-term totals. Add columns (d), (f), and (g) of line 20. Enter here and on line 2. | 21 | | | ▨ | | |

Part V — Long-Term Capital Gains and Losses—Assets Held More Than One Year (Continuation of Part II)

(a)	(b)	(c)	(d)	(e)	(f)	(g)
22						

23 Long-term totals. Add columns (d), (f), and (g) of line 22. Enter here and on line 10. | 23 | | | ▨ | | |

Portfolio Problem (Harold A. and Maude L.)   Name _____   A-25

SCHEDULE SE (Form 1040) Department of the Treasury Internal Revenue Service	Self-Employment Tax ▶ See Instructions for Schedule SE (Form 1040). ▶ Attach to Form 1040.	OMB No. 1545-0074 **1993** Attachment Sequence No. 17
Name of person with **self-employment** income (as shown on Form 1040)	Social security number of person with **self-employment** income ▶	

Who Must File Schedule SE
You must file Schedule SE if:
- Your wages (and tips) subject to social security AND Medicare tax (or railroad retirement tax) were less than $135,000; **AND**
- Your net earnings from self-employment from other than church employee income (line 4 of Short Schedule SE or line 4c of Long Schedule SE) were $400 or more; **OR**
- You had church employee income of $108.28 or more. Income from services you performed as a minister or a member of a religious order **is not** church employee income. See page SE-1.

Note: Even if you have a loss or a small amount of income from self-employment, it may be to your benefit to file Schedule SE and use either "optional method" in Part II of Long Schedule SE. See page SE-3.

Exception. If your only self-employment income was from earnings as a minister, member of a religious order, or Christian Science practitioner, **AND** you filed Form 4361 and received IRS approval not to be taxed on those earnings, **DO NOT** file Schedule SE. Instead, write "Exempt–Form 4361" on Form 1040, line 47.

May I Use Short Schedule SE or MUST I Use Long Schedule SE?

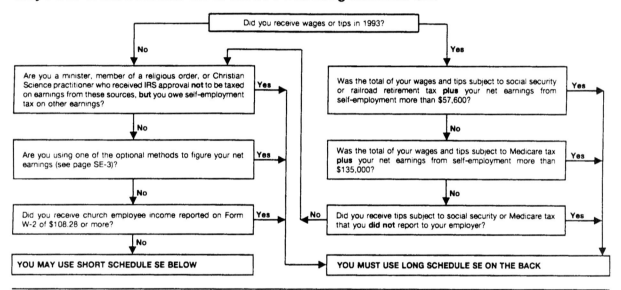

Section A—Short Schedule SE. Caution: *Read above to see if you can use Short Schedule SE.*

1	Net farm profit or (loss) from Schedule F, line 36, and farm partnerships, Schedule K-1 (Form 1065), line 15a	1
2	Net profit or (loss) from Schedule C, line 31; Schedule C-EZ, line 3; and Schedule K-1 (Form 1065), line 15a (other than farming). Ministers and members of religious orders see page SE-1 for amounts to report on this line. See page SE-2 for other income to report	2
3	Combine lines 1 and 2	3
4	**Net earnings from self-employment.** Multiply line 3 by 92.35% (.9235). If less than $400, **do not** file this schedule; you do not owe self-employment tax . . . . ▶	4
5	**Self-employment tax.** If the amount on line 4 is: • $57,600 or less, multiply line 4 by 15.3% (.153) and enter the result. • More than $57,600 but less than $135,000, multiply the amount in excess of $57,600 by 2.9% (.029). Then, add $8,812.80 to the result and enter the total. • $135,000 or more, enter $11,057.40. Also enter on **Form 1040, line 47. (Important:** You are allowed a deduction for **one-half** of this amount. Multiply line 5 by 50% (.5) and enter the result on **Form 1040, line 25.)**	5

For Paperwork Reduction Act Notice, see Form 1040 instructions.   Cat. No. 11358Z   Schedule SE (Form 1040) 1993

Copyright © 1994 by Harcourt Brace & Company. All rights reserved.

A-26 Portfolio Problem (Harold A. and Maude L.)

Schedule SE (Form 1040) 1993 — Attachment Sequence No. **17** — Page **2**

Name of person with **self-employment** income (as shown on Form 1040) | Social security number of person with **self-employment** income ▶

Section B—Long Schedule SE

Part I — Self-Employment Tax

Note: *If your only income subject to self-employment tax is church employee income, skip lines 1 through 4b. Enter -0- on line 4c and go to line 5a. Income from services you performed as a minister or a member of a religious order* **is not** *church employee income. See page SE-1.*

A If you are a minister, member of a religious order, or Christian Science practitioner **AND** you filed Form 4361, but you had $400 or more of **other** net earnings from self-employment, check here and continue with Part I . . . . . ▶ ☐

1. Net farm profit or (loss) from Schedule F, line 36, and farm partnerships, Schedule K-1 (Form 1065), line 15a. **Note:** *Skip this line if you use the farm optional method. See page SE-3* . . | **1** |
2. Net profit or (loss) from Schedule C, line 31; Schedule C-EZ, line 3; and Schedule K-1 (Form 1065), line 15a (other than farming). Ministers and members of religious orders see page SE-1 for amounts to report on this line. See page SE-2 for other income to report. **Note:** *Skip this line if you use the nonfarm optional method. See page SE-3* . . . . | **2** |
3. Combine lines 1 and 2 . . . . | **3** |
4a. If line 3 is more than zero, multiply line 3 by 92.35% (.9235). Otherwise, enter amount from line 3 | **4a** |
  b. If you elected one or both of the optional methods, enter the total of lines 17 and 19 here . . | **4b** |
  c. Combine lines 4a and 4b. If less than $400, **do not** file this schedule; you do not owe self-employment tax. **Exception.** If less than $400 and you had church employee income, enter -0- and continue . ▶ | **4c** |
5a. Enter your church employee income from Form W-2. **Caution:** *See page SE-1 for definition of church employee income* . . . . | **5a** |
  b. Multiply line 5a by 92.35% (.9235). If less than $100, enter -0- . . . . | **5b** |
6. **Net earnings from self-employment.** Add lines 4c and 5b . . . . | **6** |
7. Maximum amount of combined wages and self-employment earnings subject to social security tax or the 6.2% portion of the 7.65% railroad retirement (tier 1) tax for 1993 . . . . | **7** | 57,600 | 00
8a. Total social security wages and tips (from Form(s) W-2) and railroad retirement (tier 1) compensation . . . . | **8a** |
  b. Unreported tips subject to social security tax (from Form 4137, line 9) | **8b** |
  c. Add lines 8a and 8b . . . . | **8c** |
9. Subtract line 8c from line 7. If zero or less, enter -0- here and on line 10 and go to line 12a ▶ | **9** |
10. Multiply the **smaller** of line 6 or line 9 by 12.4% (.124) . . . . | **10** |
11. Maximum amount of combined wages and self-employment earnings subject to Medicare tax or the 1.45% portion of the 7.65% railroad retirement (tier 1) tax for 1993 . . . . | **11** | 135,000 | 00
12a. Total Medicare wages and tips (from Form(s) W-2) and railroad retirement (tier 1) compensation . . . . | **12a** |
  b. Unreported tips subject to Medicare tax (from Form 4137, line 14) . | **12b** |
  c. Add lines 12a and 12b . . . . | **12c** |
13. Subtract line 12c from line 11. If zero or less, enter -0- here and on line 14 and go to line 15 . | **13** |
14. Multiply the **smaller** of line 6 or line 13 by 2.9% (.029) . . . . | **14** |
15. **Self-employment tax.** Add lines 10 and 14. Enter here and on **Form 1040, line 47. (Important:** You are allowed a deduction for **one-half** of this amount. Multiply line 15 by 50% (.5) and enter the result on **Form 1040, line 25.)** . . . . | **15** |

Part II — Optional Methods To Figure Net Earnings (See page SE-3.)

Farm Optional Method. You may use this method **only** if **(a)** Your gross farm income[1] was not more than $2,400 **or (b)** Your gross farm income[1] was more than $2,400 and your net farm profits[2] were less than $1,733.

16. Maximum income for optional methods . . . . | **16** | 1,600 | 00
17. Enter the **smaller** of: two-thirds (⅔) of gross farm income[1] (not less than zero) **or** $1,600. Also, include this amount on line 4b above . . . . | **17** |

Nonfarm Optional Method. You may use this method **only** if **(a)** Your net nonfarm profits[3] were less than $1,733 and also less than 72.189% of your gross nonfarm income,[4] **and (b)** You had net earnings from self-employment of at least $400 in 2 of the prior 3 years. **Caution:** *You may use this method no more than five times.*

18. Subtract line 17 from line 16 . . . . | **18** |
19. Enter the **smaller** of: two-thirds (⅔) of gross nonfarm income[4] (not less than zero) **or** the amount on line 18. Also, include this amount on line 4b above . . . . | **19** |

[1] From Schedule F, line 11, and Schedule K-1 (Form 1065), line 15b.
[2] From Schedule F, line 36, and Schedule K-1 (Form 1065), line 15a.
[3] From Schedule C, line 31; Schedule C-EZ, line 3; and Schedule K-1 (Form 1065), line 15a.
[4] From Schedule C, line 7; Schedule C-EZ, line 1; and Schedule K-1 (Form 1065), line 15c.

Copyright © 1994 by Harcourt Brace & Company. All rights reserved.

Portfolio Problem (Harold A. and Maude L.) Name _____ A-27

Form 2106
Department of the Treasury
Internal Revenue Service

Employee Business Expenses

▶ See separate instructions.

▶ Attach to Form 1040.

OMB No 1545-0139

1993

Attachment Sequence No. 54

Your name	Social security number	Occupation in which expenses were incurred

Part I Employee Business Expenses and Reimbursements

STEP 1 Enter Your Expenses

		Column A Other Than Meals and Entertainment	Column B Meals and Entertainment
1	Vehicle expense from line 22 or line 29		////
2	Parking fees, tolls, and transportation, including train, bus, etc., that **did not** involve overnight travel		////
3	Travel expense while away from home overnight, including lodging, airplane, car rental, etc. **Do not** include meals and entertainment		////
4	Business expenses not included on lines 1 through 3. **Do not** include meals and entertainment		////
5	Meals and entertainment expenses (see instructions)	////	
6	**Total expenses.** In Column A, add lines 1 through 4 and enter the result. In Column B, enter the amount from line 5		

Note: *If you were not reimbursed for any expenses in Step 1, skip line 7 and enter the amount from line 6 on line 8.*

STEP 2 Enter Amounts Your Employer Gave You for Expenses Listed in STEP 1

7	Enter amounts your employer gave you that were **not** reported to you in box 1 of Form W-2. Include any amount reported under code "L" in box 13 of your Form W-2 (see instructions) . . .		

STEP 3 Figure Expenses To Deduct on Schedule A (Form 1040)

8	Subtract line 7 from line 6		
	Note: *If both columns of line 8 are zero, stop here. If Column A is less than zero, report the amount as income on Form 1040, line 7, and enter -0- on line 10, Column A.*	////	////
9	Enter 20% (.20) of line 8, Column B	////	
10	In Column A, enter the amount from line 8. In Column B, subtract line 9 from line 8		
11	Add the amounts on line 10 of both columns and enter the total here. **Also, enter the total on Schedule A (Form 1040), line 19.** (Qualified performing artists and individuals with disabilities, see the instructions for special rules on where to enter the total.) . . . . ▶		

For Paperwork Reduction Act Notice, see instructions.   Cat. No. 11700N   Form **2106** (1993)

Copyright © 1994 by Harcourt Brace & Company. All rights reserved.

Form 2106 (1993) Page 2

Part II — Vehicle Expenses (See instructions to find out which sections to complete.)

Section A.—General Information

		(a) Vehicle 1	(b) Vehicle 2
12	Enter the date vehicle was placed in service	/ /	/ /
13	Total miles vehicle was driven during 1993	miles	miles
14	Business miles included on line 13	miles	miles
15	Percent of business use. Divide line 14 by line 13	%	%
16	Average daily round trip commuting distance	miles	miles
17	Commuting miles included on line 13	miles	miles
18	Other personal miles. Add lines 14 and 17 and subtract the total from line 13	miles	miles

19 Do you (or your spouse) have another vehicle available for personal purposes? ☐ Yes ☐ No

20 If your employer provided you with a vehicle, is personal use during off duty hours permitted? ☐ Yes ☐ No ☐ Not applicable

21a Do you have evidence to support your deduction? ☐ Yes ☐ No

21b If "Yes," is the evidence written? ☐ Yes ☐ No

Section B.—Standard Mileage Rate (Use this section only if you own the vehicle.)

22 Multiply line 14 by 28¢ (.28). Enter the result here and on line 1. (Rural mail carriers, see instructions.) 22

Section C.—Actual Expenses

		(a) Vehicle 1	(b) Vehicle 2
23	Gasoline, oil, repairs, vehicle insurance, etc.		
24a	Vehicle rentals		
b	Inclusion amount (see instructions)		
c	Subtract line 24b from line 24a		
25	Value of employer-provided vehicle (applies only if 100% of annual lease value was included on Form W-2—see instructions)		
26	Add lines 23, 24c, and 25		
27	Multiply line 26 by the percentage on line 15		
28	Depreciation. Enter amount from line 38 below		
29	Add lines 27 and 28. Enter total here and on line 1		

Section D.—Depreciation of Vehicles (Use this section only if you own the vehicle.)

		(a) Vehicle 1	(b) Vehicle 2
30	Enter cost or other basis (see instructions)		
31	Enter amount of section 179 deduction (see instructions)		
32	Multiply line 30 by line 15 (see instructions if you elected the section 179 deduction)		
33	Enter depreciation method and percentage (see instructions)		
34	Multiply line 32 by the percentage on line 33 (see instructions)		
35	Add lines 31 and 34		
36	Enter the limitation amount from the table in the line 36 instructions		
37	Multiply line 36 by the percentage on line 15		
38	Enter the smaller of line 35 or line 37. Also, enter this amount on line 28 above		

Copyright © 1994 by Harcourt Brace & Company. All rights reserved.

Portfolio Problem (Harold A. and Maude L.)   Name _____   A-29

Form 2119 — Sale of Your Home

Form **2119**
Department of the Treasury
Internal Revenue Service

▶ Attach to Form 1040 for year of sale.
▶ See separate instructions.   ▶ Please print or type.

OMB No. 1545-0072
1993
Attachment Sequence No. **20**

Your first name and initial. If a joint return, also give spouse's name and initial.   Last name   Your social security number

Fill in Your Address Only If You Are Filing This Form by Itself and Not With Your Tax Return

Present address (no., street, and apt. no., rural route, or P.O. box no. if mail is not delivered to street address)   Spouse's social security number

City, town or post office, state, and ZIP code

Part I — General Information

1. Date your former main home was sold (month, day, year) ▶ **1** ___/___/___
2. Have you bought or built a new main home? ☐ Yes ☐ No
3. Is or was any part of either main home rented out or used for business? If "Yes," see instructions ☐ Yes ☐ No

Part II — Gain on Sale—Do not include amounts you deduct as moving expenses.

4. Selling price of home. Do not include personal property items you sold with your home   **4**
5. Expense of sale (see instructions)   **5**
6. Amount realized. Subtract line 5 from line 4   **6**
7. Adjusted basis of home sold (see instructions)   **7**
8. **Gain on sale.** Subtract line 7 from line 6   **8**

Is line 8 more than zero?
— Yes ▶ If line 2 is "Yes," you **must** go to Part III or Part IV, whichever applies. If line 2 is "No," go to line 9.
— No ▶ **Stop** and attach this form to your return.

9. If you haven't replaced your home, do you plan to do so within the **replacement period** (see instructions)? ☐ Yes ☐ No
   • If line 9 is "Yes," stop here, attach this form to your return, and see **Additional Filing Requirements** in the instructions.
   • If line 9 is "No," you **must** go to Part III or Part IV, whichever applies.

Part III — One-Time Exclusion of Gain for People Age 55 or Older
By completing this part, you are electing to take the one-time exclusion (see instructions). If you are not electing to take the exclusion, go to Part IV now.

10. Who was age 55 or older on the date of sale?   ☐ You ☐ Your spouse ☐ Both of you
11. Did the person who was age 55 or older own and use the property as his or her main home for a total of at least 3 years (except for short absences) of the 5-year period before the sale? If "No," go to Part IV now   ☐ Yes ☐ No
12. At the time of sale, who owned the home?   ☐ You ☐ Your spouse ☐ Both of you
13. Social security number of spouse at the time of sale if you had a different spouse from the one above. If you were not married at the time of sale, enter "None" ▶ **13**
14. **Exclusion.** Enter the **smaller** of line 8 or $125,000 ($62,500 if married filing separate return). Then, go to line 15   **14**

Part IV — Adjusted Sales Price, Taxable Gain, and Adjusted Basis of New Home

15. If line 14 is blank, enter the amount from line 8. Otherwise, subtract line 14 from line 8   **15**
    • If line 15 is zero, stop and attach this form to your return.
    • If line 15 is more than zero and line 2 is "Yes," go to line 16 now.
    • If you are reporting this sale on the installment method, stop and see the instructions.
    • All others, stop and **enter the amount from line 15 on Schedule D, col. (g), line 4 or line 12.**
16. Fixing-up expenses (see instructions for time limits)   **16**
17. If line 14 is blank, enter amount from line 16. Otherwise, add lines 14 and 16   **17**
18. **Adjusted sales price.** Subtract line 17 from line 6   **18**
19a. Date you moved into new home (month, day, year) ▶ ___/___/___ **b** Cost of new home   **19b**
20. Subtract line 19b from line 18. If zero or less, enter -0-   **20**
21. **Taxable gain.** Enter the **smaller** of line 15 or line 20   **21**
    • If line 21 is zero, go to line 22 and attach this form to your return.
    • If you are reporting this sale on the installment method, see the line 15 instructions and go to line 22.
    • All others, **enter the amount from line 21 on Schedule D, col. (g), line 4 or line 12,** and go to line 22.
22. **Postponed gain.** Subtract line 21 from line 15   **22**
23. **Adjusted basis of new home.** Subtract line 22 from line 19b   **23**

Sign Here Only If You Are Filing This Form by Itself and Not With Your Tax Return

Under penalties of perjury, I declare that I have examined this form, including attachments, and to the best of my knowledge and belief, it is true, correct, and complete.

▶ Your signature _____   Date _____
▶ Spouse's signature _____   Date _____
If a joint return, both must sign.

For Paperwork Reduction Act Notice, see separate instructions.   Cat. No. 11710J   Form **2119** (1993)

✺ Printed on recycled paper

Copyright © 1994 by Harcourt Brace & Company. All rights reserved.

A-30   Portfolio Problem (Harold A. and Maude L.)

Form **2441**
Department of the Treasury
Internal Revenue Service

Child and Dependent Care Expenses

▶ Attach to Form 1040.
▶ See separate instructions.

OMB No. 1545-0068
1993
Attachment Sequence No. **21**

Name(s) shown on Form 1040 | Your social security number

You need to understand the following terms to complete this form: **Dependent Care Benefits, Earned Income, Qualified Expenses,** and **Qualifying Person(s).** See **Important Terms** on page 1 of the Form 2441 instructions. Also, if you had a child born in 1993 and line 32 of Form 1040 is less than $23,050, see **A Change To Note** on page 2 of the instructions.

Part I — Persons or Organizations Who Provided the Care—You must complete this part.
(If you need more space, use the bottom of page 2.)

1	(a) Care provider's name	(b) Address (number, street, apt. no., city, state, and ZIP code)	(c) Identifying number (SSN or EIN)	(d) Amount paid (see instructions)

2 Add the amounts in column (d) of line 1 . . . . **2**

3 Enter the number of **qualifying persons** cared for in 1993 . . . . ▶

Did you receive **dependent care benefits?**
— NO ⟶ Complete only Part II below.
— YES ⟶ Complete Part III on the back now.

Part II — Credit for Child and Dependent Care Expenses

4 Enter the amount of **qualified expenses** you incurred and paid in 1993. DO NOT enter more than $2,400 for one qualifying person or $4,800 for two or more persons. If you completed Part III, enter the amount from line 25 . . . . **4**

5 Enter YOUR **earned income** **5**

6 If married filing a joint return, enter YOUR SPOUSE'S earned income (if student or disabled, see instructions); **all others,** enter the amount from line 5 . . . . **6**

7 Enter the **smallest** of line 4, 5, or 6 . . . . **7**

8 Enter the amount from Form 1040, line 32 . . . . **8**

9 Enter on line 9 the decimal amount shown below that applies to the amount on line 8

If line 8 is—		Decimal amount is	If line 8 is—		Decimal amount is
Over	But not over		Over	But not over	
$0	10,000	.30	$20,000	22,000	.24
10,000	12,000	.29	22,000	24,000	.23
12,000	14,000	.28	24,000	26,000	.22
14,000	16,000	.27	26,000	28,000	.21
16,000	18,000	.26	28,000	No limit	.20
18,000	20,000	.25			

9   × .

10 Multiply **line 7** by the decimal amount on line 9. Enter the result. Then, see the instructions for the amount of credit to enter on Form 1040, line 41 . . . . **10**

Caution: If you paid $50 or more in a calendar quarter to a person who worked in your home, you must file an employment tax return. Get **Form 942** for details.

For Paperwork Reduction Act Notice, see separate instructions.   Cat. No. 11862M   Form **2441** (1993)

Copyright © 1994 by Harcourt Brace & Company. All rights reserved.

Portfolio Problem (Harold A. and Maude L.)   Name _____   A-31

Form 3903
Department of the Treasury
Internal Revenue Service

Moving Expenses
▶ Attach to Form 1040.
▶ See separate instructions.

OMB No. 1545-0062
1993
Attachment Sequence No. 62

Name(s) shown on Form 1040 | Your social security number

Caution: *If you are a member of the armed forces, see the instructions before completing this form.*

1 Enter the number of miles from your **old home** to your **new workplace** 1
2 Enter the number of miles from your **old home** to your **old workplace** 2
3 Subtract line 2 from line 1. Enter the result but not less than zero. . . . . ▶ 3

If line 3 is 35 or more miles, complete the rest of this form. Also, see **Time Test** in the instructions. If line 3 is less than 35 miles, you may not deduct your moving expenses.

Part I   Moving Expenses

Note: *Any payments your employer made for any part of your move (including the value of any services furnished in kind) should be included on your W-2 form. Report that amount on **Form 1040, line 7**. See **Reimbursements** in the instructions.*

Section A—Transportation of Household Goods

4 Transportation and storage for household goods and personal effects 4

Section B—Expenses of Moving From Old To New Home

5 Travel and lodging **not** including meals 5
6 Total meals 6
7 Multiply line 6 by 80% (.80) 7
8 Add lines 5 and 7 8

Section C—Pre-move Househunting Expenses and Temporary Quarters
(for any 30 days in a row after getting your job)

9 Pre-move travel and lodging **not** including meals 9
10 Temporary quarters expenses **not** including meals 10
11 Total meal expenses for both pre-move househunting and temporary quarters 11
12 Multiply line 11 by 80% (.80) 12
13 Add lines 9, 10, and 12 13

Section D—Qualified Real Estate Expenses

14 Expenses of (check one) **a** ☐ selling or exchanging your old home, or ⎫
                            b ☐ if renting, settling an unexpired lease.   ⎭ 14
15 Expenses of (check one) **a** ☐ buying your new home, or ⎫
                            b ☐ if renting, getting a new lease. ⎭ 15

Part II   Dollar Limits and Moving Expense Deduction

Note: *If you and your spouse moved to separate homes, see the instructions.*

16 Enter the **smaller** of:
   • The amount on line 13, or
   • $1,500 ($750 if married filing a separate return and at the end of ⎫ . . 16
     1993 you lived with your spouse who also started work in 1993). ⎭
17 Add lines 14, 15, and 16 17
18 Enter the **smaller** of:
   • The amount on line 17, or
   • $3,000 ($1,500 if married filing a separate return and at the end ⎫ 18
     of 1993 you lived with your spouse who also started work in 1993). ⎭
19 Add lines 4, 8, and 18. Enter the total here and on Schedule A, line 18. This is your **moving expense deduction** . . . . ▶ 19

For Paperwork Reduction Act Notice, see separate instructions.   Cat. No. 12490K   Form **3903** (1993)

Printed on recycled paper

Copyright © 1994 by Harcourt Brace & Company. All rights reserved.

Portfolio Problem (Harold A. and Maude L.) Name _____ A-33

Form **4562**	**Depreciation and Amortization**	OMB No. 1545-0172
Department of the Treasury Internal Revenue Service	(Including Information on Listed Property) ▶ See separate instructions. ▶ Attach this form to your return.	**1993** Attachment Sequence No. **67**

Name(s) shown on return | Identifying number

Business or activity to which this form relates

Part I — Election To Expense Certain Tangible Property (Section 179) (Note: *If you have any "Listed Property," complete Part V before you complete Part I.*)

1	Maximum dollar limitation (If an enterprise zone business, see instructions.)	1	$17,500
2	Total cost of section 179 property placed in service during the tax year (see instructions)	2	
3	Threshold cost of section 179 property before reduction in limitation	3	$200,000
4	Reduction in limitation. Subtract line 3 from line 2, but do not enter less than -0-	4	
5	Dollar limitation for tax year. Subtract line 4 from line 1, but do not enter less than -0-. (If married filing separately, see instructions.)	5	

	(a) Description of property	(b) Cost	(c) Elected cost
6			

7	Listed property. Enter amount from line 26.	7	
8	Total elected cost of section 179 property. Add amounts in column (c), lines 6 and 7	8	
9	Tentative deduction. Enter the smaller of line 5 or line 8	9	
10	Carryover of disallowed deduction from 1992 (see instructions)	10	
11	Taxable income limitation. Enter the smaller of taxable income or line 5 (see instructions)	11	
12	Section 179 expense deduction. Add lines 9 and 10, but do not enter more than line 11	12	
13	Carryover of disallowed deduction to 1994. Add lines 9 and 10, less line 12 ▶	13	

Note: *Do not use Part II or Part III below for listed property (automobiles, certain other vehicles, cellular telephones, certain computers, or property used for entertainment, recreation, or amusement). Instead, use Part V for listed property.*

Part II — MACRS Depreciation For Assets Placed in Service ONLY During Your 1993 Tax Year (Do Not Include Listed Property)

(a) Classification of property	(b) Month and year placed in service	(c) Basis for depreciation (business/investment use only—see instructions)	(d) Recovery period	(e) Convention	(f) Method	(g) Depreciation deduction
14 General Depreciation System (GDS) (see instructions):						
a 3-year property						
b 5-year property						
c 7-year property						
d 10-year property						
e 15-year property						
f 20-year property						
g Residential rental property			27.5 yrs.	MM	S/L	
			27.5 yrs.	MM	S/L	
h Nonresidential real property				MM	S/L	
				MM	S/L	
15 Alternative Depreciation System (ADS) (see instructions):						
a Class life					S/L	
b 12-year			12 yrs.		S/L	
c 40-year			40 yrs.	MM	S/L	

Part III — Other Depreciation (Do Not Include Listed Property)

16	GDS and ADS deductions for assets placed in service in tax years beginning before 1993 (see instructions)	16	
17	Property subject to section 168(f)(1) election (see instructions)	17	
18	ACRS and other depreciation (see instructions)	18	

Part IV — Summary

19	Listed property. Enter amount from line 25.	19	
20	Total. Add deductions on line 12, lines 14 and 15 in column (g), and lines 16 through 19. Enter here and on the appropriate lines of your return. (Partnerships and S corporations—see instructions)	20	
21	For assets shown above and placed in service during the current year, enter the portion of the basis attributable to section 263A costs (see instructions)	21	

For Paperwork Reduction Act Notice, see page 1 of the separate instructions.   Cat. No. 12906N   Form **4562** (1993)

Copyright © 1994 by Harcourt Brace & Company. All rights reserved.

Form 4562 (1993) Page 2

Part V — Listed Property—Automobiles, Certain Other Vehicles, Cellular Telephones, Certain Computers, and Property Used for Entertainment, Recreation, or Amusement

For any vehicle for which you are using the standard mileage rate or deducting lease expense, complete only 22a, 22b, columns (a) through (c) of Section A, all of Section B, and Section C if applicable.

Section A—Depreciation and Other Information (Caution: See instructions for limitations for automobiles.)

22a Do you have evidence to support the business/investment use claimed? ☐ Yes ☐ No   **22b** If "Yes," is the evidence written? ☐ Yes ☐ No

(a) Type of property (list vehicles first)	(b) Date placed in service	(c) Business/investment use percentage	(d) Cost or other basis	(e) Basis for depreciation (business/investment use only)	(f) Recovery period	(g) Method/ Convention	(h) Depreciation deduction	(i) Elected section 179 cost
23 Property used more than 50% in a qualified business use (see instructions):								
		%						
		%						
		%						
24 Property used 50% or less in a qualified business use (see instructions):								
		%				S/L –		
		%				S/L –		
		%				S/L –		

25 Add amounts in column (h). Enter the total here and on line 19, page 1. . . . . . **25**

26 Add amounts in column (i). Enter the total here and on line 7, page 1 . . . . **26**

Section B—Information Regarding Use of Vehicles—If you deduct expenses for vehicles:
- Always complete this section for vehicles used by a sole proprietor, partner, or other "more than 5% owner," or related person.
- If you provided vehicles to your employees, first answer the questions in Section C to see if you meet an exception to completing this section for those vehicles.

	(a) Vehicle 1		(b) Vehicle 2		(c) Vehicle 3		(d) Vehicle 4		(e) Vehicle 5		(f) Vehicle 6	
27 Total business/investment miles driven during the year (DO NOT include commuting miles)												
28 Total commuting miles driven during the year												
29 Total other personal (noncommuting) miles driven												
30 Total miles driven during the year. Add lines 27 through 29.												
	Yes	No	Yes	No	Yes	No	Yes	No	Yes	No	Yes	No
31 Was the vehicle available for personal use during off-duty hours?												
32 Was the vehicle used primarily by a more than 5% owner or related person?												
33 Is another vehicle available for personal use?												

Section C—Questions for Employers Who Provide Vehicles for Use by Their Employees
Answer these questions to determine if you meet an exception to completing Section B. **Note:** *Section B must always be completed for vehicles used by sole proprietors, partners, or other more than 5% owners or related persons.*

	Yes	No
34 Do you maintain a written policy statement that prohibits all personal use of vehicles, including commuting, by your employees?		
35 Do you maintain a written policy statement that prohibits personal use of vehicles, except commuting, by your employees? (See instructions for vehicles used by corporate officers, directors, or 1% or more owners.)		
36 Do you treat all use of vehicles by employees as personal use?		
37 Do you provide more than five vehicles to your employees and retain the information received from your employees concerning the use of the vehicles?		
38 Do you meet the requirements concerning qualified automobile demonstration use (see instructions)? . .		

Note: *If your answer to 34, 35, 36, 37, or 38 is "Yes," you need not complete Section B for the covered vehicles.*

Part VI — Amortization

(a) Description of costs	(b) Date amortization begins	(c) Amortizable amount	(d) Code section	(e) Amortization period or percentage	(f) Amortization for this year
39 Amortization of costs that begins during your 1993 tax year:					

40 Amortization of costs that began before 1993 . . . . **40**

41 Total. Enter here and on "Other Deductions" or "Other Expenses" line of your return . . . **41**

Portfolio Problem (Harold A. and Maude L.)   Name _____ A-35

Form **4684**	**Casualties and Thefts**	OMB No. 1545-0177
Department of the Treasury Internal Revenue Service	▶ See separate instructions. ▶ Attach to your tax return. ▶ Use a separate Form 4684 for each different casualty or theft.	**1993** Attachment Sequence No. 26

Name(s) shown on tax return | Identifying number

SECTION A—Personal Use Property (Use this section to report casualties and thefts of property **not** used in a trade or business or for income-producing purposes.)

1   Description of properties (show type, location, and date acquired for each):
   Property **A** ....
   Property **B** ....
   Property **C** ....
   Property **D** ....

Properties (Use a separate column for each property lost or damaged from one casualty or theft.)

		A	B	C	D
2	Cost or other basis of each property				
3	Insurance or other reimbursement (whether or not you filed a claim). See instructions				
	Note: *If line 2 is more than line 3, skip line 4.*				
4	Gain from casualty or theft. If line 3 is **more than** line 2, enter the difference here and skip lines 5 through 9 for that column. See instructions if line 3 includes insurance or other reimbursement you did not claim, or you received payment for your loss in a later tax year				
5	Fair market value **before** casualty or theft				
6	Fair market value **after** casualty or theft				
7	Subtract line 6 from line 5				
8	Enter the **smaller** of line 2 or line 7				
9	Subtract line 3 from line 8. If zero or less, enter -0-				

10	Casualty or theft loss. Add the amounts on line 9. Enter the total	10	
11	Enter the amount from line 10 or $100, whichever is **smaller**	11	
12	Subtract line 11 from line 10	12	
	Caution: *Use only one Form 4684 for lines 13 through 18.*		
13	Add the amounts on line 12 of all Forms 4684	13	
14	Combine the amounts from line 4 of all Forms 4684	14	
15	• If line 14 is **more than** line 13, enter the difference here and on Schedule D. Do not complete the rest of this section (see instructions). • If line 14 is **less than** line 13, enter -0- here and continue with the form. • If line 14 is **equal to** line 13, enter -0- here. Do not complete the rest of this section.	15	
16	If line 14 is **less than** line 13, enter the difference	16	
17	Enter 10% of your adjusted gross income (Form 1040, line 32). Estates and trusts, see instructions	17	
18	Subtract line 17 from line 16. If zero or less, enter -0-. Also enter result on Schedule A (Form 1040), line 17. Estates and trusts, enter on the "Other deductions" line of your tax return	18	

For Paperwork Reduction Act Notice, see page 1 of separate instructions.   Cat. No. 129970   Form **4684** (1993)

Copyright © 1994 by Harcourt Brace & Company. All rights reserved.

Portfolio Problem (Harold A. and Maude L.) Name _____ A-37

Form **4797**	**Sales of Business Property**	OMB No. 1545-0184
Department of the Treasury Internal Revenue Service	(Also Involuntary Conversions and Recapture Amounts Under Sections 179 and 280F(b)(2)) ▶ Attach to your tax return. ▶ See separate instructions.	**1993** Attachment Sequence No. 27

Name(s) shown on return | Identifying number

1 Enter here the gross proceeds from the sale or exchange of real estate reported to you for 1993 on Form(s) 1099-S (or a substitute statement) that you will be including on line 2, 11, or 22 . . . . **1**

Part I — Sales or Exchanges of Property Used in a Trade or Business and Involuntary Conversions From Other Than Casualty or Theft—Property Held More Than 1 Year

(a) Description of property	(b) Date acquired (mo., day, yr.)	(c) Date sold (mo., day, yr.)	(d) Gross sales price	(e) Depreciation allowed or allowable since acquisition	(f) Cost or other basis, plus improvements and expense of sale	(g) LOSS ((f) minus the sum of (d) and (e))	(h) GAIN ((d) plus (e) minus (f))
2							

3 Gain, if any, from Form 4684, line 39 . . . . **3**
4 Section 1231 gain from installment sales from Form 6252, line 26 or 37 . . . . **4**
5 Section 1231 gain or (loss) from like-kind exchanges from Form 8824 . . . . **5**
6 Gain, if any, from line 34, from other than casualty or theft **6**
7 Add lines 2 through 6 in columns (g) and (h) . . . . **7** (   )
8 Combine columns (g) and (h) of line 7. Enter gain or (loss) here, and on the appropriate line as follows: . . . **8**

  Partnerships—Enter the gain or (loss) on Form 1065, Schedule K, line 6. Skip lines 9, 10, 12, and 13 below.
  S corporations—Report the gain or (loss) following the instructions for Form 1120S, Schedule K, lines 5 and 6. Skip lines 9, 10, 12, and 13 below, unless line 8 is a gain and the S corporation is subject to the capital gains tax.
  All others—If line 8 is zero or a loss, enter the amount on line 12 below and skip lines 9 and 10. If line 8 is a gain and you did not have any prior year section 1231 losses, or they were recaptured in an earlier year, enter the gain as a long-term capital gain on Schedule D and skip lines 9, 10, and 13 below.

9 Nonrecaptured net section 1231 losses from prior years (see instructions) **9**
10 Subtract line 9 from line 8. If zero or less, enter -0-. Also enter on the appropriate line as follows (see instructions): **10**
  S corporations—Enter this amount (if more than zero) on Schedule D (Form 1120S), line 13, and skip lines 12 and 13 below.
  All others—If line 10 is zero, enter the amount from line 8 on line 13 below. If line 10 is more than zero, enter the amount from line 9 on line 13 below, and enter the amount from line 10 as a long-term capital gain on Schedule D.

Part II — Ordinary Gains and Losses

11 Ordinary gains and losses not included on lines 12 through 18 (include property held 1 year or less):

12 Loss, if any, from line 8 . . . . **12**
13 Gain, if any, from line 8, or amount from line 9 if applicable **13**
14 Gain, if any, from line 33 . . . . **14**
15 Net gain or (loss) from Form 4684, lines 31 and 38a **15**
16 Ordinary gain from installment sales from Form 6252, line 25 or 36 . . . . **16**
17 Ordinary gain or (loss) from like-kind exchanges from Form 8824 . . . . **17**
18 Recapture of section 179 expense deduction for partners and S corporation shareholders from property dispositions by partnerships and S corporations (see instructions) **18**
19 Add lines 11 through 18 in columns (g) and (h) . . . . **19** (   )
20 Combine columns (g) and (h) of line 19. Enter gain or (loss) here, and on the appropriate line as follows: . . . **20**
  a For all except individual returns: Enter the gain or (loss) from line 20 on the return being filed.
  b For individual returns:
    (1) If the loss on line 12 includes a loss from Form 4684, line 35, column (b)(ii), enter that part of the loss here and on line 20 of Schedule A (Form 1040). Identify as from "Form 4797, line 20b(1)." See instructions . . . . **20b(1)**
    (2) Redetermine the gain or (loss) on line 20, excluding the loss, if any, on line 20b(1). Enter here and on Form 1040, line 15 . **20b(2)**

For Paperwork Reduction Act Notice, see page 1 of separate instructions.   Cat. No. 13086I   Form **4797** (1993)

Form 4797 (1993) Page 2

Part III — Gain From Disposition of Property Under Sections 1245, 1250, 1252, 1254, and 1255

21	(a) Description of section 1245, 1250, 1252, 1254, or 1255 property:	(b) Date acquired (mo., day, yr.)	(c) Date sold (mo., day, yr.)
A			
B			
C			
D			

	Relate lines 21A through 21D to these columns ▶		Property A	Property B	Property C	Property D
22	Gross sales price (Note: See line 1 before completing.)	22				
23	Cost or other basis plus expense of sale	23				
24	Depreciation (or depletion) allowed or allowable	24				
25	Adjusted basis. Subtract line 24 from line 23	25				
26	Total gain. Subtract line 25 from line 22	26				
27	**If section 1245 property:**					
a	Depreciation allowed or allowable from line 24	27a				
b	Enter the **smaller** of line 26 or 27a	27b				
28	**If section 1250 property:** If straight line depreciation was used, enter -0- on line 28g, except for a corporation subject to section 291.					
a	Additional depreciation after 1975 (see instructions)	28a				
b	Applicable percentage multiplied by the **smaller** of line 26 or line 28a (see instructions)	28b				
c	Subtract line 28a from line 26. If residential rental property or line 26 is not more than line 28a, skip lines 28d and 28e	28c				
d	Additional depreciation after 1969 and before 1976	28d				
e	Enter the **smaller** of line 28c or 28d	28e				
f	Section 291 amount (corporations only)	28f				
g	Add lines 28b, 28e, and 28f	28g				
29	**If section 1252 property:** Skip this section if you did not dispose of farmland or if this form is being completed for a partnership.					
a	Soil, water, and land clearing expenses	29a				
b	Line 29a multiplied by applicable percentage (see instructions)	29b				
c	Enter the **smaller** of line 26 or 29b	29c				
30	**If section 1254 property:**					
a	Intangible drilling and development costs, expenditures for development of mines and other natural deposits, and mining exploration costs (see instructions)	30a				
b	Enter the **smaller** of line 26 or 30a	30b				
31	**If section 1255 property:**					
a	Applicable percentage of payments excluded from income under section 126 (see instructions)	31a				
b	Enter the **smaller** of line 26 or 31a	31b				

Summary of Part III Gains. Complete property columns A through D, through line 31b before going to line 32.

32	Total gains for all properties. Add columns A through D, line 26	32	
33	Add columns A through D, lines 27b, 28g, 29c, 30b, and 31b. Enter here and on line 14	33	
34	Subtract line 33 from line 32. Enter the portion from casualty or theft on Form 4684, line 33. Enter the portion from other than casualty or theft on Form 4797, line 6	34	

Part IV — Recapture Amounts Under Sections 179 and 280F(b)(2) When Business Use Drops to 50% or Less
See instructions for Part IV.

			(a) Section 179	(b) Section 280F(b)(2)
35	Section 179 expense deduction or depreciation allowable in prior years	35		
36	Recomputed depreciation (see instructions)	36		
37	Recapture amount. Subtract line 36 from line 35. See instructions for where to report	37		

Portfolio Problem (Harold A. and Maude L.)   Name _____   A-39

Form **6252**	**Installment Sale Income**	OMB No. 1545-0228
Department of the Treasury Internal Revenue Service	▶ See separate instructions. ▶ Attach to your tax return. Use a separate form for each sale or other disposition of property on the installment method.	**1992** Attachment Sequence No. **79**
Name(s) shown on return		Identifying number

1 Description of property ▶ ....
2a Date acquired (month, day, and year) ▶ __/__/__ b Date sold (month, day, and year) ▶ __/__/__
3 Was the property sold to a related party after May 14, 1980? See instructions . . . . ☐ Yes ☐ No
4 If the answer to question 3 is "Yes," was the property a marketable security? If "Yes," complete Part III. If
   "No," complete Part III for the year of sale and for 2 years after the year of sale. . . . . ☐ Yes ☐ No

Part I   **Gross Profit and Contract Price.** Complete this part for the year of sale only.

5	Selling price including mortgages and other debts. Do not include interest whether stated or unstated	5	
6	Mortgages and other debts the buyer assumed or took the property subject to, but not new mortgages the buyer got from a bank or other source . .	6	
7	Subtract line 6 from line 5	7	
8	Cost or other basis of property sold	8	
9	Depreciation allowed or allowable	9	
10	Adjusted basis. Subtract line 9 from line 8	10	
11	Commissions and other expenses of sale.	11	
12	Income recapture from Form 4797, Part III. See instructions . .	12	
13	Add lines 10, 11, and 12	13	
14	Subtract line 13 from line 5. If zero or less, do not complete the rest of this form	14	
15	If the property described on line 1 above was your main home, enter the total of lines 16 and 24 from Form 2119. Otherwise, enter -0-	15	
16	**Gross profit.** Subtract line 15 from line 14	16	
17	Subtract line 13 from line 6. If zero or less, enter -0-	17	
18	**Contract price.** Add line 7 and line 17	18	

Part II   **Installment Sale Income.** Complete this part for the year of sale and any year you receive a payment or have certain debts you must treat as a payment on installment obligations.

19	Gross profit percentage. Divide line 16 by line 18. For years after the year of sale, see instructions	19	
20	**For year of sale only**—Enter amount from line 17 above; otherwise, enter -0-	20	
21	Payments received during year. See instructions. Do not include interest whether stated or unstated	21	
22	Add lines 20 and 21	22	
23	Payments received in prior years. See instructions. Do not include interest whether stated or unstated	23		
24	**Installment sale income.** Multiply line 22 by line 19	24	
25	Part of line 24 that is ordinary income under recapture rules. See instructions	25	
26	Subtract line 25 from line 24. Enter here and on Schedule D or Form 4797. See instructions	26	

Part III   **Related Party Installment Sale Income.** Do not complete if you received the final payment this tax year.

27 Name, address, and taxpayer identifying number of related party ....
....
28 Did the related party, during this tax year, resell or dispose of the property ("second disposition")? . . . ☐ Yes ☐ No
29 If the answer to question 28 is "Yes," complete lines 30 through 37 below unless one of the following conditions is met. Check only the box that applies.
  a ☐ The second disposition was more than 2 years after the first disposition (other than dispositions of marketable securities). If this box is checked, enter the date of disposition (month, day, year) ▶ __/__/__
  b ☐ The first disposition was a sale or exchange of stock to the issuing corporation.
  c ☐ The second disposition was an involuntary conversion where the threat of conversion occurred after the first disposition.
  d ☐ The second disposition occurred after the death of the original seller or buyer.
  e ☐ It can be established to the satisfaction of the Internal Revenue Service that tax avoidance was not a principal purpose for either of the dispositions. If this box is checked, attach an explanation. See instructions.

30	Selling price of property sold by related party	30	
31	Enter contract price from line 18 for year of first sale	31	
32	Enter the **smaller** of line 30 or line 31	32	
33	Total payments received by the end of your 1992 tax year. Add lines 22 and 23	33	
34	Subtract line 33 from line 32. If zero or less, enter -0-	34	
35	Multiply line 34 by the gross profit percentage on line 19 for year of first sale	35	
36	Part of line 35 that is ordinary income under recapture rules. See instructions	36	
37	Subtract line 36 from line 35. Enter here and on Schedule D or Form 4797. See instructions	37	

For Paperwork Reduction Act Notice, see separate instructions.   Cat. No. 13601R   Form **6252** (1992)
1993 form not available at press time.

Copyright © 1994 by Harcourt Brace & Company. All rights reserved.

Portfolio Problem (Martha P. Neilson)   Name_____   A-43

Form 1040A — Department of the Treasury—Internal Revenue Service
U.S. Individual Income Tax Return 1993   IRS Use Only—Do not write or staple in this space.

OMB No. 1545-0085

Label (See page 15.)

Use the IRS label. Otherwise, please print or type.

L A B E L   H E R E

- Your first name and initial | Last name
- If a joint return, spouse's first name and initial | Last name
- Home address (number and street). If you have a P.O. box, see page 16. | Apt. no.
- City, town or post office, state, and ZIP code. If you have a foreign address, see page 16.

Your social security number

Spouse's social security number

For Privacy Act and Paperwork Reduction Act Notice, see page 4.

Presidential Election Campaign Fund (See page 16.)
Do you want $3 to go to this fund? . . . .
If a joint return, does your spouse want $3 to go to this fund?   Yes | No

Note: *Checking "Yes" will not change your tax or reduce your refund.*

Check the box for your filing status
(See page 16.)
Check only one box

1 ☐ Single
2 ☐ Married filing joint return (even if only one had income)
3 ☐ Married filing separate return. Enter spouse's social security number above and full name here. ▶ _____
4 ☐ Head of household (with qualifying person). (See page 17.) If the qualifying person is a child but not your dependent, enter this child's name here. ▶ _____
5 ☐ Qualifying widow(er) with dependent child (year spouse died ▶ 19___). (See page 18.)

Figure your exemptions
(See page 19.)

If more than seven dependents, see page 22

6a ☐ **Yourself.** If your parent (or someone else) can claim you as a dependent on his or her tax return, **do not** check box 6a. But be sure to check the box on line 18b on page 2.
b ☐ **Spouse**
c **Dependents:**

(1) Name (first, initial, and last name)	(2) Check if under age 1	(3) If age 1 or older, dependent's social security number	(4) Dependent's relationship to you	(5) No. of months lived in your home in 1993

No. of boxes checked on 6a and 6b _____

No. of your children on 6c who:
• lived with you _____
• didn't live with you due to divorce or separation (see page 22) _____

Dependents on 6c not entered above _____

d If your child didn't live with you but is claimed as your dependent under a pre-1985 agreement, check here . . . . . . ▶ ☐
e Total number of exemptions claimed.

Add numbers entered on lines above _____

Figure your total income

Attach Copy B of your Forms W-2 and 1099-R here.

If you didn't get a W-2, see page 24

If you are attaching a check or money order, put it on top of any Forms W-2 or 1099-R

7   Wages, salaries, tips, etc. This should be shown in box 1 of your W-2 form(s). Attach Form(s) W-2. | 7
8a **Taxable** interest income (see page 25). If over $400, also complete and attach Schedule 1, Part I. | 8a
b   **Tax-exempt** interest. DO NOT include on line 8a. 8b
9   Dividends. If over $400, also complete and attach Schedule 1, Part II. | 9
10a Total IRA distributions. 10a | 10b Taxable amount (see page 26). | 10b
11a Total pensions and annuities. 11a | 11b Taxable amount (see page 26). | 11b
12 Unemployment compensation (see page 30). | 12
13a Social security benefits. 13a | 13b Taxable amount (see page 30). | 13b
14 Add lines 7 through 13b (far right column). This is your **total income**. ▶ 14

Figure your adjusted gross income

15a Your IRA deduction (see page 32). 15a
b   Spouse's IRA deduction (see page 32). 15b
c   Add lines 15a and 15b. These are your **total adjustments**. 15c
16 Subtract line 15c from line 14. This is your **adjusted gross income**.
    If less than $23,050 and a child lived with you, see page 63 to find out if you can claim the "Earned income credit" on line 28c. ▶ 16

Cat. No. 11327A   1993 Form 1040A page 1

Copyright © 1994 by Harcourt Brace & Company. All rights reserved.

1993 Form 1040A page 2

Name(s) shown on page 1 | Your social security number

Figure your standard deduction, exemption amount, and taxable income

17 Enter the amount from line 16. — 17

18a Check if:
- ☐ You were 65 or older ☐ Blind
- ☐ Spouse was 65 or older ☐ Blind

Enter number of boxes checked ▶ 18a ☐

b If your parent (or someone else) can claim you as a dependent, check here. . . . . ▶ 18b ☐

c If you are married filing separately and your spouse files Form 1040 and itemizes deductions, see page 36 and check here ▶ 18c ☐

19 Enter the **standard deduction** shown below for your filing status. **But if you checked any box on line 18a or b,** go to page 36 to find your standard deduction. **If you checked box 18c,** enter -0-.
- Single—$3,700
- Head of household—$5,450
- Married filing jointly or Qualifying widow(er)—$6,200
- Married filing separately—$3,100   19

20 Subtract line 19 from line 17. If line 19 is more than line 17, enter -0-. 20

21 Multiply $2,350 by the total number of exemptions claimed on line 6e. 21

22 Subtract line 21 from line 20. If line 21 is more than line 20, enter -0-. This is your **taxable income.** ▶ 22

Figure your tax, credits, and payments

If you want the IRS to figure your tax, see the instructions for line 22 on page 37.

23 Find the tax on the amount on line 22. Check if from:
☐ Tax Table (pages 50–55) or   ☐ Form 8615 (see page 38).   23

24a Credit for child and dependent care expenses. Complete and attach Schedule 2.   24a

b Credit for the elderly or the disabled. Complete and attach Schedule 3.   24b

c Add lines 24a and 24b. These are your **total credits.**   24c

25 Subtract line 24c from line 23. If line 24c is more than line 23, enter -0-.   25

26 Advance earned income credit payments from Form W-2.   26

27 Add lines 25 and 26. This is your **total tax.** ▶ 27

28a Total Federal income tax withheld. If any tax is from Form(s) 1099, check here. ▶ ☐   28a

b 1993 estimated tax payments and amount applied from 1992 return.   28b

c **Earned income credit.** Complete and attach Schedule EIC.   28c

d Add lines 28a, 28b, and 28c. These are your **total payments.** ▶ 28d

Figure your refund or amount you owe

29 If line 28d is more than line 27, subtract line 27 from line 28d. This is the amount you **overpaid.**   29

30 Amount of line 29 you want **refunded to you.**   30

31 Amount of line 29 you want **applied to your 1994 estimated tax.**   31

32 If line 27 is more than line 28d, subtract line 28d from line 27. This is the **amount you owe.** For details on how to pay, including what to write on your payment, see page 42.   32

33 Estimated tax penalty (see page 43). Also, include on line 32.   33

Sign your return

Under penalties of perjury, I declare that I have examined this return and accompanying schedules and statements, and to the best of my knowledge and belief, they are true, correct, and accurately list all amounts and sources of income I received during the tax year. Declaration of preparer (other than the taxpayer) is based on all information of which the preparer has any knowledge.

Your signature | Date | Your occupation

Keep a copy of this return for your records.

Spouse's signature. If joint return, BOTH must sign. | Date | Spouse's occupation

Paid preparer's use only

Preparer's signature ▶ | Date | Check if self-employed ☐ | Preparer's social security no.

Firm's name (or yours if self-employed) and address ▶ | E.I. No. | ZIP code

Portfolio Problem (Martha P. Neilson) Name_____ A-45

Schedule 1 (Form 1040A)
Department of the Treasury—Internal Revenue Service
Interest and Dividend Income for Form 1040A Filers
1993
OMB No 1545-0085

Name(s) shown on Form 1040A | Your social security number

Part I
Interest income
(See pages 25 and 56.)

Note: *If you received a Form 1099–INT, Form 1099–OID, or substitute statement from a brokerage firm, enter the firm's name and the total interest shown on that form.*

1 List name of payer. If any interest is from a seller-financed mortgage and the buyer used the property as a personal residence, see page 56 and list this interest first. Also, show that buyer's social security number and address.

	Amount
1	

2 Add the amounts on line 1.   **2**
3 Excludable interest on series EE U.S. savings bonds issued after 1989 from Form 8815, line 14. You MUST attach Form 8815 to Form 1040A.   **3**
4 Subtract line 3 from line 2. Enter the result here and on Form 1040A, line 8a.   **4**

Part II
Dividend income
(See pages 25 and 57.)

Note: *If you received a Form 1099–DIV or substitute statement from a brokerage firm, enter the firm's name and the total dividends shown on that form.*

5 List name of payer

	Amount
5	

6 Add the amounts on line 5. Enter the total here and on Form 1040A, line 9.   **6**

For Paperwork Reduction Act Notice, see Form 1040A instructions.   Cat. No. 12075R   1993 Schedule 1 (Form 1040A) page 1

Copyright © 1994 by Harcourt Brace & Company. All rights reserved.

A-46 Portfolio Problem (Martha P. Neilson)   Name _____

Form 8615
Department of the Treasury
Internal Revenue Service

**Tax for Children Under Age 14
Who Have Investment Income of More Than $1,200**
▶ See instructions below and on back.
▶ Attach ONLY to the child's Form 1040, Form 1040A, or Form 1040NR.

OMB No. 1545-0998
1992
Attachment Sequence No. **33**

General Instructions

Purpose of Form. For children under age 14, investment income (such as taxable interest and dividends) over $1,200 is taxed at the parent's rate if the parent's rate is higher than the child's rate. If the child's investment income is more than $1,200, use this form to figure the child's tax.

Investment Income. As used on this form, "investment income" includes all taxable income other than earned income as defined on page 2. It includes income such as taxable interest, dividends, capital gains, rents, royalties, etc. It also includes pension and annuity income and income (other than earned income) received as the beneficiary of a trust.

Who Must File. Generally, Form 8615 must be filed for any child who was under age 14 on January 1, 1993, and who had more than $1,200 of investment income. If neither parent was alive on December 31, 1992, do not use Form 8615. Instead, figure the child's tax in the normal manner.

Note: *The parent may be able to elect to report the child's interest and dividends on his or her return. If the parent makes this election, the child will not have to file a return or Form 8615. For more details, see the instructions for Form 1040 or Form 1040A, or get **Form 8814**,*

Parents' Election To Report Child's Interest and Dividends.

Additional Information. For more details, get Pub. 929, Tax Rules for Children and Dependents.

Incomplete Information for Parent. If a child's parent or guardian cannot obtain the information needed to complete Form 8615 before the due date of the child's return, reasonable estimates of the parent's taxable income or filing status and the net investment income of the parent's other children may be made. The appropriate line(s) of Form 8615 must be marked "Estimated." For more details, see Pub. 929.

(Instructions continue on back.)

Child's name shown on return	Child's social security number
A Parent's name (first, initial, and last). **Caution:** *See instructions on back before completing.*	**B** Parent's social security number

C Parent's filing status (check one):
☐ Single   ☐ Married filing jointly   ☐ Married filing separately   ☐ Head of household   ☐ Qualifying widow(er)

Step 1 **Figure child's net investment income**

1	Enter child's investment income, such as taxable interest and dividend income. See instructions. If this amount is $1,200 or less, **stop here**; do not file this form	1
2	If the child DID NOT itemize deductions on Schedule A (Form 1040 or Form 1040NR), enter $1,200. If the child ITEMIZED deductions, see instructions	2
3	Subtract line 2 from line 1. If the result is zero or less, **stop here**; do not complete the rest of this form but ATTACH it to the child's return	3
4	Enter child's **taxable** income from Form 1040, line 37; Form 1040A, line 22; or Form 1040NR, line 35 . .	4
5	Enter the **smaller** of line 3 or line 4 here . . . . ▶	5

Step 2 **Figure tentative tax based on the tax rate of the parent listed on line A**

6	Enter parent's **taxable** income from Form 1040, line 37; Form 1040A, line 22; Form 1040EZ, line 5; or Form 1040NR, line 35. If the parent transferred property to a trust, see instructions . .	6
7	Enter the total, if any, of the net investment income from Forms 8615, line 5, of ALL OTHER children of the parent. **Do not** include the amount from line 5 above	7
8	Add lines 5, 6, and 7	8
9	Tax on line 8 based on the **parent's** filing status. See instructions. If from Schedule D, enter amount from line 22 of that Schedule D here ▶ _____	9
10	Enter parent's tax from Form 1040, line 38; Form 1040A, line 23; Form 1040EZ, line 7; or Form 1040NR, line 36. If from Schedule D, enter amount from line 22 of that Schedule D here ▶ _____	10
11	Subtract line 10 from line 9. If line 7 is blank, enter on line 13 the amount from line 11; skip lines 12a and 12b	11
12a	Add lines 5 and 7	12a	
b	Divide line 5 by line 12a. Enter the result as a decimal (rounded to two places)	12b	× .
13	Multiply line 11 by line 12b . . . . ▶	13

Step 3 **Figure child's tax**

Note: If lines 4 and 5 above are the same, go to line 16.

14	Subtract line 5 from line 4	14	
15	Tax on line 14 based on the **child's** filing status. See instructions. If from Schedule D, enter amount from line 22 of that Schedule D here ▶ _____	15
16	Add lines 13 and 15	16
17	Tax on line 4 based on the **child's** filing status. See instructions. If from Schedule D, check here ▶ ☐	17
18	Enter the **larger** of line 16 or line 17 here and on Form 1040, line 38; Form 1040A, line 23; or Form 1040NR, line 36. Be sure to check the box for "Form 8615" even if line 17 is more than line 16 . ▶	18

For Paperwork Reduction Act Notice, see back of form.   Cat. No. 64113U   Form **8615** (1992)

1993 form not available at press time.

Copyright © 1994 by Harcourt Brace & Company. All rights reserved.

Portfolio Problem (Harriet T. Neilson)   Name _____ A-47

Form 1040

Department of the Treasury—Internal Revenue Service
U.S. Individual Income Tax Return 1993

For the year Jan. 1–Dec. 31, 1993, or other tax year beginning _____, 1993, ending _____, 19 ___ | OMB No. 1545-0074

IRS Use Only—Do not write or staple in this space

Label (See instructions on page 12.)
Use the IRS label. Otherwise, please print or type.

L A B E L H E R E	Your first name and initial	Last name	Your social security number
	If a joint return, spouse's first name and initial	Last name	Spouse's social security number
	Home address (number and street). If you have a P.O. box, see page 12	Apt. no.	**For Privacy Act and Paperwork Reduction Act Notice, see page 4.**
	City, town or post office, state, and ZIP code. If you have a foreign address, see page 12.		

Presidential Election Campaign (See page 12.)
Do you want $3 to go to this fund? . . . .
If a joint return, does your spouse want $3 to go to this fund? . . . .

Yes | No | Note: Checking "Yes" will not change your tax or reduce your refund.

Filing Status
(See page 12.)
Check only one box.

1. ☐ Single
2. ☐ Married filing joint return (even if only one had income)
3. ☐ Married filing separate return. Enter spouse's social security no. above and full name here. ▶ _____
4. ☐ Head of household (with qualifying person). (See page 13.) If the qualifying person is a child but not your dependent, enter this child's name here. ▶ _____
5. ☐ Qualifying widow(er) with dependent child (year spouse died ▶ 19 ___). (See page 13.)

Exemptions
(See page 13.)

6a ☐ **Yourself.** If your parent (or someone else) can claim you as a dependent on his or her tax return, **do not** check box 6a. But be sure to check the box on line 33b on page 2.

b ☐ **Spouse**

No. of boxes checked on 6a and 6b _____

c **Dependents:**

(1) Name (first, initial, and last name)	(2) Check if under age 1	(3) If age 1 or older, dependent's social security number	(4) Dependent's relationship to you	(5) No. of months lived in your home in 1993

If more than six dependents, see page 14.

No. of your children on 6c who:
- lived with you _____
- didn't live with you due to divorce or separation (see page 15) _____

Dependents on 6c not entered above _____

d If your child didn't live with you but is claimed as your dependent under a pre-1985 agreement, check here ▶ ☐

e Total number of exemptions claimed . . . .

Add numbers entered on lines above ▶ _____

Income

Attach Copy B of your Forms W-2, W-2G, and 1099-R here.

If you did not get a W-2, see page 10.

If you are attaching a check or money order, put it on top of any Forms W-2, W-2G, or 1099-R.

7	Wages, salaries, tips, etc. Attach Form(s) W-2	7	
8a	Taxable interest income (see page 16). Attach Schedule B if over $400	8a	
b	Tax-exempt interest (see page 17). DON'T include on line 8a	8b	
9	Dividend income. Attach Schedule B if over $400	9	
10	Taxable refunds, credits, or offsets of state and local income taxes (see page 17)	10	
11	Alimony received	11	
12	Business income or (loss). Attach Schedule C or C-EZ	12	
13	Capital gain or (loss). Attach Schedule D	13	
14	Capital gain distributions not reported on line 13 (see page 17)	14	
15	Other gains or (losses). Attach Form 4797	15	
16a	Total IRA distributions . 16a ___ b Taxable amount (see page 18)	16b	
17a	Total pensions and annuities 17a ___ b Taxable amount (see page 18)	17b	
18	Rental real estate, royalties, partnerships, S corporations, trusts, etc. Attach Schedule E	18	
19	Farm income or (loss). Attach Schedule F	19	
20	Unemployment compensation (see page 19)	20	
21a	Social security benefits 21a ___ b Taxable amount (see page 19)	21b	
22	Other income. List type and amount—see page 20 ___	22	
23	Add the amounts in the far right column for lines 7 through 22. This is your **total income** ▶	23	

Adjustments to Income
(See page 20.)

24a	Your IRA deduction (see page 20)	24a	
b	Spouse's IRA deduction (see page 20)	24b	
25	One-half of self-employment tax (see page 21)	25	
26	Self-employed health insurance deduction (see page 22)	26	
27	Keogh retirement plan and self-employed SEP deduction	27	
28	Penalty on early withdrawal of savings	28	
29	Alimony paid. Recipient's SSN ▶ ___	29	
30	Add lines 24a through 29. These are your **total adjustments** ▶	30	

Adjusted Gross Income

31 Subtract line 30 from line 23. This is your **adjusted gross income**. If this amount is less than $23,050 and a child lived with you, see page EIC-1 to find out if you can claim the "Earned Income Credit" on line 56 . . . . ▶ | 31 | |

Cat. No. 11320B   Form **1040** (1993)

Copyright © 1994 by Harcourt Brace & Company. All rights reserved.

Form 1040 (1993)   Page **2**

Tax Computation (See page 23.)	32	Amount from line 31 (adjusted gross income)	32
	33a	Check if: ☐ **You** were 65 or older, ☐ Blind; ☐ **Spouse** was 65 or older, ☐ Blind. Add the number of boxes checked above and enter the total here ▶ 33a	
	b	If your parent (or someone else) can claim you as a dependent, check here ▶ 33b ☐	
	c	If you are married filing separately and your spouse itemizes deductions or you are a dual-status alien, see page 24 and check here ▶ 33c ☐	
	34	Enter the larger of your: { **Itemized deductions** from Schedule A, line 26, **OR** **Standard deduction** shown below for your filing status. **But if you checked any box on line 33a or b**, go to page 24 to find your standard deduction. If you checked **box 33c**, your standard deduction is zero. • Single—$3,700 • Head of household—$5,450 • Married filing jointly or Qualifying widow(er)—$6,200 • Married filing separately—$3,100 }	34
	35	Subtract line 34 from line 32	35
	36	If line 32 is $81,350 or less, multiply $2,350 by the total number of exemptions claimed on line 6e. If line 32 is over $81,350, see the worksheet on page 25 for the amount to enter	36
If you want the IRS to figure your tax, see page 24.	37	**Taxable income.** Subtract line 36 from line 35. If line 36 is more than line 35, enter -0-	37
	38	Tax. Check if from **a** ☐ Tax Table, **b** ☐ Tax Rate Schedules, **c** ☐ Schedule D Tax Worksheet, or **d** ☐ Form 8615 (see page 25). Amount from Form(s) 8814 ▶ **e** _____	38
	39	Additional taxes (see page 25). Check if from **a** ☐ Form 4970 **b** ☐ Form 4972	39
	40	Add lines 38 and 39 ▶	40
Credits (See page 25.)	41	Credit for child and dependent care expenses. Attach Form 2441	41
	42	Credit for the elderly or the disabled. Attach Schedule R	42
	43	Foreign tax credit. Attach Form 1116	43
	44	Other credits (see page 26). Check if from **a** ☐ Form 3800 **b** ☐ Form 8396 **c** ☐ Form 8801 **d** ☐ Form (specify) _____	44
	45	Add lines 41 through 44	45
	46	Subtract line 45 from line 40. If line 45 is more than line 40, enter -0- ▶	46
Other Taxes	47	Self-employment tax. Attach Schedule SE. Also, see line 25	47
	48	Alternative minimum tax. Attach Form 6251	48
	49	Recapture taxes (see page 26). Check if from **a** ☐ Form 4255 **b** ☐ Form 8611 **c** ☐ Form 8828	49
	50	Social security and Medicare tax on tip income not reported to employer. Attach Form 4137	50
	51	Tax on qualified retirement plans, including IRAs. If required, attach Form 5329	51
	52	Advance earned income credit payments from Form W-2	52
	53	Add lines 46 through 52. This is your **total tax** ▶	53
Payments Attach Forms W-2, W-2G, and 1099-R on the front.	54	Federal income tax withheld. If any is from Form(s) 1099, check ▶ ☐	54
	55	1993 estimated tax payments and amount applied from 1992 return	55
	56	**Earned income credit.** Attach Schedule EIC	56
	57	Amount paid with Form 4868 (extension request)	57
	58a	Excess social security, Medicare, and RRTA tax withheld (see page 28)	58a
	b	Deferral of additional 1993 taxes. Attach Form 8841	58b
	59	Other payments (see page 28). Check if from **a** ☐ Form 2439 **b** ☐ Form 4136	59
	60	Add lines 54 through 59. These are your **total payments** ▶	60
Refund or Amount You Owe	61	If line 60 is more than line 53, subtract line 53 from line 60. This is the amount you **OVERPAID** ▶	61
	62	Amount of line 61 you want **REFUNDED TO YOU** ▶	62
	63	Amount of line 61 you want **APPLIED TO YOUR 1994 ESTIMATED TAX** ▶ 63	
	64	If line 53 is more than line 60, subtract line 60 from line 53. This is the **AMOUNT YOU OWE.** For details on how to pay, including what to write on your payment, see page 29	64
	65	Estimated tax penalty (see page 29). Also include on line 64 65	

Sign Here
Keep a copy of this return for your records.

Under penalties of perjury, I declare that I have examined this return and accompanying schedules and statements, and to the best of my knowledge and belief, they are true, correct, and complete. Declaration of preparer (other than taxpayer) is based on all information of which preparer has any knowledge.

Your signature	Date	Your occupation
Spouse's signature. If a joint return, BOTH must sign.	Date	Spouse's occupation

Paid Preparer's Use Only

Preparer's signature	Date	Check if self-employed ☐	Preparer's social security no.
Firm's name (or yours if self-employed) and address		E.I. No.	
		ZIP code	

Portfolio Problem (Harriet T. Neilson)   Name _____ A-49

Schedules A&B (Form 1040) 1993   OMB No. 1545-0074   Page 2

Name(s) shown on Form 1040. Do not enter name and social security number if shown on other side.   Your social security number

Schedule B—Interest and Dividend Income

Attachment Sequence No. 08

Part I Interest Income

(See pages 16 and B-1.)

Note: *If you had over $400 in taxable interest income, you must also complete Part III.*

Interest Income	Amount
1 List name of payer. If any interest is from a seller-financed mortgage and the buyer used the property as a personal residence, see page B-1 and list this interest first. Also show that buyer's social security number and address ▶	1

Note: If you received a Form 1099-INT, Form 1099-OID, or substitute statement from a brokerage firm, list the firm's name as the payer and enter the total interest shown on that form.

2 Add the amounts on line 1	2
3 Excludable interest on series EE U.S. savings bonds issued after 1989 from Form 8815, line 14. You MUST attach Form 8815 to Form 1040	3
4 Subtract line 3 from line 2. Enter the result here and on Form 1040, line 8a ▶	4

Part II Dividend Income

(See pages 17 and B-1.)

Note: *If you had over $400 in gross dividends and/or other distributions on stock, you must also complete Part III.*

Dividend Income	Amount
5 List name of payer. Include gross dividends and/or other distributions on stock here. Any capital gain distributions and nontaxable distributions will be deducted on lines 7 and 8 ▶	5

Note: If you received a Form 1099-DIV or substitute statement from a brokerage firm, list the firm's name as the payer and enter the total dividends shown on that form.

6 Add the amounts on line 5	6
7 Capital gain distributions. Enter here and on Schedule D* .	7	
8 Nontaxable distributions. (See the inst. for Form 1040, line 9.)	8	
9 Add lines 7 and 8 . . . . ▶	9
10 Subtract line 9 from line 6. Enter the result here and on Form 1040, line 9 . ▶	10

*If you received capital gain distributions but do not need Schedule D to report any other gains or losses, see the instructions for Form 1040, lines 13 and 14.

Part III Foreign Accounts and Trusts

(See page B-2.)

If you had over $400 of interest or dividends OR had a foreign account or were a grantor of, or a transferor to, a foreign trust, you must complete this part.   Yes | No

11a At any time during 1993, did you have an interest in or a signature or other authority over a financial account in a foreign country, such as a bank account, securities account, or other financial account? See page B-2 for exceptions and filing requirements for Form TD F 90-22.1 . . . .

  b If "Yes," enter the name of the foreign country ▶ ....

12 Were you the grantor of, or transferor to, a foreign trust that existed during 1993, whether or not you have any beneficial interest in it? If "Yes," you may have to file Form 3520, 3520-A, or 926 .

For Paperwork Reduction Act Notice, see Form 1040 instructions.   Schedule B (Form 1040) 1993

Copyright © 1994 by Harcourt Brace & Company. All rights reserved.

A-50 Portfolio Problem (Harriet T. Neilson)   Name _____

SCHEDULE E
(Form 1040)
Department of the Treasury
Internal Revenue Service

Supplemental Income and Loss
(From rental real estate, royalties, partnerships,
S corporations, estates, trusts, REMICs, etc.)
▶ Attach to Form 1040 or Form 1041.   ▶ See Instructions for Schedule E (Form 1040).

OMB No. 1545-0074

1993

Attachment Sequence No. **13**

Name(s) shown on return | Your social security number

Part I **Income or Loss From Rental Real Estate and Royalties** Note: *Report income and expenses from your business of renting personal property on* **Schedule C** *or* **C-EZ** *(see page E-1). Report farm rental income or loss from* **Form 4835** *on page 2, line 39.*

1 Show the kind and location of each **rental real estate property**:	2 For each rental real estate property listed on line 1, did you or your family use it for personal purposes for more than the greater of 14 days or 10% of the total days rented at fair rental value during the tax year? (See page E-1.)	Yes	No
A	A		
B	B		
C	C		

Income:		Properties			Totals
		A	B	C	(Add columns A, B, and C.)
3 Rents received	3				3
4 Royalties received	4				4
Expenses:					
5 Advertising	5				
6 Auto and travel (see page E-2) .	6				
7 Cleaning and maintenance . . .	7				
8 Commissions	8				
9 Insurance	9				
10 Legal and other professional fees	10				
11 Management fees	11				
12 Mortgage interest paid to banks, etc. (see page E-2)	12				12
13 Other interest	13				
14 Repairs	14				
15 Supplies	15				
16 Taxes	16				
17 Utilities	17				
18 Other (list) ▶	18				
19 Add lines 5 through 18	19				19
20 Depreciation expense or depletion (see page E-2)	20				20
21 Total expenses. Add lines 19 and 20	21				
22 Income or (loss) from rental real estate or royalty properties. Subtract line 21 from line 3 (rents) or line 4 (royalties). If the result is a (loss), see page E-2 to find out if you must file **Form 6198**. . .	22				
23 Deductible rental real estate loss. **Caution:** *Your rental real estate loss on line 22 may be limited. See page E-3 to find out if you must file* **Form 8582**.	23	( )	( )	( )	
24 **Income.** Add positive amounts shown on line 22. **Do not** include any losses					24
25 **Losses.** Add royalty losses from line 22 and rental real estate losses from line 23. Enter the total losses here					25 ( )
26 **Total rental real estate and royalty income or (loss).** Combine lines 24 and 25. Enter the result here. If Parts II, III, IV, and line 39 on page 2 do not apply to you, also enter this amount on Form 1040, line 18. Otherwise, include this amount in the total on line 40 on page 2					26

For Paperwork Reduction Act Notice, see Form 1040 instructions.   Cat. No. 11344L   Schedule E (Form 1040) 1993

Copyright © 1994 by Harcourt Brace & Company. All rights reserved.

Portfolio Problem (Harriet T. Neilson) Name _____ A-51

Schedule R
(Form 1040)
Department of the Treasury
Internal Revenue Service

Credit for the Elderly or the Disabled

▶ Attach to Form 1040. ▶ See separate instructions for Schedule R.

OMB No. 1545-0074

1993

Attachment Sequence No. **16**

Name(s) shown on Form 1040 | Your social security number

You may be able to use Schedule R to reduce your tax if by the end of 1993:
- You were age 65 or older, **OR**
- You were under age 65, you retired on **permanent and total** disability, and you received taxable disability income.

But you must also meet other tests. See the separate instructions for Schedule R.

Note: *In most cases, the IRS can figure the credit for you. See page 25 of the Form 1040 instructions.*

Part I — Check the Box for Your Filing Status and Age

If your filing status is:	And by the end of 1993:	Check only one box:
Single, Head of household, or Qualifying widow(er) with dependent child	1 You were 65 or older 1	☐
	2 You were under 65 and you retired on permanent and total disability . . . 2	☐
Married filing a joint return	3 Both spouses were 65 or older 3	☐
	4 Both spouses were under 65, but only one spouse retired on permanent and total disability 4	☐
	5 Both spouses were under 65, and both retired on permanent and total disability 5	☐
	6 One spouse was 65 or older, and the other spouse was under 65 and retired on permanent and total disability 6	☐
	7 One spouse was 65 or older, and the other spouse was under 65 and **NOT** retired on permanent and total disability 7	☐
Married filing a separate return	8 You were 65 or older and you lived apart from your spouse for all of 1993 . . 8	☐
	9 You were under 65, you retired on permanent and total disability, and you lived apart from your spouse for all of 1993 9	☐

If you checked box 1, 3, 7, or 8, skip Part II and complete Part III on the back. All others, complete Parts II and III.

Part II — Statement of Permanent and Total Disability (Complete **only** if you checked box 2, 4, 5, 6, or 9 above.)

IF: 1 You filed a physician's statement for this disability for 1983 or an earlier year, or you filed a statement for tax years after 1983 and your physician signed line B on the statement, **AND**

2 Due to your continued disabled condition, you were unable to engage in any substantial gainful activity in 1993, check this box . . . . ▶ ☐

- If you checked this box, you do not have to file another statement for 1993.
- If you **did not** check this box, have your physician complete the following statement.

Physician's Statement (See instructions at bottom of page 2.)

I certify that _____
                Name of disabled person

was permanently and totally disabled on January 1, 1976, or January 1, 1977, **OR** was permanently and totally disabled on the date he or she retired. If retired after December 31, 1976, enter the date retired. ▶ _____

Physician: Sign your name on **either** line A or B below.

A The disability has lasted or can be expected to last continuously for at least a year . . . . . _____
  Physician's signature   Date

B There is no reasonable probability that the disabled condition will ever improve . . . . . _____
  Physician's signature   Date

Physician's name _____ Physician's address _____

For Paperwork Reduction Act Notice, see Form 1040 instructions.   Cat. No. 11359K   Schedule R (Form 1040) 1993

Copyright © 1994 by Harcourt Brace & Company. All rights reserved.

Schedule R (Form 1040) 1993 Page **2**

Part III Figure Your Credit

10 If you checked (in Part I):   Enter:
    Box 1, 2, 4, or 7 . . . . $5,000
    Box 3, 5, or 6 . . . . $7,500   } **10**
    Box 8 or 9 . . . . $3,750
    Caution: *If you checked box 2, 4, 5, 6, or 9 in Part I, you **MUST** complete line 11 below. All others, skip line 11 and enter the amount from line 10 on line 12.*

11 If you checked:
    • Box 6 in Part I, add $5,000 to the taxable disability income of the
      spouse who was under age 65. Enter the total.
    • Box 2, 4, or 9 in Part I, enter your taxable disability income.   } **11**
    • Box 5 in Part I, add your taxable disability income to your spouse's
      taxable disability income. Enter the total.
    TIP: For more details on what to include on line 11, see the instructions.

12 • If you completed line 11, look at lines 10 and 11. Enter the
      smaller of the two amounts.   } **12**
    • All others, enter the amount from line 10.

13 Enter the following pensions, annuities, or disability income that you
    (and your spouse if filing a joint return) received in 1993:
  a Nontaxable part of social security benefits, and
    Nontaxable part of railroad retirement benefits treated as   } . . . **13a**
    social security. See instructions.
  b Nontaxable veterans' pensions, and
    Any other pension, annuity, or disability benefit that is   } . . . **13b**
    excluded from income under any other provision of law.
    See instructions.
  c Add lines 13a and 13b. (Even though these income items are not
    taxable, they **must** be included here to figure your credit.) If you did
    not receive any of the types of nontaxable income listed on line 13a
    or 13b, enter -0- on line 13c **13c**

14 Enter the amount from Form 1040, line 32   **14**
15 If you checked (in Part I): Enter:
    Box 1 or 2 . . . . $7,500
    Box 3, 4, 5, 6, or 7 . . . $10,000   }   **15**
    Box 8 or 9 . . . . $5,000
16 Subtract line 15 from line 14. If line 15 is
    more than line 14, enter -0- **16**

17 Divide line 16 above by 2 . . . . **17**

18 Add lines 13c and 17 . . . . **18**

19 Subtract line 18 from line 12. If line 18 is more than line 12, stop here; you **cannot** take the
    credit. Otherwise, go to line 21 . . . . **19**

20 Decimal amount used to figure the credit . . . . **20**   × .15

21 Multiply line 19 above by the decimal amount (.15) on line 20. Enter the result here and on Form
    1040, line 42. **Caution:** *If you file Schedule C, C-EZ, D, E, or F (Form 1040), your credit may be
    limited. See the instructions for line 21 for the amount of credit you can claim* **21**

Instructions for Physician's Statement

Taxpayer
If you retired after December 31, 1976, enter the date you retired in the space provided in Part II.

Physician
A person is permanently and totally disabled if **both** of the following apply:
 1. He or she cannot engage in any substantial gainful activity because of a physical or mental condition, and

 2. A physician determines that the disability has lasted or can be expected to last continuously for at least a year or can lead to death.

Copyright © 1994 by Harcourt Brace & Company. All rights reserved.

Portfolio Problem (Harriet T. Neilson) Name_____ A-53

Form 4562
Department of the Treasury
Internal Revenue Service

Depreciation and Amortization
(Including Information on Listed Property)
▶ See separate instructions. ▶ Attach this form to your return.

OMB No. 1545-0172
1993
Attachment Sequence No. 67

Name(s) shown on return | Identifying number

Business or activity to which this form relates

Part I — Election To Expense Certain Tangible Property (Section 179) (Note: If you have any "Listed Property," complete Part V before you complete Part I.)

1	Maximum dollar limitation (If an enterprise zone business, see instructions.)	1	$17,500
2	Total cost of section 179 property placed in service during the tax year (see instructions)	2	
3	Threshold cost of section 179 property before reduction in limitation	3	$200,000
4	Reduction in limitation. Subtract line 3 from line 2, but do not enter less than -0-	4	
5	Dollar limitation for tax year. Subtract line 4 from line 1, but do not enter less than -0-. (If married filing separately, see instructions.)	5	

(a) Description of property	(b) Cost	(c) Elected cost
6		

7	Listed property. Enter amount from line 26.	7	
8	Total elected cost of section 179 property. Add amounts in column (c), lines 6 and 7	8	
9	Tentative deduction. Enter the smaller of line 5 or line 8	9	
10	Carryover of disallowed deduction from 1992 (see instructions)	10	
11	Taxable income limitation. Enter the smaller of taxable income or line 5 (see instructions)	11	
12	Section 179 expense deduction. Add lines 9 and 10, but do not enter more than line 11	12	
13	Carryover of disallowed deduction to 1994. Add lines 9 and 10, less line 12 ▶	13	

Note: Do not use Part II or Part III below for listed property (automobiles, certain other vehicles, cellular telephones, certain computers, or property used for entertainment, recreation, or amusement). Instead, use Part V for listed property.

Part II — MACRS Depreciation For Assets Placed in Service ONLY During Your 1993 Tax Year (Do Not Include Listed Property)

(a) Classification of property	(b) Month and year placed in service	(c) Basis for depreciation (business/investment use only—see instructions)	(d) Recovery period	(e) Convention	(f) Method	(g) Depreciation deduction
14 General Depreciation System (GDS) (see instructions):						
a 3-year property						
b 5-year property						
c 7-year property						
d 10-year property						
e 15-year property						
f 20-year property						
g Residential rental property			27.5 yrs.	MM	S/L	
			27.5 yrs.	MM	S/L	
h Nonresidential real property				MM	S/L	
				MM	S/L	
15 Alternative Depreciation System (ADS) (see instructions):						
a Class life					S/L	
b 12-year			12 yrs.		S/L	
c 40-year			40 yrs.	MM	S/L	

Part III — Other Depreciation (Do Not Include Listed Property)

16	GDS and ADS deductions for assets placed in service in tax years beginning before 1993 (see instructions)	16	
17	Property subject to section 168(f)(1) election (see instructions)	17	
18	ACRS and other depreciation (see instructions)	18	

Part IV — Summary

19	Listed property. Enter amount from line 25.	19	
20	Total. Add deductions on line 12, lines 14 and 15 in column (g), and lines 16 through 19. Enter here and on the appropriate lines of your return. (Partnerships and S corporations—see instructions)	20	
21	For assets shown above and placed in service during the current year, enter the portion of the basis attributable to section 263A costs (see instructions)	21	

For Paperwork Reduction Act Notice, see page 1 of the separate instructions. Cat. No. 12906N Form **4562** (1993)

Copyright © 1994 by Harcourt Brace & Company. All rights reserved.

Portfolio Problem Optional Extension 1   Name_____   A-55

Form **6251**	**Alternative Minimum Tax—Individuals**	OMB No. 1545-0227
Department of the Treasury Internal Revenue Service	▶ See separate instructions. ▶ Attach to Form 1040 or Form 1040NR.	**1993** Attachment Sequence No. **32**
Name(s) shown on Form 1040		Your social security number

Part I — Adjustments and Preferences

1	If you itemized deductions on Schedule A (Form 1040), go to line 2. If you did not itemize deductions, enter your standard deduction from Form 1040, line 34, and skip to line 6	1
2	Medical and dental expenses. See instructions	2
3	Taxes. Enter the amount from Schedule A, line 8	3
4	Certain interest on a home mortgage not used to buy, build, or improve your home	4
5	Miscellaneous itemized deductions. Enter the amount from Schedule A, line 24	5
6	Refund of taxes. Enter any tax refund from Form 1040, line 10 or 22	6 ( )
7	Investment interest. Enter difference between regular tax and AMT deduction	7
8	Post-1986 depreciation. Enter difference between regular tax and AMT depreciation	8
9	Adjusted gain or loss. Enter difference between AMT and regular tax gain or loss	9
10	Incentive stock options. Enter excess of AMT income over regular tax income	10
11	Passive activities. Enter difference between AMT and regular tax income or loss	11
12	Beneficiaries of estates and trusts. Enter the amount from Schedule K-1 (Form 1041), line 8	12
13	Tax-exempt interest from private activity bonds issued after 8/7/86	13

14	Other. Enter the amount, if any, for each item and enter the total on line 14.
	  a Charitable contributions g Long-term contracts
	  b Circulation expenditures h Loss limitations
	  c Depletion i Mining costs
	  d Depreciation (pre-1987) j Pollution control facilities
	  e Installment sales k Research and experimental
	  f Intangible drilling costs l Tax shelter farm activities
	                     m Related adjustments
		14

15	**Total Adjustments and Preferences.** Combine lines 1 through 14 ▶	15

Part II — Alternative Minimum Taxable Income

16	Enter the amount from **Form 1040, line 35.** If less than zero, enter as a (loss) ▶	16
17	Net operating loss deduction, if any, from Form 1040, line 22. Enter as a positive amount	17
18	If Form 1040, line 32, is over $108,450 (over $54,225 if married filing separately), enter your itemized deductions limitation, if any, from line 9 of the worksheet for Schedule A, line 26	18 ( )
19	Combine lines 15 through 18 ▶	19
20	Alternative tax net operating loss deduction. See instructions	20
21	**Alternative Minimum Taxable Income.** Subtract line 20 from line 19. (If married filing separately and line 21 is more than $165,000, see instructions.) ▶	21

Part III — Exemption Amount and Alternative Minimum Tax

22 **Exemption Amount.** (If this form is for a child under age 14, see instructions.)

If your filing status is:	And line 21 is not over:	Enter on line 22:	
Single or head of household	$112,500	$33,750	
Married filing jointly or qualifying widow(er)	150,000	45,000	22
Married filing separately	75,000	22,500	

If line 21 is **over** the amount shown above for your filing status, see instructions.

23	Subtract line 22 from line 21. If zero or less, enter -0- here and on lines 26 and 28 ▶	23
24	If line 23 is $175,000 or less ($87,500 or less if married filing separately), multiply line 23 by 26% (.26). Otherwise, see instructions	24
25	Alternative minimum tax foreign tax credit. See instructions	25
26	Tentative minimum tax. Subtract line 25 from line 24 ▶	26
27	Enter your tax from Form 1040, line 38 (plus any amount from Form 4970 included on Form 1040, line 39), minus any foreign tax credit from Form 1040, line 43	27
28	**Alternative Minimum Tax.** (If this form is for a child under age 14, see instructions.) Subtract line 27 from line 26. If zero or less, enter -0-. Enter here and on Form 1040, line 48 ▶	28

For Paperwork Reduction Act Notice, see separate instructions.   Cat. No. 13600G   Form **6251** (1993)

Copyright © 1994 by Harcourt Brace & Company. All rights reserved.

Excerpt From Form 6251 Instructions

Page 2

Line 2—Medical and Dental Expenses

If you do not have an entry on line 1 of Schedule A (Form 1040), skip Form 6251, line 2, and go to Form 6251, line 3. Otherwise, if **none** of the adjustments and preferences on lines 6, 7 (from investment interest on Schedule E (Form 1040)), 8 through 13, 14b through 14l, 17, and 20 apply to you, enter on Form 6251, line 2, the smaller of Schedule A, line 4, or 2.5% of Form 1040, line 32. If **any** of these adjustments and preferences apply to you, complete the **Medical and Dental Expenses Worksheet** on this page. Before you start the worksheet, complete Form 6251, lines 6, 7 (if you deducted investment interest on Schedule E), 8 through 13, 14b through 14m, 17, and 20.

Medical and Dental Expenses Worksheet—Line 2 (keep for your records)

1. Enter the amount from Schedule A, line 1 . . . . . 1. _____
2. Complete the ATAGI worksheet on page 6 for purposes of this line, and enter the ATAGI from line 7 . . . . 2. _____
3. Multiply line 2 above by 10% (.10). If zero or less, enter -0- 3. _____
4. Enter the amount from Schedule A, line 4 . . . . . 4. _____
5. Subtract line 3 from line 1. If zero or less, enter -0- . . 5. _____
6. Subtract line 5 from line 4. Enter the result on Form 6251, line 2 . . . . 6. _____

Page 6

Line 14m—Related adjustments.

If you have an entry on line 6, 7 (if you deducted investment interest on Schedule E (Form 1040)), 8 through 13, 14b through 14l, or a net operating loss deduction (for the AMT or regular tax), you must refigure any related items that are affected by adjustments or preferences or by adjusted gross income (AGI). Figure the difference between the AMT and regular tax amount for each item. Combine the amounts for all your related adjustments and enter the total on line 14m. Keep a copy of all computations for your records, including any AMT carryover and basis amounts.

Items that may be affected by other adjustments or preferences include:
- Section 179 expense deduction.
- Expenses for business use of your home deduction.
- Self-employed health insurance deduction.
- IRA, SEP, or Keogh plan deduction.

Items that are affected by AGI must be refigured using alternative tax adjusted gross income (ATAGI) from line 7 of the worksheet on this page instead of AGI. (But do not refigure your deduction for medical and dental expenses or charitable contributions because those items are refigured on lines 2 and 14a.) These items include:
- Taxable social security benefits (Form 1040, line 21b).
- Excludable savings bond interest (Form 8815, line 14).

Alternative Tax Adjusted Gross Income (ATAGI) Worksheet (keep for your records)

1. Enter the amount from Form 1040, line 32 . . . . . 1. _____
2. Enter the amount from Form 6251, line 6. . . . . . 2. (_____)
3. If you deducted investment interest on Schedule E, enter the part of the adjustment on Form 6251, line 7, that is allocable to Schedule E . . . . 3. _____
4. Combine lines 8 through 13, 14b through 14l, and 17 of Form 6251 . . . . 4. _____
5. Figure the adjustments for line 14m and enter the combined total of those adjustments (do not include an adjustment for personal casualty or theft losses or the item for which you are completing this worksheet) . . . . 5. _____
6. Enter the amount, if any, from Form 6251, line 20 . . . 6. (_____)
7. **ATAGI.** Combine lines 1 through 6 . . . . 7. _____

- IRA deductions (Form 1040, lines 24a and 24b).
- Personal casualty or theft losses (Form 4684, line 18).

Example. On your Schedule C (Form 1040) you have a net profit of $9,000 before figuring your section 179 expense deduction (and you do not report any other business income on your return). During the year, you purchased a business asset for $10,000 for which you elect to take the section 179 expense deduction. You also have an AMT depreciation adjustment of $700 for other business assets depreciated on your Schedule C. Your section 179 expense deduction for the regular tax is limited to your net profit (before any section 179 expense deduction) of $9,000. The $1,000 excess is a section 179 expense deduction carryforward for the regular tax. But, for the AMT, your net profit is $9,700, so you are allowed a section 179 expense deduction of $9,700 for the AMT. You have a section 179 expense deduction carryforward of $300 for the AMT. You would include a $700 negative adjustment on line 14m because your section 179 expense deduction for the AMT is $700 greater than your allowable regular tax deduction. In the following year when you use the $1,000 regular tax carryforward, you would have a $700 positive adjustment for the AMT because your AMT carryforward is only $300.

Portfolio Problem Optional Extension 2   Name_____ A-57

Form **941**
(Rev. January 1994)
Department of the Treasury
Internal Revenue Service

4141

Employer's Quarterly Federal Tax Return
▶ See separate instructions for information on completing this return.
Please type or print.

Proof as of August 1993 (subject to change)

Enter state code for state in which deposits made ▶ ☐ (see page 2 of instructions).

Name (as distinguished from trade name)   Date quarter ended

Trade name, if any   Employer identification number

Address (number and street)   City, state, and ZIP code

OMB No. 1545-0029

T	
FF	
FD	
FP	
I	
T	

If address is different from prior return, check here ▶ ☐

IRS Use

[boxes labeled 1 1 1 1 1 1 1 1 2 3 3 3 3 3 4 4 4
         5 5 5 6 7 8 8 8 8 8 9 9 10 10 10 10 10 10 10 10 10]

If you do not have to file returns in the future, check here ▶ ☐ (and enter) date final wages paid ▶
If you are a seasonal employer, see **Seasonal employers** on page 2 and check here (see instructions) ▶ ☐

1 Number of employees (except household) employed in the pay period that includes March 12th ▶
2 Total wages and tips subject to withholding, plus other compensation **2**
3 Total income tax withheld from wages, tips, and sick pay **3**
4 Adjustment of withheld income tax for preceding quarters of calendar year **4**
5 Adjusted total of income tax withheld (line 3 as adjusted by line 4—see instructions) . . **5**
6a Taxable social security wages . . . . $ _____ × 12.4% (.124) = **6a**
 b Taxable social security tips . . . . $ _____ × 12.4% (.124) = **6b**
7 Taxable Medicare wages and tips . . . . . $ _____ × 2.9% (.029) = **7**
8 Total social security and Medicare taxes (add lines 6a, 6b, and 7) Check here if wages are not subject to social security and/or Medicare tax . . . . ▶ ☐ **8**
9 Adjustment of social security and Medicare taxes (see instructions for required explanation)
   Sick Pay $ _____ ± Fractions of Cents $ _____ ± Other $ _____ = **9**
10 Adjusted total of social security and Medicare taxes (line 8 as adjusted by line 9—see instructions) **10**
11 **Total taxes** (add lines 5 and 10) **11**
12 Advance earned income credit (EIC) payments made to employees, if any **12**
13 Net taxes (subtract line 12 from line 11). **This should equal line 17, column (d) below** (or line D of Schedule B (Form 941)) **13**
14 Total deposits for quarter, including overpayment applied from a prior quarter **14**
15 **Balance due** (subtract line 14 from line 13). Pay to Internal Revenue Service **15**
16 **Overpayment,** if line 14 is more than line 13, enter excess here ▶ $ _____
   and check if to be: ☐ Applied to next return OR ☐ Refunded.

• **Monthly depositors:** Complete line 17, columns (a) through (d) and check here . . . . ▶ ☐
• **Semiweekly depositors:** Complete Schedule B and check here . . . . ▶ ☐
• **All filers:** If line 13 is less than $500, you need not complete line 17 or Schedule B.

17	Monthly Summary of Federal Tax Liability.			
	(a) First month liability	(b) Second month liability	(c) Third month liability	(d) Total liability for quarter

Sign Here Under penalties of perjury, I declare that I have examined this return, including accompanying schedules and statements, and to the best of my knowledge and belief, it is true, correct, and complete.

Signature ▶ _____   Print Your Name and Title ▶ _____   Date ▶ _____

For Paperwork Reduction Act Notice, see page 1 of separate instructions.   Cat. No. 17001Z   Form **941** (Rev. 1-94)

1993 form not available at press time.

Copyright © 1994 by Harcourt Brace & Company. All rights reserved.

A-58 Portfolio Problem Optional Extension 2   Name _____

Form **940**
Department of the Treasury
Internal Revenue Service

Employer's Annual Federal Unemployment (FUTA) Tax Return

▶ For Paperwork Reduction Act Notice, see separate instructions.

OMB No. 1545-0028

1992

T	
FF	
FD	
FP	
I	
T	

If incorrect, make any necessary change. ▶

Name (as distinguished from trade name)   Calendar year

Trade name, if any

Address and ZIP code   Employer identification number

	Yes	No
A Are you required to pay unemployment contributions to only one state?	☐	☐
B Did you pay all state unemployment contributions by February 1, 1993? (If a 0% experience rate is granted check "Yes.")	☐	☐
C Were all wages that were taxable for FUTA tax also taxable for your state's unemployment tax?	☐	☐
D Did you pay all wages in a state other than Michigan?	☐	☐

If you answered "No" to any of these questions, you must file Form 940. If you answered "Yes" to all the questions, you may file Form 940-EZ which is a simplified version of Form 940. You can get Form 940-EZ by calling 1-800-TAX-FORM (1-800-829-3676).

If you will not have to file returns in the future, check here, complete, and sign the return . . . . ▶ ☐
If this is an Amended Return, check here . . . . ▶ ☐

Part I   Computation of Taxable Wages

1 Total payments (including exempt payments) during the calendar year for services of employees . **1**

2 Exempt payments. (Explain each exemption shown, attach additional sheets if necessary.) ▶ _____   Amount paid **2**

3 Payments of more than $7,000 for services. Enter only amounts over the first $7,000 paid to each employee. Do not include payments from line 2. The $7,000 amount is the Federal wage base. Your state wage base may be different. **Do not use the state wage limitation** **3**

4 Total exempt payments (add lines 2 and 3) **4**

5 **Total taxable wages** (subtract line 4 from line 1) . . . . ▶ **5**

6 Additional tax resulting from credit reduction for unrepaid advances to the State of Michigan. Enter the wages included on line 5 for Michigan and multiply by .011. (See the separate Instructions for Form 940.) Enter the credit reduction amount here and in Part II, line 5:
   Michigan wages _____ × .011 = ... ▶ **6**

Form 940 (1992)   Page **2**

Part II   Tax Due or Refund

1 Gross FUTA tax. Multiply the wages in Part I, line 5, by .062 . . . . **1**
2 Maximum credit. Multiply the wages in Part I, line 5, by .054 . . | **2** |
3 Computation of tentative credit:

(a) Name of state	(b) State reporting number(s) as shown on employer's state contribution returns	(c) Taxable payroll (as defined in state act)	(d) State experience rate From	To	(e) State experience rate	(f) Contributions if rate had been 5.4% (col. (c) x .054)	(g) Contributions payable at experience rate (col. (c) x col. (e))	(h) Additional credit (col. (f) minus col.(g)). If 0 or less, enter 0.	(i) Contributions actually paid to state

3a Totals . . . ▶
3b Total tentative credit (add line 3a, columns (h) and (i) only—see instructions for limitations on late payments) ▶

4 **Credit:** Enter the smaller of the amount in Part II, line 2, or line 3b . **4**
5 Enter the amount from Part I, line 6 . . . . **5**
6 **Credit allowable** (subtract line 5 from line 4). (If zero or less, enter 0.) **6**
7 **Total FUTA tax** (subtract line 6 from line 1) **7**
8 Total FUTA tax deposited for the year, including any overpayment applied from a prior year . . **8**
9 **Balance due** (subtract line 8 from line 7). This should be $100 or less. Pay to the Internal Revenue Service . . . . ▶ **9**
10 **Overpayment** (subtract line 7 from line 8). Check if it is to be: ☐ **Applied to next return,** or ☐ **Refunded** . . . . ▶ **10**

Part III   Record of Quarterly Federal Tax Liability for Unemployment Tax (Do not include state liability)

Quarter	First	Second	Third	Fourth	Total for year
Liability for quarter					

Under penalties of perjury, I declare that I have examined this return, including accompanying schedules and statements, and to the best of my knowledge and belief, it is true, correct, and complete, and that no part of any payment made to a state unemployment fund claimed as a credit was or is to be deducted from the payments to employees.

Signature ▶ _____   Title (Owner, etc.) ▶ _____   Date ▶ _____

1993 form not available at press time.

Copyright © 1994 by Harcourt Brace & Company. All rights reserved.

APPENDIX B

Tax Rate Schedules

1993 Tax Rate Schedules

Single—Schedule X

If the amount on Form 1040, line 37 is: Over—	But not over—	Enter on Form 1040, line 38		of the amount over—
$0	$22,100	... 15	%	$ 0
22,100	53,500	$ 3,315.00 + 28	%	22,100
53,500	115,000	12,107.00 + 31	%	53,500
115,000	250,000	31,172.00 + 36	%	115,000
250,000	...	79,772.00 + 39.6%		250,000

Schedule Y-1—Use if your filing status is Married filing jointly or Qualifying widow(er)

If the amount on Form 1040, line 37, is: Over—	But not over—	Enter on Form 1040, line 38		of the amount over—
$0	$36,900	... 15	%	$ 0
36,900	89,150	$ 5,535.00 + 28	%	36,900
89,150	140,000	20,165.00 + 31	%	89,150
140,000	250,000	35,928.50 + 36	%	140,000
250,000	...	75,528.50 + 39.6%		250,000

Schedule Y-2—Use if your filing status is Married filing separately

If the amount on Form 1040, line 37, is: Over—	But not over—	Enter on Form 1040, line 38		of the amount over—
$0	$18,450	... 15	%	$ 0
18,450	44,575	$ 2,767.50 + 28	%	18,450
44,575	70,000	10,082.50 + 31	%	44,575
70,000	125,000	17,964.25 + 36	%	70,000
125,000	...	37,764.25 + 39.6%		125,000

Schedule Z—Use if your filing status is Head of household

If the amount on Form 1040, line 37, is: Over—	But not over—	Enter on Form 1040, line 38		of the amount over—
$0	$29,600	... 15	%	$ 0
29,600	76,400	$ 4,440.00 + 28	%	29,600
76,400	127,500	17,544.00 + 31	%	76,400
127,500	250,000	33,385.00 + 36	%	127,500
250,000	...	77,485.00 + 39.6%		250,000

1993 Exemption, Standard Deduction, and Phaseout Amounts

Exemption deduction	$ 2,350
Standard deduction:	
Basic amounts:	
Single	$ 3,700
Married -filing jointly	6,200
Married-filing separately	3,100
Head of household	5,450
Minimum standard deduction	$ 600
Additional standard deduction for persons age 65 or older or legally blind:	
Single or head of household	$ 900
Married	700
Phaseout of personal exemption deduction Begins at adjusted gross income of:	
Single	$108,450
Married-filing jointly	162,700
Married-filing separately	81,350
Head of household	135,600
Phaseout of itemized deductions begins at adjusted gross income of:	
Married-filing separately	$ 54,225
All other returns	108,450

1994 Tax Rate Schedules

Single — Schedule X

If the amount on Form 1040, line 37 is: Over—	But not over—	Enter on Form 1040, line 38	of the amount over—
$0	$22,750	... 15 %	$ 0
22,750	55,100	$ 3,412.50 + 28 %	22,750
55,100	115,000	12,470.50 + 31 %	55,100
115,000	250,000	31,039.50 + 36 %	115,000
250,000	...	79,639.50 + 39.6%	250,000

Schedule Y-1—Use if your filing status is Married filing jointly or Qualifying widow(er)

If the amount on Form 1040, line 37, is: Over—	But not over—	Enter on Form 1040, line 38	of the amount over—
$0	$38,000	... 15 %	$ 0
38,000	91,850	$ 5,700.00 + 28 %	38,000
91,850	140,000	20,778.00 + 31 %	91,850
140,000	250,000	35,704.50 + 36 %	140,000
250,000	...	75,304.50 + 39.6%	250,000

Schedule Y-2—Use if your filing status is Married filing separately

If the amount on Form 1040, line 37, is: Over—	But not over—	Enter on Form 1040, line 38	of the amount over—
$0	$19,000	... 15 %	$ 0
19,000	45,925	$ 2,850.00 + 28 %	19,000
45,925	70,000	10,389.00 + 31 %	45,925
70,000	125,000	17,852.25 + 36 %	70,000
125,000	...	37,652.25 + 39.6%	125,000

Schedule Z—Use if your filing status is Head of household

If the amount on Form 1040, line 37, is: Over—	But not over—	Enter on Form 1040, line 38	of the amount over—
$0	$30,500	... 15 %	$ 0
30,500	76,400	$ 4,575.00 + 28 %	30,500
78,700	127,500	18,071.00 + 31 %	78,700
127,500	250,000	33,199.00 + 36 %	127,500
250,000	...	77,299.00 + 39.6%	250,000

1994 Exemption, Standard Deduction, and Phaseout Amounts

Exemption deduction	$ 2,450
Standard deduction:	
Basic amounts:	
Single	$ 3,800
Married-filing jointly	6,350
Married-filing separately	3,175
Head of household	5,600
Minimum standard deduction	$ 600
Additional standard deduction for persons age 65 or older or legally blind:	
Single or head of household	$ 950
Married	750
Phaseout of personal exemption deduction	
Begins at adjusted gross income of:	
Single	$118,800
Married-filing jointly	167,700
Married-filing separately	83,850
Head of household	139,750
Phaseout of itemized deductions begins at adjusted gross income of:	
Married-filing separately	$ 55,900
All other returns	111,800

APPENDIX J

Tax Law Changes Effective in 1994

CHAPTER 1

IV. PHASEOUT OF THE PERSONAL EXEMPTION DEDUCTION MADE PERMANENT

The personal exemption phaseout computation was originally enacted by Congress as a temporary measure, applicable only to the tax years 1991 through 1996. As part of the 1993 Act, Congress has permanently extended this phaseout computation.

CHAPTER 2

No changes are first effective in 1994.

CHAPTER 3

IV. SOCIAL SECURITY BENEFITS SUBJECT TO POTENTIALLY HIGHER TAXES

Taxpayers with large amounts of "provisional income" (i.e., adjusted gross income plus tax-exempt income plus one-half of social security benefits) may find that a larger portion of social security payments received are subject to tax after 1993. Those taxpayers with provisional income at or below $34,000 (single taxpayers) or $44,000 (married-filing jointly) will still compute the taxable portion of social security under the 1993 rules (e.g., the lesser of (1) 50% of the social security or (2) 50% of the excess of provisional income over the $25,000 (single) or $32,000 (married-filing jointly) threshold amounts).

For tax years beginning after 1993, taxpayers with provisional incomes exceeding $34,000 (single) or $44,000 (married-filing jointly) will be subject to a new 85% threshold computation. Specifically, the portion of social security taxable to such taxpayers will be the *lesser* of

(1) 85% of the total social security benefits received, or
(2) 85% of the excess of provisional income over $34,000 (single) or $44,000 (married-filing jointly), plus the *lesser* of (a) the amount includable under 1993 law, or (b)$4,500 ($6,000 for married-filing jointly).

Note that the $4,500 and $6,000 amounts in the second computation are simply 50% of the $9,000 and $12,000 increases in the old threshold amounts of $25,000 and $32,000. This insures that the amount includable from the increased threshold amounts will not be greater than under prior law (with the 50% threshold).

✓ **Example.** Aaron and Suzanne Stein file a joint return in 1993. Their 1993 income consists of $35,000 taxable interest, $20,000 taxable dividends, and $14,000 social security. The Stein's provisional income under 1993 law would be $62,000, or $35,000 + $20,000 + $7,000 (50% of the social security received). One-half of the excess of provisional income ($62,000) over the 1993 base of $32,000 would be $15,000, and since this exceeds 50% of the social security benefits received ($7,000), only $7,000 of the social security benefits are taxable in 1993.

✓ **Example.** Assume the same facts as in the previous example, except that the tax year is 1994. The portion of the Stein's social security benefits taxable in 1994 is $11,900, the *lesser* of

(1) $14,000 × .85 = $11,900
(2) [($62,000 - $44,000) × .85) + $6,000* = $21,300

* Less than the $7,000 includable under 1993 law.

CHAPTER 4

II RENTAL REAL ESTATE ACTIVITIES

See Part III of Chapter 7 for a discussion of the changes in the treatment of rental real estate activites for persons devoting substantial time to these activities.

III CHARITABLE CONTRIBUTION SUBSTANTIATION RULES

Taxpayers who make a contribution to a charitable organization of $250 or more will no longer be able to take a deduction for the contribution unless they obtain "contemporaneous written substantiation" from that organization. Contemporaneous substantiation is defined as substantiation received on or before the earlier of (1) the due date (including extensions) for filing the return or (2) the date on which the return is filed. Information supplied as part of this substantiation includes (1) the amount of cash given or a description of other property contributed, (2) whether the organization provided any goods or services to the donor in return for the contribution, and (3) a good-faith estimate of the value of any goods or services identified in (2).

The Internal Revenue Service has clarified that the $250 threshold applies to a single donation and that multiple donations made at various times during the year do not have to be aggregated for purposes of these substantiation rules.

✓ Example. Joy Bond gives $10 a week for 50 weeks to her church. Although the *total* exceeds $250, the substantiation requirements would not have to be met since no *single* contribution is $250 or more. If she felt generous at year-end and gave $500 to her church in one donation, she would be required to obtain the contemporaneous written substantiation.

IV CHANGES IN THE MOVING EXPENSE DEDUCTION

Taxpayers' deductions for moving expenses will be limited to (1) the expenses incurred in moving their household goods and personal effects to a new residence from the old residence and (2) traveling expenses to a new residence from the old residence. Traveling expenses are redefined to exclude all meal expenses. As a result, taxpayers will no longer be able to deduct any meal expense or any indirect moving costs—premove house hunting expenses, temporary living expenses, and costs of obtaining a new residence and disposing of the old residence—as moving expenses.

Taxpayers will also have to meet an increased mileage requirement. The new residence will have to be at least 50 miles farther than the old residence was from the previous place of employment or moving expenses will not be deductible.

The one bright spot in these changes is that the moving expense deduction reverts to an "above the line" deduction; that is, it is a deduction *for* AGI. Thus, taxpayers who do not itemize their deductions can still benefit from this modified moving expense deduction.

V INCREASE IN DISALLOWED PORTION OF MEAL AND ENTERTAINMENT EXPENSES

The disallowed portion of business meals and entertainment is increased from 20% to 50%. Thus, taxpayers' deductions are limited to 50% of these expenses rather than the 80% previously allowed.

V DISALLOWANCE OF THE DEDUCTION FOR CLUB DUES

Taxpayers will no longer be able to deduct *any* portion of club dues or membership fees regardless of the club's business use by the taxpayer. This applies to all clubs organized for "business, pleasure, recreation, or other social purpose."

V RESTRICTION ON DEDUCTIBILITY OF RELATED-PARTY TRAVEL EXPENSES

Taxpayers will no longer be able to deduct travel expenses for their spouses, dependents, or other individuals accompanying the taxpayer unless that person(s) (a) is an employee of the taxpayer, (b) has a bona fide business purpose for accompanying the taxpayer, and (c) would otherwise be able to deduct the expenses.

V REDUCTION OF ITEMIZED DEDUCTIONS FOR HIGH-INCOME TAXPAYERS MADE PERMANENT

When originally enacted in 1990, the reduction in itemized deductions for high-income taxpayers was to expire at the end of the 1996 tax year. This reduction has now been made a permanent part of the tax structure and high-income taxpayers will be required to calculate a reduction in their itemized deductions every year unless the law is changed again.

VI MOVING EXPENSES DEDUCTIBLE FOR AGI

As mentioned above, the modified moving expense deduction will now become a deduction *for* AGI along with contributions to IRAs and alimony paid.

CHAPTER 5

I MODIFICATION OF THE EARNED-INCOME CREDIT

There are two major changes in the earned-income credit for tax years beginning after 1993. The earned-income credit reverts to a single credit; that is, the additional credits for a child born during the current tax year and for health insurance are repealed. A reduced earned-income credit is available for low-income individuals who do not have a qualifying child living with them. To be eligible for the reduced earned-income credit without a qualifying child, the taxpayer's principal residence must be in the United States for over one-half of the tax year, the taxpayer (or spouse, if married) must be at least 25 years of age (but less than 65 years of age) by the end of the current tax year, and the taxpayer cannot be claimed as a dependent on the return of another.

The format for determing the modified earned credit remains the same as the format for determining the basic earned income credit of prior years; however, the income limitations, phaseout income amounts, and credit and phaseout percentages have been modified. These amounts are as follows:

Tax Year	Number of Children	Credit Percentage and Earned Income Limit	Phaseout Percent and Income Limit*
1994	0	7.65 $4,000	7.65 $4,000
	1	26.3 $7,750	15.98 $11,000
	2 or more	30.0 $8,425	17.68 $11,000
1995	0	7.65 $4,000†	7.65 $5,000†
	1	34.0 $6,000†	15.98 $11,000†
	2 or more	36.0 $8,425†	20.22 $11,000†
1996	0	7.65 $4,000†	7.65 $5,000†
	1	34.0 $6,000†	15.98 $11,000*
	2 or more	40.0 $8,425†	21.06 $11,000†

*Adjusted gross income or earned income, if greater.
†Adjusted for inflation for tax years after 1994.

☑ **Example.** John Jacobs is a single parent with one qualifying child in tax year 1994. He has $9,800 of earned income and an AGI of $12,500. His earned-income credit is

```
  $ 7,750
  ×  26.3
  $ 2,038   Tentative credit

  $12,500
  -11,000
  $ 1,500   Excess Income

  $ 1,500
  × 15.98
  $   240   Phaseout amount

  $ 2,038
  -   240
  $ 1,798   Credit amount
```

VI SIMPLIFIED ESTIMATED TAX PAYMENT REQUIREMENTS FOR HIGHER-INCOME INDIVIDUALS

Taxpayers with adjusted gross incomes in excess of $150,000 ($75,000 married-filing separately) may now use a simplified method for determining their estimated tax payments for the current tax year to avoid underpayment penalties. These taxpayers may avoid penalties by paying 110% of the prior year's tax liability as their estimated tax payment. Taxpayers with adjusted gross incomes of $150,000 or less will still be able to use the payment of 100% of the prior year's tax liability.

> ✓ **Example.** Amy Wetherill expects taxable income of $220,000 in 1994. Her tax liability for 1993 was $24,550 on taxable income of $138,000 in 1993. Amy's withholding and estimated payments must total $27,005 ($24,550 × 1.10) in order to avoid underpayment penalties for 1994.

CHAPTER 6
CHAPTER APPENDIX: SPECIAL MARK-TO-MARKET RULES FOR SECURITIES DEALERS

New Sec. 475 accelerates income recognition by securities dealers by requiring such dealers to "mark to market" any securities held as inventory on the inventory date. (These rules do not apply to securities clearly labeled as investments under the rules discussed in the Appendix.) Generally, this means that any unrealized gains (the difference between a security's fair market value and its cost basis) must be included in gross income *before* the gain is realized in a market transaction. Any gain or loss realized when the security is actually sold is then adjusted for the previous mark-to-market.

> ✓ **Example.** Amy Madison, a registered securities dealer, has 1,000 shares of Beale Corporation stock in her 1994 ending inventory. She had purchased the stock for $9,000 and it is worth $14,000 on the inventory date (December 31st). Amy must include a $5,000 mark-to-market gain in her 1994 gross income.

> ✓ **Example.** Assume the same facts as in the previous example. If Amy sells the 1,000 shares of Beale Corporation stock in 1995 for $16,000, her reportable gain is $2,000 ($16,000 amount realized less the $9,000 adjusted basis less the $5,000 gain previously taxed in 1994 under the mark-to-market rules).

CHAPTER 7

III MODIFICATION OF RENTAL REAL ESTATE ACTIVITIES AS PASSIVE ACTIVITIES

Prior to 1994, all rental real estate activity was, by definition, a passive activity. While certain exceptions existed for rental activities of short duration and/or those for which substantial services were performed as part of the rental, persons who spent a majority of their time in rental real estate not qualifying under these exceptions were treated in the same manner as taxpayers with little or no time commitment to the activity; that is, their income or loss from the activity was passive regardless of the total time spent. Now, taxpayers who are in a "real property business" may classify that activity as active.

This newly added exception applies to taxpayers who (1) spend more than one-half of the total time spent on personal service trades or businesses in real property trades or businesses in which the taxpayer materially participates and (2) perform more than 750 hours of services in these same trades or businesses. A real property trade or business is defined as "real property development, redevelopment, construction, reconstruction, acquisition, conversion, rental, operation, management, leasing, or brokerage trade or business."

If a husband and wife file a joint tax return, they *may not* aggregate their activities to meet this exception; one or the other of them must *separately* qualify. Moreover, personal services performed as an employee cannot be treated as related to a real estate trade or business unless the employee owns 5% or more of the real estate trade or business. Closely-held C corporations may qualify under this exception if more than 50% of their gross receipts are from real estate trades or businesses in which they materially participate during the tax year.

CHAPTER 8

I LIMITS ON DEDUCTIBILITY OF EXECUTIVE COMPENSATION

For tax years after 1993, Congress has imposed an "automatic standard" of reasonableness on the deductibility of compensation to certain key executives (generally, the chief executive officer and the four other highest-paid executives) in publicly-held corporations. In general, the maximum corporate deduction is established at $1 million per year for each covered executive.

However, corporations may be able to justify a larger deduction if the compensation is based on the attainment of certain performance goals that are set by a compensation committee of the Board of Directors, approved by a majority of the shareholders, and are certified as having been met by the compensation committee. For purposes of these rules, the compensation committee must consist of at least two or more directors who are not officers or employees of the company. This performance goal exception may prove to be an administrative nightmare for the IRS when conducting an audit of affected companies.

I DISALLOWANCE OF ADDITIONAL LOBBYING EXPENSE DEDUCTIONS

Although most lobbying expenses were not deductible under prior law, an exception applied for those lobbying expenses related to attempts to influence legislation that directly related to a taxpayer's trade or business. In general, such expenditures that attempt to influence federal or state legislation will no longer be deductible for tax years after 1993. This disallowance provision also applies to that portion of dues paid to trade associations or other groups that relate to lobbying activities.

The disallowance rule does not apply to expenditures attempting to influence legislation at the local government level (e.g., city or county governments). Also, a *de minimis* rule allows a taxpayer to deduct up to $2,000 of "in-house" lobbying expenses (those not paid to professional lobbyists or associations).

V REMOVAL OF THE FICA MEDICARE TAX EARNINGS CAP

For years after 1993, the FICA medicare tax earnings cap (set at $135,000 for 1993) will be removed. A cap will still be in place for the FICA social security tax (set at $57,600 for 1993 and $60,000 for 1994). Thus, self-employment earnings after 1993 will be fully subject to the 2.9% medicare tax.

CHAPTER APPENDIX: REMOVAL OF MEDICARE TAX EARNINGS CAP ALSO APPLIES TO EMPLOYEES

The removal of the cap also applies to the earnings of employees for purposes of withholdings and employer taxes (as discussed in the Appendix).

CHAPTER 9

V CREDIT FOR SOCIAL SECURITY TAXES PAID ON EMPLOYEE CASH TIPS

A credit for the excess employer social security taxes paid on cash tips reported by the employee to the employer is added to the general business credit. Excess employer social security taxes are .0765 (the employer's FICA tax rate) times reported tips in excess of the amount considered wages paid at the minimum wage rate to the employee.

> ☑ **Example.** Jerry Burger worked ten hours a week during the last 30 weeks of 1994 at a restaurant. He was paid an hourly rate of $2.50 and was permitted to keep all of his tips. The applicable minimum wage rate was $4.25 per hour. Jerry reported a total of $875 in tips to his employer during that period. The employer paid .0765 FICA tax on Jerry's total income of $2,375, or $181.69. Jerry's minimum wage during the period would be $1,275 (10 × 30 × $4.25). The employer's excess social security taxes would be $84.15 [$181.69 − (.0765 × $1275)].

This credit is limited to the excess social security taxes paid by employers on tips received by employees from customers served food and/or beverages for consumption at the place where they were served. It would not apply, however, to other types of services, such as baggage handling by bellhops, for which tips are normally received.

To avoid a double benefit, the employer is not permitted a deduction for taxes paid on any excess social security taxes for which the credit is claimed. Employers may, however, elect *not* to claim the credit on a year-by-year basis.

This credit is a part of the general business credit and would be combined with other general business credits on Form 3800. Any part of the credit not used in the current tax year *may not be carried back* to any tax year prior to the enactment of this credit.

APPENDIX K

Instructions for Commonly Used Tax Forms

Section 4.

Line Instructions for Form 1040

Name, Address, and Social Security Number (SSN)

Why Use the Label? The mailing label on the front of the instruction booklet is designed to speed processing at Internal Revenue Service Centers and prevent common errors that delay refund checks. But do not attach the label until you have finished your return. Cross out any errors and print the correct information. Add any missing items such as your apartment number.

Caution: *If the label is for a joint return and the SSNs are not listed in the same order as the first names, show the SSNs in the correct order.*

Besides your name, address, and SSN, the label contains various code numbers and letters. The diagram below explains what these numbers and letters mean.

Address Change. If the address on your mailing label is not your current address, cross out your old address and print your new address. If you move after you file your return, see page 35.

Name Change. If you changed your name because of marriage, divorce, etc., be sure to report this to your local Social Security Administration office before filing your return. This prevents delays in processing your return and issuing refunds. It also safeguards your future social security benefits. If you received a mailing label, cross out your former name and print your new name.

Deceased Taxpayer. See **Death of Taxpayer** on page 35.

What if I Do Not Have a Label? If you didn't receive a label, print or type the information in the spaces provided. But if you are married filing a separate return, do not enter your husband's or wife's name here. Instead, show his or her name on line 3.

Social Security Number. Enter your SSN in the area marked "Your social security number." If you are married, enter your husband's or wife's SSN in the area marked "Spouse's social security number." Be sure the SSN you enter agrees with the SSN on your social security card. Also, check that your SSN is correct on your Forms W-2 and 1099. See page 35 for more details.

If you don't have an SSN, get **Form SS-5** from your local Social Security Administration (SSA) office or call the SSA toll free at 1-800-772-1213. Fill it in and return it to the SSA. If you do not have an SSN by the time your return is due, enter "Applied for" in the space for the SSN.

Nonresident Alien Spouse. If your spouse is a nonresident alien and you file a joint return, your spouse must get an SSN. But if your spouse cannot get an SSN because he or she had no income from U.S. sources, enter "NRA" in the space for your spouse's SSN. If you file a separate return and your spouse has no number and no income, enter "NRA."

P.O. Box. If your post office does not deliver mail to your home and you have a P.O. box, show your box number instead of your home address.

Foreign Address. If your address is outside the United States or its possessions or territories, fill in the line for "City, town or post office, state, and ZIP code" in the following order: city, province or state, postal code, and the name of the country. **Do not** abbreviate the country name.

Presidential Election Campaign Fund

Congress set up this fund to help pay for Presidential election campaign costs. The fund reduces candidates' dependence on large contributions from individuals and groups and places candidates on an equal financial footing in the general election. If you want $3 of your tax to go to this fund, check the "Yes" box. If you are filing a joint return, your spouse may also have $3 go to the fund. If you check "Yes," your tax or refund will not change.

Filing Status

In general, your filing status depends on whether you are considered single or married. The filing statuses are listed below. The ones that will usually give you the lowest tax are listed last.

- Married filing a separate return
- Single
- Head of household
- Married filing a joint return or Qualifying widow(er) with dependent child

If more than one filing status applies to you, choose the one that will give you the lowest tax.

Line 1

Single

You may check the box on line 1 if **any** of the following was true on December 31, 1993:

- You were never married, or
- You were legally separated, according to your state law, under a decree of divorce or of separate maintenance, or
- You were widowed before January 1, 1993, and did not remarry in 1993.

If you had a child living with you, you may be able to take the earned income credit on line 56. See page EIC-1 to find out if you can take the credit.

Line 2

Married Filing Joint Return

You may check the box on line 2 if **any** of the following is true:

- You were married as of December 31, 1993, even if you did not live with your spouse at the end of 1993, or

Your Mailing Label—What Does It Mean?

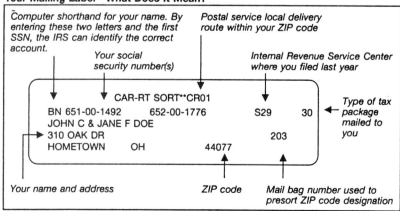

- 12 -

- Your spouse died in 1993 and you did not remarry in 1993, or
- Your spouse died in 1994 before filing a 1993 return. For details on filing the joint return, see **Death of Taxpayer** on page 35.

A husband and wife may file a joint return even if only one had income or if they did not live together all year. However, both must sign the return and both are responsible. This means that if one spouse does not pay the tax due, the other may have to.

If you file a joint return for 1993, you may not, after the due date for filing that return, amend that return to file as married filing a separate return.

Nonresident Aliens and Dual-Status Aliens. You may be able to file a joint return. Get **Pub. 519**, U.S. Tax Guide for Aliens, for details.

Line 3

Married Filing Separate Return

If you file a separate return, you will generally pay more tax. But you may want to figure your tax both ways (married filing joint and married filing separate) to see which filing status is to your benefit. If you file a separate return, **all** the following apply.

- You cannot take the standard deduction if your spouse itemizes deductions.
- You cannot take the credit for child and dependent care expenses in most cases.
- You cannot take the earned income credit.
- You cannot exclude the interest from series EE U.S. savings bonds issued after 1989, even if you paid higher education expenses in 1993.
- You cannot take the credit for the elderly or the disabled unless you lived apart from your spouse for all of 1993.
- You may have to include in income up to one-half of any social security or equivalent railroad retirement benefits you got in 1993.
- Generally, you report only your own income, exemptions, deductions, and credits. Different rules apply to people who live in community property states. See page 15.

But you may be able to file as head of household if you had a child living with you and you lived apart from your spouse during the last 6 months of 1993. See **Married Persons Who Live Apart** on this page.

Line 4

Head of Household

This filing status is for **unmarried** individuals who provide a home for certain other persons. (Some **married persons who live apart** may also qualify. See below.) You may check the box on line 4 **only if** you were unmarried or legally separated as of December 31, 1993. But **either** 1 or 2 below must apply to you.

1. You paid over half the cost of keeping up a home that was the main home for all of 1993 of your **parent** whom you can claim as a dependent. Your parent did not have to live with you in your home; or

2. You paid over half the cost of keeping up a home in which you lived and in which one of the following also lived for more than half of the year (if half or less, see the **Exception** later):

- Your **unmarried** child, adopted child, grandchild, great-grandchild, etc., or stepchild. This child does not have to be your dependent. But in this case, enter the child's name in the space provided on line 4.
- Your **married** child, adopted child, grandchild, great-grandchild, etc., or stepchild. This child must be your dependent. But if your married child's other parent claims him or her as a dependent under the rules for **Children of Divorced or Separated Parents** on page 14, this child does not have to be your dependent. Enter this child's name on line 4.
- Your **foster** child, who must be your dependent.
- Any other relative you can claim as a dependent. For the definition of a relative, see **Test 1** on page 14. But for this purpose, the **Exception** at the end of that test doesn't apply.

Note: *You cannot file as head of household if your child, parent, or relative described above is your dependent under the rules on page 14 for Person Supported by Two or More Taxpayers.*

Married Persons Who Live Apart. Even if you were not divorced or legally separated in 1993, you may be able to file as head of household. You may check the box on line 4 if **all five** of the following apply.

1. You **must** have lived apart from your spouse for the **last 6 months** of 1993.

2. You file a separate return from your spouse.

3. You paid over half the cost of keeping up your home for 1993.

4. Your home was the main home of your child, adopted child, stepchild, or foster child for more than half of 1993 (if half or less, see the **Exception** later).

5. You claim this child as your dependent or the child's other parent claims him or her under the rules for **Children of Divorced or Separated Parents** on page 14. If this child is not your dependent, be sure to enter the child's name on line 4.

Note: *If all five of the above apply, you may also be able to take the credit for child and dependent care expenses and the earned income credit. You can take the standard deduction even if your spouse itemizes deductions. For more details, see the instructions for these topics.*

Keeping Up a Home. To find out what is included in the cost of keeping up a home, get **Pub. 501**, Exemptions, Standard Deduction, and Filing Information.

If you used payments you received under the **Aid to Families With Dependent Children (AFDC)** program or **other public assistance** programs to pay part of the cost of keeping up your home, you **cannot** count them as money you paid. But you must include them in the total cost of keeping up your home to figure if you paid over half of the cost.

Dependents. To find out if someone is your dependent, see the instructions for line 6c.

Exception. You can count temporary absences such as for school, vacation, or medical care as time lived in the home.

If the person for whom you kept up a home was born or died in 1993, you may still file as head of household as long as the home was that person's main home for the part of the year he or she was alive.

Line 5

Qualifying Widow(er) With Dependent Child

You may check the box on line 5 and use joint return tax rates for 1993 if **all five** of the following apply.

1. Your spouse died in 1991 or 1992 and you did not remarry in 1993.

2. You have a child, stepchild, adopted child, or foster child whom you can claim as a dependent.

3. This child lived in your home for all of 1993. Temporary absences, such as for vacation or school, count as time lived in the home.

4. You paid over half the cost of keeping up your home for this child.

5. You could have filed a joint return with your spouse the year he or she died, even if you didn't actually do so.

Do not claim an exemption for your spouse.

If your spouse died in 1993, you may not file as qualifying widow(er) with dependent child. Instead, see the instructions for line 2.

If you can't file as qualifying widow(er) with dependent child, read the instructions for line 4 to see if you can file as head of household. You must file as single if you can't file as qualifying widow(er) with dependent child, married filing a joint return, or head of household.

Exemptions

For each exemption you can take, you generally can deduct $2,350 on line 36.

Line 6a

Yourself

Check the box on line 6a **unless** your parent (or someone else) can claim you as a dependent on his or her tax return. For example, if your parents (or someone else) could claim you as a dependent on their return but they chose not to claim you, **do not** check the box on line 6a.

Line 6b

Spouse

If you file a joint return and your spouse cannot be claimed as a dependent on another person's return, check the box on line 6b. If you file a separate return, you can take an exemption for your spouse only if your spouse is not filing a return, had no income, and cannot be claimed as a dependent on another person's return.

If you were divorced or legally separated at the end of 1993, you cannot take an exemption for your former spouse. If your divorce was not final (an interlocutory decree), you are considered married for the whole year.

Death of Your Spouse. If your spouse died in 1993 and you did not remarry by the end of 1993, check the box on line 6b if you could have taken an exemption for your spouse on the date of death. For other filing instructions, see **Death of Taxpayer** on page 35.

Nonresident Alien Spouse. If your filing status is married filing separately, you can take an exemption for your nonresident alien spouse only if your spouse had no income from U.S. sources and is not the dependent of another person. If you can take an exemption for your spouse, check the box on line 6b and enter "NRA" to the right of the word "Spouse."

Line 6c

Dependents

You can take an exemption for each of your dependents who was alive during some part of 1993. This includes a baby **born** in 1993 or a person who **died** in 1993. Get **Pub. 501,** Exemptions, Standard Deduction, and Filing Information, for more details. Any person who meets **all five** of the following tests qualifies as your dependent.

Test 1—Relationship

The person must be your relative. But see **Exception** at the end of **Test 1.** The following are considered your relatives:

- Your child, stepchild, adopted child; a child who lived in your home as a family member if placed with you by an authorized placement agency for legal adoption; or a foster child (any child who lived in your home as a family member for the whole year).
- Your grandchild, great-grandchild, etc.
- Your son-in-law, daughter-in-law.
- Your parent, stepparent, parent-in-law.
- Your grandparent, great-grandparent, etc.
- Your brother, sister, half brother, half sister, stepbrother, stepsister, brother-in-law, sister-in-law.
- If related by blood, your aunt, uncle, nephew, niece.

Any relationships established by marriage are not treated as ended by divorce or death.

Exception. A person who lived in your home as a family member for the entire year can also be considered a dependent. But the relationship must not violate local law.

Test 2—Married Person

If the person is married and files a joint return, you cannot take an exemption for the person. However, if the person and the person's spouse file a joint return only to get a refund of all tax withheld, you may be able to claim him or her if the other four tests are met. See Pub. 501 for details.

Test 3—Citizen or Resident

The person must be **one** of the following:
- A U.S. citizen or resident alien, or
- A resident of Canada or Mexico, or
- Your adopted child who is not a U.S. citizen but who lived with you all year in a foreign country.

Test 4—Income

Generally, the person's gross income must be less than $2,350. Gross income does not include nontaxable income, such as welfare benefits or nontaxable social security benefits.

Income earned by a permanently and totally disabled person for services performed at a sheltered workshop school is generally not included for purposes of the income test. See Pub. 501 for details.

Exception for Your Child. Your child can have gross income of $2,350 or more if:

1. Your child was **under age 19** at the end of 1993, **or**

2. Your child was **under age 24** at the end of 1993 **and** was a **student.**

Your child was a **student** if he or she—

- Was enrolled as a full-time student at a school during any 5 months of 1993, or
- Took a full-time, on-farm training course during any 5 months of 1993. The course had to be given by a school or a state, county, or local government agency.

A **school** includes technical, trade, and mechanical schools. It does not include on-the-job training courses or correspondence schools.

Test 5—Support

The general rule is that you had to provide over half the person's total support in 1993. If you file a joint return, support can come from either spouse. If you remarried, the support provided by your new spouse is treated as support coming from you. For exceptions to the support test, see **Children of Divorced or Separated Parents** and **Person Supported by Two or More Taxpayers** on this page.

Support includes food, a place to live, clothing, medical and dental care, and education. It also includes items such as a car and furniture, but only if they are for the person's own use or benefit. In figuring total support:

- Use the actual cost of these items, but figure the cost of a place to live at its fair rental value.
- Include money the person used for his or her own support, even if this money was not taxable. Examples are gifts, savings, social security and welfare benefits, and other public assistance payments. This support is treated as **not** coming from you.

Total support **does not** include items such as income tax, social security and Medicare tax, life insurance premiums, scholarship grants, or funeral expenses.

If you care for a foster child, see Pub. 501 for special rules that apply.

Children of Divorced or Separated Parents. Special rules apply to determine if the support test is met for children of divorced or separated parents. The rules also apply to children of parents who lived apart from each other during the last 6 months of the year, even if they do not have a separation agreement. For these rules, a **custodial parent** is the parent who had custody of the child for most of the year. A **noncustodial parent** is the parent who had custody for the shorter period or who did not have custody at all. See Pub. 501 for the definition of custody.

The general rule is that the custodial parent is treated as having provided over half of the child's total support if both parents together paid over half of the child's support. This means that the custodial parent can claim the child as a dependent if the other dependency tests are also met.

But if you are the noncustodial parent, you are treated as having provided over half of the child's support and can claim the child as a dependent if both parents together paid over half of the child's support, the other dependency tests are met, and **either** 1 or 2 below applies:

1. The custodial parent agrees not to claim the child's exemption for 1993 by signing **Form 8332** or a similar statement. But you (as the noncustodial parent) **must** attach this signed Form 8332 or similar statement to your return. Instead of attaching Form 8332, you can attach a copy of certain pages of your divorce decree or separation agreement if it went into effect after 1984 (see **Children Who Didn't Live With You Due to Divorce or Separation** on page 15), **or**

2. Your divorce decree or written separation agreement went into effect before 1985 and it states that you (the noncustodial parent) can claim the child as a dependent. But you must have given at least $600 for the child's support in 1993. Also, you must check the pre-1985 agreement box on line 6d. This rule does not apply if your decree or agreement was changed after 1984 to say that you cannot claim the child as your dependent.

Person Supported by Two or More Taxpayers. Even if you did not pay over half of another person's support, you might still be able to claim him or her as a dependent if **all five** of the following apply.

1. You and one or more other eligible person(s) together paid over half of another person's support.

2. You paid over 10% of that person's support.

3. No one alone paid over half of that person's support.

4. Tests 1 through 4 on this page are met.

5. Each eligible person who paid over 10% of support completes **Form 2120,** Multiple Support Declaration, and you attach these forms to your return. The form states that only you will claim the person as a dependent for 1993.

An **eligible person** is someone who could have claimed another person as a dependent except that he or she did not pay over half of that person's support.

Columns (1) through (5)

After you have figured out who you can claim as a dependent, fill in the columns on line 6c. If you have more than six dependents, attach a statement to your return. Give the same information as in columns (1) through (5) for each dependent.

Column (1). Enter the name of each dependent.

Column (2). If your dependent was under age 1 on December 31, 1993, put a checkmark in column (2).

Column (3). Any dependent age 1 or older must have a social security number (SSN). You must enter that SSN in column (3). If you do not enter it or if the SSN is wrong, you may have to pay a $50 penalty.

Your dependent can get an SSN by filing **Form SS-5** with your local Social Security Administration (SSA) office. It usually takes about 2 weeks to get an SSN. If your dependent won't have an SSN when you are ready to file your return, ask the SSA to give you a receipt. When you file your return, enter "Applied for" in column (3). If the SSA gave you a receipt, attach a copy of it to your return. If your dependent lives in Canada or Mexico, see Pub. 501 for details on how to get an SSN.

Column (4). Enter your dependent's relationship to you. For example, if the dependent is your child, enter "son" or "daughter."

Column (5). Enter the number of months your dependent lived with you in 1993. Do not enter more than 12. Count temporary absences such as school or vacation as time lived in your home. If your dependent was born or died in 1993, enter "12" in this column. If your dependent lived in Canada or Mexico during 1993, don't enter a number. Instead, enter "CN" or "MX," whichever applies.

Children Who Didn't Live With You Due to Divorce or Separation. If you are claiming a child who didn't live with you under the rules on page 14 for **Children of Divorced or Separated Parents,** enter the total number of such children on the line to the right of line 6c labeled "No. of your children on 6c who: didn't live with you due to divorce or separation." If you put a number on this line, you **must** do one of the following **each** year you claim this child as a dependent.

● **Check the box on line 6d** if your divorce decree or written separation agreement went into effect before 1985 and it states that you can claim the child as your dependent.

● Attach **Form 8332** or similar statement to your return. If your divorce decree or separation agreement went into effect after 1984 and it unconditionally states that you can claim the child as your dependent, you may attach a copy of the following pages from the decree or agreement instead of Form 8332:

1. Cover page (enter the other parent's SSN on this page),
2. The page that unconditionally states you can claim the child as your dependent, and
3. Signature page showing the date of the agreement.

Note: *You must attach the required information even if you filed it in an earlier year.*

Other Dependent Children. Enter the total number of children who did not live with you for reasons other than divorce or separation on the line labeled "Dependents on 6c not entered above." Include dependent children who lived in Canada or Mexico during 1993.

Income

Examples of Income You Must Report

The following kinds of income must be reported on Form 1040, or related forms and schedules, in addition to the types of income listed on Form 1040, lines 7 through 21b. You may need some of the forms and schedules mentioned below.

● Scholarship and fellowship grants (see the instructions for line 7).
● Awards and endowments.
● Prizes (including contests, raffles, lotteries, gambling winnings, etc.)
● Lump-sum distributions (Form 4972). (See page 19.)
● Distributions from Simplified Employee Pension (SEP) and Defined Employee Contribution (DEC) plans.
● Accumulation distributions from trusts (Form 4970).
● Tier 2 and supplemental annuities under the Railroad Retirement Act.
● Life insurance proceeds from a policy you cashed in if the proceeds are more than the premiums you paid.
● Amounts received in place of wages from accident and health plans (including sick pay and disability pensions) if your employer paid for the policy.
● Gains from the sale or exchange (including barter) of real estate, securities, coins, gold, silver, gems, or other property (Schedule D or Form 4797).
● Gain from the sale or exchange of your main home (Schedule D and Form 2119).
● Director's fees.
● Fees received as an executor or administrator of an estate.
● Earned income, such as wages and tips, from sources outside the United States (Form 2555 or Form 2555-EZ).
● Unearned income, such as interest, dividends, and pensions, from sources outside the United States unless exempt by law or a tax treaty.
● Original issue discount (Schedule B).
● Bartering income (fair market value of goods or services you received in return for your services).
● Your share of income from S corporations, partnerships, estates, trusts, etc. (Schedules B, D, or E.)
● Embezzled or other illegal income.

U.S. Citizens Living Abroad

Generally, foreign source income must be reported. Get **Pub. 54,** Tax Guide for U.S. Citizens and Resident Aliens Abroad, for more details.

Examples of Income Not To Be Reported

Do not include the following types of income when you decide if you must file a return.

● Welfare benefits.
● Disability retirement payments and other benefits paid by the Department of Veterans' Affairs.
● Workers' compensation benefits, insurance, damages, etc., for injury or sickness. Punitive damages received in cases not involving physical injury or sickness usually must be reported as income. Get **Pub. 525,** Taxable and Nontaxable Income.
● Supplemental security income (SSI) payments.
● Child support.
● Money or property that was inherited, willed to you, or received as a gift.
● Dividends on veterans' life insurance.
● Life insurance proceeds received because of a person's death.
● Amounts you received from insurance because you lost the use of your home due to fire or other casualty to the extent the amounts were more than the cost of your normal expenses while living in your home. Reimbursements for normal living expenses must be reported as income.
● Certain amounts received as a scholarship grant (see the instructions for line 7).
● Cancellation of certain student loans if, under the terms of the loan, the student performs certain professional services for any of a broad class of employers. Get **Pub. 520,** Scholarships and Fellowships.

Community Property States

Community property states are Arizona, California, Idaho, Louisiana, Nevada, New Mexico, Texas, Washington, and Wisconsin.

If you and your spouse lived in a community property state, you must follow state law to determine what is community income and what is separate income. However, different rules could apply if:

● You and your spouse lived apart all year,
● You do not file a joint return, and
● None of the community income you earned was transferred to your spouse.

For details, get **Pub. 555,** Federal Tax Information on Community Property.

Line 7

Wages, Salaries, Tips, etc.

Show the total of all wages, salaries, fees, commissions, tips, bonuses, supplemental unemployment benefits, and other amounts you were paid before taxes, insurance, etc., were taken out. For a joint return, be sure to include your spouse's income on line 7.

Include in this total:

● The amount that should be shown in box 1 on **Form W-2.** Report all wages, salaries, and tips you received, even if you do not have a Form W-2.
● Corrective distributions of excess salary deferrals.
● Corrective distributions of excess contributions and excess aggregate contributions to a retirement plan.
● Disability pensions if you have not reached the minimum retirement age set by your employer.

Note: *Disability pensions received after you reach your employer's minimum retirement age and other pensions shown on Form 1099-R (other than payments from an IRA) are reported on lines 17a and 17b of Form 1040. Payments from an IRA are reported on lines 16a and 16b.*

● Payments by insurance companies, etc., not included on Form W-2. If you received sick pay or a disability payment from anyone other than your employer, and it is not included in the wages shown on Form W-2, include it on line 7. Attach a statement showing the name and address of the payer and amount of sick pay or disability income. Get **Form W-4S** for details on withholding of Federal income tax from your sick pay.
● Fair market value of meals and living quarters if given by your employer as a matter of your choice and not for your employer's convenience. Don't report the value of meals given to you at work if they were provided for your employer's convenience. Also, don't report the value of living quarters you had to accept on your employer's business premises as a condition of employment.

- Strike and lockout benefits paid by a union from union dues. Include cash and the fair market value of goods received. Don't report benefits that were gifts.
- Any amount your employer paid for your moving expenses, including the value of services furnished in kind, that is not included in box 1 on Form W-2.

Note: *You must report on line 7 all wages, salaries, etc., paid for your personal services, even if the income was signed over to a trust (including an IRA), another person, a corporation, or a tax-exempt organization.*

For more details on reporting income received in the form of goods, property, meals, stock options, etc., get **Pub. 525**, Taxable and Nontaxable Income.

Tip Income. Be sure to report all tip income you actually received, even if it is not included in box 1 of your W-2 form(s). You must report as income the amount of allocated tips shown on your W-2 form(s) unless you can prove a smaller amount with adequate records. Allocated tips should be shown in box 8 of your W-2 form(s). They are not included in box 1 of your W-2 form(s). For details on allocated tips, get **Pub. 531**, Reporting Tip Income.

Use **Form 4137,** Social Security and Medicare Tax on Unreported Tip Income, to figure any social security and Medicare tax on unreported or allocated tips. See the instructions for line 50.

Statutory Employees. If you were a statutory employee, the "Statutory employee" box in box 15 of your W-2 form should be checked. Statutory employees include full-time life insurance salespeople, certain agent or commission drivers and traveling salespeople, and certain homeworkers.

If you are deducting business expenses as a statutory employee, report the amount shown in box 1 of your W-2 form and your expenses on Schedule C or C-EZ. If you are not deducting business expenses, report your income on line 7.

Employer-Provided Vehicle. If you used an employer-provided vehicle for both personal and business purposes and 100% of the annual lease value of the vehicle was included in the wages box (box 1) of your W-2 form, you may be able to deduct the business use of the vehicle on Schedule A. But you must use **Form 2106,** Employee Business Expenses, to do so. The total annual lease value of the vehicle should be shown in either box 12 or 14 of your W-2 form or on a separate statement. For more details, get **Pub. 917,** Business Use of a Car.

Excess Salary Deferrals. If you chose to have your employer contribute part of your pay to certain retirement plans (such as a 401(k) plan or the Federal Thrift Savings Plan) instead of having it paid to you, the "Deferred compensation" box in box 15 of your W-2 form should be checked. The amount deferred should be shown in box 13. The total amount that may be deferred for 1993 under **all** plans is generally limited to $8,994 for each person. But a different limit may apply if amounts were deferred under a tax-sheltered annuity plan or an eligible plan of a state or local government or tax-exempt organization. For details, get **Pub. 575**, Pension and Annuity Income (Including Simplified General Rule). Any amount deferred in excess of these limits must be reported on Form 1040, line 7.

Caution: *You may not deduct the amount deferred. It is not included as income in box 1 of your W-2 form.*

Dependent Care Benefits (DCB). If you received benefits for 1993 under your employer's dependent care plan, you may be able to exclude part or all of them from your income. But you must use **Form 2441,** Child and Dependent Care Expenses, to do so. The benefits should be shown in box 10 of your W-2 form(s). First, fill in Parts I and III of Form 2441. Include any taxable benefits from line 20 of that form on Form 1040, line 7. On the dotted line next to line 7, enter "DCB."

Caution: *If you have a child who was born in 1993 and you earned less than $23,050, you may be able to take the extra credit for a child born in 1993 on Schedule EIC. But you cannot take the extra credit and the exclusion of dependent care benefits for the same child. To find out which would benefit you more, see A Change To Note in the Instructions for Form 2441.*

Scholarship and Fellowship Grants. If you received a scholarship or fellowship that was granted **after** August 16, 1986, part or all of it may be taxable even if you didn't receive a W-2 form. If you were a degree candidate, the amounts you used for expenses other than tuition and course-related expenses are taxable. For example, amounts used for room, board, and travel are taxable. If you were not a degree candidate, the full amount of the scholarship or fellowship is taxable.

Include the taxable amount not reported on a W-2 form on line 7. Then, enter "SCH" and the taxable amount not reported on a W-2 form on the dotted line next to line 7.

Line 8a

Taxable Interest Income

Report **all** of your taxable interest income on line 8a even if it is $400 or less. If the total is over $400 or any of the other conditions listed at the beginning of the Schedule B instructions (see page B-1) apply to you, fill in Schedule B first.

The payer should send you a **Form 1099-INT** or, if applicable, a **Form 1099-OID** for this interest. A copy of the form is also sent to the IRS.

Report any interest you received or that was credited to your account so you could withdraw it, even if it wasn't entered in your passbook. Interest credited in 1993 on deposits that you could not withdraw because of the bankruptcy or insolvency of the financial institution may not have to be included in your 1993 income. For details, get **Pub. 550,** Investment Income and Expenses.

Caution: *Be sure each payer of interest income has your correct social security number. Otherwise, the payer may withhold 31% of the interest (backup withholding). You may also be subject to penalties.*

Examples of Taxable Interest Income You Must Report

Report interest from:

- Accounts (including certificates of deposit and money market accounts) with banks, credit unions, and savings and loan associations.
- Building and loan accounts.
- Notes, loans, and mortgages. Special rules apply to loans with below-market interest rates. See Pub. 550.
- Tax refunds. Report only the interest on them as interest income.
- Insurance companies if paid or credited on dividends left with the company.
- Bonds and debentures. Also, arbitrage bonds issued by state and local governments after October 9, 1969. (Report interest on other state and local bonds and securities on line 8b.) Also, report as interest on line 8a any gain on the disposition of certain market discount bonds to the extent of the accrued market discount. See Pub. 550 for details. For taxable bonds acquired after 1987, reduce your interest income on the bonds by the amount of any amortizable bond premium (see page B-1). **Do not** deduct the premium as interest expense on Schedule A.
- U.S. Treasury bills, notes, and bonds.
- U.S. savings bonds. The interest is the yearly increase in the value of the bond. Interest on series E or EE bonds can be reported using method **a** or **b** below:

  a. Report the total interest when you cash the bonds, or when they reach final maturity and no longer earn interest, **or**

  b. Each year report on your return the yearly increase in the bonds' value.

  If you change to method **b,** report the entire increase in all your bonds from the date they were issued. Each year after report only the yearly increase. You may not change to method **a** unless you complete **Form 3115** and attach it to your tax return. See Pub. 550 for details.

Note: *If you get a 1993 Form 1099-INT for U.S. savings bond interest that includes amounts you reported before 1993, see Pub. 550.*

- Original issue discount (OID). This is the difference between the issue price of a debt instrument and the stated redemption price at maturity. If the instrument was issued at a discount after May 27, 1969 (or for certain noncorporate instruments, after July 1, 1982), include in your interest income the discount for the part of the year you held it. The taxable OID may be more or less than the amount shown on Form 1099-OID.

  If you bought a corporate debt instrument at original issue and held it for all of 1993 or the part of 1993 that it was outstanding, include in interest income the OID from Form 1099-OID. Get **Pub. 1212,** List of Original Issue Discount Instruments, to figure the taxable OID for other corporate debt instruments and noncorporate debt instruments (such as zero coupon U.S. Treasury-backed securities).

  If you had OID for 1993 but did not receive Form 1099-OID, or if the price you paid for the instrument is more than the issue price plus accumulated OID, see Pub. 1212. It provides total OID on the instruments listed and gives computational information.

  Also, include in your interest income any other periodic interest shown on Form 1099-OID.

Line 8b

Tax-Exempt Interest

If you received any tax-exempt interest income, such as from municipal bonds, report it on line 8b. Include any exempt-interest dividends from a mutual fund or other regulated investment company. **Do not** include interest earned on your IRA.

Line 9

Dividend Income

Dividends are distributions of money, stock, or other property that corporations pay to stockholders. They also include dividends you receive through a partnership, an S corporation, or an estate or trust. Payers include nominees or other agents. The payer should send you a **Form 1099-DIV.** A copy of this form is also sent to the IRS.

If your total gross dividends are over $400, first fill in Schedule B (see page B-1). Gross dividends should be shown in box 1a of Form 1099-DIV. Also, fill in Schedule B if you received, as a nominee, dividends that actually belong to someone else. If you don't have to fill in Schedule B, include on line 9 only ordinary dividends and any investment expenses that should be shown in box 1e of Form 1099-DIV.

Caution: *Be sure each payer of dividends has your correct social security number. Otherwise, the payer may withhold 31% of the dividend income (backup withholding). You may also be subject to penalties.*

Dividends Include:

Ordinary dividends. These should be shown in box 1b of Form 1099-DIV.

Capital gain distributions. These should be shown in box 1c of Form 1099-DIV. If you have other capital gains or losses, also enter your capital gain distributions on Schedule D. If you don't need Schedule D to report any other gains or losses, see the instructions for lines 13 and 14.

Nontaxable distributions. Some distributions are nontaxable because they are a return of your cost. They will not be taxed until you recover your cost. You must reduce your cost (or other basis) by these distributions. After you get back all of your cost (or other basis), you must report these distributions as capital gains. For details, get **Pub. 550,** Investment Income and Expenses. Nontaxable distributions should be shown in box 1d of Form 1099-DIV.

Note: *Generally, payments from a money market fund are dividends.*

Do Not Report as Dividends

• Dividends on insurance policies. These are a partial return of the premiums you paid. Do not include them in income until they exceed the total of all net premiums you paid for the contract. Remember to report on line 8a any interest on dividends left with an insurance company.

• Amounts paid on deposits or accounts from which you could withdraw your money, such as mutual savings banks, cooperative banks, and credit unions. Remember to report these amounts as interest on line 8a.

• Alaska Permanent Fund dividends. Report these amounts on line 22 instead.

Line 10

Taxable Refunds, Credits, or Offsets of State and Local Income Taxes

If you received a refund, credit, or offset of state or local income taxes in 1993 that you paid and deducted before 1993, part or all of this amount may be taxable. You may receive **Form 1099-G,** or similar statement, showing the refund.

If you chose to apply part or all of the refund to your 1993 estimated state or local income tax, the amount applied is considered income you received in 1993.

If, in the year you paid the tax, you **(a)** did not itemize deductions on Schedule A (Form 1040), or **(b)** filed Form 1040A or Form 1040EZ, **none** of your refund is taxable.

If the refund was for a tax you paid in 1992 and you itemized deductions on Schedule A (Form 1040) for 1992, use the worksheet below to see if any of your refund is taxable.

Exceptions. See **Recoveries** in **Pub. 525,** Taxable and Nontaxable Income, instead of using the worksheet below if **any** of the following applies:

• You received a refund in 1993 that is for a tax year other than 1992.

• You received a refund other than an income tax refund, such as a real property tax refund, in 1993 of an amount deducted or credit claimed in an earlier year.

• Your 1992 adjusted gross income was more than $905,250 (more than $805,250 if head of household; more than $585,250 if single; more than $452,625 if married filing separately).

• Your 1992 taxable income was less than zero.

• You made your last payment of 1992 estimated state or local income tax in 1993.

• You owed alternative minimum tax in 1992.

• You could not deduct the full amount of credits you were entitled to in 1992 because the total credits exceeded the tax shown on your 1992 Form 1040, line 40.

• You could be claimed as a dependent by someone else in 1992.

Line 11

Alimony Received

Enter amounts received as alimony or separate maintenance. You must let the person who made the payments know your social security number. If you don't, you may have to pay a $50 penalty. For details, get **Pub. 504,** Divorced or Separated Individuals.

If you received payments under a divorce or separation instrument executed after 1984, see the instructions for line 29 on page 23 for the rules that apply in determining whether these payments qualify as alimony.

Line 12

Business Income or (Loss)

If you operated a business or practiced your profession as a sole proprietor, report your income and expenses on Schedule C or Schedule C-EZ. Enter on line 12 your net profit or (loss) from Schedule C or your net profit from Schedule C-EZ.

Lines 13 and 14

Capital Gain or (Loss)

Enter on line 13 your capital gain or (loss) from Schedule D. If you received **capital gain distributions** (reported to you on **Form 1099-DIV** or a substitute statement) but do not need Schedule D for other capital transactions, enter those distributions on line 14.

Exception. Report your capital gain distributions on Schedule D and use the **Schedule D Tax Worksheet** in the instructions for Schedule D to figure your tax if your taxable

- 17 -

income (Form 1040, line 37) is **more than** $89,150 ($53,500 if single; $76,400 if head of household; or $44,575 if married filing separately).

Line 15
Other Gains or (Losses)

If you sold or exchanged assets used in a trade or business, see the Instructions for **Form 4797**. Enter on line 15 the ordinary gain or (loss) from Part II of Form 4797.

Lines 16a and 16b
IRA Distributions

Use lines 16a and 16b to report payments (distributions) you received from your individual retirement arrangement (IRA). These include regular distributions, early distributions, rollovers, and any other money or property you received from your IRA account or annuity. You should get a **Form 1099-R** showing the amount of your distribution.

If you made any nondeductible contributions to your IRA for 1993 or an earlier year or you rolled your IRA distribution over into another IRA, see below. **Do not** use lines 16a and 16b to report a rollover from a qualified employer's plan to an IRA. Instead, see the instructions for lines 17a and 17b.

IRA distributions that you must include in income are taxed at the same rate as other income. You may not use the special averaging rule for lump-sum distributions from qualified employer plans.

If your IRA distribution is fully taxable, enter it on line 16b; **do not** make an entry on line 16a. If only part is taxable, enter the total distribution on line 16a and the taxable part on line 16b.

Caution: *If you received an early distribution and the total distribution was not rolled over or you received an excess distribution, you may have to pay additional tax. See the instructions for line 51 for details.*

Nondeductible Contributions. If you made nondeductible contributions for any year, part of your IRA distribution may be nontaxable. Get **Form 8606** to figure the taxable part of your IRA distribution. If you made any nondeductible contributions for 1993, you may need to make a special computation. Get **Pub. 590**, Individual Retirement Arrangements (IRAs), for details. Enter the total distribution on line 16a and the taxable part on line 16b.

Rollovers. A rollover is a tax-free transfer of cash or other assets from one retirement program to another. Use lines 16a and 16b to report a rollover from one IRA to another IRA. Enter the total distribution on line 16a. If the total on line 16a was rolled over, enter zero on line 16b. If the total was not rolled over, enter the part not rolled over on line 16b. But if you ever made nondeductible contributions to any of your IRAs, use Form 8606 to figure the taxable part to enter on line 16b. For more details, see Pub. 590.

Lines 17a and 17b
Pensions and Annuities

Use lines 17a and 17b to report pension and annuity payments you received, including disability pensions received after you reach the minimum retirement age set by your employer. Disability pensions received before you reach your employer's minimum retirement age are reported on line 7. Also, use lines 17a and 17b to report payments (distributions) from profit-sharing plans, retirement plans, and employee-savings plans. See **Rollovers** below and **Lump-sum Distributions** on page 19 for details.

You should receive a **Form 1099-R** showing the amount of your pension or annuity. Attach Form 1099-R to Form 1040 if any Federal income tax was withheld from your pension or annuity.

Do not use lines 17a and 17b to report corrective distributions of excess salary deferrals, excess contributions, or excess aggregate contributions from retirement plans. Instead, see the instructions for line 7. Also, **do not** use lines 17a and 17b to report any social security or railroad retirement benefits shown on **Forms SSA-1099** and **RRB-1099**. Instead, see the instructions for lines 21a and 21b.

Caution: *Certain transactions, such as loans against your interest in a qualified plan, may be treated as taxable distributions and may also be subject to additional taxes. For details, get Pub. 575, Pension and Annuity Income (Including Simplified General Rule).*

Fully Taxable Pensions and Annuities

If your pension or annuity is fully taxable, enter it on line 17b; **do not** make an entry on line 17a. Your pension or annuity payments are fully taxable if **either** of the following applies:

1. You did not contribute to the cost of your pension or annuity, or

2. You used the 3-Year Rule and you got your entire cost back tax free before 1993.

Fully taxable pensions and annuities also include military retirement pay shown on Form 1099-R. For details on military disability pensions, get **Pub. 525**, Taxable and Nontaxable Income. If you received a **Form RRB-1099-R**, get Pub. 575 to see how to report your benefits.

Partially Taxable Pensions and Annuities

If your pension or annuity is partially taxable and your Form 1099-R does not show the taxable part, you must use the General Rule to figure the taxable part. The General Rule is explained in **Pub. 939**, Pension General Rule (Nonsimplified Method). But if your annuity starting date (defined later) was **after** July 1, 1986, you may be able to use the Simplified General Rule (explained later) to figure the taxable part of your pension or annuity.

If you choose to, you may submit a ruling request to the IRS before the due date of your return (including extensions) and the IRS will figure the taxable part for you for a $50 fee. For details, see Pub. 939.

If your Form 1099-R shows a taxable amount, you may report that amount on line 17b. But you may use the General Rule or, if you qualify, the Simplified General Rule to see if you can report a lower taxable amount.

Once you have figured the taxable part of your pension or annuity, enter that amount on line 17b and the total on line 17a.

Annuity Starting Date. Your annuity starting date is the later of the first day of the first period for which you received a payment from the plan, or the date on which the plan's obligations became fixed.

Simplified General Rule. Using this method will usually result in at least as much of the pension or annuity being tax free each year as under the General Rule or as figured by the IRS. You qualify to use this simpler method if **all four** of the following apply.

1. Your annuity starting date was **after** July 1, 1986.

2. The pension or annuity payments are for **(a)** your life or **(b)** your life and that of your beneficiary.

3. The pension or annuity payments are from a qualified employee plan, a qualified employee annuity, or a tax-sheltered annuity.

4. At the time the pension or annuity payments began, either you were under age 75 or, if you were 75 or older, the number of years of guaranteed payments was fewer than 5.

If you qualify, use the worksheet on page 19 to figure the taxable part of your pension or annuity. But if you received U.S. Civil Service retirement benefits and you chose the lump-sum credit option, use the worksheet in **Pub. 721**, Tax Guide to U.S. Civil Service Retirement Benefits, instead of the one on page 19. If you are a beneficiary entitled to a death benefit exclusion, add the exclusion to the amount you enter on line 2 of the worksheet even if you received a Form 1099-R showing a taxable amount. The payer of the annuity cannot add the death benefit exclusion to your cost when figuring the taxable amount. Attach a signed statement to your return stating that you are entitled to a death benefit exclusion. For more details on the Simplified General Rule, see Pub. 575 or Pub. 721.

Age at Annuity Starting Date. If you are the retiree, use your age on the annuity starting date. If you are the survivor of a retiree, use the retiree's age on his or her annuity starting date. If you are the beneficiary of an employee who died, get Pub. 575. If there is more than one beneficiary, see Pub. 575 or Pub. 721 to figure each beneficiary's taxable amount.

Changing Methods. If your annuity starting date was **after** July 1, 1986, you may be able to change from the General Rule to the Simplified General Rule (or the other way around). For details, see Pub. 575 or Pub. 721.

Death Benefit Exclusion. If you are the beneficiary of a deceased employee or former employee, amounts paid to you by, or on behalf of, an employer because of the death of the employee may qualify for a death benefit exclusion of up to $5,000. If you are entitled to this exclusion, add it to the cost of the pension or annuity. Special rules apply if you are the survivor under a joint and survivor's annuity. For details, see Pub. 575.

Rollovers. A rollover is a tax-free transfer of cash or other assets from one retirement program to another. Use lines 17a and 17b to report a rollover, including a direct rollover, from one qualified employer's plan to another or to an IRA.

Enter on line 17a the total distribution before income tax or other deductions were withheld. This amount should be shown in box 1 of **Form 1099-R.** If the total on line 17a (minus any contributions that were taxable to you when made) was rolled over, either directly or within 60 days of receiving the distribution, enter zero on line 17b. Otherwise, subtract the amount that was rolled over and any contributions that were taxable to you when made from the total on line 17a. Enter the result on line 17b. Special rules apply to partial rollovers of property. For more details on rollovers, including distributions under qualified domestic relations orders, see Pub. 575.

Lump-Sum Distributions. If you received a lump-sum distribution from a profit-sharing or retirement plan, your Form 1099-R should have the "Total distribution" box in box 2b checked. If you received an early distribution from a qualified retirement plan and the total amount was not rolled over, you may owe an additional tax. You may also owe an additional tax if you received an excess distribution from a qualified retirement plan. For details, see the instructions for line 51.

Enter the total distribution on line 17a and the taxable part on line 17b. But you may pay less tax on the distribution if you were born before 1936, you meet certain other conditions, and you choose to use **Form 4972,** Tax on Lump-Sum Distributions, to figure the tax on any part of the distribution. You may also be able to use Form 4972 if you are the beneficiary of a deceased employee who was born before 1936 and was age 50 or older on the date of death. For details, get Form 4972.

If you use Form 4972 to figure the tax on any part of your distribution, do not include that part of the distribution on line 17a or 17b of Form 1040.

Line 18

Rental Real Estate, Royalties, Partnerships, S Corporations, Trusts, etc.

Use Schedule E to report income or losses from rental real estate, royalties, partnerships, S corporations, estates, trusts, and REMICs. Enter on line 18 your total income or (loss) from Schedule E.

Line 19

Farm Income or (Loss)

Use Schedule F to report farm income and expenses. Enter on line 19 your net profit or (loss) from Schedule F.

Line 20

Unemployment Compensation

Enter on line 20 any unemployment compensation (insurance) you received. By January 31, 1994, you should receive a **Form 1099-G** showing the total amount paid to you during 1993. This amount should be in box 1.

If you received an overpayment of unemployment compensation in 1993 and you repaid any of it in 1993, subtract the amount you repaid from the total amount you received. Enter the result on line 20. Also, enter "Repaid" and the amount you repaid on the dotted line next to line 20. If, in 1993, you repaid unemployment compensation that you included in gross income in an earlier year, you may deduct the amount repaid on Schedule A, line 20. But if the amount repaid was more than $3,000, see **Repayments** in Pub. 525, Taxable and Nontaxable Income, for details on how to report the repayment.

Do not include on line 20 any supplemental unemployment benefits received from a company-financed supplemental unemployment benefit fund. Instead, report these benefits on line 7.

Caution: *If you expect to receive unemployment compensation in 1994, which may cause you to owe tax when you file your return next year, you may need to make estimated tax payments during 1994. See* **Income Tax Withholding and Estimated Tax Payments for 1994** *on page 35.*

Lines 21a and 21b

Social Security Benefits

Social security and equivalent railroad retirement benefits you received may be taxable in some instances. Social security benefits include any monthly benefit under title II of the Social Security Act or the part of a tier 1 railroad retirement benefit treated as a social security benefit. Social security benefits do not include any supplemental security income (SSI) payments.

By January 31, 1994, you should receive a **Form SSA-1099** showing in box 3 the total social security benefits paid to you in 1993. Box 4 will show the amount of any benefits you repaid in 1993. If you received railroad retirement benefits treated as social security, you should receive a **Form RRB-1099.** For more details, get **Pub. 915,** Social Security Benefits and Equivalent Railroad Retirement Benefits.

Caution: *Do not use lines 21a and 21b to report any railroad retirement benefits shown on* **Form RRB-1099-R.** *Instead, see the instructions for lines 17a and 17b.*

To find out if any of your benefits are taxable, first complete Form 1040, lines 7 through 20, 22, and 30 if they apply to you. Then, complete the worksheet on page 20. However, **do not** use the worksheet if any of the following applies to you:

- You made IRA contributions for 1993 and you were covered by a retirement plan at work or through self-employment. Instead, use the worksheets in **Pub. 590,** Individual Retirement Arrangements (IRAs), to see if any of your social security benefits are taxable and to figure your IRA deduction.

- You repaid any benefits in 1993 and your total repayments (box 4) were more than your total benefits for 1993 (box 3). **None** of your benefits are taxable for 1993. In addition, you may be able to take an itemized deduction for part of the excess repayments if they were for benefits you included in gross income in an earlier year. See Pub. 915.

- You file **Form 2555,** Foreign Earned Income, **Form 2555-EZ,** Foreign Earned Income Exclusion, **Form 4563,** Exclusion of Income for Bona Fide Residents of American Samoa, **Form 8815,** Exclusion of Interest From Series EE U.S. Savings Bonds Issued After 1989, or you exclude income from sources within Puerto Rico. Instead, use the worksheet in Pub. 915.

Simplified General Rule Worksheet—Lines 17a and 17b (keep for your records)

1. Enter the total pension or annuity payments received this year. Also, enter this amount on Form 1040, line 17a . . . . . . 1. _____

2. Enter your cost in the plan at the annuity starting date plus any death benefit exclusion . . . . 2. _____

3. Age at annuity starting date (see page 18):

	Enter:
55 and under	300
56–60	260
61–65	240
66–70	170
71 and older	120

   3. _____

4. Divide line 2 by the number on line 3 . 4. _____

5. Multiply line 4 by the number of months for which this year's payments were made. If your annuity starting date was **before** 1987, also enter this amount on line 8; skip lines 6 and 7. Otherwise, go to line 6 . . . 5. _____

6. Enter the amount, if any, recovered tax free in years after 1986 . . . . 6. _____

7. Subtract line 6 from line 2 . . . . . 7. _____

8. Enter the **smaller** of line 5 or line 7 . . . . 8. _____

9. **Taxable amount.** Subtract line 8 from line 1. Enter the result, but not less than zero. Also, enter this amount on Form 1040, line 17b. If your Form 1099-R shows a larger amount, use the amount on this line instead of the amount from Form 1099-R . 9. _____

Note: *If you had more than one partially taxable pension or annuity, figure the taxable part of each separately. Enter the total of the taxable parts on Form 1040, line 17b. Enter the total pension or annuity payments received in 1993 on Form 1040, line 17a.*

Social Security Benefits Worksheet—Lines 21a and 21b (keep for your records)

If you are married filing separately and you **lived apart** from your spouse for all of 1993, enter "D" to the left of line 21a.

1. Enter the total amount from **box 5** of **all** your **Forms SSA-1099** and **Forms RRB-1099** (if applicable) . . . . 1. _____

   Note: *If line 1 is zero or less, stop here; none of your social security benefits are taxable. Otherwise, go to line 2.*

2. Divide line 1 above by 2 . . . . 2. _____
3. Add the amounts on Form 1040, lines 7, 8a, 9 through 15, 16b, 17b, 18 through 20, and line 22. Do not include here any amounts from box 5 of Forms SSA-1099 or RRB-1099 . . . 3. _____
4. Enter the amount from Form 1040, line 8b . . . . . . 4. _____
5. Add lines 2, 3, and 4 . . . . 5. _____
6. Enter the total adjustments from Form 1040, line 30 . . . 6. _____
7. Subtract line 6 from line 5 . . . . 7. _____
8. Enter on line 8 the amount shown below for your filing status:
   - Single, Head of household, or Qualifying widow(er), enter $25,000
   - Married filing jointly, enter $32,000
   - Married filing separately, enter -0- ($25,000 if you **lived apart** from your spouse for all of 1993)

   8. _____

9. Subtract line 8 from line 7. If zero or less, enter -0- . . . . 9. _____
   - If line 9 is zero, stop here. None of your social security benefits are taxable. Do not enter any amounts on lines 21a or 21b. But if you are married filing separately and you **lived apart** from your spouse for all of 1993, enter -0- on line 21b. Be sure you entered "D" to the left of line 21a.
   - If line 9 is more than zero, go to line 10.
10. Divide line 9 above by 2 . . . . 10. _____
11. **Taxable social security benefits.**
    - First, enter on Form 1040, line 21a, the amount from line 1.
    - Then, enter the **smaller** of line 2 or line 10 here and on Form 1040, line 21b . . . . 11. _____

Note: *If part of your benefits are taxable for 1993 and they include benefits paid in 1993 that were for an earlier year, you may be able to reduce the taxable amount shown on the worksheet. Get Pub. 915 for details.*

Line 22

Other Income

Use line 22 to report any other income not reported on your return or other schedules. See examples later. List the type and amount of income. If necessary, show the required information on an attached statement. For more details, see **Miscellaneous Taxable Income** in Pub. 525, Taxable and Nontaxable Income.

Do not report any income from self-employment on line 22. If you had any income from self-employment, you **must** use Schedule C, C-EZ, or F, even if you do not have any business expenses. You may also have to file **Schedule SE,** Self-Employment Tax. Your payments of self-employment tax contribute to your coverage under the social security system. Social security coverage provides you with retirement and medical insurance (Medicare) benefits.

Examples of income to report on line 22 are:

- Prizes and awards.
- Gambling winnings. Proceeds from lotteries, raffles, etc., are gambling winnings. You must report the full amount of your winnings on line 22. You cannot offset losses against winnings and report the difference. If you had any gambling losses, you may take them as an itemized deduction on Schedule A. But you cannot deduct more than the winnings you report.
- Amounts received for medical expenses or other items, such as real estate taxes, that you deducted in an earlier year if they reduced your tax. See Pub. 525 for details on how to figure the amount to report.
- Amounts recovered on bad debts that you deducted in an earlier year.
- Fees received for jury duty and precinct election board duty. You may be able to deduct part or all of your jury duty pay. See the instructions for line 30.
- Fees received as a nonprofessional fiduciary, such as an executor or administrator of the estate of a deceased friend or relative. But fees related to active participation in the operation of the estate's business or the management of an estate that required extensive management activities over a long period of time are subject to self-employment tax. Report these fees on Schedule C or C-EZ.
- Alaska Permanent Fund dividends.
- Income from line 5 of **Form 8814,** Parents' Election To Report Child's Interest and Dividends.
- Refund of overpaid mortgage interest if you deducted the interest in an earlier year and it reduced your tax. To figure the amount to report, see Pub. 525.
- Income from the rental of personal property if you were not in the business of renting such property. (See the instructions for line 30 to report your expenses.) Otherwise, report the income and expenses on Schedule C or C-EZ.
- Income from an activity not engaged in for profit. See **Not-for-Profit Activities** in Pub. 535, Business Expenses, for more details.

Net Operating Loss. If you had a net operating loss in an earlier year to carry forward to 1993, include it as a negative amount on line 22. Attach a statement showing how you figured the amount. Get Pub. 536, Net Operating Losses, for more details.

Line 23

Total Income

Enter the total of the amounts in the far right column for lines 7 through 22. If any of these amounts are negative, first add all the positive amounts. Next, add all the negative amounts. Then, subtract the total of the negative amounts from the total of the positive amounts and enter the result on line 23. If the result is negative, enter it in (parentheses).

Adjustments to Income

Lines 24a and 24b

IRA Deduction

If you made contributions to an Individual Retirement Arrangement (IRA) for 1993, you may be able to take an IRA deduction. Read the instructions below and on the next page to see if you can take an IRA deduction and, if you can, which worksheet to use to figure it. Enter your IRA deduction on line 24a. If you file a joint return, enter your spouse's deduction on line 24b. You should receive a statement by May 31, 1994, that shows all contributions to your IRA for 1993.

Caution: *You may not deduct contributions to a 401(k) plan or the Federal Thrift Savings Plan. These amounts are not included as income in box 1 of your W-2 form.*

If you were age 70½ or older at the end of 1993, you cannot deduct any contributions made to your IRA for 1993 or treat them as nondeductible contributions.

Note: *If you file Form 2555, Foreign Earned Income, or Form 2555-EZ, Foreign Earned Income Exclusion, get Pub. 590 to figure your IRA deduction.*

Were You Covered by a Retirement Plan?

If you were covered by a retirement plan (qualified pension, profit-sharing (including 401(k)), annuity, Keogh, SEP, etc.) at work or through self-employment, your IRA deduction may be reduced or eliminated. But you can still make contributions to an IRA even if you can't deduct them. In any case, the income earned on your IRA contributions is not taxed until it is paid to you.

The "Pension plan" box in box 15 of your W-2 form should be checked if you were covered by a plan at work even if you were not vested in the plan. You are also covered by a plan if you were self-employed and had a Keogh or SEP retirement plan.

If you were covered by a retirement plan and you file **Form 8815**, Exclusion of Interest From Series EE U.S. Savings Bonds Issued After 1989, get Pub. 590 to figure the amount, if any, of your IRA deduction.

Special Rule for Married Individuals Who File Separate Returns. If you were not covered by a retirement plan but your spouse was, **you** are considered covered by a plan unless you **lived apart** from your spouse for all of 1993. See the chart on this page. It will tell you if you can take the deduction and, if you can, which worksheet to use.

Not Covered by a Retirement Plan. If you (and your spouse if filing a joint return) were not covered by a plan, use **Worksheet 1** on this page to figure your deduction.

Covered by a Retirement Plan. If you (or your spouse if filing a joint return) were covered by a plan, see the chart on this page. It will tell you if you can take the deduction and, if you can, which worksheet to use.

Nondeductible Contributions. You can make nondeductible contributions to your IRA even if you are allowed to deduct part or all of your contributions. Your nondeductible contribution is the difference between the total allowable contributions to your IRA and the amount you deduct.

Example. Your filing status is single and you paid $2,000 into your IRA. You were covered by a retirement plan and your modified AGI is over $35,000 (all wages). You can't deduct the $2,000. But you can treat it as a nondeductible contribution.

Use **Form 8606** to report all contributions you treat as nondeductible. If you don't, you may have to pay a $50 penalty. Also, use it to figure the basis (nontaxable part) of your IRA. If you and your spouse each make nondeductible contributions, each of you must complete a separate Form 8606.

Read the following list before you fill in your IRA worksheet.

- You will first need to complete Form 1040 through line 23, lines 25 through 29, and figure any write-in amount for line 30.
- If you made contributions to your IRA in 1993 that you deducted for 1992, **do not** include them in the worksheet.
- If you received a distribution from a nonqualified deferred compensation plan, get Pub. 590 to figure your IRA deduction. The distribution should be shown in box 11 of your W-2 form.
- Your IRA deduction can't be more than the total of your wages and other earned income minus any deductions on Form 1040, lines 25 and 27. For purposes of the IRA deduction, alimony payments received under certain divorce or separation instruments are considered earned income. For more details, see Pub. 590.
- If the total of your IRA deduction on Form 1040 plus any nondeductible contribution on your Form 8606 is less than your total IRA contributions for 1993, see Pub. 590 for special rules.
- You must file a joint return to deduct contributions to your nonworking spouse's IRA. A **nonworking spouse** is one who had no wages or other earned income in 1993, or a

working spouse who chooses to be treated as having no earned income for figuring the deduction.

- Do not include rollover contributions in figuring your deduction. See the instructions for lines 16a and 16b on page 18 for more details on rollover contributions.
- Do not include trustee's fees that were billed separately and paid by you for your IRA. These fees can be deducted only as an itemized deduction on Schedule A.

- If married filing a joint return and both spouses worked and had IRAs, figure each spouse's deduction separately using columns (a) and (b) of the worksheet.

Line 25

One-Half of Self-Employment Tax

If you had income from self-employment and you owe self-employment tax, first fill in

Chart for People Covered by a Retirement Plan*—Lines 24a and 24b

In this chart, **modified AGI** (adjusted gross income) is the amount on Form 1040, line 23, minus the total of any deductions claimed on Form 1040, lines 25 through 29 and any amount you entered on the dotted line next to line 30.

If you (or your spouse if filing jointly) **were covered by a retirement plan and—**

Your filing status is:	And your modified AGI is:	You can take:
Single, Head of household, or Married filing separately and **lived apart** from your spouse for all of 1993	$25,000 or less	Full IRA deduction (use **Worksheet 1** on this page)
	Over $25,000 but less than $35,000	Partial IRA deduction (use **Worksheet 2** on page 22)
	$35,000 or more	No IRA deduction (but see Nondeductible Contributions)
Married filing jointly or Qualifying widow(er)	$40,000 or less	Full IRA deduction (use **Worksheet 1** on this page)
	Over $40,000 but less than $50,000	Partial IRA deduction (use **Worksheet 2** on page 22)
	$50,000 or more	No IRA deduction (but see Nondeductible Contributions)
Married filing separately and lived with your spouse at any time during 1993	Over -0- but less than $10,000	Partial IRA deduction (use **Worksheet 2** on page 22)
	$10,000 or more	No IRA deduction (but see Nondeductible Contributions)

* If married filing separately and you were not covered by a plan but your spouse was, **you** are considered covered by a plan unless **you lived apart** from your spouse for all of 1993.

IRA Worksheet 1—Lines 24a and 24b (keep for your records)

	(a) Your IRA	(b) Your working spouse's IRA
1. Enter IRA contributions you made, or will make by April 15, 1994, for 1993. But **do not** enter more than $2,000 in either column . . . . . . 1.	_____	_____
2. For each person, enter wages and other earned income from Form 1040, minus any deductions on Form 1040, lines 25 and 27. Do not reduce wages by any loss from self-employment . . 2.	_____	_____
3. Enter the **smaller** of line 1 or line 2. Enter on Form 1040, line 24a, the amount from line 3, column (a), you choose to deduct. Enter on Form 1040, line 24b, the amount, if any, from line 3, column (b), you choose to deduct. If filing a joint return and contributions were made to your nonworking spouse's IRA, go to line 4 . . . . 3.	_____	_____

	Nonworking spouse's IRA
4. Enter the **smaller** of line 2, column (a), or $2,250 . . . . . 4.	_____
5. Enter the amount from line 3, column (a) . . . . 5.	_____
6. Subtract line 5 from line 4 . . . . 6.	_____
7. Enter IRA contributions made, or that will be made by April 15, 1994, for 1993 for your nonworking spouse. But **do not** enter more than $2,000 . . . . 7.	_____
8. Enter the **smaller** of line 6 or line 7. Enter on Form 1040, line 24b, the amount from line 8 you choose to deduct . . . . 8.	_____

IRA Worksheet 2—Lines 24a and 24b (keep for your records)

1. If you checked Filing Status box:
   - 1 or 4, enter $35,000
   - 2 or 5, enter $50,000
   - 3, enter $10,000 ($35,000 if you **lived apart** from your spouse for all of 1993)

   1. _____

2. Enter the amount from Form 1040, line 23 . . . . . .   2. _____

3. Add amounts on Form 1040, lines 25 through 29, and any amount you entered on the dotted line next to line 30 . .   3. _____

4. Subtract line 3 from line 2. If the result is equal to or more than the amount on line 1, none of your IRA contributions are deductible. Stop here. If you want to make a nondeductible IRA contribution, see Form 8606 . . . .   4. _____

5. Subtract line 4 from line 1. **If the result is $10,000 or more, stop here and use Worksheet 1** . . . .   5. _____

6. Multiply line 5 above by 20% (.20). If the result is not a multiple of $10, round it up to the next multiple of $10 (for example, round $490.30 to $500). If the result is $200 or more, enter the result. But if it is less than $200, enter $200. Go to line 7 .   6. _____

	(a) Your IRA	(b) Your working spouse's IRA
Deductible IRA contributions		
7. For each person, enter wages and other earned income from Form 1040, minus any deductions on Form 1040, lines 25 and 27. Do not reduce wages by any loss from self-employment . . 7.	_____	_____
8. Enter IRA contributions you made, or will make by April 15, 1994, for 1993. But **do not** enter more than $2,000 in either column . . . . 8.	_____	_____
9. Enter the **smallest** of line 6, 7, or 8. This is the most you can deduct. Enter on Form 1040, line 24a, the amount from line 9, column (a), you choose to deduct. Enter on Form 1040, line 24b, the amount, if any, from line 9, column (b), you choose to deduct. If line 8 is more than line 9, go to line 10 . . . . 9.	_____	_____
Nondeductible IRA contributions		
10. Subtract line 9 from the **smaller** of line 7 or line 8. Enter on line 1 of your Form 8606 the amount from line 10 you choose to make nondeductible 10.	_____	_____

If filing a joint return and contributions were made to your nonworking spouse's IRA, go to line 11.

Deductible IRA contributions for nonworking spouse

11. Enter the **smaller** of line 7, column (a), or $2,250 . . . .   11. _____

12. Add the amount on line 9, column (a), to the part of line 10, column (a), that you choose to make nondeductible . . .   12. _____

13. Subtract line 12 from line 11. If the result is zero or less, stop here. You cannot make deductible or nondeductible IRA contributions for your nonworking spouse . . . . . .   13. _____

14. Enter the **smallest** of (a) IRA contributions made, or that will be made by April 15, 1994, for 1993 for your nonworking spouse; (b) $2,000; or (c) the amount on line 13 . . . .   14. _____

15. Multiply line 5 above by 22.5% (.225). If the result is not a multiple of $10, round it up to the next multiple of $10. If the result is $200 or more, enter the result. But if it is less than $200, enter $200 . . . .   15. _____

16. Enter the amount from line 9, column (a) . . . .   16. _____

17. Subtract line 16 from line 15 . . . .   17. _____

18. Enter the **smaller** of line 14 or line 17 . . . .   18. _____

19. Enter the **smallest** of line 6, 7, or 18. This is the most you can deduct. Enter on Form 1040, line 24b, the amount from line 19 you choose to deduct. If line 14 is more than line 19, go to line 20 . . . .   19. _____

Nondeductible IRA contributions for nonworking spouse

20. Subtract line 19 from line 14. Enter on line 1 of your spouse's Form 8606 the amount from line 20 that you choose to make nondeductible . . . .   20. _____

Schedule SE. Then, enter on Form 1040, line 25, one-half of the self-employment tax shown on line 5 of Short Schedule SE or line 15 of Long Schedule SE, whichever applies.

Line 26

Self-Employed Health Insurance Deduction

If you were self-employed and had a net profit for the year, or if you received wages in 1993 from an S corporation in which you were a more than 2% shareholder, you may be able to deduct part of the amount paid for health insurance on behalf of yourself, your spouse, and dependents. But if you were also eligible to participate in any subsidized health plan maintained by your or your spouse's employer for any month or part of a month in 1993, amounts paid for health insurance coverage for that month cannot be used to figure the deduction. For example, if you were eligible to participate in a subsidized health plan maintained by your spouse's employer from September 30 through December 31, you cannot use amounts paid for health insurance coverage for September through December to figure your deduction. For more details, get **Pub. 535,** Business Expenses.

If you qualify to take the deduction, use the worksheet on page 23 to figure the amount you can deduct. But if either of the following applies, **do not** use the worksheet. Instead, see Pub. 535 to find out how to figure your deduction.

- You had more than one source of income subject to self-employment tax.
- You file **Form 2555,** Foreign Earned Income, or **Form 2555-EZ,** Foreign Earned Income Exclusion.

Caution: *If you can file Schedule EIC, Earned Income Credit, you may also be able to claim the health insurance credit on that schedule. If you do claim that credit,* **do not** *use the worksheet on page 23. Instead, get* **Pub. 596,** *Earned Income Credit, to figure your self-employed health insurance deduction.*

Line 27

Keogh Retirement Plan and Self-Employed SEP Deduction

If you are self-employed or a partner, deduct payments to your Keogh (HR 10) plan or simplified employee pension (SEP) plan on line 27. Deduct payments for your employees on Schedule C or F.

Caution: *You must be self-employed to claim the Keogh deduction. There are two types of Keogh plans:*

- A **defined-contribution plan** has a separate account for each person. Benefits are based on the amount paid to each account.
- Payments to a **defined-benefit plan** are determined by the funds needed to give a specific benefit at retirement. If you deduct payments to this kind of plan, enter "DB" next to line 27.

Get **Pub. 560,** Retirement Plans for the Self-Employed, for more details, including limits on the amount you can deduct.

Self-Employed Health Insurance Deduction Worksheet—Line 26
(keep for your records)

1. Enter the total amount paid in 1993 for health insurance coverage for 1993 for you, your spouse, and dependents. But do not include amounts for any month you were eligible to participate in an employer-sponsored health plan . . . . 1. _____
2. Percentage used to figure the deduction . . . . 2. _____ × .25
3. Multiply line 1 by the percentage on line 2 . . . . 3. _____
4. Enter your net profit and any other earned income* from the business under which the insurance plan is established, minus any deductions you claim on Form 1040, lines 25 and 27 . . . 4. _____
5. **Self-employed health insurance deduction.** Enter the **smaller** of line 3 or line 4 here and on Form 1040, line 26. DO NOT include this amount in figuring any medical expense deduction on Schedule A (Form 1040). . . . . 5. _____

* *Earned income* includes net earnings and gains from the sale, transfer, or licensing of property you created. It does not include capital gain income. If you were a more than 2% shareholder in an S corporation, earned income is your wages from that corporation.

Line 28

Penalty on Early Withdrawal of Savings

The **Form 1099-INT** or, if applicable, **Form 1099-OID** given to you by your bank or savings and loan association will show the amount of any penalty you were charged because you withdrew funds from your time savings deposit before its maturity. Enter this amount on line 28. Be sure to include the interest income on Form 1040, line 8a.

Line 29

Alimony Paid

You can deduct periodic payments of alimony or separate maintenance made under a court decree. You can also deduct payments made under a written separation agreement or a decree for support. Don't deduct lump-sum cash or property settlements, voluntary payments not made under a court order or a written separation agreement, or amounts specified as child support.

For details, call Tele-Tax (see page 30) and listen to topic 452 or get **Pub. 504,** Divorced or Separated Individuals.

Caution: *You must enter the recipient's social security number (SSN) in the space provided on line 29. If you don't, you may have to pay a $50 penalty and your deduction may be disallowed.*

If you paid alimony to more than one person, enter the SSN of one of the recipients. Show the SSN(s) and the amount paid to the other recipient(s) on an attached statement. Enter your total payments on line 29.

Divorce or Separation Instruments Executed After 1984. Generally, you may deduct any payment made in cash to, or on behalf of, your spouse or former spouse under a divorce or separation instrument executed after 1984 if **all four** of the following apply.

1. The instrument does not prevent the payment from qualifying as alimony.
2. You and your spouse or former spouse did not live together when the payment was made if you were separated under a decree of divorce or separate maintenance.
3. You are not required to make any payment after the death of your spouse or former spouse.
4. The payment is not treated as child support.

These rules also apply to certain instruments modified after 1984. Other rules apply if your annual payments decreased by more than $15,000. For details, see Pub. 504.

Line 30

Total Adjustments

Add lines 24a through 29 and enter the total on line 30. Also, include in the total on line 30 any of the following adjustments.

Qualified Performing Artists. If you are a qualified performing artist, include in the total on line 30 your performing-arts-related expenses from line 11 of **Form 2106,** Employee Business Expenses. Enter the amount and "QPA" on the dotted line next to line 30.

Jury Duty Pay Given to Employer. If you reported jury duty pay on line 22 and you were required to give your employer any part of that pay because your employer continued to pay your salary while you served on the jury, include the amount you gave your employer in the total on line 30. Enter the amount and "Jury pay" next to line 30.

Forestation or Reforestation Amortization. If you can claim a deduction for amortization of the costs of forestation or reforestation and you do not have to file Schedule C, C-EZ, or F for this activity, include your deduction in the total on line 30. Enter the amount and "Reforestation" on the dotted line next to line 30.

Repayment of Sub-Pay Under the Trade Act of 1974. If you repaid supplemental unemployment benefits (sub-pay) that you previously reported in income because you became eligible for payments under the Trade Act of 1974, include in the total on line 30 the amount you repaid in 1993. Enter the amount and "Sub-pay TRA" on the dotted line next to line 30. Or, you may be able to claim a credit against your tax instead. Get **Pub. 525,** Taxable and Nontaxable Income, for more details.

Contributions to Section 501(c)(18) Pension Plans. If you chose to have your employer contribute part of your pay to a pension plan exempt from tax under Internal Revenue Code section 501(c)(18), the amount contributed should be identified with code H in box 13 of your W-2 form. You may deduct the amount contributed subject to the limits explained under **Excess Salary Deferrals** on page 16. Include your deduction in the total on line 30. Enter the amount and "501(c)(18)" next to line 30.

Deduction for Clean-Fuel Vehicles. If you can take this deduction for a vehicle placed in service after June 30, 1993, that uses a clean-burning fuel, include the amount of your deduction in the total on line 30. But if you are claiming part of your deduction on Schedule C, C-EZ, E, or F, subtract that part from your total deduction and include only the balance on line 30. Enter the amount and "Clean-Fuel" on the dotted line next to line 30. **Clean-burning fuels** are natural gas, liquefied natural gas, liquefied petroleum (LP) gas, hydrogen, electricity, and fuels containing at least 85% alcohol (including methanol or ethanol) or ether.

Expenses From the Rental of Personal Property. If you reported income from the rental of personal property on line 22, include the total of your deductible expenses related to that income in the total on line 30. Enter the amount and "PPR" on the dotted line next to line 30.

Adjusted Gross Income

Line 31

If line 31 is less than zero, you may have a net operating loss that you can carry to another tax year. If you carry the loss back to earlier years, see **Form 1045,** Application for Tentative Refund. If you do not wish to carry back a net operating loss, you may elect to carry the loss over to future years. You must attach the election to your return. For more details, get **Pub. 536,** Net Operating Losses.

Tax Computation

Line 33a

If you were age 65 or older or blind, check the appropriate boxes on line 33a. If you were married and checked the box on line 6b on page 1 of Form 1040 and your spouse was age 65 or older or blind, also check the appropriate boxes for your spouse. Then, add the number of boxes checked on line 33a. Enter the total in the box provided on line 33a. You need this total to use the **Standard Deduction Chart for People Age 65 or Older or Blind** on page 24.

Age. If you were age 65 or older on January 1, 1994, check the "65 or older" box on your 1993 return.

Blindness. If you were completely blind as of December 31, 1993, attach a statement to your return describing this condition. If you were partially blind, you must attach a statement certified by your eye doctor or registered optometrist that:

● You can't see better than 20/200 in your better eye with glasses or contact lenses, or

- Your field of vision is 20 degrees or less.

If your eye condition is not likely to improve beyond the conditions listed above, attach a statement certified by your eye doctor or registered optometrist to this effect. Keep a copy of this statement for your records. If you attached this statement in a prior year, attach a note saying that you have already filed a statement.

Line 33b

If your parent (or someone else) can claim you as a dependent on his or her return (even if that person chose not to claim you), check the box on line 33b. Use the **Standard Deduction Worksheet for Dependents** on this page to figure your standard deduction.

Line 33c

If your spouse itemizes deductions on a separate return or if you were a dual-status alien, check the box on line 33c. But if you were a dual-status alien and you file a joint return with your spouse who was a U.S. citizen or resident at the end of 1993 and you and your spouse agree to be taxed on your combined worldwide income, **do not** check the box.

If you check this box, you **cannot** take the standard deduction. If you have any itemized deductions, such as state and local income taxes, your Federal income tax will be less if you itemize your deductions.

Line 34

Itemized Deductions or Standard Deduction

Your Federal income tax will be less if you take the **larger** of:

- Your itemized deductions, or
- Your standard deduction.

The standard deduction has increased for most people. Even if you itemized last year, be sure to see if the standard deduction will benefit you in 1993.

Itemized Deductions. To figure your itemized deductions, fill in **Schedule A**.

If your itemized deductions are larger than your standard deduction, attach Schedule A and enter on Form 1040, line 34, the amount from Schedule A, line 26.

Standard Deduction. Most people can find their standard deduction by looking at line 34 of Form 1040. But if you checked **any** of the boxes on **lines 33a or 33b**, use the chart or worksheet on this page that applies to you to figure your standard deduction. Also, if you checked the box on **line 33c**, your standard deduction is zero, even if you were age 65 or older or blind.

If your standard deduction is larger than your itemized deductions, enter your standard deduction on line 34.

Itemizing for State Tax or Other Purposes. If you itemize even though your itemized deductions are less than your standard deduction, enter "IE" (itemized elected) next to line 34.

Standard Deduction Chart for People Age 65 or Older or Blind—Line 34

If someone can claim you as a dependent, use the worksheet below instead.

Enter the number from the box on line 33a of Form 1040 ▶ ☐ **Caution:** *Do not use the number of exemptions from line 6e.*

If your filing status is:	And the number in the box above is:	Your standard deduction is:
Single	1	$4,600
	2	5,500
Married filing jointly or Qualifying widow(er)	1	$6,900
	2	7,600
	3	8,300
	4	9,000
Married filing separately	1	$3,800
	2	4,500
	3	5,200
	4	5,900
Head of household	1	$6,350
	2	7,250

Standard Deduction Worksheet for Dependents—Line 34 (keep for your records)

Use this worksheet **only** if someone can claim you as a dependent.

1. Enter your **earned income** (defined below). If none, enter -0-   1. _____
2. Minimum amount 2. 600.00
3. Enter the **larger** of line 1 or line 2 . . . .   3. _____
4. Enter on line 4 the amount shown below for your filing status:
   - Single, enter $3,700
   - Married filing separately, enter $3,100
   - Married filing jointly or Qualifying widow(er), enter $6,200
   - Head of household, enter $5,450

   4. _____
5. Standard deduction.
   a. Enter the **smaller** of line 3 or line 4. If under 65 and not blind, stop here and enter this amount on Form 1040, line 34. Otherwise, go to line 5b . . . .   5a. _____
   b. If 65 or older or blind, multiply $900 ($700 if married filing jointly or separately, or qualifying widow(er)) by the number on Form 1040, line 33a . . . .   5b. _____
   c. Add lines 5a and 5b. Enter the total here and on Form 1040, line 34 . . . .   5c. _____

Earned income includes wages, salaries, tips, professional fees, and other compensation received for personal services you performed. It also includes any amount received as a scholarship that you must include in your income. Generally, your earned income is the total of the amount(s) you reported on Form 1040, lines 7, 12, and 19, minus the amount, if any, on line 25.

The IRS Will Figure Your Tax and Some of Your Credits

If you want, we will figure your tax for you. If you have paid too much, we will send you a refund. If you did not pay enough, we'll send you a bill. We won't charge you interest or a late payment penalty if you pay within 30 days of the notice date or by the due date for your return, whichever is later.

We can figure your tax if you meet **all five** of the conditions described below:

1. All of your income for 1993 was from wages, salaries, tips, interest, dividends, taxable social security benefits, unemployment compensation, IRA distributions, pensions, or annuities.
2. You do not itemize deductions.
3. You do not file any of the following forms:

Schedule D, Capital Gains and Losses.
Form 2555, Foreign Earned Income.
Form 2555-EZ, Foreign Earned Income Exclusion.
Form 4137, Social Security and Medicare Tax on Unreported Tip Income.
Form 4970, Tax on Accumulation Distribution of Trusts.
Form 4972, Tax on Lump-Sum Distributions.
Form 6198, At-Risk Limitations.
Form 6251, Alternative Minimum Tax—Individuals.
Form 8615, Tax for Children Under Age 14 Who Have Investment Income of More Than $1,200.
Form 8814, Parents' Election To Report Child's Interest and Dividends.

4. Your taxable income (line 37) is less than $100,000.
5. You do not want any of your refund applied to next year's estimated tax.

Deduction for Exemptions Worksheet—Line 36 (keep for your records)

Use this worksheet **only** if the amount on Form 1040, line 32, is more than the dollar amount shown on line 3 below for your filing status. If the amount on Form 1040, line 32, is equal to or less than the dollar amount shown on line 3, multiply $2,350 by the total number of exemptions claimed on Form 1040, line 6e, and enter the result on line 36.

1. Multiply $2,350 by the total number of exemptions claimed on Form 1040, line 6e . . . . 1. _____
2. Enter the amount from Form 1040, line 32 . . 2. _____
3. Enter on line 3 the amount shown below for your filing status:
   - Married filing separately, enter $81,350
   - Single, enter $108,450
   - Head of household, enter $135,600
   - Married filing jointly or Qualifying widow(er), enter $162,700

   3. _____
4. Subtract line 3 from line 2. If zero or less, **stop here**; enter the amount from line 1 above on Form 1040, line 36 . . . . 4. _____

   *Note: If line 4 is more than $122,500 (more than $61,250 if married filing separately), **stop here**; you **cannot** take a deduction for exemptions. Enter -0- on Form 1040, line 36.*
5. Divide line 4 by $2,500 ($1,250 if married filing separately). If the result is not a whole number, round it up to the next higher whole number (for example, round 0.0004 to 1) . . . . . . 5. _____
6. Multiply line 5 by 2% (.02) and enter the result as a decimal amount . . . . 6. _____
7. Multiply line 1 by line 6 . . . . 7. _____
8. **Deduction for exemptions.** Subtract line 7 from line 1. Enter the result here and on Form 1040, line 36 . . . . 8. _____

To have us figure your tax, please do the following:

- Fill in the parts of your return through line 37 that apply to you.
- If you are filing a joint return, use the space under the words "Adjustments to Income" on the front of your return to separately show your taxable income and your spouse's taxable income.
- Read lines 39 through 59. Fill in the lines that apply to you, but do not fill in the total lines. Please be sure to fill in line 54 for Federal income tax withheld. See the instructions below if you want us to figure your credit for the elderly or the disabled or your earned income credit.
- Fill in and attach any forms or schedules asked for on the lines you completed.
- Sign and date your return (both spouses must sign a joint return) and enter your occupation(s).
- Mail your return by April 15, 1994.

We will figure the following credits too:

Credit for the Elderly or the Disabled. If you can take this credit, attach **Schedule R** to your return and enter "CFE" on the dotted line next to line 42. Check the box on Schedule R for your filing status and age, and fill in lines 11 and 13 of Part III if applicable. Also, fill in Part II if applicable.

Earned Income Credit (EIC). Read the instructions that begin on page EIC-1 to see if you can take this credit. If you can, fill in page 1 of Schedule EIC and attach it to your return. Enter "EIC" on the dotted line next to line 56.

Line 38

Tax

To figure your tax, use one of the following methods.

Tax Table. If your taxable income is less than $100,000, you **must** use the Tax Table to find your tax unless you are required to use **Form 8615** or you use the **Schedule D Tax Worksheet** (see below). Be sure you use the correct column in the Tax Table. After you have found the correct tax, enter that amount on line 38.

Tax Rate Schedules. You must use the Tax Rate Schedules to figure your tax if your taxable income is $100,000 or more unless you are required to use **Form 8615** or you use the **Schedule D Tax Worksheet**.

Schedule D Tax Worksheet. If you had a net capital gain, your tax may be less if you figure it using the worksheet in the instructions for Schedule D.

Form 8615. Form 8615 must generally be used to figure the tax for any child who was under age 14 on January 1, 1994, and who had more than $1,200 of investment income, such as taxable interest or dividends. But if neither of the child's parents was alive on December 31, 1993, do not use Form 8615 to figure the child's tax.

Note: If you are filing Form 8814, Parents' Election To Report Child's Interest and Dividends, include in your total for line 38 the tax from Form 8814, line 8. Also, enter that tax in the space provided next to line 38.

Line 39

Additional Taxes

Check the box(es) on line 39 to report any additional taxes from:

Form 4970, Tax on Accumulation Distribution of Trusts, or

Form 4972, Tax on Lump-Sum Distributions.

Credits

Line 41

Credit for Child and Dependent Care Expenses

You may be able to take this credit if you paid someone to care for your child **under age 13** or your dependent or spouse who could not care for himself or herself. But to do so, the care must have been provided so that you (and your spouse if you were married) could work or look for work and you must have had income from a job or through self-employment.

Use **Form 2441** to figure the credit. If you received any dependent care benefits for 1993, you must file Form 2441 to figure the amount of the benefits you may exclude from your income even if you cannot take the credit. For more details, including special rules for divorced or separated parents, see the Instructions for Form 2441 and **Pub. 503,** Child and Dependent Care Expenses.

*Note: If the care was provided in your home, both you and the employee may have to pay a share of the social security and Medicare tax on the employee's wages. You may also have to pay Federal unemployment tax, which is for your employee's unemployment insurance. For details, get **Pub. 926,** Employment Taxes for Household Employers.*

Line 42

Credit for the Elderly or the Disabled

You may be able to take this credit and reduce your tax if by the end of 1993:

- You were age 65 or older, **or**
- You were under age 65, you retired on **permanent and total** disability, and you had taxable disability income in 1993.

Even if you meet one of the above conditions, you generally cannot take the credit if you are:

- Single, head of household, or qualifying widow(er), and the amount on Form 1040, line 32, is $17,500 or more; or you received $5,000 or more of nontaxable social security or other nontaxable pensions.
- Married filing jointly, only one spouse is eligible for the credit, and the amount on Form 1040, line 32, is $20,000 or more; or you received $5,000 or more of nontaxable social security or other nontaxable pensions.
- Married filing jointly, both spouses are eligible for the credit, and the amount on Form 1040, line 32, is $25,000 or more; or you received $7,500 or more of nontaxable social security or other nontaxable pensions.

- Married filing separately, you lived apart from your spouse all year, and the amount on Form 1040, line 32, is $12,500 or more; or you received $3,750 or more of nontaxable social security or other nontaxable pensions.

For more details, see the separate instructions for Schedule R and **Pub. 524**, Credit for the Elderly or the Disabled. If you want the IRS to figure the credit for you, see **The IRS Will Figure Your Tax and Some of Your Credits** on page 24.

Line 43

Foreign Tax Credit

Form 1116 explains when you can take this credit for payment of income tax to a foreign country. Also, get **Pub. 514**, Foreign Tax Credit for Individuals.

Line 44

Other Credits

Complete line 44 if you can take any of the following credits.

General Business Credit. If you have two or more of the following general business credits, a general business credit carryforward, or a general business credit (other than the low-income housing credit) from a passive activity, you must also complete **Form 3800** to figure the total credit. Include on line 44 the amount from Form 3800 and check box **a** on line 44. If you have only one general business credit, include on line 44 the amount of the credit from the form. Also, check box **d** on line 44 and enter the form number for that credit.

Form 3468, Investment Credit. This credit was generally repealed for property placed in service after 1985. For exceptions, see Form 3468.

Form 5884, Jobs Credit. If you are a business employer who hires people who are members of special targeted groups, you may be able to take this credit. Use Form 5884 to figure the credit.

Form 6478, Credit for Alcohol Used as Fuel. If you sold straight alcohol (or an alcohol mixture) at retail or used it as fuel in your trade or business, get Form 6478 to see if you can take this credit. For more details, get **Pub. 378**, Fuel Tax Credits and Refunds.

Form 6765, Credit for Increasing Research Activities. You may be able to take a credit for research and experimental expenditures paid or incurred in carrying on your trade or business. Get Form 6765 for details.

Form 8586, Low-Income Housing Credit, and Schedule A (Form 8609), Annual Statement. If you owned a building that was part of a low-income housing project, you may be able to take this credit. Use Form 8586 and Schedule A (Form 8609) to figure the credit. Also, complete and attach **Form 8609**, Low-Income Housing Credit Allocation Certification.

Form 8826, Disabled Access Credit. If you paid or incurred expenses to make your business accessible to or usable by individuals with disabilities, get Form 8826 to see if you can take this credit.

Form 8830, Enhanced Oil Recovery Credit. You may be able to take a credit of 15% of your enhanced oil recovery costs. Get Form 8830 for details.

Form 8835, Renewable Electricity Production Credit. If you owned a facility that produced electricity from qualified energy resources and the facility was placed in service after 1992, get Form 8835 to see if you can take this credit.

Mortgage Interest Credit (Form 8396). If you were issued a mortgage credit certificate by a state or local government under a qualified mortgage credit certificate program to buy, rehabilitate, or improve your main home, get Form 8396 to see if you can take this credit. If you can, check box **b** on line 44. For more details, get **Pub. 530**, Tax Information for First-Time Homeowners.

Credit for Prior Year Minimum Tax (Form 8801). If you paid alternative minimum tax in an earlier year, get Form 8801 to see if you can take this credit. If you can, check box **c** on line 44. For more details, get **Pub. 909**, Alternative Minimum Tax for Individuals.

Qualified Electric Vehicle Credit (Form 8834). If you placed a new electric vehicle in service after June 30, 1993, get Form 8834 to see if you can take this credit. If you can, check box **d** on line 44 and enter the form number.

Line 45

Add amounts on lines 41 through 44 and enter the total on line 45.

Nonconventional Source Fuel Credit. A credit is allowed for the sale of qualified fuels produced from a nonconventional source. See Internal Revenue Code section 29 for a definition of qualified fuels, details on figuring the credit, and other special rules. Attach a separate schedule showing how you figured the credit. Include the credit in the total on line 45. Enter the amount and "FNS" on the dotted line next to line 45.

Other Taxes

Line 47

Self-Employment Tax

If you had self-employment income in 1993 and earned under $135,000 in wages from which social security, Medicare, or railroad retirement (RRTA) tax was withheld, you may owe self-employment tax. Get **Schedule SE** and its instructions to see if you owe this tax. If you do, enter the tax on line 47.

Line 48

Alternative Minimum Tax

The tax law gives special treatment to some kinds of income and allows special deductions and credits for some kinds of expenses. If you benefit from these provisions, you may have to pay at least a minimum amount of tax through the alternative minimum tax. This tax is figured on **Form 6251**, Alternative Minimum Tax—Individuals. Use the worksheet on page 27 to see if you should complete Form 6251.

Exception. If you claimed or received any of the items listed below, **don't** use the worksheet on page 27. Instead, fill in Form 6251.
1. Accelerated depreciation in excess of straight-line.
2. Income from the exercise of incentive stock options.
3. Tax-exempt interest from private activity bonds (including exempt-interest dividends from a regulated investment company to the extent derived from private activity bonds).
4. Intangible drilling costs.
5. Depletion.
6. Circulation expenditures.
7. Research and experimental expenditures.
8. Mining exploration and development costs.
9. Amortization of pollution-control facilities.
10. Income or (loss) from tax shelter farm activities.
11. Income or (loss) from passive activities.
12. Income from long-term contracts figured under the percentage-of-completion method.
13. Income from installment sales of certain property.
14. Interest paid on a home mortgage **not** used to buy, build, or substantially improve your home.
15. Investment interest expense.
16. Foreign tax credit.
17. Net operating loss deduction.

Caution: Form 6251 should be filled in for a child under age 14 if the total of the child's adjusted gross income from Form 1040, line 32, is more than the sum of $1,000 plus the child's earned income.

Line 49

Recapture Taxes

Complete line 49 if you owe any of the following taxes.

Recapture of Investment Credit. If you disposed of investment credit property or changed its use before the end of its useful life or recovery period, you may owe this tax. See **Form 4255** for details. If you owe this tax, check box **a** and include the tax on line 49.

Recapture of Low-Income Housing Credit. If you disposed of property (or there was a reduction in the qualified basis of the property) on which you took the low-income housing credit, you may owe this tax. See **Form 8611** for details. If you owe this tax, check box **b** and include the tax on line 49.

Recapture of Federal Mortgage Subsidy. If you sold your home in 1993 and it was financed (in whole or part) from the proceeds of any tax-exempt qualified mortgage bond or you claimed the mortgage interest credit, you may owe this tax. See **Form 8828** for details. If you owe this tax, check box **c** and include the tax on line 49.

Worksheet To See If You Should Fill In Form 6251—Line 48 (keep for your records)

1. Enter the amount from Form 1040, line 35 . . . . 1. _____
2. If you itemized deductions on Schedule A, go to line 3. Otherwise, enter your standard deduction from Form 1040, line 34, and go to line 5. . . . . 2. _____
3. Enter the **smaller** of the amount on Schedule A, line 4, or 2.5% of the amount on Form 1040, line 32 . . . . 3. _____
4. Add lines 8 and 24 of Schedule A and enter the total . . . 4. _____
5. Add lines 1 through 4 above . . . . 5. _____
6. Enter $45,000 ($22,500 if married filing separately; $33,750 if single or head of household) . . . . 6. _____
7. Subtract line 6 from line 5. If zero or less, **stop here**; you don't need to fill in Form 6251 . . . . 7. _____
8. Enter $150,000 ($75,000 if married filing separately; $112,500 if single or head of household) . . . . 8. _____
9. Subtract line 8 from line 5. If zero or less, enter -0- here and on line 10 and go to line 11 . . . . 9. _____
10. Multiply line 9 by 25% (.25) and enter the result but do not enter more than line 6 above . . . . 10. _____
11. Add lines 7 and 10. If the total is over $175,000 ($87,500 if married filing separately), **stop here** and fill in Form 6251 to see if you owe the alternative minimum tax . . . . 11. _____
12. Multiply line 11 by 26% (.26) . . . . 12. _____

Next: If line 12 is more than the amount on Form 1040, line 38, fill in Form 6251 to see if you owe the alternative minimum tax. If line 12 is equal to or less than the amount on Form 1040, line 38, **do not** fill in Form 6251.

Line 50

Social Security and Medicare Tax on Tip Income Not Reported to Employer

If you received tips of $20 or more in any month and you did not report the full amount to your employer, or your W-2 form(s) shows allocated tips that you are including in your income, you must pay the social security and Medicare or railroad retirement (RRTA) tax on the unreported tips. If you reported the full amount to your employer but the social security and Medicare or RRTA tax was not withheld, you must pay it unless the rules discussed under **Uncollected Employee Social Security and Medicare or RRTA Tax on Tips** (line 53) apply.

To figure the social security and Medicare tax, get **Form 4137**, Social Security and Medicare Tax on Unreported Tip Income. Enter the tax on line 50.

To pay the RRTA tax, contact your employer. Your employer will collect the tax.

Be sure all your tips are reported as income on Form 1040, line 7.

Caution: *You may be charged a penalty equal to 50% of the social security and Medicare tax due on tips you received but did not report to your employer.*

Line 51

Tax on Qualified Retirement Plans, Including IRAs

You may owe this tax if any of the following apply:

1. You received any early distributions from a qualified retirement plan (including your IRA), annuity, or modified endowment contract (entered into after June 20, 1988).
2. You received any excess distributions from a qualified retirement plan.
3. You made excess contributions to your IRA.
4. You had excess accumulations in a qualified retirement plan.

If any of the above apply, get **Form 5329** and its instructions to see if you owe this tax and if you must file Form 5329. Enter the tax from Form 5329 on line 51. However, if *only* item 1 above applies to you **and** distribution code 1 is shown in box 7 of your **Form 1099-R,** you do not have to file Form 5329. Instead, multiply the taxable amount of the distribution by 10% (.10) and enter the result on line 51. The taxable amount of the distribution is the part of the distribution you reported on line 16b or line 17b of Form 1040 or on Form 4972. Also, enter "No" on the dotted line next to line 51 to indicate that you do not have to file Form 5329. **But** if distribution code 1 is incorrectly shown in box 7, you must file Form 5329.

Caution: *Be sure to include on line 16b or line 17b of Form 1040 or on Form 4972, whichever applies, the taxable part of any early distributions you received.*

Line 52

Advance Earned Income Credit Payments

Enter the total amount of advance earned income credit (EIC) payments you received. These payments should be shown in box 9 of your W-2 form(s). See Schedule EIC to figure the earned income credit you can actually take.

Line 53

Total Tax

Add lines 46 through 52 and enter the total on line 53. Also, include in the total on line 53 any of the following that applies.

Section 72(m)(5) Excess Benefits Tax. If you are or were a 5% owner of a business and you received a distribution of excess benefits from a qualified pension or annuity plan, you may have to pay a penalty tax of 10% of the distribution. Get **Pub. 560** for more details. Include this penalty tax in your total for line 53. Enter the amount of this tax and the words "Section 72(m)(5)" on the dotted line next to line 53.

Uncollected Employee Social Security and Medicare or RRTA Tax on Tips. If you did not have enough wages to cover the social security and Medicare or railroad retirement (RRTA) tax due on tips you reported to your employer, the amount of tax due should be identified with codes **A** and **B** in box 13 of your Form W-2. Include this tax in the total for line 53. Enter the amount of this tax and the words "Uncollected Tax" on the dotted line next to line 53.

Uncollected Employee Social Security and Medicare or RRTA Tax on Group-Term Life Insurance. If you had group-term life insurance through a former employer, you may have to pay social security and Medicare or RRTA tax on part of the cost of the life insurance. The amount of tax due should be identified with codes **M** and **N** in box 13 of your Form W-2. Include this tax in the total for line 53. Enter the amount of this tax and the words "Uncollected Tax" on the dotted line next to line 53.

Golden Parachute Payments. Golden parachute payments are certain payments made by a corporation to key employees to compensate them if control of the corporation changes. If you received an excess parachute payment (EPP), you must pay a tax equal to 20% of this excess payment. Enter the amount and "EPP" on the dotted line next to line 53.

If you received a **Form W-2** that includes a parachute payment, the amount of tax on any excess payment should be identified with code **K** in box 13 of Form W-2. (Box 2 of Form W-2 should also include any amount withheld for this tax.) Include this tax in the total for line 53. Enter the amount of this tax and "EPP" on the dotted line next to line 53.

If you received a **Form 1099-MISC** that includes a parachute payment, any excess payment will be separately identified on the form. Multiply the excess payment by 20% to figure the amount to include in the total for line 53. Enter the amount and "EPP" on the dotted line next to line 53.

Payments

Line 54

Federal Income Tax Withheld

Add the amounts shown as Federal income tax withheld on your **Forms W-2, W-2G,** and **1099-R.** Enter the total on line 54. The amount withheld should be shown in box 2 of Form W-2 or W-2G, and in box 4 of Form 1099-R. If line 54 includes amounts withheld as shown on Form 1099-R, check the box on line 54. Be sure to attach the Form 1099-R.

Backup Withholding. If you received a 1993 Form 1099 showing Federal income tax withheld (backup withholding) on dividends, interest income, or other income you received, include the amount withheld in the total on line 54. This should be shown in box 2 of Form 1099-DIV and box 4 of the other 1099 forms. Be sure to check the box on line 54.

Line 55

1993 Estimated Tax Payments

Enter on this line any payments you made on your estimated Federal income tax (**Form 1040-ES**) for 1993. Include any overpayment from your 1992 return that you applied to your 1993 estimated tax.

If you and your spouse paid joint estimated tax but are now filing separate income tax returns, either of you can claim all of the amount paid. Or you can each claim part of it. Get **Pub. 505**, Tax Withholding and Estimated Tax, for details on how to divide your payments. Be sure to show both social security numbers (SSNs) in the space provided on the separate returns. If you or your spouse paid separate estimated tax but you are now filing a joint income tax return, add the amounts you each paid. Follow these instructions even if your spouse died in 1993 or in 1994 before filing a 1993 return.

Divorced Taxpayers. If you were divorced during 1993 and you made joint estimated tax payments with your former spouse, enter your former spouse's SSN in the space provided on the front of Form 1040. If you were divorced and remarried in 1993, enter your present spouse's SSN in the space provided on the front of Form 1040. Also, under the bold heading "Payments" to the left of line 55, enter your former spouse's SSN, followed by "DIV."

Name Change. If you changed your name because of marriage, divorce, etc., and you made estimated tax payments using your former name, attach a statement to the front of Form 1040 explaining all the payments you and your spouse made in 1993, the service center where you made the payments, and the name(s) and SSN(s) under which you made the payments.

Line 56

Earned Income Credit

If the amount on line 31 is less than $23,050 and a child lived with you, you may be able to take this credit. See page EIC-1 to find out if you can take this credit. If you can, use **Schedule EIC** to figure the credit. If you want the IRS to figure the credit for you, see the instructions for Schedule EIC.

Note: *If you got advance earned income credit (EIC) payments in 1993, report these payments on line 52. If you are eligible, you may be able to get advance EIC payments in 1994 by filing* **Form W-5** *with your employer.*

Line 57

Amount Paid With Form 4868 (Extension Request)

If you filed **Form 4868** to get an automatic extension of time to file Form 1040, enter the amount you paid with that form. Also, include any amounts paid with **Form 2688** or **Form 2350**.

Line 58a

Excess Social Security, Medicare, and RRTA Tax Withheld—More Than One Employer

Excess Social Security and Medicare Tax Withheld. If you had more than one employer for 1993 and your total wages were over $57,600, your employers may have withheld too much social security tax. If your total wages were over $135,000, your employers may have withheld too much Medicare tax. If so, you can take a credit for the excess amount on line 58a. Use the worksheet on this page to figure the excess amount.

If any one employer withheld more than $3,571.20 of social security tax, or more than $1,957.50 of Medicare tax, you must ask that employer to refund the excess to you. You cannot claim it on your return.

Excess Railroad Retirement (RRTA) Tax Withheld. If you had more than one railroad employer for 1993 and your total compensation was over $57,600, your employers may have withheld too much tier 1 tax. If your total compensation was over $42,900, your employers may have withheld too much tier 2 tax. If so, you can take a credit for the excess amount on line 58a. Get **Pub. 505**, Tax Withholding and Estimated Tax, to figure the excess amount. **Do not** use the worksheet on this page.

If any one employer withheld more than $3,571.20 of tier 1 RRTA tax, more than $1,957.50 of tier 1 Medicare tax, or more than $2,102.10 of tier 2 tax, you must ask that employer to refund the excess to you. You cannot claim it on your return.

Line 58b

Deferral of Additional 1993 Taxes

If your taxable income on Form 1040, line 37, is over $140,000 (over $115,000 if single; over $127,500 if head of household; over $70,000 if married filing separately) and you do not owe the alternative minimum tax on Form 1040, line 48, you may be able to elect to defer part of the tax shown on line 53. Get **Form 8841** for details. Enter the amount from Form 8841 on line 58b.

Line 59

Other Payments

Regulated Investment Company Credit. Include on this line the total amount of the credit from **Form 2439**, Notice to Shareholder of Undistributed Long-Term Capital Gains. Be sure to attach Copy B of Form 2439 and check box **a** on line 59.

Credit for Federal Tax Paid on Fuels. If you can take a credit for tax on gasoline, diesel fuel, and other fuels used in your business, or for certain diesel-powered cars, vans, and light trucks, attach **Form 4136**. Include the credit on line 59 and check box **b**.

Line 60

Total Payments

Add lines 54 through 59 and enter the total. Also, include on line 60 any credit for overpaid windfall profit tax from Form 6249. Write the amount and "OWPT" on the dotted line next to line 60. Attach Forms 6249 and 6248.

Excess Social Security and Medicare Tax Withheld Worksheet—Line 58a (keep for your records)

If you are filing a joint return, you must figure any excess tax withheld separately for each spouse. DO NOT combine amounts of both husband and wife.

Caution: *Do not use this worksheet if* **any** *RRTA tax was withheld from your pay. Instead, get* **Pub. 505** *to figure the excess amount.*

1. Add all social security tax withheld but not more than $3,571.20 for each employer. This tax should be shown in box 4 of your W-2 forms. Enter the total here . . . . 1. _____
2. Enter any uncollected social security tax on tips or group-term life insurance included in the total on Form 1040, line 53 . . 2. _____
3. Add lines 1 and 2. If $3,571.20 or less, enter -0- on line 5 and go to line 6 . . . . 3. _____
4. Social security tax limit 4. 3,571.20
5. Subtract line 4 from line 3. . . . . 5. _____
6. Add all Medicare tax withheld but not more than $1,957.50 for each employer. This tax should be shown in box 6 of your W-2 forms. Enter the total here . . . . 6. _____
7. Enter any uncollected Medicare tax on tips or group-term life insurance included in the total on Form 1040, line 53 . . . 7. _____
8. Add lines 6 and 7. If $1,957.50 or less, enter -0- on line 10 and go to line 11 . . . . 8. _____
9. Medicare tax limit 9. 1,957.50
10. Subtract line 9 from line 8. . . . . 10. _____
11. **Excess social security and Medicare tax withheld.** Add lines 5 and 10. Enter the total here and on Form 1040, line 58a . 11. _____

Refund or Amount You Owe

Line 61

Amount Overpaid (If line 60 is more than line 53)

Subtract line 53 from line 60 and enter the result on line 61. If line 61 is under $1, we will send a refund only on written request.

Note: *If the amount you overpaid is large, you may want to decrease the amount of income tax withheld from your pay. See* **Income Tax Withholding and Estimated Tax Payments for 1994** *on page 35.*

Injured Spouse Claim. If you file a joint return and your spouse has not paid child or spousal support payments or certain Federal debts such as student loans, all or part of the overpayment on line 61 may be used to pay the past due amount. But **your** part of the overpayment may be refunded to you if **all three** of the following apply:

1. You are not required to pay the past due amount.
2. You received and reported income (such as wages, taxable interest, etc.) on the joint return.
3. You made and reported payments (such as Federal income tax withheld from your wages or estimated tax payments) on the joint return.

If **all three** of the above apply to you and you want your part of the amount on line 61 refunded to you, complete **Form 8379,** Injured Spouse Claim and Allocation. Write "Injured Spouse" in the upper left corner of Form 1040 and attach Form 8379. If you have already filed your return for 1993, file Form 8379 by itself to get your refund.

Note: *You may also be able to file an injured spouse claim for prior years. See Form 8379 for details.*

Line 63

Applied to 1994 Estimated Tax

Subtract line 62 from line 61 and enter the result on line 63. This is the amount that will be applied to your estimated tax for 1994. We will apply this amount to your account unless you request us to apply it to your spouse's account. The request should include your spouse's social security number.

Line 64

Amount You Owe (If line 53 is more than line 60)

Subtract line 60 from line 53 and enter the result on line 64. This is the amount you owe. Attach to the front of your return a check or money order payable to the Internal Revenue Service for the full amount due when you file. Write your name, address, social security number (SSN), daytime phone number, and "1993 Form 1040" on your payment. Be sure to attach your payment on top of any Forms W-2, 1099-R, etc., on the front of your return.

You do not have to pay if line 64 is under $1.

Do not include any estimated tax payment in your check or money order. Mail any estimated tax payment in an envelope separate from the one you use to pay the tax due on Form 1040.

Note: *If you owe tax for 1993, you may need to (a) increase the amount of income tax withheld from your pay or (b) make estimated tax payments for 1994. See* **Income Tax Withholding and Estimated Tax Payments for 1994** *on page 35.*

Installment Payments. If you cannot pay the full amount shown on line 64 with your return, you may ask to make monthly installment payments. However, you will be charged interest and a late payment penalty on the tax not paid by April 15, even if your request to pay in installments is granted. To limit the interest and penalty charges, pay as much of the tax as possible with your return. But before requesting an installment agreement, you should consider other less costly alternatives, such as a bank loan.

To ask for an installment agreement, attach to the front of your return either a completed **Form 9465,** Installment Agreement Request, or your own written request. You can get Form 9465 by calling 1-800-TAX-FORM (1-800-829-3676). A written request should include your name, address, SSN, the amount shown on line 64, the amount you paid with your return, and the amount and date you can pay each month. It should also include the tax year and the form number (Form 1040). You should receive a response to your request for installments within 30 days. But if you file your return after March 31, it may take us longer to reply.

Line 65

Estimated Tax Penalty

If line 64 is at least $500 and it is more than 10% of the tax shown on your return, you may owe this penalty. For most people, the "tax shown on your return" is the amount on line 53 minus the total of any amounts shown on line 56 and Forms 8828, 4137, 4136, and 5329 (Parts II, III, and IV only). Also, the penalty may be due if you underpaid your 1993 estimated tax liability for any payment period. Get **Form 2210** (or **Form 2210-F** for farmers and fishermen) to see if you owe the penalty. If so, use the form to figure the amount. Because Form 2210 is complicated, if you want, the IRS will figure the penalty for you and send you a bill.

In certain situations, you may be able to lower your penalty. See **Lowering the Penalty** later.

Exceptions to the Penalty. You will not owe the penalty if **either** of the following applies:

1. You had no tax liability for 1992, you were a U.S. citizen or resident for all of 1992, AND your 1992 tax return was for a tax year of 12 full months, or
2. The total of lines 54, 55, and 58 on your 1993 return is at least as much as your 1992 tax liability, AND your 1992 tax return was for a tax year of 12 full months. Your estimated tax payments for 1993 must have been made on time and for the required amount.

Caution: *Item 2 above may not apply if your 1993 adjusted gross income (AGI) on Form 1040, line 32: (a) is over $75,000 (over $37,500 if married filing separately), AND (b) exceeds your 1992 AGI by more than $40,000 (more than $20,000 if married filing separately). If these conditions apply to you, see Form 2210 and its instructions for details.*

Figuring the Penalty. If the **Exceptions** above do not apply and you choose to figure the penalty yourself, use Form 2210 (or Form 2210-F). Enter the penalty on Form 1040, line 65. Add the penalty to any tax due and enter the total on line 64. If you are due a refund, subtract the penalty from the overpayment you show on line 61. **Do not** file Form 2210 with your return. Instead, keep it for your records.

If you leave line 65 blank, the IRS will figure the penalty and send you a bill. We will not begin to charge you interest on the penalty until 10 days after the date of the bill.

Lowering the Penalty. In the following situations, you may be able to lower the amount of your penalty.

- You claim a waiver.
- Your income varied during the year and you use the annualized income installment method to figure your required payments.
- You had Federal income tax withheld from your wages and you treat it as being paid when it was actually withheld (instead of in four equal amounts).

If any of the situations above apply to you, complete Form 2210 (or Form 2210-F) to see if your penalty can be lowered. If so, you **must** file Form 2210 (or Form 2210-F) with your return. For more details, see the Instructions for Form 2210 (or Form 2210-F).

Sign Your Return

Form 1040 is not considered a valid return unless you sign it. If you are filing a joint return, your spouse must also sign. Be sure to date your return and enter your occupation(s). If you have someone prepare your return, you are still responsible for the correctness of the return. If you are filing a joint return with your deceased spouse, see **Death of Taxpayer** on page 35.

Child's Return. If your child cannot sign the return, sign your child's name in the space provided. Then, add "By (your signature), parent for minor child."

Paid Preparers Must Sign Your Return. Generally, anyone you pay to prepare your return must sign it. A preparer who is required to sign your return must sign it by hand in the space provided (signature stamps or labels cannot be used) and give you a copy of the return for your records. Someone who prepares your return for you but does not charge you should not sign your return.

Section 8.

Instructions for Schedules to Form 1040

Instructions for Schedule A, Itemized Deductions

Use Schedule A to figure your itemized deductions. Your Federal income tax will be less if you take the **larger** of your itemized deductions or your standard deduction.

If you itemize, you may deduct part of your medical and dental expenses and unreimbursed employee business expenses, and amounts you paid for certain taxes, interest, contributions, and miscellaneous expenses. You may also deduct certain moving expenses and casualty and theft losses.

Medical and Dental Expenses

Before you can figure your deduction for medical and dental expenses, you must fill in Form 1040 through line 32. If the amount on Form 1040, line 32, is less than $23,050 and a child lived with you, see the instructions on page EIC-1 to find out if you may also claim the health insurance credit on **Schedule EIC**, Earned Income Credit. If you can, figure your health insurance credit before you figure your deduction for medical and dental expenses.

You may deduct only the part of your medical and dental expenses that is more than 7.5% of the amount on Form 1040, line 32.

Additional Information. Pub. 502, Medical and Dental Expenses, discusses the types of expenses that may and may not be deducted. It also explains when you may deduct capital expenses and special care expenses for disabled persons.

Examples of Medical and Dental Payments You May Deduct

To the extent you were not reimbursed, you may deduct what you paid for:
- Prescription medicines and drugs, or insulin.
- Medical doctors, osteopathic doctors, dentists, eye doctors, chiropractors, podiatrists, psychiatrists, psychologists, physical therapists, acupuncturists, and psychoanalysts (medical care only).
- Medical examinations, X-ray and laboratory services, insulin treatment, and whirlpool baths your doctor ordered.
- Nursing help. If you paid someone to do both nursing and housework, you may deduct only the cost of the nursing help.
- Hospital care (including meals and lodging), clinic costs, and lab fees.
- The supplemental part of Medicare insurance (Medicare B).
- Medical treatment at a center for drug or alcohol addiction.
- Medical aids such as hearing aid batteries, braces, crutches, wheelchairs, and guide dogs including the cost of maintaining them.
- Lodging expenses (but not meals) paid while away from home to receive medical care in a hospital or a medical care facility that is related to a hospital. **Do not** include more than $50 a night for each eligible person.
- Ambulance service and other travel costs to get medical care. If you used your own car, you may claim what you spent for gas and oil to go to and from the place you received the care; or you may claim 9 cents a mile. Add parking and tolls to the amount you claim under either method.

Examples of Medical and Dental Payments You May Not Deduct

- The basic cost of Medicare insurance (Medicare A).
Note: *If you were 65 or older but not entitled to social security benefits, you may deduct premiums you voluntarily paid for Medicare A coverage.*
- Cosmetic surgery unless the procedure was necessary to improve a deformity resulting from, or directly related to, a congenital abnormality, an injury from an accident or trauma, or a disfiguring disease.
- Life insurance or income protection policies.
- The Medicare tax on your wages and tips or the Medicare tax paid as part of the self-employment tax.
- Nursing care for a healthy baby. But you may be able to claim the child and dependent care credit; get **Form 2441** for details.
- Illegal operations or drugs.
- Nonprescription medicines or drugs.
- Travel your doctor told you to take for rest or a change.
- Funeral, burial, or cremation costs.

Line 1

Medical and Dental Expenses

Enter the total of your medical and dental expenses, after you reduce these expenses by any payments received from insurance or other sources. See **Reimbursements** on this page. Include the amount you paid for insurance premiums for medical and dental care, after you reduce that amount by—
- Any self-employed health insurance deduction you claimed on Form 1040, line 26, and
- Any health insurance credit you claimed on Schedule EIC, line 16.

When you figure your deduction, include medical and dental bills you paid for:
- Yourself.
- Your spouse.
- All dependents you claim on your return.
- Your child whom you do not claim as a dependent because of the rules explained on page 14 for **Children of Divorced or Separated Parents.**
- Any person that you could have claimed as a dependent on your return if that person had not received $2,350 or more of gross income or had not filed a joint return.

Example. You provided over half of your mother's support but may not claim her as a dependent because she received wages of $2,350 in 1993. You may include on line 1 any medical and dental expenses you paid in 1993 for your mother.

Reimbursements. If your insurance company paid the provider directly for part of your expenses, and you paid only the amount that remained, include on line 1 ONLY the amount you paid. If you received a reimbursement in 1993 for medical or dental expenses you paid in 1993, reduce your 1993 expenses by this amount. If you received a reimbursement in 1993 for prior year medical or dental expenses, do not reduce your 1993 expenses by this amount. But if you deducted the expenses in the earlier year and the deduction reduced your tax, you must include the reimbursement in income on Form 1040, line 22. See Pub. 502 for details on how to figure the amount to include in income.

Cafeteria Plans. Do not include on line 1 insurance premiums paid by an employer-sponsored health insurance plan (cafeteria plan) unless the premiums are included in box 1 of your W-2 form(s). Also, do not include any other medical and dental expenses paid by the plan unless the amount paid is included in box 1 of your W-2 form(s).

Taxes You Paid

Taxes You May Not Deduct

- Federal income and excise taxes.
- Social security, Medicare, and railroad retirement (RRTA) taxes.
- Customs duties.
- Federal estate and gift taxes. But see the instructions for line 25 on page A-5.

A-1

- Certain state and local taxes, including: general sales tax, tax on gasoline, car inspection fees, assessments for sidewalks or other improvements to your property, tax you paid for someone else, and license fees (marriage, driver's, dog, etc.).

Line 5

State and Local Income Taxes

Include on this line the state and local income taxes listed below:

- State and local income taxes withheld from your salary during 1993. Your W-2 form(s) will show these amounts. Forms W-2G, 1099-R, and 1099-MISC may also show state and local income taxes withheld.
- State and local income taxes paid in 1993 for a prior year, such as taxes paid with your 1992 state or local income tax return. **Do not** include penalties or interest.
- State and local estimated tax payments made during 1993, including any part of a prior year refund that you chose to have credited to your 1993 state or local income taxes.
- Mandatory contributions you made to the following state disability funds:
1. California Nonoccupational Disability Benefit Fund.
2. New Jersey Nonoccupational Disability Benefit Fund.
3. New York Nonoccupational Disability Benefit Fund.
4. Rhode Island Temporary Disability Benefit Fund.

Do not reduce your deduction by:

- Any state or local income tax refund or credit you expect to receive for 1993, or
- Any refund of, or credit for, prior year state and local income taxes you actually received in 1993. Instead, see the instructions for Form 1040, line 10.

Line 6

Real Estate Taxes

Include taxes you paid on real estate you own that was not used for business, but only if the taxes are based on the assessed value of the property. Also, the assessment must be made uniformly on property throughout the community, and the proceeds must be used for general community or governmental purposes. **Pub. 530** explains the deductions homeowners may take. **Do not** include—

- Real estate taxes deducted elsewhere such as on Schedule C, C-EZ, E, or F, or
- Itemized charges for services to specific property or persons (for example, a $20 monthly charge per house for trash collection, a $5 charge for every 1,000 gallons of water consumed, or a flat charge for mowing a lawn that had grown higher than permitted under a local ordinance), or
- Charges for improvements that tend to increase the value of your property (for example, an assessment to build a new sidewalk). The cost of a property improvement is added to the basis of the property. However, a charge is deductible if it is used only to maintain an existing public facility in service (for example, a charge to repair an existing sidewalk, and any interest included in that charge).

If your mortgage payments include your real estate taxes, you may deduct only the amount the mortgage company actually paid to the taxing authority in 1993.

If you sold your home in 1993, any real estate tax charged to the buyer should be shown in box 5 of **Form 1099-S**, Proceeds From Real Estate Transactions. This amount is considered a refund of real estate taxes you received in 1993. See **Refunds and Rebates** next.

Refunds and Rebates. If you received a refund or rebate in 1993 of real estate taxes you paid in 1993, reduce your deduction by the amount of the refund or rebate. If you received a refund or rebate in 1993 of real estate taxes you paid in an earlier year, do not reduce your deduction by this amount. Instead, you must include the refund or rebate in income on Form 1040, line 22, if you deducted the real estate taxes in the earlier year and the deduction reduced your tax. **Pub. 525**, Taxable and Nontaxable Income, tells you how to figure the amount to include in income.

Line 7

Other Taxes

If you had any deductible tax not listed on Schedule A, line 5 or 6, list the type and amount of tax. Enter one total on line 7.

Examples of taxes to include on line 7 are:

- Personal property tax, but only if it is an annual tax based on value alone. For example, if part of the fee you paid for the registration of your car was based on the car's value and part was based on its weight, you may deduct only the part based on the car's value.
- Tax you paid to a foreign country or U.S. possession. But you may want to take a credit for the tax instead of a deduction. Get **Pub. 514** for details.

Interest You Paid

Include interest you paid on nonbusiness items only; **do not** include any amount deducted elsewhere such as on Schedule C, C-EZ, E, or F. Whether your interest expense is treated as investment interest, personal interest, or business interest depends on how and when you used the loan proceeds. Get **Pub. 535**, Business Expenses, for details.

In general, if you paid interest in 1993 that includes amounts that apply to any period after 1993, you may deduct only the amount that applies for 1993.

Interest You May Not Deduct

- Personal interest, such as interest paid on car loans, student loans, life insurance loans, credit cards, charge accounts, etc.
- Interest paid on your debts by others, such as mortgage interest subsidy payments made by a government agency.
- Interest on certain loans against your interest in a 401(k) plan or a tax-sheltered annuity plan that were made, renewed, renegotiated, modified, or extended after 1986. Get **Pub. 575**, Pension and Annuity Income (Including Simplified General Rule), for details.
- Interest paid for tax-exempt income. This includes interest on money you borrowed to buy or carry wholly tax-exempt securities. It also includes interest paid to buy or carry obligations or shares, or to make deposits or other investments, to the extent any interest income received from the investment is tax exempt.
- Interest on a debt to buy a single-premium life insurance or endowment contract.
- Interest on any kind of business transaction. Use Schedule C, C-EZ, E, or F to deduct business interest expenses.

See Pub. 535 for more details.

Lines 9a and 9b

Home Mortgage Interest

A **home mortgage** is any loan that is secured by your main home or second home. It includes first and second mortgages, home equity loans, and refinanced mortgages.

A **home** may be a house, condominium, cooperative, mobile home, boat, or similar property. It must provide basic living accommodations including sleeping space, toilet, and cooking facilities.

Limit on Home Mortgage Interest. The amount of home mortgage interest you may deduct depends on the date you took out the mortgage, how you used the proceeds, and the amount of the mortgage.

If all of your home mortgages fit into one or more of **Categories 1, 2,** and **3** (explained later), you may deduct all of your home mortgage interest on line 9a or 9b, whichever applies. If one or more of your mortgages does not fit into any of the three categories, get **Pub. 936,** Home Mortgage Interest Deduction, to figure the amount of interest you may deduct.

If you had **more than one home** at the same time (a main home and a second home), the dollar limits in **Categories 2** and **3** apply to the total mortgages on both homes. See Pub. 936 for more details.

Category 1. Mortgages taken out **on or before October 13, 1987.** How you used the proceeds of these mortgages does not matter. This category includes **line-of-credit mortgages** you had on October 13, 1987. But if you borrowed additional amounts on this line-of-credit after October 13, 1987, the additional amounts fit into **Category 2** or **3** (or **2** and **3** if a **mixed-use mortgage**—explained later).

This category also includes mortgages you had on October 13, 1987, that you **refinanced** after that date. But if you refinanced for more than the balance of the old mortgage, only the part of the new mortgage equal to the amount you owed on the old mortgage at the time you refinanced it fits into this category. The part of the new mortgage that is more than the balance of the old mortgage fits into **Category 2** or **3** (or **2** and **3** if a **mixed-use mortgage**—explained later).

Category 2. Mortgages taken out **after October 13, 1987, to buy, build, or improve your home,** but only if these mortgages plus any mortgages in **Category 1** above totaled $1 million or less throughout 1993. The limit

A-2

is $500,000 or less if married filing separately.

Category 3. Mortgages taken out **after October 13, 1987, other than to buy, build, or improve your home,** but only if these mortgages totaled $100,000 or less throughout 1993. The limit is $50,000 or less if married filing separately. An example of this type of mortgage is a home equity loan you used to pay off credit card bills, to buy a car, or to pay tuition costs.

Note: *If the total amount of all mortgages exceeds the fair market value of the home, additional limits apply. See Pub. 936 for details.*

Mixed-Use Mortgages. If you took out a mortgage after October 13, 1987 (including refinancing for more than what you owed or borrowing additional amounts on a line-of-credit mortgage you had on October 13, 1987) and used the proceeds for purposes described in both **Categories 2** and **3** earlier, you have a mixed-use mortgage. The mortgage proceeds used to buy, build, or improve the home fit into **Category 2** and the rest of the proceeds fit into **Category 3.**

Line 9a. Enter on line 9a mortgage interest and points reported to you on **Form 1098,** Mortgage Interest Statement. If you did not receive a Form 1098, enter the interest on line 9b and any deductible points on line 10.

If you paid $600 or more of mortgage interest (including points paid to buy your main home), the recipient will generally send you a Form 1098, or similar statement, by January 31, 1994. This form shows the total interest and points the recipient received from you during 1993. It also shows any refund of overpaid interest. Do not reduce your deduction by the refund. Instead, see the instructions for Form 1040, line 22.

If you paid more interest to financial institutions than is shown on Form 1098, see Pub. 936 to find out if you can deduct the additional interest. If you can, attach a statement explaining the difference and write "See attached" next to line 9a.

Note: *If you are claiming the mortgage interest credit (see the instructions for Form 1040, line 44), subtract the amount shown on line 3 of Form 8396 from the total deductible interest you paid on your home mortgage. Enter the result on line 9a.*

Line 9b. If the recipient was not a financial institution or you did not receive a Form 1098 from the recipient, report your deductible mortgage interest on line 9b.

If you bought your home from the recipient, be sure to show that recipient's name, identifying no., and address on the dotted lines next to line 9b. If the recipient is an individual, the identifying no. is his or her social security number (SSN). Otherwise, it is the employer identification no. You must also let the recipient know your SSN. If you don't show the required information about the recipient and let the recipient know your SSN, you may have to pay a $50 penalty.

If you and at least one other person (other than your spouse if filing a joint return) were liable for and paid interest on the mortgage, and the other person received the Form 1098, attach a statement to your return showing the name and address of that person. Next to line 9b, write "See attached."

Line 10

Points Not Reported on Form 1098

Generally, points charged **only** for the use of money are deductible over the life of your mortgage.

Exception. You may deduct points (including loan origination fees on a loan used to buy your main home) in the year paid if:

• The loan was used to **buy or improve your main home,** and

• The loan was secured by your main home, and

• It is customary to charge points in the area where the loan was made, and

• The points paid did not exceed the points usually charged in that area, and

• The points are computed as a percentage of the amount of the loan, and

either you provided funds (see below) at the time of closing at least equal to the points charged if the loan was used to **buy** your main home,

or you paid the points with funds other than those obtained from the lender if the loan was used to **improve** your main home.

Funds provided by you include down payments, escrow deposits, earnest money applied at closing, and other amounts actually paid at closing. They do not include amounts you borrowed as part of the overall transaction.

Note: *Points paid on a loan to buy your main home include loan origination fees designated on VA and FHA loans.*

Refinancing. If you paid points to refinance your mortgage, get **Pub. 936,** Home Mortgage Interest Deduction.

Line 11

Investment Interest

Investment interest is interest paid on money you borrowed that is allocable to property held for investment. It does not include any interest allocable to a passive activity.

Complete and attach **Form 4952,** Investment Interest Expense Deduction, to figure your deduction.

Exception. You do not have to file Form 4952 if **all four** of the following apply:

1. Your only investment income was from interest or dividends.

2. You have no other deductible expenses connected with the production of the interest or dividends.

3. Your investment interest expense is not more than your investment income.

4. You have no carryovers of investment interest expense from 1992.

Note: *Alaska Permanent Fund dividends, including those reported on **Form 8814,** Parents' Election To Report Child's Interest and Dividends, are not investment income.*

For more details, get **Pub. 550,** Investment Income and Expenses.

Gifts to Charity

You may deduct contributions or gifts you gave to organizations that are religious, charitable, educational, scientific, or literary in purpose. You may also deduct what you gave to organizations that work to prevent cruelty to children or animals. Examples of these organizations are:

• Churches, temples, synagogues, mosques, Salvation Army, Red Cross, CARE, Goodwill Industries, United Way, Boy Scouts, Girl Scouts, Boys and Girls Clubs of America, etc.

• Fraternal orders, if the gifts will be used for the purposes listed above.

• Veterans' and certain cultural groups.

• Nonprofit schools, hospitals, and organizations whose purpose is to find a cure for, or help people who have, arthritis, asthma, birth defects, cancer, cerebral palsy, cystic fibrosis, diabetes, heart disease, hemophilia, mental illness or retardation, multiple sclerosis, muscular dystrophy, tuberculosis, etc.

• Federal, state, and local governments if the gifts are solely for public purposes.

If you do not know whether you may deduct what you gave to an organization, check with that organization or with the IRS.

Caution: *If you contributed to a charitable organization and also received a benefit from it, you may deduct only the amount that is more than the value of the benefit you received. For more details, get **Pub. 526,** Charitable Contributions.*

Contributions You May Deduct

Contributions may be in cash (keep canceled checks, receipts, or other reliable written records showing the name of the organization and the date and amount given), property, or out-of-pocket expenses you paid to do volunteer work for the kinds of organizations described earlier. If you drove to and from the volunteer work, you may take 12 cents a mile or the actual cost of gas and oil. Add parking and tolls to the amount you claim under either method. But don't deduct any amounts that were repaid to you.

Limit on the Amount You May Deduct. Get Pub. 526 to figure the amount of your deduction if **any** of the following applies:

• Your cash contributions or contributions of ordinary income property are more than 30% of the amount shown on Form 1040, line 32.

• Your gifts of capital gain property are more than 20% of the amount shown on Form 1040, line 32.

• You gave gifts of property that increased in value or gave gifts of the use of property.

You May Not Deduct as Contributions

• Travel expenses (including meals and lodging) while away from home unless there was no significant element of personal pleasure, recreation, or vacation in the travel.

• Political contributions.

• Dues, fees, or bills paid to country clubs, lodges, fraternal orders, or similar groups.

• Cost of raffle, bingo, or lottery tickets.

• Cost of tuition.

• Value of your time or services.

• Value of blood given to a blood bank.

• The transfer of a future interest in tangible personal property (generally, until the entire interest has been transferred).

A-3

- Gifts to individuals, foreign organizations, and groups that are run for personal profit.
- Gifts to groups whose purpose is to lobby for changes in the laws.
- Gifts to civic leagues, social and sports clubs, labor unions, and chambers of commerce.
- Value of any benefit, such as food, entertainment, or merchandise, that you received in connection with a contribution to a charitable organization.

Example. You paid $100 to a charitable organization to attend a fund-raising dinner. To figure the amount of your deductible charitable contribution, subtract the value of the dinner from the total amount you paid. If the value of the dinner was $40, your deductible contribution is $60.

Line 13

Contributions by Cash or Check

Enter the total contributions you made in cash or by check (including out-of-pocket expenses).

Line 14

Other Than by Cash or Check

Enter your contributions of property. If you gave used items, such as clothing or furniture, deduct their fair market value at the time you gave them. Fair market value is what a willing buyer would pay a willing seller when neither has to buy or sell and both are aware of the conditions of the sale.

If the amount of your deduction is more than $500, you must complete and attach **Form 8283**, Noncash Charitable Contributions. For this purpose, the "amount of your deduction" means your deduction BEFORE applying any income limits that could result in a carryover of contributions. If your total deduction is over $5,000, you may also have to get appraisals of the values of the donated property. See Form 8283 and its instructions for details.

Recordkeeping. If you gave property, you should keep a receipt or written statement from the organization you gave the property to, or a reliable written record, that shows the organization's name and address, the date and location of the gift, and a description of the property. For each gift of property, you should also keep reliable written records that include:

- How you figured the property's value at the time you gave it. If the value was determined by an appraisal, you should also keep a signed copy of the appraisal.
- The cost or other basis of the property if you must reduce it by any ordinary income or capital gain that would have resulted if the property had been sold at its fair market value.
- How you figured your deduction if you chose to reduce your deduction for gifts of capital gain property.
- Any conditions attached to the gift.

Note: *If your total deduction for gifts of property is over $500, or if you gave less than your entire interest in the property, or if you made a "qualified conservation contribution" under Internal Revenue Code section 170(h),* your records should contain additional information. See Pub. 526 for details.

Line 15

Carryover From Prior Year

Enter any carryover of contributions that you could not deduct in an earlier year because they exceeded your adjusted gross income limit. See Pub. 526 for details on how to figure a carryover.

Casualty and Theft Losses

Line 17

Use line 17 to report casualty or theft losses of property that is not trade or business, income-producing, or rent or royalty property. Complete and attach **Form 4684**, Casualties and Thefts, to figure the amount of your loss to enter on line 17.

Losses You May Deduct

You may be able to deduct part or all of each loss caused by theft, vandalism, fire, storm, or similar causes, and car, boat, and other accidents. You may also be able to deduct money you had in a financial institution but lost because of the insolvency or bankruptcy of the institution.

You may deduct nonbusiness casualty or theft losses only to the extent that—

1. The amount of **each** separate casualty or theft loss is more than $100, and
2. The total amount of **all** losses during the year is more than 10% of the amount shown on Form 1040, line 32.

Special rules apply if you had both gains and losses from nonbusiness casualties or thefts. See Form 4684 for details.

Additional Information. For more details, get **Pub. 547,** Nonbusiness Disasters, Casualties, and Thefts. It also has information about Federal disaster area losses.

Losses You May Not Deduct

- Money or property misplaced or lost.
- Breakage of china, glassware, furniture, and similar items under normal conditions.
- Progressive damage to property (buildings, clothes, trees, etc.) caused by termites, moths, other insects, or disease.

Use line 20 of Schedule A to deduct the costs of proving that you had a property loss. Examples of these costs are appraisal fees and photographs used to establish the amount of your loss.

Moving Expenses

Line 18

Employees and self-employed persons (including partners) can deduct certain moving expenses.

You can take this deduction if you moved in connection with your job or business and your new workplace is at least 35 miles farther from your old home than your old home was from your old workplace. If you had no former workplace, your new workplace must be at least 35 miles from your old home. If you meet these requirements, call Tele-Tax (see page 30) and listen to topic 504 or get **Pub. 521,** Moving Expenses. Complete and attach **Form 3903,** Moving Expenses, to figure the amount to enter on line 18. If you began work at a new workplace outside the United States or its possessions, get **Form 3903-F,** Foreign Moving Expenses.

Miscellaneous Deductions

Most miscellaneous deductions cannot be deducted in full. Instead, you must subtract 2% of your adjusted gross income from the total. You figure the 2% limit on line 23.

The 2% limit generally applies to job expenses you paid for which you were not reimbursed. These expenses are reported on line 19. The limit also applies to certain expenses you paid to produce or collect taxable income. These expenses are reported on line 20.

Miscellaneous deductions that are not subject to the 2% limit are reported on line 25. See the instructions for line 25.

Additional Information. For more details, get **Pub. 529,** Miscellaneous Deductions.

Examples of Expenses You May Not Deduct

- Political contributions.
- Personal legal expenses.
- Lost or misplaced cash or property. But see **Casualty and Theft Losses** on this page.
- Expenses for meals during regular or extra work hours.
- The cost of entertaining friends.
- Expenses of going to or from your regular workplace.
- Education you need to meet minimum requirements for your job or that will qualify you for a new occupation.
- Travel expenses for employment away from home if that period of employment exceeds 1 year.
- Travel as a form of education.
- Expenses of attending a seminar, convention, or similar meeting unless it is related to your employment.
- Expenses of adopting a child, including a child with special needs.
- Fines and penalties.
- Expenses of producing tax-exempt income.

Line 19

Unreimbursed Employee Expenses

Enter the total job expenses you paid for which you were not reimbursed. But you MUST fill in and attach **Form 2106,** Employee Business Expenses, if **either** of the following applies:

1. You claim any travel, transportation, meal, or entertainment expenses for your job, OR
2. Your employer paid you for any of your job expenses reportable on line 19.

these expenses, you must use Form 2106 for all of your job expenses.

- Union dues.
- Safety equipment, small tools, and supplies you needed for your job.
- Uniforms your employer said you must have, and which you may not usually wear away from work.
- Protective clothing required in your work, such as hard hats, safety shoes, and glasses.
- Physical examinations your employer said you must have.
- Dues to professional organizations and chambers of commerce.
- Subscriptions to professional journals.
- Fees to employment agencies and other costs to look for a new job in your present occupation, even if you do not get a new job.
- Business use of part of your home but only if you use that part exclusively and on a regular basis in your work and for the convenience of your employer. For details, including limits that apply, see Tele-Tax (topic no. 309) on page 28 or get **Pub. 587,** Business Use of Your Home.
- Educational expenses you paid that were required by your employer, or by law or regulation, to keep your salary or job. In general, you may also include the cost of keeping or improving skills you must have in your job. For more details, see Tele-Tax (topic no. 313) on page 28 or get **Pub. 508,** Educational Expenses. Some educational expenses are not deductible. See **Examples of Expenses You May Not Deduct** on this page.

Line 20

Other Expenses

Enter the total amount you paid to produce or collect taxable income, manage or protect property held for earning income, and for tax preparation fees. But **do not** include any expenses deducted elsewhere such as on Schedule C, C-EZ, E, or F. List the type and amount of each expense on the dotted lines next to line 20. If you need more space, attach a statement showing the type and amount of each expense. Enter one total on line 20.

Examples of expenses to include on line 20 are:

- Tax return preparation fees, including fees paid for filing your return electronically.
- Safe deposit box rental.
- Certain legal and accounting fees.
- Clerical help and office rent.
- Custodial (e.g., trust account) fees.
- Your share of the investment expenses of a regulated investment company.
- Certain losses on nonfederally insured deposits in an insolvent or bankrupt financial institution. For details, including limits on the amount you may deduct, see Pub. 529.
- Deduction for repayment of amounts under a claim of right if $3,000 or less.

Line 25

Other Miscellaneous Deductions

Enter your total miscellaneous deductions that are not subject to the 2% AGI limit. List the type and amount of each expense on the dotted lines next to line 25. If you need more space, attach a statement showing the type and amount of each expense. Enter one total on line 25. Only the expenses listed below can be deducted on line 25:

- Gambling losses to the extent of gambling winnings. Report gambling winnings on Form 1040, line 22.
- Federal estate tax on income in respect of a decedent.
- Amortizable bond premium on bonds acquired before October 23, 1986.
- Deduction for repayment of amounts under a claim of right if more than $3,000. See Pub. 525 for details.
- Certain unrecovered investment in a pension. Get **Pub. 575,** Pension and Annuity Income (Including Simplified General Rule), for details.
- Impairment-related work expenses of a disabled person.

For more details on these expenses, see Pub. 529.

Total Itemized Deductions

Line 26

People with higher incomes may not be able to deduct all of their itemized deductions. If the amount on Form 1040, line 32, is more than $105,250 (more than $52,625 if married filing separately), use the worksheet on this page to figure the amount you may deduct.

Itemized Deductions Worksheet—Line 26 (keep for your records)

1. Add the amounts on Schedule A, lines 4, 8, 12, 16, 17, 18, 24, and 25 . . . . 1. _____
2. Add the amounts on Schedule A, lines 4, 11, and 17, plus any gambling losses included on line 25 . . . . 2. _____
   Caution: *Be sure your total gambling losses are clearly identified on the dotted line next to line 25.*
3. Subtract line 2 from line 1. If the result is zero, **stop here;** enter the amount from line 1 above on Schedule A, line 26 . . . 3. _____
4. Multiply line 3 above by 80% (.80) . . . 4. _____
5. Enter the amount from Form 1040, line 32 5. _____
6. Enter $105,250 ($52,625 if married filing separately) . . . . 6. _____
7. Subtract line 6 from line 5. If the result is zero or less, **stop here;** enter the amount from line 1 above on Schedule A, line 26 . . 7. _____
8. Multiply line 7 above by 3% (.03) . . . 8. _____
9. Enter the **smaller** of line 4 or line 8 . . . . 9. _____
10. **Total itemized deductions.** Subtract line 9 from line 1. Enter the result here and on Schedule A, line 26 . . . . . . 10. _____

A-5

Instructions for Schedule C, Profit or Loss From Business

Use Schedule C to report income or loss subject to self-employment tax from a business you operated or a profession you practiced as a sole proprietor. Also, use Schedule C to report wages and expenses you had as a statutory employee. An activity qualifies as a business if your primary purpose for engaging in the activity is for income or profit and you are involved in the activity with continuity and regularity. For example, a sporadic activity or a hobby does not qualify as a business. To report income from a nonbusiness activity, see the Instructions for Form 1040, line 22.

Small businesses and statutory employees with gross receipts of $25,000 or less and expenses of $2,000 or less may be able to file **Schedule C-EZ,** Net Profit From Business, instead of Schedule C. See Schedule C-EZ to find out if you qualify to file it.

This activity may subject you to state and local taxes and other requirements such as business licenses and fees. Check with your state and local governments for more information.

General Instructions

Changes To Note

- **Deduction for Clean-Fuel Vehicle Refueling Property.** A deduction may be claimed in Part V of Schedule C for part of the cost of qualified clean-fuel vehicle refueling property placed in service after June 30, 1993. See **Pub. 535,** Business Expenses, for more details.
- **New Part IV, Information on Your Vehicle.** New Part IV has been added to Schedule C to simplify the reporting of business vehicle information for sole proprietors by eliminating the requirement to file Form 4562 for this purpose. You can use Part IV instead of Form 4562 if you are claiming the standard mileage rate, you lease your vehicle, or your vehicle is fully depreciated. However, if Form 4562 must be filed for any other reason, you must continue to use Part V of Form 4562 to report vehicle information.

Other Schedules and Forms You May Have To File

Schedule A to deduct interest, taxes, and casualty losses not related to your business.
Schedule E to report rental real estate and royalty income or (loss) that is **not** subject to self-employment tax.
Schedule F to report profit or (loss) from farming.
Schedule SE to pay self-employment tax on income from any trade or business.
Form 4562 to claim depreciation on assets placed in service in 1993, to claim amortization that began in 1993, or to report information on listed property.
Form 4684 to report a casualty or theft gain or loss involving property used in your trade or business or income-producing property.
Form 4797 to report sales, exchanges, and involuntary conversions (other than from a casualty or theft) of trade or business property.
Form 8594 to report certain purchases or sales of groups of assets that constitute a trade or business.
Form 8824 to report like-kind exchanges.
Form 8829 to claim expenses for business use of your home.

Heavy Vehicle Use Tax

If you use certain highway trucks, truck-trailers, tractor-trailers, or buses in your trade or business, you may have to pay a Federal highway motor vehicle use tax. Get **Form 2290,** Heavy Vehicle Use Tax Return, to see if you owe this tax.

Information Returns

You may have to file information returns for wages paid to employees, certain payments of fees and other nonemployee compensation, interest, rents, royalties, real estate transactions, annuities, and pensions. You may also have to file an information return if you sold $5,000 or more of consumer products to a person on a buy-sell, deposit-commission, or other similar basis for resale. For more information, get the **Instructions for Forms 1099, 1098, 5498, and W-2G.**

If you received cash of more than $10,000 in one or more related transactions in the course of your trade or business, you may have to file **Form 8300.** For details, get **Pub. 1544,** Reporting Cash Payments of Over $10,000.

Tax Shelter

If you claim or report any deduction, loss, credit, other tax benefit, or income on Schedule C or C-EZ from an interest purchased or otherwise acquired in a tax shelter that is required to be registered, you **must** file **Form 8271** with your return.

Additional Information

Get **Pub. 334,** Tax Guide for Small Business, for more details on business income and expenses.

Specific Instructions

Filers of Form 1041

Do not complete the block labeled "Social security number." Instead, enter your employer identification number (EIN) on line D.

Line A

Describe the business or professional activity that provided your principal source of income reported on line 1. If you owned more than one business, you must complete a separate Schedule C for each business. Give the general field or activity and the type of product or service. If your general field or activity is wholesale or retail trade, or services connected with production services (mining, construction, or manufacturing), also give the type of customer or client. For example, "wholesale sale of hardware to retailers" or "appraisal of real estate for lending institutions."

Line B

Enter on this line the four-digit code that identifies your principal business or professional activity. See page C-6 for the list of codes.

Line D

You need an employer identification number (EIN) only if you had a Keogh plan or were required to file an employment, excise, fiduciary, or alcohol, tobacco, and firearms tax return. If you need an EIN, file **Form SS-4,** Application for Employer Identification Number.

If you do not have an EIN, leave line D blank. **Do not** enter your SSN.

Line E

Enter your business address. Show a street address instead of a box number. Include the suite or room number, if any. If you conducted the business from your home located at the address shown on Form 1040, page 1, you do not have to complete this line.

Line F

You must use the cash method on your return unless you kept account books. If you kept such books, you can use the cash method or the accrual method. However, if inventories are required, you must use the accrual method for sales and purchases. Special rules apply to long-term contracts. See Internal Revenue Code section 460 for details. The method used must clearly reflect your income.

If you use the **cash method,** show all items of taxable income actually or constructively received during the year (in cash, property, or services). Income is constructively received when it is credited to your account or set aside for you to use. Also, show amounts actually paid during the year for deductible expenses.

If you use the **accrual method,** report income when you earn it and deduct expenses when you incur them even if you do not pay them during the tax year.

Accrual-basis taxpayers are put on a cash basis for deducting business expenses owed to a related cash-basis taxpayer. Other rules determine the timing of deductions based on economic performance. Get **Pub. 538,** Accounting Periods and Methods.

To change your accounting method (including treatment of inventories), you must usually first get permission from the IRS. In general, file **Form 3115** within the first 180 days of the tax year in which you want to make the change.

Line G

Your inventories can be valued at:
- Cost,
- Cost or market value, whichever is lower, or
- Any other method approved by the IRS.

Line I

Participation, for purposes of the seven material participation tests listed below, generally includes any work you did in connection with an activity if you owned an interest in the activity at the time you did the work. The capacity in which you did the work does not matter. However, work is not treated as participation if it is work that an owner would not customarily do in the same type of activity and one of your main reasons for doing the work was to avoid the disallowance of losses or credits from the activity under the passive activity rules.

Work you did as an investor in an activity is not treated as participation unless you were directly involved in the day-to-day management or operations of the activity. Work done as an investor includes:

1. Studying and reviewing financial statements or reports on operations of the activity.

2. Preparing or compiling summaries or analyses of the finances or operations of the activity for your own use.

3. Monitoring the finances or operations of the activity in a nonmanagerial capacity.

Participation by your spouse during the tax year in an activity you own can be counted as your participation in the activity. This applies even if your spouse did not own an interest in the activity and whether or not you and your spouse file a joint return for the tax year.

Material Participation. For purposes of the passive activity rules, you materially participated in the operation of this trade or business activity during 1993 if you meet any of the following seven tests:

1. You participated in the activity for more than 500 hours during the tax year.

2. Your participation in the activity for the tax year was substantially all of the participation in the activity of all individuals (including individuals who did not own any interest in the activity) for the tax year.

3. You participated in the activity for more than 100 hours during the tax year, and you participated at least as much as any other person for the tax year. This includes individuals who did not own any interest in the activity.

4. The activity is a significant participation activity for the tax year, and you participated in all significant participation activities for more than 500 hours during the year. An activity is a "significant participation activity" if it involves the conduct of a trade or business, you participated in the activity for more than 100 hours during the tax year, and you did not materially participate under any of the material participation tests (other than this test 4).

5. You materially participated in the activity for any 5 of the prior 10 tax years.

6. The activity is a personal service activity in which you materially participated for any 3 prior tax years. A personal service activity is an activity that involves performing personal services in the fields of health, law, engineering, architecture, accounting, actuarial science, performing arts, or consulting, or any other trade or business in which capital is not a material income-producing factor.

7. Based on all the facts and circumstances, you participated in the activity on a regular, continuous, and substantial basis during the tax year. But you do not meet this test if you participated in the activity for 100 hours or less during the tax year. Your participation in managing the activity does not count in determining if you meet this test if any person (except you) —

a. Received compensation for performing management services in connection with the activity, or

b. Spent more hours during the tax year than you spent performing management services in connection with the activity (regardless of whether the person was compensated for the services).

If you meet any of the above tests, check the "Yes" box on line I.

If you **do not** meet any of the above tests, check the "No" box on line I. This business is a **passive activity.** If you have a loss from this business, see **Limit on Losses** below. If you have a profit from this business activity but have current-year losses from other passive activities or you have prior-year unallowed passive activity losses, see the instructions for **Form 8582,** Passive Activity Loss Limitations.

Exception for Oil and Gas. If you are filing Schedule C to report income and deductions from an oil or gas well in which you own a working interest directly or through an entity that does not limit your liability, check the "Yes" box on line I. The activity of owning the working interest is not a passive activity regardless of your participation in the activity.

Limit on Losses. If you checked the "No" box on line I and you have a loss from this business, you may have to use Form 8582 to figure your allowable loss, if any, to enter on Schedule C, line 31. Generally, you can deduct losses from passive activities only to the extent of income from passive activities.

For more details, get **Pub. 925,** Passive Activity and At-Risk Rules.

Line J

If you started or acquired this business in 1993, check the box on line J.

Also, check the box if you are reopening or restarting this business after temporarily closing it, and you did not file a 1992 Schedule C or C-EZ for this business.

Part I. Income

Line 1

Enter gross receipts or sales from your business. Be sure to include on this line amounts you received in your trade or business as shown on Form(s) **1099-MISC.**

Statutory Employees. If you received a Form W-2 and the "Statutory employee" box in box 15 of that form was checked, report your income and expenses related to that income on Schedule C or C-EZ. Enter your statutory employee income from box 1 of Form W-2 on line 1 of Schedule C or C-EZ, and **check the box** on that line. Social security and Medicare tax should have been withheld from your earnings; therefore, you do not owe self-employment tax on these earnings.

Statutory employees include full-time life insurance agents, certain agent or commission drivers and traveling salespersons, and certain homeworkers.

If you had both self-employment income and statutory employee income, **do not** combine these amounts on a single Schedule C or C-EZ. In this case, you must file two Schedules C. You cannot use Schedule C-EZ.

Installment Sales. Generally, the installment method may not be used to report income from the sale of **(a)** personal property regularly sold under the installment method, or **(b)** real property held for resale to customers. But the installment method may be used to report income from sales of certain residential lots and timeshares if you elect to pay interest on the tax due on that income after the year of sale. See Internal Revenue Code section 453(l)(2)(B) for details. If you make this election, include the interest on Form 1040, line 53. Also write "453(l)(3)" and the amount of the interest on the dotted line to the left of line 53.

If you use the installment method, attach a schedule to your return. Show separately for 1993 and the 3 preceding years: gross sales, cost of goods sold, gross profit, percentage of gross profit to gross sales, amounts collected, and gross profit on amounts collected.

Line 2

Enter on line 2 such items as returned sales, rebates, and allowances from the sales price.

Line 6

Report on line 6 amounts from finance reserve income, scrap sales, bad debts you recovered, interest (such as on notes and accounts receivable), state gasoline or fuel tax refunds you got in 1993, credit for Federal tax paid on gasoline or other fuels claimed on your 1992 Form 1040, and other kinds of miscellaneous business income. Include amounts you received in your trade or business as shown on **Form(s) 1099-PATR.**

If the business use percentage of any listed property (defined in the instructions for line 13) decreased to 50% or less in 1993, report on this line any recapture of excess depreciation, including any section 179 expense deduction. Use **Form 4797,** Sales of Business Property, to figure the recapture. Also, if the business use percentage drops to 50% or less on leased listed property (other than a vehicle), include on this line any inclusion amount. Get **Pub. 534,** Depreciation, to figure the amount.

Part II. Expenses

Capitalizing Costs of Property. If you produced real or tangible personal property or acquired property for resale, certain expenses attributable to the property must be included in inventory costs or capitalized. In addition to direct costs, producers of inventory property must also include part of certain indirect costs in their inventory. Purchasers of personal property acquired for resale must include part of certain indirect costs in inventory only if the average annual gross receipts for the 3 prior tax years exceed $10 million. Also, you must capitalize part of the indirect costs that benefit real or tangible personal property constructed for use in a trade or business, or noninventory property produced for sale to customers. Reduce the amounts on lines 8–26 and Part V by amounts capitalized. For more details, see **Pub. 538.**

Exception for Creative Property. If you are an artist, author, or photographer, you may be exempt from the capitalization rules. However, your personal efforts must have created (or reasonably be expected to create) the property. This exception does not apply to any expense related to printing, photographic plates, motion picture films, video tapes, or similar items. These expenses are subject to the capitalization rules. For more details, see Pub. 538.

Line 9

Caution: *Cash method taxpayers cannot take a bad debt deduction unless the amount was previously included in income.*

Include debts and partial debts from sales or services that were included in income and are definitely known to be worthless. If you later collect a debt that you deducted as a bad debt, include it as income in the year collected.

For more details, get **Pub. 535,** Business Expenses.

Line 10

You can deduct the actual cost of running your car or truck, or take the standard mileage rate. You **must** use actual costs if you did not own the vehicle or if you used more than one vehicle simultaneously in your business (such as in fleet operations).

If you deduct actual costs, include on line 10 the business portion of expenses for gasoline, oil, repairs, insurance, tires, license plates, etc. Show depreciation on line 13 and rent or lease payments on line 20a.

If you want to take the standard mileage rate, multiply the number of business miles by 28 cents a mile. Add to this amount your parking fees and tolls, and enter the total on line 10.

If you claim car and truck expenses, you must provide certain information on the use of your vehicle by completing:

• Part IV of Schedule C, or Part III of Schedule C-EZ, if **(a)** you are claiming the standard mileage rate, you lease your vehicle, or your vehicle is fully depreciated, and **(b)** you are not required to file Form 4562. If you used more than one vehicle during the year, attach your own schedule with the information requested in Part IV of Schedule C, or Part III of Schedule C-EZ, for each additional vehicle.

• Part V of **Form 4562,** Depreciation and Amortization, if you are claiming depreciation on your vehicle or you are required to file Form 4562 for any other reason (see the instructions for line 13 below).

For more details, get **Pub. 917,** Business Use of a Car.

Line 12

Enter your deduction for depletion on this line. If you have timber depletion, attach **Form T.** See Pub. 535 for details.

Line 13

Depreciation and Section 179 Expense Deduction. Depreciation is the annual deduction allowed to recover the cost or other basis of business or investment property with a useful life of more than 1 year. You can also depreciate improvements made to leased business property. However, stock in trade, inventories, and land are not depreciable.

Depreciation starts when you first use the property in your business or for the production of income. It ends when you take the property out of service, deduct all your depreciable cost or other basis, or no longer use the property in your business or for the production of income.

For property placed in service after 1980, see the Instructions for Form 4562 to figure the amount of depreciation to enter on line 13. For property placed in service before 1981, figure depreciation from your own books and records and enter the total on line 13.

You may also choose under Internal Revenue Code section 179 to expense part of the cost of certain property you bought in 1993 for use in your business. See the Instructions for Form 4562 for more information.

You must complete and attach Form 4562 **only if:**

• You are claiming depreciation on property placed in service during 1993, or

• You are claiming depreciation on listed property (defined below), regardless of the date it was placed in service, or

• You are claiming a section 179 expense deduction.

If you acquired depreciable property for the first time in 1993, get **Pub. 946,** How To Begin Depreciating Your Property. For a more comprehensive guide on depreciation, get **Pub. 534,** Depreciation.

Listed property generally includes, but is not limited to:

• Passenger automobiles weighing 6,000 pounds or less.

• Any other property used for transportation if the nature of the property lends itself to personal use, such as motorcycles, pick-up trucks, etc.

• Any property used for entertainment or recreational purposes (such as photographic, phonographic, communication, and video recording equipment).

• Cellular telephones or other similar telecommunications equipment placed in service after 1989.

• Computers or peripheral equipment.

Exception. Listed property does not include photographic, phonographic, communication, or video equipment used exclusively in your trade or business or at your regular business establishment. It also does not include any computer or peripheral equipment used exclusively at a regular business establishment and owned or leased by the person operating the establishment. For purposes of these exceptions, a portion of your home is treated as a regular business establishment only if that portion meets the requirements under Internal Revenue Code section 280A(c)(1) for deducting expenses attributable to the business use of a home.

If the business use percentage of any listed property decreased to 50% or less in 1993, you may have to recapture excess depreciation, including any section 179 expense deduction. Get **Form 4797** and its instructions for details.

Line 14

Deduct contributions to employee benefit programs that are not an incidental part of a pension or profit-sharing plan included on line 19. Examples are accident and health plans, group-term life insurance, and dependent care assistance programs.

Do not include on line 14 any contributions you made on your behalf as a self-employed person to an accident and health plan or for group-term life insurance. You may be able to deduct on Form 1040, line 26, part of the amount you paid for health insurance on behalf of yourself, your spouse, and dependents, even if you do not itemize your deductions. See the Form 1040 instructions on page 22 for more details.

Line 15

Deduct premiums paid for business insurance on line 15. Deduct on line 14 amounts paid for employee accident and health insurance.

Do not deduct amounts credited to a reserve for self-insurance or premiums paid for a policy that pays for your lost earnings due to sickness or disability.

For more details, see Pub. 535.

Lines 16a and 16b

Interest Allocation Rules. The tax treatment of interest expense differs depending on its type. For example, home mortgage interest and investment interest are treated differently. "Interest allocation" rules require you to allocate (classify) your interest expense so it is deducted (or capitalized) on the correct line of your return and gets the right tax treatment. These rules could affect how much interest you are allowed to deduct on Schedule C or C-EZ.

Generally, you allocate interest expense by tracing how the proceeds of the loan were used. See Pub. 535 for details.

If you paid interest in 1993 that applies to future years, deduct only the part that applies to 1993.

If you paid interest on a debt secured by your main home and any of the proceeds from that debt were used in connection with your trade or business, see Pub. 535 to figure the amount that is deductible on Schedule C or C-EZ.

If you have a mortgage on real property used in your business (other than your main home), enter on line 16a the interest you paid for 1993 to banks or other financial institutions for which you received a **Form 1098,** Mortgage Interest Statement. If you didn't receive a Form 1098, enter the interest on line 16b.

If you paid $600 or more of mortgage interest, the recipient should send you a Form 1098 or similar statement showing the total interest received from you during 1993. This statement must be sent to you by January 31, 1994. If you paid more mortgage interest to financial institutions than is shown on Form 1098, or similar statement, see Pub. 535 to find out if you can deduct the additional interest. If you can, enter the amount on line 16a. Attach a statement to your return explaining the difference. Write "See attached" in the left margin next to line 16a.

If you and at least one other person (other than your spouse if you file a joint return) were liable for and paid interest on the mortgage and the other person received the Form 1098, report your share of the interest on line 16b. Attach a statement to your return showing the name and address of the person who received the Form 1098. In the left margin next to line 16b, write "See attached."

Do not deduct interest you paid or accrued on debts allocable to investment property. This interest is generally deducted on **Schedule A.** For details, get **Pub. 550,** Investment Income and Expenses.

Line 17

Include on this line fees for tax advice related to your business and for preparation of the tax forms related to your business.

Line 19

Enter your deduction for contributions to a pension, profit-sharing, or annuity plan, or plans for the benefit of your employees. If the plan includes you as a self-employed person, enter contributions made as an employer on your behalf on Form 1040, line 27, not on Schedule C.

Generally, you must file one of the following forms if you maintain a pension, profit-sharing, or other funded-deferred compensation plan. The filing requirement is not affected by whether or not the plan qualified under the Internal Revenue Code, or whether or not you claim a deduction for the current tax year.

Form 5500. Complete this form for each plan with 100 or more participants.

Form 5500-C/R or 5500-EZ. Complete the applicable form for each plan with fewer than 100 participants.

There is a penalty for failure to timely file these forms.

For more information, get **Pub. 560,** Retirement Plans for the Self-Employed.

Lines 20a and 20b

If you rented or leased vehicles, machinery, or equipment, enter on line 20a the business portion of your rental cost. But if you leased a vehicle for a term of 30 days or more, you may have to reduce your deduction by an amount called the **inclusion amount.**

You may have to do this if—

The lease term began:	And the vehicle's fair market value on the first day of the lease exceeded:
During 1993	$14,300
During 1992	13,700
During 1991	13,400
After 1986 but before 1991	12,800

If the lease term began after June 18, 1984, but before January 1, 1987, see **Pub. 917** to find out if you have an inclusion amount.

See Pub. 917 to figure your inclusion amount.

Enter on line 20b amounts paid to rent or lease other property, such as office space in a building.

Line 21

Deduct the cost of repairs and maintenance. Include labor, supplies, and other items that do not add to the value or increase the life of the property. Do not deduct the value of your own labor. Do not deduct amounts spent to restore or replace property; they must be capitalized.

Line 23

You can deduct the following taxes:

• State and local sales taxes imposed on you as the seller of goods or services. If you collected this tax from the buyer, you must also include the amount collected in gross receipts or sales on line 1.

• Real estate and personal property taxes on business assets.

• Social security and Medicare taxes paid to match required withholding from your employees' wages. Also, Federal unemployment tax paid. To deduct one-half of your self-employment tax, see the Instructions for Form 1040, line 25, on page 21.

• Federal highway use tax.

Do not deduct:

• Federal income taxes.

• Estate and gift taxes.

• Taxes assessed to pay for improvements, such as paving and sewers.

• Taxes on your home or personal use property.

• State and local sales taxes on property purchased for use in your business. Instead, treat these taxes as part of the cost of the property.

• State and local sales taxes imposed on the buyer that you were required to collect and pay over to the state or local governments. These taxes are not included in gross receipts or sales nor are they a deductible expense. However, if the state or local government allowed you to retain any part of the sales tax you collected, you must include that amount as income on line 6.

• Other taxes not related to your business.

Line 24a

Enter your expenses for lodging and transportation connected with overnight travel for business while away from your tax home. Generally, your tax home is your main place of business regardless of where you maintain your family home. You cannot deduct expenses paid or incurred in connection with employment away from home if that period of employment exceeds 1 year.

Do not include expenses for meals and entertainment on this line. Instead, see the instructions for lines 24b and 24c below.

You cannot deduct expenses for attending a foreign convention unless it is directly related to your trade or business and it is as reasonable for the meeting to be held outside the North American area as within it. These rules apply to both employers and employees. Other rules apply to luxury water travel.

For more details, get **Pub. 463,** Travel, Entertainment, and Gift Expenses.

Lines 24b and 24c

On line 24b, enter your total business meal and entertainment expenses. Include meals while traveling away from home for business. Instead of the actual cost of your meals while traveling away from home, you may use the standard meal allowance. For more details, see Pub. 463.

Business meal expenses are deductible only if they are **(a)** directly related to or associated with the active conduct of your trade or business, **(b)** not lavish or extravagant, and **(c)** incurred while you or your employee is present at the meal.

You cannot deduct any expense paid or incurred for a facility (such as a yacht or hunting lodge) used for any activity usually considered entertainment, amusement, or recreation.

There are exceptions to these rules as well as other rules that apply to sky-box rentals and tickets to entertainment events. See Pub. 463.

Generally, you may deduct **only** 80% of your business meal and entertainment expenses, including meals incurred while traveling away from home on business. However, you may fully deduct meals and entertainment furnished or reimbursed to an employee if you properly treat the expense as wages subject to withholding. You may also fully deduct meals and entertainment provided to a nonemployee to the extent the expenses are includible in the gross income of that person and reported on Form 1099-MISC.

Figure how much of the amount on line 24h is subject to the 80% limit. Then, multiply that amount by 20% (.20) and enter the result on line 24c.

Line 25

Deduct only utility expenses paid or incurred for your trade or business.

Local Telephone Service. If you used your home phone for business, do not deduct the base rate (including taxes) of the first phone line into your residence. But you can deduct expenses for any additional costs you incurred for business that are more than the cost of the base rate for the first phone line. For example, if you had a second line, you can deduct the business percentage of the charges for that line, including the base rate charges.

Line 26

Enter the total salaries and wages (other than salaries and wages deducted elsewhere on your return) paid or incurred for the tax year minus any jobs credit you claimed on **Form 5884,** Jobs Credit. Do not include amounts paid to yourself.

Caution: *If you provided taxable fringe benefits to your employees, such as personal use of a car, do not deduct as wages the amount applicable to depreciation and other expenses claimed elsewhere.*

Line 30

Business Use of Your Home. You may be able to deduct certain expenses for business use of your home, subject to limitations. Generally, any amount not allowed as a deduction for 1993 because of the limitations can be carried over to 1994. You must attach **Form 8829,** Expenses for Business Use of Your Home, if you claim this deduction.

For details, see the Instructions for Form 8829, and get **Pub. 587,** Business Use of Your Home.

Line 31

If you have a loss, the amount of loss you can deduct this year may be limited. Go on to line 32 before entering your loss on line 31. If you answered "No" to Question I on Schedule C, also see the Instructions for Form 8582. Enter the net profit or **deductible** loss here. Combine this amount with any profit or loss from other businesses, and enter the total on Form 1040, line 12, and Schedule SE, line 2. Fiduciaries should enter the total on Form 1041, line 3.

If you have a net profit on line 31, this amount is earned income and may qualify you for the earned income credit if you meet certain conditions. See page EIC-1 for more details.

Statutory Employees. If you are filing Schedule C to report income and expenses as a statutory employee, include your net profit or deductible loss from line 31 with other Schedule C amounts on Form 1040, line 12. However, **do not** report this amount on Schedule SE, line 2. If you are required to file Schedule SE because of other self-employment income, see the instructions for Schedule SE.

Line 32

At-Risk Rules. Generally, if you have **(a)** a business loss, and **(b)** amounts in the business for which you are **not at risk,** you will have to complete **Form 6198,** At-Risk Limitations, to figure your allowable loss.

The at-risk rules generally limit the amount of loss (including loss on the disposition of assets) you can claim to the amount you could actually lose in the business.

Check **box 32b** if you have amounts for which you are not at risk in this business, such as the following.

- Nonrecourse loans used to finance the business, to acquire property used in the business, or to acquire the business, that are not secured by your own property (other than property used in the business). However, there is an exception for certain nonrecourse financing borrowed by you in connection with holding real property.
- Cash, property, or borrowed amounts used in the business (or contributed to the business, or used to acquire the business) that are protected against loss by a guarantee, stop-loss agreement, or other similar arrangement (excluding casualty insurance and insurance against tort liability).
- Amounts borrowed for use in the business from a person who has an interest in the business, other than as a creditor, or who is related, under Internal Revenue Code section 465(b)(3), to a person (other than you) having such an interest.

If all amounts are at risk in this business, check **box 32a** and enter your loss on line 31. But if you answered "No" to Question I, you may need to complete **Form 8582** to figure your allowable loss to enter on line 31. See the Instructions for Form 8582 for more details.

If you checked **box 32b,** get Form 6198 to determine the amount of your deductible loss and enter that amount on line 31. But if you answered "No" to Question I, your loss may be further limited. See the Instructions for Form 8582. If your at-risk amount is zero or less, enter zero on line 31. Be sure to attach Form 6198 to your return. If you checked box 32b and you do not attach Form 6198, the processing of your tax return may be delayed.

Statutory employees. Include your deductible loss with other Schedule C amounts on Form 1040, line 12. **Do not** include this amount on Schedule SE, line 2.

Any loss from this business not allowed for 1993 because of the at-risk rules is treated as a deduction allocable to the business in 1994. For more details, see the Instructions for Form 6198 and **Pub. 925.**

Part III. Cost of Goods Sold

If you engaged in a trade or business in which the production, purchase, or sale of merchandise was an income-producing factor, merchandise inventories must be taken into account at the beginning and end of your tax year.

Note: *Certain direct and indirect expenses must be capitalized or included in inventory. See the instructions for Part II.*

Part V. Other Expenses

Include all ordinary and necessary business expenses not deducted elsewhere on Schedule C. List the type and amount of each expense separately in the space provided. Enter the total on lines 46 and 27. Do not include the cost of business equipment or furniture, replacements or permanent improvements to property, or personal, living, and family expenses. Do not include charitable contributions. For more details on business expenses, see Pub. 535.

Amortization. Include amortization in this part. For amortization that begins in 1993, you must complete and attach **Form 4562.**

You may amortize:

- The cost of pollution-control facilities.
- Amounts paid for research and experimentation.
- Certain business startup costs.
- Qualified forestation and reforestation costs.
- Amounts paid to acquire, protect, expand, register, or defend trademarks or trade names.
- Goodwill and certain other intangibles.

In general, you **may not** amortize real property construction period interest and taxes. Special rules apply for allocating interest to real or personal property produced in your trade or business.

At-Risk Loss Deduction. Any loss from this activity that was not allowed as a deduction last year because of the at-risk rules is treated as a deduction allocable to this activity in 1993.

Capital Construction Fund. Do not claim on Schedule C or C-EZ the deduction for amounts contributed to a capital construction fund set up under the Merchant Marine Act of 1936. To take the deduction, reduce the amount that would otherwise be entered as taxable income on Form 1040, line 37, by the amount of the deduction. In the margin to the left of line 37, write "CCF" and the amount of the deduction. For more information, get **Pub. 595,** Tax Guide for Commercial Fishermen.

Disabled Access Credit and the Deduction for Removing Barriers to Individuals with Disabilities and the Elderly. You may be able to claim a tax credit of up to $5,000 for eligible expenditures paid or incurred in 1993 to provide access to your business for individuals with disabilities. Get **Form 8826,** Disabled Access Credit, for more details. You can also deduct up to $15,000 of costs paid or incurred in 1993 to remove architectural or transportation barriers to individuals with disabilities and the elderly. However, you cannot take both the credit and the deduction on the same expenditures.

Principal Business or Professional Activity Codes

Locate the major category that best describes your activity. Within the major category, select the activity code that most closely identifies the business or profession that is the principal source of your sales or receipts. **Enter this 4-digit code on line B of Schedule C or C-EZ.** For example, real estate agent is under the major category of **"Real Estate,"** and the code is **"5520."**

Note: *If your principal source of income is from farming activities, you should file **Schedule F** (Form 1040), Profit or Loss From Farming.*

Agricultural Services, Forestry, Fishing
Code
- 1990 Animal services, other than breeding
- 1933 Crop services
- 2113 Farm labor & management services
- 2246 Fishing, commercial
- 2238 Forestry, except logging
- 2212 Horticulture & landscaping
- 2469 Hunting & trapping
- 1974 Livestock breeding
- 0836 Logging
- 1958 Veterinary services, including pets

Construction
- 0018 Operative builders (for own account)

Building Trade Contractors, Including Repairs
- 0414 Carpentering & flooring
- 0455 Concrete work
- 0273 Electrical work
- 0299 Masonry, dry wall, stone, & tile
- 0257 Painting & paper hanging
- 0232 Plumbing, heating, & air conditioning
- 0430 Roofing, siding, & sheet metal
- 0885 Other building trade contractors (excavation, glazing, etc.)

General Contractors
- 0075 Highway & street construction
- 0059 Nonresidential building
- 0034 Residential building
- 3889 Other heavy construction (pipe laying, bridge construction, etc.)

Finance, Insurance, & Related Services
- 6064 Brokers & dealers of securities
- 6080 Commodity contracts brokers & dealers; security & commodity exchanges
- 6148 Credit institutions & mortgage bankers
- 5702 Insurance agents or brokers
- 5744 Insurance services (appraisal, consulting, inspection, etc.)
- 6130 Investment advisors & services
- 5777 Other financial services

Manufacturing, Including Printing & Publishing
- 0679 Apparel & other textile products
- 1115 Electric & electronic equipment
- 1073 Fabricated metal products
- 0638 Food products & beverages
- 0810 Furniture & fixtures
- 0695 Leather footwear, handbags, etc.
- 0836 Lumber & other wood products
- 1099 Machinery & machine shops
- 0877 Paper & allied products
- 1057 Primary metal industries
- 0851 Printing & publishing
- 1032 Stone, clay, & glass products
- 0653 Textile mill products
- 1883 Other manufacturing industries

Mining & Mineral Extraction
- 1537 Coal mining
- 1511 Metal mining
- 1552 Oil & gas
- 1719 Quarrying & nonmetallic mining

Real Estate
- 5538 Operators & lessors of buildings, including residential
- 5553 Operators & lessors of other real property
- 5520 Real estate agents & brokers
- 5579 Real estate property managers
- 5710 Subdividers & developers, except cemeteries
- 6155 Title abstract offices

Services: Personal, Professional, & Business Services

Amusement & Recreational Services
- 9670 Bowling centers
- 9688 Motion picture & tape distribution & allied services
- 9597 Motion picture & video production
- 9639 Motion picture theaters
- 8557 Physical fitness facilities
- 9696 Professional sports & racing, including promoters & managers
- 9811 Theatrical performers, musicians, agents, producers, & related services
- 9613 Video tape rental
- 9837 Other amusement & recreational services

Automotive Services
- 8813 Automotive rental or leasing, without driver
- 8953 Automotive repairs, general & specialized
- 8839 Parking, except valet
- 8896 Other automotive services (wash, towing, etc.)

Business & Personal Services
- 7658 Accounting & bookkeeping
- 7716 Advertising, except direct mail
- 7682 Architectural services
- 8318 Barber shop (or barber)
- 8110 Beauty shop (or beautician)
- 8714 Child day care
- 7872 Computer programming, processing, data preparation & related services
- 7922 Computer repair, maintenance, & leasing
- 7286 Consulting services
- 7799 Consumer credit reporting & collection services
- 8755 Counseling (except health practitioners)
- 7732 Employment agencies & personnel supply
- 7518 Engineering services
- 7773 Equipment rental & leasing (except computer or automotive)
- 8532 Funeral services & crematories
- 7633 Income tax preparation
- 7914 Investigative & protective services
- 7617 Legal services (or lawyer)
- 7856 Mailing, reproduction, commercial art, photography, & stenographic services
- 7245 Management services
- 8771 Ministers & chaplains
- 8334 Photographic studios
- 7260 Public relations
- 8733 Research services
- 7708 Surveying services
- 8730 Teaching or tutoring
- 7880 Other business services
- 6882 Other personal services

Hotels & Other Lodging Places
- 7237 Camps & camping parks
- 7096 Hotels, motels, & tourist homes
- 7211 Rooming & boarding houses

Laundry & Cleaning Services
- 7450 Carpet & upholstery cleaning
- 7419 Coin-operated laundries & dry cleaning
- 7435 Full-service laundry, dry cleaning, & garment service
- 7476 Janitorial & related services (building, house, & window cleaning)

Medical & Health Services
- 9274 Chiropractors
- 9233 Dentist's office or clinic
- 9217 Doctor's (M.D.) office or clinic
- 9456 Medical & dental laboratories
- 9472 Nursing & personal care facilities
- 9290 Optometrists
- 9258 Osteopathic physicians & surgeons
- 9241 Podiatrists
- 9415 Registered & practical nurses
- 9431 Offices & clinics of other health practitioners (dieticians, midwives, speech pathologists, etc.)
- 9886 Other health services

Miscellaneous Repair, Except Computers
- 9019 Audio equipment & TV repair
- 9035 Electrical & electronic equipment repair, except audio & TV
- 9050 Furniture repair & reupholstery
- 2881 Other equipment repair

Trade, Retail—Selling Goods to Individuals & Households
- 3038 Catalog or mail order
- 3012 Selling door to door, by telephone or party plan, or from mobile unit
- 3053 Vending machine selling

Selling From Showroom, Store, or Other Fixed Location

Apparel & Accessories
- 3921 Accessory & specialty stores & furriers for women
- 3939 Clothing, family
- 3772 Clothing, men's & boys'
- 3913 Clothing, women's
- 3756 Shoe stores
- 3954 Other apparel & accessory stores

Automotive & Service Stations
- 3558 Gasoline service stations
- 3319 New car dealers (franchised)
- 3533 Tires, accessories, & parts
- 3335 Used car dealers
- 3517 Other automotive dealers (motorcycles, recreational vehicles, etc.)

Building, Hardware, & Garden Supply
- 4416 Building materials dealers
- 4457 Hardware stores
- 4473 Nurseries & garden supply stores
- 4432 Paint, glass, & wallpaper stores

Food & Beverages
- 0612 Bakeries selling at retail
- 3086 Catering services
- 3095 Drinking places (bars, taverns, pubs, saloons, etc.)
- 3079 Eating places, meals & snacks
- 3210 Grocery stores (general line)
- 3251 Liquor stores
- 3236 Specialized food stores (meat, produce, candy, health food, etc.)

Furniture & General Merchandise
- 3988 Computer & software stores
- 3970 Furniture stores
- 4317 Home furnishings stores (china, floor coverings, drapes)
- 4119 Household appliance stores
- 4333 Music & record stores
- 3996 TV, audio & electronic stores
- 3715 Variety stores
- 3731 Other general merchandise stores

Miscellaneous Retail Stores
- 4812 Boat dealers
- 5017 Book stores, excluding newsstands
- 4853 Camera & photo supply stores
- 3277 Drug stores
- 5058 Fabric & needlework stores
- 4655 Florists
- 5090 Fuel dealers (except gasoline)
- 4630 Gift, novelty, & souvenir shops
- 4838 Hobby, toy, & game shops
- 4671 Jewelry stores
- 4895 Luggage & leather goods stores
- 5074 Mobile home dealers
- 4879 Optical goods stores
- 4697 Sporting goods & bicycle shops
- 5033 Stationery stores
- 4614 Used merchandise & antique stores (except motor vehicle parts)
- 5884 Other retail stores

Trade, Wholesale—Selling Goods to Other Businesses, etc.

Durable Goods, Including Machinery Equipment, Wood, Metals, etc.
- 2634 Agent or broker for other firms—more than 50% of gross sales on commission
- 2618 Selling for your own account

Nondurable Goods, Including Food, Fiber, Chemicals, etc.
- 2675 Agent or broker for other firms—more than 50% of gross sales on commission
- 2659 Selling for your own account

Transportation, Communications, Public Utilities, & Related Services
- 6619 Air transportation
- 6312 Bus & limousine transportation
- 6676 Communication services
- 6395 Courier or package delivery
- 6361 Highway passenger transportation (except chartered service)
- 6536 Public warehousing
- 6114 Taxicabs
- 6510 Trash collection without own dump
- 6635 Travel agents & tour operators
- 6338 Trucking (except trash collection)
- 6692 Utilities (dumps, snow plowing, road cleaning, etc.)
- 6551 Water transportation
- 6650 Other transportation services

- 8888 **Unable to classify**

Instructions for Schedule D, Capital Gains and Losses

Additional Information. Get **Pub. 544**, Sales and Other Dispositions of Assets, and **Pub. 550**, Investment Income and Expenses, for more details.

General Instructions

Changes To Note

- Schedule D has been simplified for 1993. We hope you will find it easier to use. We no longer ask for information on the election not to use the installment method and have also discontinued the requirement to reconcile on Schedule D bartering income reported on Forms 1099-B. In addition, the computation of tax using the maximum capital gains rate and carryovers of short-term and long-term capital losses are no longer figured on page 2 of Schedule D. Instead, we have added worksheets on page D-4 that you can use to make these computations. As a result of these changes, we were able to use page 2 of Schedule D as a continuation sheet for transactions reported on lines 1 and 9. The continuation sheet used in previous years, Schedule D-1 (Form 1040), is now obsolete.
- If you sold publicly traded securities at a gain after August 9, 1993, you may be able to postpone all or part of the gain if you bought stock or a partnership interest in a specialized small business investment company during the 60-day period that began on the day you sold the securities. For more details, see page D-2.

Purpose of Schedule

Use Schedule D to report:
- The sale or exchange of a capital asset.
- Gains from involuntary conversions (other than from casualty or theft) of capital assets not held for business or profit.
- Capital gain distributions not reported on Form 1040, line 14.
- Nonbusiness bad debts.

Other Forms You May Have To File

Use **Form 4797**, Sales of Business Property, to report the following:
- The sale or exchange of property used in a trade or business; depreciable and amortizable property; oil, gas, geothermal, or other mineral property; and section 126 property.
- The involuntary conversion (other than from casualty or theft) of property used in a trade or business and capital assets held for business or profit.
- The disposition of noncapital assets other than inventory or property held primarily for sale to customers in the ordinary course of your trade or business.

Use **Form 4684**, Casualties and Thefts, to report involuntary conversions of property due to casualty or theft.

Use **Form 8824**, Like-Kind Exchanges, if you made one or more like-kind exchanges. See **Exchange of Like-Kind Property** on page D-2.

Capital Asset

Most property you own and use for personal purposes, pleasure, or investment is a capital asset. For example, your house, furniture, car, stocks, and bonds are capital assets.

A capital asset is any property held by you **except** the following:

1. Stock in trade or other property included in inventory or held for sale to customers.
2. Accounts or notes receivable for services performed in the ordinary course of your trade or business or as an employee, or from the sale of any property described in **1**.
3. Depreciable property used in your trade or business even if it is fully depreciated.
4. Real property (real estate) used in your trade or business.
5. Copyrights, literary, musical, or artistic compositions, letters or memoranda, or similar property: (a) created by your personal efforts; (b) prepared or produced for you (in the case of letters, memoranda, or similar property); or (c) that you received from someone who created them or for whom they were created, as mentioned in (a) or (b), in a way (such as by gift) that entitled you to the basis of the previous owner.
6. U.S. Government publications, including the Congressional Record, that you received from the government, other than by purchase at the normal sales price, or that you got from someone who had received it in a similar way, if your basis is determined by reference to the previous owner's basis.

Short-Term or Long-Term

Separate your capital gains and losses according to how long you held or owned the property. The holding period for long-term capital gains and losses is more than 1 year. The holding period for short-term capital gains and losses is 1 year or less.

To figure the holding period, begin counting on the day after you received the property and include the day you disposed of it. Use the trade dates for date acquired and date sold for stocks and bonds traded on an exchange or over-the-counter market.

If you disposed of property that you acquired by inheritance, report the disposition as a long-term gain or loss, regardless of how long you held the property.

A nonbusiness bad debt must be treated as a short-term capital loss. See Pub. 550 under **Nonbusiness Bad Debts** for what qualifies as a nonbusiness bad debt and how to enter it on Schedule D.

Limit on Capital Losses

For 1993, you may deduct capital losses up to the amount of your capital gains plus $3,000 ($1,500 if married filing separately). Capital losses that exceed this amount are carried forward to later years.

Losses That Are Not Deductible

Do not deduct a loss from the direct or indirect sale or exchange of property between any of the following.

- Members of a family.
- A corporation and an individual owning more than 50% of the corporation's stock (unless the loss is from a distribution in complete liquidation of a corporation).
- A grantor and a fiduciary of a trust.
- A fiduciary and a beneficiary of the same trust.
- A fiduciary and a beneficiary of another trust created by the same grantor.
- An individual and a tax-exempt organization controlled by the individual or the individual's family.

See Pub. 544 for more details on sales and exchanges between related parties.

If you dispose of **(a)** an asset used in an activity to which the at-risk rules apply, or **(b)** any part of your interest in an activity to which the at-risk rules apply, and you have amounts in the activity for which you are not at risk, get the instructions for **Form 6198**, At-Risk Limitations. If the loss is allowable under the at-risk rules, it may then be subject to the passive activity rules. Get **Form 8582**, Passive Activity Loss Limitations, and its instructions to see how to report capital gains and losses from a passive activity.

Items for Special Treatment and Special Cases

The following items may require special treatment:

- Transactions by a securities dealer.
- Wash sales of stock or securities (including contracts or options to acquire or sell stock or securities). See Pub. 550 for details.
- Bonds and other debt instruments. See Pub. 550 for details.
- Certain real estate subdivided for sale which may be considered a capital asset.
- Gain on the sale of depreciable property to a more than 50% owned entity, or to a trust of which you are a beneficiary.

- Gain on the disposition of stock in an Interest Charge Domestic International Sales Corporation.
- Gain on the sale or exchange of stock in certain foreign corporations.
- Transfer of property to a foreign corporation as paid-in surplus or as a contribution to capital, or to a foreign trust or partnership.
- Transfer of property to a partnership that would be treated as an investment company if it were incorporated.
- Sales of stock received under a qualified public utility dividend reinvestment plan. See Pub. 550 for details.
- Transfer of appreciated property to a political organization.
- Loss on the sale, exchange, or worthlessness of small business (section 1244) stock.
- In general, no gain or loss is recognized on the transfer of property from an individual to a spouse or a former spouse if the transfer is incident to a divorce. Get **Pub. 504,** Divorced or Separated Individuals.
- Amounts received on the retirement of a debt instrument generally are treated as received in exchange for the debt instrument.
- Any loss on the disposition of converted wetland or highly erodible cropland that is first used for farming after March 1, 1986, is reported as long-term capital loss on Schedule D, but any gain is reported as ordinary income on Form 4797.
- Gifts of property and inherited property. See Pub. 544.
- Amounts received by shareholders in corporate liquidations.
- Cash received in lieu of fractional shares of stock as a result of a stock split or stock dividend. See Pub. 550.
- Mutual fund load charges may not be taken into account in determining gain or loss on certain dispositions of stock in mutual funds if reinvestment rights were exercised. For details, get **Pub. 564,** Mutual Fund Distributions.
- Deferral of gain on conflict-of-interest dispositions by certain members of the Executive Branch of the Federal Government under section 1043. See Form 8824.

Short Sales

A short sale is a contract to sell property you borrowed for delivery to a buyer. At a later date, you either buy substantially identical property and deliver it to the lender or deliver property that you held but did not want to transfer at the time of the sale. Usually, your holding period is the amount of time you actually held the property eventually delivered to the lender to close the short sale. However, if you held substantially identical property for 1 year or less on the date of the short sale, or if you acquire property substantially identical to the property sold short after the short sale but on or before the date you close the short sale, your gain when closing the short sale is a short-term capital gain. If you held substantially identical property for more than 1 year on the date of a short sale, any loss realized on the short sale is a long-term capital loss, even if the property used to close the short sale was held 1 year or less.

Gain or Loss From Options

Report on Schedule D gain or loss from the closing or expiration of an option that is not a section 1256 contract, but that is a capital asset in your hands.

If a purchased option expired, enter the expiration date in column (c), and write "**EXPIRED**" in column (d).

If an option that was granted (written) expired, enter the expiration date in column (b), and write "**EXPIRED**" in column (e).

Fill in the other columns as appropriate. See Pub. 550 for more details.

Exchange of Like-Kind Property

A "like-kind exchange" occurs when you exchange business or investment property for property of a like kind. Complete and attach Form 8824 to your return for each exchange.

For exchanges of capital assets, include the gain or loss from Form 8824, if any, on line 4 or line 12 in column (f) or (g).

Sale or Exchange of Capital Assets Held for Personal Use

Gain from the sale or exchange of this property is a capital gain. Report it on Schedule D, Part I or Part II. Loss from the sale or exchange of this property is not deductible. But if you had a loss from the sale or exchange of real estate held for personal use (other than your main home), you must report the transaction on Schedule D even though the loss is not deductible.

For example, you have a loss on the sale of a vacation home that is not your main home. Report it on line 1 or 9, depending on how long you owned the home. Complete columns (a) through (e). Because the loss is not deductible, write "Personal Loss" across columns (f) and (g).

Rollover of Gain From the Sale of Publicly Traded Securities Into Specialized Small Business Investment Companies

If you sold publicly traded securities after August 9, 1993, you may be able to postpone all or part of the gain on that sale if you bought common stock or a partnership interest in a specialized small business investment company (SSBIC) during the 60-day period that began on the day of the sale. An SSBIC is any partnership or corporation licensed by the Small Business Administration under section 301(d) of the Small Business Investment Act of 1958. You must recognize gain on the sale to the extent the proceeds from the sale exceed the cost of your SSBIC stock or partnership interest purchased during the 60-day period that began on the date of the sale (and not previously taken into account). The gain you postpone is limited to $50,000 a year and $500,000 during your lifetime. (Reduce these dollar amounts by one-half if you are married filing separately.) The basis of your SSBIC stock or partnership interest is reduced by any postponed gain.

If you choose to postpone gain, report the entire gain realized on the sale on line 1 or 9. Directly below the line on which you reported the gain, enter in column (a) "SSBIC Rollover" and in column (f) the amount of the postponed gain. Also attach a schedule showing (a) how you figured the postponed gain, (b) the name of the SSBIC in which you purchased common stock or a partnership interest, (c) the date of that purchase, and (d) your new basis in that SSBIC stock or partnership interest.

Disposition of Partnership Interest

A sale or other disposition of an interest in a partnership may result in ordinary income. Get **Pub. 541,** Tax Information on Partnerships.

Long-Term Capital Gains From Regulated Investment Companies

Include on line 12 the amount on **Form 2439,** Notice to Shareholder of Undistributed Long-Term Capital Gains, that represents your share of the undistributed capital gains of a regulated investment company. Enter on Form 1040, line 59, the tax paid by the company shown on Form 2439. Add to the basis of your stock the excess of the amount included in income over the amount of the credit. See Pub. 550 for more details.

Capital Gain Distributions

Enter on line 14 capital gain distributions paid to you during the year as a long-term capital gain, regardless of how long you held your investment. See Pub. 550 for more details.

Sale of Your Home

Use **Form 2119,** Sale of Your Home, to report the sale of your main home whether or not you bought another one. You must file Form 2119 for the year in which you sell your main home, even if you have a loss or you postpone or defer all or part of your gain.

Installment Sales

If you sold property (other than publicly traded stocks or securities) at a gain and you will receive a payment in a tax year after the year of sale, you must report the sale on the installment method unless you elect not to do so.

Use **Form 6252,** Installment Sale Income, to report the sale on the installment method. Also use Form 6252 to report any payment received in 1993 from a sale made in an earlier year that you reported on the installment method.

To elect out of the installment method, report the full amount of the gain on Schedule D on a timely filed return (including extensions).

Section 1256 Contracts and Straddles

Use **Form 6781,** Gains and Losses From Section 1256 Contracts and Straddles, to report these transactions. Include the amounts from Form 6781 on lines 4 and 12.

Form 1099-A, Acquisition or Abandonment of Secured Property

If you received a Form 1099-A from your lender, you may have gain or loss to report because of the acquisition or abandonment. See Pub. 544 for details.

Specific Instructions

Parts I and II

Column (b)

Date Acquired

Enter in this column the date the asset was acquired. Use the trade date for stocks and bonds traded on an exchange or over-the-counter market. For stock or other property sold short, enter the date the stock or property was delivered to the broker or lender to close the short sale.

If you disposed of property that you acquired by inheritance, report it on line 9 and write **"INHERITED"** in column (b) instead of the date you acquired the property.

If you sold a block of stock (or similar property) that was acquired through several different purchases, you may report the sale on one line and write **"VARIOUS"** in column (b). However, you still must report the short-term gain or loss on the sale in Part I and the long-term gain or loss on the sale in Part II.

Column (c)

Date Sold

Enter in this column the date the asset was sold. Use the trade date for stocks and bonds traded on an exchange or over-the-counter market. For stock or other property sold short, enter the date you sold the stock or property you borrowed to open the short sale transaction.

Column (d)

Sales Price

Enter in this column either the gross sales price or the net sales price from the sale. If you sold stocks or bonds and you received a Form 1099-B or similar statement from your broker that shows gross sales price, enter that amount in column (d). But if Form 1099-B (or your broker) indicates that gross proceeds minus commissions and option premiums were reported to the IRS, enter that net amount in column (d). If the net amount is entered in column (d), do not include the commissions and option premiums in column (e).

You should not have received a Form 1099-B (or substitute statement) for a transaction merely representing the return of your original investment in a nontransferrable obligation, such as a savings bond or a certificate of deposit. But if you did, report the amount shown on Form 1099-B (or substitute statement) in both columns (d) and (e).

Caution: *Be sure to add all sales price entries on lines 1 and 9, column (d), to amounts on lines 2 and 10, column (d). Enter the totals on lines 3 and 11.*

Column (e)

Cost or Other Basis

In general, the cost or other basis is the cost of the property plus purchase commissions and improvements, minus depreciation, amortization, and depletion. If you inherited the property, got it as a gift, or received it in a tax-free exchange, involuntary conversion, or "wash sale" of stock, you may not be able to use the actual cost as the basis. If you do not use the actual cost, attach an explanation of your basis.

You should not have received a Form 1099-B (or substitute statement) for a transaction merely representing the return of your original investment in a nontransferrable obligation, such as a savings bond or a certificate of deposit. But if you did, report the amount shown on Form 1099-B (or substitute statement) in both columns (d) and (e).

When selling stock, adjust your basis by subtracting all the nontaxable distributions you received before the sale. Also adjust your basis for any stock splits. See Pub. 550 for details on how to figure your basis in stock that split while you owned it.

The basis of property acquired by gift is generally the basis of the property in the hands of the donor. The basis of property acquired from a decedent is generally the fair market value at the date of death.

Increase the cost or other basis of an original issue discount (OID) debt instrument by the amount of OID that has been included in gross income for that instrument.

If a charitable contribution deduction is allowed because of a bargain sale of property to a charitable organization, the adjusted basis for purposes of determining gain from the sale is the amount which has the same ratio to the adjusted basis as the amount realized has to the fair market value.

Increase your cost or other basis by any expense of sale, such as broker's fees, commissions, state and local transfer taxes, and option premiums before making an entry in column (e), unless you reported the net sales price in column (d).

For more details, get **Pub. 551**, Basis of Assets.

Lines 1 and 9

Enter all sales and exchanges of capital assets, including stocks, bonds, etc., and real estate (if not reported on Form 2119, 4684, 4797, 6252, 6781, or 8824). Include these transactions even if you did not receive a Form 1099-B or 1099-S (or substitute statement) for the transaction. You can use abbreviations to describe the property as long as the abbreviations are based on the descriptions of the property as shown on Form 1099-B or 1099-S (or substitute statement).

Use lines 20 and 22 on page 2 of Schedule D if you need more space to list transactions for lines 1 and 9. You may use as many copies of page 2 of Schedule D as you need. Enter on Schedule D, lines 2 and 10, columns (d), (f), and (g) the combined totals of all your copies of page 2 of Schedule D.

Caution: *Add the following amounts reported to you for 1993 on Forms 1099-B and 1099-S (or on substitute statements):*

1. *Proceeds from transactions involving stocks, bonds, and other securities, and*

2. *Gross proceeds from real estate transactions not reported on another form or schedule.*

*If this total is **more** than the total of lines 3 and 11, attach a statement explaining the difference.*

Part III

Line 18

The maximum tax rate on net capital gain (the smaller of line 17 or 18 of Schedule D) that you did not elect to treat as investment income on Form 4952, line 4e, is 28%. If both lines 17 and 18 are gains, and Form 1040, line 37, is over $89,150 ($53,500 if single; $76,400 if head of household; $44,575 if married filing separately), use the **Schedule D Tax Worksheet** on this page to figure your tax; otherwise, use the Tax Table or Tax Rate Schedules, whichever applies.

Line 19

If line 18 is a (loss), enter on line 19 and as a (loss) on Form 1040, line 13, the **smaller** of these losses: **(a)** the (loss) on line 18; **or (b)** ($3,000) or, if your filing status is married filing separately, ($1,500). For example, if the (loss) on line 18 is ($1,000), you would enter ($1,000) on Form 1040, line 13, because that is the smaller loss.

If the loss on line 19 is a smaller loss than the loss on line 18, **or** Form 1040, line 35, is a loss, use the **Capital Loss Carryover Worksheet** on this page to figure your short-term and long-term capital loss carryovers to 1994. You will need these amounts to complete your 1994 Schedule D, so be sure to keep the worksheet for your records.

Schedule D Tax Worksheet (keep for your records)

Use this worksheet to figure your tax **only** if both lines 17 and 18 of Schedule D are gains, **and:**

Your filing status is:	AND	Form 1040, line 37, is over:	Your filing status is:	AND	Form 1040, line 37, is over:
Single		$53,500	Married filing separately		$44,575
Married filing jointly or qualifying widow(er)		$89,150	Head of household		$76,400

1. Enter the amount from Form 1040, line 37 . . . . 1. _____
2. **Net capital gain.** Enter the **smaller** of Schedule D, line 17 or line 18 . . . . 2. _____
3. If you are filing Form 4952, enter the amount from Form 4952, line 4e . . . . 3. _____
4. Subtract line 3 from line 2. If zero or less, stop here; you cannot use this worksheet to figure your tax. Instead, use the Tax Table or Tax Rate Schedules, whichever applies . . . . 4. _____
5. Subtract line 4 from line 1 . . . . 5. _____
6. Enter: $22,100 if single; $36,900 if married filing jointly or qualifying widow(er); $18,450 if married filing separately; or $29,600 if head of household . . . . 6. _____
7. Enter the **greater** of line 5 or line 6 . . . . 7. _____
8. Subtract line 7 from line 1 . . . . 8. _____
9. Figure the tax on the amount on line 7. Use the Tax Table or Tax Rate Schedules, whichever applies . . . . 9. _____
10. Multiply line 8 by 28% (.28) . . . . 10. _____
11. Add lines 9 and 10 . . . . 11. _____
12. Figure the tax on the amount on line 1. Use the Tax Table or Tax Rate Schedules, whichever applies . . . . 12. _____
13. **Tax.** Enter the **smaller** of line 11 or line 12 here and on Form 1040, line 38. Check the box for Schedule D Tax Worksheet. 13. _____

Capital Loss Carryover Worksheet (keep for your records)

Use this worksheet to figure your capital loss carryovers from 1993 to 1994 if Schedule D, line 19, is a loss and **(a)** that loss is a smaller loss than the loss on Schedule D, line 18, **or (b)** Form 1040, line 35, is a loss.

1. Enter the amount from Form 1040, line 35. If a loss, enclose the amount in parentheses . . . . 1. _____
2. Enter the loss from Schedule D, line 19, as a positive amount 2. _____
3. Combine lines 1 and 2. If zero or less, enter -0- . . . . 3. _____
4. Enter the **smaller** of line 2 or line 3 . . . . 4. _____

Note: *If line 8 of Schedule D is a loss, go to line 5; otherwise, skip lines 5 through 9.*

5. Enter the loss from Schedule D, line 8, as a positive amount 5. _____
6. Enter the gain, if any, from Schedule D, line 17 . . . . 6. _____
7. Enter the amount from line 4 . . . . . 7. _____
8. Add lines 6 and 7 . . . . 8. _____
9. **Short-term capital loss carryover to 1994.** Subtract line 8 from line 5. If zero or less, enter -0- . . . . 9. _____

Note: *If line 17 of Schedule D is a loss, go to line 10; otherwise, skip lines 10 through 14.*

10. Enter the loss from Schedule D, line 17, as a positive amount 10. _____
11. Enter the gain, if any, from Schedule D, line 8 . . . . 11. _____
12. Subtract line 5 from line 4. If zero or less, enter -0- . . . . 12. _____
13. Add lines 11 and 12 . . . . 13. _____
14. **Long-term capital loss carryover to 1994.** Subtract line 13 from line 10. If zero or less, enter -0- . . . . 14. _____

Instructions for Schedule SE, Self-Employment Tax

Use Schedule SE to figure the tax due on net earnings from self-employment. The Social Security Administration uses the information from Schedule SE to figure your benefits under the social security program. This tax applies no matter how old you are, and even if you are already getting social security or Medicare benefits.

Additional Information. Get **Pub. 533**, Self-Employment Tax, for more details.

General Instructions

A Change To Note

For 1993, the maximum amount of self-employment income subject to social security tax is $57,600. The maximum amount subject to Medicare tax for 1993 is $135,000.

Who Must File Schedule SE

You must file Schedule SE if:

1. You were self-employed, and your net earnings from self-employment from other than church employee income were $400 or more (or you had church employee income of $108.28 or more—see **Employees of Churches and Church Organizations** on this page), AND

2. You did not have wages (and tips) of $135,000 or more that were subject to social security and Medicare tax (or railroad retirement tax).

Who Is Subject to Self-Employment Tax?

Self-Employed Persons

You are subject to SE tax if you had net earnings as a self-employed person. If you are in business for yourself, or you are a farmer, for example, you are self-employed.

Your share of certain partnership income and your guaranteed payments are also subject to SE tax. See **Partnership Income or Loss** on page SE-2.

Employees of Churches and Church Organizations

If you had church employee income of $108.28 or more, you may be subject to SE tax. **Church employee income** is wages you received as an employee (other than as a minister or member of a religious order) from a church or qualified church-controlled organization that has a certificate in effect electing exemption from employer social security and Medicare taxes.

Ministers and Members of Religious Orders

You are subject to SE tax on salaries and other income for services you performed as a minister or member of a religious order, unless you received approval from the IRS for an exemption from SE tax. See **Who Is Not Subject to Self-Employment Tax?** on this page. If you are subject to SE tax, include this income on line 2 of either Short or Long Schedule SE. But do not report it on line 5a of Long Schedule SE; it is not considered church employee income. Also include on line 2:

- The rental value of a home or an allowance for a home furnished to you (including payments for utilities), and
- The value of meals and lodging provided to you, your spouse, and your dependents for your employer's convenience.

If you were a duly ordained minister who was an employee of a church and you are subject to SE tax, the unreimbursed business expenses that you incurred as a church employee are allowed only as an itemized deduction for income tax purposes. Subtract the allowable amount from your SE earnings when figuring SE tax.

If you were a U.S. citizen or resident alien serving outside the United States as a minister or member of a religious order and you are subject to SE tax, you may not reduce your net earnings by the foreign housing exclusion or deduction.

For more details, get **Pub. 517**, Social Security and Other Information for Members of the Clergy and Religious Workers.

U.S. Citizens Employed by Foreign Governments or International Organizations

You are subject to SE tax if you are a U.S. citizen employed by a foreign government (or, in certain cases, by a wholly-owned instrumentality of a foreign government or an international organization under the International Organizations Immunities Act) in the United States, Puerto Rico, Guam, American Samoa, the Commonwealth of the Northern Mariana Islands, or the Virgin Islands. Report income from this employment on Schedule SE (Section A or B), line 2. If you are employed elsewhere by a foreign government or an international organization, those earnings are not subject to SE tax.

U.S. Citizens or Resident Aliens Living Outside the United States

If you are a self-employed U.S. citizen or resident alien living outside the United States, in most cases you are subject to SE tax. You may not reduce your foreign earnings from self-employment by your foreign earned income exclusion.

Who Is Not Subject to Self-Employment Tax?

In most cases, you are subject to SE tax on net earnings you received as a minister, a member of a religious order who has not taken a vow of poverty, or a Christian Science practitioner. But you will not be subject to SE tax on those net earnings if you filed **Form 4361**, Application for Exemption From Self-Employment Tax for Use by Ministers, Members of Religious Orders and Christian Science Practitioners, and you received approval from the IRS for an exemption from paying SE tax. In this case, if you have no other income subject to SE tax, write "Exempt–Form 4361" on Form 1040, line 47. However, if you have other earnings of $400 or more subject to SE tax, see line A at the top of Long Schedule SE.

Note: If you have ever filed Form 2031 to elect social security coverage on your earnings as a minister, you cannot revoke that election now.

If you have conscientious objections to social security insurance because of your membership in and belief in the teachings of a religious sect recognized as being in existence at all times since December 31, 1950, and which has provided a reasonable level of living for its dependent members, you are not subject to SE tax if you got IRS approval by filing **Form 4029**, Application for Exemption From Social Security and Medicare Taxes and Waiver of Benefits. In this case, do not file Schedule SE. Instead, write "Form 4029" on Form 1040, line 47.

See Pub. 517 for more details.

More Than One Business

If you were a farmer and had at least one other business or you had two or more businesses, your net earnings from self-employment are the combined net earnings from all of your businesses. If you had a loss in one business, it reduces the income from another. Figure the combined SE tax on one Schedule SE.

Joint Returns

Show the name of the spouse with SE income on Schedule SE. If both spouses have SE income, each must file a separate Schedule SE. If one spouse qualifies to use Short Schedule SE, and the other has to use Long Schedule SE, both can use one Schedule SE. One spouse should complete the front and the other the back.

Include the total profits or losses from all businesses on Form 1040, as appropriate. Enter the combined SE tax on Form 1040, line 47.

Community Income

In most cases, if any of the income from a business (including farming) is community income, all of the income from that business is SE earnings of the spouse who carried on the business. The facts in each case will determine which spouse carried on the business. If you and your spouse are partners in a partnership, see **Partnership Income or Loss** below.

If you and your spouse had community income and file separate returns, attach Schedule SE to the return of the spouse with the SE income. Also attach Schedule(s) C, C-EZ, or F.

Caution: *Community income included on Schedule(s) C, C-EZ, or F must be divided for income tax purposes on the basis of the community property laws.*

Fiscal Year Filers

If your tax year is a fiscal year, use the tax rate and earnings base that apply at the time the fiscal year begins. Do not prorate the tax or earnings base for a fiscal year that overlaps the date of a rate or earnings base change.

Specific Instructions

Read the chart on page 1 of Schedule SE to see if you can use **Section A,** Short Schedule SE, or if you must use **Section B,** Long Schedule SE. For either section, you need to know what to include as net earnings from self-employment. Read the instructions below to see what to include as net earnings and how to fill in lines 1 and 2 of either Short or Long Schedule SE. Enter all negative amounts in parentheses.

Net Earnings From Self-Employment

What Is Included in Net SE Earnings?

In most cases, net earnings include your net profit from a farm or nonfarm business. If you were a partner in a partnership, see the instructions below.

Partnership Income or Loss

If you were a general or limited partner in a partnership, include on line 1 or line 2, whichever applies, the amount from line 15a of Schedule K-1 (Form 1065). If you were a general partner, reduce this amount before entering it on Schedule SE by any section 179 expense deduction claimed, unreimbursed partnership expenses claimed, and depletion claimed on oil and gas properties. If you reduce the amount you enter on Schedule SE, attach an explanation.

If you were a general partner, the amount reported by the partnership on line 15a of Schedule K-1 should include your share of partnership income or loss subject to SE tax and any guaranteed payments the partnership made to you for services or for the use of capital. If you were a limited partner, the amount reported on line 15a of Schedule K-1 should include only guaranteed payments for services you actually rendered to or on behalf of the partnership.

Income or loss from a partnership engaged solely in the operation of a group investment program is not included in net SE earnings for either a general or limited partner.

If you were married and both you and your spouse were partners in a partnership, each of you is subject to SE tax on your own share of the partnership income. Each of you must file a Schedule SE and report the partnership income or loss on **Schedule E** (Form 1040), Part II, for income tax purposes.

SE income belongs to the person who is the member of the partnership and cannot be treated as SE income by the nonmember spouse even in community property states.

If a partner dies and the partnership continues, include in SE income the deceased's distributive share of the partnership's ordinary income or loss through the end of the month in which he or she dies. See Internal Revenue Code section 1402(f).

Share Farming

You are considered self-employed if you produced crops or livestock on someone else's land for a share of the crops or livestock produced (or a share of the proceeds from the sale of them). This applies even if you paid another person (an agent) to do the actual work or management for you. Report your net earnings for income tax purposes on **Schedule F** (Form 1040) and for SE tax purposes on Schedule SE. For more details, get **Pub. 225,** Farmer's Tax Guide.

Other Income and Losses Included in Net Earnings From Self-Employment

- Rental income from a farm if, as landlord, you participated materially in the production or management of the production of farm products on this land. This income is farm earnings. To determine whether you participated materially in farm management or production, do not consider the activities of any agent who acted for you. The material participation tests are explained in Pub. 225.
- Cash or a payment-in-kind from the Department of Agriculture for participating in a land diversion program.
- Payments for the use of rooms or other space when you also provided substantial services. Examples are hotel rooms, boarding houses, tourist camps or homes, parking lots, warehouses, and storage garages.
- Income from the retail sale of newspapers and magazines if you were age 18 or older and kept the profits.
- Amounts received by current or former self-employed insurance agents that are:

1. Paid after retirement but calculated as a percentage of commissions received from the paying company before retirement;

2. Renewal commissions; or

3. Deferred commissions paid after retirement for sales made before retirement.

- Income as a crew member of a fishing vessel with a crew of normally fewer than 10 people. See Pub. 595.
- Fees as a state or local government employee if you were paid only on a fee basis and the job was not covered under a Federal-state social security coverage agreement.
- Interest received in the course of any trade or business, such as interest on notes or accounts receivable.
- Fees and other payments received by you for services as a director of a corporation.
- Recapture amounts under sections 179 and 280F that you included in gross income because the business use of the property dropped to 50% or less. Do not include amounts you recaptured on the disposition of property. See **Form 4797,** Sales of Business Property.
- Fees you received as a professional fiduciary. This may also apply to fees paid to you as a nonprofessional fiduciary if the fees relate to active participation in the operation of the estate's business, or the management of an estate that required extensive management activities over a long period of time.
- Gain or loss from section 1256 contracts or related property by an options or commodities dealer in the normal course of dealing in or trading section 1256 contracts.

Income and Losses Not Included in Net Earnings From Self-Employment

- Salaries, fees, etc., subject to social security or Medicare tax that you received for performing services as an employee, including services performed as a public official (except as a fee basis government employee as explained earlier under **Other Income and Losses Included in Net Earnings From Self-Employment**) or as an employee or employee representative under the railroad retirement system.
- Income you received as a retired partner under a written partnership plan that provides for lifelong periodic retirement payments if you had no other interest in the partnership and did not perform services for it during the year.
- Income from real estate rentals (including rentals paid in crop shares), if you did not receive the income in the course of a trade or business as a real estate dealer. This includes cash and crop shares received from a tenant or sharefarmer. Report this income on Schedule E.
- Dividends on shares of stock and interest on bonds, notes, etc., if you did not receive the income in the course of your trade or business as a dealer in stocks or securities.
- Gain or loss from:

1. The sale or exchange of a capital asset;

2. The sale, exchange, involuntary conversion, or other disposition of property unless the property is stock in trade or other property that would be includible in inventory, or held primarily for sale to customers in the ordinary course of the business; or

3. Certain transactions in timber, coal, or domestic iron ore.

- Net operating losses from other years.

Statutory Employee Income. If you were a statutory employee (see page 14 for a definition) and filed Schedule C or C-EZ to report your income and expenses, **do not** include the net profit or (loss) from line 31 of that Schedule C (or the net profit from line 3 of Schedule C-EZ) on line 2 of Short or Long Schedule SE. But if you file Long Schedule

SE, be sure to include statutory employee social security wages and tips from Form W-2 on line 8a, and statutory employee Medicare wages and tips from Form W-2 on line 12a.

Optional Methods

How Can the Optional Methods Help You?

Social Security Coverage. The optional methods may give you credit toward your social security coverage even though you have a loss or a small amount of income from self-employment.

Earned Income Credit. Using the optional methods may qualify you to claim the earned income credit or give you a larger credit if your net SE earnings (determined without using the optional methods) are less than $1,600. Figure the earned income credit with and without using the optional methods to see if the optional methods will benefit you.

Child and Dependent Care Credit. The optional methods may also help you qualify for this credit or give you a larger credit if your net SE earnings (determined without using the optional methods) are less than $1,600. Figure this credit with and without using the optional methods to see if the optional methods will benefit you.

Note: Using the optional methods may give you the benefits described above but they may also increase your self-employment tax.

Farm Optional Method

You may use this method to figure your net earnings from farm self-employment if your gross farm income was $2,400 or less **OR** your gross farm income was more than $2,400 but your net farm profits (defined below) were less than $1,733. There is no limit on how many years you can use this method.

Under this method, you report on line 17, Part II, two-thirds of your gross farm income, up to $1,600, as your net earnings. This method can increase or decrease your net SE farm earnings even if the farming business resulted in a loss.

You may change the method after you file your return. For example, you can change from the regular to the optional method or from the optional to the regular method.

For a farm partnership, figure your share of gross income based on the partnership agreement. With guaranteed payments, your share of the partnership's gross income is your guaranteed payments plus your share of the gross income after it is reduced by all guaranteed payments of the partnership. If you are a limited partner, include only guaranteed payments for services you actually rendered to or on behalf of the partnership.

Net farm profits is the total of the amounts from Schedule F (Form 1040), line 36, and Schedule K-1 (Form 1065), line 15a, from farm partnerships.

Nonfarm Optional Method

You may be able to use this method to figure your net earnings from nonfarm self-employment if your nonfarm profits (defined below) were less than $1,733, and also less than 72.189% of your gross nonfarm income. To use this method, you also must be regularly self-employed. You meet this requirement if your actual net earnings from self-employment were $400 or more in 2 of the 3 years preceding the year you use the nonfarm method. The net earnings of $400 or more could be from either farm or nonfarm earnings or both. The net earnings include your distributive share of partnership income or loss subject to SE tax. Use of the nonfarm optional method from nonfarm self-employment is limited to 5 years. The 5 years do not have to be consecutive.

Under this method, you report on line 19, Part II, two-thirds of your gross nonfarm income, up to $1,600, as your net earnings. But **you may not report less than your actual net earnings** from nonfarm self-employment.

You may change the method after you file your return. For example, you can change from the regular to the optional method or from the optional to the regular method.

Figure your share of gross income from a nonfarm partnership in the same manner as a farm partnership. See **Farm Optional Method** above for details.

Net nonfarm profits is the total of the amounts from Schedule C (Form 1040), line 31 (or Schedule C-EZ (Form 1040), line 3), and Schedule K-1 (Form 1065), line 15a, from other than farm partnerships.

Using Both Optional Methods

If you can use both methods, you may report less than your total actual net earnings from farm and nonfarm income, but you **cannot** report less than your actual net earnings from nonfarm SE income alone.

If you use both methods to figure net earnings, you **cannot** report more than $1,600 of net SE earnings.

1993 Instructions for Form 4562

Department of the Treasury
Internal Revenue Service

Depreciation and Amortization
(Including Information on Listed Property)

Section references are to the Internal Revenue Code, unless otherwise noted.

General Instructions

Paperwork Reduction Act Notice

We ask for the information on this form to carry out the Internal Revenue laws of the United States. You are required to give us the information. We need it to ensure that you are complying with these laws and to allow us to figure and collect the right amount of tax.

The time needed to complete and file this form will vary depending on individual circumstances. The estimated average time is:

Recordkeeping . . . . 36 hr., 50 min.
Learning about the law or the form . . . . 4 hr., 40 min.
Preparing and sending the form to the IRS . . . . 5 hr., 28 min.

If you have comments concerning the accuracy of these time estimates or suggestions for making this form more simple, we would be happy to hear from you. You can write to both the IRS and the Office of Management and Budget at the addresses listed in the instructions for the tax return with which this form is filed.

Changes To Note

The Revenue Reconciliation Act of 1993 made the following changes:

- Beginning in 1993, the maximum section 179 expense deduction for most taxpayers has been increased from $10,000 to $17,500. A larger section 179 expense deduction may be claimed by enterprise zone businesses placing qualified zone property in service after 1993. In addition, only 50% of the cost of section 179 property that is also qualified zone property is taken into account when figuring the reduction in the maximum section 179 expense deduction for an enterprise zone business. See the instructions for lines 1 and 2 for more details.

- The recovery period for nonresidential real property placed in service after May 12, 1993 (with limited exceptions), has been increased from 31.5 to 39 years. See the instructions for column (d) of lines 14a through 14h for more details.

- Certain computer software may now be depreciated using the straight line method over a 36-month period. See the instructions for line 18 for more details.

- Goodwill and certain other intangibles may now be amortized over a 15-year period. See the instructions for line 39 for more details.

- Shorter recovery periods apply to qualified Indian reservation property placed in service after 1993. See the instructions for column (d) of lines 14a through 14h for more details.

Purpose of Form

Use Form 4562 to claim your deduction for depreciation and amortization; to make the election to expense certain tangible property (section 179); and to provide information on the business/investment use of automobiles and other listed property.

Who Must File

Except as otherwise noted, complete and file Form 4562 if you are claiming:

- Depreciation for property placed in service during the 1993 tax year;
- A section 179 expense deduction (which may include a carryover from a previous year);
- Depreciation on any vehicle or other listed property (regardless of when it was placed in service);
- A deduction for any vehicle reported on a form other than **Schedule C (Form 1040)**, Profit or Loss From Business, or **Schedule C-EZ (Form 1040)**, Net Profit From Business;
- Any depreciation on a corporate income tax return (other than Form 1120S); or
- Amortization of costs that begins during the 1993 tax year.

However, **do not** file Form 4562 to report depreciation and information on the use of vehicles if you are an employee deducting job-related vehicle expenses using either the standard mileage rate or actual expenses. Instead, use **Form 2106**, Employee Business Expenses, for this purpose.

You should prepare and submit a separate Form 4562 for each business or activity on your return. If more space is needed, attach additional sheets. However, complete only one Part I in its entirety when computing your allowable section 179 expense deduction.

Definitions

Depreciation

Depreciation is the annual deduction allowed to recover the cost or other basis of business or income-producing property with a determinable useful life of more than 1 year. However, land is not depreciable.

Depreciation starts when you first use the property in your business or for the production of income. It ends when you take the property out of service, deduct all your depreciable cost or other basis, or no longer use the property in your business or for the production of income.

If you acquired depreciable property for the first time in 1993, get Pub. 946, How To Begin Depreciating Your Property. For a more comprehensive guide on depreciation, get **Pub. 534**, Depreciation. For information on claiming depreciation on a car, get **Pub. 917**, Business Use of a Car.

Amortization

Amortization is similar to the straight line method of depreciation in that an annual deduction is allowed to recover certain costs over a fixed period of time. You can amortize such items as the costs of starting a business, goodwill and certain other intangibles, reforestation, and pollution control facilities. For additional information, get **Pub. 535**, Business Expenses.

Listed Property

For a definition of "listed property" see **Part V—Listed Property** on page 5.

Recordkeeping

Except for Part V (relating to listed property), the IRS does not require you to submit detailed information with your return regarding the depreciation of assets placed in service in previous tax years. However, the information needed to compute your depreciation deduction (basis, method, etc.) must be part of your permanent records.

Because Form 4562 does not provide for permanent recordkeeping, you may use the depreciation worksheet on page 8 to assist you in maintaining depreciation records. However, the worksheet is designed only for Federal income tax purposes. You may need to keep additional records for accounting and state income tax purposes.

Certification of Business Use Requirement for Aircraft Exempt From Luxury Tax

If you purchased a new aircraft in 1991 or 1992 that was exempt from the 10% Federal luxury tax **solely** because at least 80% of your use of the aircraft (measured in hours of flight time) would be for business purposes, you must attach a statement to your income tax return for each of the 2 tax years ending after the date the aircraft was placed in service. On this statement, you must certify that at least 80% of your use of the aircraft during the tax year was in a trade or business. If you fail to make this certification, you must pay a tax equal to the luxury tax that would have been imposed on the purchase of the aircraft if the business use exemption had not applied. In addition, interest is imposed on the tax from the date of purchase of the aircraft.

If you do not pay the tax when due because you failed to meet this requirement, no depreciation may be claimed on the aircraft for any tax year.

See the instructions for **Form 720**, Quarterly Federal Excise Tax Return, for more information on paying the tax and interest due.

Specific Instructions

Part I—Election To Expense Certain Tangible Property (Section 179)

Note: *An estate or trust cannot make this election.*

You may elect to expense part of the cost of certain tangible personal property used in your trade or business and certain other property described in Pub. 534. To do so, you must have purchased the property (as defined in section 179(d)(2)) and placed it in service during the 1993 tax year.

The election must be made with:

1. The original return you file for the tax year the property was placed in service (whether or not you file your return on time), or

2. An amended return filed no later than the due date (including extensions) for your return for the tax year the property was placed in service.

Once made, the election (and the selection of the property you elect to expense) may not be revoked without IRS consent.

Cat. No. 12907Y

If you elect this deduction, reduce the amount on which you figure your depreciation or amortization deduction by the section 179 expense deduction.

Section 179 property does **not** include:

1. Property used 50% or less in your trade or business,

2. Property held for investment (section 212 property), or

3. Property you lease to others (if you are a noncorporate lessor) **unless (a)** you manufactured or produced the property or **(b)** the term of the lease is less than 50% of the property's class life, and for the first 12 months after the property is transferred to the lessee, the sum of the deductions related to the property that are allowed to you solely under section 162 (except rents and reimbursed amounts) is more than 15% of the rental income from the property.

The section 179 expense deduction is subject to two separate limitations, both of which are figured in Part I:

1. A dollar limitation and

2. A taxable income limitation.

In the case of a partnership, these limitations apply to the partnership and each partner. In the case of an S corporation, these limitations apply to the S corporation and each shareholder. In the case of a controlled group, all component members are treated as one taxpayer.

Line 1

For an enterprise zone business, the maximum section 179 expense deduction is increased by the **smaller** of **(a)** $20,000, or **(b)** the cost of section 179 property that is also qualified zone property (including such property placed in service by your spouse, even if you are filing a separate return. Cross out the preprinted entry on line 1 and enter in the margin the larger amount if your business is an enterprise zone business. For the definitions of enterprise zone business and qualified zone property, see sections 1397B and 1397C.

Line 2

Enter the cost of all section 179 property placed in service during the tax year. Be sure to include amounts from any listed property from Part V. Also include any section 179 property placed in service by your spouse, even if you are filing a separate return.

For an enterprise zone business, include on this line only 50% of the cost of section 179 property that is also qualified zone property.

Line 5

If line 5 is zero, you cannot elect to expense any property; skip lines 6 through 11, enter zero on line 12, and enter the carryover of disallowed deduction from 1992, if any, on line 13.

If you are married filing separately, you and your spouse must allocate the dollar limitation for the tax year between you. To do so, multiply the total limitation that you would otherwise enter on line 5 by 50%, unless you and your spouse elect a different allocation. If you and your spouse elect a different allocation, multiply the total limitation by the percentage you elect. If a different allocation is elected, the sum of the percentages you and your spouse elect must equal 100%. Do not enter on line 5 more than your share of the total dollar limitation.

Line 6

Caution: *Do not include any listed property on line 6.*

Column (a).—Enter a brief description of the property for which you are making the election (e.g., truck, office furniture, etc.).

Column (b).—Enter the cost of the property. If you acquired the property through a trade-in, do not include any undepreciated basis of the assets you traded in. Get **Pub. 551,** Basis of Assets, for more information.

Column (c).—Enter the amount that you elect to expense. You do not have to elect to expense the entire cost of the property. You can depreciate the amount you do not elect to expense. See the line 14 and line 15 instructions.

To report your share of a section 179 expense deduction from a partnership or an S corporation, instead of completing columns (a) and (b), write "from Schedule K-1 (Form 1065)" or "from Schedule K-1 (Form 1120S)" across the columns.

Line 9

The tentative deduction represents the amount you may expense in 1993 or carry over to 1994. If this amount is less than the taxable income limitation on line 11, you may expense the entire amount. If this amount is more than line 11, you may expense in 1993 only an amount equal to line 11. Any excess may be carried over to 1994.

Line 10

The carryover of disallowed deduction from 1992 is the amount of section 179 property, if any, elected to be expensed in previous years, but not allowed as a deduction due to the taxable income limitation. If you filed Form 4562 for 1992, enter the amount from line 13 of your 1992 Form 4562. For additional information, see Pub. 534.

Line 11

The section 179 expense deduction is further limited to the "taxable income" limitation under section 179(b)(3).

If you are an individual, enter the smaller of line 5 or the aggregate taxable income from any trade or business actively conducted by you, computed without regard to any section 179 expense deduction, the deduction for one-half of self-employment taxes under section 164(f), or any net operating loss deduction. Include in aggregate taxable income the wages, salaries, tips, and other compensation you earned as an employee (not reduced by unreimbursed employee business expenses). If you are married filing a joint return, combine the aggregate taxable incomes for both you and your spouse.

For a partnership, enter the smaller of line 5 or the aggregate of the partnership's items of income and expense described in section 702(a) from any trade or business actively conducted by the partnership (other than credits, tax-exempt income, the section 179 expense deduction, and guaranteed payments under section 707(c)).

For an S corporation, enter the smaller of line 5 or the aggregate of the corporation's items of income and expense described in section 1366(a) from any trade or business actively conducted by the corporation (other than credits, tax-exempt income, the section 179 expense deduction, and the deduction for compensation paid to the corporation's shareholder-employees).

For a corporation (other than an S corporation), enter the smaller of line 5 or the corporation's taxable income before the net operating loss deduction and special deductions (excluding items not derived from a trade or business actively conducted by the corporation).

If you have to apply another Code section that has a limitation based on taxable income, see Regulations section 1.179-2(c)(5) for rules for applying the taxable income limitation under section 179 in such a case.

You are considered to actively conduct a trade or business if you meaningfully participate in the management or operations of the trade or business. A mere passive investor is not considered to actively conduct a trade or business.

Line 12

The limitations on lines 5 and 11 apply to the taxpayer, and not to each separate business or activity. Therefore, if you have more than one business or activity, you may allocate your allowable section 179 expense deduction among them. To do so, write "Summary" at the top of Part I of the separate Form 4562 you are completing for the aggregate amounts from all businesses or activities. Do not complete the rest of that form. On line 12 of the Form 4562 you prepare for each separate business or activity, enter the amount allocated to the business or activity from the "Summary." No other entry is required in Part I of the separate Form 4562 prepared for each business or activity.

Part II—MACRS Depreciation For Assets Placed in Service ONLY During Your 1993 Tax Year

Note: *The term "Modified Accelerated Cost Recovery System" (MACRS) includes the General Depreciation System and the Alternative Depreciation System. Generally, MACRS is used to depreciate any tangible property placed in service after 1986. However, MACRS does not apply to films, videotapes, and sound recordings. See section 168(f) for other exceptions.*

Depreciation may be an adjustment for alternative minimum tax purposes. For details, get **Form 4626,** Alternative Minimum Tax—Corporations; **Form 6251,** Alternative Minimum Tax—Individuals; or Schedule H of **Form 1041,** U.S. Fiduciary Income Tax Return.

Lines 14a Through 14h—General Depreciation System (GDS)

Note: *Use lines 14a through 14h only for assets placed in service during the tax year beginning in 1993 and depreciated under the General Depreciation System, except for automobiles and other listed property (which are reported in Part V).*

Column (a).—Determine which property you acquired and placed in service during the tax year beginning in 1993. Then, sort that property according to its classification (3-year property, 5-year property, etc.) as shown in column (a) of lines 14a through 14h. The classifications for some property are shown below. For property not shown, see **Determining the classification** on page 3.

• **3-year property** includes **(a)** a race horse that is more than 2 years old at the time it is placed in service and **(b)** any horse (other than a race horse) that is more than 12 years old at the time it is placed in service.

• **5-year property** includes **(a)** automobiles; **(b)** light general purpose trucks; **(c)** typewriters, calculators, copiers, and duplicating equipment; **(d)** any semi-conductor manufacturing equipment; **(e)** any computer or peripheral equipment; **(f)** any section 1245 property used in connection with research and experimentation; and **(g)** certain energy property specified in section 168(e)(3)(B)(vi).

- **7-year property** includes (a) office furniture and equipment; (b) appliances, carpets, furniture, etc., used in residential rental property; (c) railroad track; and (d) any property that does not have a class life and is not otherwise classified.

- **10-year property** includes (a) vessels, barges, tugs, and similar water transportation equipment; (b) any single purpose agricultural or horticultural structure (see section 168(i)(13)); and (c) any tree or vine bearing fruit or nuts.

- **15-year property** includes (a) any municipal wastewater treatment plant and (b) any telephone distribution plant and comparable equipment used for 2-way exchange of voice and data communications.

- **20-year property** includes any municipal sewers.

- **Residential rental property** is a building in which 80% or more of the total rent is from dwelling units.

- **Nonresidential real property** is any real property that is neither residential rental property nor property with a class life of less than 27.5 years.

- **50-year property** includes any improvements necessary to construct or improve a roadbed or right-of-way for railroad track that qualifies as a railroad grading or tunnel bore under section 168(e)(4).

There is no separate line to report 50-year property. Therefore, attach a statement showing the same information as required in columns (a) through (g). Include the deduction in the line 20 "Total" and write "See attachment" in the bottom margin of the form.

Determining the classification.—If your depreciable property is **not** listed above, determine the classification as follows: First, find the property's class life. The class life of most property can be found in the Table of Class Lives and Recovery Periods in Pub. 534. Next, use the following table to find the classification in column (b) that corresponds to the class life of the property in column (a).

(a) Class life (in years) (See Pub. 534)	(b) Classification
4 or less	3-year property
More than 4 but less than 10	5-year property
10 or more but less than 16	7-year property
16 or more but less than 20	10-year property
20 or more but less than 25	15-year property
25 or more	20-year property

Column (b).—For lines 14g and 14h, enter the month and year the property was placed in service. If property held for personal use is converted to use in a trade or business or for the production of income, treat the property as being placed in service on the date of conversion.

Column (c).—To find the basis for depreciation, multiply the cost or other basis of the property by the percentage of business/investment use. From that result, subtract any section 179 expense deduction, deduction for removal of barriers to the disabled and the elderly, disabled access credit, and enhanced oil recovery credit. See section 50(c) to determine the basis adjustment for investment credit property.

Column (d).—Determine the recovery period from **Table 1** below, unless either **1** or **2** below applies:

1. You make an irrevocable election to use the 150% declining balance method of depreciation for 3-, 5-, 7-, or 10-year property (excluding any tree or vine bearing fruit or nuts). The election applies to all property within the classification for which it is made that was placed in service during the tax year. If you elect this method, you must use the recovery period under the Alternative Depreciation System (ADS) discussed in the line 15 instructions. You will not have an adjustment for alternative minimum tax purposes on the property for which you make this election.

2. You acquired qualified Indian reservation property (as defined in section 168(j)(4)) that you placed in service after 1993. Use **Table 2** for qualified Indian reservation property placed in service after 1993.

Note: *Qualified Indian reservation property does not include property placed in service for purposes of conducting class I, II, or III gaming activities.*

Table 1—Recovery Period for Most Property

In the case of:	The applicable recovery period is:
3-year property	3 yrs.
5-year property	5 yrs.
7-year property	7 yrs.
10-year property	10 yrs.
15-year property	15 yrs.
20-year property	20 yrs.
Residential rental property	27.5 yrs.
Nonresidential real property placed in service before May 13, 1993	31.5 yrs.
Nonresidential real property placed in service after May 12, 1993	*39 yrs.
Railroad gradings and tunnel bores	50 yrs.

*The recovery period is 31.5 years for property you placed in service before 1994, if you started construction on the property before May 13, 1993, or you had a binding written contract to buy or build it before that date.

Table 2—Recovery Period for Qualified Indian Reservation Property Placed in Service After 1993

In the case of:	The applicable recovery period is:
3-year property	2 yrs.
5-year property	3 yrs.
7-year property	4 yrs.
10-year property	6 yrs.
15-year property	9 yrs.
20-year property	12 yrs.
Nonresidential real property	22 yrs.

Column (e).—The applicable convention determines the portion of the tax year for which depreciation is allowable during a year property is either placed in service or disposed of. There are three types of conventions (discussed below). To select the correct convention, you must know when you placed the property in service and the type of property.

Half-year convention (HY).—This convention applies to all property reported on lines 14a through 14f, unless the mid-quarter convention applies. It does not apply to residential rental property, nonresidential real property, and railroad gradings and tunnel bores. It treats all property placed in service (or disposed of) during any tax year as placed in service (or disposed of) on the mid-point of such tax year.

Mid-quarter convention (MQ).—If the aggregate bases of property subject to depreciation under section 168 and placed in service during the last 3 months of your tax year exceed 40% of the aggregate bases of property subject to depreciation under section 168 and placed in service during the entire tax year, the mid-quarter, instead of the half-year, convention applies.

The mid-quarter convention treats all property placed in service (or disposed of) during any quarter as placed in service (or disposed of) on the mid-point of such quarter. However, no depreciation is allowed under this convention for property that is placed in service and disposed of within the same tax year.

In determining whether the mid-quarter convention applies, **do not** take into account:

- Property that is being depreciated under the pre-1987 rules;
- Any residential rental property, nonresidential real property, or railroad gradings and tunnel bores; and
- Property that is placed in service and disposed of within the same tax year.

Mid-month convention (MM).—This convention applies ONLY to residential rental property, nonresidential real property (lines 14g or 14h), and railroad gradings and tunnel bores. It treats all property placed in service (or disposed of) during any month as placed in service (or disposed of) on the mid-point of such month.

Enter "HY" for half-year; "MQ" for mid-quarter; or "MM" for mid-month convention.

Column (f).—Applicable depreciation methods are prescribed for each classification of property. Except for property for which you elected to use the 150% declining balance method and any tree or vine bearing fruit or nuts, the applicable method for 3-, 5-, 7-, and 10-year property is the 200% declining balance method, switching to the straight line method in the first tax year that maximizes the depreciation allowance.

For 15- and 20-year property, property used in a farming business, and property for which you elected to use the 150% declining balance method, the applicable method is the 150% declining balance method, switching to the straight line method in the first tax year that maximizes the depreciation allowance.

For residential rental property, nonresidential real property, any railroad grading or tunnel bore, or any tree or vine bearing fruit or nuts, the only applicable method is the straight line method.

You may also make an irrevocable election to use the straight line method for all property within a classification that is placed in service during the tax year.

Enter "200 DB" for 200% declining balance; "150 DB" for 150% declining balance; or "S/L" for straight line.

Column (g).—To compute the depreciation deduction you may use optional Tables A through E on page 7. To do this, multiply the applicable rate from the appropriate table by the property's **unadjusted** basis (column (c)) (see Pub. 534 for complete tables). Or you may compute the deduction yourself by completing the following steps:

Step 1.—Determine the depreciation rate as follows:

- If you are using the 200% or 150% declining balance method in column (f), divide the declining balance rate (use 2.00 for 200 DB or 1.50 for 150 DB) by the number of years in the recovery period in column (d). For example, for property depreciated using the 200 DB method over a recovery period of 5 years, divide 2.00 by 5 for a rate of 40%.

- If you are using the straight line method, divide 1.00 by the remaining number of years in the recovery period as of the beginning of the tax year (but not less than one). For example, if there are 6½ years remaining in the recovery period as of the beginning of the year, divide 1.00 by 6.5 for a rate of 15.38%.

Note: *If you are using the 200% or 150% DB method, be sure to switch to the straight line rate in the first year that the straight line rate exceeds the declining balance rate.*

Step 2.—Multiply the percentage rate determined in Step 1 by the property's unrecovered basis (basis for depreciation (as defined in column (c)) reduced by all prior year's depreciation).

Step 3.—For property placed in service or disposed of during the current tax year, multiply the result from Step 2 by the applicable decimal amount from the tables below (based on the convention shown in column (e)).

Half-year (HY) convention	. . . . 0.5

Mid-quarter (MQ) convention

Placed in service (or disposed of) during the:	Placed in service	Disposed of
1st quarter	0.875	0.125
2nd quarter	0.625	0.375
3rd quarter	0.375	0.625
4th quarter	0.125	0.875

Mid-month (MM) convention

Placed in service (or disposed of) during the:	Placed in service	Disposed of
1st month	0.9583	0.0417
2nd month	0.8750	0.1250
3rd month	0.7917	0.2083
4th month	0.7083	0.2917
5th month	0.6250	0.3750
6th month	0.5417	0.4583
7th month	0.4583	0.5417
8th month	0.3750	0.6250
9th month	0.2917	0.7083
10th month	0.2083	0.7917
11th month	0.1250	0.8750
12th month	0.0417	0.9583

Short tax years.—See Pub. 534 for rules on how to compute the depreciation deduction for property placed in service in a short tax year.

Lines 15a Through 15c—Alternative Depreciation System (ADS)

Note: *Lines 15a through 15c should be completed for assets, other than automobiles and other listed property, placed in service ONLY during the tax year beginning in 1993 and depreciated under the Alternative Depreciation System. Depreciation on assets placed in service in prior years is reported on line 16.*

Under ADS, depreciation is computed by using the applicable depreciation method, the applicable recovery period, and the applicable convention. The following types of property **must** be depreciated under ADS:

• Any tangible property used predominantly outside the United States,

• Any tax-exempt use property,

• Any tax-exempt bond financed property,

• Any imported property covered by an executive order of the President of the United States, and

• Any property used predominantly in a farming business and placed in service during any tax year in which you made an election under section 263A(d)(3).

Instead of depreciating property under GDS (line 14), you may make an irrevocable election with respect to any classification of property for any tax year to use ADS. For residential rental and nonresidential real property, you may make this election separately for each property.

Column (a).—Use the following rules to determine the classification of the property under ADS:

• **Class life.** Under ADS, the depreciation deduction for most property is based on the property's class life, which can be found in the Table of Class Lives and Recovery Periods in Pub. 534. Use line 15a for all property depreciated under ADS, except for property that does not have a class life, residential rental and nonresidential real property, and railroad gradings and tunnel bores.

Note: *See section 168(g)(3)(B) for a special rule for determining the class life for certain property.*

• **12-year.** Use line 15b for property that does not have a class life.

• **40-year.** Use line 15c for residential rental and nonresidential real property.

• **Railroad gradings and tunnel bores** are 50-year property under ADS. There is no separate line to report 50-year property. Therefore, attach a statement showing the same information as required in columns (a) through (g). Include the deduction in the line 20 "Total" and write "See attachment" in the bottom margin of the form.

Column (b).—For 40-year property, enter the month and year it was placed in service or was converted to use in a trade or business or for the production of income.

Column (c).—See the instructions for line 14, column (c).

Column (d).—On line 15a, enter the property's class life.

Column (e).—Under ADS, the applicable conventions are the same as those used under GDS. See the instructions for line 14, column (e).

Column (f).—Under ADS, the only applicable method is the straight line method.

Column (g).—The depreciation deduction is computed in the same manner as under GDS except you must apply the straight line method over the ADS recovery period and use the applicable convention.

Part III—Other Depreciation

Note: *Do not use Part III for automobiles and other listed property. Instead, report this property in Part V on page 2 of Form 4562.*

Line 16

For tangible property placed in service after 1986 and depreciated under MACRS (including tangible property placed in service after July 31, 1986, for which you elected to use MACRS), enter the GDS and ADS deductions for the current year. To compute the deductions, see the instructions for column (g), line 14.

Line 17

Report property that you elect, under section 168(f)(1), to depreciate under the unit-of-production method or any other method not based on a term of years (other than the retirement-replacement-betterment method).

Attach a separate sheet showing **(a)** a description of the property and the depreciation method you elect that excludes the property from ACRS or MACRS; and **(b)** the depreciable basis (cost or other basis reduced, if applicable, by salvage value, any section 179 expense deduction, deduction for removal of barriers to the disabled and the elderly, disabled access credit, and enhanced oil recovery credit). See section 50(c) to determine the basis adjustment for investment credit property.

Line 18

Enter the total depreciation you are claiming for the following types of property (except listed property and property subject to a section 168(f)(1) election):

• ACRS property (pre-1987 rules);

• Property placed in service before 1981;

• Certain public utility property, which does not meet certain normalization requirements;

• Certain property acquired from related persons;

• Property acquired in certain nonrecognition transactions;

• Certain sound recordings, movies, and videotapes; and

• Intangible property, other than section 197 intangibles, including:

1. Computer software. Use the straight line method over 36 months for software acquired after August 10, 1993. You may also elect this method for software acquired after July 25, 1991. The amortization of section 197 intangibles is also included in this election. See the line 39 instructions for more details.

2. Any right to receive tangible property or services under a contract or granted by a governmental unit (not acquired as part of a business).

3. Any interest in a patent or copyright (not acquired as part of a business).

4. Mortgage servicing rights. Use the straight line method over 108 months for rights acquired after August 10, 1993. You may also elect this method for rights acquired after July 25, 1991. The amortization of section 197 intangibles is also included in this election. See the line 39 instructions for more details.

See section 167(f) for more details.

For ACRS property, unless you use an alternate percentage, multiply the property's unadjusted basis by the applicable percentage as follows:

• 5-year property—4th and 5th years (21%);

• 10-year property—4th through 6th years (10%), 7th through 10th years (9%);

• 15-year public utility property—4th year (8%), 5th and 6th years (7%), 7th through 15th years (6%);

• 15-year, 18-year, and 19-year real property and low-income housing—Use the tables in Pub. 534.

If you elected an alternate percentage for any ACRS property, use the straight line method over the recovery period you chose in the prior year. See Pub. 534 for more information and tables.

Include any amounts attributable to the Class Life Asset Depreciation Range (CLADR) system. If you previously elected the CLADR system, you must continue to use it to depreciate assets left in your vintage accounts. You must continue to meet recordkeeping requirements.

Prior years' depreciation, plus current year's depreciation, can never exceed the depreciable basis of the property.

The basis and amounts claimed for depreciation should be part of your permanent books and records. **No attachment is necessary.**

Part IV—Summary

Line 20

A partnership or S corporation does not include any section 179 expense deduction (line 12) on this line. Any section 179 expense deduction is passed through separately to the partners and shareholders on the appropriate line of their Schedules K-1.

Line 21

If you are subject to the uniform capitalization rules of section 263A, enter the increase in basis from costs that are required to be capitalized. For a detailed discussion of who is subject to these rules, which costs must be capitalized, and allocation of costs among activities, see Temporary Regulations section 1.263A-1T.

Part V—Listed Property

Taxpayers claiming the standard mileage rate, actual vehicle expenses (including depreciation), or depreciation on other listed property must provide the information requested in Part V, regardless of the tax year the property was placed in service. However, filers of Form 2106 and Schedule C-EZ (Form 1040) report this information on those forms and not in Part V. Also Schedule C (Form 1040) filers who are claiming the standard mileage rate or actual vehicle expenses (except depreciation), and who are not required to file Form 4562 for any other reason, report vehicle information in Part IV of Schedule C and not on Form 4562.

Listed property generally includes, but is not limited to:

- Passenger automobiles weighing 6,000 pounds or less.
- Any other property used for transportation if the nature of the property lends itself to personal use, such as motorcycles, pick-up trucks, etc.
- Any property used for entertainment or recreational purposes (such as photographic, phonographic, communication, and video recording equipment).
- Cellular telephones (or other similar telecommunications equipment).
- Computers or peripheral equipment.

Exception. Listed property does not include (a) photographic, phonographic, communication, or video equipment used exclusively in a taxpayer's trade or business or at the taxpayer's regular business establishment; (b) any computer or peripheral equipment used exclusively at a regular business establishment and owned or leased by the person operating the establishment; or (c) an ambulance, hearse, or vehicle used for transporting persons or property for hire. For purposes of the preceding sentence, a portion of the taxpayer's home is treated as a regular business establishment only if that portion meets the requirements under section 280A(c)(1) for deducting expenses attributable to the business use of a home. (However, for any property listed under (a) above, the regular business establishment of an employee is his or her employer's regular business establishment.)

Section A—Depreciation and Other Information

Lines 23 and 24

Qualified business use.—For purposes of determining whether to use line 23 or line 24 to report your listed property, you must first determine the percentage of qualified business use for each property. Generally, a qualified business use is any use in your trade or business. However, it does not include:

- Any investment use;
- Leasing the property to a 5% owner or related person;
- The use of the property as compensation for services performed by a 5% owner or related person; or

- The use of the property as compensation for services performed by any person (who is not a 5% owner or related person), unless an amount is included in that person's income for the use of the property and, if required, income tax was withheld on that amount.

As an exception to the general rule, if at least 25% of the total use of any aircraft during the tax year is for a qualified business use, the leasing or compensatory use of the aircraft by a 5% owner or related person is considered a qualified business use.

Determine your percentage of qualified business use in a manner similar to that used to figure the business/investment use percentage in column (c). Your percentage of qualified business use may be smaller than the business/investment use percentage.

For more information, see Pub. 534.

Column (a).—List on a property-by-property basis all of your listed property in the following order:

1. Automobiles and other vehicles; and
2. Other listed property (computers and peripheral equipment, etc.).

In column (a), list the make and model of automobiles, and give a general description of other listed property.

If you have more than five vehicles used 100% for business/investment purposes, you may group them by tax year. Otherwise, list each vehicle separately.

Column (b).—Enter the date the property was placed in service. If property held for personal use is converted to business/investment use, treat the property as placed in service on the date of conversion.

Column (c).—Enter the percentage of business/investment use. For automobiles and other vehicles, this is determined by dividing the number of miles the vehicle is driven for trade or business purposes or for the production of income during the year (not to include any commuting mileage) by the total number of miles the vehicle is driven for all purposes. Treat vehicles used by employees as being used 100% for business/investment purposes if the value of personal use is included in the employees' gross income, or the employees reimburse the employer for the personal use.

Employers who report the amount of personal use of the vehicle in the employee's gross income, and withhold the appropriate taxes, should enter "100%" for the percentage of business/investment use. For more information, see Pub. 917. For listed property, (such as computers or video equipment), allocate the use based on the most appropriate unit of time the property is actually used. See Temporary Regulations section 1.280F-6T.

If during the tax year you convert property used solely for personal purposes to business/investment use, figure the percentage of business/investment use only for the number of months the property is used in your business or for the production of income. Multiply that percentage by the number of months the property is used in your business or for the production of income, and divide the result by 12.

Column (d).—Enter the property's actual cost or other basis (unadjusted for prior years' depreciation). If you traded in old property, your basis is the adjusted basis of the old property (figured as if 100% of the property's use had been for business/investment purposes) plus any additional amount you paid for the new property. For a vehicle, reduce your basis by any diesel-powered highway vehicle credit, qualified electric vehicle credit, or deduction for clean-fuel vehicles you claimed. For property purchased after 1986, add to your basis any sales tax paid on the property.

If you converted the property from personal use to business/investment use, your basis for depreciation is the smaller of the property's adjusted basis or its fair market value on the date of conversion.

Column (e).—Multiply column (d) by the percentage in column (c). From that result, subtract any section 179 expense deduction and half of any investment credit taken before 1986 (unless you took the reduced credit). For automobiles and other listed property placed in service after 1985 (i.e., transition property), reduce the depreciable basis by the entire investment credit.

Column (f).—Enter the recovery period. For property placed in service after 1986 and used more than 50% in a qualified business use, use the table in the line 14, column (d) instructions. For property placed in service after 1986 and used 50% or less in a qualified business use, depreciate the property using the straight line method over its ADS recovery period. The ADS recovery period is 5 years for automobiles and computers.

Column (g).—Enter the method and convention used to figure your depreciation deduction. See the instructions for line 14, columns (e) and (f). Write "200 DB," "150 DB," or "S/L" for the depreciation method, and "HY," "MM," or "MQ," for half-year, mid-month, or mid-quarter conventions, respectively. For property placed in service before 1987, write "PRE" if you used the prescribed percentages under ACRS. If you elected an alternate percentage, enter "S/L."

Column (h).—See **Limitations for automobiles** below before entering an amount in column (h).

If the property is used more than 50% in a qualified business use (line 23), and the property was placed in service after 1986, figure column (h) by following the instructions for line 14, column (g). If placed in service before 1987, multiply column (e) by the applicable percentages given in the line 18 instructions for ACRS property. If the recovery period for the property ended before your tax year beginning in 1993, enter your unrecovered basis, if any, in column (h).

If the property is used 50% or less in a qualified business use (line 24), and the property was placed in service after 1986, figure column (h) by dividing column (e) by column (f) and using the same conventions as discussed in the instructions for line 14, column (e). The amount in column (h) cannot exceed the property's unrecovered basis. For automobiles placed in service after June 18, 1984, and before your tax year beginning in 1988, enter your unrecovered basis, if any, in column (h).

For computers placed in service after June 18, 1984, and before 1987, multiply column (e) by 8.333%.

For property placed in service before 1987 that was disposed of during the year, enter zero.

Limitations for automobiles.—The depreciation deduction plus section 179 expense deduction for automobiles is limited for any tax year. The limitation depends on when you placed the property in service. Use Table F on page 7 to determine the limitation. For any automobile you list on line 23 or 24, the total of columns (h) and (i) for that automobile cannot exceed the limit shown in Table F.

Note: These limitations are further reduced when the business/investment use percentage (column (c)) is less than 100%. For example, if an automobile placed in service in 1993 is used

Page 5

60% for business/investment purposes, then the first year depreciation plus section 179 expense deduction is limited to 60% of $2,860, which is $1,716.

Column (i).—Enter the amount you choose to expense for section 179 property used more than 50% in a qualified business use (subject to the limitations for automobiles noted above). Refer to the Part I instructions to determine if the property qualifies under section 179. Be sure to include the total cost of such property (50% of the cost if qualified zone property placed in service by an enterprise zone business) on line 2, page 1.

Recapture of depreciation and section 179 expense deduction.—If any listed property was used more than 50% in a qualified business use in the year it was placed in service, and used 50% or less in a later year, you may have to recapture in the later year part of the depreciation and section 179 expense deduction. Use **Form 4797**, Sales of Business Property, to figure the recapture amount.

Section B—Information Regarding Use of Vehicles

The information requested in Questions 27 through 33 must be completed for each vehicle identified in Section A.

Employees must provide their employers with the information requested in Questions 27 through 33 for each automobile or vehicle provided for their use.

Employers providing more than five vehicles to their employees, who are not more than 5% owners or related persons, are not required to complete Questions 27 through 33 for such vehicles. Instead, they must obtain this information from their employees, check "Yes" to Question 37, and retain the information received as part of their permanent records.

Section C—Questions for Employers Who Provide Vehicles for Use by Their Employees

For employers providing vehicles to their employees, a written policy statement regarding the use of such vehicles, if initiated and kept by the employer, will relieve the employee of keeping separate records for substantiation.

Two types of written policy statements will satisfy the employer's substantiation requirements under section 274(d): **(a)** a policy statement that prohibits personal use including commuting; and **(b)** a policy statement that prohibits personal use except for commuting.

Line 34

A policy statement that prohibits personal use (including commuting) must meet the following conditions:

• The vehicle is owned or leased by the employer and is provided to one or more employees for use in the employer's trade or business;

• When the vehicle is not used in the employer's trade or business, it is kept on the employer's business premises, unless it is temporarily located elsewhere (e.g., for maintenance or because of a mechanical failure);

• No employee using the vehicle lives at the employer's business premises;

• No employee may use the vehicle for personal purposes, other than de minimis personal use (e.g., a stop for lunch between two business deliveries); and

• Except for de minimis use, the employer reasonably believes that no employee uses the vehicle for any personal purpose.

Line 35

A policy statement that prohibits personal use (except for commuting) is NOT available if the commuting employee is an officer, director, or 1% or more owner. This policy must meet the following conditions:

• The vehicle is owned or leased by the employer and is provided to one or more employees for use in the employer's trade or business and is used in the employer's trade or business;

• For bona fide noncompensatory business reasons, the employer requires the employee to commute to and/or from work in the vehicle;

• The employer establishes a written policy under which the employee may not use the vehicle for personal purposes, other than commuting or de minimis personal use (e.g., a stop for a personal errand between a business delivery and the employee's home);

• Except for de minimis use, the employer reasonably believes that the employee does not use the vehicle for any personal purpose other than commuting; and

• The employer accounts for the commuting use by including an appropriate amount in the employee's gross income.

For both written policy statements, there must be evidence that would enable the IRS to determine whether use of the vehicle meets the conditions stated above.

Line 38

An automobile is considered to have qualified demonstration use if the employer maintains a written policy statement that:

• Prohibits its use by individuals other than full-time automobile salesmen;

• Prohibits its use for personal vacation trips;

• Prohibits storage of personal possessions in the automobile; and

• Limits the total mileage outside the salesmen's normal working hours.

Part VI—Amortization

Each year you may elect to deduct part of certain capital costs over a fixed period. If you amortize property, the property you amortize does not qualify for the election to expense certain tangible property or depreciation.

For individuals reporting amortization of bond premium for bonds acquired before October 23, 1986, do not report the deduction here. See the instructions for Schedule A (Form 1040).

For taxpayers (other than corporations) claiming a deduction for amortization of bond premium for bonds acquired after October 22, 1986, but before January 1, 1988, the deduction is treated as interest expense and is subject to the investment interest limitations. Use **Form 4952**, Investment Interest Expense Deduction, to compute the allowable deduction.

For taxable bonds acquired after 1987, the amortization offsets the interest income. Get **Pub. 550**, Investment Income and Expenses.

Line 39

Complete line 39 only for those costs for which the amortization period begins during your tax year beginning in 1993.

Column (a).—Describe the costs you are amortizing. You may amortize:

• Pollution control facilities (section 169, limited by section 291 for corporations).

• Certain bond premiums (section 171).

• Research and experimental expenditures (section 174).

• The cost of acquiring a lease (section 178).

• Qualified forestation and reforestation costs (section 194).

• Business start-up expenditures (section 195).

• Organizational expenditures for a corporation (section 248) or partnership (section 709).

• Optional write-off of certain tax preferences over the period specified in section 59(e).

• Section 197 intangibles, which generally include:

   1. Goodwill,

   2. Going concern value,

   3. Workforce in place,

   4. Business books and records, operating systems, or any other information base,

   5. Any patent, copyright, formula, process, design, pattern, knowhow, format, or similar item,

   6. Any customer-based intangible (e.g., composition of market or market share),

   7. Any supplier-based intangible,

   8. Any license, permit, or other right granted by a governmental unit,

   9. Any covenant not to compete entered into in connection with the acquisition of a business, and

   10. Any franchise (other than a sports franchise), trademark, or trade name.

Section 197 intangibles acquired after August 10, 1993, must be amortized over 15 years starting with the month the intangibles were acquired. You may also elect to amortize section 197 intangibles acquired after July 25, 1991, over the same period. If you make this election, it applies to all property acquired after July 25, 1991. In addition to section 197 intangibles, the election requires that you depreciate computer software and mortgage servicing rights under the special rules in section 167(f) (as discussed in the line 18 instructions). Once made, the election may not be revoked without IRS consent.

Note: *Section 197 will not apply to an acquisition of property under a binding contract in effect on August 10, 1993, and all times thereafter until you acquired the property, if you elect to exclude the property from this provision.*

Column (b).—Enter the date the amortization period begins under the applicable Code section.

Column (c).—Enter the total amount you are amortizing. See the applicable Code section for limits on the amortizable amount.

Column (d).—Enter the Code section under which you amortize the costs.

Column (f).—Compute the amortization deduction by:

   1. Dividing column (c) by the number of months over which the costs are to be amortized, and multiplying the result by the number of months in the amortization period included in your tax year beginning in 1993; or

   2. Multiplying column (c) by the percentage in column (e).

Attach any other information the Code and regulations may require to make a valid election. See Pub. 535 for more information.

Line 40

Enter the amount of amortization attributable to those costs for which the amortization period began before 1993.

	If the recovery period is:			
Year	3 yrs.	5 yrs.	7 yrs.	10 yrs.
1	33.33%	20.00%	14.29%	10.00%
2	44.45%	32.00%	24.49%	18.00%
3	14.81%	19.20%	17.49%	14.40%
4	7.41%	11.52%	12.49%	11.52%
5		11.52%	8.93%	9.22%
6		5.76%	8.92%	7.37%
7			8.93%	6.55%
8			4.46%	6.55%

Table B—General and Alternative Depreciation System   Method: 150% declining balance switching to straight line   Convention: Half-year

	If the recovery period is:					
Year	5 yrs.	7 yrs.	10 yrs.	12 yrs.	15 yrs.	20 yrs.
1	15.00%	10.71%	7.50%	6.25%	5.00%	3.750%
2	25.50%	19.13%	13.88%	11.72%	9.50%	7.219%
3	17.85%	15.03%	11.79%	10.25%	8.55%	6.677%
4	16.66%	12.25%	10.02%	8.97%	7.70%	6.177%
5	16.66%	12.25%	8.74%	7.85%	6.93%	5.713%
6	8.33%	12.25%	8.74%	7.33%	6.23%	5.285%
7		12.25%	8.74%	7.33%	5.90%	4.888%
8		6.13%	8.74%	7.33%	5.90%	4.522%

Table C—General Depreciation System   Method: Straight line   Convention: Mid-month   Recovery period: 27.5 years

	The month in the 1st recovery year the property is placed in service:											
Year	1	2	3	4	5	6	7	8	9	10	11	12
1	3.485%	3.182%	2.879%	2.576%	2.273%	1.970%	1.667%	1.364%	1.061%	0.758%	0.455%	0.152%
2–8	3.636%	3.636%	3.636%	3.636%	3.636%	3.636%	3.636%	3.636%	3.636%	3.636%	3.636%	3.636%

Table D—General Depreciation System   Method: Straight line   Convention: Mid-month   Recovery period: 31.5 years

	The month in the 1st recovery year the property is placed in service:											
Year	1	2	3	4	5	6	7	8	9	10	11	12
1	3.042%	2.778%	2.513%	2.249%	1.984%	1.720%	1.455%	1.190%	0.926%	0.661%	0.397%	0.132%
2–7	3.175%	3.175%	3.175%	3.175%	3.175%	3.175%	3.175%	3.175%	3.175%	3.175%	3.175%	3.175%
8	3.175%	3.174%	3.175%	3.174%	3.175%	3.174%	3.175%	3.175%	3.175%	3.175%	3.175%	3.175%

Table E—General Depreciation System   Method: Straight line   Convention: Mid-month   Recovery period: 39 years

	The month in the 1st recovery year the property is placed in service:											
Year	1	2	3	4	5	6	7	8	9	10	11	12
1	2.461%	2.247%	2.033%	1.819%	1.605%	1.391%	1.177%	0.963%	0.749%	0.535%	0.321%	0.107%
2–39	2.564%	2.564%	2.564%	2.564%	2.564%	2.564%	2.564%	2.564%	2.564%	2.564%	2.564%	2.564%

Table F—Limitations for Automobiles

Date Placed in Service	Year of Deduction			
	1st Tax Year	2nd Tax Year	3rd Tax Year	4th & Later Tax Years
June 19–Dec. 31, 1984				$6,000
Jan. 1–April 2, 1985				$6,200
April 3, 1985–Dec. 31, 1986				$4,800
Jan. 1, 1987–Dec. 31, 1990				$1,475
Jan. 1–Dec. 31, 1991			$2,550	$1,575
Jan. 1–Dec. 31, 1992		$4,400	$2,650	$1,575
Jan. 1–Dec. 31, 1993	$2,860	$4,600	$2,750	$1,675
After Dec. 31, 1993	*	*	*	*

* The limitations for automobiles placed in service after Dec. 31, 1993, will be published in the Internal Revenue Bulletin. These amounts were not available at the time these instructions were printed.

Page 7

Depreciation Worksheet

Description of Property	Date Placed in Service	Cost or Other Basis	Business/ Investment Use %	Section 179 Deduction	Depreciation Prior Years	Basis for Depreciation	Method/ Convention	Recovery Period	Rate or Table %	Depreciation Deduction

Appendix K K-45

1993  Department of the Treasury
Internal Revenue Service

Instructions for Form 4797
Sales of Business Property
(Also Involuntary Conversions and Recapture Amounts Under Sections 179 and 280F(b)(2))
Section references are to the Internal Revenue Code unless otherwise noted.

Paperwork Reduction Act Notice

We ask for the information on this form to carry out the Internal Revenue laws of the United States. You are required to give us the information. We need it to ensure that you are complying with these laws and to allow us to figure and collect the right amount of tax.

The time needed to complete and file this form will vary depending on individual circumstances. The estimated average time is:

Recordkeeping . . . . . 30 hr., 8 min.
Learning about the law
or the form . . . . . 11 hr., 29 min.
Preparing the form . . . . 17 hr., 7 min.
Copying, assembling, and
sending the form to the IRS . 1 hr., 20 min.

If you have comments concerning the accuracy of these time estimates or suggestions for making this form more simple, we would be happy to hear from you. You can write to both the IRS and the Office of Management and Budget at the addresses listed in the instructions for the tax return with which this form is filed.

General Instructions
Purpose of Form

Use Form 4797 to report:

• The sale or exchange of property used in your trade or business; depreciable and amortizable property; oil, gas, geothermal, or other mineral properties; and section 126 property.

• The involuntary conversion (from other than casualty or theft) of property used in your trade or business and capital assets held in connection with a trade or business or a transaction entered into for profit.

• The disposition of noncapital assets other than inventory or property held primarily for sale to customers in the ordinary course of your trade or business.

• The recapture of section 179 expense deductions for partners and S corporation shareholders from property dispositions by partnerships and S corporations.

• The computation of recapture amounts under sections 179 and 280F(b)(2), when the business use of section 179 or listed property drops to 50% or less.

Other Forms To Use

• Use **Form 4684**, Casualties and Thefts, to report involuntary conversions from casualties and thefts.

• Use **Form 8824**, Like-Kind Exchanges, for each exchange. A "like-kind exchange" occurs when you exchange business or investment property for property of a like kind. For exchanges of property used in a trade or business (and other noncapital assets), enter the gain or (loss) from Form 8824, if any, on line 5 or 17.

• If you sold property on which you claimed investment credit, get **Form 4255**, Recapture of Investment Credit, to see if you must recapture some or all of the credit.

Special Rules

Installment sales.—If you sold property at a gain and you will receive a payment in a tax year after the year of sale, you must report the sale on the installment method unless you elect not to do so.

Use **Form 6252**, Installment Sale Income, to report the sale on the installment method. Also use Form 6252 to report any payment received in 1993 from a sale made in an earlier year that you reported on the installment method.

To elect out of the installment method, report the full amount of the gain on a timely filed return (including extensions).

Get **Pub. 537**, Installment Sales, for more details.

Recapture of preproductive expenses.—If you elected out of the uniform capitalization rules of section 263A, any plant that you produce is treated as section 1245 property. For dispositions of plants reportable on Form 4797, enter the recapture amount taxed as ordinary income on line 24 of Form 4797. Get **Pub. 225**, Farmer's Tax Guide, for more details.

Involuntary conversion of property.—You may not have to pay tax on a gain from an involuntary or compulsory conversion of property. Get **Pub. 544**, Sales and Other Dispositions of Assets, for details.

At-risk rules.—If you report a loss on an asset used in an activity for which you are not at risk, in whole or in part, see the instructions for **Form 6198**, At-Risk Limitations. Also, get **Pub. 925**, Passive Activity and At-Risk Rules. Losses from passive activities are first subject to the at-risk rules and then to the passive activity rules.

Passive loss limitations.—If you have an overall loss from passive activities, and you report a loss on an asset used in a passive activity, use **Form 8582**, Passive Activity Loss

Examples of Items To Be Reported on This Form—Where To Make First Entry

	(a) Type of property	(b) Held 1 year or less	(c) Held more than 1 year
1	Depreciable trade or business property:		
a	Sold or exchanged at a gain	Part II	Part III (1245, 1250)
b	Sold or exchanged at a loss	Part II	Part I
2	Depreciable residential rental property:		
a	Sold or exchanged at a gain	Part II	Part III (1250)
b	Sold or exchanged at a loss	Part II	Part I
3	Farmland held less than 10 years upon which soil, water, or land clearing expenses were deducted:		
a	Sold at a gain	Part II	Part III (1252)
b	Sold at a loss	Part II	Part I
4	Disposition of cost-sharing payment property described in section 126	Part II	Part III (1255)
5	Cattle and horses used in a trade or business for draft, breeding, dairy, or sporting purposes:	Held less than 24 months	Held 24 months or more
a	Sold at a gain	Part II	Part III (1245)
b	Sold at a loss	Part II	Part I
c	Raised cattle and horses sold at a gain	Part II	Part I
6	Livestock other than cattle and horses used in a trade or business for draft, breeding, dairy, or sporting purposes:	Held less than 12 months	Held 12 months or more
a	Sold at a gain	Part II	Part III (1245)
b	Sold at a loss	Part II	Part I
c	Raised livestock sold at a gain	Part II	Part I

Cat. No. 13087T

Limitations, to see how much loss is allowed before entering it on Form 4797.

Unused passive activity credits are not allowable when you dispose of your interest in an activity. However, if you dispose of your entire interest in an activity, you may elect to increase the basis of the credit property by the original basis reduction of the property to the extent that the credit has not been allowed because of the passive activity rules. No basis adjustment may be elected on a partial disposition of your interest in an activity. See Pub. 925 for details.

Transfer of appreciated property to political organizations.—Treat a transfer of property to a political organization as a sale of property on the date of transfer if the property's fair market value when transferred is more than your adjusted basis. Apply the ordinary income or capital gains provisions as if a sale had actually occurred. See section 84.

Allocation of purchase price.—If you acquire or dispose of assets that constitute a trade or business, the buyer and seller must allocate the total purchase price using the "residual method" and must file **Form 8594,** Asset Acquisition Statement.

Form 1099-A, Acquisition or Abandonment of Secured Property.—If you receive a Form 1099-A from your lender, you may have gain or loss to report because of acquisition or abandonment. See Pub. 544 for details.

Specific Instructions

To show losses, enclose figures in (parentheses).

Part I

Section 1231 transactions are:

- Sales or exchanges of real or depreciable property used in a trade or business and held for more than 1 year. To figure the holding period, begin counting on the day after you received the property and include the day you disposed of it.
- Cutting of timber that the taxpayer elects to treat as a sale or exchange under section 631(a).
- Disposal of timber with a retained economic interest treated as a sale under section 631(b).
- Disposal of coal (including lignite) or domestic iron ore with a retained economic interest that is treated as a sale under section 631(c).
- Sales or exchanges of cattle and horses, regardless of age, used in a trade or business by the taxpayer for draft, breeding, dairy, or sporting purposes and held for 24 months or more from acquisition date.
- Sales or exchanges of livestock other than cattle and horses, regardless of age, used by the taxpayer for draft, breeding, dairy, or sporting purposes and held for 12 months or more from acquisition date.

Note: *Livestock does not include poultry.*

- Sales or exchanges of unharvested crops. See section 1231(b)(4).
- Involuntary conversions of trade or business property or capital assets held in connection with a trade or business or a transaction entered into for profit, and kept more than 1 year.

These conversions may result from **(a)** part or total destruction, **(b)** theft or seizure, or **(c)** requisition or condemnation (whether threatened or carried out). If any recognized losses were from involuntary conversions from fire, storm, shipwreck, or other casualty, or from theft, and they exceed the recognized gains from the conversions, do not include them when figuring your net section 1231 losses.

Section 1231 transactions **do not** include:

- Sales or exchanges of inventory or property held primarily for sale to customers.
- Sales or exchanges of copyrights, literary, musical, or artistic compositions, letters or memoranda, or similar property **(a)** created by your personal efforts, **(b)** prepared or produced for you (in the case of letters, memoranda, or similar property), or **(c)** that you received from someone who created them or for whom they were created, as mentioned in **(a)** or **(b)**, in a way (such as by gift) that entitled you to the basis of the previous owner.
- Sales or exchanges of U.S. Government publications, including the Congressional Record, that you received from the Government, other than by purchase at the normal sales price, or that you got from someone who had received it in a similar way, if your basis is determined by reference to the previous owner's basis.

Line 9—Nonrecaptured net section 1231 losses.—Part or all of your section 1231 gains on line 8 may be taxed as ordinary income instead of receiving long-term capital gain treatment. These net section 1231 gains are treated as ordinary income to the extent of the "nonrecaptured section 1231 losses." The nonrecaptured losses are net section 1231 losses deducted during the 5 preceding tax years that have not yet been applied against any net section 1231 gain for determining how much gain is ordinary income under these rules.

Example. If you had net section 1231 losses of $4,000 and $6,000 in 1988 and 1989 and net section 1231 gains of $3,000 and $2,000 in 1992 and 1993, line 8 would show the 1993 gain of $2,000, and line 9 would show nonrecaptured net section 1231 losses of $7,000 ($10,000 net section 1231 losses minus the $3,000 that was recaptured because of the 1992 gain). The $2,000 gain on line 8 is all ordinary income and would be entered on line 13 of Form 4797. For recordkeeping purposes, the $4,000 loss from 1988 is all recaptured ($3,000 in 1992 and $1,000 in 1993) and you have $5,000 left to recapture from 1989 ($6,000 minus the $1,000 recaptured this year).

Figuring the prior year losses.—You had a net section 1231 loss if section 1231 losses exceeded section 1231 gains. Gains are included only to the extent taken into account in computing gross income. Losses are included only to the extent taken into account in computing taxable income except that the limitation on capital losses does not apply. See Pub. 544 for more details.

Line 10.—For recordkeeping purposes, if line 10 is zero, the amount on line 8 is the amount of net section 1231 loss recaptured in 1993. If line 10 is more than zero, you have recaptured in 1993 all of your net section 1231 losses from prior years.

Part II

If a transaction is not reportable in Part I or Part III and the property is not a capital asset reportable on Schedule D, report the transaction in Part II.

If you receive ordinary income from a sale or other disposition of your interest in a partnership, get **Pub. 541,** Tax Information on Partnerships.

Line 11.—Report other ordinary gains and losses, including property held 1 year or less, on this line.

Section 1244 (small business) stock.—Individuals report ordinary losses from the sale or exchange (including worthlessness) of section 1244 (small business) stock on line 11. The maximum amount that may be treated as an ordinary loss is $50,000 ($100,000, if married filing a joint return). Gains from the sale or exchange of section 1244 stock (and losses in excess of the maximum amount that may be treated as an ordinary loss) are reported on Schedule D.

If you claim a section 1244 stock loss, you **must** file a statement with your return that specifies:

1. The address of the corporation that issued the stock;

2. The manner in which you acquired the stock;

3. The amount and type of consideration you gave in exchange for the stock; and

4. If you acquired the stock in a nontaxable transaction in exchange for property other than money, the type of property and the adjusted basis and fair market value of the property on the date it was transferred to the corporation.

If you do not file this statement with your return, ordinary loss treatment under section 1244 may not be allowed.

Be sure to keep adequate records to distinguish section 1244 stock from any other stock owned in the same corporation. Get **Pub. 550,** Investment Income and Expenses, for more information.

Line 18.—Enter any recapture of section 179 expense deduction included on Schedule K-1 (Form 1065), line 23, and on Schedule K-1 (Form 1120S), line 23, but only if it is due to a disposition. Include it only to the extent that you took a deduction for it in an earlier year. See instructions for Part IV if you have section 179 recapture when the business use percentage of the property dropped to 50% or less.

Line 20b(1).—You must complete this line if there is a gain on Form 4797, line 3; a loss on Form 4797, line 12; and a loss on Form 4684, line 35, column (b)(ii). Enter on this line and on Schedule A (Form 1040), line 20, the **smaller** of the loss on Form 4797, line 12; or the loss on Form 4684, line 35, column (b)(ii). To figure which loss is smaller, treat both losses as positive numbers.

Part III

Part III is used to compute recapture of depreciation and certain other items that must be reported as ordinary income on the disposition of property. Fill out lines 21 through 26 to determine the gain on the disposition of the property. If you have more than four properties to report, use additional forms. For more details on depreciation recapture, see Pub. 544.

Note: *If the property was sold on the installment sale basis, see the Instructions for Form 6252 before completing this part. Also, if you have both installment sales and noninstallment sales, you may want to use a separate Form 4797, Part III, for each installment sale and one Form 4797, Part III, for the noninstallment sales.*

Line 22.—The gross sales price includes money, the fair market value of other property received, and any existing mortgage or other debt the buyer assumes or takes the property subject to. For casualty or theft gains, include insurance or other reimbursement you received or expect to receive for each item. Include on this line your insurance coverage, whether or not you are submitting a claim for reimbursement.

For section 1255 property disposed of in a sale, exchange, or involuntary conversion, enter the amount realized. For section 1255 property disposed of in any other way, enter the fair market value.

Line 23.—Be sure to reduce the cost or other basis of the property by the amount of any qualified electric vehicle credit, diesel-powered highway vehicle credit, enhanced oil recovery credit, or disabled access credit.

However, **do not** reduce the cost or other basis on this line by any of the following amounts:

1. Deductions allowed or allowable for depreciation, amortization, depletion, or preproductive expenses;

2. The section 179 expense deduction;

3. The downward basis adjustment under section 50(c) (or the corresponding provision of prior law);

4. The deduction for qualified clean-fuel vehicle property or refueling property; or

5. Deductions claimed under section 190, 193, or 1253(d)(2) or (3) (as in effect before the enactment of P.L. 103-66).

Instead, include these amounts on line 24. They will be used to determine the property's adjusted basis on line 25.

Line 24.—For a taxpayer other than a partnership or an S corporation, complete the following steps to figure the amount to enter on line 24:

Step 1.—Add the following amounts:

1. Deductions allowed or allowable for depreciation, amortization, depletion, or preproductive expenses;

2. The section 179 expense deduction;

3. The downward basis adjustment under section 50(c) (or the corresponding provision of prior law);

4. The deduction for qualified clean-fuel vehicle property or refueling property; and

5. Deductions claimed under section 190, 193, or 1253(d)(2) or (3) (as in effect before the enactment of P.L. 103-66).

Step 2.—From the step 1 total, **subtract** the following amounts:

1. Any investment credit recapture amount if the basis of the property was reduced for the tax year the property was placed in service under section 50(c)(1) (or the corresponding provision of prior law). See section 50(c)(2) (or the corresponding provision of prior law).

2. Any section 179 or 280F(b)(2) recapture amount included in gross income in a prior tax year because the business use of the property dropped to 50% or less.

3. Any qualified clean-fuel vehicle property or refueling property deduction you were required to recapture because the property ceased to be eligible for the deduction.

You may have to include depreciation allowed or allowable on another asset (and recompute the basis amount for line 23) if you use its adjusted basis in determining the adjusted basis of the property described on line 21. An example is property acquired by a trade-in. See Regulations section 1.1245-2(a)(4).

Partnerships should enter the deductions allowed or allowable for depreciation, amortization, or depletion on line 24. Enter the section 179 expense deduction on Form 1065, Schedule K, line 22. Partnerships should make the basis adjustment required under section 50(c) (or the corresponding provision of prior law). Partners adjust the basis of their interest in the partnership to take into account the basis adjustments made at the partnership level.

S corporations should enter the deductions allowed or allowable for depreciation, amortization, or depletion on line 24. Enter the section 179 expense deduction on Form 1120S, Schedule K, line 21, but only if the corporation disposed of property acquired in a tax year beginning after 1982. S corporations should make the basis adjustment required under section 50(c) (or the corresponding provision of prior law). Shareholders adjust the basis in their stock in the corporation to take into account the basis adjustments made at the S corporation level under section 50(c) (or the corresponding provision of prior law).

Line 25.—For section 1255 property, enter the adjusted basis of the section 126 property disposed of.

Line 27—Section 1245 property.—Section 1245 property is depreciable (or amortizable under section 185 (repealed) or 1253(d)(2) or (3) (as in effect before the enactment of P.L. 103-66)) and is one of the following:

- Personal property.

- Elevators and escalators placed in service before 1987.

- Real property (other than property described under tangible real property below) subject to amortization or deductions under section 169, 179, 185 (repealed), 188 (repealed), 190, 193, or 194.

- Tangible real property (except buildings and their structural components) if it is used in any of the following ways:

1. As an integral part of manufacturing, production, extraction, or furnishing transportation, communications, or certain public utility services.

2. As a research facility in these activities.

3. For the bulk storage of fungible commodities (including commodities in a liquid or gaseous state) used in these activities.

- A single purpose agricultural or horticultural structure (as defined in section 168(i)(13)).

- A storage facility (not including a building or its structural components) used in connection with the distribution of petroleum or any primary petroleum product.

- Any railroad grading or tunnel bore (as defined in section 168(e)(4)).

See section 1245(b) for exceptions and limits involving the following:

- Gifts.
- Transfers at death.
- Certain tax-free transactions.
- Certain like-kind exchanges, involuntary conversions, etc.
- Sales or exchanges to carry out FCC policies, and exchanges to comply with SEC orders.
- Property distributed by a partnership to a partner.
- Transfers to tax-exempt organizations where the property will be used in an unrelated business.
- Timber property.

See the following sections for special rules:

- Section 1245(a)(4) for player contracts and section 1056(c) for information required from the transferor of a franchise of any sports enterprise if the sale or exchange involves the transfer of player contracts.

- Section 1245(a)(5) (repealed) for property placed in service before 1987, when only a portion of a building is section 1245 recovery property.

- Section 1245(a)(6) (repealed) for qualified leased property placed in service before 1987.

Line 28—Section 1250 property.—Section 1250 property is depreciable real property (other than section 1245 property). ACRS deductions under section 168 are subject to recapture under section 1245, except for the following, which are treated as section 1250 property if the property was placed in service before 1987:

- 15-, 18-, or 19-year real property and low-income housing that is residential rental property.

- 15-, 18-, or 19-year real property and low-income housing that is used mostly outside the United States.

- 15-, 18-, or 19-year real property and low-income housing for which a straight line election was made.

- Low-income rental housing described in clause (i), (ii), (iii), or (iv) of section 1250(a)(1)(B). See instructions for line 28b.

Section 1250 recapture applies when an accelerated depreciation method was used.

The section 1250 recapture rules **do not** apply to dispositions of 27.5-year (or 40-year, if elected) residential rental property or 22-, 31.5-, or 39-year (or 40-year, if elected) nonresidential real property placed in service after 1986 (or after July 31, 1986, if the election is made).

See section 1250(d) for exceptions and limits involving the following:

- Gifts.
- Transfers at death.
- Certain tax-free transactions.
- Certain like-kind exchanges, involuntary conversions, etc.
- Sales or exchanges to carry out FCC policies, and exchanges to comply with SEC orders.

- Property distributed by a partnership to a partner.
- Disposition of a main home.
- Disposition of qualified low-income housing.
- Transfers of property to tax-exempt organizations where the property will be used in an unrelated business.
- Dispositions of property as a result of foreclosure proceedings.

Special rules:
- For additional depreciation attributable to rehabilitation expenditures, see section 1250(b)(4).
- If substantial improvements have been made, see section 1250(f).

Line 28a.—Enter the additional depreciation for the period after 1975. **Additional depreciation** is the excess of actual depreciation over depreciation figured using the straight line method. For this purpose, do not reduce the basis under section 50(c)(1) (or the corresponding provision of prior law) in figuring straight line depreciation.

Line 28b.—Use 100% as the percentage for this line, except for low-income rental housing described in clause (i), (ii), (iii), or (iv) of section 1250(a)(1)(B). For this type of low-income rental housing, see section 1250(a)(1)(B) for the percentage to use.

Line 28d.—Enter the additional depreciation after 1969 and before 1976. If the straight line depreciation is more than the actual depreciation after 1969 and before 1976, reduce line 28a by the amount the straight line depreciation exceeds actual depreciation, but not by more than the amount on line 28a.

Line 28f—Corporations subject to section 291.—The amount treated as ordinary income under section 291 is 20% of the excess, if any, of the amount that would be treated as ordinary income if such property were section 1245 property, over the amount treated as ordinary income under section 1250. If you used the straight line method of depreciation, the ordinary income under section 291 is 20% of the amount figured under section 1245.

Line 29—Section 1252 property.—Partnerships should skip this section. Partners should enter on the applicable lines of Part III amounts subject to section 1252 according to instructions from the partnership.

You may have ordinary income on the disposition of certain farmland held more than 1 year but less than 10 years.

Refer to section 1252 to determine if there is ordinary income on the disposition of certain farmland for which deductions were allowed under sections 175 (soil and water conservation) and 182 (land clearing) (repealed). Skip line 29 if you dispose of such farmland during the 10th or later year after you acquired it.

Gain from disposition of certain farmland is subject to ordinary income rules under section 1252 before being considered under section 1231 (Part I).

When filling out line 29b, enter 100% of line 29a on line 29b, except as follows:
- 80% if the farmland was disposed of within the 6th year after it was acquired.
- 60% if disposed of within the 7th year.
- 40% if disposed of within the 8th year.
- 20% if disposed of within the 9th year.

Line 30—Section 1254 property.—If you had a gain on the disposition of oil, gas, or geothermal property placed in service before 1987, you must treat all or part of the gain as ordinary income. Include on line 24 of Form 4797 any depletion allowed (or allowable) in determining the adjusted basis of the property.

If you had a gain on the disposition of oil, gas, geothermal, or other mineral properties (section 1254 property) placed in service after 1986, you must recapture all expenses that were deducted as intangible drilling costs, depletion, mine exploration costs, and development costs, under sections 263, 616, and 617.

Exception. Property placed in service after 1986 and acquired under a written contract entered into before September 26, 1985, and binding at all times thereafter is treated as placed in service before 1987.

Note: In the case of a corporation that is an integrated oil company, amounts amortized under section 291(b)(2) are treated as a deduction under section 263(c) when completing line 30a.

Line 30a.—If the property was placed in service before 1987, enter the total expenses after 1975 that:
- Were deducted by the taxpayer or any other person as intangible drilling and development costs under section 263(c). (Previously expensed mining costs that have been included in income upon reaching the producing state are not taken into account in determining recapture.); and
- Would have been reflected in the adjusted basis of the property if they had not been deducted.

If the property was placed in service after 1986, enter the total expenses that:
- Were deducted under section 263, 616, or 617 by the taxpayer or any other person; and
- Which, but for such deduction, would have been included in the basis of the property; plus
- The deduction under section 611 that reduced the adjusted basis of such property.

If you disposed of a portion of section 1254 property or an undivided interest in it, see section 1254(a)(2).

Line 31—Section 1255 property.—For line 31a, use 100% if the property is disposed of less than 10 years after receipt of payments excluded from income. Use 100% minus 10% for each year, or part of a year, that the property was held over 10 years after receipt of the excluded payments. Use zero if 20 years or more.

Part IV

Section 179 property—column (a).—If you took a section 179 expense deduction for property placed in service after 1986 (other than listed property, as defined in section 280F(d)(4)), and the business use of the property was reduced to 50% or less this year, complete column (a) of lines 35 through 37 to figure the recapture amount.

Listed property—column (b).—If you have listed property that you placed in service in a prior year and the business use dropped to 50% or less this year, figure the amount to be recaptured under section 280F(b)(2). Complete column (b), lines 35 through 37. Get Pub. 917, Business Use of a Car, for more details on recapture of excess depreciation.

Note: If you have more than one property subject to the recapture rules, use separate statements to figure the recapture amounts and attach the statements to your tax return.

Line 35.—In column (a), enter the section 179 expense deduction claimed when the property was placed in service. In column (b), enter the depreciation allowable on the property in prior tax years. Include any section 179 expense deduction you took as depreciation.

Line 36.—In column (a), enter the depreciation that would have been allowable on the section 179 amount from the year it was placed in service through the current year. Get Pub. 534, Depreciation. In column (b), enter the depreciation that would have been allowable if the property had not been used more than 50% in a qualified business. Figure the depreciation from the year it was placed in service until the current year. See Pub. 534 and Pub. 917.

Line 37.—Subtract line 36 from line 35 and enter the recapture amount as "other income" on the same form or schedule on which you took the deduction. For example, if you took the deduction on Schedule C (Form 1040), report the recapture amount as other income on Schedule C (Form 1040).

Note: If you filed Schedule C or F (Form 1040) and the property was used in both your trade or business and for the production of income, the portion attributable to your trade or business is subject to self-employment tax. Allocate the amount on line 37 before entering the recapture amount on the appropriate schedule.

Be sure to increase the basis of the property by the recapture amount.

Index to Internal Revenue Code Section

Sec. 1(i), 2-33
Sec. 1(i)(1), 2-33
Sec. 1(i)(1)(A), 2-33
Sec. 1(i)(1)(B), 2-33
Sec. 1(i)(1)(B)(i), 2-33
Sec. 1(i)(1)(B)(ii), 2-33
Sec. 1(i)(3), 2-34
Sec. 1(i)(3)(A), 2-34
Sec. 1(i)(3)(A)(i), 2-34
Sec. 1(i)(3)(A)(ii), 2-34
Sec. 21(a)(1), 5-16
Sec. 21(a)(2), 5-17
Sec. 21(c), 5-17
Sec. 21(c)(1), 5-17
Sec. 21(c)(2), 5-17
Sec. 22(a), 5-9
Sec. 22(b), 5-9
Sec. 22(b)(1), 5-9
Sec. 22(b)(2), 5-9
Sec. 27(a), 5-22
Sec. 32(a), 5-2
Sec. 32(a)(1), 5-2
Sec. 32(a)(2), 5-2
Sec. 41(a), 9-44
Sec. 41(a)(1), 9-44
Sec. 41(a)(1)(A), 9-44
Sec. 41(a)(1)(B), 9-44
Sec. 41(a)(2), 9-44
Sec. 42(a), 9-47
Sec. 42(a)(1), 9-47
Sec. 42(a)(2), 9-47
Sec. 42(b)(2)(A), 9-47
Sec. 42(b)(2)(B), 9-47
Sec. 42(b)(2)(B)(i), 9-47
Sec. 42(b)(2)(B)(ii), 9-47
Sec. 46(a), 9-37
Sec. 46(a)(1), 9-37
Sec. 46(a)(2), 9-37
Sec. 46(a)(3), 9-37
Sec. 51(a), 9-41
Sec. 51(b)(1), 9-41
Sec. 51(b)(2), 9-41
Sec. 51(b)(3), 9-41
Sec. 55(a), 7-2
Sec. 55(a)(1), 7-2
Sec. 55(a)(2), 7-2
Sec. 55(b), 7-2
Sec. 55(b)(1), 7-2
Sec. 55(b)(1)(A), 7-2
Sec. 55(b)(1)(B), 7-2
Sec. 55(b)(2), 7-2
Sec. 55(b)(2)(A), 7-2
Sec. 55(b)(2)(B), 7-2

Sec. 55(d), 7-12
Sec. 55(d)(1), 7-12
Sec. 55(d)(1)(A), 7-12
Sec. 55(d)(1)(A)(i), 7-12
Sec. 55(d)(1)(A)(ii), 7-12
Sec. 55(d)(1)(B), 7-12
Sec. 55(d)(1)(B)(i), 7-12
Sec. 55(d)(1)(B)(ii), 7-12
Sec. 55(d)(1)(C), 7-12
Sec. 55(d)(1)(C)(i), 7-12
Sec. 55(d)(1)(C)(ii), 7-12
Sec. 55(d)(3), 7-12
Sec. 55(d)(3)(A), 7-12
Sec. 55(d)(3)(B), 7-12
Sec. 55(d)(3)(C), 7-12
Sec. 61, 2-2
Sec. 63(b), 1-17
Sec. 63(b)(1), 1-17
Sec. 63(b)(2), 1-17
Sec. 63(c)(5), 1-20
Sec. 71(f)(1), 2-28
Sec. 71(f)(1)(A), 2-28
Sec. 71(f)(1)(B), 2-28
Sec. 72(a), 2-18
Sec. 72(b), 2-18
Sec. 72(b)(2), 2-20
Sec. 72(b)(3), 2-21
Sec. 72(b)(3)(A)(i), 2-21
Sec. 72(b)(3)(A)(ii), 2-21
Sec. 79(a), 3-13
Sec. 79(a)(1), 3-13
Sec. 79(a)(2), 3-13
Sec. 85(a), 3-10
Sec. 86(a), 3-22
Sec. 86(a)(1), 3-22
Sec. 86(a)(2), 3-22
Sec. 101(a)(1), 3-3
Sec. 101(b), 3-2
Sec. 101(b)(1), 3-2
Sec. 101(b)(2), 3-2
Sec. 101(b)(2)(A), 3-2
Sec. 102(a), 3-1
Sec. 102(b), 3-1
Sec. 102(b)(1), 3-1
Sec. 102(b)(2), 3-1
Sec. 103(a), 2-10
Sec. 105(a), 3-9
Sec. 105(a)(1), 3-9
Sec. 105(a)(2), 3-9
Sec. 105(b), 3-9
Sec. 106, 3-8
Sec. 117(a), 3-5
Sec. 119(a), 3-14

Sec. 119(a)(1), 3-14
Sec. 119(a)(2), 3-14
Sec. 121(a), 6-41
Sec. 121(a)(1), 6-41
Sec. 121(a)(2), 6-41
Sec. 121(b), 6-41
Sec. 121(b)(1), 6-41
Sec. 121(b)(2), 6-41
Sec. 132(a), 3-17
Sec. 132(a)(1), 3-17
Sec. 132(a)(2), 3-17
Sec. 132(a)(3), 3-17
Sec. 132(a)(4), 3-17
Sec. 162(a), 4-37, 8-1
Sec. 162(a)(2), 4-37
Sec. 163(d)(1), 4-12
Sec. 163(h), 4-8
Sec. 163(h)(1), 4-8
Sec. 163(h)(2), 4-8
Sec. 163(h)(2)(A), 4-8
Sec. 163(h)(2)(B), 4-8
Sec. 163(h)(2)(D), 4-8
Sec. 163(h)(3), 4-8
Sec. 163(h)(3)(A), 4-8
Sec. 163(h)(3)(A)(i), 4-8
Sec. 163(h)(3)(A)(ii), 4-8
Sec. 163(h)(3)(B), 4-9
Sec. 163(h)(3)(B)(i), 4-9
Sec. 163(h)(3)(B)(i)(I), 4-9
Sec. 163(h)(3)(B)(i)(II), 4-9
Sec. 163(h)(4)(A)(i), 4-9
Sec. 163(h)(4)(A)(i)(I), 4-9
Sec. 163(h)(4)(A)(i)(II), 4-9
Sec. 164(a), 4-14
Sec. 164(a)(1), 4-14
Sec. 164(a)(2), 4-14
Sec. 164(a)(3), 4-14
Sec. 165(a), 4-26, 8-5
Sec. 165(c), 4-25, 6-2, 8-5
Sec. 165(c)(1), 6-2, 8-5
Sec. 165(c)(2), 6-2, 8-5
Sec. 165(c)(3), 6-2, 8-5
Sec. 165(h), 4-27
Sec. 165(h)(1), 4-27
Sec. 165(h)(2), 4-27
Sec. 165(h)(2)(A), 4-27
Sec. 165(h)(2)(A)(i), 4-27
Sec. 165(h)(2)(A)(ii), 4-27
Sec. 166(a)(1), 8-45
Sec. 166(a)(2), 8-45
Sec. 167(a), 8-18
Sec. 167(a)(1), 8-18
Sec. 167(a)(2), 8-18

S-1

Sec. 168(a), 8-23
Sec. 168(a)(1), 8-23
Sec. 168(a)(2), 8-23
Sec. 168(a)(3), 8-23
Sec. 168(b)(5), 8-26
Sec. 168(g)(2), 8-26
Sec. 168(g)(2)(A), 8-26
Sec. 168(g)(2)(B), 8-26
Sec. 168(g)(2)(C), 8-26
Sec. 170(a), 4-17
Sec. 170(a)(1), 4-17
Sec. 170(b), 4-18
Sec. 170(b)(1), 4-19
Sec. 170(b)(1)(A), 4-19
Sec. 170(b)(1)(A)(i), 4-19
Sec. 170(b)(1)(A)(viii), 4-19
Sec. 170(b)(1)(B), 4-20
Sec. 170(b)(1)(B)(i), 4-20
Sec. 170(b)(1)(B)(ii), 4-20
Sec. 172(a), 9-51
Sec. 172(b)(1)(A), 9-51
Sec. 172(c), 9-54
Sec. 172(d)(1), 9-54
Sec. 172(d)(2), 9-54
Sec. 172(d)(3), 9-54
Sec. 172(d)(4), 9-54
Sec. 172(d)(4)(C), 9-54
Sec. 183(d), 8-4
Sec. 212, 8-2
Sec. 212(1), 8-2
Sec. 212(2), 8-2
Sec. 212(3), 8-2
Sec. 213(a), 4-3
Sec. 215, 4-56
Sec. 215(a), 4-57
Sec. 215(b), 4-57
Sec. 217(a), 4-29
Sec. 217(b), 4-32
Sec. 217(b)(1), 4-32
Sec. 217(b)(1)(A), 4-32
Sec. 217(b)(1)(B), 4-32
Sec. 217(b)(1)(C), 4-32
Sec. 217(b)(1)(D), 4-32
Sec. 217(b)(1)(E), 4-32
Sec. 217(c)(3), 4-33
Sec. 217(c)(3)(A), 4-33
Sec. 217(c), 4-29
Sec. 217(c)(1), 4-29
Sec. 217(c)(1)(A), 4-29
Sec. 217(c)(1)(B), 4-29
Sec. 217(c)(2)(A), 4-29
Sec. 217(c)(2)(B), 4-29
Sec. 219(a), 4-59
Sec. 219(b), 4-59
Sec. 219(b)(1), 4-59
Sec. 219(b)(1)(A), 4-59
Sec. 219(b)(1)(B), 4-59
Sec. 248(a), 10-34
Sec. 274(a)(1), 4-41
Sec. 274(a)(1)(A), 4-41
Sec. 274(n)(1), 4-44
Sec. 274(n)(1)(A), 4-44
Sec. 274(n)(1)(B), 4-44
Sec. 280A(a), 4-47
Sec. 280A(c)(1), 4-47
Sec. 280A(c)(1)(A), 4-47
Sec. 280A(c)(1)(B), 4-47
Sec. 280A(c)(1)(C), 4-47
Sec. 280F(b)(2), 8-28
Sec. 316(a), 2-15
Sec. 316(a)(1), 2-15
Sec. 316(a)(2), 2-15
Sec. 351(a), 10-21
Sec. 351(b), 10-24
Sec. 351(b)(1), 10-24
Sec. 351(b)(1)(A), 10-24
Sec. 351(b)(1)(B), 10-24
Sec. 351(b)(2), 10-24
Sec. 402(d)(4)(A), 7-16
Sec. 402(d)(4)(A)(i), 7-16
Sec. 402(d)(4)(A)(ii), 7-16
Sec. 402(d)(4)(A)(iii), 7-16
Sec. 402(d)(4)(B), 7-17
Sec. 402(e)(1)(A), 7-18
Sec. 402(e)(1)(B), 7-18
Sec. 402(e)(1)(B)(i), 7-18
Sec. 402(e)(1)(B)(ii), 7-18
Sec. 404(a)(3), 8-39
Sec. 446(c), 2-5
Sec. 446(c)(1), 2-5
Sec. 446(c)(2), 2-5
Sec. 446(c)(3), 2-5
Sec. 446(c)(4), 2-5
Sec. 453(a), 6-27
Sec. 453(b)(1), 6-27
Sec. 453(b)(2), 6-27
Sec. 453(c), 6-30
Sec. 453(d)(1), 6-28
Sec. 453(d)(2), 6-28
Sec. 611(a), 8-43
Sec. 702(b), 10-9
Sec. 702(c), 10-9
Sec. 703(a), 10-10
Sec. 703(a)(1), 10-10
Sec. 703(a)(2), 10-10
Sec. 703(a)(2)(A), 10-10
Sec. 703(a)(2)(B), 10-10
Sec. 703(a)(2)(C), 10-10
Sec. 703(a)(2)(D), 10-10
Sec. 703(a)(2)(E), 10-10
Sec. 703(a)(2)(F), 10-10
Sec. 709(b)(1), 10-12
Sec. 721(a), 10-3
Sec. 722, 10-4
Sec. 723, 10-5
Sec. 761(a), 10-2
Sec. 1001(a), 6-3
Sec. 1001(b), 6-3
Sec. 1001(c), 6-2
Sec. 1012, 6-6
Sec. 1014(a), 6-7
Sec. 1014(a)(1), 6-7
Sec. 1014(a)(2), 6-7
Sec. 1015(a), 6-9
Sec. 1031(a)(1), 9-2
Sec. 1031(b), 9-5
Sec. 1031(d), 9-7
Sec. 1032(a), 10-27
Sec. 1033(a), 9-10
Sec. 1033(a)(1), 9-10
Sec. 1033(a)(2), 9-10
Sec. 1034(a), 6-35
Sec. 1044(a), 9-9
Sec. 1044(a)(1), 9-9
Sec. 1044(a)(2), 9-9
Sec. 1211(b), 6-15
Sec. 1211(b)(1), 6-15
Sec. 1211(b)(2), 6-15
Sec. 1221, 6-13
Sec. 1221(1), 6-13
Sec. 1221(2), 6-13
Sec. 1221(3), 6-13
Sec. 1221(4), 6-13
Sec. 1221(5), 6-13
Sec. 1222(3), 6-15
Sec. 1231(a), 9-17
Sec. 1231(a)(1), 9-17
Sec. 1231(a)(1)(A), 9-17
Sec. 1231(a)(1)(B), 9-17
Sec. 1231(a)(2), 9-17
Sec. 1231(a)(2)(A), 9-17
Sec. 1231(a)(2)(B), 9-17
Sec. 1231(a)(3), 9-21
Sec. 1231(a)(3)(A), 9-21
Sec. 1231(a)(3)(A)(i), 9-21
Sec. 1231(a)(3)(A)(ii), 9-21
Sec. 1231(a)(3)(A)(ii)(I), 9-21
Sec. 1231(a)(3)(A)(ii)(II), 9-21
Sec. 1231(a)(3)(B), 9-21
Sec. 1231(a)(4)(C), 9-21
Sec. 1231(a)(4)(C)(i), 9-21
Sec. 1231(a)(4)(C)(ii), 9-21
Sec. 1231(b), 9-16
Sec. 1231(b)(1), 9-16
Sec. 1231(b)(1)(A), 9-16
Sec. 1231(b)(1)(B), 9-16
Sec. 1231(b)(1)(C), 9-16
Sec. 1231(b)(1)(D), 9-16
Sec. 1245(a), 9-27
Sec. 1245(a)(1), 9-27
Sec. 1245(a)(3), 9-27
Sec. 1245(a)(3)(A), 9-27
Sec. 1245(a)(3)(B), 9-27
Sec. 1245(a)(3)(D), 9-27
Sec. 1245(a)(3)(E), 9-27
Sec. 1250(a), 9-31
Sec. 1250(a)(1), 9-31
Sec. 1250(a)(1)(A), 9-31
Sec. 1250(a)(1)(A)(i), 9-31
Sec. 1250(a)(1)(A)(ii), 9-31
Sec. 1250(a)(1)(B), 9-31
Sec. 1250(a)(1)(B)(v), 9-31
Sec. 1361(b)(1), 10-45
Sec. 1361(b)(1)(A), 10-46
Sec. 1361(b)(1)(B), 10-46
Sec. 1361(b)(1)(C), 10-46
Sec. 1361(b)(1)(D), 10-46
Sec. 1362(b)(1), 10-47
Sec. 1362(b)(1)(A), 10-47
Sec. 1362(b)(1)(B), 10-47
Sec. 3102(a), 8-57
Sec. 3301, 8-68
Sec. 3301(1), 8-68
Sec. 3301(2), 8-68
Sec. 6654, 5-26
Sec. 6654(a)(1), 5-26
Sec. 6654(a)(2), 5-26
Sec. 6654(a)(3), 5-26
Sec. 6654(c)(2), 5-26
Sec. 7805(a), 1-5

Topic Index

Accelerated Cost Recovery System. *See* ACRS
Accrual basis, used with inventories, 8-11–8-12
ACRS (Accelerated Cost Recovery System), 8-18–8-19
  personalty under, 8-31
  realty under, 8-32
Adjusted basis of property, 6-6–6-12
  adjustments subsequent to acquisition, 6-11–6-12
    capital improvements, 6-11
    capital recoveries, 6-12
  of gift property, 6-9–6-10
  of gift property, dual basis for, 6-9
  and holding period, 6-6
  of inherited property, 6-7–6-8
    as long-term asset, 6-8
    fair market values, 6-8
  of personal property converted to business use, 6-10–6-11
  of purchased property, 6-7
Adjusted gross income (AGI), 1-11–1-12
  affected by capital gains and losses, 6-18
  deductions for, 1-10–1-11, 6-18
  deductions from, 1-11–1-12
  limitation in itemized deductions, 4-1
  limitation on donated capital-gain property, 4-20–4-21
  limits for charitable contributions, 4-19
AGI. *See* Adjusted basis of property
Alimony, 2-26–2-31
  as deduction, 2-26
  as deduction for AGI, 4-57–4-59
  eligibility requirements, 4-57
  exclusions from, 4-58
  federal tax definition of, 2-26
  recapture rule for, 2-27–2-28
  as taxable income, 2-26
  wherewithal-to-pay principal with, 2-26
Allocable parental tax, 2-33–2-39
  computing, 2-35–2-37
  limitations on, 2-34
Alternative minimum tax (AMT), 7-1, 7-2–7-3. *See also* Alternative minimum taxable income (AMTI)
Alternative minimum tax (AMT)
  calculating, 7-13
  credit, 7-13–7-14

Alternative minimum taxable income (AMTI), 7-2–7-12. *See also* Alternative minimum tax
  adjustments to determine, 7-6–7-11
  exemption for, 7-11–7-12
Amended tax returns, 7-29
  and statute of limitations, 7-29–7-31
Amortization, 8-42–8-43
AMT. *See* Alternative Minimum Tax
AMTI. *See* Alternative minimum taxable income
Annuities, 2-18–2-23
  defined, 2-18
  excluded from gross income, 2-19–2-22
  excluded from gross income, exclusion ratio formula, 2-19–2-20
  as income, 2-18–2-22
Annuity calculations, 2-41–2-44
  for joint and survivor annuities, 2-43–2-44
  for joint annuities, 2-43
  for ordinary life annuities, 2-41

Bonds, interest as income, 2-10–2-12
Break-even rate of return for a taxable investment formula, 3-29
Business and trade
  alcohol fuels credit, 9-48
  business energy credit, 9-38–9-40
  capital gains and losses, 9-16–9-27
  corporate charitable contributions, 10-32–10-33
  corporations, 10-1–10-2
  credit for qualified summer youth employees, 9-42–9-43
  deductibility limits of meals and entertainment, 4-45
  deductions for retirement plans, 8-38–8-41
  depreciation recapture provisions, 9-27–9-32
  disabled access credit, 9-48
  educational expenses, as deductions, 4-49–4-51
  enhanced oil recovery credit, 9-49
  entertainment expenses, as deductions, 4-41, 4-44
  expenses as deductions, 8-6
  expenses vs. hobby expenses, 8-4–8-5
  general business credit, 9-34–9-36
  home office expense, as deduction,
4-47–4-49
  investment in SSBICs, 9-9
  investment tax credit, 9-36–9-37
  involuntary conversion of property, 9-10–9-16
  like-kind exchanges, 9-2–9-9
    basis of property received, 9-7
    boot provision for nonqualifying property, 9-4–9-5
    deferred exchanges, 9-8–9-9
    property eligible for nonrecognition, 9-2
    property exceptions, 9-3–9-4
    three-party exchanges, 9-8
  low-income housing credit, 9-46–9-48
  net operating loss (NOL) deductions, 9-50–9-58
  nonrecognition of gains, 9-1–9-16
  partnerships, 10-1, 10-3–10-20
  realized gains and losses, 9-4
  reforestation credit, 9-40
  regular investment tax credit 9-56–9-59
  rehabilitation credit, 9-37–9-38
  reimbursed expenses as deductions, 4-45–4-47
  renewable electricity production credit, 9-49
  replacement for lost property, 9-13
  research expenditures credit, 9-44–9-46
  S corporations, 10-2, 10-46–10-58
  sole proprietorships, 10-1
  targeted jobs credit, 9-40–9-43
  tax credits, 9-33–9-50

Capital assets. *See also* Capital gains and losses
  capital gains from, 6-13–6-14
  defined, 6-13–6-14
  worthless securities as, 6-45–6-46
    franchises, 6-47
    patents, 6-47
    sales of subdivided realty, 6-46–6-47
    Section 1244 stock, 6-46
    securities owned by securities dealers, 6-46
    trademarks, 6-47
    trade names, 6-47
Capital gains and losses, 6-13–6-14. *See also* Gains and losses
  business assets, 9-16–9-27
  and charitable contributions, 4-19–4-20

Capital gains and losses (continued)
conversion of ordinary income to, 6-49–6-50
corporate, 10-34–10-35
deferral of on sale of personal residence, 6-35–6-41
deferral of recognition for installment sales, 6-27–6-34
deferral of recognition for installment sales, calculations required, 6-29–6-32
exclusion of small business stock from, 6-49
long-term, 1-8, 4-19, 6-15
long-term, tax treatment of, 6-16–6-18
netting process, 6-15–6-20
one-time elective exclusion of on sale of personal residence, 6-41–6-44
reporting, 6-20–6-21
short-term, tax treatment of, 6-15–6-16
Charitable contributions
of appreciated property, 7-10
of capital-gain property, 4-19–4-20
corporate, 10-32–10-33
as deductions, 4-17–4-24
percentage limitation of AGI, 4-19
to private charities, 4-17
to public charities, 4-17
Charitable contributions to private non-operating foundations, 4-21
Child and dependent care credit
AGI limitations, 5-18
calculation of, 5-18
eligibility for, 5-16
eligible dependent, defined, 5-16
expenses qualifying for, 5-16–5-17
maximum expenses eligible, 5-18
Community property income, 2-32–2-33
Congress
and amendment of Internal Revenue Code, 1-2
and history of U.S. income tax, 1-2
Conversion transaction, 6-49–6-50
Corporations, 10-1
alternative minimum tax exemption, 7-12
AMT (alternative minimum tax) of, 10-41–10-43
capital losses, taxation of, 10-35
charitable contribution deductions, 10-32–10-33
depreciation recapture on property transferred to, 10-27
dividend received deduction, 10-33–10-34
dividend received deduction, income limitation for, 10-34
expenses as adjustment to AMTI, 7-8
forming, 10-21–10-24
forming, tax consequences on shareholders, 10-22–10-24
income, taxation of, 10-30–10-45
investment in, 6-49
nonrecognition provision for sale or transfer of stock, 10-27–10-28
organizational expenses, taxation of, 10-35–10-36

property received, basis in, 10-28
shareholders
basis in stock and property, 10-25–10-27
distributions to, 10-44–10-45
recognized gains of, 10-24–10-25
taxable income, 10-32
tax rate schedule, 10-30–10-31
tax return filing requirements, 10-36–10-41
Cost of goods sold
and changes in inventory, 8-11–8-13
defined, 8-10–8-11
estimated by periodic system, 8-15
Credit for the elderly and permanently disabled, 5-9–5-15
AGI limitations for, 5-12–5-15
eligibility requirements, 5-9

Deductions 1-10–1-12. *See also* Personal exemption deductions; Itemized deductions
for AGI, 1-10–1-11, 4-1, 4-57–4-61, 8-9, 8-47, 8-48
from AGI, 1-11–1-12, 4-1
itemized, 1-11–1-12
personal exemption, 1-11
standard, 1-11–1-12
amortization, 8-42–8-43
for bad debt, 8-46–8-47
business educational expenses, 4-49–4-51
business entertainment expenses, 4-41, 4-44–4-47
business expenses vs. hobby expenses, 8-4–8-5
corporate charitable contributions, 10-32–10-33
criteria for eligibility, 8-2–8-3
depletion, 8-43–8-45
depreciation, 8-18–8-19
disallowed, 8-3–8-6
dividends received by corporations, 10-33–10-34
for employee contributions to retirement plans, 8-39
employee salaries and wages, 8-47–8-48
for employer contributions to retirement plans, 8-40
for health insurance premiums, 8-47–8-48
and hobby loss rule, 8-5
home office expense, 4-47–4-49
investment property interest, 4-11–4-12
for Keogh plan, 8-36–8-38, 8-40–8-41
net operating loss (NOL), 9-50–9-58
for partnership activities, 8-9
passive losses, 7-23–7-25
percentage depletion, 7-10
rental income expenses, 8-6–8-9
repair expenses, 8-47
royalty income expenses, 8-6–8-9
for S corporation shareholders, 8-9
self-employment tax, 8-47–8-48
for sole proprietors, 8-49–8-55
timing of, 8-3

types of losses eligible, 8-5–8-6
Dependent
eligibility tests, 1-27–1-35
citizenship test, 1-28
exceptions to, 1-31–1-34
filing status test, 1-34
gross income test. 1-28
relationship test, 1-29
support test, 1-30–1-34
relative qualified as, 1-23–1-24
Depletion
accelerated, 7-11
cost method of, 8-43–8-44
defined, 8-44
percentage, 7-10
percentage method of, 8-44–8-45
Depreciation, 8-18–8-19. *See also* ACRS and MACRS
as adjustment to AMTI, 7-8
Asset Depreciation Range (ADR) system for, 8-22
declining-balance method for, 8-20
defined, 8-19
maximum rates for (table), 8-21
rates for, 8-21–8-22
recapture of excess, of real property, 9-31–9-32
recapture on property transferred to corporations, 10-27
recapture provisions for business property, 9-27–9-32
salvage value for, 8-19
straight-line method for, 8-20
sum-of-the-years' digits method for, 8-20
useful life of property for, 8-19–8-20
Dividends, 2-15–2-18
as capital gain distribution, 2-15
defined, 2-15
as income, 2-15–2-16
as nontaxable income, 2-15–2-16
reporting as income, 2-16–2-18

Earned income, 1-19
Earned-income credit, 5-2–5-8
advance payments of, 5-6–5-7
affected by AGI limit, 5-4–5-5
calculation of, 5-4–5-5
eligibility requirements, 5-3
eligibility requirements, for qualifying child, 5-3
as refundable credit, 5-6
supplemental young-child credit, 5-8
supplemental young-child credit, child or dependent care credit affected by, 5-8
Employees, retirement plans for, 8-38
Employment taxes, 8-57–8-69
federal income tax, 8-57, 8-58
FICA contributions, 8-57
FUTA contributions, 8-57, 8-68
percentage method to determine, 8-60
social security taxes, 8-57–8-58
using form 941, 8-57–8-67
wage bracket method to determine, 8-64

Estimated tax payments
  for individuals, 5-26–5-30
  for individuals, penalties for under-
    payment, 5-30
Exclusions. *See* Taxable income, exclu-
    sions from

Federal courts, as tax authority, 1-5
Filing status, 1-21–1-24
  head of household, 1-23–1-24
    individual qualified as, 1-23
    provision of household, 1-23
  married-filing jointly, 1-21–1-22
  married-filing separately, 1-22
  single, 1-21
  widow or widower, 1-24
Five-year forward averaging, 7-1
  computations for, 7-18–7-20
  election limitations, 7-17–7-18
  eligibility, 7-15–7-17
Foreign tax credit, 5-22–5-23, 7-12–7-13
Formula
  addition to basis for gift tax, 6-10
  alternative minimum tax, 7-3
  basis of like-kind property received,
    9-7–9-8
  break-even rate of return for a taxable
    investment, 3-29
  Corporate AMT, 10-41–10-43
  corporate tax, 10-29
  estimate cost of goods sold with peri-
    odic inventory system, 8-15
  exclusion ratio for annuities, 2-19
  maximum foreign tax credit, 5-23

Gains and losses. *See also* Adjusted basis of
    property; Capital gains and losses
  as adjustments to AMTI, 7-9
  income recognition from, 9-17–9-26
  measuring amount realized, 6-3–6-5
  nonrecognition of, 9-1–9-15
    property eligible for, 9-3
    property exceptions, 9-3
  realization criterion, 6-2
  realized, 9-4
  recognition of, for partnership distribu-
    tions, 10-18–10-19
  recognized, boot received from corpo-
    rations, 10-24–10-25
Gross income, 1-10, 2-1–2-9
  interest as part of, 2-10–2-11
  inventory changes reflected in,
    8-11–8-13
Gross receipts, 1-8

Health insurance credit, 5-9

Income. *See also* specific types of income
  accountant's definition of, 2-2
  economist's definition of, 2-1–2-2
  foreign-earned, 5-22–5-23
  interest as part of, 2-10–2-12
  from property, 2-31–2-32
  ordinary, conversion of, 6-48–6-49
  property as, 2-3
  from services, 2-31–2-32
  services as, 2-3

Income realization, 9-1
Income recognition, 9-1–9-2
  like-kind exchanges, 9-2–9-9
  like-kind exchanges, property eligible
    for nonrecognition, 9-3
  replacement of lost property, 9-13
Income recognition, gains and losses,
    9-65
Income reporting period
  calendar year, 2-4
  fiscal year, 2-4
Individual return
  with Form 1040, 1-49
  with Form 1040A, 1-39, 1-41
  with Form 1040EZ, 1-39
Individual tax computation, 1-8–1-16. *See
    also* Gross receipts; Exclusions;
    Adjusted gross income (AGI);
    Taxable income; Tax Liability
  example, 1-9
Individual retirement accounts. *See* IRA
Interest, 2-10–2-12
  as adjustment to AMTI, 7-7
  defined, 2-10
  excluded from gross income, 2-10–2-12
  for investment property, as deduction,
    4-11–4-12
  as part of gross income, 2-10–2-11
  personal, as deduction, 4-7, 4-13
  for qualified residence, as deduction,
    4-8–4-11
    for acquisition indebtedness, 4-9
    for home equity indebtedness, 4-10
  reporting as income, 2-16–2-18
  tax exempt, as adjustment to AMTI,
    7-10
Internal Revenue Code (IRC), 1-1
  amendment of, 1-2–1-4
  as tax authority, 1-4
  of 1913, 1-2
  of 1986, 1-2
Internal Revenue Service (IRS)
  as tax authority, 1-5
  and statute of limitations, 7-30–7-31
Inventory
  accrual basis with, 8-11–8-12
  average cost method for, 8-15
  changes affecting gross income,
    8-11–8-12
  cost method of valuing, 8-13–8-14
  defined, 8-10
  first-in, first-out (FIFO) method for,
    8-15–8-17
  goods included in, 8-13
  last-in, first-out (LIFO) method for,
    8-16–8-17
  market method of valuing, 8-14
  periodic system of tracking, 8-11, 8-15
  perpetual system of tracking, 8-11
Investments in small business stock, 6-48
IRA (Individual Retirement Account), 8-41
IRA (Individual Retirement Accounts)
  contributions qualifying for deduction
    for AGI, 4-59–4-61
  maximum contribution, 4-59
  maximum deduction, 4-60

IRS. *See* Internal Revenue Service
Itemized deductions, 4-52–4-53. *See also*
    Deductions
  as adjustment to AMTI, 7-6–7-8
  business entertainment expenses, 4-45
  business transportation expenses,
    4-39–4-43
  business travel expenses, 4-37–4-39
  charitable contributions, 4-17–4-24
  home office expenses, 4-48
  medical expenses, 4-3–4-6
    insurance reimbursement for, 4-6
    qualifying dependent for, 4-3
  moving expenses, 4-28–4-35
    expenses eligible, 4-32–4-34
    qualifying for, 4-28–4-32
  personal casualty losses, 4-25–4-28
    computation of, 4-27–4-28
    insurance reimbursement for,
      4-26–4-27
  property taxes, 4-14–4-17
  qualified residence interest, 4-8–4-11
  reduction of, for high-income tax-
    payers, 4-52–4-53
  state and local income taxes, 4-14–4-15
  state and local sales taxes, 4-16
  for taxes paid on foreign-earned
    income, 5-22
  theft losses, 4-25–4-28
    computation of, 4-27–4-28
    insurance reimbursement for, 4-27

Keogh plan, 8-36–8-38, 8-40–8-41
Kiddie tax. *See* Allocable parental tax

Long-term assets
  defined by holding period, 6-6
  inherited property as, 6-8
Losses. *See* Gains and losses; Capital
    gains and losses
Lump-sum distributions. *See also* Five-
    year forward averaging
Lump-sum distributions, minimum distri-
    bution allowances, 7-20–7-21

MACRS (Modified Accelerated Cost
    Recovery System), 8-18–8-19,
    8-22–8-29. *See also* ACRS
  ADS for, 8-26–8-27
  deductions computations for, 8-24
  listed property rules for, 8-28
  luxury auto limitations for, 8-28
  mid-quarter convention for cost recov-
    ery for, 8-25
  mid-year convention for cost recovery
    for, 8-24
  personalty under, 8-23–8-29
  realty under, 8-29–8-30
  straight-line recovery method for, 8-26
Medical expenses, 4-3–4-6
  insurance reimbursement for, 4-6
  qualifying dependent for deduction, 4-3
Modified Accelerated Cost Recovery
    System. *See* MACRS

Net operating loss (NOL), 9-50–9-58

1991 Estimated Tax Worksheet, 5-24

Partnerships, 10-1
  adjustments of partners' bases, 10-15
  allocations for contributed property, 10-13
  basis in contributed property, 10-4
  distribution of cash, taxation of, 10-18
  distribution of noncash property, taxation of, 10-18
  effects of liabilities on partner's basis, 10-5–10-7
  expenses as adjustment to AMTI, 7-8
  filing tax returns, 10-14–10-15
  formation, 10-3
  holding period of partnership assets, 10-7
  income, taxation of, 10-10–10-11
  organizational expenses, taxation of, 10-12
  payments to partners, taxation of, 10-12–10-13
  recapture of depreciation of transferred assets, 10-7
  retiring a partner, 10-20
  sale of interest in, 10-19–10-20
  sales of contributed assets, 10-7
  taxable year, 10-18
  transactions with partners, 10-8
Passive activities. *See also* Passive losses
  defined, 7-23–7-25
  rental activities as, 7-24–7-25
Passive losses, 7-23–7-24. *See also* Passive activities
  for passive activities, 7-23–7-24
  rental activity exception, 7-26
  reporting rules, 7-25
Personal exemption deductions, 1-27–1-38. *See also* Deductions
  as adjustment to AMTI, 7-6
  annual adjustments for inflation in, 1-37
  phaseout of, 1-34–1-36
  for qualified dependent, 1-28–1-34

Rents, 2-24–2-25
  constructive-receipt doctrine with, 2-24
  defined, 2-24
  excluded from taxable income, 2-25
  as taxable income, 2-24–2-25
Retirement plans, Keogh plan, 8-35–8-37
Revenue Act of 1913, 1-2
Revenue Reconciliation Act of 1990, 7-1, 7-10
Revenue Reconciliation Act of 1993, 1-13, 6-49, 7-1, 7-10, 10-31

S corporations, 10-2
  formation of, 10-46
  income, treatment of, 10-49
  qualifications to become, 10-47
  shareholders
    distributions to, 10-57–10-58
    stock bases, 10-48–10-49
  tax return reporting requirements, 10-49–10-57

Self-employed individuals. *See also* Sole proprietors
  deduction for self-employment tax, 8-48
  deductions for health insurance premiums, 8-47–8-48
  deductions for retirement plans for, 8-36–8-41
  defined contribution plan, 8-38–8-39
  Keogh plan for, 8-36–8-41
Self-employment tax, 8-49, 8-55
Short-term assets, defined by holding period, 6-6
Short-term capital gains and losses, bad debt as, 8-46–8-47
Sixteenth Amendment, 1-2
Small business, investment in, 6-49
Sole proprietors, tax-reporting procedures for, 8-49–8-55
Sole proprietorships, 10-1
Standard deduction, 1-17–1-21. *See also* Deductions
  as adjustment to AMTI, 7-6
  additional amounts, 1-18–1-19
  annual adjustments for inflation, 1-37
  for dependents with unearned income, 1-19–1-20
  limits on, 1-19
  for married-filing separately, 1-19
State and local income taxes, 4-15
Supreme Court, and history of U.S. income tax, 1-2

Taxable income, 1-12–1-14, 2-2–2-4. *See also* Taxable income, exclusions from; and Income
  accident and health plan benefits, 3-9–3-10
  adjustments to for AMTI, 7-6–7-12
  for corporations, 10-30
  employee dependent care assistance, 3-16–3-17
  employee educational assistance, 3-15–3-16
  employee fringe benefits, 3-17–3-21
  employee group legal services, 3-16–3-17
  employee meals and lodging, 3-14–3-15
  employee medical reimbursement, 3-15–3-16
  exclusions from, 1-9–1-10
  foreign earned income, 3-24–3-25
  forgiveness of debt, 3-26
  foreign-earned income, 5-22
  gift property, 3-1–3-3
  group-term life insurance, 3-13–3-14
  inheritance property, 3-1–3-2
  lawsuit damages, 3-11
  life insurance proceeds, 3-3–3-4
  loans, interest free or below market, 3-26–3-27
  long-term capital gain, 2-3
  measuring the value of, 3-28–3-29
  measuring the value of, break-even rate of return for a taxable investment formula, 3-29
  military payments, 3-25

  prizes and awards, 3-4–3-5
  property as, 6-4–6-5
  public assistance payments, 3-25
  scholarships and fellowships, 3-5–3-7
  services as, 6-4
  short-term capital gain, 2-3
  social security payments, 3-22–3-24
  tax benefit rule, 3-27–3-28
  unemployment compensation, 3-10–3-11
  worker's compensation, 3-10
Tax accounting methods, 2-5
  accrual method, 2-6
  cash method, 2-5–2-6
  claim-of-right doctrine, 2-8–2-9
  constructive-receipt doctrine, 2-7
  hybrid method, 2-6
  wherewithal-to-pay principal, 2-7
Tax authority, sources of, 1-4–1-7
  Constitution, 1-4
  federal courts, 1-5
    circuit courts of appeal, 1-5
    U.S. Claims Court, 1-5
    U.S. District Court, 1-5
    U.S. Tax Court, 1-5
  Internal Revenue Code, 1-4
  Internal Revenue Service, 1-5
  Treasury Department, 1-5
  U.S. Supreme Court, 1-5
Tax credits, 5-1, 9-33
  alcohol fuels credit, 9-48
  for AMT, 7-13–7-14
  business energy credit, 9-38–9-40
  child and dependent care credit, 5-16–5-20
  credit for qualified summer youth employees, 9-42–9-43
  disabled access credit, 9-48
  earned-income credit, 5-2–5-8, 5-10–5-11
  for the elderly and permanently disabled, 5-9, 5-12–5-15
  enhanced oil recovery credit, 9-49
  foreign, 7-12
  foreign tax credit, 5-22–5-23
  general business credit, 9-33–9-36
  health insurance credit, 5-9–5-10
  investment tax credit, 9-36–9-37
  low-income housing credit, 9-46–9-48
  reforestation credit, 9-40
  regular investment tax credit 9-56–9-58
  rehabilitation credit, 9-37–9-38
  renewable electricity production credit, 9-49
  research expenditures credit, 9-44–9-46
  targeted jobs credit, 9-40–9-44
Tax form 940, Employer's Annual Federal Unemployment (FUTA) Tax Return, 8-69
Tax form 941, Employer's Quarterly Federal Tax Return, 8-66
Tax form 1040 (or 1040A), Schedule EIC, Earned Income Credit, 5-10–5-11
Tax form 1040, U.S. Individual Income Tax Return, 1-50–1-51
  Schedule A, Itemized Deductions, 4-4, 4-10, 4-15, 4-18, 4-30, 4-34, 4-41, 4-52, 4-54

Schedule B, Interest and Dividend Income, 2-17–2-18
Schedule C, Profit or Loss from Business, 8-50–8-51
Schedule D, Capital Gains and Losses, 6-22–6-25
Schedule E, Supplemental Income and Loss, 8-7–8-8
Schedule R, Credit for the Elderly or the Disabled, 5-13
Tax form 1040, Schedule SE, Self-Employment Tax, 8-53–8-54
Tax form 1040, Social Security Benefits Worksheet, 3-23
Tax form 1040A, U.S. Individual Income Tax Return, 1-42–1-48
Tax form 1040-ES, Payment of Estimated Tax, 5-27
Tax form 1040EZ, Income Tax Return for Single Filers with no Dependents, 1-40
Tax form 1045, Application for Tentative Refund, 9-57
Tax form 1065, U.S. Partnership Return of Income, 10-16–10-17
Tax form 1065, Schedule K-1, Partner's Share of Income, Credits, Deductions, etc., 10-50–10-51
Tax form 1099-B, Proceeds from Broker and Barter Exchange Transactions, 6-26
Tax form 1099-Div, Dividend Income, 2-19
Tax form 1099-Int, Interest Income, 2-19
Tax form 1116, Foreign Tax Credit, 5-24–5-25
Tax form 1120, U.S. Corporation Income Tax Return, 10-38–10-39
Tax form 1120-A, U.S. Corporation Short-Form Income Tax Return, 10-40
Tax form 1120S, U.S. Income Tax Return for an S Corporation, 10-50–10-51
Tax form 2106, Employee Business Expenses, 4-42–4-43, 4-46
Tax form 2119, Sale of Your Home, 6-41
Tax form 2119, with Sec. 121 election, 6-44
Tax form 2120, Multiple Support Declaration, 1-31
Tax form 2210, 5-31
Tax form 2441, Child and Dependent Care Expenses, 5-19
Tax form 3468, Investment Credit, 9-39
Tax form 3903, Moving Expenses, 4-35
Tax form 4562, Depreciation and Amortization, 8-34–8-35
Tax form 4626, Alternative Minimum Tax–Corporations, 10-43
Tax form 4684, Casualties and Thefts, 4-31
Tax form 4797, Sales of Business Property, 9-29–9-30
Tax form 4972 (for ten-year averaging), 7-22
Tax form 4972, Tax on Lump-Sum Distributions, 7-19
Tax form 5884, Jobs Credit, 9-41
Tax form 6252, Installment Sale Income, 6-32
Tax form 6765, Credit for Increasing Research Activities, 9-45
Tax form 8283, Noncash Charitable Contributions, 4-23–4-24
Tax form 8332, Release of Claim to Exemption for Child of Divorced or Separated Parents, 1-33
Tax form 8582, Passive Activity Loss Limitations, 7-27
Tax form 8615, Exclusion of Interest from Series EE U.S. Savings Bonds Issued after 1989, 2-38
Tax form 8815, Tax for Children under Age 14 Who Have Investment Income of More Than $1,100, 2-13–2-14
Tax form 8814, Parent's Election to Report Child's Interest and Dividends, 2-40
Tax form 8824, Like-Kind Exchanges, 9-6
Tax form 8829, Expenses for Business Use of Your Home, 4-50
Tax form SS-4, Application for Employer Identification number, 8-58
Tax form W-2, Wage and Tax Statement, 1-41
Tax form W-2P, Statement for Recipients of Annuities, Pensions, Retired Pay, or IRA Payments, 2-23
Tax form W-3, Transmittal of Income Tax Statements, 8-67
Tax form W-4, Employee Withholding Allowance Certificate, 8-61–8-62
Tax form W-5, Earned Income Credit Advance Payment Certificate, 5-6
Tax liability
  computation of, 1-13
  computation of, use of tax tables, 1-13
  credits against, 1-14–1-15
  prepayments of, 1-15
Taxpayers
  penalty provisions applicable to, 1-52, 1-54, 5-30, 7-32–7-34
  responsibilities of, 1-52
  subject to interest charges, 7-32
Tax preference items, as adjustments to AMTI, 7-10–7-11
Tax preparers
  penalty provisions applicable to, 1-53, 1-54
  responsibilities of, 1-52
Tax rate schedules, 1-12
Tax Reform Act of 1986, 7-1
Tax return
  appeals process, 5-32–5-34
  audit process, 5-32–5-34
Tax returns. See also Amended returns; Tax authority, sources of
Tax returns
  corporate filing requirements, 10-36–10-37
  filing for extensions, 7-28–7-29
  filing for partnerships, 10-14–10-15
  requirements for filing, 1-24
Tax tables, 1-13
Treasury Department, as tax authority, 1-4

U.S. Constitution, as tax authority, 1-4
U.S. income tax, history of, 1-2
U.S. president, as tax authority, 1-4
Unearned income, 1-20
Uniform Partnership Act, 10-1